AF772056

AAAI–90

Proceedings Eighth National Conference on Artificial Intelligence

Volume One

Sponsored by the
American Association for
Artificial Intelligence

July 29, 1990 – August 3, 1990

AAAI Press / The MIT Press
Menlo Park • Cambridge • London

First MIT Press edition, 1990

Copublished and distributed by The MIT Press, Massachusetts Institute of Technology, Cambridge, Massachusetts, and London, England.

ISBN 0-262-51057-X

Contents

Volume One

Volume Two

Foreword

This volume comprises the written record of research presented at the Eighth National Conference on Artificial Intelligence. The American Association for Artificial Intelligence (AAAI), the sponsor of this conference, is a technical society whose principal goal is to promote research in the field, primarily through its annual national conference. Thus, this volume is to some extent a capsule summary of the current scientific state of AI.

We have endeavored to produce an interesting conference of the highest technical quality. AAAI has always prided itself on its careful reviewing process and its consistent high standards for acceptance of submitted papers. Each of the 926 papers submitted to the conference was read by at least two members of the Program Committee, which, as you will note (p. v), is a sizable body of well-respected and technically expert researchers. After all of the papers were read, the entire Program Committee met face to face, and each paper was discussed until a final decision was agreed upon (where necessary, additional reviews were obtained from other members of the committee). Ultimately, 161 papers were accepted for presentation at the conference and for publication in these proceedings.

Because of the continuing growth of research activity in AI and the associated increase in the number of papers submitted, this year's Program Committee was the largest ever assembled for the National Conference. The successful operation of the Program Committee depended on the hard work of the Area Chairs, who took responsibility for recruiting reviewers in each area and for coordinating the review process. Another essential ingredient of the review process was the wisdom and hard work contributed by the AAAI office staff (p. v). Finally, each Co-Chair was assisted by an Associate Chair, who helped in all phases of the process. We wish to thank the staff, the associate chairs, the area chairs, and all members of the Program Committee for their efforts.

In addition to technical papers, the conference also includes a collection of invited talks and panels. Peter Friedland took responsibility for collecting nominations, tallying votes by the Area Chairs, and inviting the speakers and panels. To the extent possible, we have included written versions of these talks and panels in these proceedings.

In sum, you hold in your hands a volume of the highest-quality short papers on current research in AI. As these papers demonstrate, research in artificial intelligence continues its vigorous and exciting growth. We hope you enjoy this most challenging of intellectual adventures.

Tom Dietterich
William Swartout
Program Co-Chairmen, AAAI-90

Organization of the American Association for Artificial Intelligence

1990 National Conference on Artificial Intelligence Program Committee

Program Cochairs

Thomas Dietterich, *Oregon State University*
William Swartout, *University of Southern California—ISI*

Associate Chairs

Hussein Almuallim, *Oregon State University*
Cecile Paris, *University of Southern California—ISI*

Program Committee

James Allen, *University of Rochester*
Kevin Ashley, *Learning R & D Center*
James Bennett, *Coherent Thought*
Hans Berliner, *Carnegie Mellon University*
Ronald J. Brachman, *AT&T Bell Laboratories*
Rodney Brooks, *Massachusetts Institute of Technology*
Bruce Buchanan, *University of Pittsburgh*
Wray Buntine, *NASA Ames Research Center*
B. Chandrasekaran, *Ohio State University*
Greg Clemenson, *IntelliCorp*
Daniel Corkill, *University of Massachusetts*
Bruce D'Ambrosio, *Oregon State University*
Thomas Dean, *Brown University*
Gerald DeJong, *University of Illinois*
Johan de Kleer, *Xerox Palo Alto Research Center*
Jon Doyle, *Massachusetts Institute of Technology*
Mark Drummond, *NASA Ames Research Center*
Michael Dyer, *University of California at Los Angeles*
Thomas Ellman, *Rutgers University*
David Etherington, *AT&T Bell Laboratories*
Brian Falkenhainer, *Xerox Palo Alto Research Center*
Ron Fearing, *University of California at Berkeley*
Jerry Feldman, *ICSI*
Douglas Fisher, *Vanderbilt University*
Kenneth Forbus, *University of Illinois at Urbana-Champaign*
Eugene Freuder, *University of New Hampshire*
Peter Friedland, *NASA Ames Research Center*
John Grefensette, *Naval Center AI Research*
Ramanathan Guha, *MCC*
Walter Hamscher, *Price-Waterhouse Technology Centre*
Barbara Hayes-Roth, *Stanford University*
Julia Hirschberg, *AT&T Bell Laboratories*
Graeme Hirst, *University of Toronto*
Eric Horvitz, *Stanford University*
John Hotchkiss, *Symbolics Inc.*
Michael Huhns, *MCC*
David Israel, *SRI International*
Paul Jacobs, *General Electric Corporation*
Leo Joskowicz, *IBM, T. J. Watson Research Center*
Leslie Kaelbling, *Teleos Research*
Robert Kasper, *University of Southern California—ISI*
Henry Kautz, *AT&T Bell Laboratories*
Phil Klahr, *Inference Corporation*
Janet Kolodner, *Georgia Institute of Technology*
Kurt Konolige, *SRI International*
Richard Korf, *University of California at Los Angeles*
Benjamin Kuipers, *University of Texas at Austin*
Vipin Kumar, *University of Minnesota*
Peter Ladkin, *University of California at Berkeley*
Philip Laird, *NASA Ames Research Center*
Amy Lansky, *NASA Ames Research Center*
Jim Little, *University of British Columbia*
Robert Mac Gregor, *University of Southern California—ISI*
Alan Mackworth *University of British Columbia*
Pattie Maes, *Massachusetts Institute of Technology*
Jitendra Malik, *University of California at Berkeley*
Thomas Malone, *Massachusetts Institute of Technology*
William Mark, *Lockheed AI Center*
David McAllester, *Massachusetts Institute of Technology*
John McDermott, *Digital Equipment Corporation*
Kathleen McKeown, *Columbia University*
Daniel Miranker, *University of Texas at Austin*
Tom Mitchell, *Carnegie Mellon University*
Sanjay Mittal, *Xerox Palo Alto Research Center*
Johanna Moore, *University of Pittsburgh*
Robert Neches, *University of Southern California—ISI*
Peter Patel-Schneider, *AT&T Bell Laboratories*
Ramesh Patil, *Massachusetts Institute of Technology*
Judea Pearl, *University of California at Los Angeles*
Edwin Pednault, *AT&T Bell Laboratories*
Raymond Perrault, *SRI International*

David Plaisted, *University of North Carolina at Chapel Hill*
David Poole, *University of British Columbia*
Edwina Rissland, *University of Massachusetts*
Stuart Russell, *University of California at Berkeley*
Elisha Sacks, *Princeton University*
Jeffrey Schlimmer, *Carnegie Mellon University*
James Schmolze, *Tufts University*
Alberto Segre, *Cornell University*
Ross Shachter, *Stanford University*
Lokendra Shastri, *University of Pennsylvania*
Yoav Shoham, *Stanford University*
Howard Shrobe, *Symbolics*
Reid Simmons, *Carnegie Mellon University*
Elliot Soloway, *University of Michigan*
Mark Stickel, *SRI International*
Devika Subramanian, *Cornell University*
Prasad Tadepalli, *Oregon State University*
Paul Utgoff, *University of Massachusetts*
Kurt VanLehn, *Carnegie Mellon University*
Marc Vilain, *The MITRE Corporation*
Richard Waters, *Massachusetts Institute of Technology*
Jay Weber, *Lockheed*
Daniel Weld, *University of Washington*
Michael Wellman, *WRDC/TXI*
David Wilkins, *SRI International*
Yorick Wilks, *New Mexico State University*
Brian Williams, *Xerox Palo Alto Research Center*
Mike Williams, *IntelliCorp*

Auxiliary Reviewers

Kenneth Basye
Mark Boddy
Robert Cassels
Lisa Dent
Kurt Eiselt
Ashok Goel
Klaus Gross
Anshul Gupta
Keiji Kanazawa
Diane Litman
Andre Ljolje
Ambuj Mahanti
Bernard Nadel
Tony Plate
Ashwin Ram
Michael Redmond
Steve Robinson
Enrique Ruspini
Shashi Shekhar
Munindar P. Singh
Richard Sproat
Jaydeep Srivastava
Ming Tan

AAAI Officials

President
Daniel G. Bobrow, Xerox Palo Alto Research Center

President-elect
Patrick Hayes, Xerox Palo Alto Research Center

Past President
Raj Reddy, Carnegie Mellon University

Secretary-Treasurer
Bruce Buchanan, University of Pittsburgh

Councilors (through 1990)
William J. Clancey, Institute for Research on Learning
Richard Duda, San Jose State University
Hector Levesque, University of Toronto
Kathleen McKeown, Columbia University

Councilors (through 1991)
Elaine Rich, MCC
Geoffrey Hinton, University of Toronto
Wendy Lehnert, University of Massachusetts
Reid Smith, Schlumberger Laboratory of Computer Science

Councilors (through 1992)
Kenneth Forbus, *University of Illinois at Urbana-Champaign*
Howard Shrobe, Symbolics
William Swartout, University of Southern California—ISI
J. Martin Tenenbaum, Schlumberger

Standing Committees

Conference Chair
Howard Shrobe, Symbolics

Finance Chair
Bruce Buchanan, University of Pittsburgh

Publications Chair
William J. Clancey, Institute for Research on Learning

Scholarship Chair
Barbara Hayes-Roth, Stanford University

Symposium Chair
Peter Patel-Schneider, AT&T Bell Laboratories

Workshop Cochair
Peter Hart, Syntelligence

Workshop Cochair
Kathy McKeown, Columbia University

AI in Medicine Subgroup Liaison
Gordon Banks, University of Pittsburgh

AI in Manufacturing Subgroup Liaison
Karl Kempf, Intel

AI and the Law Subgroup Liaison
Edwina Rissland, University of Massachusetts

AI and Business Subgroup Liaison
Dan O'Leary, University of Southern California

AA

PROGR

Sunday, July 29

Registration: **Hynes Convention Center, Hall B 7:30 am—6:00 pm**

Workshops: 8:00 am—6:00 pm

Monday, July 30

Registration: **Hynes Convention Center, Hall B 7:30 am—6:00 pm**

MA Tutorials: 9:00 am—1:00 pm

Workshops: 8:00 am—6:00 pm

Tuesday, July 31

Registration: **Hynes Convention Center, Hall B 7:30 am—6:00 pm**

Workshops: 8:00 am—6:00 pm

Exhibit Program: Hynes Convention Cen

AI On-Line: Hynes Convention Center 9:30 am—11:30 am

Technical Session: Plenary Address 8:30 am—10:40 am

Introduction—Raj Reddy, Past President AAAI
AAAI Presidental Address—Daniel G. Bobrow, Xerox Palo Alto Research Center, "Dimensions of Interaction: Looking Towards an Interaction Level"
Invited Speaker—Samuel Fuller, Vice President, Corporate Research & Architectures, Digital Equipment Corporation, "Why Is It So Hard Moving AI To Reality"

Technical Session: 11:00 am—12:40 pm

Invited Speaker—Ronald Brachman, AT&T Bell Laboratories, "The Future of Knowledge Representation"
Automated Reasoning: Distributed and Parallel Systems
Machine Learning: Knowledge Based Inductive Learning
Commonsense Reasoning: Reasoning with Mulitple Models
Cognitive Modelling: Case-Based Reasoning

Wednesday, August 1

Registration: **Hynes Convention Center, Hall B 7:30 am—6:00 pm**

Workshops: 8:00 am—6:00 pm

Exhibit Program: Hynes Convention Center, Halls C & D 10:00 am—6:00 pm

Technial Session: 8:30 am—10:10 am

Invited Speaker—Jon Doyle, Massachusetts Institute of Technology, "Rationality & Its Roles in Reasoning"
Intelligent Multi-Media Interfaces
Machine Learning: Learning & Problem Solving
Automated Reasoning: Constraint Satisfaction Problems I
Vision
Automated Reasoning: Theorem Proving I & Program Synthesis

Technical Session: 11:00 am—12:40 pm

Invited Panel—"User Modeling & User Interfaces"
Automated Reasoning: Evidential Reasoning
Machine Learning: Inductive Learning II & Relational and Probabilistic Models
Automated Reasoning: Planning I
Knowledge Representation: Inheritance
Theorem Proving II: Term Rewriting

Thursday, August 2

Registration: **Hynes Convention Center, Hall B 7:30 am—6:00 pm**

Workshops: 8:00 am—6:00 pm

Exhibit Program: Hynes Convention Center, Halls C & D 10:00 am—5:00 pm

Technical Session: 8:30 am—10:10 pm

Invited Speaker—David McAllester, Massachussetts Institute of Technology, "Truth Maintance Systems"
Natural Language: Interpretation
Machine Learning: Inductive Learning II
Robotics: Robot Planning
Knowledge Representation: Representation & Uncertainty

Technical Session: 11:00 am—12:40 pm

Highlights from the Innovative Applications of Artificial Intelligence Conference, May 1-3, 1990, Part I
Intelligent Interfaces of Plan Recognition
Commonsense Reasoning: Model Based Diagnosis of Design I
Automated Reasoning: Planning II
Knowledge Representation: Complexity & Expressiveness

Friday, August 3

Registration: **Hynes Convention Center, Hall B 7:30 am—11:30 am**

Technical Session: 8:30 am—10:10 am

Invited Speaker—David Waltz, Thinking Machines Corp., "Massively Parallel AI"
Commonsense Reasoning: Model-Based Diagnosis II
Machine Learning: Generalization & Specialization
Robotics: Intelligent Mobile Robots
Knowledge Representation: Architectures

Technical Session: Plenary Address 11:00 am—12:40 pm

Introduction—Daniel G. Bobrow, President AAAI
Invited Speaker—Craig Fields, Department of Defense, "AI & the National Technological Infrastructure"

90

EDULE

2:00 pm—6:00 pm

2:00 pm—6:00 pm

12:00 pm—7:00 pm

cal Session: 2:10 pm—3:50 pm

Panel—"AI & Software Engineering: Will the Twain er Meet?"
Language: Discourse
e Learning: Connectionist Methods
edge Representation: Causality & Introspection
ated Reasoning: Truth Maintenance Systems

Technical Session: 4:40 pm—6:40 pm

Invited Speaker—David Haussler, University of California, Santa Cruz, "Probably Approximately Correct Learning"
Automated Reasoning: Distributed AI
Knowledge Acquistion & Expert Systems Design Methodologies
Knowledge Representation: Temporal & Spatial Reasoning
Automated Reasoning: Search

Reception

Copley Marriott
7:00 pm—9:00 pm

e: 1:30 pm—3:30 am

WP Tutorials: 2:00 pm—6:00 pm

Laboratory Tours:

7:00 pm-10:00 pm

ical Session: 2:10 pm—3:50 pm

ghts from the Innovative Applications of Artificial ligence Conference, May 1-3, 1990, Part II
Speaker—Stanley Rosenschein, Teleos Research, asoning and Acting Real Time"
onsense Reasoning: Qualitative Modelling of sical Systems
ne Learning: Discovery & Learning Robots
ated Reasoning: Constraint Satisfaction Problems III
edge Representation: Default Representations

Technical Session: 4:40 pm—6:20 pm

AI and Education
Machine Learning: Speed Up Learning
Automated Reasoning: Planning III
Knowledge Representation: Data Bases & Connectionism

Papers

Automated Reasoning

Planning

Search

Theorem Proving and Program Synthesis

Truth Maintenance Systems

Cognitive Modeling

Case-Based Reasoning

Commonsense Reasoning

Model-Based Diagnosis and Design

Qualitative Modeling of Physical Systems

Reasoning with Multiple Models

Education and AI

Intelligent Interfaces

Multimedia

Plan Recognition

Knowledge Acquisition

Expert System Design Methodologies

Knowledge Representation

Causality and Introspection

Complexity and Expressiveness

Connectionism

Default Representations

Learning and Problem Solving

Natural Language

Discourse

Interpretation

Robotics

Vision

Invited Talks & Panels

Panel: AI and Software Engineering

Panel: User Modeling and User Interfaces

Papers

Automated Reasoning

Complexity of K-Tree Structured Constraint Satisfaction Problems

Eugene C. Freuder[1]

Department of Computer Science
University of New Hampshire
Durham, New Hampshire 03824

Abstract

Trees have played a key role in the study of constraint satisfaction problems because problems with tree structure can be solved efficiently. It is shown here that a family of generalized trees, k-trees, can offer increasing representational complexity for constraint satisfaction problems, while maintaining a bound on computational complexity linear in the number of variables and exponential in k. Additional results are obtained for larger classes of graphs known as partial k-trees. These methods may be helpful even when the original problem does not have k-tree or partial k-tree structure. Specific tradeoffs are suggested between representational power and computational complexity.

1 Introduction

A *constraint satisfaction problem* (*CSP*) involves finding values for variables subject to constraints on what combinations of values are allowed. Constraint satisfaction problems occur widely in artificial intelligence. Recently they have received particular attention in the domains of scheduling and temporal reasoning.

Judea Pearl has observed that a primary advantage of viewing AI problems in CSP terms is our ability to identify certain "islands of tractability" among CSP problems, classes of problems that admit efficient solution. The significance of such classes is increased by techniques for "massaging" problems outside these classes to fit into or utilize these classes.

Up until now there has been one major tractable island, the class of tree structured problems. In this paper I identify a "chain" of such islands, generalizations of tree structures, which considerably expand the "tractable topography" of the CSP world. The tractability of these classes varies inversely with the representational complexity of the problems in the class, but the solution effort is always linear in the number of problem variables.

We will restrict our attention here to binary constraint satisfaction problems, in which the given constraints involve two variables. (Non-binary CSPs are shown to be "reducible" to binary CSPs in [Rossi, Dhar, Petrie, 89].) A binary CSP can be represented by a *constraint network*, in which the nodes represent variables and the links represent constraints.

The general constraint satisfaction problem is NP-complete. However, tree structured problems (those with tree structured constraint networks) have a worst case complexity bound that is linear in the number of problem variables [Mackworth and Freuder, 84]. If there are n variables, and no variable has more than d values to choose from, a tree structured CSP can be solved in $O(nd^2)$ time [Dechter and Pearl, 88].

K-trees [Beineke and Pippert, 71; Rose, 74] generalize trees. Trees are 1-trees. The central result of this paper is the demonstration that CSPs whose constraint networks are k-trees can be solved in $O(nd^{k+1})$ time. Note that we are saying that the complexity of a k-tree structured CSP is bounded by a linear function in the number of variables as long as we maintain the original k-tree structure and d bound when increasing the size of the problem.

Further results are described briefly for larger classes of graphs known as k-chordal graphs and partial k-trees. Partial k-trees are characterized in a manner that generalizes the characterization of forests in [Freuder, 82].

Methods have been developed to utilize tree structures in solving general CSPs [Dechter and Pearl, 88]. K-trees now provide us with a range of "target" structures of increasing complexity that we can consider utilizing in similar fashion.

Jeavons has introduced the issue of the expressive power of constraint networks [Jeavons, 89]. I show that the class of partial p-tree structured networks have less expressive power than the class of partial q-tree structured networks for p less than q. Combined with the complexity bounds indicated above, this suggests a tradeoff between computational complexity and expressive power [Levesque and Brachman, 1985].

Another tradeoff arises in utilizing k-trees as target structures in a *partial* constraint satisfaction process [Freuder, 89]. Any CSP can be solved in time exponential in k by removing enough constraints to give the problem a k-tree structure. In the worst case this would necessitate removing a number of constraints equal to the number of edges in a complete graph of n-k vertices.

The 2-tree case is of some special interest. "Minimum

1. This material is based in part upon work supported by the National Science Foundation under Grant No. IRI-8601209 and Grant No. IRI-8913040.

IFI networks" are 2-trees [Wald and Coburn, 83]. "Regular width-2 constraint graphs" are partial 2-trees; this paper improves on the $O(n^3d^3)$ complexity bound for regular width-2 CSPs reported in [Dechter and Pearl, 88]. "Series-parallel graphs" are partial 2-trees [Arnborg, 85].

Many of the basic concepts used here have been rediscovered in different forms in different fields at different times. This is a testimony to their importance, but makes issues of attribution and terminology difficult. [Dechter and Pearl, 88] provides useful background from an AI CSP perspective; [Arnborg, 85] provides useful background from the perspective of work on combinatorial graph algorithms.

The complexity results exploit the connection between CSP theory and combinatorial graph theory. Some background material in these areas is presented in section 2 along with examples of k-trees. The complexity bounds are derived in section 3. Section 4 discusses representational complexity and suggests how k-trees can be utilized even when the original problem does not have k-tree structure. Section 5 summarizes the results.

2 Background

2.1 Constraint Satisfaction Problems

A *binary constraint satisfaction problem* (*binary CSP*) consists of a set of variables, each with a domain of potential values, and a set of binary constraints, which specify pairs of allowable variable values. In a *constraint graph* variables are represented as vertices and constraints as edges.

The n-queens problem is often used as a CSP example. This problem involves placing n queens on an n by n chessboard such that no two queens attack one another. In the constraint graph for this problem each pair of vertices is connected by an edge.

A *solution* to a CSP is an assignment of one value to each of the problem variables such that any pair of values satisfies (is allowed by) the constraint between the corresponding variables. A constraint graph for a CSP *represents* the set of solutions to the CSP. Two constraint graphs are *equivalent* if they represent the same set of solutions.

An *ordered constraint graph* [Freuder, 82] is a constraint graph together with an ordering of the vertices, $v_1 \ldots v_n$. The *width* [Freuder, 82] *of a vertex* in an ordered constraint graph is the number of edges from that vertex back to vertices preceding it in the ordering. The *width of an ordered constraint graph* is the maximal width of its vertices and the *width of a constraint graph* is the minimal width of all the ordered constraint graphs obtained by utilizing every ordering of the vertices.

The well-known backtrack search process is a standard method for solving CSPs. An ordering of the variables of a CSP is *backtrack-free* [Freuder, 82] if backtrack search using that variable order can always find a value for a variable consistent with previous choices of values for variables.

Dechter and Pearl present an *adaptive-consistency* procedure [Dechter and Pearl, 88], which transforms an ordered constraint graph, O, into an equivalent ordered constraint graph, I, with a backtrack-free variable order. I is called the *induced graph* of O. The width of I is called the *induced width of the ordered constraint graph* O. Define the *induced width of a constraint graph* G to be the minimal induced width of all the ordered constraint graphs of G.

The adaptive-consistency procedure from [Dechter and Pearl, 88] is shown below:

```
Adaptive-consistency(X1,...,Xn)
begin
    for r=n to 1 by -1 do
    compute PARENTS(Xr)
    perform Consistency(Xr, PARENTS(Xr))
    connect by arcs
      all elements in PARENTS(Xr)
      (if they are not yet connected)
end
```

The X_i are variables in an ordered constraint graph. PARENTS(X_i) returns the set of variables preceding X_i in the ordering that are connected to X_i by an edge in the graph. (Notice that the procedure may add edges to the graph.) The procedure Consistency(v,S) records a constraint on all the variables of S (if S has j variables, this will be a j-ary constraint). The constraint permits an assignment of values to the variables of S only if the assignment is consistent with at least one (consistent) value for v. To determine consistency Dechter and Pearl specify that all constraints be used (old or new) that involve v and a subset (possibly empty) of variables from S. The algorithm basically works to enforce a backtrack-free ordering by adding constraints that prevent one from making choices that will lead to inconsistency.

Define the *adaptive-consistency level* achieved by the adaptive-consistency procedure to be one greater than the maximum size of the PARENTS sets encountered during the running of the algorithm.

An $O(\exp(W^*(\pi)+1))$ bound is given in [Dechter and Pearl, 88] for adaptive-consistency, where $W^*(\pi)$ is the induced width of the constraint graph with ordering π. The bound on the algorithm can be expressed as $O(nd^{W^*(\pi)+1})$. On each of n-1 passes through the outer loop the consistency procedure needs to check that there is a value for X_r consistent with any consistent assignment of values to the parents of X_r. There are at most $W^*(\pi)$ parents. There are at most $d^{W^*(\pi)+1}$ combinations of values for the parents together with X_r. For each of these there are at most $2^{W^*(\pi)}$ constraints to check that involve X_r and some (possibly empty) set of parents.

2.2 Combinatorial Graph Theory

A *graph*, G=(V,E), consists of a set of vertices, V, and a set of edges, E, where each edge is a two-element subset of V. An edge is *incident* to the two vertices in the edge. Two vertices are *adjacent* if they belong to the same edge. A *complete* graph is one that contains all possible edges. The *subgraph* of a graph G *induced by* a subset of vertices V' from G, written G(V'), consists of the vertices V' together with all edges in G incident only to vertices in V'.

Define the *neighborhood* of a vertex v as the set of vertices adjacent to v, and the *degree* of v as the number of vertices in its neighborhood.

A graph G is a *k-tree* [Beineke and Pippert, 71; Rose, 74] if:

1. G has k vertices and is complete

or

2. a. there is a vertex, v, of degree k, whose neighborhood induces a complete graph

   and

   b. the graph obtained by removing v and all edges incident to it from G is a k-tree.

A *simplicial* vertex of a k-tree is one that satisfies part 2 of the definition. Call the complete graph of k vertices the *trivial k-tree.*

K-trees are structures that can be built as follows: start with a complete graph of k vertices; each time you add a new vertex add an edge between it and k previous vertices that already form a complete subgraph (each pair of vertices is joined by an edge). For example, 1-trees are just trees, and can be built as follows: start with a single vertex, connect each new vertex to one of the previous vertices.

The constraint graph for the n-queens problem is an n-tree; it is also an (n-1)-tree. For example the constraint graph for the 4-queens problem (place 4 non-attacking queens on a 4 by 4 board) is a 3-tree: it can be viewed as a complete graph of 3 vertices (a triangle) plus a fourth vertex connected to each of those three.

Now consider the following variation on the n-queens problem, which I will call the n/m-queens problem. The n/m-queens problem requires only that a given queen cannot attack (or be attacked by) any queen in the previous m rows. The n/m-queens problem has an m-tree constraint graph. The 4/2-queens problem has a 2-tree constraint graph.

A *partial graph* of G consists of the vertices of G and a subset of the edges of G. A subgraph of G is a partial graph of an induced subgraph of G. A *partial k-tree* [Arnborg, 86], is a subgraph of a k-tree; the k-tree is termed an *embedding* of the partial k-tree. Partial 1-trees are forests. Any graph is a partial k-tree for sufficiently large k.

I define a *weak k-tree* as the class of graphs that result when "k" is replaced by "≤k" and "k-tree" by "weak k-tree" in the k-tree definition. The weak k-trees are the k-chordal graphs [Chandrasekharan and Hedetniemi, 88].

3 Computational Complexity

Tree structured problems have been solved with backtrack-free search by achieving a consistency level greater than their width. (Partial) k-tree structured problems are solved here with backtrack-free search by achieving an adaptive consistency level greater than their induced width.

3.1 K-Trees

Dechter and Pearl point out, citing [Arnborg, Corneil and Proskurowski, 87], that determing the induced width, W*, of a constraint graph is an NP-complete problem. However, we will see that for k-trees W*=k (except for the trivial k-tree with k vertices, for which W*=k-1). If the constraint graph is a k-tree it can be recognized as such, if necessary, and an ordered constraint graph with induced width k can be obtained, in O(n) time (regarding k as a constant). Adaptive-consistency can then obtain an equivalent ordered constraint graph with a backtrack-free variable ordering in $O(nd^{k+1})$ time. The backtrack-free search can be completed in O(nd) time. Taken together this provides the promised $O(nd^{k+1})$ bound for solving k-tree structured CSPs.

Arnborg (citing [Rose, 70]) states that k-trees "are easily recognized by a procedure which successively deletes vertices with completely connected neighborhoods" [Arnborg, 85]. I present here an algorithm that performs this recognition for a graph G, and returns an ordering of G with induced width k (k-1 if G is the trivial k-tree) in time linear in the number of vertices, n, for a fixed k.

Algorithm W:

Input: A constraint graph G and an integer k.

Output: If G is a k-tree, the algorithm returns an ordering of G with induced width k (k-1 for the trivial k-tree); if G is not a k-tree the algorithm reports failure.

1. Determine the degree of each vertex, store that number with the vertex, and place all the degree k vertices in a queue K. Sum the vertex degrees as you proceed; if and when the sum exceeds $2n\text{-}k\text{-}k^2$ (twice the number of edges in a k-tree), report failure.
2. For i = 1 to n-k
   - If K is empty, report failure.
   - If K is not empty:
     - Take a vertex v from K.
     - If the graph G(N) induced by the neighborhood N of v is not complete, report failure.
     - If G(N) is complete:
       - record v as the (n-i+1)th vertex in the ordering, remove v and its incident edges from G, subtract one from the degree count associated with the vertices in N and place vertices that now have degree k in the K queue.
3. If G is now a complete graph (of k vertices) choose the remaining vertices in any order to complete the vertex ordering. If G is not complete, report failure.

Theorem 1. A k-tree constraint graph with n vertices

can be recognized as a k-tree, and an ordered constraint graph of induced width k found (k-1 for the trivial k-tree), in O(n) time.

Proof. Algorithm W does the job. If G is the trivial k-tree, step 3 produces a width k-1 ordering. Adaptive-consistency will not change this width (there are no edges to add). If G is a k-tree with more than k vertices, for any vertex v with degree k the graph induced by the neighborhood of v must be complete, because the definition of k-trees implies that every vertex in a k-tree of more than k nodes is connected to at least k others that induce a complete graph. Any k-tree vertex with a neighborhood that induces the complete graph of k vertices is simplicial [Arnborg, 85; Rose, 70]. Therefore, by part 2 of the k-tree definition, if G is a k-tree it remains one after each pass through step 2. If G is a k-tree after step 2 it must satisfy part 1 of the definition and be the complete graph of k vertices. The ordering produced is such that the parent set of each vertex will already induce a complete graph, therefore adaptive-consistency does not change the width, which remains k.

A k-tree has k(k-1)/2+(n-k)k edges (count the edges as you apply the definition). That and the use of the K queue are the keys to maintaining an $O(nk^2)$ complexity bound for the algorithm. •

Theorem 2. The induced width, W*, of a non-trivial k-tree is k; for the trivial k-tree, W*=k-1. The induced width of a k-tree is equal to its width.

Proof. The trivial k-tree is the complete graph with k vertices, for which the width and the induced width are obviously equal to k-1. Now consider the non-trivial case. Theorem 1 demonstrates that W*≤k. The width of a graph is obviously ≤ its induced width and thus ≤ k. A k-tree with more than k vertices includes a complete graph of k+1 vertices, and regardless of how they are ordered the last one will have k parents. This demonstrates that the width and therefore the induced width are both ≥ k. Thus the width equals the induced width equals k. •

Theorem 3. Given an induced graph I, with induced width k, of an ordered constraint graph of a k-tree structured CSP; the CSP has n variables each with a domain of at most d values. A backtrack-free search using the ordering of I can be conducted with time bound O(nd).

Proof. The adaptive consistency procedure ensures that the ordering of the induced graph is backtrack-free [Dechter and Pearl, 88]. Thus to instantiate each of the n variables, we need at worst try each of the d possible values. For each value we need check at most 2^k constraints involving that variable and subsets of its parents. •

Theorem 4. A k-tree structured CSP can be solved in time $O(nd^{k+1})$.

Proof. Given a constraint graph G for the CSP we can use algorithm W to obtain an ordered constraint graph O with induced width k in O(n) time (Theorem 1). We can then apply adaptive-consistency to obtain an equivalent induced graph in $O(nd^{k+1})$ time, as discussed in section 2. Finally we can carry out a backtrack-free search in O(nd) time (Theorem 3). •

If we do not assume k to be a constant, we can derive an $O(n(2d)^{k+1})$ bound, taking into account the analysis of adaptive consistency presented in section 2.1.

3.2 Partial K-Trees

This section will sketch some extensions of the k-tree results to partial k-trees. It also contains a characterization of partial k-trees in terms of induced width.

Theorem 4 holds for weak k-trees. (As we will see below weak k-trees are partial k-trees; see also [Chandrasekharan and Hedetniemi, 1988]) The key observation (similar to one made by Arnborg, citing Rose [Arnborg, 85; Rose, 70]) is that the basic idea behind Theorem 1 of deleting vertices whose neighborhoods induce a complete graph still works. We can obtain an O(n) bound by modifying Algorithm W to maintain in place of the queue K a queue C of vertices whose adjacent vertices induce a complete graph of ≤k vertices.

If we have an embedding of a partial k-tree in a k-tree, we can go on to use the above methods on the embedding. Every partial k-tree with at least k vertices can be embedded in a k-tree without adding vertices [Arnborg, 86]. Even if we are given an embedding with more vertices than we started with we can simply throw away the extra and still have a weak k-tree (picture an ordering with induced width k, now throw away the extra vertices).

There is unfortunately no similar analog of Algorithm W known for easily recognizing partial k-trees and finding an embedding. There is an $O(n^{k+2})$ algorithm for doing so [Arnborg, 87], and more efficient methods are known for k=2 [Wald and Coburn, 83] and k=3 [Arnborg, 86] (and, of course, for k=1).

Theorem 2 can be extended to the following characterization of partial k-trees, which generalizes the characterization in [Freuder, 82] of forest-structured constraint graphs (partial 1-trees) as those with width≤1. Forests are 1-trees and the width of a 1-tree is equal to its induced width. (Compare with Arnborg's Theorem 3.1(iv) involving the "dimension" concept in [Arnborg, 85].)

The following theorem also serves to identify exactly when we can "induce" width ≤ k, namely when we start with a partial k-tree. K-tree embedding in that case provides a method for obtaining an ordered constraint graph with this induced width. Adaptive consistency, obtained with no more than $O(nd^{k+1})$ effort, then leads to backtrack-free search.

Theorem 5. A constraint graph has induced width≤k iff it is a partial k-tree.

Proof. If the graph has fewer than k vertices the theorem is trivial; assume there are at least k vertices. Suppose the graph, G, is a partial k-tree. It can be embedded in a k-tree with the same vertices. The k-tree will have width k. The partial k-tree's width will be, if anything, less.

Suppose G has induced width w≤k. Let I be an induced graph of an ordered constraint graph of G with induced width w. G is a partial graph of I. I is a weak k-tree. We will see that it can be extended to a k-tree by adding further edges (if necessary), i.e that weak k-trees are partial graphs of k-trees.

First add edges as needed so that the first k vertices in the ordering will induce a complete graph. If the graph has only k vertices we are done. If not add edges to connect the next vertex to the first k, if necessary. This k+1st vertex will now have a parent set that induces the complete graph of k vertices. I will demonstrate inductively that edges can be added as needed so that any remaining vertices will have such parent sets. The resulting graph will clearly satisfy the k-tree definition.

Assume that edges have been added as needed so that the first i vertices in the ordering after the initial k each have a set of parents that induces the complete graph of k vertices. Consider the i+1st vertex, v. Its parent set induces a complete graph (we have a weak k-tree). If its parent set contains k vertices, this step is complete. If its parents all lie within the first k vertices, simply add edges to connect v to all of the first k vertices. Otherwise, consider the parent set of the parent vertex, p, of v that is closest to v in the ordering. The vertex p will have a parent set that induces a complete graph of k vertices, and that parent set will already include the other parents of v. Simply add edges to connect v with as many of the parents of p as needed to bring the total number of parents of v up to k. The resulting set of parents for v will induce a complete graph of k vertices, as they are all in the complete graph of k+1 vertices induced by p and its parents. •

4 Representational Complexity

The representational complexity of k-trees can be analyzed in ways that suggest tradeoffs between representational power and computational complexity. Problems that do not have (partial) k-tree structure for a given k may still be viewed, in whole or in part, in (partial) k-tree terms.

4.1 Representational Power

It is of course in some sense obvious that 2-trees are more "representationally complex" than trees (1-trees), that representational complexity increases with increasing k. Thus the complexity bounds obtained for (partial) k-trees can be viewed as either a) expanding the range of problems for which we can guarantee a relatively efficient solution or b) expanding the representational complexity we can permit in formulating our problems while still maintaining relatively efficient bounds on the effort required to solve the problems.

In temporal reasoning, consideration has been given to restricting the expressive power of the relational language in order to guarantee computational tractability [van Beek, 89]. The results in this paper suggest another means of trading expressivity for tractability, namely restricting expressibility to k-tree structures. For example, by analogy with the n/m-queens example, one could ensure a partial k-tree structure in the constraint graph of the temporal relations in a narrative by insisting that no event could be temporally compared with any event more than k events previous in the narrative. Similar restrictions could be imposed to ensure tractability in scheduling problems.

A more precise notion of representational power permits a more formal analysis. Jeavons [Jeavons, 89] has raised the issue of the "expressive power" of constraint networks. He develops methods for actually counting the number of different solution sets that certain classes of constraint graphs can represent. The following theorem makes a qualitative rather than quantitative statement about the expressive power of partial k-trees.

Theorem 6. Let S_k be the set of solution sets represented by partial k-tree structured constraint graphs. S_p is a proper subset of S_q for p<q.

Proof. Since a partial p-tree is a partial q-tree (Theorem 5) clearly S_p is a subset of S_q. I will construct a partial q-tree structured constraint graph that represents a solution set that cannot be represented by a partial p-tree structured constraint graph.

Consider the following constraint graph, G, with q+1 vertices. G is complete. The complete graph with q+1 vertices is a q-tree. Each variable represented has a domain of q+1 values, the numbers 1 through q+1. A constraint $c(v_i,v_j)$ between variables v_i and v_j specifies that any pair of values is allowed except the pair (i,j).

I will show that the complete graph with q+1 vertices is the only graph that can be used to represent the solution set, S, of this CSP. Therefore, since the complete graph of q+1 vertices cannot be a partial p-tree no partial p-tree can represent S.

Suppose we remove an edge, e, from G, between v_i and v_j for some i and j. Now the constraint c(i,j) cannot be present to prevent solutions that include i for v_i and j for v_j. How can we make up for that? We cannot. No pairs can be removed from the other constraints, as all those pairs are allowed in solutions in the solution set. Adding pairs, or removing other constraints (edges), can only, if anything, increase the number of solutions; CSPs are monotonic in that respect. There are no new constraints to add. Thus the complete graph with q+1 vertices is the only constraint graph that can represent S. •

4.2 Reduction

Various methods have been proposed for expanding the applicability of tree structures in constraint satisfaction problem solving. These methods suggest analogous techniques for utilizing (partial) k-tree structures, even when the original problem does not have such structure. (Of course, the additional complexity permitted by k-tree structure, as opposed to tree structure, should decrease the need for reduction techniques.)

For example, Dechter and Pearl have observed that if we remove enough vertices from an arbitrary constraint graph (along with edges incident to the vertices) we will be left with a tree or forest structure [Dechter and Pearl, 88]. They have studied how arbitrary CSPs can thus be reduced to CSPs with tree (or forest) structure by removing or instantiating variables that comprise a "cycle-cutset" for the constraint graph.

Analogous methods can be used to reduce arbitrary CSPs to k-trees or partial k-trees. In particular, partial 2-trees can be characterized as graphs that do not contain a subgraph homeomorphic to K_4, the complete graph of 4 vertices (i.e. no subgraph is K_4 or K_4 plus additional degree-two vertices) [Arnborg, 85]. Thus we could utilize "K_4-cutsets" to reduce constraint graphs to partial 2-trees.

The cycle-cutset work can be viewed as providing complexity bounds for CSPs in terms of how close their constraint graphs are to having tree or forest structure. In general the complexity of a CSP can be analyzed in terms of the number of variables whose removal would leave a (partial) k-tree structure. For example, the constraint graph for the 4-queens problem can be reduced to a tree by removing two of the four vertices; it can be reduced to a 2-tree by removing a single vertex.

Closeness to k-tree structure can also be measured in terms of constraints. Freuder [Freuder, 89] discusses partial constraint satisfaction problems, which involve weakening the original problem in order to solve an overconstrained problem, or solve a properly constrained problem faster. The following theorem provides an upper bound on how many constraints we have to ignore in order to force a problem into a k-tree structure, thus ensuring that we can solve it in time linear in the number of variables and only exponential in k.

Theorem 7. Any constraint graph, G, can be made into a k-tree structured constraint graph by removing at most a number of edges (constraints) equal to the number of edges in a complete graph of n-k vertices.

Proof. As indicated earlier the number of edges in a k-tree is $k(k-1)/2+(n-k)k$. Suppose G is a complete graph with n vertices. It then has $n(n-1)/2$ edges. We can make G into a k-tree by removing $(n(n-1)/2)-(k(k-1)/2+(n-k)k)=(n-k)(n-k-1)/2$ edges, i.e. the number of edges in a complete graph with n-k vertices. If G is not complete we can first add edges to make it complete (these will correspond to the trivial constraint that allows all pairs, which is normally not included in the constraint graph). We can form a k-tree by removing edges as before (only in the worst case will they all be edges of the original graph). •

For example, the constraint graph for the 4-queens problem can be reduced to a tree by removing three edges. It can be reduced to a 2-tree by removing a single edge.

5 Conclusion

1. The $O(nd^2)$ bound on the complexity of tree structured CSPs generalizes to an $O(nd^{k+1})$ bound for k-trees.

2. CSPs with partial k-tree structure (and every CSP has partial k-tree structure for some k) can be solved in $O(nd^{k+1})$ time once a k-tree embedding has been found (which may require $O(n^{k+2})$ time).

3. The identification of graphs with width ≤1 as forests generalizes to the identification of graphs with induced width ≤k as partial k-trees.

4. Representational power increases with increasing k for partial k-trees.

5. Reduction methods can be used to broaden the applicability of (partial) k-tree results.

Acknowledgments. This work profited from discussion with Pilar de la Torre and Raymond Greenlaw.

References

[Arnborg, 85] Efficient algorithms for combinatorial problems on graphs with bounded decomposability - a survey, *BIT* 25: 2-23.

[Arnborg and Proskurowski, 86] Characterization and recognition of partial 3-trees, *Siam J. Alg. Disc. Meth.* 7(2).

[Arnborg, Corneil and Proskurowski, 87] Complexity of finding embeddings in a *k*-tree, *Siam J. Alg. Disc. Meth.* 8(2).

[Beineke and Pippert, 71] Properties and characterizations of *k*-trees, *Mathematika* 18: 141-151.

[Chandrasekharan and Hedetniemi, 88] Fast parallel algorithms for tree decomposing and parsing partial k-trees, *Proc. of the 26th Annual Allerton Conference on Comm., Cont. and Comp.*, Urbana-Champaign, Illinois.

[Dechter and Pearl, 88] Network-based heuristics for constraint-satisfaction problems, *Art. Int.* 34(1).

[Freuder, 82] A sufficient condition for backtrack-free search, *JACM* 29(1).

[Freuder, 89] Partial constraint satisfaction, *IJCAI-89*.

[Jeavons, 89] The expressive power of constraint networks, Dept. of C.S., Univ. of London, UK.

[Levesque and Brachman, 85] A fundamental tradeoff in knowledge representation and reasoning (revised version), in *Readings in Knowledge Representation*, Brachman and Levesque, editors, Morgan Kaufmann, Los Altos, CA.

[Mackworth and Freuder, 84] The complexity of some polynomial network consistency algorithms for constraint satisfaction problems, *Art. Int.* 25(1).

[Rose, 70] Triangulated graphs and the elimination process, *Journal of Mathematical Analysis and Applications* 32: 597-609.

[Rose, 74] On simple characterizations of k-trees, *Discrete Math* 7: 317-322.

[Rossi, Dhar and Petrie, 89] On the equivalence of constraint satisfaction problems, MCC Technical Report ACT-AI-222-89. MCC, Austin, Texas 78759.

[van Beek, 89] Approximation algorithms for temporal reasoning, *IJCAI-89*.

[Wald and Colbourn, 83] Steiner trees, partial 2-trees, and minimum IFI networks, *Networks* 13: 159-167.

Tree Decomposition with Applications to Constraint Processing

Itay Meiri, Rina Dechter † and Judea Pearl

Cognitive Systems Laboratory
Computer Science Department
University of California
Los Angeles, CA 90024
itay@cs.ucla.edu, dechter@techsel.bitnet, judea@cs.ucla.edu

Abstract

This paper concerns the task of removing redundant information from a given knowledge base, and restructuring it in the form of a tree, so as to admit efficient problem solving routines. We offer a novel approach which guarantees the removal of all redundancies that hide a tree structure. We develop a polynomial time algorithm that, given an arbitrary constraint network, generates a precise tree representation whenever such a tree can be extracted from the input network; otherwise, the fact that no tree representation exists is acknowledged, and the tree generated may serve as a good approximation to the original network.

1. Introduction

This paper concerns the problem of finding computationally attractive structures for representing constraint-based knowledge.

It has long been recognized that sparse constraint networks, especially those that form trees, are extremely efficient both in storage space and in query processing. A densely-specified network may hide such a desirable structure, and the challenge is to identify and remove redundant links until the natural structure underlying the knowledge base is recovered. The general issue of removing redundancies has been investigated in the literature of relational databases [Maier 1983, Dechter 1987], as well as in the context of constraint networks [Dechter and Dechter 1987]. This paper offers a novel approach which guarantees the removal of all redundancies that hide a tree structure.

* This work was supported in part by the National Science Foundation Grant # IRI 8815522 and an Air Force Grant # AFOSR 880177

† Current address: Computer Science Department, Technion - Israel Institute of Technology, Haifa 32000, Israel.

Formally, the problem addressed is as follows. Given a constraint network, find whether it can be transformed into a tree-structured network without loss of information; if the answer is positive find such a tree, if the answer is negative, acknowledge failure.

This paper develops a polynomial time algorithm that, given an arbitrary network, generates a tree representation having the following characteristics:

1. The tree represents the network exactly whenever such a tree can be extracted from the input network, and

2. If no tree representation exists, the fact is acknowledged, and the tree generated may serve as a good approximation to the original network.

The algorithm works as follows. We examine all triplets of variables, identify the redundancies that exist in each triplet, and assign weights to the edges in accordance with the redundancies discovered. The algorithm returns a maximum-spanning-tree relative to these weights.

An added feature of the algorithm is that when the tree generated is recognized as an approximation, it can be further tightened by adding edges until a precise representation obtains. This technique may be regarded as an alternative redundancy-removal scheme to the one proposed in [Dechter and Dechter 1987], accompanied with polynomial complexity and performance guarantees.

2. Preliminaries and nomenclature

We first review the basic concepts of constraint satisfaction [Montanari 1974, Mackworth 1977, Dechter and Pearl 1987].

A **network of binary constraints** consists of a set of variables $\{X_1, \ldots, X_n\}$ and a set of binary constraints on the variables. The **domain** of variable X_i, denoted by D_i, defines the set of values X_i may assume. A **binary constraint,** R_{ij}, on variables X_i and X_j, is a subset of the Cartesian product of their domains (i.e., $R_{i,j} \subseteq D_i \times D_j$); it specifies the permitted pairs of values for X_i and X_j.

A binary constraint R is **tighter** than R' (or conversely R' is more **relaxed** than R), denoted by $R \subseteq R'$, if every pair of values allowed by R is also allowed by R'. The most relaxed constraint is the **universal** constraint which allows all pairs of the Cartesian product.

A tuple that satisfies all the constraints is called a **solution.** The set of all solutions to network R constitutes a relation, denoted by $rel(R)$, whose attributes are the variables names. Two networks with the same variable set are **equivalent** if they represent the same relation.

A binary CSP is associated with a **constraint graph,** where node i represents variable X_i, and an edge between nodes i and j represents a **direct constraint,** R_{ij}, between them, which is not the universal constraint. Other constraints are **induced** by paths connecting i and j. The constraint induced on i and j by a path of length m through nodes $i_0 = i, i_1, \ldots, i_m = j$, denoted by $R_{i_0, i_1, \ldots, i_m}$, represents the **composition** of the constraints along the path. A pair of values $x \in D_{i_0}$ and $y \in D_{i_m}$ is allowed by the path constraint, if there exists a sequence of values $v_1 \in D_{i_1}, \ldots, v_{m-1} \in D_{i_{m-1}}$ such that $R_{i_0,i_1}(x, v_1), R_{i_1,i_2}(v_1, v_2), \ldots,$ and $R_{i_{m-1},i_m}(v_{m-1}, y)$.

A network whose direct constraints are tighter than any of its induced path constraints is called **path consistent**. Formally, a path P of length m through nodes $i_0, i_1, \ldots, i_m$ is consistent, if and only if $R_{i_0,i_m} \subseteq R_{i_0,i_1,\ldots,i_m}$. Similarly, arc (i,j) is consistent if for any value $x \in D_i$, there exists a value $y \in D_j$ such that $R_{ij}(x,y)$. A *network* is arc and path consistent if all its arcs and paths are consistent. Any network can be converted into an equivalent arc and path consistent form in time $O(n^3)$(1) [Mackworth and Freuder 1985]. In this paper we assume all networks are arc and path consistent.

Not every relation can be represented by a binary constraint network. The best network that approximates a given relation is called the **minimal network**; its constraints are the projections of the relation on all pairs of variables, namely, each pair of values allowed by the minimal network participates in at least one solution. Thus, the minimal network displays the tightest constraints between every pair of variables. Being a projection of the solution set, the minimal network is always arc and path consistent.

(1) Actually, the complexity is $O(n^3k^3)$, where k is the domain size; however, for simplicity, we assume the domain size is constant.

3. Problem statement

We now define the **tree decomposability problem**. First, we introduce the notion of **tree decomposition.**

Definition. A network R is **tree decomposable** if there exists a tree-structured network T, on the same set of variables, such that R and T are equivalent (i.e., represent the same relation). T is said to be a **tree decomposition** of R, and the relation ρ represented by R is said to be tree decomposable (by T). R is **tree reducible** if there exists a tree T such that R is decomposable by T, and for all $(i,j) \in T$, $T_{ij} = R_{ij}$, namely the constraints in T are taken *unaltered* from R.

The **tree decomposability problem** for networks is defined as follows. Given a network R, decide if R is tree decomposable. If the answer is positive find a tree decomposition of R, else, acknowledge failure. The **tree reducibility problem** is defined in a similar way. A related problem of decomposing a relation was treated in [Dechter 1987], and will be discussed in Section 6.

Example 1. Consider a relation ρ_1 shown in Figure 1. The minimal network is given by

$$M_{A,B} = M_{A,C} = M_{B,C} = \{00, 11\}$$

$$M_{A,D} = M_{B,D} = M_{C,D} = \{00, 10, 11\},$$

where constraints are encoded as lists of permitted pairs. Any tree containing two edges from $\{AB, AC, BC\}$ is a tree decomposition of M; for example, $T_1 = \{AB, AC, AD\}$ and $T_2 = \{AB, BC, BD\}$. M is also tree reducible, since the link constraints in these trees are identical to the corresponding constraints in M.

A	B	C	D
0	0	0	0
1	1	1	0
1	1	1	1

Figure 1. ρ_1 – a tree-decomposable relation.

Example 2. Consider a relation ρ_2 shown in Figure 2. $T = \{AB, AC, AD, AE\}$ is the only tree decomposition of

ρ_2.

A	B	C	D	E
0	1	1	0	0
0	1	1	0	1
0	1	1	1	0
0	1	1	1	1
1	0	0	1	1
1	0	1	1	1
1	1	0	1	1
1	1	1	1	1

Figure 2. ρ_2 – a tree-decomposable relation.

The rest of the paper is organized as follows. Sections 4 and 5 describe the tree decomposition scheme, while Section 6 presents extensions and ramifications of this scheme. Proofs of theorems can be found in [Meiri, Dechter and Pearl 1990].

4. Tree decomposition schemes

Tree decomposition comprises two subtasks: searching for a skeletal spanning tree, and determining the link constraints on that tree. If the input network is minimal, the second subtask is superfluous because, clearly, the link constraints must be taken unaltered from the corresponding links in the input network, namely, decomposability coincides with reducibility. We shall, therefore, first focus attention on minimal networks, and postpone the treatment of general networks to Section 6. Our problem can now be viewed as searching for a tree skeleton through the space of spanning trees. Since there are n^{n-2} spanning trees on n vertices (Cayley's Theorem [Even 1979]), a method more effective than exhaustive enumeration is required.

The notion of **redundancy** plays a central role in our decomposition schemes. Consider a consistent path $P = i_0, i_1, \ldots, i_m$. Recall that the direct constraint R_{i_0,i_m} is tighter than the path constraint $R_{i_0,i_1,\ldots,i_m}$. If the two constraints are identical we say that edge (i,j) is **redundant** with respect to path P; it is also said to be redundant in the cycle C consisting of nodes $\{i_0, i_1, \ldots, i_m\}$. If the direct constraint is strictly tighter than the path constraint, we say that (i,j) is **nonredundant** with respect to P (or nonredundant in C). Another interpretation of redundancy is that any instantiation of the variables $\{i_0, i_1, \ldots, i_m\}$ which satisfies the constraints along P is allowed by the direct constraint R_{i_0,i_m}. Conversely, nonredundancy implies that there exists at least one instantiation which violates R_{i_0,i_m}.

Definition. Let T be a tree, and let $e = (i,j) \notin T$. The unique path in T connecting i and j, denoted by $P_T(e)$, is called the **supporting path** of e (relative to T). The cycle $C_T(e) = P_T(e) \cup \{e\}$ is called the **supporting cycle** of e (relative to T).

Theorem 1. Let $G = (V,E)$ be a minimal network. G is decomposable by a tree T if and only if every edge in $E - T$ is redundant in its supporting cycle.

Theorem 1 gives a method of testing whether a network G is decomposable by a given tree T. The test takes $O(n^3)$ time, as there are $O(n^2)$ edges in $E - T$, and each redundancy test is $O(n)$.

Illustration. Consider Example 1. Tree $T_1 = \{AB, AC, AD\}$ is a tree decomposition, since edges BC, BD and CD are redundant in triangles $\{A, B, C\}$, $\{A, B, D\}$ and $\{A, C, D\}$, respectively. On the other hand, $T_2 = \{AD, BD, CD\}$ is not a tree decomposition since edge AB is nonredundant in triangle $\{A, B, D\}$ (indeed, the tuple $(A = 1, B = 0, C = 0, D = 0)$ is a solution of T_2, but is not part of ρ_1).

An important observation about redundant edges is that they can be deleted from the network without affecting the set of solutions; the constraint specified by a redundant edge is already induced by other paths in the network. This leads to the following decomposition scheme. Repeatedly select an edge redundant in some cycle C, delete it from the network, and continue until there are no cycles in the network. This algorithm, called TD-1, is depicted in Figure 3.

Algorithm TD-1

1. $N \leftarrow E$;
2. while there are redundant edges in N do
3. select an edge e which is redundant in some cycle C, and
4. $N \leftarrow N - \{e\}$
5. end;
6. if N forms a tree then G is decomposable by N
7. else G is not tree decomposable;

Figure 3. TD-1 – A tree decomposition algorithm.

Theorem 2. Let G be a minimal network. Algorithm TD-1 produces a tree T if and only if G is decomposable by T.

To prove Theorem 2, we must show that if the network is tree decomposable, *any* sequence of edge removals will generate a tree. A phenomenon which might prevent the algorithm from reaching a tree structure is that of a **stiff cycle**, i.e., one in which every edge is nonredundant (e.g. cycle $\{B, D, C, E\}$ in Example 2). It can be shown, however, that one of the edges in such a cycle must be redundant in another cycle.

The proof of Theorem 2 rests on the following three lemmas, which also form the theoretical basis to Section 5.

Lemma 1. Let G be a path consistent network and let $e = (i_0, i_m)$ be an edge redundant in cycle $C = \{i_0, i_1, \ldots, i_m\}$. If $C' = \{i_0, i_1, \ldots, i_k, i_{k+l}, \ldots, i_m\}$ is an interior cycle created by chord (i_k, i_l), then e is redundant in C'.

Lemma 2. Let G be a minimal network decomposable by a tree T, and let $e \in T$ be a tree edge redundant in some cycle C. Then, there exists an edge $e' \in C$, $e' \notin T$, such that e is redundant in the supporting cycle of e'.

Lemma 3. Let G be a minimal network decomposable by a tree T. If there exist $e \in T$ and $e' \notin T$ such that e is redundant in the supporting cycle of e', then G is decomposable by $T' = T - \{e\} \cup \{e'\}$.

Algorithm TD-1, though conceptually simple, is highly inefficient. The main drawback is that in Step 3 we might need to check redundancy against an exponential number of cycles. In the next section we show a polynomial algorithm which overcomes this difficulty.

5. Tree, triangle and redundancy labelings

In this section we present a new tree decomposition scheme, which can be regarded as an efficient version of TD-1, whereby the criterion for removing an edge is essentially precomputed. To guide TD-1 in selecting redundant edges, we first impose an ordering on the edges, in such a way that nonredundant edges will always attain higher ranking than redundant ones. Given such ordering, we do not remove edges of low ranking, but apply the dual method instead, and construct a tree containing the preferred edges by finding a maximum weight spanning tree (MWST) relative to the given ordering. This idea is embodied in the following scheme.

Definition Let $G = (V,E)$ be a minimal network. A **labeling** w of G is an assignment of weights to the edges, where the weight of edge $e \in E$ is denoted by $w(e)$. w is said to be a **tree labeling** if it satisfies the following condition. If G is tree decomposable, then G is decomposable by tree T if and only if T is a MWST of G with respect to w.

Finding a tree labeling essentially solves the tree decomposability problem, simply following the steps of algorithm TD-2 shown in Figure 4. TD-2 stands for a family of algorithms, each driven by a different labeling. Steps 2-4 can be implemented in $O(n^3)$: Step 2 can use any MWST algorithm, such as the one by Prim, which is $O(n^2)$ (see [Even 1979]); Steps 3-4, deciding whether G is decomposable by T, are $O(n^3)$ as explained in Section 4.

Algorithm TD-2

1. $w \leftarrow$ tree labeling of G;
2. $T \leftarrow$ MWST of G w.r.t. w;
3. test whether G is decomposable by T;
4. if the test fails G is not tree decomposable;

Figure 4. TD-2 – A polynomial tree decomposition algorithm.

We now turn our attention to Step 1, namely computing a tree labeling. This will be done in two steps. We first introduce a necessary and sufficient condition for a labeling to qualify as a tree labeling, and then synthesize an $O(n^3)$ algorithm that returns a labeling satisfying this condition. As a result, the total running time of TD-2 is bounded by $O(n^3)$.

Definition. Let $G = (V,E)$ be a minimal network. A labeling w of G is called a **redundancy labeling**, if it satisfies the following condition. For any tree T and any two edges, $e' \in E - T$ and $e \in T$, such that e is on the supporting cycle $C_T(e')$ of e', if G is decomposable by T then

$$(i)\ w(e') \leq w(e). \quad (1)$$

$$(ii)\ e \text{ is redundant in } C_T(e') \text{ whenever } w(e') = w(e). \quad (2)$$

Theorem 3. Let w be any labeling of a minimal network G. w is a tree labeling if and only if w is a redundancy labeling.

The merit of Theorem 3 is that it is often easier to test for redundancy labeling than for the ultimate objective of tree labeling. Having established this equivalence, the next step is to construct a labeling that satisfies conditions

(1) and (2).

Definition. A labeling w of network G is a **triangle labeling**, if for any triangle $t = \{e_1, e_2, e_3\}$ the following conditions are satisfied.

(*i*) If e_1 is redundant in t then

$$w(e_1) \le w(e_2)\ ,\ w(e_1) \le w(e_3). \tag{3}$$

(*ii*) If e_1 is redundant in t and e_2 is nonredundant in t then

$$w(e_1) < w(e_2). \tag{4}$$

Conditions (3) and (4) will be called **triangle constraints.**

Illustration. Consider the minimal network of Example 2. Analyzing redundancies relative to all triangles leads to the triangle constraints depicted in Figure 5. Each node in the figure represents an edge of the minimal network, and an arc $e_1 \rightarrow e_2$ represents the triangle constraint $w(e_1) < w(e_2)$ (for clarity, all arcs from bottom layer to top layer were omitted). It so happens that only strict inequalities were imposed in this example. A triangle labeling w can be easily constructed by assigning the following weights:

$$w(AB) = w(AC) = w(AD) = w(AE) = 3$$

$$w(BD) = w(BE) = w(CD) = w(CE) = 2$$

$$w(BC) = w(DE) = 1.$$

Note that the tree $T = \{AB, AC, AD, AE\}$, which decomposes the network, is a MWST relative to these weights, a property that we will show to hold in general.

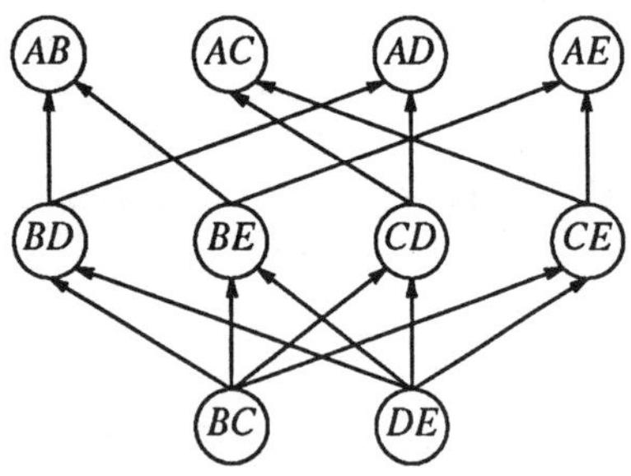

Figure 5. Triangle constraints for Example 2.

Clearly, conditions (3) and (4) are easier to verify as they involve only test on triangles. In Theorem 5 we will indeed show that they are sufficient to constitute a redundancy labeling, hence a tree labeling. Moreover, a labeling satisfying (3) and (4) is easy to create primarily because, by Theorem 4, such a labeling is guaranteed to exist for any path consistent (hence minimal) network. Note that this is by no means obvious, because there might be two sets of triangles imposing two conflicting constraints on a pair (a,b) of edges; one requiring $w(a) \le w(b)$, and the other $w(a) > w(b)$.

Theorem 4. Any path consistent network admits a triangle labeling.

The idea behind triangle labelings is that all redundancy information necessary for tree decomposition can be extracted from individual triangles rather than cycles. By Lemma 1, if an edge is redundant in a cycle, it must be redundant in some triangle. Contrapositively, if an edge is nonredundant in all triangles, it cannot be redundant in any cycle, and thus must be included in any tree decomposition. To construct a tree decomposition, we must therefore include all those necessary edges (note that they attain the highest ranking) and then, proceed by preferring edges which are nonredundant relative to others. The correctness of the next theorem rests on these considerations.

Theorem 5. Let G be a minimal network, and let w be a labeling of G. If w is a triangle labeling then it is also a redundancy labeling.

By Theorems 3 and 5, if the network is minimal any triangle labeling is also a tree labeling. What remains to be shown is that, given any minimal network $G = (V,E)$, a triangle labeling can be formed in $O(n^3)$ time. Algorithm TLA, shown in Figure 6, accomplishes this task.

Algorithm TLA

1. create an empty directed graph $G_1 = (V_1, E_1)$ with $V_1 = E$;
2. for each triangle $t = \{e_i, e_j, e_k\}$ in G do
3.   if edge e_i is redundant in t then add arcs $e_i \rightarrow e_j$ and $e_i \rightarrow e_k$ to G_1;
4. $G_2 = (V_2, E_2) \leftarrow$ superstructure of G_1;
5. compute a topological ordering w for V_2;
6. for $i := 1$ to $|V_2|$ do
7.   for each edge e in C_i do
8. $w(e) \leftarrow w(C_i)$;

Figure 6. TLA – an algorithm for constructing a triangle labeling.

Let us consider the TLA algorithm in detail. First, it constructs a graph, G_1, that displays the triangle constraints. Each node in G_1 represents an edge of G, and arc

$u \rightarrow v$ stands for a triangle constraint $w(u) \leq w(v)$ or $w(u) < w(v)$. The construction of G_1 (Steps 1-3) takes $O(n^3)$ time, since there are $O(n^3)$ triangles in G, and the time spent for each triangle is constant.

Consider a pair of nodes, u and v, in G_1. It can be verified that if they belong to the same strongly-connected component (i.e., they lie on a common directed cycle), their weights must satisfy $w(u) = w(v)$. If they belong to two distinct components, but there exists a directed path from u to v, their weights must satisfy $w(u) < w(v)$. These relationships can be effectively encoded in the *superstructure* of G_1 [Even 1979]. Informally, the superstructure is formed by collapsing all nodes of the same strongly-connected component into one node, while keeping only arcs that go across components. Formally, let $G_2 = (V_2, E_2)$ be the superstructure of G_1. Node $C_i \in G_2$ represents a strongly-connected component, and a directed arc $C_i \rightarrow C_j$ implies that there exists an edge $u \rightarrow v$ in G_1, where $u \in C_i$ and $v \in C_j$. Identifying the strongly connected components, and consequently constructing the superstructure (Step 4), takes $O(n^3)$ (a time proportional to the number of edges in G_1 [Even 1979]).

It is well-known that the superstructure forms a DAG (directed acyclic graph), moreover, the nodes of the DAG can be topologically ordered, namely they can be given distinct weights w, such that if there exists an arc $i \rightarrow j$ then $w(i) < w(j)$. This can be accomplished (Step 5) in time proportional to the number of edges, namely $O(n^3)$. Finally, recall that each node in G_2 stands for a strongly-connected component, C_i, in G_1, which in turn represents a set of edges in G. If we assign weight $w(C_i)$ to these edges (Steps 6-8), w will comply with the triangle constraints, and thus will constitute a triangle labeling. Since all steps are $O(n^3)$, the entire algorithm is $O(n^3)$.

Illustration. Consider Example 1. There are two strongly-connected components in G_1:

$$C_1 = \{AD, BD, CD\}$$

and

$$C_2 = \{AB, AC, BC\}.$$

There are edges going only from C_1 to C_2. Thus, assigning weight 1 to all edges in C_1 and weight 2 to all edges in C_2 constitutes a triangle labeling. Consider Example 2, for which G_1 is shown in Figure 5. Note that $G_2 = G_1$, that is, every strongly-connected component consists of a single node. Assigning weights in the ranges 1-2, 3-6 and 7-10 to the bottom, middle and top layers, respectively, constitutes a triangle labeling.

6. Extensions and Ramifications

6.1. Decomposing a relation

Given a relation ρ, we wish to determine whether ρ is tree decomposable. We first describe how TD-2 can be employed to solve this problem, and then compare it with the solution presented in [Dechter 1987].

We start by generating the minimal network M from ρ. We then apply TD-2 to solve the decomposability problem for M. If M is not tree decomposable, ρ cannot be tree decomposable; because otherwise, there would be a tree T satisfying $\rho = rel(T) \subset rel(M)$, violating the minimality of M [Montanari 1974]. If M is decomposable by the generated tree T, we still need to test whether $rel(T) = \rho$ (note that M may not represent ρ precisely). This can be done by comparing the sizes of the two relations; ρ is decomposable by T if and only if $|\rho| = |rel(T)|$. Generating M takes $O(n^2 |\rho|)$ operations, while $|T|$ can be computed in $O(n)$ time [Dechter and Pearl 1987]; thus, the total time of this method is $O(n^2 |\rho|)$.

An alternative solution to the problem was presented in [Dechter 1987]. It computes for each edges a numerical measure, w, based on the frequency that each pair of values appears in the relation. First, the following parameters are computed:
$n(X_i = x_i)$ = number of tuples in ρ in which variable X_i attains value x_i.
$n(X_i = x_i, X_j = x_j)$ = number of tuples in ρ in which both $X_i = x_i$ and $X_j = x_j$.
Then, each edge $e = (i,j)$ is assigned the weight

$$w(e) = \sum_{x_i, x_j \in X_i, X_j} n(x_i, x_j) \log \frac{n(x_i, x_j)}{n(x_i) n(x_j)}. \quad (5)$$

It has been shown that this labeling, w, is indeed a tree labeling, also requiring $O(n^2 |\rho|)$ computational steps.

Comparing the two schemes, our method has three advantages. First, it does not need the precision required by the log function. Second, it offers a somewhat more effective solution in cases where ρ is not available in advance but is observed incrementally through a stream of randomly arriving tuples. Finally, it is conceptually more appealing, since the removal of each edge is meaningfully justified in terms of being redundant.

6.2. Reducing a network

Given an arc and path consistent network R, we wish to

determine whether R is tree reducible. This problem admits TD-2 directly, since it can be shown that any path consistent network is tree reducible only when it is minimal. Thus, if TD-2 returns failure, we are assured that R is not tree reducible (though it could still be tree decomposable).

6.3. Removing redundancies from a network

Given a network R (not necessarily tree decomposable), we wish to to remove as many redundant edges as possible from the network. Our scheme provides an effective heuristics, alternative to that of [Dechter and Dechter 1987]. We first apply the TD-2 algorithm and, in case the tree generated does not represent the network precisely, we add nonredundant edges until a precise representation obtains.

6.4. Approximating a Network

Given a network R, find a tree network which constitutes a good approximation of R. The tree T generated by TD-2 provides an upper bound of R, as it enforces only a subset of the constraints. The quality of this approximation should therefore be evaluated in terms of the tightness, or specificity, of T.

Conjecture: The tree T generated by TD-2 is **most specific** in the following sense: no other tree T', extracted form the network, satisfies $rel(T') \subset rel(T)$.

Although we could find no proof yet, the conjecture has managed to endure all attempts to construct a counterexample.

7. Conclusions

We have addressed the problem of decomposing a constraint network into a tree. We have developed a tractable decomposition scheme which requires $O(n^3)$ time, and solves the problem for minimal networks. The technique maintains its soundness when applied to an arbitrary network, and is guaranteed to find a tree decomposition if it can be extracted from the input network without altering the link constraints. The main application of our scheme lies in preprocessing knowledge bases and transforming them into a very effective format for query processing. Other applications are in guiding backtrack search by tree relaxation of subproblems. Finally, we envision this technique to be useful in inductive learning; especially, for learning and generalizing concepts where instances are observed sequentially. The tree generated by TD-2 provides one of the simplest descriptions consistent with the observed data, and at the same time it is amenable to answer queries of subsumption and extension.

References

Dechter A. and Dechter R. 1987. Removing Redundancies in Constraint Networks. In Proceeding of AAAI-87, Seattle, WA.

Dechter R. 1987. Decomposing a Relation into a Tree of Binary Relations. In Proceedings of 6th Conference on Principles of Database Systems, San Diego, CA, 185-189. To appear in *Journal of Computer and System Science*, Special Issue on the Theory of Relational Databases.

Dechter R. and Pearl J. 1987. Network-Based Heuristics for Constraint Satisfaction Problems. *Artificial Intelligence* 34(1), 1-38.

Even S. 1979. *Graph Algorithms*. Computer Science Press, Rockville, Md.

Freuder E. C. 1982. A Sufficient Condition of Backtrack-Free Search, *JACM* 29(1), 24-32.

Mackworth A. K. 1977. Consistency in Networks of Relations. *Artificial Intelligence* 8(1), 99-118.

Mackworth A. K. and Freuder E. C. 1985. The Complexity of Some Polynomial Network Consistency Algorithms for Constraint Satisfaction Problems. *Artificial Intelligence* 25(1), 65-74.

Maier D. 1983. *The Theory of Relational Databases*. Computer Science Press, Rockville, Md.

Meiri I., Dechter R. and Pearl J. 1990. Tree Decompositions with Applications to Constraint Processing. Technical Report R-146, Cognitive Systems Lab., University of California, Los Angeles.

Montanari U. 1974. Networks of Constraints: Fundamental Properties and Applications to Picture Processing. *Information Sciences* 7, 95-132.

Solving Large-Scale Constraint Satisfaction and Scheduling Problems Using a Heuristic Repair Method

Steven Minton[1] **Mark D. Johnston**[2] **Andrew B. Philips**[1] **Philip Laird**[3]

[1]Sterling Federal Systems
NASA Ames Research Center
Mail Stop: 244-17
Moffett Field, CA 94035

[2]Space Telescope Science Institute
3700 San Martin Drive
Baltimore, MD 21218

[3]AI Research Branch
NASA Ames Research Center
Mail Stop: 244-17
Moffett Field, CA 94035

Abstract

This paper describes a simple heuristic method for solving large-scale constraint satisfaction and scheduling problems. Given an initial assignment for the variables in a problem, the method operates by searching though the space of possible repairs. The search is guided by an ordering heuristic, the *min-conflicts heuristic*, that attempts to minimize the number of constraint violations after each step. We demonstrate empirically that the method performs orders of magnitude better than traditional backtracking techniques on certain standard problems. For example, the one million queens problem can be solved rapidly using our approach. We also describe practical scheduling applications where the method has been successfully applied. A theoretical analysis is presented to explain why the method works so well on certain types of problems and to predict when it is likely to be most effective.

Introduction

One of the most promising general approaches for solving combinatorial search problems is to generate an initial, suboptimal solution and then to apply local *repair* heuristics. Techniques based on this approach have met with empirical success on many problems, including the traveling salesman and graph partitioning problems[11]. Such techniques also have a long tradition in AI, most notably in problem-solving systems that operate by debugging initial solutions [20,22]. This idea can be extended to constraint satisfication problems in a straightforward manner. Our method takes an initial, inconsistent assignment for the variables in a constraint satisfaction problem (CSP) and incrementally repairs constraint violations until a consistent assignment is achieved. The method is guided by a simple ordering heuristic for repairing constraint violations: select a variable that is currently participating in a constraint violation, and choose a new value that minimizes the number of outstanding constraint violations.

The work described in this paper was inspired by a surprisingly effective neural network developed by Adorf and Johnston for scheduling the use of the Hubble Space Telescope[2,13]. Our heuristic CSP method was distilled from an analysis of the network, and has the virtue of being extremely simple. It can be implemented very efficiently within a symbolic CSP framework, and combined with various search strategies. This paper includes empirical studies showing that the method performs extremely well on some standard problems, such as the n-queens problem, to the extent that the method can quickly find solutions to the one million queens problem. We also describe initial work on large-scale scheduling applications which suggests that the method has important practical implications as well. The final contribution of this paper is a theoretical analysis that describes how various problem characteristics affect the performance of the method.

Previous Work: The GDS Network

By almost any measure, the Hubble Space Telescope scheduling problem is a complex task [24,19,12]. Between ten thousand and thirty thousand astronomical observations per year must be scheduled, subject to a vast variety of constraints involving time-dependent orbital characteristics, power restrictions, priorities, movement of astronomical bodies, stray light sources, etc. Because the telescope is an extremely valuable resource with a limited lifetime, efficient scheduling is a critical concern. An initial scheduling system, developed in FORTRAN using traditional programming methods, highlighted the difficulty of the problem; it was estimated that it would take over three weeks for the system to schedule one week of observations. A more successful constraint-based system was then developed to augment the original system. At its heart is a neural network developed by Johnston and Adorf, the Guarded Discrete Stochastic (GDS) network, which searches for a schedule[2,13].

From a computational point of view, the network is interesting because Johnston and Adorf found that it performs well on a variety of tasks, in addition to the space telescope scheduling problem. For example, the network performs significantly better on the n-queens problem than previous heuristic methods. The n-queens problem requires placing n queens on an $n \times n$ chessboard so that no two queens share a row, column or diagonal. The network has been used to solve problems of up to 1024 queens, whereas previous methods discussed in the literature[21] encounter difficulties with problems that are ten times smaller. Later in this paper we describe how our analysis of the GDS network enabled us to build a simple heuristic algorithm that performs even better.

The GDS network is a modified Hopfield network[9]. The most significant modification is that the main network is coupled asymmetrically to an auxiliary network of *guard neurons* which restricts the configurations that the network can assume. This modification enables the network to rapidly find a solution for many problems, even when the network is simulated on a serial machine. The disadvantage is that convergence to a stable configuration is no longer guaranteed. Thus, the network can fall into a local minimum involving a group of unstable states among which it will oscillate. In practice, however, if the network fails to converge after some number of neuron state transitions, it can simply be stopped and started over. [1]

To illustrate the network architecture and updating scheme, let us consider how the network is used to solve binary constraint satisfaction problems. A problem consists of n variables, $X_1 \ldots X_n$, with domains $D_1 \ldots D_n$, and a set of binary constraints. Each constraint $C_\alpha(X_j, X_k)$ is a subset of $D_j \times D_k$ specifying incompatible values for a pair of variables.[2] To solve a CSP using the network, each variable is represented by a separate set of neurons, one neuron for each of the variable's possible values. Each neuron is either "on" or "off", and in a solution state, every variable will have exactly one of its corresponding neurons "on", representing the value of that variable. Constraints are represented by inhibitory (i.e., negatively weighted) connections between the neurons. To insure that every variable is assigned a value, there is a guard neuron for each set of neurons representing a variable; if no neuron in the set is on, the guard neuron will provide an excitatory input that is large enough to turn one on. (Due to the way the connection weights are set up, it is unlikely that the guard neuron will turn on more than one neuron.) The network is updated on each cycle by randomly picking a set of neurons that represents a variable, and flipping the state of the neuron in that set whose input is ***most inconsistent*** with its current output (if any). When all neurons' states are consistent with their input, a solution is achieved.

The Min-Conflicts Heuristic

Why does the GDS network perform so much better than traditional backtracking methods on tasks such as the n-queens? In addressing this question, we began with a number of competing hypotheses (some of which were suggested by Adorf and Johnston[2]). For instance, one hypothesis was that the systematic nature of the search carried out by backtracking is the source of its problems, as compared to the stochastic nature of the search carried out by the network. Specifically, if solutions in the backtracking space are clustered together (with correspondingly high inter-cluster distances), then a completely randomized search of the space can be more effective than systematic backtracking. However, although tasks such as n-queens are in fact solved more efficiently using randomized algorithms (such as Las Vegas algorithms [4]), our studies indicate that the performance of the GDS network is far too good to be explained by this hypothesis.

As it turns out, the key to the network's performance appears to be that when it chooses a neuron to update, it chooses the neuron whose state is most inconsistent with its input. Thus, from a constraint satisfaction perspective, the network will "deassign" a variable's current value only if it is inconsistent with other variables. Furthermore, when a new value is later assigned, the network will choose the value that minimizes the number of other variables that it is inconsistent with. This idea is captured by the following heuristic:

> **Min-Conflicts heuristic:**
> *Given:* A set of variables, a set of binary constraints, and an assignment specifying a value for each variable. Two variables *conflict* if their values violate a constraint.
> *Procedure:* Select a variable that is in conflict, and assign it a value that minimizes the number of conflicts.[3] (Break ties randomly.)

We have found that the network's behavior can be approximated by a symbolic system that uses the min-

[1] The emphasis in Johnston and Adorf's work is to produce a computational architecture that can efficiently solve CSP problems, as opposed to modeling cognitive or neural behavior. Our discussion necessarily ignores many aspects of Johnston and Adorf's work, which is described in detail elsewhere[13,2].

[2] This paper only considers the task of finding a single solution, that is, finding an assignment for each of the variables which satisfies the constraints.

[3] In general, the heuristic attempts to minimize the number of other variables that will need to be repaired. For binary CSPs, this corresponds to minimizing the number of conflicting variables. For general CSPs, where a single constraint may involve several variables, the exact method of counting the number of variables that will need to be repaired depends on the particular constraint. The space telescope scheduling problem is a general CSP, whereas most of the other tasks described in this paper are binary CSPs.

conflicts heuristic for hill-climbing. The hill-climbing system starts with an initial assignment generated in a preprocessing phase. At each choice point, the heuristic chooses a variable that is currently in conflict and reassigns its value, until a solution is found. The system thus searches the space of possible assignments, favoring assignments with fewer total conflicts. Of course, the hill-climbing system can become "stuck" in a local maximum, in the same way that the network may become "stuck" in a local minimum. In the next section we present empirical evidence to support our claim that the min-conflicts heuristic is responsible for the network's effectiveness.

One of the virtues of extracting the heuristic from the network is that the heuristic can be used with a variety of different search strategies in addition to hill-climbing. For example, we have found that informed backtracking can be an effective strategy when used in the following manner. Given an initial assignment generated in a preprocessing phase (as described above), an informed backtracking program employs the min-conflicts heuristic to order the choice of variables and values to consider, as described in figure 1. Initially the variables are all on a list of VARS-LEFT, and as they are repaired, they are pushed onto a list of VARS-DONE. The program attempts to find a sequence of repairs, such that no variable is repaired more than once. If there is no way to repair a variable in VARS-LEFT without violating a previously repaired variable (a variable in VARS-DONE), the program backtracks.

It should be clear that the informed backtracking algorithm is simply a basic backtracking algorithm augmented with the min-conflicts heuristic to order its choice of which variable and value to attend to. This illustrates an important point. The informed backtracking program incrementally extends a consistent partial assignment (i.e., VARS-DONE), in the same manner as a basic backtracking program, but in addition, uses information from the initial assignment (i.e., VARS-LEFT) to bias its search. The next section documents the degree to which this information is useful.

```
Procedure INFORMED-BACKTRACK (VARS-LEFT VARS-DONE)
  If all variables are consistent,
    then solution found, STOP.
  Let VAR = a variable in VARS-LEFT
    that is in conflict.
  Remove VAR from VARS-LEFT.
  Push VAR onto VARS-DONE.
  Let VALUES = list of possible values for VAR
    ordered in ascending order according to number
    of conflicts with variables in VARS-LEFT.
  For each VALUE in VALUES, until solution found:
    If VALUE does not conflict with any variable
         that is in VARS-DONE, then
      Assign VALUE to VAR.
      Call INFORMED-BACKTRACK(VARS-LEFT VARS-DONE)
    end if
  end for
 end procedure

Begin program
 Let VARS-LEFT = list of all variables,
                 each assigned an initial value.
 Let VARS-DONE = nil
 Call INFORMED-BACKTRACK(VARS-LEFT VARS-DONE)
End program
```

Figure 1: Informed Backtracking Using the Min-Conflicts Heuristic

Experimental Results

This section has two purposes. First, we evaluate the performance of the min-conflicts heuristic on some standard tasks using a variety of search strategies. Second, we show that the heuristic, when used with a hill-climbing strategy, approximates the behavior of the GDS network.

We have employed the following search strategies with the min-conflicts heuristic:

1. Hill-climbing: This strategy most closely replicates the behavior of the GDS network. The disadvantage is that a hill-climbing program can get caught in local maxima, in which case it will not terminate.
2. Informed backtracking: As described earlier, this strategy is a basic backtracking strategy, augmented with the min-conflicts heuristic for ordering the assignment of variables and values. Because the min-conflicts heuristic repairs the initial assignment, it can also be viewed as backtracking in the space of possible repairs. One advantage of this strategy is that it is complete – if there is a solution, it will eventually be found; if not, failure will be reported. Unfortunately, this is of limited significance for large-scale problems because terminating in a failure can take a very long time. A second advantage is that the strategy can be augmented with pruning heuristics which cut off unpromising branches. This can be very useful, as documented in the next section.
3. Best-first search: This strategy keeps track of multiple assignments (each corresponding to a leaf in the search tree). On each cycle it picks the assignment with the fewest constraint violations and considers the set of repairs that can be applied to that assignment. We have found that best-first search (of which A^* is one variation) is generally expensive to employ on large-scale problems due to the cost of maintaining multiple assignments.

The N-Queens Problem

The n-queens problem, originally posed in the 19th century, has become a standard benchmark for testing backtracking and CSP algorithms. In a sense, the problem of finding a single solution was "solved" in the 1950's by the discovery of a pair of patterns that can

Strategy	$n = 10^1$	$n = 10^2$	$n = 10^3$	$n = 10^4$	$n = 10^5$	$n = 10^6$
Basic Backtrack†	53.8	4473 (70%)	88650 (13%)	*	*	*
Most Constrained Backtrack†	17.4	687 (96%)	22150 (81%)	*	*	*
MinConflicts Hill-Climbing‡	57.0	55.6	48.8	48.5	52.8	48.3
MinConflicts Backtrack‡	46.8	25.0	30.7	27.5	27.8	26.4

† = number of backtracks, ‡ = number of repairs
$*$ = exceeded computational resources (100 runs required > 12 hours on a SPARCstation1)

Table 1: Number of Backtracks/Repairs for N-Queens Algorithms

be instantiated in linear time to yield a solution[1]. Nevertheless, the problem has remained relatively "hard" for heuristic search methods. Several studies of the n-queens problem [21,8,14] have compared heuristic backtracking methods such as search rearrangement backtracking (e.g., most-constrained first), forward checking, dependency-directed backtracking, etc. However, no previously identified heuristic search method has been able to consistently solve problems involving hundreds of queens within a reasonable time limit.

On the n-queens problem, Adorf and Johnston [2] reported that the probability of the GDS network converging increases with the size of the problem. For large problems, e.g., $n > 100$ (where n is the number of queens), the network almost certainly converges. Moreover, the median number of cycles required for convergence is only about $1.16n$. Since it takes $O(n)$ time to execute a transition (i.e., picking a neuron and updating its connections), the expected time to solve a problem is (empirically) approximately $O(n^2)$. The network has been used to solve problems with as many as 1024 queens, which takes approximately 11 minutes in Lisp on a TI Explorer II. For larger problems, memory becomes a limiting factor because the the network requires approximately $O(n^2)$ space. (Although the number of non-zero connections is $O(n^3)$, some connections are computed dynamically rather than stored).

To compare the network with our min-conflicts approach, we constructed a hill-climbing program that operates as follows. An initial assignment is created in a preprocessing phase using a greedy algorithm that iterates through the rows, placing each queen on the column where it conflicts with the fewest previously placed queens (breaking ties randomly). In the subsequent repair phase, the program keeps repairing the assignment until a solution is found. To make a repair, the program selects a queen that is in conflict and moves it to a different column in the same row where it conflicts with the fewest other queens (breaking ties randomly). Interestingly, we found that this program performs significantly better than the network. For $n \geq 100$ the program has never failed to find a solution. Moreover, the required number of repairs appears to remain *constant* as n increases. After further analysis, however, we found the hill-climbing program performs better than the network because the hill-climbing program's preprocessing phase invariably produces an initial assignment that is "close" to a solution, in that the number of conflicting queens in the initial assignment grows extremely slowly (from a mean of 3.1 for $n = 10$ to a mean of 12.8 for $n = 10^6$). Once this difference was eliminated, by starting the network in an initial state produced by our preprocessing algorithm, the network and the hill-climbing program performed quite similarly. We note, however, that the network requires $O(n^2)$ space, as compared to the $O(n)$ space required by the hill-climbing program, which prevented us from running very large problems on the network.

Table 1 compares the efficiency of our hill-climbing program and several backtracking programs. Each program was run 100 times for n increasing from 10 to one million. Each entry in the table shows the mean number of queens moved, where each move is either a backtrack or a repair, depending on the program. A bound of $n \times 100$ queen movements was employed so that the experiments could be conducted in a reasonable amount of time; If the program did not find a solution after moving $n \times 100$ queens, it was terminated and credited with $n \times 100$ queen movements. For the cases when this occurred, the corresponding table entry indicates in parentheses the percentage of times the program completed successfully. The first row shows the results for a basic backtracking program. For $n \geq 1000$, the program was completely swamped. The second row in the table shows the results for informed backtracking using the "most-constrained first" heuristic. This program is a basic backtracking program that selects the row that is most constrained when choosing the next row on which to place a queen. In an empirical study of the n-queens problem, Stone and Stone [21] found that this was by far the most powerful heuristic for the n-queens problem out of several described earlier by Bitner and Reingold[3]. The program exhibited highly variable behavior. At $n = 1000$, the program found a solution on only 81% of the runs, but three-quarters of these successful runs required fewer than 100 backtracks. Unfortunately, for $n > 1000$, one hundred runs of the program required considerably more than 12 hours on a SPARCstation1, both because the mean number of backtracks grows rapidly and because the "most-constrained first" heuristic takes $O(n)$

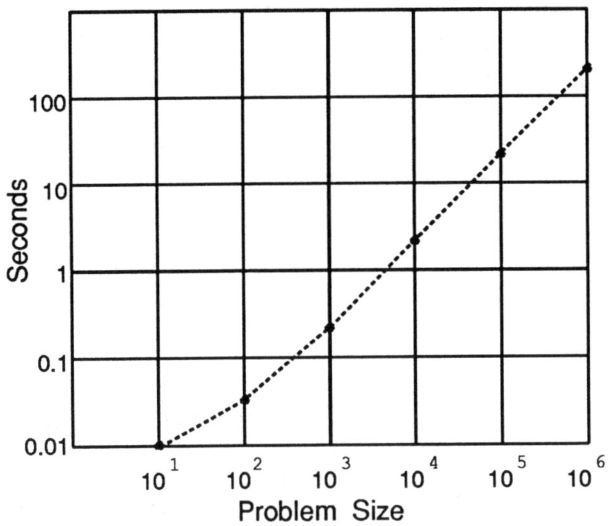

Figure 2: Mean Solution Time for Hill-Climbing Program on N-Queens Problem

time to select the next row after each backtrack. Thus we were prevented from generating sufficient data for $n > 1000$. The next row in the table shows the results for hill-climbing using the min-conflicts heuristic. As discussed above, this algorithm performed extremely well, requiring only about 50 repairs regardless of problem size. The final row shows the results for an informed backtracking program that used the min-conflicts heuristic as described in the previous section. We augmented this program with a pruning heuristic that would initiate backtracking when the number of constraint violations along a path began to increase significantly. However, for $n \geq 100$, this program never backtracked (i.e., no queen had to be repaired more than once). The results are better than those for the hill-climbing program (although there is little room for improvement) primarily because the hill-climbing program tends to repair the same queen again and again.

We note that for the two programs using the min-conflicts heuristic, each repair requires $O(n)$ time in the worst case. However, this is a relatively minor price to pay. Since the number of repairs remains approximately constant as n grows, the average runtime of the program is approximately linear. This is illustrated by figure 2, which shows the average runtime for the hill-climbing program. In terms of realtime performance, this program solves the million queens problem in less than four minutes on a SPARCstation1. (The algorithm can also be optimized for large problems, in which case the solution time is less than a minute and a half.)

Scheduling Applications

A scheduling problem involves placing a set of tasks on a time line, subject to temporal constraints, resource constraints, preferences, etc. The space telescope scheduling problem, as discussed earlier, is a complex problem on which traditional backtracking and operations research techniques perform poorly. The problem can be considered a constraint optimization problem where we must maximize both the number and the importance of the constraints that are satisfied. In practice, the GDS network has performed quite well using a relatively simple approach. The network, in effect, attempts to satisfy as many "important" constraints as possible; less "important" constraints, or preferences, are used to break ties during the update procedure. Naturally, a similar approach can be used with the min-conflicts heuristic. As usual, we minimize the number of conflicts, but rather than breaking ties randomly, the preference constraints are used to break ties. (Due to space limitations, we only report our main results here. See [18] for a more in-depth discussion of this application.)

The min-conflicts heuristic under hill-climbing has been shown to be at least as effective as the GDS network on representative data sets provided by the Space Telescope Sciences Institute. Moreover, because the min-conflicts heuristic is so simple, the scheduling program was easy to code and is extremely efficient.[4] While this may be regarded as just an implementation issue, we believe that the clear and simple formulation of the method was a significant enabling factor. We are currently experimenting with a variety of different search strategies that can be combined with the min-conflicts heuristic. Although this study is not yet complete, we expect that the improvements in speed we have observed will eventually translate into better schedules, since the search process can explore a larger number of acceptable schedules.

The min-conflicts method has also been tested on data on the Space Shuttle Payload Scheduling problem, another complex, real-world scheduling problem. Preliminary results show that the method performs far better than a backtracking CSP program that was previously built for this task[26]. Additional corroboration comes from a parallel study by Zweben[25], who has investigated a related method for repairing schedules using simulated annealing. In general, it appears that repair-based methods fare quite well on this problem. An additional bonus, as Zweben has pointed out, is that repair-based methods can also be used for dynamic rescheduling. In many domains this capability is important because unexpected events may require frequent schedule revision.

Other Applications

The min-conflicts and/or GDS network have also been tried on a variety of other problems with good (but

[4] The scheduling program runs at least an order of magnitude faster than the network, although some of the improvement is due to factors such as programming language differences. This makes a precise comparison difficult.

preliminary) results, including the randomly generated problems described by Dechter and Pearl [6,2] and conjunctive precondition matching problems[17]. We are currently cataloging the types of applications for which our method works well.

We have also compared the performance of the GDS network and the min-conflicts heuristic on graph 3-colorability, a well-studied NP-complete problem. In this problem, we are given an undirected graph with n vertices. Each vertex must be assigned one of three colors subject to the constraint that no neighboring vertices be assigned the same color. Adorf and Johnston found that the performance of the network depended greatly on the connectivity of the graph. On sparsely connected graphs (with average vertex degree 4) the network performed poorly, becoming caught in local minima with high probability. On densely connected graphs the network converged rapidly to a solution.

We have repeated Adorf and Johnston's experiments with our hill-climbing program, and found similar results. We have also experimented with variations of informed backtracking using the min-conflicts heuristic. Our most effective program is an informed backtracking program that records the assignment with the least conflicts found so far. When the number of backtracks exceeds a (dynamically adjusted) threshold, the search process is restarted using this best assignment. We have found that performance is further improved by adding heuristics for selecting which vertex to repair, and that, as in the n-queens problem, it helps to have a good initial assignment, which can also be produced using additional heuristics. This illustrates the well-known principle that combining multiple heuristics can improve performance significantly.

In this domain, certain heuristic methods are known to produce excellent results. For instance, Brelaz's k-colorability algorithm [5] employs two strong heuristics (forms of "most-constrained first") and it outperforms our informed backtracking algorithm. Turner [23] has shown that this algorithm will optimally color "almost all" random k-colorable graphs without backtracking, so its dominance is not surprising.

Summary of Experimental Results

For all of the tasks discussed in the previous section, we have found that the behavior of the GDS network can be approximated by hill-climbing with the min-conflicts heuristic. To this extent, we have a theory that explains the network's behavior. Obviously, there are certain practical advantages to having "extracted" the heuristic from the network. First, the heuristic is very simple, and so can be programmed extremely efficiently, especially if done in a task-specific manner. Second, the heuristic can then be used in combination with different search strategies and task-specific heuristics. This is a significant factor for most practical applications.

Insofar as the power of the heuristic is concerned, our experimental results are encouraging. On the n-queens problem the min-conflicts heuristic clearly outperforms heuristics that have previously been investigated. Furthermore, the heuristic has already been applied successfully to real-world scheduling problems.

We have also considered variations of the min-conflicts heuristic, such as repairing the variable that participates in the *most* conflicts first. In general, we have found that minor variations of the heuristic do not affect performance significantly, as long as the heuristic tends to decrease the number of variables that are inconsistent.

Analysis

The previous section showed that the min-conflicts heuristic is extremely effective on some tasks, such as placing queens on a chessboard, and less effective on other tasks, such as coloring sparsely connected graphs. In this section, we analyze how the parameters of a task influence the effectiveness of the heuristic. Consider a CSP with n variables, where each variable has k possible values. We restrict our consideration to a simplified model where every variable is subject to exactly c binary constraints, and we assume that there is only a single solution to the problem, that is, exactly one satisfying assignment. We address the following question: What is the probability that the min-conflicts heuristic will make a mistake when it assigns a value to a variable that is in conflict? We define a mistake as choosing a value that will have to be changed again before the solution is found. We note that for our informed backtracking program, a mistake of this sort early in the problem-solving process may prove fatal, as it may require an exponential amount of search to recover from its mistake.

For any assignment of values to the variables, there will be a set of d variables whose values will have to be changed to convert the assignment into the solution. We can regard d as a measure of distance to the solution. The key to our analysis is the following observation. Given a variable V to be repaired, only one of its k possible values will be good[5] and the other $k-1$ values will be bad (i.e., mistakes). Whereas the good value may conflict with at most d other variables in the assignment, a bad value may conflict with as many as c other variables. Thus, as d shrinks, the min-conflicts heuristic should be less likely to make a mistake when it repairs V. In fact, if each of the $k-1$ bad values has more than d conflicts, then the min-conflicts heuristic cannot make a mistake – it will select the good value when it repairs this variable, since the good value will have fewer conflicts than any bad value.

[5] Although a variable is in conflict, its current value may actually be the good value. This can happen when the variable with which it conflicts has a bad value. In this paper we have defined the min-conflicts heuristic so that it can choose *any* possible value for the variable, including its initial value.

We can use this idea to bound the probability of making a mistake when variable V is repaired. Let V' be a variable related to V by a constraint. We assume that a bad value for V conflicts with V' with probability p, independent of the variables V and V'. Let N_b be a random variable representing the number of conflicts for an arbitrary one of the $k-1$ bad values for V. Thus, the expected value for N_b is pc. Since we are interested in the behavior of the min-conflicts heuristic as d shrinks, let us suppose that d is less than pc. Then, to bound the probability that N_b is less than d, we can use Hoeffding's inequality, which states that after c trials, the probability that a random variable is sc less than the mean is bounded by e^{-2s^2c}. With $s = (pc - d)/c$, the relative distance between pc and d, we obtain:

$$Pr(N_b < d) \leq e^{-2(pc-d)^2/c}$$

To account for the fact that a mistake can occur if *any* of the $k-1$ bad values has d or fewer conflicts, we bound the probability of making a mistake on any of them by multiplying by $k-1$:

$$Pr(mistake) \leq (k-1)e^{-2(pc-d)^2/c}$$

Note that as c (the number of constraints per variable) becomes large, the probability of a mistake approaches zero, if all other parameters remain fixed. This analysis thus offers an explanation as to why 3-coloring densely connected graphs is relatively easy. We also see that as d becomes small, a mistake is also less likely, explaining our empirical observation that having a "good" initial assignment is important. Additionally, we note that as p increases or k decreases, the probability of a mistake also shrinks.

The analysis makes several simplifying assumptions, including the assumption that only a single solution exists. In the n-queens problem, it appears that the number of possible solutions grows rapidly with n [21]. To explain the excellent performance of the min-conflicts heuristic on the n-queens problem, it seems necessary to take this additional fact into account; we note that for n-queens the bounds derived above are relatively weak. (In n-queens, each row is represented by a variable, so that $c = n$, and $p \approx 2.5/n$, since any two rows constrain each other along a column and either one or two diagonals. Therefore, pc remains approximately constant as n grows.)

Discussion

The heuristic method described in this paper can be characterized as a *local search* method[11], in that each repair minimizes the number of conflicts for an individual variable. Local search methods have been applied to a variety of important problems, often with impressive results. For example, the Kernighan-Lin method, perhaps the most successful algorithm for solving graph-partitioning problems, repeatedly improves a partitioning by swapping the two vertices that yield the greatest cost differential. The much-publicized simulated annealing method can also be characterized as a form of local search[10]. However, it is well-known that the effectiveness of local search methods depends greatly on the particular task. We are currently comparing the algorithm's performance with alternative techniques on a variety of tasks.

There is also a long history of AI programs that use repair or debugging strategies to solve problems, primarily in the areas of planning and design[22,20]. These programs have generally been quite successful, although the repair strategies they employ may be domain specific. In comparison, the min-conflicts heuristic is a completely general, domain-independent approach. Of course, any domain-independent heuristic is likely to fail in certain cases, precisely because of its lack of domain-specific expertise.

In fact, it is easy to imagine problems on which the min-conflicts heuristic will fail. The heuristic is poorly suited to problems with a few highly critical constraints and a large number of less important constraints. For example, consider the problem of constructing a four-year course schedule for a university student. We may have an initial schedule which satisfies almost all of the constraints, except that a course scheduled for the first year is not actually offered that year. If this course is a prerequisite for subsequent courses, then many significant changes to the schedule may be required before it is fixed. In general, if repairing a constraint violation requires completely revising the current assignment, then the min-conflicts heuristic will offer little guidance. This intuition is partially captured by the analysis presented in the previous section, which shows how the effectiveness of the heuristic is inversely related to the distance to a solution.

The problems investigated in this paper, especially the n-queens problem, tend to be relatively uniform, in that the likelihood of such critical constraints existing is low. In the space telescope scheduling problem, constraint preprocessing techniques[16] are applied to reduce the likelihood that any particular constraint will be highly critical. For example, by taking the transitive closure of temporal constraints (e.g. the "after" relation) and representing each inferred constraint explicitly, critical constraints can be transformed into sets of constraints. This works well because the min-conflicts heuristic will be less likely to violate a set of constraints than a single constraint. In some cases, we expect that more sophisticated techniques will be necessary to identify critical constraints[7]. To this end, we are currently evaluating abstraction and explanation-based learning techniques that have worked well for planning systems[15,17].

Conclusions

This paper has two primary contributions. First, we have analyzed a very successful neural network algorithm and shown that an extremely simple heuristic is responsible for its effectiveness. Second, we have demonstrated that this heuristic can be incorporated into symbolic CSP programs with excellent results.

Acknowledgements

The authors wish to thank Hans-Martin Adorf, Richard Franier, and Don Rosenthal for their assistance on this research project, and Peter Cheeseman, Monte Zweben, John Bresina, Megan Eskey, Mark Drummond, Eric Raymond, Oren Etzioni, Craig Knoblock and Bernadette Kowalski for their comments and advice, and for their company during late-night dinners. The Space Telescope Science Institute is operated by the Association of Universities for Research in Astronomy for NASA.

References

[1] B. Abramson and M. Yung. Divide and conquer under global constraints: a solution to the n-queens problem. *Journal of Parallel and Distributed Computing*, 61:649–662, 1989.

[2] H.M. Adorf and M.D. Johnston. A discrete stochastic neural network algorithm for constraint satisfaction problems. In *Proceedings of the International Joint Conference on Neural Networks*, San Diego, CA, 1990.

[3] J. Bitner and E.M. Reingold. Backtrack programming techniques. *Communications of the ACM*, 18:651–655, 1975.

[4] G. Brassard and P. Bratley. *Algorithmics - Theory and Practice.* Prentice Hall, Englewood Cliffs, NJ, 1988.

[5] D. Brelaz. Almost all k-colorable graphs are easy to color. *Journal of Algorithms*, 9:63–82, 1988.

[6] R. Dechter and J. Pearl. Network-based heuristics for constraint satisfaction problems. *Artificial Intelligence*, 34:1–38, 1988.

[7] M.S. Fox, N. Sadeh, and C. Baykan. Constrained heuristic search. In *Proceedings IJCAI-89*, Detroit, MI, 1989.

[8] R.M. Haralick and G.L. Elliot. Increasing tree search efficiency for constraint satisfaction problems. *Artificial Intelligence*, 14:263–313, 1980.

[9] J.J. Hopfield. Neural networks and physical systems with emergent collective computational abilities. In *Proceedings of the National Academy of Sciences*, 1982.

[10] D.S. Johnson, C.R. Aragon, L.A. McGeoch, and C. Schevon. Optimization by simulated annealing: an experimental evaluation, Part II. *To appear in Journal of Operations Research*, 1990.

[11] D.S. Johnson, C.H. Papadimitrou, and M. Yannakakis. How easy is local search? *Journal of Computer and System Sciences*, 37:79–100, 1988.

[12] M.D. Johnston. Automated telescope scheduling. In *Proceedings of the Symposium on Coordination of Observational Projects*, Cambridge University Press, 1987.

[13] M.D. Johnston and H.M. Adorf. Learning in stochastic neural networks for constraint satisfaction problems. In *Proceedings of NASA Conference on Space Telerobotics*, Pasadena, CA, January 1989.

[14] N. Keng and D.Y.Y. Yun. A planning/scheduling methodology for the constrained resource problem. In *Proceedings IJCAI-89*, Detroit, MI, 1989.

[15] C.A. Knoblock. Learning hierarchies of abstraction spaces. In *Proceedings of the Sixth International Conference on Machine Learning*, Ithica, N.Y., 1989.

[16] A.K. Mackworth. Consistency in networks of relations. *Artificial Intelligence*, 8:98–118, 1977.

[17] S. Minton. Empirical results concerning the utility of explanation-based learning. In *Proceedings AAAI-88*, Minneapolis, MN, 1988.

[18] S. Minton, A.B. Philips, M. Johnston, and P. Laird. *The Min-Conflicts Heuristic: Experimental and Theoretical Results.* Technical Report forthcoming, NASA Ames Artificial Intelligence Research Branch, 1990.

[19] N. Muscettola, S.F. Smith, G. Amiri, and D. Pathak. *Generating Space Telescope Observation Schedules.* Technical Report CMU-RI-TR-89-28, Carnegie Mellon University, Robotics Institute, 1989.

[20] R.G. Simmons. A theory of debugging plans and interpretations. In *Proceedings AAAI-88*, Minneapolis, MN, 1988.

[21] H.S. Stone and J.M. Stone. Efficient search techniques - an empirical study of the n-queens problem. *IBM Journal of Research and Development*, 31:464–474, 1987.

[22] G. J. Sussman. *A Computer Model of Skill Acquisition.* American Elsevier, New York, 1975.

[23] J.S. Turner. New methods to color the vertices of a graph. *Communications of the ACM*, 22:251–256, 1979.

[24] M. Waldrop. Will the Hubble space telescope compute? *Science*, 243:1437–1439, 1989.

[25] M. Zweben. *A Framework for Iterative Improvement Search Algorithms Suited for Constraint Satisfaction Problems.* Technical Report RIA-90-05-03-1, NASA Ames Research Center, AI Research Branch, 1990.

[26] M. Zweben and M. Eskey. Constraint satisfaction with delayed evaluation. In *Proceedings IJCAI-89*, Detroit, MI, 1989.

Dynamic Constraint Satisfaction Problems

Sanjay Mittal and **Brian Falkenhainer**
System Sciences Laboratory
Xerox Palo Alto Research Center
3333 Coyote Hill Road, Palo Alto CA 94304

Abstract

Constraint satisfaction (CSP) is a powerful and extensively used framework for describing search problems. A CSP is typically defined as the problem of finding consistent assignment of values to a fixed set of variables given some constraints over these variables. However, for many synthesis tasks such as configuration and model composition, the set of variables that are relevant to a solution and must be assigned values changes dynamically in response to decisions made during the course of problem solving. In this paper, we formalize this notion as a *dynamic constraint satisfaction problem* that uses two types of constraints. *Compatibility constraints* correspond to those traditionally found in CSPs, namely, constraints over the values of variables. *Activity constraints* describe conditions under which a variable may or may not be actively considered as a part of a final solution. We present a language for expressing four types of activity constraints in terms of variable values and variables being considered. We then describe an implemented algorithm that enables tight interaction between constraints about variable activity and constraints about variable values. The utility of this approach is demonstrated for configuration and model composition tasks.

1 Introduction

Constraint satisfaction is a powerful and extensively used framework for expressing and solving search problems. A variety of general techniques have been developed for finding a consistent assignment of values to a predefined set of variables [3; 8; 9; 12; 11]. The variables typically have preenumerated domains of discrete values, and a set of constraints over subsets of these variables limit their possible values.

In contrast, for synthesis tasks such as configuration, design, or model composition, the constraint problem is of a more dynamic nature where any of the elements of the constraint problem (i.e., variables, domains, constraints) might change as the search progresses. For example, selecting the type of hard disk controller for a computer configuration is only relevant when a hard disk has been chosen as the form of secondary storage. Installing a floppy disk drive would require solving for a different set of variables and constraints.

A common approach in such cases is to embed general constraint satisfaction mechanisms within a larger task-specific problem solving architecture. In this coupled mode of problem-solving, the problem solver makes decisions about which variables and constraints are relevant in order to define a problem solvable by some constraint satisfaction mechanism. For example, in the Cossack expert system for configuration [6],the problem solver created variables in response to requirements specifying some functional aspects of a desired configuration. Consistent choices were assigned to these variables by selecting a component and propagating constraints associated with the selected component. Separate mechanisms were used for creating variables and processing constraints on them. Similarly, the Mapsee-2 and Mapsee-3 programs for understanding sketch maps [16] have a control cycle that alternates between creating a new variable for each image element (a chain of edges in the Mapsee terminology) and propagating constraints between existing variables to find consistent interpretations for the image elements. However, experience with Cossack and Mapsee-2 suggests that this separation becomes cumbersome and inefficient when decisions about which variables are relevant interact closely with decisions about consistent value assignments.

In this paper, we identify a specialized but useful class of dynamic problems that we call *dynamic constraint satisfaction problems* (DCSP). For this class of problems, we propose a more integrated approach that extends the notion of constraint satisfaction problems to include constraints about the variables considered in each solution. When a variable must be included, we say that it is *active*. By expressing the conditions under which variables are and are not active, standard CSP methods can be extended to make inferences about variable activity as well as their possible value assignments.

The key characteristic of such dynamic constraint problems is that constraints on introducing or removing variables from a potential solution closely interact with constraints on consistent assignment of values to some already identified set of variables. This property distinguishes our model of DCSP from other "dynamic" formalisms such as incremental constraint satisfaction methods that can handle a changing set of variables [17] or constraints [7], but cannot themselves reason about the activity of a variable. Similarly, constraint logic programming [10] naturally allows variables to be dynamically introduced but provides no special support for efficiently reasoning about variable activity.

We begin by considering how to formalize configuration as a constraint satisfaction problem. This provides the motivation for the formal definition of dynamic CSPs. We describe a simple language for stating constraints about the activity of problem variables in a form that is usable within an extended constraint satisfaction framework. This enables introduction and removal of variables and constraints during search. Further, it provides a useful framework in which to express certain kinds of knowledge for synthesis problems. Examples from configuration and model composition tasks are used to illustrate the use of our language. Finally, we describe an implemented search algorithm for solving DCSPs that is tuned to this specialized language. We close by describing some extensions in progress.

2 Modeling configuration as constraint satisfaction

A constraint satisfaction problem (CSP) is typically specified by a set of variables $V = \{v_1, \cdots, v_n\}$ and a set of constraints C on subsets of V limiting the values that may be assigned in a consistent manner [11; 12]. Each variable v_i has an associated domain $D_i = \{d_{i1}, \cdots, d_{in_i}\}$ which identifies its set of possible values. The constraint satisfaction task is to find assignments of values for $\{v_1, \cdots, v_n\}$ that simultaneously satisfy all the constraints C.

We shall motivate the ideas behind this paper by considering how to formalize a configuration task as defined in [14] as a CSP. In that paper, it was shown that many configuration domains satisfy two important properties. One, the functional roles played by a component in a configured artifact are known ahead of time. Two, for each functional role, one can identify a set of components as the "key" for each role, i.e., one of these "key components" are always needed for implementing the corresponding functional role. For example, in a computer domain, the functional roles include instruction execution, program memory, secondary storage, display, and printing. The key components for these functions respectively include microprocessor chip, memory chip, hard disk or floppy disk, display terminal, and printer.

One can model such configuration tasks as a CSP by making additional simplifying assumptions such as: (1) there are a fixed set of functional roles to be decided in a configured artifact; (2) there is a one-to-one association between functional roles and the components that function in that role; and (3) there is a fixed set of components for each functional role. In the CSP model, we create a variable for each functional role and the components associated with that functional role constitute the domain of these variables. Constraints are used to represent compatibility and selection knowledge.

The model presented above is rather simplistic, since only assumption (3) above is valid. Assumption (2) is generally invalid, since the mapping between functional roles and actual available components is typically many-to-many. For example, in order to provide secondary storage one not only needs a disk drive but also a drive controller, bus connection, and some associated driver software. Here the crucial problem is not just the additional components that are needed but the fact that *different components for the same functional role often need non-identical sets of additional components.* Similarly, some of the available components often provide more than one function. For example, the motherboard on a PC often implements many functions such as the microprocessor, co-processor, program memory, basic I/O system, and assorted other functions. The problem is not just the multiplicity of functions but the fact that such *multi-function components often provide non-identical sets of functions.*

One can use the "key component" idea to partially solve this problem. Essentially, retain the mapping described above but keep in mind that the mapping is only partial, i.e., the component associated with a functional role may only partially provide that function and other components (or functional roles) may be needed to complete the requirements. One can express these additional requirements by dynamically introducing "new" variables and constraints in the solution as a result of selecting a partially satisfying component C for a functional role R. The model of dynamic CSP presented in this paper formalizes this insight by extending CSP to allow constraints on both the values of a variable and "relevance" to a solution. It is important to point out that the language presented here is more general than the initial motivation. In particular, as will become apparent from the examples discussed later in the paper, the same constraint type can be used to represent many different kinds of domain knowledge. Furthermore, the CSP extensions require new methods for solving the problem and also create opportunities for additional heuristics for controlling search.

3 Dynamic constraint satisfaction problems

In CSPs, the sets V, D_i, and C are fixed and known beforehand. Each solution must contain an assignment for every variable in V. In DCSPs, there is also some set of variables V. However, unlike for a CSP, not all variables have to be assigned a value to solve the problem. Some variables and their value assignments render other variables irrelevant, thus indicating that effort should not be spent considering values and constraints for these irrelevant variables.

Because the set of variables requiring assignment is not fixed by the problem definition, we distinguish between variables that appear in the solution and those that do not. A variable is called *active* when it must be part of the solution. The statement that v_i is active is represented by the proposition $active{:}v_i$; the statement that v_i is not active is represented by $\neg active{:}v_i$. A variable v_i is assigned one of its possible values $\{d_{i1}, \cdots, d_{in_i}\}$ if and only if it is active:

$$active{:}v_i \leftrightarrow v_i = d_{i1} \vee \cdots \vee v_i = d_{in_i}$$

DCSPs can themselves post constraints about which variables are active. Thus, a DCSP explicitly constructs each *active*:v_i and every solution to a DCSP only assigns values to variables that are also active.

A dynamic CSP specifies a non-empty set of *initial variables* V_I that must appear in all solutions (i.e., for all v_i in V_I, *active*:v_i always holds). The set of active variables appearing in each solution will always be a superset of V_I. A problem not requiring additional variables reduces to a conventional CSP with $V = V_I$.

To concisely represent the conditions under which a variable and its associated domain become relevant to forming a solution, we extend the notion of constraint to include a set of *activity constraints* C^A affecting variable activity. These constrain a variable to be active or not active based on other variables' activity and value assignments. There are several activity constraint types described in section 4. The simplest of these is logically equivalent to:

$$P(v_1,\cdots,v_n) \rightarrow active{:}v_j$$

where $v_j \notin \{v_1,\cdots,v_n\}$ and P is a predicate over variables and their possible values.

To distinguish between activity constraints and traditional constraints over variable values, we call the standard set of CSP constraints *compatibility constraints*, represented by C^C. Due to the active variable distinction, we must also revise the conditions under which a compatibility constraint is satisfied. Take $P(v_i,v_j,v_k)$ to represent a compatibility constraint over variables v_i, v_j, and v_k. It is treated as being logically equivalent to:

$$active{:}v_i \wedge active{:}v_j \wedge active{:}v_k \rightarrow P(v_i,v_j,v_k)$$

Thus, if one of the variables in a constraint is not active, the constraint is trivially satisfied; if all of the variables in a constraint are active, it has the standard meaning and we say that the constraint is *active*. For efficiency reasons, we make these two cases explicit within the problem solver so that only active constraints need be checked.

We can now define a dynamic constraint satisfaction problem as follows:

Given:

- A set of variables V representing all variables that may potentially become active and appear in a solution. (This list need not be explicitly preenumerated, although our algorithm does not currently handle that case.)
- A non-empty set of *initial variables* $V_I = \{v_1,\cdots,v_k\}$, which is a subset of V.
- A set of discrete, finite domains $D_1,\cdots,D_k$, with each domain $D_i = \{d_{i1},\cdots,d_{ik_i}\}$ representing the set of possible values for each variable v_i in V.
- A set of *compatibility constraints* C^C on subsets of V limiting the values they may take on.
- A set of *activity constraints* C^A on subsets of V specifying constraints between the activity and possible values of problem variables.

Find:

- All solutions, where a solution is an assignment $\mathcal{A}$ which meets two criteria:
    1. The variables and assignments in $\mathcal{A}$ satisfy $C^C \cup C^A$.
    2. No subset of $\mathcal{A}$ is a solution.

This definition extends the standard definition of CSP by introducing activity constraints and identifying a subset of the possible variables as initial variables. Note that the choice of initial variables is important for defining the problem. Keeping everything else the same, we can create different problems simply by changing V_I.[1] Also note that because activity may be affected by value assignments, each possible solution may contain a different set of variables.

Consider the following simple dynamic CSP. We are given the variables v_1, v_2, v_3, v_4 with domains $D_1 = \{a,b\}$, $D_2 = \{c,d\}$, $D_3 = \{e,f\}$, and $D_4 = \{g,h\}$. Further, we are given initial variables $V_I = \{v_1,v_2\}$ and constraints:

$$\begin{array}{l} v_1 = a \rightarrow v_2 = d \\ v_1 = b \rightarrow v_2 = c \\ v_2 = c \wedge v_3 = e \rightarrow v_4 = h \\ v_1 = b \rightarrow active : v_3 \\ v_3 = e \rightarrow active : v_4 \end{array}$$

This problem has three solutions:

$$\begin{array}{c} v_1 = a,\ v_2 = d \\ v_1 = b,\ v_2 = c,\ v_3 = f \\ v_1 = b,\ v_2 = c,\ v_3 = e,\ v_4 = h \end{array}$$

4 Activity constraints

In applying the dynamic CSP framework to several application tasks, we have found it useful to define a specialized language for expressing four types of activity constraints. This language is useful for compactly representing selection and composition constraints in synthesis tasks. Additionally, separating these different activity constraints into distinct types also improves search efficiency by adding finer control over constraint propagation within our algorithm.

4.1 Require variable constraint

The most fundamental activity constraint is the *require variable* (RV), which establishes a variable's activity based on an assignment of values to a set of active variables. RV constraints have the form:

$$P(v_1,\cdots,v_j) \underset{\text{RV}}{\Longrightarrow} v_k \qquad (\text{where } v_k \notin \{v_1,\cdots,v_j\})$$

This notation is logically equivalent to:

$$P(v_1,\cdots,v_j) \rightarrow active{:}v_k$$

[1]This flexibility in reusing the knowledge base is often quite useful in the class of problems that have provided the motivation for the ideas presented here.

where $P(v_1,\cdots,v_j)$ is a predicate over the possible values of variables. When $P(v_1,\cdots,v_j)$ is both active (i.e., $v_1,\cdots,v_j$ are all active) and satisfied, v_k must be active. A contradiction results if it is inconsistent for v_k to be active.

One use of RV constraints is to represent conditional requirements in synthesis tasks.

4.2 Always Require

The *always require variable* (ARV) constraint extends the basic notion of a require constraint to require a variable's activity based on the activity of other variables, independent of their current value. ARV constraints have the form:

$$v_1 \wedge \cdots \wedge v_j \underset{\text{ARV}}{\Longrightarrow} v_k \qquad (\text{where } v_k \notin \{v_1,\cdots,v_j\})$$

This form handles the special case where all choices for v_1 through v_j require v_k. While logically equivalent to

$$\{v_1{=}d_{11} \vee \cdots \vee v_1{=}d_{1n_1}\} \wedge \cdots \wedge \{v_j{=}d_{j1} \vee \cdots \vee v_j{=}d_{jn_j}\} \rightarrow active{:}v_k$$

the special form is more compact and can lead to more efficient search. The search method presented in section 6 takes advantage of the form of ARV constraints to make v_k active as soon as v_1 through v_j become active, without waiting for particular value assignments to v_1 through v_j.

Note that the initial variables in the definition of a DCSP could alternatively be expressed as a set of ARV constraints whose conditions are "true". Thus, a given DCSP can be easily modified by simply changing such top-level ARV constraints.

4.3 Require Not

In addition to stating when variables must be in the problem space, some tasks require the ability to state when variables must not be in the problem space. For example, selecting a convertible body frame for a car is inconsistent with **any** type of sunroof. The *require not* (RN) constraint states an inconsistency between an assignment of values to a set of active variables and another variable being active. RN constraints have the form:

$$P(v_1,\cdots,v_n) \underset{\text{RN}}{\Longrightarrow} v_j \qquad (\text{where } v_j \notin \{v_1,\cdots,v_n\})$$

They are logically equivalent to

$$P(v_1,\cdots,v_n) \rightarrow \neg active{:}v_j$$

For some applications, this constraint is more efficiently reexpressed as an inconsistency (c.f. ATMS *NoGood* [1]):

$$P(v_1,\cdots,v_n) \wedge active{:}v_j \rightarrow \bot$$

where $\bot$ represents false.

RN constraints are particularly useful for expressing an incompatibility between variables without knowing if the variables will ever be active. This situation often arises when a given DCSP can be incrementally modified by simply adding a few other variables to the initial set.

4.4 Always Require Not

Analogous to the always require constraint, the *always require not* (ARN) constraint extends the basic notion of a require not constraint to rule out a variable's activity based on the activity of other variables, independent of their current value. ARN constraints have the form:

$$v_1 \wedge \cdots \wedge v_n \underset{\text{ARN}}{\Longrightarrow} v_j \qquad (\text{where } v_j \notin \{v_1,\cdots,v_n\})$$

and are logically equivalent to

$$active{:}v_1 \wedge \cdots \wedge active{:}v_n \rightarrow \neg active{:}v_j$$

or the corresponding NoGood.

5 Examples

The DCSP framework is being applied to two independent research problems. The first is concerned with configuration and automated design tasks [6; 14]. The second is concerned with composing the most appropriate model of a physical system given some query [4; 5]. In this section, we demonstrate our approach on some simplified examples taken from each.

5.1 Configuration

The following simple example of a DCSP has been formulated from a car configuration task (adapted from [13]). There are eight variables, of which three are in the initial variable set. Notice that the activity constraints have been used to represent many different kinds of domain knowledge such as packaging, functional requirements, structural decomposition, and incompatibilities. Similarly, compatibility constraints represent functional, structural, and packaging concerns.

Variable	**Domain**	
Package	{luxury, deluxe, standard}	*Initial var*
Frame	{convertible, sedan, hatchBack}	*Initial var*
Engine	{small, med, large}	*Initial var*
Battery	{small, med, large}	
Sunroof	{sr1,sr2}	
AirConditioner	{ac1,ac2}	
Glass	{tinted,not-tinted}	
Opener	{auto,manual}	

Activity constraints

1. Package=luxury $\underset{\text{RV}}{\Longrightarrow}$ Sunroof
2. Package=luxury $\underset{\text{RV}}{\Longrightarrow}$ AirConditioner
3. Package=deluxe $\underset{\text{RV}}{\Longrightarrow}$ Sunroof
4. Sunroof=sr2 $\underset{\text{RV}}{\Longrightarrow}$ Opener
5. Sunroof=sr1 $\underset{\text{RV}}{\Longrightarrow}$ AirConditioner
6. Sunroof $\underset{\text{ARV}}{\Longrightarrow}$ Glass
7. Engine $\underset{\text{ARV}}{\Longrightarrow}$ Battery
8. Opener $\underset{\text{ARV}}{\Longrightarrow}$ Sunroof
9. Glass $\underset{\text{ARV}}{\Longrightarrow}$ Sunroof
10. Sunroof=sr1 $\underset{\text{RN}}{\Longrightarrow}$ Opener
11. Frame=convertible $\underset{\text{RN}}{\Longrightarrow}$ Sunroof
12. Battery= small & Engine=small $\underset{\text{RN}}{\Longrightarrow}$ AirConditioner

Compatibility constraints

13. Package=standard $\rightarrow$ AirConditioner$\neq$ac2

14. Package=luxury → AirConditioner≠ac1
15. Package=standard → Frame≠convertible
16. Opener=auto & AirConditioner=ac1 → Battery=med
17. Opener=auto & AirConditioner=ac2 → Battery=large
18. Sunroof=sr1 & AirConditioner=ac2 → Glass≠Tinted

For this problem the smallest solutions have only four variables (Package, Frame, Engine, and Battery) and the largest have all eight. The description of a car configuration knowledge base given above would be augmented by additional constraints that represent user requirements before solving the problem. Thus, notice that changing the set of initial variables (e.g., by making `Sunroof` another initial variable) creates a somewhat different problem with different solutions, which may not simply be subsets of the solution set of the original problem.

5.2 Model composition

Compositional modeling is a method for reasoning about modeling assumptions and automatically composing the most appropriate model of a physical system for a given analytic query [4; 5]. The model composition problem is to synthesize the simplest model that is relevant to the needs of the task and consistent with the operating conditions of the system. This model must contain the parameters of interest, be able to show specified information about those parameters at a specified degree of accuracy, and minimize "cost" by reducing extraneous detail and computational effort. Many choices must be made, including the parts of the system to consider, their structural decomposition, the phenomena to consider, and how they should be modeled (e.g., what approximations can be applied).

In the compositional modeling framework, the system's models of various domains consists of a set of *elementary domain models*, each describing some fundamental piece of the domain's physics, such as processes (e.g., liquid flow), devices (e.g., transistor), and objects (e.g., container). Each elementary model is conditioned on a set of modeling assumptions stating their range of applicability and underlying approximations. Reasoning focuses on choosing among the set of possible modeling assumptions, which enable a corresponding set of elementary models, rather than reasoning about each elementary model individually. Model composition consists of four steps:

1. *Query analysis.* A query specifies a set of parameters of interest. Thus, a minimal requirement is that all of these parameters be modeled. Additionally, these parameters directly suggest further constraints. For example, a query about the level of liquid in a container indicates that a macroscopic, "contained fluids" view is called for as opposed to a microscopic "particle dynamics" view.

2. *Object expansion.* The query directly indicates a set of objects to consider, but additional objects may need to be considered to capture all relevant interactions.

3. *Candidate completion.* Some choices of simplifying assumptions raise new choices in turn. For example, considering liquid flowing through a pipe requires a decision about whether to model the fluid as compressible or incompressible.

4. *Candidate evaluation and selection.* Finally, each candidate is evaluated and the "best" candidate is selected.

Choices made during the first two stages are fully determined by the query. The DCSP framework is being used to express and solve the third stage, in which additional choices made relevant by the query must be made. In describing the possible modeling assumptions for a domain, some collections of assumptions represent mutually exclusive, alternative ways to model the same aspect of an object or phenomenon. To represent this important relationship, some assumptions are organized into sets called ***assumption classes.*** Each assumption class has a name c_i representing a DCSP variable; its domain is the set of assumptions in that class. The analytic query entails a set of minimal required modeling assumptions, which identify V_I, a DCSP's initial variables. The dynamic constraint satisfaction task is to extend this initial set to identify a set of modeling assumptions corresponding to a coherent and parsimonious model.

For example, consider the task of determining an appropriate set of modeling assumptions for analyzing the flow of water through a pipe connecting two containers. There are 7 variables, with the initial variable set consisting of V_I ={Precision, Can-Geometry}.[2]

Assumption Class	**Domain**
Precision	{qualitative,quantitative}
Can-Geometry	{quantity(level), ¬quantity(level)}
Can-Capacity	{finite-cans, infinite-cans}
Ontology	{energy-flows, contained-fluids, particle-dynamics}
Fluid-Density	{incompressible, compressible}
Fluid-Viscosity	{inviscid, viscous, non-newtonian}
Flow-Structure	{laminar, turbulent}

Activity constraints

Can-Geometry $\underset{ARV}{\Longrightarrow}$ Can-Capacity
Fluid-Viscosity=viscous $\underset{RV}{\Longrightarrow}$ Flow-Structure
Fluid-Viscosity=inviscid $\underset{RN}{\Longrightarrow}$ Flow-Structure
Precision=quantitative & Ontology=contained-fluids
$\underset{RV}{\Longrightarrow}$ Flow-Structure
Ontology=contained-fluids $\underset{RV}{\Longrightarrow}$ Fluid-Density
Ontology=particle-dynamics $\underset{RN}{\Longrightarrow}$ Fluid-Density
Ontology=particle-dynamics $\underset{RN}{\Longrightarrow}$ Can-Capacity

Compatibility constraints

Can-Geometry=quantity(level)
→ Ontology=contained-fluids
Flow-Structure=turbulent → Fluid-Viscosity≠inviscid

[2] A more sophisticated set of representations is used in the modeling work than shown here. We have highly simplified the representation descriptions in an effort to gain clarity.

Can-Capacity=finite-cans
→ Can-Geometry=quantity(level)

Given a query about the changing levels of the two containers, these constraints elaborate the query as needed to ensure that the resulting model is coherent. For example, asking about the changing fluid levels requires a model that represents a macroscopic view of liquids and their containers.

6 Algorithm and Implementation

6.1 ATMS-based Implementation

We have implemented the dynamic CSP framework as a specialized problem solver integrated with an *assumption-based truth maintenance system* (ATMS) [1]. The algorithm is designed to use our specialized language and is summarized in Figure 1. It enables constraints about variable activity (the *problem space*) to interact with constraints about variable values (the *solution space*), producing the two problem solving levels shown in Figure 2.

The algorithm consists of a main *choose / propagate* cycle based largely on [2]. Each choose step selects an active, unassigned variable and assigns it a value that has not been previously ruled out. Each propagate step checks the constraints relevant to the new variable value assignment and propagates their consequences and dependencies. Constraint checking is ordered to take advantage of the differing scope of each constraint type. ARV and ARN constraints are checked first because they have the largest scope (i.e., they apply to variable activity, encompassing all their possible value assignments). RV and RN are checked second, because they affect a variable's activity, independent of its possible values. Finally, compatibility constraints are examined to see if the new variable value assignment is consistent. A constraint is "run" when it becomes active. Due to ATMS caching, each constraint need only be run once. Constraints that never become active during the course of problem solving are never checked. Search for each solution terminates when all active variables have been consistently assigned a value (i.e., there are no more variables for the choose step). Other variables do not appear in the solution.

Here we informally show that the algorithm is sound, which requires showing that each solution generated meets the criteria specified in section 3. The first criterion, that each solution satisfies all the constraints in $C^C \cup C^A$, is easy to show since each time a value is assigned to an active variable, all the constraints activated by that assignment are checked before the next choose.

The second criterion states that each solution must be minimal in the sense that there should be no other solution that is a superset of another. Since a solution is described by a set of variables and their associated value assignments, a proof of minimality requires proving two properties for each solution. One, no variable is assigned a value unless it is active. Two, a variable

Figure 1: Dynamic constraint satisfaction algorithm.

```
procedure DCSP (V_I)

V ← V_I
SOLUTION ← empty
Check all applicable activity and compatibility constraints
if CONTRADICTION(V, SOLUTION),
   then return fail (initial problem statement is inconsistent)
BACKUP? ← false

while V is not empty
      if BACKUP? or CONTRADICTION(V, SOLUTION)
        then backtrack and change V and SOLUTION.
             if backtracking fails,
               then return fail.
             BACKUP? ← false

      else if there is an active ARV constraint c_i
         then run c_i and add newly activated variables to V
      else if there is an active ARN constraint c_i
         then run c_i
      else if there is an active RV constraint c_i
         then run c_i and add newly activated variables to V
      else if there is an active RN constraint c_i
         then run c_i
      else if there is an active compatibility constraint c_i
         then run c_i
      else v_i ← SELECT&DELETE(V) {choose next variable}
           value(v_i) ← CHOOSE(v_i)      {choose an assignment}
           if value(v_i) is NULL,
             then BACKUP? ←true
             else add value(v_i) to SOLUTION

return SOLUTION
```

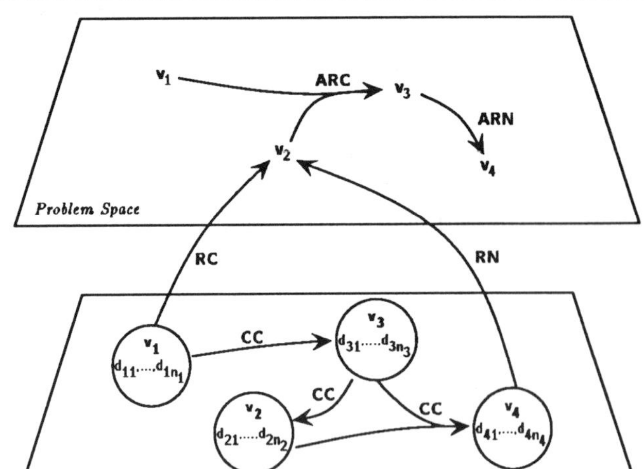

Figure 2: A dynamic constraint satisfaction network.

is made active if and only it has well-founded support from the initial set of active variables. It is easy to see that the first property holds since the only variables that are assigned values are those that have been made active by a previous step in the main loop. The second property, i.e., well-founded support for active variables can be seen to hold for our algorithm based on the following observations. *One*, at any time through the loop in the algorithm, a new variable *v* is made active if and only if there are some active activity constraints that justify it and there is no active activity constraint that contradicts *v*'s activity. This ensures that a variable becomes active if and only if it has well-founded support. In other words, all active variables in a solution are required either by the initial variables or by explicitly chosen value assignments. *Two*, the only place where a choice is made (i.e., a branch in the search space) is in the assignment of a value to a variable. Each such choice generates a potentially different solution. Notice that in the language described so far, there is no disjunction over required variable constraints. While such disjunctive activity constraints will be necessary for expressing some types of domain knowledge, finding minimal solutions in the presence of such constraints can be very expensive. We are exploring heuristics that will work in some special cases. Also see [15] for an alternative formulation of disjunctive require constraints in some cases.

6.2 Example Trace

Here we briefly show a partial trace of our algorithm solving the car configuration example described in section 5.1. The algorithm does not commit to any heuristics for selecting the next variable or choosing a value for the selected variable. For this trace assume that a "smallest domain size" heuristic is used to select variables and the "first value" heuristic is used to choose variable values. We show the active variables and value assignments in bold font, constraint propagation and value choices in italics, and explanatory comments in roman. We have also shortened the names of the variables to the first letter.

V_I = {P,F,E}
C7 runs (ARV making B active)
V = {P,F,E,B}
Choose P=luxury
C1 runs (RV making S active)
V = {P=luxury,F,E,B,S}
C6 runs (ARV making G active)
V = {P=luxury,F,E,B,S,G}
C2 runs (RV making A active)
V = {P=luxury,F,E,B,S,G,A}
C9 runs, (ARV on S - no change to the active variables)
V = {P=luxury,F,E,B,S,G,A}
C14 runs (constraint between P and A, creating nogood{P=luxury, A=ac1}
Choose A=ac2
Choose F=convertible
V = {P=luxury,F=convertible,E,B,S,G,A=ac2}
C11 runs (RN on S, leading to a contradiction (C1 & C11))
Backup to the previous choice point
Choose F=sedan
V = {P=luxury,F=sedan,E,B,S,G,A=ac2}
Choose E=small
Choose B=small
V = {P=luxury,F=sedan,E=small,B=small, S,G,A=ac2}
C12 runs (RN on A, leading to a contradiction on AirConditioner activity (C2 & C12))
Backup to the previous choice point
Choose B=medium
V = {P=luxury,F=sedan,E=small,B=medium, S,G,A=ac2}
Choose S=sr1
V = {P=luxury,F=sedan,E=small,B=medium, S=sr1,G,A=ac2}
C5 runs (RV on A - no change to the active variables)
C10 runs (RN on O - no immediate effect)
C18 runs, creating nogood{S=sr1, A=ac2, G=tinted}
Choose G=not-tinted
V = {P=luxury,F=sedan,E=small,B=medium, S=sr1,G=not-tinted,A=ac2}
This is one of the possible solutions. Others can be found by backtracking.

6.3 Backtracking Implementation

A subset of our language (only the RV and CC constraints) has also been implemented by extending a conventional backtrack-search CSP framework [13]. The basic algorithm is similar to the one shown in Figure 1 with the major difference that each time an active variable is assigned a value, we use forward checking to propagate all active compatibility constraints.

This implementation was also used for making some comparisons between solving a DCSP directly using the method presented here versus solving a logically equivalent "static" CSP. The latter was obtained by introducing a new distinguished value called "null" in the domains of all variables and by appropriate transformations of all constraints such that they are trivially satisfied if one or more variables have a "null" value. In the examples that we tried, the DCSP version outperformed the "static" CSP version in all the performance metrics we measured (total time, number of backtracks, constraint checks and total variable assignments). Even on simple problems the difference in constraint checks, the metric most commonly used in the literature, was quite significant. A more detailed comparison will be presented in an extended version of this paper.

7 Discussion

In this paper we showed how to extend a constraint satisfaction framework to include constraints on activity of variables. With these extensions, we described a core language for compactly representing selection and composition constraints in synthesis tasks. We also described an algorithm that efficiently finds minimal (non-redundant) solutions to such dynamic CSPs.

We believe that the combination of the DCSP version of a problem and our method for solving such problems is effective for two reasons. One, by creating distinct kinds of constraints, we can tune a search engine to take advantage of these distinctions in focussing the search. Two, in the DCSP version most of the variables and constraints are initially "not active". Thus, the constraint graph for the problem starts out by being very sparsely connected. It is filled only as the result of choices made by the search engine. Theoretical and empirical results [3; 8; 9] based on analyses of constraint graphs clearly show a close correspondence between the search effort and connectivity (e.g., width) of variables in the problem. The DCSP version (when relevant) "hides" many of the variables and constraints. Clearly more work is needed here, especially in terms of precise mathematical analysis that can quantify this intuition.

We are also developing improved heuristics for choosing the next active variable (e.g., most supported) or choosing a value from the domain of these variables (e.g., based on how many variables are activated by a choice). We are also looking at heuristics that help with disjunctive require constraints.

The language we have presented is only a subset of what will eventually be needed for modelling the relationships that are important in synthesis tasks. For example, referring back to the discussion in section 2, note that we need to express constraints of the form that a component may also provide additional functional roles or that it cannot be part of a configured solution by itself, i.e., without some other parent component. We have already alluded to the need for expressing disjunctive activity constraints, the simplest examples arising in cases where a component's requirements can be satisfied by disjunctive functional roles. Our methodology has been to identify language primitives for expressing some domain relationships and then examine their implications for our search method both in terms of efficiency of search and minimality of solutions found. We expect to report progress on developing a more complete language in the next paper.

8 Acknowledgments

Felix Frayman and Harley Davis made important contributions in defining the basic notion of a dynamic CSP in the context of formalizing configuration tasks. We are grateful to Dan Bobrow, Johan deKleer, Vijay Saraswat, and Mark Shirley for in-depth discussions and comments on earlier drafts of this paper.

References

[1] de Kleer, J. An assumption-based TMS. *Artificial Intelligence*, 28(2), March 1986.

[2] de Kleer, J. and Williams, B. Back to backtracking: Controlling the ATMS. In *Proceedings of AAAI-86*, August, 1986.

[3] Dechter, R. J and Pearl, J. Network-based heuristics for constraint-satisfaction problems. *Artificial Intelligence*, 34(1):1–38, December 1987.

[4] Falkenhainer, B and Forbus, K. D. Setting up large-scale qualitative models. In *Proceedings of AAAI-88*, August 1988.

[5] Falkenhainer, B and Forbus, K. D. Compositional modeling: Finding the right model for the job. (*submitted for publication*), January 1990.

[6] Frayman, F and Mittal, S. Cossack: A Constraints-Based Expert System for Configuration Tasks. In Sriram, D and Adey, R. A, editors, *Knowledge Based Expert Systems in Engineering: Planning and Design*. Computational Mechanics Publications,pp. 143–166, August 1987.

[7] Freeman-Benson, B. N., Maloney, J., Borning, A. An Incremental Constraint Solver *Communications of the ACM*, 33(1):54–63, January 1990.

[8] Freuder, E. C. A sufficient condition for backtrack-free search. *Journal of ACM*, 29(1):24–32, 1982.

[9] Freuder, E. C. A sufficient condition for backtrack-bounded search. *Journal of ACM*, 32(4):755–761, 1985.

[10] Joxan, J. and Lassez. J. Constraint Logic Programming Technical Report, IBM Thomas J. Watson Res. Ctr., Yorktown Hts., NY, USA, October 1986

[11] Mackworth, A. K. Consistency in networks of relations. *Artificial Intelligence*, 8:99–118, 1977.

[12] Mackworth, A. K. Constraint Satisfaction. In Shapiro, S. C. (ed.), *Encyclopedia of Artificial Intelligence*, Vol. I, 2nd edition,John Wiley & Sons, New York, 1990

[13] Mittal, S and Davis, H. Representing and solving hierarchical constraint problems. SSL Technical report, Xerox PARC, 1989.

[14] Mittal, S. and Frayman, F. Towards a Generic Model of Configuration Tasks. *Proceedings IJCAI-89*, Detroit, Michigan, August 1989.

[15] Mittal, S. Reasoning about Resource Constraints in Configuration Tasks. SSL Technical report, Xerox PARC, 1990

[16] Mulder, J., A. Mackworth, W. S. Havens Knowledge Structuring and Constraint Satisfaction: The Mapsee Approach. *IEEE Trans. on Pattern Analysis and Machine Intelligence*, 10(6):866–879, November 1988.

[17] Seidel, R. A New Method for Solving Constraint Satisfaction Problems. *Proc. IJCAI-81*, pages 338–342, Vancouver, Canada, August 24-28, 1981.

The Complexity of Constraint Satisfaction in Prolog

Bernard A. Nadel

Department of Computer Science
Wayne State University
Detroit, Michigan, 48202
ban@cs.wayne.edu

Abstract

We obtain here the complexity of solving a type of Prolog problem which Genesereth and Nilsson have called *sequential constraint satisfaction.* Such problems are of direct relevance to relational database retrieval as well as providing a tractable first step in analyzing Prolog problem-solving in the general case. The present paper provides the first analytic expressions for the expected complexity of solving sequential constraint satisfaction problems. These expressions provide a basis for the formal derivation of heuristics for such problems, analogous to the theory-based heuristics obtained by the author for traditional constraint satisfaction problem-solving. A first application has been in providing a formal basis for Warren's heuristic for optimally ordering the goals in a conjunctive query. Due to the incorporation of "constraint looseness" into the analysis, the expected complexity obtained here has the useful property that it is usually quite accurate even for individual problem instances, rather than only for the assumed underlying problem class as a whole. Heuristics based on these results can be expected to be equally instance-specific. Preliminary results for Warren's heuristic have shown this to be the case.

1. Introduction

Two areas of major interest in Artificial Intelligence are *constraint satisfaction* problem solving and the logic programming language *Prolog.* Recently there has been considerable interest in the relationship between these two areas [4] [14] [16] [17] [18]. This paper grew out of a study of this relationship. It treats one of the simplest types of Prolog problems, which Genesereth and Nilsson [2] call *sequential constraint satisfaction problems.* These involve a database consisting of no rules, but only of facts all of which are ground, and a query which is a conjunction of positive literals containing variables. Strategies for ordering the conjunctive queries have been studied in [15] and [19].

The present paper provides the first analytic expressions for the expected complexity of solving such problems. The analysis is based on a division of the problem class into what we call *small classes*, defined in section 2. These classes, and the assumed probability model defined in section 3, are analogs for Prolog of those used in the author's earlier analyses of the complexity of traditional constraint satisfaction problem-solving [6], [8], [12]. As opposed to the *big classes* which were also used in prior work (but which are not defined here), most instances of a small classes have remarkably similar complexity values.

This *homogeneity* property is the result of taking into account "constraint tightness" (in terms of S_j or R_j below) in defining small classes. As a result of small class homogeneity, the expected case complexity for a given small class is likely to be a good estimate of the "exact case" complexity of most individual instances in the small class. This makes the expected case results much more practical by allowing them to be used for complexity prediction on an instance-by-instance basis, independent of the applicable probability distribution, if any, rather than only for a small class as a whole, under the assumed distribution.

The expected complexity for solving sequential constraint satisfaction problems is obtained in section 4, in terms of the expected number of nodes in the Prolog search tree for finding all solutions of a problem in a small class. Extensions of the results are discussed briefly in section 5. A simple running example is used throughout.

The complexity expressions obtained here provide a formal basis for the derivation of heuristics for solving this kind of Prolog problem, analogous to the theory-based derivation of heuristics (for choosing a good algorithm, search ordering and even problem representation) which has been possible for regular constraint satisfaction problem-solving [3] [6] [7] [8] [9] [12] [13]. A first example of this for our Prolog problems has been in providing a formal basis for Warren's intuitively motivated heuristic for optimally ordering the goals in a conjunctive query [19]. The instance-specificity of the complexity results here is expected to carry over to the theory-based heuristics derived from them. Preliminary results for Warren's heuristic show this to be the case. By generalizing the problem class under consideration (in particular, allowing databases with rules and variables) it should be possible to obtain similar instance-specific, theory-based guidance for Prolog problem solving in general.

2. Sequential Constraint Satisfaction Problems and Small Classes

To analyze the complexity of solving sequential constraint satisfaction problems it is convenient to divide[1] the space of all possible databases for such problems into what we class small classes. The expected complexity derived will be over the databases of a small class, each database arising with equal probability as described in the next section.

Associated with a small class is an underlying set $Z = \{z_1, z_2, \ldots, z_n\}$ of n variables, each having a finite domain $d_{z_i} = \{1, 2, \ldots, m_{z_i}\}$ of m_{z_i} candidate values. We denote the domain values as integers here for convenience, but the results apply for values that are arbitrary Prolog ground terms. Variables z_i will sometimes be called ***domain variables*** or ***formal variables*** to distinguish them from ***logical variables*** which appear in the queries to be asked with respect to a database.

There is a set $P = \{p_1, p_2, \ldots, p_K\}$ of K predicate symbols, each having an associated *fact template*

$$p_j(z_{i_1}, z_{i_2}, \ldots, z_{i_{A_j}}) \tag{1}$$

which specifies its ***arguments variables*** $z_{i_k} \in Z$ and their corresponding argument positions. The order of arguments in a template is usually, but not necessarily, in increasing order of the argument variable indices. A fact template is analogous to a *relation schema* in relational database theory [5]. It is *not* the same thing as a literal used in a query of the Prolog database, although they are related as discussed below. $Z_j = \{z_{i_1}, z_{i_2}, \ldots, z_{i_{A_j}}\}$ and $A_j = |Z_j|$ are respectively the ***argument set*** and ***arity*** of p_j. We may assume without loss of generality that the set Z of all variables is given by $Z = \bigcup_{j=1}^{K} Z_j$.

Each database of the small class consists only of ground facts for each of the predicate symbols p_j. The fact templates serve to specify the form and range of these facts. Specifically, facts for p_j must have the form

$$p_j(\bar{z}_{i_1}, \bar{z}_{i_2}, \ldots, \bar{z}_{i_{A_j}})$$

where $\bar{z}_{i_k}$ is a value chosen only from the domain of the argument variable z_{i_k} occurring for that position in the fact template. Each fact $p_j(\bar{Z}_j)$ thus corresponds to an A_j-tuple $\bar{Z}_j$ from the cartesian product D_j of the domains of the arguments of p_j. Cartesian product D_j and its size M_j are given respectively by $D_j = \bigtimes_{z_i \in Z_j} d_{z_i}$ and $M_j = \prod_{z_i \in Z_j} m_{z_i}$.

For each p_j there is a parameter S_j, called the ***satisfiability*** of p_j, which specifies how many facts for p_j are in the database. The quantity $R_j = S_j/M_j$ we call the ***satisfiability ratio*** for p_j. Of course S_j and R_j respectively satisfy $0 \le S_j \le M_j$ and $0 \le R_j \le 1$. R_j is the fraction of possible tuples (formable from the domains of the corresponding argument variables) which actually correspond to facts in the database for p_j. Considering the goals of a conjunctive query as constraints to be simultaneously satisfied, R_j is a measure of the looseness of the constraint corresponding to the p_j goal.

The required S_j facts for p_j can correspond to any size-S_j subset of D_j and hence there are $\binom{M_j}{S_j}$ ways to choose the facts for p_j. Since such a choice of S_j facts is required for each p_j, $1 \le j \le K$, the number of sequential constraint satisfaction databases scsd in a small class is

$$|\mathrm{SCSD}(n, \mathbf{m}, K, \mathbf{Z}, \mathbf{S})| = \prod_{j=1}^{K} \binom{M_j}{S_j}.$$

Here $\mathrm{SCSD}(n, \mathbf{m}, K, \mathbf{Z}, \mathbf{S})$ denotes the generic small class characterized by n problem variables, set $\mathbf{m} = \{m_{z_1}, m_{z_2}, \ldots, m_{z_n}\}$ of domain sizes, K predicate symbols, set $\mathbf{Z} = \{Z_1, Z_2, \ldots, Z_K\}$ of predicate argument sets and set $\mathbf{S} = \{S_1, S_2, \ldots, S_K\}$ of predicate satisfiabilities.

[1] This division is not a partition however, since a given database may be considered as a member of an infinite number of small classes, as implied in section 5 and discussed more fully in [11].

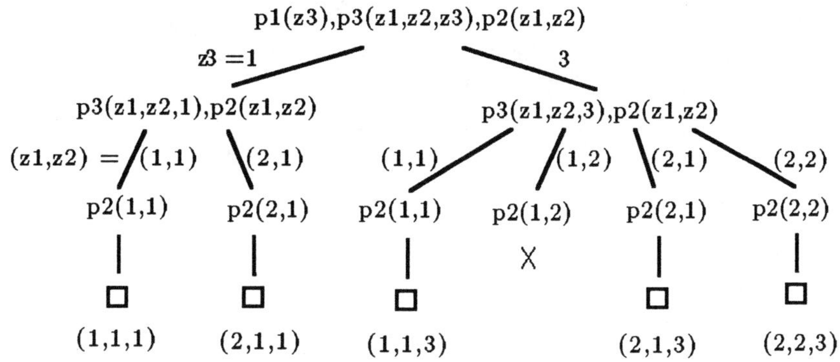

k	N_k	$\bar{N}_k$		
0	1	1	=	1
1	2	$1 \cdot (3 \cdot \frac{2}{3})$	=	2
2	6	$2 \cdot (4 \cdot \frac{10}{12})$	=	$6\frac{2}{3}$
3	5	$6\frac{2}{3} \cdot (1 \cdot \frac{3}{4})$	=	5
	14			$14\frac{2}{3}$

Fig. 1: The Prolog search tree for the scsp of solving query (2) with respect to our example database.

For example, consider the set $Z = \{z_1, z_2, z_3\}$ of $n = 3$ underlying domain variables, having domains $d_{z_1} = d_{z_2} = \{1, 2\}$ and $d_{z_3} = \{1, 2, 3\}$ of respective sizes $m_{z_1} = m_{z_2} = 2$ and $m_{z_3} = 3$. Let's say the database consists of facts for $K = 3$ predicate symbols p_1, p_2, p_3, with respective fact templates $p_1(z_3)$, $p_2(z_1, z_2)$, $p_3(z_1, z_2, z_3)$ and satisfiabilities $S_1 = 2$, $S_2 = 3$, $S_3 = 10$. The cartesian products for the three predicates therefore have respective sizes $M_1 = m_{z_3} = 3$, $M_2 = m_{z_1} \times m_{z_2} = 4$ and $M_3 = m_{z_1} \times m_{z_2} \times m_{z_3} = 12$. Thus the number of databases in the small class is $\binom{M_1}{S_1} \times \binom{M_2}{S_2} \times \binom{M_3}{S_3} = \binom{3}{2} \times \binom{4}{3} \times \binom{12}{10} = 792$. The following is one of these 792 possible Prolog databases:

$p_1(1)$. $p_1(3)$. $p_2(1,1)$. $p_2(2,1)$. $p_2(2,2)$.
$p_3(1,1,1)$. $p_3(1,1,2)$. $p_3(1,1,3)$. $p_3(1,2,2)$. $p_3(1,2,3)$.
$p_3(2,1,1)$. $p_3(2,1,2)$. $p_3(2,1,3)$. $p_3(2,2,2)$. $p_3(2,2,3)$.

As required by the corresponding fact templates, the values for the single argument of p_1 come from the domain of z_3, the values for the first and second arguments of p_2 are respectively from the domains of z_1 and z_2, and the first, second and third argument values for p_3 are respectively from the domains of z_1, z_2 and z_3.

A sequential constraint satisfaction problem *scsp* is a sequential constraint satisfaction database *scsd* plus an associated conjunctive query Q such as

$$?\!-\ p_1(z_3), p_3(z_1, z_2, z_3), p_2(z_1, z_2). \qquad (2)$$

The z_i here are logical variables, not necessarily related to the domain variables of the same name used to define the small class. Figure 1 shows the Prolog search tree for solving this query with respect to the above database. Success nodes, indicated by $\Box$, are labelled by the corresponding 3-tuple solution for the logical variables in the order (z_1, z_2, z_3). In the following sections we derive the expected case complexity of answering such queries with respect to the databases of a small class. The analysis is for the case, as in figure 1, where *all* solutions of a query are sought.

3. Probability Model

The probability model we assume for the databases of a small class is very straight-forward: each selection of S_j tuples from the cartesian product D_j of the j-th constraint is equally likely, and such a selection is made independently for each predicate p_j, $1 \le j \le K$. As such, each database scsd in a small class SCSD is equally likely, with probability $P(\text{scsd}) = |\text{SCSD}|^{-1} = \prod_{j=1}^{K} \binom{M_j}{S_j}^{-1}$.

4. Expected Complexity

For the generic small class SCSD$(n, \mathbf{m}, K, \mathbf{Z}, \mathbf{S})$ described above, our analysis considers only queries which are a conjunction, in any order, of K positive literals, one for each small class predicate symbol p_j. These literals contain logical variables. In practice, logical variables are not necessarily named z_i as are the domain variables in terms of which a small class is defined. Nor is there necessarily a one to one correspondence between logical variables in the set of query literals and domain variables in the set of fact templates. For example, given our previous example small class, such a correspondence is lacking for query

$$?\!-\ p_1(z_1), p_2(z_1, z_3), p_3(z_3, z_1, z_2) \qquad (3)$$

even though this is a perfectly legal query. However, for the following analysis we assume queries for which such a one to one correspondence does exist. For simplicity we may then assume that logical variables have the same names as their corresponding domain variables. Therefore, if in the small class definition, a predicate has associated fact template as in (1), then we assume an "isomorphic" corresponding literal

$$p_j(Z_j) = p_j(z_{i_1}, z_{i_2}, \ldots, z_{i_{A_j}}), \tag{4}$$

in the query, the z_i here of course being logical variables. As in (4), we may therefore also use Z_j to denote the set of logical variables of the p_j query literal, as well as for the set of domain variables in the p_j fact template.

To allow for an arbitrary permutation π of conjunctions (literals) in the query, we write p^j and Z^j respectively for the predicate symbol and the argument set of the j-th literal in the query. The queries we consider are thus of the form

$$?\text{-}\ p^1(Z^1), p^2(Z^2), \ldots, p^K(Z^K) \tag{5}$$

where $p^j = p_{\pi(j)}$ and $Z^j = Z_{\pi(j)}$ (and similarly for all predicate-related quantities: $D^j = D_{\pi(j)}$, $M^j = M_{\pi(j)}$, $S^j = S_{\pi(j)}$, $R^j = R_{\pi(j)}$). Query (2) used in figure 1 is of the form given by (4) and (5), assumed in our analysis. It corresponds to permutation $\pi = \left(\begin{smallmatrix} 1 & 2 & 3 \\ 1 & 3 & 2 \end{smallmatrix}\right)$ and we have $p^1 = p_{\pi(1)} = p_1$, $p^2 = p_{\pi(2)} = p_3$ and $p^3 = p_{\pi(3)} = p_2$, and analogously $Z^1 = Z_1$, $Z^2 = Z_3$ and $Z^3 = Z_2$. Another query of the form covered by our analysis is

$$?\text{-}\ p_2(z_1, z_2), p_1(z_3), p_3(z_1, z_2, z_3).$$

corresponding to permutation $\pi = \left(\begin{smallmatrix} 1 & 2 & 3 \\ 2 & 1 & 3 \end{smallmatrix}\right)$.

As our measure of complexity for solving sequential constraint satisfaction problems in Prolog we use the number of nodes in the Prolog search tree for finding all solutions. We include the root node and the success nodes $\square$. Variations on this measure may be appropriate for different implementations of Prolog, but in general these variations should be closely related to the fundamental measure used here and be derivable by a similar analysis.

Counting the root node as being at level $k = 0$, the search tree for solving a scsp has levels $k = 0, 1, \ldots, K$, as for example in figure 1. Since the number of nodes N in a search tree can of course be expressed as the sum of the number of nodes N_k at each level k of the tree we have $N = \sum_{k=0}^{K} N_k$. Taking the expectation of both sides we have that the expected number of nodes in a Prolog search tree for instances of a small class of K predicates is the sum of the expected number $\bar{N}_k$ of nodes at each level,

$$\bar{N} = \sum_{k=0}^{K} \bar{N}_k. \tag{6}$$

We now obtain a recursive, then non-recursive, expression for $\bar{N}_k$. The nodes at level k arise as children of those at level $k-1$. These children of a node are generated by unifying in all ways the leftmost literal at a level $k-1$ node with the corresponding facts in the database. The leftmost literal at a level $k-1$ node is the p^k literal (that corresponding to predicate symbol p^k) and each node at level $k-1$ potentially has a child for each combination of values that can be assigned to the uninstantiated variables of that literal. The set of *instantiated* variables is the same for the leftmost literal of each level $k-1$ node, and is the union $I^{(k)} = \bigcup_{j=1}^{k-1} Z^j$ of the argument sets of the initial-query literals $p^1(Z^1)$ to $p^{k-1}(Z^{k-1})$, since these literals have all been solved at preceding levels. The set of *uninstantiated* variables of the p^k literal at a level $k-1$ node is thus $U^{(k)} = Z^k - I^{(k)}$, the set difference between the argument set for the literal and the instantiated variables so far.

By definition of the parent small class, there are m_{z_i} à priori possible values for variable z_i. Each uninstantiated variable $z_i \in U^{(k)}$ of the p^k literal at a level $k-1$ node has such an associated domain, and hence

$$m^{(k)} = \prod_{z_i \in U^{(k)}} m_{z_i} \tag{7}$$

children are à priori possible for a level $k-1$ node by unifying each uninstantiated variable in all ways against facts in the database. However, also by definition of the parent small class, only some fraction $R^k = S^k/M^k$ of the possible M^k tuples of the cartesian product D^k correspond to database facts for p^k. Thus only this fraction of the maximum M^k unifications are possible (the actual number of possible unifications being $S^k = R^k M^k$) for the initial-query literal $p^k(Z^k)$. Even though in general the p^k literal at level $k-1$ is not $p^k(Z^k)$, but is $p^k(Z^k)$ with some argument variables $z_i \in Z^k$ already instantiated, the same fraction R^k nevertheless governs how many unifications are possible on average for the p^k literal at level $k-1$ against database facts, given an arbitrary assignment of values to its instantiated variables. But due to the instantiation of some variables of the p^k literal, this fraction is now out of $m^{(k)}$ possibilities rather than all M^k.

The average number of children (or average branching factor) of a level $k-1$ node is therefore $m^{(k)}R^k$. The average number of nodes at level k is thus $\bar{N}_k = \bar{N}_{k-1}m^{(k)}R^k$, the average number of nodes at the previous level by their average branching factor. We have then the following recurrence for the expected number of nodes at level k in the Prolog search tree

$$\bar{N}_k = \begin{cases} 1 & \text{if } k=0 \\ \bar{N}_{k-1}m^{(k)}R^k & \text{if } 1 \le k \le K \end{cases} \tag{8}$$

which, by induction, has the closed-form solution

$$\bar{N}_k \;=\; \prod_{j=1}^{k} m^{(j)}\,R^j \;=\; \prod_{j=1}^{k}\Big[\prod_{z_i\in U^{(j)}} m_{z_i}\Big]\,R^j. \tag{9}$$

A product over no terms (i.e. when $k=0$) is considered to equal 1 (cf. $x^0 = 1$). Similarly in (7), if there are no uninstantiated argument variables for the p^k literal at level $k-1$ then $m^{(k)} = 1$. By (6) and (9), the expected total number of nodes in a Prolog search tree is

$$\bar{N} = \sum_{k=0}^{K}\prod_{j=1}^{k} m^{(j)}R^j = \sum_{k=0}^{K}\prod_{j=1}^{k}\Big[\prod_{z_i\in U^{(j)}} m_{z_i}\Big]R^j \tag{10}$$

Note that for $k=K$, expression (9) must be the expected number of solutions for an instance of a small class — a result which (unlike $\bar{N}_k$ for $k<K$) is of course independent of the ordering of the K conjuncts in the initial query. Since by assumption, Z is the set of all variables appearing in the K literals of the initial query, and the set of uninstantiated variables at the leftmost literal over all levels must be Z, we have from (9) when $k=K$, that the expected number of solutions is

$$\bar{S} = \Big[\prod_{z_i\in Z} m_{z_i}\Big]\Big[\prod_{j=1}^{K} R_j\Big].$$

Figure 1 includes a table at the right showing the number of nodes N_k at each level k for the particular problem instance being solved and also the corresponding expected number of nodes $\bar{N}_k$ by (8) at level k for the small class to which the instance belongs. For example, in calculating the expected number of nodes $\bar{N}_2$ at level $k=2$, there are 2 uninstantiated variables, z_1 and z_2, in the leftmost $p^2 = p_3$ literal at the preceding level $k=1$. We thus have $m^2 = m_{z_1} \times m_{z_2} = 4$, and from the initial specification of the small class we have $R^2 = R_3 = S_3/M_3 = 10/12$. Thus $(4 \cdot \frac{10}{12})$ is the second factor in the expression for $\bar{N}_2$ in the table of figure 1. By (8), the first factor is $\bar{N}_1$ from the preceding line of the table.

5. Applications and Extensions

Due to the preliminary nature of the work and also because of space restrictions, we only sketch here the ways in which the above complexity results may be applied and extended. This section is based on [11] where these issues have been addressed in more detail.

The above complexity expressions are for finding all solutions to a conjunctive query against databases of an arbitrary small class, where the databases are all equally likely. As such, our complexities are exact *expected case* results. However, we have found them also to be good approximations to the *exact case* complexity of solving most individual instances of a given small class.

Experiments have shown that most instances of a small class have a similar complexity of solution, and so the expected case complexity for a small class is close to that of most subsumed instances. Specifically, we have found that about 85% of the instances in a small class have (exact-case) complexity of solution within 15% of the expected complexity for their small class value. It is in this sense that we say that small classes are ***homogeneous***. Homogeneity is an unusual and very useful property of problem subclasses. It was first observed for the essentially same kind of small classes (called *c-classes* in [12]) used in our analyses of traditional (non-Prolog) methods for solving constraint satisfaction problems [6] [8] [12].

The key to obtaining homogeneity for constraint satisfaction problems is the use of the R_j "constraint looseness" parameters in defining small classes. Problem instances whose corresponding "constraints" have equal looseness are usually sufficiently alike, given equality of the other parameters used in defining a small class, that their complexities of solution are also close. Small class homogeneity allows our expected case complexity to be used — as in figure 1 — as a good estimate for individual instances of the corresponding small class. As such, the results can be applied irrespective of the actual probability distribution or grouping of instances that occurs in practice. The notion of homogeneity and its importance is studied more fully in [10].

However our analysis assumed a query of quite restricted form; in particular we required literals to be isomorphic to the fact templates defining the small class (see (4)). More general kinds of queries are certainly possible, such as that in (3). Our results do not give the *expected* complexity for solving such queries.

However, in approximating the *exact* case complexity for a specific problem instance our results may be applied even for these different kinds of queries. The reason is simply because when only a single instance is of interest, no particular parent small class has been specified. The latter may therefore be chosen as convenient for the purposes of the computation. In particular, we are free to choose the parent small class so that the database query of interest satisfies the required assumptions of the analysis. The procedure is quite straight-forward, as given in [11]. Having chosen an appropriate parent small class, the corresponding parameter values are inserted into (10). Due to homogeneity, the resulting expected complexity for the small class is likely to be a good approximation for the original instance even though the small class is only a "nominal" parent of the instance. In this way small class homogeneity allows our results to be used to approximate well the *exact* case complexity of most scsp instances, even for conjunctive queries not of the type assumed for the *expected* case analysis per se.

The next logical step is to consider ways in which our results may guide problem solving so as to *minimize* complexity, rather than just *predicting* the complexity. Warren in [19] has proposed a heuristic for ordering the conjuncts in a query: rank the literals according to increasing cost, where cost of a literal (he calls them *goal predicates*) is defined as "the total size (i.e. number of tuples) of the relation corresponding to the goal predicate, divided by the product of the sizes of the domains of each instantiated argument position". It is not obvious why his cost measure, and its use in this way, is appropriate. However it becomes clear when the relation to our analysis is established. In our notation Warren's cost for the k-th literal in a query is

$$\begin{aligned} S^k / \prod_{z_i \in I^{(k)}} m_{z_i} &= S^k / \prod_{z_i \in Z^k - U^{(k)}} m_{z_i} \\ &= S^k \Big[\prod_{z_i \in U^{(k)}} m_{z_i} \Big] / M^k \\ &= \Big[\prod_{z_i \in U^{(k)}} m_{z_i} \Big] R^k \\ &= m^{(k)} R^k \end{aligned}$$

This is just the branching factor from (8). In other words, Warren's heuristic can be interpreted as

1. implicitly assuming that the instance of interest is a member of its natural parent small class, uniformly distributed according to our probability model above

2. choosing the next literal using a "greedy" approach of minimizing the expected (over the parent small class) branching factor, and hence the expected number (over the parent small class) of nodes at the next level

3. implicitly taking advantage of small class homogeneity in using the result obtained with respect to the parent small class as appropriate to the initial instance itself.

Our experiments [1] have shown Warren's heuristic to usually lead to the optimal, or a near optimal, conjunct ordering in terms of minimizing the expected total number of nodes $\bar{N}$ for the assumed parent small class of a given instance. Moreover, as a result of small class homogeneity, the actual total number of nodes N for a given instance is usually close to $\bar{N}$ for its parent small class, so that the conjunct ordering which minimizes $\bar{N}$ also tends to minimize N for the instance.

However, Warren's heuristic does not *always* succeed in minimizing $\bar{N}$ of a small classes, let alone in minimizing N of an individual member instance. More accurate heuristics are however implicit in our results above. One just needs to use (10) more completely, rather than in the incomplete greedy manner in which it was implicitly used by Warren. We are currently investigating such improved theory-based heuristic guidance in solving sequential constraint satisfaction problems [1]. Moreover, by generalizing the problem class under consideration (in particular, to allow databases with rules and variables) it should be similarly possible to obtain a formal basis for instance-specific, theory-based optimization of Prolog problem solving in general.

References

[1] Chugh K., *Theory-based heuristics for constraint satisfaction in Prolog*, Computer Science Dept., Wayne State University, Detroit, Michigan, M. Sc. thesis, 1990, to appear.

[2] Genesereth M. R., and Nilsson N. J., "Logical Foundations of Artificial Intelligence", *Morgan Kaufmann*, Los Altos, California., 1987.

[3] Haralick R. M. and Elliot G. L., "Increasing tree search efficiency for constraint satisfaction problems", *Artificial Intelligence*, vol. 14, 1980, pp. 263-313.

[4] Jaffar J. and Lassez J.-L., "Constraint logic programming", *Proc. 14-th ACM Conference on Principles of Programming Languages*, Munich, West Germany, January, 1987.

[5] Maier D., *The Theory of Relational Databases*, Computer Science Press, Rockville, Maryland, 1983.

[6] Nadel B. A., *The Consistent Labeling Problem and its Algorithms: Towards Exact-Case Complexities and Theory-Based Heuristics*, Computer Science Dept., Rutgers University, New Brunswick, N. J., May 1986, Ph. D. dissertation.

[7] Nadel B. A., "Representation selection for constraint satisfaction: a case study using n-queens", *IEEE Expert*, vol. 5, #3, June 1990.

[8] Nadel B. A., "The complexity of Backtracking and Forward Checking: search-order and instance specific results", submitted for publication. Also in technical report CSC-88-002, Dept. Computer Science, Wayne State University, Detroit, Michigan.

[9] Nadel B. A., "Constraint satisfaction algorithms", *Computational Intelligence*, vol. 5, no. 4, November 1989, pp. 188-224. A preliminary version appeared as "Tree search and arc consistency in constraint satisfaction algorithms", in *Search in Artificial Intelligence*, edited by L. Kanal and V. Kumar, Springer-Verlag, 1988.

[10] Nadel B. A., "Precision complexity analysis: a case study using insertion sort", submitted for publication. Available as technical report CSC-88-008, 1988, Dept. Computer Science, Wayne State University, Detroit, Michigan.

[11] Nadel B. A., "The complexity of constraint satisfaction in Prolog", technical report CSC-89-004, 1989, Dept. Computer Science, Wayne State University, Detroit, Michigan.

[12] Nudel B. A., "Consistent-labeling problems and their algorithms: expected-complexities and theory-based heuristics", *Artificial Intelligence (Special Issue on Search and Heuristics)*, vol. 21, nos. 1 and 2, March 1983, pp. 135-178. Also in book: *Search and Heuristics*, Ed. J. Pearl, North-Holland, Amsterdam, 1983.

[13] Nudel B. A., "Solving the general consistent labeling (or constraint satisfaction) problem: Two algorithms and their expected complexities", *Proc. Nat. Conf. on Artificial Intelligence (AAAI)*, Washington D.C., August 1983, pp. 292-296.

[14] Rossi F., "Constraint satisfaction problems in logic programming" SIGART Newsletter of the ACM, October 1988, pp. 24-28.

[15] Smith D. E. and Genesereth M. R., "Ordering conjunctive queries", *Artificial Intelligence*, vol. 26, no. 3, 171-215, 1985.

[16] Van Hentenryck P. and Dincbas M., "Domains in logic programming", *Proc. Fifth Nat. Conf. on Artificial Intelligence (AAAI)*, Philadelphia, Pennsylvania, August 1986.

[17] Van Hentenryck P., *Consistency Techniques in Logic Programming*, Universitaires Notre-Dame de la Paix, Namur, Belgium, July 1987, Ph. D. dissertation.

[18] Van Hentenryck P., "A theoretical framework for consistency techniques in logic programming", *Proc. International Joint Conference on Artificial Intelligence (IJCAI)*, August 1987, pp. 2-8.

[19] Warren D., "Efficient processing of interactive relational database queries expressed in logic", *Proc. Seventh Conf. on Very Large Data Bases*, Cannes, France, 272-282, August 1981.

An Algebraic Approach to Conflict Resolution in Planning

Qiang Yang *
Department of Computer Science
University of Waterloo
Waterloo, Ont. Canada, N2L 3G1
qyang@watdragon.waterloo.edu

Abstract

This paper presents an algebra for conflict resolution in nonlinear planning. A set of conflicts in a plan is considered as a constraint network. Each node in the network represents a conflict, and is associated with a set of alternative ways for resolving it. Thus, resolving conflicts in a plan corresponds to selecting a set of consistent resolution methods so that, after they are applied to the plan, every conflict can be removed. The paper discusses the represenional issues related to the conflict resolution, presents an algebra for resolving conflicts, and illustrates that some modified algorithms for preprocessing networks of constraints can greatly enhance the efficiency of conflict resolution.

Introduction

Many planners can be considered as search in a space of possible plans [Chapman, 1985; Sacerdoti, 1977; Stefik, 1981; Tate, 1977; Wilkins, 1988]. A major contributing factor to the branching factor in this space is the number of alternative ways for resolving a set of conflicts in a plan. Since search efficiency is greatly affected by the branching factor in the search space, reducing the number of ways for resolving a set of conflicts is an important way for improving planning efficiency.

Unfortunately, most existing planning systems [Chapman, 1985; Sacerdoti, 1977; Stefik, 1981; Tate, 1977; Wilkins, 1988] spend little or no effort in analyzing conflicts in an intermediate plan, in order to reduce the number of ways for resolving them. Usually there is more than one conflict to be introduced to a given plan as a result of some planning activity. These planners will simply generate a set of resolution methods for each conflict, and either commit to one of them in a depth-first manner, or generate the set of all possible successor states, in a breadth-first way. However, as we will show later in the paper, some of the conflict resolution methods can be proven to be either not applicable to the current plan, or related to other methods in such a way that they are redundant. In most of the existing planning systems, a great deal of computational overhead can be spent on these "useless" branches. It would be desirable to reduce the number of alternative ways in many circumstances through an analysis of conflicts in a plan.

Without any analysis at all on the inter-relations among the conflicts can be considered as one extreme on a spectrum of search control, while doing a complete analysis in order to minimize the number of possible alternatives can be considered as the other extreme on that spectrum. Certainly, it may not be advantageous to do a complete analysis over doing no analysis in improving planning efficiency, since there may exist some middle points on the spectrum that are better than either extreme. However, without knowing both ends of the spectrum well, it is hard to make an intelligent decision on how much analysis is needed. It is the purpose of this paper to investigate various ways for minimizing the number of alternative methods for resolving a given set of conflicts.

In particular, this paper presents a *conflict algebra* for analyzing methods for resolving a set of conflicts in nonlinear plans. Modified versions of the preprocessing algorithms for network-based constraint satisfaction problems (CSP) can be used for efficient application of the algebra. The modified algorithms take into account a wider range of possible constraints, so that it is possible to prune from the constraint network not only values that are inconsistent, but also those that can be proven "redundant." Interestingly, these algorithms can be applicable to large classes of problem domains rather than just the planning domain, and in this respect, part of the results in this paper should also be of interest to researchers in CSP area.

Below we discuss how conflicts in a plan are represented. Then we consider the details of the conflict algebra, and show how to apply it to planning. This is followed by a discussion of the algorithms for preprocessing a constraint network.

*This work was supported in part by an interim research grant from the Faculty of Mathematics at the University of Waterloo.

Conflicts and Conflict Resolutions

Preliminaries

A plan consists of a set of operators, a set of precedence constraints on the operators, and a set of codesignation constraints on the binding of variables of the operators. Each operator o is defined in terms of a set of preconditions, P_o, and a set of effects E_o. Two special operators, start and finish, exist in any plan, representing the initial and goal situations, respectively. The operator, start (finish), has a set of empty preconditions (effects), and has as its effects (preconditions) the set of conditions true in the initial (goal) situation.

Let P be a plan. We adopt the notational convention of [Chapman, 1985] for precedence and codesignation constraints. Thus, $a \prec b$ denotes that the operator a precedes operator b in P, and $p \approx q$ or $p \not\approx q$ denotes that p and q are constrained to codesignate or noncodesignate in P, respectively. If for two variables x and y, $x \approx y$, then x and y are constrained to be bound to the same constant. Moreover, we also assume both the definitions and graphical notation of *necessarily* ($\Box$) and *possibly* ($\Diamond$) in [Chapman, 1985].

Below we formally define conflicts. To do this, we first define *precondition establishment*:operator a is said to establish a condition p for operator b, or Est(a, b, p), if and only if (i) p is a precondition for b, (ii) $\Box(a \prec b)$, (iii) $\exists u \in E_a$ such that $\Box(u \approx p)$, and (iv) $\forall a'$ such that $\Box(a \prec a' \prec b)$ and $\forall u' \in E_{a'}$, $\neg\Box(u' \approx p)$. That is, no other operators necessarily between a and b necessarily assert p.

In [Hertzberg and Horz, 1989], a is called a *producer* of p for b, while b is called a *user* of p. If for every operator b in a plan and for every precondition p of b, there exists an operator a such that Est(a, b, p), then P is said to be *well-formed* [Hertzberg and Horz, 1989]. Note that a well-formed plan is not necessarily a correct plan, since some operators may exist that can possibly deny certain preconditions.

In this paper, we make the same assumptions as [Hertzberg and Horz, 1989]. That is,

(1) All plans are well-formed.
(2) The *locality assumption* holds. That is, every operator must specify all the domain conditions it may change, and every change is independent of the situation before the operator is applied.
(3) The STRIPS assumption holds. That is, conditions change only if mentioned in the effects some operators in a plan.

Although the conflict resolution methods to be introduced below become inadequate without these assumptions, the preprocessing algorithms later in the paper are independent of them.

Conflicts in a Plan

Let P and U be operators in a plan such that Est(P, U, p). Suppose there is another operator N in the plan such that (i) N can possibly be between P and U, and (ii) $\exists\neg q \in E_N$ such that $\Diamond(q \approx p)$. Then N is called a *clobberer* of p for U, and tuple $\langle P, U, N, p, q\rangle$ is called a *conflict* in the plan. To distinguish from other forms of conflicts in a plan, such as consumable resources, we call the conflicts defined above as *deleted-condition conflicts.* In this paper, we only consider deleted-condition conflicts.

Hertzberg et. al. [Hertzberg and Horz, 1989] have shown that all deleted-condition conflicts in a well-formed plan are compositions of four types of conflicts listed below:

(1) Linear Conflict (LN(P,U,N,p,q)) if N is between P and U.
(2) Left Fork (LF(P,U,N,p,q)) if U is after P and N, and P and N are unordered in the plan.
(3) Right Fork (RF(P,U,N,p,q)) if P precedes both U and N, and the latter two are unodered in the plan.
(4) Parallel Conflict (PR(P,U,N,p,q)) if P precedes U, and N is unordered with both operators.

A plan is *correct*, if its set of operators is partially ordered by the precedence constraints, it is well-formed, and it is free of conflicts.

Conflict Resolution Methods

To resolve a conflict, a planner imposes various kinds of constraints. Chapman [Chapman, 1985] formulated a necessary and sufficient goal achievement criterion, known as the necessary modal truth criterion, or MTC. He also provided a set of sufficient procedural interpretations of the MTC, which includes "promotion," "demotion," "establishments," "separation," and "introducing white knights." These methods can be considered as various alternative constraints one can impose on a plan for resolving a given conflict. A simplified version of the above methods is listed below: Let $\langle P, U, N, p, q\rangle$ be a conflict. Then the following constraints are sufficient for resolving it:

(1) promotion of clobberer: $U \prec N$,
(2) demotion of clobberer: $N \prec P$,
(3) separation: $p \not\approx q$,
(4) demotion and establishment : for some W, where W is either an existing operator in the plan, or an inserted operator, and for some $r \in E_W$, $N \prec W \prec U$ and $r \approx p$.

Now consider how to resolve each type of conflict in a well-formed plan. We use $+$ for logical disjunction, and $\cdot$ for conjunction. Let r_{de} represent the establishment and demotion methods. That is,

$$r_{de} = (N \prec W \prec U) \cdot (r \approx p),$$

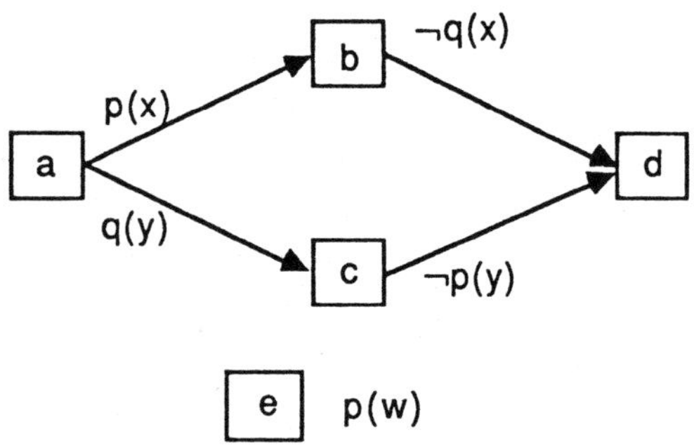

Figure 1: An example plan with two conflicts. The literals $p(x), q(y)$, etc., are the effects of the operator immediately before them.

where $r \in E_W$ and W is an operator. Let R_{de} be the disjunction of all r_{de}. Then

$$\begin{aligned} LN(P,U,N,p,q) &= (p \not\approx q) + R_{de}, \\ LF(P,U,N,p,q) &= (N \prec P) + (p \not\approx q) + R_{de}, \\ RF(P,U,N,p,q) &= (U \prec N) + (p \not\approx q) + R_{de}, \\ PR(P,U,N,p,q) &= LF(P,U,N,p,q) \\ &\quad + RF(P,U,N,p,q). \end{aligned}$$

where '=' means "can be resolved by."

As an example, consider the plan shown in Figure 1. The set of precedence constraints in this plan is:

$$P = \{a \prec b, a \prec c, b \prec d, c \prec d, a \prec d\}.$$

Suppose that Est$(a, b, p(x))$, and Est$(a, c, q(y))$, then there are two conflicts in this plan, C_1 and C_2, where $C_1 = RF(a, b, c, p(x), p(y)) = r_{11} + r_{12} + R$, $r_{11} = (b \prec c)$, $r_{12} = (x \not\approx y)$, and $R = r_{13} \cdot r_{14} \cdot r_{15}$, with $r_{13} = (c \prec e)$, $r_{14} = (e \prec b)$, and $r_{15} = (w \approx x)$. $C_2 = RF(a, c, b, q(y), q(x)) = r_{21} + r_{22}$, where $r_{21} = (c \prec b)$, and $r_{22} = (x \not\approx y)$.

Relations Among Conflicts

Above we have shown that all conflicts in a well-formed plan can be resolved using a set of resolution methods, represented in a concise form. If all the conflicts in a plan are found, then each conflict will be automatically associated with a set of alternative resolution methods, and the set of all conflicts can be represented in a conjunction of disjunctive normal form. The purpose of representing the conflict resolution methods is to find one or all constraints that can resolve the conflicts in a plan. Each consistent set of constraints that can resolve all the conflicts is called a solution. Below we consider the relationship between different conflict resolution methods.

Let R_1 and R_2 be two precedence constraints. R_1 *subsumes* R_2, or $S(R_1, R_2)$, if and only if $\{R_1\} \bigcup B(P) \supset R_2$, where $B(P)$ is the set of precedence (co-designation) constraints in P. Likewise for codesignation and non-codesignation constraints.

Intuitively, R_1 subsumes R_2 if imposing R_1 will guarantee that R_2 is also imposed. Thus, R_2 is considered to be weaker than R_1. For example, let $r_1 = (b \prec c)$, and $r_2 = (a \prec d)$. If $\{(a \prec b), (c \prec d)\} \in B(P)$, then $S(r_1, r_2)$. As another example, let $r_1 = (x \approx y)$ and $r_2 = (y \not\approx z)$. If $(x \not\approx z) \in C(P)$ then $S(r_1, r_2)$.

Imposing a set of constraints on a plan may result in an incorrect plan. With the assumptions in this paper, such incorrect plans are signaled by inconsistent constraints of the form $a \prec a$ or $x \not\approx x$, for some operator a and variable x. Below, we use "Fail" for such situations.

Two constraints R_1 and R_2 are inconsistent, or $I(R_1, R_2)$, if and only if

$$\{R_1, R_2\} \bigcup C(P) \bigcup B(P) \supset Fail.$$

Intuitively, R_1 and R_2 are inconsistent if imposing R_1 and R_2 together will result in a contradiction in a plan. For example, if $r_1 = (a \prec b)$, and $r_2 = (b \prec a)$, then $I(r_1, r_2)$. Also consider an example of inconsistent codesignation constraints. If $r_1 = (x \approx y)$ and $r_2 = (u \approx v)$, and $\{(x \approx u), (y \not\approx v)\} \in C(P)$, then $I(r_1, r_2)$.

Having the above definitions, we now can prove the following theorems:

Theorem 1 *If* $S(R_1, R)$, $S(R_2, R')$, *and* $I(R, R')$, *then* $I(R_1, R_2)$.

Intuitively, this theorem says that if the weaker constraints implied by two constraints are inconsistent, then they are inconsistent themselves.

Theorem 2 *If* $S(R_1, R_2)$, $S(R_2, R_3)$,*then* $S(R_1, R_3)$.

This says the subsumption relation is transitive. We also require that S is reflexive. However, the inconsistency relation is not transitive.

Algebraic Rules

The disjunction and conjunction operations can be considered as algebraic operations, with special semantics. For example, the meaning of a conjunction $R_1 \cdot R_2$ in a disjunctive normal form representation of a conflict is that it is sufficient to impose both R_1 and R_2 for removing some conflicts. The meaning of disjunction $R_1 + R_2$ is that either R_1 or R_2 is sufficient for resolving some conflicts. Given the precise meaning of these operations, we can prove that "·" and "+" satisfy the rules of boolean algebra, as well as the following set of rules:

Rule 1 *If* $S(R_1, R_2)$ *then* $R_1 \cdot R_2 = R_1$.

Rule 2 *If $S(R_1, R_2)$ and u is any constraint, then $R_1 \cdot u + R_2 = R_2$.*

Rule 3 *If $S(R_1, R_2)$ and $S(R_1, R_3)$, then $S(R_1, R_2 \cdot R_3)$, and $S(R_1, R_2 + R_3)$.*

Rule 4 *If $R = R_1 \cdot R_2$, then $S(R, R_1)$ and $S(R, R_2)$.*

Consider the plan shown in Figure 1. Analysis of the conflicts establishes the following relationships: $I(r_{11}, r_{21})$ $S(r_{12}, r_{22})$, $S(r_{22}, r_{12})$, and $S(R, r_{21})$.

Expanding $C_1 \cdot C_2$ we get

$$\begin{aligned}
& r_{11} \cdot r_{21} + r_{11} \cdot r_{22} + r_{12} \cdot r_{21} \\
& +r_{12} \cdot r_{22} + R \cdot r_{21} + R \cdot r_{22} \\
= \; & r_{11} \cdot r_{22} + r_{12} \cdot r_{21} + r_{12} \cdot r_{22} \\
& +R \cdot r_{21} + R \cdot r_{22} && (I(r_{11}, r_{21})) \\
= \; & r_{11} \cdot r_{22} + r_{12} \cdot r_{21} + r_{12} \\
& +R \cdot r_{21} + R \cdot r_{22} && (Rule1) \\
= \; & r_{12} + R \cdot r_{21} + R \cdot r_{22} && (Rule2) \\
= \; & r_{12} + R \cdot r_{21} + R && (Rule1) \\
= \; & r_{12} + R && (Rule2)
\end{aligned}$$

Thus, using algebraic rules we are able to reduce the number of backtracking points from 6 to 2.

Pruning using CSP Techniques

A set of conflicts can be considered as a constraint network, where each conflict is a node, and the consistency relations between the conflicts are arcs in the network. Each node has a set of values to choose from, each value being an alternate conflict resolution method. Thus, a conflict resolution problem can be considered as a constraint satisfaction problem (CSP). In particular, the goal of a conflict resolution problem in planning is either to find out the set of all consistent values, or to find out just one value.

As in CSP, we would like to enforce arc and path consistency of the network. The degree of constraints in such a network of conflicts can be the size of the network. To see this, consider the following example. Each node N_i in the network contains a primitive precedence constraint $a_i \prec a_{i+1}$, for $i = 0, \ldots, n-1$. Also, node N_n contains a value $a_n \prec a_0$. Thus, if no two a_i are identical, then no proper subset of the set of these values is inconsistent, while the set of values when considered together is. This particular network is constrained by n-ary constraints. It follows that ensuring arc and path consistencies is not sufficient for global consistency in general.

Important difference exists between this particular CSP and a traditional one, because of the existence of subsumption relations between the different values of a node. Using this relation, redundant backtrack points can be quickly discovered, and removed. The set of rules that enable this ability is what we call "pruning rules." Below, we consider path consistency and redundancy removal separately.

Path Consistency

The first type of pruning is the same as a traditional definition for arc and path-consistency in CSP: Let C_1 and C_2 be two nodes in a constraint network. If for some $R \in C_1$ such that $\forall R' \in C_2$ $I(R, R')$ holds, then R can be pruned from C_1.

If all the values of C_1 are pruned,then the network has no solution. This type of pruning is called "inconsistency pruning."

New relations concerning inconsistency can also be obtained when considering groups of nodes greater than two. The most commonly known such algorithms for establishing new relations are the path-consistency algorithms. We present a modified path consistency algorithm based on algorithm PC-2 in [Mackworth and Freuder, 1985]. As in PC-2, this algorithm returns an updated set of inconsistency relations, possibly implemented in a matrix form. The difference here is that upon termination, a list Q of arcs that are modified during the execution of the entire algorithm is returned. This list is used for further removal of redundant values or nodes in the network, and we will discuss this in detail in the next subsection.

The function PC is listed below. In PC, Related-Paths(i, k, j) is a function which returns a set of length-2 paths that might have their consistency affected by a change in the consistency of (i, k, j). Likewise, REVISE$((i, k, j))$ returns true if $I(i, j)$ is modified due to path inconsistency. Both functions are defined in [Mackworth, 1981].

```
Function PC(Q')
begin
   Q := emptyset;
   while Q' is not empty, do
         begin
           select and delete a path (i, k, j) from Q';
           if REVISE((i,k,j)) then
             begin
               Q' := Q' ∪ Related-Paths(i, k, j);
               Q := Q ∪ {(i, j)}
             end; (if)
         end; (while)
         return Q
end
```

Redundancy Removal

More pruning can be achieved using subsumption relations among constraints. Note that the redundancy as defined below is caused by the subsumption and the inconsistency relations, instead of the latter alone. Thus, our results here are fundamentally different from that in [Dechter and Dechter, 1977].

Theorem 3 *Suppose $\exists R_2 \in C_2$, such that $\forall R_1 \in C_1$, $S(R_1, R_2)$. Then C_2 can be pruned from the network, without affecting the set of solutions.*

Note that this theorem is different from inconsistent pruning. It says that if some value of C_2 is subsumed by all values of C_1, then C_2 is subsumed by C_1, in the sense that any solution for C_1 must also be a solution for C_2. This type of pruning can be called "subsumption pruning."

Subsumption relations also allow for the removal of individual values.

Theorem 4 *If $\exists R_2 \in C_2$, such that $\forall R_1 \in C_1$, either*

1. $\exists R_2' \in C_2$, such that $R_2 \neq R_2'$ and $S(R_1, R_2')$, or

2. $I(R_1, R_2)$,

then R_2 can be pruned from C_2, without affecting the solution of the network.

Removal of nodes or values in some node is called *redundancy removal.* This is different from inconsistency removal. If a node becomes empty after applying the inconsistency pruning rule, then the whole network is inconsistent. In planning, this means that the current plan corresponds to a dead end in the search space. On the other hand, if a node is made empty by applying the subsumption theorems, then it simply means that the removed node is redundant, and has no direct relation with the consistency of the whole network.

Algorithm RR (Redundancy Removal), listed below, is an implementation of the above two redundancy-pruning theorems. In the function RR, the list Q, which is returned at the end, contains length-2 paths which have changes in their domains because of the redundancy pruning. Q will be used for checking more possible inconsistency pruning.

```
Function REVISE-RR((i,j))
begin
   DELETE := false
   for each R ∈ C_i do
        if for all R' ∈ C_j such that
          either I(R', R) or S(R', R'') for some R'' ∈ C_i
            such that R ≠ R'', then
            begin
              delete R from C_i;
              DELETE := true
            end;
        if C_i becomes empty, then
            delete it from the network;
        return DELETE
end

Function RR(Q')
begin
   Q := emptyset;
   while Q' is not empty, do
           begin
             select and delete any arc (i, j) from Q';
             INC := {(k, i) | k ≠ i, k ≠ j}
             if REVISE-RR((i,j)) then
               begin
                 Q' := Q' ⋃ INC;
                 Q := Q ⋃ Related-Paths((i, j, i))
               end;(if)
           end;(while)
           return Q
end
```

Combining Path Consistency and Redundancy Pruning

When both inconsistency and redundancy pruning are done, the outcome of modifying one relation can possibly affect the status of the other. For example, removing a redundant value from a node can produce further inconsistency, and thus, the two types of pruning have to be used interchangeably. The basic idea is to interleave the two algorithms PC and RR, until no changes can possibly be made. Algorithm PP (Pre-Processing), listed below, achieves this purpose. It can be shown that the algorithm PP has a worst case complexity of $O(k^5n^3)$, where k is the number of values in a node, and n is the number of nodes in the network.

```
Procedure PP
begin
   Q := {(i, j, k) | ¬(i = j = k)};
   PC(Q);
   if any node is deleted, then return(fail);
   Q := {(i, j) | (i, j) ∈ arcs(G), i ≠ j};
   Q :=RR(Q);
   while Q is not empty, do
         begin
           Q := PC(Q);
           if any node is deleted, then return(fail);
           Q := RR(Q);
         end;
end
```

Example

Now consider again the example given in Figure 1. We start with the set of relations among the constraints: $I(r_{11}, r_{21})$, $S(r_{12}, r_{22})$, and $S(r_{22}, r_{12})$, and $S(R, r_{21})$. Now apply the pruning rules. By Theorem 4, r_{11} can be pruned from C_1. Thus, after updating, $C_1 = r_{12} + R$. By Theorem 3, the node C_2 can be pruned. Thus, what is left is $C_1 = r_{12} + R$. The number of backtracking points for planning is again reduced form six to two. Therefore, using preprocessing techniques, one can simplify the constraint network while avoiding an exponential number of algebraic expansions.

Applying the Algebraic and CSP Techniques to Planning

A typical planning session can be considered as iterations of several steps:

(1) Select a condition to be achieved and some operators for achieving it. Insert these operators into the plan, possibly with certain precedence

and codesignation constraints.
(2) Activate a conflict detection routine, and compute the set of all conflicts introduced by the inserted operators and constraints.
(3) Impose a set of conflict resolution constraints for resolving one or more conflicts. Save the rest of the alternative conflict resolution methods as backtrack points.

After step 2 is done, the conflict algebra can be applied for simplifying the conflict resolution methods. The resultant methods can be represented in a disjunctive normal form. One or more disjuncts can then be chosen to be imposed on the plan, and the rest saved as backtrack points.

Conclusion

This paper proposes to analyze conflicts in a plan in order to reduce the number of backtracking points in a planner's search space. In particular, a set of algebraic rules, together with a set of preprocessing algorithms are presented for simplifying a set of conflict resolution methods. Via subsumption relationship between constraint to be imposed on a plan, the algorithms are able to not only remove inconsistent choices, but also those that are redundant. Furthermore, these algorithms are applicable to a class of constraint satisfaction problems in which subsumption relations are involved.

With the theoretical foundation of this paper, we intend to further explore the amount of analysis of conflicts necessary for a planner's best performance. Such exploration will have to involve a considerable amount of experimentation. We will also look for other kinds of relations in a constraint network, similar to subsumption ones, in order to allow more powerful preprocessing algorithms to be designed.

Acknowledgments. Thanks to Peter Van Beek for many useful comments.

References

[Allen and Koomen, 1983] J. Allen and J Koomen. Planning using a temporal world model. In *Proceedings of the 8th IJCAI*, pages 741–747, 1983.

[Allen, 1984] James F. Allen. Towards a general theory of action and time. *Artificial Intelligence*, 23(2):123–154, 1984.

[Chapman, 1985] David Chapman. Planning for conjunctive goals. AI Technical Report 802, Massachusetts Institute of Technology, 1985.

[Charniak and McDermott, 1985] Eugene Charniak and Drew McDermott. *Introduction to Artificial Intelligence.* Addison-Wesley Publishing Company, 1985.

[Dean and Boddy, 1988] T. Dean and M. Boddy. Reasoning about partially ordered events. *Artificial Intelligence*, 36:375–399, 1988.

[Dechter and Dechter, 1977] A. Dechter and R. Dechter. Removing redundancies in constraint networks. In *Proceedings of the 6th AAAI*, pages 105–109, 1977.

[Dechter and Pearl, 1987] R. Dechter and J. Pearl. Network-based heuristics for constraint-satisfaction problems. *Artificial Intelligence*, 34, 1987.

[Hertzberg and Horz, 1989] Hertzberg and Horz. Towards a theory of conflict detection and resolution in nonlinear plans. In *Proceedings of the 11th IJCAI*, pages 937–942, Detroit, Michigan, 1989.

[Mackworth and Freuder, 1985] A.K. Mackworth and E.C. Freuder. The complexity of some polynomial network consistency algorithms for constraint satisfaction problems. *Artificial Intelligence*, 125:65–74, 1985.

[Mackworth, 1981] A.K. Mackworth. Consistency in networks of relations. In Webber and Nilsson, editors, *Readings in Artificial Intelligence*, pages 69–78. Morgan Kaufmann Publishers Inc., 1981.

[Sacerdoti, 1977] Earl Sacerdoti. *A Structure for Plans and Behavior.* American Elsevier, 1977.

[Stefik, 1981] Mark Stefik. Planning with constraints. *Artificial Intelligence*, 16(2):111–140, 1981.

[Tate, 1977] Austin Tate. Generating project networks. In *Proceedings of the 5th IJCAI*, pages 888–893, 1977.

[Van Beek and Cohen, 1989] P. Van Beek and R. Cohen. Approximation algorithms for temporal reasoning. Technical Report CS-89-12, Department of Computer Science, University of Waterloo, 1989.

[Vilain and Kautz, 1986] M. Vilain and H. Kautz. Constraint propagation algorithms for temporal reasoning. In *Proceedings of the 5th AAAI*, pages 337–382, 1986.

[Wilkins, 1988] David Wilkins. *Practical Planning: Extending the Classical AI Planning Paradigm.* Morgan Kaufmann, CA, 1988.

[Yang and Tenenberg, 1990] Qiang Yang and Josh Tenenberg. Abtweak: Abstracting a nonlinear, least commitment planner. Department of Computer Science, University of Waterloo, Technical Report No. cs-90-09, 1990.

[Yang, 1990] Qiang Yang. Formalizing planning knowledge for hierarchical planning. *Computational Intelligence*, 6, 1990.

Some Applications of Graph Bandwidth to Constraint Satisfaction Problems

Ramin Zabih
Computer Science Department
Stanford University
Stanford, California 94305

Abstract

Bandwidth is a fundamental concept in graph theory which has some surprising applications to a class of AI search problems. Graph bandwidth provides a link between the syntactic structure of a constraint satisfaction problem (CSP) and the complexity of the underlying search task. Bandwidth can be used to define a new class of easy CSP's, namely those that have limited constraint graph bandwidth. These CSP's can be solved in polynomial time, essentially by divide and conquer. This in turn suggests that bandwidth provides a mathematical measure of the decomposability of a search problem. In addition, bandwidth supplies a measure for comparing different search orderings for a given CSP. Statistical analysis suggests that backtracking with small bandwidth orderings leads to a more efficient search than that obtained under orderings with larger bandwidths. Small bandwidth orderings also limit the pruning that can be done by intelligent backtracking. If small bandwidth orderings are indeed advantageous, then a large number of heuristics developed in numerical analysis to find such orderings may find applicability to solving constraint satisfaction problems.

1 Introduction

The bandwidth of an ordering of a graph is the maximum distance between two adjacent vertices, and the bandwidth of a graph is its minimum bandwidth under any ordering.[1] Bandwidth is one of the basic concepts in graph theory, and is related to almost every other mathematical property that graphs possess [Zinn *et al.*, 1982]. It is nonetheless surprising to discover some strong connections between graph bandwidth and a class of search problems encountered in AI.

The search problems known as constraint satisfaction problems (CSP's) have an associated constraint graph. The vertices of the graph consist of the variables of the search problem, and there is an edge between two vertices if there is a (non-trivial) constraint between those variables.

[1] These definitions will be made more precise in section 3.

The bandwidth of the constraint graph is strongly related to the complexity of the underlying constraint satisfaction problem. In particular, there is evidence for two claims.

- The bandwidth of the constraint graph of a constraint satisfaction problem serves as a measure of its decomposability.
- The bandwidth of a search ordering provides a measure of its quality, as backtracking with a small bandwidth ordering generally results in a smaller search tree.

The first claim is supported by a proof that any problem of limited bandwidth can be solved in polynomial time, essentially by divide and conquer. The second claim is supported by statistical analysis, and by evidence that small bandwidth orderings have additional important properties related to intelligent backtracking. If small bandwidth orderings are indeed useful, then the large body of heuristics that has been developed by numerical analysts for finding such orderings may prove to be useful for solving CSP's.

After a brief review of constraint satisfaction problems, section 3 formally defines bandwidth and relates it to some other graph-theoretic notions in the CSP literature. Section 4 proves that any CSP whose bandwidth can be limited is solvable in polynomial time. Section 5 presents statistical data which suggests that small bandwidth orderings are generally superior, as well as describing some preliminary results about the interaction between such orderings and intelligent backtracking.

2 Constraint Satisfaction Problems

A constraint satisfaction problem (CSP) has a set of variables and a domain of values,

$$V = \{v_1, v_2, \ldots, v_n\} \text{ the set of variables, } \|V\| = n,$$
$$D = \{d_1, d_2, \ldots, d_m\} \text{ the set of values, } \|D\| = d.$$

Every variable v_i must be assigned a value d_k.

A CSP also consists of some constraints saying which assignments are compatible. Most interesting problems are *binary* CSP's, where the constraints involve pairs of variables. Such a constraint is a (proper) subset of $D \times D$ consisting of the simultaneously permitted assignments. A binary CSP has an associated constraint graph $G = (V, E)$, where

$$E = \{ (v_i, v_j) \mid \text{there is a contraint between } v_i \text{ and } v_j \}.$$

Note that the constraint graph hides a great deal of the information about the search problem, particularly the tightness of the constraints.

The constraint graph G may be assumed to be connected, as otherwise each connected component can be considered separately. Many standard combinatorial problems are binary CSP's, including graph coloring and the n-queens problem.

3 Graph Definitions

Given a graph G with n vertices, an ordering h is a one-to-one map from the vertices of G to the set $\{1, \ldots, n\}$. The bandwidth of a vertex v under an ordering h is the maximum value of $|h(v) - h(w)|$ over all vertices w connected to v. The bandwidth of a graph under an ordering is the maximum bandwidth of any vertex, and the bandwidth of a graph is its minimum bandwidth under any ordering. The bandwidth of G under h will be written as $B(G, h)$.

3.1 Relating bandwidth and other graph properties

There are many notions akin to bandwidth which have been developed in the CSP literature. It is straightforward to determine the relationship between bandwidth and three graph properties: front length (introduced by [Seidel, 1981]), width [Freuder, 1982], and induced width [Dechter and Pearl, 1987].

Seidel [1981] defines an invasion of G to be a sequence of subgraphs $G_1, \ldots, G_n$ where G_i is a subgraph of G_{i+1} with i vertices and where $G_n = G$. For a given invasion, a front F_i consists of the vertices in G_i that are adjacent (in G) to vertices not in G_i. The front length of an invasion is the maximum size of F_i. There is an invasion associated with any ordering h, defined by $G_1 = h^{-1}(1)$, $G_{i+1} = G_i \cup h^{-1}(i+1)$. The front length of G under the invasion associated with h will be written as $F(G, h)$.

Freuder [1982] defines the width of a vertex v under an ordering h to be the number of vertices that are connected to v which occur earlier than v under h. The width of a graph under an ordering is the maximum width of any vertex. The width of G under h will be written as $W(G, h)$.

Dechter and Pearl [1987] construct the induced graph of G under an ordering h by processing G's vertices in the order $\{h^{-1}(n), \ldots, h^{-1}(1)\}$, and adding an edge between any two neighbors of a vertex v that precede v under h. The induced graph of G under h will be written as G^h.

It is straightforward to analyze the relationships among these quantities. First, for a fixed ordering h, define

$$P_i \stackrel{\text{def}}{=} \{h^{-1}(i - B(G,h)), \ldots, h^{-1}(i-1)\}$$

(assuming $h^{-1}(j) = h^{-1}(1)$ if $j < 1$ for simplicity). The important property of P_i is the following: if there is an edge between v and w, where v occurs before $h(i)$ and w does not, then $v \in P_i$.

Theorem 3.1 *For any graph G and ordering h $B(G, h) \geq F(G, h)$.*

Proof: Consider a front F_i in the invasion defined by h. Clearly $F_i \subseteq P_{i+1}$. But $\|P_{i+1}\| \leq B(G, h)$. □

Theorem 3.2 *For any graph G and ordering h $B(G, h) \geq W(G, h)$.*

Proof: All of the previous vertices that $v = h(i)$ is connected to must be in P_i. □

Theorem 3.3 *For any graph G and ordering h $B(G, h) \geq W(G^h, h)$.*

Proof: The edges added when $v = h(i)$ is processed will be between two elements of P_i. Adding such edges will never increase the bandwidth, so $B(G^h, h) = B(G, h)$. Applying theorem 3.2 with G replaced by G^h gives the desired result. □

Note that the above three inequalities cannot be made strict (i.e., it is invalid to replace '$\geq$' by '$>$').

Theorem 3.4 *There exists a graph G and an ordering h such that $B(G, h) = F(G, h) = W(G, h) = W(G^h, h)$.*

Proof: Consider a graph G that is a triangle. Then, for any ordering h, $B(G, h) = F(G, h) = W(G, h) = W(G^h, h) = 2$. □

4 Limited Bandwidth CSP's

There is no technical definition of what it means for a search problem to be "local" or "nearly decomposable". The intuition behind these terms, however, is that certain search problems can be solved piece by piece, without taking the entire problem into consideration at each point in the search. Coloring a long and narrow graph is an example of such a search problem.

There are several reasons to believe that the bandwidth of a CSP's constraint graph reflects the locality of the search problem. First, note that edges in the constraint graph measure strong interactions between variables. If there is no edge between two variables, then assigning one a value can have no (direct) effect upon the other, so the lack of an edge reflects a sort of independence. If the CSP has limited bandwidth, each vertex in the constraint graph can have no more than a bounded number of neighbors. This suggests that small bandwidth graphs should be solvable by only worrying about a small subset of the variables at any instant.

Additional anecdotal evidence to support this conclusion can be obtained by visual inspection of graphs of various bandwidths. Graphs with small bandwidths tend to look long and thin. The highest bandwidth graph, on the other hand, is the complete graph where there is an edge between every pair of vertices.

A stronger argument can be made on the basis of the claim that nearly decomposable search problems should be easy to solve. In particular, it should be possible to solve them efficiently by solving their subparts more or less independently (gluing the subparts back together into a solution by divide and conquer or by dynamic programming). It turns out that any CSP of limited bandwidth can be solved in polynomial time by dynamic programming.

4.1 Solving bandwidth-limited CSP's in polynomial time

The basic strategy is to find an ordering with minimal bandwidth, and then to use this ordering to solve the CSP. In general, determining the bandwidth of a graph is an NP-complete problem [Papadimitriou, 1976]. However, if the graph's bandwidth is no larger than b, a minimal bandwidth ordering can be found in time $O(n^b)$ and also space $O(n^b)$. This can be done via an algorithm of Saxe [1980] as improved by Gurari and Sudborough [1984].

Given an ordering h with bandwidth no larger than b, the CSP can then be solved via dynamic programming. There are three possible algorithms, with slightly different bounds. Because of the relationships between bandwidth, front length and induced width that are proven in section 3, either Seidel's or Dechter and Pearl's method may be used. In addition, Fernández-Baca has recently produced an algorithm that makes explicit use of bandwidth [Fernández-Baca, 1988]. However, Dechter and Pearl's algorithm gives the bound that seems likely to be lowest in practice.

Dechter and Pearl [1987] show how to solve a CSP under an ordering h with induced width $w = W(G^h, h)$ in time $O(d^{w+1})$ and space $O(d^w)$. Applying theorem 3.3, $w \leq b$. Combining this with Saxe's algorithm gives the desired result.

Theorem 4.1 *Any CSP whose constraint graph's bandwidth is no larger than b can be solved in time $O(n^b + d^{b+1})$ and space $O(n^b + d^b)$.*

One corollary of this theorem is a very simple proof of a result first discovered by Monien and Sudborough [1985].

Corollary 4.2 *Any graph of limited bandwidth can be colored in polynomial time.*

5 Small Bandwidth Orderings

Since small bandwidth CSP's are easy to solve, the obvious generalization would be to claim that small bandwidth orderings are generally efficient. In fact, the method for solving small bandwidth CSP's described above first finds a small bandwidth ordering (by Saxe's algorithm), and next uses that ordering to solve the search problem. This suggests that there is something special about small bandwidth orderings.

$B(G,h)$	N	Tree size
8	84	15832 ± 1255
9	628	18271 ± 528
10	1850	19855 ± 379
11	2793	21733 ± 382
12	2908	22703 ± 405

Figure 1: Average tree size for a graph-coloring problem, with 99% confidence intervals.

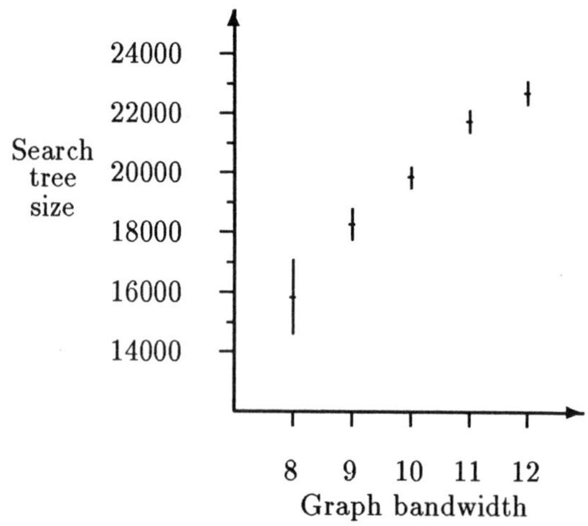

Figure 2: Average tree size as a function of ordering bandwidth, with 99% confidence intervals.

There is both empirical and theoretical evidence that small bandwidth orderings have special properties. Empirically, there is statistical evidence that using small bandwidth orderings for backtrack search is advantageous. There are also theoretical evidence that links small bandwidth orderings with intelligent backtracking.

5.1 Empirical results

Statistical analysis of some preliminary experimental results suggest that small bandwidth orderings are indeed advantageous. The problem that has been examined is the graph-coloring problem described in [Bruynooghe and Pereira, 1984]. This CSP has 1176 solutions. Depth-first search (sometimes referred to as backtracking, or chronological backtracking) has been run on the problem several thousand times, under orderings with different bandwidths.

Figure 1 shows the average number of nodes in the search tree as a function of the bandwidth of the ordering, together with the 99% confidence intervals. The graph in figure 2 presents the same data in a slightly more readable form. The data supports the hypothesis that the search trees resulting from small bandwidth orderings are significantly smaller than those resulting from orderings with greater bandwidth.

More precisely, the data suggests that as the bandwidth of the ordering increases, the search tree gets larger. Furthermore each increment in bandwidth results in a corresponding increase in search tree size which is statistically significant at the 99% confidence level. For this problem at least, it is not merely the case that the very smallest bandwidth orderings are better han the very largest.

Of course, one would like to have evidence from more than one problem. The large number of trial runs necessary to obtain statistically significant results, however, makes this something of a challenge.

5.2 Ordering bandwidth and intelligent backtracking

Why should it be advantageous to use a small bandwidth ordering? Suppose that a CSP is solved by chronological backtracking under an ordering with bandwidth b. Such a process will construct a search tree in the standard manner: the nodes of the search tree will consist of labelings which assign values to some subset of the variables, the root node will consist of the empty labeling, and the children of a node will assign a value to one variable that was not assigned a value by the parent node. Assuming that the CSP is solved under a fixed ordering, each level in the search tree will correspond to a single variable which is assigned a value at that depth in the tree.[2] Some of the leaf nodes of the search tree will be solutions to the CSP; the remaining leaf nodes are failures, because all the possible values of some unassigned variable are incompatible with the values of the variables that have been assigned values.

At a given node of this search tree, the corresponding labeling will have assigned values to certain variables. However, only the most recent b variables to have been assigned values can have any effect on the remainder of the search. Any variables that were assigned values earlier will have no edges in the constraint graph connecting them to variables that do not yet have values, and hence will have no effect.

More precisely, consider two labelings at the same level in the search tree. If these two labelings assign the same values to the most recent b variables, then the subtrees underneath the two labelings will be isomorphic. This is the property that the dynamic programming schemes mentioned in section 4.1 exploit.

This is also an advantageous property for doing chronological backtracking. In a small bandwidth ordering, at any point in the search the only variables that matter are a small number of recent ones.

When using backtrack search, the decision actually responsible for a failure can occur significantly before the failure itself is detected. This is a well-known malady of backtracking which can lead to extremely poor performance. The greater the number of intervening decisions, the worse backtracking performs.

Various schemes have been proposed to solve this problem. These schemes mostly work by invoking some sort of failure analysis to determine where responsibility for a failure lies. The results of this analysis are then used to discard portions of the search tree which can be shown to contain no solution.

The two most popular such schemes are *dependency-directed backtracking* [Stallman and Sussman, 1977] and *intelligent backtracking* [Bruynooghe, 1981]. The major difference involves how much pruning of the search tree is done. Dependency-directed backtracking achieves a much greater reduction in search tree size, at the cost of a potentially exponential use of storage space. Intelligent backtracking uses very little space, but does less pruning.

Researchers who have studied dependency-directed backtracking or intelligent backtracking have generally suspected that these schemes have some relationship with search order. For instance, it is very difficult to construct an example of a problem where dependency-directed backtracking is helpful without requiring that the problem be solved in a particular order. There is usually some other ordering which solves the problem without running into this problem. One example is the sample problem described by [de Kleer, 1986, page 136].

Suppose that a search problem is being solved by chronological backtracking under an ordering with bandwidth b. At any point in the search, only the last b variables that have been assigned values matter. A failure occurs because all the values at a particular variable v_i have been eliminated. The responsible variables must be among the last b to be assigned values, as no other variables have an edge connecting them with v_i.

This strongly suggests that the number of intervening decisions between the choice responsible for a failure and the failure itself should be bounded by b. It is possible to prove a theorem that supports this intuition.

The theorem applies to intelligent backtracking schemes, which are in fairly wide use in the PROLOG community. Bruynooghe [1981] gives one intelligent backtracking algorithm for solving CSP's. There are numerous other very similar schemes, such as that given in [Bruynooghe and Pereira, 1984]. The statement of the theorem, which applies to all these schemes, is as follows.

If a CSP is searched in a fixed order using intelligent backtracking, the bandwidth of that ordering provides

[2] It is rather straightforward to extend all of the results in this paper to rearrangement search strategies such as [Purdom *et al.*, 1981]. The bandwidth of a dynamic search ordering is simply the maximum of the bandwidths of the orderings used down any branch of the search tree.

a bound on the amount of the search tree that intelligent backtracking will prune. This bound holds at almost all nodes in the search tree; the only exception is when intelligent backtracking declares the problem to be insolvable. It is possible to prove restrictions on the nodes in the search tree where these exceptions can occur, in terms of the k-consistency [Freuder, 1978] of the original CSP.

This theorem and some related results will be discussed in detail in a forthcoming paper. They provide an interesting relationship between search ordering and intelligent backtracking. Intelligent backtracking and search order are clearly not orthogonal. Choosing a good (i.e., small bandwith) ordering reduces the advantages of using intelligent backtracking. A reasonable explanation would be that choosing a small bandwidth ordering ameliorates the problem that intelligent backtracking is designed to solve. This explanation is consistent with the statistical evidence that small bandwidth orderings are useful for (chronological) backtracking.

5.3 Bandwidth and adjacency

One final interesting property of small bandwidth orderings is their relationship to the "adjacency" heuristic. This is one of the simplest and most standard ordering heuristics, which is especially common for graph-coloring problems. Adjacency simply means that the ordering starts at one edge of the graph and looks at new vertices that are adjacent (i.e., connected) to a vertex that has already been examined.

The adjacency heuristic is clearly related to minimizing ordering bandwidth. A small bandwidth ordering, by definition, will examine all of a vertex v's neighbors soon after it examines v. It is not always the case that a small bandwidth ordering will next examine a vertex adjacent to those already examined. However, it is usually true, and in any event the next vertex will be close to the previously examined vertices.

5.4 Consequences

If it is indeed true that small bandwidth orderings are in general efficient, then there is a large set of algorithms developed by numerical analysts that can be applied to CSP's. Bandwidth minimization, as mentioned, is NP-complete. However, because it is an important problem in the field of numerical analysis, many heuristic procedures for finding small bandwidth orderings have been developed. Most of these have relatively low time overhead. [Zinn *et al.*, 1982] surveys some of these algorithms; perhaps the most popular one is [Gibbs *et al.*, 1976].

These algorithms can be applied to CSP's to yield small bandwidth orderings. The CSP may then be solved using chronological backtracking under that ordering; or, as an alternative, it can be solved using the dynamic programming methods mentioned in section 4.1.

6 Conclusions

Graph bandwidth has been defined and shown to have applicability to CSP's. Bandwidth provides a new class of tractably solvable constraint satisfaction problems, and a possible measure of CSP decomposability. In addition, the bandwidth is an important characteristic of a search ordering. Small bandwidth orderings seem to result in a statistically significant increase in backtracking efficiency, and these orderings are also related to intelligent backtracking and to adjacency.

6.1 Acknowledgements

Johan de Kleer, David McAllester and Joe Weening contributed to this research. The author is supported by a fellowship from the Fannie and John Hertz Foundation.

References

[Bruynooghe and Pereira, 1984] Maurice Bruynooghe and Luis Pereira. Deduction revision by intelligent backtracking. In J. A. Campbell, editor, *Implementations of Prolog*, chapter 3, pages 196–215. Ellis Horwood, Chichester, 1984.

[Bruynooghe, 1981] Maurice Bruynooghe. Solving combinatorial search problems by intelligent backtracking. *Information Processing Letters*, 12(1):36–39, 1981.

[de Kleer, 1986] Johan de Kleer. An assumption-based TMS. *Artificial Intelligence*, 28(2):127–162, March 1986.

[Dechter and Pearl, 1987] Rina Dechter and Judea Pearl. Network-based heuristics for constraint-satisfaction problems. *Artificial Intelligence*, 34(1):1–38, December 1987.

[Fernández-Baca, 1988] David Fernández-Baca. Nonserial dynamic programming formulations of satisfiability. *Information Processing Letters*, 27:323–326, May 1988.

[Freuder, 1978] Eugene Freuder. Synthesizing constraint expressions. *Communications of the Association for Computing Machinery*, 21:958–966, 1978.

[Freuder, 1982] Eugene Freuder. A sufficient condition for backtrack-free search. *Journal of the Association for Computing Machinery*, 29(1):24–32, January 1982.

[Gibbs *et al.*, 1976] Norman Gibbs, William Poole, and Paul Stockmeyer. An algorithm for reducing the bandwidth and profile of a sparse matrix. *SIAM Journal of Numerical Analysis*, 13(2), April 1976.

[Gurari and Sudborough, 1984] Eitan Gurari and Ivan Sudborough. Improved dynamic programming algorithms for bandwidth minimization and the mincut linear arrangement problem. *Journal of Algorithms*, 5:531–546, December 1984.

[Monien and Sudborough, 1985] Burkhard Monien and Ivan Sudborough. Bandwidth constrained NP-complete problems. *Theoretical Computer Science*, 41:141–167, 1985.

[Papadimitriou, 1976] Christos Papadimitriou. The NP-completeness of the bandwidth minimization problem. *Computing*, 16:263–270, 1976.

[Purdom *et al.*, 1981] Paul Purdom, Cynthia Brown, and Edward Robertson. Backtracking with multi-level dynamic search rearrangement. *Acta Informatica*, 15:99–114, 1981.

[Saxe, 1980] James Saxe. Dynamic programming algorithms for recognizing small bandwidth graphs in polynomial time. *SIAM Journal on Algebraic and Discrete Methods*, 1(4):363–369, December 1980.

[Seidel, 1981] Raimund Seidel. A new method for solving constraint satisfaction problems. In *Proceedings of IJCAI-81, Vancouver, BC*, pages 338–342, August 1981.

[Stallman and Sussman, 1977] Richard Stallman and Gerald Jay Sussman. Forward reasoning and dependency directed backtracking in a system for computer-aided circuit analysis. *Artificial Intelligence*, 9:135–196, 1977.

[Zinn *et al.*, 1982] P. Z. Zinn, J. Chvátalová, A. K. Dewdney, and N. E. Gibbs. The bandwidth problem for graphs and matrices — a survey. *Journal of Graph Theory*, 6(3):223–254, 1982.

An Organizational Approach to Adaptive Production Systems

Toru Ishida **Makoto Yokoo**
NTT Communications and
Information Processing Laboratories
1-2356, Take, Yokosuka-shi, 238-03, Japan
ishida/yokoo%nttkb.ntt.jp@relay.cs.net

Les Gasser
Computer Science Department
University of Southern California
Los Angeles, CA 90089-0782
gasser@pollux.usc.edu

Abstract

Recently-developed techniques have improved the performance of production systems several times over. However, these techniques are not yet adequate for continuous problem solving in a dynamically changing environment. To achieve adaptive real-time performance in such environments, we use an *organization of distributed production system agents*, rather than a single monolithic production system, to solve problems. *Organization self-design* is performed to satisfy real-time constraints and to adapt to changing resource requirements. When overloaded, individual agents *decompose* themselves to increase parallelism, and when the load lightens the agents *compose* with each other to free hardware resources. In addition to increased performance, generalizations of our composition/decomposition approach provide several new directions for organization self-design, a pressing concern in Distributed AI.

Introduction

To improve the efficiency of production systems, high-speed matching algorithms, such as RETE [Forgy, 1982], TREAT [Miranker, 1987], and optimization algorithms [Ishida, 1988] have been investigated. Two kinds of parallel processing techniques have also been proposed: *parallel matching* [Stolfo, 1984; Gupta *et al.*, 1985; Acharya *et al.*, 1989] to speed-up matching processes and *parallel firing* [Ishida *et al.*, 1985; Ishida, 1990; Tenorio *et al.*, 1985; Moldvan, 1986] to reduce the total number of sequential production cycles. The motive for all of these studies is to speed up production systems several times over. However, these techniques are not yet adequate for continuous problem solving systems.

Typical examples can be found in *real-time expert systems*, where new techniques are required to adapt the systems to dynamically changing environments [Laffey *et al.*, 1988]. To satisfy real-time constraints, various *agent-centered approaches* are currently being studied. Lesser *et al.* [1988] discussed *approximate processing techniques.* Hayes-Roth *et al.* [1989] introduced *adaptive intelligent systems* that reason about and interact with other dynamic entities in real-time. These approaches attempt to meet deadlines by improving the decision-making of individual agents. In this paper we take an *organization-centered approach*, where problems are solved by a society of distributed problem-solving agents. This approach aims to achieve adaptive real-time performance through reorganization of the society. In addition to improving adaptability, our technique provides several insights and general mechanisms for organizational adaptation, a pressing concern in DAI [Gasser *et al.*, 1989a]. Moreover, it has the advantage of being grounded in a well-understood body of theory and practice: parallel production systems.

To explore the effectiveness of the organization-centered approach, we are studying the adaptive load balancing problem in which a particular problem solver shares a collection of processor resources with other problem solvers (and so has an opportunity for adapting its levels of resource use). Problem solving requests arrive at the organization continuously, at variable rates. Meaningful results are required within a (possibly changing) time limit. When the problem-solver is embedded in an open community of other problem solvers, it does not suffice to simply decompose to maximal parallelism – the collective must adapt itself to take advantage of resources as needed, *but it must also adaptively free up resources for others while continuing to operate.*

To achieve this goal, we first extended *parallel production systems*, where global control exists, into *distributed production systems*, with distributed control. We then introduced *organization self-design* (OSD) [Corkill, 1982; Durfee *et al.*, 1987; Gasser *et al.*, 1989a,b] into these distributed production systems. In previous research, reorganization mechanisms typically changed agent roles or inter-agent task ordering. In this paper, we added new reorganization primitives: *composition and decomposition of agents.* When problem solving requests arrive frequently, and make it difficult for the organization to meet its deadlines, agents autonomously *decompose* themselves so that parallelism increases. In contrast, when the organizational load decreases, two agents *compose* (combine with each other) to save hardware resources. As a result, both real-time constraints and efficient resource utilization are satisfied through composition and decomposition of the agents.

Production Systems

To establish our terminology, we give a brief overview of production systems. A *production system* is defined by a set of *rules* or *productions* called *production memory (PM)*, together with an assertion database called *working memory (WM)* that contains a set of *working memory elements (WMEs)*. Each rule comprises a conjunction of *condition elements* called the *left-hand side (LHS)* of the rule, and a set of actions called the *right-hand side (RHS)*. *Positive condition elements* are satisfied when a matching WME exists, and *negative condition elements* are satisfied when no matching WME is found. An *instantiation* of the rule is a set of WMEs that satisfy the positive condition elements. The RHS specifies assertions to be added to or deleted from the WM[1].

A *data dependency graph of production systems* [Ishida *et al.*, 1985; Ishida, 1990] is constructed from the following four primitives:

A *production node*, which represents a set of instantiations. Production nodes are shown as circles in Figure 1 and 2.

A *working memory node*, which represents a set of WMEs. Working memory nodes are shown as squares in Figure 1 and 2.

A *directed edge from a production node to a working memory node*, which represents the fact that a production node modifies a working memory node. More precisely, the edge labeled '+' ('-') indicates that a WME in a working memory node is added (deleted) by firing an instantiation in a production node.

A *directed edge from a working memory node to a production node*, which represents the fact that a production node refers to a working memory node. More precisely, the edge labeled '+' ('-') indicates that a WME in a working memory node is referenced by positive (negative) condition elements when creating an instantiation in a production node.

Interference exists among rule instantiations when the result of parallel execution of the rules is different from the results of sequential executions applied in any order; it must be avoided by synchronization.

Figure 1 shows an example of OPS5 rules and their data dependency graph. In this example, if either `ruleA` or `ruleB` is fired first it destroys the other rule's

[1]In this paper, we assume that each WME contains unique information. Operations adding duplicated WMEs are ignored.

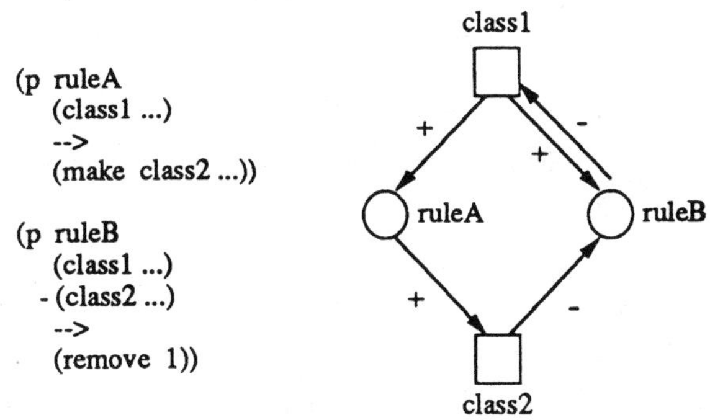

Figure 1: Data Dependency Graph

preconditions; therefore, interference may occur when firing both rules in parallel. If the two rules are distributed to different agents, the agents have to synchronize to prevent firing those rules in parallel.

Distributed Production Systems

Overview

A *distributed production system* is defined as a set of production system agents, each of which contains and fires some of the problem solving rules of the overall system. Each agent comprises the following three components:

A *problem solver*, which continuously repeats the *problem solving cycle* described later in this section. In parallel production systems, multiple rules are simultaneously fired but globally synchronized at the conflict resolution phase [Ishida *et al.*, 1985; Ishida, 1990]. In distributed production systems, on the other hand, rules are asynchronously fired by distributed agents. Since no global control exists, interference among the rules is prevented by local synchronization between individual agents.

Problem solving knowledge, contained in the PMs and WMs. For simplifying the following discussion, we assume no overlap between PMs in different agents, and assume the union of all PMs in the organization is sufficient to solve the given problem. Each agent's WM contains only WMEs that match the LHS of that agent's rules. Since the same condition elements can appear in different rules, the WMs in different agents may overlap. The union of WMs in an organization logically represents all the facts necessary to solve the given problem. In practice, since agents asynchronously fire rules, WMs can be temporarily inconsistent.

Organizational knowledge, representing relationships among agents. Each agent knows only about the others with whom it has data dependency or interference relationships (called its *neighbors*—see below). Since agents asynchronously perform reorganization, organizational knowledge can be temporarily inconsistent across agents.

Organizational Knowledge

Organizational knowledge consists of the following three elements:

Dependencies:
Each agent knows which rules in the organization have data dependency relationships with its own rules. We say that **ruleA** *depends on* **ruleB** if **ruleA** refers to a working memory node that is changed by **ruleB**. We describe this as **depends(ruleA, ruleB)**. The data dependency knowledge of **agentP** is represented as:

$$DEPENDENCY_{agentP} = \{(\mathtt{ruleA},\ \mathtt{ruleB}) \mid (\mathtt{ruleA} \in PM_{agentP} \vee \mathtt{ruleB} \in PM_{agentP}) \wedge \mathtt{depends(ruleA,\ ruleB)}\}$$

Interference:
Each agent knows which rules in the organization may interfere with its own rules. Various interference analysis techniques are reported in [Ishida, 1990]. We describe the interference of **ruleA** and **ruleB** as **interfere(ruleA, ruleB)**. The interference knowledge of **agentP** is represented as:

$$INTERFERENCE_{agentP} = \{(\mathtt{ruleA},\ \mathtt{ruleB}) \mid (\mathtt{ruleA} \in PM_{agentP} \vee \mathtt{ruleB} \in PM_{agentP}) \wedge \mathtt{interfere(ruleA,\ ruleB)}\}$$

Though an individual agent's execution cycle is sequential, potential interference among its own rules is analyzed for future distribution of those rules.

Locations:
Each agent, say **agentP**, knows the location of rules, say **ruleA**, appearing in its own data dependency and interference knowledge. We describe this as **appears(ruleA, agentP)**. The neighbor knowledge of **agentP** is represented as:

$$LOCATION_{agentP} = \{(\mathtt{ruleA},\ \mathtt{agentQ}) \mid \mathtt{appears(ruleA,\ agentP)} \wedge \mathtt{ruleA} \in PM_{agentQ}\}$$

Figure 2 illustrates the organizational knowledge of **agentP**. For example, since **ruleA** and **ruleB** interfere with each other, **agentP** has to synchronize with **agentQ** when executing **ruleA**. Also, **ruleA**'s WM modification has to be transferred to **agentS**. We call **agentQ** a *neighbor* of **agentP** when **agentQ** has data dependency or interference relationships with **agentP**. From this definition, as illustrated in Figure 2, **agentP**'s organizational knowledge refers only to its *neighbors*.

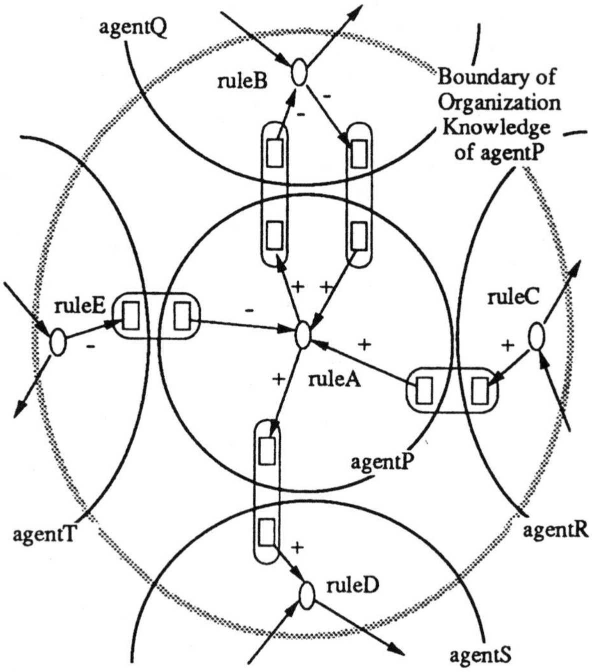

indicates the same working memory node duplicatively stored in different agents.

DEPENDENCY$_{agentP}$ = {(ruleA, ruleC) (ruleD, ruleA) (ruleA, ruleE)}
INTERFERENCE$_{agentp}$ = {(ruleA, ruleB)}
LOCATION$_{agentP}$ = {(ruleA, agentP) (ruleB, agentQ) (ruleC, agentR) (ruleD, agentS) (ruleE, agentT)}

Figure 2: Organizational Knowledge

Problem Solving Cycle

We define a *problem solving cycle of distributed production system agents* by extending the conventional *Match-Select-Act cycle* to accommodate inter-agent data transfers and synchronization. Temporary inter-agent inconsistency caused by distribution is handled locally using temporary synchronization via *rule deactivation*. (We assume the preservation of message ordering.) The cycle is:

1. *Process messages:*
When receiving a *synchronization request message* (e.g., **deactivate(ruleA)**), return an *acknowledgment message* and deactivate the corresponding rule (**ruleA**) until receiving a *synchronization release message* (**activate (ruleA)**). When receiving a *WM modification message*, update the local WM to reflect the change made in the other agent's WM.

2. *Match:*
For each rule, determine whether the LHS matches the current WM.

3. *Select:*
Choose one instantiation of a rule (e.g., `ruleB`) that is not deactivated.

4. *Request synchronization:*
Using interference knowledge, send synchronization request messages (`deactivate(ruleB)`) to the agents requiring synchronization. Await acknowledgment from all synchronized agents[2]. After complete acknowledgment, handle all WM modification messages that have arrived during synchronization. If the selected instantiation is thereby canceled, send synchronization release messages and restart the problem solving cycle.

5. *Act:*
Fire the selected rule instantiation (`ruleB`). Using the data dependency knowledge of `agentP`, inform dependent agents with WM modification messages.

6. *Release synchronization:*
Send synchronization release messages (`activate (ruleB)`) to all synchronized agents.

Organization Self-Design (OSD)

Reorganization Requests

To start reorganization, two kinds of *reorganization requests* are sent to all agents of the organization. *Decomposition requests* are issued when the organization cannot meet deadlines. *Composition requests* are issued to release resources when the organization-wide load is light. For these purposes, the behavior of the organization must be continuously observed.

Decomposition requests initiate division in heavily-loaded agents. Decomposition continues until parallelism increases, response times are shortened, and decomposition requests disappear. Conversely, composition requests initiate combining each two lightly-loaded agents into one. Composition continues until the organization's load increases and composition requests disappear. Both kinds of requests can be issued simultaneously.

Reorganization Process

To control the reorganization processes, we added to each agent an *organization self-designer*, which performs reorganization at the end of each problem solving cycle. We describe below how one agent (e.g., `agentP`) decomposes itself into two agents(e.g., `agentP` and `agentQ`). During reorganization, rules, WMEs, dependency and interference knowledge are transferred from `agentP` to `agentQ`, but not modified. Location knowledge is modified and changes are propagated to other agents.

1. *Create a new agent:*
`agentP` creates a new agent, `agentQ`, which immediately starts problem solving cycles.

2. *Select rules to be transferred:*
`agentP` selects *active* rules to be transferred (e.g., `ruleA`) to `agentQ`. `agentP` sends synchronization request messages (`deactivate(ruleA)`) to `agentQ`. Currently, half of the active rules are arbitrarily selected and transferred, but we are refining a theory of rule selection based on maximizing intra-agent rule dependencies and minimizing inter-agent communication.

3. *Request synchronization:*
`agentP` sends synchronization request messages to *neighbors* for all rules that have data dependency or interference relationships with rules to be transferred (e.g., `deactivate(ruleB)` is sent if `depends(ruleA, ruleB)`, `depends(ruleB, ruleA)` or `interfere(ruleA, ruleB)`)[3]. `agentP` waits for complete acknowledgment (resolving deadlock as before).

4. *Transfer rules:*
`agentP` transfers rules (`ruleA`) to `agentQ`, updates its own location knowledge, and propagates any changes to its *neighbors*.

5. *Transfer WMEs:*
`agentP` copies WMEs that match the LHS of the transferred rules (`ruleA`) to `agentQ`[4]. A bookkeeping process follows in both agents to eliminate duplicated or unneeded WMEs.

6. *Transfer dependency and interference knowledge:*
`agentP` copies its dependency and interference knowledge to `agentQ`. Both agents do bookkeeping to eliminate duplicated or unneeded organizational knowledge[5].

7. *Release synchronization:*
`agentP` sends synchronization release messages (`activate(ruleA)` to `agentQ` and `activate(ruleB)` to all synchronized *neighbors*). This ends reorganization.

---

[2] Deadlock is a possibility. When acknowledge messages are not received, synchronization release messages are sent and the problem solving cycle is restarted.

[3] This is to assure that WM modification and synchronization request messages related to rules to be transferred are not sent to agentP during the reorganization process.

[4] More precisely, to avoid reproducing once-fired instantiations, not only WMEs but also conflict sets are transferred to `agentQ`. Before transferring the conflict sets, however, agentP has to maintain its WM by handling the WM modification messages that have arrived during the synchronization process.

[5] Unneeded data dependency and interference knowledge are the tuples that include none of the agents' rules. Unneeded location knowledge is the tuples that include none of the rules that appear in the agents' data dependency and interference knowledge.

An agent (e.g., **agentP**) can compose with another agent by a similar process. First, **agentP** sends *composition request messages* to its *neighbors.* If some agent, say **agentQ**, acknowledges, **agentP** transfers all rules and organizational knowledge to **agentQ** and destroys itself. The transfer method is the same as that for decomposition.

During the reorganization process, neighboring agents deactivate rules that have data dependency or interference relationships with transferred rules. However, neighboring agents can concurrently perform other activities including firing and transferring rules that are not deactivated. This localization helps agents to modify the organization incrementally.

Experimental Evaluation

To evaluate the effectiveness of our approach, we implemented a simulation environment and solved the *Waltz labeling problem*: 36 rules solve the problem that appears in Figure 3-17 in [Winston, 1977] with 80 rule firings.

At initiation, only one agent, with all problem-solving and organizational knowledge, exists in the organization. We assume the organization knowledge for the initial agent is prepared by analyzing its problem solving knowledge before execution. Problem-solving requests continuously arrive at the agent; older pending requests are processed with higher priority. The load of each agent is represented by a *firing ratio*: the ratio of the number of rule firings to the number of problem solving cycles. Reorganization is performed as follows. (Global parameters are adjustable.)

When the organization cannot solve a problem within a predefined time limit, say 20 problem solving cycles, decomposition requests are sent to the organization. We use experimentally-generated firing ratio thresholds to trigger reorganization. Agents whose firing ratio is greater than 80% start decomposing. Upon decomposition, rules are arbitrary divided and distributed between two agents. When the organization-wide ratio is less than 60%, composition requests are sent to the organization. Agents whose firing ratio is less than 30% compose with each other. These thresholds were experimentally found to provide a good balance between adaptiveness and sensitivity, but further study is warranted.

Figure 3 shows the simulation results. The line chart indicates response times normalized by problem solving cycles, and the step chart represents the number of agents in the organization. In Figure 3(a), problem solving requests arrive at constant intervals. In Figure 3(b), the frequency of requests is changed periodically. From these figures, we can conclude the following:

Adaptiveness of the organization:

In Figure 3(a), the organization reaches a stable state. Since several composition and decomposition cycles are performed, the firing ratios of the resulting agents are equalized. In Figure 3(b), we can see

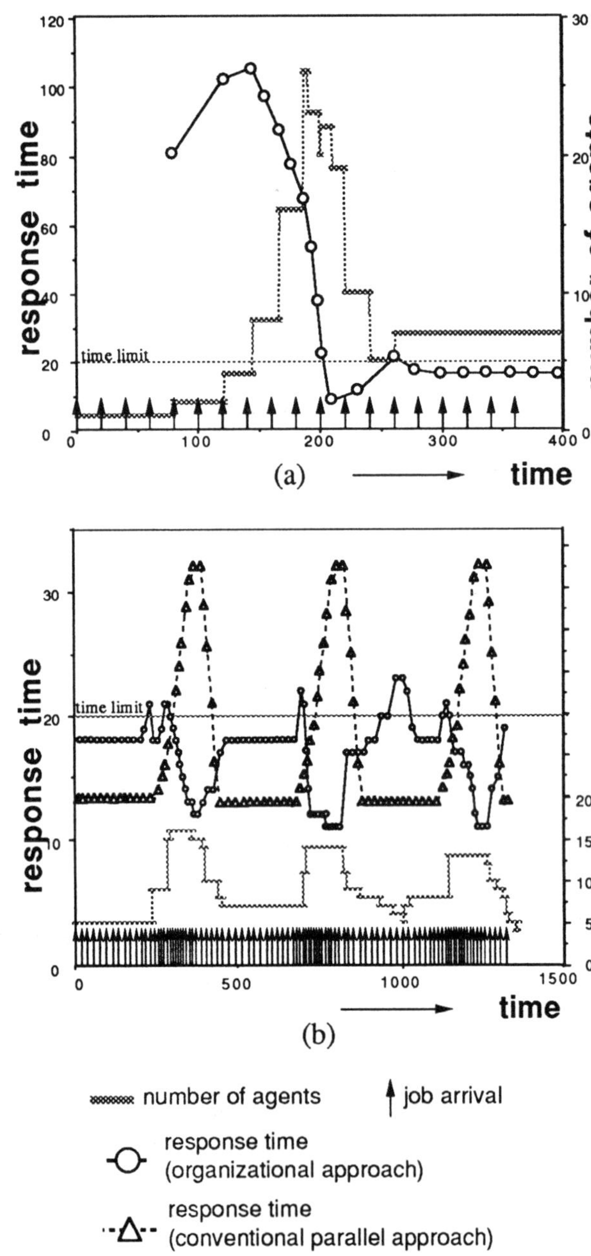

Figure 3: Simulation Results

the number of agents at the busiest peak slightly decreases over time. Both charts show that the society of agents has gradually adapted to the situation through repeated reorganization.

Real-time problem solving:
The average number of agents in Figure 3(b) is 8.95. We compared the organization response times to the performance of 9 permanent agents with no self-design (which is the conventional parallel production system approach, shown as the dashed line in Figure 3(b)). Differences between the dashed and solid lines demonstrate how the organizational approach is effective for adaptive real-time problem solving. However, the effect of reorganization lags the change in problem load. To improve the capability to meet deadlines, time limits must be set shorter than actual deadlines, and load increases must be detected as early as possible.

Efficient resource utilization:
In Figure 3(b), the number of required agents varies from 4 to 17. It is obvious that the organizational approach is more economical than the conventional parallel approach that permanently reserves 17 agents. The resource saving effect of the organizational approach is also supported by the fact that 9 permanent agents (which require almost the same processing resources as the organizational approach) cannot meet deadlines.

Conclusion

Techniques for building problem-solving systems that can adapt to changing problem solving requests and deadlines are of great interest. This paper has presented an approach that relies on reorganization of a collection of problem-solvers to track changes in deadlines and problem solving requests. It exploits an adaptive trade-off of parallelism for time by making new agents and continually reallocating problem-solving knowledge. The importance of this approach goes beyond the adaptive performance we have illustrated.

With additional decision-making meta-knowledge, this approach can become a more general organization self-design technique. It also has the advantage of being grounded in a well-understood body of theory and practice: parallel production systems. In the current version, composition/decomposition decisions are made solely on the basis of firing ratios, and the choice of rules to transfer is made arbitrarily. Allocation decisions could instead be based on the semantics of rules (i.e., distribution based on the kinds of tasks that need more resources). Partial knowledge transfer among *existing* agents can be combined with composition and decomposition to provide a flexible and distributed task-sharing system.

Within our existing formulation, avenues for future research include the implementation and the evaluation of this approach on actual message passing multiprocessor systems, evaluating the impact of reorganization overheads, finer threshold sensitivity analyses, techniques for incrementally acquiring reorganization strategy in more dynamic contexts, and applying this approach to adaptively overcoming local faults and inconsistency among agents.

Acknowledgments

The basic ideas in this paper were elaborated during Les Gasser's visit at NTT Communications and Information Processing Laboratories. The authors wish to thank Kunio Murakami and Ryohei Nakano for their support to our joint research project, and Nick Rouquette for helpful comments.

References

[Acharya *et al.*, 1989] A. Acharya and M. Tambe, "Production Systems on Message Passing Computers: Simulation Results and Analysis," *International Conference on Parallel Processing*, pp. 246-254, 1989.

[Corkill, 1982] D.D. Corkill, *A Framework for Organizational Self-Design in Distributed Problem Solving Networks*, PhD Dissertation, COINS-TR-82-33, University of Massachusetts, 1982.

[Durfee *et al.*, 1987] E. H. Durfee and V. R. Lesser, "Using Partial Global Plans to Coordinated Distributed Problem Solvers," *IJCAI-87*, pp. 875-883, 1987.

[Forgy, 1982] C. L. Forgy, "A Fast Algorithm for the Many Pattern / Many Object Pattern Match Problem," *Artificial Intelligence*, Vol. 19, pp. 17-37, 1982.

[Gasser *et al.*, 1989a] L. Gasser and M. N. Huhns, "Themes in Distributed AI Research," in L. Gasser and M. N. Huhns, Editors, *Distributed Artificial Intelligence*, Volume II, London:Pitman, 1989.

[Gasser *et al.*, 1989b] L. Gasser, N. Rouquette, R. Hill and J. Lieb, "Representing and Using Organizational Knowledge in DAI Systems," in L. Gasser and M. N. Huhns, Editors, *Distributed Artificial Intelligence*, Volume II, London:Pitman, pp. 55-78, 1989.

[Gupta *et al.*, 1988] A. Gupta, C. L. Forgy, D. Kalp, A. Newell and M. Tambe, "Parallel OPS5 on the Encore Multimax," *International Conference on Parallel Processing*, pp. 271-280, 1988.

[Hayes-Roth *et al.*, 1989] B. Hayes-Roth, R. Washington, R. Hewett, M. Hewett and A. Seiver, "Intelligent Monitoring and Control," *IJCAI-89*, pp. 243-249, 1989.

[Ishida *et al.*, 1985] T. Ishida and S. J. Stolfo, "Towards Parallel Execution of Rules in Production

System Programs," *International Conference on Parallel Processing*, pp. 568-575, 1985.

[Ishida, 1988] T. Ishida, "Optimizing Rules in Production System Programs," *AAAI-88*, pp. 699-704, 1988.

[Ishida, 1990] T. Ishida, "Methods and Effectiveness of Parallel Rule Firing," *IEEE Conference on Artificial Intelligence Applications*, pp. 116-122, 1990.

[Laffey *et al.*, 1988] T. J. Laffey, P. A. Cox, J. L. Schmidt, S. M. Kao, and J. Y. Read, "Real-Time Knowledge-Based Systems," *AI Magazine*, Vol. 9, No. 1, pp. 27-45, 1988.

[Lesser *et al.*, 1988] V. R. Lesser, J. Pavlin and E. H. Durfee, "Approximate Processing in Real Time Problem Solving," *AI Magazine*, Vol. 9, No. 1, pp. 49-61, 1988.

[Miranker, 1987] D. P. Miranker, "TREAT: A Better Match Algorithm for AI Production Systems," *AAAI-87*, pp. 42-47, 1987.

[Moldovan, 1986] D. I. Moldovan, "A Model for Parallel Processing of Production Systems," *IEEE International Conference on Systems, Man, and Cybernetics*, pp. 568-573, 1986.

[Stolfo, 1984] S. J. Stolfo, "Five Parallel Algorithms for Production System Execution on the DADO Machine," *AAAI-84*, pp. 300-307, 1984.

[Tenorio *et al.*, 1985] F. M. Tenorio and D. I. Moldovan, "Mapping Production Systems into Multiprocessors," *International Conference on Parallel Processing*, pp. 56-62, 1985.

[Winston, 1977] P. H. Winston, *Artificial Intelligence*, Addison-Wesley, 1977.

The Design of a Marker Passing Architecture for Knowledge Processing

Wing Lee and Dan Moldovan

Department of Electrical Engineering - Systems
University of Southern California 90089-1115
Los Angeles, California
wlee@gringo.usc.edu, moldovan@gringo.usc.edu

Abstract

Knowledge processing is very demanding on computer architectures. Knowledge processing generates subcomputation paths at an exponential rate. It is memory intensive and has high communication requirements. Marker passing architectures are good candidates to solve knowledge processing problems. In this paper, we justify the design decisions made for the Semantic Network Array Processor (SNAP). Important aspects of SNAP are: the instruction set, markers, relations, propagation rules, interconnection network, and granularity. These features are compared to those in NETL and the Connection Machine.

1 Basic Operations in Knowledge Processing

The computations that are typical of knowledge processing require the generation of numerous computation paths that all could potentially be followed in parallel. The process of spawning a number of relatively independent subcomputations, each of which may spawn other subcomputations, is called *bifurcation.* Bifurcation processes appear to be important for a wide range of knowledge based systems. On a serial computer, the bifurcation of independent subprocesses leads to large computational demands. Even a parallel computer does not have the hardware resources to examine all of the parallel paths of a problem. The problem with using current parallel computers is that the problems bifurcate into multiple computation paths that share a considerable amount of context.

[0]This research has been funded by the National Science Foundation Grant No. MIP-89/02426

Another basic operation in knowledge processing is *inheritance.* Inheritance is the mechanism which locates properties attached to concepts within a certain "distance". Often, the inheritance is not obvious, or deals with conflicting properties.

Recognition is also important in knowledge processing. It deals with the ability to recognize concepts or situations in the knowledge base. Although similar to ordinary pattern matching, this problem is far more complex. For example, the properties may not be available locally and may have to be extracted via inheritance, or the exact pattern may not exist and the best match must be determined.

Classification is the process of placing a concept in the knowledge hierarchy. Once placed, it is very easy to retrieve information about the concept. However, classifying a concept is a non-trivial task. It involves comparing the properties of the new concept with properties of all the concepts in the knowledge base.

Unification is the process of generalizing two patterns to form a new pattern that match what both input patterns would have matched. For example, unification may be used to match an inference rule with a knowledge base to determine the applicability of that inference rule.

In *probabilistic reasoning,* probabilities are attached to concepts in the semantic network. The probabilites are modified by interactions with other nodes. Thresholding is used to filter out hypotheses

Problem	Operation
Bifurcation	Control the bifurcation process
Inheritance	Find all nodes connected to a node via some combination of relations
	Find the paths connecting two nodes
	Find the implicit properties of a concept
Recognition	Locate entities in the knowledge base that best match a set of features
	Find the pattern that best matches a given pattern
Classification	Place a pattern at the most appropriate place in the knowledge base
Unification	Bind concepts with compatible concepts in the knowledge base
Probablistic Reasoning	Associate numerical values to parts of the knowledge base
	Compute the strength of hypotheses and compare measures
Learning	Change the values of nodes or links according to some learning algorithm

Table 1: Important Problems and Operations in Knowledge Processing

that have low probabilities.

Learning is the ability of a system to adapt to a problem domain. Commonly, learning involves assigning weights to concepts or links, and being able to change the weights to match the characteristics of the problem domain.

Table 1 lists some of the important problems and operations in knowledge processing. Some other important aspectgs of knowledge representation and reasoning are described in [Brachman, 1988].

2 SNAP Design

2.1 Marker-Passing Architectures

Marker passing architectures provide efficient implementation of the operations indentified previously [Hendler, 1988],[Moldovan, 1989]. However, the class of marker passing architectures has been relatively unexplored. This is due primarly because knowledge processing operations and algorithms have not really been identifed.

Our design approach was to build a machine that would achieve efficient performance for the operations we described earlier and for a set of Natural Language parsing algorithms. In the rest of this paper, we will be describing some of the features of SNAP. In order to better understand these features, we will be comparing them with the features of two other architectures for knowledge processing: NETL and the Connection Machine.

SNAP is a parallel machine consisting of a central controller and a 16K processing nodes. A SNAP node is capable of storing a single fact, concept, rule pattern, etc. The nodes in the network connect to other nodes in the network by a way of relations. Each relation type denotes a different relationship between concepts (nodes). The primary means of computation in SNAP is the processing of markers.

NETL [Fahlman 1979] was one of the first architectures for knowledge processing. It consisted of a central controller and a collection of very simple processing nodes. NETL had 8 different node types and 8 link types for connecting nodes together. A physical wire served as the connection between two nodes. The computation model in NETL was marker-passing, with the controller playing an active role in the movement of markers. Although NETL was never built, it served as the basis for several architectures, including the Connection Machine and SNAP.

The **Connection Machine** [Hillis, 1985] was originally developed as an implementation of Fahlman's NETL. The Connection Machine is a fine-grained array processor with programmable connections between nodes. It consists of 64K single-bit processors, with each processor having 4K bits of memory and a serial ALU. The processors operate in SIMD fashion, with messages being the method of communication.

2.2 Relations

The knowledge base in SNAP is built upon relations between nodes. SNAP can support 64 user-defined relations. The user can extend the number of relations by using nodes to act as relations. This construct is called a Relation-node. Relation-nodes are not as efficent as the primitive relation, but they effectively enable the user to have as many relations as needed. Relations in SNAP also have a weight associated with them. The weight can represent the strength of the link, the cost of traversing the link, etc. Associating weights with relations is essential for implementing reasoning mechanisms such as probabilistic reasoning.

In NETL, relations are pre-defined. Thus, the knowledge base has to be defined using the 8 link types (VC, EQ, CANCEL, CANVC, SPLIT, EXFOR, EXIN, SCOPE). This puts a severe constraint on the type of knowledge that can be represented. NETL has no mechanism for extending the number of relations beyond these 8. In addition, NETL relations cannot carry weights. In fact, NETL has no numeric capabilities at all.

The relations in the Connection Machine are more general than those in both NETL and SNAP. Like SNAP, the relations are all user-definable. Unlike SNAP, the Connection Machine has no limit in the number of relations. However, the total amount of memory available to the node for storage is limited to 4K bits. In SNAP, we felt that 64 relations was more than adequate for most applications, and that it was not worth the hardware resources to extend beyond 64. We provided the Relation-node construct to support those cases where more than 64 relations are needed.

2.3 Markers and Value Passing

SNAP is a marker-passing architecture. The nodes in SNAP communicate by way of messages. The effect of a message at a destination node is to manipulate a marker and possibly generate more messages. Each SNAP node is capable of simultaneously storing up to 24 markers. Each marker consists of a bit indicating whether the node possesses that marker, a value register and a pointer register. The value register can store either data, the current strength of the marker, a probability, etc. A marker also contains a pointer value. This pointer value identifies the node that originated the marker. The marker pointer allows the same marker to be used for different hypothesis. The pointer "colors" the marker so that we can identify which hypothesis it refers to. The marker pointer also enables the easy creation of new relations between nodes. This can be used to solidify a hypothesis, or be the end result of a series of computations (classification of a concept is one example where the creation/deletion of links is the end result).

We created markers of this type to support probabilistic reasoning. Probabilistic reasoning requires the passing of not only markers but also values. The values contain the probabilities and cost associated with the network. They must be included in the marker messages that are sent between nodes. Otherwise, the system has no way to modify the probabilities in the network. Probabilistic reasoning has important applications in the areas of speech recognition and translation and natural language understanding.

The markers in SNAP differ from those in NETL and the Connection Machine. NETL markers consist of only a single bit. No pointer or value is associated with the marker. Consequently, NETL cannot distinguish between two or more hypotheses using the same marker nor can it support probabilistic reasoning. The Connection Machine is able to associate a pointer and value with a marker. However, this is a software construct and is not nearly as efficent in utilizing these features as the built-in hardware in SNAP.

2.4 Propagation Rules

SNAP nodes are capable of communicating with other nodes by way of messages. Each message type has a built-in "propagation rule" which determines the path messages take (i.e. on which relation links to place the messages on). When a destination node receives a message, it sets a marker, performs a corresponding action, and, depending on the propagation rule, can "propagate" the message to other nodes. Thus, propagation rules permit the transfer and bifurcation of messages to occur without intervention from the central controller. This allows many different message types, with different propagation rules, to travel in the network simultaneously.

In the SNAP design we felt that it was important to implement in hardware some key propagation rules. The five propagation rules listed below give the programmer considerable freedom to direct how markers are to be propagated.

1. SEQ(R1, R2): the SEQUENCE propagation rule allows the marker to propagate through R1 once, then to R2 once.

2. SPREAD(R1, R2): the SPREAD propagation rule allows the marker to traverse through a chain of R1 links. For each cell in the R1 path, if there exist any R2, the marker switches to R2 link and continues to propagate until the end of the R2 link.

3. COMB(R1, R2): the COMBine propagation rule allows the marker to propagate to all R1 R2 links without limitation.

4. END-SPREAD(R1, R2): This propagation rule is the same as SPREAD except that it marks only the last cells in the paths.

5. END-COMB(R1, R2): This propagation rule is the same as COMB except that it marks only the last cells in the paths.

By comparison, the propagation rules in NETL are primitive. Markers can propagate on only one relation type making a propagation rule like Combination difficult to achieve. In addition, the NETL controller plays an active role in monitoring and controlling the propagation of markers. Consequently, only one type of marker can be propagating in the network.

In the Connection Machine, the propagation rules can be quite flexible, which allows the Connection Machine to easily implement the SNAP propagation rules. However, the propagation rules in the Connection Machine are software mechanisms. This creates several drawbacks. First, marker propagation in the Connection Machine occurs much more slowly than in SNAP. In SNAP, the marker propagation and processing is built into the hardware. Second, since the Connection Machine must execute instructions to process markers, marker propagation must occur in the foreground. Thus, the Connection Machine cannot perform any other function during this time. In the majority of cases, only a small portion of the network participates in marker propagation, the rest of the network is idle. In SNAP, however, marker propagation occurs in the background. Consequently, the SNAP nodes that are not busy processing markers are free to do other things. Finally, because marker processing in the Connection Machine is software based, the Connection Machine can propagate only one type of marker at a time. A different type of marker would require a different set of software instructions, which would not be able to execute at the same time as the first marker instructions. In order to solve most problems, several different markers are typically required. SNAP, therefore can acheive results with less effort and time than the Connection Machine.

2.5 Instruction Set

We have designed for SNAP a set of 21 powerful instructions specific to knowledge processing for SNAP. These instructions are executed by the processing nodes and are divided into 6 groups: Node Maintenance, Search, Logical, Marker, Marker-Auxiliary, and Data Retrival. We felt that the instructions in these 6 groups represent the core functions required for knowledge processing. The Node Maintenance instructions (CREATE, DELETE, SET-COLOR) are used for loading and modifying the knowledge base. The Search instructions (SEARCH and SEARCH-COLOR) are used to select a node or a group of nodes in the array. The Logical functions (AND, OR, NOT) are used to manipulate the markers within a node. The Marker instructions (MARKER, MARKER-ADD, MARKER-SUB, MARKER-MULT, and MARKER-DIVIDE) introduce a marker into the network. Each of the Marker instructions has a propagation rule associated with it to provide decentralized control. In addition, an arithmetic function can be associated with a marker to enable manipulation of the numeric values in the marker value and the relation weight registers. This enables SNAP to support a wide range of numeric applications, including probabilistic reasoning and learning. The Marker-Auxiliary functions (CLEAR-MARKER, STOP-MARKER, CLEAR-STOP-MARKER, EQUATE, and CLEAR-EQUATE) are used to modify the operation of the Marker instructions. The STOP-MARKER enables a node to "eat" a marker and prevent it from propagating. This is an important mechanism for controlling the flow of markers and preventing the movement of markers into undesired areas. The EQUATE instruction enables a relation to be treated as if it were another relation type during marker propagation. The CLEAR instructions are used to reset the marker portions of nodes. Finally, the Data Retrieval (COLLECT, COLLECT-RELATION, COLLECT-MARKER) are used to obtain information from the nodes. For a more detailed look at the SNAP instruction set see [Moldovan 1989].

In NETL, there is no real instruction set per se. The nodes in NETL are very simple. Control of markers is governed by the NETL controller. Reasoning on NETL is done by retrieving patterns from the knowledge base.

The nodes in the Connection Machine have a basic instruction set. They can be combined to form higher level instructions like those in SNAP. For example, [Chung 1989] created an instruction set similar to SNAP's when he programmed some knowledge processing examples on the Connection Machine.

Our approach was to spend more hardware to create more complex primitive instructions. This allows us to perform basic knowledge processing operations in a minimal amount of time.

2.6 Granularity of a SNAP Chip

In SNAP, we have packaged 32 nodes into a single custom-designed chip. Each node can have an average of 10 relations. We placed these two limitations on SNAP to reduce the cost and to save space. The advances in VLSI techonology in the last decade have enabled us to place more logic onto a chip. Consequently, we felt it would be much easier to build a machine with 512 chips than it would be to build one with 16K chips. With the amount of logic that each node takes, we have estimated that 32 nodes and 320 total relations would easily fit onto a chip.

There is a tradeoff in terms of placing more nodes onto a chip. Each SNAP chip has only 4 data ports for communication with other chip. With 32 nodes in a chip, the data ports can become a bottleneck in the system. [Kim, 1989] has done some preliminary analysis into this area.

In both NETL and the Connection Machine, each chip consisted of only one node.

2.7 Interconnection Network

The SNAP interconnection network is used to connect the SNAP chips together. It is used to enable message passing between nodes. The SNAP interconnection network is a modified bus hypercube. A 16K network is made up of 512 SNAP chips. Each chip has 4 data ports for communication with other chips and a router for determining the message path. Messages in SNAP are 50 bits long and are sent as five 10-bit packets. The maximum number of intermediate chips a SNAP message must pass through is 3. More details on the SNAP interconnection network can be found in [Moldovan 1989]. The network has been software simulated and compared with other networks [Lee 1989]. The results show that the network performs favorably when compared to the performance of other networks.

The interconnection network in NETL is vastly different. In NETL, all connections between nodes are point to point. A physical wire is placed between two nodes that share a relation. Thus, NETL messages can travel very fast. However, a network of this type is unfeasible. In a dense network (more than a hundred nodes) it is almost impossible to place a physical wire between two nodes and be able to remove it later. A network where we cannot delete links can only support monotonic reasoning; in almost all cases, this is unacceptable.

The Connection Machine has special routing chips for sending messages. This frees the nodes from having to participate in message routing. In a 64K Connection Machine, there are 4K routers, with each router servicing 16 nodes. The routers are arranged in a 12-dimensional hypercube and can process 1-bit at a time. In SNAP, we chose not to create a special router chip, because we felt that incorporating the routing function into the node chip was a better alternative. Unlike the Connection Machine, marker propagation in SNAP can proceed in the background without intervention from the controller. Thus an integrated router fits right into that concept. In the Connection Machine, however, actual instructions have to be executed to process a message. Incorporating the routing function in the node would further complicate the long process of marker propagation.

3 Simulation Results

We have built a simulator of SNAP to test some of the concepts we have discussed in this paper. We have run several examples on the SNAP simulator. Table 2 summarizes the simulation results for these examples. Example 1 is a non-obvious inheritance problem involving 30 concepts (nodes). Example

	SNAP		CM	Tcm/
	Cycle	Time	Time	Tsnap
Example1 Inheritance	387	59.8us	202ms	3380
Example2 Inheritance	2888	446us	519ms	1163
Example3 Recognition	329	50.8us	379ms	7460
Example4 Classification	366	56.5us	NA	

Table 2: Comparsion between SNAP and Connection Machine

2 is a inheritance problem over an imaginary two-dimensional 10 × 10 network. Example 3 deals with recognition with multiple properties. Example 4 is a small classification problem [Lipkis, 1983]. A complete description of the examples can be found in [Moldovan 1990].

Some of these examples have been implemented on the Connection Machine at USC-ISI. Those times are listed along with the SNAP times in Table 2. Note, for SNAP we considered the speed to be the same clock as the Connection Machine (6.47443 MHz).

4 Conclusions

SNAP combines several features which collectively make SNAP a powerful knowledge processing engine. Some of these features are: a powerful instruction set implemented in hardware, marker passing architecture, associative array processing, and a modified hypercube interconnection network. The instruction set has been carefully designed to provide hardware implementation of the most often used knowledge processing operations. Special attention has been given to marker propagation rules.

The results shown in Table 2 between SNAP and the Connection Machine are not suprising considering the differences between the two machines described in this paper. The fundamental reason for the superior performance of SNAP is that it implements in hardware features that require software instructions in the Connection Machine.

References

Brachman, R. [1988]. "The basics of knowledge representation and reasoning", *AT&T Technical Journal*, 67:1, 7-24.

Chung, S., Moldovan, D. and Tung, Y. [1989]. "Reasoning on the Connection Machine", Technical Report CENG-89-13. University of Southern California Department of EE Systems.

Fahlman, S. [1979]. "NETL: A system for representing and using real-world knowledge". The MIT Press, Cambridge, MA.

Hendler, J. [1988] "Integrating Marker-Passing and Problem-Solving". Lawerence Erlbaum Associates, Inc.

Hillis, W. [1985] "The Connection Machine". The MIT Press, Cambridge, MA.

Kim, J. and Moldovan, D. [1989]. "Parallel Classificaton for Knowledge Representation on SNAP". *Proceedings of the 1990 International Conference on Parallel Processing.* Department of Electrical Engineering Systems, Univ. of Southern California.

Lee, W. "Bandwidth Analysis of Message Passing Networks". Technical Report CENG 89-24, Department of Electrical Engineering-Systems. University of Southern California.

Lipkis, T. and Schmolze, J. [1983]. "Classification in the KL-ONE knowledge representation system", *Proceedings of the Eighth International Joint Conference on Artificial Intelligence*, Vol. 1, 330-332.

Moldovan, D., Lee, W., and Lin, C. [1989]. "SNAP: A Marker-Propagation Architecture for Knowledge Processing", Technical Report No: 89-10. Department of Electrical Engineering Systems, Univ. of Southern California.

Moldovan, D., Lee, W., Lin, C., and Chung, S. [1990]. "Parallel Knowledge Processing on SNAP". *Proceedings of the 1990 International Conference on Parallel Processing.*

A Parallel Asynchronous Distributed Production System*

James G. Schmolze and **Suraj Goel**
Department of Computer Science
Tufts University / Medford, MA 02155 / USA
E-mail: schmolze@cs.tufts.edu

Abstract

To speed up production systems, many researchers have turned to parallel implementations. We describe a system called PARS that executes production rules in parallel. PARS is novel because it (1) executes many rules simultaneously, (2) runs in a highly asynchronous fashion, and (3) runs on a distributed memory machine. Item (1) improves available concurrency over systems that only perform the MATCH step in parallel. Item (2) reduces bottlenecks over synchronous parallel production systems. Item (3) makes the techniques more available given the lower cost of distributed versus shared memory machines. The two main problems regarding correctness, namely serialization and the maintenance of consistent distributed databases, are addressed and solved. Estimates of the effectiveness of this approach are also given.

Introduction

Production systems have been effective vehicles for implementing expert systems. The terminology of production systems and the usual serial execution model are presented in Figure 1. Unfortunately, large production systems are often slow and many will require substantial speed improvements. To speed them up, researchers have studied parallel implementations, with much of that research focusing on OPS5 [Forgy, 1981].

Since most cpu time in OPS5 is spent in the MATCH step (over 90% according to [Forgy, 1979]), many efforts (e.g., [Gupta, 1983; Stolfo, 1984; Gupta, 1986; Miranker, 1987; Oflazer, 1987]) have tried to make parallel that one step while leaving the system to continue executing only one rule at a time. Overall, the maximum speedups realized by these approaches are about ten times the fastest sequential version of OPS5, no matter how many processors are used [Gupta, 1986].

To gain additional speedup, several researchers have investigated systems that execute many rules simultaneously. We call these systems *multiple rule execution systems*. When two or more rule instantiations execute simultaneously in one of these systems, we say they *co-execute*. Multiple rule execution systems have two important problems. (1) The order of rule execution is difficult to control. (2) The results produced may not be producible under any serial execution scheme, i.e., the final results may not be *serializable*.

[Boulanger, 1988] and [Morgan, 1988] each take this approach and each offers a way to control partially the order of rule execution. However, neither guarantees

Production Memory: A set of rules or productions.

Working Memory (WM): A set of facts.

Working Memory Element (WME): Each fact in the WM is a WME. Each is a ground literal consisting of a class name plus a sequence of arguments.

Condition Element (CE): A test found in a rule.

Left-Hand Side (LHS): A sequence of CEs associated with a rule that determine when the rule matches against a specific sequence of WMEs.

Action: An operation performed when the rule executes. Usually adds or removes a WME.

Right-Hand Side (RHS): A sequence of actions associated with a rule that determines what to do when the rule is executed.

Basic Loop: The following loop is executed until no matches are found in the first step.

MATCH: For each rule, determine all sequences of WMEs that match its LHS. Each match results in an *instantiation*, which consists of the rule plus the sequence of WMEs matching the unnegated condition elements (CEs) of its LHS. A single rule may have many instantiations.

SELECT: Choose exactly one instantiation according to some predefined *conflict resolution strategy*.

ACT: Perform the actions on the RHS of the rule for the selected instantiation.

Figure 1: Terminology and Serial Execution Model for Production Systems

*This work was supported in part by the National Science Foundation under grant number IRI-8800163.

serializable results. In contrast, [Ishida and Stolfo, 1985; Moldovan, 1986; Pasik, 1989; Schmolze, 1989; Ishida, 1990] do not address the issue of controlling the order of rule execution, but each guarantees serializability. In addition, each takes advantage of parallel matching algorithms, thereby gaining additional speedup.

All of the above multiple rule execution systems are designed to operate ***synchronously***, i.e., all processors execute each step together. To obtain good speedup, the work must be effectively distributed for each of the three steps. This is likely to prove difficult since resources must be allocated to solve three different distribution problems. Unfortunately, no efforts along this line have been reported to date. Only the MATCH step has so far been studied in this fashion.

An alternative is to execute a multiple rule execution system in a highly ***asynchronous*** fashion. This eliminates the time wasted in synchronous systems where some processors are forced to wait for other processors to finish the current step. The distribution problem is still challenging in an asynchronous system, but it is simplified to one distribution problem. Some preliminary work on an asynchronous parallel production system is reported in [Miranker *et al.*, 1989].

Herein, we address the problem of executing a multiple rule execution system that operates asynchronously on a distributed memory machine. The advantages of this approach follow.

- We obtain speedup over serial and parallel-match-only systems by executing all steps in parallel.
- We obtain speedup over synchronous parallel systems by a reduction of bottlenecks and a simplification of the distribution problem.
- We take advantage of distributed memory technology, which is less expensive and more accessible than shared-memory technology given today's market.[1]

This work is related to distributed database (DDBMS) technology, the main difference being the source of the transactions. For DDBMSs, they come from users, and are highly unpredictable. For production systems (PSs), they come from the rules and WM, and are more predictable. Thus, special techniques that take advantage of off-line rule analysis can yield considerable improvement. Sellis *et al* [Sellis *et al.*, 1987; Raschid *et al.*, 1989] take a database approach by delaying certain transactions using locks in order to guarantee serializability. However, they do not take strong advantage of off-line rule analysis, and their system can cause deadlock, whose detection and resolution may require considerable resources. Given that, it is appropriate to pursue other approachs such as ours.

[1]Furthermore, Gupta and Tambe [Gupta and Tambe, 1989] have argued that distributed memory machines are good choices for production systems.

The remainder of this paper describes the design problems we faced, solutions to those problems, and estimates of the effectiveness of our solutions.

The Execution Model

We assume a distributed memory machine with a set of processors, $\mathcal{P}$, and a fast interconnection network between them. Any processor can communicate with any other, either directly or through intermediaries. We are given a set of rules, $\mathcal{R}$, a set of class names, $\mathcal{C}$, that comprise all the classes used in $\mathcal{R}$, and an initial working memory, WM_0. Each WME belongs to exactly one class in $\mathcal{C}$. Each processor uses the same execution model and each is capable of storing rules and WMEs.

For simplicity, we use a static distribution. Each rule in $\mathcal{R}$ is assigned to exactly one processor from $\mathcal{P}$. For each rule r on each processor p, we store on p all classes of WMEs that could match a CE of r's LHS. If a CE in r has a variable appearing as the class, then all classes in $\mathcal{C}$ are stored on p. By storing a class c on p, we mean that all WMEs whose class is c are stored on p. Thus, classes that appear on the LHS of several rules may be stored in several processors.

Each processor p executes a variant of the basic loop for serial systems, as explained below. Each executes the loop at its own pace in an asynchronous fashion.

MATCH: In performing the MATCH step, p only examines the rules and WMEs stored locally. Since all WMEs that could affect the matching of each rule (i.e., all WMEs affecting its LHS) are stored on the same processor as the rule, no matches are missed. We use the TREAT match algorithm [Miranker, 1987].

SELECT: The SELECT step is also performed using only local data. As we will explain later, certain rules may be temporarily disabled and instantiations of such rules are ignored here. Since we do not guarantee any particular overall order of rule execution, each processor arbitrarily selects an instantiation whose rule is not currently disabled. If there are none, p returns to the MATCH step. Otherwise, p goes to the DISABLE step. Assume for now that p selects an instantiation of rule r.

DISABLE: Before executing the selected instantiation, some synchronization must occur. As we will discuss later, we guarantee serializability by prohibiting the co-execution of certain pairs of rules. Thus, in this step, p requests certain other processors to ***disable*** certain other rules, namely, those rules that cannot co-execute with r. If some of those rules are currently executing, then their execution is completed, after which their processor disables them. p waits until it receives messages verifying that all appropriate rules are disabled. While waiting, it is possible that p received new actions from elsewhere that invalidated the selected instantiation or that another processor disabled *r* (*p* responds immediately to such requests). Thus, *p* checks this, and if so, *p* does not execute the instantiation and jumps to ENABLE. Otherwise, *p* goes to ACT.

ACT: The ACT step also requires communication since some of the actions may add or remove WMEs that are stored on other processors. In such cases, the actions are forwarded as appropriate. After actions are sent, the processor waits for acknowledgements from all recipients before re-acknowledging and proceeding. The reasons for this will become clear when we later explain our solution to the inconsistency problem. Thus, at the completion of this step, all processors who store the affected WMEs have taken the actions into account. Actions that affect the local WM are taken immediately.

ENABLE: Rules on other processors that were previously disabled in the DISABLE step are re-enabled. *p* now returns to MATCH.

Processors accept messages from other processors at the start of the MATCH step and while waiting during the DISABLE step. Even though some synchronization is needed in the DISABLE and ACT steps, it comprises a reasonably small portion of the basic cycle time (MATCH consumes the most) and thus leaves the system highly asynchronous.

We define the *period of the execution* of an instantiation *i* as extending from the time that the commitment to execute *i* is made to the later of either (1) the time that *i*'s local actions are taken, or (2) the time that all acknowledgements have been received regarding the delivery of *i*'s actions. (A commitment to execute *i* is made in the DISABLE step, not the SELECT step.) We say that a set of instantiations *co-execute* iff their periods of execution overlaps.

In addition, we have an algorithm that is guaranteed to determine when all processors have no instantiations. When this occurs, all processors are terminated.

The Serialization Problem

The parallel execution of a set of instantiations is serializable if the result produced by the parallel system could be produced by executing the same instantiations in some serial order. The goal of serialization is to ensure that every execution sequence by our parallel system is serializable.

There are three causes of non-serializability in our parallel model. The first cause is *disabling*. We say that one instantiation *disables* another if executing the first causes the second to no longer match. This occurs iff the first adds (removes) a WME that the second matched negatively (positively). If we co-execute a pair of instantiations where each disables the other, the result is not serializable because, in a serial system, one instantiation would execute but not both. In general, when given a set of instantiations, not all should co-execute if there is a cycle of disabling relations among them.

P1: +(A <x>), −(C <y>) → +(C <x>), +(D <x>)
P2: +(B <x>), −(C <y>) → +(C <x>), +(E <x>)

For example, assume that we execute rules P1 and P2 rules from an initial WM of {(A 1),(B 2)}. Here, both rules match and, if co-executed, produce {(A 1),(B 2),(C 1),(D 1),(C 2),(E 2)}. However, no serial execution can produce this result. If P1 alone were executed from the original WM, the result would be {(A 1),(B 2),(C 1),(D 1)}, in which P2 no longer matches. Similarly, if P2 were executed alone from the original WM, the result would be {(A 1),(B 2),(C 2),(E 2)}, in which P1 no longer matches.

We solve this problem by preventing the co-execution of any set of instantiations that have a cycle of disabling relations among them.

The second cause is *clashing*. We say that one instantiation *clashes* with another if, when executed, one would add a WME that the other would remove. If (a) two instantiations clash and (b) one rule can disable the other, then we might obtain non-serializable results.

P1: +(A <x>), −(C <y>) → +(C <x>), +(D <x>)
P3: +(D <x>), −(C <y>) → −(D <x>), +(E <x>)

For example, rules P1 and P3 would match in {(A 1),(D 1)}, but executing P1 will disable P3. Thus, there are two possible serial orders. We can execute P1 and not P3, or we can execute P3 followed by P1. If the two are co-executed, then the result must be identical to that resulting from executing P3 followed by P1. Since P3 deletes (D 1) while P1 adds it, (D 1) must be in the final WM. Therefore, if these two rules are co-executed, the result must be {(A 1),(C 1),(D 1),(E 1)}.

In our parallel model, we cannot make this guarantee because our control of the order of rule execution is not sufficiently fine. Instead, we solve the problem by prohibiting the co-execution of such pairs of instantiations.

The third cause arises from temporary inconsistencies in the distributed WM. We deal with this problem two sections hence.

Solution to the Serialization Problem

If the execution of two instantiations do not overlap in time, i.e., they do not co-execute, then serialization is guaranteed. Namely, an appropriate serial order simply has the first before the second. We therefore concern ourselves only with sets of instantiations that co-execute. For now, we assume a consistent WM.

We solve the serialization problem by: (1) determining pairs of rules whose instantiations should not co-execute (we say that any such pair of rules are to be

1. Collect all pairs of rules from our set of rules, $\mathcal{R}$, that possibly clash and, for each pair, add an edge to an undirected graph called *RSynch*. *RSynch* has a node for each rule in $\mathcal{R}$ and will eventually have an edge between each distinct pair A and B iff A and B must be synchronized.
2. Construct *RDO*($\mathcal{R}$). Then, construct a modified subgraph of *RDO*($\mathcal{R}$), called *M-RDO*. We start with *RDO*($\mathcal{R}$) and, for each edge from A to B in *RSynch*, remove any edge from A to B or from B to A in *RDO*($\mathcal{R}$).
3. Construct an acyclic sub-graph of *M-RDO* called *A-RDO*. The goal is to remove only edges from *M-RDO* in producing *A-RDO*, and to remove as few edges as possible since each edge removed will create a rule synchronization. We begin *A-RDO* with a node for each rule but no edges. We maintain a reachability matrix, M, for *A-RDO* such that $M[r_j,r_k]$ is true iff there is a directed path from r_j to r_k. We examine each edge, e, from *M-RDO* in turn. Let e go from r_j to r_k. If adding e to *A-RDO* would not create a cycle, we add e to *A-RDO* and update M. Otherwise, we add an edge from r_j to r_k in *RSynch* and, if there is an edge from r_k to r_j in *M-RDO*, we remove it. Afterwards, *A-RDO* is an acyclic sub-graph of *M-RDO* and, for all edges e in *M-RDO* but not in *A-RDO*, the undirected version of e appears in *RSynch*.
4. We synchronize each pair of distinct rules that have an edge between them in *RSynch*.

Figure 2: Off-Line Algorithm to Identify Rules to Synchronize

synchronized [2]), and (2) enforcing these rule synchronizations. We work at the rule, not the instantiation, level because the latter requires too much communication for our hardware model.

We say that one rule *possibly disables* another if any instantiation of the first can disable any instantiation of the second. We define *possibly clashes* in a corresponding fashion. Off-line tests for these two inter-rule relations are given in [Schmolze, 1989].[3] We define a directed graph, called *RDO*($\mathcal{R}$), that represents the *rule disabling order*. For each rule in $\mathcal{R}$, there is a node in *RDO*($\mathcal{R}$). For each A and B in $\mathcal{R}$ where B possibly disables A, there is an edge from A to B in *RDO*($\mathcal{R}$) (note the reversal of A and B). This comprises all of *RDO*($\mathcal{R}$). Also, we define *Rules*($\mathcal{I}$) as the set of rules that have an instantiation in $\mathcal{I}$.

Theorem 1: [4] *The co-execution of a set of instantiations, $\mathcal{I}$, in our parallel model, is serializable if*

1. *RDO(Rules($\mathcal{I}$)) is acyclic except for self loops,*
2. *rules that have self loops in RDO(Rules($\mathcal{I}$)) have only one instantiation in $\mathcal{I}$,*
3. *no two distinct rules in Rules($\mathcal{I}$) can possibly clash,*
4. *rules that possibly clash with themselves have only one instantiation in $\mathcal{I}$, and*
5. *the WM is consistent.*

Since each rule appears on exactly one processor in our model, we cannot have two instantiations of the same rule co-executing. Thus, conditions 2 and 4 are met. We meet condition 3 by synchronizing every pair of rules that possibly clash. We meet condition 1 by identifying a near-minimum number of pairs of rules to synchronize such that, for any set $\mathcal{I}$ of instantiations to co-execute, *RDO*(*Rules*($\mathcal{I}$)) is acyclic. The rules requiring synchronization are identified using the off-line algorithm in Figure 2. The output is a set of pairs of rules that must be synchronized. Condition 5 is assumed for now and dealt with in the next section.

Our method of enforcing rule synchronization was given in the explanation of our execution model. To reduce the work in enforcing these synchronizations, and to prevent deadlock, we take several additional steps. First, we remove from this set of pairs of rules to synchronize any pair where both are on the same processor. No synchronization is needed between such pairs as only one can execute at a time.

Second, we recognize that in order for two rules to synchronize, only one of them needs to initiate the needed disabling. Let A and B be such a pair and let A be the one to initiate the disabling. When B's processor wishes to execute B, it simply does so as long as B is not disabled. When A's processor wishes to execute A, it first disables B, then executes A, and finally re-enables B.

If we think of the pairs of rules to synchronize as an undirected graph, this simplification has the effect of directing each edge. In this case, the undirected edge between A and B becomes a directed edge from A to B, indicating that A can execute only if B is disabled. However, cycles in this directed graph can lead to deadlock. For example, let A require that B be disabled, B require that C be disabled and C require that A be disabled. Let all three are on separate processors and let A, B and C each be selected for execution at the same time. Disabling messages go out from each processor and each waits for acknowledgements before responding to the disable request it receives, leading to deadlock.

[2] We borrow this term from [Ishida and Stolfo, 1985] who first proposed this approach to solving the serialization problem. Our solution represents an improvement over their method along with an adjustment made for our parallel model, which differs from theirs. See [Schmolze, 1989] for a complete discussion.

[3] In essence, r_1 possibly disables r_2 if an add (remove) action of r_1 unifies with a negative (positive) CE of r_2. r_1 possibly clashes with r_2 if an add (remove) action of r_1 unifies with a remove (add) action of r_2.

[4] The proof can be found in [Schmolze, 1989].

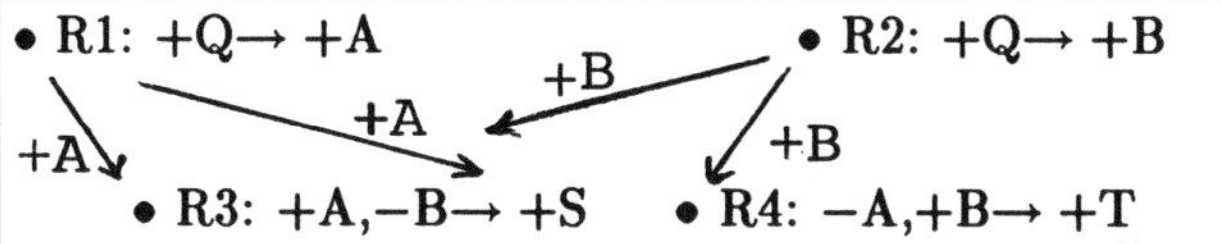

Figure 3: Temporary Inconsistencies Can Cause Non-Serializable Effects

Fortunately, this is easily solved because we can always take an undirected graph that has no self loops and direct each edge such that there are no cycles. To do so, number the M nodes from 1 to M. Go through each edge and direct it from the lower numbered node to the higher numbered one. Since there no self loops, this is an unambiguous choice.[5]

As a result, synchronization is simplified and deadlock free. Moreover, the results of our parallel system are serializable with respect to both disablings and clashes. In fact, we expect only very small delays from the needed synchronizations.[6]

Temporary Database Inconsistencies

Given that our WM is distributed, temporary WM inconsistencies can occur while actions are being sent, which can lead to non-serializable effects. For an example, we offer a case with four rules as shown in Figure 3. Here, R1 and R2 match if there is a WME of class Q and they add WMEs of classes A and B, respectively. R3 matches if there is some WME of class A and no WMEs of class B, and it adds a WME of class S. R4 matches if there are no WMEs of class A and some WME of class B, and it adds a WME of class T. We assume there are no other rules.

Let us examine all serial orders that can arise from an initial WM of {Q}. Both R1 and R2 match, but R3 and R4 do not. Let R1 execute, which adds an A WME. Now, R3 matches as well as R2. Let R3 execute, which adds an S WME. Only R2 matches, so we execute it, which adds a B WME. R4 never matched and still does not due to the presence of the the A WME. Thus, our first serial order is (1) R1, R3 followed by R2. There are three other serial orders, namely, (2) R2, R4 followed by R1, (3) R2 followed by R1, and finally, (4) R1 followed by R2. However, there is no serial order in which all four rules execute.

Unfortunately, with temporary WM inconsistencies in our parallel model, all four rules *can* execute. Assume that each of these rules is on its own processor. Let R1 and R2 co-execute and let each send out its respective action at the same time. Furthermore, let the time of message delivery be small between R1 and R3 and between R2 and R4. Conversely, let the time of delivery be large between R1 and R4 and between R2 and R3. Thus, R3 will receive the +A action from R1 before receiving the $+B$ action from R2. Let us assume that after receiving the +A and before receiving the +B, R3's processor commits to execute R3 (remember, the processors run asynchronously). Note that no rule synchronization is necessary here since there are no possible disabling cycles and no possible clashes. In a similar fashion, R4 receives the +B action before the +A action, and during the interim period, R4's processor commits to executing R4. As a result, we get all four rules executing, which is not serializable.

Solution to the Inconsistency Problem

We solve this problem by incorporating a double acknowledgement protocol when sending actions. The protocol for the *sender* of actions is as follows.

1. Send actions to all appropriate processors.
2. Wait for all recipients to acknowledge receipt of the actions.
3. Send re-acknowledgements to all recipients.

The protocol for the *receiver* of actions is as follows.

1. Send an acknowledgement to the original sender.
2. Disable all rules affected by the actions.
3. Continue with the basic loop.
4. Upon re-acknowledgement from the original sender, re-enable the rules disabled by the actions.

The basic idea here is that the original receipt of actions from another processor indicates that certain WMEs will be added or removed. However, to prevent inconsistency problems, the receiver prevents the use of this information until it is sure that *all* appropriate processors have received it. It is sure of this upon receipt of the re-acknowledgement.

The rules disabled by the receiver are those rules having CEs that might test either positively or negatively for the WMEs affected by the action. The reason the receiver disables and re-enables rules is that, while waiting for re-acknowledgements, it can continue with its basic loop.[7]

For an example, we return to Figure 3 when R1 and R2 are about to send out their respective actions to both R3 and R4's processors. R3's processor receives the +A action, disables rule R3 since it tests for a WME of class A, and sends an acknowledgement to R1's processor. At about the same time, R4's processor receives the +B action, disables rule R4, and

[5]If there were a loop, it must involve at least two nodes, and thus must have an edge from a higher numbered node to a lower numbered node, which is impossible.□

[6]We note that I/O should also be serialized. We accomplish this by assigning all rules that perform I/O to a single processor. Thus, only one I/O rule executes at a time.

[7]In an alternative design, the processor could simply wait for the re-acknowledgements instead of continuing on with its basic loop. It thus would not need to disable and re-enable rules. However, this alternative is wasteful of time, so we reject it.

	No. Non I/O Rules	I&S	PARS
Mapper	77	13.2	6.9
ToruWaltz	31	15.2	6.9
Weighted Average		13.8	6.9
Avg. Improvement Over I&S		1.0	2.0

Table 1: Comparison of Number of Synchronizations per Rule

	No. of CS's	Avg. CS Size	I&S	PARS N=8	PARS N=32
Mapper	340	20.3	1.2	2.6	3.1
ToruWaltz	207	47.2	1.0	2.2	4.7
Weighted Average	273.5	30.5	1.1	2.4	4.1
Improvement Over I&S			1.0	2.2	3.7

Table 2: Concurrency Estimates using Number of Co-Executions Available

sends an acknowledgement to R2's processor. Similar activities occur when R3's processor receives the +B action and when R4's processor receives the +A action. Soon thereafter, R1's processor has received the two acknowledgements it wants, and so it sends out re-acknowledgements. At about the same time, R2 does the same. Note that each of the rules R3 and R4 have been disabled twice. Thus, neither is re-enabled until both re-acknowledgements are received. By the time this occurs, both R3 and R4's processors have received both actions so, in this case, neither R3 nor R4 execute.

As a result, we have a protocol that prevents non-serializable effects due to temporary inconsistencies in our distributed WM. The cost of this guarantee is that additional messages must be sent and, for certain periods of time, certain rules are disabled. However, these periods are short as they last only long enough for an acknowledgement and re-acknowledgement messages to be sent. Overall, we estimate this to be a reasonably small fraction of the basic cycle time, leading to a small cost for this guarantee.

Assessment of Effectiveness

An implementation of PARS is currently under construction, so we are not able to report on actual speedups realized. Instead, we estimate speedup in terms of increased numbers of co-executing instantiations.

We applied our rule analysis method to two production systems that are commonly used as benchmarks for parallel production systems. These systems are (1) the Manhattan Mapper [Lerner and Cheng, 1983], which provides travel schedules for trips through Manhattan, and (2) ToruWaltz, which applies Dave Waltz's constraint propagation algorithm to identify objects from line drawings [Waltz, 1975]. First, we measured the number of pairs of rules to be synchronized. Second, we examined a number of conflict sets from serial execution traces and determined how many instantiations would co-execute in our system if it were running synchronously.

We compare our system to that of Ishida and Stolfo's (I&S) [Ishida and Stolfo, 1985] as their's is the most influential work in the area of multiple rule execution systems. Thus, we are comparing a synchronous version of our approach to another synchronous system.

Table 1 compares the number of rules to be synchronized for the method of I&S versus ours. As shown in the table, we improve upon their method by having each rule synchronize with, on the average, about half the number of rules that I&S require. Table 2 compares the number of instantiations that could co-execute in our sample traces. For 8 processors, our system co-executes over twice as many instantiations than does I&S. For 32 processors, our system co-executes almost four times as many. While this demonstrates improvement, it does not take into account the cost of our differing execution model, including message passing times. We are thus optimistic that our system will show notable improvements in speedup. However, final results must await actual run times.

Conclusions

We presented a parallel production system called PARS. Novel about PARS is that it (1) executes many rules simultaneously, (2) runs mostly asynchronously, and (3) uses a distributed memory machine. Its advantages are that it (1) improves the available concurrency over serial and match-only parallel approaches by having multiple rule executions, (2) reduces a number of bottlenecks found in synchronous multiple rule execution systems, (3) simplifies the distribution problem over these synchronous systems, and (4) makes the techniques more generally available by using lower cost distributed versus shared memory machines.

PARS guarantees that the final results it produces are serializable. However, like other similar systems, PARS does not guarantee any particular order of rule execution. To help with this, we have added non-OPS5 control constructs. Unfortunately, space does not allow their presentation here (but see [Schmolze, 1988]).[8]

Overall, the speedups estimated for PARS are better than those for other similar systems. However, these speedups are not spectacular. This arises from the

[8]Space also does not allow us to present our distribution algorithm (but see [Goel, 1990]).

benchmarks having been written for serial systems. In the future, we will write and use more appropriate benchmarks. We will experiment with variations of the strategies presented herein, including dynamic distribution schemes. We will incorporate rule decomposition strategies (e.g., [Pasik and Stolfo, 1987; Pasik, 1989]). Finally, we will continue to design new control strategies for multiple rule execution systems.

Acknowledgements

Many thanks go to the students who have contributed either ideas or programs to the development of PARS, which includes David Cheung, Michael Futeran, Eric Gothelf, Kiran Shah, David Yates, and the 1987 class of CSC 280. In addition, special thanks goes to Dan Miranker et al for making the OPS5C system available to us for use in the PARS implementation.

References

[Boulanger, 1988] Albert Boulanger. The Modification of a Rule-based Diagnostic System for Routinized Parallelism on the Butterfly Parallel Computer. Technical Report 6713, BBN Laboratories Inc., Camb., MA, January 1988.

[Forgy, 1979] C.L. Forgy. *On the Efficient Implementation of Production Systems.* PhD thesis, Dept. of Computer Science, Carnegie Mellon Univ., Pittsburg, PA, 1979.

[Forgy, 1981] C.L. Forgy. OPS5 User's Manual. Technical Report CMU-CS-81-135, Dept. of Computer Science, Carnegie Mellon Univ., 1981.

[Goel, 1990] Suraj Goel. Rule Partitioning for Parallel Production Systems. Technical Report 90–2, Dept. of Computer Science, Tufts Univ., Medford, MA, 1990. In preparation.

[Gupta and Tambe, 1989] A. Gupta and M. Tambe. Suitability of Message Passing Machines for Implementing Production Systems. In *Proc. of AAAI-88*, St. Paul, Minnesota, August 1989. American Assoc. for Artificial Intelligence.

[Gupta, 1983] A. Gupta. Implementing OPS5 Production Systems on DADO. Technical Report CMU-CS-84-115, Dept. of Computer Science, Carnegie Mellon Univ., December 1983.

[Gupta, 1986] A. Gupta. *Parallelism in Production Systems.* PhD thesis, Dept. of Computer Science, Carnegie Mellon Univ., March 1986. (Also appears as Technical Report CMU-CS-86-122).

[Ishida and Stolfo, 1985] T. Ishida and S.J. Stolfo. Towards the Parallel Execution of Rules in Production System Programs. In *Proc. of the International Conference on Parallel Processing*, 1985.

[Ishida, 1990] Toru Ishida. Methods and Effectiveness of Parallel Rule Firing. In *Proc. of the 6th IEEE Conference on Artificial Intelligence Applications*, March 1990.

[Lerner and Cheng, 1983] M. Lerner and J. Cheng. The Manhattan Mapper Expert Production System. Technical report, Dept. of Computer Science, Columbia Univ., May 1983.

[Miranker *et al.*, 1989] Daniel P. Miranker, Chin-Ming Kuo, and James C. Browne. Parallelizing Transformations for a Concurrent Rule Execution Language. Technical Report TR-89-30, Dept. of Computer Science, Univ. of Texas at Austin, Austin, Texas, October 1989.

[Miranker, 1987] D. P. Miranker. *TREAT: A New and Efficient Match Algorithm for AI Production Systems.* PhD thesis, Dept. of Computer Science, Columbia Univ., 1987. (Also appears as Report No. TR-87-03, Dept. of Computer Science, Univ. of Texas at Austin, 1987.).

[Moldovan, 1986] Dan I. Moldovan. A Model for Parallel Processing of Production Systems. In *Proc. of IEEE International Conerence. on Systems, Man and Cybernetics*, pages 568–573, Atlanta, GA, 1986. IEEE.

[Morgan, 1988] Keith Morgan. BLITZ: A Rule-Based System for Massively Parallel Architectures. In *Proc. of 1988 ACM*, Snowbird, Utah, July 1988. ACM Conference for Lisp and Functional Programming.

[Oflazer, 1987] K. Oflazer. *Partitioning in Parallel Processing of Production Systems.* PhD thesis, Dept. of Computer Science, Carnegie Mellon Univ., 1987. (Also appears as Tech. Rep. CMU-CS-87-114, March 1987.).

[Pasik and Stolfo, 1987] Alexander J. Pasik and Salvatore J. Stolfo. Improving Production system Performance on Parallel Architectures by Creating Constrained Copies of Rules. Technical Report CUCS-313-87, Columbia Univ., New York, New York, 1987.

[Pasik, 1989] Alexander J. Pasik. *A Methodology for Programming Production Systems and its Implications on Parallelism.* PhD thesis, Columbia Univ., New York, 1989.

[Raschid *et al.*, 1989] Louiqa Raschid, Timos Sellis, and Chih-Chen Lin. Exploiting concurrency in a DBMS Implementation for Production Systems. Technical Report CS-TR-2179, Dept. of Computer Science, Univ. of Maryland, College Park, MD, January 1989.

[Schmolze, 1988] James G. Schmolze. An Asynchronous Parallel Production System with Distributed Facts and Rules. In *Proc. of AAAI-88 Workshop on Parallel Algorithms for Machine Intelligence and Pattern Recognition*, St. Paul, Minn., August 1988.

[Schmolze, 1989] James G. Schmolze. Guaranteeing Serializable Results in Synchronous Parallel Production Systems. Technical Report 89-5, Dept. of Computer Science, Tufts Univ., Medford, MA, October 1989.

[Sellis *et al.*, 1987] Timos Sellis, Chih-Chen Lin, and Louiqa Raschid. Implementing Large Production Systems in a DBMS Environment: Concepts and Algorithms. Technical Report CS-TR-1960, Dept. of Computer Science, Univ. of Maryland, College Park, MD, December 1987.

[Stolfo, 1984] S.J. Stolfo. Five Parallel Algorithms for Production System Execution on the DADO Machine. In *Proc. of the AAAI-84*. American Assoc. for Artificial Intelligence, 1984.

[Waltz, 1975] D.L. Waltz. Understanding Line Drawings of Scenes with Shadows. In P. Winston, editor, *The Psychology of Computer Vision*, pages 19–91. McGraw Hill, New York, NY., 1975.

Distributed Truth Maintenance

David Murray Bridgeland and Michael N. Huhns
Microelectronics and Computer Technology Corporation
Artificial Intelligence Laboratory
3500 West Balcones Center Drive
Austin, TX 78759-6509
bridgeland@mcc.com

Abstract

In this paper we define the concept of logical consistency of belief among a group of computational agents that are able to reason nonmonotonically. We then provide an algorithm for truth maintenance that guarantees local consistency for each agent and global consistency for data shared by the agents. Furthermore, we show the algorithm to be complete, in the sense that if a consistent state exists, the algorithm will either find it or report failure. The algorithm has been implemented in the *RAD* distributed expert system shell.

Introduction

Two trends have recently become apparent out of the widespread use of knowledge-based systems: 1) systems are being developed for larger and more complicated domains, and 2) there are attempts to use several small systems in concert when their application domains overlap. Both of these trends argue for knowledge-based systems to be developed in a distributed fashion, where modules are constructed to interact productively. The individual modules then are characteristic of intelligent agents. The interconnected agents can cooperate in solving problems, share expertise, work in parallel on common problems, be developed modularly, be fault tolerant through redundancy, represent multiple viewpoints and the knowledge of multiple experts, and be reusable. Additional motivations are presented in (Huhns, 1987) and (Gasser and Huhns, 1989). But in order for these agents to coordinate their activities and cooperate in solving mutual problems, it is essential that they be able to communicate with each other. Further, in order for them to interact intelligently and efficiently, we believe that the agents must be able to assess and maintain the integrity of the communicated information, as well as of their own knowledge.

Knowledge Base Integrity

There are many desirable properties for the knowledge base of an expert system or agent, such as completeness, conciseness, accuracy, and efficiency. For an agent that can reason nonmonotonically, there are additional properties used to describe the *integrity* of the agent's knowledge base: stability, well-foundedness, and logical consistency. A *stable* state of a knowledge base is one in which 1) each knowledge base element that has a valid justification is believed, and 2) each knowledge base element that lacks a valid justification is disbelieved. A *well-founded* knowledge base permits no set of its beliefs to be mutually dependent. A *logically-consistent* knowledge base is one that is stable at the time that consistency is determined and in which no logical contradiction exists. Depending on how beliefs, justifications, and data are represented, a consistent knowledge base may be one in which no datum is both believed and disbelieved (or neither), or in which no datum and its negation are both believed. These concepts are often extended to include other types of contradictions.

In addition, any algorithm that attempts to maintain well-founded stable states of a knowledge base, such as one of the many algorithms for truth maintenance (Doyle, 1979; de Kleer, 1986; Martins and Shapiro, 1988; McAllester, 1980; Russinoff, 1985), should be *complete*, in the sense that if a well-founded stable state exists, the algorithm will either find it or report failure. In general, we desire each agent in a multiagent environment to have a complete algorithm for maintaining the integrity of its own knowledge base.

However, the above definitions of properties for a single knowledge base are insufficient to characterize the multiple knowledge bases in such a multiagent environment. When agents that are nonmonotonic reasoners exchange beliefs and then make inferences based on the exchanged beliefs, then new concepts of knowledge-base integrity are needed. In addition, the relevant concept of global truth maintenance becomes especially problematic if agents must compute their beliefs locally, based on beliefs communicated and justified externally. The next sections extend the above definitions to the multiagent case.

The JTMS

We presume that each agent has a problem-solving component, separate from its knowledge base, that makes inferences and supplies the results to the knowledge base. Our discussion applies to the set of beliefs that are held and maintained in this knowledge base. In particular, we focus on the systems for maintaining beliefs known as truth-maintenance systems (TMS) (Doyle, 1979).

TMSs are a common way to achieve knowledge base integrity in a single agent system, because they deal with the frame problem, they deal with atomicity, and they lead to efficient search. Furthermore, the justification networks they create can be used for nonmonotonic reasoning, problem-solving explanations to a user, explanation-based learning, and multiagent negotiation. Our research is based on a justification-based TMS, in which every datum has a set of justifications and an associated status of IN (believed) or OUT (disbelieved).

In the example considered below, an initial state of a distributed knowledge base is given and presumed consistent. Our goal is to construct a consistent extension of this state or determine that no such extension exists. The distributed TMS (DTMS) algorithm presented for this task is most often invoked to restore consistency when a consistent state is disrupted by altering the justification for a datum.

Consistent Beliefs among Agents

Consider a network of many agents, each with a partially-independent system of beliefs. The agents interact by exchanging data, either unsolicited or in response to a query. Each agent has two kinds of data in its knowledge base:

Shared Data Beliefs that the agent has shared with another agent sometime in the past.

Private Data Beliefs that the agent has never shared with another agent.

A private datum might become a shared datum by being told to another agent, or by being the answer to some other agent's query. Once shared with other agents, a datum can never again be private. Each shared datum is shared by a subset of the agents in the network—precisely those that have either sent or received assertions about the datum.

We extend the concept of knowledge-base consistency stated above by defining four degrees of consistency and well-foundedness that are possible in a multiagent system.

Inconsistency: one or more agents are individually inconsistent, i.e., at least one agent has a private datum without a valid justification and labeled IN, or a private datum with a valid justification and labeled OUT.

Local Consistency: each agent is locally consistent, i.e., no private OUT datum has a valid justification, and each private IN datum has a valid justification. However, there may be global inconsistency among agents: there may be a shared datum that one agent believes to be IN and another believes to be OUT.

Local-and-Shared Consistency: each agent is locally consistent and each agent is mutually consistent about any data shared with another agent, i.e., each shared datum is either IN in all the agents that share it or OUT in those agents. There is, however, no global consistency.

Global Consistency: the agents are both individually and mutually consistent, i.e., their beliefs could be merged into one large knowledge base without the status of any datum necessarily changing.

In the absence of interagent communication, and presuming the local environment of each agent is consistent, then Local Consistency should hold. The introduction of interagent communication, however, tends to drive the system towards Inconsistency, because the agents might receive data that conflict with their current beliefs. The mechanism for truth maintenance we describe below enables each agent then to strive for Local-and-Shared Consistency. The presumption here is that the shared data are the most important, because they affect the problem solving of another agent, and so special effort should be made to maintain their consistency.

Although our goal is to maintain Local-and-Shared Consistency, we at times allow the system to fall short of this goal in order to permit agents to have different viewpoints. In this case, one agent may hold a belief that is known to be contrary to the belief of a second agent. The agents do not attempt to resolve this dispute if resolution would result in their being individually inconsistent. A consequence of this is that these agents should then not believe any data originating from each other, unless that agent can prove that its belief for that data is independent of the disputed data.

Ill-Foundedness: individual agents have beliefs that are internally ill-founded.

Local Well-Foundedness: individual agents have beliefs that are internally well-founded; however, there may be shared data that are IN but have no valid justifications in any agent.

Local-and-Shared Well-Foundedness: individual agents have beliefs that are internally well-founded, and every IN shared datum has a valid justification in some agent; however, there may be ill-founded circularities of beliefs among groups of agents.

Global Well-Foundedness: every datum has a globally valid justification and no set of data, whether local to an agent or distributed among a group of agents, is mutually dependent.

A Multiagent TMS

In the classical TMS, a datum can be either IN or OUT. For the DTMS, we refine the IN status to two substatuses: INTERNAL and EXTERNAL. An INTERNAL datum is one that is believed to be true, and that has a valid justification. An EXTERNAL datum is believed to be true, but need not have a valid justification. Intuitively, the justification of an EXTERNAL datum is "so-and-so told me." Hence, only a shared datum can be EXTERNAL. For Local-and-Shared Well-Foundedness, a shared datum must be INTERNAL to at least one of the agents that shares it and either INTERNAL or EXTERNAL to the rest of the agents.

In the only complete justification-based TMS labeling algorithm (Russinoff, 1985), Russinoff takes a generate and test approach, first unlabeling a collection of data, then attempting to relabel that collection. On failure to relabel, a superset of the last unlabeled collection is unlabeled. We take a similar approach in the DTMS. Since new data in one agent can change not only the status of that agent's beliefs, but also that of other agents, our unlabeling and subsequent labeling will sometimes involve multiple agents.

The support status of a shared datum is jointly maintained by several agents. Hence, a single agent is generally not free to change the status of a shared datum on its own accord. It must coordinate with the other agents so that they are all consistent on the status of the datum. Central to the DTMS then is the single agent operation of **label-wrt**. **label-wrt** is a variation of classical TMS labeling in which the statuses of some data—though unlabeled—are fixed by external requirements.

More precisely, **label-wrt** is given a network of data. Some of the data have statuses of IN, OUT, INTERNAL, or EXTERNAL. Other data are unlabeled. For each shared datum, there is a *desired* label of either OUT, INTERNAL, or EXTERNAL. **label-wrt** either finds a consistent well-founded labeling of the network that satisfies the shared data requirements, or it reports failure. Space prohibits a presentation of an algorithm to implement **label-wrt**. Our approach is a variation of Russinoff's well-founded and complete labeling algorithm (Russinoff, 1985).

Algorithm Schema

The DTMS is a double generate and test. Relabeling is invoked by the addition or removal of a justification. When invoked, the DTMS does the following three things:

1. Unlabel some data, including the newly justified datum and presumably its consequences. This unlabeled data set might be confined to a single agent or it might span several agents. If a shared datum is unlabeled in some agent, it must be unlabeled in all the agents that share it.
2. Choose labelings for all the unlabeled shared data, as defined above.
3. Label each of the affected agents with respect to the requirements imposed by the shared data, invoking **label-wrt** as described above. If any of the affected agents fails to label, then backtrack. Either choose different labelings for the shared data (step 2), or unlabel a different set of data (step 1).

This schema will be refined later, but some nice properties emerge at this abstract level:

- Any labeling found by the DTMS will have Local-and-Shared Consistency and Well-Foundedness.
- If the two generate steps are exhaustive, the DTMS is complete: it will find a labeling should one exist.

Note that these properties are true both of the DTMS algorithm described in this paper, and any other algorithm that conforms to this schema.

Unlabeling

When the DTMS algorithm is invoked, it starts by unlabeling a collection of data. This collection may be confined to a single agent or it may span many agents. However, it must meet the following constraints:

1. It must include the datum that originally acquired the new justification.
2. A shared datum that is unlabeled in one agent must be unlabeled in all the agents that share it.
3. On failure to label the collection, it must generate a new collection of unlabeled data. To guarantee completeness, the generation must be exhaustive: it must eventually generate a collection sufficiently large that failure to label it means the whole network cannot be labeled.

Using only these constraints, unlabeling is underconstrained: many algorithms satisfy. For example, on any status change one could unlabel all data in all agents. This global unlabeling satisfies all the constraints and is also quite simple, but also is too inefficient for practical use. The global unlabeling does reveal two DTMS principles that motivate the more complex algorithm presented later:

Principle 1 *Belief changes should be resolved with as few agents as possible.*

Principle 2 *Belief changes should be resolved by changing as few beliefs as possible.*

Most belief changes can be resolved by changing things only "downstream" of the new justification, i.e., those data that directly or indirectly depend on the datum newly justified. It is sometimes necessary to move "upstream" as well, and relabel data that directly or indirectly support the status of the newly justified datum. Consider the knowledge base for a single agent shown in Figure 1 (Russinoff, 1985). Here, datum Q acquires the new justification shown in dotted lines. If only P and Q are reassigned, the system is forced to report an unsatisfiable circularity. In order to restore stability, the status of the data upstream from P must

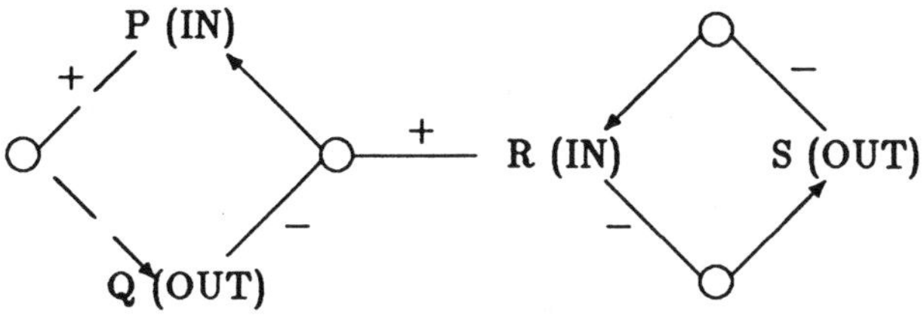

Figure 1: Relabeling upstream data to resolve an odd loop

be changed: if the system makes S OUT and R IN, both P and Q can be OUT.

Principle 3 *Belief changes should be resolved downstream if possible; upstream relabeling should be minimized.*

The above principles motivate the algorithm **unlabel**. It attempts to minimize both the involvement of other agents and the unlabeling of upstream data, but prefers the former to the latter. **Unlabel** is invoked on a list containing either the newly justified datum, when **unlabel** is first invoked, or the unlabeled data that could not be labeled on a previous invocation. **Unlabel** attempts to find yet to be unlabeled private data downstream of those already labeled. If there are none, it looks for shared data downstream, unlabeling those in all the agents that share them, and also unlabeling private data downstream of the shared data. Finally, if there are no shared data downstream that are yet to be unlabeled, it unlabels data just upstream of all the downstream data, and all private data downstream of that. If there is nothing yet to be unlabeled upstream, **unlabel** fails and, in fact, the data admit no Local-and-Shared Consistent and Well-Founded labeling.

Consider the DTMS network in Figure 2. There are two agents, Agent 1 and Agent 2, and they share the datum T. As in Figure 1, the initial labeling shown in the diagram is perturbed by the addition of the new dotted justification. Agent 1 initially unlabels just the changed datum and private data downstream, P and Q, but there is no consistent relabeling. Hence, Agent 1 unlabels all shared data downstream of P and Q, and all private data downstream from there: P, Q, both Ts, and U. Again labeling fails. Since there is no further shared data downstream, Agent 1 and Agent 2 unlabel upstream and privately downstream from there: P, Q, Ts, U, R, and S. Now labeling succeeds (with S and U IN and everything else OUT). Had labeling failed, **Unlabel** would not be able to unlabel more data, and would report that the network is inconsistent.

Distributed System Issues To be implemented, the **unlabel** algorithm needs to be distributed. This is straightforward if each agent keeps track of which data are currently unlabeled and reports to other agents only whether yet to be unlabeled data became unlabeled. Upstream and downstream messages mention only which shared datum is affected, and the corresponding acknowledgements report only whether new data were unlabeled.

When a group of agents are labeling, their beliefs are in a state not suitable for reasoning. Hence, queries from other agents must be queued until labeling is complete. However, if two agents share a datum, and are involved in separate unlabeling tasks (i.e., initiated by different changes to beliefs), deadlock could occur. Fortunately, the separate unlabeling tasks can be combined into a single one, with a corresponding combination of the subsequent labeling.

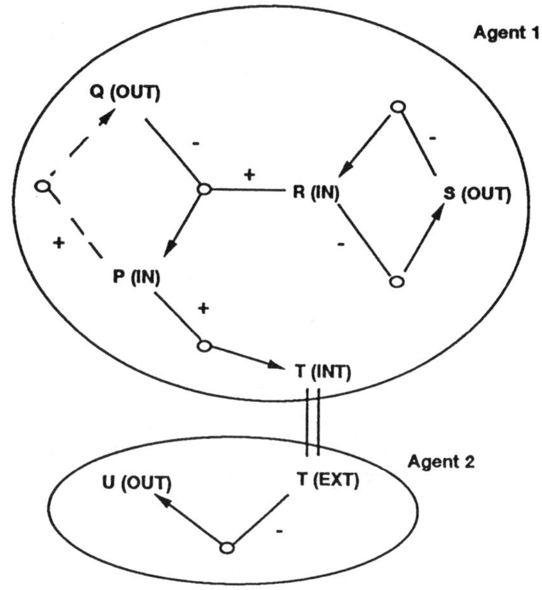

Figure 2: A DTMS network before relabeling

Labeling

Once an area of data is unlabeled, the DTMS must pick candidate labels for the shared data, such that each datum is either OUT in all the agents that share it, or INTERNAL in at least one agent and INTERNAL or EXTERNAL in the rest. Any exhaustive means of picking will guarantee completeness. The following Prolog code shows one means:

```
label-shared([], Shared-labels, Shared-labels).

label-shared([Agent|Agents], So-far, Final) <--
  label-one-shared(Agent, So-far, New),
  label-shared(Agents, New, Final).
```

label-shared relates its first argument—a list of agents—and its third argument—a list of shared data and their labels. The second argument is used to pass commitments about labels for shared data to recursive calls to **label-shared**. The relation calls **label-one-shared**, attempting to assign labels to a single agent that are consistent with those already assigned to others. If it finds such an assignment, it recursively attempts to find labels for the other agents. On failure, it bactracks and looks for alternatives to the previous single-agent labeling.

This algorithm could be implemented on a fully connected multiagent system by having each agent responsible for generating labels that are consistent with others already generated, as in **label-one-shared**, and implementing the recursive nature of **label-shared** with a message passed depth-first from agent to agent. This message needs to contain a list of agents already visited, so that none are revisited, and a list of the already labeled shared data. Also, before an agent passes a message to another, it needs to record its state for future backtracking. The shared-data labeling fits into the larger labeling process as follows:

```
label(Agents) <--
  label-shared(Agents, [], Shared),
  label-private(Agents, Shared).

label-private([],Shared).

label-private([Agent|Agents],Shared) <--
  local-shared(Agent, Shared, Local-Shared),
  label-wrt(Agent, Local-Shared),
  label-private(Agents, Shared).
```

The private labeling follows the shared data labeling. The private data are labeled one agent at a time. First the relation **local-Shared** extracts the shared labels relevant to a single agent from the list of all the shared labels. Then **label-wrt** attempts to label the private data consistently with the shared data. Any failure to label causes backtracking. This algorithm will find a Local-and-Shared Consistent and Well-Founded labeling of an unlabeled area in a collection of agents.

Unfortunately, this algorithm has poor computational performance. If there is no consistent labeling of the agents, the DTMS will generate all shared data labelings and attempt to label each privately. The performance can be improved by interleaving the labeling of the shared data and the private data. Failure in a single agent to find a private labeling consistent with the labels of the shared data will then cause earlier backtracking:

```
label(Agents) <-- label-internal(Agents, []).

label-internal([], Shared).

label-internal([Agent|Agents], So-far) <--
  label-one-shared(Agent, So-far, New),
  local-shared(Agent, New, Local-shared),
  label-wrt(Agent, Local-shared),
  label-internal(Agents, New).
```

Label-internal could be implemented by a message passed depth-first from agent to agent. This message needs to contain a list of the agents visited so far, and a record of the labels given so far to the shared data.

Consider again Figure 2. R, S, P, Q, U, and both Ts have now been unlabeled. Agent 1 chooses labels for T and attempts to label his private data in a consistent manner. If Agent 1 chooses `INTERNAL` as T's label, he finds there is no labeling of his private data to make T internally justified. A next attempt with `EXTERNAL` is consistent (with S `IN` and everything else `OUT`), and Agent 1 passes his label of T to Agent 2. Agent 2 must then label T `INTERNAL`, but finds there is no way to label U. Agent 2 then backtracks and Agent 1 tries a final attempt to label T, this time as `OUT`. This succeeds with S `IN` and everything else `OUT`, and Agent 2 can also label T `OUT` by labeling U `IN`.

Optimizations

This DTMS algorithm admits several local optimizations:

1. An agent can forgo the labeling of its unlabeled shared data by **label-one-shared** and instead label everything that is unlabeled with **label-wrt**. This requires a more sophisticated **label-wrt** that can generate `INTERNAL` and `EXTERNAL` labels for the shared data, as well as `IN` and `OUT` labels for the private data.
2. An agent can keep a record of label attempts, caching for each combination of shared data labels whether it succeeded or failed to find a private labeling. A call to **label-wrt** will first consult the cache, thus avoiding redundant work. Ordering the shared data and then indexing the combinations in a discrimination net seems to be a good implementation for this cache.
3. In the above algorithm, only one agent is active at a time. However, there is something productive that the other agents can do: fill in their label caches by attempting to find private labelings for shared data combinations not yet examined. In fact, this effort could be guided by other agents. If agent 1 shares data with agents 2, 3, and 4, when agent 1 passes a label-internal message to agent 2, it could advise agents 3 and 4 about its decisions on the labels of shared data. Then other agents could work only on that portion of their caches that are consistent with agent 1's decision.

Discussion

There have been many other attempts to develop systems of cooperating agents or knowledge sources. Early attempts, based on the blackboard model, involved agents with independent knowledge bases. The independence was achieved by restricting agent interactions to modifications of a global data structure—a blackboard—and by minimizing overlap in the agents' knowledge. Later systems allowed richer agent interactions and overlapping knowledge, but the agents were required to have consistent knowledge and to reason monotonically. This led to representational problems, because different experts in the same domain often have different perspectives and *conflicting* knowledge, making it difficult to construct a coherent problem-solving system for that domain. Earlier solutions were to allow inconsistent knowledge bases; this enabled the conflicting knowledge to be represented, but it did not confront the problem of how to resolve the conflicts.

Other researchers have explored negotiation as a means to mediate among conflicting agents. These systems have involved either monotonic reasoners, such as (Sycara, 1989), or nonmonotonic, but memoryless, reasoners, such as (Zlotkin and Rosenschein, 1989), i.e., reasoners that simply discard old solutions and re-solve in the face of conflicts.

Another approach is to consider the research efforts in multiple-context truth-maintenance systems (de Kleer, 1986; Martins and Shapiro, 1988) from a distributed viewpoint. These systems manipulate belief spaces, or contexts, in order to remove inconsistent ones. One might imagine each belief space represented by a different agent, who then maintains it. However, in this model, the belief spaces themselves do not interact and, in fact, the belief revision system treats each space separately.

A notable exception to this is the work of (Mason and Johnson, 1989), who developed a distributed assumption-based TMS. In this system, agents interact by exchanging data, with their associated assumption sets, and NOGOODS, i.e., bad assumption sets. The agents maintain separate belief spaces and may disagree about an exchanged datum. The agents therefore have Local-and-Shared Well-Foundedness, but only Local Consistency.

The system presented herein, although an improvement in that it achieves Local-and-Shared Consistency, nevertheless suffers from several deficiencies:

- First, by not supporting some form of explicit negation or reasons for disbelief in a datum, the system allows an agent with less information to dominate an agent with more. For example, if two agents each have an identical justification for belief in a shared datum, and one agent learns a fact that invalidates its justification, the other agent's still-valid justification will be sufficient for both to continue believing in the datum.
- Second, our algorithm can involve significant computational overhead if the agents have shared a large amount of data, if the data have many connections to the rest of the agents' belief networks, and if the status of their beliefs changes frequently.
- Third, we believe unsatisfiable circularities are more likely in a distributed system.

We are currently investigating the likelihood and severity of these deficiencies in real-world application domains. We are also developing a mechanism for negotiation that uses the beliefs supplied by our DTMS.

The above algorithm has been implemented in the *RAD* distributed expert system shell, which includes a framework within which computational agents can be integrated. RAD is a first step toward cooperative distributed problem solving among multiple agents. It provides the low-level communication and reasoning primitives necessary for beneficial agent interactions, but it does not yet guarantee successful and efficient cooperation. The next steps will require increased intelligence and capabilities for each agent, resulting in more sophisticated agent interactions occurring at a higher level.

References

Johan de Kleer. An Assumption-Based TMS, Extending the ATMS, and Problem Solving with the ATMS. *Artificial Intelligence*, 28(2):127–224, March 1986.

Jon Doyle. A Truth Maintenance System. *Artificial Intelligence*, 12(3):231–272, 1979.

Les Gasser and Michael N. Huhns. *Distributed Artificial Intelligence, Volume II.* Pitman Publishing, London, 1989.

Michael N. Huhns. *Distributed Artificial Intelligence.* Pitman Publishing, London, 1987.

Joao P. Martins and Stuart C. Shapiro. A Model for Belief Revision. *Artificial Intelligence*, 35(1):25–79, May 1988.

Cindy L. Mason and R. R. Johnson. Datms: A Framework for Distributed Assumption Based Reasoning. In Les Gasser and Michael N. Huhns, editors, *Distributed Artificial Intelligence, Volume II*, pages 293–317. Pitman Publishing, London, 1989.

David A. McAllester. An Outlook on Truth Maintenance. AI Memo No. 551, Artificial Intelligence Laboratory, MIT, Cambridge, MA, August 1980.

David M. Russinoff. An Algorithm for Truth Maintenance. MCC Technical Report No. ACA-AI-062-85, Microelectronics and Computer Technology Corporation, Austin, TX, April 1985.

Katia Sycara. Multiagent Compromise Via Negotiation. In Les Gasser and Michael N. Huhns, editors, *Distributed Artificial Intelligence, Volume II*, pages 119–137. Pitman Publishing, London, 1989.

Gilad Zlotkin and Jeffrey S. Rosenschein. Negotiation and Task Sharing among Autonomous Agents in Cooperative Domains. In *Proceedings IJCAI-89*, pages 912–917, Detroit, MI, August 1989.

DARES: A Distributed Automated REasoning System *

S. E. Conry and **D. J. MacIntosh**† and **R. A. Meyer**
Clarkson University
Potsdam, NY 13699
conry @ sun.soe.clarkson.edu

Abstract

In many domains of interest to distributed artificial intelligence, the problem solving environment may be viewed as a collection of loosely coupled intelligent agents, each of which reasons based on its own incomplete knowledge of the state of the world. No agent has sufficient knowledge to solve the problem at hand so that coordinated cooperative problem solving is required to satisfy system goals. In this paper, we present DARES, a distributed reasoning system in which agents have the ability to focus their attention on selective information interchange to facilitate cooperative problem solving. The experimental results we present demonstrate that agents in a loosely coupled network of problem solvers can work semi-independently, yet focus their attention with the aid of relatively simple heuristics when cooperation is appropriate. These results suggest that we have developed an effective cooperation strategy which is largely independent of initial knowledge distribution.

Introduction

In this paper we present DARES, the Distributed Automated REasoning System we have used to investigate the role of knowledge in distributed problem solving. Automated reasoning has been used successfully in a wide variety of applications since Robinson's 1965 paper [8]. Automated reasoning remains an area of active research, with interest focused on such areas as development of more efficient strategies [10] and parallel architectures designed to perform automated reasoning in near linear time [1, 2]. Our interest is in issues that arise in distributed environments where no agent has complete knowledge. In these environments, successful problem solving requires that an agent ultimately be able to reason based on knowledge that was initially known only to other agents.

DARES is an automated reasoning system for distributed environments which gives an agent the ability to reason beyond the limitations of its local knowledge. DARES' environment can be viewed as a collection of distributed agents which cooperate to perform automated reasoning about the domain. Many concurrent reasoning tasks may proceed simultaneously, and an agent may be involved in solving any subset of the complete set of tasks. Since the domain is distributed, there is no global view. Each agent has its own knowledge of the domain expressed in the first order predicate calculus.

When a reasoning task is assigned to a group of agents, each agent begins working towards a solution based on its local knowledge. However, since reasoning tasks are distributed among the agents, and each agent has incomplete knowledge, any one of these agents may soon discover that it cannot solve the reasoning task without acquiring further knowledge. DARES provides these agents with a mechanism for importing knowledge in an intelligent manner, so that there is no attempt by an agent to acquire complete knowledge. Instead, an agent in need of external information assesses its local solution space and heuristically makes requests based on its local progress.

At other times during the reasoning process, an agent may decide that its local efforts do not indicate that progress is being made. When this situation arises, an agent will make a knowledge importation request based on this negative assessment, in an attempt to import information that will help to provide insight and direction to its local efforts.

Thus, we see that DARES requires agents to assess their local reasoning efforts in order to determine whether or not nonlocal knowledge is needed. When a knowledge request is made, the informational content of the request is based upon this assessment. This decision making intelligence inherent in DARES is what allows it to perform automated reasoning about distributed domains that other systems have not yet achieved.

---

*This work was supported, in part, by the Air Force Systems Command, Rome Air Development Center, Griffiss Air Force Base, New York 13441-5700, and the Air Force Office of Scientific Research, Bolling AFB, DC 20332 under Contract No. F30602-85-C-0008. This contract supports the Northeast Artificial Intelligence Consortium (NAIC).

†Current address: BP America, Cleveland, OH 44128

System Architecture

In a loosely coupled distributed system, an agent spends most of its cpu time in computation as opposed to communication. Since theorem proving by nature is computationally intensive, we have chosen a loosely coupled implementation for our distributed theorem prover. Each theorem prover agent spends most of its time performing binary resolution [1], with the balance spent on problem assessment and communication. Problem assessment helps determine what course of action to take next to further the proof locally. Communication between agents generally falls into one of the following categories: (i) a request is sent to one or more agents for information; (ii) an agent returns information in response to a request.

The architecture for our theorem proving agent has been tailored to suit the characteristics of the problem solving environment mentioned above (i.e. loosely coupled, multiple concurrent tasks). The architecture of a single theorem proving agent is composed of several processes attached to a communications network. The problem solving system is then comprised of several nodes, each having this agent architecture. In each agent there is one mail process, and the remaining processes are each associated with a distinct problem solving activity. Each process in an agent has equal priority and active processes compete for cpu time in a round robin fashion. Under normal circumstances, every theorem prover process is active. The mail process is typically in a wait state and becomes active when new mail is received via the communications channel. Each theorem prover process in an agent has its own environment and is associated with one automated reasoning task identified by a unique tag. Theorem prover processes working on the same reasoning task in different agents throughout the network bear the same tag. In addition, no two theorem prover processes for a given agent may work on the same theorem. It need not be the case that every agent works on every theorem.

Distributed Theorem Proving Strategies

As is the case with single agent theorem provers, distributed theorem proving exhibits exponential behavior. It turns out, however, that some of the strategies used in classical theorem proving to help minimize the number of resolvents generated can also be used in the distributed case to reduce the content of information exchanged between agents. Development of these of strategies is essential, since the performance of distributed theorem proving can be greatly enhanced by them. If the computational effort in replying to a request is significant, it may have not been worth making the request in the first place. Similarly, in information-intensive domains requests that receive a bombardment of replies can be counterproductive.

Figure 1 is a flow diagram which depicts a high level view of our approach to distributed theorem proving. DARES is based on a traditional saturation level type theorem prover.

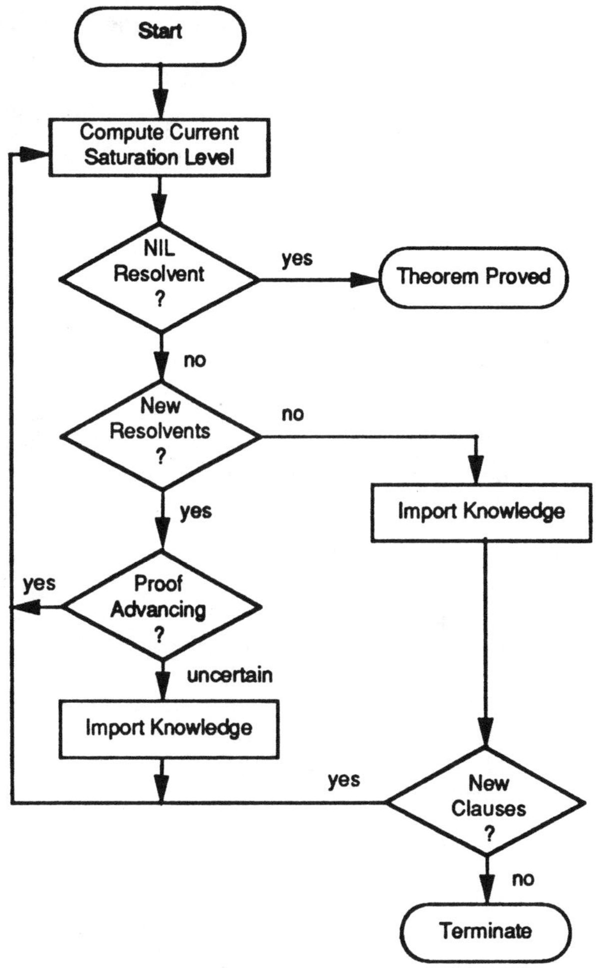

Figure 1: Distributed automated reasoning flow diagram.

We have previously noted that in our distributed environment no one agent can achieve the task at hand by itself. Therefore, we do not terminate the resolution process simply because the current resolution level has failed to generate new resolvents. In fact, reaching this point triggers a theorem prover agent to attempt to import relevant information from other agents as shown in Figure 1. If an agent is successful in importing new knowledge, the resolution process continues. Otherwise the distributed theorem proving pro-

[1] The binary resolution performed by each agent in DARES uses a tautology and subsumption reduction strategy to minimize the number of resolvents generated, and it uses the set of support strategy to limit its search space. Furthermore, the set of resolvents generated by each level of resolution is sorted by length, so that shorter clauses are resolved first during the next level.

cess terminates with no conclusion being drawn about the current theorem.

It is not sufficient just to wait for local resolution to halt prior to importing new knowledge, since mechanical theorem proving in general may not terminate when dealing with incomplete knowledge. Therefore, as shown in Figure 1, our system must evaluate whether or not progress is being made locally towards a solution. The *Forward Progress* test is made at the conclusion of each resolution level to heuristically determine whether the proof has advanced towards a NIL resolvent. This test cannot give a definitive answer. It can only say "Yes, progress has been made," or that it "does not know." On this basis, local resolution moves to the next level only if the Forward Progress test concludes that progress has been made. Otherwise, nonlocal knowledge is imported just as if the current level had failed to produce new resolvents.

Forward Progress Heuristic

Given a negated theorem and a set of axioms that is adequate for establishing that theorem, a single agent with complete knowledge will, given enough time, eventually determine that the theorem is valid by producing a NIL resolvent. However, when the same axiom set and theorem are distributed over several agents, it is possible that no agent will have sufficient local knowledge to establish the result. It is therefore possible for each agent under this circumstance, without a Forward Progress heuristic, to perform resolution forever and not prove a theorem that conventional systems have no difficulty in proving.

The purpose of our Forward Progress heuristic is to guarantee that no agent in our system will enter a mode in which it can perform resolution forever, without eventually attempting to import nonlocal knowledge that may lead to an inconsistency. This safeguard gives DARES the ability to prove any theorem that conventional systems can prove given the same set of global system knowledge. What the Forward Progress heuristic does not do is to give DARES any advantage over the single agent case when the single agent is faced with nontermination.

When it is apparent that an agent is not progressing, the Forward Progress heuristic triggers the importation of nonlocal information in order to increase the agent's knowledge relative to the task at hand. Experimental data indicate that this heuristic does indeed enhance system performance, even when a DARES agent is not faced with nontermination.

In defining the Forward Progress heuristic, we make use of two related heuristics: the *Proof Advancing heuristic* and the *Monotonic Search heuristic.* The Proof Advancing heuristic is the component of the Forward Progress heuristic which is used to detect local advancement. This heuristic either detects advancement, or is uncertain whether or not the proof is advancing. The Monotonic Search heuristic is the mechanism that the Forward Progress heuristic relies upon if uncertainty about proof advancement persists.

The *Proof Advancing heuristic* is determined at each level of resolution by examination of the newly generated resolvents. A resolvent R is said to be *advancing the proof* if

(a) given two clauses C and D with literal length c and d respectively, the clause length r of R is less than $(c+d)-2$,

or

(b) R is a single literal,

or

(c) R was generated from a single literal clause.

If any resolvent generated at saturation level i advances the proof, then we say the Proof Advancing heuristic is *satisfied* at level i.

In general, when two clauses are resolved using binary resolution, the resolvents will always have length no greater than the sum of the lengths of the two parent clauses, minus the two literals which are consumed by the resolution process. Condition (a) in the Proof Advancing heuristic considers a proof to be advancing whenever a resolvent is generated with length less than this upper bound. Conditions (b) and (c) in the Proof Advancing heuristic definition recognize that some resolvents are desirable even though their length equals the upper bound. For example, when a single literal clause C is resolved with clause D of length n, the resolvent has length $c+d-2=1+n-2=n-1$. The importance of these resolvents are recognized by the *Unit Preference* [11] strategy.

Whenever condition (a), (b), and/or (c) occurs during resolution, the proof is considered to be *advancing.* If none of these occur, we do not know if the proof is making progress. If it is not clear whether or not a proof is advancing, and this uncertainty persists, some mechanism for forcing a knowledge request is required. This is where the Monotonic Search heuristic comes into play.

The *Monotonic Search heuristic* is defined as follows: Let α_n be the total number of distinct predicate symbols found in the set of newly generated resolvents at saturation level n. The search for a proof is said to be *monotonic* at level i if for $i>1$, $\alpha_{i-1}>\alpha_i$.

The *Forward Progress heuristic* is used to detect an apparent lack of forward progress in the proof. This lack of progress is defined in terms of the Proof Advancing and Monotonic Search heuristics.

A proof is said to exhibit an apparent lack of *forward progress* at saturation level i if

(1) the Proof Advancing heuristic is not satisfied at saturation level $i-1$,

and

(2) the Proof Advancing heuristic is not satisfied at saturation level i,

and

(3) the search is not monotonic at level i.

The Forward Progress heuristic guarantees that if proof advancement is uncertain and the number of predicate symbols is nondecreasing in successive levels of resolution, a knowledge request is made. (Whenever the number of predicate symbols is a decreasing function in successive levels of resolution, the number of predicate symbols must eventually shrink to zero. If this situation occurs, it will be detected by the *New Resolvents* test (refer to Figure 1), since a scenario involving zero predicate symbols can only occur if the current level of resolution fails to generate new resolvents.)

Priority Set

In our environment, when an agent has reached a point where it is evident that new information must be acquired in order to continue problem solving, it formulates a *Priority Set P*.

Definition A *Priority Set P* has the form $P = \{C_1, ..., C_n\}$ where each C_i for $0 < i \leq n$ is a clause heuristically determined to have a high likelihood of furthering the proof towards a NIL resolvent. P is said to have length n, where n is the number of clauses in P.

The heuristic we use to determine the *likelihood* of a clause extracts some ideas found in two conventional resolution strategies: *Set of Support* [12] and *Unit Preference* [11]. However, our heuristic is more than just a combination of these two strategies. Our importation heuristic determines a *likelihood* that a clause will be relevant in furthering a proof towards a NIL resolvent. This heuristic is based on clause length and clause ancestry. Clauses whose ancestry do not lead back to the negated theorem have no *likelihood* and are assigned the value of 0. Clauses having an ancestry link to the negated theorem have a *likelihood* whose value is the reciprocal of the clause length. Single literal clauses with a negated theorem ancestry have the maximum likelihood of 1.

As a first cut in distributed theorem proving, one could simply form the Priority Set P using all clauses possessing maximum likelihood. Then P could be sent to all agents, with each agent being requested to return any clause that can resolve with one or more members in P. Unfortunately, P could potentially be large, requiring significant processing on behalf of each agent receiving the request. A better strategy would be to first remove any clause in P which is subsumed by another clause in P, as any reduction in the size of P reduces the overhead other agents incur while processing the request.

Though use of subsumption in this way reduces the size of P, it still has the potential of being relatively large. An alternative approach makes use of a Minimal Literal Set L_{min} derived from P that is defined as follows:

Definition Let each clause C_i in a Priority Set P of length n be of the form $C_i = \{L_{i1}, ..., L_{im_i}\}$ where L_{ij} is a literal, and:

1. $1 \leq i \leq n$;
2. $m_i > 0$ and is the number of literals in clause i;
3. $1 \leq j \leq m_i$.

Then the *Priority Literal Set L* is defined to be the union of literals found in clauses $C_1, ..., C_n$ and has the form $L = C_1 \cup ... \cup C_n$.

Definition Given L, the Priority Literal Set for $P = \{C_1, ..., C_n\}$, we define L_{min}, the *Minimum Priority Literal Set* for P as follows:

$L_{min} = L - L'$, where $L' = \{L_{jk} \in L \mid$ there is a literal L_{pq} in L, such that L_{jk} is subsumed by $L_{pq}\}$.

After computing the Minimal Priority Literal Set L_{min} from the Priority Set P, the agent could transmit L_{min} to other agents and request knowledge about clauses they may have that resolve with one or more literals in L_{min}. If this were done, an agent responding to this request would then systematically attempt to perform resolution with each literal in L_{min} against its local clause set, complementing each L_{min} literal and attempting to unify it with a literal in each of its local clauses. Recognizing this fact, in an attempt to minimize the effort of an agent replying to a request, the requesting agent complements each literal in L_{min} prior to making the request. We call the resulting set the Minimum Priority Negated Literal Set and define it as follows:

Definition Given a Minimum Priority Literal Set $L_{min} = \{Q_1, ..., Q_n\}$ of length n, where each Q_i is a literal for $0 < i \leq n$, then the *Minimum Priority Negated Literal Set* NL_{min} has the form $NL_{min} = \{R_1, ..., R_n\}$, where each $R_i = \neg Q_i$ for $0 < i \leq n$.

After computing the Minimal Priority Negated Literal Set NL_{min} from the Priority Set P, the agent transmits NL_{min} to other agents and requests knowledge about clauses they may have that unify with one or more literals in NL_{min}.

Up to now we have concentrated on explaining how an agent determines when a request needs to be made, and how it formulates the content of the request. We have said nothing about what happens if the first attempt to import knowledge fails, nor have we given much insight into the procedure followed by an agent replying to the request.

The first thing the requesting agent does is to determine the range of likelihoods possible for its clause set. Beginning with the clauses having highest likelihood, the agent computes its Minimum Literal Priority Set and broadcasts a request based on this set. This set is a function of likelihood ($NL_{min}(l)$). If the request based on maximum likelihood fails to import nonlocal knowledge, the likelihood constraint is relaxed to its next possible value and the agent makes another request. This process continues until the requesting agent is successful in importing knowledge, or the agent has exhausted its clause set.

We have found that it is beneficial for agents replying to knowledge requests to also incorporate a likelihood dependency. When an agent makes a request with a high likelihood, the knowledge requested is specific in nature and it should receive information back which is also relatively specific. As requests are made based upon lower likelihoods, we have observed that the requested information encompasses a wider spectrum and is more general in nature.

In DARES, we have incorporated a simple strategy into request processing which links the likelihood of a request to the scope of the search space that an agent considers when making its reply. We require that the likelihood l, used to formulate $NL_{min}(l)$, be used to determine which clauses in a theorem prover's environment are to be considered when evaluating the request. In order for a clause to be deemed a candidate for consideration, it must have length no greater than the maximum length of any clause found in the Priority Set used to generate $NL_{min}(l)$.

When a clause satisfies the requirements of the request, it is tagged to be considered later as part of the reply. The significance of tagging potential clauses during the unification process is twofold: once a clause is tagged, it is never again considered when subsequent requests are made by the same agent with respect to the current theorem under investigation. Secondly, subsumption is used among the tagged clauses to minimize what is returned to the requesting agent. This tagging mechanism helps avoid redundancy in what is returned in response to subsequent requests. In addition, tagging can be viewed as an aggregation of knowledge about other agents' activities (not unlike the behavior evident in the scientific community metaphor [3, 4, 5, 9]), although DARES makes no specific use of this information at this time.

Experimental Results

There are three key issues which have been addressed in our experiments using DARES. They are:

1. How is DARES' problem solving behavior affected as the number of active agents is varied?
2. How are anomalies in system behavior which result from particular knowledge distributions minimized, so that DARES' automated reasoning behavior is not misconstrued?
3. What affect does the amount of shared knowledge throughout the network have on system performance?

In order to measure the amount of shared knowledge among agents in a distributed reasoning network, we introduce the notion of a *relevant axiom* and the *Redundancy Factor*.

Very simply, an axiom is considered *relevant* if it can be used in some proof of the current reasoning task. If S is a clause set and P a logical consequence of S, then in general there may be more than one subset of S from which P can be deduced. We do not address this issue here. Instead, we presume that each and every clause in S is required in order to derive P.

The *Redundancy Factor (R)* of a network is a global measure of the amount of relevant knowledge shared among the agents. When no relevant knowledge is shared between agents, the Redundancy Factor is 0. When every agent has complete relevant knowledge the network Redundancy Factor is 1. For distributions falling within these boundaries, we define the Redundancy Factor to be:

$$R = \frac{\sum_{i=1}^{k}(m_i - C)}{k(N - C)} \tag{1}$$

where
- k = number of active agents
- N = number of relevant axioms for the reasoning task
- C = $\frac{N}{k}$
- m_i = number of local axioms known to agent i
- R = is the Redundancy Factor

Each of our experiments corresponds to one distributed reasoning task. For every experiment, data is collected over a wide range of values for each system parameter. As these parameters are varied, each new run begins with a different random distribution of knowledge for the same task. For each distribution, there are three constraints that must be met. First, each active agent must initially be given at least one axiom. Secondly, multiple copies of an axiom are not permitted in an agent's local environment. (But n copies of an axiom may exist across several agents.) Lastly, the total number of axioms distributed throughout the system must equal the number specified by the current Redundancy Factor.

There are two data collection parameters in each experiment: k and r. Parameter k corresponds to the number of agents actively engaged in the reasoning task, and r is the Redundancy Factor. Given a theorem to prove which is comprised of M axioms and N negated theorem clauses, the experiment is done utilizing k agents, where k is varied between 1 and M. For each value of k, the knowledge distribution is varied between 0 and 100% Redundancy.

We minimize the effects that a particular knowledge distribution has on general behavior, by performing many passes at a given data point (k, r), with each pass having a different distribution. Likewise, the behavioral characteristics of DARES can be determined by performing many different experiments, where each experiment is based on a unique automated reasoning task. In fact, this has been done. The results presented here are based upon analysis of many different experiments. The figures incorporated in this paper reflect the results from one experiment as a vehicle for demonstrating DARES' distributed automated reasoning behavior.

The performance characteristics for a typical experiment are given in Figure 2. These characteristics are normalized to the nondistributed case, in which a single agent performs the complete reasoning task alone.

The two system parameters for DARES' data collection experiment, k and r, correspond to the "Number of Agents" and "Redundancy Factor" axes in Figure 2, respectively. Since DARES performs distributed automated reasoning approximately one order of magnitude faster than its nondistributed counterpart, we have taken the natural log of the elapsed time data for the experiment. Furthermore, we have normalized this data so that the single agent case has a value of unity. The Redundancy Factor axis has been scaled by a factor of 10 for legibility.

In general, when there is a very high level of redundancy among the agent's local knowledge, DARES' runtime rapidly begins to approach that of the single agent. This behavior can be attributed to a very low interaction rate among agents, since each agent has sufficient local knowledge to advance the proof to near completion. The Forward Progress heuristic detects this advancement and does not initiate any knowledge importation requests. Instead, local advancement continues until resolution fails to generate any new resolvents. It is at this point that a knowledge request is made to import nonlocal information.

We observe that requests made in high redundancy environments tend to be very specific in nature, since an agent has advanced the proof nearly to completion prior to making the request. We have also observed that when a request of this sort is made, the knowledge sought is readily available in the network. This is a direct consequence of the other agents having near complete knowledge, and of the fact that they have had ample time to advance their local efforts.

In general, we find that as the number of agents in a network increases, replies to knowledge requests tend to have better informational content. This relationship between network size and reply content is a direct consequence of simply having more agents in the network to query, each agent having a different local perspective derived from its differing initial knowledge distribution. In Figure 2 the effect of this relationship is evident in the high redundancy areas. Note that as the number of agents increases, the slope associated with the rapid approach towards the single agent case becomes steeper and the width of these peaks decreases.

Figure 2 also suggests that performing distributed theorem proving is best done by many agents possessing little redundancy. In this situation, each agent can be viewed as a specialist. At the start of the distributed theorem proving process, each agent advances its part of the proof as far as it can before making a knowledge request. At the time such a request is made, the agent has begun to concentrate its efforts on its local advancement and imports knowledge relative to this acquired focus. Since redundancy is low, we see the agents becoming specialized in different areas, which reduces search space overlap between agents and leads to enhanced system performance.

Although system performance is best with many agents in a low redundancy environment, there is only a small increase in system performance as the number of agents is increased. What we see happening as network size becomes larger, is that initial knowledge importation requests occur earlier. These requests are based on less local effort and are more general in nature, thus leading to the initial importation of larger volumes of knowledge. Therefore, agents in smaller networks acquire a focus sooner than agents in larger networks. However, as the distributed effort nears completion, we see larger networks outperforming smaller ones, since requested information near the end of the proof is more readily available in larger networks due to network size and the local efforts of more agents. It appears that the performance of larger networks near the end of the proof is sufficient to offset the advantage smaller networks have at the start, thus we see a slight improvement in system performance as network size increases.

The behavioral characteristics displayed in Figure 2 reflect DARES' general runtime characteristics. This surface plot was generated from data recorded by DARES and represents the average value of all passes made for each data point. The validity of our conclusions is supported by a comparison of the characteristics of both the lower and upper bound surfaces. These surfaces are shown in Figures 3 and 4 respectively.

The lower bound characteristic surface is a plot of the minimum runtime over all passes made for a given data point. Note that there are no major discrepancies in the plateau regions between the general and minimum surfaces. In fact, the smoothness of the plateau in the average value surface suggests that we have indeed minimized dependencies associated with particular distributions.

The upper bound characteristic surface shown in Figure 4 is a plot of the maximum of all runtimes recorded by DARES for a given data point. This plot also has (to a limited degree) the same general shape as the average time characteristic surface in Figure 2. However, the most notable feature of this surface is that it is very *spiked*. This is a demonstration of how sensitive distributed automated reasoning is to its knowledge distribution. Each one of the peaks (spikes) represents reduced system performance directly related to the knowledge distribution used.

There are two important observations to be made with respect to the upper bound surface: First, since its overall shape is basically that of the average time surface, we have further evidence supporting the hypothesis that the average time characteristics do represent those of general behavior; Secondly, the noise in this plot indicates how a *relatively poor distribution*

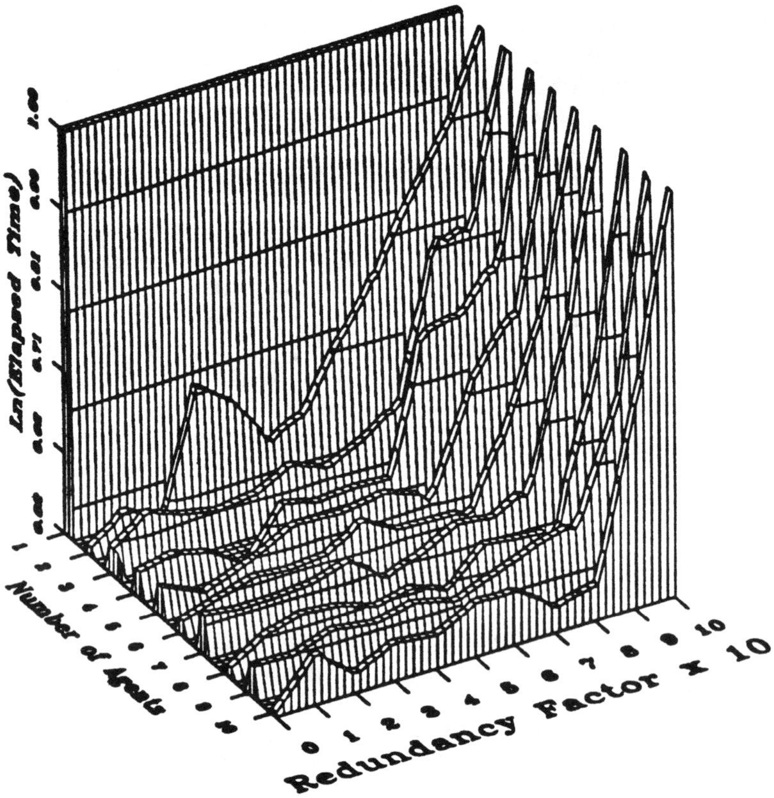

Figure 2: Performance Characteristics for an Experiment.

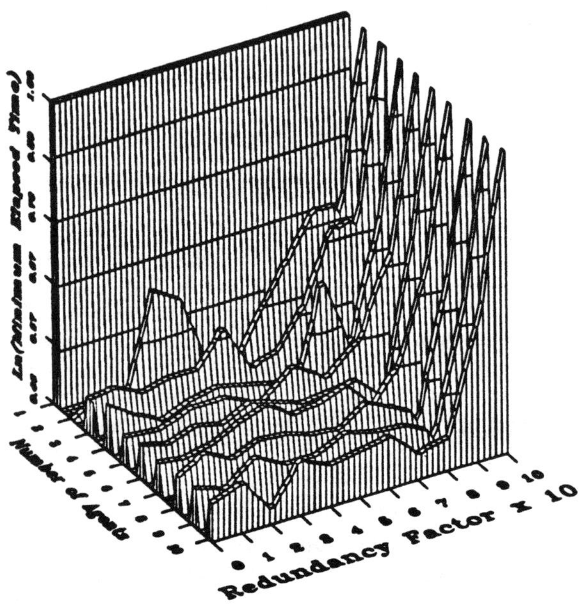

Figure 3: Lower Bound Time Characteristics

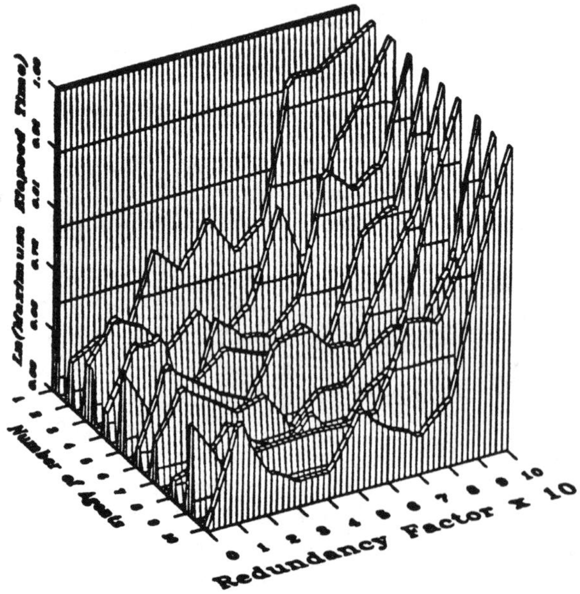

Figure 4: Upper bound time characteristics

can affect system performance. But more importantly, it demonstrates that DARES in its worst case environment performs automated reasoning at a reasonable rate relative to the that of the nondistributed case.

Concluding Remarks

In this paper, we have described DARES, our distributed automated reasoning system. Experiments with DARES have provided us with enhanced insight into the role of knowledge in distributed problem solving. We have seen cases in which performance can be very sensitive to initial knowledge distribution, but the average case statistics indicate that one must be unlucky to encounter such a distribution when knowledge is randomly distributed.

More importantly, the experimental results we have presented demonstrate that agents in a loosely coupled network of problem solvers can work semi-independently, yet focus their attention with the aid of relatively simple heuristics when cooperation is appropriate. These results suggest that we have developed an effective cooperation strategy which is largely independent of initial knowledge distribution.

DARES has been implemented in a distributed testbed facility, SIMULACT [6], that runs on a network of Lisp machines. SIMULACT has provided a well instrumented environment in which applications of this kind are easily developed and maintained. A number of additional experiments have been performed using DARES [7], but discussion of these experiments is beyond the scope of this paper.

References

[1] P. E. Allen, S. Bose, E. M. Clarke, and S. Michaylov. PARTHENON: A parallel theorem prover for non-horn clauses. In *9th International Conference on Automated Deduction*, pages 764–765. Springer-Verlag, May 1988.

[2] M. P. Cline. *A Fast Parallel Algorithm for N-ary Unification with A.I. Applications*. PhD thesis, Clarkson University, Potsdam, NY 13676, April 1989.

[3] M. S. Fox. An organizational view of distributed systems. *IEEE Transactions on Systems, Man, and Cybernetics*, SMC-11(1):70–80, January 1981.

[4] W. A. Kornfeld and C. E. Hewitt. The scientific community metaphor. *IEEE Transactions on Systems, Man, and Cybernetics*, SMC-11(1):24–33, January 1981.

[5] V. R. Lesser and D. D. Corkill. Functionally accurate, cooperative distributed systems. *IEEE Transactions on Systems, Man, and Cybernetics*, SMC-11(1):81–96, January 1981.

[6] D. J. MacIntosh and S. E. Conry. SIMULACT: A generic tool for simulating distributed systems. In *Proceedings of the Eastern Simulation Conference*, pages 18–23, Orlando, Florida, April 1987. The Society for Computer Simulation. (also available as NAIC Technical Report TR-8713).

[7] D. J. MacIntosh. *Distributed Automated Reasoning: The Role of Knowledge in Distributed Problem Solving*. PhD thesis, Clarkson University, Potsdam, NY 13699, December 1989.

[8] J. A. Robinson. A machine-oriented logic based on the resolution principle. *Journal of the Association for Computing Machinery*, 12(1):23–41, January 1965.

[9] R. G. Smith and R. Davis. Frameworks for cooperation in distributed problem solving. *IEEE Transactions on Systems, Man, and Cybernetics*, SMC-11(1):61–70, January 1981.

[10] L. Wos. *Automated Reasoning: 33 Basic Research Problems*. Prentice-Hall, Engelwood Cliffs, NJ., 1988.

[11] L. Wos, R. Overbeek, E. Lusk, and J. Boyle. *Automated Reasoning: Introduction and Applications*. Prentice-Hall, Engelwood Cliffs, NJ., 1984.

[12] L. Wos and G. A. Robinson. Paramodulation and set of support. In *Proceedings of the IRIA Symposium on Automatic Demonstration*, pages 267–310. Springer-Verlag, 1968.

A Hierarchical Protocol for Coordinating Multiagent Behaviors

Edmund H. Durfee and Thomas A. Montgomery
Department of Electrical Engineering and Computer Science
University of Michigan
Ann Arbor, Michigan 48109
durfee@caen.engin.umich.edu, monty@caen.engin.umich.edu

Abstract

We describe how a behavior hierarchy can be used in a protocol that allows AI agents to discover and resolve interactions flexibly. Agents that initially do not know with whom they might interact use this hierarchy to exchange abstractions of their anticipated behaviors. By comparing behaviors, agents iteratively investigate interactions through more focused exchanges of successively detailed information. They can also modify their behaviors along different dimensions to either avoid conflicts or promote cooperation. We explain why our protocol gives agents a richer language for coordination than they get through exchanging plans or goals, and we use a prototype implementation to illustrate our protocol. We argue that our hierarchical protocol for coordinating behaviors provides a powerful representation for negotiation and can act as a common foundation for integrating theories about plans and organizations.

Introduction

In a world inhabited by numerous active systems (agents), the agents often must engage in cooperative and competitive behavior in order to achieve their goals. To decide how they should behave, they need to know how agents with whom they might interact might behave. Just as important, they need to avoid expending their limited reasoning resources on studying how agents with whom they will not interact might behave. If potential interactions between agents can be predicted because each has some predefined role (due, for example, to commonly known organizational constraints [Corkill and Lesser, 1983; Durfee *et al.*, 1987] or to functional or geographical relationships [Conry *et al.*, 1988]), then channeling detailed information about planned actions is straightforward. On the other hand, if agents are ignorant about with whom they might interact, then they need to narrow down the possibilities before they exchange detailed information, otherwise they might swamp the communication channels and each other. Mobile robots on a warehouse floor, for example, can have an ever-changing group of neighbors, and when plotting collision-free paths for the near future should identify and converse only with their current neighbors.

We introduce a hierarchical protocol for this type of problem. In our protocol, an agent represents its anticipated behavior at numerous levels of abstraction. When it must decide with whom it might interact, the agent blindly broadcasts its most abstract behavioral information rather than details about its planned actions. Then, as an agent receives abstract information from others, it compares anticipated behaviors to decide with whom it might interact, and then exchanges more detailed information with only those agents. In essence, the protocol allows the agents to engage in a dialogue in which they can move between different levels of detail about behavior, feeling each other out to discover who they can safely ignore and how they should change their behaviors based on anticipated interactions with agents that they cannot ignore.

Our protocol advances the field of distributed artificial intelligence (DAI) in two ways. The obvious way is that it adds to DAI's arsenal of coordination techniques, permitting a form of coordination that has been unavailable. By enlarging the set of coordination techniques, we both extend the range of coordination problems that we can solve and learn more about the nature of intelligent coordination. The more subtle but potentially far-reaching contribution of our protocol is that it introduces the use of behaviors into multi-agent coordination. Behaviors subsume the more traditional representations of goals and plans, and even blur the boundaries between plans and organizations. As a result, our protocol has the potential to integrate diverse theories and mechanisms for intelligent planning and organizational design. We return to these possibilities in the concluding section. First, we outline our protocol, relate our protocol to other research, and describe a preliminary implementation of the protocol and experimental results.

[0]This research was sponsored, in part, by the University of Michigan under a Rackham Faculty Research Grant, and by a Bell Northern Research Postgraduate Award.

The Protocol

At the heart of our protocol is the concept of a *behavior hierarchy*. To define what this hierarchy is, we first indicate what it is not. It is not a plan hierarchy, where plans are represented in varying levels of detail and detailed subplans are linked to their more abstract counterparts. Similarly, it is not a goal hierarchy, that links goals and their subgoals for a given task. Although plan and goal hierarchies are useful for deciding on actions to achieve results, they only describe limited aspects of an agent's behavior. For example, plan hierarchies emphasize *how* to do things: At the abstract levels are vague, encompassing instructions, while the detailed levels prescribe specific actions. Alternatively, goal hierarchies emphasize *what* to do: At the abstract levels are broad objectives, and at the detailed levels are specific, atomic goals.

A behavior hierarchy subsumes plan and goal hierarchies because it represents the what and how of agents, and also the who, when, where, and why. That is, an entry in the behavior hierarchy represents *who* are behaving in a particular way, *what* they are trying to achieve, *when* they are behaving this way, *where* they are behaving this way, *how* they are acting to accomplish this behavior, and *why* they have initiated this behavior. Each of these 6 aspects represents a different dimension for composition or decomposition.[1] In fact, we might have hierarchies for each dimension, as well as for the overall behavior. Example partial hierarchies are shown in Figure 1. Note that moving between entries in a behavior hierarchy can involve moving along several separate dimensions simultaneously.

Our protocol currently assumes that all agents use the same language to describe the different behavioral dimensions. The agents thus can map a received behavior into their local representations; in essence, the behavioral dimensions describe a 6-dimensional space, and an agent can find the region in this space that a received behavior occupies. From this mapping, an agent can recognize potential behavioral interactions when behaviors' regions overlap or are proximal. The ability to recognize interacting behaviors and to move along dimensions to find alternative interactions is at the core of our protocol.

With this representation in mind, we now present a generalized version of the protocol; a more detailed description for a particular application is given later. An agent with its own tasks (or a group of agents with group tasks) forms a behavior hierarchy representing a decomposition of the tasks along the dimensions that are appropriate given the tasks and the environment. Agents then exchange information at the highest level of abstraction, and map received information into their local behavior hierarchy. By inspecting

[1] Other dimensions might be incorporated into the representation in the future. However, the 6 currently included were an obvious initial choice.

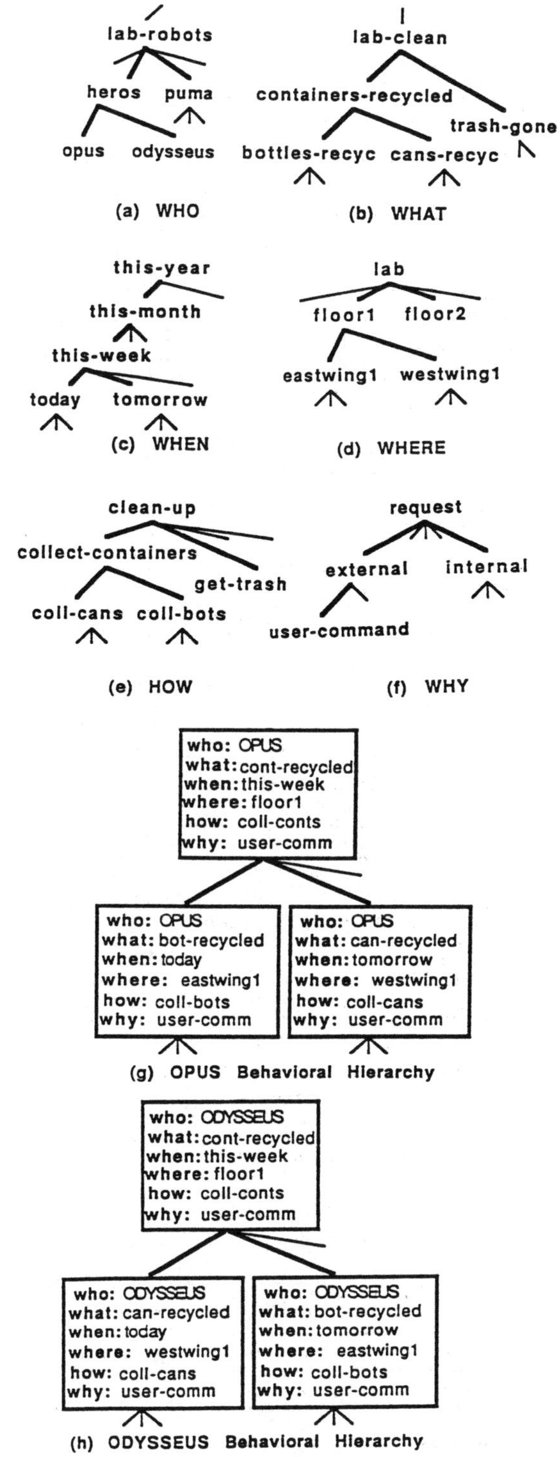

In (a) is a partial personnel hierarchy, (b) is a partial goal hierarchy, (c) is a partial temporal hierarchy, (d) is a partial spatial hierarchy, (e) is a partial plan hierarchy, and (f) is a motivation hierarchy. In (g) and (h) are partial behavior hierarchies for robots OPUS and ODYSSEUS, respectively.

Figure 1: Example Partial Hierarchies

relationships between behaviors along the different dimensions, an agent can recognize potential negative interactions (such as resource conflicts) with another agent. For example, if the robot Opus, with the behavior hierarchy in Figure 1g, receives from Odysseus its most abstract behavior (Figure 1h), then it finds a potential conflict along the when and where dimensions. The robots will be on the same floor in the same time interval, and thus could collide.

When an agent recognizes a potential negative interaction, it has two alternatives. One choice is to modify its own behaviors such that the interaction is avoided. To do this, it searches through alternative values along the behavioral dimensions that lead to acceptable, but no longer interacting, behaviors.[2] For example, Opus might modify its behavior so that it works on the floor next-week instead. The other choice an agent has is to refine its view of the potential interaction, so as to identify more specifically how the behaviors are interacting, or possibly to discover upon closer inspection that there is no interaction. To pursue this choice, the agents move down to the next level of the hierarchy and exchange only the behavioral information that is relevant to the potential interaction. When it receives new behavioral information at less abstract levels, an agent maps this information into its hierarchy and the process repeats. For example, at the more detailed level, Opus learns that he and Odysseus will be working in different wings, and so no collision is possible (Figures 1g and 1h). If they discover that their behaviors do not, in fact, interact, the agents discontinue their communications. Thus, agents that are not interacting discover this with minimal communication of more detailed information.

Agents can also interact positively, and at times might change their behaviors to capitalize on positive interactions. For example, Opus and Odysseus might decide that one of them could achieve the goals of both. Opus might extend its behaviors for today and tomorrow along the "what" dimension (to "containers-recycled") and along the "how" dimension (to "collect-containers"), while Odysseus is now free to pursue other behaviors. In our protocol, an agent has a choice between modifying its behavior at the current level of abstraction to improve interactions, or exchanging information to probe more deeply into positive interactions and establish them at a more detailed level. Detailed exchanges can lead to crisper coordination. For example, if Odysseus wants to meet Opus to cart away the containers collected in the morning, then going to more detailed levels allows them to decide more specifically when and where to meet.

This outline of our protocol leaves many unanswered questions. Some deal with the agents' knowledge: Where does the hierarchical knowledge come from? How can we ensure consistency between agents? How do we represent constraints that moving along one dimension might impose on other dimensions? Other questions deal with effectively using the protocol: When should agents initiate an exchange of abstract behavioral information? How do agents decide which of them should modify their behavior to avoid negative or promote positive interactions? How do agents decide which dimensions of their behavior to modify? What happens when modifying an interaction with some agents introduces new interactions with other agents? Can the protocol guarantee convergence? What are the computational and communication costs of the protocol? Answering these questions is an ongoing effort, and our initial answers to some of them are only a first step. Before discussing these, we relate our protocol to prior research.

[2]Searching hypothetical behaviors is similar to searching hypothetical cases for argumentation [Ashley, 1988].

Relationship to Other Research

Our protocol addresses problems where the spatial and functional relationships between agents change over time. These issues also arise in the air-traffic control problems studied at Rand [Cammarata *et al.*, 1983; Steeb *et al.*, 1988]. Unlike our protocol, the Rand approach involves centralizing authority. Specifically, in their approach a group of potentially interacting aircraft engage in a discussion to choose a group leader. Once chosen, the leader collects detailed information from each group member, designs a group plan to avoid negative interactions (aircraft collisions), and then tells each aircraft what it should do. Although the leader could send processing tasks to group members during the planning phase [Steeb *et al.*, 1986], control is centralized.

The Contract-Net protocol [Davis and Smith, 1983] provides a mechanism by which autonomous agents negotiate to assign tasks among themselves to balance load and connect tasks with the agents that are most suited to pursuing them. The view taken by Contract-Net is that interactions between agents are due to mutually agreed upon task assignments; unlike our protocol, the Contract-Net protocol does not anticipate that agents might independently take actions that could lead to unintended interactions.

The multistage negotiation protocol developed by Conry and her colleagues [Conry *et al.*, 1988] does address the need to identify and recover from resource conflicts. Developed in the context of a distributed network management task, their approach first propagates information about tasks (circuits to complete) through the network, so that each subnetwork controller can enumerate the possible ways it can assign its resources. The controllers then engage in an iterative dialogue where they tentatively choose combinations of assignments, exchange information to detect constraint violations (overburdened channels that connect their subnetworks), and eventually converge on a consistent set of assignments (even if it means neglecting low-priority tasks). Unlike our protocol, multistage negotiation assumes a fixed topography that controllers use to guide communication. Also, their approach assumes that the agents can enumerate *all* of the possible resource assignments, and so the protocol is a constraint labeling process. In our protocol, the space of possible behaviors can be intractable, so the search for acceptable combinations of behaviors involves modifying behaviors on the fly.

In the partial global planning framework [Durfee and Lesser, 1987; Durfee, 1988] local plans are exchanged to recognize larger goals to work toward, and then the actions taken to achieve these goals are reordered to improve group performance. In the context of our new protocol, the information about *what* each problem solver is doing (the results it is trying to develop) is mapped into a hierarchy of goals in order to identify more encompassing results, and then the *how* and *when* of the plans are revised to improve group problem solving. Thus, partial global planning is subsumed by our new protocol. In addition, to avoid the overhead of unconstrained exchanges of the plans, partial global planning insists that the agents have static organizational knowledge, which essentially dictates who each agent should exchange plan information with. Our protocol assumes no such knowledge because agents instead broadly exchange abstract behavioral information and use this to focus more detailed information appropriately. Our approach also differs from recent efforts to more generally classify plan and goal interactions [Decker and Lesser, 1989; von Martial, 1989] because of our extension to agent behaviors, not just plans and goals.

Lansky has developed a formalism for specifying behavioral information about agents, and has investigated its use for multi-agent domains [Lansky, 1985]. Her use of the term "behavioral" and ours differ, in that she considers behavior in terms of the constraints on possible relationships between actions, whereas we see behavior in terms of (possibly underspecified) information about the who, what, when, where, how, and why of activity in the world. These views are not incompatible, and her formalisms could be incorporated into our approach. Davis [Davis, 1981] also has enumerated many of the issues involved in coordinating multiagent behavior. While Davis' treatment is at a conceptual level, we have moved toward an experimental investigation.

Implementation and Experiments

As a preliminary test of our new protocol, we have been investigating the general problem of detecting and resolving resource conflicts. As a representative example of this problem, consider an application where several mobile robots move in common areas and between these areas through shared doorways. The common space, and especially the space in and around the doorways, represents important resources for which the robots might contend.

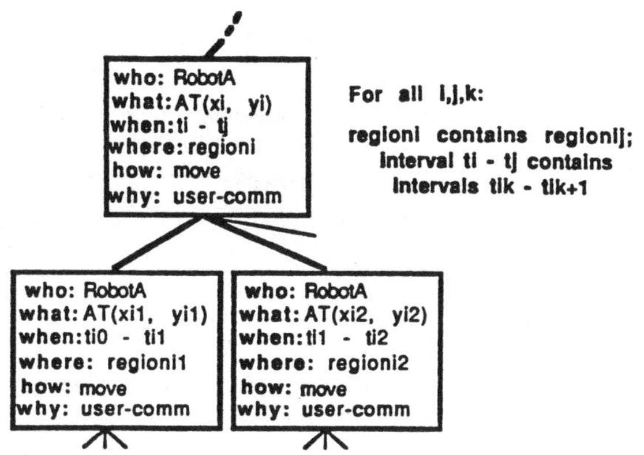

Figure 2: A Robot's Partial Behavior Hierarchy

We have implemented and evaluated our protocol using a simulation of this application. A partial, generalized behavior hierarchy for the application is shown in Figure 2. What sets this type of hierarchy apart from more typical plan/goal decomposition hierarchies is that the representation at one level summarizes the information in the lower levels. For example, in a typical plan/goal decomposition, a desire to move to a goal location might be decomposed into a sequence of intermediate locations to achieve, which might be further decomposed, and so on. In that type of decomposition, an entry at one level only reflects the *expected end result* of the levels below it, and *not* the behavior of the agent in achieving this result. In contrast, the spatial (where) information of an entry in our behavior hierarchy is computed as the smallest region that subsumes the regions below it, just as the temporal (when) interval is the shortest interval that includes all of the intervals below it. As a result, an entry essentially describes where the robot might be (as opposed to where it is going) over an interval of time.

The robots are currently limited to knowing how to move, who they are individually (they have no concept of coalitions), and that commands come from external sources. They plan paths to goal locations by finding a sequence of intermediate locations that avoid obstacles, and represent spatial regions as rectangular areas. They use knowledge about their movement speeds to compute the time needed to move between locations. If they decide that their behaviors might lead to collisions, the agents can search along either the temporal or spatial dimensions to change their behaviors.

Using the Protocol

To implement the protocol for our experiments, we have made several assumptions to promote structured communication and algorithmic convergence. First, we assume that each robot is given a unique authority value, so that robots can decide, when their plans are equally ranked, whose should get priority. Second, we assume that there are distinct intervals during which behavioral information is exchanged and modified. Third, we assume that robots modify their behaviors either by introducing delays in their actions or by choosing alternative routes. This choice is currently based on a user-supplied parameter.

The process begins by each robot broadcasting a message indicating who it is and what goal it wants to pursue. After enough time elapses, the robots build a list of robots sorted by their goal priorities. When robots have equal priority goals, they are sorted by their unique authority values. Because robots develop identical lists, the highest authority (superior) robot knows who it is. This robot broadcasts its most abstract behavioral information to the other (inferior) robots, who in turn broadcast theirs back to acknowledge receipt. Each of the inferior robots compares its local information with what it has received, and checks for conflict. This is simply computed by determining whether it expects to be in an overlapping region at an overlapping time interval. If no conflict is possible, it sends an empty message back to the superior who records that no conflict exists.

If a conflict exists, the inferior can either resolve it or more fully explore it. It can resolve the conflict by either delaying its activities until after the superior has completed its own, or by moving through another spatial region (if possible). Alternatively, it can explore the conflict by comparing its more detailed anticipated behavior (at the next level of the hierarchy) with what it knows of the superior, and then sending information about those aspects of its behavior that might be conflicting back to the superior. The superior compares these with its more detailed behaviors, and sends back only the more detailed behaviors that might interact. This process continues until either the inferior resolves the conflict at some level or it discovers on closer inspection that no conflict will occur. Either way, it sends an empty message back to the superior who records that no conflict exists anymore.

When the superior has heard from all inferiors that no conflicts exists, it passes control to the next robot in the pecking order. The process repeats, and the new superior interacts with the remaining inferiors to remove conflicts. When done, the process repeats again, and so on. At each repetition, the set of inferiors decreases, until no inferiors remain. At this point, all of the conflicts have been removed.

However, there is one wrinkle: When an inferior modifies its behaviors to avoid conflicting with the current superior, it might introduce behaviors that conflict with previous superiors. For this reason, before an inferior sends a message to the current superior indicating that no conflict exists anymore, it first communicates with previous superiors to ensure no new conflict has been introduced. If a new conflict has occurred, the inferior uses the same techniques as before to resolve the conflict with the previous superior, and then checks for new conflicts with the current superior. We can guarantee that we will not enter infinite loops of refinement because of our assumption that a robot changes its behavior either by introducing delays (always postponing actions) or by choosing a route that no superior has chosen. Using temporal modification, the robots could at worst serialize their actions so that no parallelism remains. Fortunately, such worst-case scenarios need seldom occur. Using spatial modification, the robots at worst pursue very roundabout routes.

When the last robot in the pecking order is given control, it knows that all conflicts have been resolved and broadcasts this fact to the others. The robots synchronize and then begin carrying out their planned activities. As each completes its activities, it again broadcasts this fact (along with its next goal's priority) to the others; when all have completed their activities, the protocol is initiated again for the next goals.

This is just one possible implementation of the protocol, and is primarily intended to test the implications of communicating at different levels of the behavior hierarchy. To maintain computational tractability, to ensure convergence, and to guarantee that conflicts will be resolved ahead of time (which typically requires that some agent ultimately has authority), this implementation assumes a total order on the agents and restricts how agents can modify their behaviors. We are developing more robust implementations in which new agents can join in at any time, agents can recover if one of them fails during the protocol process, and agents can dynamically allocate authority based on current circumstances.

Experiments

To investigate the performance of this implementation of our protocol, we simulated 2 environments in MICE (the Michigan Intelligent Coordination Experiment testbed [Durfee and Montgomery, 1989]). The first environment consists of 2 robots in 2 rooms that are joined by 2 doorways. Each doorway is only large enough for one robot (Figure 3a). The second environment consist of 3 robots in 2 rooms joined by 1 doorway (Figure 3b). In these environments, if the robots attempt to occupy the same location at the same time, they "bounce off" each other and return to their previous locations. Robots require 1 simulated time unit to move in any direction.

Each robot has its own distinct blackboard-based architecture, implemented in GBB [Corkill *et al.*, 1986]. The robots are given appropriate knowledge sources for planning paths to goal positions, for building behaviors based on these plans, for exchanging information at various levels of their behavior hierarchy, and for modifying behaviors along temporal and spatial dimensions to avoid potential collisions.

Communication delay between robots is 1 simulated time unit. To measure the protocol's communication overhead, we record the number of behaviors exchanged. Similarly, to measure the computa-

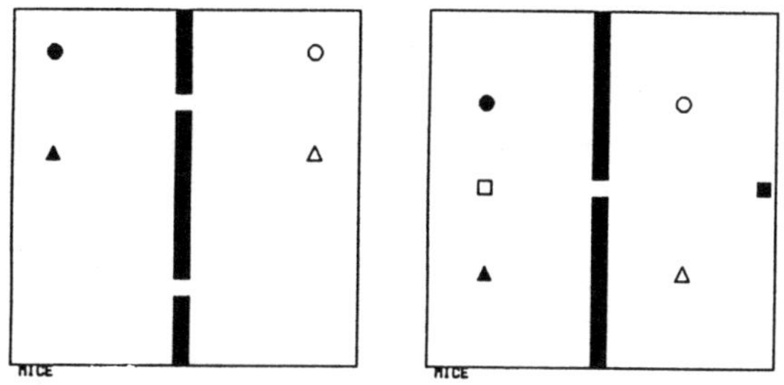

(a) (b)

In (a), RobotA (solid circle) is trying to get to the location marked with a hollow circle, RobotB (solid triangle) to the hollow triangle. In (b), RobotC (solid square) is also trying to get to the location marked with the hollow square.

Figure 3: Experimental Scenarios in MICE

tional overhead, we use MICE's capabilities for charging robots for time spent reasoning in the following way. As it compares behavioral information, a robot keeps track of how many comparisons between local and received behaviors it makes. For every n comparisons (where n is a user-modifiable parameter), it tells MICE to increment its clock by 1 simulated time unit. We also measure the simulated time spent carrying out the activities (from the earliest time an agent begins moving to the latest time an agent arrives at its goal destination), and the overall time to achieve all of the goals. For simplicity, we only give each robot one goal.

In our first set of experiments, consider the 2 robot case (Figure 3a). Unhindered, each robot requires 22 time units to move from start to goal locations. The results of our experiments are given in Table 1. Without any exchange of behavioral information (experiment 1), the robots spend a small amount of time initializing their plans. The time that robots spend moving to their goal destinations, however, is infinite, because the robots perpetually collide at the doorway.

When we allow the exchange of behavioral information, the robots can successfully make it to their goal destinations. First, consider the case where robots can make 5 comparisons of behaviors per simulated time unit. In experiment 2, the robots resolve potential conflicts between their most abstract behaviors. The overall expected regions of movement for the robots overlap at the doorway, so RobotB (the lower authority robot) changes the timing of its activities so that it does not begin moving anywhere in its overall region until RobotA expects to have finished. In essence, the robots have serialized their activities (with 1 extra time unit imposed between their activities to ensure no overlap).

In experiment 3, we make the robots resolve potential conflicts at an intermediate level. At this level,

Table 1: Experiment Summary.

Ex	En	M	Cps	Rs	Ex	TP	TA	Done
1	a	-	-	none	0	5	∞	∞
2	a	t	5	abs	2	10	45	55
3	a	t	5	int	9	16	35	51
4	a	t	5	det	16	77	24	101
5	a	t	50	abs	2	10	45	55
6	a	t	50	int	9	13	35	48
7	a	t	50	det	16	23	24	47
8	a	s	5	abs	2	10	32	42
9	a	s	5	int	8	14	32	46
10	a	s	5	det	13	47	32	79
11	a	s	50	abs	2	10	32	42
12	a	s	50	int	8	13	32	45
13	a	s	50	det	13	17	32	49
14	a′	-	-	none	0	5	22	27
15	a′	t	5	abs	2	10	43	53
16	a′	t	5	int	8	15	33	48
17	a′	t	5	det	7	33	22	55
18	a′	t	50	abs	2	10	43	53
19	a′	t	50	int	8	13	33	46
20	a′	t	50	det	7	15	22	37
21	a′	s	5	abs	2	10	32	42
22	a′	s	5	int	7	14	32	46
23	a′	s	5	det	7	33	22	55
24	a′	s	50	abs	2	10	32	42
25	a′	s	50	int	7	13	32	45
26	a′	s	50	det	7	15	22	37
27	b	-	-	none	0	5	∞	∞
28	b	t	5	abs	6	14	63	77
29	b	t	5	int	23	27	54	81
30	b	t	5	det	68	178	25	203
31	b	t	20	abs	6	14	63	77
32	b	t	20	int	23	21	54	75
33	b	t	20	det	68	65	25	90
34	b	t	50	abs	6	14	63	77
35	b	t	50	int	23	21	54	75
36	b	t	50	det	68	44	25	69

Abbreviations

Ex:	Experiment number
En:	Environment
M:	Modification (temporal or spatial)
Cps:	Comparisons per simulated time unit
Res:	Level where behavior conflicts are resolved: ABStract, INTermediate, or DETailed.
Ex:	Number of behaviors exchanged
TP:	Time for planning non-conflicting behaviors
TA:	Elapsed time for robot activities
Done:	Time at which all robot goals achieved

each has broken its overall behavior into 3 parts: to get in front of the door, to get to the other side of the door, and to get to the goal location. In the initial, abstract behavior exchange, they detect the potential conflict, and so RobotB requests intermediate information from RobotA. At first, RobotB changes its activities so that it will not begin its first intermediate behavior (going to the door) until RobotA begins its second behavior (entering the door). However, because RobotA's second behavior includes being in front of the door, and because this overlaps with the region of RobotB's first behavior, RobotB further delays its first behavior until RobotA has actually moved through the door. RobotB propagates the effects of this delay on the rest of its behaviors, and because subsequent time intervals are modified, no further conflicts between the robots' behaviors exist. The data shows that resolving potential conflicts at this level incurs more communication and further delays the start of the plans (compared to experiment 2), but results in more movement parallelism in the robots' actions. As a result, the overall time to achieve the goals is lower.

In experiment 4, the robots exchange abstract, then intermediate, and finally fully detailed behaviors (down to locations they will occupy at specific times). Based on this information, RobotB again modifies the intervals of its behaviors, but this time recognizes that it need not delay from the very start. Instead, it determines that trying to get in front of the door is what conflicts with RobotA, and delays this detailed behavior. Propagating this change removes all other conflicts. The movements of the robots in this case have substantial parallelism so the time spent carrying out the plans is reduced, but the amount of communication and the time spent resolving the conflicting plans is much greater. In fact, the overall time is much worse than the previous 2 experiments.

Experiments 5-7 are the same as 2-4, except the number of comparisons per simulated time unit is 50. This serves to make computation cheaper with respect to movement, but does not change the quality of coordination. The implication of this change is that exerting computational effort to increase parallel movement is more worthwhile, so resolving conflicts at more detailed levels is better.

In experiments 8-13, RobotB resolves the conflict along the spatial dimension by moving through the further doorway. This results in identical plans regardless of the level at which the conflicts are resolved, because once RobotB plans its new path, the robots' behaviors no longer interact at any level of abstraction. To save on overhead, resolving conflicts at less detailed levels is thus better.

Experiments 14-26 are the same as 1-13, but now RobotA starts slightly closer to the door (environment a′). As a result, the robots' actions will not conflict, and the best results are achieved without any coordination (experiment 14). When the robots coordinate at the abstract and intermediate levels, they cannot ensure that no conflict will occur, so they modify their plans either temporally (experiments 15, 16, 18, 19) or spatially (experiments 21, 22, 24, 25). At the detailed level, the robots recognize that no resolution is needed, but only after substantial investment of effort. Sometimes this effort is worthwhile (experiments 20, 26) while at other times it is not (experiments 17, 23).

Finally, experiments 27-36 are based on the 3 robot environment (Figure 3b). Without any conflict avoidance, the robots once again perpetually collide at the doorway (experiment 27). The addition of a third robot can dramatically increase the amount of information exchanged at the detailed and intermediate levels. As a result, when robots can do only 5 comparisons per simulated time unit (experiments 28-30), resolving conflicts at the abstract level is better than the intermediate level which is better than the detailed level. As the number of comparisons per simulated time unit increases (experiments 31-36), first the intermediate and then the detailed levels are best. Note that the time spent resolving conflicts at more detailed levels is always greater regardless of comparisons allowed per time unit, because of the communication delay. Several messages might be in transit at the same time, however, so the time spent resolving conflicts can be less than the number of behaviors exchanged (such as in experiments 35 and 36).

In summary, these experiments highlight the fact that different circumstances demand different amounts of communication and coordination. Sometimes not communicating or coordinating is best (experiment 14), but at other times such a strategy can be catastrophic (experiments 1 and 27). Sometimes it is more cost effective to coordinate at a high-level, because it involves less overhead and results in relatively acceptable coordination (such as in experiments 8, 11, 21, and 28). Coordinating at detailed levels has advantages in situations where the chances for parallelism are greater (such as in experiments 7 and 36), or where the robots can only ensure that they will not conflict when the examine their behaviors in detail (such as in experiment 26). And coordinating at an intermediate level is sometimes the best policy (such as in experiments 3 and 32). In short, conflicts should be resolved at different levels in different cases. Unlike previous protocols that work at a single level of detail, our new protocol allows the robots to coordinate at different levels flexibly.

The experiments also point toward further research directions. Issues in mediating between different perspectives (which our current implementation avoids by imposing a total ordering on agents) and in deciding along what dimensions and at what level to resolve conflicts (recall our current implementation depends on user-supplied parameters) are focuses of our current research. In addition, using other dimensions for resolving conflicts (or promoting cooperation) is important, and we are exploring issues in getting agents to adopt each other's (or joint) goals or having them choose methods that achieve their goals in non-conflicting ways. The challenge in this research is in exploiting the richness of the behavior hierarchy while heuristically restricting the search among behaviors to maintain computational tractability.

Conclusions

As we have demonstrated experimentally, our protocol allows a form of coordination that is well suited to domains where interacting agents do not know, *a priori*, with whom they will interact. This is accomplished through a dialogue between the agents in which they are free to exchange information at different levels of abstraction about their anticipated behavior. In essence, this dialogue is a rudimentary form of negotiation between the agents: Although our specific implementation identified which agent involved in a conflict should modify its behavior, our protocol admits to more flexible (and arguably more computationally expensive) encounters, where each agent involved in a conflict moves along some of its behavioral dimensions until a compromise is found that eliminates the conflict and yet allows each agent to retain important behavioral attributes. Our work thus paves the way for a new investigation into intelligent negotiation.

Another observation that we have made is that the dimensions of our behavior hierarchy correspond to problem decomposition directions found in human organizations [Malone, 1987]. If we decompose a behavior along the *what* dimension, for example, we are decomposing based on results (or products) of behavior, which leads to a *product hierarchy*. Similarly, decomposing along the *how* dimension leads to a type of *functional hierarchy*. From other dimensions, we see personnel hierarchies, temporal hierarchies, spatial hierarchies, and even motivational hierarchies. We are intrigued by the possible relationship between our approach and organizational theory, and indeed are working toward experiments where groups of robots team up and represent their overall behavior in the behavior hierarchy. As a result, groups (or organizations) of individuals are viewed as single entities, and can negotiate as a unit; yet, by traversing the hierarchy the behaviors of individuals are still represented. Based on these insights, we are currently exploring how to integrate organizational and planning theories within our single protocol.

References

[Ashley, 1988] Kevin D. Ashley. *Modelling Legal Argument: Reasoning with Cases and Hypotheticals.* PhD thesis, University of Massachusetts, February 1988.

[Cammarata *et al.*, 1983] Stephanie Cammarata, David McArthur, and Randall Steeb. Strategies of cooperation in distributed problem solving. In *Proceedings of the Eighth International Joint Conference on Artificial Intelligence*, pages 767–770, Karlsruhe, Federal Republic of Germany, August 1983.

[Conry *et al.*, 1988] Susan E. Conry, Robert A. Meyer, and Victor R. Lesser. Multistage negotiation in distributed planning. In Alan H. Bond and Les Gasser, editors, *Readings in Distributed Artificial Intelligence*, pages 367–384. Morgan Kaufman, 1988.

[Corkill and Lesser, 1983] Daniel D. Corkill and Victor R. Lesser. The use of meta-level control for coordination in a distributed problem solving network. In *Proceedings of the Eighth International Joint Conference on Artificial Intelligence*, pages 748–756, Karlsruhe, Federal Republic of Germany, August 1983.

[Corkill *et al.*, 1986] Daniel D. Corkill, Kevin Q. Gallagher, and Kelly E. Murray. GBB: A generic blackboard development system. In *Proceedings of the National Conference on Artificial Intelligence*, pages 1008–1014, Philadelphia, Pennsylvania, August 1986.

[Davis and Smith, 1983] Randall Davis and Reid G. Smith. Negotiation as a metaphor for distributed problem solving. *Artificial Intelligence*, pages 63–109, 1983.

[Davis, 1981] Randall Davis. A model for planning in a multiagent environment: Steps toward principles for teamwork. AI Working Paper 217, Artificial Intelligence Laboratory, Massachusetts Institute of Technology, Cambridge, Massachusetts 02139, June 1981.

[Decker and Lesser, 1989] Keith S. Decker and Victor R. Lesser. Some initial thoughts on a generic architecture for cdps network control. In *Proceedings of the 1989 Distributed AI Workshop*, pages 73–94, September 1989.

[Durfee and Lesser, 1987] Edmund H. Durfee and Victor R. Lesser. Using partial global plans to coordinate distributed problem solvers. In *Proceedings of the Tenth International Joint Conference on Artificial Intelligence*, pages 875–883, Milan, Italy, August 1987.

[Durfee and Montgomery, 1989] Edmund H. Durfee and Thomas A. Montgomery. MICE: A flexible testbed for intelligent coordination experiments. In *Proceedings of the 1989 Distributed AI Workshop*, pages 25–40, September 1989.

[Durfee *et al.*, 1987] Edmund H. Durfee, Victor R. Lesser, and Daniel D. Corkill. Coherent cooperation among communicating problem solvers. *IEEE Transactions on Computers*, C-36(11):1275–1291, November 1987.

[Durfee, 1988] Edmund H. Durfee. *Coordination of Distributed Problem Solvers.* Kluwer Academic Publishers, 1988.

[Lansky, 1985] Amy L. Lansky. Behavioral specification and planning for multiagent domains. Technical Report 360, SRI International, Menlo Park CA, 1985.

[Malone, 1987] Thomas W. Malone. Modeling coordination in organizations and markets. *Management Science*, 33(10):1317–1332, 1987.

[Steeb *et al.*, 1986] R. Steeb, S. Cammarata, S. Narain, J. Rothenburg, and W. Giarla. Cooperative intelligence for remotely piloted vehicle fleet control. Technical Report R-3408-ARPA, Rand Corporation, October 1986.

[Steeb *et al.*, 1988] R. Steeb, S. Cammarata, F. Hayes-Roth, P. Thorndyke, and R. Wesson. Architectures for distributed air-traffic control. In Alan H. Bond and Les Gasser, editors, *Readings in Distributed Artificial Intelligence*, pages 90–101. Morgan Kaufman, 1988.

[von Martial, 1989] Frank von Martial. Multiagent plan relationships. In *Proceedings of the 1989 Distributed AI Workshop*, pages 59–72, September 1989.

On Acting Together

Hector J. Levesque*
Dept. of Computer Science
University of Toronto
Toronto, Ont. M5S 1A4
hector@ai.toronto.edu

Philip R. Cohen
AI Center and CSLI
SRI International
Menlo Park, CA 94025
pcohen@ai.sri.com

José H. T. Nunes
Dept. of Computer Science
University of Toronto
Toronto, Ont. M5S 1A4
nunes@ai.toronto.edu

Abstract

Joint action by a team does not consist merely of simultaneous and coordinated individual actions; to act together, a team must be aware of and care about the status of the group effort as a whole. We present a formal definition of what it could mean for a group to jointly commit to a common goal, and explore how these joint commitments relate to the individual commitments of the team members. We then consider the case of joint intention, where the goal in question involves the team performing some action. In both cases, the theory is formulated in a logical language of belief, action, and time previously used to characterize individual commitment and intention. An important consequence of the theory is the types of communication among the team members that it predicts will often be necessary.

Introduction

What is involved when a group of people decide to do something *together*? Joint action by a team involves more than just the union of simultaneous individual actions, even when those actions are coordinated. We would not say that there is any *team work* involved in ordinary automobile traffic, even though the drivers act simultaneously and are coordinated (one hopes) by the traffic signs and rules of the road. But when a group of drivers decide to do something together, such as driving somewhere as a *convoy*, it appears that the group acts as a single agent with beliefs, goals, and intentions of its own, over and above the individual ones. In this paper, we present a formal model of these mental properties of a group, and especially how joint intentions to act affect and are affected by (and ultimately reduce to) the mental states of the participants.

In previous work, we have presented a belief-desire-intention model of the mental states of individuals in which intentions are seen as internal commitments to perform an action while in a certain mental state. To achieve a degree of realism required for successful autonomous behaviour, we model individual agents as situated in a dynamic, multi-agent world, as possessing neither complete nor correct beliefs about the world or the other agents, as having changeable goals and fallible actions, and as subject to interruption from external events. Whereas the model is sufficient to predict planning, replanning, and communication [Cohen and Levesque, in press; Cohen and Levesque, 1990], it does so only from the perspective of each individual agent, by constraining the rational balance that agents maintain among their own beliefs, goals, commitments, intentions, and actions. This paper extends our previous work and characterizes joint intentions as shared commitments to perform an action (typically composite) while the group is in a certain shared mental state.

Although we do not explore how these ideas can be applied in computational systems that reason about action, we take the research presented here to be essential groundwork. Some account of joint action is obviously needed to at least describe (or form plans containing) coordinated activities such as jointly lifting a heavy object or writing a paper, as well as pure group activities like games, plays, and dances. The theory also provides a basis for formalizing the type of agreement and commitment underlying legal contracts and treaties. In addition, it allows us to make sense of mundane utterances like "Uh-huh," "OK," "Right," "Go on," "Now" and others, that pepper all our natural dialogues. These can be seen as attempts to establish and maintain the mutual beliefs necessary to the achievement of joint intentions. Indeed, one of the main goals of this theory is to predict and interpret the sort of linguistic activity that arises when agents cooperate. A companion paper [Cohen *et al.*, 1990] will provide details of the application of the theory to dialogue.

In the rest of this paper, we discuss the problem of joint action in general, and then build a formal theory of joint commitment based on the same primitives as the individual case. We then examine some of the properties of joint commitment, and use it to define a simple form of joint intention. Finally, we discuss why it is rational for agents to form joint commitments at all.

*Fellow of the Canadian Institute for Advanced Research

A Convoy Example

If team behaviour is more than coordinated individual behaviour, how does it work? When is it necessary? When should agents communicate? What should they communicate? These questions are perhaps best answered by considering what would happen in the case of a convoy example *without* the right sort of joint intention.

Consider two agents, A and B, driving somewhere together, with A leading the way until B knows his[1] way home. Assume that both agents have this as their intention, and furthermore, that these individual intentions are mutually believed to hold. In other words, it is mutually known to both agents that each will do his part (if he can) as long as the other agent does likewise. Will this work?

This is essentially the model of joint intention proposed by Tuomela and Miller [1988] and by Grosz and Sidner [in press]. We feel that it runs into difficulties in cases where it is possible for one of the agents to come to believe (privately) that the intention either has been achieved or is impossible to achieve. We assume that in such a situation, a rational agent has no choice but to abandon the goal. For example, if A comes to realize that he was mistaken and in fact does not know where B lives, the intention to lead B must be given up. The trouble is that there is nothing in the agreement to stop A from just speeding away, ignoring a puzzled B behind him. Conversely, if B comes to realize that he now knows his way home, the goal has been satisfied according to him, and there is nothing to stop him from pulling over to enjoy the scenery, without regard to how A might interpret his action.

But the real problem with this characterization of joint intention is that it does not work even if both parties behave with the utmost of consideration for the other, and even if these private beliefs of failure or success do not arise. As long as these beliefs are thought to be *possible*, what can happen is that one agent may come to believe that something like this is happening to the other! For example, if A makes a turn, B could very well (falsely) conclude that A is no longer able to lead him, and so make other plans for getting home. Conversely, if B is forced to pull over (for example, because of difficulties with his car), A could simply conclude that B now knows the way, and continue driving without him. At a deeper level of misunderstanding, even if each agent does not misinterpret the other's actions, he has no way of knowing that the other agent will not misinterpret his! Even if A is indeed prepared to stop in case B does, B might not realize this, and not want to pull over in case A takes it to mean that B now knows his way home. This can continue indefinitely to deeper and deeper levels. Overall then, with the potential for this kind of misunderstanding, even with the best of intentions, nothing is holding the collective behaviour together. Individual intentions do not a convoy make.

So what do we expect from a convoy? Among other things, robustness against misunderstandings like those above: A will signal when it is time to get started, A and B will endeavor to keep each other within sight and not pull over privately, A will not take actions that he believes would render B's intentions impossible to achieve, B will signal when he knows his way, and without such a signal, A will still assume B is following. Of course, A and B do not need to explicitly agree to these actions; they should be consequences of what it means to act together. Before examining a definition of joint action that has these properties, we review the individual case.

[1]We use masculine adjectives and pronouns throughout, but they should be read as "his," "her" or "its" (for robots), as the reader desires.

Individual Commitment and Intention

The account of intention given in [Cohen and Levesque, 1990] is formulated in a modal language that has the usual connectives of a first-order language with equality, as well as operators for the propositional attitudes and for talking about sequences of events: (BEL x p) and (GOAL x p) say that x has p as a belief and goal respectively; (MB x y p) says that x and y mutually believe that p holds; (AGT $x_1 \ldots x_n$ e) says that $x_1 \ldots x_n$ are the only agents for the sequence of events e; $e_1 \leq e_2$ says that e_1 is an initial subsequence of e_2; and finally, (HAPPENED a), (HAPPENING a), and (HAPPENS a) say that a sequence of events describable by an action expression a has just happened, is happening now, or will happen next, respectively. An action expression here is built from variables ranging over sequences of events using the constructs of dynamic logic: a;b is action composition; a|b is nondeterministic choice; a||b is concurrent occurrence of a and b; p? is a test action; and finally, a* is repetition. The usual programming constructs like IF/THEN actions and WHILE loops can easily be formed from these.[2]

A few comments on how formulas of this language are semantically interpreted. BEL and GOAL are given a possible-world semantics, where a world is modeled as a function mapping each time point to a set of primitive event types (the events happening simultaneously at that point in time). We assume that each agent has perfect introspection about both his beliefs and goals, that beliefs are consistent, and that goals are consistent with each other and with what is believed. Sentences are evaluated at both a world and a current time point on that world. The truth value of sentences with HAPPENED, HAPPENING, and HAPPENS differ only with re-

[2]Test actions occur frequently in our analysis, yet are potentially confusing. The expression p?;a should be read as "action a with p holding initially," and analogously for a;p?. Note specifically that an agent can perform these without ever knowing the truth value of p.

spect to the position of the current time point: immediately after, straddled by, and immediately before the action, respectively. We will also use the following syntactic abbreviations:

Actions:

$$(\mathsf{DONE}\ x_1 \ldots x_n\ a) \stackrel{\text{def}}{=} (\mathsf{HAPPENED}\ a) \wedge (\mathsf{AGT}\ x_1 \ldots x_n\ a)$$

$$(\mathsf{DOING}\ x_1 \ldots x_n\ a) \stackrel{\text{def}}{=} (\mathsf{HAPPENING}\ a) \wedge (\mathsf{AGT}\ x_1 \ldots x_n\ a)$$

$$(\mathsf{DOES}\ x_1 \ldots x_n\ a) \stackrel{\text{def}}{=} (\mathsf{HAPPENS}\ a) \wedge (\mathsf{AGT}\ x_1 \ldots x_n\ a).$$

Eventually: $\Diamond p \stackrel{\text{def}}{=} \exists e\ (\mathsf{HAPPENS}\ e;p?)$.
There is something that happens, including the empty sequence of events, after which p holds, *i.e.*, p is true at some point in the future.

Always: $\Box p \stackrel{\text{def}}{=} \neg\Diamond\neg p$.
The wff p is true from now on.

Until: $(\mathsf{UNTIL}\ p\ q) \stackrel{\text{def}}{=}$
$\forall c\ (\mathsf{HAPPENS}\ c;\neg q?) \supset \exists a\ (a \leq c) \wedge (\mathsf{HAPPENS}\ a;p?)$.
Until the wff p is true, the wff q will remain true.

With these definitions in place, we can say what it means for an agent x to be (fanatically) committed to achieving a goal p: he should believe that p is false, but want it to be true at some point, and continue to want it to be true until he believes that it is true, or that it will never be true. Thus we have the following definition:[3]

Definition 1 $(\mathsf{PGOAL}\ x\ p\ q) \stackrel{\text{def}}{=}$

$$(\mathsf{BEL}\ x\ \neg p) \wedge (\mathsf{GOAL}\ x\ \Diamond p) \wedge$$
$$(\mathsf{UNTIL}\ [(\mathsf{BEL}\ x\ p) \vee (\mathsf{BEL}\ x\ \Box\neg p) \vee (\mathsf{BEL}\ x\ \neg q)]\ (\mathsf{GOAL}\ x\ \Diamond p))$$

The extra condition q here (which we will occasionally omit) is simply a reason x may have for keeping the goal. It is most often used in an expression such as (PGOAL x p (GOAL x q)) to express a commitment to p as a *subgoal* relative to q.[4] Finally, we define what it means for x to intend to do an action a:

Definition 2 $(\mathsf{INTEND}\ x\ a\ q) \stackrel{\text{def}}{=}$

$$(\mathsf{PGOAL}\ x\ (\mathsf{DONE}\ x\ [\mathsf{UNTIL}\ (\mathsf{DONE}\ x\ a)\ (\mathsf{BEL}\ x\ (\mathsf{DOING}\ x\ a))]?;a)\ q)$$

So an agent intends to do an action if he has a persistent goal to have done that action, and moreover, to have done it believing throughout that he was doing it. It is therefore a commitment to do the action *deliberately*. Typically such a goal would arise within a subgoal-supergoal chain as a decision to do an action a to achieve a goal p by getting into a mental state where a would be done knowingly.[5] If the chain is something like

$$(\mathsf{PGOAL}\ x\ p) \wedge$$
$$(\mathsf{PGOAL}\ x\ (\mathsf{HAPPENED}\ a)\ (\mathsf{GOAL}\ x\ \Diamond p)) \wedge$$
$$(\mathsf{PGOAL}\ x\ (\mathsf{DONE}\ x\ a)\ (\mathsf{GOAL}\ x\ \Diamond(\mathsf{HAPPENED}\ a))) \wedge$$
$$(\mathsf{INTEND}\ x\ a\ (\mathsf{GOAL}\ x\ \Diamond(\mathsf{DONE}\ x\ a))),$$

then the goal could be given up if the agent discovers that a was performed somehow without his realizing it (or any other goal higher in the chain was achieved).

Joint Commitment

How should the definition of persistent goal and intention be generalized to the case where a group is acting like a single agent? Restricting ourselves to two agents here (and throughout), a first attempt at a definition for JPG, *joint persistent goal*, would be to replace belief in the definition of PGOAL by mutual belief, and replace (GOAL x ◇p) by mutual belief in the goal as in

Definition attempt: $(\mathsf{JPG}\ x\ y\ p\ q) \stackrel{\text{def}}{=}$

$$(\mathsf{MB}\ x\ y\ \neg p) \wedge (\mathsf{MG}\ x\ y\ p) \wedge$$
$$(\mathsf{UNTIL}\ [(\mathsf{MB}\ x\ y\ p) \vee (\mathsf{MB}\ x\ y\ \Box\neg p) \vee (\mathsf{MB}\ x\ y\ \neg q)]\ (\mathsf{MG}\ x\ y\ p)),$$

where

$$(\mathsf{MG}\ x\ y\ p) \stackrel{\text{def}}{=} (\mathsf{MB}\ x\ y\ (\mathsf{GOAL}\ x\ \Diamond p) \wedge (\mathsf{GOAL}\ y\ \Diamond p)).$$

This has the effect of treating x and y together as a single agent, but otherwise leaving the notion of persistent goal unchanged.

However, the definition is not quite right: it will only work in cases where neither agent can come to believe *privately* that the goal p has succeeded or is impossible.[6] To see why, suppose that x alone comes to believe that p is impossible; x must drop the goal, and so (MG x y p) must be false; but this mutual goal was supposed to persist until there was a certain mutual belief, and as there is as yet none, there cannot have been a JPG to start with.

So joint commitment cannot be just a version of individual commitment where a team is taken to be the agent, for the simple reason that the team members may diverge in their beliefs. If an agent comes to think a goal is impossible, then he must give up the goal, and fortunately knows enough to do so, since he believes it is impossible. But when a member of a team finds out a goal is impossible, the team as a whole must again give up the goal, but *the team does not necessarily know enough to do so.* Although there will no longer be mutual belief that the goal is achievable, there need not be mutual belief that it is *unachievable.* Moreover, we cannot simply stipulate that a goal can be dropped when there is no longer mutual belief since that would allow agreements to be dissolved as soon as there was uncertainty about the state of the other team members.

[3] This is slightly different from the one appearing in [Cohen and Levesque, 1990].

[4] A better way to do this would be to allow for a dynamically evolving set of *priorities*, and to allow an agent to drop a goal if it is found to conflict with one of higher priority.

[5] An alternative but less effective choice would be to blunder about at random, checking periodically to see whether or not the action had been done.

[6] We thank Henry Kautz for this observation.

This was precisely the problem with the failed convoy discussed above. Rather, we must insist on arriving at mutual belief, that is, at an agreement that the goal is impossible to achieve, before commitments can be discharged. Any team member who discovers privately that a goal is impossible (or has been achieved) should be left with a goal to make this fact known to the team as a whole, which, in effect, is what introspection does in the individual case.

We therefore define the state of a team member x nominally working on p relative to another member y as follows:

Definition 3 (WG x y p) $\stackrel{\text{def}}{=}$

$$[\neg(\text{BEL x p}) \wedge (\text{GOAL x} \Diamond\text{p})] \quad \vee$$
$$[(\text{BEL x p}) \wedge (\text{GOAL x} \Diamond(\text{MB x y p}))] \quad \vee$$
$$[(\text{BEL x} \Box\neg\text{p}) \wedge (\text{GOAL x} \Diamond(\text{MB x y} \Box\neg\text{p}))]$$

This form of "weak goal" involves three mutually exclusive cases: either x has $\Diamond$p as a goal, or thinks that p is true and wants to make that mutually believed,[7] or similarly for p never being true.

If a team is jointly committed to achieving p, the team members cannot assume of each other that they have p as a goal, but only that they have p as a *weak* goal; each member has to allow that any other member may have discovered privately that p is impossible and be in the process of making that known to the team as a whole.

A further possibility (that we will not deal with) is for an agent to discover that it is impossible to make the status of p known to the group as a whole, for example, when communication is impossible. For simplicity, we assume that once an agent comes to think that p is unachievable, he never changes his mind, and that it is always possible to achieve the correct mutual belief. Among other things, this restricts joint persistent goals to conditions where there will eventually be agreement among the team members regarding its achievement or impossibility.[8]

So the final definition of JPG replaces MG in the last clause of the previous definition by a weaker version:

Definition 4 (JPG x y p q) $\stackrel{\text{def}}{=}$

$$(\text{MB x y} \neg\text{p}) \wedge (\text{MG x y p}) \wedge$$
$$(\text{UNTIL } [(\text{MB x y p}) \vee (\text{MB x y} \Box\neg\text{p}) \vee (\text{MB x y} \neg\text{q})] \; (\text{WMG x p}))$$

where

$$(\text{WMG x y p}) \stackrel{\text{def}}{=} (\text{MB x y (WG x y p)} \wedge (\text{WG y x p})).$$

[7] More accurately, we should say here that his goal is making it mutually believed that p *had been* true, in case p can become false again.

[8] Actually, agents do have the option of using the escape clause q to get around this difficulty. For example, ¬q could say that there was an unresolvable disagreement of some sort, or just claim that an expiry date had been reached. In this case, mutual belief in ¬q amounts to an agreement to dissolve the commitment regardless of the status of p.

Properties of Joint Commitment

The first thing to observe about this definition of JPG is that like its flawed predecessor, it also generalizes the concept of PGOAL, in that it reduces to the individual case when the two agents are the same:

Theorem 1

$$\models (\text{JPG x x p}) \equiv (\text{PGOAL x p})$$

The proof is that if x has a weak goal that persists until he believes it to be true or impossible, he must also have an ordinary goal that persists.

It can also be shown that like the previous account, this definition of joint commitment implies individual commitments from the team members:

Theorem 2

$$\models (\text{JPG x y p}) \supset (\text{PGOAL x p}) \wedge (\text{PGOAL y p}).$$

To see why x has p as a persistent goal, imagine that at some point in the future x does not believe that p is true or impossible to achieve. Then there is no mutual belief either, and so p must still be a weak goal. But under these circumstances, this means that p must still be a real goal. Consequently, p persists as a goal until x believes it to be satisfied or impossible to achieve.

So if two agents agree to do something, they become individually committed to achieving it. This was stated by Searle as one of the major puzzles of joint intention [Searle, in press]: given that joint intentions do not reduce to the conjunction of individual ones, where do the individual intentions come from (since ultimately, it is the individuals who act)? In the Grosz and Sidner formulation, joint intentions are *defined* in terms of individual ones. But as we saw earlier, their definition had a drawback given the possibility of private discoveries about the status of the goal. With our definition, however, an agent cannot give up the goal just because he suspects that the other agent has given it up (or suspects that the other suspects that he has, and so on). Until they know the status of the goal itself, they cannot drop it.

So what *does* happen when one agent x discovers privately that p is impossible to achieve?[9] First observe that the agent must now drop the goal of achieving p, and so the PGOAL and the JPG must be false as well. This is as it should be: we would not want to say that the agents continue to be jointly committed to achieving p, since one of them has now given it up.

But (and this is the important point) the fact that there is no longer a joint commitment does not mean that the collective behaviour falls apart. Since there is as yet no mutual belief that p is impossible, we know that the (WMG x y p) must persist. This means that (WG x y p) must persist, and (GOAL x $\Diamond$(MB x y $\Box\neg$p)) must persist too, since (BEL x $\Box\neg$p) is true and will remain true. So although the original JPG no longer

[9] Similar considerations apply when one of agents discovers that the goal has been achieved, or when the agent thinks that something like this is happening to the other.

holds, because of the UNTIL clause in that JPG, the goal to eventually achieve mutual belief persists until it is achieved. This goal is therefore a PGOAL:

Theorem 3

$$\models \text{(JPG x y p)} \wedge \ldots \supset$$
$$\text{(UNTIL [(MB x y p)} \vee \text{(MB x y } \Box\neg\text{p)]}$$
$$\text{[(BEL x (}\Box\neg\text{p)}\wedge\neg\text{(MB x y } \Box\neg\text{p))} \supset$$
$$\text{(PGOAL x (MB x y } \Box\neg\text{p))])}$$

The ellipsis here is some condition that is sufficient to guarantee that x will not change his mind about the impossibility of p. The simplest and strongest such condition is $\Box$[(BEL x $\Box\neg$p) $\supset$ $\Box$(BEL x $\Box\neg$p)], but others are possible.

Similarly, when agent x discovers privately that p has been achieved, the goal of making p mutually believed persists until the JPG is discharged:

Theorem 4

$$\models \text{(JPG x y p)} \wedge \ldots \supset$$
$$\text{(UNTIL [(MB x y p)} \vee \text{(MB x y } \Box\neg\text{p)]}$$
$$\text{[(BEL x p}\wedge\neg\text{(MB x y p))} \supset$$
$$\text{(PGOAL x (MB x y p))])}$$

To summarize: once a JPG has been established, if one of the agents comes to believe that the goal has been achieved or is impossible, the individual commitment to achieve p is replaced by a new commitment to make the status of p mutually believed.

This has two very important consequences. First, this PGOAL to attain mutual belief predicts that *communication* will take place as this is typically how mutual belief is attained, unless there is co-presence to begin with. To satisfy a contract, in other words, it is not enough to satisfy the agreed upon goal (or to find it to be unsatisfiable), one must be prepared to *show* the other that it has been satisfied. This explains why contracts normally have concrete *deliverables*, and why it would be strange to have a contract requiring one of the parties to merely think about something.

Second, if there is a joint commitment, agents can count on the commitment of the other members, first to the goal in question, and then, if necessary, to the communication of the status of the goal. We do not merely require the agent to work on the goal while he believes the other agent to be doing the same, since in many natural cases, one agent will lose track of what the other is up to. Instead, he must work on a goal until there is mutual belief regarding the status of the goal. As we discuss below, what makes this at least reasonable is the fact that an agent can rely on the other to let him know if he is wasting his time on an impossible goal.

Let us reexamine the convoy example in the light of these theorems. First, we introduce some (simplistic) notation:

$$\text{(know-way y)} \overset{\text{def}}{=} \exists \text{z (BEL y (way-home y z)).}$$

$$\text{(done-convoy x y)} \overset{\text{def}}{=} \text{(DONE x y}$$
$$\text{(WHILE } \neg\text{(know-way y) [(leads x);(follows y)]))}$$

The expression (know-way y) is intended to say that y knows his way home, and (done-convoy x y) says that x and y have just done the iterative action consisting of x leading and y following (whatever that means) until y knows his way home.

If x and y are jointly committed to doing the convoy action, we can show that if y comes to know his way home, he cannot simply ignore x and go home; he remains committed to making it mutually believed that he knows his way home (for example, by signalling):

Theorem 5

$$\models \text{(JPG x y (done-convoy x y))} \wedge \ldots \supset$$
$$\text{(UNTIL [(MB x y (done-convoy x y))}$$
$$\vee \text{ (MB x y } \Box\neg\text{(done-convoy x y))]}$$
$$\text{[(BEL y (know-way y)} \wedge$$
$$\neg\text{(MB x y (know-way y)))} \supset$$
$$\text{(PGOAL y (MB x y (know-way y)))])}$$

All that is needed to show that this theorem follows from Theorem 4 is the fact that the worlds where y knows his way home are precisely the worlds where the WHILE loop has just ended (after perhaps zero iterations). More complex properties of the convoy depend on a joint commitment to more than just the proper completion of the WHILE loop, as in joint intention, which we now turn to.

Joint Actions

Given the notion of joint commitment, we define JI, *joint intention*, as the obvious generalization of individual intention:

Definition 5 $\text{(JI x y a q)} \overset{\text{def}}{=}$

$$\text{(JPG x y}$$
$$\text{(DONE x y}$$
$$\text{[UNTIL (DONE x y a)}$$
$$\text{(MB x y (DOING x y a))]?;a)}$$
$$\text{q)}$$

So joint intention is a joint commitment to do an action while mutually believing (throughout the execution of the action, that is) that the agents are doing it. Space permits us only to sketch broadly some of the implications of this definition.

Typically, the a in question will be a composite action involving parts to be done by each agent alone. For example, a could be $a_x;a_y$ or $a_x \| a_y$, where a_x is some action to be performed by x alone, and similarly for a_y. Since both parties are committed to getting *all* of a done, both parties care about the other's actions and so will not intentionally do something that would make them impossible. If one agent does his part, but sees that the other agent has difficulty doing his, this definition predicts that the first agent will want to *redo* his part, to get the whole thing right. If there are turns to be played, each agent will have to make sure that the other knows when it is his turn, perhaps by a signal of some sort. In fact, neither agent is committed to his part of the bargain in isolation; individual intentions to do one's part do *not* follow from a joint intention to do a composite action. Acting alone could very well be ineffectual (as in lifting a piano) or worse (as in the "coordinated attack" problem [Halpern and Fagin, 1985]). An agent that discovers that his partner's action is impossible may refuse to do his part, even if it remains possible to do so. These properties suggest that an agent's commitments to another's actions will need to be treated quite similar to his commitments to his own. Both will need to be part of his plans, for example, even though only his own intentions lead him to act.

The other feature of joint intention is that the action needs to be performed in a certain shared mental state. The main consequence of this is that it predicts that communication will be used to ensure that both parties are aware throughout the execution of a that the action is being done. In addition to signals that transfer control when taking turns (noted above), one would expect to see a signal at the start of the action (like "Ready"), and various reassuring confirmation signals (like "Uh-huh") to make sure the initial mutual belief does not dissipate over time [Cohen *et al.*, 1990].

Conclusion

In our previous work, we discussed individual actions and intentions in terms of the rational balance agents maintain among their beliefs, goals, and commitments. We conclude here by discussing why we feel it is *rational* for agents to enter into joint commitments. Our account predicts (perhaps counterintuitively) that an agent will persist in trying to achieve a goal even if he happens to believe the other agent is in the process of informing him of why he had to give it up. Why is this persistence a better strategy than letting the other agent do all the work or dropping the goal as soon as there is uncertainty in the air? There are two reasons. First, the agent knows that he will eventually be told by his partner if he is working on a futile goal. If in fact he is doing more than he strictly needs to, he at least knows that his partner is committed to rescuing him. Second, if he were to take the more conservative strategy and quit immediately, or even if there were suspicions to that effect, the collective behaviour would fall apart and doom the project. This is not unlike the classical Prisoner's Dilemma problem where if both agents fail to cooperate and choose the *locally optimal* strategy, the global result is unacceptable to both parties. It is the mutual commitment to a non-conservative form of behaviour that binds the team together.

Of course the *real* problem in interpersonal affairs is trying to arrive a truly shared commitment. If one of the parties is suspicious of the goals of the other, then by our definition, there is no joint commitment, even if the other party thinks there is. International treaties are most often predicated on *verifiability*, that is, on ways to assuage suspicions as they arise. But suspicion at any level (even a belief that the other party believes that *you* are suspicious) implies that there is no mutual belief that the goals of the treaty are shared. Thus, there is no joint commitment, and like the failed convoy example, the treaty will not be robust in difficult situations. Sad, but true. What it takes to build *trust* in potentially adversarial situations is perhaps the single most delicate aspect of multi-agent interaction. Our account of joint commitment obviously does not provide criteria for avoiding deception or for recognizing true commitment when it exists; but it does state precisely what one is trying to recognize, and what believing in a commitment amounts to.

Acknowledgments

This research was supported by a grant from the National Aeronautics and Space Administration to SRI International, subcontracted from Stanford University, for work on "Intelligent Communicating Agents," and by a contract from ATR International to SRI International. The Toronto authors were supported in part by a grant from the Natural Sciences and Engineering Research Council of Canada.

References

[Cohen and Levesque, 1990] P. R. Cohen and H. J. Levesque. Intention is choice with commitment. *Artificial Intelligence*, 42(3), 1990.

[Cohen and Levesque, in press] P. R. Cohen and H. J. Levesque. Rational interaction as the basis for communication. In P. R. Cohen, J. Morgan, and M. E. Pollack, editors, *Intentions in Communication*. M.I.T. Press, Cambridge, Massachusetts, in press.

[Cohen *et al.*, 1990] P. R. Cohen, H. J. Levesque, J. Nunes, and S. L. Oviatt. Task-oriented dialogue as a consequence of joint activity, in preparation, 1990.

[Grosz and Sidner, in press] B. Grosz and C. Sidner. Plans for discourse. In P. R. Cohen, J. Morgan, and M. E. Pollack, editors, *Intentions in Communication*. M.I.T. Press, Cambridge, Massachusetts, in press.

[Halpern and Fagin, 1985] J. Y. Halpern and R. Fagin. A formal model of knowledge, action, and communication in distributed systems: Preliminary report. In *Proceedings of the 4th ACM Conference on Principles of Distributed Computing*, New York City, New York, 1985. Association for Computing Machinery.

[Searle, in press] J. R. Searle. Collective intentionality. In P. R. Cohen, J. Morgan, and M. E. Pollack, editors, *Intentions in Communication*. M.I.T. Press, Cambridge, Massachusetts, in press.

[Tuomela and Miller, 1988] R. Tuomela and K. Miller. We-intentions. *Philosophical Studies*, 53:367–389, 1988.

Negotiation and Conflict Resolution in Non-Cooperative Domains

Gilad Zlotkin*
Jeffrey S. Rosenschein
Computer Science Department, Hebrew University
Givat Ram, Jerusalem, Israel
gilad@humus.huji.ac.il, jeff@humus.huji.ac.il

Abstract

In previous work [Zlotkin and Rosenschein, 1989a], we have developed a negotiation protocol and offered some negotiation strategies that are in equilibrium. This negotiation process can be used only when the "negotiation set" (NS) is not empty. Domains in which the negotiation sets are never empty are called cooperative domains; in general *non-cooperative* domains, the negotiation set is sometimes empty.

In this paper, we present a theoretical negotiation model for rational agents in general non-cooperative domains. Necessary and sufficient conditions for cooperation are outlined. By redefining the concept of utility, we are able to enlarge the number of situations that have a cooperative solution. An approach is offered for conflict resolution, and it is shown that even in a conflict situation, partial cooperative steps can be taken by interacting agents (that is, agents in fundamental conflict might still agree to cooperate up to a certain point).

A Unified Negotiation Protocol is developed that can be used in all cases. It is shown that in certain borderline cooperative situations, a partial cooperative agreement (i.e., one that does not achieve all agents' goals) might be preferred by all agents, even though there exists a rational agreement that would achieve all their goals.

Introduction

The subject of negotiation has been of continuing interest in the distributed artificial intelligence (DAI) community [Smith, 1978; Rosenschein and Genesereth, 1985; Durfee, 1988; Malone *et al.*, 1988; Sycara, 1988; Sycara, 1989; Kuwabara and Lesser, 1989; Conry *et al.*, 1988]. The operation of cooperating, intelligent autonomous agents would be greatly enhanced if they were able to communicate their respective desires and compromise to reach mutually beneficial agreements. The work described in this paper follows the general direction of [Rosenschein and Genesereth, 1985; Zlotkin and Rosenschein, 1989a] in treating negotiation in the spirit of game theory, while altering game theory assumptions that are irrelevant to DAI.

Previous work [Zlotkin and Rosenschein, 1989a] discussed inter-agent negotiation protocols and negotiation strategies that were in equilibrium, but could only be used if the so-called "negotiation set" [Harsanyi, 1977] was not empty. Cooperative domains are those in which NS is never empty; in this paper, we present a theoretical negotiation model for general *non-cooperative* domains (where NS might be empty).

General Definitions

Two autonomous agents A and B share the same world; this world is in some initial state s. Each agent wants the world to satisfy a set of goal conditions.

Definition 1 Goals

- *The* goal *of agent* $i \in \{A, B\}$, g_i, *is a set of predicates that agent* i *wants the world to satisfy.*
- G_i *stands for the set of world states that satisfy all the predicates in* g_i.

Both agents have the same set of operations OP that they can perform. An operation o in OP moves the world from one state to another; it is a function o: ST $\rightarrow$ ST where ST is the set of all possible world states.

Definition 2 Plans

- *A* one-agent plan *to move the world from state* s *to state* f *in* ST *is a list* $[o_1, o_2, \ldots, o_n]$ *of operations from* OP *such that* $f = o_n(o_{n-1}(\ldots o_1(s)\ldots))$.
- *A* joint plan *to move the world from state* s *to state* f *in* ST *is a pair of one-agent plans* (P_A, P_B) *and a schedule.*

A schedule is a partial order over the union of actions in the two one-agent plans. It specifies that some actions cannot be taken until other actions are completed; because it is a *partial* order, it of course allows

*Supported in part by the Leibniz Center for Research in Computer Science.

simultaneous actions by different agents. If the initial state of the world is s and each agent i executes plan P_i according to the schedule, then the final state of the world will be f. We will sometimes write J to stand for a joint plan (P_A, P_B).

Definition 3 Costs

- *There exists a* cost function, Cost: OP $\rightarrow \mathbb{N}$.
- *For each one-agent plan* $P = [o_1, o_2, \ldots, o_n]$, Cost($P$) *is defined to be* $\sum_{k=1}^{n} \text{Cost}(o_k)$.
- *For each joint plan* $J = (P_A, P_B)$, $\text{Cost}_i(J)$ *is defined to be* $\text{Cost}(P_i)$.

Note that cost is a function over an operation—it is independent of the state in which the operation is carried out. This definition, however, is not critical to the subsequent discussion. Our theory is insensitive to the precise definition of any single operation's cost. What is important is the ability of an agent to measure the cost of a one-agent plan, and the cost of one agent's part of a joint multi-agent plan.

Definition 4 Best Plans

- $s \rightarrow f$ *is the minimal* Cost *one-agent plan that moves the world from state* s *to state* f. *If a plan like this does not exist, then* $s \rightarrow f$ *is undefined.*
- $s \rightarrow F$ *(where* s *is a world state and* F *is a set of world states) is the minimal* Cost *one-agent plan that moves the world from state* s *to one of the states in* F*:*

$$\text{Cost}(s \rightarrow F) = \min_{f \in F: s \rightarrow f \text{ is defined}} \text{Cost}(s \rightarrow f)$$

Example: The Blocks World Domain

There is a table and a set of blocks. A block can be on the table or on some other block, and there is no limit to the height of a stack of blocks. However, on the table there are only a bounded number of slots into which blocks can be placed. There are two operations in this world: PickUp(i) — Pick up the top block in slot i (can be executed whenever slot i is not empty), and PutDown(i) — Put down the block which is currently being held into slot i. An agent can hold no more than one block at a time. Each operation costs 1.[1]

Underlying Assumptions

In [Zlotkin and Rosenschein, 1989a], we introduced several assumptions that are in force for our discussion here as well (the final two assumptions were implicit in previous work):[2]

1. **Utility Maximizer:** *Each agent wants to maximize his expected utility.*
2. **Complete Knowledge:** *Each agent knows all relevant information.*
3. **No History:** *There is no consideration given by the agents to the past or future; each negotiation stands alone.*
4. **Fixed Goals:** *Though the agents negotiate with one another over operations, their goals remain fixed.*
5. **Bilateral Negotiation:** *In a multi-agent encounter, negotiation is done between a pair of agents at a time.*

Deals and the Negotiation Set

The agents negotiate on a joint plan that brings the world to a state that satisfies both agents' goals.

Definition 5 Deals

- *A* Pure Deal *is a joint plan* (P_A, P_B) *that moves the world from state* s *to a state in* $G_A \cap G_B$.
- *A* Deal *is a mixed joint plan* $(P_A, P_B){:}\,p$; $0 \leq p \leq 1 \in \mathbb{R}$.

The semantics of a Deal is that the agents will perform the joint plan (P_A, P_B) *with probability* p*, or the symmetric joint plan* (P_B, P_A) *with probability* $1 - p$.

- *If* $\delta = (J{:}\,p)$ *is a* Deal, *then* $\text{Cost}_i(\delta)$ *is defined to be* $p\text{Cost}_i(J) + (1-p)\text{Cost}_j(J)$ *(where* j *is* i*'s opponent).*
- *If* δ *is a* Deal, *then* $\text{Utility}_i(\delta)$ *is defined to be* $\text{Cost}(s \rightarrow G_i) - \text{Cost}_i(\delta)$.

The utility for an agent from a deal is simply the difference between the cost of achieving his goal alone and his expected part of the deal.

- *A* Deal δ *is* individual rational *if, for all* i, $\text{Utility}_i(\delta) \geq 0$.
- *A* Deal δ *is* pareto optimal *if there does not exist another* Deal *which dominates it—there does not exist another* Deal *which is better for one of the agents and not worse for the other.*
- *The* negotiation set NS *is the set of all the deals that are both individual rational and pareto optimal.*

These definitions of an individual rational deal, a pareto optimal deal, and the negotiation set NS are standard definitions from game theory and bargaining theory (see, for example, [Luce and Raiffa, 1957; Nash, 1950; Harsanyi, 1977]).

[1] Note that actions are relative to the current state, and don't name a particular block for manipulation. This emphasizes the role of the schedule in ensuring that the two agents move the correct blocks at the correct times.

[2] See [Zlotkin and Rosenschein, 1990b] for a discussion of how the Fixed Goals assumption can be relaxed. The relaxation of the Complete Knowledge assumption, in specific circumstances, was treated in [Zlotkin and Rosenschein, 1989a]. Future work will further examine the consequences of removing one or more of these assumptions, such as the No History assumption and the Bilateral Negotiation assumption.

Conditions for Cooperation

A necessary condition for NS to be non-empty is that there is no contradiction between the two agents' goals, i.e., $G_A \cap G_B \neq \emptyset$.[3] This condition is not sufficient, however, because even when there is no contradiction between agents' goals, there may still be a *conflict* between them. In such a conflict situation, any joint plan that satisfies the union of goals will cost one agent (or both) more than he would have spent achieving his own goal in isolation (that is, no deal is individual rational).

Example: The initial state can be seen at the left in Figure 1. g_A is "The Black block is at slot 2 but not on the table" and g_B is "The White block is at slot 1 but not on the table".

In order to achieve his goal alone, each agent has to execute one PickUp and then one PutDown; $\text{Cost}(s \rightarrow G_i) = 2$. The two goals do not contradict each other, because there exists a state in the world which satisfies them both, as can be seen on the right side of Figure 1. There does not exist a joint plan that moves the world from the initial state to a state that satisfies the two goals with total cost less than 8—that is, no deal is individual rational.

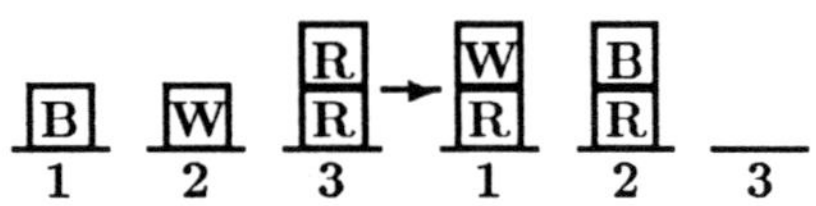

Figure 1: Conflict exists even though union of goals is achievable

The existence of a joint plan that moves the world from its initial state s to a state in $G_A \cap G_B$ is a necessary condition for NS to be non-empty. When this condition is not true, we will call it a *conflict* situation. Ways in which this conflict can be resolved will be discussed in the Conflict Resolution section below.

Definition 6 Sum and Min Conditions

- *A joint plan J will be said to satisfy the* sum condition *if*

$$\sum_{i \in \{A,B\}} \text{Cost}(s \rightarrow G_i) \geq \sum_{i \in \{A,B\}} \text{Cost}_i(J).$$

- *A joint plan J will be said to satisfy the* min condition *if*

$$\min_{i \in \{A,B\}} \text{Cost}(s \rightarrow G_i) \geq \min_{i \in \{A,B\}} \text{Cost}_i(J).$$

Theorem 1 *There exists a joint plan that moves the world from its initial state s to a state in $G_A \cap G_B$ and also satisfies the sum and the min conditions, if and only if* $\text{NS} \neq \emptyset$.

[3]All the states that exist in the intersection of the agents' goal sets might, of course, not be reachable given the domain of actions that the agents have at their disposal. See [Zlotkin and Rosenschein, 1989b] for an example of a domain in which such a situation can occur.

Proof. For the proof of this theorem and subsequent theorems, see [Zlotkin and Rosenschein, 1990a]. □

When the conditions of Theorem 1 are true, we will say that the situations are cooperative.

Redefinition of Utility

In non-conflict situations, if neither the min nor the sum conditions are true, then in order for the agents to cooperatively bring the world to a state in $G_A \cap G_B$, at least one of them will have do more than if he were alone in the world and achieved only his own goals. Will either one of them agree to do extra work? It depends on how important each g_i is to agent i, i.e., how much i is willing to pay in order to bring the world to a state in G_i.

The Worth of a Goal

Definition 7 *Let W_i be the maximum* expected *cost that agent i is willing to pay in order to achieve his goal g_i.*

We assume that such an upper bound exists. There may be situations and domains in which there is no limit to the cost that an agent is willing to pay in order to achieve his goal—he would be willing to pay *any* cost (see [Zlotkin and Rosenschein, 1989b]). That situation, however, is beyond the scope of this paper.

The declaration of Utility can be usefully altered as follows:

Definition 8 *If δ is a deal, then* $\text{Utility}_i(\delta)$ *is defined to be* $W_i - \text{Cost}_i(\delta)$.

The utility for an agent of a deal is the difference between W_i and the cost of his part of the deal. If an agent achieves his goal alone, his utility is the difference between the worth of the goal and the cost that he pays to achieve the goal.

Theorem 2 *If in Definition 6 we change every occurrence of* $\text{Cost}(s \rightarrow G_i)$ *to W_i, then Theorem 1 is still true.*

Types of Interactions

Before the redefinition of utility, we had two possible situations for agent interaction: *conflict* and *cooperative*. A conflict situation implied a contradiction between the agents' goals, or a cost to achieving the union of their goals that was so high, no deal was individual rational.

Now that utility has been redefined, we have three possible situations for agent interaction: conflict, *compromise*, and cooperative.

- A *conflict* situation is one in which (as before) the negotiation set is empty—no individual rational deals exist.
- A *compromise* situation is one where there are individual rational deals. However, agents would prefer to be alone in the world, and to accomplish their

goals alone. Since they are forced to cope with the presence of other agents, they will agree on a deal. All of the deals in NS are better for both agents than leaving the world in its initial state s.

- A *cooperative* situation is one in which there exists a deal in the negotiation set that is preferred by both agents over achieving their goals alone. Here, every agent welcomes the existence of the other agents.

When the negotiation set is not empty, we can distinguish between compromise and cooperative situations using the following criterion. If for all i, $W_i \leq \text{Cost}(s \rightarrow G_i)$ and $\text{NS} \neq \emptyset$, then it is a cooperative situation; otherwise, it is a compromise situation.[4]

Conflict Resolution

What can be done when the agents are in a conflict situation?

If we dropped Assumption 3 ("No History"), then we could offer some mechanism in which agents can "buy their freedom" by making a promise to their opponent regarding future actions. In this case, they will negotiate over the price of freedom. A discussion of altering utilities through promises, however, is beyond the scope of this paper.

A simpler solution would be for the agents to flip a coin in order to decide who is going to achieve his goal and who is going to be disappointed. In this case they will negotiate on the probabilities (weightings) of the coin toss. If they run into a conflict during the negotiation (fail to agree on the coin toss weighting), the world will stay in its initial state s.[5]

Utility for agent i in general is the difference between the worth for i of the final state of the world and the cost that i spends in order to bring the world to its final state.

If agent i wins the coin toss, then he can reach his goal. In this case, his utility is W_i (the worth of his goal) minus the cost he has to spend in order to bring the word to a state that satisfies his goal. If agent i loses the coin toss, his opponent is going to bring the world to a state that satisfies his opponent's goal. This state will not satisfy g_i (otherwise it would not be a conflict situation). The final state of the world in this case is worth 0 to agent i, but he is not going to spend *anything* to bring the world to this state, so his total utility in the case where he loses the coin toss is 0.

If the agents agree to flip a coin with weighting q, then the utility for agent i of such a deal is $q_i(W_i - \text{Cost}(s \rightarrow G_i))$, where $q_A = q; q_B = 1 - q$.

Example: There is one block at slot 1. g_A is "The block is at slot 2" and g_B is "The block is at slot 3"; $W_A = 12$, and $W_B = 22$. The agents will agree here on the deal that will give them the same utility—to flip a coin with weighting $\frac{2}{3}$. This deal will give them each a utility of $\frac{20}{3}$.[6]

Cooperation in Conflict Resolution

The agents may find that, instead of simply flipping a coin in a conflict situation, it is better for them to cooperatively reach a new world state (not satisfying either of their goals) and *then* to flip the coin in order to decide whose goal will ultimately be satisfied.

Example: One agent wants the block currently in slot 1 to be in slot 2; the other agent wants it to be in slot 3. In addition, both agents share the goal of swapping the two blocks currently in slot 4 (i.e., reverse the stack's order). See the left side of Figure 2. Assume that $W_A = W_B = 12$. The cost for an agent of achieving his goal alone is 10. If the agents decide to flip a coin in the initial state, they will agree on a weighting of $\frac{1}{2}$, which brings them a utility of 1 (i.e., $\frac{1}{2}(12 - 10)$). If, on the other hand, they decide to do the swap cooperatively (at cost of 2 each), bringing the world to the state shown on the right of Figure 2, and *then* flip a coin, they will still agree on a weighting of $\frac{1}{2}$, which brings them an overall utility of 4 (i.e., $\frac{1}{2}(12 - 2 - 2)$).

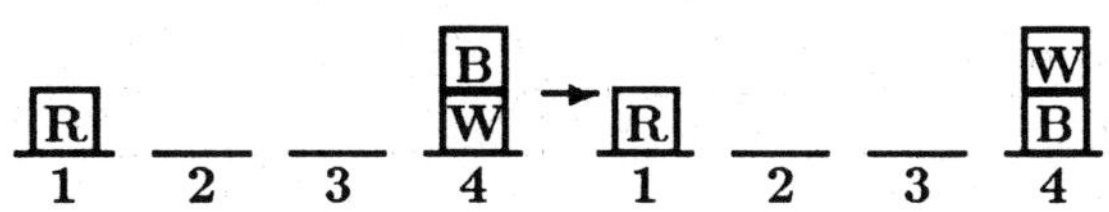

Figure 2: Cooperation up to a certain point

Definition 9 *A* Semi-Cooperative Deal *is a tuple (t, J, q) where t is a world state, J is a mixed joint plan that moves the world from the initial state s to state t, and $0 \leq q \leq 1 \in \mathbb{R}$ is the weighting of the coin toss—the probability that agent A will achieve his goal.*

The semantics of such a deal is that the two agents will perform the mixed joint plan J, and will bring the world to state t; then, in state t, they will flip a coin with weighting q in order to decide who continues the plan towards their own goal.

Definition 10

$$\begin{aligned}\text{Utility}_i(t, J, q) &= q_i(W_i - \text{Cost}_i(J) - \text{Cost}(t \rightarrow G_i)) \\ &\quad -(1 - q_i)\text{Cost}_i(J) \\ &= q_i(W_i - \text{Cost}_i(t \rightarrow G_i)) - \text{Cost}_i(J)\end{aligned}$$

[4] An example of a compromise situation can be found in Figure 1 when W_i is greater than 4.

[5] There is a special case where the initial state s already satisfies one of the agent's goals, let's say agent A (s cannot satisfy both goals since then we would not have a conflict situation). In this case, the only agreement that can be reached is to leave the world in state s. Agent A will not agree to any other deal and will cause the negotiation to fail.

[6] We have $\frac{2}{3}(12 - 2) = \frac{1}{3}(22 - 2) = \frac{20}{3}$.

Unified Negotiation Protocol (UNP)

In cooperative and compromise situations, the agents negotiate on deals that are mixed joint plans, $J:p$ (cooperative deals). In a conflict situation, the agents negotiate on deals of the form (t, J, q) (semi-cooperative deals).

We would like to find a Unified Negotiation Protocol (UNP) that the agents can use in any situation. The main benefit would be that the agents would not have to know (or even to agree), prior to the negotiation process, on the type of situation that they are in. Determining whether the situation is cooperative or not may be difficult. An agent may not have full information at the beginning of a negotiation; he may gain more information during the negotiation, for example, from the deals that his opponents are offering, and from computations he himself is doing in order to generate the next offered deal. Agents may only know near the end of a negotiation just what kind of situation they are in.

The semi-cooperative deals (t, J, q) are general enough so that, with some minor changes in the definition of utility, they may be used in the Unified Negotiation Protocol. A *cooperative* deal which is a mixed joint plan $J:p$ can also be represented as $(J(s), J:p, 0)$ where $J(s)$ is the final world state resulting from the joint plan J when the initial state is s. $J(s)$ is in $G_A \cap G_B$, so the result of the coin flip at state $J(s)$ does not really matter (since none of the agents would want to change the state of the world anyway).

What we advocate is for agents to negotiate always using semi-cooperative deals. A cooperative agreement can still be reached (when the situation is cooperative) because the cooperative deals are a subset of the semi-cooperative deals.

Definition 11

- *If (t, J, q) is a semi-cooperative deal, then f_i will be defined as the final state of the world when agent i wins the coin toss in state t. $f_i = (t \rightarrow G_i)(t) \in G_i$.*
- *$W_i(f_j) = W_i$ when $f_j \in G_i$, otherwise it is 0.*
- $\text{Utility}_i(t, J, q) = q_i(W_i - \text{Cost}_i(t \rightarrow G_i)) + (1 - q_i)W_i(f_j) - \text{Cost}_i(J)$
- *Two deals d_1, d_2 (cooperative or semi-cooperative) will be said to be* equivalent *if* $\forall i$ $\text{Utility}_i(d_1) = \text{Utility}_i(d_2)$. *The calculation of the utility of each deal is done according to the type of the deal (cooperative or semi-cooperative).*

Theorem 3 *If* $\forall i$ $W_i \geq \text{Cost}(s \rightarrow G_i)$, *then* $\text{NS} \neq \emptyset$.

If $W_i < \text{Cost}(s \rightarrow G_i)$ then agent i cannot even achieve his goal alone. This does not necessarily mean that NS is empty—Theorem 3 stated in the opposite direction is not true.

Theorem 4 *For a semi-cooperative deal* $(t, J, q) \in$ NS, *if there exists an i such that $f_i \in G_A \cap G_B$, then this semi-cooperative deal is equivalent to some cooperative deal.*

It is easy to see that whenever $f_A, f_B \notin G_A \cap G_B$, then the definition of utility in Definition 10 is the same as that in Definition 11.

UNP in a Cooperative Situation

In a cooperative situation, there is always an individual rational cooperative deal, where both agents' goals are satisfied. One might expect that in such a situation, even if the agents use the Unified Negotiation Protocol, they will agree on a semi-cooperative deal that is equivalent to the cooperative deal, i.e., both goals would be achieved. Surprisingly, this is not the case: there might exist a semi-cooperative deal that dominates all cooperative deals and does *not* achieve both agents' goals. See the example below.

It turns out that this is a borderline situation, brought about because W_i is low. As long as W_i is high enough, any semi-cooperative deal that agents agree on in a cooperative situation will be equivalent to a cooperative deal.

Example: The initial situation in Figure 3 consists of 5 duplications of the example from Figure 1, in slots 1 to 15. In addition, two slots (16 and 17) each contain a stack of 2 blocks. g_A is "Black blocks are in slots 2, 5, 8, 11 and 14 but not on the table; the blocks in slots 16 and 17 are swapped" (i.e., each tower is reversed). g_B is "White blocks are in slots 1, 4, 7, 10 and 13 but not on the table; the blocks in slots 16 and 17 are swapped".

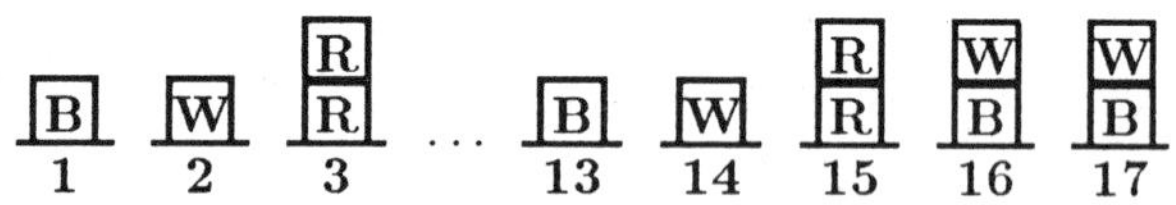

Figure 3: Semi-Cooperative Agreement in a Cooperative Situation

For all i, $\text{Cost}(s \rightarrow G_i) = 26 = (2 \times 5) + (8 \times 2)$. Let J be the minimal cost joint plan that achieves both goals. The cooperative deal $J:\frac{1}{2}$ satisfies the min and the sum conditions, because for all i, $\text{Cost}_i(J:\frac{1}{2}) = 24 = \frac{1}{2}((8 \times 5) + (4 \times 2))$. This situation is cooperative. For all i, $\text{Utility}_i(J:\frac{1}{2}) = 26 - 24 = 2$. Let t be the state where the blocks in slots 16 and 17 are swapped, and the other slots are unchanged. Let T be the minimal cost joint plan that moves the world to state t. For all i, $\text{Utility}_i(t, T:\frac{1}{2}, \frac{1}{2}) = \frac{1}{2}(26 - (2 \times 5)) - (2 \times 2) = 4$. The semi-cooperative deal $(t, T:\frac{1}{2}, \frac{1}{2})$ thus dominates the cooperative deal $J:\frac{1}{2}$ even though it is a cooperative situation.

Conclusions

We have presented a theoretical negotiation model that encompasses both cooperative and conflict situations. Necessary and sufficient conditions for cooperation were outlined. By redefining the concept of utility, a new boundary type of interaction, a *compromise* situation, was demarcated. A solution was offered for conflict resolution, and it was shown that even in a conflict situation, partial cooperative steps can be taken by interacting agents. A Unified Negotiation Protocol was developed that can be used in all cases, whether cooperative, compromise, or conflict. It was shown that in certain borderline cooperative situations, a partial cooperative agreement (i.e., one that does not achieve all agents' goals) might be preferred by all agents.

References

[Conry *et al.*, 1988] Susan E. Conry, Robert A. Meyer, and Victor R. Lesser. Multistage negotiation in distributed planning. In Alan H. Bond and Les Gasser, editors, *Readings in Distributed Artificial Intelligence*, pages 367–384. Morgan Kaufmann Publishers, Inc., San Mateo, California, 1988.

[Durfee, 1988] Edmund H. Durfee. *Coordination of Distributed Problem Solvers.* Kluwer Academic Publishers, Boston, 1988.

[Harsanyi, 1977] John C. Harsanyi. *Rational Behavior and Bargaining Equilibrium in Games and Social Situations.* Cambridge University Press, Cambridge, 1977.

[Kuwabara and Lesser, 1989] Kazuhiro Kuwabara and Victor R. Lesser. Extended protocol for multistage negotiation. In *Proceedings of the Ninth Workshop on Distributed Artificial Intelligence*, pages 129–161, Rosario, Washington, September 1989.

[Luce and Raiffa, 1957] R. Duncan Luce and Howard Raiffa. *Games and Decisions.* John Wiley & Sons, Inc., New York, 1957.

[Malone *et al.*, 1988] Thomas W. Malone, Richard E. Fikes, and M. T. Howard. Enterprise: A market-like task scheduler for distributed computing environments. In B. A. Huberman, editor, *The Ecology of Computation*, pages 177–205. North-Holland Publishing Company, Amsterdam, 1988.

[Nash, 1950] John F. Nash. The bargaining problem. *Econometrica*, 28:155–162, 1950.

[Rosenschein and Genesereth, 1985] Jeffrey S. Rosenschein and Michael R. Genesereth. Deals among rational agents. In *Proceedings of the Ninth International Joint Conference on Artificial Intelligence*, pages 91–99, Los Angeles, California, August 1985.

[Smith, 1978] Reid G. Smith. *A Framework for Problem Solving in a Distributed Processing Environment.* PhD thesis, Stanford University, 1978.

[Sycara, 1988] Katia P. Sycara. Resolving goal conflicts via negotiation. In *Proceedings of the Seventh National Conference on Artificial Intelligence*, pages 245–250, St. Paul, Minnesota, August 1988.

[Sycara, 1989] Katia P. Sycara. Argumentation: Planning other agents' plans. In *Proceedings of the The Eleventh International Joint Conference on Artificial Intelligence*, pages 517–523, Detroit, Michigan, August 1989.

[Zlotkin and Rosenschein, 1989a] Gilad Zlotkin and Jeffrey S. Rosenschein. Negotiation and task sharing among autonomous agents in cooperative domains. In *Proceedings of the The Eleventh International Joint Conference on Artificial Intelligence*, pages 912–917, Detroit, Michigan, August 1989. The International Joint Conference on Artificial Intelligence.

[Zlotkin and Rosenschein, 1989b] Gilad Zlotkin and Jeffrey S. Rosenschein. Negotiation and task sharing in a non-cooperative domain. In *Proceedings of the Ninth Workshop on Distributed Artificial Intelligence*, pages 307–327, Rosario, Washington, September 1989.

[Zlotkin and Rosenschein, 1990a] Gilad Zlotkin and Jeffrey S. Rosenschein. Negotiation and conflict resolution in non-cooperative domains. Technical Report 90-6, Computer Science Department, Hebrew University, Jerusalem, Israel, 1990.

[Zlotkin and Rosenschein, 1990b] Gilad Zlotkin and Jeffrey S. Rosenschein. Negotiation and goal relaxation. Technical report, Computer Science Department, Hebrew University, Jerusalem, Israel, 1990. In preparation.

Probabilistic Semantics for Cost Based Abduction*

Eugene Charniak and **Solomon E. Shimony**
Computer Science Department
Box 1910, Brown University
Providence, RI 02906
ec@cs.brown.edu and ses@cs.brown.edu

Abstract

Cost-based abduction attempts to find the best explanation for a set of facts by finding a minimal cost proof for the facts. The costs are computed by summing the costs of the assumptions necessary for the proof plus the cost of the rules. We examine existing methods for constructing explanations (proofs), as a minimization problem on a DAG. We then define a probabilistic semantics for the costs, and prove the equivalence of the cost minimization problem to the Bayesian network MAP solution of the system.

Introduction

The deductive nomological theory of explanation has it that an explanation is a proof of what is to be explained from knowledge of the world plus a set of assumptions. While there are well known problems with the theory [McDermott, 1987], it is nevertheless an attractive one for people in AI, since it ties something we know little about (explanation) to something we as a community know quite a bit more about (theorem proving).

From an AI viewpoint the *real* problems with the deductive nomological theory are not the abstract ones of the philosopher, but rather the immediate one that there are many possible sets of assumptions, which together with our knowledge of the world would serve to explain (prove) the desired fact. Somehow, a choice between the sets must be made. Several researchers ([Kautz and Allen, 1986], [Genesereth, 1984]), have used the above technique and graded assumption sets by a) only allowing some formulas to be assumed, and b) preferring sets with the minimum number of assumptions. Obviously, these simplifying assumptions are severely limiting.

Cost-based abduction is the obvious generalization of these theorem proving techniques. It allows any formula to be assumed, and assigns all assumed formulas a non-negative real number cost. The best explanation is then the proof with the minimum cost (a formal definition of cost-based abduction will be given in the next section). Something very similar to what we are calling "cost-based abduction" has been proposed and implemented by Hobbs and Stickel [Hobbs and Stickel, 1988], and it appears to be a promising method for handling abductive problems. However, their scheme has one immediate drawback; at the present moment the "costs" have no adequate semantics: for Hobbs and Stickel they are simply numbers pulled out of a hat.

In what follows we will provide a probabilistic semantics for cost-based abduction, according to the following outline. First, we will formalize a cost-based proof (explanation) of some facts as an augmented DAG, and exploit the similarity of the DAG to a belief network (Bayesian network, [Pearl, 1988]) to define a probability distribution using the topology of the DAG plus the costs. A major theorem of the paper will show that the maximum a-posteriori (MAP) assignment of truth values to the network corresponds to the minimal cost proof[1]. In the discussion these results will be explained in a more intuitive fashion.

Appelt, in [Appelt, 1990], has attempted to give a semantics for the Hobbs-Stickel cost scheme. We will discuss the Hobbs-Stickel approach in more detail, and show why Appelt's semantics is not adequate. Lastly, we will briefly mention our practical experience with an implementation of cost-based abduction.

DAG Representation for Rule Systems

A rule based system with assumability costs has rules of the form:

$$R: \quad p_1 \wedge p_2 \wedge \ldots \wedge p_n \quad \rightarrow \quad q$$

with costs $c(p_i)$ for each conjunct, and a cost $c(R)$ for applying the rule. A conjunct has the same cost in all the rules where it appears on the left hand side (LHS). The cost of proving q with this rule is the cost of all the conjuncts assumed, plus the cost of the rule. For

*This work has been supported in part by the National Science Foundation under grants IST 8416034 and IST 8515005 and Office of Naval Research under grant N00014-79-C-0529. We also wish to thank Robert Goldman for helpful comments about the semantics, and Randy Calistri for proof reading earlier versions of this paper.

[1] A MAP assignment is the way to set the values of all random variables such that their joint probability is highest.

the rest of this section and the next one, we assume without loss of generality that all rule costs are 0. We can do this by adding a p_0 (that appears nowhere else) to the LHS, with a cost $c(p_0) = c(R)$. We want to find a minimal cost proof for some fact set $\mathcal{E}$ ("the evidence").

We now formalize the minimum cost proof problem as a minimization problem on a weighted AND/OR DAG (acronym WAODAG). We use a three valued logic (values $\{T, F, U\}$), augmented by symbols for keeping track of assumed nodes, versus implied nodes. The values we actually use are $Q = \{T^A, T, U, F^A, F\}$, where U stands for undetermined (intuitively: either true or false), T for true, F for false, and the A superscript stands for "assumed". We use $u \searrow v$ to say that u is an immediate parent of v.

Definition 1 *A WAODAG is a 4-tuple (G, c, r, s), where:*

1. G is a connected directed acyclic graph, $G = (V, E)$.
2. c is a function from $\{V \times Q\}$ to the non-negative reals, called the *cost function.* For values T, F, U, we have zero cost. $c(v) \equiv c(v, T^A)$.
3. r is a function from V to {AND, OR}, called the *label.* A node labeled AND is called an AND node, etc.
4. s is an AND node with outdegree 0 (*evidence* node).

Definition 2 *A truth assignment for a WAODAG is a function f from V to Q. A truth assignment is a (possibly partial)* model *iff the following conditions hold:*

1. If v is a root node (a node with in-degree 0) then $f(v) \in \{T^A, U, F^A\}$.
2. If v is a non-root node, then it can only be assigned values consistent with its parents and its label (AND or OR), and if its parents do not uniquely determine the node's truth value, it can have any value in $\{T^A, F^A, U\}$.

The exact details of consistency are pursued in [Charniak and Shimony, 1990], but should be obvious from the well-known definitions of AND and OR in 3-valued logic. Note that in our DAG, an OR node is true if at least one of its *parents* is true, as in belief networks, but *not* as commonly used for search AND/OR trees. A non-root node may still be assumed true if its parents determine that it has to be true.

Intuitively, an assignment is a model if the AND/OR constraints are obeyed. A node v where $f(v) = T^A$ in an assignment, is called an *assumed true* node relative to the assignment. Likewise for other values of $f(v)$.

Definition 3 *A model for a WAODAG is* satisfying *iff* $f(s) \in \{T^A, T\}$.

Definition 4 *The cost of an assignment $\mathcal{A}$ for a WAODAG is the sum*

$$C = \sum_{v \in V} c(v, f(v))$$

The Best Selection Problem is the problem of finding a minimal cost (possibly not unique) satisfying model for a given WAODAG. The Given Cost Selection Problem is that of finding a satisfying model with cost less than or equal to a given cost. Note that in a partial model, assuming a node false is useless, as such an assumption cannot contribute towards a satisfying model.

Theorem 1 *The Given Cost Selection Problem is NP-complete.*

The theorem is easily proved via a reduction from Vertex Cover (see [Garey and Johnson, 1979]). We present the complete proof in [Charniak and Shimony, 1990]. The Best Selection Problem is clearly at least as hard as the Given Cost Selection Problem, because if we had a minimal cost satisfying model, we can find its cost in $O(|V|)$, and give an answer to the Given Cost Selection Problem. Thus, the Best Selection Problem is NP-hard.

We will now make the connection between the graphs and the rule based system. We assume that exactly all possibly relevant rule and fact instances are given. How that may be achieved is beyond the scope of this paper.

Theorem 2 *The Best Selection Problem subsumes the problem of finding a minimal cost proof for the rule-based system with assumability costs, assuming that the rule based system is acyclic.*

Informal proof: by constructing a WAODAG (i.e. constructing the graph G, and assigning labels and costs) for the rule instance set, as follows:

1. For each literal in any rule[2] R's LHS, construct OR node v, and set $c(v, T^A)$ to the cost of the literal in the system. For each literal appearing only on the RHS of rules, construct an OR node v, with $c(v, T^A) = \infty$.
2. For each LHS of a rule R, construct and AND node v with $c(v, T^A) = \infty$, make it a parent of the node constructed for the literal on the RHS of R (in step 1), and make it a child of all the nodes constructed for the literals in the LHS of R.
3. Construct an AND node s, with parent nodes corresponding to the facts to be proved.

Example: Given the rule instances in the table, used for word-sense disambiguation in natural language, with rb=river-bank(bank1), sb=savings-bank(bank1), w=water(water5), p=plant(plant7), we want to explain the evidence: say(bank1)∧say(water5).

	Rules	Literal	Cost
R_1 :	sb → say(bank1)	rb	3
R_2 :	rb → say(bank1)	sb	2
R_3 :	rb ∧ w → say(water5)	w	2
R_4 :	p ∧ w → say(water5)	p	4

[2]We assume that literals with the same name in different rules are the same literal.

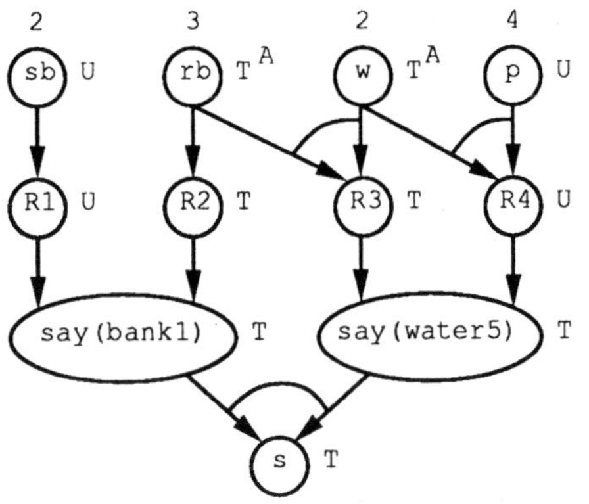

Figure 1: WAODAG for our example rules

Using the above construction, we get the WAODAG in figure 1, with best partial model (total cost 5) shown.

Definition 5 *A root-only assignment for a WAODAG is an assignment where only root nodes may be assumed (i.e. have values in $\{F^A, T^A\}$).*

It is possible to force root-only assignments for a WAODAG to be globally minimal by setting the cost of all non-root nodes to infinity (in practice, it suffices to set a cost greater than the sum of the root costs). We now show that given an WAODAG D, we can create another WAODAG D', such that the semantics of minimal models is not changed, i.e. if a non-root node is selected in D, some corresponding new root node is selected in D'.

Proof: by construction, as follows ($D' = D$ initially):

1. For each AND node v with cost $c(v, T^A) < \infty$ in D', construct an OR node w in D', and a new root node u, where $c(u, T^A) = c(v, T^A)$, and make both $v \searrow w$ and $u \searrow w$. Transfer all the children[3] of v to w.
2. For each OR node v with cost $c(v, T^A) < \infty$, create a new root-node u, with $c(u, T^A) = c(v, T^A)$. Make $u \searrow v$.
3. For all non-root nodes v in D', set $c(v, T^A) = \infty$.

It is clear that each time a node is selected in a minimal cost model of D to be assumed true, the node constructed from it in D' will be assumed true in some root-only minimal cost model for D'.

Definition 6 *An assignment (or model) is* complete *iff* $\forall v \in V,\ f(v) \neq U$.

A variant of the Best Selection Problem is one of selecting a minimal cost *complete* model. Clearly, if the cost of assuming a node false is 0 for all nodes, the solution will be exactly the same as for the partial model Best Selection Problem. However, in our semantics we intend to treat assumability costs as negative logarithms of probabilities (so that summing costs is akin to multiplying probabilities), and we want $P(f(v) = F^A) = 1 - P(f(v) = T^A)$ to hold for all root nodes. Thus, the cost of assuming a node v false is:

$$c(v,\ F^A) = -log(1 - e^{-c(v,\ T^A)})$$

Probabilistic Semantics for WAODAGs

We now provide a probabilistic semantics for the cost based abduction system. We construct a boolean belief network out of the weighted AND/OR DAG, and show the correspondence between the solution to the Best Selection Problem and finding the most likely explanation for a given fact (or set of facts).

We assume that the rule based system is in the WAODAG format with root-only assignment. We now construct a belief network from the given WAODAG, and show that a minimal cost satisfying complete model for the WAODAG corresponds to a maximum-probability assignment of root-nodes given the evidence in the belief network (where the evidence is exactly the set of facts to be proved using the rule system).

From a WAODAG D we construct a belief network B as follows:

1. B has exactly the nodes and arcs of D. Thus, we use the same name for a node of B and the corresponding node of D. Nodes retain their labels[4].
2. Each root node v in B has a prior probability of $e^{-c(v,\ T^A)}$.
3. The node s is the "evidence node", i.e. the event of node s being true is the evidence $\mathcal{E}$.

Defining an assignment for the network analogously with the WAODAG assignment, we assume, without loss of generality, that we are only interested in assignment to the set of root nodes[5]. We want to find the "best" satisfying model $\mathcal{A}$, which assigns values from $\{T^A,\ F^A,\ U\}$ to the set of all root nodes, i.e. the assignment that maximizes $P(\mathcal{A} \mid \mathcal{E})$. An assignment of U to a root node means that it is omitted from the calculation of joint probabilities, as $P(v_i = U) = 1$. Intuitively, we are searching for the most probable explanation for the given evidence. This can be done by running a Bayesian network algorithm for finding Bel* on the root nodes, as defined in [Pearl, 1988]. We now show the following result:

Theorem 3 *In a boolean belief network B constructed as above, a satisfying complete model $\mathcal{A}$ that maximizes*

[3] If the AND node is s, create a new sink AND node, s', and make $w \searrow s'$.

[4] A belief network AND node has a 1 in its conditional distribution array for the case of all parents being true, and 0 elsewhere. An OR node is defined analogously.

[5] Maximizing the probability over assignments to root nodes is equivalent to finding the MAP, when we allow only *complete* models, because a complete assignment for the root nodes induces a unique model for all other nodes.

$P(\mathcal{A} \mid \mathcal{E})$ will also be a minimal cost satisfying complete model for D.

Proof: In a belief network, all root nodes (given no evidence) are mutually independent. Thus, for any assignment of values to root nodes, $\mathcal{A} = (a_1, a_2, ..., a_n)$, where $a_i = (v_i, q_i)$ and $q_i \in \{F^A, T^A\}$[6].

$$P(a_1, a_2, ..., a_n) = P(a_1)\, P(a_2) \, ... \, P(a_n)$$

However, we also have (by definition of conditional probabilities):

$$P(\mathcal{A} \mid \mathcal{E}) = \frac{P(\mathcal{E} \mid \mathcal{A})P(\mathcal{A})}{P(\mathcal{E})}$$

But as $P(\mathcal{E} \mid \mathcal{A}) = 1$ when the assignment is a satisfying model (because all nodes are strict OR and AND nodes), and 0 otherwise, and $P(\mathcal{E})$ is a constant, we can eliminate everything but $P(\mathcal{A})$ from the maximization. Also, we have:

$$P(\mathcal{A}) = \prod_{i=1}^{n} P(a_i) = \prod_{i=1}^{n} e^{-c(a_i)} = e^{-\sum_{i=1}^{n} c(a_i)}$$

Since e^x is monotonically increasing in x, we see that maximizing $P(\mathcal{A} \mid \mathcal{E})$ is equivalent to minimizing the cost of the assignment, Q.E.D.

We now generalize the DAG so that nodes can have any gating function[7]. The definition of a model is extended in the obvious way.

Theorem 4 *Given a gate-only belief network, with a single evidence node, the problem of finding the most probable complete satisfying model given the evidence is equivalent to finding a minimal cost complete model for the weighted gated DAG.*

Proof: The proof of theorem 3 relies only on the fact that the probability of the evidence given a satisfying model is 1, and 0 given any other complete model. Thus, we can use exactly the same proof here.

If we want to find the best *partial* model, and are only interested in satisfying models, the above theorem still holds. It is no longer true, however, that finding the minimum cost model is equivalent to finding the MAP over the entire belief net.

Evaluation of Cost Based Abduction

In essence, the theorems of the last two section serve to define not one scheme of cost-based abduction, but four. The most obvious distinction is between Theorems 3 and 4. The first restricts itself to WAODAGs, while the second generalizes to arbitrary gating functions. There are two things to keep in mind about this distinction. First, if one is using a standard theorem prover, as found in typical rule-based systems, the theorem prover will itself only generate AND/OR DAGS. So unless one is willing to add capabilities to the theorem prover, arbitrary gates are pointless. Also, since AND/OR gates do not require the labels F^A and F, they are marginally simplier to implement. (However, as we will note in the section on implementation, we found that we needed the capabilities of arbitrary gates for our domain.).

The second distinction is between partial and complete models. The distinction here is whether we simply assign costs to those facts which we must assume true (or false) to make the proof work, or go on to make decisions about every fact in the domain, whether or not it plays a role in the proof. Intuitively the former makes more sense. Unfortunately, our theorem (that we would get the MAP assignment) is only true for complete models, and counterexamples exist for non-complete models. Also, the minimal cost complete model will *not* agree, in general, with the minimal cost partial model, even if we compare only the sets of nodes assumed. However, the minimal solution of the complete model problem will be a nearly minimal solution for the partial model, provided a) there is no other complete model with nearly the same cost as the minimum, and b) the cost for assuming nodes false is low. These are reasonable assumptions in many cases. For example, the probabilistic semantics presented in [Charniak and Goldman, 1988] is characterized by low prior probabilities, thus low costs for assuming nodes false.

Lastly, a further word is required about the relation between the costs and the probabilities. In our definition of cost-based abduction there were three sorts of entities which received costs: rules, root nodes, and interior nodes. By the time we reached theorems 3 and 4, however, we had reduced this to one, by showing that rule and interior node costs could be replaced by added root node costs. But how do these transformations affect our interpretation of what the costs mean in terms of probabilities?

Things are most obvious for root nodes. As stated earlier, the cost of assuming a root node must be $-log(P(node))$. For rules and interior nodes, however, things are slightly more complex. The cost of a rule got moved to the cost of a new root node. Suppose for rule R we add the new root node R'. We can, of course, say that the cost of a rule must be $-log(P(R'))$. However, R' does not correspond to anything in our model of the world (it is merely a mathematical fiction designed to make the proof simpler). We need to define the cost in terms of elements of our world model. Thus, suppose R is the rule:

$$p_1 \wedge ... \wedge p_n \rightarrow q$$

and we will denote the AND node corresponding to its left-hand side as $A_R{}'$. We will refer to the AND node without the added cost root attached as A_R.

[6] Additionally, we use the a_i's to denote the event of node v_i having value q_i.

[7] Gate nodes are any probabilistic nodes which have only entries of 1 and 0 in their conditional distribution arrays.

Suppose that the other rules which can prove q are R_1, ..., R_n with the corresponding AND nodes (without attached cost roots) $A_{R_1}, ..., A_{R_n}$. It is easy to see that $P(q \mid A_R \wedge \neg A_{R_1} \wedge \ldots \wedge \neg A_{R_n}) = P(R')$. That is, the cost of a rule is minus log probability of its consequent being true given that a) its antecedent is true, and b) none of the other ways of proving (or assuming) the consequent are true.

Analogously, we can show that the cost of assuming an interior OR node v is $-log(P(v \mid$ all the ways of proving it are false$))$. Finally, since in practice there is never a need for assuming an AND node, we will ignore it here. The above analysis only holds when we are considering complete assignments. When partial assignments are allowed, a case may be made for setting the cost of assuming an interior OR node to $(-log(P(v)))$, because if non of its parents are assigned (i.e. we are not *proving* the node, just *assuming* it), then presumably the probability of the node reverts to its prior probability. Given that the notion of partial MAP's is not well defined in the literature, we defer the solution to this problem to future research. We believe, however, that decision theoretic methods may have to be applied in the latter case.

Appelt's Semantics for Hobbs-Stickel

In [Hobbs and Stickel, 1988], Hobbs and Stickel have proposed a scheme very similar to what we have proposed. In their scheme, the initial facts to be explained are each assigned an assumption cost c_i. All inference rules are of the form:

$$p_1^{w_1} \wedge \ldots \wedge p_n^{w_n} \rightarrow q$$

The cost of the p_i's are then given by $cost(p_i) = w_i \; cost(q)$.

However, if two separate portions of the proof-tree require the same assumption, the proof is only charged once for the assumption (and is charged the minimum of the two costs being charged for the fact).

Hobbs and Stickel point out that $C = \sum_{i=1}^{n} w_i$ does not have to equal 1. If $C < 1$ then the system will prefer to assume p_1, ..., p_n, since that will be less expensive than assuming q. They refer to this as *most-specific abduction*. On the other hand, if $C > 1$, then, everything else being equal, the system will tend to just assume q (*least-specific abduction*). Note, however, that even with least-specific abduction, cost sharing on common assumptions can make a more specific scenario cost less. Hobbs and Stickel believe that least-specific abduction (with cost sharing) is the way to go, at least for the abductive problems they are concerned with (natural language comprehension). In general we agree with this assessment.

As we have noted, Hobbs and Stickel did not give a semantics for their weights, and Appelt in [Appelt, 1990] is concerned with overcoming this deficit. Appelt takes as his starting point Selman and Kautz's theory of default reasoning [Selman and Kautz, 1989] called *model preference theory*. In this theory a default rule $p \rightarrow q$ is interpreted as meaning that in all models in which p is true, the models in which q is also true are to be preferred. Appelt, in the spirit of abduction, reverses this by saying that a rule $p^{w_p} \rightarrow q$ where $w_p < 1$ is to be interpreted as a model preference among those models which have q for those which have p was well. However, it is possible to have another rule $r^{w_r} \rightarrow s$ (where $w_r < 1$), but where p and r are not compatible. Thus if s is also in our model we must choose which rules to use. Appelt specifies that if $w_p < w_r$ then use $p \rightarrow q$, and vice versa. Appelt calls this scheme *weighted abduction*.

The most obvious difference between Hobbs-Stickel, and weighted abduction is that the former use rules of the form:

$$p_1^{w_1} \wedge \ldots \wedge p_n^{w_n} \rightarrow q$$

where weighted abduction only has rules of the form $p^{w_p} \rightarrow q$. We assume that what Appelt has in mind is recasting the Hobbs Stickel rules as $(p_1 \wedge \ldots \wedge p_n)^{w_p} \rightarrow q$. With $w_p = \sum_i w_i$. Assuming this is correct, there are two immediate problems with Appelt's semantics. First, it only handles the case where the sum of the w_i's is less than 1. This is what Hobbs and Stickel call more-specific abduction. But as they note, less-specific abduction seems to be the more important case, and Appelt says nothing about it[8]. Secondly, Appelt can give no obvious guidance to how to apportion w_p into the individual w_i's required by Hobbs-Stickel.

But even if we restrict ourselves to finding the single w_p, and also restrict ourselves to more-specific abduction, it would seem that Appelt's semantics gives little guidance when trying to judge if a number is "right". Suppose we have a system with a group of w's for various rules $\{w_a, w_b \ldots w_y\}$ and we now want to add a rule with the number w_z, and we want to know what w_z should be. Following Appelt we will look for models in which the rules w_a, w_b, ... w_y are used but where the rule Z conflicts with their use. In each case we see which rule takes precedence. But this is not sufficient. Suppose we have a model in which A and B are used but where Z makes both unusable. Since costs are additive we have several possibilities: $\{A + B > Z$, but $A < Z\}$, $\{B < Z$ but $A + B < Z\}$, etc. Depending on the numbers, in some cases we should prefer using rules A and B together over Z, in other cases not. But this is not sufficient either, what about $A + C$, and $A + B + C$, and $B + C$, etc. In fact, the number of models which need to be checked grows exponentially with the number of costs in the system.

[8] In his talk at the Symposium on Abduction 1990, Appelt has extended the scheme for *some* cases where the weights sum to more than 1. We doubt, however, whether this extension can be generalized.

Implementation

As we have showed in this paper, anything that can be done with cost-based abduction can also be done by probabilistic methods. One might then ask, why not use the more standard probability theory? The reason would have to be that the standard probabilistic methods are computationally expensive. Evaluating general belief nets is NP-hard. Unfortunately, as we saw in Theorem 1, so is the minimal cost proof problem. However, as the mathematics is quite a bit simpler for minimal cost proofs, one might hope that the constant in front is a lot less. Also, thinking in terms of minimal-cost proofs suggests different ways of looking for solutions. There are well known techniques for doing best first search on AND/OR search spaces, and this looks like an obvious application.

We have implemented a best-first search scheme for finding minimal cost proofs. We have applied it to the work described in [Charniak and Goldman, 1988], which uses belief nets to make abductive decisions on problems that come up in natural language understanding, such as noun-phrase reference, or plan recognition. Thus, we had a ready-made source of networks and probabilities upon which we could test the system, and a benchmark (the speed of our current probabilistic methods).

The approach seems to have some promise. We were able to adapt our networks to the new scheme with little difficulty. (Of the four versions of cost-based abduction mentioned above, we found that complete models did not seem to be required for our networks, but we did need general gates, and not just WAODAGs.). Because we did not use MAP labelings in our earlier work, but rather decided what to believe on the basis of the probability of individual statements, we simulated this by looking for multiple MAP solutions when there were several within some epsilon of each other, and only believing the statements which were in all of them. For the examples we have tried it on, this gave the same results as our belief network calculations.

After minor tuning, our cost algorithm seems to be running significantly faster than the belief-network updating scheme we were using. However, we have not yet done formal timing comparisons between them, and at the moment both the cost algorithm, and the belief-network updating scheme, are very sensitive to efficiency measures. Thus it is unclear how much the timing will prove. It does, however, seem safe to say that cost-based abduction deserves serious consideration.

We should note that this speed-up occurs despite the fact that we do not have a good admissible heuristic cost estimator for our best-first search. We are using the simplest heuristic imaginable – at any point in a partial proof, we assume that the final cost of the proof will be the costs incurred to date. This is a very poor estimator because the bulk of a proof's cost comes from the root assumptions, and they are not found until the end. We are currently exploring other estimator possibilities, such as logic minimization approaches and factoring in assumption costs earlier in the search.

Conclusion

We have shown that cost-based abduction can be given an adequate semantics based upon probability theory, and that under the appropriate circumstances it is guaranteed to find the best MAP assignment of truth values to the propositions in our theory. Initial experiments with the model show that it does produce results consistent with full blown posterior probability calculation, and does so quickly compared to our current probabilistic methods. However, further experimentation is clearly required.

References

[Appelt, 1990] Douglas E. Appelt. A theory of abduction based on model preference. In *Proceedings of the AAAI Symposium on Abduction*, 1990.

[Charniak and Goldman, 1988] Eugene Charniak and Robert Goldman. A logic for semantic interpretation. In *Proceedings of the AAAI Conference*, 1988.

[Charniak and Shimony, 1990] Eugene Charniak and Solomon E. Shimony. Probabilistic semantics for rule based systems. Technical Report CS-90-02, Computer Science Department, Brown University, February 1990.

[Garey and Johnson, 1979] M. R. Garey and D. S. Johnson. *Computers and Intractibility, A Guide to the Theory of NP-completeness*, page 190. W. H. Freeman and Co., 1979.

[Genesereth, 1984] Michael R. Genesereth. The use of design descriptions in automated diagnosis. *Artificial Intelligence*, pages 411–436, 1984.

[Hobbs and Stickel, 1988] Jerry R. Hobbs and Mark Stickel. Interpretation as abduction. In *Proceedings of the 26th Conference of the ACL*, 1988.

[Kautz and Allen, 1986]
Henry A. Kautz and James F. Allen. Generalized plan recognotion. In *Proceedings of the Fifth Conference of AAAI*, August 1986.

[McDermott, 1987] Drew V. McDermott. Critique of pure reason. *Computational Intelligence*, 3:151–60, November 1987.

[Pearl, 1988] J. Pearl. *Probabilistic Reasoning in Intelligent Systems: Networks of Plausible Inference.* Morgan Kaufmann, San Mateo, CA, 1988.

[Selman and Kautz, 1989] Bart Selman and Henry Kautz. The complexity of model-preference default theories. In Reinfrank et. al., editor, *Non-Monotonic Reasoning*, pages 115–130. Springer Verlag, Berlin, 1989.

Two views of belief: Belief as generalized probability and belief as evidence

Joseph Y. Halpern
Ronald Fagin
IBM Almaden Research Center
San Jose, CA 95120
email: halpern@ibm.com, fagin@ibm.com

Abstract

Belief functions are mathematical objects defined to satisfy three axioms that look somewhat similar to the axioms defining probability functions. We argue that there are (at least) two useful and quite different ways of understanding belief functions. The first is as a generalized probability function (which technically corresponds to the *lower envelope* or infimum of a family of probability functions). The second is as a way of representing *evidence*. Evidence, in turn, can be understood as a mapping from probability functions to probability functions. It makes sense to think of *updating* a belief if we think of it as a generalized probability. On the other hand, it makes sense to *combine* two beliefs (using, say, Dempster's *rule of combination*) only if we think of the belief functions as representing evidence. Many previous papers have pointed out problems with the belief function approach; the claim of this paper is that these problems can be explained as a consequence of confounding these two views of belief functions.

1 Introduction

A *belief function* is a function that assigns to every subset of a given set S a number between 0 and 1. Intuitively, the belief in a set (or event) A is meant to describe a lower bound on the degree of belief of an agent that A is actually the case. The corresponding upper bound is provided by a *plausibility function*. The idea of a belief function was introduced by Dempster [Dem67, Dem68] (he uses the terms *lower probability* for belief and *upper probability* for plausibility), and then put forth as a framework for reasoning about uncertainty in Shafer's seminal work *A Mathematical Theory of Evidence* [Sha76a]. Since then belief functions have become a standard tool in expert systems applications (see, for example, [Abe88, Fal88, LU88, LG83]).

While belief functions have an attractive mathematical theory and many intuitively appealing properties, there has been a constant barrage of criticism directed against them, going back to when they were first introduced by Dempster (see the discussion papers that appear after [Dem68], particularly the comments of Smith, Aitchison, and Thompson). The fundamental concern seems to be how we should interpret belief functions. This point is made in a particularly sharp way by Diaconis and Zabell [Dia78, DZ82]. They consider the *three prisoners problem*, and show that applying the the belief function approach to this problem, particularly Dempster's *rule of combination* (which is a rule for combining two belief functions to produce a new belief functions) leads to counterintuitive results. Other authors have shown that the belief function approach leads to counterintuitive or incorrect answers in a number of other situations (see, for example, [Ait68, Bla87, Hun87, Lem86, Pea88, Pea89]).

In this paper, we argue that all these problems stem from a confounding of two different views of belief functions: the first is as a generalized probability function, while the second is as a representation of evidence. In the remainder of this introduction, we briefly sketch these two views.

Formally, a belief function can be defined as a function satisfying three axioms (just as a *group* is a mathematical object satisfying a certain set of axioms). These axioms can be viewed as a weakening of the axioms that characterize probability functions. From that point of view, it seems reasonable to try to understand a belief function as a generalized probability function. There are in fact many ways of relating belief functions to probability functions (see, e.g., [Dem67, Dem68, FH89b, FH89a, Kyb87, Rus87, Sha79]). The approach we focus on here is a well-known one, going back to [Dem67], where a belief function is viewed as the *lower envelope* of a family of probability functions: the belief in a set A is the infimum of the probability of A, where the infimum is taken over all probability functions in the family.

This view of a belief function as a generalized probability function is quite different from the view taken by Shafer in [Sha76a]. Here, belief is viewed as a representation of *evidence*. The more evidence we have to support a particular proposition, the greater our belief in that proposition.

Now the question arises as to what exactly evidence is, and how it relates to probability (if at all). Notice that if we start with a probability function and then we get some evidence, then we can *update* our original probability function to take this evidence into account. If the evidence comes in the form of an observation of some event B, then this updating is typically done by moving to the conditional probability. Starting with a probability function Pr, we update it to get the (conditional) probability function $Pr(\cdot|B)$. This suggests that evidence can be viewed as a function that takes as an argument a probability function and returns an updated probability function. By using ideas that already appear in [Sha76a], it can be shown that a belief function can in fact be viewed as representing evidence in this sense.

This point is perhaps best understood in terms of an example. Imagine we toss a coin that is either a fair coin or a double-headed coin. We see k heads in a row. Intuitively, that should provide strong evidence in favor of the coin being a double-headed coin. And, indeed, if we encode this evidence as a belief function following the methodology suggested in [Sha76a], we find that the larger k is, the stronger our belief that the coin is double-headed. On the other hand, seeing k heads in a row tells us nothing about the probability that the coin is double-headed. For example, if we know that *a priori*, the probability of the coin being fair is .9999 and $k = 8$, then it is still quite probable that the coin is fair. Once we are given a prior probability on the coin being fair then, using conditional probability, we can compute the probability that the coin is fair given that we have observed k heads. If we use Shafer's method, then it can be shown that the conditional probability is exactly the result of using the rule of combination to combine the prior probability with the belief function that encodes our evidence (the fact that we have seen k heads). Thus, the belief function provides us a way of updating the probability function, that is, with a way of going from a prior probability to a posterior (conditional) probability.

Once we decide to view belief functions as representations of evidence, we must tackle the question of *how* to go about representing evidence using belief functions. A number of different representations have been suggested in the literature. We have already mentioned the one due to Shafer; still others have been suggested by Dempster and Smets [Dem68, Sha82]. Walley [Wal87] compares a number of representations of evidence in a general framework. In the full paper we review his framework, and present a slight strengthening of one of his results, showing that perhaps the best representation is given by a certain belief function that is also a probability function, in that it is the only representation satisfying certain reasonable properties that acts correctly under the combination of evidence.

Both of the viewpoints discussed here give us a way of understanding belief in terms of well-understood ideas of probability theory. (Indeed, the distinction between the approaches is closely related to the well-known distinction in probability theory between *absolute beliefs* and *belief updates*; see [HH86] for discussion and further references.) However, as we show by example, these two viewpoints result in very different ways of modelling situations (although, if we do things right, we expect to reach the same conclusions no matter which viewpoint we take!). The major difference between the viewpoints is how they treat new evidence. If we view belief as a generalized probability, then it makes sense to *update* beliefs but not *combine* them. On the other hand, if we view beliefs as a representation of evidence, then it makes sense to combine them, but not update them. This suggests that the rule of combination is appropriate only when we view beliefs as representations of evidence. A way of updating beliefs, appropriate when we view beliefs as generalized probabilities, is described in [FH89a]. It seems that all the examples showing the counterintuitive nature of the rule of combination arise from an attempt to combine two beliefs that are really being viewed as generalized probabilities.

The confusion between the two views seems prevalent throughout the literature. For example, in [LG83], belief functions are used to represent the evidence of sensors; yet, they are introduced as generalized probabilities. That is, it is argued that a belief function which assigns $Bel(A) = 1/3$ and $Pl(A) = 2/3$ is appropriate to represent the fact that a reading on a sensor gives us uncertain information about the true probability of A, and all that can be said about the probability of A is that it is between $1/3$ and $2/3$. Yet these belief functions which are viewed as generalized probabilities are combined using the rule of combination. As our results suggest, this may lead to inappropriate representations of evidence.

In the remainder of the report, we give a brief overview of our results. The reader is encouraged to consult the full paper [HF89] for details.

2 Belief as generalized probability

A belief function on a set S is a function $Bel: 2^S \rightarrow [0,1]$ satisfying:

B0. $Bel(\emptyset) = 0$

B1. $Bel(A) \geq 0$

B2. $Bel(S) = 1$

B3. $Bel(A_1 \cup \ldots \cup A_k) \geq \sum_{I \subseteq \{1,\ldots,k\}, I \neq \emptyset} (-1)^{|I|+1} Bel(\bigcap_{i \in I} A_i)$.

For every set A, we define $Pl(A)$, the ***plausibility of** A*, as $Pl(A) = 1 - Bel(\overline{A})$ (where we use $\overline{A}$ to denote the complement of A). It is not hard to show (using B1, B2, and B3) that $Pl(A) \geq Bel(A)$ for every set A. Intuitively, we can view the interval $[Bel(A), Pl(A)]$ as providing lower and upper bounds on the "likelihood" or probability of A. There are a number of ways of making this precise. We focus on one that goes back to [Dem67].

Given a set $\mathcal{P}$ of probability functions all defined on a sample space S, define the ***lower envelope*** of $\mathcal{P}$ to be the function f such that for each $A \subseteq S$, we have $f(A) = \inf\{Pr(A) : Pr \in \mathcal{P}\}$. We have the corresponding definition of ***upper envelope*** of $\mathcal{P}$. It was already known to Dempster [Dem67] that a belief function can be viewed as a lower envelope. More formally, let Bel be a belief function defined on S, and let Pr be a probability function on S. We say that Pr is ***consistent with** Bel* if $Bel(A) \leq Pr(A) \leq Pl(A)$ for each $A \subseteq S$. Intuitively, Pr is consistent with Bel if the probabilities assigned by Pr are consistent with the intervals $[Bel(A), Pl(A)]$ given by the belief function Bel. Let $\mathcal{P}_{Bel}$ be the set of all probability functions consistent with Bel. The next theorem tells us that the belief function Bel is the lower envelope of $\mathcal{P}_{Bel}$ and Pl is the upper envelope.

Theorem 2.1: *Let Bel be a belief function on S. Then for all $A \subseteq S$, we have*

$$Bel(A) = \inf_{Pr \in \mathcal{P}_{Bel}} Pr(A)$$
$$Pl(A) = \sup_{Pr \in \mathcal{P}_{Bel}} Pr(A).$$

We remark that the converse to Theorem 2.1 does not hold: not every lower envelope is a belief function (see [Dem67, Kyb87, Bla87, Pea89] for counterexamples).

If we start with a probability function Pr and then get some new evidence B, we update it to the conditional probability function $Pr(\cdot|B)$. Analogously, we can update a belief function viewed as a lower envelope by taking the lower envelope of the family of probability functions. Thus, we define:

$$Bel(A|B) = \inf_{Pr \in \mathcal{P}_{Bel}} Pr(A|B)$$
$$Pl(A|B) = \sup_{Pr \in \mathcal{P}_{Bel}} Pr(A|B).$$

It is not hard to see that the infimum and supremum above are not well-defined unless $Bel(B) > 0$; therefore, we define $Bel(A|B)$ and $Pl(A|B)$ only if $Bel(B) > 0$. It is also straightforward to check that if Bel is actually the probability function Pr, and A and B are measurable sets with respect to Pr, then $Bel(A|B) = Pr(A|B)$. Thus, our definition of conditional belief generalizes that of conditional probability.

As shown in [FH89a], there are elegant closed form expressions for conditional belief and plausibility.

Theorem 2.2: *If Bel is a belief function on S such that $Bel(B) > 0$, we have*

$$Bel(A|B) = \frac{Bel(A \cap B)}{Bel(A \cap B) + Pl(\overline{A} \cap B)}$$
$$Pl(A|B) = \frac{Pl(A \cap B)}{Pl(A \cap B) + Bel(\overline{A} \cap B)}.$$

In order to argue that this is a reasonable way to update belief functions, we must also show that, just as the conditional probability function is a probability function, the conditional belief function is a belief function. Fortunately, we have the following result from [FH89a]:

Theorem 2.3: *Let Bel be a belief function defined on S and Pl the corresponding plausibility function. Let $B \subseteq S$ be such that $Bel(B) > 0$. Then $Bel(\cdot|B)$ is a belief function and $Pl(\cdot|B)$ is the corresponding plausibility function.*

Our definition of conditional belief and plausibility is quite different from that given by Dempster. He defines

$$Bel(A||B) = \frac{Bel(A \cup \overline{B}) - Bel(\overline{B})}{1 - Bel(\overline{B})}.$$

$Bel(\cdot||B)$ is indeed a belief function, and the corresponding plausibility function satisfies

$$Pl(A||B) = \frac{Pl(A \cap B)}{Pl(B)}.$$

For the remainder of this paper, we call this the ***DS notion of conditioning***. While this definition has a reasonable motivation (which we discuss in the next section), it is well known to occasionally give counterintuitive answers. In [FH89a], the DS notion is carefully compared to our notion of conditioning. Our notion is shown to give reasonable answers in the cases where the DS notion does not. The discrepancy between the two notions can be explained by analyzing both in terms of conditional probability; the DS notion can be shown to correspond to a somewhat unusual updating process. (The reader is encouraged to consult [FH89a] for more details.)

3 Belief as evidence

Up to now we have viewed belief as a generalized probability. This does *not* seem to be the view of belief that Shafer espouses in [Sha76a]. He talks of belief as being a representation of a body of *evidence*. To say that $Bel(A) = p$ is to say that, as a result of the evidence encoded by Bel, the agent has a degree of belief p in the proposition represented by the set A.

From this point of view, it makes sense to *combine* two belief functions Bel_1 and Bel_2. The resulting belief function Bel is meant to represent the combined evidence encoded by each of Bel_1 and Bel_2 separately. In order to combine two or more independent pieces of evidence, Shafer suggests the use of Dempster's *rule of combination*. For reasons of space, we omit the definition of the rule of combination in this abstract; details can be found in [Sha76a]. The reader not familiar with it should still be able to follow our main points. We denote by $Bel_1 \oplus Bel_2$ the belief function obtained by combining the belief functions Bel_1 and Bel_2 using Dempster's rule of combination.

Shafer presents many examples of the intuitively appealing nature of the rule of combination in [Sha76a]. He also shows that in some sense we can use the rule of combination to capture the idea of updating a belief function as the result of learning new evidence. The effect of learning B can be captured by the belief function $Learn^B$, which assigns belief 1 to every superset of B, and belief 0 to every set which is not a superset of B. It is this idea of learning that is used to define the DS notion of conditional belief. In fact, it can be shown that $Bel(\cdot||B) = Bel \oplus Learn^B$; i.e., $Bel(\cdot||B)$ is the result of combining Bel with the belief function that corresponds to learning B.

This definition may seem quite natural. If we view Bel as a representation of evidence, then a case can be made that $Bel(\cdot||B)$ represents that body of evidence that results from combining the evidence encoded by Bel with the evidence that B is actually the case. On the other hand, if we view Bel as a generalized probability distribution, we can no longer expect that the rule of combination should correspond to a natural updating process. In fact, as shown in [FH89a], it does not. The key point here is that updating and combining are different processes; what makes sense in one context does not necessarily make sense in the other.

The discussion above suggests that, whatever evidence is, evidence and probability are different. They are related though. A probability function gets updated as a result of evidence. This suggests that one way we can represent evidence is as an update function. As we shall see, belief functions can indeed be viewed as update functions. The idea is that given a belief function Bel and a prior probability Pr, we transform this to a posterior probability Pr' by using the rule of combination. That is, we can consider the mapping $Pr \mapsto Pr' = Pr \oplus Bel$. *A priori*, it is not clear that this mapping does anything interesting. Clearly, for this mapping to have the "right" properties, we need to consider how to represent evidence as a belief function.

3.1 Representing evidence

In most of the examples given in [Sha76a], subjective degrees of belief are assigned to various events in the light of evidence. Although Shafer shows that the degrees of belief seem to have reasonable qualitative behavior when the evidence is combined, there is no external notion of "reasonable" against which we can evaluate how reasonable these numbers are. The one place where there is an external of reasonableness comes in the area that Shafer terms *statistical evidence*. In this case, we have numbers provided by certain conditional probabilities. A prototypical example of this type of situation is given by the following coin-tossing situation.

Imagine a coin is chosen from a collection of coins, each of which is either biased towards heads or biased towards tails. The coins biased towards heads land heads with probability 2/3 and tails with probability 1/3, while those biased towards tails land tails with probability 2/3 and heads with probability 1/3. We start tossing the coin in order to determine its bias. We observe that the first k tosses result in heads. Intuitively, the more heads we see without seeing a tail, the more evidence we have that the coin is in fact biased towards heads. How should we represent this evidence in terms of belief functions?

Suppose that we have a space $S = \{BH, BT\}$, where BH stands for *biased towards heads*, and BT stands for *biased towards tails*. Let Bel_h be the belief function on S that captures the evidence in favor of BH and BT as a result of seeing the coin land heads once. We would certainly expect that $Bel_h(BH) > Bel_h(BT)$, since seeing the coin lands heads provides more evidence in favor of the coin being biased towards heads than it does in favor of the coin being biased towards tails. But what numeric values should we assign to $Bel_h(BH)$ and $Bel_h(BT)$? According to a convention introduced by Shafer [Sha76a, Chap. 11] (discussed in detail in the full paper), we should take $Bel_h(BH) = 1/2$ and $Bel_h(BT) = 0$. By symmetry, the belief function Bel_t representing the evidence of the coin landing tails satisfies $Bel_t(BH) = 0$ and $Bel_t(BT) = 1/2$. Note that $Pl_h(BH) = 1$ and $Pl_h(BT) = 1/2$. Thus, the ratio $Pl_h(BH) : Pl_h(BT) = 2 : 1$, which is precisely the ratio of the probability of the observation *heads* given BH (namely, 2/3) to the probability of *heads* given BT (namely, 1/3). We will make use of this fact later.

If we assume that our observations are independent, then it seems reasonable to expect that the belief function which represents the observation of k heads should correspond in some sense to combining the evidence of observing one head k times. Let $Bel_h^k = Bel_h \oplus \cdots \oplus Bel_h$ (k times); it can be shown that $Bel_h^k(BT) = 0$ and $Bel_h^k(BH) = (2^k - 1)/2^k$. This seems qualitatively reasonable. If we see k heads in a row, then it is much more likely that the coin is biased towards heads than that it is biased towards tails. It is also easy to compute that

$$(Bel_h \oplus Bel_t)(BH) = (Bel_h \oplus Bel_t)(BT) = 1/3.$$

Again, it seems reasonable that if we see heads followed by tails, we should have no more evidence in favor of the coin being biased towards heads than it being biased towards heads (although the particular choice of 1/3 as the appropriate amount of evidence may seem somewhat mysterious).

What do these numbers tell us about the probability that the coin is biased towards heads or biased towards tails? Without knowing something about how the coin is chosen, probability theory does not give us much guidance. For example, if the coin was chosen at random from a collection of 1,000,000 coins only one of was biased towards heads and all the rest biased towards tails, then even after seeing 10 heads in a row, we would still say that it is extremely likely that the coin is biased towards tails.

Now suppose that we know that the coin was chosen at random from a collection with proportion α of coins biased towards heads and $1-\alpha$ of coins biased towards tails. By definition,

$$Pr(BH|k \text{ heads}) = Pr(BH \wedge k \text{ heads})/Pr(k \text{ heads}).$$

A straightforward computation now shows that the conditional probability is $2^k\alpha/(1+(2^k-1)\alpha)$. As expected, this probability approaches 1 as k gets larger.

Let Bel be the belief function that describes the initial probability; thus $Bel(BH) = \alpha$ and $Bel(BT) = 1-\alpha$. If we define $Bel_1 = Bel \oplus Bel_h$ and $Bel_k = Bel \oplus Bel_h^k$, then a straightforward computation shows $Bel_1 = Pr(\cdot|heads)$ and $Bel_k = Pr(\cdot|k\ heads)$. By combining the prior with the belief function that represents the evidence, we get the posterior. The same phenomenon occurs if we combine the prior with Bel_t.

Judging by this example, Shafer's definition of Bel_h and Bel_t has two very interesting properties, namely:

- when we combine Bel_h with a prior on $S = \{BH, BT\}$, we get the conditional (posterior) probability on S given that heads is observed.
- Bel_h^k in some sense represents the evidence encoded observing k heads, and $Bel_h \oplus Bel_t$ represents the evidence encoded by observing heads and then tails, in that if we combine these belief functions with the prior, we get the appropriate conditional probability.

3.2 Choosing the right representation

Obviously, we now want to know whether these properties hold not just for certain observations made in this coin-tossing example, but in general. The answer is yes, and the appropriate theorems that show this can already be found in [Sha76a]. We review Shafer's theorems in the full paper in detail, as well as his way of representing evidence. The upshot is that ***any*** belief functions Bel_h and Bel_t can be used to represent the observations *heads* and *tails* respectively and will satisfy the two properties above, provided that the ratio of $Pl_h(BH) : Pl_h(BT) = 2:1 = Pr(heads|BH) : Pr(heads|BT)$, and $Pl_t(BH) : Pl_t(BT) = 1:2 = Pr(tails|BH) : Pr(tails|BT)$. (As we observed above, Shafer's representation indeed has this property.)

There are other reasonably motivated representation schemes with these properties, besides the one suggested by Shafer. One is suggested by Dempster [Dem68] (see [Sha76b] for a comparison between his approach and that of Dempster). Yet another is defined by Smets (see [Sha82] for a discussion of Smets' representation). We consider a fourth reasonable choice (also considered in [Sha82]), which we would claim is perhaps the most natural of all; namely, to consider the unique belief function that satisfies the condition stated above that is also a probability function.

In our coin-tossing example, let Pr_h and Pr_t represent the probabilistic belief function that captures the observations of *heads* and *tails* respectively. In order to get $Pr_h(BH) : Pr_h(BT) = 2:1$, we must have $Pr_h(BH) = 2/3$, $Pr_h(BT) = 1/3$. Similarly, we have $Pr_t(BH) = 1/3$, $Pr_t(BT) = 2/3$. Although Pr_h and Pr_t can be viewed as probability functions, they should not be thought of as representing the probability of BH or BT in any sense corresponding to the frequentist or subjectivist interpretation of probability. Rather, these are encodings of the evidence for BH and BT given the observations *heads* and *tails* respectively.[1] It is easy to check that,

[1] They are, in fact, closely related to the *likelihood* functions introduced by R. A. Fisher. We discuss the relationship in more detail in the full paper. See also [Hac65] for further discussion of likelihoods.

for example, we have $Pr_h^k(BH) = 2^k/(2^k+1)$ and $Pr_h^k(BT) = 1/(2^k+1)$, where $Pr_h^k = Pr_h \oplus \cdots \oplus Pr_h$ (k times). Again, the more heads we see, the greater the evidence that the coin is biased towards heads. And if we combine this with a prior Pr such that $Pr(BH) = \alpha$, then an easy computation shows that $(Pr \oplus Pr_h^k)(BH) = 2^k\alpha/(1+(2^k-1)\alpha)$. Thus, $(Pr \oplus Pr_h^k)(BH) = Pr(BH|k\ heads)$. This shows that (at least in this example) the probabilistic representation of evidence has the same properties we observed with Shafer's representation.

There is one additional property we might require of a representation of evidence. Suppose that we make k independent observations. It seems that this should be equivalent to making one joint observation. In our coin-tossing example, we might expect that observing heads and then observing tails should be identical to making the joint observation $(heads, tails)$. Unfortunately, as Shafer already observed [Sha76a, p. 249–250], his representation does *not* have this property in general. Returning to our coin tossing example, recall that $(Bel_h \oplus Bel_t)(BH) = 1/3$. As we show in the full paper, it follows from Shafer's definitions that if $Bel_{(h,t)}$ is the belief function that represents the joint observation "heads followed by tails", then $Bel_{(h,t)}(BH) = 0$. Thus $Bel_h \oplus Bel_t \neq Bel_{(h,t)}$.

The fact that Shafer's approach to representing evidence does not represent a joint observation in the same way that it represents the combination of the individual observations has disturbed a number of authors [Dia78, Sei81, Wil78]. In fact, in a later paper [Sha82], Shafer has indicated that he is inclined to agree that this property is unacceptable. In the full paper we focus on this problem in more detail. We show that the probabilistic representation of evidence discussed above does satisfy it. Moreover, we show that if we make one reasonable assumption, then the probabilistic representation of evidence is the *only* representation that satisfies this additional property. Roughly speaking, our assumption says that all that matters is the *relative* likelihood of observations. In terms of our coin-tossing example, this means that all that matters is the ratio of $Pr(heads|BH) : Pr(heads|BT)$, and not the actual values of the conditional probabilities. Of the representations mentioned above, this assumption is satisfied by Shafer's representation and by the probabilistic representation, but is *not* satisfied by either Dempster's representation or Smets' representation. For a more general discussion of the issue of representing belief, the reader is encouraged to consult [Wal87].

4 Examples

Depending on which of the two views of belief functions we take, we will model a situation in very different ways. For example, it is typically assumed that lack of information about an event E should be modelled by the vacuous belief function Bel, so that $Bel(E) = 0$ and $Pl(E) = 1$. While this way of modelling the lack of information is consistent with the view of belief as a generalized probability (intuitively, our information is consistent with E having any probability between 0 and 1), it is *not* in general consistent with the view of belief as evidence. To take a simple example, suppose we have two fair coins, call them coin A and coin B. Someone tosses one of the two coins and announces that it lands heads. Intuitively, we now have no evidence to favor the coin being either coin A or coin B. Taking the view of belief as generalized probability, we would have $Bel(A \text{ tossed}) = 0$ and $Pl(A \text{ tossed}) = 1$. However, taking the view of belief as evidence and using the probabilistic representation of belief, we get $Bel(A \text{ tossed}) = Pl(A \text{ tossed}) = 1/2$. Lack of information is not being represented by the vacuous belief function under this viewpoint.

In general, starting with a (belief function representing a) prior, if we get new evidence, we can either update the prior, or combine it with a belief function representing the evidence. As we already saw in the coin-tossing example of Section 3, we get the same answer no matter how we do it (although the intermediate comptuations are quite different), providing we represent the evidence appropriately. The one thing we must be careful not to do is to represent the evidence as a generalized probability, and then combine it with the prior.

To understand this issue, consider the following slightly simplified version of a puzzle appearing in [Hun87]: Suppose that we have 100 agents, all holding a lottery ticket, numbered 00 to 99. Suppose that agent a_1 holds ticket number 17. Assume that the lottery is fair, so, *a priori*, the probability that a given agent will win is 1/100. We are then told that the first digit of the winning ticket is 1. Straightforward probability arguments show that the probability that the winning ticket is 17 given that the first digit of the winning ticket is 1 is 1/10; thus, agent 1's probability of winning in light of the new information is 1/10.

How can we represent this information using belief functions? Hunter essentially considers two belief functions on the space $S = \{a_1, \ldots, a_{100}\}$, where $Bel(a_i)$ represents the belief that a_i wins. It seems reasonable to represent the information that the lottery is fair by the belief function Bel_1 where $Bel_1(\{a_i\}) = Pl_1(\{a_i\}) = 1/100$, for $i = 1, \ldots, 100$. (Note that this belief function is actually a probability function.)

Now how should we represent the second piece of information? Hunter suggests representing it by the belief function Bel_2 which is the lower envelope of the set $\mathcal{P}$ of probability functions on S that assign $\{a_1\}$ probability 1/10. Thus, we have $Bel_2(\{a_1\}) = 1/10$ and $Bel_2(\{a_2, \ldots, a_{100}\}) = 9/10$, but $Bel_2(A) = 0$ if A is a strict subset of $\{a_2, \ldots, a_{100}\}$.

Hunter then considers the result of combining these two belief functions by using the rule of combination. In the light of our previous discussion, it should not be surprising that the result does not seem to represent the combined evidence at all. In fact, an easy computation shows that the result of combining Bel_1 and Bel_2 is a probability function that places probability 1/892 on a_1 winning, and probability 9/892 on a_i winning, for $i = 2, \ldots, 100$. It certainly does not seem appropriate that the evidence that a_1's probability of winning is 1/10, when combined with the information that the lottery is fair, should decrease our belief that a_1 will win and, in fact, result is a belief that any other agent is 9 times as likely to win as a_1!

There may be some objections to the appropriateness of the use of the rule of combination here (these are discussed in the full paper), but as the discussion in the previous section suggests, the real problem here is that we are trying to use the rule of combination with a belief function that is meant to represent a generalized probability. The point is that Bel_2 does not represent the evidence appropriately. In order to apply the techniques discussed in the previous section for representing the evidence, we need to know the likelihood, for each agent a_i, that the first digit of the winning number is 1, given the hypothesis that a_i wins the lottery. In the case of a_1, it is easy to compute this probability: since a_1's number is 17, the probability that the first digit of the winning number is 1 given that a_1 wins is 1. In the case of the other agents, we cannot compute this probability at all, since we do not know what their lottery numbers are.

In order to deal with this problem, first consider a fixed assignment A of lottery numbers to agents, so that $A(i)$ is the lottery number of a_i. We assume (as is the case in the story) that $A(1) = 17$. With respect to this fixed assignment, it is easy to see that there are 10 agents a_i for which the probability that the first digit of the winning number is 1 given that a_i wins is 1; namely, all those agents a_i such that the first digit of $A(i)$ is 1. For every other agent a_i, the probability that the first digit of the winning number is 1 given that a_i wins is 0. Using the probabilistic representation of evidence discussed in the previous section, we would thus represent the evidence that the first digit of the winning lottery number is 1 by the belief function Bel_2^A such that the mass function $m_2^A(\{a_i\}) = 1/10$ for each agent a_i such that the first digit of $A(i)$ is 1 (note that, in particular, this includes a_1), and $m_2^A(\{a_i\}) = 0$ if the first digit of $A(i)$ is not 1. It is now easy to check that $Bel_1 \oplus Bel_2^A = Bel_2^A$. Thus, independent of the assignment A of lottery numbers, we have $(Bel_1 \oplus Bel_2^A)(\{a_1\}) = 1/10$, as expected. (We would get essentially the same results using the other representations discussed in the previous section.)

In the full paper, we also consider in detail the puzzle of of Mr. Jones' murderer, introduced in [SK89]. Our analysis of this puzzle can also be applied to the three prisoners problem (this problem is analyzed under the viewpoint of beliefs as generalized probabilities in [FH89a]).

Acknowledgements: This paper benefitted from discussions with numerous people, including Fahiem Bacchus, Alan Bundy, Dan Hunter, Ben Grosof, Ric Horvitz, Judea Pearl, Tom Strat, Moshe Vardi, and Larry Wasserman.

References

[Abe88] S. Abel. The sum-and-lattice-points method based on an evidential-reasoning system applied to the real-time vehicle guidance problem. In *Uncertainty in Artificial Intelligence 2*, pages 365–370, 1988.

[Ait68] J. Aitchison. Discussion on Professor Dempster's paper. *Journal of the Royal Statistical Society, Series B*, 30:234–237, 1968.

[Bla87] P. Black. Is Shafer general Bayes? In *Proc. Third AAAI Uncertainty in Artificial Intelligence Workshop*, pages 2–9, 1987.

[Dem67] A. P. Dempster. Upper and lower probabilities induced by a multivalued mapping. *Annals of Mathematical Statistics*, 38:325–339, 1967.

[Dem68] A. P. Dempster. A generalization of Bayesian inference. *Journal of the Royal Statistical Society, Series B*, 30:205–247, 1968.

[Dia78] P. Diaconis. Review of "A Mathematical Theory of Evidence". *Journal of the American Statistical Society*, 73(363):677–678, 1978.

[DZ82] P. Diaconis and S. L. Zabell. Updating subjective probability. *Journal of the American Statistical Society*, 77(380):822–830, 1982.

[Fal88] B. Falkenhainer. Towards a general-purpose belief maintenance system. In *Uncertainty in Artificial Intelligence 2*, pages 125–131, 1988.

[FH89a] R. Fagin and J. Y. Halpern. A new approach to updating beliefs. Research Report RJ 7222, IBM, 1989. A revised version will appear in May, 1990.

[FH89b] R. Fagin and J. Y. Halpern. Uncertainty, belief, and probability. In *Eleventh International Joint Conference on Artificial Intelligence (IJCAI-89)*, pages 1161–1167, 1989. An expanded version of this paper appears as IBM Research Report RJ 6191, April 1988.

[Hac65] I. Hacking. *Logic of Statistical Inference.* Cambridge University Press, 1965.

[HF89] J. Y. Halpern and R. Fagin. Two views of belief: Belief as generalized probability and belief as evidence. Research Report RJ 7221, IBM, 1989. A revised version will appear in May, 1990.

[HH86] E. Horvitz and D. Heckerman. The inconsistent use of measures of certainty in artificial intelligence research. In L. N. Kanal and J. F. Lemmer, editors, *Uncertainty in Artificial Intelligence*, pages 137–151. North-Holland, 1986.

[Hun87] D. Hunter. Dempster-Shafer vs. probabilistic logic. In *Proc. Third AAAI Uncertainty in Artificial Intelligence Workshop*, pages 22–29, 1987.

[Kyb87] H. E. Kyburg, Jr. Bayesian and non-Bayesian evidential updating. *Artificial Intelligence*, 31:271–293, 1987.

[Lem86] J. F. Lemmer. Confidence factors, empiricism, and the Dempster-Shafer theory of evidence. In L. N. Kanal and J. F. Lemmer, editors, *Uncertainty in Artificial Intelligence*, pages 167–196. North-Holland, 1986.

[LG83] J. D. Lowrance and T. D. Garvey. Evidential reasoning: an implementation for multisensor integration. Technical Report TN 307, SRI International, 1983.

[LU88] Z. Li and L. Uhr. Evidential reasoning in a computer vision system. In *Uncertainty in Artificial Intelligence 2*, pages 403–412, 1988.

[Pea88] J. Pearl. *Probabilistic Reasoning in Intelligent Systems.* Morgan Kaufmann, 1988.

[Pea89] J. Pearl. Reasoning with belief functions: a critical assessment. Technical Report R-136, UCLA, 1989.

[Rus87] E. H. Ruspini. The logical foundations of evidential reasoning. Research Note 408, revised version, SRI International, 1987.

[Sei81] T. Seidenfeld. Statistical evidence and belief functions. *PSA 1978*, 2:478–489, 1981.

[Sha76a] G. Shafer. *A Mathematical Theory of Evidence.* Princeton University Press, 1976.

[Sha76b] G. Shafer. A theory of statistical evidence. In W. L. Harper and C. A. Hooker, editors, *Foundations of Probability Theory, Statistical Inference, and Statistical Theories of Science, Vol. II.* Reidel, 1976.

[Sha79] G. Shafer. Allocations of probability. *Annals of Probability*, 7(5):827–839, 1979.

[Sha82] G. Shafer. Belief functions and parametric models (with commentary). *Journal of the Royal Statistical Society, Series B*, 44:322–352, 1982.

[SK89] P. Smets and R. Kennes. The transferable belief model: comparison with Bayesian models, unpublished manuscript. 1989.

[Wal87] P. Walley. Belief function representations of statistical evidence. *Annals of Statistics*, 18(4):1439–1465, 1987.

[Wil78] P. M. Williams. On a new theory of epistemic probability (review of "A Mathematical Theory of Evidence"). *The British Journal for the Philosophy of Science*, 29:357–387, 1978.

The Belief Calculus and Uncertain Reasoning

Yen-Teh Hsia*

IRIDIA, Université Libre de Bruxelles
50 av. F. Roosevelt, CP 194/6
1050, Brussels, Belgium
r01509@bbrbfu01.bitnet

Abstract

We formulate the Dempster-Shafer formalism of belief functions [Shafer 76] in the spirit of logical inference systems. Our formulation (called the belief calculus) explicitly avoids the use of set-theoretic notations. As such, it serves as an alternative for the use of the Dempster-Shafer formalism for uncertain reasoning.

1. Introduction

Traditionally, the "syntax" of the Dempster-Shafer (D-S) formalism [Shafer 76] has been set-theoretic in nature (e.g., [Gordon and Shortliffe 84; Kong 86; Shafer et al. 87; Yen 89]). In some cases, propositions may be used for belief specifications (e.g., [Smets 88; Zarley et al. 88]). However, to date, there is no purely logic-oriented formulation of this formalism.

Set-theoretic notations are appropriate when we are concerned with general theory rather than applications. But on the other hand, we might also find it difficult to use set-theoretic notations in some application domains. To overcome this notational disadvantage of the D-S formalism, we give an alternative formulation of belief functions in this paper. Our formulation (called the belief calculus) is developed along the lines of natural deduction systems, and it explicitly avoids the use of set-theoretic notations. This differs from the previous research [Ruspini 87; Fagin and Halpern 89] in which the main concern was the "structure" or semantics of the D-S formalism and not its syntax.

To show how the belief calculus may be used for uncertain reasoning, we give three examples. These examples model different real world situations, and they address issues such as independent random variables, belief dependency structures, and "distinct" sources of evidence.

The remainder of this paper is organized as follows. In Section 2, we describe the belief calculus. In Section 3, we show how the belief calculus may be used for uncertain reasoning. In Section 4, we discuss some related issues. Finally, Section 5 concludes.

* This work was supported in part by the DRUMS project funded by the Commission of the European Communities under the ESPRIT II-Program, Basic Research Project 3085.

2. The Belief Calculus

The multivariate formalism. Our formulation of the D-S formalism starts with the multivariate formalism [Kong 86]. That is, we assume that different aspects of the world that are of interests to us are already appropriately formulated as questions or *variables* (e.g., "Is the entity capable of flying?", "Can the object be used to cross the river?" etc). Each of these variables is associated with a set of mutually exclusive and exhaustive values (called the *frame* of the variable) representing all possible answers to the question. A *boolean variable* is one that has an associated frame of {Yes, No}.

Propositions. Primitive propositions (i.e., atoms) are of the form "SomeVariable = SomeValue". From propositions, we build compound propositions using five logical connectives (with the usual semantics): ¬ (not), ∨ (or), ∧ (and), → (if ... then), ↔ (if and only if).

As a basic requirement of the multivariate formalism, we assume that, for every variable and its associated frame, there is a corresponding *mutual exclusion axiom.* For example, if the frame of the variable A is {h, m, l}, then the mutual exclusion axiom associated with A and its frame is '((A = h) ∧ ¬(A = m) ∧ ¬(A = l)) ∨ (¬(A = h) ∧ (A = m) ∧ ¬(A = l)) ∨ (¬(A = h) ∧ ¬(A = m) ∧ (A = l))'. We use $\mathbb{ME}$ to denote the set of all mutual exclusion axioms. For convenience, we also use 'A' as an abbreviation for 'A = Yes' whenever A is a boolean variable (and '¬A' will be logically equivalent to 'A = No' under $\mathbb{ME}$).

Let $A_1, A_2, \ldots, A_N$ be all variables, and let $\Theta_1, \Theta_2, \ldots, \Theta_N$ be their respective frames. A *valuation* is an assignment of an element of Θ_i ($1 \leq i \leq N$) to A_i for every i (i.e., an assignment of a value-vector to the variable-vector $<A_1, A_2, \ldots, A_N>$). A proposition P is said to be true under a valuation V if P is true when all variables occurring in P are replaced with their corresponding values in V; otherwise P is said to be false under V.

Formally, a valuation is defined as an assignment of values to all variables. But when the situation permits, we also use the word 'valuation' to mean a (partial) valuation of all variables occurring in some proposition.

Example 1. "(PLACE = Africa) $\rightarrow$ (TEMP = high)" is a proposition. It is false under the valuation <PLACE, TEMP> = <Africa, medium> and true under the valuation <PLACE, TEMP> = <Europe, medium>.

A *contingent proposition*, then, is a proposition that is true under one valuation but false under another valuation. A *valid proposition* (or tautology), denoted as 'T', is a proposition that is true under every valuation, while an *unsatisfiable proposition*, denoted as 'F', is a proposition that is false under every valuation (and a *satisfiable proposition* is true under at least one valuation).

Beliefs. A *belief* is a formula specified in the following format:

$$P_1\ (m_1) \vee P_2\ (m_2) \vee \ldots \vee P_n\ (m_n)$$
where
$$\forall\ i\ (1 \le i \le n),\quad P_i \text{ is a satisfiable proposition and } 0 < m_i \le 1,$$
$$\text{and } \sum m_i = 1. \qquad (1)$$

As a convention, if 'T' appears in formula (1), it is usually specified at the end (i.e., as P_n). "T (1)" is called *the vacuous belief.*

Intuitively, each m_i (called the "m-value" of P_i) in formula (1) represents the amount of belief we specifically "allocate" to P_i. That is, formula (1) may be interpreted to mean the following: the world, as we understand it, is such that P_1 holds (with the amount of belief m_1 being allocated to it), *or* P_2 holds (with the amount of belief m_2 being allocated to it), ..., *or* P_n holds (with the remaining amount of belief m_n being allocated to it). This is why we use the symbol '$\vee$' to delimit the 'P_i (m_i)' of a belief. However, this symbol '$\vee$' is not to be confused with the usual logical symbol '$\vee$' that occurs within a proposition.

In the following, we use the term 'intuitive belief' (or 'intuitive beliefs') to denote the intuitive belief(s) we have in mind, and we also use the word 'belief' (or 'beliefs') to denote a formula (or formulas).

Belief sets. We may be able to come up with one single belief (i.e., one formula) which appropriately formalizes our intuitive belief in (almost) every way. However, this is not a very easy task in general, and it may be argued whether the specification of such a joint belief is always necessary.

As human problem solvers, we are often capable of identifying various "independent" aspects of a problem. Once such aspects have been identified, we can then specify a (unique) belief for each of these aspects and use some kind of inference mechanism to "combine" the specified (independent) beliefs. This philosophy is embodied in the D-S formalism. Accordingly, the belief calculus works with sets of beliefs (called belief sets)[1]; when using this calculus for reasoning, we first try to infer a singleton set (containing the combined belief) from the given belief set.

A *belief set* $\mathbb{B}$ is a non-empty set of beliefs. In notation,

$$\mathbb{B} = \{\mathbf{b}_1; \mathbf{b}_2; \ldots ; \mathbf{b}_r\}, \text{ where}$$
$$r \ge 1, \text{ and } \forall\ i\ (1 \le i \le r),\ \mathbf{b}_i \text{ is a belief.}$$

(We use ';' to delimit the specified beliefs. This specification of beliefs does not mean that the beliefs are implicitly ordered.)

We now give the inference rules of the belief calculus[2]. The first three rules are trivial. (Notation: Throughout this paper, we use '|- P' to mean that "the proposition P is provable in the propositional calculus from the set of mutual exclusion axioms $\mathbb{ME}$".)

1. Commutation:

$$\frac{\{\ldots \vee P_i\ (m_i) \vee \ldots \vee P_j\ (m_j) \vee \ldots; \mathbf{b}_2; \mathbf{b}_3; \ldots ; \mathbf{b}_r\}}{\{\ldots \vee P_j\ (m_j) \vee \ldots \vee P_i\ (m_i) \vee \ldots; \mathbf{b}_2; \mathbf{b}_3; \ldots ; \mathbf{b}_r\}}$$

2. Addition:

$$\frac{\vdash (P \leftrightarrow R),\quad \{\ldots \vee P\ (m_i) \vee \ldots \vee R\ (m_j) \vee \ldots; \mathbf{b}_2; \mathbf{b}_3; \ldots ; \mathbf{b}_r\}}{\{\ldots \vee P\ (m_i + m_j) \vee \ldots \vee \ldots; \mathbf{b}_2; \mathbf{b}_3; \ldots ; \mathbf{b}_r\}}$$

3. Substitution:

$$\frac{\vdash (P \leftrightarrow R),\ \{\ldots \vee P\ (m) \vee \ldots ; \mathbf{b}_2; \mathbf{b}_3; \ldots ; \mathbf{b}_r\}}{\{\ldots \vee R\ (m) \vee \ldots ; \mathbf{b}_2; \mathbf{b}_3; \ldots ; \mathbf{b}_r\}}$$

We also need a fourth rule for inferring combined beliefs ($\oplus$ is defined below).

4. Combination[3]:

$$\frac{\{\mathbf{b}_1; \mathbf{b}_2; \mathbf{b}_3; \ldots ; \mathbf{b}_r\},\ \mathbf{b}_1 \oplus \mathbf{b}_2 = \mathbf{b}_c}{\{\mathbf{b}_c; \mathbf{b}_3; \ldots ; \mathbf{b}_r\}}$$

The combination operator $\oplus$. Let $\mathfrak{B}$ denote the set of all beliefs. The combination operator $\oplus$ (read as "Dempster's combination") is a partial function that maps from $\mathfrak{B} \times \mathfrak{B}$ to $\mathfrak{B}$.

Intuitively, $\oplus$ (e.g., $\big(A\ (.8) \vee (\neg A)\ (.2)\big) \oplus \big(A\ (.5) \vee B\ (.3) \vee T\ (.2)\big)$) may be thought of as a two step process.

The first step is to apply the (*independence*) assumption that allocating p_i to P_i in the first belief *and* allocating r_j to R_j in the second belief *should mean* allocating $p_i{*}r_j$ to

[1] with singleton sets as special cases.

[2] The belief calculus is formulated along the lines of natural deduction systems. However, due to space limitations, we only describe the inference mechanism of this system.

[3] This is the only inference rule (in the context of the belief calculus) that can be used to reduce the number of beliefs in a belief set.

$P_i \wedge R_j$ in the combined belief (e.g., $((A \wedge A)\ (.4) \vee (A \wedge B)\ (.24) \vee (A \wedge T)\ (.16) \vee (\neg A \wedge A)\ (.1) \vee (\neg A \wedge B)\ (.06) \vee (\neg A \wedge T)\ (.04))$).

The second step is to apply the (*coherence*) assumption that the two beliefs that are being combined are meant to be coherent; this is done by taking away all "pairs" containing unsatisfiable propositions (e.g., $(\neg A \wedge A)\ (.1)$) and redistributing their m-values (e.g., .1) to the remaining propositions by proportions (e.g., $((A \wedge A)\ (.444) \vee (A \wedge B)\ (.267) \vee (A \wedge T)\ (.178) \vee (\neg A \wedge B)\ (.067) \vee (\neg A \wedge T)\ (.044))$). This step is also known as "renormalization".

Formally, $\oplus$ is defined as follows. (Notation: Let S be an ordered set of "pairs" $(P_1\ (m_1), P_2\ (m_2), \ldots, P_n\ (m_n))$, then by '$\vee$ S', we mean the formula '$P_1\ (m_1) \vee P_2\ (m_2) \vee \ldots \vee P_n\ (m_n)$'.)

$(P_1\ (p_1) \vee P_2\ (p_2) \vee \ldots \vee P_M\ (p_M)) \oplus$
$(R_1\ (r_1) \vee R_2\ (r_2) \vee \ldots \vee R_N\ (r_N))$
$=$

if $\exists\ (i, j) \in \{1, \ldots, M\} \times \{1, \ldots, N\}$
such that $P_i \wedge R_j$ is satisfiable,
then
$\vee\ \{(P_i \wedge R_j)\ (p_i{*}r_j / (1 - \Sigma_{(h,k) \in S}\, p_h{*}r_k))\ |$
S is the maximum subset of
$\{1, \ldots, M\} \times \{1, \ldots, N\}$ such that
$\forall\ (h,k) \in S, \vdash ((P_h \wedge R_k) \leftrightarrow F)$,
and
$(i, j) \in (\{1, \ldots, M\} \times \{1, \ldots, N\}) \setminus S$
}[4],
otherwise undefined.

$\oplus$ is an associative operation (i.e., $(\mathbf{b}_1 \oplus \mathbf{b}_2) \oplus \mathbf{b}_3$, if defined, is the same as $\mathbf{b}_1 \oplus (\mathbf{b}_2 \oplus \mathbf{b}_3)$). If we use $\underline{\oplus}$ to denote "$\oplus$ without renormalization", then $\underline{\oplus}$ is obviously associative; but more importantly, $\mathbf{b}_1 \oplus \mathbf{b}_2 \oplus \ldots \oplus \mathbf{b}_r$ (whatever the order of combinations is), if defined, is the same as $\mathbf{b}_1\ \underline{\oplus}\ \mathbf{b}_2\ \underline{\oplus} \ldots \underline{\oplus}\ \mathbf{b}_r$ followed by one single renormalization.

Also, r beliefs $\mathbf{b}_1, \mathbf{b}_2, \ldots, \mathbf{b}_r$ are said to be *incompatible* whenever $\mathbf{b}_1 \oplus \mathbf{b}_2 \oplus \ldots \oplus \mathbf{b}_r$ (whatever the order of combinations is) is undefined.

Example 2. $(A\ (1)) \oplus ((\neg A)\ (1))$ is undefined.

The calculus. The belief set $\mathbb{B}_2$ is *Dempster-Shafer provable from* the belief set $\mathbb{B}_1$, denoted as '$\mathbb{B}_1 \vdash_{DS} \mathbb{B}_2$', if $\mathbb{B}_2$ can be inferred from $\mathbb{B}_1$ after a finite number of applications of the (four) inference rules.

We are now ready to define the overall belief BEL in an arbitrary proposition. Let $\mathfrak{BS}$ be the set of all belief sets and $\mathfrak{P}$ be the set of all propositions. BEL is a partial function from $\mathfrak{BS} \times \mathfrak{P}$ to [0, 1], defined as follows (let $\mathbb{B}$ be a belief set and R be a proposition.)

$\mathrm{BEL}(\mathbb{B}, R) = \Sigma_{\vdash (P_i \to R)}\, m_i$

where $\mathbb{B} \vdash_{DS} \{P_1\ (m_1) \vee P_2\ (m_2) \vee \ldots \vee P_n\ (m_n)\}$.

/* i.e., we must first deduce a singleton from $\mathbb{B}$ */

Clearly, BEL($\mathbb{B}$, R) will be undefined (for every proposition R) whenever the beliefs contained in $\mathbb{B}$ are incompatible.

Note that, even if BEL($\mathbb{B}$, R) is defined for some contingent proposition R, it can still be zero. This simply means that we have no idea whether R holds in the world (because we are not aware of anything that logically supports it). But having no (intuitive) belief in R does not necessarily mean that we have any (intuitive) belief in $\neg$R (i.e., BEL($\mathbb{B}$, $\neg$R) > 0), because our degree of belief in a proposition ($\neg$R in this case), as defined by BEL, is always dependent on whether we are aware of anything that logically supports it and not on whether we are ignorant of anything supporting its negation (i.e., R). This is one of the characteristics of the D-S formalism.

Example 3. $\mathrm{BEL}(\{(A \to B)\ (1)\}, B) = 0$.

Example 4.
$\{A\ (.8) \vee (\neg A)\ (.2);\ A\ (.5) \vee B\ (.3) \vee T\ (.2)\}$
/* i.e., $\mathbb{B}$ */
$\vdash_{DS} \{(A \wedge A)\ (.444) \vee (A \wedge B)\ (.267) \vee (A \wedge T)\ (.178) \vee (\neg A \wedge B)\ (.067) \vee (\neg A \wedge T)\ (.044)\}$
Combination
$\vdash_{DS} \{A\ (.444) \vee (A \wedge B)\ (.267) \vee A\ (.178) \vee (\neg A \wedge B)\ (.067) \vee \neg A\ (.044)\}$
Substitution
$\vdash_{DS} \{A\ (.622) \vee (A \wedge B)\ (.267) \vee (\neg A \wedge B)\ (.067) \vee \neg A\ (.044)\}$
Addition

Therefore
BEL($\mathbb{B}$, A) = .622 + .267 = .889, and BEL($\mathbb{B}$, $\neg$A) = .067 + .044 = .111.

Relating to the "usual" formulation. To see the relation between the belief calculus and the usual set-theoretic formulation of belief functions [Shafer 76], consider the following mapping: let $A_1, A_2, \ldots, A_N$ be all the variables, and let $\Theta_1, \Theta_2, \ldots, \Theta_N$ be their respective frames. Then each proposition P corresponds to exactly one subset of the joint frame $\Theta_1 \times \Theta_2 \times \ldots \times \Theta_N$ (i.e., the set of all "total" valuations that make P true). Similarly, for each subset of the joint frame, there is a corresponding set of logically equivalent propositions. Let S_P be the subset of the joint frame that corresponds to the proposition P and let S_R be the subset of the joint frame that corresponds to the proposition R, then: $\vdash (P \to R)$ if and only if $S_P \subseteq S_R$; $S_P \cup S_R$ corresponds to $P \vee R$; $S_P \cap S_R$ corresponds to $P \wedge R$; and $\Theta_1 \times \Theta_2 \times \ldots \times \Theta_N \setminus S_P$ corresponds to $\neg$P. This

[4]We assume these '$P_i \wedge R_j$' are lexicographically ordered in (i, j).

provides a straightforward translation between the language of the belief calculus and the language of the usual set-theoretic formulation of belief functions.

Example 5. We now use the belief calculus notations to describe the idea of combining the ATMS [de Kleer 86a] with belief functions (e.g., [Laskey and Lehner 89]). Let $\mathfrak{J} = \{P_1, P_2, ..., P_n\}$ be the set of (boolean) propositional clauses that have been transmitted to the ATMS (premises are specified in $\mathfrak{J}$ as "→ C" or "→ ¬C")[5]. Let $\{A_1, A_2, ..., A_k\}$ be a distinguished set of primitives (i.e., assumptions) such that either A_i or $\neg A_i$ (or both) occurs in $\mathfrak{J}$. Furthermore, let $\mathbb{B}$ contain the following (and only the following) beliefs: (a) for each P_i, "P_i (1)" is in $\mathbb{B}$, (b) for each A_i, "A_i (m) ∨ $\neg A_i$ (1-m)" is in $\mathbb{B}$[6]. Then for any literal B (i.e., a primitive Q or its negation ¬Q) occurring in $\mathfrak{J}$, we can compute BEL($\mathbb{B}$, B) using the nogoods and the label associated with B as a basis. For more details, see [D'Ambrosio 87, 88; Laskey and Lehner 88, 89; Provan 89a, 89b].

3. Uncertain Reasoning

The specification of independent beliefs. The D-S formalism encourages the use of the following methodology: we first identify the "independent" aspects of the problem at hand; and then we specify a belief for each of the identified aspects. Therefore, the purpose of this section is to show how we can use the belief calculus for uncertain reasoning *once the independent aspects of the problem at hand have been identified.*

Example 6. (adapted from [Kong 86]) Two sites A and B are connected by a one-way valve which, when working, allows water to flow from A to B. The probability that this valve is working (i.e., not blocked) is p_1. Similarly, sites B and C are connected by a one-way valve (with a working probability of p_2). These two valves work independently. We have no information as to whether there is any water going into A or B or C, but we are interested in whether there is any water in each site. Therefore, we formulate the working of the two valves as two independent random variables, and $\mathbb{B}$ = {V1Working (p_1) ∨ ¬V1Working (1-p_1); (V1Working → (WaterA → WaterB)) (1); V2Working (p_2) ∨ ¬V2Working (1-p_2); (V2Working → (WaterB → WaterC)) (1)}, and the values of BEL($\mathbb{B}$, WaterA), BEL($\mathbb{B}$, WaterB) and BEL($\mathbb{B}$, WaterC) are zero at the moment.

Suppose we just learned that <WaterB> = <Yes>. Then BEL($\mathbb{B}$ ∪ {WaterB (1)}, WaterB) = 1, BEL($\mathbb{B}$ ∪ {WaterB (1)}, WaterC) = p_2, and BEL($\mathbb{B}$ ∪ {WaterB (1)}, WaterA) remains zero.

Belief dependency structures. In general, the uncertainties we want to specify may be intuitively related. When this is the case, we can no longer formulate these uncertainties as independent random variables. Nevertheless, we can try to work out a dependency structure (in a sense similar to the idea of the Bayesian causal trees [Pearl 86]) among the variables, and we make sure that the way a variable (e.g., A) depends on a valuation of other variables (e.g., (B = Yes) ∧ (C = h)) is independent of the ways this same variable (i.e., A) depends on other valuations of these other variables (i.e., (B = Yes) ∧ (C = m); (B = No) ∧ (C = l); etc.). This is the rational behind the following technique which uses a method described in [Smets 78] for specifying a belief set from independent conditional beliefs:

Let $\mathcal{A}_0 = \{A_1, A_2, ... , A_N\}$ (e.g., {Bird, Penguin, Fly}) be a set of variables. We first specify a set $\mathfrak{C}$ of categorical beliefs about these variables (e.g., $\mathfrak{C}$ = {(Penguin → Bird ∧ ¬Fly) (1)}). Then, we recursively apply the following three steps until the variables contained in $\mathcal{A}_i$ ($i \geq 0$) do not directly "depend on" each other.

Step 1: From $\mathcal{A}_i$ (e.g., $\mathcal{A}_0$), we identify exactly one variable[7] A (e.g., Fly) and also a subset $\mathfrak{B}_i$ of $\mathcal{A}_i$\{A} so that A directly "depends on" the valuation of the elements of $\mathfrak{B}_i$ (e.g., $\mathfrak{B}_0$ = {Bird, Penguin} is a subset of {Bird, Penguin, Fly}\{Fly} so that Fly directly depends on the valuation of the two variables Bird and Penguin).

Step 2: For *each and every* logically possible valuation of the elements of $\mathfrak{B}_i$ (e.g., <Bird, Penguin> = <Yes, No>; <Bird, Penguin> = <Yes, Yes>; <Bird, Penguin> = <No, No>), we assess an independent belief about the valuation of A (e.g., we assess the belief "(Fly = Yes) (.9) ∨ ((Fly = Yes) ∨ (Fly = No)) (.1)" for the valuation <Bird, Penguin> = <Yes, No>). If this assessed belief is non-vacuous and non-categorical, we (need to) translate it into the following belief:[8]

("the valuation" → A's value is in ValueSet1) (m_1) ∨
("the valuation" → A's value is in ValueSet2) (m_2) ∨
...
("the valuation" → A's value is in ValueSetM) (m_M),

(e.g., "(Bird ∧ ¬Penguin → (Fly = Yes)) (.9) ∨ (Bird ∧ ¬Penguin → (Fly = Yes) ∨ (Fly = No)) (.1)",
or simply, "(Bird ∧ ¬Penguin → Fly) (.9) ∨ T (.1)").

---

[5]The ATMS actually uses a (positive) primitive to represent the negation of another (positive) primitive [de Kleer 86b]. However, for simplicity, we can think of the ATMS as if it accepted a negated primitive directly.

[6]A more general specification will be to specify exactly one of the following for A_i : "A_i (m_1) ∨ T (1-m_1)", "$\neg A_i$ (m_1) ∨ T (1-m_1)", or "A_i (m_1) ∨ $\neg A_i$ (m_2) ∨ T (1-m_1-m_2)" (the specification of "T (1-m_1-m_2)" is optional).

[7]Actually, we can identify more than one variable if we want. Here, just for simplicity, we restrict it to be one.

[8]This translation is based on the principle of minimum specificity [Dubois and Prade 86].

Step 3: Let $\mathcal{A}_{i+1}$ be $\mathcal{A}_i \backslash \{A\}$ (e.g., $\mathcal{A}_1$ = {Bird, Penguin, Fly}\{Fly} = {Bird, Penguin}).

Once we get to $\mathcal{A}_{final}$, we can, if we want, specify a (non-vacuous) belief for each of the variables remaining in $\mathcal{A}_{final}$ (e.g., $\mathcal{A}_{final} = \mathcal{A}_2$ = {Bird}, and we have the option of specifying a belief such as "Bird (.7) ∨ T (.3)" for the variable Bird; however, we prefer to have "T (1)" for Bird in this case).

Example 8. The belief set

$\mathbb{B}$ = {(Penguin → Bird ∧ ¬Fly) (1);
(Bird ∧ ¬Penguin → Fly) (.9) ∨ T (.1);
(Bird → ¬Penguin) (.95) ∨ T (.05);}

is obtained from the following "constraints":

valuation	belief about some variable
Bird ∧ ¬Penguin	Fly (.9) ∨ T (.1)
Bird ∧ Penguin	¬Fly (1)
¬Bird ∧ ¬Penguin	T (1)
¬Bird ∧ Penguin	(logically impossible)
Bird	¬Penguin (.95) ∨ T (.05)
¬Bird	¬Penguin (1)

Therefore, BEL($\mathbb{B}$ ∪ {Bird (1)}, ¬Penguin) = .95, BEL($\mathbb{B}$ ∪ {Bird ∧ ¬Penguin (1)}, Fly) = .9, BEL($\mathbb{B}$ ∪ {Bird ∧ ¬Penguin (1)}, ¬Fly) = 0, etc.

In addition, BEL($\mathbb{B}$, ¬Penguin) = .95, BEL($\mathbb{B}$, Bird) = 0, BEL($\mathbb{B}$ ∪ {Bird (1)}, Fly) = .855, BEL($\mathbb{B}$ ∪ {Bird (1)}, ¬Fly) = 0, BEL($\mathbb{B}$ ∪ {Fly (1)}, ¬Penguin) = 1.0, BEL($\mathbb{B}$ ∪ {Fly (1)}, Bird) = 0, BEL($\mathbb{B}$ ∪ {Fly (1)}, ¬Bird) = 0, etc.

"Distinct" sources of evidence. We sometimes encounter the following situation[9]: (1) there are one or more sources that provide us with information, and each source has full confidence in the information it provides; (2) the information provided by each source directly "indicts" some elements of the frame of the "main variable" (i.e., the one we are interested in); (3) we can make a reliability estimation for each of these sources[10]; (4) the reliabilities of the sources are independent.

When we are in this kind of situation, we can put our evidence about each particular source into a unique group, and we specify a belief dependency structure according to each group of (related) evidence. The resulting belief set, then, consists of several belief dependency structures intersecting on the main variable.

Example 7. Our friend is ill, and doctors can not pinpoint the problem. Since it may involve life and death, we bring our friend to two doctors B and C that are famous in this area. It is reasonable to assume that these two doctors are independent in making their diagnoses (because they received their trainings in different medical doctrines, they live in different cities, they do not confer to each other, etc.). We also did some background study about the two doctors. Therefore we know that B is extremely busy, B has more authority in this area than C does, and C has a reputation of always doing his best for his patients. Also, our actual experience with the two doctors seems to confirm this background information. We are interested in the reliabilities of the two doctors. We are also concerned that B's being busy may mean that B does not spend enough time examining our friend's case. Therefore we formulate our knowledge about the two doctors as two belief sets $\mathbb{B}_1$ and $\mathbb{B}_2$, with each $\mathbb{B}_i$ containing our (intuitive) beliefs about a doctor:

$\mathbb{B}_1$ = {(AuthorityB ∧ BusyB) (1);
(BusyB → LessCaseStudyB) (.8) ∨
(BusyB → ¬LessCaseStudyB) (.2);
AuthorityB ∧ LessCaseStudyB → ReliableB) (.7) ∨
AuthorityB ∧ LessCaseStudyB → ¬ReliableB) (.3);
(AuthorityB ∧ ¬LessCaseStudyB → ReliableB) (.95) ∨
(AuthorityB ∧ ¬LessCaseStudyB → ¬ReliableB) (.05)}

$\mathbb{B}_2$ = {(SemiAuthorityC ∧ ReputationC) (1);
(SemiAuthorityC ∧ ReputationC → ReliableC) (.8) ∨
(SemiAuthorityC ∧ ReputationC → ¬ReliableC) (.2)}

After diagnosis, doctor B determines with full confidence that the patient has either illness X or illness Y. Also after diagnosis, doctor C determines with full confidence that the patient has either illness Y or illness Z. It is a medical fact that a person can not have any two of these three illnesses at the same time. Therefore we let the frame of (the main variable) Illness to be {X, Y, Z, OTHER}, and we specify three more categorical beliefs:

$\mathbb{B}_3$ = {(BSaysXY ∧ CSaysYZ) (1);
(BSaysXY ∧ ReliableB → (Illness = Y) ∨ (Illness = Z)) (1);
(CSaysYZ ∧ ReliableC → (Illness = Y) ∨ (Illness = Z)) (1)}.

With $\mathbb{B} = \mathbb{B}_1 \cup \mathbb{B}_2 \cup \mathbb{B}_3$, we get: BEL($\mathbb{B}$, (Illness = X)) = 0; BEL($\mathbb{B}$, (Illness = Z)) = 0; BEL($\mathbb{B}$, (Illness = Y)) = .6; BEL($\mathbb{B}$, (Illness = X) ∨ (illness = Y)) = .75; BEL($\mathbb{B}$, (Illness = Y) ∨ (Illness = Z)) = .8; BEL($\mathbb{B}$, (Illness = X) ∨ (Illness = Y) ∨ (Illness = Z)) = .95, etc.

4. Discussion

Appropriateness of the notation. The belief calculus serves as a (notational) alternative for the the use of the D-S formalism for uncertain reasoning. As such, the appropriateness of the belief calculus (as a notation) will have to depend on the application domain, and there may well be situations in which set-theoretic notations are more appropriate.

[9]The author thanks Nic Wilson and Philippe Smets for arriving at this characterization of distinctness.

[10]A source is reliable (with respect to the information it provides) if the information it provides is indeed true.

However, it may be worthwhile to point out a superficial but nevertheless important "difference" between the (uses of the) two notations: with the belief calculus, we can sometimes explicitly specify what our evidence is and how this evidence induces beliefs; whereas with the usual set-theoretic notations, the evidence is generally regarded as "outside of" our specifications of beliefs.

Tractability. The computational complexity of the belief calculus is exponential with respect to the number of variables in a belief set, and there are ways for improving the speed of this computation (e.g., [Kennes and Smets 90; Shafer et al. 87; Wilson 89]).

We might also look at this complexity problem from a different perspective: if we treat propositional provability (which is well known for its NP-completeness!) as the basic operator, then the complexity of the belief calculus is exponential with respect to the number of beliefs in a belief set. Thus, if we have many variables but only a few beliefs in a belief set, then a deduction-based approach such as ATMS + D-S (see [Provan 89b] for a complexity analysis of ATMS + D-S) may turn out to be a more attractive way for computing BEL.

5. Conclusion

We formulated the D-S formalism along the lines of natural deduction systems. This formulation (called the belief calculus) allows us to infer beliefs from beliefs without ever appealing to the use of set-theoretic notations.

To show how the belief calculus may be used for uncertain reasoning, we gave three examples. These examples suggested different ways for modelling real world situations.

Acknowledgements. The author thanks Mike Clarke, Robert Kennes, Alessandro Saffiotti, Philippe Smets, and Nic Wilson for stimulating discussions, and two anonymous referees for very helpful comments.

References

D'Ambrosio, B. (1987). Truth maintenance with numeric certainty estimates. *Proceedings of the Third IEEE Conference on AI Applications*, Orlando, Florida, 244-249.

D'Ambrosio, B. (1988). A hybrid approach to reasoning under uncertainty. *International Journal of Approximate Reasoning*, **2**, 1, 29-45.

de Kleer, J. (1986a). An assumption-based truth maintenance system. *Artificial Intelligence*, **28**, 2, 127-162.

de Kleer, J. (1986b). Extending the ATMS. *Artificial Intelligence*, **28**, 2, 163-196.

Dubois, D. and Prade, H. (1986). The principle of minimum specificity as a basis for evidential reasoning. In *Uncertainty in Knowledge-Based Systems* (Bouchon and Yager eds.), Springer-Verlag, Berlin, 75-84.

Fagin, R. and Halpern, J. Y. (1989). Uncertainty, belief, and probability. *Proceedings of the Eleventh International Joint Conference on Artificial Intelligence*, Detroit, Michigan, Aug. 20-25, 1161-1167.

Gordon, J. and Shortliffe, E. H. (1984). The Dempster-Shafer theory of evidence. In *Rule-Based Expert Systems: The MYCIN Experiments of the Stanford Heuristic Programming Project* (Buchanan and Shortliffe eds.), Addison-Wesley, Reading, Mass., 272-292.

Kennes, R. and Smets, P. (1990). Fast algorithms for Dempster-Shafer theory. (submitted for publication).

Kong, A. (1986). Multivariate belief functions and graphical models. Doctoral dissertation, Department of Statistics, Harvard University.

Laskey, K. B. and Lehner, P. E. (1988). Belief maintenance: An integrated approach to uncertainty management. *Proceedings of the Seventh AAAI Conference*, Saint Paul, Minnesota, Aug. 21-26, 210-214.

Laskey, K. B. and Lehner, P. E. (1989). Assumptions, beliefs and probabilities. *Artificial Intelligence*, **41**, 1, 65-77.

Pearl, J. (1986). Fusion, propagation, and structuring in belief networks. *Artificial Intelligence*, **29**, 241-288.

Provan, G. (1989a). An analysis of ATMS-based techniques for computing Dempster-Shafer belief functions. *Proceedings of the Eleventh International Joint Conference on Artificial Intelligence*, Detroit, Michigan, Aug. 20-25, 1115-1120.

Provan, G. (1989b). A logic-based analysis of Dempster Shafer theory. Technical Report 89-08, Computer Science Dept., University of British Columbia.

Ruspini, E. H. (1987). Epistemic logics, probability, and the calculus of evidence. *Proceedings of the Tenth International Joint Conference on Artificial Intelligence.*

Shafer, G. (1976). *A Mathematical Theory of Evidence.* Princeton University Press.

Shafer, G., Shenoy, P. P. and Mellouli, K. (1987). Propagating belief functions in qualitative Markov trees. *International Journal of Approximate Reasoning*, **1**, 349-400.

Smets, P. (1978). Un modèle mathématico-statistique simulant le processus du diagnostic médical. Doctoral dissertation, Université Libre de Bruxelles, Bruxelles.

Smets, P. (1988). Belief functions. In *Non-Standard Logics for Automated Reasoning* (P. Smets, E. H. Mamdani, D. Dubois and H. Prade eds.). Academic Press, London.

Wilson, N. (1989). Justification, computational efficiency and generalisation of the Dempster-Shafer theory.

Yen, J. (1989). Gertis: A Dempster-Shafer approach to diagnosing hierarchical hypotheses. *Communications of the ACM*, **32**, 5, 573-585.

Zarley, D., Hsia, Y.-T., and Shafer, G. (1988). Evidential reasoning using DELIEF. *Proceedings of the Seventh AAAI Conference*, St. Paul, Minnesota, **1**, 205-209.

Symbolic Probabilistic Inference in Belief Networks

Ross D. Shachter, Engineering-Economic Systems Dept. Stanford University Stanford, CA 94305-4025 shachter@sumex-aim.stanford.edu

Bruce D'Ambrosio, and Department of Computer Science Oregon State University Corvallis, OR 97331-3902 dambrosio@cs.orst.edu

Brendan A. Del Favero Engineering-Economic Systems Dept. Stanford University Stanford, CA 94305-4025 a.apollo@macbeth.stanford.edu

Abstract

The Symbolic Probabilistic Inference (SPI) Algorithm [D'Ambrosio, 1989] provides an efficient framework for resolving general queries on a belief network. It applies the concept of dependency-directed backward search to probabilistic inference, and is incremental with respect to both queries and observations. Unlike most belief network algorithms, SPI is goal directed, performing only those calculations that are required to respond to queries. The directed graph of the underlying belief network is used to develop a tree structure for recursive query processing. This allows effective caching of intermediate results and significant opportunities for parallel computation. A simple preprocessing step ensures that, given the search tree, the algorithm will include no unnecessary distributions. The preprocessing step eliminates dimensions from the intermediate results and prunes the search path.

1. Introduction

Belief networks, directed graphical structures representing the probabilistic dependency among a set of variables, are an increasingly popular knowledge representation for uncertain reasoning. Much of their success is due to a growing body of methods for evaluating queries and performing probabilistic inference. The most popular methods [Jensen et al., 1990; Kim and Pearl, 1983; Lauritzen and Spiegelhalter, 1988; Pearl, 1986] gain much of their performance by efficient precomputation of simple queries in response to new observations.

The Symbolic Probabilistic Inference Algorithm (SPI) [D'Ambrosio, 1989; D'Ambrosio and Shachter, 1990], on the other hand, is a goal-driven method, which can respond to arbitrary conditional or conjunctive queries. SPI is incremental with respect to both queries and observations. It uses the structural information in the belief network graph to construct a search tree of efficiently evaluable factored symbolic expressions, which allows parallel computation and caching of intermediate results. By incorporating an efficient preprocessing step and recognizing when we do not need a full joint distribution, it can achieve additional savings in search and computation.

Section 2 presents an overview of SPI and the key concepts which underlie it, while Section 3 is a formal presentation of the framework and proofs of the correctness of SPI. The details of the algorithm are presented in Section 4, and conclusions and extensions are in Section 5.

2. Overview

SPI reorganizes the nodes in a belief network into a tree structure for query processing by a procedure in which every node is visited at most twice. Queries are directed to the root of the tree, which in turn generates queries for its subtrees and so forth until the response to a particular query can be determined and returned to the next higher level. Once a node has responses from all of its subtrees it can compute its own response. This process continues until the root of the tree returns a response for the original query. The performance of SPI depends critically on the organization of this search tree.

There is a condition on the construction of the search tree: if there is an arc between two nodes in the original belief network, then one node must be the root of a subtree containing the other. In other words, there can be no arcs in the belief net between nodes that are in parallel subtrees. Conversely, whenever two nodes are "separated" by higher root nodes, they can and should be placed in different subtrees. (Two nodes are said to be <u>separated</u> by a set if every undirected path between the nodes contains an element from the set.)

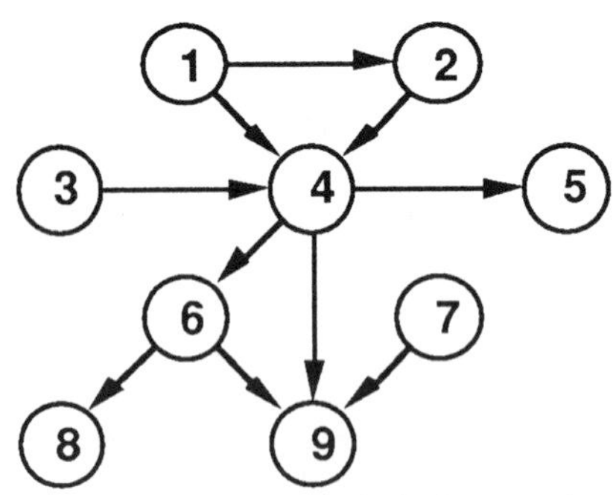

Figure 1. Example belief network.

For example, consider the belief network shown in Figure 1, containing nodes numbered 1 through 9. Any node can be chosen to be the root of a search tree, but node 4 seems like a promising choice, since it separates the other nodes into four subtrees, $\{1, 2\}$, $\{3\}$, $\{5\}$, and $\{6, 7, 8, 9\}$. A possible search tree for this network is shown in Figure 2a. Some other search trees for the network are drawn in Figure 2b and 2c. There are many different configurations for the subtree {6, 7, 8, 9} in a tree rooted by node 4. Several of these are shown in Figures 2d, 2e, 2f, and 2g. Note that in the tree drawn in Figure 2e, node 7 roots one of the subtrees for node 6. There is no requirement that a subtree root, such as node 7, have an arc in the belief network to one of its higher level roots. The only requirement is that, since there is an arc (7, 9) in the belief net, node 9 must either be higher or lower than node 7 in the tree.

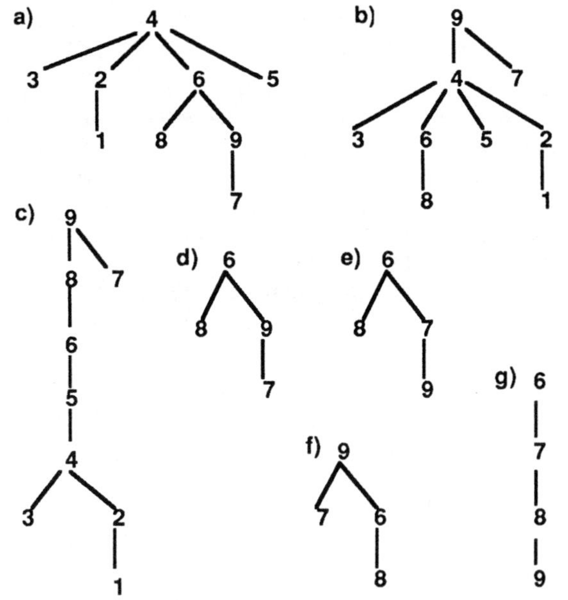

Figure 2. Possible search trees for the network in Fig. 1.

In general, there are many alternate tree structures possible for a given belief network. We would like to choose a structure that facilitates optimal performance for the anticipated queries. Since the processing in parallel subtrees is independent, it can be performed in parallel and using independent information. This suggests that a good heuristic might be to branch wherever possible and as high as possible in the tree. One rule of thumb might be to select that root node for which the largest subtree is as small as possible. In this respect the tree drawn in Figure 2a is better than the ones in 2b and 2c.

We can illustrate the basic concepts underlying SPI with a few simple examples. Corresponding to each node j in the belief network is a conditional probability distribution π_j for the variable X_j, conditioned on j's parents. The joint probability distribution for all of the variables is obtained in factored form by multiplying their conditional distributions,

$$P\{X_1=x_1, \ldots, X_9=x_9\}$$
$$= P\{X_1=x_1\}\, P\{X_2=x_2 \mid X_1=x_1\} \ldots P\{X_9=x_9 \mid X_{4,6,7}=x_{4,6,7}\}$$
$$= \pi_1(x_1)\, \pi_2(x_{1,2}) \ldots \pi_9(x_{4,6,7,9}),$$

where $x_{4,6,7,9}$ is a vector whose components are symbolically matched to the proper dimensions.

Suppose that we want to find $P\{X_1\}$. Of course, this is simply stored in π_1, but we can find it by using the more general method of summing over the joint distribution,

$$P\{X_1=x_1\} = \Sigma_{x_{2,\ldots,9}} P\{X_1=x_1, \ldots, X_9=x_9\}$$
$$= \Sigma_{x_{2,\ldots,9}} \pi_1(x_1)\, \pi_2(x_{1,2}) \ldots \pi_9(x_{4,6,7,9}).$$

Now we can recognize that π_1 does not vary in the summation, and thus it can be brought out of the sum. Using the property that conditional distributions sum to 1, we can eliminate each of the distributions in turn to obtain

$$P\{X_1=x_1\}$$
$$= \pi_1(x_1)\, \Sigma_{x_{2,\ldots,9}} \pi_2(x_{1,2}) \ldots \pi_9(x_{4,6,7,9})$$
$$= \pi_1(x_1).$$

In a similar way we can find $P\{X_1 \mid X_2\}$, which can easily be computed[1] from $P\{X_1, X_2\}$,

$$P\{X_1=x_1, X_2=x_2\}$$
$$= \Sigma_{x_{3,\ldots,9}} P\{X_1=x_1, \ldots, X_9=x_9\}$$
$$= \pi_1(x_1)\, \pi_2(x_{1,2}).$$

This approach can also be applied to more complex problems, such as $P\{X_5 \mid X_2\}$,

$$P\{X_{5,2}=x_{5,2}\}$$
$$= \Sigma_{x_{1,3,4,6,7,8,9}} P\{X_1=x_1, \ldots, X_9=x_9\}$$
$$= \Sigma_{x_{1,3,4,6,7,8,9}} \pi_1(x_1)\, \pi_2(x_{1,2})\, \pi_9(x_{4,6,7,9})$$
$$= \Sigma_{x_{1,3,4}} \pi_1(x_1)\, \pi_2(x_{1,2})\, \pi_3(x_3)\, \pi_4(x_{1,2,3,4})\, \pi_5(x_{4,5}).$$

We are unable to simplify this final expression any more by distributing terms. To compute any further, we must use the actual numbers. Nonetheless, it does still pay to order the terms so as to minimize the number of calculations and the size of intermediate results [D'Ambrosio and Shachter, 1990].

Suppose that X_3 has been observed with value x^*_3. The solution for $P\{X_5, X_2 \mid X_3 = x^*_3\}$ is similar to the one above, except that the specific value for x_3 can be substituted into all of the distributions and it should not be summed,

$$P\{X_{5,2}=x_{5,2} \mid X_3=x^*_3\}$$
$$= \Sigma_{x_{1,4}} \pi_1(x_1)\, \pi_2(x_{1,2})\, \pi_3(x^*_3)\, \pi_4(x_{1,2,4}, x^*_3)\, \pi_5(x_{4,5}).$$

Finally, suppose that we want to find $P\{X_5 \mid X_4\}$. We could easily obtain this from $P\{X_5, X_4\}$, but we can save work if we recognize the difference between the two

---

[1] A conditional probability is defined as $P\{X_1=x_1 | X_2=x_2\} = P\{X_1=x_1, X_2=x_2\} / \Sigma_{y_1} P\{X_1=y_1, X_2=x_2\}$.

queries. The former is simply the distribution, $P\{ X_5=x_5 \mid X_4=x_4 \} = \pi_5(x_{4,5})$, while the latter requires multiplication and summation. In general, we can recognize cases in which we can obtain the conditional more easily that the joint distribution.

The operations shown in these examples correspond exactly to those in SPI. There are three basic operators: product of distributions, summation of a distribution over a set of variables, and substitution of an observed value into a distribution. We can apply these operators both symbolically and numerically. Symbolic operations help us recognize when we can apply the distributive law to pull a factor out of a summation. On the other hand, we must sooner or later evaluate to numbers. If we maintain a cache of numerical results, we can avoid repeating their calculation.

3. Framework and Notation

In this section, we provide a formal description of the framework for the algorithm, and prove the fundamental results underlying it.

We assume that we are given a fully specified belief network, which contains a directed acyclic graph on a set of nodes N. Each node j corresponds to a random variable X_j, which can take on a finite number of possible values $x_j \in \Omega_j$ with conditional probability distribution π_j. As a convention, a lower case letter represents a single node while an upper case letter represents a set of nodes, so that X_J denotes the vector of variables indexed by the set J. Therefore, the conditional distribution π_j for node j can be expressed in terms of its parents or conditional predecessors C(j),

$$\pi_j (x_{j \cup C(j)}) = P\{ X_j = x_j \mid X_{C(j)} = x_{C(j)} \}.$$

If the node j has no parents, $C(j) = \emptyset$ and π_j is an unconditional probability distribution. Distribution π_j has dimensions D(j),

$$D(j) = j \cup C(j),$$

and we can think of the distribution as a nonnegative function, $\pi_j\colon \Omega_{D(j)} \rightarrow \boldsymbol{R}$. We can extend the definition of node conditional distributions and their dimensions to apply to sets so that

$$D(J) = \cup_{j \in J} D(j),$$

and

$$\pi_J (x_{D(J)}) = \Pi_{j \in J}\ \pi_j(x_{D(j)}).$$

We say that there is an undirected path or chain between nodes i and j if we can get from node i to node j in the network along arcs ignoring their direction. When there is a chain between two nodes, they are said to be connected; otherwise they are disconnected. Clearly, if node i is connected to node j, then node i will be connected to node k if and only if j is connected to k. We can therefore identify the maximal connected sets of nodes, called components. If there is some set S such that every chain between nodes i and j contains a node from S, S is said to separate i and j. Any set of nodes disjoint from S can be partitioned into maximal sets which are the components separated by S.

A structure on a set of nodes is said to be a tree if exactly one of the nodes is identified as its root and the others are partitioned into subtrees, which are themselves trees. In SPI, all of the nodes are organized into a search tree. For each node i, let T(i) be the nodes in the subtree rooted at node i and let S(i) be the roots of all subtrees containing i. The components of T(i) \ {i} [2] separated by S(i) form the subtrees of T(i), and the roots of those subtrees are given by R(i). For example, in the tree drawn in Figure 2a, T(6) = {6, 8, 9, 7 }, S(6) = { 4, 6 }, and R(6) = { 8, 9 }. If there are separate components in the original belief network, one can create a "fictitious node" 0 with no arcs, so $D(0) = \emptyset$ and $\pi_0 = 1$. Each of the components is then a subtree in T(0).

As stated earlier, the search tree has one restriction on its organization. If there is an arc between nodes i and j in the belief network then either $i \in S(j)$ or $j \in S(i)$. This is enforced automatically by including all (conditionally) connected nodes in the same subtree. There is still tremendous flexibility in the construction of the search tree, since the choice of root node for any tree is arbitrary.

Generalized Distributions

A nonnegative function $Q\colon \Omega_{J \cup K} \rightarrow \boldsymbol{R}$ will be called a (generalized) distribution for J given K if it can be normalized to compute $P\{ X_J \mid X_K \}$, namely,

$$P\{ X_J = x_J \mid X_K = x_K \} = Q(x_J, x_K) / \Sigma_{y_J \in \Omega_J} Q(y_J, x_K) .$$

Although the generalized distribution contains sufficient information to compute the conditional distribution, it might not have enough to compute the joint distribution $P\{ X_{J \cup K} \}$. We define three operators on these distributions: product, summation, and substitution. Given distributions Q_1 and Q_2 on sets J_1 and J_2, the conformal product of the distributions is given by

$$Q = \langle *, Q_1, Q_2 \rangle$$

where $Q\{ x_{J_1 \cup J_2} \} = Q_1\{ x_{J_1} \} Q_2\{ x_{J_2} \}$.

The summation over dimensions K is $Q = \langle \Sigma, K, Q_1 \rangle$ where $Q\{ x_{J \setminus K} \} = \Sigma_{x_K \in \Omega_K} Q_1(x_J)$.

Lastly, the substitution of observation x^*_i in dimension i is $Q = \langle \downarrow, i, x^*_i, Q_1 \rangle$ where $Q(x_{J_1 \setminus \{i\}}) = Q_1\{ X_i = x^*_i, X_{J_1 \setminus \{i\}} = x_{J_1 \setminus \{i\}} \}$.

Note that the product increases the dimension of the resulting distribution, while the summation and substitution decrease it. Processing time is proportional to the size of the distributions, which are exponential in the number of dimensions, so it is advantageous to postpone performing the product operation as long as possible, and instead to perform summation and substitution as soon as possible.

We can represent a distribution either by the actual

[2] The symbol "\" is set subtraction, $A \setminus B = \{ j \in A : j \notin B \}$.

function, or by a symbolic expression of operators applied to distributions. Symbolic manipulation to the expression allows us to reorder terms to reduce computation time. Of course, at any time, the expression can be evaluated to obtain the numerical distribution. The key to reordering operations is given by the following lemma, which just states the distributive law for addition and multiplication of real numbers in terms of the notation for SPI.

<u>Lemma 1. Distributive Law for Distributions</u>

Given distributions Q_1 and Q_2 on sets J_1 and J_2

$$\langle \Sigma, K, \langle *, Q_1, Q_2 \rangle \rangle$$
$$= \langle \Sigma, K \cap J_1, \langle *, Q_1, \langle \Sigma, K \cap (J_2 \setminus J_1), Q_2 \rangle \rangle.$$

The lemma states that instead of summing after multiplying two distributions, we can sum one distribution over dimensions for which the other distribution does not vary before multiplying the distributions. Since this reduces the number of dimensions processed in the outer sum, it can lead to substantial savings. We will try to exploit this property whenever possible in evaluating a query. Consider the search tree shown in Figure 3, in which A, B, and C are now sets of nodes. This represents the general case in SPI, in which B is a subtree, C is the union of B's sibling subtrees, if any, and A is the remainder of the nodes N in the network. If we want to find $P\{X_M\}$ for some subset M of N, then the distributive law can be applied to this search tree, by the following theorem.

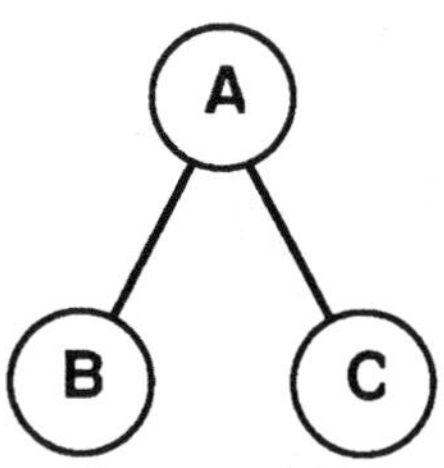

Figure 3. General Network for the Proof of SPI.

<u>Theorem 1.</u>

Given an arbitrary subset M of N, and a partition of N into sets A, B, and C, such that B and C are separated by A, then the generalized distribution

$Q(x_M) = P\{X_M = x_M\}$ is

$$Q = \langle \Sigma, M' \setminus M, \langle *, \pi_A, \langle *, \langle \Sigma, B \setminus M', \pi_B \rangle, \langle \Sigma, C \setminus M', \pi_C \rangle \rangle \rangle \rangle,$$

where $M' = M \cup D(A)$.

<u>Proof:</u>

Q can be obtained by summing all variables except M from the joint distribution, which is just the product of the node distributions,

$$Q = \langle \Sigma, N \setminus M, P\{X_N\} \rangle$$
$$= \langle \Sigma, N \setminus M, \langle *, \pi_A, \langle *, \pi_B, \pi_C \rangle \rangle \rangle.$$

Since dimensions D(A) appear in distributions π_A we cannot pull π_A out of the sum for D(A). Nonetheless, the construction of the search tree ensures that $D(B) \cap D(C) \subseteq D(A)$, so three applications of Lemma 1 yield

$$Q = \langle \Sigma, M' \setminus M, \langle *, \pi_A, \langle \Sigma, \emptyset, \langle *, \langle \Sigma, B \setminus M', \pi_B \rangle, \langle \Sigma, C \setminus M', \pi_C \rangle \rangle \rangle \rangle \rangle.$$

In general, the response to a query is a generalized distribution and not necessarily a full joint distribution. Suppose that the desired distribution has dimensions M and is obtained by multiplying the distributions in nodes L, where $D(L) = M \cup L$. The resulting distribution, $P\{X_{M \cap L} \mid X_{M \setminus L}\}$, is then obtained by summing over $L \setminus M$. For example, Theorem 1 is the special case for which L = N. The search tree in Figure 3 can now be applied to the conditional case.

<u>Theorem 2.</u>

Given arbitrary subsets M and L of N such that $D(L) = M \cup L$, and a partition of N into sets A, B, and C, such that B and C are separated by A, then the generalized distribution

$Q(x_M) = P\{X_{M \cap L} = x_{M \cap L} \mid X_{M \setminus L} = x_{M \setminus L}\}$ is

$$Q = \langle \Sigma, M' \setminus M, \langle *, \pi_{A \cap L}, \langle *, \langle \Sigma, B \cap L \setminus M', \pi_{B \cap L} \rangle, \langle \Sigma, C \cap L \setminus M', \pi_{C \cap L} \rangle \rangle \rangle \rangle,$$

where $M' = L \cap [M \cup D(A \cap L)]$.

<u>Proof</u>:

Because $D(L) = M \cup L$, summation and product yield

$$Q = \langle \Sigma, L \setminus M, \langle *, \pi_{A \cap L}, \langle *, \pi_{B \cap L}, \pi_{C \cap L} \rangle \rangle \rangle$$
$$= \langle \Sigma, M' \setminus M, \langle *, \pi_{A \cap L}, \Sigma, \emptyset, \langle *, \langle \Sigma, B \cap L \setminus M', \pi_{B \cap L} \rangle, \langle \Sigma, C \cap L \setminus M', \pi_{C \cap L} \rangle \rangle \rangle \rangle,$$

by the same logic as Theorem 1.

Incorporating Evidence

Evidence is entered in the system in the form of exact observations of the values of variables. The set of variables which have been observed is denoted by E. Suppose that X_i has been observed with the value x^*_i. The substitution operator $\langle \downarrow, i, x^*_i, Q \rangle$ can now be applied to any distribution Q to incorporate that evidence into the distribution. There is no longer any need to sum out dimension i and, in fact, it would be an error to do so. Because dimension i can no longer be summed over and the substitution operator eliminates all instances of it, it can be freely distributed within all products, down to the node distributions themselves. This substitution at each node distribution can be performed at every computation, but it is much simpler to substitute for dimension i in every distribution in which it appears whenever its observation is reported. Those distributions in which dimension i appears belong to node i and its children. Therefore, the node distributions π_j for those nodes should be modified by

$$\pi_j(x_{D(j) \setminus E}) \leftarrow \pi_j(x_{D(j) \setminus E}, x^*_i) = \langle \downarrow, i, x^*_i, \pi_j \rangle.$$

Once the evidence has been incorporated into the node distributions, all of our earlier results can be applied, using the new dimensions of the distributions. For example, suppose that a desired distribution has dimensions M and is obtained by multiplying the distributions in nodes L, where $D(L) = M \cup L \cup E$ and $M \cap E = \emptyset$. This is a straightforward extension of Theorem 2.

Corollary 1.

Given arbitrary subsets M and L of N such that $D(L) = M \cup L \cup E$ and $M \cap E = \emptyset$, and a partition of N into sets A, B, and C, such that B and C are separated by A, then the generalized distribution

$$Q(x_M) = P\{ X_{M \cap L} = x_{M \cap L}, X_{E \cap L} = x^*_{E \cap L} \mid X_{M \setminus L} = x_{M \setminus L}, X_{E \setminus L} = x^*_{E \setminus L} \}$$ is

$$Q = \langle \Sigma, M' \setminus M, \langle *, \pi_{A \cap L}, \langle *, \langle \Sigma, B \cap L \setminus (E \cup M'), \pi_{B \cap L} \rangle, \langle \Sigma, C \cap L \setminus (E \cup M'), \pi_{C \cap L} \rangle \rangle \rangle \rangle,$$

where $M' = (L \setminus E) \cap [M \cup D(A \cap L)]$.

4. The Symbolic Probabilistic Inference Algorithm

We can now present a complete description of SPI in terms of the framework developed in the previous section, given a belief network and a search tree.

The general form of query received by SPI is of the form $P\{ X_J \mid X_K, X_E = x^*_E \}$, where x^*_E are the recorded observations. This query is transformed and sent to the highest root node in the search tree. When that node has obtained a response to all of its queries from its subtrees, it returns a generalized distribution for J given K, which can then be normalized to the desired result.

The query actually sent to the highest root node consists of the set of node distributions L needed to respond to the query and the dimensions M of the desired response. The sets L and M can be computed by an algorithm which runs in time linear in the number of nodes and arcs in the belief network graph [Geiger et al., 1989; Geiger et al., 1990; Shachter, 1988; Shachter, 1990]. This algorithm operates on a copy of the graph: after deleting all outgoing arcs from $K \cup E$ and deleting all nodes which are neither in nor ancestors of $J \cup K \cup E$, the set L is those nodes connected to J and $M = (J \cup K) \cap D(L)$.[3] These sets satisfy $D(L) = M \cup L \cup E$ and $M \cap E = \emptyset$. The formulae are efficient and simple to implement. We refer the reader to the above-cited literature for more explanation.

The response from the search tree will be a generalized distribution Q for J given K satisfying

$$P\{ X_J = x_J \mid X_K = x_K, X_E = x^*_E \} = Q(x_M) / \Sigma_{y_J \in \Omega_J} Q(y_J, x_{M \setminus J}).$$

The heart of the SPI algorithm can now be described. At any node i, a request arrives for a distribution to be obtained by multiplying the distributions in nodes L and summing over dimensions $L \setminus (E \cup M)$, which must therefore have dimensions $W = M \cup [D(L) \setminus (L \cup E)]$. The node's response is a generalized distribution Q for $W \cap L$ given $W \setminus L$,

$$Q(x_W) = P\{ X_{W \cap L} = x_{W \cap L}, X_{E \cap L} = x^*_{E \cap L} \mid X_{W \setminus L} = x_{W \setminus L}, X_{E \setminus L} = x^*_{E \setminus L} \}.$$

Of course, if such a distribution had been computed earlier and cached, it could be returned immediately. Usually, however, it will be necessary to send requests to the subtrees below this node in order to compute the response.

The recursive step of the SPI request is shown in Figure 4. The first three **if** statements check whether there is a cached result and whether the main processing block can be avoided by recognizing two important special cases. The main processing block in general has been verfied by Corollary 1.

```
algorithm Request ( i, L, M )
begin
  if ( L, M ) is cached at this node
  then Qi ← cached result
  else if L = Ø
       then Qi ← 1
  else if L = {i}
       then Qi ← πi
  else begin main processing block
    if i ∈ L
    then M' ← ( L \ E ) ∩ [ M ∪ D( i ) ]
    else M' ← M ;
    Qi ← 1 ;
    for r ∈ R(i)
       Qi ← ⟨ *, Qi, Request (r, L∩T(r), M'∩T(r)) ⟩ ;
    if i ∈ L
    then Qi ← ⟨ Σ, M' \ M, ⟨ *, πi, Qi ⟩ ⟩ ;
    if caching of result is desired
    then cache result Qi for (L, M) ;
  end main processing block ;
  return Qi ;
end ;
```

Figure 4. The recursive ***request*** *procedure for each node in the SPI algorithm.*

The query nature of SPI is designed to allow caching of responses at each node. Whenever an observation is received for node i, and the substitution operation performed on the distribution of node i and its children, all caches above node i and its children in the search tree become suspect, and should be removed from the caches. Alternatively, a check similar to the algorithm for determining the original M set could be performed to recognize for which cached expressions the new evidence is relevant, and only those expressions need be removed from the cache [Shachter, 1990].

The cache management scheme can exploit the generalized distributions being returned. Suppose that the

[3] We assume without loss of generality that E, K, and J are disjoint. If they are not, then the response can be computed using E, K\E, and J\(K∪E), with an additional check for consistency among the overlapping values.

distribution Q_c, the response to a request (L_c, M_c), has been cached. Q_c can serve as the response to a subsequent request (L, M) with the same dimensions, provided that $L \subseteq L_c$, since in that case Q_c has "too much" information. On the other hand, if $L \supset L_c$, then a new response must be computed, and it might as well replace Q_c in the cache.

Examples

Suppose that SPI were applied to the query P{ $X_5 \mid X_2$ } for the belief network in Figure 1 using the search tree in Figure 2a. The following results would be obtained:

$J \leftarrow \{5\}, K \leftarrow \{2\}, E \leftarrow \emptyset$;
$Q \leftarrow$ Request(4, {1,2,3,4,5}, {2,5}) ;
$Q_4 \leftarrow \langle \Sigma, \{1,3,4\}, \langle *, \pi_4,$ Request(2, {1,2}, {1,2}),
Request(3, {3}, {3}),
Request(5, {5}, {5}),
Request(6, Ø, Ø) $\rangle\rangle$;
$Q_2 \leftarrow \langle \Sigma, \emptyset, \langle *, \pi_2,$ Request(1, {1}, {1}) $\rangle\rangle$;
$Q_1 \leftarrow \pi_1$; $Q_3 \leftarrow \pi_3$; $Q_5 \leftarrow \pi_5$; and $Q_6 \leftarrow 1$.

Now, suppose that observations were made of $X_6 = x^*_6$ and $X_9 = x^*_9$. The caches for nodes 8, 9, 6, and 4 would be invalidated and $E \leftarrow \{6,9\}$;
$\pi_6 \leftarrow \langle \downarrow, 6, x^*_6, \pi_6 \rangle$; $\pi_8 \leftarrow \langle \downarrow, 6, x^*_6, \pi_8 \rangle$; and
$\pi_9 \leftarrow \langle \downarrow, 9, x^*_9, \pi_9 \rangle$.
In response to query P{ $X_2 \mid X_6 = x^*_6, X_9 = x^*_9$ }:
$J \leftarrow \{2\}, K \leftarrow \emptyset$;
$Q \leftarrow$ Request(4, {1,2,3,4,6,7,9}, {1}) ;
$Q_4 \leftarrow \langle \Sigma, \{1,3,4\}, \langle *, \pi_4,$ Request(2, {1,2}, {1,2}),
Request(3, {3}, {3}),
Request(5, Ø, Ø),
Request(6, {6,7,9}, Ø) $\rangle\rangle$;
$Q_2 \leftarrow$ cached result from above ;
$Q_6 \leftarrow \langle \Sigma, \emptyset, \langle *, \pi_6,$ Request(8, Ø, Ø),
Request(9, {7,9}, {Ø}) $\rangle\rangle$;
$Q_9 \leftarrow \langle \Sigma, \{7\}, \langle *, \pi_9,$ Request(7, {7}, {7}) $\rangle\rangle$;
$Q_3 \leftarrow \pi_3$; $Q_5 \leftarrow 1$, $Q_7 \leftarrow \pi_7$; and $Q_8 \leftarrow 1$;

5. Conclusions and Extensions

In this paper, we have presented the Symbolic Probabilistic Inference Algorithm along with a proof of its correctness. SPI is a goal-driven rather than data-driven algorithm, which performs a variation of dependency-directed backward search in response to arbitrary conditional queries.

There are many ways that SPI can be refined for practical implementation. The most significant issue is the construction of the search tree. A promising approach appears to be recursive decomposition, in which the search tree is made as balanced and shallow as possible [Cooper, 1990; Fiduccia and Mattheyses, 1982]. This not only allows for parallel processing along the independent branches, but means that observations will invalidate the fewest possible caches.

Given a search tree, there are still difficult (NP-hard) decisions to made, since there can be significant benefit to postponing evaluation of an expression, maintaining it in symbolic rather than numeric form. For example, if one factor in a distribution product shares none of the dimensions being summed over, then that factor can be pulled out of the sum as in Lemma 1. It might also be worthwhile to reorder the factors in the product before performing the summation [D'Ambrosio, 1989; D'Ambrosio and Shachter, 1990] .

There are additional interesting tradeoffs between symbolic and numeric computations of intermediate results. By evaluating expressions completely at nodes, caches can be created to prevent repeated computations. Sometimes, however, postponing those evaluations can lead to improved factoring opportunities. Finally, the search tree can be constructed dynamically in response to queries, yielding the most efficient search structure, but eliminating caching opportunities. Much needs to be learned about the relative benefits of such customized query-processing versus maintaining the accumulated information.

6. Acknowledgements

We benefited greatly from the comments of Greg Cooper, Mike Fehling, Eric Horvitz, Perry McCarty, Ramesh Patil, and Mike Wellman.

7. References

Cooper, G. G. (1990). Bayesian belief-network inference using recursive decomposition (KSL 90-05). Knowledge Systems Laboratory, Stanford University.

D'Ambrosio, B. (1989). Symbolic probabilistic inference in belief nets . Department of Computer Science, Oregon State University.

D'Ambrosio, B. and Shachter, R. D. (1990). Factoring Heuristics for Generalized SPI. Conference on Uncertainty in Artificial Intelligence, Boston, submitted.

Fiduccia, C. M. and Mattheyses, R. M. (1982). A linear-time heuristic for improving network reliability. Nineteenth Design Automation Conference, Las Vegas.

Geiger, D., Verma, T., and Pearl, J. (1989). d-separation: from theorems to algorithms. Fifth Workshop on Uncertainty in Artificial Intelligence, University of Windsor, Ontario, 118-125.

Geiger, D., Verma, T., and Pearl., J. (1990). Identifying independence in Bayesian networks. *Networks*, to appear.

Jensen, F. V., Olesen, K. G., and Andersen, S. K. (1990). An algebra of Bayesian belief universes for knowledge based systems. *Networks*, to appear.

Kim, J. H. and Pearl, J. (1983). A computational model for causal and diagnostic reasoning in inference engines. 8th International Joint Conference on Artificial Intelligence, Karlsruhe, West Germany.

Lauritzen, S. L. and Spiegelhalter, D. J. (1988). Local computations with probabilities on graphical structures and their application to expert systems. *J. Royal Statist. Soc. B*, 50(2), 157-224.

Pearl, J. (1986). Fusion, propagation and structuring in belief networks. *Artificial Intelligence*, 29(3), 241-288.

Shachter, R. D. (1988). Probabilistic Inference and Influence Diagrams. *Operations Research*, 36(July-August), 589-605.

Shachter, R. D. (1990). An Ordered Examination of Influence Diagrams. *Networks*, to appear.

An Approach to Reasoning About Continuous Change for Applications in Planning

Thomas Dean* **Greg Siegle**
Department of Computer Science
Brown University
Box 1910, Providence, RI 02912

Abstract

There are many planning applications that require an agent to coordinate its activities with processes that change continuously over time. Several proposals have been made for combining a temporal logic of time with the differential and integral calculus to provide a hybrid calculus suitable for planning applications. We take one proposal and explore some of the issues involved in implementing a practical system that derives conclusions consistent with such a hybrid calculus. Models for real-valued parameters are specified as systems of ordinary differential equations, and constructs are provided for reasoning about how these models change over time. For planning problems that require projecting the consequences of a set of events from a set of initial conditions and causal rules, a combination of numerical approximation and symbolic math routines and a simple default reasoning strategy provide for an efficient inference engine.

Introduction

Many problems in planning, scheduling, and decision support require reasoning about processes that change continuously over time (*e.g.*, determining how long to leave a valve open in order to fill a container without causing it to overflow, or when to schedule the delivery of parts after the start of a machining process so as to minimize the total time spent in fabrication). While there has been some research involving continuous change (*e.g.*, [Hendrix, 1973]), much of the work on temporal reasoning in artificial intelligence has focused on discrete change [Allen, 1984, McDermott, 1982, Shoham, 1988]. Recently, however, researchers [Sandewall, 1989, Rayner, 1989] have noted that the differential and integral calculus provide us with a perfectly good means of reasoning about continuous change. Sandewall [1989] describes a hybrid calculus that combines an interval temporal logic with the differential calculus. In this paper, we discuss some of the issues involved in implementing a variant of Sandewall's hybrid calculus useful for applications in planning.

*This work was supported in part by a National Science Foundation Presidential Young Investigator Award IRI-8957601 with matching funds from IBM, and by the Advanced Research Projects Agency of the Department of Defense and was monitored by the Air Force Office of Scientific Research under Contract No. F49620-88-C-0132.

Discrete and Continuous Change

Following [McDermott, 1982] and [Shoham, 1988], we treat time points as primitive and reason about intervals in terms of points. Time points are notated `t` or `t`i, $i \in \mathbf{Z}$ (*e.g.*, `t1`, `t2`). Variables ranging over time points are notated t or t_i, $i \in \mathbf{Z}$ (*e.g.*, t_1, t_2). We introduce a binary relation, $\preceq$, on time points indicating temporal precedence. If `t1` and `t2` are time points, then $\langle$`t1,t2`$\rangle$ is an interval. We use the notation `holds(t1,t2,p)` to indicate that the proposition `p` is true throughout the interval $\langle$`t1,t2`$\rangle$. For instance,

`holds(t1,t2,temp(room32)>72°)`

is meant to represent the fact that the temperature in a particular room is greater than 72° throughout the interval $\langle$`t1,t2`$\rangle$. We use the abbreviation `holds`(t,φ) for `holds`(t,t,φ), and $\Box\varphi$ to indicate that φ is always true.

In order to reason about discrete change, the logic has to be extended to deal with the problems that arise due to the frame and qualification problems. As an expedient, we adopt Shoham's semantics of chronological minimization [Shoham, 1988], noting that, while not appropriate for all types of temporal reasoning, chronological minimization is entirely satisfactory for the simple sort of projection problems that arise in many planning applications.

In this paper, we are primarily interested in reasoning about quantities that change continuously as functions of time. Rather than invent new machinery within our temporal logic, we will import into the logic as much of the differential calculus as is needed for our planning applications. Our treatment here roughly follows that of Sandewall [1989].

First, we introduce a set, U, of real-valued parameters closed under the differential operator, ∂. If $u \in U$, then $\partial^n u \in U$, where $\partial^n u$ is the nth partial derivative of u with respect to time. We can trivially extend the syntax to represent statements about the values of parameters at various time points. For instance,

$$\texttt{holds(t1,t2,}y = 3.1472\texttt{)}$$

is meant to indicate that the parameter y has the value of 3.1472 throughout the interval $\langle \texttt{t1,t2} \rangle$. By restricting y to remain constant throughout the interval $\langle \texttt{t1,t2} \rangle$, we also restrict ∂y to remain 0 throughout the same interval.

To guarantee this intended meaning, we have to augment the semantics somewhat. In addition to a set of parameters U, we assume that each interpretation includes a function $Q : (\mathbf{R} \times U) \rightarrow \mathbf{R}$, where we employ the set of real numbers, $\mathbf{R}$, for the set of time points as well as for the set of all parameter values.

Since we will find it convenient on occasion to model abrupt changes in the value of parameters as they change over time, we introduce the notion of a *breakpoint*. We assume that a physical process is modeled using a set of differential equations that describe continuous changes in the parameters over intervals of time, and a set of axioms that determine what equations are appropriate over what intervals. Breakpoints are times at which the axioms signal a change in the differential equations used to model a given quantity or set of quantities. Generally, at a breakpoint there is a discontinuity in some time varying parameter.

We have to augment the semantics to account for the behavior of parameters with respect to breakpoints. Each interpretation must include a set of breakpoints $S \subset \mathbf{R}$, so that for all $u \in U$, $Q(t, u)$ is continuous over every interval not containing an element of S, and for all $t \notin S$, $\frac{du}{dt} = Q(t, \partial u)$. Strange things can happen at breakpoints, but not so strange that we will allow a parameter to take on two different values. To avoid such anomalies, we will have to introduce some additional machinery.

At time t_0, we have a set of differential equations and a set of initial values for all of the parameters; these equations and initial values are known to hold until some indeterminate time t_1, at which point a breakpoint occurs and the axioms determine a new set of differential equations and a new set of "initial" values. In order to establish breakpoints and the values for parameters immediately following breakpoints, we need to refer to the values of parameters "just before" and "just after" breakpoints. To do so, we define the left and right limits of a parameter x at time t as:

$$\lim_{\tau \rightarrow t^-} Q(\tau, x) = Q(t, x^l) \quad \text{and} \quad \lim_{\tau \rightarrow t^+} Q(\tau, x) = Q(t, x^r)$$

A *discontinuity* occurs at t with regard to a parameter x whenever the left and right limits are not equal:

$$Q(t, x^l) \neq Q(t, x^r)$$

As long as there are no discontinuities, the differential equations tell us exactly how the parameters vary with time. The axioms tell us when breakpoints occur and what differential equations and initial conditions should be used to model processes between breakpoints. Discontinuities play a role in reasoning about real-valued quantities analogous to the role played by clippings in reasoning about the persistence of propositions. Just as the axioms do not rule out spurious models resulting from unexplained clippings, neither do they rule out models resulting from unexplained discontinuities.

Suppose that we have two objects moving toward one another along a horizontal line. Assume that the surface is frictionless, the objects are represented as identical point masses, and there are no external forces acting on the objects. Let x_1 and x_2 represent the parameters corresponding to the position of the first and second objects, respectively, as measured from some reference on the horizontal line. At time 0, the first object is located at position 0, and the second object is located 10 meters to the right. A positive velocity indicates movement to the right. We make use of the standard conventions for notating position (x), velocity ($\partial x = \dot{x}$), and acceleration ($\partial^2 x = \ddot{x}$). Here are the axioms indicating the initial conditions:

$\texttt{holds(0,}x_1 = 0\texttt{)}$	$\texttt{holds(0,}x_2 = 10\texttt{)}$
$\texttt{holds(0,}\dot{x}_1 = 2\texttt{)}$	$\texttt{holds(0,}\dot{x}_2 = -3\texttt{)}$
$\texttt{holds(0,}\ddot{x}_1 = 0\texttt{)}$	$\texttt{holds(0,}\ddot{x}_2 = 0\texttt{)}$

where velocity is in units of meters per second. The next axiom determines the new velocities immediately following a collision breakpoint.

$$\Box((x_1 = x_2) \wedge ((\dot{x}_1 - \dot{x}_2) > 0)) \supset ((\dot{x}_1^l = \dot{x}_2^r) \wedge (\dot{x}_2^l = \dot{x}_1^r))$$

For the most part, the propositions corresponding to equations involving the parameters in U are constantly changing. In order for us to make useful predictions, however, certain equations have to persist over intervals of time. Suppose you are told that at time t_0, $x = 0$, $\dot{x} = 2$, and $\ddot{x} = 0$. If $x = 0$ persists, then there will be discontinuities in $\dot{x}$ and $\ddot{x}$. If $\ddot{x} = 0$ persists, then $\dot{x} = 2$ has to persist or be discontinuous in order to avoid a discontinuity in $\dot{x}$, and x is completely determined by $\dot{x} = 2$. However, if none of $x = 0$, $\dot{x} = 2$, or $\ddot{x} = 0$ persist, there need not be a discontinuity in any one of x, $\dot{x}$, or $\ddot{x}$, but neither is there any way of predicting the changes in x over time. In this example, we force an interpretation by stating that the accelerations for the two objects are always 0: $\Box((\ddot{x}_1 = 0) \wedge (\ddot{x}_2 = 0))$.

Using Sandewall's extension of Shoham's chronological minimization, there is a single discontinuity in the acceleration of the objects two seconds after time 0, after which the objects, having exchanged velocities, head in opposite directions forever. We assume that the values of parameters are established in intervals not containing breakpoints by differential equations. In the following, we distinguish propositions corresponding to real-valued parameters taking on specific values (*e.g.*, $\ddot{x} = 2$) from propositions corresponding to truth-valued parameters (*e.g.*, `on(furnace17)`).

In the previous example, $\Box((\ddot{x}_1 = 0) \wedge (\ddot{x}_2 = 0))$ serves as the model for x_1 and x_2. In other cases, it may be convenient to infer a change in a model that persists over some indeterminate interval of time, just as we are able to infer changes in propositions that persist over intervals of time. To handle this sort of inference, we introduce a particular type of proposition $\texttt{models}(x, m)$ where x is a real-valued parameter and m is a model for x. If m is an nth-order differential equation, then it is assumed that the nth-order equation determines all higher-order derivatives, and all lower-order derivatives are known as part of the initial conditions. By stipulating $\Box(\ddot{x} = 0)$, we implicitly indicated $\texttt{holds(0,models(}x, \ddot{x} = 0\texttt{))}$ and that $x = 0$ and $\dot{x} = 2$ were the initial conditions at 0. Propositions of the form $\texttt{models}(x, m)$ persist according to standard chronological minimization.

Suppose that we want to reason about the temperature in a room heated by a furnace, and suppose that the furnace is controlled by a thermostat set to 70°. To make the example more interesting, suppose further that the thermostat has a 4° differential (*i.e.*, the furnace starts heating when the temperature drops to 68° and stops when the temperature climbs to 72°). To represent parameters "dropping to" (↓) or "climbing to" (↑) certain values, we define $\texttt{trans}(\downarrow, u, v)$ (similarly for ↑) where $u \in U$ and $v \in \mathbf{R}$ as follows:

$$\texttt{holds}(t, \texttt{trans}(\downarrow, u, v)) \equiv$$
$$Q(t,u) = v \ \wedge\ \exists t' \prec t, \forall t' \prec t'' \prec t, Q(t'', u) > Q(t, u)$$

Propositions of the form $\texttt{trans}([\downarrow \mid \uparrow], u, v)$ are used to represent point events of the sort that trigger changes.

To model changes in the room's temperature when the furnace is off, we use Newton's law of cooling

$$\frac{dr}{dt} = -\kappa_1(r - a)$$

where r is the temperature of the room, a is the temperature outside the room, and κ_1 depends on the insulation surrounding the room. To model changes in the room's temperature when the furnace is running, we use

$$\frac{dr}{dt} = \kappa_2(f - r) - \kappa_1(r - a)$$

where f is the temperature of the furnace when it is running, and κ_2 depends on the heat flow characteristics of the furnace. The following axioms describe the temperature in the room over time.

$$\Box(\texttt{trans}(\uparrow, r, 72°) \wedge \texttt{on(furnace17)}) \supset \texttt{models}(r, \partial r^r = -\kappa_1(r - a))$$

$$\Box(\texttt{trans}(\downarrow, r, 68°) \wedge \texttt{on(furnace17)}) \supset \texttt{models}(r, \partial r^r = \kappa_2(f - r) - \kappa_1(r - a))$$

Suppose that we are interested in the temperature in the room over the interval from time 0 to time 10. We are told that the temperature outside is 32° throughout this interval, and that at time 0 the room is 75° with the furnace on but currently not heating. We represent these facts as follows:

$\texttt{holds(0,}r = 75°\texttt{)}$ $\quad$ $\texttt{holds(0,}\partial r = -\kappa_2(r - a)\texttt{)}$

$\texttt{holds(0,10,}a = 32°\texttt{)}$ $\quad$ `holds(0,on(furnace17))`

With a little extra work (*e.g.*, in order to eliminate certain unintended models, we have to take steps to avoid simultaneous cause and effect), we can obtain the following inferences. The temperature drops off exponentially[1] from 75° to 68° at which point the furnace starts heating and continues until the temperature reaches 72°, after which the furnace toggles on and off forever with the temperature always between 68° and 72°.

Note that we can always substitute a set of models that persist over different intervals of time for a single model that is true for all time but with additional parameters that make the model behave differently over different intervals of time. In the furnace example, we might state that $\Box(\partial r = \kappa_2(f - a) - \kappa_1(r - a))$ and then have rules that govern the value of f over different intervals of time. The choice of whether to vary the model or employ a single model and vary the parameters of the model is a matter of preference. The system described in the next section supports either approach.

Projection Involving Continuous Change

In this section, we discuss the issues involved in building a temporal inference engine for reasoning about continuously changing quantities. We consider only a limited form of temporal reasoning called *projection* that can be performed by making a single sweep forward in time inferring at each point what things change and what things remain the same. Following [Dean and McDermott, 1987], we distinguish between a general type of event or proposition (*e.g.*, "the furnace came on") and a specific instance of a general type (*e.g.*, "the furnace came on at noon"). The latter are referred to as *time tokens* or simply *tokens*. A token associates a general type of event or proposition with a specific interval of time over which the event is said to occur or the proposition hold. Tokens are notated $\texttt{token}(t, i)$ where t is a type and i is an interval; $\texttt{begin}(i)$ and $\texttt{end}(i)$ indicate the begin and end points respectively of the interval i. Projection uses a set of initial tokens and causal rules

[1] The behavior of the system can be described in terms of a piecewise continuous function in which the specific solutions for each piece are given, alternately, by $r(t) = 32° + (r_0 - 32°)e^{-\kappa t}$ and $r(t) = C + (r_0 - C)e^{-(\kappa_2+\kappa_1)t}$ where $C = \frac{\kappa_2 500° + \kappa_1 32°}{\kappa_1 + \kappa_2}$, r_0 is the initial temperature of the room for that particular piece and t is the time elapsed from the beginning of that piece.

corresponding to events and propositions to generate additional tokens corresponding to the consequences of the events. Metric constraints are handled as in [Dean and McDermott, 1987]

We require that the interval corresponding to a token persist no further than the first subsequent interval corresponding to a token of a *contradictory type*. For any proposition type φ, φ and $\neg\varphi$ are said to be contradictory. Additional contradictory types have to be explicitly asserted. For instance, the assertion

```
contradicts(location(X,Y),location(X,Z)) ← Y≠Z.
```

indicates that any two tokens of type `location`(*arg1*, *arg2*) are contradictory if their first arguments are the same, and their second arguments are different. The process of modifying the bounds on token intervals corresponding to propositions to ensure that tokens of contradictory types do not overlap is referred to as *persistence clipping*.

Causal rules for reasoning about discrete change are of the form `project`(*antecedent_conditions*, *trigger_event*, *delay*, *consequent_effects*) to indicate that, if an event of type *trigger event* occurs, and the *antecedent conditions* hold at the outset of the interval associated with *trigger event*, then the *consequent effects* are true after an interval of time determined by *delay*. The trigger event is specified as a type, the antecedent conditions and consequent effects are specified as types or conjunctions of types, and the delay is optional defaulting to ϵ, a positive infinitesimal. As an example `project(¬on(furnace17), toggle(switch42), on(furnace17))` indicates that, if the switch on the furnace is toggled at a time when the furnace is not on, then, after a delay of ϵ, it will come on. The basic algorithm for persistence clipping and projecting the consequences of events is described in [Dean and McDermott, 1987]; in the following, we extend that algorithm to handle continuous change.

Let U be a set of real-valued parameters, and P be a set of boolean-valued propositional variables.[2] In addition, we introduce two mappings $Q : \mathbf{R} \times U \rightarrow 2^{\mathbf{R}}$ and $V : \mathbf{R} \times P \rightarrow 2^{\{true,false\}}$. The task of projection is to determine Q and V for some closed interval of $\mathbf{R}$. We begin by considering the completely determined case in which both Q and V map to singleton sets (*i.e.*, $Q : \mathbf{R} \times U \rightarrow \mathbf{R}$ and $V : \mathbf{R} \times P \rightarrow \{true, false\}$).

At the initial time point, we assume that the values of all parameters and propositional variables are known. In addition, we are given a set of events specified to occur at various times over the time interval of interest. We assume a set of projection rules as before. In addition, we assume a set of modeling rules for parameters in U. A modeling rule is just a special sort of projection rule; the basic form is the same as that introduced earlier in this section, the only difference being that the delay is always assumed to be ϵ, and the consequent effects consist of parameter assignments in the form of ordinary differential equations with constant coefficients (*e.g.*, $\partial u = 2$, or $\partial^2 u = 3\partial u + 5u + 4$).

The projection rule from the last section for reasoning about the temperature of the room in the case that the furnace is on but not running is encoded as follows,

$$\texttt{project(on(furnace17),trans(}\uparrow, r, 72^o\texttt{),}\ \texttt{models(}r, \partial r^r = -\kappa_1(r-a)\texttt{)).}$$

To make sure that persistence clipping is handled correctly, we state that a given parameter can have only one model at a time.

```
contradicts(models(X,M1),models(X,M2)) ← M1≠M2.
```

Now we can state the basic algorithm for performing projection given some set of initial conditions and a projection interval $\langle t_s, t_f\rangle$. To simplify the description of the algorithm, we assume that all events are point events (*i.e.*, if e is a type corresponding to the occurrence of an event, $\texttt{token}(e,k) \supset (\texttt{begin}(k) = \texttt{end}(k))$), and all events described in the initial conditions begin after t_s. Let $\mathcal{A}$ be the set of all currently active process models (*i.e.*, all m such that $\texttt{holds}(t_c, \texttt{models}(x,m))$ for some x). Let $\mathcal{E}$ be the set of pending events (*i.e.*, the set of all events, $\texttt{token}(e,k)$, generated so far such that $t_c \prec \texttt{begin}(k)$). Let C be the set of current conditions (*i.e.*, all $u^r = v$ such that there exists $m \in \mathcal{A}$ such that $\texttt{holds}(t_c, \texttt{models}(x,m))$, $u = \partial^n x$ for some n, and $\texttt{holds}(t_c, u^r = v)$.

In the cases that we are interested in, we can recast a set of ordinary differential equations and their initial conditions as a system of first-order differential equations. We can then solve these equations using numerical methods based on the Taylor expansion (*e.g.*, the Runge-Kutta methods [Ralston and Rabinowitz, 1978]) and various forms of linear and nonlinear extrapolation (*e.g.*, the Adams-Bashforth and Adams-Moulton methods [Shampine and Gordon, 1975]). In the following, we assume the ability to generate solutions to ordinary differential equations efficiently, and refer to the procedure for generating such solutions as the *extrapolation procedure*. Given a set of initial conditions and a projection interval $\langle t_s, t_f\rangle$ projection is carried out by the following algorithm.

1. Set t_c to be t_s.
2. Set $\mathcal{E}$ to be the set of events specified in the initial conditions.
3. Using $\mathcal{A}$, C, and the extrapolation procedure, find t_n corresponding to the earliest point in time following t_c such that the trigger for some projection rule is satisfied or t_f whichever comes first. If $t_n \neq t_f$, then t_n could be the time of occurrence of the earliest event in $\mathcal{E}$, or it could be earlier, corresponding to the solution of a set of simultaneous equations (*e.g.*, $((x_1 = x_2) \wedge ((\dot{x}_1 - \dot{x}_2) > 0))$).

[2] It should be noted that, despite the presence of variables and complex terms in our rules, the underlying logic is purely propositional.

4. If $t_n = t_f$, then quit, else set t_c to be t_n.
5. Find all of the projection rules with the trigger found in Step 3.
6. For each rule found in Step 5 whose antecedent conditions are satisfied, create tokens corresponding to the types of the consequent effects, except in the case of consequent effects corresponding to parameter assignments (*e.g.*, $x_1^\tau = x_2^\tau$). Constrain the new tokens according to the delay specified in the corresponding rule, and add them to the database.
7. For each token added in Step 6 whose type corresponds to an event, add it to $\mathcal{E}$.
8. For each token added in Step 6 whose type does not correspond to an event, find all tokens of a contradictory type that begin before the newly added token and constrain them to end before the beginning of the new token.
9. If the trigger found in Step 3 corresponds to the type of an event token in $\mathcal{E}$ whose time of occurrence is t_c, remove it from $\mathcal{E}$.
10. Use the consequent effects corresponding to parameter assignments found in Step 6 and the results of extrapolation to determine $\mathcal{C}$. The parameter assignments corresponding to the consequent effects of projection rules take precedence over the extrapolation results. $\mathcal{A}$ is also updated at this time.
11. Go to Step 3.

The above algorithm has been implemented in Prolog and C. We use C-Prolog as a front end and database for storing projection rules. The extrapolation procedure employs Runge-Kutta methods and is written in C. Differential equations are specified using the notational conventions of Maple.[3] Prolog routines are used to preprocess the differential equations converting each one into a system of first-order equations. We assume that all equations are 5th order or less, and that they can be rewritten so that the highest-order term is algebraically isolated on the left-hand side of the equation. The system can make use of analytic solutions when available, but, for the planning problems we are concerned with, the extrapolation routine is more than accurate enough. It is also generally faster to use the extrapolation routine written in C than the analytic solver written in Prolog.

To get a better idea of how the program works, consider the following simple benchmark problem. Figure 1 depicts a pipe leading into a holding tank used to fill portable tanks that are positioned beneath a second pipe leading out of the holding tank. There are rotary valves mounted on the pipes that restrict the flow of

[3]Maple is a widely distributed symbolic math package developed by the Symbolic Computation Group in the Department of Computer Science at the University of Waterloo, Waterloo, Ontario.

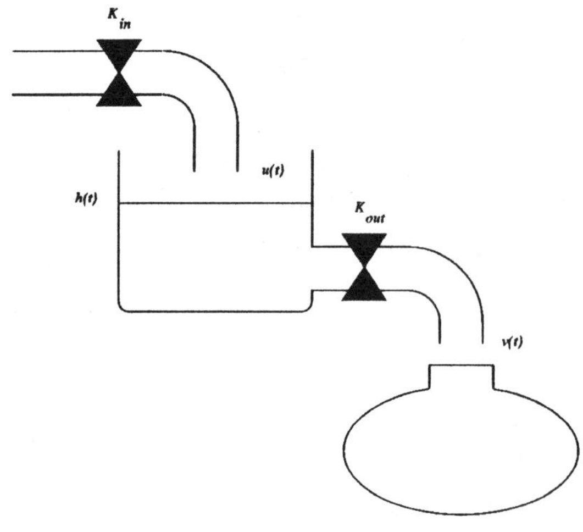

Figure 1: Reasoning about fluid flow

```
% Constants:             % Initial conditions:     % Discrete events:
constant(area,5).        holds(0,u=0).             occurs(1,turn(θin,15)).
constant(height,3).      holds(0,v=0).             occurs(2,turn(θout,90)).
constant(volume,2).      holds(0,h=0).             occurs(5,turn(θin,45)).
constant(kin,5).         holds(0,θin=0).           occurs(10,turn(θin,-60)).
constant(kout,3).        holds(0,θout=0).          occurs(11,turn(θout,-90)).

% Static models:
holds(T,models(r,r(t)=kin*θin(t)/(kout*θout(t)))).
holds(T,models(u,diff(u(t),t) = kin*θin(t))).
holds(T,models(v,diff(v(t),t) = kout*θout(t)*h(t))).
holds(T,models(sp,sp(t)=sp1(t)+sp2(t))).
holds(T,models(θin,diff(θin(t),t)=0)).
holds(T,models(θout,diff(θout(t),t)=0)).
holds(T,models(P,_=C)) :- constant(P,C).

% Dynamic models:
holds(T,models(h,diff(h(t),t)=(kin*θin(t)-kout*θout(t)*h(t))/area)) :-
      holds(T,h < height).
project(always,trans(up,h,height),models(h,diff(h(t),t)=0)).
project(always,trans(down,r,height),
      models(h,diff(h(t),t)=(kin*θin(t)-kout*θout(t)*h(t))/area)).
holds(T,models(sp1,sp1(t)=0)) :- holds(T,h < height).
project(always,trans(up,h,height),models(sp1,sp1(t)=u(t))).
project(always,trans(down,r,height),models(sp1,sp1(t)=0)).
holds(T,models(sp2,sp2(t)=0)) :- holds(T,v < volume).
project(always,trans(up,v,volume),models(sp2,sp2(t)=v(t))).
```

Figure 2: Prolog clauses for the fluid-flow problem

fluid; the valves vary from 0° to 90°. We are interested in the consequences of a plan involving a sequence of adjustments to the two valves. In particular, we are interested in the volume of the fluid in the portable tank after the output valve is finally closed, and the total amount of fluid spilled from either the holding tank or the portable tank during the filling process.

Let K_{in} be the flow rate of the input valve in cubic meters per degree minute, K_{out} be the flow rate of the output valve in square meters per degree minute, H be the height of the holding tank in meters, A be the surface area of the portable tank, and V be its total volume. In addition to these constants, we have the following state variables (functions of time): h is the height of the fluid in the holding tank, θ_{in} is the angle of the input valve, θ_{out} is the angle of the output valve, u is the total volume of fluid to have entered the holding tank, and v is the total volume of fluid to have left the holding tank. Initially, we have $h(0) = u(0) = v(0) = 0$, $\partial u = K_{in}\theta_{in}$, and $\partial v = K_{out}\theta_{out}h$, where θ_{in} and θ_{out} are determined by the plan being evaluated. As long as $h < H$, we have $\partial h = (K_{in}\theta_{in} - K_{out}\theta_{out}h)/A$. If $\texttt{trans}(\uparrow, h, H)$, then we have $\partial h = 0$, and, if $\texttt{trans}(\downarrow, r, H)$ where $r = K_{in}\theta_{in}/K_{out}\theta_{out}$, we are back to $\partial h = (K_{in}\theta_{in} - K_{out}\theta_{out}h)/A$. To determine the total amount of fluid spilled, we have to set up rules to handle the various possibilities for $h < H$ and $v < V$. The complete Prolog representation is shown in Figure 2. During projection, every time that `h` rises to `height`, `r` falls to `height`, or `v` rises to `volume`, the conditions for certain projection rules shown in Figure 2 are met, and these rules are used to generate tokens specifying new models for various parameters.

For many planning problems, it is convenient to define a special function of time for evaluating alternative plans. In our simple example, this evaluation function is `sp(t)` which is the sum of the fluid spilled from either tank during the evaluation interval. If the plan consists of the five discrete events shown in Figure 2 and the evaluation interval is $\langle 0, 12 \rangle$, then we can evaluate the plan using the query `holds(12,sp=S)` which returns with `S` bound to 1.37. The response time is negligible for this query. The algorithm is guaranteed to terminate if the projection interval is finite. The complexity of projection is largely determined by the set of causal rules. For the sorts of rules we have encountered in our planning problems, projection is at worst a small polynomial in the size of the set of rules and initial conditions.

Conclusion

The current implementation of our hybrid calculus is convenient to use and remarkably fast for a prototype system. It still lacks much of functionality of our previous temporal database systems [Dean, 1989]. The current system has only limited ability to reason about uncertainty in either the time of occurrence of events or the initial values of parameters. However, uncertainty is difficult to handle even with discretely changing parameters and boolean variables [Dean and Boddy, 1988], and it appears that many of the techniques we have developed for handling uncertainty involving discrete change also apply in the continuous case.

The primary advantage of the hybrid system described in this paper over most temporal reasoning systems is its increased expressiveness and precision. It is clearly possible to model continuous processes using discrete approximations, but such approximations are often clumsy to formulate and sacrifice precision in order to achieve a reasonable level of performance. In our hybrid system, physical phenomena that are naturally modeled as continuous processes can be done so in a mathematical language designed for that purpose, and discrete processes can be modeled using first-order temporal logic which is well suited for that purpose. The use of numerical methods for solving systems of ordinary differential equations gives the modeler a great deal of flexibility, and provides more than ample precision for the modeling tasks we have encountered so far. In addition, for projection problems of the sort encountered in many planning applications, our system subscribes to Sandewall's semantics up to the precision of the underlying numerical methods. Finally, and perhaps most importantly, we are now able to easily reason about planning problems that were impossible or at least prohibitively complicated to do so previously.

References

[Allen, 1984] James Allen. Towards a general theory of action and time. *Artificial Intelligence*, 23:123–154, 1984.

[Brachman *et al.*, 1989] Ronald J. Brachman, Hector J. Levesque, and Raymond Reiter, editors. *Proceedings of the First International Conference on Principles of Knowledge Representation and Reasoning*. Morgan-Kaufman, Los Altos, California, 1989.

[Dean and Boddy, 1988] Thomas Dean and Mark Boddy. Reasoning about partially ordered events. *Artificial Intelligence*, 36(3):375–399, 1988.

[Dean and McDermott, 1987] Thomas Dean and Drew V. McDermott. Temporal database management. *Artificial Intelligence*, 32(1):1–55, 1987.

[Dean, 1989] Thomas Dean. Using temporal hierarchies to efficiently maintain large temporal databases. *Journal of the ACM*, 36(4):687–718, 1989.

[Hendrix, 1973] Gary Hendrix. Modeling simultaneous actions and continuous processes. *Artificial Intelligence*, 4:145–180, 1973.

[McDermott, 1982] Drew V. McDermott. A temporal logic for reasoning about processes and plans. *Cognitive Science*, 6:101–155, 1982.

[Ralston and Rabinowitz, 1978] A. Ralston and P. Rabinowitz. *A First Course in Numerical Analysis*. McGraw-Hill, New York, 1978.

[Rayner, 1989] Manny Rayner. Did newton solve the "extended prediction problem?". In Brachman et al. [1989], pages 381–385.

[Sandewall, 1989] Erik Sandewall. Combining logic and differential equations for describing real-world systems. In Brachman et al. [1989], pages 412–420.

[Shampine and Gordon, 1975] L. F. Shampine and M. K. Gordon. *Computer Solution of Ordinary Differential Equations*. W. H. Freeman and Company, 1975.

[Shoham, 1988] Yoav Shoham. *Reasoning About Change: Time and Causation from the Standpoint of Artificial Intelligence*. MIT Press, Cambridge, Massachusetts, 1988.

Anytime Synthetic Projection: Maximizing the Probability of Goal Satisfaction

Mark Drummond* and **John Bresina**†
Sterling Federal Systems
AI Research Branch, NASA Ames Research Center
Mail Stop: 244-17, Moffett Field, CA 94035

Abstract

This paper presents a projection algorithm for incremental control rule synthesis. The algorithm synthesizes an initial set of goal-achieving control rules using a combination of situation probability and estimated remaining work as a search heuristic. This set of control rules has a certain probability of satisfying the given goal. The probability is incrementally increased by synthesizing additional control rules to handle "error" situations the execution system is likely to encounter when following the initial control rules. By using situation probabilities the algorithm achieves a computationally effective balance between the limited robustness of triangle tables and the absolute robustness of universal plans.

Introduction

We are interested in a continuum of plan-guided systems, from those that can operate entirely off-line, where complete plans are produced in advance and later used by independently competent execution systems, to those systems that are embedded in the situations for which their plans are generated. These embedded systems are especially interesting since they must close the loop between plan formation and plan execution in their environment. For an embedded system, simply generating a plan is not enough; such a system must instead incrementally coerce its environment to conform with its goals. The key tasks for an embedded system are resource-bounded incremental plan synthesis and reactive behavior using appropriate plans in a closed-loop fashion.

The work presented in this paper extends existing theory in the areas of temporal projection, anytime algorithms, and plan synthesis for embedded systems. The goals of this paper are to: 1) define the syntax and semantics of behavioral constraints and provide a search heuristic for their satisfaction; 2) define the probability of behavioral constraint satisfaction; 3) describe a synthetic temporal projection algorithm with anytime properties which heuristically maximizes the probability of behavioral constraint satisfaction.

The next section provides relevant background information. The synthetic temporal projection algorithm is then presented by way of a simple example. The paper concludes with a discussion of connections to related research.

Background

Realistic planning and control problems suggest the need for temporally extended goals of *maintenance* and *prevention*, in addition to the traditional planning goals of *achievement*. Our approach employs a language of *behavioral constraints* which is based on a branching temporal logic (*cf* Drummond, 1989). As an example, consider the following behavioral constraint, or BC.

```
(and
  (prevent (and (drunk driver)
                (has-car-keys driver))
           7 12)
  (achieve (or  (at-home me)
                (have-companion me))
           ?t1))
```

This BC represents a conjunction of two temporally extended goals: the first goal must be false from time 7 through time 12 and the second goal must be true at some arbitrary time in the future. Behavioral constraint semantics are defined in terms of possible behaviors that are synthesized by our temporal projection algorithm. Intuitively, we say that a given projection path w satisfies a behavioral constraint β if and only if all of the formulas in β are true in w over the required time intervals. See appendix A for more details on BC syntax and semantics.

We define a *behavioral constraint strategy* (or BC strategy) to be a partial order over a set of behavioral constraints. The partial order, denoted by "$\prec$",

*This work has been partially supported by the Artificial Intelligence Research Program of the Air Force Office of Scientific Research.

†Also affiliated with the Computer Science Department at Rutgers University.

indicates both execution and problem solving precedence. Behavioral constraint strategies for a given behavioral constraint are produced using domain- and problem-specific planning expertise. The BC strategy constructed for a given BC indicates a set of subproblems for the projector to satisfy and an order in which to satisfy them. This process is beyond the scope of this paper; please refer to Bresina and Drummond (1990) for more information. The way in which BC strategies are used by the projector is made clear in the next section.

In order to project future possible courses of action our projector needs a *causal theory* for each domain of application. A causal theory is a set of operators which defines both the *actions* that the system can take and the exogenous *events* that can occur in the application environment. The difference between actions and events is simply this: actions can be chosen for execution by the control system under construction (*e.g.*, move in a direction) while the occurrence of events is determined by the system's environment (*e.g.*, a gust of wind). From the perspective of the projector however, actions and events are similar, and both can be characterized as a situation to situation transition.

The projector explores various possible futures by repeatedly finding enabled operators and applying them to produce new hypothetical situations. The projector creates a directed acyclic graph, where each node denotes a domain situation and each arc is labelled with a domain operator. Projection associates a duration with each operator application and uses this to calculate a time stamp for the resulting situation.

A path in a projection graph denotes a future possible behavior. Projection paths which satisfy a given behavioral constraint are compiled into a set of Situated Control Rules (SCRs) similar to the way that a STRIPS plan is transformed into a triangle table (Fikes *et al.*, 1972). The SCRs indicate to the reaction component those actions which will "lead to" the eventual satisfaction of its current behavioral constraint. SCRs are used by the reaction component as a set of local instructions constituting a control program.

See Bresina and Drummond (1990) and Drummond (1989) for more details about our overall architecture. The algorithm described in this paper does not critically depend on the architecture, so many irrelevant details have been suppressed. Our temporal projection algorithm can be used by a variety of systems, in a range of architectures.

The Projection Algorithm

This section presents our anytime synthetic projection algorithm. We start with a description of the algorithm in operation and then present ways to control the search that is inherent in this approach.

The *project* algorithm accepts a behavioral constraint and domain causal theory; it attempts to maximize the probability that the reaction component will satisfy the behavioral constraint. Our algorithm is based on the heuristic search paradigm which makes it hard to guarantee that the actual *maximum* probability will be found. Instead, as is typically done with heuristic search algorithms, we claim only that our algorithm attempts to maximize the probability of goal satisfaction, which we refer to as *heuristic maximization.*

To simplify the presentation we characterize the projector's causal theory as a single function called *transition.* The function *transition* (s) maps a situation description s to a set of triples $< s_i, p_i, o_i >$ such that $p(s_i \mid s, o_i) = p_i$, where the conditional probability expression has the following interpretation. If o_i denotes an action, then p_i is the probability that s_i will be the resulting situation if o_i is executed in situation s. If o_i denotes an event, then p_i is the probability that s_i will be the resulting situation if o_i occurs in situation s. For a given s, we assume that the possible transitions are mutually exclusive. Notice that this definition of *transition*(s) makes the Markov assumption by ignoring the particular sequence of operators used to produce s. It is difficult to achieve a complete specification of all possible situation transitions in a realistic domain, and the automatic incremental improvement of the transition function specification is part of our future research agenda.

See figure 1 for an abstract projection graph example. The behavioral constraint strategy $\beta_1 \prec \beta_2$ has been selected as an appropriate way to satisfy β. This BC strategy indicates that a path which satisfies β_1 composed with a path which satisfies β_2 will constitute a path which satisfies β.

Project first calls *traverse* to find a single path that satisfies $\beta_1 \prec \beta_2$ from its "current" situation, s_1. *Traverse* uses the function *transition* to create situations reachable under the application of a single operator from s_1. Not all possible transitions are considered: a filter is used to select a subset of the most probable transitions, and only these are used to produce new successors to s_1. In our example only s_2 survives the probability filter. The number of survivors under this winnowing operation is determined by a filter-width parameter, corresponding to the filter selection function in Ow and Morton's (1986) *filtered beam search.*

A heuristic value is calculated for each successor situation based on the situation's probability and an estimate of the remaining work required to satisfy β_1 from that situation. (This estimation function is explained in more detail below.) Another winnowing process is used to select a subset of these situations that have the highest heuristic value. For our example, this set contains only s_2. In general, however, this set will contain a subset of all possible frontier search nodes in the developing projection graph. The number of elements in this set is limited by a beam-width parameter, corresponding to Ow and Morton's (1986) beam selection function. This set of frontier nodes is passed on to a

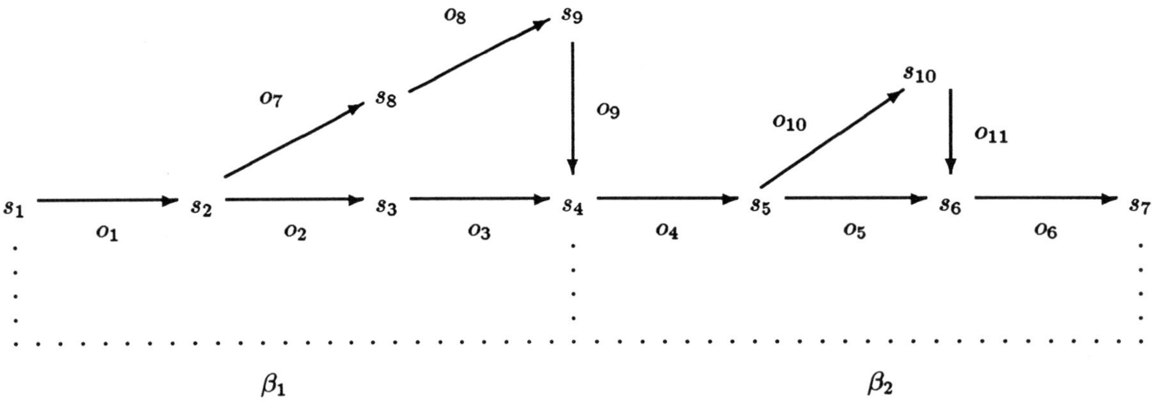

Figure 1: A Simple Projection Graph Example

recursive call of *traverse*.

Traverse continues to extend projection paths by selecting possible transitions until it finds a path which satisfies β_1. In the figure, the first satisfactory path discovered is $s_1o_1s_2o_2s_3o_3s_4$. Situated Control Rules are now compiled for each situation in this path. The reaction component will thus be given a set of rules of the form: IF s_i AND β_1 THEN o_i, for $i = 1, 2, 3$. At this point, *traverse* focuses its search for a solution path to β_2 in the subspace anchored at s_4. This is accomplished by collapsing the set of frontier nodes to the singleton set $\{s_4\}$. Such a collapse has the effect of requiring any solution path for β_2 to start in the situation terminating the satisfactory path for β_1. Winnowing the set of possibilities in this way helps to control the projector's search by reducing the number of alternative situations in the expanding search frontier.

We call this strategy *cut-and-commit*, and it is one aspect of the algorithm's anytime operation. The conditions under which this approach is advisable are discussed below.

Traverse continues its search to satisfy β by finding a projection path which satisfies β_2 from s_4. In our figure, the eventual satisfactory path for β_2 is $s_4o_4s_5o_5s_6o_6s_7$. This path is passed to the SCR compiler producing another set of SCRs for the satisfaction of β_2. The probability for the path s_1 through s_7 can be calculated from $p(s_{i+1}|s_i, o_i)$, $i = 1, \ldots, 6$ (as defined below). This number gives us a lower bound on the probability that the reaction component will satisfy β. Assuming that there is still time before the reaction component must take action, we can increase this probability by finding additional paths which also satisfy β. Each additional path will serve to increase the lower bound on the reaction component's probability of satisfying β.

Robustify is our algorithm for finding additional projection paths. The algorithm finds high-probability deviations from the single existing solution path and calls *traverse* to find alternative paths which recover from each deviation. A deviation is a transition in a situation which produces a new situation from which there does not yet exist a satisfactory path. For example, when *robustify* is applied to the path $s_1o_1s_2o_2s_3o_3s_4$, it finds that the transition to s_8 via operator o_7 has a high probability of occurring in s_2. *Traverse* is used to recover from this deviation by synthesizing an alternate path, $s_1o_1s_2o_7s_8o_8s_9o_9s_4$, which also satisfies β_1. Similarily, *robustify* finds that the transition from s_5 to s_{10} via o_{10} has high probability and calls *traverse* to synthesize the path $s_4o_4s_5o_{10}s_{10}o_{11}s_6o_6s_7$. Each additional path serves to increase the probability that β will be satisfied by increasing the probability that each of its component constraints, β_1 and β_2, will be satisfied.

Situated Control Rules are compiled for each new subpath synthesized by *traverse*; in our example, new SCRs are created for s_2, s_8, s_9, s_5, and s_{10}. This incremental *deviate-and-recover* strategy is another aspect of the algorithm's anytime operation. As each new path is found, SCRs are given to the reaction component to help it deal with ever more of the possible domain situations in which it might find itself.

Controlling the Search

Situation probability and estimated remaining work were used in *traverse* to define a heuristic evaluation function. The heuristic value for a situation s, with respect to a BC β, is computed as: $h(s,\beta) = \text{K}1 \cdot p(s) + \text{K}2 \cdot rwt(s,\beta)$, where $p(s)$ is the probability of situation s and $rwt(s,\beta)$ is the estimated remaining work required to satisfy β from s. The user-provided weights, K1 and K2, determine the relative importance of low-cost and high-probability in the computation of h and, hence, affect the type of solutions synthesized by *traverse*. These parameters must be tuned as required for each domain of application. This section gives def-

$rw(s, (and\, \beta_1 \ldots \beta_n))$	$=$	$\sum_{i=1}^{n} rw(s, \beta_i)$
$rw(s, (or\, \beta_1 \ldots \beta_n))$	$=$	$\min_{i=1}^{n} rw(s, \beta_i)$
$rw(s, (maintain\, \psi\, \tau_s\, \tau_e))$	$=$	$\text{KW} \cdot \textit{min-true}\ (\psi, s) \cdot (\tau_e - \tau_n) + \textit{min-false}\ (\psi, s) \cdot (\text{CW} + \text{KW} \cdot (\tau_e - \tau_s))$
$rw(s, (prevent\, \psi\, \tau_s\, \tau_e))$	$=$	$\text{KW} \cdot \textit{min-true}\ (\psi, s) \cdot (\tau_e - \tau_n) + \textit{min-false}\ (\psi, s) \cdot (\text{CW} + \text{KW} \cdot (\tau_e - \tau_s))$
$rw(s, (maintain\, \psi\, \varphi\, \varphi))$	$=$	$\text{KW} \cdot \textit{min-true}\ (\psi, s) + \text{CW} \cdot \textit{min-false}\ (\psi, s)$
$rw(s, (prevent\, \psi\, \varphi\, \varphi))$	$=$	$\text{KW} \cdot \textit{min-true}\ (\psi, s) + \text{CW} \cdot \textit{min-false}\ (\psi, s)$

Table 1: Definition of $rw(s, \beta)$

initions for estimated remaining work and path probability, and more clearly explains the role of behavioral constraint strategies in controlling search.

Estimated remaining work

For planners concerned only with conjunctive goals of achievement, a heuristic based on situation difference gives reasonable results (Nilsson, 1980); to handle behavioral constraints we have generalized the notion of situation difference to that of *remaining work per time.*

Our heuristic uses two global parameters, KW (*k*eep *w*ork) and CW (*c*hange *w*ork), which relate predicate truth value to work. The parameter KW denotes the minimum work per unit time to keep the truth value of a predicate constant. The parameter CW denotes the minimum number of work units required to change the truth value of a predicate. We assume that facts change instantaneously and CW estimates the minimum work required to change the truth value of a randomly selected predicate. A user must set these parameters as required for each application domain.

We define the remaining work per time $rwt(s, \beta)$ to be $rw(s, \beta)/rt(s, \beta)$; where $rw(s, \beta)$ is the remaining work necessary to satisfy β from s and $rt(s, \beta)$ is the remaining time in which to do the work. The remaining time can be easily estimated from β and s. Let s be a situation, and let τ_n be the time stamp of s. The numerator of our equation, $rw(s, \beta)$, can then be defined as shown in table 1.

The function *min-true*(ψ, s) gives the minimum number of predicates in the formula ψ that are true in situation s. Similarly, *min-false*(ψ, s) gives the minimum number of false predicates. These terms, together with CW and KW, produce an optimistic estimate of the amount of remaining work.

For example, consider the evaluation of $rw(s, (maintain\ \psi\ \ \tau_s\ \tau_e))$. The formula ψ must be maintained from time point τ_s through time point τ_e, from situation s with time stamp τ_n. The appropriate definition in table 1 has two terms: the first term describes the work required to keep the minimum number of true predicates in ψ true from τ_n through τ_e; the second term deals with the work required to change the minimum number of false predicates in ψ to be true, and the work required to keep these predicates true from τ_s through τ_e. The classical situation difference heuristic is a degenerate form of these measures, where work is measured in the number of predicates that must be made true and where there is no cost for keeping predicates true over time.

Goal Satisfaction Probability

Our description of *traverse* depended on the ability to combine individual transition probabilities into aggregate projection path probabilities; this section explains how this is accomplished.

Let $G = (S, T)$ be a projection graph, where S is a set of possible situations and T is a set of situation-to-situation transitions; let $s \in S$ be a particular situation, and let $w = s_1 o_1 s_2 o_2 \ldots o_{n-1} s_n$ be a path in G. The *path probability* of w is defined to be the product of the transition probabilities in w: $p(w) = p(s_1) \cdot \Pi_{i=1}^{n-1} p(s_{i+1} \mid s_i, o_i)$.

For a situation s, the *situation probability* is defined as the sum of the path probabilities of all paths from the unique starting situation of G, ss, to s: $p(s) = \sum p(w)$ summed over $\{w : w = s_1 o_1 \ldots o_{n-1} s_n$ is a path in G, $s_1 = ss$, and $s_n = s\}$.

Finally, we can define the probability that a behavioral constraint, β, is satisfied by a projection graph, G, as the sum of the probabilities of all paths in G anchored at the unique starting situation ss which satisfy β: $p(\beta \mid G) = \sum p(w)$ summed over $\{w : w = s_1 o_1 \ldots o_{n-1} s_n$ is a path in G, $s_1 = ss$, and w satisfies $\beta\}$.

The probability that the reaction component will satisfy a BC β under the guidance of the SCRs compiled from a projection graph G is bounded below by $\mathrm{p}(\beta \mid G)$. The probability $\mathrm{p}(\beta \mid G)$ is a lower bound because the reaction component might have access to other SCRs relevant to β which cover situations that are not in G.

Behavioral Constraint Strategies

As mentioned above, a behavioral constraint strategy is a partial order over a set of behavioral constraints. A given BC strategy controls search by giving the projector a set of behavioral constraints to satisfy and an order in which to satisfy them. A BC strategy is satisfied when each of its component constraints is satisfied in an order consistent with the given partial order.

To make this idea more precise, let $(\Gamma, \prec)$ be a BC strategy, where Γ contains n behavioral constraints; let Θ be the set of all total orders over Γ compatible with

$\prec$. The objective for *traverse* is to synthesize a path $w = w^1 \circ w^2 \circ \cdots \circ w^n$, such that there exists a total order $\theta \in \Theta$ where for each w^i, w^{i+1} in w, there exists $\beta \prec \beta' \in \theta$ such that w^i satisfies β and w^{i+1} satisfies β'. Furthermore, each $\beta \in \Gamma$ must be satisfied by one w^i in w. The "$\circ$" operator represents path composition defined as follows: $w \circ w' = s_1 o_1 s_2 o_2 \ldots s_i e'_1 s'_2 e'_2 \ldots s'_j$, where $w = s_1 o_1 s_2 o_2 \ldots s_i$ and $w' = s'_1 e'_1 s'_2 e'_2 \ldots s'_j$, if the union of s_i and s'_1 is consistent, else $w \circ w'$ is undefined.

Consider the simple example used above where the BC strategy is $\beta_1 \prec \beta_2$. In the ideal case, for each path w^1 that satisfies β_1, there exists a path w^2 that satisfies β_2 such that $w^1 \circ w^2$. In this case, our cut-and-commit strategy will never be forced to backtrack over the first solution found for β_1, and the policy of immediate SCR compilation is risk-free. However, it is not always possible to construct such ideal BC strategies. More typically only a subset of the paths which satisfy β_1 can be extended to also satisfy β_2. In this case, the projector might have to backtrack to find another solution to β_1. If such backtracking occurs, then (at least some of) the SCRs that were compiled from a rejected solution to β_1 are not appropriate in the context of $\beta_1 \prec \beta_2$. However, they may be appropriate in the context of another BC strategy and hence could still prove useful.

In this paper, we do not address what the reactor does when more than one SCR is applicable. This issue is part of our current research effort; we are developing a SCR conflict resolution strategy based on the BC strategy context for which an SCR is appropriate in combination with the transition probability and the remaining work estimates associated with an SCR. In our ongoing research on the interaction between the projector and the automatic production of behavioral constraint strategies, one future topic will be techniques for assessing and reducing the risk of backtracking over the inter-behavioral constraint "cut" points.

Discussion

A triangle table (Fikes *et al.*, 1972) is analogous to what you get after running *traverse* only once, a universal plan (Schoppers, 1987) is analogous to what you get by doing exhaustive search of the space of possible domain situations. A triangle table is like a set of SCRs designed to deal with each situation in a sequence of situations, and a universal plan is like a set of SCRs which has 100% coverage of the space of situations. Ginsberg (1989) has argued against the practicality of universal plans. He has suggested that for "cognitive tasks", a system should be able to enhance its performance by expending additional mental resources. Our projection algorithm does exactly this. Under our approach, additional computation time serves to increase the probability of goal satisfaction.

There are various architectures addressing the real-time embedded control problem. Representative approaches include Brooks' (1985) *subsumption architecture*, Nilsson's *action nets* (Nilsson, *et al.*, 1990), Maes' (1990) spreading activation approach, and the *situated automata* of Rosenschein and Kaelbling (Rosenschein, 1989; Rosenschein & Kaelbling 1986; Kaelbling, 1987a,b, 1988). Each of these approaches gives a designer a language and methodology for specifying a control system.

Brooks' (1985) *subsumption architecture* provides an elegant way of organizing the functional components of an embedded control system. The subsumption architecture "model" of embedded execution is richer than our simple IF–THEN Situated Control Rule view. However, we are able to synthesize SCRs automatically from a given behavioral constraint and causal theory describing a particular application domain. To our knowledge, Brooks has not yet addressed the automatic synthesis of subsumption architecture instances.

Nilsson's *action nets* (Nilsson, *et al.*, 1990) provide another methodology and language for the description of embedded systems. Nilsson's view of closed-loop homeostatic servo mechanisms is appealing, and early results are promising. Our work differs in providing a more expressive language of behavioral constraints and by using information about situation probability to control search.

Maes' (1990) system employs a spreading activation approach for dynamic action selection and can be viewed as a form of on-line action synthesis. The behavior of Maes' algorithm depends on a number of global parameters which are set by the user based on (among other factors) characteristics of the environment and the specific goal to be achieved. Hence, if the nature of the environment changes or if the desired goal changes, the user will need to re-tune the parameters. Our work differs by explicitly searching through the space of possible futures. A behavioral constraint is one of the algorithm's inputs; hence, changes in the system's goals are taken into account automatically. Changes in the nature of the environment would be reflected in the transition probabilities; hence, updated probabilities would appropriately influence the projection search.[1]

The most closely related work is that of Rosenschein and Kaelbling (Rosenschein, 1989; Rosenschein & Kaelbling 1986; Kaelbling, 1987a,b, 1988). Kaelbling's GAPPS system is a compiler which translates goal reduction expressions into directly executable circuits. However, a person writing GAPPS goal reductions must essentially do their own temporal projection; that is, it is the person's responsibility to guarantee that the rules, once sequenced, will "lead to" goal satisfaction. In contrast, our approach defines a temporal projection mechanism which sorts out the effects

[1] We have not yet implemented the automatic update of transition probabilities.

of various action sequences automatically. Of course, we potentially pay a greater computational cost by carrying out this search. Additionally, the GAPPS system, and the REX language on which it is based, have a great deal to say about bounded reaction time in terms of the circuits synthesized from higher-level expressions. We are not currently addressing this issue.

We stress the *synthetic* nature of our projector to distinguish it from *analytic* projection (Dean & McDermott, 1987; Hanks, 1990). An analytic projector is used by a planner to validate plans while a synthetic projector combines operator selection and validation in the same algorithm. The analytic/synthetic distinction is largely one of perspective, since it is possible to view a planner–analytic projector pair as a complete system which performs synthetic projection.

Hanks (1990) greatly extended the capabilities of temporal projection systems by adding information regarding probability. Dean and Kanazawa (1988) also use similar information. The techniques of Hanks, Dean and Kanazawa can be used to judge the probability that a given fact will be true at an arbitrary point in the future. We can imagine providing such an inferential facility, but for now, we permit only calculations of individual situation probability. The algorithms of Hanks, Dean and Kanazawa can perform more powerful inferences.

Dean and Boddy (1988) have characterized an *anytime algorithm* as one which can be asked for an answer at any point, where the algorithm's answers are expected to improve the longer it is allowed to run. Our use of *traverse* and *robustify* satisfy this characterization, in the sense that a set of SCRs is available for the reactor at any point in time, and in the sense that the set of SCRs "improves" over time by incrementally increasing goal satisfaction probability. We have identified two ways in which a synthetic temporal projection algorithm can be considered "anytime": first, by using our cut-and-commit search strategy based on behavioral constraint strategies; and second, by recursively employing our deviate-and-recover strategy to manage probable errors.

Our cut-and-commit approach ameliorates the complexity of the projection search. To see this, suppose that the average branching factor in the projection is b, and suppose that an eventual solution path is of length n. This means that breadth-first search would have to project, in the worst case, $b^{n+1} - 2$ many situations to find a successful path. Suppose that the projector's BC strategy is totally ordered and is of length c. In the worst case, the number of situations that *traverse* must project is $c \cdot b^{(n/c)+1} - 2c$. As c approaches n, the number of situations we must consider falls off dramatically. This assumes, of course, that no backtracking occurs. As c increases, the projection takes on the shape of a series of small trees connected end-to-end, rather than one large tree running from start to finish. The larger c is, the smaller the computation's anytime "grain size" becomes.

We have designed and implemented a simulator for an experimental domain called the Reactive Tile World. The Reactive Tile World exhibits exogenous events and temporally extended goals of maintenance and prevention. We are in the process of empirically validating our projection algorithm on a suite of Reactive Tile World test problems.

Acknowledgements

Other members of the ERE group, namely, Rich Levinson, Andy Philips, Nancy Sliwa, and Keith Swanson have helped us develop these ideas; discussions with Mark Boddy, Leslie Kaelbling, Stan Rosenschein, and Steve Hanks have been useful. Thanks to John Allen, Hamid Berenji, Guy Boy, Peter Cheeseman, Smadar Kedar, Phil Laird, and Amy Lansky for useful comments on a previous draft. Final responsibility for all errors and omissions rests, of course, with the authors. Thanks also to Peter Friedland for providing an excellent research environment at NASA Ames.

Appendix A: Behavioral Constraint Syntax and Semantics

A behavioral constraint (BC) is an expression constructed according to the following grammar. We use the symbol β to stand for an arbitrary BC and the symbol | to indicate alternatives.

$$
\begin{array}{lll}
\beta & \rightarrow & (\mathit{and}\ \beta_1\, \beta_2\ \ldots\ \beta_n)\ \mid\ (\mathit{or}\ \beta_1\, \beta_2\ \ldots\ \beta_n) \\
\beta & \rightarrow & (\mathit{maintain}\ \psi\ \tau_1\ \tau_2)\ \mid\ (\mathit{prevent}\ \psi\ \tau_1\ \tau_2) \\
\beta & \rightarrow & (\mathit{maintain}\ \psi\ \varphi\ \varphi)\ \mid\ (\mathit{prevent}\ \psi\ \varphi\ \varphi) \\
\psi & \rightarrow & (\mathit{and}\ \psi_1\, \psi_2 \ldots\ \psi_n)\ \mid\ (\mathit{or}\ \psi_1\, \psi_2 \ldots\ \psi_n) \\
\psi & \rightarrow & \mathit{predicate}
\end{array}
$$

We use ψ to denote a formula, τ to denote a time point constant, and φ to denote a time point variable. Time points are natural numbers. A variable is indicated by a question-mark, for instance: $?t$. All variables are implicitly existentially quantified. We currently use time point variables only to express those goals of "achievement" or "destruction" which are not required to occur at a predetermined point in time; these goals are given the following syntactic forms: $(\mathit{maintain}\ \psi\ \varphi\ \varphi) \equiv (\mathit{achieve}\ \psi\ \varphi)$ and $(\mathit{prevent}\ \psi\ \varphi\ \varphi) \equiv (\mathit{destroy}\ \psi\ \varphi)$.

Behavioral constraint semantics are defined in terms of projection graph paths. Let $w = s_1 o_1 s_2 o_2 \ldots o_{n-1} s_n$ be a projection graph path; let $ts\,(s)$ denote the time stamp of situation s; and let β be a behavioral constraint. Then w satisfies β under the following conditions.

$$
\begin{array}{lll}
w & \models & (\mathit{and}\ \beta_1 \ldots \beta_n) \\
 & \text{iff} & \forall i \in \{1 \ldots n\} :\ w \models \beta_i \\
w & \models & (\mathit{or}\ \beta_1 \ldots \beta_n) \\
 & \text{iff} & \exists i \in \{1 \ldots n\} :\ w \models \beta_i \\
w & \models & (\mathit{maintain}\ \psi\ \tau_1\ \tau_2) \\
 & \text{iff} & \exists s_i \in w :\ ts(s_i) \leq \tau_1 \text{ and } s_i \models \psi \\
 & & \quad \text{and } \forall s_j \in w, j > i : \\
 & & \quad\quad s_j \models \psi \text{ or } ts(s_j) > \tau_2 \\
w & \models & (\mathit{prevent}\ \psi\ \tau_1\ \tau_2) \\
 & \text{iff} & \exists s_i \in w :\ ts(s_i) \leq \tau_1 \text{ and } s_i \not\models \psi \\
 & & \quad \text{and } \forall s_j \in w, j > i : \\
 & & \quad\quad s_j \not\models \psi \text{ or } ts(s_j) > \tau_2 \\
w & \models & (\mathit{maintain}\ \psi\ \varphi\ \varphi) \\
 & \text{iff} & \exists s_i \in w :\ s_i \models \psi \\
w & \models & (\mathit{prevent}\ \psi\ \varphi\ \varphi) \\
 & \text{iff} & \exists s_i \in w :\ s_i \not\models \psi \\
s & \models & (\mathit{and}\ \psi_1 \ldots \psi_n) \\
 & \text{iff} & \forall i \in \{1 \ldots n\} :\ s \models \psi_i \\
s & \models & (\mathit{or}\ \psi_1 \ldots \psi_n) \\
 & \text{iff} & \exists i \in \{1 \ldots n\} :\ s \models \psi_i \\
s & \models & \mathit{predicate} \\
 & \text{iff} & \mathit{predicate} \in s
\end{array}
$$

References

[1] Bresina, J., and Drummond, M. 1990. Integrating Planning and Reaction: A Preliminary Report. *Proceedings of the 1990 AAAI Spring Symposium Series* (session on Planning in Uncertain, Unpredictable, or Changing Environments).

[2] Bresina, J., Marsella, S., and Schmidt, C. 1986. REAPPR – Improving Planning Efficiency via Expertise and Reformulation. Rept. LCSR-TR-82, LCSR, Rutgers University, June.

[3] Brooks, R. 1985. A Robust Layered Control System for a Mobile Robot. Technical Report 864, Artificial Intelligence Laboratory, Massachusetts Institute of Technology, Cambridge, Massachusetts.

[4] Dean, T., and Boddy, M. 1988. An Analysis of Time-Dependent Planning. *AAAI-88*. pp. 49–54.

[5] Dean, T., and Kanazawa, K. 1989. A Model for Projection and Action. *Proceedings of IJCAI-89*. pp. 985–990.

[6] Dean, T., and McDermott, D. 1987. Temporal Database Management. *AI Journal*. Vol. 32(1). pp. 1–55.

[7] Drummond, M. 1989. Situated Control Rules. *Proceedings of Conference on Principles of Knowledge Representation & Reasoning*. Toronto, Canada.

[8] Ginsberg, M. 1989. Universal Planning: An (Almost) Universally Bad Idea. *AI Magazine*, Vol. 10, No. 4. pp. 40–44.

[9] Hanks, S. 1990. Projecting Plans for Uncertain Worlds. Yale University, CS Department, YALE/CSD/RR#756.

[10] Fikes, R., Hart, P., and Nilsson, N. 1972. Learning and Executing Generalized Robot Plans. *AI Journal*, Vol 3, pp. 251–288.

[11] Fikes, R. and Nilsson. N. 1971. STRIPS: A New Approach to the Application of Theorem Proving to Problem Solving. *AI Journal*, Vol. 2, pp. 189–208.

[12] Kaelbling, L. 1987a. An Architecture for Intelligent Reactive Systems. *Reasoning About Actions and Plans*. M. Georgeff and A. Lansky, Eds., Morgan Kauffman.

[13] Kaelbling, L. 1988. Goals as Parallel Program Specifications. *Proceedings of the Seventh National Conference on Artificial Intelligence*. St. Paul, Minnesota.

[14] Maes, P. 1990. How To Do the Right Thing. *Connection Science Journal*. (Special Issue on Hybrid Systems. J. Hendler, editor).

[15] Nilsson, N., Moore, R., and Torrance, M., ACT-NET: An Action Network Language and its Interpreter. Draft paper, Stanford Computer Science Department, February 1990.

[16] Nilsson, N. 1980. *Principles of Artificial Intelligence*. Tioga Publishing Company, CA.

[17] Ow, P. and Morton, T. 1986. Filtered Beam Search in Scheduling. Working paper, Graduate School of Industrial Administration, Carnegie-Melon University.

[18] Rosenschein, S. 1989. Synthesizing Information-Tracking Automata from Environment Descriptions. *Proceedings of Conference on Principles of Knowledge Representation & Reasoning*. Toronto, Canada.

[19] Rosenschein, S. and Kaelbling, L. 1986. The Synthesis of Digital Machines with Provable Epistemic Properties. *Proceedings of Workshop on Theoretical Aspects of Knowledge*. Monterey, CA (March 13-14).

[20] Schoppers, M. 1987. Universal Plans for Reactive Robots in Unpredictable Environments. *Proceedings of the Tenth International Conference on Artificial Intelligence*. pp. 1039–1046, Milan, Italy.

Incremental, Approximate Planning

Charles Elkan
Department of Computer Science
University of Toronto*

ABSTRACT: This paper shows how using a nonmonotonic logic to describe the effects of actions enables plausible plans to be discovered quickly, and then refined if time permits. Candidate plans are found by allowing them to depend on unproved assumptions. The nonmonotonic logic makes explicit which antecedents of rules have the status of default conditions, and they are the only ones that may be left unproved, so only plausible candidate plans are produced. These are refined incrementally by trying to justify the assumptions on which they depend. The new planning strategy has been implemented, with good experimental results.

1 Introduction

Because of uncertainty and because of the need to respond rapidly to events, the traditional view of planning (deriving from STRIPS [Fikes *et al.*, 1972] and culminating in TWEAK [Chapman, 1987]) must be revised drastically. That much is conventional wisdom nowadays. One point of view is that planning should be replaced by some form of improvisation [Brooks, 1987]. However an improvising agent is doomed to choose actions whose optimality is only local. In many domains, goals can only be achieved by forecasting the consequences of actions, and choosing ones whose role in achieving a goal is indirect. Thus traditional planners must be improved, not discarded.

This paper addresses the issue of how to design a planner that is incremental and approximate. An approximate planner is one that can find a plausible candidate plan quickly. An incremental planner is one that can revise its preliminary plan if necessary, when allowed more time.

It is not clear how existing planning strategies can be made approximate and incremental. We therefore first outline a strategy for finding guaranteed plans using a new formalism for specifying planning problems, and then show how to extend this guaranteed strategy to make it approximate and incremental.

Our approach draws inspiration from work on abductive reasoning. A plan is an explanation of how a goal is achievable: a sequence of actions along with a proof that the sequence achieves the goal. An explanation is abductive (as opposed to purely deductive) if it depends on assumptions that are not known to be justified. We find approximate plans by allowing their proofs of correctness to depend on unproved assumptions. Our planner is incremental because, given more time, it refines and if necessary changes a candidate plan by trying to justify the assumptions on which the plan depends.

The critical issue in abductive reasoning is to find plausible explanations. Our planning calculus uses a nonmonotonic logic that makes explicit when an antecedent of a rule has the epistemological status of a default condition. The distinguishing property of a default condition is that it may plausibly be assumed. These antecedents are those that are allowed to be left unjustified in an approximate plan. Concretely, every default condition in the planning calculus expresses either a claim that an achieved property of the world persists, or that an unwanted property is not achieved. Thus the approximate planning strategy only proposes reasonable candidate plans.

Sections 2 and 3 below present the formalism for specifying planning problems and the strategy for finding guaranteed plans. In Section 4 the strategy is extended to become approximate and incremental. Section 5 contains experimental results, and finally Section 6 discusses related and future work.

2 The planning formalism

Different formal frameworks for stating planning problems vary widely in the complexity of the problems they can express. Using modal logics or reification, one can reason about multiple agents, about the temporal prop-

*For correspondence: Department of Computer Science, University of Toronto, Toronto M5S 1A4, Canada, (416) 978-7797, cpe@ai.toronto.edu.

erties of actions, and about what agents know [Moore, 1985; Konolige, 1986; Cohen and Levesque, 1990]. The simplest planning problems can be solved by augmented finite state machines [Brooks *et al.*, 1988], whose behaviour can be specified in a propositional logic. The planning problems considered here are intermediate in complexity. They cannot be solved by an agent reacting immediately to its environment, because they require maintaining an internal theory of the world, in order to project the indirect consequences of actions. On the other hand, they involve a single agent, and they do not require reasoning about knowledge or time.

Our nonmonotonic logic for specifying this type of planning problem is called the PERFLOG calculus.[1] Technically, the calculus is the language of locally stratified definite clauses with the minimal model semantics of [Przymusiński, 1987] and certain "laws of nature" presented below. The PERFLOG calculus is distinctive in that it has a well-defined first-order semantics *and* it is practically usable for planning. Other proposed planning formalisms with a well-defined semantics either do not have first-order expressiveness (for example the TWEAK calculus [Chapman, 1987]), or else they use logics for which simple proof procedures capable of inventing plans are not known (for example the circumscriptive calculus of [Lifschitz and Rabinov, 1989]).

The Yale shooting problem [Hanks and McDermott, 1986] is at the simple end of the spectrum of planning problems for which the PERFLOG calculus is appropriate. It serves here to introduce the calculus by example. We start with the laws of nature mentioned above. In the following rules, think of s as denoting a state of the world, of a as denoting an action, and of $do(s, a)$ as denoting the state resulting from performing the action a in the initial state s. Finally, think of p as denoting a contingent property that holds in certain states of the world: a fluent.

$$\forall a, s, p \;\; causes(a, s, p) \rightarrow holds(p, do(s, a)) \qquad (1)$$

$$\forall a, s, p \;\; holds(p, s) \wedge \neg cancels(a, s, p) \rightarrow holds(p, do(s, a)). \qquad (2)$$

The rules (1) and (2) are frame axioms. Rule (1) captures the commonsense notion of causation, and rule (2) expresses the commonsense "law of inertia": a fluent p holds after an action a if it holds before the action, and the action does not cancel the fluent. Note that since in addition to a, one argument of *causes* and of *cancels* is s, the results of an action (that is, the fluents it causes and cancels) may depend on the state in which the action is performed, and not just on which action it is.

[1] PERFLOG is an abbreviation for "performance-oriented perfect model logic."

Given rules (1) and (2), a particular planning domain is specified by writing axioms that mention the actions and fluents of the domain, and say which actions cause or cancel which fluents. In the world of the Yale shooting problem, there are three fluents, *loaded*, *alive*, and *dead*, and three actions, *load*, *wait*, and *shoot*. The relationships of these fluents and actions are specified by the following axioms:

$$\forall s \;\; causes(load, s, loaded) \qquad (3)$$

$$\forall s \;\; holds(loaded, s) \rightarrow causes(shoot, s, dead) \qquad (4)$$

$$\forall s \;\; holds(loaded, s) \rightarrow cancels(shoot, s, alive) \qquad (5)$$

$$\forall s \;\; holds(loaded, s) \rightarrow cancels(shoot, s, loaded). \qquad (6)$$

The initial state of the world s_0 is specified by saying which fluents are true in it:

$$holds(alive, s_0). \qquad (7)$$

According to the nonmonotonic semantics of PERFLOG collections of rules,

$$holds(dead, do(do(do(s_0, load), wait), shoot))$$

is entailed by rules (1)–(7). The Yale shooting problem is thus solved.

The advantages and disadvantages of the PERFLOG calculus will be discussed in a forthcoming paper. It can be extended to match the expressiveness of competing proposed nonmonotonic logics for reasoning about action. For the purposes of this paper, what is most important is that the calculus is usable for inventing plans, not just for specifying when a plan is correct. Given clauses (1)–(7) and the query $\exists p \; holds(dead, p)$?, the planning strategy of the next section quickly produces the answer substitution $p = do(do(x, load), shoot)$. (The variable x in the generated plan indicates that it works whatever the initial situation.)

3 Finding guaranteed plans

The previous section showed how to state the relationships between the actions and fluents of a planning domain as a PERFLOG set of axioms. This section describes a strategy for inventing plans using such a set of axioms; the next section extends the strategy to be approximate and incremental.

A PERFLOG set of axioms is general logic program, and our planning strategy is a four-point extension of the standard PROLOG procedure for answering queries against a logic program.

Iterative deepening. The standard PROLOG strategy can be viewed as depth-first exploration of an and/or tree representing the space of potential proofs of the query posed by the user. Each or-node corresponds to a subgoal[2] that must be unified with the head of some clause, and each and-node corresponds to the body of a clause. The root of the tree, always an or-node, is the user's query. Depth-first exploration can be implemented many times more efficiently than other exploration patterns, but it is liable to get lost on infinite paths. These paths can be cut off by imposing a depth bound. The idea of iterative deepening is to repeatedly explore a search space depth-first, each time with an increased depth bound [Stickel and Tyson, 1985].

Conspiracy numbers. Iterative deepening algorithms differ in how the depth of a node is defined. The conspiracy idea underlies the best known way of defining depth in and/or trees. A conspiracy for a partially explored and/or tree is a minimal (with respect to subsets) set of subgoal leafs such that if all the subgoals in the conspiracy have compatible answer substitutions, then an answer substitution exists for the root goal of the tree. Suppose that for each member of a conspiracy, whether it has an answer substitution is a statistically independent event. Even so, as the conspiracy gets larger, heuristically the chance that all the members have compatible answer substitutions decreases as if these events were negatively correlated. Thus a good definition of the depth of a leaf node is the size of the smallest conspiracy to which it belongs. Conspiracy sizes can be computed efficiently [Elkan, 1989].

Negation-as-failure. The strategy described so far applies to positive subgoals only. Given a negated goal, the negation-as-failure idea is to attempt to prove the un-negated version of the goal. If this attempt succeeds, the negated goal is taken as false. If no proof exists for the un-negated goal, then the negated goal is taken as true. Negation-as-failure is combined with iterative deepening by using the conspiracy depth measure to limit searches for proofs of un-negated notional subgoals corresponding to negated actual subgoals. If the and/or tree representing the space of possible proofs of a notional subgoal is completely explored, without finding a proof, then the corresponding actual negated subgoal is taken as true. If a proof of the notional subgoal is found, then the actual negated subgoal is taken as false. If exploration of the possible proofs of the notional subgoal is cut off by the current depth bound, it remains unknown whether or not the notional subgoal is provable, so for soundness the actual negated subgoal must be taken as false.

Freezing and constructive negation. Negation-as-failure only works on ground negated subgoals. Suppose the unit clauses $p(a)$ and $q(b)$ are given, and consider the query $\exists x\ \neg p(x) \wedge q(x)$?. This query should have one answer, $x = b$, but the strategy described so far produces no answer: naive negation-as-failure attempts to prove $p(x)$, succeeds, deems $\neg p(x)$ to be false, and fails on the whole query. The solution to this problem is to apply negation-as-failure to ground negated subgoals only. When a negated subgoal is encountered, it is postponed until it becomes ground. Concretely, in the example above $\neg p(x)$ is delayed, and $q(x)$ is solved, obtaining the substitution $x = b$. Now $\neg p(x)[x \mapsto b]$ is revived, and proved. This process is called freezing [Naish, 1986]. If postponement is not sufficient to ground a negated subgoal, then an auxiliary subgoal is introduced to generate potential answers. This process is called constructive negation [Foo *et al.*, 1988].

The performance of the planning strategy just described could be improved significantly, notably by caching subgoals once they are proved or disproved [Elkan, 1989]. Nevertheless it is already quite usable. More important as a basis for further work, it is sound and complete.

Lemma: The guaranteed planning strategy is sound.
Proof: Negation-as-failure is sound under the completion semantics for general logic programs [Clark, 1978]. The perfect model semantics allows a subclass of the class of models allowed by the completion semantics. Therefore given a query of the form $\exists p\ holds(\sigma, p)$?, if the strategy above returns with the answer substitution $p = \pi$, then $holds(\sigma, \pi)$ is true, and π is a correct plan. ∎

Completeness is a more delicate issue. In general, perfect models may be non-recursively enumerable [Apt and Blair, 1988], and all sufficiently expressive non-monotonic logics have non-computable entailment relations. However PERFLOG theories all have a similar structure, using the same three fundamental predicates, so their completion and perfect model semantics essentially coincide, and the strategy above is complete.

4 Finding plausible plans

This section describes modifications to the strategy of the previous section that make it approximate and incremental. In the same way that the guaranteed planning strategy is in fact a general query-answering procedure, the incremental planning strategy is really a general procedure for forming and revising plausible explanations using a default theory.

Any planning strategy that produces plans relying on unproved assumptions is *ipso facto* unsound, but by its incremental nature the strategy below tends to soundness: with more time, candidate plans are either proved to be valid, or changed.

Approximation. The idea behind finding approximate plans is simple: an explanation is approximate

[2] Here and in similar contexts, 'goal' refers to a literal for which an answer substitution is wanted.

if it depends on unproved assumptions. Strategies for forming approximate explanations can be distinguished according to the class of approximate explanations that each may generate. One way to define a class of approximate explanations is to fix a certain class of subgoals as the only ones that may be taken as assumptions. Looking at the PERFLOG formalism, there is an obvious choice of what subgoals to allow to be assumptions. Negated subgoals have the epistemological status of default conditions: the nonmonotonic semantics makes them true unless they are forced to be false. It is reasonable to assume that a default condition is true unless it it is provably false.

There is a second, procedural, reason to allow negated subgoals to be assumed, but not positive subgoals. Without constructive negation, negated subgoals can only be answered true or false. Negation-as-failure never provides an answer substitution for a negated subgoal. Therefore unproved negated subgoals in an explanation never leave "holes" in the answer substitution induced by the explanation. Concretely, a plan whose correctness proof depends on unproved default conditions will never change because those defaults are proved to hold.

In more detail, the guaranteed planning strategy is modified as follows. When a negated subgoal becomes ground, the proof of its notional positive counterpart is attempted. If this attempt succeeds or fails within the current depth bound, the negated subgoal is taken as false or true, respectively, as before. However, if the depth bound is reached during the attempted proof, then the negated subgoal is given the status of an assumption.

Incrementality. An approximate explanation can be refined by trying to prove the assumptions it depends on. If an assumption is proved, the explanation thereby becomes "less approximate". As just mentioned, proving an assumption never causes a plan to change. On the other hand, if an assumption is disproved, the approximate plan is thereby revealed to be invalid, and it is necessary to search for a different plan.

Precisely, any negated subgoal is allowed to be assumed initially. Each iteration of iterative deepening takes place with an increased depth bound. For each particular (solvable) planning problem, there is a certain minimum depth bound at which one or more approximate plans can first be found. Each of these first approximate plans depends on a certain set of assumptions. In later iterations, only subsets of these sets are allowed to be assumed. This restriction has the effect of concentrating attention on either refining the already discovered approximate plans, or finding new approximate plans that depend on fewer assumptions.

```
% rules for how the world evolves

holds(P,do(S,A)) :-
        causes(A,S,P).
holds(P,do(S,A)) :-
        holds(P,S), not(cancels(A,S,P)).

% the effects of actions

causes(pounce(lion,X),S,eats(lion,X)) :-
        can(pounce(lion,X),S).
can(pounce(X,Y),S) :-
        holds(in(X,L),S), holds(in(Y,L),S),
        not(call(X = Y)),
        not(Z,holds(eats(X,Z),S)).
causes(jump(X),S,in(X,arena)) :-
        can(jump(X),S), holds(in(X,cage),S).
can(jump(lion),S) :-
        holds(eats(lion,centurion),S).
cancels(drop(X,Y),S,eats(X,Y)) :-
        can(drop(X,Y),S).
can(drop(X,Y),S) :-
        holds(eats(X,Y),S).
holds(in(X,H),S) :-
        holds(eats(lion,X),S),
holds(in(lion,H),S).

% the initial state of the world

holds(in(christian,arena),s0).
holds(in(lion,cage),s0).
holds(in(centurion,cage),s0).
```

Figure 1: The theory of a lion and a Christian.

5 Experimental results

Implementing the planning strategies described above is straightforward, because the PERFLOG calculus is based on directed clauses. In general, it is insufficiently realized how efficiently logics with this basis, both monotonic and nonmonotonic, can be automated. The state of the art in PROLOG implementation is about nine RISC cycles per logical inference [Mills, 1989]. Any PERFLOG theory could be compiled into a specialized incremental planner running at a comparable speed.

The experiment reported here uses a classical planning domain: a lion and a Christian in a stadium. The goal is for the lion to eat the Christian. Initially the lion is in its cage with a centurion, and the Christian is in the arena. The lion can jump from the cage into the arena only if it has eaten the centurion. The lion eats a person by pouncing, but it cannot pounce while it is already eating. The PERFLOG theory in Figure 1 describes this domain formally.

Using the guaranteed planning strategy of Section 3, the query `holds(eats(lion,christian),P)?` is first solved with conspiracy depth bound 19, in 4.75 seconds.[3] The plan found is

```
P = do(do(do(do(s0,pounce(lion,centurion)),
                 jump(lion)),
              drop(lion,centurion)),
           pounce(lion,christian)).
```

Using the approximate planning strategy of Section 4, the same query is solvable in 0.17 seconds, with conspiracy depth bound 17. The candidate plan found is

```
P = do(do(do(s0,pounce(lion,centurion)),
              jump(lion)),
           pounce(lion,christian)).
```

This plan depends on the assumption that no `Z` exists such that

```
holds(eats(lion,Z),do(do(s0,pounce(lion,centurion)),
                       jump(lion))).
```

Although the assumption is false and the plan is not correct, it is plausible. Note also that the first two actions it prescribes are the same as those of the correct plan: the approximate plan is an excellent guide to immediate action.

6 Discussion

The strategy for incremental, approximate planning uses simplifying assumptions in a principled way: first the planner searches for a plan assuming that default conditions hold, then it attempts to prove that they do hold. The idea of relying on assumptions that are left unproven appears in [Feldman and Rich, 1986] and elsewhere. This paper shows how a formal nonmonotonic logic determines reasonable potential assumptions, and how iterative deepening can be used to modulate the effort expended on checking these assumptions. The point that default theories suggest how to focus inference is made independently in [Ginsberg, 1990]. To accommodate arbitrary sources of knowledge about plausible assumptions, our implementation allows the user to say explicitly what must always be proved, and what may sometimes be left unproved, as in [Chien, 1989].

From a knowledge-level point of view, approximate planning is a type of hierarchical planning. Each maximum conspiracy size defines a different abstraction space in which to search for plans. In each space the available actions and their effects are the same. However, the lower the maximum conspiracy size, the more each action is stripped of its difficult-to-check preconditions. Abstraction spaces defined in this way have the advantage that the execution of any plan invented using them can be initiated immediately if it is necessary to act instantly. Other hierarchical planners typically construct plans using abstract actions that must be elaborated before they can be executed [Knoblock, 1989].

Selecting good simplifying assumptions is a type of abductive inference. Abduction mechanisms have been investigated a great deal for the task of plan recognition, not so much for the task of inventing plans, and not at all for the task of inventing plausible plans. These three different tasks lead to different choices of what facts may be assumed. In the work of [Shanahan, 1989] for example, properties of the initial state of the world may be assumed. In our work, the facts that may be assumed say either that an established property of the world persists, or that an unestablished property does not hold.

An incremental approximate planner is an "anytime algorithm" for planning in the sense of [Dean and Boddy, 1988]. Anytime planning algorithms have been proposed before, but not for problems of the traditional type treated in this paper. For example, the real-time route planner of [Korf, 1987] is a heuristic graph search algorithm, and the route improvement algorithm of [Boddy and Dean, 1989] relies on an initial plan that is guaranteed to be correct.

For future work, one important direction is to quantify how an approximate plan is improved by allowing more time for its refinement. Another problem is to find a planning strategy that is focused as well as approximate and incremental. A focused strategy would be one that concentrated preferentially on finding the first step in a plan–what to do *next*.

[3] All times are for an implementation in CProlog, running on a Silicon Graphics machine rated at 20 MIPS.

References

[Apt and Blair, 1988] Krzysztof R. Apt and Howard A. Blair. Arithmetic classification of perfect models of stratified programs. In Kenneth Bowen and Robert Kowalski, editors, *Fifth International Conference and Symposium on Logic Programming*, volume 2, pages 765–779, Seattle, Washington, August 1988. MIT Press.

[Boddy and Dean, 1989] Mark Boddy and Thomas Dean. Solving time-dependent planning problems. In *Proceedings of the Eleventh International Joint Conference on Artificial Intelligence*, pages 979–984, August 1989.

[Brooks *et al.*, 1988] Rodney A. Brooks, Jonathan H. Connell, and Peter Ning. Herbert: A second generation mobile robot. MIT AI Memo 1016, January 1988.

[Brooks, 1987] Rodney A. Brooks. Planning is just a way of avoiding figuring out what to do next. Technical Report 303, Artificial Intelligence Laboratory, MIT, September 1987.

[Chapman, 1987] David Chapman. Planning for conjunctive goals. *Artificial Intelligence*, 32:333–377, 1987.

[Chien, 1989] Steve A. Chien. Using and refining simplifications: Explanation-based learning of plans in intractable domains. In *Proceedings of the Eleventh International Joint Conference on Artificial Intelligence*, pages 590–595, 1989.

[Clark, 1978] Kenneth. L. Clark. Negation as failure. In Hervé Gallaire and Jack Minker, editors, *Logic and Databases*, pages 293–322. Plenum Press, New York, 1978.

[Cohen and Levesque, 1990] Philip R. Cohen and Hector J. Levesque. Intention is choice with commitment. *Artificial Intelligence*, 42(2–3):213–261, 1990.

[Dean and Boddy, 1988] Thomas Dean and Mark Boddy. An analysis of time-dependent planning. In *Proceedings of the National Conference on Artificial Intelligence*, pages 49–54, August 1988.

[Elkan, 1989] Charles Elkan. Conspiracy numbers and caching for searching and/or trees and theorem-proving. In *Proceedings of the Eleventh International Joint Conference on Artificial Intelligence*, pages 341–346, August 1989.

[Feldman and Rich, 1986] Yishai A. Feldman and Charles Rich. Reasoning with simplifying assumptions: A methodology and example. In *Proceedings of the National Conference on Artificial Intelligence*, pages 2–7, August 1986.

[Fikes *et al.*, 1972] Richard E. Fikes, Peter E. Hart, and Nils J. Nilsson. Learning and executing generalized robot plans. *Artificial Intelligence*, 3:251–288, 1972.

[Foo *et al.*, 1988] Norman Y. Foo, Anand S. Rao, Andrew Taylor, and Adrian Walker. Deduced relevant types and constructive negation. In Kenneth Bowen and Robert Kowalski, editors, *Fifth International Conference and Symposium on Logic Programming*, volume 1, pages 126–139, Seattle, Washington, August 1988. MIT Press.

[Ginsberg, 1990] Matthew L. Ginsberg. Defaults and hierarchical problem solving. In *Preprints of the Third International Workshop on Nonmonotonic Reasoning*, Lake Tahoe, May/June 1990.

[Hanks and McDermott, 1986] Steve Hanks and Drew McDermott. Default reasoning, nonmonotonic logics, and the frame problem. In *Proceedings of the National Conference on Artificial Intelligence*, pages 328–333, August 1986.

[Knoblock, 1989] Craig A. Knoblock. Learning hierarchies of abstraction spaces. In *Proceedings of the Sixth International Workshop on Machine Learning*, pages 241–245. Morgan Kaufmann Publishers, Inc., 1989.

[Konolige, 1986] Kurt Konolige. *A Deduction Model of Belief.* Pitman, 1986.

[Korf, 1987] Richard E. Korf. Real-time path planning. In *Proceedings of the DARPA Knowledge-Based Planning Workshop*, 1987.

[Lifschitz and Rabinov, 1989] Vladimir Lifschitz and Arkady Rabinov. Things that change by themselves. In *Proceedings of the Eleventh International Joint Conference on Artificial Intelligence*, pages 864–867, 1989.

[Mills, 1989] Jonathan W. Mills. A pipelined architecture for logic programming with a complex but single-cycle instruction set. In *Proceedings of the IEEE First International Tools for AI Workshop*, September 1989.

[Moore, 1985] Robert C. Moore. A formal theory of knowledge and action. In *Formal Theories of the Commonsense World.* Ablex, 1985.

[Naish, 1986] Lee Naish. *Negation and Control in* PROLOG. Number 238 in Lecture Notes in Computer Science. Springer Verlag, 1986.

[Przymusiński, 1987] Teodor C. Przymusiński. On the declarative semantics of stratified deductive databases and logic programs. In Jack Minker, editor, *Foundations of Deductive Databases and Logic Programming*, pages 193–216, Los Altos, California, 1987. Morgan Kaufmann Publishers, Inc.

[Shanahan, 1989] Murray Shanahan. Prediction is deduction but explanation is abduction. In *Proceedings of the Eleventh International Joint Conference on Artificial Intelligence*, pages 1055–1060, 1989.

[Stickel and Tyson, 1985] Mark E. Stickel and W. M. Tyson. An analysis of consecutively bounded depth-first search with applications in automated deduction. In *Proceedings of the Ninth International Joint Conference on Artificial Intelligence*, pages 1073–1075, August 1985.

Admissible Criteria For Loop Control In Planning

Roy Feldman and **Paul Morris**
IntelliCorp
1975 El Camino Real West
Mountain View, CA 94040
feldman@intellicorp.com morris@intellicorp.com

Abstract

We introduce methods for identifying operator preconditions that need not be expanded further. The methods are proved to be *admissible* , that is, they will not cause a solution to be missed when one exists. In certain cases, the methods also identify operator reformulations that increase the number of nonexpandable preconditions. This approach provides effective loop control in common situations. Moreover, the computation required can be performed during a precompilation of the operators in a domain; thus, there is no significant additional run-time overhead during planning.

Introduction

A major challenge facing the builder of a generative planner is to prevent undesired looping behavior. This is most clearly seen in "vicious circle" situations. For example, a planner, given the problem of opening a car door when the keys are locked in the car, may loop indefinitely in trying to find a solution. A more subtle form of the syndrome can occur during backtracking search. In these situations, time is wasted in considering partial solutions that involve unnecessary digressions. For example, a planner may consider going from one place to another by irrelevant circuitous routes.

Missing a solution due to infinite looping can be avoided by a breadth-first search, such as used by Tweak [Chapman 1987]. However, this kind of search is impractical for many types of problems, and in any event the efficiency issue remains.

Clearly, a planner needs some way of determining when a subgoal should not be expanded further. The danger of any pruning criterion, however, is that for some problems it may prevent any solution from being found, even when a solution exists. What is needed is a guarantee that the criterion allows at least one solution to be found for every solvable problem. A pruning strategy with this property is called *admissible* by Drummond and Currie [Drummond & Currie 1989].

Similar difficulties with looping can arise in backward-chaining inference systems. Smith, et al. [Smith, Genesereth & Ginsberg 1986] show that the common idea of failing a subgoal that is identical to one of its ancestors is an admissible strategy for inference systems. A similar approach has been used for loop control in planning (e.g., [Rich 1983, p. 258]). Unfortunately, as shown below, this strategy is not admissible for planning systems. Nonlinear planning can be formulated as an inference task via Chapman's modal truth criterion [Chapman 1987]. However, failing repetitive subgoals in the inferential problem appears to have little practical significance for the planning problem.

An alternative approach to loop control in planning was introduced by Tate [Tate 1976; Tate 1977]. In his NONLIN system, certain preconditions of operators are designated as *hold* conditions (called *usewhen* conditions in [Tate 1977]). Hold conditions are not allowed to be expanded. The difficulty here is that the user is required to specify these, and no guidance is provided for selecting them. If the user's intuition is faulty, the strategy will be inadmissible. Furthermore, as we will see presently, for some ways of specifying the operators in a domain, there may not be any admissible hold conditions that provide adequate loop control.

Nevertheless, the concept of a nonexpandable precondition will form the basis of our approach. We will present a way of determining when a precondition may admissibly be made nonexpandable. Moreover, the method automatically reformulates the operators in certain cases in order to increase the number of such determinations.

In following sections, we first show the inadmissibility in planning of failing subgoals that are identical to an ancestor. Then we present a formalization of plan graphs that serves as a framework for our approach. Next we introduce a structure called the *predecessor graph* that provides information about allowable operator sequences of length 2. Finally, we show how to use

This research was sponsored by a joint project of the Defense Advanced Research Projects Agency and the National Aeronautics and Space Administration under contract F30602-88-C-0045.

this graph to identify admissibly nonexpandable preconditions. The proofs are contained in the appendix.

Robot Recharging Problem

In this section, we present an example that resists existing methods of loop control. In particular, it shows the inadmissibility of failing a goal that is identical to an ancestor. The operator representation we will give for the problem, although a natural one, is also not amenable to control with hold conditions. We will see later that successful loop control requires a reformulation of one of the operators.

The example, called the "robot recharging problem," was first described in [Morris 1984]. A robot is capable of holding a unit of charge. As long as it is charged, the robot may move around. We assume that moving uses a negligible amount of energy. The robot also needs to fix a hole in its body. We assume this uses up all its energy, so that the robot becomes discharged. The robot is initially at location A. There is a power source at location B where the robot can recharge. The goals of the robot are to fix the hole and be charged.

The following is the STRIPS representation of the domain.

FIX
Preconditions and delete conditions:
CHARGED, HOLE
Add conditions: UNCHARGED, NO-HOLE
RECHARGE
Preconditions: AT(B), UNCHARGED
Delete condition: UNCHARGED
Add condition: CHARGED
GO
Preconditions: CHARGED, AT(?X)
Delete condition: AT(?X)
Add condition: AT(?Y)

Initial state: AT(A), CHARGED, HOLE
Goals: CHARGED, NO-HOLE

Obviously, the robot must first go to location B. Only then can it perform its task and still be able to recharge. However, if we examine the structure of this plan, we see that AT(B) is a subgoal of CHARGED. When AT(B) is expanded by a GO action, this introduces a further subgoal of CHARGED, which is identical to the ancestor goal. Note that if we fail this subgoal, the problem will not be solved. (It may be helpful to refer to figure 1 below.)

If we use no loop control method, the problem can be solved. Consider, however, the closely related problem where the robot is uncharged in the initial state. This has no solution. Without some loop control criterion, a planner faced with this problem will loop endlessly. The challenge is to find some method that cuts off the search in the second situation, but not in the first.

The most obvious candidates for hold conditions are the UNCHARGED precondition in RECHARGE, the AT(?X) in GO, and the HOLE in FIX. Unfortunately, these are not sufficient to terminate looping in the second situation, since there is a cycle through the AT(B) precondition of RECHARGE and the CHARGED precondition of GO. Intuitively, it seems as if the AT(B) in RECHARGE might be a hold condition. However, we saw above that constructing the plan in the first situation requires AT(B) to be expanded.

Notice that the need for the GO action indirectly results from the presence of the NO-HOLE goal, but this is not reflected in the goal ancestor path. Interestingly, the methods we will consider have the effect of reformulating the operators in a way that diverts the ancestor path to this goal.

Plan Graphs

We use the general framework of nonlinear planning introduced by Sacerdoti [Sacerdoti 1977] and Tate [Tate 1977]. Planning proceeds in stages. At each stage, a goal is selected to work on. The planner satisfies the goal either by matching it to an already achieved fact, or by introducing a new action into the plan. In the former case, we say the goal is *linked* to the matching fact. In the latter case, we say the goal is *expanded.*

The possible actions are determined by a set of STRIPS operators [Nilsson 1980]. However, we require that the operators be formulated so that they are never applied in situations where one of their delete conditions is already false, or where one of their add conditions is already true; i.e., none of the adds or deletes are no-ops. This is not a severe restriction. First, operators that are constructed in practice generally have this property. Second, an operator that does not can always be replaced by several more specialized operators that do satisfy the restriction. We also require that the operators be formulated to avoid the need for *coincident* solutions, that is, where two preconditions, or two add conditions, of the same operator become instantiated in such a way that they coincide. Again, this can be accomplished by using more specialized operators, if necessary.

We associate each action with two sets of facts: the *before-facts*, consisting of the delete conditions and undeleted preconditions; and the *after-facts*, comprised of the add conditions and undeleted preconditions. This division may be viewed as a relational production [Vere 1977] representation of the action.

A *plan graph* is a graphical representation of a plan that shows how the after-facts of various actions contribute to the before-facts of other actions. Formally, a plan graph is a directed acyclic multigraph where the nodes are labeled with actions, and the edges are labeled with facts. The labeling on an edge connecting two actions must belong to the after-facts of the first action and the before-facts of the second. There is also a distinguished START action whose after-facts

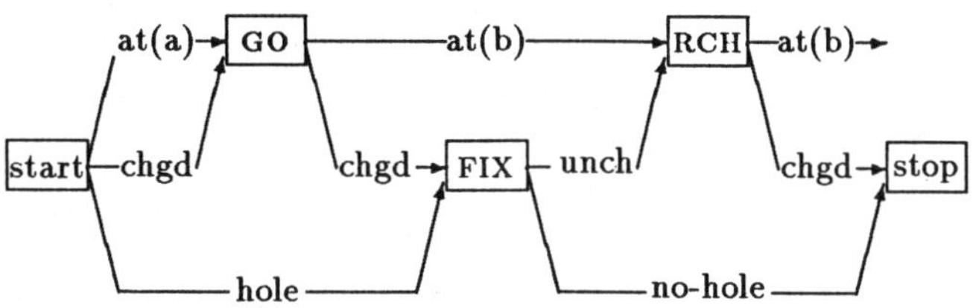

Figure 1: Plan Graph For Robot Problem

supply the initial facts for the plan, and a STOP action whose before-facts include the atomic top-level goals. Figure 1 shows the plan graph for a solution to the robot problem.

For linguistic convenience, we blur the distinction between a node and the action it is labeled with. For example, we may speak of the "before-facts" of a node, and the "incoming edges" of an action.

The following concepts will be useful in the subsequent discussion.

Note that every directed acyclic multigraph determines a partial order on its nodes and edges. Given a plan graph, we say a node or edge *precedes* another node or edge if it precedes it in this partial order. Furthermore, we say a node or edge is *parallel* to a second node or edge if neither precedes the other.

A plan graph is *complete* if the before-facts of each action in the plan are supplied by after-facts of other actions, i.e., if the incoming edges to each action cover all of the before-facts. This corresponds to a situation where there are no remaining unsolved goals. Unless otherwise stated, in the remainder of this paper, we will assume plan graphs are complete. Also, unless otherwise clear from the context, we restrict our attention to plan graphs that are *conflict-free* in the following sense: no edge is parallel to an action that deletes the fact that the edge is labeled with. This is closely related to the usual concept of plan conflict (e.g., [Tate 1976]).

It is never necessary for two incoming edges to an action to be labeled with the same fact, since we can simply drop one of the edges without affecting the completeness of the plan. Expressed in terms of planning, a goal is satisfied by linking to a single matching fact. However, traditional approaches to planning allow a fact to satisfy more than one goal. Thus, it is possible for two outgoing edges from an action to be labeled with the same fact. We will call this a *collision.* The following result indicates that collisions are not essential, and could be excluded without seriously impairing a planner.

Theorem 1 *For every conflict-free plan graph, there is a collision-free plan graph with the same actions that solves the same problem.*

In light of theorem 1, *we assume from now on that the plan graphs are collision-free.* This restriction turns out to be very useful for proving results about plan graphs.

Note that the theorem shows it is admissible to adopt an approach to planning where a fact that is linked to a goal is "used up" by the goal, i.e., becomes unavailable for linking by another goal. In the case where the consuming goal corresponds to a precondition of an action that remains true after the action, the fact is "put back" as a postcondition of the action. This approach to planning has been studied in [Morris 1984].

We now introduce a notion that is related to the concept of primary cut introduced by Drummond and Currie [Drummond & Currie 1989]. We will say a set of edges is *parallel* if every edge in the set is parallel to every other edge in the set. A *cut* of a plan graph is a maximal parallel set of edges, i.e., a parallel set of edges that is not a subset of any other parallel set of edges.

The following theorem (actually, its corollary) is central to reasoning about plan graphs.

Theorem 2 *For every cut, there is a reachable state of the domain that contains each fact in the labeling of the cut. Moreover, no two edges in the cut are labeled with the same fact.*

Corollary 2.1 *Edges that are parallel cannot have the same label or contradictory labels. A node cannot be parallel to an edge whose label coincides with or conflicts with one of its before-facts or after-facts.*

To apply the corollary, we need to reason about inconsistencies. In principle, any domain constraints could be used for this purpose. However, we have found the most useful constraints to be exclusive-or relationships. Inconsistencies based on such constraints can be efficiently determined. In [Morris & Feldman 1989], a method is presented for automatically extracting candidate exclusive-or relationships from operator descriptions.

The Predecessor Graph

Obviously, not every combination of actions is possible or useful. We now address the question of what actions can appear next to each other in a plan graph.

Given a plan graph, we will say a node A is an *immediate predecessor* of a node B if A precedes B, and there is no other node C such that A precedes C and C precedes B. We are interested in necessary conditions for a node to be an immediate predecessor.

It is easy to see that if A is an immediate predecessor of B, then some outgoing edge of A must be an incoming edge of B. (The converse is not necessarily true: A could be connected by an edge to B without being an immediate predecessor, since there may be a second route from A to B.) Corollary 2.1 provides additional requirements. Note that the after-facts of A must be

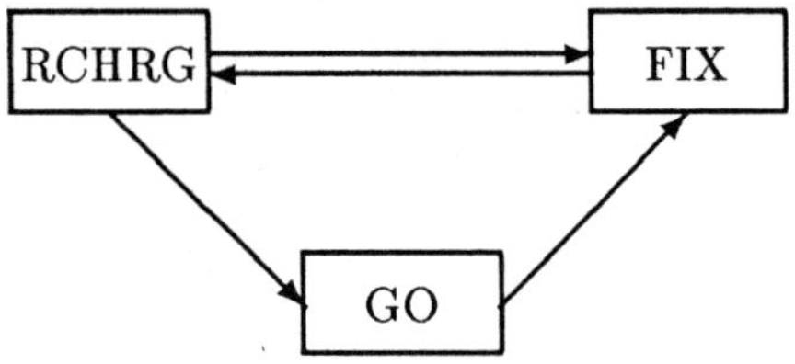

Figure 2: Predecessor Graph For Robot Problem

consistent with the before-facts of B; otherwise, we would have parallel contradictory edges.

This requirement allows us to completely rule out certain combinations of operators. For example in the robot recharging problem, no instance of GO can be an immediate predecessor of RECHARGE because the CHARGED precondition of the former conflicts with the UNCHARGED precondition of the latter. Similarly, FIX cannot immediately precede GO or itself, and RECHARGE cannot immediately precede itself.

Certain other combinations, although not impossible, can be ruled out as not being sensible. Suppose, for example, an action A is immediately preceded by its exact inverse B. Since the actions are inverses, there is an exact match between the after-facts of B and the before-facts of A. Corollary 2.1 then implies that every outgoing edge of A must be an incoming edge of B and vice versa; otherwise we would have parallel edges with the same label. It follows that the plan graph could be simplified by excising the portion from A to B and directly joining the resulting dangling edges.

There are no inverses in the robot problem. However, a further example of a non-sensible situation occurs when a two operator combination is subsumed by a single operator. Suppose in the robot problem that GO is immediately preceded by itself. The binding of ?Y in the earlier instance of GO must match the binding of ?X in the other; otherwise the consistency requirement is violated. But then the after-facts of the earlier instance coincide with the before-facts of the other, and all the edges from the former must connect to the latter. It follows that the portion of the plan graph containing the two GOs can be replaced by a single GO. Thus, we can assume that GO does not immediately precede itself.

After using the techniques above to eliminate various combinations, we are left with a set of combinations that have not been ruled out. We can form a graph of the operators that reflects these. We call this the *predecessor graph*. Figure 2 shows the predecessor graph for the robot problem.

The predecessor graph can often be annotated with constraints on bindings that arise from the immediate predecessor relationship. For example, if GO is immediately preceded by RECHARGE, then uniqueness of location requires that the variable ?X in GO be bound to B.

The above uses consistency analysis to rule out potential operator combinations in forming the predecessor graph. Other applications of consistency analysis in planning appear in the work of Irani and Cheng [Irani & Cheng 1987], and Drummond and Currie [Drummond & Currie 1989].

Loop Control

We now consider how to use the predecessor graph to determine nonexpandable preconditions. The method is based on results in this section.

We define a plan graph to be *minimal* if it contains no unnecessary actions, i.e., there is no other plan graph that solves the same problem with a proper subset of the actions. To prove admissibility of a pruning criterion, it is enough to show that every minimal plan graph can be constructed within the bounds of the criterion.

The following concept will also be useful. We say an operator A is *guarded* by one of its preconditions G if, for every minimal plan graph in which A occurs, the before-fact of A corresponding to G is an after-fact or a before-fact of every immediate predecessor of A.

Our first theorem on loop control involves a special case of A being guarded by G.

Theorem 3 *It is admissible not to expand a precondition G of an operator A if, for every minimal plan graph in which A occurs, the before-fact of A corresponding to G is a before-fact of every immediate predecessor of A.*

Intuitively, theorem 3 is used to make a operator precondition nonexpandable by way of deferral. If a precondition G meets the conditions of the theorem, it means that the expansion of any of the sibling preconditions of G are guaranteed to introduce a precondition identical to G. Thus, G can be expanded later. Our next result presents an alternative means of determining nonexpandability.

Theorem 4 *It is admissible not to expand a deleted precondition G of an operator A if A is guarded by G and, for every minimal plan graph in which A appears, the facts added by A are contained in the before-facts of every immediate predecessor of A.*

Moreover, this criterion and that of theorem 3 are simultaneously admissible.

The proof of theorem 4 is based on showing the expansion of the precondition is unnecessary because either some other goal can be expanded to introduce the same action, or any possible expansion will produce a non-minimal plan graph.

The following examples show how these theorems may be used. Our first example is a formalization of the car keys problem. We have the following operator descriptions.

OPEN-CAR-DOOR
Preconditions: DOOR-CLOSED, HAVE-KEYS
Delete condition: DOOR-CLOSED
Add condition: DOOR-OPEN
GET-KEYS-FROM-CAR
Preconditions: KEYS-IN-CAR, DOOR-OPEN
Delete condition: KEYS-IN-CAR
Add condition: HAVE-KEYS

In this example, consistency analysis shows that neither operator can have any immediate predecessor, i.e., all operator sequences of length 2 are impossible. Thus, every precondition can admissibly be made nonexpandable. This gives us the loop control we need.

Our next example is the robot problem. Consider the AT(?X) precondition of GO. The only immediate predecessor of GO is RECHARGE, which has AT(B) as a precondition. We noted earlier that when GO is immediately preceded by RECHARGE the ?X in GO must be bound to B. Thus, the precondition is also a precondition of every possible immediate predecessor. We conclude by theorem 3 that AT(?X) is admissibly nonexpandable for this domain.

Also, consider the UNCHARGED precondition of RECHARGE. The only immediate predecessor is FIX. Thus, UNCHARGED guards RECHARGED. Note that the only fact added by RECHARGE is CHARGED. This is among the preconditions of FIX. Moreover, UNCHARGED is deleted by RECHARGE. Thus, by theorem 4, it is a nonexpandable precondition.

We would like to make the AT(B) precondition of RECHARGE nonexpandable. However, as things stand the method does not apply, since the immediate predecessor, FIX, does not have AT(?X) as a precondition. Indeed, we noted earlier that with this operator representation, AT(B) needs to be expanded to solve the robot problem.

Observe, however, that if we include AT(?X) as an additional precondition in the FIX operator, then the criterion of the theorem is satisfied, and AT(B) can be made a nonexpandable precondition of RECHARGE. Moreover, it is admissible to augment the FIX operator in this way, since every state must satisfy some instance of AT(?X). The reason why the robot problem is now solvable is that the AT(?X) precondition of FIX can be expanded instead. Note that we have shifted the goal ancestor path for the expansion of AT(?X) so that it now leads to the NO-HOLE top-level goal. Intuitively, the problem with the original representation was that the expansions were not correctly motivated. Figure 3 shows the reformulated plan graph for this problem.

This technique of modifying the operators can be made systematic. In general, we may need to replace the immediate predecessor operator with several operators that are augmented with the different members of some exclusive-or set that includes the precondition under consideration. (If no better exclusive-or set is available, the fact and its negation can be used.) Note that consistency requirements ensure that of the replacement operators, only the one corresponding to the precondition is an immediate predecessor.

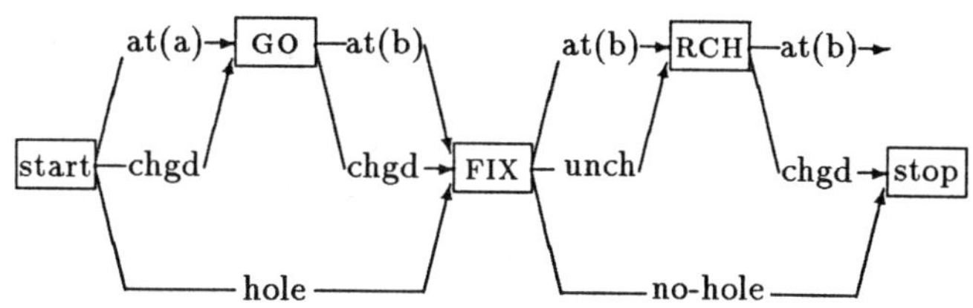

Figure 3: Reformulated Plan Graph

It is easy to see that the modification procedure can be applied to make any precondition nonexpandable provided that no immediate predecessor has the precondition as an add condition.

Observe that all the preconditions of RECHARGE are now nonexpandable. It can be verified that every potential loop in the robot problem passes through the RECHARGE operator. Thus, no loops remain.

It is important to note that the methods provide only sufficient conditions for admissible nonexpandability, and it is not true in general that they will prevent all loops. We can think of theorem 3 as eliminating goal repetitions where a goal is an immediate subgoal of itself. Theorem 4 applies to goals that repeat after two steps. Slightly larger repetition intervals can be handled by combining operators as necessary to reduce the repetition distance. However, in the blocks world, for example, there can be repetitions with an indefinite number of intervening goals, and neither theorem applies in this case. Nevertheless, the results here appear to cover many of the intuitive examples of hold conditions.

Closing Remarks

One of the features which distinguishes modern work in AI from that of earlier periods is an increasing concern for rigorous analysis and deeper understanding of the techniques studied. Previous loop control methods in planning may be classified as engineering art. Indeed, loop control is an important, but neglected issue in generative planning. We have presented provably correct methods that are effective in common situations. An important observation that follows from the results in this paper is that operator descriptions may need to be reformulated in order to facilitate control. The methods of the paper can be used to identify useful reformulations.

A system that identifies nonexpandable preconditions based on the theorems in the paper has been successfully implemented. Our present implementation uses a full theorem prover (the Boyer-Moore theorem prover [Boyer & Moore 1979]) to reason about inconsistency, which limits its applicability. However, in practice, less costly reasoning about exclusive-or relationships should be sufficient. Note also that the reasoning is performed during a precompilation of the operators in a domain, so the cost is amortized over all problem-solving in that domain.

Nonexpandability is only part of the content of the hold condition idea of Tate; the other part is a determination that linking need not be delayed until side effects of other operators are available. This property is called *effective isolation* in [Morris 1984]. The predecessor graph may also be useful for determinations of effective isolation, and current work is exploring this.

Acknowledgment We thank Bob Filman for suggestions to improve the presentation.

Appendix: Proofs

Theorem 1: For every conflict-free plan graph, there is a collision-free plan graph with the same actions that solves the same problem.

Proof: Suppose an action has two outgoing edges labeled with the same fact F. If the two edges are received by a single action, then one edge is redundant and can be removed. Otherwise, the edges must be received by different actions. At least one of these, say A, is not preceded by the other, B. If the plan is conflict-free, then the receiving action A cannot delete the fact F, since it is parallel to the edge that goes to B. Thus, F must also occur as an after-fact of A. Now the original F-labeled edge to B can be replaced by an edge from A to B. If there is already an outgoing edge from A labeled with F, then the above process can be repeated. Note that each repetition moves the collision closer to the STOP node. Ultimately, either it disappears, or a redundancy occurs among the incoming edges to the STOP node and can be removed.

Theorem 2: For every cut, there is a reachable state of the domain that contains each fact in the labeling of the cut. Moreover, no two edges in the cut are labeled with the same fact.

Proof: We say a node precedes a cut if it precedes some edge in the cut. The theorem will be proved by induction on the number of nodes that precede a cut.

Note that the outgoing edges from the START node constitute a cut that is preceded only by the START node itself. We call this the *initial cut*. Clearly, the result holds for the initial cut.

Now consider some other cut. Let A be a node preceding the cut that is maximally close to the cut, i.e., A does not precede any other node that precedes the cut. Let e be any outgoing edge of A. We show e must belong to the cut. Suppose otherwise. Then e cannot precede any edge in the cut; otherwise there would be another node between A and the cut. Also, e cannot be preceded by any edge in the cut. If it did, then A could not precede the cut. Thus, e is parallel to every edge in the cut. But this contradicts the definition of a cut, which requires it to be a maximal parallel set of edges.

We have shown that every outgoing edge of A belongs to the cut. Let us call this cut C. Now consider the set of edges obtained from C by replacing the outgoing edges of A with its incoming edges. It is not hard to verify that this is also a cut, which we will call C'. By the inductive hypothesis, the labels of edges in C' are free of duplicates, and are contained in some reachable state. The preconditions of A are satisfied in that state. Thus, the state resulting from applying A is also reachable. This state contains the facts corresponding to edges in C. This proves the first part of the result.

Note that the only way that applying A could produce a duplicate edge (we are assuming no collisions among the outgoing edges of A) would be if one of its outgoing edges had the same label as an edge common to the two cuts. But then A would be applicable in a situation where one of its add conditions is already true, contrary to our restriction on operators. This shows the second part of the result.

Corollary 2.1: Edges that are parallel cannot have the same label or contradictory labels. A node cannot be parallel to an edge whose label coincides with or conflicts with one of its before-facts or after-facts.

Proof: If two edges are parallel, then there is some cut that contains them both. By the theorem, the cut has no duplicate labels. Furthermore, the labels are contained in some reachable state, so they cannot be contradictory.

Now suppose a node A is parallel to an edge e. It is easy to see that the incoming and outgoing edges of A must also be parallel to e. Thus, the only case we need to consider is that of an unused after-fact. Note that the plan graph can be modified to include the after-fact as a top level goal without changing any of the labels. Then, the previous reasoning can be applied to the after-fact. The result follows.

Lemma 1 *Suppose A is guarded by a precondition G. Consider some minimal plan graph in which A occurs. Let e be the incoming edge to A that corresponds to G, and let B be the node of which e is an outgoing edge. Then B is an immediate predecessor of A, and is the only immediate predecessor of A in the plan graph.*

Proof: Clearly, B is a predecessor of A. Suppose there is some other node C that is an immediate predecessor of A. Then C has either an after-fact or a before-fact that matches the label of e. Clearly, e is parallel to C, leading to a violation of corollary 2.1. Thus, there cannot be any other immediate predecessor. It follows that B must be the immediate predecessor of A.

Theorem 3: It is admissible not to expand a precondition G of an operator A if, for every minimal plan graph in which A occurs, the before-fact of A corresponding to G is a before-fact of every immediate predecessor of A.

Proof: Consider a minimal plan graph in which A occurs. There must be some incoming edge e of A that corresponds to G. Suppose the edge e comes from another node B. By the statement of the theorem, A is guarded by G. Hence, by lemma 1, B must be an immediate predecessor of A.

By hypothesis, B has a before-fact that coincides with the label of e, and so e does not correspond to an add condition of B. It follows that during planning, B could not have been introduced into the plan as an expansion of G, i.e., it must have resulted from the expansion of some other goal (or be the START node). Thus, it is safe to make G nonexpandable.

Theorem 4: It is admissible not to expand a deleted precondition G of an operator A if A is guarded by G and, for every minimal plan graph in which A appears, the facts added by A are contained in the before-facts of every immediate predecessor of A.

Moreover, this criterion and that of theorem 3 are simultaneously admissible.

Proof: In the following, We use the term *add-fact* to describe an after-fact that corresponds to an add condition. Similarly, *delete-fact* is a before-fact that corresponds to a delete condition.

Consider any minimal plan graph in which a node B occurs. Let $\mathcal{E}$ be the set of outgoing edges of B that correspond to add-facts of B, and let $\mathcal{A}$ be the set of nodes that receive the edges in $\mathcal{E}$.

Each edge e in $\mathcal{E}$ corresponds to a precondition G of some node A in $\mathcal{A}$. We claim that at least one such G is not made nonexpandable by the criterion of the theorem. Assume otherwise. We will show that this leads to a contradiction. We note here that the assumption implies that every edge from an add-fact of B leads to a delete-fact of the connected node.

We proceed by showing all the outgoing edges of the nodes in the set $\mathcal{A} \cup \{B\}$ (other than internal edges) can be replaced by equivalent incoming edges. This will allow all the nodes in the set to be excised, contradicting the minimality of the plan graph.

By lemma 1, B is an immediate predecessor of each node in $\mathcal{A}$. It follows that the edges being considered for replacement are all parallel to each other. By corollary 2.1, their labels are all different. Thus, there is no danger of two outgoing edges competing for a replacement among the incoming edges, so it is sufficient to show that the edges can be replaced individually.

There are three cases to be considered: outgoing edges of (nodes in) $\mathcal{A}$ that correspond to add-facts; other outgoing edges of $\mathcal{A}$; and outgoing edges of B that do not go to $\mathcal{A}$.

If e corresponds to an add-fact of some A in $\mathcal{A}$, then by the condition of the theorem, it can be replaced by an equivalent incoming edge e' to B.

If e is an outgoing edge of some A, but does not correspond to an add-fact, then there must be an incoming edge e' of A that has the same label. If e' is not an internal edge, then e can simply be replaced by e'. Otherwise, e' is an outgoing edge of B. Since its label is not a delete-fact of A, it is not an add-fact of B (by the assumption; see above). Thus, there must be an incoming edge e'' of B with the same label as e'. In this case e can be replaced by e''.

If e is an outgoing edge of B that does not go to some A, then it is not in $\mathcal{E}$. It follows that it is not an add-fact of B. Thus, there is some incoming edge e' of B with the same label, and we can replace e with e'.

This proves our claim. Thus, at least one edge in $\mathcal{E}$ must correspond to a precondition G that does not satisfy the criterion of the theorem. When the plan has been constructed up to the after-facts of B, this G can be expanded to introduce B into the plan.

Note that the G exhibited here corresponds to an add-fact of B; thus, B does not have an equivalent before-fact. It follows that G is not made nonexpandable by the criterion of theorem 3.

References

Boyer, R. S., and Moore, J.S. *A Computational Logic.* Academic Press, 1979.

Chapman, D. Planning for conjunctive goals. *Artificial Intelligence*, 32:333–378, July 1987.

Drummond, D., and Currie, K. Goal ordering in partially ordered plans. In *Proc. IJCAI-89*, pages 960–965, Detroit, Michigan, 1989.

Irani, Keki B., and Cheng J. Subgoal ordering and goal augmentation for heuristic problem solving. In *Proc. IJCAI-87*, pages 1018–1024, Milan, Italy, 1987.

Morris P., and Feldman, R. Automatically derived heuristics for planning search. In *Second Irish Conference on Artificial Intelligence and Cognitive Science*, Dublin, Ireland, 1989. Proceedings to appear in Springer-Verlag Brit. Comp. Soc. Workshop Series.

Morris, P. H. *A Resource Oriented Formalism for Plan Generation.* PhD thesis, University of California, Irvine, 1984.

Nilsson, N. J. *Principles of Artificial Intelligence.* Tioga Publishing Company, Palo Alto, Ca., 1980.

Rich, E. *Artificial Intelligence* McGraw-Hill, 1983.

Sacerdoti, E. D. *A Structure for Plans and Behavior.* Elsevier North-Holland, 1977.

Smith, D. E.; Genesereth, M. R.; and Ginsberg, M.L. Controlling recursive inference. *Artificial Intelligence*, 30(3):343–389, 1986.

Tate, A. *Project Planning Using A Hierarchic Non-Linear Planner.* Research Report 25, Dept. of Artificial Intelligence, Univ. of Edinburgh, Aug. 1976.

Tate, A. Generating project networks. In *Proc. IJCAI-77*, pages 888–893, Cambridge, Ma., 1977.

Vere S.A. Relational production systems. *Artificial Intelligence*, 8:47–68, 1977.

Practical Temporal Projection

Steve Hanks*
Department of Computer Science and Engineering, FR-35
University of Washington
hanks@cs.washington.edu

Abstract

Temporal projection—predicting future states of a changing world—has been studied mainly as a formal problem. Researchers have been concerned with getting the concepts of causality and change right, and have ignored the practical issues surrounding projection. In planning, for example, when the effects of a plan's actions depend on the prevailing state of the world and that state of the world is not known with certainty, projecting the plan may generate an exponential number of possible outcomes. This problem has traditionally been eliminated by (1) restricting the domain so the world state is always known, and (2) by restricting the action representation so that either the action's *intended effect* is realized or the action cannot be projected at all. We argue against these restrictions and instead present a system that (1) represents and reasons about an uncertain world, (2) supports a representation that allows context-sensitive action effects, and (3) generates projections that reflect only the *significant* or *relevant* outcomes of the plans, where relevance is determined by the planner's queries about the resulting world state.

Introduction

Temporal projection consists of taking (1) a model of some world, and (2) the description of a particular series of events that happen in the world, and trying to predict the world's state after the events occur. In the planning community the events generally comprise a plan to be executed and the world model is a set of rules describing the effects of the actions that make up the plan.[1]

Temporal projection has been studied extensively in the literature on planning and acting,[2] but mainly as a formal problem: one starts with a logic that purports to capture notions involving time, action, change and causality, and argues that the inferences the logic licenses are the intuitively correct ones.

This paper takes a somewhat different view, arguing that temporal projection is an interesting *practical* problem. We argue that computing the possible outcomes of a plan, even if formally well understood, is computationally intractable, and thus one must restrict one's attention to the "important" or "significant" outcomes. This is especially true in domains for which the agent lacks perfect knowledge, and in which forces not under the agent's control can change the world—in other words, any interesting domain.[3]

We present an implemented framework for plan projection, which is actually part of a system that maintains the agent's *world model*—a network of beliefs that are both dynamic and tentative. This paper will focus on how commitments to act (potential plans) change the model; the planning process, conversely, is concerned with how the model guides the agent's choice of action.

We first discuss briefly a subsystem that performs probabilistic temporal reasoning—computing the likelihood that a proposition will be true at some point in time. We next motivate and present a representation for action and demonstrate the exact nature of the projection problem, then proceed to sketch our algorithm. We end by discussing the system's performance.

Probabilistic Temporal Reasoning

Central to the problem of predicting a plan's outcomes is determining the truth of various propositions (*e.g.* an action's preconditions) at some point in time (*e.g.* the time at which the action is to be executed). Since the

*This paper describes part of the author's thesis work at Yale University, advised by Drew McDermott and supported in part by DARPA grant DAAA15-87-K-0001. Thanks to Dan Weld and Tony Barrett for comments on this paper.

[1] Projection is a central problem in the area of qualitative physics as well. We will be concentrating on the area of planning and acting, but believe the problems we raise, and perhaps the solutions as well, are equally valid applied to QP situations. See, for example, [Kuipers and Chiu 1987]

[2] There are simply too many references to cite here, given the space limitations. An interested but uninformed reader might start with the relevant papers in [Ginsberg 1987] and work forward from there.

[3] See [Chapman 1987] for some discouraging results, even for artificially restricted domains.

agent will typically lack perfect information about the world (past, present, or future) we need some mechanism to express its uncertainty regarding the states of these propositions. We are using probabilities to represent this uncertainty, thus are concerned with computing the quantity P("φ true at time t"), where φ is some proposition and t is a time point. We will abbreviate this notation to $P(\varphi_t)$.

Three sorts of evidence get used in the computation: (1) reports from the sensors about φ's state, (2) symbolic causal rules of the form "if event E occurs while some fact P is true, then φ will become true at the next instant in time," and (3) background information (prior probabilities) about φ, E, P, and so on.

Uncertainty can come from a number of sources: (1) one can doubt whether the sensor reported correctly on φ's state, (2) one can be unsure as to whether a relevant event E actually occurred at some point in time, and (3) one can lack confidence in the causal rules: perhaps the rules mentioning φ aren't *really* necessary and sufficient predictors of φ's state changes. Our representation for propositions, rules, and the like takes into account all of these factors.

Important computational problems arise in implementing this approach: a tremendous amount of evidence must be brought to bear in computing the probability. Sensory observations of φ might extend arbitrarily far back into the past, as do the relevant causal rules (since they are implicitly quantified over all time points). Most of this evidence, however, will not affect φ's probability significantly.

Although computing φ's exact probability requires considering a potentially infinite amount of information, we might expect that under the right circumstances—sensors that are reasonably reliable and changes that occur reasonably infrequently—we can compute a good approximation of the probability using only a few pieces of evidence. The question is how good need a "good" approximation be?

The application program (planner) provides this information in the form of a *probability threshold* τ, indicating that it doesn't care what φ's probability is, but only to what side of τ the probability falls. A "good" approximation is therefore one that reports correctly with respect to the threshold. [Hanks 1988] presents a heuristic algorithm for limiting the search for evidence, the limit depending on how close the current estimate is to the threshold. The program also computes probabilities for joint events (logical conjunction), and monitors the database for new information that might invalidate the current approximation. Details of this subsystem appear in [Hanks 1988] and [Hanks 1990]. The projector invokes the probability-calculation subsystem by posing a *probabilistic query*—a question of the form "$P(\varphi_t) > \tau$?" The answer is returned in a data structure, called a *belief*, which is an assertion about which side of the threshold the probability lies (given current evidence).

Action representation

The typical action representation in the literature on action and planning (*e.g.* [Fikes and Nilsson 1971], [Lifschitz 1987], [Ginsberg and Smith 1988]) describes an action as a mapping from *preconditions* into *effects*. A good example is the "start the car" scenario, usually used to motivate the qualification problem: if there is fuel in the tank, the starter is working, ..., and there is no potato obstructing the tailpipe, then turning the key causes the engine to start.[4] A planner or projector faced with the hypothetical execution of such an action would first try to infer the action's preconditions; if they turn out to be true the effects would be noted in the resulting world state; if false, the action is said to be infeasible, and the planner could not reason about subsequent execution of the plan.

What's troublesome here is the planner's inability to reason about the action in cases where the precondition is false: in no sense is the action of turning the key of a car with, say, an obstructed tailpipe *impossible* or *meaningless*, yet that is what is implied by these systems' failure to project further.

In fact the action will have predictable effects even if the tailpipe is obstructed: it will take some time, wear down the battery, make some noise, perhaps generate a spark. It turns out that one particular effect, the engine running, will not be realized, and it may be the case that in some situations that's the only effect the planner is interested in, but it does not mean that executing the action is meaningless. What these systems have done is confused the notion of an action being *meaningful* or *conceivable* with the notion of an action's achieving its intended effect.[5] The former is rightfully a property of the action's definition, but the latter depends on the situation at hand. Actions will typically have a variety of effects depending on the circumstances, and it may be impossible to predict ahead of time which of those effects will turn out to be important.

If our representation for actions and plans is to support clever detection of planning bugs (*e.g.* trying to start the engine too many times thus running down the battery, or generating a spark in a gas-filled room) or innovative planning or plan recognition (running the car to warm the garage or to light the headlights without taxing the battery) we must associate intention or relevance with the *situation* rather than with the action's *definition*.

Consider as an alternative the code in Figure 1.[6] It is intended to represent the action "drive the truck

[4]The point is that there are myriad preconditions to any action—too many to verify explicitly.

[5]Pednault's ADL [1988a] is an exception, since it explicitly allows for context-dependent effects. In [Pednault 1988b] he notes various computational problems associated with using the representation for planning or projection.

[6]This is a simplified version of an action based on the robot-truck world of [Firby and Hanks 1987].

```
(action (travel R L1 L2)
  (if (not (loc TRUCK L1))
(A)     (outcomes INFEASIBLE)
        (if (< FUEL-LEVEL 10)
(B)         (outcomes (loc TRUCK ON-ROAD)
                      (status TRUCK OUT-OF-GAS)
                      (consume FUEL 10)
                      (duration 0 60))
            (if (not (muddy R))
(C)             (outcomes (loc TRUCK L2)
                          (consume FUEL 10 15)
                          (duration 45 60))
                (if (chance 0.25)
(D)                 (outcomes (loc TRUCK ON-ROAD)
                              (status TRUCK STUCK)
                              (muddy TRUCK)
                              (consume FUEL 0 30)
                              (duration 0 75))
(E)                 (outcomes (loc TRUCK L2)
                              (muddy TRUCK)
                              (consume FUEL 25 30)
                              (duration 50 75]
```

Figure 1: Traveling on a dirt road

down road R from location L1 to location L2. The code describes a mapping from state descriptions to sets of *outcomes*.[7] Note that actions can still be infeasible, as outcome set (A) indicates, but the idea is that it is truly meaningless to contemplate a trip starting at location L1 if you are not at location L1. Running out of gas or getting stuck in the mud may be inconvenient, may even be impossible (probability 0) under some circumstances, but it is not inconceivable.

The feasible outcome set (D) indicates that as a result of executing the **travel** action the truck is somewhere on the road, stuck in the mud, has used up some quantity of fuel less than 30 gallons, and somewhat less than 70 time units will have passed.

An outcome set's *label*, the conjunction of all the **if** propositions leading to it, describes states of the world in which the outcome set will be realized. Set (D), for example, will be realized if the action is executed when the world satisfies the the following condition:

$$\texttt{(loc TRUCK L1)} \wedge \texttt{(not (< FUEL-LEVEL 10))} \wedge \texttt{(muddy R)} \wedge \texttt{(chance 0.25)}$$

The action's **if-then-else** form ensures that the labels for different outcome sets will be mutually exclusive and that the labels for *all* an action's outcome sets will be exhaustive. Therefore exactly one set's label will be true at any point in time, so no matter when the action is executed exactly one set of outcomes will be realized. Of course we may not know what that state of the world is, even after the action is executed.[8]

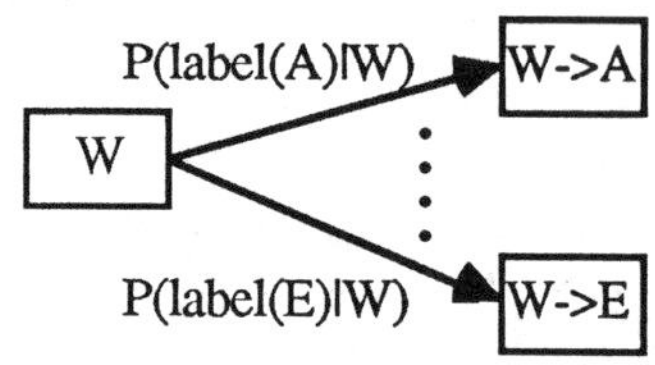

Figure 2: Projecting a single action

An outcome set's label is a formula that can be posed as a probabilistic query (given a time point representing the proposed time of execution). We can therefore compute a probability distribution over the outcome sets relative to a time point, asking, for each outcome set (X), "what is the probability that (X)'s label will be true?"

We can then view the process of projecting a single action as building a tree as pictured in Figure 2. Nodes are states of the worlds, and each arc represents the possibility that a particular outcome set will be realized, given that the world is in a state like that of its parent node. The probability associated with an arc, *e.g.* P(**label(A)**|W) is the probability that outcome set A's label will be true, and thus its outcomes will be realized, given that the world is in state W at execution time. W→A is then the state of the world resulting from the action's outcome set A being realized in world W.[9]

Scenarios and Projection

To project a sequence of actions $A_1, A_2, \ldots,$ we just iterate the process of single-action projection: we project action A_{i+1}, in *each* of the world states resulting from the execution of A_i. Projecting a plan therefore results in a directed tree which branches forward in time. We call this tree a *scenario* structure, and each path through the tree a *chronicle*. Each chronicle has an associated probability, and the probabilities of all chronicles in a scenario must sum to 1.

Figure 4(a) shows the structure generated by projecting the sequence **(load O1); (load O2); (travel BR L3 L4)** whose action descriptions appear in Figure 3. The **load** actions—load an object into the cargo bay—have a 0.1 chance of failing, but take 1 time unit in either case; BR is a bridge that will collapse if the truck is carrying two or more items when it crosses.

The projection problem manifests itself in the proliferation of chronicles: a plan with n actions each containing an average of m outcome sets will gener-

[7] Outcomes are essentially the same as the "effects" above, but extended to allow reasoning about sets, continuous quantities, passing time, and so on.

[8] We account for an action's having indeterminate effects by introducing the chance predicate, *e.g.* Figure 1 outcome set (D), whose real truth value is never known, but whose probability can easily be computed.

[9] The projector can also account for the possibility that other relevant events occur while the action is executing, but that process is beyond the scope of this paper.

```
(action (load ?x)
  (if (not (reachable ?x))
(F)     (outcomes INFEASIBLE)
        (if (chance 0.9)
(G)         (outcomes (holding ?x)
                      (duration 1))
(H)         (outcomes (duration 1)))))

(action (travel BR L3 L4)
  (if (not (loc TRUCK L3)
(I)       (outcomes INFEASIBLE)
        (if (>= (card CARGO) 2)
(J)       (outcomes (loc TRUCK RAVINE)
                    (status TRUCK MANGLED)
                    (duration 0 7))
(K)       (outcomes (loc TRUCK L4)
                    (duration 3 7))))
```

Figure 3: More action code

ate roughly m^n chronicles. Although we can obviously do some pruning of the tree, by eliminating zero-probability and infeasible chronicles for example, an impractical number of feasible and possible chronicles remain.[10]

Figure 4(a) shows an exhaustive projection of the plan above. Every arc in the tree has a single outcome set associated with it, so the tree branches with every possible outcome for every possible action. We can reduce proliferation of the tree by instead associating a *set* of outcome sets with each arc. The intuition is that the distinctions noted by outcome sets *within* each set are irrelevant, while the distinctions between outcomes in *different* sets are significant.

Referring back to the **travel** action in Figure 1, suppose that we care only about whether the truck reaches its destination L2. In that case we don't care about the distinctions implied by outcomes sets **(A) (B)** and **(D)**, nor about the distinctions between **(C)** and **(E)**. So we form two sets and produce two branches in the tree instead of five. We call each of these groupings a *bundle*. Each arc in the scenario tree has an associated bundle, which contains one or more outcome sets.

Bundling outcome sets speeds the process of computing label probabilities as well, in that the label associated with a bundle (the disjunction of its member's labels) may be much simpler than the individual labels. As an extreme case suppose we are only interested in whether Figure 1's action is feasible or not. In that case we put **(A)** in one bundle and the rest of the outcome sets in another. Computing the probability of the second bundle (which has four members) is simply a matter of evaluating **(loc TRUCK L1)**. Note that as long as we assign each outcome set to exactly one

[10]We have been testing the program with examples in which $n = 10$ and $m = 6$, which gives rise to some 6×10^7 chronicles in the worst case. Pruning infeasible and impossible chronicles gets rid of some $\frac{3}{4}$ of them, but that still leaves more than ten million.

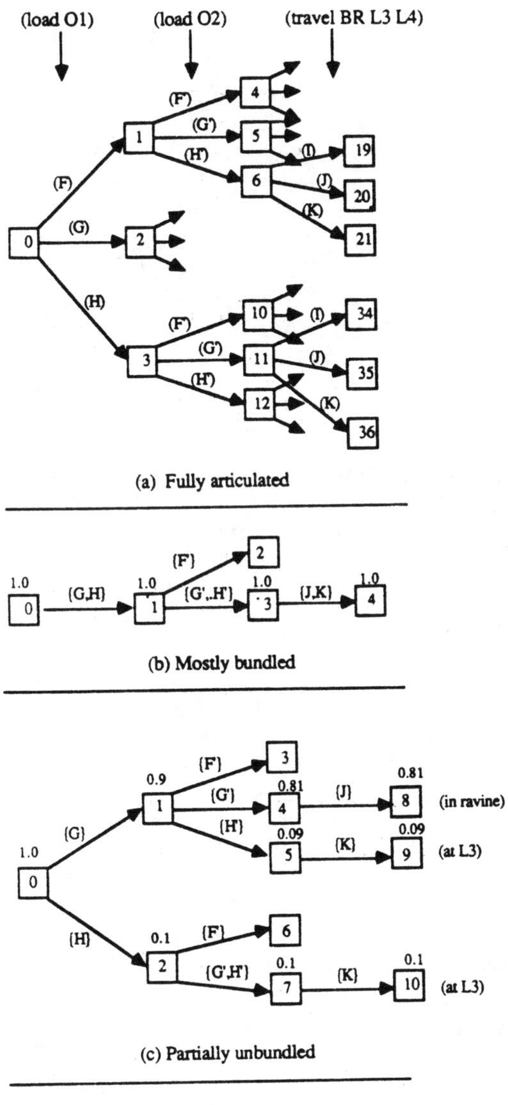

Figure 4: Bundled and unbundled scenario trees

bundle, the bundles still partition the set of possible execution-time situations, and thus their probabilities sum to 1.

The problem with bundling outcome sets is that we can make less precise predictions. When we project an action across a bundle of outcome sets we can infer only the weakest conclusion allowed by all members of that bundle. If we construct the bundle {(C),(E)} from Figure 1, for example, we can conclude that the truck will be at L2, but we can only make vague predictions about the fuel consumption (between 10 and 30 gallons), and the action's duration, and we cannot predict whether or not the truck will be muddy. But then again we may not care.

Practical projection, then, is a process of balancing the need for parsimony in the scenario tree and speed in computing chronicle probabilities against the need to make precise predictions about what the world will be like after the plan is executed. The former argues for keeping much of the tree's structure implicit by forming a few large bundles; the latter argues for representing the tree explicitly. Obviously we want to make explicit the "important" or "significant" or "relevant" distinctions in the tree and leave the rest implicit. But how do we determine which distinctions these are?

The answer is that we can use the probabilistic temporal queries, which may be posed by the planner or generated as the projector computes a chronicle's probabilities: the projector wants to articulate exactly enough of the tree to give the best possible answers to the queries it receives. Of course the nature of these queries will not be known in advance, so the projector must be able to articulate the tree more fully—to "unbundle" outcome sets—on demand.

To see how the process works, consider again the sequence (load O1); (load O2); (travel BR L3 L4). The planner additionally supplies the projector with a time point at which to begin, initial assumptions (the truck is at L3, objects O1 and O2 are reachable, the cargo bay is empty, and the fuel tank is full), and a probability threshold. Chronicles whose probabilities fall below this threshold will be abandoned, at least initially.

The projector proceeds to project each action in sequence, assuming that the only distinction the planner is interested in is between feasible and infeasible outcomes. The initial projection appears in Figure 4(b).[11] The projector returns the (single) chronicle representing a feasible plan completion: the chronicle ending in node 4. At this point we can say little about where the truck is or what it is carrying.

Now suppose the planner poses the query "is the truck at L3?" The projector notes that the current tree yields an ambiguous answer to this question, but that splitting the bundle {(J),(K)} would result in a more precise answer. In the process of splitting that bundle it needs to compute label probabilities for (J) and (K), leading it to ask "(>= (card CARGO) 2)?" So the projector poses that query with respect to node 3. Once again the answer is ambiguous: currently we can predict only that the cargo bay will contain between 0 and 2 items, but two bundles, {(G), (H)} and {(G'), (H')} contribute to the ambiguity, so the projector considers the possibility of splitting them. Details of when and how the projector splits a bundle of outcome sets appear in [Hanks 1990, Chapter 4].

When all the splitting completes, queries get answered, and projection finishes, the tree appears as in Figure 4(c). Now there are three feasible chronicles, each of which answers unambiguously the question "is the truck at L3?"[12] The probability for a query Q is the sum $\sum_c P(Q \mid c)P(c)$ where c varies over all chronicles. The probability for "is the truck at L3" is therefore roughly 0.19. The probability of "is the truck at L3 and carrying both O1 and O2" would be 0, and could be computed without further splitting.

[11] We have pruned away 0-probability outcomes, like one in which O1 instantaneously becomes unreachable, or the truck inexplicably gets moved away from L3. Node 2 represents a situation in which somebody removes object O2 during the time that O1 was being loaded, but it has a small enough probability that it is not projected further.

[12] Node 8, Figure 4(c) says "no," 9 and 10 say "yes."

Maintaining the world model

Our system performs three main functions: answering probabilistic queries, projecting plans, and monitoring the database for information that would change existing beliefs. It is interesting to note how closely interrelated the three processes are: adding plans causes label probabilities to be computed, which gives rise to queries. A query may demand that the scenario tree be split, thus causing more projection, and so on. A query may also cause previously abandoned chronicles, like the ones ending in Nodes 3 and 6, Figure 4(c), to be projected further. New information, like relevant sensor reports, may cause beliefs to change, plan commitments to be rethought, new queries to be posed, and new plans to be projected.

The system can thus be regarded as maintaining the planner's world model, one in which evidence takes the form of plan commitments and sensor reports, and aspects of the model are revealed through the *belief* data structures.

Performance

It is hard to make precise general statements about the projector's performance. The worst case, involving a complete articulation of the tree, is exponential both in the number of actions and in the average number of outcome sets per action. In general the tree proliferates to the extent the planner asks questions about plan outcomes that depend on propositions whose state the projector cannot predict definitively (with probabilities near 0 or 1). So performance depends on the queries, both their types and their thresholds, and on the underlying probabilistic model.

A more interesting question is whether the projector always produces the splits necessary, and *only* the splits necessary, to answer a particular query. If it fails to make a necessary split it will report an overly vague answer to a query; if it makes unnecessary splits it will report the correct answer but do so inefficiently. We address this question in [Hanks 1990], but the short answer is that the projector will never fail to make a relevant split in the tree, but will sometimes make unnecessary splits. The decision whether to split an arc is made locally at that arc, but we cannot always determine locally whether a split is really necessary given other splits that might be made. Superfluous splitting does not seem to be a problem in practice, however.

We have implemented the projector and tested it on fairly complex examples, involving 15 or so plan steps including conditionals, loops, and information-gathering actions. Each projection took about 4 minutes on average, but we have reason to believe that more powerful computing equipment and superficial code optimizations would cut this figure in half. We were surprised to learn that most of the time was spent in the temporal database manager module (which maintains the network of time points and constraints), so improving its efficiency will significantly improve performance as well.

Conclusion

Systems for action and planning have made stringent assumptions about the domains in which they operate and the nature of the actions they manipulate. They typically assume that no events occur apart from those the planner intends, and that an action either achieves its intended effect or cannot be meaningfully executed.

These assumptions together mask an important practical problem: when the effects of one's actions depend on the state of the world at execution time, and when one is uncertain about that world state, one faces an explosion of possible plan outcomes. The hope is that most of these outcomes can be dismissed as uninteresting, improbable, or both.

We have presented a system to manage the process of hypothetical reasoning about actions and plans. The system builds a "scenario tree," tracing the possible outcomes of a plan, but tries to keep as much of the tree's structure implicit as possible, thus avoiding the explosion of possible plan outcomes. It uses the planner's queries as a guide to what aspects of the world, thus what outcomes of the plans, are important and deserve explicit consideration.

References

[Chapman 1987] David Chapman. Planning for conjunctive goals. *Artificial Intelligence*, 32(3):333–378, 1987.

[Fikes and Nilsson 1971] Richard Fikes and Nils J. Nilsson. STRIPS: A new approach to the application of theorem proving to problem solving. *Artificial Intelligence*, 2(3):189–208, 1971.

[Firby and Hanks 1987] R. James Firby and Steven Hanks. The simulator manual. Technical Report 563, Yale University, Department of Computer Science, November 1987.

[Ginsberg and Smith 1988] Matthew L. Ginsberg and David E. Smith. Reasoning about action I: A possible worlds approach. *Artificial Intelligence*, 35(2):165–196, 1988.

[Ginsberg 1987] Matthew L. Ginsberg, editor. *Readings in Nonmonotonic Reasoning.* Morgan-Kaufmann, 1987.

[Hanks 1988] Steven Hanks. Representing and computing temporally scoped beliefs. In *Proceedings AAAI*, pages 501–505, 1988.

[Hanks 1990] Steven Hanks. Projecting plans for uncertain worlds. Technical Report 756, Yale University, Department of Computer Science, January 1990.

[Kuipers and Chiu 1987] Benjamin Kuipers and Charles Chiu. Taming intractible branching in qualitative simulation. In *Proceedings IJCAI*, pages 1079–1085, 1987. Also appears in [Weld and de Kleer 1989].

[Lifschitz 1987] Vladimir Lifschitz. Formal theories of action. In Frank Brown, editor, *The Frame Problem in Artificial Intelligence: Proceedings of the 1987 Workshop.* Morgan-Kaufmann, 1987.

[Pednault 1988a] Edwin P.D. Pednault. Extending conventional planning techniques to handle actions with context-dependent effects. In *Proceedings AAAI*, pages 55–59, 1988.

[Pednault 1988b] Edwin P.D. Pednault. Synthesizing plans that contain actions with context-dependent effects. *Computational Intelligence*, 4(4):356–372, 1988.

[Weld and de Kleer 1989] Daniel S. Weld and Johan de Kleer, editors. *Readings in Qualitative Reasoning about Physical Systems.* Morgan-Kaufmann, 1989.

Synthesis of Reactive Plans for Multi-Path Environments*

F. Kabanza
Université de Liège
Institut Montéfiore B28
4000 Liège Sart-Tilman; Belgium
U519026@BLIULG11.bitnet

Abstract

We describe a planner that works on the description of a multi-path environment and generates a conditional plan. The resulting plan is guaranteed to fulfill its goal whatever path of the description the environment follows during the plan execution.

Introduction

Classical planning systems [Fikes *et al.*, 1971; Cohen and Feigenbaum, 1982; Wilkins, 1984] assume that the planning agent operates in a static environment (world). That is, at every moment of time, the world is in a given state and that state remains unchanged until an action is performed by the agent.

Yet most interesting environments in which an intelligent agent is expected to operate are not static. Most realistic worlds are changing and nondeterministic. The assumption that the world remains static between successive actions of the agent no longer holds. Furthermore, the agent usually has only nondeterministic information on how the world is going to evolve.

Recent work has considered the problem of planning in such environments. Allen and Koomen [Allen and Koomen, 1983] use an interval temporal logic to model the past, the present, and the future knowledge of the agent. The changes of the environment and the nondeterminism of its behavior are conveyed by formulas of the logic. McDermott [McDermott, 1982] uses a branching structure (tree of chronsets) to represent a nondeterministic future. Pednault [Pednault, 1987] uses a STRIP-like representation of actions to model some changing worlds, especially in motion problems for which one can give a prediction of the state of the world after an action. Lansky [Lansky, 1987] uses a point-based logic and an event-based representation of states to express synchronization properties between agents in a multiagent domain. Dean [Dean, 1987] describes a framework for scheduling tasks with imposed deadline constraints. In that approach, the planner can use statistical information to predict the future.

In this paper, we also consider the problem of planning in a multi-path environment. We introduce a planning method that is inspired by recent developments in program synthesis from temporal logic specifications [Abadi *et al.*, 1989; Pnueli and Rosner, 1989a; Pnueli and Rosner, 1989b]. The multi-path environment is viewed as a tree of states, which we call a *world-automaton*. Each path in the tree represents a possible behavior of the environment. We call *environment* knowledge the knowledge represented by the world-automaton. We assume that the planner has no control over this tree and that he cannot predict which path the world is actually going to follow. The *operational* knowledge of the plan is given by a set of actions. The planning problem can now be stated as follows: given an environment characterized by a world-automaton, an operational knowledge, an initial state, and a goal, find a (conditional) plan that is guaranteed to achieve the goal whatever path of the world-automaton the environment actually follows.

To handle this problem, one first needs a formalism for describing the environment knowledge. One could give the set of world states and the transition relation between these states, but such a description would be tedious and hence prone to error in complex environments. Instead, we use propositional branching time temporal logic (CTL [Emerson and Clarke, 1982]). For instance, let us assume that the world-automaton is specified by the CTL formula "$\exists\Box$guard $\wedge$ $\forall\Diamond$dark" stating that it might be the case that there is always a guard present and that it will definitely end up being dark. Consider the goal "**rob**($20 million) from Bank" and an initial state where it is not dark. Then the plan that is generated should work whether a guard is present or not, though it can wait for darkness to appear since this is guaranteed to happen.

The problem of generating the plan is related to that of synthesizing a reactive module as described in [Rosenschein, 1989; Pnueli and Rosner, 1989a; Pnueli and Rosner, 1989b]. A reactive program is one that continuously interacts with its environment dur-

*The following text presents research results of the Belgian National incentive-program for fundamental research in artificial intelligence initiated by the Belgian State - Prime Minister's Office - Science Policy Programming. The scientific responsibility is supported by its author.

ing execution. The environment controls some variables, the program others. The synthesis problem consists in building a program that satisfies a given specification (expressed in temporal logic) for all possible behaviors of the environment (also expressed in temporal logic). This is done by first building a formula expressing the statement : "for any execution of the environment, there is an execution of the program that satisfies the specification". One then uses a decision procedure to generate a model for this formula. One could adapt the algorithms of [Pnueli and Rosner, 1989a; Pnueli and Rosner, 1989b] to the synthesis of plans. Unfortunately these methods are of very high computational complexity (double exponential), which makes them of limited use in practice.

The approach we follow proceeds in three steps. First, we generate a description of the world-automaton from the CTL formula describing the environment. This can be done with the algorithms described in [Emerson and Clarke, 1982; Emerson and Halpern, 1985; Manna and Wolper, 1984] and summarized in [Wolper, 1989]. Then, from this world-automaton, the operational knowledge, and the goal, we build a graph representing a synchronization of the executions of the agent and of the environment. A node of this graph represents an action that has to be executed by the agent. A transition between two nodes is labeled by an event of the world-automaton, that is, of the environment. Finally, we extract the desired plan from this graph. This approach allows us to exploit classical heuristic methods (as in SIPE [Wilkins, 1984]) to only explore a fragment of the search space of possible action sequences.

In the next section, we start with a formal description of world-automata and plans. We then discuss the specification language and the algorithm that automatically generates the world-automaton from a CTL specification. The following section describes the planner. The last section is devoted to other features of the planner and to possible extensions.

Describing Environment Knowledge and Plans

Actions, Events, Goals, and Strategies

Actions are described, as in classical systems such as STRIPS or SIPE [Fikes *et al.*, 1971; Wilkins, 1984], essentially by their precondition and their effect. However, we also allow an exclusive disjunction as the effect of an action to represent an effect that depends on the state in which the action is applied. We will call actions with disjunctive effects *disjunctive actions*. The action $NULL$ means "do nothing".

Goals are also described, as in classical systems, by a set of propositions. But in addition, we allow *conditional goals* of the form $p \rightarrow a$, where p is a proposition and a is an action. Such a goal means "do a every time p is true".

A *strategy* is a set of linearly ordered goals. The order must be safe, that is, if a goal g_1 precedes a goal g_2, then all actions leading to g_1 have to be performed before any action for g_2 during execution. Therefore a goal is a special strategy. Strategies are more or less similar to Chapman's "cognitive cliches" [Chapman and Agre, 1987].

Environment Knowledge and Plans

A world-automaton is a tuple $W = (Q, E, \gamma, next, q)$, where

$Q = \{q_1, \ldots q_n\}$ is a set of states;

$E = \{NOTH, e_1, \ldots e_m\}$ is a set of events (the event $NOTH$ is a special event indicating that nothing (interesting) happens in the environment);

$\gamma : Q \rightarrow E$ is a function mapping states to events;

$next : Q \rightarrow 2^Q$ is the transition relation between states;

$q \in Q$ is the initial state.

The fact that there is only one initial state is not restrictive. If an automaton has many initial states we can make them the successors of an initial state with event $NOTH$. An execution of a world-automaton is defined as in classical automata theory. We start in the initial state q. The first event to appear is $\gamma(q)$. Being in state q_i means that the event $\gamma(q_i)$ is the last one to have occurred.

The *environment knowledge* is described by a world-automaton. The possible executions of this automaton constitute an infinite tree. Each path of this tree describes a possible behavior of the environment. Henceforth, we will use the terms "execution", "behavior", and "path" of the environment interchangeably.

The *plans* we generate are also represented by world-automata. An automaton representing a plan contains both the actions (events) of the environment and those of the planning agent. To execute a plan, an agent performs the actions in the plan that are his own and waits for the environment to perform all other actions.

Events can be generic, that is, have many possible instances. But, at any moment, only one instance of an event may happen. For example, the event $on(a, x)$ has $on(a, table)$ and $on(a, b)$ among its instances. In the world-automaton, a transition happens when any instance of the corresponding event happens.

Example 1 Suppose we have to build a reactive plan for robot *Agent2* stacking on table $T2$ parts produced on a separate table $T1$ by another robot *Agent1*. Agent1 produces parts by groups of four: blocks a, b, c and d. It stacks each block on a separate rack appropriate for its type. When a rack is occupied, the agent waits until it becomes clear. The block b is always produced just after the block a, and d is always produced just after c. In figures and in formulas, we abbreviate "rack i" by r_i.

The environment knowledge for Agent2 is thus the production activity of Agent1. It is described by the world-automaton of Figure 1. A part of the plan that our method generates for Agent2 is given in Figure 2. In this figure, all actions that have to be performed by Agent2 are prefixed by *ad*.

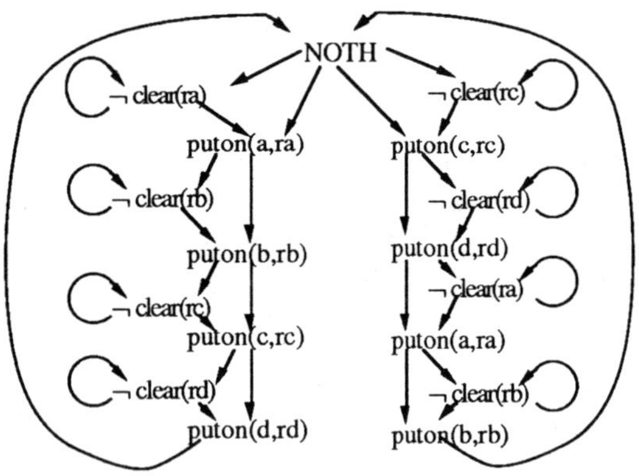

Figure 1: Environment for Agent2

∎

Specifying the World-Automaton

We use propositional branching time temporal logic (CTL) to describe the environment. This logic is formally defined in [Emerson and Clarke, 1982; Wolper, 1989]. We only introduce it informally here.

CTL formulas are built from atomic propositions, boolean connectives, and eight temporal operators. A temporal operator is a path quantifier directly followed by a modality operator. The path quantifiers are $\forall$ meaning "for all execution paths", and $\exists$ meaning "there is an execution path". The modality operators are $\Diamond$ ("eventually"), $\Box$ ("always"), $\bigcirc$ ("next") and U "until". They are all unary, except U which is binary. Proposional formulas (i.e. without temporal operator) are the basic CTL formulas. Any formula built by prefixing a CTL formula with a temporal operator is also a CTL formula. Examples of CTL formulas are : $\exists\Diamond accepted \wedge \forall(\neg presented\, U\, accepted)$.

Formulas are interpreted over infinite trees of propositions. They can be naturally interpreted over world-automata.

- A formula is satisfied by an interpretation if it is satisfied by the initial state of the interpretation.
- A proposition is satisfied by a state if it is true (in the classical sense) of the event of that state.
- $\exists \bigcirc f$ means *"possibly next f"*. Its dual $\forall \bigcirc f$ means *"surely next f"*.
- $\exists\Diamond f$ means *"possibly f will happen"*. Its dual $\forall\Diamond f$ means *"surely eventually f"*.
- $\exists\Box f$ means *"possibly it is the case that always f"*, whereas $\forall\Box f$ means *"surely always f"*.
- $\exists(fUg)$ means *"possibly it is the case that f holds until g"*, and $\forall(fUg)$ means *"surely f holds until g"*

For instance, the world-automaton of Figure 2 satisfies the formula $\exists\Diamond puton(d, rd)$.

Generating the World-Automaton

We use the algorithm of [Emerson and Clarke, 1982] to generate the world-automaton from a CTL specification. The worst case complexity of the algorithm is exponential in the size of the formula. However, with an implementation that uses all possible optimizations, it often gives good results.

Example 2 The following formulas are the bulk of the specification from which the world-automaton for *Agent2* (Figure 1) has been generated.

1. A block is produced if its rack is empty
   $\forall\Box(puton(a, r_a) \supset clear(r_a))$
   (Similar axioms for b, c and d.)
2. Every time r_a is empty, a will eventually be produced
   $\forall\Box(clear(r_a) \supset \forall\Diamond puton(a, r_a))$
   (A similar axiom is given for r_c.)
3. The order of block production: when a is produced, the following block must be b
   $\forall\Box(puton(a, r_a) \supset$
   $\quad \forall(\neg(puton(a, r_a) \vee puton(c, r_c) \vee puton(d, r_d))$
   $\quad\quad U\, puton(b, r_b)))$
   (Similarly for c and d.)
4. At each cycle we do not know the first block to be produced
   $\exists\Diamond puton(a, r_a) \wedge \exists\Diamond puton(c, r_c)$

∎

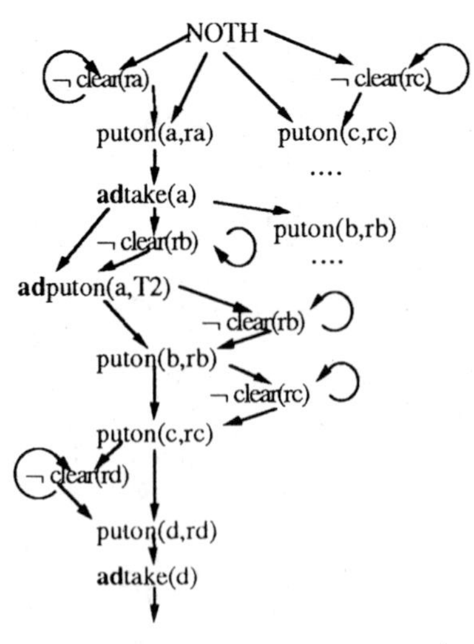

Figure 2: Plan for Agent2

The Planner

The General Idea

We start with the following data: a world-automaton, an operational knowledge, and a strategy (set of goals). From this, we first build an intermediate structure. This structure is a directed graph whose nodes are labeled with actions of the operational knowledge and whose transitions are labeled with events of the world-automaton. This graph represents a synchronization of the agent trying to complete the goals with the environment: at a node of the graph, the agent executes the associated action; it then waits for an event labeling a transition from that node. When the event happens, the agent goes to the node indicated by the transition labeled by the event, executes the action corresponding to that node, and waits again. Actions of the graph are chosen by the planner so that they lead to the goals.

It then remains to extract a plan from the constructed graph. As mentioned in the knowledge description section, the plan has the form of a world-automaton. Hence, it can be used as input for another planning agent.

Building the graph is thus the core of the algorithm. We associate the following additional information to each node of the graph: a state of the world-automaton, a goal to be completed within the node, and a stack of strategies to be performed by descendants of the node (the part of the initial strategy that still has to be completed). Recall that the strategy is the goal of the agent.

We build the graph starting from a state in which the associated node of the world-automaton is the initial state of that automaton, the strategy is the overall goal, and the action is $NULL$. The graph is then built incrementally as follows.

- A graph node with no successor and with a nonempty strategy is chosen.
- An action whose precondition is satisfied and that reduces the distance from the goal is chosen (nondeterministically).
- Successor nodes are constructed for each possible action: the action chosen for the agent and all possible environment actions.

Of course, backtracking is used to implement the nondeterministic choices. Also, goal-reduction is used: when the precondition of the chosen action cannot be satisfied, we attempt to apply goal reduction to the action. If this is impossible, we look ahead in the world-automaton to see if more promising states are coming up and we wait for them; if this is not the case, we backtrack.

The Algorithm

In this paper, we sketch the planning algorithm with the following restrictions: there are no conditional goals, no generic events, and the operational knowledge does not contain disjunctive actions.

The planning algorithm operates in one of two modes: wait and reduce. In the wait mode, it is searching the world-automaton for an event to happen. In the reduce mode, it is trying to find an action that fulfills a goal. We use the following convention for variables: s and s' for nodes of the graph, e for events of the world-automaton. S is the set of nodes of the graph and E is the set of events of the environment. The data-structures used by the planning algorithm are:

- The world-automaton $(Q, E, \gamma, next, q_0)$;
- The intermediate structure (graph) in which:

  S is a set of nodes of the graph,
  $succ : (S \times E) \rightarrow S$ is the graph transition function.
  The information associated with each node s consists of: an action $action(s)$, a world-automaton state $was(s)$, a goal $G(s)$, and a strategy $stack(s)$;
- The variable $Mode$ that takes values W (wait) and R (reduce);
- The event waited upon when in mode W is *waited-event*.

A sketch of construction of the intermediate graph is given in Figure 3.

The *goal-reduction* is any of the heuristics available in AI [Wilkins, 1984], used to decompose a goal into primitive subgoals. Any of these heuristics can be applied since we have the same problem: find a sequence of actions to complete a goal $G(s)$ from an initial state q_0, given a set of actions (the operational knowledge).

Nodes can be fused when they are defined by the same elements (action, stack,...). Hence loops might be introduced. The planning algorithm has to check that the loops that are introduced are safe. This is done with techniques similar to those used to check that *eventuality formulas* are satisfied when building models of temporal logic formulas [Emerson and Clarke, 1982; Manna and Wolper, 1984].

The plan is extracted from the intermediate structure as follows. First build a new structure from the intermediate structure, by introducing between two successive nodes a new node labeled with the transition label between those nodes. The plan is induced from that last structure by skipping $NULL$ actions and $NOTH$ events.

Example 3 Consider the environment knowledge of Example 1. Suppose we are given the following operational knowledge:

Actions

$take(x)$	precond:	$on(x, z) \wedge clear(x)$
	add-list:	$have(x) \wedge clear(z)$
$puton(x, y)$	precond:	$have(x) \wedge clear(y)$
	add-list:	$on(x, y)$.

The goal of Agent2 is to arrange blocks on a different table $T2$, as follows:

$$on(a, T2) \wedge on(d, a) \wedge on(b, d) \wedge on(c, b).$$

Construct-Intermed-Struct(strategy)

Create an initial node s with $G(s) = NULL$, $stack(s)$= strategy, and $was(s) = q_0$.

Set $Mode$ to R.

Repeat

Select a node s with $stack(s)$ not empty and with no successors. If there is no such node, break from the loop.

If $Mode{=}W$ **then:**

Check if $was(s)$ =*waited-event*. If so, set $Mode$ to R. If not, set $action(s)$ to $NULL$; for each event e successor of $was(s)$, create the node $succ(s,e)$, set $G(succ(s,e))$ to $G(s)$, and $stack(succ(s,e))$ to $stack(s)$.

Else:

-If $G(s)$ is not an atomic action reduce it to a sequence of atomic actions by applying goal-reduction. If such a sequence can be found then update $G(s)$ and $stack(s)$ and continue.

-From now, we can assume $G(s)$ is atomic. If the precondition of $G(s)$ is not satisfied use the verification algorithm of [Clarke *et al.*, 1986] to see if the precondition of $G(s)$ can be satisfied by further states of the world-automaton; if it can, set $Mode$ to W, and set *waited-event* to the precondition of $G(s)$; else backtrack.

-If the precondition of $G(s)$ is satisfied, set $action(s)$ to $G(s)$; then determine the strategy and the stack for successors nodes : for each event successor of $was(s)$, create a new node s' of the graph and a transition, labeled by the event, from the current node to the new node s'; set $G(s')$ to the first element of $stack(s)$ and $stack(s')$ to the rest of $stack(s)$.

End of Repeat

End of Construct-Intermed-Struct

Figure 3: Constructing the intermediate structure

It is reduced to the strategy:
$take(a) \rightarrow puton(a,T2) \rightarrow take(d) \rightarrow puton(d,a) \rightarrow take(b) \rightarrow puton(b,d) \rightarrow take(c) \rightarrow puton(c,b)$.

The initial part of the plan generated is shown in Figure 2. ∎

Additional Features and Possible Extensions

The following features have also been developed: the use of past temporal formulas to express conditions of conditional goals. We keep a linear structure recording the past activity. We can then use a polynomial algorithm to verify if past preconditions of actions are satisfied on that structure. The verification algorithm is similar to that of [Clarke *et al.*, 1986]. We can also use temporal formulas to describe the effects of an action. This is a partial response to the commitment problem [Cohen and Levesque, 1987]. When an action with a temporal effect is selected at a state in the intermediate structure, we replace the sub-automaton rooted at the corresponding state in the world-automaton by a cross-poduct of the sub-automaton with an automaton representing the effects formula.

If there are paths of the world-automaton on which it is impossible for the agent to achieve its goal, there is no solution to the planning problem. However, it seems reasonable for the agent to move ahead anyway making the assumption that the path for which he cannot plan is unlikely. This implies that it would be useful to have probabilistic information for each path of the world automaton. The planner would then use that information to estimate the probability that the plan will work. Another interesting approach is for the planner to procrastinate when, for some goals, the future is very uncertain. He would delay planning for those goals until information about the future becomes more precise.

Automatic generation of environment specifications is a problem we intend to investigate, possibly using techniques similar to those in [Kautz and Allen, 1986; Kautz, 1987] to construct a prediction module.

Planning is also expected to be interleaved with the execution. During execution some information could confirm or disconfirm the current structure of the world-automaton. The planner can then determine whether or not the plan could go awry and, if necessary, replan with respect to the new environment structure.

Conclusions

We have shown how temporal logic can be fruitfully used for generating reactive plans. The problem we considered is that of planning for agents evolving in a changing and nondeterministic world. The generation algorithm is in fact a blend of goal-reduction and environment enabling, and it can be viewed in the tread of recent work done by [Bresina and Drummond, 1990].

The performance of this planner depends on the available strategies. The lower level the strategies are, the faster the plan generation is going to be. We believe the method viable if refined strategies are available. Such refined strategies are analogous to those used in human behavior. If you are told to go from *Liège* to *Brussels*, you immediately decide to take a bus to the station, where you hope to catch a train. If you know there might not be a bus, you immediately plan to take a cab. That is, you act as if you had strategies triggered by goals you have to commit to. You don't think "to be in *Brussels* I must have been in a train; to be in a train I must have been to the station, and so on." Such reasoning only appears in rather unusual situations (lost in a town, ...).

Clearly the method, as it stands now, has some limitations. The world-automaton has to be correct for the plan to be correct too. Thus there is need for some way of dealing with unpredictable events. Another limitation is the seemingly great complexity of the algorithm. With all that in mind, we expect this work will serve as a good guideline for future investigations towards a tractable planner.

Acknowledgments

I would like to thank two anonymous referees for helpful suggestions for a better presentation of this paper. I am also grateful to Marianne Baudinet, Jean-Marc Stevenne, and Pierre Wolper for careful reading of this paper and thoughtful comments. Philippe Simar helped in the typesetting of this paper. This work has been made possible only through the enthusiastic supervision of Professor Pierre Wolper, to whom I extend my thanks.

References

Abadi, M.; Lamport, L.; and Wolper, P. 1989. Realizable and unrealizable concurrent program specifications. In *Proc. 10th Int. Colloquium on Automata, Languages and Programming.* LNCS, Vol. 372, Springer-Verlag. 1–17.

Allen, J.F. and Koomen, J.F. 1983. Planning using a temporal world wodel. In Bundy, A., editor 1983, *8th IJCAI.* 741–747.

Bresina, J. and Drummond, M. 1990. Integrating planning and reaction. In *AAAI workshop on Planning in Uncertain, Unpredictable, or Changing Environments*, Stanford Univ.

Chapman, D. and Agre, P. E. 1987. Abstract reasoning as emergent from concrete activity. In Georgeff, M. P. and Lansky, A., editors 1987, *Reasonning about Actions and Plans, Proceedings of the 1986 Workshop, Timberline, Oregon.* Morgan Kaufmann. 411–424.

Clarke, E.M.; Emerson, E.A.; and Sistla, A.P. 1986. Automatic verification of finite-state concurrent systems using temporal logic specifications. *ACM Transactions on Programming Languages and Systems* 8(2):244–263.

Cohen, P. R. and Feigenbaum, E. A. 1982. *Handbook of Artificial Intelligence.* Pitman, London.

Cohen, P. R. and Levesque, H. J. 1987. Persistence, intention, and commitment. In Georgeff, M. P. and Lansky, A., editors 1987, *Reasonning about Actions and Plans, Proceedings of the 1986 Workshop, Timberline, Oregon.* Morgan Kaufmann. 297–340.

Dean, Thomas L. 1987. Intractability and time-dependent planning. In Georgeff, M. P. and Lansky, Amy, editors 1987, *Reasonning about Actions and Plans, Proceedings of the 1986 Workshop, Timberline, Oregon.* Morgan Kaufmann. 245–266.

Emerson, E.A. and Clarke, E.M. 1982. Using branching time logic to synthesize synchronization skeletons. *Science of Computer Programming* 2:241–266.

Emerson, E.A. and Halpern, J.Y. 1985. Decision procedures and expressiveness in the temporal logic of branching time. *Journal of Computer and System Sciences* 30:1–24.

Fikes, R.; Hart, P. E.; and Nilsson, N.J. 1971. STRIPS: A new approach to the application of theorem proving. *Artificial Intelligence* 2:189–208.

Kautz, H. A. and Allen, J. F. 1986. Generalized plan recognition. In *5th NCAI.* AAAI, Morgan Kaufmann. 32–37.

Kautz, H. A. 1987. A formal theory of plan recognition. Technical Report 215, Univ. of Rochester, NY.

Lansky, A. 1987. A representation of parallel activity based on events, structure, and causality. In Georgeff, M. P. and Lansky, A., editors 1987, *Reasonning about Actions and Plans, Proceedings of the 1986 Workshop, Timberline, Oregon.* Morgan Kaufmann. 123–159.

Manna, Z. and Wolper, P. 1984. Synthesis of communicating processes from temporal logic specifications. *ACM Transactions on Programming Languages and Systems* 6(1):68–93.

McDermott, D. 1982. A temporal logic for reasoning about processes and plans. *Cognitive Science* 6(2):101–155.

Pednault, E. P.D. 1987. Formulating multiagent, dynamic-world problems in the classical planning framework. In Georgeff, M. P. and Lansky, A., editors 1987, *Reasonning about Actions and Plans, Proceedings of the 1986 Workshop, Timberline, Oregon.* Morgan Kaufmann. 47–82.

Pnueli, A. and Rosner, R. 1989a. On the synthesis of a reactive module. In *16th Annual ACM Symposium on POPL*, Austin. 179–189.

Pnueli, A. and Rosner, R. 1989b. On the synthesis of an asynchronous reactive module. In *ICALP.* LNCS, Vol 372, Springer-Verlag. 652–671.

Rosenschein, S. J. 1989. Synthesizing information-tracking automata from environment descriptions. In Brachman, R. J.; Levesque, H. J.; and Reiter, R., editors 1989, *First International Conference on Principles of Knowledge Representation and Reasoning*, Toronto. Morgan Kaufmann. 386–393.

Wilkins, D. E. 1984. Domain-independant planning: Representation and plan generation. *Artificial Intelligence* 22(3):269–301.

Wolper, P. 1989. On the relation of programs and computations to models of temporal logic. In Banieqbal, B.; Barringer, H.; and Pnueli, A., editors 1989, *Proc. Temporal Logic in Specification.* LNCS, Vol. 398, Springer-Verlag. 75–123.

Mapping and Retrieval During Plan Reuse: A Validation Structure Based Approach

Subbarao Kambhampati*

Center for Design Research and Department of Computer Science
Stanford University
Bldg. 530, Duena Street, Stanford CA 94305-4026
e-mail: *rao@sunrise.stanford.edu*

Abstract

Effective mapping and retrieval are important issues in successful deployment of plan reuse strategies. In this paper we present a domain independent strategy for ranking a set of plausible reuse candidates in the order of cost of modifying them to solve a new planning problem. The cost of modification is estimated by measuring the amount of disturbance caused to the *validation structure* of a reuse candidate if it were to be reused in the new problem situation. This strategy is more informed than the typical feature based retrieval strategies, and is more efficient than the methods which require partial knowledge of the nature of the plan for the new problem situation to guide the retrieval process. We discuss the implementation of this retrieval strategy in PRIAR, a framework for flexible reuse and modification in hierarchical planning.

1. Introduction

The utility of reusing existing plans to solve new planning problems has been realized early in the planning research, and has more recently received considerable attention in case-based reasoning [6, 1]. A major obstacle to successful deployment of plan reuse schemes has been the problem of plan retrieval and mapping. Retrieving an appropriate plan that can be efficiently reused in the current problem situation, and choosing an appropriate mapping between the objects of the existing plan and the objects of the new planning problem is generally very hard [15]. The payoff from plan reuse depends crucially on both the cost of retrieval and mapping, and the the cost of modifying the retrieved plan to solve the new problem. Thus, for reuse to be effective, the similarity metrics used should be capable of evaluating the ease of modifying an existing plan to solve the new problem, rather than merely measuring surface similarity. For efficiency reasons, most typical retrieval strategies employ straight forward feature matching or domain dependent indexing schemes. Such schemes do not accurately reflect the cost of reusing the retrieved plan in the new problem situation. To be effective, such strategies should also be able to take into account the expected match between the plans for the two problem situations.

While the above limitations have been recognized, many of the proposed alternatives failed to be cost-effective as they require comparison of the solution derivations for the old and new problems (e.g., [2]). In this paper, we provide a partial solution for the retrieval and mapping problem that does not depend on any prior knowledge of the plan for solving the new problem. It makes an informed estimate of the cost of modifying a given plan to solve a new problem by analyzing how the internal dependencies of that plan will be affected in the new problem situation. It utilizes a novel representation of the internal dependency structure of the plan for this purpose. This strategy has been implemented in PRIAR, a framework for flexible reuse and modification of plans [10, 9, 11, 13].

PRIAR utilizes plan *validation structure*, a systematic internal dependency representation of hierarchically generated plans, to guide and control all phases of reuse of a given plan in a new problem situation. In PRIAR, plan modification is seen as a process of repairing the inconsistencies in the validation structure of an existing plan, when it is interpreted in a new problem situation. The cost of modification process depends upon the number and type of these inconsistencies. The retrieval strategy estimates the number inconsistencies for each reuse candidate, and rank orders the candidates based on that estimate. This ordering is facilitated through the development of the notion of the *plan kernel* of a plan. The plan kernel provides a way of encapsulating the validation dependencies between a plan and its problem specification. In the rest of the paper, we briefly discuss PRIAR's validation structure based plan reuse framework, and describe its plan kernel based ordering strategy for choosing among reuse candidates.

2. Overview of PRIAR Plan Modification Framework

2.1. Validation Structure

In PRIAR framework the building blocks of the stored plan dependency structure are validations. A validation is a 4-tuple $\langle E, n_s, C, n_d \rangle$ where the effect E of the task n_s (called source node) in the hierarchical task network (HTN) is used to satisfy (support) the condition C of task n_d (called destination node).

* The support of the Defense Advanced Research Projects Agency and the U.S. Army Engineer Topographic Laboratories under contract DACA76-88-C-0008, and that of Office of Naval Research under contract N00014-88-K-0620 are gratefully acknowledged.

For any plan synthesized by a hierarchical planner, there are a finite set of validations, corresponding to the *protection intervals* [3] that are maintained during planning; we denote this set by **V**. The individual validations are classified depending on the type of the conditions they support. Figure 1 shows the validation structure of the plan for solving the blocks world problem 3BS (shown in the figure). Validations are represented graphically as links between the effect of the source node and the condition of the destination node. (For the sake of exposition, validations supporting conditions of the type $Block(?x)$ have not been shown in the figure.) For example, $\langle On(B,C), n_{15}, On(B,C), n_G \rangle$ is a validation belonging to this plan since the condition $On(B,C)$ is required at the goal state n_G, and is provided by the effect $On(B,C)$ of node n_{15}.

The uniqueness of PRIAR framework is in the way the plan validations are stored on the HTN. Each task n in the HTN is annotated with the set of validations that are supplied by, consumed by, or necessarily preserved by the tasks belonging to the sub-reduction (hierarchical wedge) rooted at n. We call these the external effect conditions (e-conditions), external preconditions (e-preconditions) and persistence conditions (p-conditions) respectively of task n. The annotations on a node encapsulate the node's role in the validation structure of the plan. These annotations are computed efficiently for each node in the HTN in a bottom-up, breadth-first fashion at the planning time. In [10], we provide a $O(N^2)$ algorithm (where N is the length of the plan) for doing this.

Using the task annotations introduced before, PRIAR also defines the notion of the *validation state* preceding and following each primitive executable action in the plan. They specify the set of validations that should hold at each point during the plan execution for the rest of the plan to have a consistent validation structure (thereby guaranteeing its successful execution). Of particular interest for the PRIAR retrieval strategy are the validation state following the initial node in the HTN, denoted by $A^s(n_I)$, and the one preceding the goal node, denoted by $A^p(n_G)$. The former contains all validations which are provided by the initial node, n_I and the latter contains all the validations which are consumed by the goal node, n_G.

The annotated validation structure effectively provides a hierarchical explanation of correctness of the plan with respect to the planner's knowledge of the domain. In PRIAR, the validation structure is used (i) to locate the parts of the plan that would have to be modified, (ii) to suggest appropriate modification actions, (iii) to control the modification process such that it changes the existing plan minimally to make it work in the new situation, and (iv) to assist in plan mapping and retrieval.

2.2. Plan Modification via Annotation-Verification

Given a plan to be reused to fit the constraints of a new problem situation, PRIAR first maps the plan into the new problem situation. This process, known as *interpretation*, marks the differences between the plan and the problem situation. These differences in turn are seen to produce *inconsistencies* in the plan validation structure (such as missing, failing, or redundant validations). In PRIAR framework, a plan is modified in response to inconsistencies in its validation structure. PRIAR uses a process called *annotation-verification* to suggest appropriate modification to the plan for removing those inconsistencies from the validation structure of the plan. These domain independent modifications depend on the type of the inconsistencies and

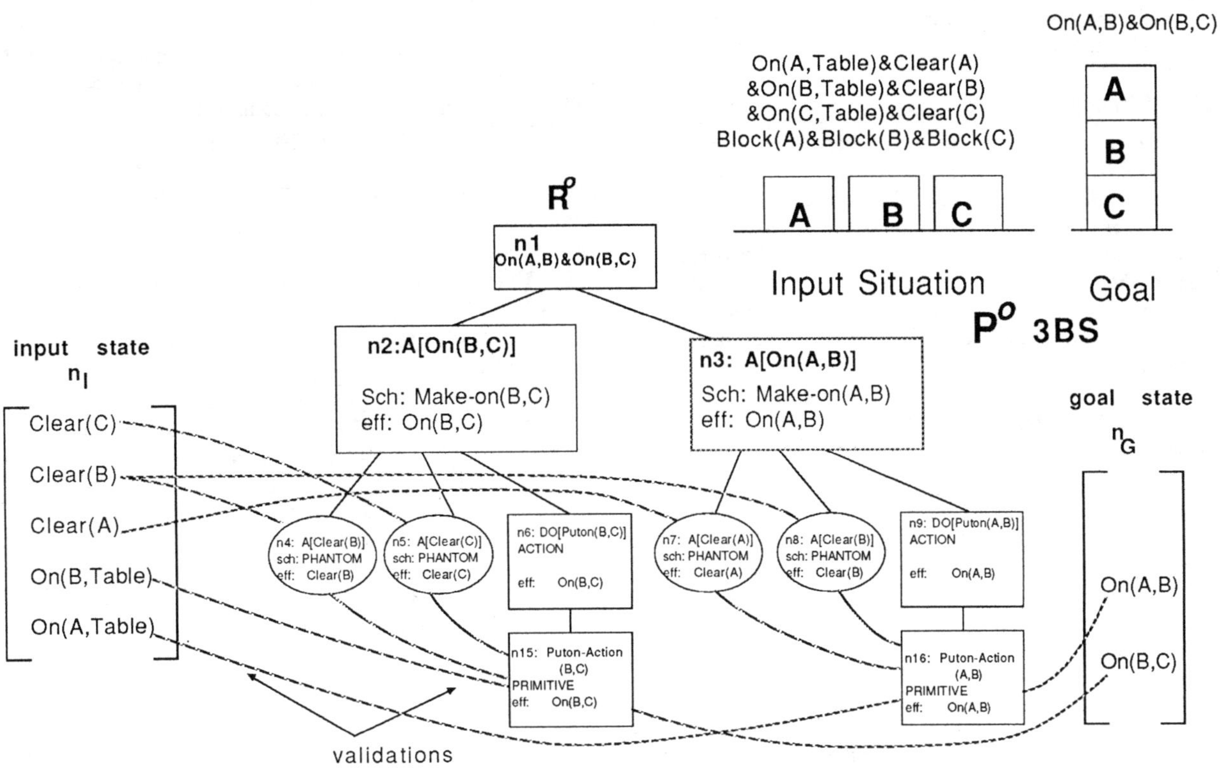

Figure 1. Validation structure of 3BS plan

involve removal of redundant parts of the plan, exploitation of any serendipitous effects of the changed situation to shorten the plan, and addition of high level refit tasks to re-establish any failing validations. At the end of the annotation-verification, which is a polynomial time process process [10], PRIAR will have a *partially reduced* plan with a *consistent* validation structure. PRIAR's hierarchical nonlinear planner accepts this partially reduced plan and produces a completely reduced HTN. The planner uses a conservative heuristic search control strategy called *task kernel-based ordering* (see [9]) to control this process of refitting, so as to localize the modification to the plan and preserve as many of its applicable portions as possible. (Further details of PRIAR modification process can be found in a companion paper [13] in this proceedings.)

3. Mapping and Retrieval in PRIAR

In this section we will assume that PRIAR is given a new problem $P^n=[I^n,G^n]$ and a set of reuse candidates $\{\langle R^o,\alpha\rangle\}$, where R^o is an existing plan, and α is a mapping between the objects of R^o and P^n. PRIAR currently performs a partial unification on the goals of R^o and P^n to get an initial set of reuse candidates. This strategy is described in [10], and is not of particular interest for the purposes of this paper. Here we will concentrate on strategies that exploit the validation structure of the plans to efficiently rank the initial set of reuse candidates in the order of the cost of modifying them to solve the new problem. The heuristic cost metric of each reuse candidate $\langle R^o,\alpha\rangle$ is computed in terms of the number and type of validations of R^o that will be failing in P^n, for the mapping α. We define the notion of *plan kernel* of a reuse candidate to facilitate efficient computation of this cost metric. The degree of match between the plan kernel of the reuse candidate and the new problem situation will be used to guide the ordering.

3.1. Plan Kernels

The plan kernel of a stored plan R^o, $PK(R^o)$, is intended to encapsulate the dependencies between R^o and the features of its input and goal specification. We will formulate it as a collection of validations of R^o that are supported by or supporting the features of the input and goal states of the plan. These validations are further divided into three categories based on the expected difficulty of re-establishing them, in the event that the input and goal state features on which they are dependent no longer hold in the new planning situation. Thus, we define it as a three tuple

$$PK(R^o) = \langle g\text{-}features,\ f\text{-}features,\ pc\text{-}features\rangle$$

where the g-features, f-features and pc-features are in turn defined as follows:

<u>g-features (Goal Features)</u>: These correspond to the validations of R^o that directly support its goals. Thus

$$g\text{-}features(PK(R^o)) = A^p(n_G)$$

(where $A^p(n_G)$ is as defined in the previous section.)

<u>f-features (Filter Features)</u>: These correspond to the validations supported by the input specification of R^o to either the filter conditions (the unachievable applicability conditions) of the plan, or the phantom nodes that achieve some main goal of R^o. Thus, a validation $v:\langle E,n_I,C,n_d\rangle$ belongs to *f-features(PK(R^o))*, iff $v \in A^s(n_I)$ and either C is a filter condition or $\exists v':\langle E',n_d,C',n_G\rangle \in A^p(n_G)$ such that $n_{d'} = n_d \wedge C=C'$

<u>pc-features (Precondition Features)</u>: These correspond to the the validations supported by the input specification of R^o that support either the preconditions of some node of R^o, or the phantom nodes achieving the preconditions of some node of R^o. In the current framework, these will essentially be all the validations of $A^s(n_I)$ that are not included in the f-features of the plan kernel. That is, *pc-features(PK(R^o))* =

$$\{v \mid v \in A^s(n_I) \wedge v \notin f\text{-}features(PK(R^o))\}$$

Based on the above definition, the plan kernel of a plan can be computed in a straightforward fashion from the initial validation state $A^s(n_I)$ and the final validation state $A^p(n_G)$ of that plan. As an example, the plan kernel of 3BS plan shown in figure 1 will be:

$$PK(3BS) = \begin{bmatrix} g\text{-}features: \begin{cases} \langle On(A,B),n_{16},On(A,B),n_G\rangle \\ \langle On(B,C),n_{15},On(B,C),n_G\rangle \end{cases} \\ f\text{-}features: \begin{cases} \langle Block(B),n_I,Block(B),n_{15}\rangle \\ \langle Block(B),n_I,Block(B),n_{16}\rangle \\ \langle Block(A),n_I,Block(A),n_{16}\rangle \\ \langle Block(C),n_I,Block(C),n_{15}\rangle \\ \langle On(B,Table),n_I,On(B,?x),n_{15}\rangle \\ \langle On(A,Table),n_I,On(A,?x),n_{16}\rangle \end{cases} \\ pc\text{-}features: \begin{cases} \langle Clear(B),n_I,Clear(B),n_4\rangle \\ \langle Clear(B),n_I,Clear(B),n_8\rangle \\ \langle Clear(C),n_I,Clear(C),n_5\rangle \\ \langle Clear(A),n_I,Clear(A),n_7\rangle \end{cases} \end{bmatrix}$$

Notice that the different features of the problem specification enter the plan kernel only by virtue of the validations that they provide to the plan. Moreover, if any features support multiple validations, they enter the plan kernel once for each of these validations. For example, the features $Block(B)$ and $Clear(B)$ enter $PK(3BS)$ more than once. Thus, the number of times a feature enters the plan kernel, and the type of validations it supports implicitly reflect the relative importance of that feature during retrieval.

3.2. Plan Kernel Based Ordering of Reuse Candidates

The degree of match between the plan kernel of a reuse candidate and the input and goal specification of a new planning problem gives a rough indication as to how much of that plan would be applicable to the new problem and as to what type of validation failures would arise when it is reused in the new problem situation. Since the refitting cost depends to a large extent on the number and type of validation failures, it is reasonable to use this match to estimate the amount of modification that would be needed for reuse. Below we describe a three layered ordering procedure to rank a set of reuse candidates with the help of their plan kernels. The procedure measures the difficulty of reusing the given plan in the new problem situation by estimating the number of inconsistencies that will arise in the validation structure of a plan because of the problem differences.

<u>Given.</u> The new problem $P^n=[I^n,G^n]$, and a set of reuse candidates $\{\langle R^o,\alpha\rangle\}$.

<u>Step 0.</u> The plan kernels of the reuse candidates are computed by translating the plan kernels of the corresponding plans, using the mapping. That is, $PK(\langle R^o,\alpha\rangle) = R^o\cdot\alpha$, where "."

refers to the operation of object substitution.

Step 1. The reuse candidates are ranked based on the number of goals of P^n that will not be supported by the g-features of the plan kernels of individual candidates. The cost function for this layer of ordering will be given by

$$\left| \left\{ g \;\middle|\; g \in G^n \wedge \left[\begin{array}{l} \nexists v : \langle E, n_d, G, n_G \rangle \in \\ \qquad g\text{-}features(PK(\langle R^o, \alpha \rangle)) \; s.t. \; G \vdash g \end{array} \right] \right\} \right|$$

(where $F \vdash f$ is true iff f can be deductively inferred from F and the domain axioms.) Based on this step, the best candidates are those which will need to achieve the least number of extra goals to be reused in the new problem situation.

Step 2. If more than one candidate is ranked best by the ordering of step 1, then the best candidates are ranked further based on the number of f-features of their plan kernels that do not hold in the input specification of the new problem. Thus the cost function for this layer is given by

$$\left| \{ v \mid v : \langle E, n_I, C, n_d \rangle \in f\text{-}features(PK(\langle R^o, \alpha \rangle)) \wedge I^n \nvdash C \} \right|$$

Step 3. Finally, the best ranked candidates in the ordering of step 2 are further ranked by the number of *pc*-features of their plan kernels that do not hold in the input state of the new problem. Thus, the cost function for this layer is given by

$$\left| \{ v : \langle E, n_I, C, n_d \rangle \mid v \in pc\text{-}features(PK(\langle R^o, \alpha \rangle)) \wedge I^n \nvdash C \} \right|$$

The best ranked reuse candidates at the end of this three layer ordering procedure are returned as the preferred candidates for reuse in solving P^n.

Remarks: Even if an old plan matches all the goals of P^n, it may still be an inappropriate candidate for solving P^n since the methods it uses to achieve those goals may not be applicable in the new problem situation. This, for example, is the case when a filter condition of the schema used to reduce the task achieving a goal in R^o is no longer true in P^n, or the phantom goal node that achieved a goal in R^o can no longer stay phantom in P^n. The ranking with respect to f-features, carried out in step 2, essentially attempts to prefer candidates which will not have validations supporting such failing filter conditions or failing phantom goals.

The implicit levels of importance attached to the validations at different layers of the plan kernel can be justified in terms of the computational effort needed for re-establishing them in the new problem situation. The main heuristic is that a significant amount of task reduction and interaction resolution would be required to generate subplans to achieve goals of the new problem that are not supported by the retrieved plan, or to replace subplans of the retrieved plan with failing filter conditions, in contrast to the effort required to reachieve the failing preconditions. The second heuristic is that in the event of filter condition failure, it is possible that to exploit some of the previous planning effort (e.g., effort expended in establishing the e-preconditions of the sub-reduction being replaced) in the new planning situation (see [10]). For this reason, the failing filter conditions are considered less costly to handle than new goals.

3.3. Example

Figure 2 shows the initial and goal state specification of 4BS1, a blocks world problem and lists four possible reuse candidates for that problem. For each reuse candidate, the figure shows the the initial and goal state specifications, the mapping between the candidate and the 4BS1 problem, and the plan kernel of the reuse candidate (as an exercise, compare the plan kernels of the reuse candidates $\langle 3BS, [A \to L, B \to K, C \to J] \rangle$ and $\langle 3BS, [A \to K, B \to J, C \to I] \rangle$ with $PK(3BS)$ specified previously). For ease of exposition, the figure shows the validations of the plan kernels only by their supporting effects. It does not include facts of type $Block(?x)$ in the specifications of the problems. Similarly, it also does not explicitly show the validations of the type $\langle Block(?x), -, -, - \rangle$.

When these four reuse candidates are ordered with the help of their plan kernels, at the first layer the g-features of the plan kernels of all the reuse candidates fail to satisfy one goal each of the new problem (4BS1). Thus, they are all deemed equally costly at this layer, and all the candidates move to the ordering at the next layer.

At this layer, the f-feature $\langle On(B, C), -, -, - \rangle$ of the plan kernel of $\langle 3BS\text{-}Phantom, [A \to L, B \to K, C \to J] \rangle$ is not preserved in the input state of the new problem (4BS1) as $I^n \nvdash On(B, C)$. (This basically means that the top level phantom goal of this reuse candidate has to be re-established if we want to use it to solve P^n.) Similarly, the f-feature $\langle Pyramid(L), -, -, - \rangle$ of the

4BS1:
Init-state(I^n): $On(I, Table)$, $On(K, Table)$, $On(L, Table)$, $On(J, L)$, $Clear(J)$, $Clear(K)$, $Clear(I)$,
Goal-state(G^n): $On(L, K)$, $On(K, J)$, $On(J, I)$

Reuse Candidates $\{\langle R^o, \alpha \rangle\}$

$\langle$**3BS-Phantom**, $[A \to L, B \to K, C \to J]\rangle$:
Init-state: $On(A, Table)$, $On(B, C)$, $On(C, Table)$, $Clear(A)$, $Clear(B)$
Goal-state: $On(A, B)$, $On(B, C)$
Plan: Put-Block-on-Block-Action(A, B)
PK(3BS-Phantom)$\cdot[A \to L, B \to K, C \to J]$:
[g-**features:** $\langle On(L, K), -, -, - \rangle$ $\langle On(K, J), -, -, - \rangle$
f-**features:** $\langle On(K, J), -, -, - \rangle$ $\langle On(L, Table), -, -, - \rangle$
pc-**features:** $\langle Clear(L), -, -, - \rangle$ $\langle Clear(K), -, -, - \rangle$]

$\langle$**3BS**, $[A \to L, B \to K, C \to J]\rangle$:
Init-state: $On(A, Table)$, $On(B, Table)$, $On(C, Table)$, $Clear(A)$, $Clear(B)$, $Clear(C)$
Goal-state: $On(A, B)$, $On(B, C)$
Plan: Put-Block-on-Block-Action(B, C)→Put-Block-on-Block-Action(A, B)
PK(3BS)$\cdot[A \to L, B \to K, C \to J]$:
[g-**features:** $\langle On(L, K), -, -, - \rangle$ $\langle On(K, J), -, -, - \rangle$
f-**features:** $\langle On(L, Table), -, -, - \rangle$ $\langle On(K, Table), -, -, - \rangle$
pc-**features:** $\langle Clear(L), -, -, - \rangle$ $\langle Clear(K), -, -, - \rangle$ $\langle Clear(J), -, -, - \rangle$]

$\langle$**3BS**, $[A \to K, B \to J, C \to I]\rangle$:
Init-state: $On(A, Table)$, $On(B, Table)$, $On(C, Table)$, $Clear(A)$, $Clear(B)$, $Clear(C)$
Goal-state: $On(A, B)$, $On(B, C)$
Plan: Put-Block-on-Block-Action(B, C)→Put-Block-on-Block-Action(A, B)
PK(3BS)$\cdot[A \to K, B \to J, C \to I]$:
[g-**features:** $\langle On(K, J), -, -, - \rangle$ $\langle On(J, I), -, -, - \rangle$
f-**features:** $\langle On(J, Table), -, -, - \rangle$ $\langle On(K, Table), -, -, - \rangle$
pc-**features:** $\langle Clear(I), -, -, - \rangle$ $\langle Clear(K), -, -, - \rangle$ $\langle Clear(J), -, -, - \rangle$]

$\langle$**3BS-Pyramid**, $[A \to L, B \to K, C \to J]\rangle$:
Init-state: $On(A, Table)$, $On(B, Table)$, $On(C, Table)$, $Clear(A)$, $Clear(B)$, $Clear(C)$, $Pyramid(A)$
Goal-state: $On(A, B)$, $On(B, C)$
Plan: Put-Block-on-Block-Action(B, C)→Put-Pyramid-on-Block(A, B)
PK(3BS-Pyramid)$\cdot[A \to L, B \to K, C \to J]$:
[g-**features:** $\langle On(L, K), -, -, - \rangle$ $\langle On(K, J), -, -, - \rangle$
f-**features:** $\langle Pyramid(L), -, -, - \rangle$ $\langle On(L, Table), -, -, - \rangle$ $\langle On(K, Table), -, -, - \rangle$
pc-**features:** $\langle Clear(K), -, -, - \rangle$ $\langle Clear(J), -, -, - \rangle$]

Figure 2. Example for Plan Kernel Based Ordering

plan kernel of the reuse candidate $\langle 3BS\text{-}Pyramid,[A \to L, B \to K, C \to J]\rangle$ is not preserved since $I^n \not\vdash Pyramid(L)$. If we want to solve 4BS1 by this reuse candidate, the sub-reduction dependent on this filter condition would have to be replaced. Further, the f-feature $\langle On(J, Table),-,-,-\rangle$[1] of the plan kernel of the reuse candidate $\langle 3BS,[A \to K, B \to J, C \to I]\rangle$ is not preserved since $I^n \not\vdash On(J, Table)$. In contrast, none of the f-features of the reuse candidate $\langle 3BS,[A \to L, B \to K, C \to J]\rangle$ fail to hold in the new problem situation. Thus, this is ranked best by the ordering based on the f-features of the plan kernel. Since this is the only best ranked candidate, the ordering at the third layer is not required and $\langle 3BS,[A \to L, B \to K, C \to J]\rangle$ is returned as the preferred reuse candidate for solving the problem 4BS1.

Notice that the plan kernel based ordering is able to discriminate among these reuse candidates even though all the candidates satisfy the same number of goals of P^n. Further, as we mentioned earlier, it is capable of discriminating among different plans as well as different mappings of the same plan. In the current example, the reuse candidates $\langle 3BS,[A \to L, B \to K, C \to J]\rangle$ and $\langle 3BS,[A \to K, B \to J, C \to I]\rangle$ correspond to two different mappings of the same (three blocks) plan. We have seen that the ordering prefers one of the mappings over the other.

3.4. Cost Overestimation in the Ordering Heuristic

A limitation of the plan kernel-based heuristic ordering strategy as discussed in the previous section is that it sometimes overestimates the cost of reusing a plan in the new situation by counting some spurious inconsistencies. This happens when parts of the reuse candidate are rendered redundant in the new problem situation. For example, when the reuse candidate supports some unnecessary goals (the goals which are satisfied by the reuse candidate but are not required in the new planning situation), some of the failing validations may actually be supporting the parts of the plan whose sole purpose is to help achieve the unnecessary goal. Such failing validations should obviously not be counted as inconsistencies, as they can eventually be removed from the HTN and thus do not have to be re-established. As an example, suppose that we are judging the appropriateness of reusing the 3BS plan, shown in figure 1, in a new problem situation where there is no match for the goal $On(A, B)$ (i.e., it is not required). In such a case, the validation $\langle Clear(A), n_I, Clear(A), n_{16}\rangle$ cannot be counted as a failure, even if $Clear(A)$ is not true in the initial state of the new problem—this validation, being an e-precondition of the node $n_3{:}A\,[On(A, B)]$, will be pruned away eventually thus making its failure inconsequential. Similar situation arises when some of the goals and sub-goals of the reuse candidate are directly satisfied in the input situation of the new problem (see p-phantom validations in [10, 13]). To avoid overestimation in these cases, the parts of the plan that are rendered redundant in the new problem situation would have to be removed, even before reuse candidates are ordered by the plan kernel based ordering. In PRIAR, this type of pruning is done only during annotation verification process, after a reuse candidate is selected (see *prune–validation* process in [10]). Thus, to eventually avoid overestimation of cost, the annotation verification procedure would have to be carried out partially before the reuse candidates are ranked by the plan kernel based ordering. Even though the annotation verification process is only a polynomial time process, we feel that using it during mapping and retrieval stage may still be too expensive. Because of this, we retained the overestimating heuristic in the current implementation of PRIAR. However, this can be changed easily if required.

3.5. Refinements to Plan Kernel Based Ordering

The *informedness* of the ordering procedure presented in section 3.2 can be further improved by exploiting the hierarchical structure of the plan. In particular, the notion of the *level* of a validation can be used as a means of differentiating further among the validations of the individual layers of the plan kernel (in terms of the estimated difficulty of re-establishing them in the event they are not preserved in the new problem situation).

The level of a validation is defined as the reduction level at which that validation is first introduced into the HTN (see [10] for the formalization of this notion). For example, in figure 1, the validation $\langle Block(A), n_I, Block(A), n_{16}\rangle$ is considered to be of a higher level than the validation $\langle On(A, Table), n_I, On(A, Table), n_{16}\rangle$, since the former is introduced into the HTN to facilitate the reduction of task n_3 while the latter is introduced during the reduction of task n_9. A useful characteristic of hierarchical planning is that its domain schemas are written in such a way that the more important conditions are established at higher levels, while the establishment of less important conditions is delegated to lower levels. Thus, the level at which a validation is first introduced into an HTN can be taken to be predictive of the importance of that validation, and the effort required to (re)establish it.[2] The validation levels can be pre-computed efficiently at the time of annotation.

To improve the informedness of the heuristic ordering, we can weight the validations of individual layers by their levels. The cost functions of the ordering procedure will then compute the weighted sum of the number of failing validations. For example, the cost function for the f-feature based ordering step in section 3.2 would now become $\sum_{\Delta} level(v)$, where $\Delta \equiv \{v{:}\langle E, n_I, C, n_d\rangle \mid v \in f\text{-}features(PK(\langle R^o, \alpha\rangle)) \wedge I^n \not\vdash C\}$. In the current example, this would mean that the failure of the validation $\langle Block(A), n_I, Block(A), n_{16}\rangle$ would be considered more costly than the failure of the validation $\langle On(A, Table), n_I, On(A, Table), n_{16}\rangle$. This is reasonable since the former necessitates the relacement of a larger sub-plan (the sub-plan rooted at n_3) than the latter (which only leads to the replacement of the sub-plan rooted at n_9; see figure 1).

4. Related Work

Research in analogical problem solving has shown that the appropriateness of reusing a previous problem's solution to solve a new problem cannot be accurately judged through a

[1] We follow the convention of [20] and classify $On(J, ?x)$ as a filter condition rather than a precondition. Some effects of the plan depend on the binding of $?x$ and one way of correctly propagating the effects when the binding of $?x$ changes is to re-reduce the corresponding task.

[2] We assume that domain schemas having this type of abstraction property have been supplied/encoded by the user in the first place. What we are doing here is to exploit the notion of importance implicit in that abstraction.

simple matching of the problem specifications. However, the alternatives, such as the one proposed by Carbonell [2] in derivational analogy, tend to be very costly, as they require that the solution derivations rather than the problem specifications be compared during retrieval. To compare derivations, the new problem would first have to be partially solved by some non-analogical methods. The retrieval method proposed here falls in the middle ground as it does essentially feature based matching, but takes the validation structure of the solution into account during the matching. This latter characteristic gives it the ability to make a more informed estimate of the importance of individual feature matches on the cost of the overall modification.

The principle motivation behind our strategy is that mapping and retrieval should be guided by the features of the existing plans that are predictive of the amount of modification required to reuse them in the new problem situation. In this sense, it has some similarities to the CHEF [6] retrieval strategy which gives importance to the features that are predictive of execution time failures and interactions. However, in contrast to CHEF, which *learns* the features predictive of the interactions (through an explanation based generalization of execution time failures), PRIAR uses the existing validation structure of the plan to decide the relative importance of the individual features. To some extent, this difference is a reflection of the differing nature of the tasks that are addressed by the two systems—while PRIAR tries to modify plans in the presence of a generative planner, and ensure correctness of the modification with respect to that planner, CHEF relies on the heuristic modification of the retrieved plans and tests the correctness through a domain model based simulation.

5. Conclusion

Our main contribution to the mapping and retrieval problem is a domain independent heuristic strategy for utilizing the validation structure of the stored plan to decide the appropriateness of reusing it in a new problem situation. The central idea is to estimate the cost of modifying the plan to solve the new problem, and prefer the candidate with least expected modification cost. The modification cost is estimated by measuring the amount of disturbance that would be caused to the validation structure of a reuse candidate in new problem situation. We have discussed the implementation of this retrieval strategy in PRIAR, a framework for flexible reuse and modification of plans. We argued that our strategy is more *informed* than the typical feature based retrieval strategies, and more *efficient* than the methods which require partial knowledge of the nature of the plan for the new problem situation to guide the retrieval process. Retrieving plans based solely on the plan kernel based ordering may still be too expensive when the plan library is very large. In such cases, the initial retrieval of candidate plans, prior to the plan kernel based ordering may have to be based on a domain dependent retrieval strategy. However, the plan kernel based ordering strategy can act in conjunction with such a gross feature-based retrieval strategy to make a more informed estimate of the utility of reusing a plan in the given problem situation.

References

1. R. Alterman, "An Adaptive Planner", *Proceedings of 5th AAAI*, 1986, 65-69.
2. J. G. Carbonell, "Derivational Analogy and its Role in Problem Solving", *Proceedings of AAAI*, Washington D.C., 1983, 64-69.
3. E. Charniak and D. McDermott, "Chapter 9: Managing Plans of Actions", in *Introduction to Artificial Intelligence*, Addison-Wesley Publishing Company, 1984, 485-554.
4. L. Daniel, "Planning: Modifying non-linear plans", DAI Working paper 24, University of Edinburgh, December 1977. (Also appears as "Planning and Operations Research," in *Artificial Intelligence: Tools, Techniques and Applications*, Harper and Row, New York, 1983).
5. R. Fikes, P. Hart and N. Nilsson, "Learning and Executing Generalized Robot Plans", *Artificial Intelligence 3* (1972), 251-288.
6. K. J. Hammond, "CHEF: A Model of Case-Based Planning", *Proceedings of 5th AAAI*, 1986, 267-271.
7. P. J. Hayes, "A Representation for Robot Plans", *Proceedings of 4th IJCAI*, 1975.
8. M. N. Huhns and R. D. Acosta, "ARGO: A System for Design by Analogy", *IEEE Expert*, Fall 1988, 53-68. (Also appears in Proc. of 4th IEEE Conf. on Appln. of AI, 1988).
9. S. Kambhampati and J. A. Hendler, "Control of Refitting during Plan Reuse", *11th International Joint Conference on Artificial Intelligence*, Detroit, Michigan, USA, August 1989, 943-948.
10. S. Kambhampati, "Flexible Reuse and Modification in Hierarchical Planning: A Validation Structure Based Approach", CS-Tech. Rep.-2334, CAR-Tech. Rep.-4698, Center for Automation Research, Department of Computer Science, University of Maryland, College Park, MD 20742, October 1989. (Ph.D. Dissertation).
11. S. Kambhampati and J. A. Hendler, "Flexible Reuse of Plans via Annotation and Verification", *Proceedings of 5th IEEE Conf. on Applications of Artificial Intelligence*, 1989, 37-44.
12. S. Kambhampati, "Mapping and Retrieval during Plan Reuse: A Validation-Structure Based Approach", *Proceedings of Eighth AAAI*, Boston, MA, 1990.
13. S. Kambhampati, "A Theory of Plan Modification", *Proceedings of Eighth AAAI*, Boston, MA, 1990.
14. J. L. Kolodner, "Maintaining Organization in a Dynamic Long-term Memory", *Cognitive Science 7* (1983), 243-280.
15. J. L. Kolodner, "Reconstructive Memory: a Computer Model", *Cognitive Science 7* (1983), 281-328.
16. J. L. Kolodner, "Case-Based Problem Solving", *Proceedings of the Fourth International Workshop on Machine Learning*, University of California, Irvine, June 1987, 167-178.
17. E. D. Sacerdoti, *A Structure for Plans and Behavior*, Elsevier North-Holland, New York, 1977.
18. R. Simmons, "A Theory of Debugging Plans and Interpretations", *Proceedings of 7th AAAI*, 1988, 94-99.
19. A. Tate, "Project Planning Using a Hierarchic Non-Linear Planner", Research Report 25, Department of AI, University of Edinburgh, 1976.
20. A. Tate, "Generating Project Networks", *Proceedings of 5th IJCAI*, 1977, 888-893.
21. D. E. Wilkins, "Domain-independent planning: representation and plan generation", *Artificial Intelligence 22* (1984), 269.
22. D. E. Wilkins, "Recovering from execution errors in SIPE", *Computational Intelligence 1* (1985).

A Theory of Plan Modification

Subbarao Kambhampati*

Center for Design Research and Department of Computer Science
Stanford University
Bldg. 530, Duena Street, Stanford CA 94305-4026
e-mail: *rao@sunrise.stanford.edu*

Abstract

We present a theory of plan modification applicable to hierarchical nonlinear planning. Our theory utilizes the validation structure of the stored plans to yield a flexible and conservative plan modification framework. The validation structure, which constitutes a hierarchical explanation of correctness of the plan with respect to the planner's own knowledge of the domain, is annotated on the plan as a by-product of initial planning. Plan modification is characterized as a process of removing inconsistencies in the validation structure of a plan when it is being reused in a new (changed) planning situation. The repair of these inconsistencies involves removing unnecessary parts of the plan and adding new non-primitive tasks to the plan to establish missing or failing validations. The resultant partially reduced plan (with a consistent validation structure) is sent to the planner for complete reduction. We discuss the development of this theory in PRIAR system, and characterize its completeness, coverage, efficiency and limitations.

1. Introduction

The ability to flexibly and conservatively modify existing plans to make them conform to the constraints of a new of changed planning situation is very useful in plan reuse, replanning and incremental planning. While the value of such capability has been acknowledged early in planning research [5, 7], the strategies developed were inflexible in that they could reuse or modify a given plan in only a limited number of situations, and could deal with only a limited variety of applicability failures. There was no general framework for conservatively modifying an existing plan to fit it to the constraints of a new problem situation. A major shortcoming with these approaches was that the stored plans did not represent enough information about the internal dependencies of the plan to permit flexible modification. For example, reuse based on macro-operators [5] built from sequences of primitive plan steps was unable to modify intermediate steps of the macro-operator, as macro-operators did not represent the intermediate decisions and dependencies corresponding to their internal steps. Even in cases where the need for the dependency information was recognized (e.g. [4, 22]), a systematic representation and utilization of such structures in plan reuse and modification was not attempted.

*The support of the Defense Advanced Research Projects Agency and the U.S. Army Engineer Topographic Laboratories under contract DACA76-88-C-0008, and that of Office of Naval Research under contract N00014-88-K-0620 are gratefully acknowledged.

We present a theory of plan modification that allows flexible and conservative modification of plans generated by a hierarchical nonlinear planner. Hierarchical planning is a prominent method of abstraction and least-commitment in domain-independent planning [3]. Our theory of plan modification proposes *validation structure* as a way of representing the internal dependencies of a hierarchical plan and provides algorithms for annotating the validation structure on the plans during plan generation. It systematically explores the utility of the annotated validation structure in guiding and controlling all the processes involved in flexible plan reuse and modification. The PRIAR plan modification system [9, 11, 10, 12] is our implementation of this theory.

The plan modification problem that is addressed in PRIAR is the following: Given (i) a planning problem P^n (specified by a partial description of the initial state I^n and goal state G^n), (ii) an existing plan R^o (generated by a hierarchical nonlinear planner), and the corresponding planning problem P^o, Produce a plan for P^n by minimally modifying R^o.

In the PRIAR reuse framework, the internal dependencies of a hierarchical plan which are relevant to guide its reuse and modification are formalized as the *validation structure* of the plan. The validation structure can be seen as a form of hierarchical explanation of correctness for the plan with respect to the planner. Individual tasks of the hierarchical plan are annotated with information about their role in the plan validation structure. PRIAR provides efficient algorithms for acquiring these annotations as a by-product of planning.

When an existing plan is being reused in a new planning situation, the applicability failures, the redundancies, and the shortcomings that may arise in the process are formally characterized as *inconsistencies* in the plan's validation structure. Reuse in the PRIAR framework is formally seen as a process of repairing the inconsistencies in the validation structure of a given plan when it is mapped into the new problem situation. Given the new problem P^n, and an *annotated* plan R^o, PRIAR's reuse process proceeds in the following steps:

(1) Mapping and Interpretation: An appropriate mapping α between the objects of $[P^o, R^o]$ and P^n is computed, and R^o is mapped into P^n with it. Next, some important differences between P^o and P^n are marked. The resulting interpreted plan, R^i, is typically a plan with an inconsistent validation structure.

(2) Annotation Verification: The inconsistencies in the validation structure of R^i are located, and appropriate repairs are suggested. The repairs include removing parts of R^i that are unnecessary and adding non-primitive tasks (called *refit tasks*) to establish any required new validations. The resulting annotation-verified plan R^a will have a consistent validation structure but is typically only partially reduced. It consists of all the applicable parts of R^i and any refit tasks which are introduced.

(3) Refitting: The refit tasks specified during the annotation verification phase constitute sub-planning problems for the hierarchical planner. The refitting process involves reducing them with the help of the planner. Conservatism is ensured through the use of a heuristic control strategy which minimizes the disturbance to the applicable parts of R^a during this process.

Computational savings stem from the fact that the cost of solving the sub-planning problems during refitting is on the average much less than the cost of solving the entire planning problem from scratch. This is supported by the results of the empirical studies in blocks world, which showed that plan modification proveds 20-98% savings (corresponding to speedup factors of 1.5 to 50) over pure generative planning.

This paper concentrates mainly on the development of the basic modification framework; the details of mapping and refitting control strategies can be found in [9, 12, 10]. The organization of this paper is as follows: Rest of this section provides some necessary preliminaries of hierarchical planning. Section 2 presents the notion of plan validation structure, explains the motivation behind remembering it along with each generated plan, and presents a scheme for annotating it on the plan. Section 3 develops the basic modification processes, and explains how they utilize the plan validation structure. Section 4 contains a discussion completeness, coverage and efficiency of PRIAR modification theory and section 5 provides a brief discussion of related work.

1.1. Preliminaries

This paper makes extensive use of the concepts of hierarchical planning paradigm. A good introduction to this methodology can be found in [3]. Some well known hierarchical planners include NOAH [17], NONLIN [20] and SIPE [21]. In hierarchical planning, a partial plan is represented as a *task network.* A task network is a 3-tuple $\langle T, O, \Pi \rangle$, where T is a collection of tasks, O defines a partial ordering over T, and Π is a set of *protection intervals.* A protection interval is a 3-tuple $\langle E, t_1, t_2 \rangle$, where $t_1, t_2 \in T$, E is an effect of t_1, and E has to necessarily persist up to t_2 [3]. Planning proceeds by selecting a task from the current task network and reducing it with the help of a task reduction schema to more concrete subtasks. This reduction may introduce some harmful interactions with the existing protection intervals, which are handled by introducing additional partial ordering relations among the tasks.

The planner cannot reduce certain distinguished tasks of the domain called *primitive tasks.* (It is assumed that the planner "knows" how to execute such tasks.) Further, if all the required effects of a task are already true in a given partial plan, then that task does not have to be reduced any further (such tasks are called *phantom goals* [3]). A task network is said to represent a *completed plan* when none of its tasks have to be reduced further.

The hierarchical development of a plan $P:\langle T, O, \Pi \rangle$ is captured by its *hierarchical task network* (abbreviated as HTN). A HTN is a 3-tuple, $\langle P:\langle T, O, \Pi \rangle, T^*, D \rangle$, where T^* is a superset of T, and D defines a set of parent-child relations among the tasks of T^*. (The immediate children of a task t are the tasks that resulted from its reduction during planning.) For convenience, we will be referring to T^*, the tasks of the HTN, also as its nodes. We shall refer to the number of leaf nodes in a HTN ($|T|$) as the length of the corresponding plan, and denote it by N_P. For the sake of uniformity, we shall assume that the HTN has two special primitive nodes $n_I, n_G \in T^*$, corresponding respectively to the input state and the goal state of the planning problem. We shall use the notation "$n_1 < n_2$" (where n_1 and n_2 are nodes of HTN) to indicate that n_1 is ordered to *precede* n_2 in the partially orderered plan represented by the HTN. Similarly, "$n_1 > n_2$" denotes that n_1 is ordered to *follow* n_2, and "$n_1 \,//\, n_2$" denotes that there is no ordering relation between the two nodes (n_1 is parallel to n_2). The set consisting of a node n and all its descendents in the HTN is called the sub-reduction of n, and is denoted by $R(n)$. Following [3, 20], we also distinguish two types of plan applicability conditions: the preconditions (such as $Clear(A)$ in the blocks world) which the planner can achieve, and the filter conditions (such as $Block(A)$ in the blocks world) which the planner cannot achieve. Finally, we shall use the notation "$F \vdash f$" to indicate that f deductively follows from the set of facts in F.

2. Validation Structure and Annotations

2.1. Validation Structure

§2.1. Validation: A *validation* is a 4-tuple $\langle E, n_s, C, n_d \rangle$, where n_s and n_d are leaf nodes belonging to the HTN, and the effect E of node n_s (called the *source*) is used to satisfy the applicability condition C of node n_d (called the *destination*). C and E are referred to as the *supported condition* and the *supporting effect* respectively of the validation. As a necessary condition for the existence of a validation v, the partial ordering among the tasks in HTN must satisfy the relation $n_s < n_d$. The *type* of a validation is defined as the type of the applicability condition that the validation supports (one of *filter condition, precondition, phantom goal*). Notice, from section 1.1 that every validation $v: \langle E, n_s, C, n_d \rangle$ corresponds to a protection interval [3] $\langle E, n_s, n_d \rangle$. This correspondence implies that there will only be a finite set of validations corresponding to a given HTN representing the development of a plan; we shall call this set **V**. (If ξ is the maximum number of applicability conditions for any action in the domain, then $|\mathbf{V}|$ is $O(\xi N_P)$ [10].)

Figure 1 shows the validation structure of the plan for solving a block stacking problem 3BS (also shown in the figure). Validations are represented graphically as links between the effect of the source node and the condition of the destination node. (For the sake of exposition, validations supporting conditions of the type $Block(?x)$ have not been shown in the figure.) For example, $\langle On(B,C), n_{15}, On(B,C), n_G \rangle$ is a validation belonging to this plan since $On(B,C)$ is required at the goal state n_G, and is provided by the effect $On(B,C)$ of node n_{15}.

§2.2. Inconsistencies and Consistency of Validation Structure: A validation $v:\langle E, n_s, C, n_d \rangle$ is considered a *failing validation* if either $E \notin effects(n_s)$ or when there exists a node $n \in$ HTN such that n possibly falls between n_s and n_d. A validation $v: \langle E, n_s, C, n_d \rangle$ is considered an *unnecessary validation* iff the node n_d does not require the condition C. (This could happen, for example, if a goal of the plan is no longer necessary in the current problem situation.) Finally, we say that there is a

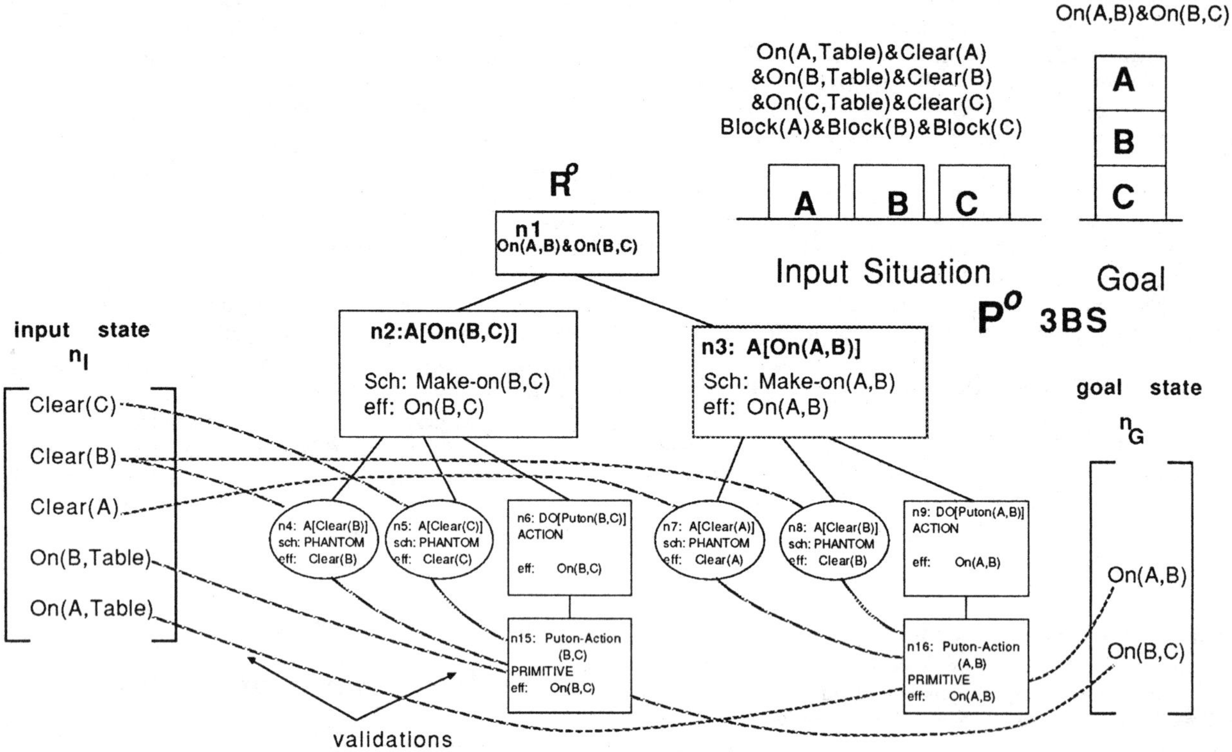

Figure 1. Validation structure of 3BS plan

missing validation corresponding to a condition, node pair $\langle C',n'\rangle$ of the HTN iff $\nexists v: \langle E, n_s, C, n_d\rangle$ *s.t.* $C=C' \wedge n_d=n'$.

The unnecessary, missing or failing validations in a HTN will be referred to as *inconsistencies* in its validation structure. An HTN is said to have a *consistent validation structure* if it does not have any inconsistencies. From these definitions, it should be clear that in a HTN with a consistent validation structure, each applicability condition of a node (including each goal of n_G) will have a non-failing validation supporting it. (Thus, a completely reduced HTN with a consistent validation structure constitutes a valid executable plan.)

2.2. Annotating Validation Structure

Having developed the notion of validation in a plan, our next concern is representing the validation structure of the plan locally as annotations on individual nodes of a HTN. The intent is to let these annotations encapsulate the role played by the sub-reduction below that node in the validation structure of the overall plan, so that they can help in efficiently gauging the effect of any modification at that node on the overall validation structure of the plan. We achieve this as follows: For each node $n \in$ HTN we define the notions of (i) *e-conditions*(n), which are the externally useful validations supplied by the nodes belonging to $R(n)$ (the sub-reduction below n) (ii) *e-preconditions*(n), which are the externally established validations that are consumed by nodes of $R(n)$, and (iii) *p-conditions*(n), which are the external validations of the plan that are required to persist over the nodes of $R(n)$.

§2.3. E-Conditions (External Effect Conditions): The e-conditions of a node n correspond to the validations supported by the effects of any node of $R(n)$ which are used to satisfy applicability conditions of the nodes that lie outside the sub-reduction. Thus, *E-conditions*(n) =

$$\{v_i: \langle E, n_s, C, n_d\rangle \mid v_i \in \mathrm{V};\ n_s \in R(n);\ n_d \notin R(n)\ \}$$

For example, the e-conditions of the node n_3 in the HTN of figure 1 contains just the validation $\langle On(A,B),\ n_{16},\ On(A,B),\ n_G\rangle$ since that is the only effect of $R(n_3)$ which is used outside of $R(n_3)$. The e-conditions provide a way of stating the externally useful effects of a sub-reduction. They can be used to decide when a sub-reduction is no longer necessary, or how a change in its effects will affect the validation structure of the parts of the plan outside the sub-reduction.

§2.4. E-Preconditions (External Preconditions): The e-preconditions of node n correspond to the validations supporting the applicability conditions of any node of $R(n)$ that are satisfied by the effects of the nodes that lie outside of $R(n)$. Thus, *E-preconditions*(n) =

$$\{v_i: \langle E, n_s, C, n_d\rangle \mid v_i \in \mathrm{V};\ n_d \in R(n);\ n_s \notin R(n)\ \}$$

For example, the e-preconditions of the node n_3 in the HTN of figure 1 will include the validations $\langle Clear(A),\ n_I,\ Clear(A),\ n_7\rangle$ and $\langle Clear(B),\ n_I,\ Clear(B),\ n_8\rangle$. The e-preconditions can be used to locate the parts of rest of the plan that will become unnecessary or redundant, if the sub-reduction below this node is changed.

§2.5. P-Conditions (Persistence Conditions): P-conditions of a node n correspond to the protection intervals of the HTN that are external to $R(n)$, and have to persist over some part of $R(n)$ for the rest of the plan to have a consistent validation structure. We define them in the following way:

A validation $v_i: \langle E, n_s, C, n_d\rangle \in \mathrm{V}$ is said to *intersect* the sub-reduction $R(n)$ below a node n (denoted by "$v \otimes R(n)$") if there exists a leaf node $n \in R(n)$ such that n possibly falls between n_s and n_d (for some total ordering of the tasks in the HTN). Using the definition of validation [10], we have $v_i: \langle E, n_s, C, n_d \rangle \otimes R(n)$ iff

$$\begin{bmatrix} \exists n' \in R(n) \; s.t. \; children(n') = \emptyset \wedge \\ (n_s < n' < n_d \vee n_s \,//\, n' \vee n_d \,//\, n') \end{bmatrix}$$

A validation $v_i: \langle E, n_s, C, n_d \rangle \in \mathbf{V}$ is considered a *p-condition* of a node n iff v_i *intersects* $R(n)$ and neither the source nor the destination of the validation belong to $R(n)$. Thus, *P-conditions*(n) =

$$\{ v_i: \langle E, n_s, C, n_d \rangle \mid v_i \in \mathbf{V};\ n_s, n_d \notin R(n);\ v_i \otimes R(n) \}$$

From this definition, it follows that if the effects of any node of the $R(n)$ violate the validations corresponding to the *p-conditions* of n, then there will be a potential for harmful interactions. As an example, the *p*-conditions of the node n_3 in the HTN of figure 1 will contain the validation $\langle On(B,C), n_{15}, On(B,C), n_G \rangle$ since the condition $On(B,C)$, which is achieved at n_{15} would have to persist over $R(n_3)$ to support the condition (goal) $On(B,C)$ at n_G. The *p*-conditions help in gauging the effect of changes made at the sub-reduction below a node on the validations external to that sub-reduction. This is of particular importance in localizing the refitting [9].

2.3. Computing Annotations

In the PRIAR framework, at the end of a planning session, the HTN showing the development of the plan is retained, and each node of the HTN is annotated with the following information: (1) *Schema*(n), the schema instance that reduced node n (2) *e-preconditions*(n) (3) *e-conditions*(n), and (4) *p-conditions*(n). The node annotations are computed in two phases: First, the annotations for the leaf nodes of the HTN are computed with the help of the set of validations, **V**, and the partial ordering relations of HTN. Next, using the relations between the annotations of a node and its children (which can be easily derived from the definitions of the previous section; see [10]), the annotations are propagated to non-leaf nodes in a bottom up breadth-first fashion. The exact algorithms are given in [10], and are fairly straightforward to understand given the development of the previous sections. The time complexity of annotation computation is $O(N_P^2)$, where N_P is the length of the plan (number of leaf nodes in the HTN).

While the procedures discussed above compute the annotations of a HTN in one-shot, often during plan modification, PRIAR needs to add and remove validations from the HTN one at a time. To handle this, PRIAR also provides algorithms to update node annotations consistently when incrementally adding or deleting validations from the HTN. These are used to re-annotate the HTN and to maintain a consistent validation structure after small changes are made to the plan. They can also be called by the planner any time it establishes or removes a new validation (or protection interval) during the development of the plan, to dynamically maintain a consistent validation structure. The time complexity of these algorithms is $O(N_P)$ [10].

3. Modification by Annotation Verification

We will now turn to the plan modification process, and demonstrate the utility of annotated validation structure in guiding plan modification. Throughout the ensuing discussion, we will be following the simple example case of modifying the plan for the three block stacking problem 3BS (*i.e.*, R^o= 3BS) shown on the left side in figure 2 to produce a plan for the four block stacking

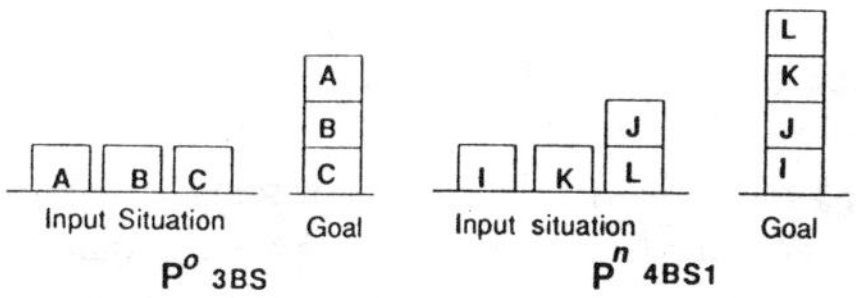

Figure 2. 3BS→4BS1 Reuse problem

problem 4BS1 (*i.e.*, P^n= 4BS1) shown on the right side. We shall refer to this as the 3BS→4BS1 example.

3.1. Mapping and Interpretation

In PRIAR, the set of possible mappings between $[P^o, R^o]$ and P^n are found through a partial unification of the goals of the two problems. There are typically several semantically consistent mappings between the two planning situations, and selecting the right mapping can considerably reduce the cost of modification. The mapping and retrieval methodology used by PRIAR [10, 12] achieves this by selecting mappings based on the number and type of inconsistencies that would be caused in the validation structure of R^o. As the details of this strategy are beyond the scope of this paper, for the purposes of this paper, we shall simply assume that such a mapping is provided to us. (It should be noted that this mapping stage will not be required if the objective is to modify an existing plan in response to changes in its own specifications.) Once a mapping α is selected, the interpreted plan R^i is constructed by mapping R^o along with its annotations into the new planning situation P^n, and marking the differences between the specifications of the old and new planning situations. These differences, marked in I^i and G^i, serve to focus the annotation verification procedure on the inconsistencies in the validation structure of the interpreted plan.

In the 3BS→4BS1 example, let us assume that the mapping strategy selects $\alpha = [A \rightarrow L, B \rightarrow K, C \rightarrow J]$ as the mapping from 3BS and 4BS1. With this mapping, $Clear(L)$ is no longer true in the input specification of 4BS1. So it will be marked *out* in I^i. The facts $On(J,L)$, $On(I,Table)$ and $Clear(I)$ are true in 4BS1 but not in 3BS, so they will be marked as *new* facts in I^i. Similarly, as $On(J,I)$ is not a goal of 3BS but is a goal of 4BS1, it will be marked as an *extra goal* in G^i. There are no *unnecessary* goals. At the end of this processing, R^i, I^i and G^i are sent to the annotation verification procedure.

3.2. Annotation Verification and Refit Task Specification

At the end of the interpretation procedure, R^i may not have a consistent validation structure (see §2.2) as the differences between the old and the new problem situations (as marked by the interpretation procedure) may be causing some inconsistencies in the validation structure of R^i. These inconsistencies will be referred to as *applicability failures*, as these are the reasons why R^i cannot be directly applied to P^n. The purpose of the annotation verification procedure is to modify R^i such that the result, R^a, will be a partially reduced HTN with a consistent validation structure.

The annotation verification procedure achieves this goal by first localizing and characterizing the applicability failures caused by the differences in I^i and G^i, and then appropriately modifying the validation structure of R^i to repair those failures.

It groups the applicability failures into one of several classes depending on the type of the inconsistencies and the type of the conditions involved in those inconsistencies. The repairs are suggested based on this classification, and involve removal of unnecessary parts of the HTN and/or addition of non-primitive tasks (called refit tasks) to establish missing and failing validations. The individual repair actions taken to repair the different types of inconsistencies are briefly described below; they make judicious use of the node annotations to modify R^i appropriately (see [10, 12] for the detailed procedures). In [10], we show that the time complexity of the annotation-verification process is polynomial ($O(|V||N_P^3|)$) in the length of the plan.

[1] Unnecessary Validations—Pruning Unrequired Parts: If the supported condition C of a validation $v:\langle E, n_s, C, n_d \rangle$ is no longer required, then v can be removed from the plan along with all the parts of the plan whose sole purpose is supplying those validations. The removal can be accomplished in a clean fashion with the help of the annotations on R^i. After removing v validation from the HTN (which will also involve incrementally re-annotating the HTN, see section 2.3), the HTN is checked for any node n_v that has no e-conditions. If such a node exists, then its sub-reduction, $R(n_v)$ has no useful purpose, and thus its nodes can be removed from the HTN. This essentially involves backtracking over the task reductions in that sub-reduction, and removing any ordering relations that were introduced as a result of those reductions. This removal turns the e-preconditions of n_v into unnecessary validations, and they are handled in the same way recursively.

[2] Missing Validations—Adding Tasks for Achieving Extra Goals: An extra goal is any goal of the new problem that is not a goal of the old plan, and thus is un-supported by any validation in R^i. The general procedure for repairing missing validations (including the extra goals, which are considered conditions of n_G) is to create a refit task of the form *Achieve*$[G]$, and to add it to the HTN in such a way that it follows the initial node n_I, and precedes the node which requires the unsupported condition (in this case n_G). Establishing a new validation in this way necessitates checking to see if its introduction leads to any new failing validations in the plan; the planner's interaction detection routines are used for this purpose. Finally, the annotations of the nodes of the HTN are updated (with the help of incremental annotation procedures) to reflect the introduction of the new validation.

[3] Failing Validations: The facts of I^i which are marked "*out*" during the interpretation process, may be supplying validations to the applicability conditions or goals of the interpreted plan R^i. The treatment of such failing validations depends upon the types of the conditions that are being supported by the validation. We distinguish three types of validation failures—validations supporting preconditions, phantom goals and filter conditions respectively—and discuss each of them in turn below[1].

(3.*i*) *Failing Precondition Validations:* If a validation supporting a precondition of some node in the HTN is found to be failing, because its supporting effect E is marked *out*, it can simply be reachieved. The procedure involves creating a refit task, n_v:*Achieve*$[E]$, to re-establish the validation v, and adding it to the HTN in such a way that it follows the source node and precedes the destination node of the failing validation. The validation structure of the plan is updated so that the failing validation will be replaced by an equivalent validation to be supplied by n_v. Finally, the annotations on the other nodes of the HTN are adjusted incrementally to reflect this change.

(3.*ii*) *Failing Phantom Validations:* If the validation supporting a phantom goal node is failing, then the node cannot remain phantom. The repair involves undoing the phantomization, so that the planner would know that it has to re-achieve that goal. Once this change is made, the failing validation is no longer required and can be removed.

(3.*iii*) *Failing Filter Condition Validations:* In contrast to the validations supporting the preconditions and the phantom goals, the validations supporting failing filter conditions cannot be reachieved by the planner. Instead, the planning decisions which introduced those filter conditions into the plan have to be undone. That is, if the validation $v:\langle E, n_s, C, n_d \rangle$ supporting a filter condition C of a node n_d is failing, and n' is the ancestor of n, whose reduction introduced C into the HTN originally, then the sub-reduction $R(n')$ has to be replaced, and n' has to be re-reduced with the help of an alternate schema instance. So as to least affect the validation structure of the rest of the HTN, any new reduction of n' is be *expected* to supply (or consume) the validations previously supplied (or consumed) by the replaced reduction. Any validations not supplied by the new reduction would have to be re-established by alternate means, and the validations not consumed by the new reduction would have to be pruned. Since there is no way of knowing what the new reduction will be until refitting time, this processing is deferred until that time.

[4] P-Phantom-Validations—Exploiting Serendipitous Effects: It is possible that some of the validations that R^i establishes via step addition can be established directly from the interpreted initial state, thus shortening the plan. Such validations, called *p–phantom validations*, are located by collecting validations whose source node is *not* n_I, and checking to see if their supporting effects are now true in the *new* facts of I^i. For each p-phantom validation, PRIAR checks to see if an equivalent validation can actually be established from the initial state, n_I without introducing new interactions (and thereby causing substantial revisions) in the plan. If so, the p-phantom validation becomes redundant, and is treated as an unnecessary validation. The parts of the plan that are currently establishing this validation are pruned from the HTN, thus effectively shortening the plan.

Example: Figure 3 shows R^a, the HTN produced by the annotation verification procedure for the 3BS→4BS1 example. The input to the annotation verification procedure is the interpreted plan R^i discussed in section 3.1. In this example, R^i contains a failing phantom validation and a missing validation corresponding to an extra goal. The goal $On(J,I)$ of G^i is an extra goal, and is not supported by any validation of the HTN. So, the refit task n_{10}:*Achieve*$[On(J,I)]$ is added to the task network, in parallel to the existing plan, such that $n_I < n_{10} < n_G$. n_{10} now supplies the validation $\langle On(J,I), n_{10}, On(J,I), n_I \rangle$ to the goal $On(J,I)$. Next, the fact $Clear(L)$, which is marked *out* in I^i, causes the validation $\langle Clear(L), n_I, Clear(L), n_7 \rangle$ supporting the phantom goal node n_7 to fail. So, the phantom goal node n_7 is converted into a refit task to be reduced. It no longer needs the failing phantom validation from n_I. Notice that the HTN shown in this figure corresponds to a partially reduced task network which consists of the applicable parts of the old plan and the two refit tasks suggested by the annotation verification

[1] In NONLIN terminology [19] the precondition validations support the "unsupervised conditions" of a schema, while the phantom goal validations support the "supervised conditions" of a schema.

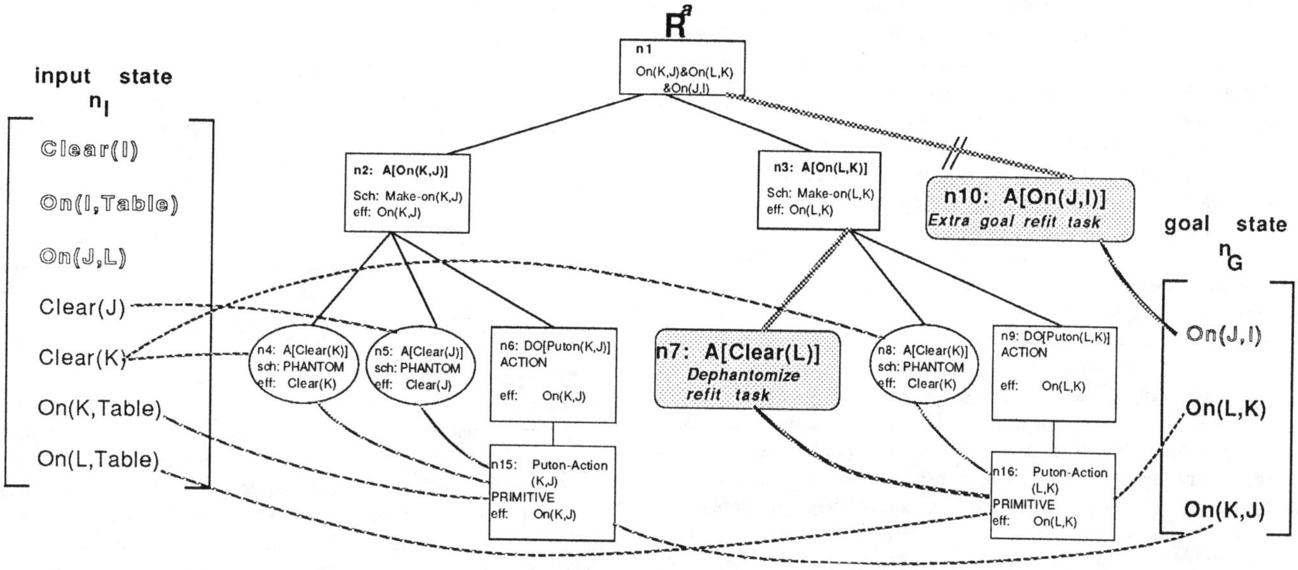

Figure 3. Annotation-Verified plan for 3BS→4BS1

procedure. It has a consistent validation structure, but it contains two unreduced refit tasks n_{10} and n_7 which have to be reduced.

3.3. Refitting

To produce an executable plan for P^n, R^a (the HTN after the annotation verification process) has to be completely reduced. This process, called refitting, essentially involves reduction of the refit tasks that were introduced into R^a during the annotation verification process. The responsibility of reducing the refit tasks is delegated to the planner by sending R^a to the planner. An important difference between refitting and from-scratch (or generative) planning is that in refitting the planner starts with an already partially reduced HTN. For this reason, solving P^n by reducing R^a is less expensive on the average than solving P^n from scratch.

The procedure used for reducing refit tasks is fairly similar to the one the planner normally uses for reducing non-primitive tasks (see section 1.1), with the following important difference. An important consideration in refitting is to minimize the disturbance to the applicable parts of R^a during the reduction of the refit tasks. To ensure this *conservatism* of refitting, the default schema selection procedure is modified in such a way that for each refit task, it selects a schema instance that is expected to give rise to the least amount of disturbance to the validation structure of R^a. The annotated validation structure of the plan helps in this selection by estimating the effect of reduction at a refit task on the rest of the plan. A detailed presentation of this heuristic control strategy is beyond the scope of this paper; the interested reader is referred to [9, 10]. Once the planer selects an appropriate schema instance in this way, it reduces the refit task by that schema instance in the normal way, detecting and resolving any interactions arising in the process.

Example: Figure 4 shows the hierarchical task reduction structure of the plan for the 4BS1 problem that PRIAR produces by reducing the annotation-verified task network (shown in Figure 3). (The top down hierarchical reductions are shown in left to right fashion in the figure. The dashed arrow lines show the temporal precedence relations developed between the nodes of the HTN.) The shaded nodes correspond to the parts of the interpreted plan R^i that survive after the annotation verification and refitting process. The white nodes represent the refit tasks added during the annotation verification process, and their subsequent reductions. In the current example, the refitting control strategy recommends that the planner reduce the refit task $A[Clear(L)]$ by putting J on I rather than putting J on *Table* or on K. This decision in turn leads to a shortened plan by allowing the extra goal refit task $A[On(J,I)]$ to be achieved by phantomization.

4. Completeness, Coverage and Efficiency

Completeness : The validation structure based modification is complete in that it will correctly handle all types of applicability failures that can arise during plan modification, and provide the planner with a partially reduced HTN with a consistent validation structure. In particular, our definition of inconsistencies (see §2.2) captures all types of applicability failures that can arise due to a change in the specification of the problem; and our annotation verification procedure provides methods to correctly modify the plan validation structure to handle each type of inconsistency (see section 3.2), without introducing any new inconsistencies into the HTN (a proof is provided in [10].)

Coverage : The validation structure developed here covers the internal dependencies of the plans produced by most traditional

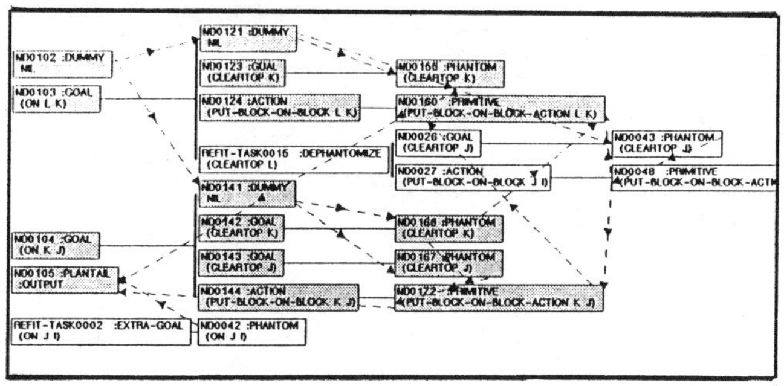

Figure 4. The plan produced by PRIAR 3BS→4BS1

hierarchical planners. The captured dependencies can be seen as a form of explanation of correctness of the plan with respect to the planner's own domain model. By ensuring the consistency of the validation structure of the modified plan, PRIAR guarantees correctness of the modified plan with respect to the planner. However, it should be noted that as the dependencies captured by the validation structure do not represent any optimality considerations underlying the plan, the optimality of modification is not guaranteed. Further, since the modification is integrated with the planner, failures arising from the incorrectness or incompleteness of the planner's own domain model will not be detected or handled by the modification theory. Of course, these should not be construed as limitations of the theory, as its goal is to improve the average case efficiency of the planner.

Flexibility and Efficiency: In the worst case, when none of the steps of R^o are applicable in the new situation, annotation verification will return a degenerate HTN containing refit tasks for all the goals of P^n. In such extreme cases PRIAR may wind up doing a polynomial amount of extra work compared to a pure generative planner. In other words, the worst case complexity of plan modification remains same as the worst case complexity of generative planning. However, on the average, PRIAR will be able to minimize the repetition of planning effort (thereby accrue possibly exponential savings in planning time) by providing the planner with a partially reduced HTN, and conservatively controlling refitting such that the already reduced (applicable) parts of R^a are left undisturbed.

The claims of flexibility and average case efficiency are also supported by the empirical evaluation experiments that were conducted on PRIAR. The plot in figure 5 shows the computational savings achieved when different blocks world problems are solved from scratch and by reusing a range of existing blocks world plans (see [10] for the details of the experimental strategy). For example, the curve marked 7BS1 shows the savings afforded by solving a particular seven-block problem by reusing several different blocks world plans (indicated on the x-axis). The relative savings over the entire corpus of experiments ranged from 30% to 98% (corresponding to speedup factors of 1.5 to 50) with the highest gains shown for the more difficult problems tested. These results also showed that as the size of P^n increases, the computational savings afforded by PRIAR stay very high for a range of reused plans with varying amount of similarity; consider, for example, the plot for the 12BS1 problem in the figure. This latter behavior lends support to the claim of flexibility of the modification framework.

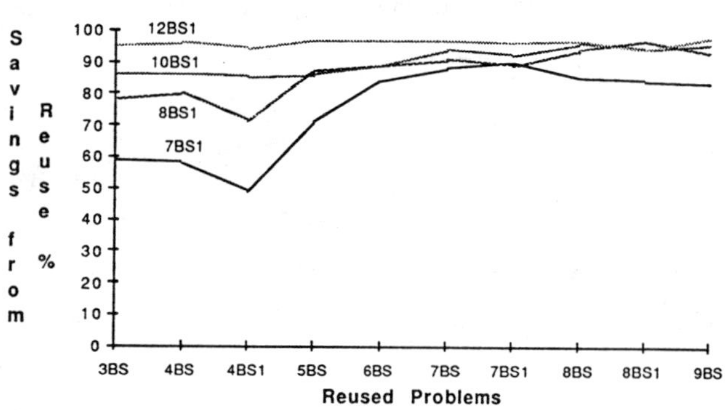

Figure 5. Variation of performance with problem size and similarity

5. Related Work

Representations of plan internal dependency structure have been used by several planners previously to guide plan modification (e.g., the triangle tables and the macro operators of [5] and [8]; the decision graphs of [7] and [4]; the plan rationale representation of [22]). However, our work is the first to systematically characterize the nature of such dependency structures and their role in plan modification. It subsumes and formalizes the previous approaches, provides a better coverage of applicability failures, and allows the reuse of a plan in a larger variety of new planning situations. Unlike the previous approaches, it also explicitly focuses on the flexibility and conservatism of the plan modification. The modification is fully integrated with the generative planning, and aims to reduce the average case cost of producing correct plans. In this sense, PRIAR's strategies are complementary to the plan debugging strategies proposed in GORDIUS [18] and CHEF [6], which use an explanation of correctness of the plan with respect to an external (deeper) domain model (generated through a causal simulation of the plan) to guide the debugging of the plan and to compensate for the inadequacies of the planner's own domain model. Similarly, PRIAR's validation structure based approach to plan modification stands in contrast to other approaches which rely on domain dependent heuristic modification of the plan (e.g. [6, 1, 16]). Our approach of grounding plan modification on validation structure guarantees the correctness of the modification with respect to planner's domain model and reduces the need for a costly modify-test-debug type approach.

6. Conclusion

Our theory of plan modification utilizes the validation structure of the stored plans to yield a flexible and conservative plan modification framework. The validation structure, which constitutes a hierarchical explanation of correctness of the plan with respect to the planner's own knowledge of the domain, is annotated on the plan as a by-product of initial planning. Plan modification is characterized as a process of removing inconsistencies in the validation structure of a plan, when it is being reused in a new (changed) planning situation. The repair of these inconsistencies involves removing unnecessary parts of the HTN, and adding new high-level tasks to it to re-establish failing validations. The resultant partially reduced HTN (with a consistent validation structure) is given to the planner for complete reduction. We discussed the development of this theory in PRIAR system, and characterized its completeness, coverage, efficiency and limitations. This theory provides unified treatment for plan modification involved in replanning, plan reuse and incremental planning.

Acknowledgements

Jim Hendler, Lindley Darden and Larry Davis have influenced the development of the ideas presented here. Jack Mostow and Austin Tate provided useful comments on previous drafts. All three AAAI referees provided very informative reviews. To all, my thanks.

References

[*Please consult the list of references under the companion article* **"Mapping and Retrieval During Plan Reuse: A Validation Structure Based Approach,"** *also in these proceedings.*]

Introducing the Tileworld: Experimentally Evaluating Agent Architectures *

Martha E. Pollack
Artificial Intelligence Center *and*
Center for the Study of Language and Information
SRI International
333 Ravenswood Ave.
Menlo Park, California 94025
pollack@ai.sri.com

Marc Ringuette
School of Computer Science
Carnegie Mellon University
Pittsburgh, Pennsylvania 15123
mnr@cs.cmu.edu

Abstract

We describe a system called Tileworld, which consists of a simulated robot agent and a simulated environment which is both dynamic and unpredictable. Both the agent and the environment are highly parameterized, enabling one to control certain characteristics of each. We can thus experimentally investigate the behavior of various meta-level reasoning strategies by tuning the parameters of the agent, and can assess the success of alternative strategies in different environments by tuning the environmental parameters. Our hypothesis is that the appropriateness of a particular meta-level reasoning strategy will depend in large part upon the characteristics of the environment in which the agent incorporating that strategy is situated. We describe our initial experiments using Tileworld, in which we have been evaluating a version of the meta-level reasoning strategy proposed in earlier work by one of the authors [Bratman *et al.*, 1988].

Introduction

Recently there has been a surge of interest in systems that are capable of intelligent behavior in dynamic, unpredictable environments. Because agents inevitably have bounded computational resources, their deliberations about what to do take time, and so, in dynamic environments, they run the risk that things will change while they reason. Indeed, things may change in ways that undermine the very assumptions upon which the reasoning is proceeding. The agent may begin a deliberation problem with a particular set of available options, but, in a dynamic environment, new options may arise, and formerly existing options disappear, during the course of the deliberation. An agent that blindly pushes forward with the original deliberation problem, without regard to the amount of time it is taking or the changes meanwhile going on, is not likely to make rational decisions.

One solution that has been proposed eliminates explicit execution-time reasoning by compiling into the agent all decisions about what to do in particular situations [Agre and Chapman, 1987, Brooks, 1987, Kaelbling, 1988]. This is an interesting endeavor, but its ultimate feasibility for complex domains remains an open question.

An alternative is to design agents that perform explicit reasoning at execution time, but manage that reasoning by engaging in *meta-level reasoning*. Within the past few years, researchers in AI have provided theoretical analyses of meta-level reasoning, often applying decision-theoretic notions to it [Boddy and Dean, 1989, Horvitz, 1987, Russell and Wefald, 1989]. In addition, architectural specifications for agents performing meta-level reasoning have been developed [Bratman *et al.*, 1988], and prototype systems that engage in meta-level reasoning have been implemented [Cohen *et al.*, 1989, Georgeff and Ingrand, 1989]. The project we describe in this paper involves the implementation of a system for experimentally evaluating competing theoretical and architectural proposals.

More specifically, we have been constructing a system called Tileworld, which consists of a simulated robot agent and a simulated environment which is both dynamic and unpredictable. Both the agent and the environment are highly parameterized, enabling one to control certain characteristics of each. We can thus experimentally investigate the behavior of various meta-level reasoning strategies by tuning the parameters of the agent, and can assess the success of alternative strategies in different environments by tuning the environmental parameters. Our hypothesis is that the appropriateness of a particular meta-level reasoning strategy will depend in large part upon the characteristics of the environment in which the agent incorporating that strategy is situated. We shall describe below how the parameters of our simulated environment correspond to interesting characteristics of real, dynamic environments.

*This research was supported by the Office of Naval Research under Contract No. N00014-89-C-0095, by a contract with the Nippon Telegraph and Telephone Corporation and by a gift from the System Development Foundation.

```
# # # # # # # # # # # # # # # # # # # #
#     T   T         T       T         #
#       #                   2 2     T #
#       #                   2         #
#       # # 5               T         #
#     # # # 5 T                       #
#         # 5   T         a         T #
#       T                             #
#         T     T             T T     #
#               # T # T   T           #
#       T       # # # #               #
#     #           # #         T       #
#     #   T   T   T       T           #
#     #                       #       #
#                         T   #   #   #
#     T                   # # # # #   #
#     # # # # #                       #
#     #                     T T       #
#                   T           T   T #
# # # # # # # # # # # # # # # # # # # #
```

a = *agent*, # = *obstacle*, T = *tile*, < *digits* > = *hole*

Figure 1: A Typical Tileworld Starting State

In our initial experiments using Tileworld, we have been evaluating a version of the meta-level reasoning strategy proposed in earlier work by one of the authors [Bratman *et al.*, 1988]. However, the Tileworld can be used to evaluate a range of competing proposals, such as the ones mentioned above: agents instantiating many alternative proposals can readily be imported into the Tileworld environment.

The Tileworld Environment

The Tileworld is a chessboard-like grid on which there are agents, tiles, obstacles, and holes. An agent is a unit square which is able to move up, down, left, or right, one cell at a time, and can, in so doing, move tiles. A tile is a unit square which "slides": rows of tiles can be pushed by the agent. An obstacle is a group of grid cells which are immovable. A hole is a group of grid cells, each of which can be "filled in" by a tile when the tile is moved on top of the hole cell; the tile and particular hole cell disappear, leaving a blank cell. When all the cells in a hole are filled in, the agent gets points for filling the hole. The agent knows ahead of time how valuable the hole is; its overall goal is to get as many points as possible by filling in holes.

Figure 1 depicts a typical Tileworld starting state. A Tileworld simulation takes place dynamically: it begins in a state which is randomly generated by the simulator according to a set of parameters, and changes continually over time. Objects (holes, tiles, and obstacles) appear and disappear at rates determined by parameters set by the experimenter, while at the same time the agent moves around and pushes tiles into holes. The dynamic aspect of a Tileworld simulation distinguishes it from many earlier domains that have been used for studying AI planning, such as blocks-world.

The Tileworld can be viewed a rough abstraction of the Robot Delivery Domain, in which a mobile robot roams the halls of an office delivering messages and objects in response to human requests. We have been able to draw a fairly close correspondence between the two domains (i.e., the appearance of a hole corresponds to a request, the hole itself corresponds to a delivery location, tiles correspond to messages or objects, the agent to the robot, the grid to hallways, and the simulator time to real time).

Features of the domain put a variety of demands on the agent. Its spatial complexity is nontrivial: a simple hill-climbing strategy can have modest success, but when efficient action is needed, more extensive reasoning is necessary. But the time spent in reasoning has an associated cost, both in lost opportunities and in unexpected changes to the world; thus the agent must make trade-offs between speed and accuracy, and must monitor the execution of its plans to ensure success. Time pressures also become significant as multiple goals vie for the agent's attention.

Of course, a single Tileworld simulation, however interesting, will give only one data point in the design space of robot agents. To explore the space more vigorously, we must be able to vary the challenges that the domain presents to the agent. We have therefore parameterized the domain, and provided "knobs" which can be adjusted to set the values of those parameters.

The knob settings control the evolution of a Tileworld simulation. Some of the knobs were alluded to earlier, for instance, those that control the frequency of appearance and disappearance of each object type. Other knobs control the number and average size of each object type. Still other knobs are used to control factors such as the shape of the distribution of scores associated with holes, or the choice between the instantaneous disappearance of a hole and a slow decrease in value (a hard bound versus a soft bound). For each set of parameter settings, an agent can be tested on tens or hundreds of randomly generated runs automatically. Agents can be compared by running them on the same set of pseudo-random worlds; the simulator is designed to minimize noise and preserve fine distinctions in performance.

The Tileworld environment is intended to provide a testbed for studying a wide range of dynamic domains and tasks to be performed in them. It exhibits spatial complexity, a central feature of many such domains; and it includes tasks of varying degrees of importance and difficulty. It is generic: although we have explored connections between Tileworld and tasks involving robot delivery, Tileworld is not tightly coupled to any particular application domain, but instead allows an experimenter to study key characteristics of whatever domain he or she is interested in, by varying parameter settings. For example, the experimenter can focus on domains in which the central characteristic is a wide distribution of task values (simulated in Tileworld by hole scores), or of task difficulty (simulated by hole size). In this regard, Tileworld differs from the Phoenix simulator [Cohen *et al.*, 1989], which is more closely tied to a particular application. Instead, the goals of the Tileworld project are closer to those of the MICE simulator [Durfee and Montgomery, 1990]. However, Tileworld is a more highly dynamic environment than MICE. Also, where MICE is used to focus on issues of real-time inter-agent coordination, Tileworld is intended as a framework for the more general investigation of intelligent behavior in dynamic environments.

Using Plans to Constrain Reasoning

The agent we have implemented and used in our experiments instantiates IRMA—the Intelligent Resource-Bounded Machine Architecture [Bratman *et al.*, 1988]. IRMA builds on observations made by Bratman [Bratman, 1987] that agents who are situated in dynamic environments benefit from having plans because their plans can constrain the amount of subsequent reasoning they need to perform. Two constraining roles of plans concern us here:

- An agent's plans focus subsequent means-end reasoning so that the agent can, in general, concentrate on elaborating its existing plans, rather than on computing all possible courses of action that might be undertaken.
- An agent's plans restrict the set of further potential courses of action to which it needs to give full consideration, by filtering out options that are inconsistent with the performance of what the agent already plans to do.

The first role of plans has always been at least implicit in the standard models of AI planning: AI planners compute means to goals that the agent already has. The second has a more dramatic effect on the architecture we are investigating: it leads to the introduction of a *filtering mechanism*, which manages execution-time reasoning by restricting deliberation, in general, to options that are compatible with the performance of already intended actions. (To have the desired effect of lessening the amount of reasoning needed, the filtering mechanism must be computationally inexpensive, relative to the cost of deliberation.)

Of course, a rational agent cannot *always* remain committed to its existing plans. Sometimes plans may be subject to reconsideration or abandonment in light of changes in belief. But if an agent constantly reconsiders its plans, they will not limit deliberation in the way they need to. Thus, an agent's plans should be reasonably stable.

To achieve stability while at the same time allowing for reconsideration of plans when necessary, the filtering mechanism should have two components. The first checks a new option for compatibility with the existing plans. The second, an override mechanism, encodes the conditions under which some portion of the existing plans is to be suspended and weighed against some other option. The filter override mechanism operates in parallel with the compatibility filter. For a new option to pass through the filter, it must either pass the compatibility check or else trigger an override by matching one of the conditions in the override mechanism. A critical task for the designer of an IRMA-agent is to construct a filter override mechanism so that it embodies the right degree of sensitivity to the problems and opportunities of the agent's environment.

The options that pass through the filter are subject to deliberation. The deliberation process is what actually selects the actions the agent will form intentions towards. In other words, it is the deliberation process that performs the type of decision-making that is the focus of traditional decision theory. The filtering mechanism thus serves to frame particular decision problems, which the deliberation process then solves.

The process of deliberation is different from means-ends reasoning in our view, and this distinction is worth discussing further. As we see it, deliberation is deciding *which* of a set of options to pursue, while means-ends reasoning is more a process of determining *how* to achieve a given goal. We see means-ends reasoning producing *options* (candidate plans to achieve a goal), which can then be the subject of deliberation.

This may be a surprising distinction to those familiar with the standard AI planning paradigm, in which the job of a planner is usually to produce the single best plan according to some set of criteria. Any deliberation which is to be done in such a system is done by the planner, and it might be argued that a planner is the best place for such reasoning. Certainly some pruning of alternatives must be done by a planner; however, there are reasons to believe that some deliberation belongs outside the planner. In some situations it is appropriate to have several means-ends reasoners with differences in solution quality and time required; these must be invoked appropriately and a single solution chosen. In other circumstances it is desirable to engage in a decision-theoretic analysis of competing alternatives. Consequently, we have maintained the distinction between deliberation and means-ends reasoning in our system.

The Tileworld Agent

In implementing an IRMA-agent for the Tileworld, we adopted a model of a robot with two sets of processing hardware. One processor executes a short control cycle (the *act cycle*), acting on previously formulated plans and monitoring the world for changes. The second processor executes a longer cycle (the *reasoning cycle*), which permits computations with lengths of up to several seconds.

The act cycle is straightforward; the agent performs

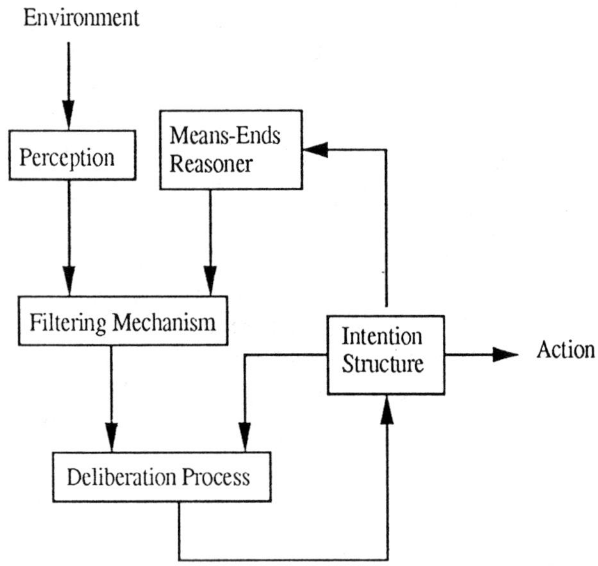

Figure 2: Tileworld Agent Architecture

those acts that have been identified during the previous reasoning cycle, monitoring for limited kinds of failures. Perception also occurs during the act cycle: the agent can access a global map of the world that indicates the locations of all objects, as well as the score and time remaining to timeout for all holes.

The reasoning cycle makes decisions about what goals to pursue and how to pursue them. The portion of the agent architecture that controls reasoning is depicted in Figure 2. Processing is aimed at maintaining the *intention structure,* a time-ordered set of tree-structured plans that represents that agent's current intentions. During any given reasoning cycle, one of two things can happen:

- Potential additions to the intention structure, called *options,* can be considered by the filtering and deliberation processes. These options can come from two sources. One, the agent may perceive environmental changes that suggest new options—in Tileworld, this occurs when new holes or tiles appear. Alternatively, options may be suggested by the means-end reasoner.
- Means-ends reasoning can be performed to produce new options that can serve as means to current intentions. The bulk of our means-ends reasoner is a special-purpose route planner.

We will concentrate here on the filtering and deliberation mechanisms. All options are in principle subject to filtering and deliberation; so far, however, we have confined such reasoning to top-level options, i.e., options to fill a particular hole.

Recall that the IRMA filtering mechanism has two parts: the compatibility filter and the filter override. An option passes the filter if it is either compatible with all existing intentions, or if it triggers an override.

Compatibility checking of top-level options, as implemented, is straightforward. A top-level option is either to fill a hole *now* or *later;* if the agent already has a current intention to fill a particular hole *now,* then an option to fill some other hole *now* is incompatible. All intentions to fill a hole *later* are compatible with each other.

The filter override must identify options that are potentially valuable enough that they warrant deliberation even if they fail the compatibility test. The simplest override mechanism compares the score of a hole being considered as an option to that of the hole currently being filled. If the difference between them equals or exceeds some threshold value v, then the new option passes the filter. The threshold value is set by a Tileworld parameter. Sometimes it may sensibly be set to a negative value: in that case, a new option could be subject to deliberation even if it involved filling a hole with a lower score than the hole currently being filled. This might be reasonable, since the new hole may, for instance, be much easier to fill. Setting the threshold value to $-\infty$ results in all options being subject to deliberation.

Recall that an option's passing the filter does not lead directly to its introduction into the intention structure: instead, it is passed to the deliberation process for more detailed consideration and comparison with the current intention. Deliberation may involve extensive analysis; deliberation strategies can be chosen in the Tileworld agent by the setting of a parameter. We currently have implemented two deliberation strategies.

The simpler deliberation module evaluates competing top-level options by selecting the one with the higher score. When there is a nonnegative threshold value in the filter, this mode of deliberation always selects the new option; with a negative threshold value, it instead always maintains the current intention. This illustrates a general point: if deliberation is extremely simple, it may be redundant to posit separate deliberation and filtering processes.

A more sophisticated deliberation strategy computes the likely value (LV) of a top-level goal. LV is an estimate of expected utility, combining information about reward (score) with information about likelihood of success. For a given option to fill a hole h, LV is computed as

$$LV(h) = \frac{score(h)}{dist(a,h) + \sum_{i=1}^{n} 2 * dist(h,t_i)}$$

where $score(h)$ is the reward for filling the hole, $dist(a,h)$ is the distance between the agent and the hole, n is the number of tiles needed to fill the hole, and $dist(h,t_i)$ is the distance from the hole to the ith closest tile. The factor of 2 occurs because the agent must traverse the interval in both directions, i.e., it must make a "round trip". If there are fewer than n

tiles available, $LV(h)$ is zero.

We intend to design additional deliberation modules, including one that performs complete means-end reasoning for all options under consideration before making its decision. Such a deliberator must not be invoked carelessly; we expect our filtering mechanism to be increasingly useful as we add more sophisticated and time-consuming deliberation components.

Preliminary Experiments

With both the simulator and the agent in place, we are in a position to conduct experimental studies of the the performance of the agent. By adjusting the Tileworld "knobs", we can control a number of domain characteristics. We can vary what we call *dynamism* (the rate at which new holes appear), *hostility* (the rate at which obstacles appear), *variability of utility* (differences in hole scores), *variability of difficulty* (differences in hole sizes and distances from tiles), and *hard/soft bounds* (holes having either hard timeouts or gradually decaying in value). There are also variables we can adjust in the agent: *act/think rate* (the relative speeds of acting and thinking), the filter's *threshold level*, and the *sophistication of the deliberation mechanism.*

Experiment 1

To begin with, we set all of these parameters to provide a baseline environment which is dynamic, variable, and moderately paced. In this environment, a competent agent can achieve reasonable scores, but is penalized for wasting time or making poor choices. We will start by comparing the simple deliberation mechanism, based on score value, with the LV evaluator, which provides a better estimate of marginal utility. For orientation, we have also included the results of a human playing the role of the agent in the same simulation; and to gain an idea of the benefit of acting in parallel with reasoning, we have included results for an agent that that acts and reasons serially.

All of these agents were tested in the baseline environment and in a similar but more rapidly changing one. In the faster environment, objects appear and disappear on the average ten times more quickly, but the agent can also move ten times more quickly. However, the agent's reasoning takes place at the same rate of speed as in the baseline case, so the opportunity cost of reasoning is correspondingly greater in the faster environment. The agents were all evaluated by taking the average score from 30 trials; the human performed 10. Each trial is a self-contained simulation with a duration of 5000 ticks of the clock, where the agent can move once per clock tick.

Speed	Score for Agent				
	LV	LV/ Serial	Simple	Simple/ Serial	Human
Normal	396	353	347	291	468
Fast	256	234	183	152	3

Experiment #1

The differences here are quite apparent. In the normal speed environment, the human subject performed best, because he had more-sophisticated planning capabilities than the robot. But in the faster environment, the human's response speed was insufficient to allow him to keep up with the pace of change.

The robot agents were better able to adjust to the more rapidly changing environments, but it is clear that the cost of reasoning is still significant for them. This is evident both from an overall decrease in score in the high-speed environment, and from the superiority of the robot agents that could reason and act in parallel.

The other distinction of note is that the LV evaluator performs better than the simple evaluator, as expected.

Experiment 2

We now move on to our initial experiments directed at understanding some of the design trade-offs in our agent. The use of Tileworld to experimentally evaluate our agent architecture is an ongoing project, and these are early results. We stress that the hypotheses presented below are preliminary; significantly more experimentation and statistical analysis of the results need to take place before we can make strong claims about the relative appropriateness of any particular agent-design strategy.

In Experiment 2, we attempt to test the usefulness of the filtering mechanism in our agent as implemented, using the LV evaluator as the deliberation component, and using the most quickly computed evaluation metric, thresholding on the score value, as the filter override mechanism. We vary the threshold from -100 to 100. Since the score for each hole ranges from 1 to 100, a threshold setting of -100 means that every new option is subject to deliberation, while a setting of 100 means that no new option will ever be considered until the currently executing plan is complete. The resulting scores are summarized in the following chart, where each value represents an average over 30 trials.

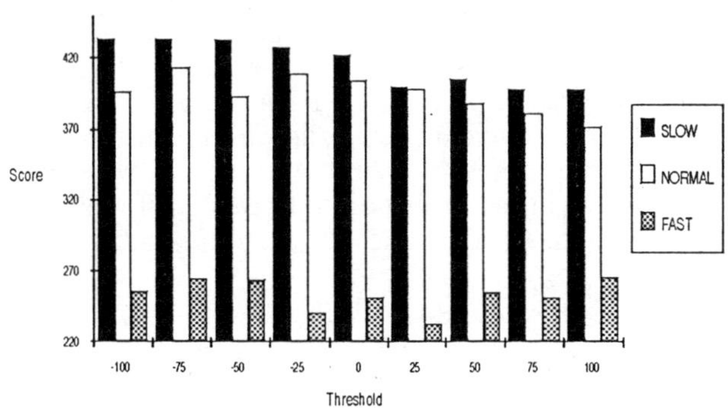

Experiment #2

At the slowest speed setting, 100 times slower than our "normal" setting, it is better to do no filtering at all. The scores achieved at this speed decrease consistently as the threshold is increased. At the normal speed setting, the effect of increased filtering still appears to be negative, but less markedly so. At a setting 10 times faster than the normal one, there seems to be little correlation between threshold level and performance, although the uncertainty in the results, which appears to be in the range of 10-20 points, prevents a sure determination. We hope, in the future, to be able to make even these relatively subtle determinations; the noise in the data comes, we believe, largely from our decision to use actual CPU-time measurements to determine reasoning time. If we wish to get the cleanest trials possible, we may need to use a time estimate that does not depend on the vagaries of the underlying machine and Lisp system. Failing that, we will need to model the uncertainty involved, and run larger trial sets.

To sum up the results of this experiment, we see that filtering is harmful at slow speeds, and even at high speeds does not give a net benefit. Our hypothesis is that the time cost of the LV evaluator is not very high, and consequently, it is usually worth taking the time to engage in extra deliberation about new opportunities. The fact that filtering is less detrimental in the faster environment leads us to hypothesize that there may be a break-even point at even faster speeds, above which filtering is useful; we intend to test for such a point. We also intend to implement more accurate (and costly) deliberation mechanisms in the near future. For these, filtering may be much more valuable; perhaps the LV-estimator is efficient enough that it can itself be used as the filter override mechanism for the more complex deliberation components.

Experiment 3

In our third experiment, we attempt to test a conjecture that the LV evaluator as described is deficient in an important way: it does not consider the time cost of means-end reasoning already performed. We modify the deliberation functions by adding a bias in favor of existing intentions, since typically at deliberation time, some means-end reasoning about how to achieve these has already taken place. This is distinct from Experiment 2, in which we adjusted the *filtering* mechanism in an attempt to save deliberation time; here we investigate a bias in the deliberation process itself with the intent of reducing the time cost of *means-end reasoning*.

We consider two cases. In the first, deliberation is done by the simple evaluator, and we apply a bias towards existing intentions equal to a fixed number of points. In the second, deliberation is done by the LV evaluator, and we apply a bias equal to a fraction of the current LV. Thus, for example, with a 100 percent bias, a newly appearing hole must have double the LV of the current one to be adopted as a new intention. The environment settings and simulation sizes are the same as for Experiment 2.

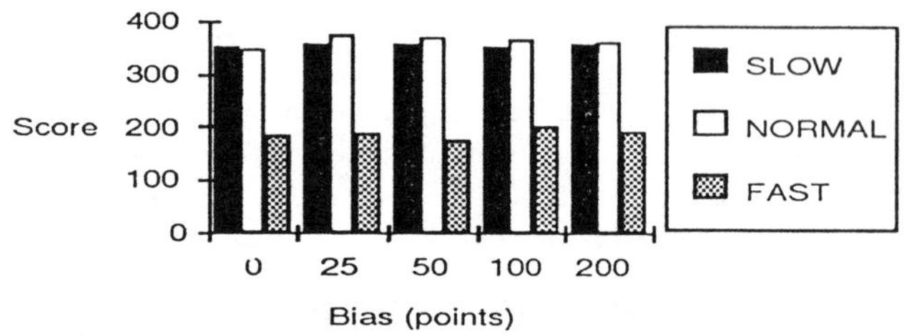

Experiment #3: Simple Evaluator

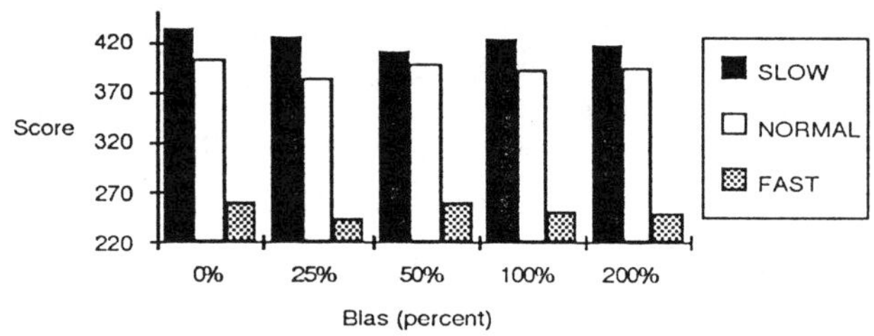

Experiment #3: LV Evaluator

As shown by the experimental results, bias in the deliberator does not appear to have a clear effect on total performance. For the simple evaluator, this isn't terribly surprising; it provides a fairly weak assessment of a hole's actual potential value in any case. We expected to see much more effect of bias on the LV evaluator, however. Two hypotheses are available to explain this. First, our test environment may have too many opportunities available, minimizing the potential cost of high bias: if the agent spends most of its time doing something with high utility, a few missed opportunities will not have a significant impact on the final score. This hypothesis can be tested in a less favorable environment. Second, it may be that means-end reasoning in the current implementation is too inexpensive, minimizing the potential benefit of high bias. This hypothesis can be tested by increasing the *size* of the environment to increase the planning time required; the addition of more complex planning routines would also provide situations in which there is a higher time cost associated with planning.

Conclusion

The experiments we have run to date have included some important milestones in the Tileworld effort. The Tileworld domain has been demonstrated, and has been shown to be a viable system for evaluating agent architectures. The Tileworld agent was demonstrated and used to test differing deliberation and filtering strategies as described in [Bratman *et al.*, 1988].

The Tileworld project is ongoing. There are a number of specific research tasks that we intend to pursue in the near future. Perhaps most importantly, we will be continuing our experimental efforts. The hypotheses we drew from our preliminary experiments suggested several obvious follow-ons, as described in the preceding section. It will be particularly useful to vary parameters other than those that control speed, for example, size of the overall space, distribution of task value and difficulty, and availability of limited resources such as tiles.

We will also implement more sophisticated deliberation algorithms, and, having done so, will attempt to identify better the principles separating the processing that is done in the filtering mechanism from that done in the deliberation procedure. In addition, we plan to implement a foveated perceptual scheme, in which the agent has access to detailed, precise information about its immediate surroundings and has only increasingly abstract, incomplete, and uncertain information about about more distant locations in its environment. Another possibility is to add learning to the system: two areas of potential benefit are in the means-ends reasoner (e.g., explanation-based learning of control rules) and in evaluations of marginal utility (e.g., empirical improvement of utility evaluations). Finally, we hope to extend the architecture to handle more difficult questions involving intention coordination. We expect that both means-end reasoning and deliberation will become much more difficult, and hence filtering much more important, when the intention structure involves more complex interactions among intentions.

More generally, we continue to investigate the larger question of how an agent should structure and control its computational effort. We believe that the architecture discussed here is a special case of a more general framework, and we are working towards a definition of that framework and its verification in our domain. We also see the Tileworld testbed as a good basis for comparison of other agent architectures proposed in the literature, and we strongly encourage other researchers to demonstrate their agents in our domain.[1]

The overall goal of our project is an improved understanding of the relation between agent design and environmental factors. In the future, when faced with a performance domain for an agent, one should be able to draw on such an understanding to choose more wisely from the wide range of implementation possibilities available.

References

[Agre and Chapman, 1987] P. E. Agre and D. Chapman. Pengi: An implementation of a theory of activity. In *Proceedings of the Sixth National Conference on Artificial Intelligence*, Seattle, WA, 1987.

[Boddy and Dean, 1989] M. Boddy and T. Dean. Solving time-dependent planning problems. In *Proceedings of the Eleventh International Joint Conference on Artificial Intelligence*, Detroit, MI, 1989.

[Bratman *et al.*, 1988] M. E. Bratman, D. J. Israel, and M. E. Pollack. Plans and resource-bounded practical reasoning. *Computational Intelligence*, 4(4), 1988.

[Bratman, 1987] M. E. Bratman. *Intention, Plans and Practical Reason.* Harvard University Press, Cambridge, MA, 1987.

[Brooks, 1987] R. A. Brooks. Planning is just a way of avoiding figuring out what to do next. Technical Report 303, MIT, Cambridge, MA, 1987.

[Cohen *et al.*, 1989] P. R. Cohen, M. L Greenberg, D. M. Hart, and A. E. Howe. Real-time problem solving in the phoenix environment. In *Proceedings of the Workshop on Real-Time Artificial Intelligence Problems*, Detroit, MI, 1989.

[Durfee and Montgomery, 1990] E. H. Durfee and T. A. Montgomery. MICE: A flexible testbed for intelligent coordination experiments. In L. Erman, editor, *Intelligent Real-Time Problem Solving: Workshop Report*, Palo Alto, CA, 1990. Cimflex Teknowledge Corp.

[Georgeff and Ingrand, 1989] M. P. Georgeff and F. F. Ingrand. Decision-making in an embedded reasoning system. In *Proceedings of the Eleventh International Joint Conference on Artificial Intelligence*, Detroit, MI, 1989.

[Horvitz, 1987] E. J. Horvitz. Reasoning about beliefs and actions under computational resource constraints. In *Proceedings of the 1987 Workshop on Uncertainty in Artificial Intelligence*, Seattle, WA, 1987.

[Kaelbling, 1988] L.P. Kaelbling. Goals as parallel program specifications. In *Proceedings of the Seventh National Conference on Artificial Intelligence*,St. Paul, MI, 1988.

[Russell and Wefald, 1989] S. J. Russell and E. H. Wefald. Principles of metareasoning. In *Proceedings of the First International Conference on Principles of Knowledge Representation and Reasoning*, Toronto, 1989.

[1]The Tileworld domain is relatively clean and portable, is written in CommonLisp, and is available electronically over the Internet from Marc Ringuette by sending electronic mail to `mnr@cs.cmu.edu`.

Getting Serious about Parsing Plans: a Grammatical Analysis of Plan Recognition

Marc Vilain

The MITRE Corporation
Burlington Road, Bedford, MA 01730
Internet: mbv@linus.mitre.org

Abstract

This paper is concerned with making precise the notion that recognizing plans is much like parsing text. To this end, it establishes a correspondence between Kautz' plan recognition formalism and existing grammatical frameworks. This mapping helps isolate subsets of Kautz' formalism in which plan recognition can be efficiently performed by parsing.

In recent years, plan recognition has emerged as one of the best-understood frameworks for analyzing goal-directed behavior. Interest in plan recognition has led to the development of diverse recognition strategies.[1] One approach suggested several times is that of parsing plan descriptions (Sidner (1985), Ross & Lewis (1987)). A plan is typically described as a sequence of steps, so interpreting some observations in terms of a plan can naturally be seen as a parsing task wherein observations are lexical tokens and plan libraries are grammars.

My aim in this paper is to explore this parsing view of plan recognition by establishing a formal correspondence between an existing plan formalism and context-free grammars. By working through the details of this correspondence, the paper explores parsing algorithms for plan recognition, and delineates classes of problems for which these algorithms are applicable and tractable.

Underlying this work is the plan recognition formalism of Henry Kautz (Kautz & Allen, 1986; Kautz, 1987). His approach is of particular interest because it is formal and well understood. It is also among the broadest of current formalisms, especially in the expressive richness of its plan representation. Finally, since general plan recognition in Kautz' framework is intractable, there is intrinsic interest in identifying those aspects of his approach that cause this intractability, and those that avoid it.

Kautz' Framework

In his dissertation work, Kautz defines a circumscriptive framework for plan recognition. He starts with a simple frame-like hierarchy of plans which is interpretable by first-order meaning postulates. Through a sequence of circumscriptive minimizations, Kautz "closes" the interpretation of the hierarchy, and thereby introduces an additional set of first-order axioms. This expanded set of axioms enables some of the normally *abductive* aspects of plan recognition to be performed through a now *deductive* process.

The Kautz plan representation

The principal component of the Kautz representation is a hierarchy of event (or plan) types. Plans are hierarchically organized according to two relations, *abstraction* and *decomposition*. The former is a subtype (or IS-A) relation; for example, in Kautz' cooking domain, the MAKE-MEAL plan abstracts the MAKE-PASTA-DISH plan. The second relation, decomposition, is borrowed from the non-linear planning literature (Sacerdoti, 1977; Wilkins, 1984, among many others), and identifies the steps making up a plan. For instance, MAKE-PASTA-DISH decomposes into a first step which is a MAKE-NOODLES plan, and a second, a MAKE-SAUCE plan. Each step is given a designator, so the MAKE-NOODLES step of MAKE-PASTA-DISH might be designated S1, and the MAKE-SAUCE step S2. For more examples, see Figure 1.

A plan hierarchy so defined is axiomatized with two meaning postulates, one per relation. For abstraction, let φ_1 and φ_2 be plans such that φ_1 abstracts φ_2. This is interpreted as

$$\forall x \;\; \varphi_1(x) \supset \varphi_2(x)$$

For decomposition, let φ be a plan with steps designated $\sigma_1 \ldots \sigma_n$, each of which is restricted to being a plan of type $\psi_1 \ldots \psi_n$. This is interpreted as

$$\forall x \;\; \varphi(x) \supset \psi_1(\sigma_1(x)) \wedge \ldots \wedge \psi_n(\sigma_n(x))$$

Finally, Kautz distinguishes an abstract plan class, END, encompassing those plans that are meaningful ends in and of themselves. MAKE-MEAL is abstracted by END, and is taken to be an independently meaningful plan. In contrast, MAKE-NOODLES is not abstracted by END, and is not considered independently meaningful — it only has meaning as a step of some other plan.

Minimal plan models

The bulk of Kautz' work formalizes the notion that plan hierarchies such as these can be treated as a complete encoding of a system's knowledge of plans. Kautz shows that a sequence of circumscriptive minimizations enforces a closed world assumption of sorts for plan hierarchies, with the effect that the hierarchies can

[1] E.g., Schmidt, Sridharan & Goodson (1978), Allen & Perrault (1980), Carberry (1983), Allen (1983), Litman (1986), Pollack (1986), Kautz (1987), Konolige & Pollack (1989), Goodman & Litman (1990).

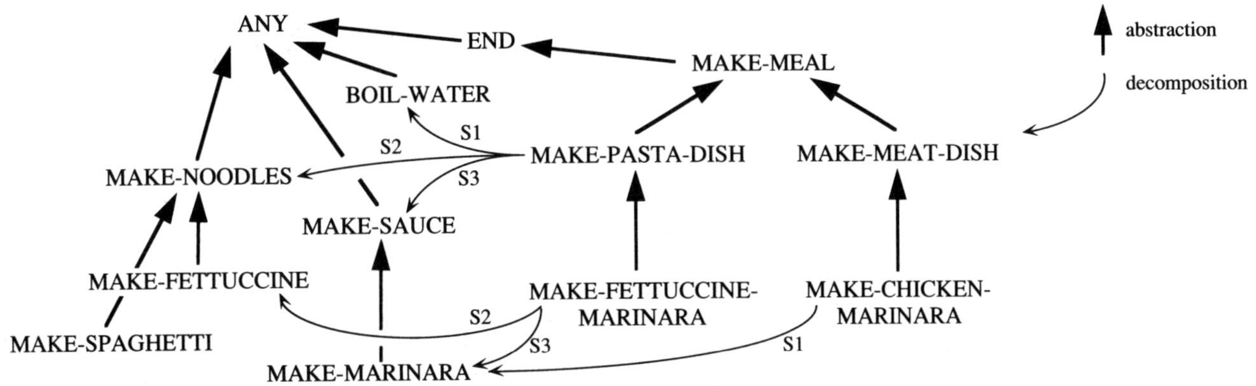

Figure 1: A plan hierarchy

be used to guide plan recognition. Briefly, the closure of a hierarchy proceeds by selecting among models of the hierarchy those models that minimize (1) the extensions of all non-leaf plan types (the hierarchy's inner nodes); (2) the extensions of all plan types but ANY, the hierarchy's root; and (3) the extensions of all non-END plan types.

In effect, the first two minimizations enforce the assumption that no abstraction relations hold over the hierarchy which aren't explicitly mentioned or derivable by transitive closure. The last minimization corresponds to assuming that non-END plans can only occur as components of some other plan. Kautz calls the resulting closed world models of a hierarchy its *covering models*.

Recognizing Kautz' plans

Since they provide a closed world encoding of the hierarchy, covering models form the foundation of the plan recognition process. The recognition problem intuitively consists of finding the most parsimonious interpretation of some observed actions, given the closed world of the hierarchy.

To formalize this notion, let H be a hierarchy described by A and D, the conjunctions of H's abstraction and decomposition axioms respectively, and let ω be a sentence describing some observations. From among the covering models of $A \wedge D \wedge \omega$, Kautz designates those models that explain ω parsimoniously as those that minimize the cardinality of END. This selects those closed world models that postulate the minimum number of end events from H that can possibly account for the observations. To extend Kautz' terminology, I will refer to these models as the minimal covering models of ω with respect to H.

Operationally, a plan recognizer doesn't manipulate models so much as plan descriptions. So in Kautz' framework, one should think of the plan recognizer's task as the mapping of an observation sentence ω to a plan sentence π that is the strongest description of the plans underlying ω, and is valid in all minimal covering models of ω with respect to the plan hierarchy.

Plan Hierarchies as Grammars

There is much similarity between Kautz' plan recognition assumptions and the assumptions underlying parsing. A parser interprets a grammar, in some sense, as a closed world; constituents can't be derived unless they're on the left hand side of a parse rule; constituents that don't derive the start symbol directly must appear in the derivation of some other constituent; *etc.* As noted above, several authors have observed that plan hierarchies can be seen as defining a grammar of plans that could be used to "parse" a string of actions.

This observation is attractive: parsing is a well-understood problem with efficient solutions, so a parsing approach to plan recognition might be expected to yield recognition strategies with better computational characteristics than those developed by Kautz. For certain classes of recognition problems, this is in fact true. With appropriate restrictions on the nature of the plan hierarchies, observations, or expected solutions, a broad class of plan recognition problems becomes tractable in a parsing framework.

Initial Plan Grammar Considerations

These tractability results are shown by constructing a mapping from Kautz' plan hierarchies to context-free grammars. Note that context-free grammatical power is not strictly necessary to encode plan hierarchies in Kautz' representation, since he nominally restricts them to being acyclic. An acyclic hierarchy does not contain any recursive plan definitions, and could in fact be encoded as a regular (finite-state) grammar. The broader context-free class is chosen here in part to allow for the possibility of recursive definitions.

Further, since a major aspect of plan recognition is recovering the plan structure underlying one's observations, the natural grammatical implementation of plan recognition is as a chart-based parser (Kay, 1980; Thompson, 1983). In particular, one can extend Earley's context-free recognition algorithm (Earley, 1970) with a chart, thus enabling it to return the structure of its

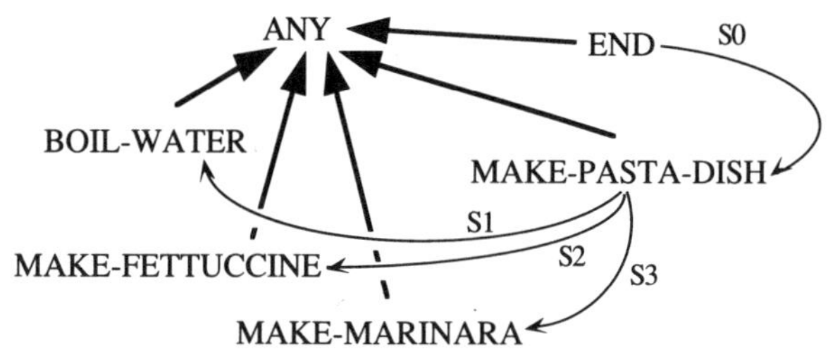

Figure 2: A very simplified hierarchy.

parses. Given such an algorithm, there is little motivation to restrict oneself to a finite-state encoding of plans. This is especially true with Earley's algorithm, since its polynomial bound on context-free recognition time reduces to a linear bound for finite-state grammars.

The complete mapping from plans into grammars is fairly involved, however. So for the sake of clarity, it is presented here as a sequence of simpler mappings into ever more expressive grammatical formalisms. As an overall simplifying assumption, I'll start by only considering solutions that neither share nor interleave steps. In other words, if more than one plan must be hypothesized to account for some observations, each plan must be fully completed before the next one can begin.

The Decomposition Grammar

The process of converting a plan hierarchy H into an equivalent grammar G starts with an encoding of the decomposition axioms. Assume for now that the description of the hierarchy contains no abstraction axioms (we can safely ignore the fact that all plan types are actually abstracted by ANY, the hierarchy's root). The hierarchy is thus entirely described by axioms of form

$$\forall x \; \varphi(x) \supset \psi_1(\sigma_1(x)) \wedge \ldots \wedge \psi_n(\sigma_n(x))$$

where φ is a plan, $\sigma_1 \ldots \sigma_n$ are its steps, and $\psi_1 \ldots \psi_n$ are the type restrictions of these steps. In general, these steps may only be partially ordered, and may even overlap if actions are modeled as having non-zero temporal extent. However, as another temporary simplification, assume that the steps of a decomposition are non-overlapping, and totally ordered according to their order in the decomposition axiom.

With these simplifications, decomposition axioms of the form shown above are mapped to parse rules of form

$$\varphi \rightarrow \psi_1 \; \cdots \; \psi_n$$

Note that the parse rule strips the names of steps from the decomposition. In addition, the following parse rule is necessary to produce the top of the parse tree, where S is the start symbol of the plan grammar.

S → END | END S

This rule introduces enough right-branching structure to account for all END plans appearing in the observations.

For example, say the cooking hierarchy in Figure 1 is simplified so as to contain only one END plan, that

Let $\Omega = \omega_1 \wedge \ldots \wedge \omega_n$ be an observation sentence where ω_i has form PLAN-TYPE$_i$(ACT$_i$).

Let *Chart*[0..n x 0..n] be an initially empty array of derived constituents.

Let *States*[0..n] be an initially empty array of intermediate parse states (dotted rules).

(1) Initialize *Chart[i-1,i]* with each PLAN-TYPE$_i$ in Ω.

(2) Add $S_{(0)}$ -> • END and $S_{(0)}$ -> • END S to *States[0]*.

(3) **For** $i \leftarrow 0$ **to** n **do**

(4) *Predict:* If $\alpha_{(j)}$ -> ⋯• $\beta\cdots$ is a dotted rule in *States[i]*, then add to *States[i]* a dotted rule $\beta_{(j)}$ -> • $\gamma\cdots$ for each rule deriving β in the grammar.

(5) *Scan:* If $\alpha_{(j)}$ -> ⋯• $\beta\,\gamma\cdots$ is in *States[i]* and β is a terminal, then if *Chart[i,i+1]* contains β, add a dotted rule of form $\alpha_{(j)}$ -> ⋯β • $\gamma\cdots$ to *States[i+1]*.

(6) *Complete:* If $\alpha_{(j)}$ -> ⋯ β • is a complete dotted rule in *States[i]*, then

(7) Add α to *Chart[j,i]*, using the AND-OR coding scheme.

(8) For each $\gamma_{(k)}$ -> ⋯• $\alpha\,\delta\cdots$ in *States[j]*, add to *States[i]* a dotted rule of form $\delta_{(i)}$ -> • $\chi\cdots$ for each rule deriving δ in the grammar.

Figure 3: Earley's algorithm.

for making fettuccine marinara. This new hierarchy (see Figure 2) would produce the following grammar.

S → END | END S
END → MAKE-PASTA-DISH
MAKE-PASTA-DISH → BOIL-WATER
MAKE-FETTUCCINE
MAKE-MARINARA

Parsing the Decomposition Grammar

As noted earlier, decomposition grammars can be applied to plan recognition with a chart-based version of Earley's algorithm. Briefly, the algorithm operates by maintaining a chart, a two-dimensional table that records the constituents spanning any two positions in the input stream.[2] If a constituent may be derived in more than one way between the same two positions, the multiple derivations are recorded as alternatives in an OR node (each derivation is itself an AND node).

Earley records partial derivations by instantiating "dotted" versions of rules. For example, A -> B C, when first applied, has a dot to the left of B ($A_{(i)}$ -> • B C). After deriving B, a new instance of the rule is created, with the dot advanced past B ($A_{(i)}$ -> B • C). The subscripted index in this notation indicates the start position of the leftmost terminal derived by the rule.

The algorithm indexes dotted rules in a set of states: if a dotted rule seeks to derive a constituent starting in some position k, the rule is added to the kth state set. When the dot is finally moved past the end of a rule, a derivation has been completed, and the derived

[2] For a sentence of length n, the chart runs from 0 to n, with each terminal spanning [i, i+1], for some i.

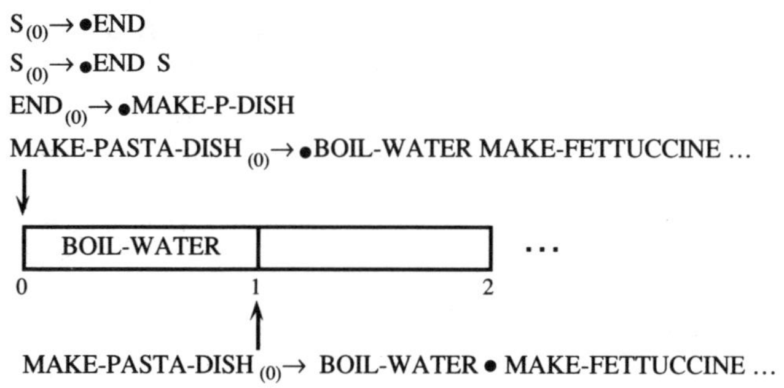

Figure 4a: States of the parser

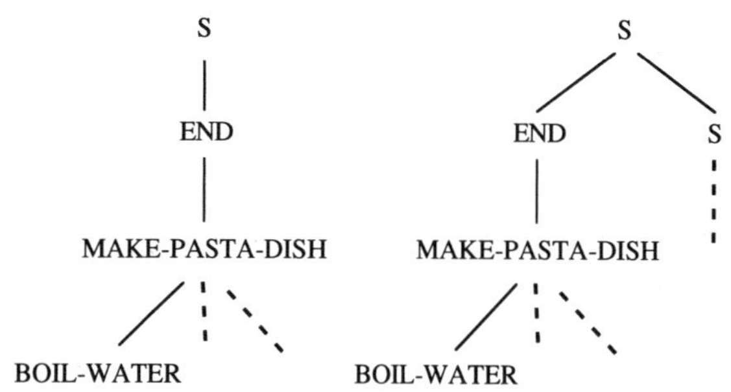

Figure 4b: Corresponding parse trees

constituent is added to cell $[i, j]$ of the chart, where i is the start index of the leftmost terminal derived by the rule, and j is the end index of the rightmost one.

The algorithm is sketched in Figure 3, with details in Earley (1970). With respect to applying the algorithm to plan recognition, three points need to be made.

First, observations are entered into the chart in a straightforward way. To be precise, say we have observed the sentence $\Omega = \omega_1 \wedge \ldots \wedge \omega_n$, where each ω_i has form PLAN-TYPE$_i$(ACT$_i$). Assuming observations are ordered and non-overlapping in time, Ω is entered into the chart by placing the terminal constituent corresponding to each PLAN-TYPE$_i$ in chart cell $[i\text{-}1, i]$.

The next point to note is that Earley's algorithm proceeds left-to-right through the input stream. Each step in the traversal computes all partial derivations that account for the input up to that point. This can be exploited to allow for incremental observations in the manner of Kautz' Incremental and Sticky Algorithms. That is, every time a new event is observed, it is added to the chart, and the main loop of the algorithm is simply restarted on the chart index for that event.

Most important, Earley is a predictive top-down parser. Thus, whenever a terminal symbol is scanned by the parser, the incomplete parse tree that ultimately derives the terminal from the start symbol is implicit in the state sets of the parser. This parse tree can be recovered from the dotted rules making up these sets.

For example, say the parser had been given the simplified cooking grammar corresponding to Figure 2, and say we had observed a BOIL-WATER action, B_1. The state of the parser and its chart would then be as shown in Figure 4a. The parser's state can be interpreted as identifying two distinct incomplete parse trees for the BOIL-WATER observation (see Figure 4b). The first derives a single END plan to account for the observation. The second tree postulates a second END plan following the first (a third would be postulated in the parser's prediction phase if the parser attempted to derive the second END plan, and so forth).

These parse trees can be interpreted as first-order sentences. For terminals, the sentential form is the observation associated with the terminal (a proposition of form PLAN-TYPE(ACT)). For non-terminals, we begin by creating for each non-terminal node an existentially quantified plan instance (ignoring the start node). The links from a node to its children in turn correspond to steps named in the decomposition axiom for the rule that derived the node. The sentential form of a parse tree t, with children $t_1 \ldots t_n$ is then the sentential forms of its children conjoined with

$$\exists \xi.\ \kappa(\xi) \wedge \sigma_1(\xi) = \xi_1 \wedge \ldots \wedge \sigma_n(\xi) = \xi_n$$

where $\xi, \xi_1, \ldots, \xi_n$ are the variables for nodes $t, t_1, \ldots, t_n$ respectively (or constants if the nodes are terminals), κ is the constituent associated with t, and the σ_i are the step names associated with the derivation of t. Multiple derivations of a constituent simply introduce into the sentential form the disjunction of their respective parses.

Under this mapping, the first parse in Figure 4b can be interpreted as:

$$\begin{aligned}&\exists\, x,y\ \text{END}(x) \wedge \text{S0}(x) = y \wedge \\ &\quad \text{MAKE-PASTA-DISH}(y) \wedge \text{S1}(y) = B_1 \wedge \\ &\quad \text{BOIL-WATER}(B_1)\end{aligned}$$

This interpretation scheme for parse trees is akin to that used by Kautz to interpret his algorithms' E-graphs.

Correctness and complexity

To prove the correctness of the plan parser, it is necessary to show that for a given hierarchy H and observation ω, the parser computes the minimal covering models of ω with respect to H. This can be accomplished in two steps.

First, the algorithm can be shown to compute the covering models of H by relying on a result from Kautz (1987). Kautz shows that the covering models of plan hierarchies with no abstraction are exactly those that satisfy all instantiations of his *component/use* axiom schema. The (slightly modified) schema is given by:

$$\begin{aligned}\forall\, x\ \varphi(x) \supset\ & \text{END}(x) \vee \\ & \exists\, y_1\ \psi_1(y_1) \wedge (\sigma_1(y_1) = x) \vee \ldots \vee \\ & \exists\, y_n\ \psi_n(y_n) \wedge (\sigma_n(y_n) = x)\end{aligned}$$

where φ is a plan type, and $\psi_1 \ldots \psi_n$ are those plan types that respectively restrict steps $\sigma_1 \ldots \sigma_n$ to be of type φ.

Extending this schema to parse trees is straightforward. In light of the sentential interpretation of parse trees, the schema can be rephrased in terms of $t, t_1,\ldots,t_n$, variables ranging over parse tree nodes:

$$\forall\, t\ \varphi(t) \supset \mathrm{END}(t) \vee \exists\, t_1 \ldots t_n\ \ \psi_1(t_1) \wedge (t_1 \Rightarrow t) \wedge \ldots \wedge \psi_n(t_n) \wedge (t_n \Rightarrow t)$$

where φ is the constituent corresponding to a plan type, and $\psi_1,\ldots,\psi_n$ are all those constituents that derive φ in the grammar. The notation $\varphi(t)$ indicates that node t has constituent type φ, and the notation $t \Rightarrow t'$ indicates that node t derives node t' in the parse tree. For the purpose of this schema, the start node S, which is only used to introduce END nodes, is once again ignored.

It is easy to see that in this form, the component/use schema is fully instantiated by Earley's algorithm. The t_i are introduced into the parse tree by the prediction step, and the derivations are recorded by the completion step. By fully instantiating the schema, the algorithm thus computes the covering models of an observation with respect to a hierarchy.

To obtain the *minimal* covering models, note that each alternative parse tree attached to the start symbol S will postulate the existence of some number of END plans. These END plans can be enumerated simply by traversing the topmost right-branching structure of the tree introduced by the rule S → END S. The minimal models are those that apply this derivation a minimal number of times. This, along with the preceding discussion, informally shows the following proposition.

Proposition 1: Under the sentential interpretation of parse trees, Earley's algorithm computes the minimal covering models of an observation ω with respect to H, a decomposition hierarchy with ordered unshared steps.

Earley (1970) shows that the run time of his recognizer for a sentence of length n is bounded by a factor of $O(n^3)$. Barton, Berwick, and Ristad (1987) note that this bound can be refined to $O(G^{\circ 2} n^3)$, where G° is the total number of possible dotted rules afforded by the grammar G.

The addition of a chart, as is done in the algorithm of Figure 3, extends Earley's recognizer into a parser, but can introduce performance degradation. Tomita (1986), for example, describes some pathological combinations of grammars and input strings that can require of his chart-based parser $O(n^5)$ space utilization, and a corresponding degradation in parse time. However, Billot and Lang (1989) suggest that by using structure sharing to implement the chart's AND-OR graphs, the space requirements for storing the chart are bounded by $O(n^3)$, while the parse times also remain cubic.

The Uses of Abstraction

The preceding results are of some interest in establishing the tractability of plan recognition for one class of plan hierarchies, those expressible without abstraction. However, the resulting formal apparatus is so impoverished as to be useless in practice.

Beyond allowing for the identification of significant abstract constructs of a domain, abstraction is used in Kautz' framework to encode three different phenomena: the multiple expansions of a plan; the isolation of substeps common to all expansions of a plan (which are then shared through inheritance); and, indeterminate observations.

Adding Abstraction to the Grammar

It is easy to extend the mapping from plan hierarchies to grammars so as to allow for abstraction in the descriptions of plan types. Abstract observations, however, impose additional considerations, which I will return to later. Assume for now that observations are given in terms of base plan types (the leaves of the plan hierarchy), and again restrict plan steps to be fully ordered and unsharable. The mapping from a hierarchy H to a grammar G proceeds from the top of the hierarchy to its leaves, distinguishing two cases:

Case 1: Say φ is a plan type decomposing into steps $\sigma_1\ldots\sigma_n$, and say φ has children $\chi_1\ldots\chi_m$. Then, for each χ_i, copy each σ_j (and its type restriction ψ_j) to the decomposition of χ_i, unless χ_i happens to further restrict σ_j. Then for each χ_i, add a rule to the grammar of form

$$\varphi \rightarrow \chi_i$$

Case 2: Say φ is a childless plan type that decomposes into (possibly inherited) steps $\sigma_1\ldots\sigma_n$, with step restrictions $\psi_1\ldots\psi_n$. Then add to the grammar a decomposition rule of form

$$\varphi \rightarrow \psi_1 \ldots \psi_n$$

Again, the root of the hierarchy (ANY) is ignored, and again, the grammar is completed by adding the initial parse rule

S → END | END S

Note that this scheme eliminates from a hierarchy the explicit decompositions of abstract actions, enforcing them implicitly by inheritance instead. Thus, returning to the plan hierarchy in Figure 1, the subhierarchy rooted at MAKE-PASTA-DISH would be encoded as

MAKE-PASTA-DISH
  → MAKE-FETTUCCINE-MARINARA
MAKE-FETTUCCINE-MARINARA
  → BOIL-WATER
    MAKE-FETTUCCINE
    MAKE-MARINARA

The grammatical treatment of abstraction introduces additional complexity to the sentential interpretation of parse trees. Indeed, one must now distinguish nodes that were introduced by abstraction parse rules from those that were introduced by decomposition parse rules. As before, say t is a node with children $t_1\ldots t_n$, and say t was introduced by a decomposition rule produced in

Case 2 of the grammatical mapping. Then the sentential form of t is that of its children conjoined with

$$\exists \xi.\ \kappa(\xi) \wedge \sigma_1(\xi) = \xi_1 \wedge \ldots \wedge \sigma_n(\xi) = \xi_n$$

For abstraction, say $\varphi \rightarrow \psi$ is a parse rule introduced to encode an abstraction axiom in Case 1 of the grammatical mapping. Let t be a node in a parse tree that derives a node t' by this rule. Then the sentential interpretation of the tree rooted at t is that of t' conjoined with the expression $\varphi(\xi)$, where ξ is the plan variable associated with the interpretation of t'.

Properties of Abstraction Grammars

The correctness and complexity properties of Earley's algorithm for decomposition grammars are easy to verify for abstraction grammars. For correctness, one must once again show that the algorithm computes the minimal covering models of some observation ω with respect to H, a hierarchy with abstraction. To begin with, Kautz (1987) showed that the covering models of a hierarchy with abstraction are precisely those that fully instantiate three axiom schemata, one of which (component/use) appeared above in a simplified form.

Disjunction: let φ be a plan type that directly abstracts types $\psi_1,\ldots, \psi_n$. Then:

$$\forall x\ \varphi(x) \supset \psi_1(x) \vee \ldots \vee \psi_n(x)$$

Exclusion: let φ_1 and φ_2 be incompatible plan types, i.e., ones for that there exists no φ_3 which is abstracted (directly or indirectly) by both φ_1 and φ_2. Then:

$$\forall x\ \neg\varphi_1(x) \vee \neg\varphi_2(x)$$

Component/use: let φ be a plan type, and let $\psi_1 \ldots \psi_n$ be all those plan types that restrict some step $\sigma_1 \ldots \sigma_n$ to be φ or a plan type compatible with φ. Then:

$$\forall x\ \varphi(x) \supset \text{END}(x) \vee \exists y_1\ \psi_1(y_1) \wedge (\sigma_1(y_1) = x) \vee \ldots \vee \exists y_n\ \psi_n(y_n) \wedge (\sigma_n(y_n) = x)$$

Under the sentential interpretation of parse trees, the disjunction schema can be recast in terms of t and t', variables ranging over nodes in the parse tree:

$$\forall t\ \varphi(t) \supset \exists t'\ (t \Rightarrow t') \wedge (\psi_1(t') \vee \ldots \vee \psi_n(t'))$$

Assuming that ω mentions only base level observations, this schema is verified by noting that a parse node corresponding to an abstract plan type φ is only introduced into the chart (during the completion step of the algorithm) if one of $\psi_1,\ldots, \psi_n$ was previously introduced into the chart.

A similar argument can be used to show that, assuming base level observations, the parser fully instantiates the exclusion schema. The argument can also be used to extend the proof of Proposition 1 in order to show that the parser fully instantiates the extended version of the component/use schema. This informally demonstrates that the algorithm computes the covering models of ω with respect to H. The minimal covering models can be obtained as before from those parses introducing fewest END nodes under S, thus showing:

Proposition 2: Under the sentential interpretation of parse trees, Earley's algorithm computes the minimal covering models of a base-level observation ω with respect to H, a hierarchy with ordered unshared steps.

As before, the time complexity of parsing an observation "sentence" is $O(G^{\circ 2} n^3)$. The G° term is related to the original hierarchy description in the following way. There is exactly one dotted rule for each abstraction axiom, and the latter's number is bounded by P, the size of the set of plan types in the hierarchy. The original decomposition axioms are also bounded in number by P, and it is easy to verify that after step inheritance, the number of corresponding dotted decomposition rules is bounded by Pd, where d is the number of steps mentioned in the longest decomposition axiom. The overall size of G° is thus $O(Pd)$.

Abstract Observations

The preceding discussion crucially relies on observed actions' not being abstract. This is a severe limitation, since abstract plan types simplify the expression of indeterminate observations. For example, in Kautz' cooking world, one might like to encode uncertainty on whether an agent is making fettuccine or spaghetti with an abstract MAKE-NOODLES observation. In grammatical terms, this amounts to allowing non-terminal categories to appear directly in the input stream.

For the plan parser to interpret these observations correctly is tricky. The problem is that to ensure that the minimal covering models are computed, the parser must expand the abstract observation into its possible specializations, and hypothesize that each may have occured. It would be appealing if this expansion could be effectuated by compiling additional parse rules out of the plan hierarchy. Unfortunately, though various naive strategies for doing so are conceivable, they all seem to have unacceptable problems.

For instance, one could allow for abstract observations to be specialized *down* the abstraction hierarchy with "reverse" abstraction rules (e.g., MAKE-PASTA-DISH → MAKE-MEAL). However, this leads directly to violations of the disjunction schema. An alternative (and equally naive) approach would produce additional decomposition rules introducing the possible abstractions of a base action, e.g.:

MAKE-FETTUCCINE-MARINARA→ MAKE-NOODLES MAKE-SAUCE

However, the number of such rules is bounded by $O(d^P)$, leading to an exponential increase in the size of the grammar and an exponential increase in parse times.

A more practical alternative is to leave the grammar unchanged, and treat an abstract observation $\varphi(e)$ disjunctively as $\vee_i\ \psi_i(e)$, where the ψ_i are those plan types that maximally specialize φ (i.e., that specialize φ and have no specializations in turn). This strategy can be seen as explicitly enforcing the disjunction axiom schema on abstract observations.

At the grammatical level, this strategy has a natural analogue in *lexical ambiguity*, the ambiguity encountered when a terminal (e.g. the English word *can*) is derivable by more than one pre-terminal (e.g. *V*, *N*, or *AUX*). In linguistic parsers the terminals in a string are usually replaced with the corresponding pre-terminals, so lexical ambiguity can be simply dealt with by adding each ambiguous pre-terminal directly into the same cell of the chart. Similarly, the plan parsing algorithm in Figure 3 can be amended to enter any abstract observation $\varphi(e)$ into its chart cell as the set of ψ_i that it abstracts. A MAKE-NOODLES observation, for example, would be entered in the chart as a set of two terminals: {MAKE-SPAGHETTI MAKE-FETTUCCINE}.

This approach to abstract observations preserves the correctness of the plan parser. As noted above, it directly enforces the disjunction schema. That the exclusion schema is enforced can be seen by noting that no two ambiguous terminal entries appear in the same parse. Consequently, under the sentential interpretation of parse trees, no two ambiguous but incompatible types can hold true of the same plan variable or plan constant. Finally, for each distinct parse, it is easy to verify that the algorithm will fully instantiate the component/use schema.

The disjunctive treatment of abstraction also maintains the polynomial tractability of the plan parser. This can be seen by noting that the $O(G^{\circ\,2}\,n^3)$ time bound on parsing an observation string of length n is obtained from a $O(G^{\circ\,2}\,n^2)$ bound on each step of the main loop of the parser (which is iterated n times). Informally, one can think of an ambiguous observation φ in position $[i\text{-}1, i]$ as temporarily "augmenting" the grammar for iteration step i. The augmentation consists of introducing a new category OBSERVED-φ and new rules of form OBSERVED-$\varphi \rightarrow \psi_i$, for each ψ_i maximally specializing φ. The abstract observation is then encoded as a token of OBSERVED-φ. This has a net effect of temporarily adding no more than P rules to the grammar at each step of the parser's main iteration, and so G° remains bounded at each step by $O(Pd)$. This leaves the overall time complexity of parsing unaffected.

The following proposition summarizes the discussion of the past few pages.

Proposition 3: There is a $O(n^3)$-time plan recognition algorithm for hierarchies with ordered, unshared steps, and for disjunctive or abstract observations.

Further Extensions

This result is of significant value, as it delineates a subset of Kautz' plan formalism for which plan recognition is tractable. The parsing approach underlying this result can in fact be extended to cover further aspects of Kautz' formalism, but unfortunately not without also sacrificing recognition tractability.

Partial Step Order

A number of recent linguistic formalisms refine the traditional phrase structure rules into two sets of rules: (1) indirect dominance (ID) rules, which specify which subconstituents may be derived by a constituent, and (2) linear precedence (LP) rules, which determine the left-to-right order of these subconstituents. This ID/LP strategy can be applied to plan hierarchies to allow for a compact encoding of partial step ordering. For example, the following two sketchy rules specify that the BOIL-WATER step of the MAKE-PASTA-DISH plan must be ordered before the MAKE-NOODLES step, but leaves all other step relations unordered.

$$\text{PASTA} \xrightarrow{\text{ID}} \text{BOIL NOODLES SAUCE} \qquad \textit{(ID rule)}$$
$$\text{BOIL} < \text{NOODLES} \qquad \textit{(LP rule)}$$

In effect, an ID rule of length n stands for an equivalent $n!$ ordered context-free rules, some of which are then eliminated if they fail to satisfy the LP rules. In principle, one could thus parse an ID/LP grammar with Earley's algorithm by first compiling it into the corresponding context-free rules. However, as the number of such rules is combinatorially explosive, the size of the resulting grammar would be correspondingly large, and parse times correspondingly lengthy. To alleviate this problem, Shieber (1983) produced a simple extension to Earley's algorithm that allows for direct parsing of ID/LP grammars, thus circumventing the combinatorial explosion produced by compilation.

Unfortunately, Shieber's parser does not escape intractability. Barton *et al.* (1987) show that ID/LP parsing is NP-complete under certain conditions. The argument is complex, but for the purposes of this paper it suffices to note that a sufficient condition for NP-completeness is the kind of lexical ambiguity used above to encode abstract observations. In fact, this NP-completeness result can easily be extended to show the following proposition (offered here without proof).

Proposition 4: Recognizing plans with abstraction and partial step order is NP-complete, regardless of recognition tactic.

This pessimistic result must be taken in perspective. Shieber's algorithm performs well in practice, and truly extreme derivational ambiguity is required to lead it to exponential performance. In fact, Barton *et al.* suggest that tractability may actually be regained by ensuring that the unordered steps of an ID decomposition are derivationally distinct. This is the case, for example, with the ID rule decomposing MAKE-PASTA-DISH, each of whose steps derives a set of constituents distinct from those derived by the others. However, a general plan distinguishability criterion has yet to be formulated.

Action Parameters

Kautz allows plans to have parameters, such as an agent. As with other aspects of plan recognition, action parameters have a grammatical analogue, in this case with unification grammars (another extension of the context-free class). Without going into details, it is straightforward to show that plan parameters and constraints on these parameters can be encoded in the unification formalism. However, parsing unification grammars is again NP-complete in the presence of derivational ambiguity (Barton *et al.* (1987)).

Plan Parsing in Perspective

There are additional aspects of Kautz' approach that may not be convincingly treated with a parsing strategy. Shared and interleaved steps are a particularly salient example of this. It is admittedly possible to formulate some kind of *type 0* or perhaps *context-sensitive* phrase structure rules to encode the sharing or interleaving of steps. However, it is not at all clear how to do so without endowing the plan formalism with enough machinery to make plan recognition intractable or even undecidable (type 0 grammars being Turing-equivalent).

Nevertheless, the main thrust of this work is not to show that all of Kautz' approach can be reformulated as parsing, as much as it is to find those aspects of his approach that become tractable when so reformulated. Beyond the immediate gains of tractability, the parsing approach does provide an operational advantage over Kautz' algorithms. Namely, it focuses recognition by predicting the existence of only those END plans sanctioned by all the observations taken together. Kautz' algorithms perform the prediction on each individual observation, independent of the others, and then combine the resulting predictions. This is computationally much more onerous, but may turn out to be unavoidable if one wants to allow for sharing and interleaving of steps.

Finally, I should note that there are many similarities between the parsing strategies described here and the plan recognition strategies in MITRE's King Kong interface (Burger & Sider, 1990). As part of our current research, my colleagues and I are investigating further extensions to King Kong that rely on parsing strategies.

Acknowledgements

This work has benefitted from discussions over the years with James Allen and Henry Kautz. Special thanks to Ellen Hays for her untiring editorial attention.

References

Allen, J. (1983). Recognizing intentions from natural language utterances. In Brady, M. & Berwick, R. (eds) *Computational Models of Discourse*. Cambridge, MA: The MIT Press.

Allen, J. & Perrault, R. (1980). Analyzing intention in dialogue. *Artificial Intelligence* **23**(2), 832-843.

Barton, G. E., Berwick, R. & Ristad, E. (1987). *Computational Complexity and Natural Language*. Cambridge, MA: The MIT Press.

Billot, S. & Lang, B. (1989). The structure of shared forests in ambiguous parsing. In *Proceedings of ACL 89*, 143-151.

Burger, J. & Sider, J. (1990). *Discourse Understanding in Expert System Interfaces*. In preparation.

Carberry, S. (1983). Tracking goals in an information seeking environment. In *Proceedings of AAAI 83*, 59-63.

Earley, J. (1970). An efficient context-free parsing mechanism. *Communications of the ACM* **13**(2), 94-102. Reprinted in Grosz et al. (1986).

Goodman, B. & Litman, D. (1990). Plan recognition for intelligent interfaces. In *Proceedings of the IEEE Conference on Artificial Intelligence Applications 1990*.

Grosz, B., Sparck Jones, K., Webber, B. L. (1986). *Readings in Natural Language Processing*. San Mateo, CA: Morgan Kaufmann.

Kay, M. (1980). *Algorithm Schemata and Data Structures in Syntactic Processing*. Tech Report CSL-80-12, Xerox PARC. Reprinted in Grosz et al. (1986).

Kautz, H. (1987). *A Formal Theory of Plan Recognition*. PhD dissertation, Dept. of Computer Science, University of Rochester. Available as Tech. Report 215.

Kautz, H. & Allen A. (1986). Generalized plan recognition. In *Proceedings of AAAI 86*, 32-37.

Konolige, K. & Pollack, M. (1989). Ascribing plans to agents — preliminary report. In *Proceedings of IJCAI 89*, 924-930.

Litman, D. (1986). Linguistic coherence: A plan-based alternative. In *Proceedings of ACL 86*, 215-223.

Pollack, M. (1986). A model of plan processing which distinguishes between the beliefs of actors and observers. In *Proceedings of ACL 86*, 207-214.

Sacerdoti, E. (1977). *A Structure for Plans and Behavior*. New York: North-Holland.

Schmidt, C. , Sridharan, N., & Goodson J. (1978). The plan recognition problem: An intersection of artificial intelligence and psychology. *Artificial Intelligence*, **11**(1), 45-83.

Shieber, S. (1983). Direct parsing of ID/LP grammars. *Linguistics and Philosophy* **7**(2), 135-154.

Sidner, C. (1985). Plan parsing for intended response recognition in discourse. *Computational Intelligence*, **1**(1), 1-10.

Thompson, H. (1983). MCHART: A flexible, modular chart parsing system. In *Proceedings of AAAI 83*, 408-410.

Tomita, M. (1986). *Efficient Parsing for Natural Language*. Boston: Kluwer Academic Publishers.

Wilkins, D. (1984). Domain-independent planning: representation and generation. *Artificial Intelligence* **22**, 269-301.

The STRIPS Assumption for Planning Under Uncertainty

Michael P. Wellman
AI Technology Office, Wright R&D Center
Wright-Patterson AFB, OH 45433
wellman@wrdc.af.mil

Abstract

The virtue of the STRIPS assumption for planning is that it bounds the information relevant to determining the effects of actions. Viewing the "assumption" as a statement about beliefs, we find that it does not actually assume anything about the world itself. We can characterize the assertion about beliefs in terms of probabilistic independence, thereby facilitating analysis of representations for planning under uncertainty. This interpretation separates the STRIPS assumption from other necessary features of a planning architecture, such as its model of persistence and its inferential policies. By isolating these factors, we can understand the role of dependence across a wide range of planners and action representations. Graphical models of dependence developed for probabilistic analysis provide a convenient tool for verifying the STRIPS assumption for a variety of planning systems. Investigation of a few representative systems reveals a Markovian event structure common to these planning models.

The Frame Problem and the STRIPS Assumption

The classic dilemma in representing and reasoning about the effects of actions is the *frame problem*, originally identified by McCarthy and Hayes [1969]. The frame problem has come to stand for a variety of computational and notational complexities arising from the apparent necessity of considering the possible change in status of every proposition for each action. Characterizations of the problem vary widely [Brown, 1987; Pylyshyn, 1987], proposed solutions even more so, but a kernel of consensus does seem to exist. AI researchers agree that part of the problem, at least, has to do with specifying the effects of actions without explicitly describing all ramifications and qualifications. In particular, we want to avoid a requirement for explicit *frame axioms* specifying the propositions *not* affected by each action.

Actual planners eschew frame axioms and restrict attention to propositions explicitly mentioned in their action specifications, a convention first applied by STRIPS [Fikes and Nilsson, 1971]. Waldinger has named this policy the "STRIPS assumption" [1977]. McDermott [1987] asserts that no program since STRIPS has been practically bothered by the frame problem, which is true if we define the problem narrowly as the need for frame axioms in the deductive planning approach. Nevertheless, building planners that perform well in complex dynamic environments is no easy task, in large part due to difficulties of representing and reasoning about change. As McDermott also points out, the frame problem *does* frustrate attempts at logical analyses of these programs and their environments, which should be relevant to the goal of designing better algorithms and representations. Much of the work on nonmonotonic logic is addressed to this issue.

Understanding the nature of the STRIPS assumption and the extent to which it circumvents the frame problem is a first step to understanding the larger issues in reasoning about actions. Previous discussions of the STRIPS assumption, including the original by Waldinger [1977], tended to encompass all of these issues, failing to distinguish the relatively small role played by this particular notational convention. While the broader views provide fuller accounts of the planners they address, their analyses are not transferable to planning frameworks that take significantly different approaches to representing and reasoning about change.

For example, Lifschitz's analysis [1986] focuses on conditions under which STRIPS's add/delete mechanism will be guaranteed to produce only valid plans. The analysis concludes essentially that STRIPS systems are sound as long as

1. the use of non-atomic sentences in operator descriptions and world models is restricted (in a precise manner described by Lifschitz), and
2. a kind of strong persistence holds, where no changes occur except as specified in add and delete lists.

These conditions (which clarify STRIPS significantly) apply to planning frameworks that adopt the same strong persistence model and forbid inference about the further consequences of specified effects. Many have been unwilling to accept these restrictions, and have worked on methods and semantic accounts of systems that go beyond them.

Research on the task of determining the implications of specified effects of actions (called the *ramification problem*), its counterpart for preconditions (the *qualification* problem), and development of models of persistence are important areas of investigation for AI planning. The point of this paper is that there is a separable aspect of the STRIPS assumption that is orthogonal to these issues, and therefore applicable across a variety of planning frameworks. Generally stated, the STRIPS assumption *per se* dictates that the effect of an action on the world model be completely determined by the direct effects explicit in its specification. By saying only that it is "completely determined," we permit the nature of the implicit effects to vary among planning systems.

I examine this interpretation below from the perspective of planning under uncertainty. Uncertainty provides further motivation for this view of the STRIPS assumption, and concepts from uncertain reasoning help to characterize it more precisely for application to existing planning frameworks.

Planning under Uncertainty

An agent plans *under uncertainty* whenever it cannot flawlessly predict the state of the environment resulting from its actions. By this definition, uncertainty is a characteristic of the agent's knowledge rather than an inherent property of the environment. Given that we are never likely to achieve perfect prediction in realistic environments, all planning is actually performed under uncertainty; planning under *certainty* is an unrealizable—albeit often useful—idealization.

The frame problem arises in planning under uncertainty just as it does in the idealized framework. Planners must employ something like the STRIPS assumption to justify leaving non-effects of an action implicit in their omission from the action's specification. However, semantic accounts of the STRIPS assumption in classical planning (e.g., STRIPS itself [Lifschitz, 1986]) do not easily map over to the uncertain case. The conventional interpretation, that planners assume that relations in the world model are unchanged unless explicitly specified, cannot literally apply to planners that admit they have incomplete knowledge about the effects of their actions on the world.

Perhaps we could modify the interpretation to assume that changes of unspecified relations are unlikely rather than impossible. The problem of this approach is identifying a particular, well-motivated, likelihood assumption that is sufficiently general for domain-independent planning. As demonstrated by some work along these lines [Dean and Kanazawa, 1988; Hanks, 1990], defining such a convention is tantamount to adopting a model of persistence and probabilistic inference. Moreover, these persistence models tend to be more varied and complicated than those proposed for planning under certainty. These differences provide further motivation for a characterization of the STRIPS assumption that does not depend on a particular model of persistence.

The essential property of the STRIPS assumption that justifies implicit treatment of non-effects is the presumption that the information specified explicitly is sufficient to describe the agent's change in belief. In other words, once the direct effects are known, knowledge of the action itself is superfluous for purposes of prediction. Thus, the STRIPS assumption is fundamentally a statement that the agent's beliefs about changes in propositions not mentioned in an action's specification are independent of the action, given those effects explicitly specified. For planning under uncertainty, we can characterize beliefs in terms of probability distributions and use the concept of probabilistic independence to formalize this interpretation of the STRIPS assumption.

Probabilistic Independence

In a state of uncertainty, an agent's beliefs are representable by a probability distribution over possible situations (which is not to say that the agent's beliefs need be encoded as such in some data structure). We take situations to be assignments on a universe of variables describing the world, including such things as what actions are performed and their consequences. Belief states are then probability distributions over this space. Note that this framework avoids imposing a temporal ontology, which, while providing essential structure for the planning problem, would also detract from the generality of our analysis of the issue at hand.

To capture the meaning of the STRIPS assumption proposed above, we need a way to express the sufficiency of explicitly specified effects to describe the full impact of an action on the agent's beliefs about the world. For this purpose, the natural concept in probability theory is *conditional independence*. We say that random variables x and y are conditionally independent given z iff

$$\Pr(x|y,z) = \Pr(x|z) \tag{1}$$

for any possible values of the variables. In other words, once the value z is known, finding out the value of y has no effect on the agent's belief about x. In this case, y is superfluous information.

The STRIPS assumption is paraphrased by a schema for equation (1). Performance of an action is represented by y, z stands for the explicit effects of y plus the "background," and x represents "everything else." The independence assertion is that for a given background, knowing the explicit effects of y provides all the information useful for predicting its implicit effects, that is, everything else. Given its explicit effects, knowledge about the action's performance is redundant.

For a satisfactory interpretation, we need a more complete account of concepts like "background" and "everything else." To understand their role in planning systems, we investigate a class of representations for actions and events based on graphical models. Graphs provide a formal language for expressing (via adjacency) the locality of explicit effects in planning representations.

Graphical Dependence Models

A *probabilistic network* (also called a *Bayesian* or *belief network* [Pearl, 1988] or *influence diagram*) is a directed acyclic graph (DAG) with nodes for the random variables connected by links indicating probabilistic relations. Associated with each node is a probability distribution for its variable given the possible values for its predecessors in the graph. Thus, a link from x to y indicates that y might depend probabilistically on x. Conversely, the absence of links restricts the dependencies that can be encoded in the network. The graphical condition for conditional independence in probabilistic networks is called *d-separation* [Geiger, 1990; Pearl *et al.*, 1989]. Two nodes x and y are d-separated by a set of nodes Z in a DAG iff for every *undirected* path between them either:

1. there is a node $z \in Z$ on the path with at least one of the incident edges leading out of z, or
2. there is a node z' on the path with both incident edges leading in, and neither z' nor any of its successors are in Z.

A dependency graph for which all d-separations are valid conditional independencies is called an *I-map*. Although any joint distribution can be represented graphically by some probabilistic network (which are all I-maps), the most efficient representations are those without superfluous links, called *minimal* I-maps.

We can characterize the independence condition underlying the STRIPS assumption in terms of these dependency graph concepts. Consider a probabilistic network with variables for all actions and events relevant to the planner. Every action node has an outgoing link exactly to those events explicitly represented as direct effects. Events may have arbitrary connections among themselves, as dictated by some world model (outside the scope of discussion here). Action nodes have no incoming links, reflecting our presumption that the planner has control over which actions are to be performed.

The STRIPS assumption is that the graph so constructed is an I-map. Let S_a be the set of event variables that action variable a directly affects, a's immediate successors in the dependency graph. By virtue of I-mapness, a is conditionally independent of any $e \notin S_a$ given e's predecessors (see, for example, [Wellman, 1990b, Lemma 4.1]). Each predecessor d of e, in turn, is either a direct effect of a or is conditionally independent given its own predecessors. Ultimately, the effect of a on e is completely determined by a's direct effects and e's relation to them. Note that we still need to describe the interaction, if any, between a and e in their joint effects.

The probabilistic STRIPS assumption does *not* require that a be conditionally independent of e given the direct effects S_a, or even by any subset of S_a. In Figure 1, for example, a and e are d-separated by $\{s, b\}$ but by no other variable set. The variable b is necessary for conditional independence of a and e even though b itself is unconditionally independent of a.

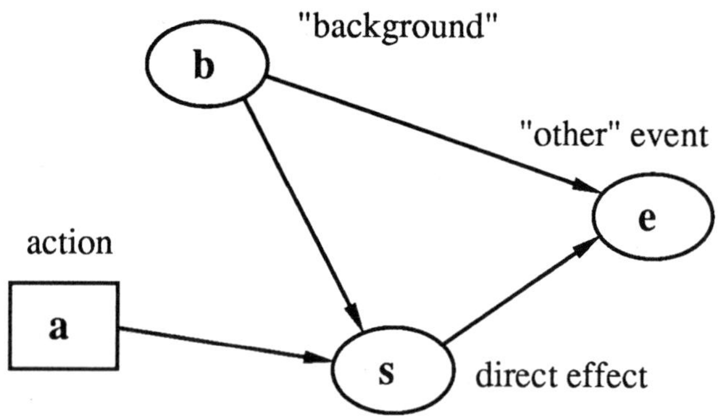

Figure 1: Action a is conditionally independent of e given $Z_a = \{s, b\}$ but not given any subset of its direct effects $S_a = \{s\}$.

If we enlarge the conditioning set to include predecessors of a's direct effects, however, we get another valid independence condition. Let $Z_a = S_a \cup B_a$, where B_a (the "background") is the set of variables that affect a's direct effects:

$$B_a = \bigcup_{s \in S_a} predecessors(s) - \{a\}.$$

The d-separation condition implies that a is conditionally independent of e given Z_a. In the graph of Figure 1, for example, the background $B_a = \{b\}$, and $Z_a = \{s, b\}$.

The dependency graph model permits us to formalize the STRIPS assumption in terms of probabilistic conditional independence. In particular, there must exist an I-map of variables in the world model where any variable e not specified as an effect of action a is not directly connected to a. Under this condition there may be a probabilistic dependency between a and e in some situations, but this can always be described in terms of a's and e's relations to S_a.

We can apply the graph construction to the informal statement of the independence condition given in the previous section. Filling in the terms, our statement is that the complete effects of an action a are fully specified by the direct effects, S_a, and the background, B_a. Everything else, e, is implicit in these variables. That is, e is conditionally independent of a given S_a and B_a. The fragment of Figure 1 can serve as a graphical schema for this pattern of relations, by interpreting the nodes as sets of variables and permitting the variables e to be connected via arbitrary paths to b and s.

Applications

The conditional independence interpretation is a valuable tool for studying specific planning systems and validating their use of the STRIPS assumption. A practical prerequisite for applying these results is identifying the relevant background context, B_a, for the various planners. Note that while planners adopt different policies regarding *how* the implicit effects are derived from the explicit effects and background, validity of the STRIPS assumption does not depend on these policies.

In the following sections I illustrate the application of the independence concepts by analyzing aspects of three planning systems. The planners examined differ in their probabilistic or deterministic representations for the effects of actions, as well as the type of temporal structure imposed on the planning environment.

SUDO-Planner

SUDO-PLANNER [Wellman, 1990a] uses *qualitative probabilistic networks* (QPNs) [Wellman, 1990b], abstractions of the models described above, for representing and reasoning about the effects of actions. When introducing actions and events of interest, the planner modifies the structure of the existing network to preserve the model's validity. One class of constructs appearing in SUDO-PLANNER's knowledge base, called *Markov influences*, specify the effect of an action on an event variable and its dependence on the previous value of that variable.

For example, consider a QPN for a medical therapy problem that includes a variable for the extent of a patient's coronary artery disease (CAD). One action considered by the planner is a coronary artery bypass graft (CABG): bypass surgery to alleviate the coronary disease. The effect of CABG is to decrease CAD (in a precise probabilistic sense [Wellman, 1990b]). Furthermore, the Markov influence specifies that the decrease is greater for patients who have more severe CAD initially. This relationship refers to the variable CAD at two distinct points in time—before and after CABG—and thus cannot be captured by simply adding CABG to the network. Instead, SUDO-PLANNER modifies the QPN by splitting CAD into two variables, CAD_1 and CAD_2. Figure 2 diagrams the result of this *mitosis* process. CABG negatively influences CAD_2, which is otherwise positively related to its value before surgery, CAD_1. The boxed minus sign indicates the synergistic interaction of CABG with CAD_1. Predecessors of the original CAD variable are connected to CAD_1, while its successors before processing the Markov influence are transferred to CAD_2.

This process has direct implications for conditional independence (which indeed was the reason for calling

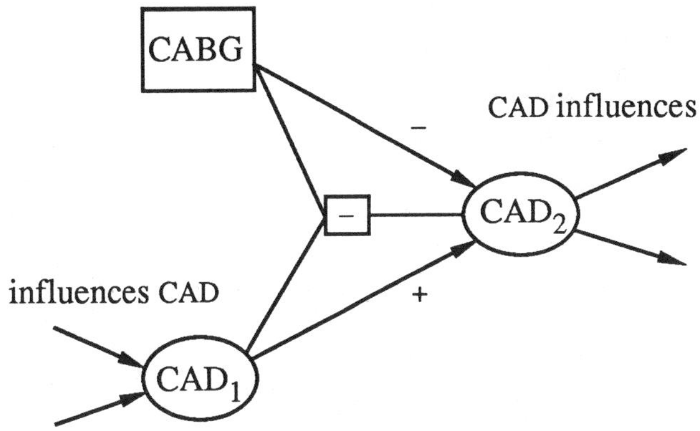

Figure 2: The Markov influence of CABG on CAD.

them *Markov* influences). Specifically, influencers of the original variable CAD are independent of CAD_2 given CAD_1, and CAD's original influences cannot depend on CAD_1 given CAD_2. (The reason is that any path between influences and influencers that circumvents the CAD_i variables must include at least one node with both incident edges leading in.) These conditions in turn imply that any variable in the network is independent of CABG given CAD_1 and CAD_2.

More generally, suppose the action a is defined exclusively by Markov influences on a set of event variables E. The STRIPS assumption dictates that the effects of a be completely captured by these influences. The corresponding independence condition is that any other event be conditionally independent of a, given $Z_a = S_a \cup B_a$, where the direct effects $S_a = E_2$, the second halves of the split event variables, and the background $B_a = E_1$, the first halves produced by SUDO-PLANNER's variable mitosis process.

Markov Influence Diagrams

Kanazawa and Dean [1989] propose a framework for planning under uncertainty based on "causal models," influence diagrams with the Markov property and some other features inessential for our purposes. In a Markov influence diagram, there is a node corresponding to every proposition of interest at every distinguished instant of time. The Markov property is enforced by permitting nodes at time t to depend only on nodes from time $t-1$. If this convention applies to actions as well, then any event at time t is d-separated from actions at time $t' < t$ by the action's direct effects (all at time $t'+1$), plus the events of time t'.

Figure 3 depicts the generic structure of a Markov influence diagram. Note that all links relate an action or event to an event at the next time point. It is possible to relax this restriction—for example, by adding auxiliary atemporal variables—as long as the regularity of temporal states is retained. See, for instance, the variant scheme described by Berzuini et al. [1989].

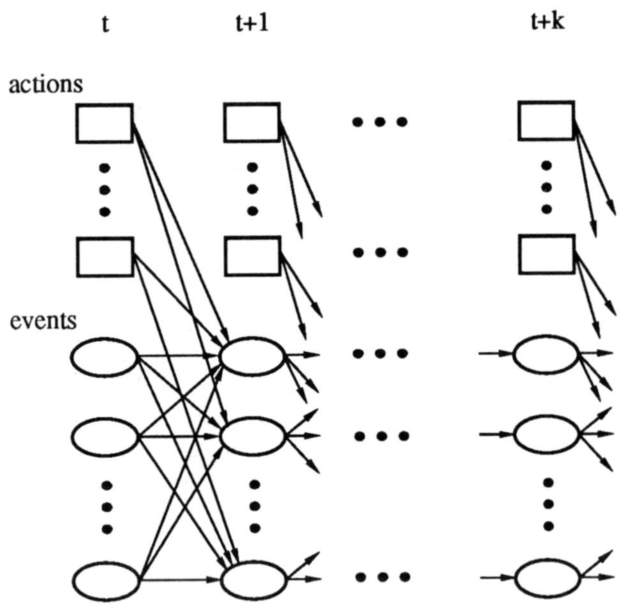

Figure 3: A schematic view of Markov influence diagrams. Actions and events at time t need not be connected to every event at $t+1$.

With respect to our statement of the STRIPS assumption, the background is (conservatively) the state of the world at the time of the action, that is, the actions and events appearing in the same column of Figure 3. The direct effects are the events from the next time point with links from the action node. In schemes for probabilistic temporal projection [Dean and Kanazawa, 1988; Hanks, 1990], these links are typically specified by a set of *causal rules* associating actions and events with their possible consequences.

STRIPS

Instantiated propositionally for a finite world, we find that a STRIPS model is actually a degenerate kind of Markov influence diagram. The Markov property follows from the linearity of the situation calculus framework [McCarthy and Hayes, 1969]. The propositions at a situation s are deterministic functions of those of the previous situation. And under Lifschitz's soundness conditions [1986], the relation of functional dependence is defined by mention in add and delete lists. The persistence model of STRIPS is that for a given proposition this function is the identity in the absence of an action performed at s affecting that proposition. Thus, the background required for any proposition is only its value in the previous situation.

In terms of dependency graphs, the STRIPS model is constructed as follows. Let a and e denote action and event types, with nodes a_t and e_t for every type in every situation t.

$$\begin{aligned} S_a &= \{e \mid e \text{ in } a\text{'s add or delete list}\}, \\ \mathit{predecessors}(e_t) &= e_{t-1} \cup \{a_{t-1} \mid e \in S_a\}. \end{aligned}$$

Most STRIPS-like systems do not specify what happens when actions are performed in situations where their preconditions do not hold. To represent "context-dependent effects" [Pednault, 1988], we need only to add events mentioned in preconditions to the background of affected events.

For deterministic variables, there is a stronger graphical criterion for conditional independence, called *D-separation* (note uppercase) [Pearl *et al.*, 1989]. Although the independence condition for STRIPS's simple graph structure is trivial, the more powerful criterion might be useful for analyzing STRIPS-like systems that permit logical and perhaps probabilistic relations among propositions.

Summary

The interpretation presented here provides a new perspective on the STRIPS assumption, constraining the semantics of a planner's knowledge base of actions and events. Essentially, it mandates that the implicit consequences of an action be completely specified by its direct effects. Although described and motivated in terms of probabilistic conditional independence, the interpretation has implications for planning systems regardless of whether they employ probabilistic representations. Moreover, it is sufficiently general to capture the principle behind the STRIPS assumption for planning systems with action-event representations considerably more expressive than that of STRIPS.

The main advantage of this approach is that it distinguishes the concept of belief dependency from the model of persistence of events in the world. It does not obviate the need for such a persistence theory, though it renders the issue orthogonal to the STRIPS assumption *per se*.

Examination of a variety of planning systems indicates that the dependency graph is a useful analytical tool for investigating the structure of relations among actions and events. When the analysis reveals regularity in this structure (as should be expected for reasonable planning architectures), general d-separation patterns can be derived, yielding constraints on the impact of actions on the agent's beliefs about the world. We can then exploit these constraints to design more efficient action representations and belief revision mechanisms.

It is not surprising that all the analyses of planning systems above appeal to some sort of Markov property. Any temporal structure on a pattern of conditional independence constitutes a Markovian form of model. This suggests that the theory of Markov models may be a good place to search for structured patterns of uncertain relationships among events over time.

The most important limitation of the analysis is that dependency graphs are an inherently propositional representation. Application to planning systems with quantified constructs (any nontrivial action and event representation) requires some instantiation mechanism. A potential solution approach is to apply the first-order axioms of conditional independence directly. This technique might be beneficial even for the propositional case, as the axiomatic theory may be stronger than the graphical [Pearl *et al.*, 1989].

References

[Berzuini *et al.*, 1989] Carlo Berzuini, Riccardo Bellazzi, and Silvana Quaglini. Temporal reasoning with probabilities. In *Proceedings of the Workshop on Uncertainty in Artificial Intelligence*, pages 14–21, Windsor, ON, 1989.

[Brown, 1987] Frank M. Brown, editor. *The Frame Problem in Artificial Intelligence: Proceedings of the 1987 Workshop*. Morgan Kaufmann, 1987.

[Dean and Kanazawa, 1988] Thomas Dean and Keiji Kanazawa. Probabilistic temporal reasoning. In *Proceedings of the National Conference on Artificial Intelligence*, pages 524–528, 1988.

[Fikes and Nilsson, 1971] Richard E. Fikes and Nils J. Nilsson. STRIPS: A new approach to the application of theorem proving to problem solving. *Artificial Intelligence*, 2:189–208, 1971.

[Geiger, 1990] Dan Geiger. Graphoids: A qualitative framework for probabilistic inference. Technical Report R-142, UCLA Computer Science Department, January 1990.

[Hanks, 1990] Steven John Hanks. Projecting plans for uncertain worlds. Technical Report 756, Yale University Department of Computer Science, January 1990.

[Kanazawa and Dean, 1989] Keiji Kanazawa and Thomas Dean. A model for projection and action. In *Proceedings of the Eleventh International Joint Conference on Artificial Intelligence*, pages 985–990, 1989.

[Lifschitz, 1986] Vladimir Lifschitz. On the semantics of STRIPS. In Michael P. Georgeff and Amy L. Lansky, editors, *Reasoning about Actions and Plans: Proceedings of the 1986 Workshop*, pages 1–9. Morgan Kaufmann, 1986.

[McCarthy and Hayes, 1969] J. McCarthy and P. J. Hayes. Some philosophical problems from the standpoint of artificial intelligence. In B. Meltzer and D. Michie, editors, *Machine Intelligence 4*, pages 463–502. Edinburgh University Press, 1969.

[McDermott, 1987] Drew McDermott. AI, logic, and the frame problem. In Brown [1987], pages 105–118.

[Pearl *et al.*, 1989] Judea Pearl, Dan Geiger, and Thomas Verma. Conditional independence and its representations. *Kybernetika*, 25:33–44, 1989.

[Pearl, 1988] Judea Pearl. *Probabilistic Reasoning in Intelligent Systems: Networks of Plausible Inference*. Morgan Kaufmann, 1988.

[Pednault, 1988] Edwin P. D. Pednault. Extending conventional planning techniques to handle actions with context-dependent effects. In *Proceedings of the National Conference on Artificial Intelligence*, pages 55–59. AAAI, 1988.

[Pylyshyn, 1987] Zenon W. Pylyshyn, editor. *The Robot's Dilemma: The Frame Problem in Artificial Intelligence*. Ablex, 1987.

[Waldinger, 1977] Richard Waldinger. Achieving several goals simultaneously. In E. Elcock and D. Michie, editors, *Machine Intelligence 8*, pages 94–136. Edinburgh University Press, 1977.

[Wellman, 1990a] Michael P. Wellman. *Formulation of Tradeoffs in Planning Under Uncertainty*. Pitman and Morgan Kaufmann, 1990.

[Wellman, 1990b] Michael P. Wellman. Fundamental concepts of qualitative probabilistic networks. *Artificial Intelligence*, 1990.

ABTWEAK: Abstracting a Nonlinear, Least Commitment Planner *

Qiang Yang
Computer Science Department
University of Waterloo
Waterloo, Ontario, Canada, N2L 3G1
qyang@watdragon.waterloo.edu.

Josh D. Tenenberg
Computer Science Department
University of Rochester
Rochester, New York, U.S.A., 14627
josh@cs.rochester.edu

Abstract

We present the system AbTweak, which extends the precondition-elimination abstraction of Abstrips to hierarchical planners using the nonlinear plan representation as defined in Tweak. We show that AbTweak satisfies the *monotonic property*, whereby the existence of a lowest level solution Π implies the existence of a highest level solution that is *structurally similar* to Π. This property enables one to prune a considerable amount of the search space without loss of completeness.

Abstracting Planning Systems

Abstraction in planning systems can be viewed as a mapping from one problem description (at a *concrete* level) to another(at the *abstract* level). There has been a considerable amount of research recently in formalizing intuitions regarding abstraction and the hierarchical problem solving strategies that abstraction gives rise to [Fikes *et al.*, 1972; Knoblock, 1988; Korf, 1985b; Nau, 1987; Sacerdoti, 1974; Tate, 1977; Tenenberg, 1988; Wilkins, 1984; Yang, 1989].

However, there has been little work in extending the formal results from linear STRIPS-like planners to richer temporal planners, such as the nonlinear planners of Sacerdoti [1977] and Chapman [1985]. The advantage of these planners over linear planners is that they allow temporal order and operator instantiations to be only partially specified through the posting of constraints; any fully specified plan consistent with these constraints is guaranteed to solve the given problem.

One particular type of abstraction that we have previously formalized [Tenenberg, 1988], involves the elimination of a subset of the predicates in the language as one ascends the abstraction hierarchy (a generalization of the precondition elimination strategy of Abstrips [Sacerdoti, 1974]). The predicates of the planning system are partitioned, which induces a partition on the preconditions of the operators, and each partition is assigned an integer value, a *criticality*. Each abstract level i is derived from the previous level by eliminating those preconditions having criticality $< i$, otherwise being identical.

We define the system AbTweak, and demonstrate in this paper that precondition-elimination abstraction can be naturally extended to nonlinear least commitment planners, and thus benefit from the advantages of both abstraction and nonlinearity. Most importantly, we show that each AbTweak system has a *monotonically expandable* abstraction space, whereby the existence of a lowest level solution Π implies the existence of a highest level solution that is structurally similar to Π. This property enables one to prune a considerable amount of the search space without loss of completeness. In addition, the abstraction space is monotonic regardless of the criticality assignment, i.e., it does not depend upon obtaining the "right" assignment of criticality values to preconditions.

We first present brief descriptions of Tweak and Abstrips, and then define AbTweak. We demonstrate that AbTweak has the monotonic property, and show how this affects search. All lemmas and theorems are presented without proofs. These proofs can be found in the longer version of this paper [Yang and Tenenberg, 1990].

Nonlinear Planning: Tweak

Chapman [1985] provides a formalization of a least commitment, nonlinear planner, Tweak. Tweak extends Strips by allowing for

1. a partial temporal ordering on the operators in a plan,

*This work was supported in part by an interim research grant to Qiang Yang, from the Faculty of Mathematics at the University of Waterloo, and by grants to Josh D. Tenenberg in part from the Air Force Systems Command, Rome Air Development Center, Griffiss Air Force Base, New York 13441-5700, and the Air Force Office of Scientific Research, Bolling AFB, DC 20332, under Contract Num. F30602-85-C-0008 which supports the Northeast Artificial Intelligence Consortium (NAIC), in part by ONR/DARPA research contract #N00014-80-C-0197, and in part by US Army Communication-Electronics Command grant #DAAB10-87-D-022.

2. partial constraints on the binding of variables (*codesignations*) of the operators.

A TWEAK plan thus represents a space of STRIPS plans: all totally ordered, fully ground plans that satisfy the ordering and codesignation constraints.

Formally, a TWEAK system is a pair $\Sigma = (L, O)$. L is a restricted language consisting of countably many predicate, constant and variable symbols, but none of the logical connectives (and, therefore, not the quantifiers). The set of *terms* of L is the constants unioned with the variables, and the set of *propositions* is all expressions of the form

$$P(x_1, \ldots, x_n),$$

where P is an n-ary predicate and the x_i are terms. The set of *literals* of L is the set of propositions unioned with the set of negations of propositions.

O is a set of operator templates (referred to simply as operators), defined in terms of preconditions and effects, with the variables in each operator standardized apart. Each precondition or effect is a literal in L. If $a \in O$ is an operator, then P_a is the set of preconditions of a, and E_a is the set of effects of a. An operator a *asserts* literal p if $p \in E_a$, and *denies* p if $\neg p \in E_a$.

Chapman [1985] did not give a formal definition of a TWEAK plan. Because this concept is very important in defining a number of others later in the paper, we formally define it below:

Definition 1 *A plan Π is a triple (A, B, C), where*

- *$A(\Pi)$ is a set of operators, defined in terms of preconditions and effects,*
- *$B(\Pi)$ is a partial ordering on A ("$\prec$"),*
- *$C(\Pi)$ is a set of codesignation and non-codesignation constraints of the form $p \approx q$ or $p \not\approx q$, where p and q are both either terms or propositions.*

If a, b are operators in $A(\Pi)$, we say $B(\Pi) \vdash (a \prec b)$ if and only if $(a \prec b)$ follows from the transitive closure of $B(\Pi)$. That is, a precedes b under every total ordering that satisfies $B(\Pi)$. If $P(x_1, \ldots, x_n)$ and $P(y_1, \ldots, y_n)$ are propositions, we say

$$C(\Pi) \vdash (P(x_1, \ldots, x_n) \approx P(y_1, \ldots, y_n))$$

if and only if each $(x_i \approx y_i)$ follows from the symmetric and transitive closure of the codesignation constraints of $C(\Pi)$. Likewise for non-codesignation.

With the above definition, we can now restate formally several terminologies used in [Chapman, 1985]. A *complete plan* is a plan where $B(\Pi)$ is a total ordering on $A(\Pi)$, and $C(\Pi)$ is such that every variable in every operator of $A(\Pi)$ codesignates with some constant. A plan *completion* refers to any complete plan that satisfies the partial constraints of a plan.

An input problem is taken to be a pair, $\rho = (I, G)$, where I is the initial state, and G is the goal state, each state consisting of a finite set of literals. A complete plan for a problem implicitly defines a sequence of states: the first element of the sequence is the given initial state, and the $i + 1^{st}$ element of the sequence is the ith state without the literals denied by the ith operator, and including the literals asserted by the ith operator. A proposition is satisfied in a state if it is an element of that state.

For simplicity, the goal G can be represented by a special operator g, where $P_g = E_g = G$. The initial state I can likewise be viewed as a special operator i, with $P_i = \emptyset$ and $E_i = I$. These two operators will be an element of each plan Π, under the constraint that, for every other operator $a \in A(\Pi)$, $(i \prec a)$ and $(a \prec g)$.

A complete plan is *correct* if all preconditions of each operator in the plan are satisfied in the state in which the operator is applied. A complete plan *solves* a problem if it is correct, and the goal is satisfied in the final state. A plan solves a problem if every completion solves the problem; similarly for correctness of plans.

In a partial plan, two terms *necessarily* codesignate, that is, unify, if they codesignate under every completion. Two terms *possibly* codesignate if they codesignate under some completion. Operator a necessarily precedes b if a precedes b under every completion. a possibly precedes b if a precedes b under some completion. We will use $\Box$ and $\Diamond$ to denote necessarily and possibly, and $\approx$, $\not\approx$, and $\prec$ to denote codesignates, non-codesignates and precedes. Necessary and possible precedence, codesignation and noncodesignation can be defined precisely, for plan P, as:

$$\begin{aligned}
\Box(a \prec b) &\iff B(\Pi) \vdash (a \prec b),\\
\Diamond(a \prec b) &\iff \neg\Box\neg(a \prec b) \iff B(\Pi) \nvdash (b \prec a),\\
\Box(p \approx q) &\iff C(\Pi) \vdash (p \approx q),\\
\Diamond(p \approx q) &\iff \neg\Box\neg(p \approx q) \iff C(\Pi) \nvdash (p \not\approx q),\\
\Box(p \not\approx q) &\iff C(\Pi) \vdash (p \not\approx q),\\
\Diamond(p \not\approx q) &\iff \neg\Box\neg(p \not\approx q) \iff C(\Pi) \nvdash (p \approx q).
\end{aligned}$$

The following definitions introduce simplifying notation.

$$\begin{aligned}
\Diamond(a \prec c \prec b) &\iff \Diamond(a \prec c) \text{ and } \Diamond(c \prec b),\\
\Box(a \prec c \prec b) &\iff \Box(a \prec c) \text{ and } \Box(c \prec b).
\end{aligned}$$

The Modal Truth Criterion

The *modal truth criterion* (MTC) defines the conditions under which an assertion will be true at a point in a partially ordered plan. Chapman [1985] provides a concise statement of the criterion that is both necessary and sufficient. A problem with his definition is that it is stated in terms of *situations*, which are not well-defined in a partially ordered and instantiated plan. For that reason, we provide a modified version of the MTC, defined in terms of operators in a plan.

Coarsely stated, a proposition p is necessarily true in the state in which operator b is applied if there exists, for every total ordering, some operator a that asserts p (adds a proposition that codesignates with p), and for which no operator between a and b asserts $\neg p$.

Definition 2 *Proposition p is necessarily true in the state in which operator b is applied in plan Π if and only if two conditions hold:*

1. *there is an operator $a \in A(\Pi)$ and $u \in E_a$, such that $\Box(a \prec b)$ and $\Box(p \approx u)$, and*
2. *for every operator $c \in A(\Pi)$ and $q \in E_c$, if $\Diamond(c \prec b)$, and $\Diamond(\neg q \approx p)$, then there is an operator $w \in A(\Pi)$ and $r \in E_w$ such that $\Box(c \prec w \prec b)$ and $C(\Pi) \cup \{(\neg q \approx p)\} \vdash (r \approx p)$.*

This last condition says that $(r \approx p)$ whenever $(\neg q \approx p)$.

AbTweak

In Abstrips, Sacerdoti developed an elegant means for generating abstract problem spaces, by assigning criticality values (an integer between 0 and k, for some small k) to preconditions, and abstracting at level i by eliminating all preconditions having criticality less than i. The formalisms for this system are straightforward, and are provided below when criticalities are assigned to the precondition literals in a Tweak system.

A k level AbTweak system is a triple $\Sigma = (L, O, crit)$, where

(1) L is a Tweak language;
(2) O is an operator set, as in Tweak, and
(3) $crit$ is a function:

$$\bigcup_{o \in O} P_o \rightarrow \{0, 1, \ldots, k-1\}.$$

Intuitively, *crit* is an assignment of criticality values to each proposition appearing in the precondition of an operator.

Let a be an operator. We take ${}_iP_a$ to be the set of preconditions of a which have criticality values of at least i:

$${}_iP_a = \{p \mid p \in P_a \text{ and } crit(p) \geq i.\},$$

and ${}_ia$ is operator a with preconditions ${}_iP_a$ and effects E_a. Let the set of all such ${}_ia$ be ${}_iO$. This defines a TWEAK system on each level i of abstraction:

$${}_i\Sigma = (L,\ {}_iO).$$

Upward Solution Property

As with Abstrips the strategy for planning with AbTweak is governed by length first search. When a problem is input, planning proceeds first at the most abstract, least constrained level. This plan is then expanded at the next lower level by inserting new operators to satisfy the re-introduced preconditions. Only after all the preconditions are satisfied on the current level does the planner pass the plan to the level below. The primary reason for using this control strategy is for solving the frame problem.

Implicit in this strategy is the assumption that short plans to solve a given problem are guaranteed to exist at the abstract level which can be successively expanded, and that search strategies exist to find such abstract plans. Our intent is to formally prove this property, and to show how it places some useful constraints on search. The intuition behind the proof is to show that if there exists a lowest (base) level solution to a problem, then this solution will also solve the problem at each higher level of abstraction, since these higher levels do not place any new constraints on the problem. Further, since there are fewer preconditions at the higher levels, one can eliminate from this plan those operators whose purpose at lower levels is solely to satisfy one of the eliminated preconditions, either directly or indirectly.

For instance, consider a plan for getting a box from one room into an adjacent room, in which the robot picks up the box, goes to the door, sets the box down, opens the door, picks up the box, and goes through the doorway. Suppose that the status of the door – whether it is open or closed – is ignored at the abstract level. In this case, since opening the door is no longer considered as a precondition, the intermediate steps of setting down and re-picking up the box are no longer necessary; their sole purpose was to free the agent's hands for the door opening. Thus, the abstract level plan is simpler than the concrete level plan.

Ascending Preserves Correctness

For notational simplicity, if Π is a plan on the base level, then for $i = 1, 2, \ldots, k-1$, let ${}_i\Pi$ represent the plan formed by replacing every occurrence of a (except i and g) in Π by ${}_ia$. As defined above, a plan Π is correct if and only if $\forall a \in A(\Pi), \forall q \in P_a$, q is necessarily true in the state in which a is applied. Removing a precondition of an operator while holding the plan fixed does not affect the necessary truth of any condition. Thus, after removing a precondition of an operator in Π, the resulting plan Π' is still correct. However, we can establish a stronger property. Namely, if Π is a plan correct at the base level, then a plan ${}_i\Pi'$ is also a correct plan on level i, where ${}_i\Pi'$ is simpler than Π in that it is ${}_i\Pi$ with possibly one or more operators removed. Thus, $A({}_i\Pi')$ is possibly smaller than $A(\Pi)$. Moreover, the constraints in ${}_i\Pi'$ are $B(\Pi)$ and $C(\Pi)$ with possibly one or more constraints removed. Thus, the plan ${}_i\Pi'$ is less constrained than Π. This will be shown by specifying the *precondition establishment* structure of the plan, that is, which operators satisfy preconditions of other operators, either directly or indirectly.

Definition 3 *Let Π be a correct plan. Let a and b be operators in $A(\Pi)$, p be a precondition of b, and u be an effect of a. Then a establishes p for b with u (Establishes(a, b, p, u)) if and only if*

1. $\Box(a \prec b)$,

2. $\Box(u \approx p)$, *and*
3. $\forall a' \in A(\Pi), \forall u' \in E_{a'}$, *if* $\Box(a \prec a' \prec b)$, *then* $\neg\Box(u' \approx p)$.

This final condition states that a must be the last such operator that necessarily precedes b which necessarily asserts precondition p.

Given this definition, it can be proven that every precondition in every operator of a correct plan has an establisher.

Lemma 4 *Let* Π *be a correct plan,* $b \in A(\Pi)$, *and* $p \in P_b$. $\exists a \in A(\Pi), \exists u \in E_a$ *such that* $\text{Establishes}(a, b, p, u)$.

Informally, a *clobberer* is an operator which possibly precedes and possibly denies the precondition of another operator in the plan. A *white knight* is another operator which necessarily re-establishes this clobbered precondition.

Definition 5 *c is a clobberer of b,* $(\text{CB}(c, b, p, q))$ *if and only if*

(1) $p \in P_b$,
(2) $q \in E_c$,
(3) $\Diamond(\neg q \approx p)$,
(4) $\exists a, u$ *such that* $\text{Establishes}(a, b, p, u)$,
(5) $\Diamond(a \prec c \prec b)$.

Definition 6 *w is a white knight for b,* $(\text{WK}(w, b, c, p, q, r))$, *if and only if*

(1) $\text{CB}(c, b, p, q)$,
(2) $r \in E_w$,
(3) $\Box(c \prec w \prec b)$, *and*
(4) $C(\Pi) \cup \{(\neg q \approx p)\} \vdash (r \approx p)$.

An operator or constraint in a plan is justified if it is subservient, directly or indirectly, to the satisfaction of the goal.

Definition 7 *Let* Π *be a plan, and* i, g *be the special operators for the initial and goal states. Then in plan* Π,

Initial/Goal justification *i and g are justified,*

Establishment justification *If b is justified, and* $\exists a, \exists u \in E_a, \exists p \in P_b$ *such that* $\text{Establishes}(a, b, p, u)$, *then*

(1) a is justified, (2) $(a \prec b)$ is justified, (3) $(u \approx p)$ is justified.

White knight justification
If $\text{WK}(w, b, c, p, q, r)$ *and b and c are justified, then w, $(c \prec w)$, and $(w \prec b)$ are justified. Moreover, let D be a minimal set of codesignation constraints such that* $D \cup \{(\neg q \approx p)\} \vdash (r \approx p)$. *Then every codesignation constraint in D is also justified.*

Separation justification *If c and b are justified, and* $\exists p \in P_b, \exists q \in E_c$ *such that* $\Box(p \not\approx \neg q)$, *then* $(p \not\approx \neg q)$ *is justified.*

Precedence Justification *If b and c are justified and* $\Box(b \prec c)$, *then* $b \prec c$ *is also justified.*

Nothing else is justified.

The justification of plan Π, $\text{Jus}(\Pi)$, is the set of operators, precedence and codesignation constraints of Π that are justified. It is obvious that the justified version of a plan is simpler than the plan itself, in the sense that the set of operators, precedence and codesignation constraints of the justified plan are a subset of those in the unjustified plan.

Lemma 8 *If* Π *is a correct plan that solves goal* G, *then* $\text{Jus}(\Pi)$ *also is a correct plan that solves* G.

The following theorem establishes the *Upward Solution Property*: if there is a solution to a problem at the base level, then the justified version of that solution at each higher level of abstraction is correct, and also solves the problem on that level. More formally,

Theorem 9 *If* Π *is a correct plan that solves G at the base level, then the justified version of* ${}_i\Pi$ *is also a correct plan that solves G on the* i^{th} *level,* $0 \leq i \leq k-1$.

Monotonic Expansion

The Upward Solution Property guarantees the existence of an abstract level solution to a problem, whenever there exists a lowest level solution. Length-first search, on the other hand, proceeds from the highest level to the lowest. Since the converse of the Upward Solution Property does not hold, one cannot be sure that an arbitrary solution obtained at the abstract level is one which can be expanded into a low level solution. It is therefore important to uncover constraints that will be helpful in plan expansion. The monotonic property is one such constraint, and was first defined by Knoblock, for linear ABSTRIPS systems [Knoblock, 1988]. We will define it here (in a slightly different form than Knoblock).

Definition 10 *Let* Π' *be a level i plan, and* Π *a level* $i-1$ *plan.* $c : A(\Pi') \mapsto A(\Pi)$ *is a correspondence function if and only if*

1. *c is* $1-1$ *and* into, *and*
2. $\forall a \in A(\Pi')$, ${}_i(c(a)) = a$.

Definition 11 *Let* Π' *be an abstract plan that solves ρ at level i,* $i > 0$. Π' *monotonically expands to level* $i-1$ *plan* Π *if and only if*

1. Π *solves ρ at level* $i-1$, *and*
2. *there exists a correspondence function* $c : \Pi' \mapsto \Pi$ *such that* $\forall a, b, p, u$ *if* $\text{Establishes}(a, b, p, u)$ *in* Π' *then* $\text{Establishes}(c(a), c(b), p, u)$ *in* Π.

Definition 12 *A k-level* ABTWEAK *system is monotonic, if and only if, for every problem ρ solvable at the concrete* (0th) *level, there exists a sequence of plans* $\Pi_{k-1}, \ldots, \Pi_0$ *such that* Π_{k-1} *solves ρ at level* $k-1$, *and for* $0 < i < k$, Π_i *monotonically expands to* Π_{i-1}.

The following Lemma can now be proven:

Lemma 13 *Every* ABTWEAK *system of k levels, for any k, is monotonic.*

Search Control

In this section, we explore the implications of the Monotonic Property on search control in ABTWEAK. We will discuss global completeness of ABTWEAK as an abstraction system, and show that ABTWEAK can backtrack on violations of higher-level establishment relations and unresolvable conflicts.

Completeness of ABTWEAK

Search for a plan with ABTWEAK proceeds in a *length-wise* fashion, by first finding a plan at the most abstract level, and then, for each lower level i, expanding the plan Π from level $i+1$ by inserting operators into Π, or imposing new constraints to satisfy the re-introduced preconditions in Π. Thus, ABTWEAK searches for a correct concrete-level plan in a space of abstract plans. In this search space, if a plan Π is not correct yet on an abstract level, then the set of state-space operators applicable to Π is the set of plan modification operations in TWEAK. On the other hand, if a plan Π is correct on level $i > 0$, then the state-space operator is simply plan expansion, which inserts all $i-1$ level preconditions to each operator in Π.

In this section, we discuss the global search control strategy for ABTWEAK. Before describing it in detail, we first explain what seems to be an obvious choice for search control, and why it is not used for ABTWEAK.

We first define what we mean by completeness, and monotonic completeness:

Definition 14 *A control strategy is* complete *if whenever there is a solution at the concrete level, the strategy will terminate by finding a solution.*

Definition 15 *A control strategy for a k-level* ABTWEAK *system is* monotonically complete *if and only if for every problem ρ solvable at the concrete (0th) level, the strategy outputs a sequence of plans $\Pi_{k-1}, \ldots, \Pi_0$ such that Π_{k-1} solves ρ at level $k-1$, and for $0 < i < k$, Π_i monotonically expands to Π_{i-1}.*

Our aim is to explore control strategies that are monotonically complete.

An intuitively obvious choice of control is to use a separate TWEAK for control on each level of abstraction, similar to the way ABSTRIPS uses STRIPS. This is especially appealing, since it is not difficult to specify complete control strategies for TWEAK, either using a complete state-space search procedure such as A*, or breadth-first search, or the procedure provided by Chapman [1985]. Using this approach, if a plan is formed on abstraction level i, then it is passed down to the level below. At level $i-1$, all the conditions of criticalities no less than $i-1$ are planned for. The process continues, until either a correct plan is formed at the base level, or it is found that a plan cannot be made correct at a level. Then the planner backtracks to the level immediately above the current one, and tries to find an alternative solution.

The fact that TWEAK is complete may lead one into believing that the above control structure is also monotonically complete. Unfortunately, this is not the case in general. The reason is that any search strategy for TWEAK will be semi-decidable, in the sense that if there is no solution, it is not guaranteed to terminate. Suppose that a plan Π is found on level $i+1$ that is not monotonically expandable, and is passed to the level i below. Then it is possible for TWEAK to run forever, without knowing it should backtrack to the level above. Incompleteness may result since there may exist a correct solution at the concrete level, and Π cannot be expanded to that solution.

Thus, although on each level of abstraction completeness is guaranteed separately, it is not ensured monotonically. A complete search strategy will be obliged to do a "diagonalizing enumeration," that is, it cannot simply pick an abstract plan, and attempt to specialize this plan further without regard to the remaining abstract solutions, but must instead do only a quanta of planning steps, and go to the next abstract solution. But, it cannot be simple minded about this either, since there may be an infinite number of abstract solutions. So, it must do some quanta on the next abstraction, and then return to the first one. That is, the enumeration must "diagonalize in two dimensions."

The above argument suggests a monotonically complete control procedure, in the sense that any state in ABTWEAK's search space may be selected next according to a complete search control strategy. Recall that ABTWEAK's search space operations include not only the plan modifications of TWEAK, but also the plan expansions. Thus, if a path exists in the original state space from the initial state to a goal state, one such path will eventually be found. Any complete search strategy will suffice for the purpose: breadth-first, A^* [Nilsson, 1980], depth-first iterative deepening[Korf, 1985a], etc.

Backtracking on Protection Violations

The monotonic property provides a powerful heuristic for guiding the search in ABTWEAK. It can be considered as a criteria for backtracking that does not sacrifice completeness. More specifically, one can backtrack on precondition-establishment violations, that is, if for some operators a and b, and literals p and u, Establishes(a, b, p, u) in a plan at abstraction level i, then at level $i-1$, if the only choices left are to insert an operator that possibly asserts $\neg p$, then ABTWEAK can backtrack without losing monotonic completeness. Thus, the causal relation between preconditions and effects should be preserved when going down abstraction levels. This effectively imposes a strong constraint on how an abstract plan should be refined at a lower level.

Backtracking on Incompleteable Plans

Sometimes no solution can be found at a particular level of abstraction. In that case, one would like to know whether a solution exists at the base level. For AbTweak, it follows from the Upward-Solution Property that if there is no solution at one level, then no solution exists at all at any lower levels of abstraction.

A related problem is whether to backtrack from an incompleteable plan. A plan Π is said to be *incompleteable* if no correct completion of Π exists, and no operators and constraints can be inserted to obtain a correct completion. One way for Π to be incompleteable is that it contains a set of clobberers of the operators in Π, and that no white knights and constraints exist to remove all of the clobbering. This situation corresponds to what is commonly known as the "unresolvable conflicts" in nonlinear planning. It can be proven that AbTweak can backtrack from an incompleteable plan without losing completeness[Yang and Tenenberg, 1990].

Conclusion

This research has been aimed at formalizing domain-independent, nonlinear planning systems that plan in hierarchies of abstraction levels. The resultant planner, AbTweak, extends the precondition-elimination methods in Abstrips for building abstraction hierarchies, and allows for least-commitment representations of plans in Tweak. We have shown that AbTweak satisfies the monotonic property, that is, as planning descends from top to concrete levels of abstraction, the precondition establishment structure of a plan need not be changed. This, to a large extent, formalizes our intuition for using abstraction in planning: that it is generally more efficient to use an abstract solution to guide search at lower levels of abstractions than without abstraction. In addition, we have demonstrated that a simplistic application of a control strategy for a single-level problem solver to each level of the abstraction hierarchy will not in general provide a complete multiple-level system. We also discussed how to ensure the monotonic completeness for AbTweak systems.

We believe that AbTweak also offers computational advantages over some of the existing hierarchical planning systems. However, to provide concrete evidence for this claim, it might take a considerable amount of experimentation. Indeed, our ongoing work is to implement AbTweak and make such computational comparisons.

Acknowledgements

We thank Craig Knoblock for many useful comments.

References

[Chapman, 1985] David Chapman. Planning for conjunctive goals. AI Technical Report 802, Massachusetts Institute of Technology, 1985.

[Fikes *et al.*, 1972] Richard Fikes, Peter Hart, and Nils Nilsson. Learning and executing generalized robot plans. *Artificial Intelligence*, 3:251–288, 1972.

[Knoblock, 1988] Craig Knoblock. A theory of abstraction for hierarchical planning. In *Proceedings of the First International Workshop in Change of Representation and Inductive Bias*, pages 53–65, 1988.

[Korf, 1985a] Richard Korf. Depth-first iterative-deepening: An optimal admissible tree search. *Artificial Intelligence*, 27:97–109, 1985.

[Korf, 1985b] Richard Korf. Planning as search: A quantitative approach. *Artificial Intelligence*, 33:65–88, 1985.

[Nau, 1987] Dana Nau. Hierarchical abstraction for process planning. In *Proceedings of Second International Conference in Applications of Artificial Intelligence in Engineering*, 1987.

[Nilsson, 1980] Nils Nilsson. *Principles of Artificial Intelligence.* Morgan Kaufmann Publishers Inc, 1980.

[Sacerdoti, 1974] Earl Sacerdoti. Planning in a hierarchy of abstraction spaces. *Artificial Intelligence*, 5:115–135, 1974.

[Sacerdoti, 1977] Earl Sacerdoti. *A Structure for Plans and Behavior.* American Elsevier, 1977.

[Tate, 1977] Austin Tate. Generating project networks. In *Proceedings of the 5th IJCAI*, pages 888–893, 1977.

[Tenenberg, 1988] Josh Tenenberg. *Abstraction in Planning.* PhD thesis, University of Rochester, Dept. of Computer Science, Rochester, NY, May 1988.

[Wilkins, 1984] David Wilkins. Domain-independent planning: Representation and plan generation. *Artificial Intelligence*, 22, 1984.

[Yang and Tenenberg, 1990] Qiang Yang and Josh Tenenberg. Abtweak: A hierarchical, least-commitment planner. Technical Report 90-09, University of Waterloo, 1990.

[Yang, 1989] Qiang Yang. *Improving the Efficiency of Planning.* PhD thesis, University of Maryland, 1989.

Search Lessons Learned from Crossword Puzzles

Matthew L. Ginsberg*
Michael Frank
Michael P. Halpin
Mark C. Torrance
Computer Science Department
Stanford University
Stanford, California 94305
ginsberg@cs.stanford.edu

Abstract

The construction of a program that generates crossword puzzles is discussed. As in a recent paper by Dechter and Meiri, we make an experimental comparison of various search techniques. The conclusions to which we come differ from theirs in some areas – although we agree that directional arc consistency is better than path-consistency or other forms of lookahead, and that backjumping is to be preferred to backtracking, we disagree in that we believe dynamic ordering of the constraints to be necessary in the solution of more difficult problems.

1 Introduction

Appearances notwithstanding, this is not a paper about crossword puzzles. It is a paper about search. More specifically, it is a paper about constraint satisfaction in large databases.

What we have done is to write a program that generates crossword puzzles by filling words into an empty frame. For frame sizes greater than 4×4, the associated search space is large enough to make brute force depth-first search impractical; heuristics must be used. The large branching factor is a consequence of the fact that any particular word can be chosen in many possible fashions – the dictionary used in this research contained some 24,000 entries. Crossword puzzle generation can therefore be used to compare the general techniques that have been proposed for solving constraint-satisfaction problems in large databases.

Crossword puzzles are fairly typical constraint-satisfaction problems; we share, for example, the constraint-satisfaction community's interest in finding a single solution to a given problem, as opposed to finding all such solutions. But crossword puzzles also tend to be far more difficult than most of the problems that have been discussed in the literature thus far. The recent work of Dechter and Meiri, for example, considers randomly-generated problems with 10-15 variables and 5 values [Dechter and Meiri, 1989]; our crosswords involved perhaps 60 variables and 7000 values.

In the next section, we discuss the general framework in which our experiments were performed. We also discuss some simple improvements to existing techniques that we developed in order to allow our program to solve more difficult crosswords.

Section 3 contains our experimental data. For each combination of the heuristics discussed in Section 2, we attempted to complete a variety of crossword frames; the average times needed to complete the search are shown, and the computational merits of the various techniques are discussed. Concluding remarks are contained in Section 4.

2 Existing work

There is very little existing work on the automatic generation of crossword puzzles; an old paper of Mazlack's [Mazlack, 1976] is the only one of which we are aware.[1] More relevant to our purposes is the work on constraint satisfaction.

As noted in [Dechter and Pearl, 1988], there are four choices to be made when solving a constraint-satisfaction problem: which variable to instantiate next, what value to use as the instantiation, how to handle backtracking, and what sort of preprocessing to do.

By a "variable," we will mean a particular word slot in the puzzle being generated; the constraints correspond to the fact that if two words intersect in a square s, they must use the same letter in that square.[2]

*This work has been supported by the Rockwell Palo Alto Laboratory.

[1]We will have little to say about Mazlack's work here. His techniques are very different from ours, and the performance of his program – even correcting for hardware advances since it was written – appears to be at least one or two orders of magnitude worse than ours.

[2]Constraint-satisfaction problems have duals, where the roles of the constraints and the variables are swapped.

Choice of variable

When choosing which variable to instantiate next (i.e., which word to fill in), one must decide whether the choice should be made when the puzzle is first examined (at "compile time") or whether it should be made dynamically as the other variables are assigned values (at "run time").

A variety of compile time heuristics have been discussed elsewhere in the literature. The so-called "cheapest-first heuristic" suggests constructing a statistical estimate of the number of choices remaining for each variable, and to then instantiate the variable that is the most constrained.[3] The "connectivity heuristic" suggests instantiating a variable that is constrained by the last variable instantiated, in order to ensure that one backtracks effectively when a dead end is reached.[4]

The best-known run time heuristic is known as "dynamic search rearrangement" and suggests that at any particular point in the search one should pick the variable that actually *is* the most constrained (by counting the number of possible solutions for each uninstantiated variable), instead of simply the one that is statistically *expected* to be the most sharply restricted as in the cheapest-first heuristic.

The two techniques that we chose to consider were the cheapest-first heuristic and its run time analog, dynamic search rearrangement. Connectivity was not considered because, as noted by Dechter and Meiri in [Dechter and Meiri, 1989], many of its advantages can be obtained by using backjumping [Gaschnig, 1979] instead of simple backtracking.

Choice of instantiation

Suppose, then, that we have selected a variable (i.e., word) to be filled next. How do we select among the possible values for it? In doing so, it is important to select one that restricts the possible choices for subsequent variables as little as possible. Why use a word with a `Q` when one with an `S` could be used instead?

In crossword puzzles, it is impractical to use this idea exactly; there are simply too many possible choices for each variable. Instead, we did the following: Suppose that we have decided to instantiate some particular variable by filling a particular word in the puzzle. The program considers the first k words that can legally fill this slot; suppose that we denote them by $w_1, \ldots, w_k$. For each w_i, the number of possibilities for each unfilled crossing word is computed, and the product of all of these values is calculated. The word actually chosen is that w_i that maximizes this product.

Of course, the behavior of this heuristic will be sensitive to the choice made for k. If $k = 1$, the first available word will be used at all times. But making k too large is also a mistake – all we really need to do is to make it large enough that one of the first k words is a fairly good choice. The time spent examining the rest of the possible words is unlikely to be justified by the small impact on the size of the subsequent search space. Some experimentation indicated that $k = 10$ was a reasonable value, and this is the value used in Section 3, where it is compared with the choice $k = 1$. The parameter k was called `min-look` in the implementation and this is how we will refer to it in Section 3.

Backtracking

When a dead end is reached (i.e., some slot is found for which there is no legal word), the program needs to backtrack and try something else. Simple chronological backtracking (backtrack to the last choice point, as in PROLOG) suffers from the problem that it may fail to address the source of the difficulty. If the program is having trouble filling the upper-left-hand corner of the puzzle, it is a mistake to make changes in a portion of the puzzle that have no effect on this problematic region.

This difficulty can be overcome using a technique known as *backjumping* [Gaschnig, 1979], which actually backs up to the source of the difficulty. It has been shown both theoretically [Dechter, 1990] and experimentally [Dechter and Meiri, 1989] that backjumping outperforms its chronological counterpart.

If no lookahead is done, backjumping can be implemented simply by always backtracking to a word that intersects a word that cannot be filled satisfactorily; the connection with the connectivity heuristic is clear in this case. If lookahead information is used as well (see the next section), then backjumping requires us to maintain, for each instantiated variable, a list of those subsequent variables that it affects in some way. This idea is obviously closely related to dependency-directed backtracking [Stallman and Sussman, 1977], although it is not quite the same because the expense of maintaining complete dependency information is avoided.

We also considered a small further improvement. Suppose that we have reached a dead end, and have decided to backjump to a particular word, w_1, that is the source of the difficulty. It is not too hard to determine what letter or letters in w_1 are causing the problem, and to then ensure that the new choice for w_1 avoids it. In conventional constraint-propagation terms, we

As Rich Korf has pointed out, the dual problem in the crossword-puzzle domain is also a natural one – the variables are the letters in the puzzle, and the constraints come from the fact that each letter sequence must be a legal English word.

[3] For example, if there are 2139 4-letter words in the dictionary, it is assumed that 2139/26 choices remain after the second letter is filled in. This is independent of whether the choice is `E` (in which case 281 completions remain) or `Q` (in which case there is in fact only 1).

[4] Thus having filled in one word, we would next fill a word that intersects it. By not jumping from one section of the puzzle to another, we ensure that chronological backtrack always considers a difficulty related to the one that actually caused the backup.

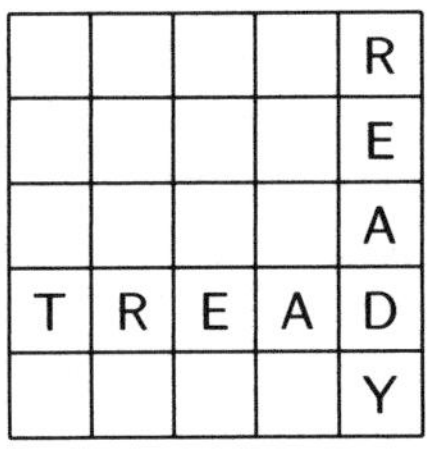

Figure 1: Is multiple lookahead worthwhile?

realize that the variable w_1 is causing trouble because of the constraints it places on a subsequent variable w_2 (or perhaps a collection of subsequent variables). Having done so, we make sure that the new choice for w_1 allows us to change our selection for w_2.

In Section 3, we will refer to the possible choices as "bt" (simple backtrack), "bj" (backjump to the relevant problem, but make no effort to ensure that the difficulty has been addressed) and "sbj" (smart backjump, ensuring that some relevant letter changes value).

Preprocessing

Finally, there is the possibility of preprocessing the data in some way that will reduce the need to backtrack in the first place. In [Dechter and Meiri, 1989], Dechter and Meiri suggest that the most effective way to do this is to preprocess the information at each node of the constraint graph in a way that ensures that when a particular variable w is instantiated, there will always be an instantiation for every other variable that shares a constraint with w. In terms of crossword puzzles, we make sure that the choice made for one word is consistent with the choices that will need to be made for the words that intersect it. This is called *directional arc-consistency* [Dechter and Pearl, 1988].

There are other possibilities as well. If we think of directional arc-consistency as a simple lookahead to depth 1, directional *path-consistency* is lookahead to depth 2, so that for the word being instantiated and every choice for a word w' that meets it, there will be a choice for every word that meets w or w'.

In a crossword puzzle, it is impractical to store all of this consistency information; there are simply too many possibilities. Indeed, this was already observed by Dechter and Meiri on the simple problems they investigate in [Dechter and Meiri, 1989].

It is possible, however, to repeat the analysis at run time, essentially doing a lookahead to a depth of greater than one when each variable is instantiated.

It seems at first that this should be a good idea. Consider the puzzle in Figure 1, for example. It might be the case that there are no two five letter words w_1 and w_2 such that w_1 ends in Y, w_2 has T as its fourth letter, and the last letter of w_2 is the same as the first letter of w_1. A two-level lookahead would notice this,

(a)

(b)

Figure 2: Test puzzles

and one of the two words in Figure 1 would be withdrawn immediately.

In practice, this does not work so well. The reason is that the computation involved is a fairly difficult one – we need to look at the possible choices for w_1, check to see which letters are still possible in which spaces (this is the expensive part, since it involves examining each of the choices for w_1), and then to use this information to prune the set of possibilities for w_2. The analysis is expensive enough that the cost incurred is not in general recovered by the associated pruning of the search space. More conventionally put, the forward branching factor for the problem is high enough that additional levels of lookahead draw conclusions no more effectively than their backward counterparts.

3 Experimental results

Frames used and raw data

In order to evaluate the usefulness of the ideas in the last section, the four puzzles appearing in Figures 2 and 3 were solved by the program. The program always used one level of lookahead (i.e., arc-consistency)

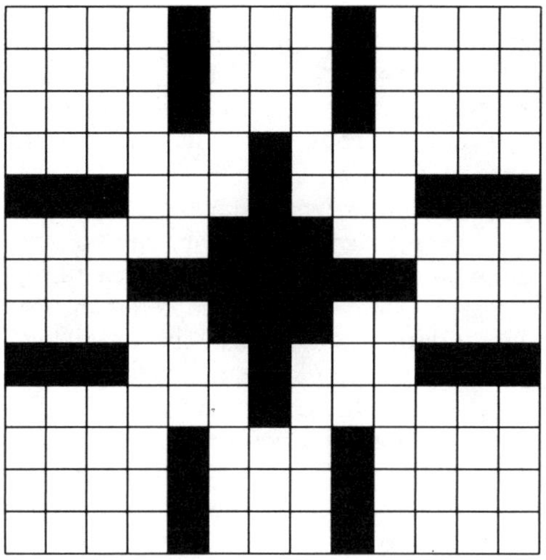

(c)

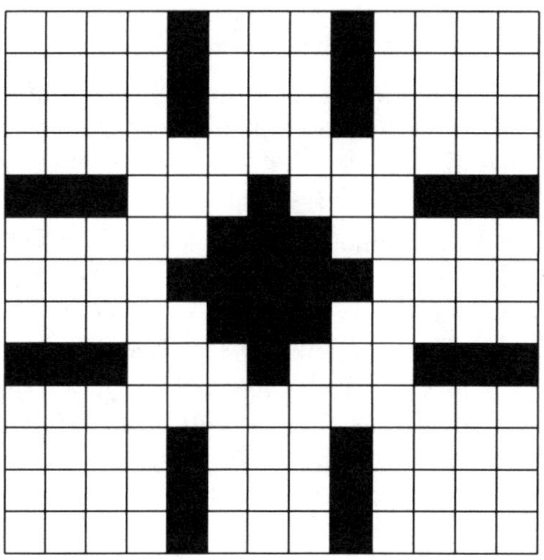

(d)

Figure 3: Test puzzles (ctd.)

and some form of the cheapest-first heuristic, since it was quickly discovered that without these, all but the simplest puzzles were intractable. The other parameters were set as follows:

1. `cheapest-first` could be either `stat`, indicating that a compile-time statistical approximation was used, or `exact`, indicating that the exact (run-time) value was used.
2. If the run-time ordering were used, `min-look` could be either 1 (always use the first acceptable word) or 10 (use the best choice among the first ten acceptable words). This calculation was not performed when the statistical ordering was used, since only dynamic information about variable orderings can be used to distinguish among words in this fashion.
3. `connected-backtrack` could be either `bt`, `bj` or `sbj`, as described in the previous section.

For each allowable selection of parameters, each of the above puzzles was solved 10 times; the dictionary was shuffled between each solution attempt to ensure that the performance of the program was not affected by a particularly fortunate or unfortunate choice of word at any point.

The results are as reported in Figure 4; the times reported are in seconds for a Symbolics 3620 with 2 megawords of memory. We feel that time of solution is a more valuable gauge of performance than the number of nodes examined or the number of backtracks (as used in [Dechter and Meiri, 1989]) because it is often possible to prune the search space but only at a prohibitive cost in terms of the time spent expanding a single node. This is the argument we made when considering lookahead to multiple depths.

For the harder puzzles, many of the choices of parameters did not lead to solutions being found within 20 minutes of CPU time, and no timing information is reported for these parameter choices. The most difficult puzzle ((d) in Figure 3) was solved in only 8 of 10 cases with `min-look` set to 1.

Analysis

As already mentioned, arc-consistency and cheapest-first were needed to solve any of the puzzles. With regard to the other choices, we observed the following:

Choice of variable Unlike the results reported by Dechter and Meiri in [Dechter and Meiri, 1989], it is apparent even for the 5×5 puzzle that runtime information plays an important role in the choice of word to be filled next. The difference in performance between the programs that used an exact version of the cheapest-first heuristic and those that used the statistical approximation available at compile time is significant in all cases; the two most difficult puzzles could not be solved at all within the twenty minute time limit unless runtime information was used.

Choice of instantiation The overhead involved in finding a word that minimally restricts the subsequent search is worthwhile only on puzzles of size 9×9 and larger, and it is not until the most difficult of the four puzzles is considered that this heuristic begins to play a significant role. This suggests that the choice of `min-look` (the number of words considered to fill a particular slot) should be closely coupled to the apparent difficulty of the puzzle being constructed.

Backtrack Backjumping (as opposed to simple backtracking) is another heuristic the value of which is only apparent on the larger puzzles; on smaller ones, the cheapest-first heuristic tends to order the words in a way that results in a particular word intersecting the word being filled next and the two techniques coincide. "Smart" backjumping is needed for puzzle (d) only – but here, it turned out to be absolutely crucial. The reason is that many of the 13-letter words have endings like "tion" and if this choice made the upper-right hand corner of the puzzle impossible to fill, it was important not to try another word with the same ending. Of course, it is not clear to what extent other constraint-satisfaction problems will share these features, but it is not unreasonable to think that they will.

Things that didn't work

It is also probably worthwhile to report on search heuristics that we tried, but that *didn't* reduce the time needed to find a solution to the puzzle.

Tree reordering while backtracking Suppose that backjumping has caused us to backtrack over a word w because it was not relevant to the problem that caused the backtrack in the first place. Is it reasonable to put w back into the puzzle before resuming the search, thereby modifying the order in which the search is conducted so that we can reuse the information that would otherwise be lost?

Unfortunately not. Just because removing w doesn't directly alleviate a particular difficulty is no reason to believe that *keeping* w won't commit us to the same problem. As an example, suppose that we put in a word w_1, then a crossword w_2, then discover that another crossword w_3 to w_1 cannot be filled satisfactorily. Provided that the choices for w_3 are not constrained by the selection of w_2, we will backtrack directly to w_1, and the above suggestion would therefore cause us to replace w_2 in the puzzle. Unfortunately, this replacement might well commit us to w_1 once again.

It may be possible to identify a limited set of situations where words that are passed over during backtracking can be safely replaced, but these situations appear to be fairly rare in practice and the cost of searching for them seems not to be justified.

Compile-time dictionary ordering We also considered the possibility of ordering the dictionary not randomly, but in a way that would prefer the use of words containing common letters.

For small puzzles, this led to significant performance improvements; the preference of common letters virtually eliminated the need to backtrack on puzzles (a) and (b). On puzzle (c), however, the performance gain was much more modest (perhaps 20%), while on puzzle (d), the performance appeared to actually *worsen* – the program was no longer able to solve the puzzle within the twenty minute time limit if `min-look` was set to 10. (For `min-look` set to 1, however, only 15 seconds were required.)

It is difficult to know what to make of such conflicting data; since the ordered dictionary can no longer be shuffled to eliminate statistical fluctuations in solution time, it is possible that the observed behavior is not reflecting the fundamental nature of the algorithm. The best explanation we can offer is the following one:

On large puzzles, where backtracking is inevitable, the ordered dictionary is likely to result in the first ten choices for any particular word being fairly similar. As a result, the program might just as well select the first word as any of the first ten; in fact, the time spent considering the others is unlikely to be repaid in practice. This is consistent with the observed behavior – the performance for an ordered dictionary with `min-look` set to 1 was uniformly better than if this parameter were set to 10. We feel this to be undesirable for the following reasons:

1. The performance of the program becomes quite brittle. If lucky, it will solve a puzzle very quickly; if unlucky, it may not solve it at all. This is the behavior that was observed on puzzle (d).
2. The program cannot improve its performance on very difficult puzzles by increasing the value of `min-look`, since this technique has been essentially invalidated by the dictionary ordering.

In addition, further experimentation showed that it was not possible to avoid this problem by segmenting the dictionary or ordering it in any other way (such as maximizing the letter differences between words appearing near each other).

We wish that we could make more definitive remarks about this technique, but cannot.

4 Conclusion

Summarizing, the conclusions that we have drawn from the experimental data in Figure 4 are the following:

1. Arc-consistency is needed if difficult constraint-satisfaction problems are to be solved effectively.
2. It is far more efficient to order variables at run time than to use the statistical information available at compile time.

3. It is important to select the instantiation for each variable carefully, although not so important that every choice should be considered in large domains.
4. Backjumping is to be preferred to simple backtracking. In addition, it is important to ensure that subsequent labels for a particular variable actually address a difficulty that was found previously in the search; this can be done without incurring the prohibitive costs involved in maintaining complete dependency information when the tree is expanded.

Acknowledgement

The first author is indebted to Greg Arnold, David Smith, Phil Stubblefield, Rich Washington and the students of his introductory artificial intelligence class for many enlightening discussions. The comments of Rich Korf and one other anonymous referee were also helpful.

References

[Dechter, 1990] Rina Dechter. Enhancement schemes for constraint processing: backjumping, learning, and cutset decomposition. *Artificial Intelligence*, 1990. To appear.

[Dechter and Meiri, 1989] Rina Dechter and Itay Meiri. Experimental evaluation of preprocessing techniques in constraint satisfaction problems. In *Proceedings of the Eleventh International Joint Conference on Artificial Intelligence*, pages 271–277, 1989.

[Dechter and Pearl, 1988] Rina Dechter and Judea Pearl. Network-based heuristics for constraint-satisfaction problems. *Artificial Intelligence*, 34:1–38, 1988.

[Gaschnig, 1979] John Gaschnig. *Performance Measurement and Analysis of Certain Search Algorithms.* Technical Report CMU-CS-79-124, Carnegie-Mellon University, 1979.

[Mazlack, 1976] Lawrence J. Mazlack. Computer construction of crossword puzzles using precedence relationships. *Artificial Intelligence*, 7:1–19, 1976.

[Stallman and Sussman, 1977] R. M. Stallman and G. J. Sussman. Forward reasoning and dependency-directed backtracking in a system for computer-aided circuit analysis. *Artificial Intelligence*, 9(2):135–196, 1977.

Puzzle	Cheapest first	min-look	Backtrack	Time (sec)
(a)	exact	1	bt	0.505
	exact	1	bj	0.533
	exact	1	sbj	0.605
	exact	10	sbj	0.607
	exact	10	bt	0.612
	stat	–	sbj	0.693
	exact	10	bj	0.719
	stat	–	bj	1.015
	stat	–	bt	1.041
(b)	exact	10	bt	2.363
	exact	10	sbj	2.453
	exact	10	bj	2.497
	exact	1	sbj	4.967
	exact	1	bt	6.327
	exact	1	bj	6.587
	stat	–	sbj	17.022
	stat	–	bj	17.170
	stat	–	bt	31.526
(c)	exact	10	sbj	11.904
	exact	10	bj	15.539
	exact	1	sbj	17.668
	exact	1	bj	17.798
(d)	exact	10	sbj	71.693
	exact	1	sbj	408.555*

* Completed on only 8 of 10 attempts

Figure 4: Test results; techniques not listed were not able to solve the puzzles in question

Iterative Broadening

Matthew L. Ginsberg* and **William D. Harvey**
Computer Science Department
Stanford University
Stanford, California 94305
ginsberg@cs.stanford.edu

Abstract

Conventional blind search techniques generally assume that the goal nodes for a given problem are distributed randomly along the fringe of the search tree. We argue that this is often invalid in practice, suggest that a more reasonable assumption is that decisions made at each point in the search carry equal weight, and show that a new search technique that we call *iterative broadening* leads to orders-of-magnitude savings in the time needed to search a space satisfying this assumption. Both theoretical and experimental results are presented.

1 Introduction

Imagine that we are searching a tree of uniform depth d using conventional depth-first search. We work our way to the fringe of the tree and check to see if we are at a goal node. Assuming that we are not, we back up a minimal amount, generate a new node at depth d, and check to see if *that* is a goal node. This process continues until we finally succeed in solving the problem at hand.

The process of depth-first search generates the fringe nodes (the nodes at depth d) in a particular order – from left to right, if we were to draw the tree in its entirety. Assuming that the goal nodes (of which there may be more than one) are randomly placed along the fringe of the search tree, this left-to-right order is a reasonable way to search the tree.

Now imagine that we are trying to solve some hard problem, say buying a birthday present for a friend. We decide to buy her a book on Tennessee walking horses, and visit a few book and tack stores looking for one but without success.

At this point, rather than continue looking for this particular gift, *we may well decide to try something else.* Even if we have good reason to believe that a book of the kind we want exists, we view our continued failure as an indication that we would be better off looking for a different gift, and end up buying her a saddle pad.

*This work has been supported by General Dynamics and by NSF under grant number DCR-8620059.

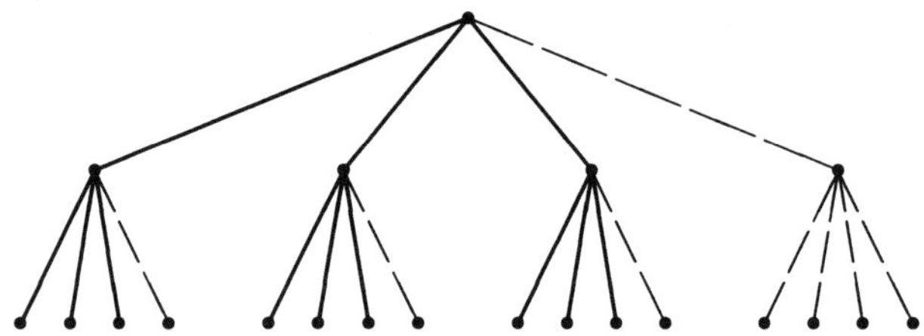

Figure 1: Search with a breadth cutoff

If all of the inference steps we might take while solving the problem were equally likely to lead to a solution, this would make no sense. But in practice, we view the fact that we have been unable to solve the problem of finding the Tennessee-walker book as evidence that the whole *idea* of getting the book is misguided. Does this idea have an analog in search generally?

It does. The reason is that it is possible to make a mistake. Going back to our tree of depth d, it is quite possible that one of the nodes at depth 1 (for example) has committed us to a course from which there is no recovery, in that this particular node has no goal nodes at all underneath it.

The way we deal with this in practice is by imposing an artificial breadth limit on our search. Thus we may try three different book stores before giving up and getting our friend something else for her birthday. What we are proposing in this paper is that blind search techniques do the same thing.

Specifically, we will suggest that depth-first search be augmented with an artificial breadth cutoff c. What this means is that when we have had to backtrack to a particular node n in the tree c times, we continue to backtrack to the previous choice point, *even if there are still unexplored children of the node n.* An example is depicted in Figure 1, where we have shown a tree with breadth 4 but a breadth cutoff of 3; the dashed lines indicate paths that have been pruned as a result.

Of course, the search with an artificial breadth cutoff will never search the entire tree; we need some way to recover if we fail to find an answer in our search to depth d. We will suggest that the most practical way to deal with this problem is to gradually increase the breadth cutoff. So we first start by searching the tree with an artificial breadth cutoff of 2, then try with a breadth cutoff of 3, and so on, until an answer is found. We will refer to this technique as "iterative broadening," borrowing terminology from Korf's notion of iterative *deepening* [Korf, 1985].

We will show in this paper that given reasonable assumptions about the distribution of the goal nodes along the fringe, this technique leads to tremendous expected savings in the amount of time needed to search the tree. The reason, roughly speaking, is that the searches with limited breadth retain a reasonable chance of finding a goal node while pruning large fractions of the complete space and enabling us to backtrack past early mistakes more effectively. Even if the preliminary searches fail to find a goal node, the time spent on them is often sufficiently small that overall performance is not much affected.

The outline of this paper is as follows: In the next section, we present a mathematical analysis of the technique, computing the utility of a search with breadth cutoff c in a space of branching factor b. In Section 3, we discuss the ratio of the time needed by our approach to that needed by the conventional one for various choices of b and d, and for various densities of goal nodes at the fringe of the tree. We present both theoretical values (which incorporate some approximations made in Section 2) and experimental results.

In Section 4, we show that the inclusion of heuristic information makes our method still more powerful, and also that it remains viable when used in combination with other search techniques (dependency-directed backtracking, etc.). Related work is discussed in Section 5.

2 Formal analysis

Suppose that our tree, of uniform branching factor b and depth d, has g successful goal nodes distributed along the fringe. What we will do is assume that decisions made at each point in the search are equally important – in other words, that there is some constant s such that if n is a node under which there is at least one goal node, then n has exactly s successful children. (We are calling a node successful if it has at least one goal node somewhere under it.) The fact that s is independent of the depth of n is the formal analog of our claim that decisions made at different depths are equally important. We assume that the s successful children are randomly distributed among the b children of n.

Since the root node is successful, it is not hard to see that there are s^d goal nodes in the tree as a whole, so that we must have $s = g^{1/d}$. In what follows, we will generally assume that s is an integer (so that we can evaluate the expressions that follow), and that $s > 1$ (so that there is more than a single goal node on the fringe).

Now suppose that we fix b, s and a breadth cutoff c. For a given depth d, we will denote the probability that the restricted-breadth search finds at least one goal node by $p(d)$, and the number of nodes examined by this search by $t(d)$. We begin by computing $\overline{p}(d) = 1 - p(d)$. What is the probability that the search *fails* to find a goal node at depth d?

For $d = 0$ (the root node), we clearly have $\overline{p}(0) = 0$. For larger d, suppose that we denote by $\mathtt{pr}(i)$ the probability that of the s successful children of a node n, exactly i of them are included in the restricted search of breadth c. Now the probability that the search to depth $d+1$ fails is given by

$$\overline{p}(d+1) = \sum_i \mathtt{pr}(i)\overline{p}(d)^i \qquad (1)$$

since in order for the search to fail, the depth d search under each of the i successful children of the root node must also fail. We sum over the various i and weight the contributions by the probability that the i successful nodes at depth 1 all actually fail.

We can evaluate $\mathtt{pr}(i)$ by noting that in order for there to be exactly i successful nodes in the restricted search, we much choose i successful nodes from the s that are available, and also $c - i$ unsuccessful nodes from the $b-s$ available. Since the total number of ways to choose the c nodes in the restricted search from the b present in the entire tree is given by $\binom{b}{c}$, it is not hard to see that

$$\mathtt{pr}(i) = \frac{\binom{s}{i}\binom{b-s}{c-i}}{\binom{b}{c}}$$

This expression, together with (1), allows us to compute $p(d)$ for various d.

What about $t(d)$, the number of nodes examined by the restricted search to depth d? We begin by defining $t_s(d)$ to be the number of nodes examined on average by the restricted search to depth d *provided that the restricted search is successful.* We immediately have

$$t(d) = [1 - \overline{p}(d)]t_s(d) + \overline{p}(d)\left(\frac{c^{d+1} - 1}{c - 1}\right) \qquad (2)$$

since the complete tree of breadth c and depth d must be searched if the restricted search fails.

We also need $\mathtt{pr}_s(i)$, the probability that exactly i of the depth 1 nodes are successful given that the restricted search succeeds. Bayes' rule gives us

$$\mathtt{pr}_s(i) = \mathtt{pr}(i|s) = \frac{\mathtt{pr}(s|i)\mathtt{pr}(i)}{\mathtt{pr}(s)} = \frac{[1 - \overline{p}(d-1)^i]\mathtt{pr}(i)}{1 - \overline{p}(d)}$$

To complete the calculation, we need to know that if we have c nodes at depth 1, of which i are successful, then the average number of these c nodes we need to examine before finding j of the successful ones is given by

$$\frac{j(c+1)}{i+1}$$

Given that the restricted search is successful, how many of the nodes do we need to examine before finding one that is successful with the breadth cutoff c? If i nodes are successful, and each successful node has a probability of failure given by $\overline{p}$, then the number of the c nodes we can expect to examine is given by

$$f(i,\overline{p}) = \sum_{j=0}^{i-1} \frac{(j+1)(c+1)}{i+1} \frac{\overline{p}^j(1-\overline{p})}{1-\overline{p}^i} \qquad (3)$$

The rationale for this expression is as follows: Each term represents the number of nodes examined assuming that the first j successful nodes fail (which happens with probability $\overline{p}$ for each) and the $j+1$st succeeds. The terms are weighted by $1/(1-\overline{p}^i)$ because $\overline{p}^i$ is the probability that none of the i nodes succeeds, and this is eliminated by our assumption that the restricted search is successful.

Given this result, the number of failing nodes examined at depth 1 is $f(i,\overline{p})-1$ and $t_s(d+1)$ is therefore:

$$1+\left[\sum_i \mathrm{pr}_s(i)f(i,\overline{p}(d))-1\right]\left(\frac{c^{d+1}-1}{c-1}\right)+t_s(d) \quad (4)$$

The first term corresponds to the fact that the root node is always examined; the final term $t_s(d)$ is the number of nodes examined below the depth 1 node that eventually succeeds. The summation is, as usual, over the number of successful children at depth 1; for each value of i, we compute the expected number of failing nodes examined at depth 1 and realize that each of these failing nodes leads to a complete search of breadth c and depth d.

Using (1) and the expression for $t_s(d+1)$ in (4), we can easily compute the probability of success and expected time taken for the first pass through the search tree, with breadth cutoff $c=2$.

Unfortunately, we cannot use these expressions to evaluate the probabilities and time taken for subsequent searches with $c=3$ and higher. The reason is that when we do the search with $c=3$, we know that the search with $c=2$ has already failed. Assuming that we do not reorder the children of the various nodes when we iterate and search the tree again, we need to take the fact that the $c=2$ search has failed into account when analyzing $c=3$.

For $f<c$, let us denote by $\overline{p}(c,f)$ the probability that the search with cutoff c fails *given that the search with cutoff f is known to fail.* Now it is obvious that

$$\overline{p}(c)=\overline{p}(c,f)\overline{p}(f)$$

so that we immediately have

$$\overline{p}(c,f)=\frac{\overline{p}(c)}{\overline{p}(f)} \qquad (5)$$

We also need to do something similar for t. We will assume (wrongly) that the expected number of nodes examined during a *successful* search to depth d is unchanged by the fact that the search with breadth cutoff f has failed. In practice, it is possible to reorder the nodes so that the expected number is less than this. However, this may not be desirable because it will abandon heuristic information present in the original order; it is because of these competing reasons that we are taking the number to be unchanged. As in (2), this leads to

$$t(c,f)=[1-\overline{p}(c,f)]t_s(d)+\overline{p}(c,f)\left(\frac{c^{d+1}-1}{c-1}\right).$$

The hard work is now done. The expected time taken to solve the problem using iterative broadening is given by

$$\sum_i \overline{p}(i-1)t(i,i-1) \qquad (6)$$

where the term being summed corresponds to the time taken by the search of breadth i, given that the previous search has failed to solve the problem.

branching factor	depth 4	7	11	15
4	1.9	5.9	19.8	59.9
6	1.7	5.8	20.2	55.2
9	1.4	4.9	17.4	46.7
12	1.2	4.1	14.6	38.7
15	1.0	3.5	12.4	32.6

Figure 2: Performance improvement for $s=2$

branching factor	depth 4	7	11	15
4	2.9	26.2	451.3	7276.6
6	3.9	30.7	292.3	1990.3
9	3.4	24.3	186.0	928.1
12	2.9	19.0	129.0	559.9
15	2.4	15.5	97.3	390.2

Figure 3: Performance improvement for $s=3$

3 Results

Theoretical

Given the results of the previous section, it is straightforward to compute the expected time taken by an iterative-broadening search and compare it to the expected time taken by a simple depth-first search (i.e., $c=b$). The tables in Figures 2 and 3 do this for $s=2$ and $s=3$ respectively and for various choices of b (branching factor) and d (depth of tree). The numbers appearing in the table are the ratios of these two times and indicate the factor saved by the new approach. (Thus the 15.5 appearing in Figure 3 for $b=15$ and $d=7$ indicates that iterative broadening will typically solve the problem 15.5 times faster than depth-first search.)

It can be seen from these figures that iterative broadening outperforms conventional search for $s \geq 2$ and $d \geq 4$. (For shallower searches, this was not always the case. The worst case examined was $s = 2, b = 15, d = 2$, when iterative broadening was 0.4 times as fast as depth-first search.) Furthermore, as the depth of search increases, so does the time saved. For large depths and branching factors, it appears that the iterative broadening technique reduces the time needed to solve the problem by an overall factor approximately linear in b and additionally reduces the effective branching factor by $s - 1$.

Note that if s were known in advance, the reduction in effective branching factor could also be achieved by working with a breadth cutoff of $b - s + 1$, since this breadth cutoff will never prune all of the goal nodes from the search space. Iterative broadening achieves this savings without advance information about the size of s. Additional savings are also obtained because of the possible success of the searches with narrower breadth cutoffs.

The large depth limit In the large d limit, it is possible to use these results to determine general conditions under which iterative broadening leads to computational speedups.

As a preliminary, we can use (4) to find the expected time needed by conventional depth-first search, obtaining for large d

$$t_{df}(d) = \frac{b^{d+1}(b-s)}{(b-1)^2(s+1)}$$

The time needed by iterative broadening is bounded by the time needed for complete searches with breadth cutoffs up to $b + s - 1$. We set $\epsilon = s - 1$ to get

$$t(d) \leq \sum_{c=2}^{b-\epsilon} \sum_{i=0}^{d} c^i \approx \frac{b^d(b - d\epsilon)}{b - \epsilon - 1}$$

Setting $t(d) = t_{df}(d)$ and solving for ϵ gives us $\epsilon = b/2d$ so that $s = 1 + \epsilon = 1 + b/2d$ and the number of goal nodes is

$$\lim_{d\to\infty} \left(1 + \frac{b}{2d}\right)^d = e^{b/2}$$

Proposition 3.1 *In the large depth limit, iterative broadening will lead to computational speedup whenever the total number of goal nodes at the fringe exceeds* $e^{b/2}$.

Experimental

In order to ensure that the approximations made in Section 2 not invalidate our theoretical results, we compared the iterative-broadening approach to conventional depth-first search on randomly generated problems. The experimental results appear in Figure 4 and are in overall agreement with our theoretical expectations.

	s				
depth	1	1.5	2	2.5	3
3	0.5	0.7	0.8	1.3	1.5
4	0.4	0.8	1.8	2.2	3.3
5	0.5	1.1	2.1	3.4	5.1
6	0.4	0.9	2.3	3.0	15.2
7	0.5	1.3	4.7	6.5	19.5

Figure 4: Performance improvement observed for branching factor 6 and small s (100 samples)

	s				
depth	1	1.5	2	2.5	3
3	0.6	0.8	1.7	1.6	2.3
4	0.7	1.1	2.7	6.6	5.4
5	0.9	1.7	4.6	8.7	11.3
6	0.9	1.5	8.8	18.5	37.9
7	1.1	2.3	12.1	17.8	45.0

Figure 5: Performance improvement observed for branching factor 6 with heuristic information (100 samples)

The experimental data also includes values for s other than 2 and 3, since in practical applications a successful node may not have a fixed number of successful children. Data is shown for $s = 1.5$ and $s = 2.5$, and $s = 1$ as well.

The case $s = 1$ is exceptional because it leads to exactly one goal node. Since this goal node is randomly located on the fringe of the search tree, the fastest search is the one that examines the fringe most rapidly, and we can therefore expect depth-first search to outperform iterative broadening in this case. At worst, iterative broadening might be a factor of b slower (since there are b possible iterations); in practice, we observed only a factor of 2. This was roughly independent of the breadth and depth of the search.

4 Heuristic information

The experimental work described in Section 3 was also extended to consider cases in which heuristic information is used to order the children of any particular node so that subnodes that are likely to lead to solutions are examined first. We simulated a fairly weak heuristic that scaled by a factor of $2(b + 1 - i)/(b + 1)$ the probability that the ith child of a successful node was itself successful. Thus the probability of the first child's success is approximately doubled and the probabilities for subsequent children are scaled by a linearly decreasing amount. The results are reported in Figure 5 and indicate that heuristic information improves the relative performance of iterative broadening with respect to standard search techniques. (In fact, for $b > 5$

and $d > 6$, iterative broadening is the technique of choice even if $s = 1$.)

These results can be understood by realizing that at any node, both search techniques examine the most likely children first. The consequences of making a mistake are different, however – if depth-first search examines an unsuccessful node near the top of the tree, it will go on to examine the entire subtree of that node at potentially devastating cost. Iterative broadening limits the fruitless search to a subtree of breadth c; the better the heuristic, the more likely it is that a goal will be encountered for small c. Even for the relatively weak heuristic used in our experiments, large relative performance improvements were obtained.

Combination with other techniques Finally, we tested the iterative-broadening technique by including it in a program designed to create crossword puzzles by filling words into an empty frame [Ginsberg *et al.*, 1990]. This program uses a variety of techniques, including a heuristic ranking of the children of the node being examined, directional arc-consistency [Dechter and Pearl, 1988], backjumping (a simple form of dependency-directed backtracking) [Gaschnig, 1979] and dynamic search rearrangement.

The results were as expected. Performance improved in almost all cases; the single exception was for a 5 × 5 puzzle containing 5 5-letter words in each direction (i.e., no black squares at all). The depth of this puzzle was shallower than for most of the others (there are only 10 words to fill in), the branching factor is very large (due to the large number of 5-letter words in the dictionary) and the solutions are quite sparse in the search space (leading to a very small value of s). As can be seen from Figures 1 and 2, all of these factors combine to reduce the effectiveness of the technique we are proposing.

5 Related work

Iterative deepening

An attractive feature of iterative broadening is that it can easily be combined with iterative deepening, the most effective known technique for searching trees where the depth of the solution nodes is unknown [Korf, 1985]. Iterative deepening works by searching the tree to progressively larger fixed depths; any of these fixed-depth searches can obviously be performed using iterative broadening instead of the simple depth-first search proposed in [Korf, 1985].

Parallel search

Kumar and Rao have recently suggested that the most effective way to search a tree of the sort we have been examining is to interleave n parallel searches for the first n children of the root node, and have shown that this technique reduces expected search time if the distribution of the goal nodes is nonuniform along the fringe of the tree.

This approach works for exactly the same reason as iterative broadening – the cost of making a mistake is minimized. Iterative broadening can be expected to lead to still further improvements, since parallel search cannot address difficulties arising from mistakes made below the first level of the search tree or from damage done if the first n children are *all* failing nodes.

6 Conclusion

Iterative broadening leads to computational speedups on search problems containing in excess of 40,000 nodes if either $s > 1.5$ (so that a successful node has, on average, at least 1.5 successful children) or there is heuristic information available indicating conditions under which a node is likely to lead to a solution. In the large depth limit, speedups can be expected whenever there are at least $e^{b/2}$ solutions to the problem in question. Since the size of the fringe grows exponentially with the difficulty of the problem (and $e^{b/2}$ doesn't), we can expect this condition to be satisfied for almost all problems that admit multiple solutions.

The speedups gained by our approach are often several orders of magnitude; this easily outweighs the cost, which appears to be at most a factor of 2. These theoretical results are confirmed by experimentation on both randomly generated small problems and the large toy problem of crossword puzzle generation.

Acknowledgement

We would like to thank Bob Floyd and Rich Korf for various helpful suggestions.

References

[Dechter and Pearl, 1988] Rina Dechter and Judea Pearl. Network-based heuristics for constraint-satisfaction problems. *Artificial Intelligence*, 34:1–38, 1988.

[Gaschnig, 1979] John Gaschnig. *Performance Measurement and Analysis of Certain Search Algorithms.* Technical Report CMU-CS-79-124, Carnegie-Mellon University, 1979.

[Ginsberg *et al.*, 1990] Matthew L. Ginsberg, Michael Frank, Michael P. Halpin, and Mark C. Torrance. Search lessons learned from crossword puzzles. In *Proceedings of the Eighth National Conference on Artificial Intelligence*, 1990.

[Korf, 1985] Richard E. Korf. Depth-first iterative deepening: An optimal admissible tree search. *Artificial Intelligence*, 27:97–109, 1985.

Path-Focused Duplication: A Search Procedure for General Matings

Sunil Issar
Carnegie Mellon University
Pittsburgh, Pennsylvania 15213-3890
si@cs.cmu.edu

Abstract

The mating paradigm for automated theorem provers was proposed by Andrews to avoid some of the shortcomings in resolution. It facilitates automated deduction in higher-order and non-classical logics. Moreover, there are procedures which translate back and forth between refutations by the mating method and proofs in a natural deduction system.

We describe a search procedure, called *path-focused duplication*, for finding refutations by the mating method. This procedure, which is a complete strategy for the mating method, addresses two crucial issues (inadequately handled in current implementations) that arise in the search for refutations: when and how to expand the search space. It focuses on a particular path that seems to cause an impasse in the search and expands the search space relative to this path in a way that allows the search to immediately resolve the impasse. The search space grows and shrinks dynamically to respond to the requirements that have arisen or have been met in the search process, thus avoiding an explosion in the size of the search space. We have implemented a prototype of this procedure and have been able to easily solve many problems that an earlier program found difficult.

Introduction

Much research in theorem proving has focused on improving the efficiency of procedures based on Robinson's resolution principle [Robinson, 1965]. The *mating* paradigm for automated theorem provers was proposed by Andrews [1981] (and a similar approach called the *connection* method was suggested by Bibel [1982]) to avoid converting a well-formed formula (wff) to clause form, which introduces redundancy and impedes analysis of the logical structure of the wff. As remarked by Stickel [1986], solutions to really hard problems will always require human assistance in specifying strategies and determining where to search for a solution; the mating method provides an attractive framework for this interaction because it retains the logical structure of the wff, and thus it is easier to see what the search is trying to achieve. According to Bibel [1988], the connection method has another advantage: *it is computationally as adequate as resolution and has the potential to do significantly better than resolution.*

The mating paradigm facilitates automated deductions in higher-order logic [Andrews, 1989] and non-classical logics [Wallen, 1990]. Refutations generated by the mating method are the underlying component of the proof presentation procedures in [Andrews, 1980; Miller, 1987; Pfenning, 1987; Pfenning and Nesmith, 1990]. These procedures translate back and forth between refutations by the mating method and proofs in a natural deduction system; the two systems can thus serve as cooperating processes, possibly in a semi-interactive environment, with each one of them trying to exploit the advantages of the other.

In this paper we focus on two crucial issues that arise in the search for refutations by the mating method: when and how to expand the search space. The procedure *path-focused duplication*, which is described later, addresses these issues. It focuses on a particular *path* that seems to cause an impasse in the search and expands the search space relative to this path; this transforms a global problem—how to expand the search space so that the search can succeed in finding a refutation—to a more specific local problem—which quantifier should we duplicate so that a particular impasse can be resolved.

As discussed in [Andrews, 1981], we cannot specify a bound on the size of the search space without sacrificing completeness, and each expansion increases the complexity of the search. (Bibel and his colleagues [Bibel *et al.*, 1983] do provide bounds for some special cases, but they also note that such bounds do not exist in general, since first-order logic is undecidable.) Search procedures for the mating method [Andrews, 1981; Bibel, 1982] have been based on the level-saturation approach [Chang and Lee, 1973]: exhaustively search for a *refutation* in a given wff before generating the expanded wff at the next level. These levels introduce artificial constraints in the search. The search procedures thus suffer from problems similar to the ones that arise in the depth-first approach, for example, the Horizon Effect [Berliner, 1973]. Since these problems are caused by the level-saturation approach, we rectify them by incorporating the expansion of the wff

This work was supported by NSF grant CCR-8702699.

intrinsically into the search process. Path-focused duplication achieves this objective by eagerly *duplicating* an expansion node whenever the search seems to have reached an impasse. This could result in extremely large wffs, but we avoid this explosion in the search space by *localizing* the duplication to the impasse that caused it. Localization is achieved by a dynamically growing and shrinking wff which responds to the requirements that have arisen or have been met in the search process.

Just as model elimination [Loveland, 1978] and set of support [Wos *et al.*, 1965] are complete strategies for resolution, path-focused duplication is a complete strategy for the mating method. Path-focused duplication facilitates the introduction of many features (such as not looking for refutations in which wffs occur more than once without sacrificing completeness) which are mentioned in [Stickel, 1982] into the mating method.

The Mating Method

We start with a brief review of the mating method [Andrews, 1981; Bibel, 1982]. As is customary in theorem proving, we will remove existential quantifiers by Skolemization. The wff can contain any connectives, but we will transform them to disjunctions and conjunctions during translation to jforms (defined below). Since the same literal (an atomic wff or the negation of an atomic wff) can occur at several places in the wff, we will assign a unique label to each occurrence of a literal in the jform. A wff W is *rectified* iff no variable occurs both bound and free in W and distinct quantifier-occurrences of W bind distinct variables. In this paper we will deal only with the wffs that are rectified. This restriction is not a drawback of our procedures; we consider the problem of how to implicitly rectify a wff to be an important implementation detail, which is adequately addressed in [Issar, 1990]. $l_1@l_2@\ldots@l_n$ is the result of concatenating the lists $l_1, l_2, \ldots, l_n$. $[n]$ denotes the set $\{i \mid 1 \leq i \leq n\}$ of positive integers.

A *jform* (junctive form) is a representation as an and/or tree for a wff of first-order logic and is defined by the following BNF expression:

$$jform = Literal \mid \bigvee_{i=1}^{n} jform_i \mid \bigwedge_{i=1}^{n} jform_i \mid <\forall x_1 x_2 \ldots x_n> jform$$

We will refer to jforms of the form $<\forall x_1 x_2 \ldots x_n>$ *jform* as *expansion nodes* and refer to $x_1, x_2, \ldots, x_n$ as the *expansion variables* at this node. The expansion variables in any jform J are the expansion variables that occur at expansion nodes in J. The terminology expansion nodes and expansion variables was introduced by Miller [1987]. We will refer to expansion nodes by the expansion variables at that node. For example, $\forall uv$ refers to the expansion node $<\forall uv>$ $\neg Quv \vee Quu$ in Figure 1. Jforms are displayed as two-dimensional diagrams called *vpforms* (vertical path forms). In a vpform the disjunctions are displayed horizontally and the conjunctions are displayed vertically.

If x is an expansion variable in a jform J, then $J[y|x]$ is the result of replacing all occurrences of x by y in J. Let M be an expansion node in J, $\{x_i \mid i \in [n]\}$ be the set of expansion variables in the subtree with root node M, $\{y_i \mid i \in [n]\}$ be a set of new variables that do not occur in J, and M' be the result of replacing x_i by y_i in M for each $i \in [n]$; then M' is a *copy* of M. Consider the jform J' that is obtained from J by replacing M with the jform $\bigwedge M M'$. We say that J' is obtained by a *duplication* from J; this duplication is almost the same as *quantifier duplication* in [Andrews, 1981]. We also say that we *duplicated* M in J and denote J' by $J + M'$. J^* is an *amplification* of a jform J iff there exists a sequence $J = J_1, J_2, \ldots, J_{m-1}, J_m = J^*$ of jforms such that J_{i+1} is obtained by a duplication from J_i for each $i \in [m-1]$.

We next illustrate these definitions with a few examples:

Example 1 $\neg[\ [\ \ Rab \wedge \forall x \forall y[Rxy \supset [Ryx \wedge Qxy]]$
$\wedge \forall u \forall v[Quv \supset Quu]]$
$\supset [Qaa \wedge Qbb]]$

The jform J_1, which is displayed as a vpform, in Figure 1 represents this wff. The labels in this jform refer to the literals that are under them. $\forall x^1 y^1$ is a copy of the expansion node $\forall xy$. J_2 is an amplification of J_1.

Example 2 $\neg[[Pa \vee Pb \vee Pc] \supset \exists x Px]$

The jform J_3 in Figure 2 represents this wff. J_4 is an amplification of J_3.

The set Paths(J) of *paths* through a jform J is defined inductively as follows:

1. $J = Literal$. Then $Paths(J) \stackrel{\text{def}}{=} \{<J>\}$.
2. $J = \bigvee_{i=1}^{n} jform_i$. Then $Paths(J) \stackrel{\text{def}}{=} \bigcup_{i=1}^{n} Paths(jform_i)$.
3. $J = \bigwedge_{i=1}^{n} jform_i$.
   Then $Paths(J) \stackrel{\text{def}}{=} \{P_1@P_2@\ldots@P_n \mid P_i \in Paths(J_i)\}$.
4. $J = <\forall x_1 \ldots x_n> jform$.
   Then $Paths(J) \stackrel{\text{def}}{=} \{<J> @P \mid P \in Paths(jform)\}$.

A *path* through a jform J is an element of the set Paths(J). We will sometimes consider a path to be an ordered set. A *partial path* through a jform J is a subset of a path through J. Our paths differ slightly from the paths in [Andrews, 1981] in that we add expansion nodes to the paths. We could as in [Pfenning, 1987] consider a path to be an element of the set of solution graphs [Nilsson, 1980] in J, but we are mainly interested in literals and expansion nodes, and thus restrict the paths to contain only these elements. To continue with our examples:

1. $<L_0, \forall xy, L_1, \forall uv, L_5, L_6>$ is a path through J_1.
2. For $i \in \{8, 9, 10\}$, let $P_i = <L_i, \forall x, L_{11}>$. Then Paths($J_3$) $= \{P_8, P_9, P_{10}\}$.
3. Paths(J_4) $= \{P@\ <\forall x_1, L_{11}^1, \forall x_2, L_{11}^2> \mid P \in Paths(J_3)\}$.

A substitution ρ is *more general* or *less specified* than a substitution ψ, denoted by $\rho \leq \psi$, iff there is a substitution ϕ such that $\phi\rho = \psi$. The relation $\leq$ is transitive. A substitution ρ is a *unifier* of a set $\mathcal{U}$ of pairs of literals iff $(t_1, t_2) \in \mathcal{U} \Rightarrow \rho t_1 = \rho t_2$. We will say that $\mathcal{U}$ is *unifiable* iff it has a unifier. ρ is the (essentially unique) *most general unifier* of $\mathcal{U}$ iff ρ is a unifier of $\mathcal{U}$ and $\rho \leq \alpha$ for any unifier α of $\mathcal{U}$.

A *connection* in a jform J is any unordered pair (L, M) of literals in J which are both on some path in J and have the property that the set $\{(\neg L, M)\}$ is unifiable. For ex-

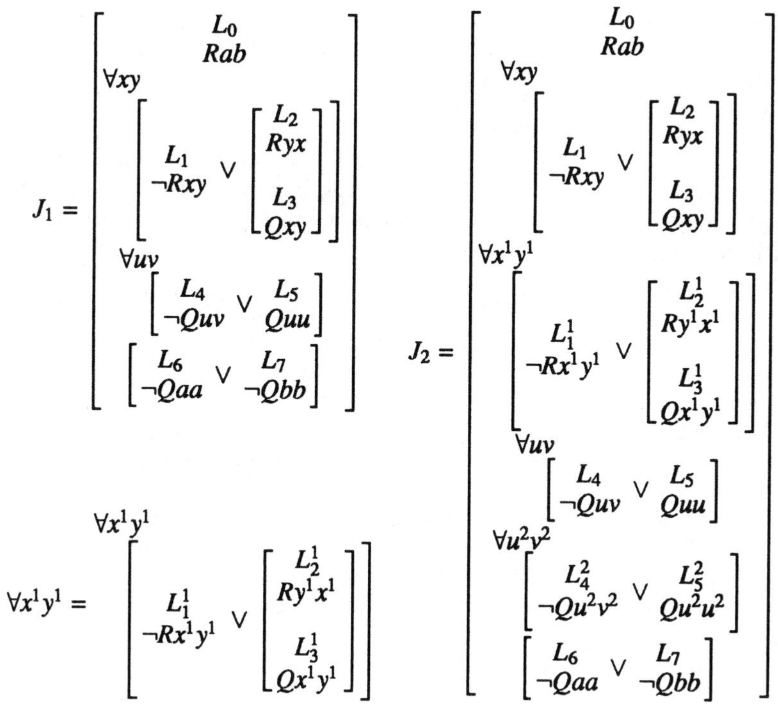

Figure 1: Vpforms for Example 1

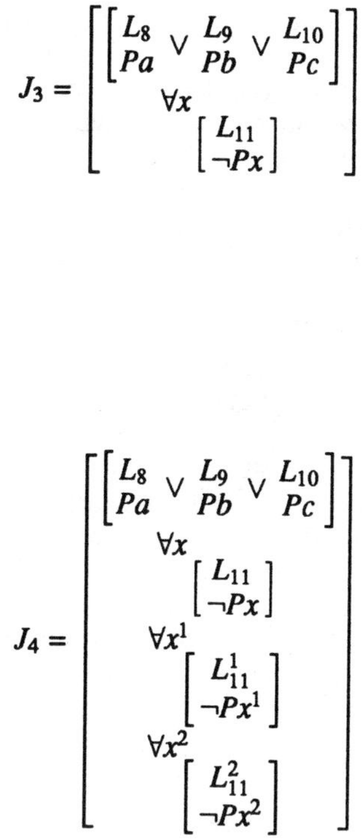

Figure 2: Vpforms for Example 2

ample, (L_5, L_7) is a connection in J_1. For any connection $C = (L, M)$, σ_C denotes the most general unifier of the set $\{(\neg L, M)\}$. A connection (L, M) in a jform J *spans* a path P through J iff both L and M are on P.

For a set $\mathcal{M}$ of connections, $\mathcal{U}_{\mathcal{M}} \stackrel{\text{def}}{=} \{(\neg L, M) \mid (L, M) \in \mathcal{M}\}$. A *mating* $\mathcal{M}$ for a jform J is a set of connections in J such that the set $\mathcal{U}_{\mathcal{M}}$ is unifiable. For example, $\mathcal{M}_1 = \{(L_0, L_1), (L_3, L_4), (L_5, L_6)\}$ is a mating for J_1 and $\{(L_{11}, L_8)\}$ is a mating for J_3. For any mating $\mathcal{M}$, $\sigma_{\mathcal{M}}$ is the most general unifier of the set $\mathcal{U}_{\mathcal{M}}$.

A mating $\mathcal{M}$ for a jform J *spans* a path P through J iff there is a connection in $\mathcal{M}$ which spans P. A mating $\mathcal{M}$ for a jform J is an *extension* of a mating $\mathcal{L}$ for J iff $\mathcal{L} \subseteq \mathcal{M}$. A mating $\mathcal{M}$ for a jform J is *p-acceptable* (*path-acceptable*) iff $\mathcal{M}$ spans all the paths through J. For example, $\{(L_{11}, L_8), (L^1_{11}, L_9), (L^2_{11}, L_{10})\}$ is a p-acceptable mating for J_4. A *refutation* for a jform J is an ordered pair $(J^*, \mathcal{M})$ such that $\mathcal{M}$ is a p-acceptable mating for the amplification J^* of J. The *mating method* for automated theorem provers is a method for finding refutations for a jform J. Andrews [1981] shows that the mating method is sound and complete:

Theorem 1 Completeness and Soundness of the Mating Method *A jform J is unsatisfiable iff there is a p-acceptable mating for some amplification J^* of J.*

Path-Focused Duplication

The task of finding a refutation in the mating method can on the basis of the definition of a refutation be naturally split in two separate subtasks:

1. *Search for a p-acceptable mating for J*: enumerate all possible matings for J until either a p-acceptable mating is found or all possible matings have been considered.
2. *Replace J by some amplification of J*: duplicate some expansion node(s) in J. We consider this duplication to be a *global duplication* because it affects the entire search as described below.

This separation is the basis for the search procedures in [Andrews, 1981; Bibel, 1982] and leads to deficiencies, some of which are outlined by Stickel [1982]. Such a search process also violates a basic principle that should be followed by the search strategies; according to Palay [1980]:

> If an action needs to be taken sometime in the search then do it immediately. If that action were postponed, unnecessary work may be performed. By taking the action immediately, certain information may be obtained that alters the current assumptions of the search, making explorations of other nodes unnecessary.

Path-focused duplication is an abstract procedure for finding refutations by the mating method, which incorporates amplifications (step 2 above) within the search process (step 1 above) itself. The above mentioned principle is the basis for this procedure: if a mating cannot be extended to span a path P in the existing search space (we say that the search seems to have reached an impasse), but some progress can be made by duplicating an expansion node, then duplicate immediately instead of postponing this action. We consider the path P to be the cause for this duplication. The search space grows and shrinks dynamically to respond to the changing requirements in the search: it grows to allow an impasse to be resolved and shrinks so that the amplification does not affect the entire search.

Let us look at the drawbacks of global duplication. The objective of the mating procedures is to span all the paths in the tree (jform). This can be done by independent processes—one for each path—which must maintain the compatibility of the substitutions for the shared variables. Each duplication increases the number of elements on some paths and in most cases the number of paths in the tree. For example, duplicating either of the expansion nodes $\forall xy$ or $\forall uv$ in J_1 doubles the number of paths in the resulting jform and each path has more literals. The global duplications thus seem to require greater overall effort, especially if there is a refutation in a smaller tree, which we did not find because we have not exhaustively searched all smaller trees. We address the resulting dilemma—should we or should we not go for global duplication— by *localizing* the duplication to the path that caused this duplication: it is as if each independent process amplifies its own copy of the tree, and the other processes are intentionally oblivious to these changes. We illustrate *localization* with an example:

Example 3 Consider the jform J_1 in Example 1. The mating $\mathcal{M}_1$ cannot be extended to span the path $Q = <L_0, \forall xy, L_2, L_3, \forall uv, L_5, L_7>$. We will then duplicate one of the expansion nodes, say $\forall xy$. The node $\forall x^1y^1$ which is a copy of $\forall xy$ is displayed in the lower left corner of Figure 1. Because we *localize* the duplication to Q, we will proceed as if the path Q has been replaced by the following two paths:

$$<L_0, \forall xy, L_2, L_3, \forall x^1y^1, L_1^1, \forall uv, L_5, L_7>$$
$$<L_0, \forall xy, L_2, L_3, \forall x^1y^1, L_2^1, L_3^1, \forall uv, L_5, L_7>$$

There are 7 other paths in J_1 that could also be extended like Q, but we will not extend them. There are 16 paths in $J_1 + \forall x^1y^1$; the effect of localization is that the search space will have only 9 paths after duplicating the expansion node $\forall xy$.

The behavior of the search is partially determined by the number and size of the paths in the search space. Duplication causes an explosion in their number. Path-focused duplication attempts to directly control the number and size of the paths in the search space without restricting quantifier duplication; this is where the strength of the procedure lies.

We next describe *path-focused duplication*, which is a procedure for finding refutations in a jform J. We use the state-space representation for this description. A state is a pair $(Open, \mathcal{M})$ where Open is the set of partial paths not spanned by the mating and $\mathcal{M}$ is the mating that is being generated. The objective of the search is to find a sequence of operations that starts from the initial state and leads to the goal state.

1. *Initial State*:
   (a) $Open = Paths(J)$.
   (b) $\mathcal{M} = \emptyset$.
2. *Goal State*: $Open = \emptyset$.
3. *Operations*. There are two operations which transform the states:
   (a) *Extension*. Select a connection C on some $P \in Open$ such that $\mathcal{U}_{\mathcal{M}\cup\{C\}}$ is unifiable.
      i. $\mathcal{M} \longleftarrow \mathcal{M} \cup \{C\}$
      ii. $Open \longleftarrow Open - \{P\}$
   (b) *Duplication*. Select an expansion node E on some $P \in Open$. Let E_i be a copy of E. This can be a new copy or a copy that was used earlier.
   $Open \longleftarrow Open - \{P\} \cup \{P@Q \mid Q \in Paths(E_i)\}$.

We illustrate path-focused duplication with an example:

Example 4 Consider the jform J_1 in Example 1 (displayed in Figure 1). We specify a partial control strategy: use first-in-first-out (FIFO) to select elements from Open, and always make a new copy of the expansion node that is selected in the duplication operation. Figure 3 shows how path-focused duplication found a refutation for J_1. Each row in Figure 3 shows the elements in *Open* after the *operation* had been applied and also lists either the *connection* that was added to $\mathcal{M}$ or the *copy* of the expansion node that was used. If the path selected in a row was already spanned by a connection added in an earlier row, then no *operation* is shown. We would get the jform J_2 (displayed in Figure 1) if the duplications implicit in step 8 and step 10 were explicitly generated. The mating $\mathcal{M}$ consists of the connections listed in the column marked *Connection*. $(J_2, \mathcal{M})$ is a refutation for the jform J_1. There are 8 paths in J_1: $<L_0, \forall xy, L_1, \forall uv, L_4, L_6>$, $<L_0, \forall xy, L_1, \forall uv, L_4, L_7>$, $<L_0, \forall xy, L_1, \forall uv, L_5, L_6>$, $<L_0, \forall xy, L_1, \forall uv, L_5, L_7>$, $<L_0, \forall xy, L_2, L_3, \forall uv, L_4, L_6>$, $<L_0, \forall xy, L_2, L_3, \forall uv, L_4, L_7>$, $<L_0, \forall xy, L_2, L_3, \forall uv, L_5, L_6>$, $<L_0, \forall xy, L_2, L_3, \forall uv, L_5, L_7>$. For $i \in [8]$, let P_i be the ith element in this sequence. Further, let $P_{81} = P_8 @ <\forall x^1y^1, L_1^1>$, $P_{82} = P_8 @ <\forall x^1y^1, L_2^1, L_3^1>$, $P_{821} = P_{82} @ <\forall u^2v^2, L_4^2>$ and $P_{822} = P_{82} @ <\forall u^2v^2, L_5^2>$. All the P_i's are partial paths in J_2.

	Operation	*Node*	*Connection*	*Open*
0.				$\{P_i \mid 1 \le i \le 8\}$
1.	Extension		(L_1, L_0)	$\{P_i \mid 2 \le i \le 8\}$
2.				$\{P_i \mid 3 \le i \le 8\}$
3.				$\{P_i \mid 4 \le i \le 8\}$
4.				$\{P_i \mid 5 \le i \le 8\}$
5.	Extension		(L_4, L_3)	$\{P_i \mid 6 \le i \le 8\}$
6.				$\{P_i \mid 7 \le i \le 8\}$
7.	Extension		(L_6, L_5)	$\{P_8\}$
8.	Duplication	$\forall x^1y^1$		$\{P_{81}, P_{82}\}$
9.	Extension		(L_1^1, L_2)	$\{P_{82}\}$
10.	Duplication	$\forall u^2v^2$		$\{P_{821}, P_{822}\}$
11.	Extension		(L_4^2, L_3^1)	$\{P_{822}\}$
12.	Extension		(L_5^2, L_7)	$\emptyset$

Figure 3: A Refutation for the Jform J_1 in Example 1

It is proved in [Issar, 1990] that path-focused duplication is a complete and sound procedure for finding refutations:

Theorem 2 *Consider any jform J.*

Soundness Theorem: *If there is a sequence of operations that starts from the initial state and leads to the goal state, then $\mathcal{M}$ is a p-acceptable mating for some amplification of J.*

Completeness Theorem: *If J is unsatisfiable, then there is a sequence of operations that starts from the initial state and leads to the goal state.*

Let us look at some advantages of path-focused duplication:

1. The number of paths considered by path-focused duplication is in most cases significantly smaller than the number of paths in the search space. For example, there are 32 paths in J_2, but path-focused duplication found a refutation by considering only 12 paths. Moreover, 10 of the 12 paths (all except P_{821} and P_{822}) were proper subsets of paths in J_2.
2. Since the effect of any duplication is local to a path, path-focused duplication can afford to be adventurous and separately try all possible duplications that might solve an impasse.
3. We can easily incorporate the set of support strategy [Wos *et al.*, 1965] into path-focused duplication: we assume that the jform is of the form $\bigwedge_{i=1}^{n} C_i$, we can identify one of the C_i's to be the *goal*, and the remaining C_i's to be the *axioms*; initialize *Open* to be the set of paths through the *goal*, and extend the *duplication* operation so that it can select the elements in the set of *axioms* also, in addition to selecting the expansion nodes. The details are provided in [Issar, 1990].
4. Path-focused duplication does not lose any advantages that might be associated with the procedures based on the level-saturation approach, since it can simulate the level-saturation procedures. The level-saturation approach specifies the copies of the expansion nodes that can be used before the search begins. If we restrict the *duplication* operation to select only these copies, then the two procedures are almost identical.

Status and Future Work

We have implemented a first-order theorem prover (without equality) based on path-focused duplication. Some of the key features in the control structure are as follows:

- Use the depth-first iterative deepening strategy to control the number of copies of an expansion node.
- Always try the extension operation before the duplication operation.
- Always make a new copy of the expansion node that is selected in the duplication operation.
- If a mating cannot be extended to a p-acceptable mating within the assigned depth, then backtrack to the last state where an alternate connection can be added.

We have tested our prover on some problems that are available in the theorem-proving literature. This program is written in CMU Common Lisp, and all experiments were performed on an IBM-RT with 12 megabytes memory. Although an earlier program for the mating method that was based on the level-saturation approach could not solve most of the benchmark problems from [Chang and Lee, 1973], our program found all of them easy. We could also easily solve the first 46 problems—most of the remaining problems are based on equality—in [Pelletier, 1986]. The table in Figure 4 presents the results for some problems: the first two problems were taken from [Andrews, 1986], the next three problems were taken from [Andrews, 1981], the sixth problem was taken from [Pelletier, 1986], and the last two problems were taken from [Stickel, 1986].

	Name	*Number of Paths*	*Number of Connections*	*Time (sec)*
1.	X2115	16	14	.11
2.	X2116	8	10	.55
3.	Thm53	8	7	.03
4.	Thm55	8	9	.05
5.	Thm56	8	7	.03
6.	Pell34	128	54	.68
7.	Has-Parts2	48	14	.35
8.	CL8	432	14	.35

Figure 4: Path-Focused Duplication

Name	*Level-saturation*		*Path-focused duplication*	
	Time (sec)	Bytes $\times 10^4$	Time (sec)	Bytes $\times 10^4$
X2115	4026.63	3×10^5	.11	.88
X2115a	5.32	17.5	.05	.39
X2116	3.32	13.0	.55	3.44
Thm53	.85	1.7	.03	.23
Thm55	3.28	8.9	.05	.35
Thm56	.82	1.5	.03	.23

Figure 5: Path-Focused Duplication vs Level-Saturation

The table in Figure 5 compares the performance of our implementation with that of an earlier program[1] which was based on the level-saturation approach. (X2115a is obtained by minimizing the scope of the quantifiers in X2115.) We use two measures for this comparison:

- *Time.* Run time for finding a refutation.
- *Space.* Number of bytes that were consed by the program as reported by Lisp.

We can get a higher-order theorem prover as in [Andrews, 1981; Pfenning, 1987], which is capable of handling equality also, by replacing the first-order unification algorithm that is used in this implementation with Huet's higher-order unification algorithm [Huet, 1975]. The implementation mentioned in this section is a prototype whose only objective is to demonstrate the effectiveness of path-focused duplication. There are many strategies described in [Issar, 1990] which can improve the performance of this program,

[1] A procedure based on the level-saturation approach is implemented in TPS [Andrews *et al.*, 1988]. We use this program for gathering data about the performance of level-saturation procedures.

but which have not been implemented yet. Some strategies, which are independent of the control structure, are as follows:

- A connection graph [Kowalski, 1975; Andrews, 1981] can be used to aid the extension operation in finding a connection on a path and the duplication operation in selecting an expansion node.
- We allow the duplication operation to select any expansion node on a path. Some of these nodes may be inappropriate because they do not have any role in the impasse that necessitated the duplication; we can restrict the duplication operation to disregard such nodes.
- The same combination of duplications may arise several times on a path. We illustrate this with an example: suppose there are three expansion nodes 1, 2, and 3 on a path; the duplication operation may try various permutations of these nodes, for example, (1, 2, 3), (1, 3, 2), and (3, 1, 2). We can restrict the duplication operation to avoid this redundancy. We have to be careful, though, because the duplication operation is not commutative, and such a restriction can affect the efficiency of the search.

There are other strategies that affect the control structure. An example of such a strategy is to use heuristic information as suggested by Stickel [1986] to perform early cutoffs within a depth and to increment the depth.

Some of the strategies in [Issar, 1990] have been implemented in a propositional theorem prover; the performance of this prover compares favorably with the performance of the resolution provers. We thus have reason to believe that these strategies will improve the performance of our first-order prover too.

Acknowledgements

First and foremost I acknowledge Professor Peter Andrews, my thesis advisor. His comments on many earlier drafts and suggestions regarding terminology helped to improve the clarity of this paper. I would also like to thank Frank Pfenning and Dan Nesmith for many discussions and for their enthusiasm about my work.

References

Andrews, Peter B.; Issar, Sunil; Nesmith, Daniel; and Pfenning, Frank 1988. The TPS theorem proving system. In *9th International Conference on Automated Deduction*, Lecture Notes in Computer Science 310. Springer-Verlag. 760–761.

Andrews, Peter B. 1980. Transforming matings into natural deduction proofs. In *5th Conference on Automated Deduction*, Lecture Notes in Computer Science 87. Springer-Verlag. 281–292.

Andrews, Peter B. 1981. Theorem proving via general matings. *Journal of ACM* 28:193–214.

Andrews, Peter B. 1986. *An Introduction to Mathematical Logic and Type Theory: To Truth Through Proof*. Academic Press.

Andrews, Peter B. 1989. On connections and higher-order logic. *Journal of Automated Reasoning* 5:257–291.

Berliner, Hans 1973. Some necessary conditions for a master chess program. In *Third International Joint Conference on Artificial Intelligence*. 77–85.

Bibel, Wolfgang; Eder, Elmar; and Fronhoefer, Bertram 1983. Towards an advanced implementation of the connection method. In *Eighth International Joint Conference on Artificial Intelligence*. 920–922.

Bibel, Wolfgang 1982. *Automated Theorem Proving*. Vieweg, Braunschweig.

Bibel, W. 1988. On the comparative complexity of resolution and the connection method. Technical Report BRC-88-6, University of British Columbia, Vancouver.

Chang, C. and Lee, R.C. 1973. *Symbolic Logic and Mechanical Theorem Proving*. Academic Press.

Huet, Gerard P. 1975. A unification algorithm for typed λ-calculus. *Theoretical Computer Science* 1:27–57.

Issar, Sunil 1990. Search strategies for general matings. Technical Report Forthcoming, Carnegie Mellon University, Pittsburgh.

Kowalski, Robert 1975. A proof procedure using connection graphs. *Journal of ACM* 22:572–595.

Loveland, Donald W. 1978. *Automated Theorem Proving: A Logical Basis*. North Holland.

Miller, Dale A. 1987. A compact representation of proofs. *Studia Logica* 46(4):347–370.

Nilsson, Nils J. 1980. *Principles of Artificial Intelligence*. Tioga Publishing Company.

Palay, Andrew J. 1980. An experimental analysis of the B* tree searching algorithm. Technical Report CMU-CS-80-106, Carnegie Mellon University, Pittsburgh.

Pelletier, Francis Jeffry 1986. Seventy five problems for testing automatic theorem provers. *Journal of Automated Reasoning* 2:191–216.

Pfenning, Frank and Nesmith, Dan 1990. Presenting intuitive deductions via symmetric simplification. In *10th International Conference on Automated Deduction*. To appear.

Pfenning, Frank 1987. *Proof Transformations in Higher-Order Logic*. Ph.D. Dissertation, Carnegie Mellon University.

Robinson, J. A. 1965. A machine-oriented logic based on the resolution principle. *Journal of ACM* 12:23–41.

Stickel, Mark E. 1982. A nonclausal connection-graph resolution theorem-proving program. In *AAAI-82 National Conference on Artificial Intelligence*. 229–233.

Stickel, Mark E. 1986. A PROLOG technology theorem prover: implementation by an extended PROLOG compiler. In *8th International Conference on Automated Deduction*, Lecture Notes in Computer Science 230. Springer-Verlag. 573–587.

Wallen, Lincoln A. 1990. *Automated Proof Search in Non-Classical Logics: Efficient Matrix Proof Methods for Modal and Intuitionistic Logics*. The MIT Press.

Wos, Lawrence; Robinson, George A.; and Carson, Daniel F. 1965. Efficiency and completeness of the set of support strategy in theorem proving. *Journal of ACM* 12:536–541.

Consistent Linear Speedups to a First Solution in Parallel State-Space Search*

Vikram A. Saletore and L. V. Kalé
Department of Computer Science,
1304 West Springfield Avenue,
University Of Illinois at Urbana–Champaign,
Urbana, Illinois 61801, USA
email: saletore@cs.uiuc.edu and kale@cs.uiuc.edu

Abstract

Consider the problem of exploring a large state-space for a goal state. Although many such states may exist, finding any one state satisfying the requirements is sufficient. All methods known until now for conducting such search in parallel fail to provide consistent linear speedups over sequential execution. The speedups vary between sublinear to superlinear and from run to run. Further, adding processors may sometimes lead to a slow-down rather than speedup, giving rise to speedup anomalies. We present prioritizing strategies which yield consistent linear speedups and requires substantially smaller memory over other methods. The performance of these strategies is demonstrated on a multiprocessor.

1 Introduction

Consider the problem of searching for a solution in a large state space, starting from a given initial state. The state space is usually structured as a tree, with operators that can transform one state 'node' to another forming arcs between different states[1]. In a large class of such problems, the computations tend to be unpredictably structured and have multiple solutions. The desired solution is usually specified by certain properties, and any state satisfying these properties is an acceptable solution. Sometimes one is interested in *optimal* solution(s) based on certain cost criteria. However, many times, one is interested in just any solution. We focus on parallel exploration of search spaces in the latter context. This is an important problem: search is a major computational paradigm in Artificial Intelligence. For AI to achieve its long term, ambitious objectives, it seems clear that it must use parallel processing techniques [Halstead 1986]. Secondly, many 'real-life' applications such as Planning (plan construction), Symbolic Integration, VLSI Test Generation, Theorem Proving, etc. require finding an *adequate* solution rather than an optimal one.

A parallel scheme must be able to *consistently* generate a solution faster than the best sequential scheme, and preferably close to P times faster, where P is the number of processors used. Also, speedups must increase monotonically with the addition of processors. Another important performance criteria is the amount of *memory* required to conduct a search, which may vary from a linear to an exponential function of the depth of the tree. With parallel processing, it may also increase proportionately to P.

2 Search Techniques

A sequential depth-first search begins by expanding the root of a pure OR tree and can be efficiently implemented using a last-in-first-out *(LIFO)* stack of active nodes. The advantage of the sequential stack based depth-first search over other search techniques is its linear storage requirement $O(BD)$ whereas for best-first and breadth-first searches, it is exponential $O(B^D)$ [Pearl 1985] for a tree with branching factor B and depth D. A parallel stack based search algorithm is an extension of the serial algorithm that uses either a shared global stack or multiple stacks.

In the *shared stack model*, all processors share a global stack. Processors pick up nodes from the shared stack and expand them and push the descendents

*This research has been supported in part by the National Science Foundation under grant number CCR-89-00988.

[1] When it is possible to go from one state to another via two distinct sequences of operators, the state-space is a graph rather than tree. However, we will confine ourselves to state-space trees in this paper.

back onto the stack. In Kumar and Rao's multiple stack model [Kumar & Rao 1987], a processor is initially given the root node. A stack splitting scheme is used to distribute work. Processors search disjoint parts of the search space using their local stack in a depth-first manner. They report speedups in [Kumar & Rao 1987] that range from 3.46 to 16.27 using 9 processors for the *first optimal* solution to a 15-Puzzle problem using Iterative Deepening A* (IDA*) [Korf 1988] algorithm [2] on a shared memory multiprocessor. The inconsistency in the speedups is due to the anomalies that exist in parallel stack based search. The reason for speedup anomalies is that the parallel search may expand fewer or more nodes than a serial search.

In a multiple stack model, since processors search disjoint parts of the search space asynchronously, anomalies are possible because a processor may find a solution by searching a smaller or larger search space than the space searched with a sequential search. In a shared stack model as all processors run asynchronously, the set of nodes that are picked up for execution and put back on the stack may be very different from run to run as well as from the one processor case. This randomness in the selection of nodes is exactly the reason for anomalies reported in [Lai & Sahni 1984]. Therefore, both *acceleration anomalies* (speedup greater than number of processors P) and *deceleration anomalies* (decrease in speedup with increase in P) are possible. Also, there is no guarantee that the work performed by the addition of a processor will contribute in finding the first solution and such work may generate more futile work for other processors.

To determine the worst case memory required for the multiple stack model, consider a search tree of uniform branching factor B and depth D. The memory needed for the search will be proportionate to the worst case sum of the individual stack lengths of all the P processors in the system. Initially a processor picks up the root node and expands into its B descendents that are put on its local stack. Idle processors will try to get untried nodes from this processor. A breadth-first search will ensue until each processor is assigned to one active node which occurs at a depth of $\lceil \log_B P \rceil$ when there are P active nodes in the system. Each processor now conducts a depth-first search of subtree of depth $(D - \lceil \log_B P \rceil)$. The maximum stack length for the system is given by:

$$Stack\ Length_{worst\ case} \approx P * D * (B - 1)$$

[2] Each iteration of the IDA* algorithm is essentially a depth-first search of the cost bounded search space such that the first solution found is also one of the optimal solutions.

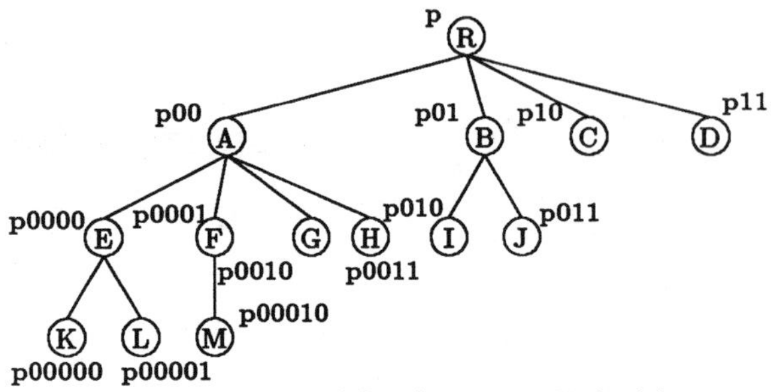

Figure 1: Or Tree with Bit Vector Priorities.

Assuming a constant node size, the memory needed for parallel search is roughly proportional to the product of P, B, and D.

For a shared stack model, a *breadth-first* search may continue until a depth of $\lceil \log_B P \rceil$ is reached. From this point onwards P processors *may* pick P nodes at level i from the stack and put $P * B$ newly created nodes at level $i + 1$ back on the stack, an increase of $P * (B - 1)$ nodes at each successive iteration. The worst case stack length for a shared stack model is given by an expression identical to the one above.

3 A Priority Based Search

We associate *priorities* with work in a parallel search and show how this would eliminate the anomalies and achieve linear speedups to a first solution. In a pure search, any of the alternatives at a choice point may lead to a solution. The alternatives may be ordered left to right, either using any local (value ordering) heuristic if available or using the default order. In a sequential depth-first search, a subtree under a node on the left is explored completely before expanding a node on the right. Thus, it gives higher priority to nodes (alternatives) on the left than the nodes on the right. In the context of first solution, the work to the right of the solution path does not contribute to the solution and therefore constitutes *wasted work*. To obtain *consistent speedups* with parallel search, we try to *focus* the search effort towards first solution by giving priorities to the alternatives at a choice point, with leftmost alternative having the highest priority (Work on other alternatives or *speculative work* can only speed up the solution to the problem if work under left subtrees fails to find a solution; otherwise, it constitutes wasted work.). Also, to mimic sequential order of node expansions, we must assign priorities such that every descendent of a leftward node has higher priority than all the descendents of rightward nodes.

A *priority bit vector* (also referred to as priority vector) is a sequence of bits of any arbitrary length. Priorities are dynamically assigned to the nodes when they are created. A node with a priority vector P_1 is de-

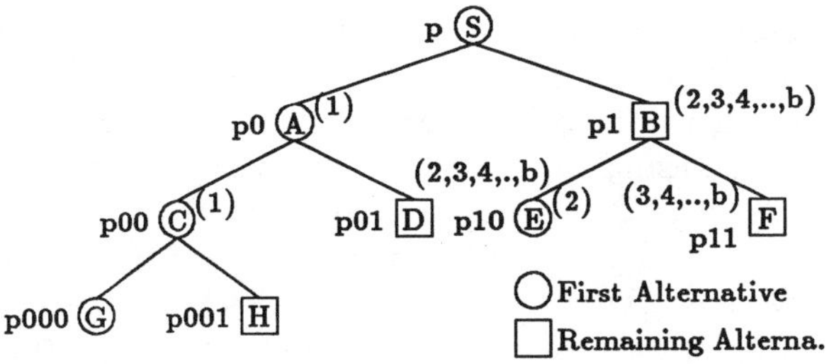

Figure 2: Binary Decomposition of a Search Tree.

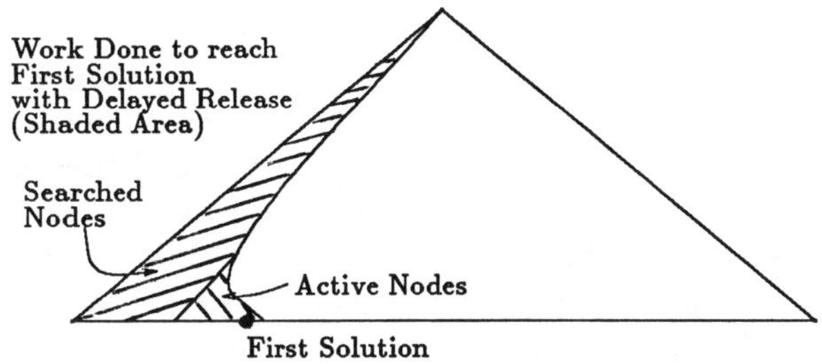

Figure 3: 'Broom Stick' sweep of a search tree.

fined to be at a higher priority than another node with priority P_2 if P_1 is *lexicographically smaller* than P_2.

Consider the OR tree in Figure 1. Let the root of this subtree R, have a priority p represented as a bit vector. The root node of the entire search space is assigned a *null* (priority bit vector of length 0) priority at the start of the search process. The m (m=4) children of the node R representing the m alternatives are assigned priority bit vectors by extending the parent's priority based on their rank. The rank of an *nth* child among its m siblings is represented as an encoding of n as a $\lceil \log m \rceil$ bit binary number. The priority vector of a child node is obtained by appending its rank to its parent's priority. Priorities assigned this way have the *prefix property*: no two children of a node have priority such that one is a prefix of the other (The idea of associating a similar sequence using path numbers with nodes of an OR trees has appeared in [Li & Wah 1986]).

Assigning bit vector priorities this way achieves two goals. (a) The relative priority (rank) of the sibling nodes preserves the left to right order of the sibling nodes. (b) Appending the priority of the child to the priority inherited from its parent ensures every descendent of a high priority node gets higher priority than all the descendents of low priority nodes. This reflects the policy that until there is no prospect of a solution from the left subtree beneath a node, the system should not spend its resources on the right subtrees, *unless* there are idle processors. I.e. if for a time period, if the work available in the left subtree is not sufficient to keep all the processors busy, the idle processors may expand the right subtrees. But as soon as high priority nodes become available in the left subtree, the processors must focus their efforts in that left subtree. For example, if two processors search the tree in Figure 1 then nodes A and B are picked up for execution once node R is expanded. When nodes A and B are expanded the processors explore nodes E and F (of higher priority) in the next cycle.

With priorities some acceleration anomalies are preserved because it is possible that when there is not enough work in the left subtree, processors that are exploring the right subtrees may find a solution faster. Also, since processing effort is always focussed leftward, the parallel search behaviour is similar to that of sequential search. This results in a decrease in wasted work and elimination of deceleration anomalies. As the wasted work is decreased to an insignificant proportion (see Section 3.2) this prioritizing strategy produces monotonic, almost linear, speedups.

The use of priorities to nodes requires the need for an efficient priority queue management, which can otherwise become a bottleneck if a large number of processors are used. We use *grain size* control to decrease the number of accesses to a shared queue and to spread the overhead of parallelisation. In terms of processing time the average grain size is defined as $\frac{Total\ Sequential\ Execution\ Time}{Total\ Number\ of\ Messages\ Processed}$. The ideal grain size for a shared memory system depends on the actual overhead involved in fetching nodes from the queue, creating parallel tasks and depositing new nodes back into the queue. Granularity control is used to determine when to stop breaking down a computation into parallel computations at a frontier node, treating it as a leaf node and executing it sequentially. A simple technique to control grain size, in state-space search, is to decide a cut-off depth beneath which the region is explored sequentially. Other techniques that attempt to gauge the size (granularity) of subtrees beneath a node are also possible. We found that such simple techniques were sufficient to prevent the priority queue from being a sequential bottleneck (see Section 4). With a large number of processors one may increase the grain size to maintain the frequency of access to the shared queue.

To retain similar speedup properties the grain size and the number of granules must both increase proportionally with the number of processors P, therefore, the overall problem size will have to increase with P^2. This can be alleviated somewhat by using concurrent heap access techniques. More important, as absolute adherence to priorities is not essential, techniques such as multiple heaps are also possible.

3.1 Binary Decomposition

The worst case stack length for *prioritized* search with a *shared queue* is given by the same expression as that for a parallel stack based search -namely $P * D * (B - 1)$. This is because there cannot be more than $P * B$ available nodes at any level in the tree, and like the single-stack, this upper bound can be realised by having the P processors pick up the leftmost P nodes at each level, in *lock-step*.

A depth-first sequential algorithm selects the current left most unexplored node at each level of the search space, backtracking to the choice point for remaining alternatives if no solution is found from the current alternative. In a parallel processing context, one can mimic this behaviour by generating the first descendent node say A in the usual manner, and *lumping* the work for generating remaining descendent nodes $(2, 3, .., b)$ into a single *lumped-node* B (see Figure 2). When this lumped-node is picked up for expansion, it generates the next sibling node E and a lumped-node F that lumps work for generating the rest of the sibling nodes $(3, 4, .., b)$. Thus, the lumped-node represents the remaining available parallelism in the subproblem in a form that is *extractable* whenever needed. This *binary decomposition* technique reduces an arbitrarily large branching factor to 2. (We have increased the depth of the tree towards right by this, but if the solution is much closer to the left in the search tree, as is frequently the case, this effect is small. Other techniques can be used to limit the depth with binary decomposition). Another advantage is that since the descendents of a node are not produced until needed, the wasted work is further reduced. (The lumped nodes are analogous to the choice-points used in OR-parallel Prolog systems e.g. [Hausman et al. 1987].).

Although we have reduced the parallelism in the initial stages of the search but once the number of nodes become greater than the number of processors, the available parallelism is more than sufficient to keep all processors busy.

3.2 Delayed Release

Although associating priorities eliminates anomalies, the memory requirement is still proportionate to P as given by the expression earlier. In both, stack and priority based models the increase in the memory usage with number of processors occurs because of the availability of large number untried alternatives at each level of the search. This *immediate availability* of parallelism at shallower levels in the search space is the major cause for increased memory usage. Notice that in the worst case all P processors pick nodes at level l, produce $B * P$ (or $2 * P$ for binary decomposition) children at level $l + 1$, and proceed to pick P nodes at level $l + 1$. To avoid the worst case, processors must *skip* intermediate levels. To achieve this, the parallelism in the problem available at shallower levels of the search space should be delayed and nodes at deeper levels of the search space should be made available to processors *first*. This *bottom-first* strategy gives rise to a search behaviour shown in Figure 3 termed the *Broom Stick* sweep. The set of searched nodes is represented in figure by a long narrow *stick* and the parallelism (active nodes) exploited at the bottom of the tree gives rise to the *broom effect*.

We achieve this *broom stick* behaviour by a technique called *Delayed Release*. The search begins at the root in the usual manner. When a node is expanded, all its children except the leftmost child are put in a list accessible only from the leftmost child. This list is local to the leftmost node and the nodes in the list are not available to other processors at the time they are generated. Also, the local list inherited by a node (parent node) is appended to the local list of its leftmost child. Therefore, each processor effectively creates only *one* child when a node is expanded, which is inserted into the shared priority queue. The search continues this way until a leaf node is encountered when all the nodes kept in the list are released as active nodes and made available to be picked up by other processors, subject to priorities, as before. This has the effect of *delaying* the availability of shallower nodes and making available the higher priority nodes to other processors from the bottom of the search space.

Figure 4 shows the state of a search tree using delayed release technique. When node R is expanded, only one *super-node* consisting of the linked list $[L_1, R_1]$ is produced. When this super-node is picked up, only the first node on the list, L_1, is expanded, and one super-node $[L_2, R_2, R_1]$ is released. Eventually, when the super-node $[A, B, R_5, R_4, R_3, R_2, R_1]$ is picked up for expansion, it is discovered that node A is a leaf, and so all the nodes in the list are released as individual nodes. Processors in the system now pick the highest priority nodes and explore the search space in a similar fashion. (Note that this delayed the expansion of the shallower, low priority node R_1.) With the current state of the search tree depicted, nodes A, B, C, D, E, R_2, and R_1 form the set of frontier nodes. The bit vector priorities ensure that the leftmost P nodes are picked up for execution. The delayed release technique achieves the following three objectives. (a) Most significantly, since processors are forced to skip node expansions at intermediate levels and focus on the nodes deeper in the tree, the wasted work is eliminated almost completely thus yielding linear speedups. (b) The memory required by the search algorithm is reduced considerably, as supported by empirical data.

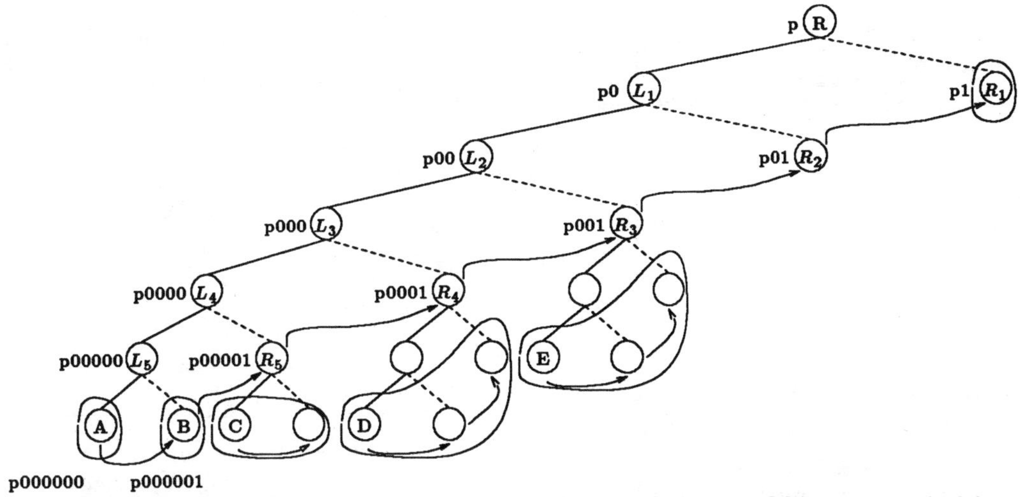

Figure 4: Tree expansion using *delayed release* technique and bit vector priorities.

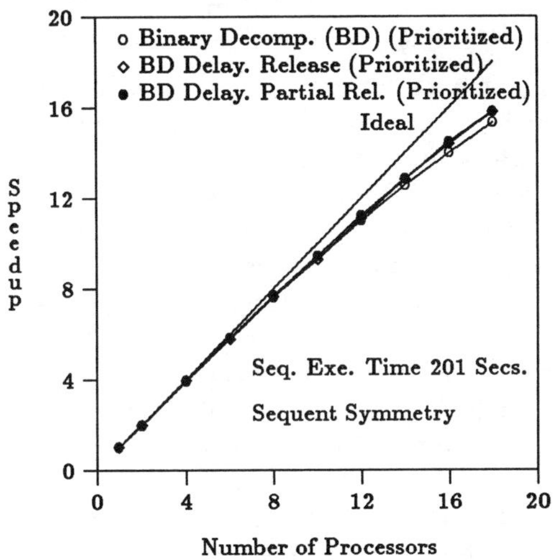

Figure 5: 126-Queens: First Solution Speedups.

(c) Since the number of active nodes in the priority queue at any time is reduced the overhead of managing the queue is reduced.

In the above strategy when a processor picks up a leaf node it releases all the nodes created and stored thus far in the local list of the leaf node. If the number of nodes released is larger than P, then the nodes in excess of P released constitute excess parallelism that can not be exploited at the time of release. In the *delayed partial release* technique, when a leaf node is encountered, the processor releases a maximum of P highest priority nodes and a single node that comprises the remaining nodes. If an idle processor cannot find other high priority nodes it expands the node comprising the excess nodes and proceeds in the usual manner. This technique does not result in a reduction in memory space, since memory space is still needed to store the *un-released* excess nodes in a list. However, since now there are even fewer entries in the queue than the *delayed release* strategy, the overhead of managing and restoring the priority queue is further reduced.

4 Multiprocessor Performance

We implemented the above search techniques for parallel search on Sequent Symmetry shared memory multiprocessor with up to 20 processors and studied their performance. The parallel search strategies were implemented using the *Chare-Kernel* [Kale 1990], a machine independent parallel programming system that currently runs on several multiprocessors. We present performance data on a few state-space search problems. Speedup performance is obtained by comparing to the best sequential program for the problem.

Nodes Expanded on Sequent Symmetry					
PEs	1 (seq)	4	8	16	18
BD	35248	35574	36164	36795	36944
BD-DR	35248	35306	35601	36229	36507
BD-DPR	35248	35357	35644	36219	36448

BD: Binary Decomposition (BD)
BD-DR: BD Delayed Release
BD-DPR: BD Delayed Partial Release

Table I: 126-Queens: Number of Nodes Expanded.

In the **N-Queens** problem the goal is to place N non-attacking Queens on a NXN chess-board. This problem has a large number of solutions where any one solution may be acceptable. We obtained performance data for the 126-Queens (N=126) problem. N was chosen to be large to show that such a large problem can be solved within a reasonable amount of memory usage and time. Binary decomposition technique of Section 3.1 was used since a complete decomposition at every level resulted in memory overflow.

The speedup plots in Figure 5 show that with bit vector priorities the wasted work is reduced resulting in linear, clearly monotonic speedups. The perfor-

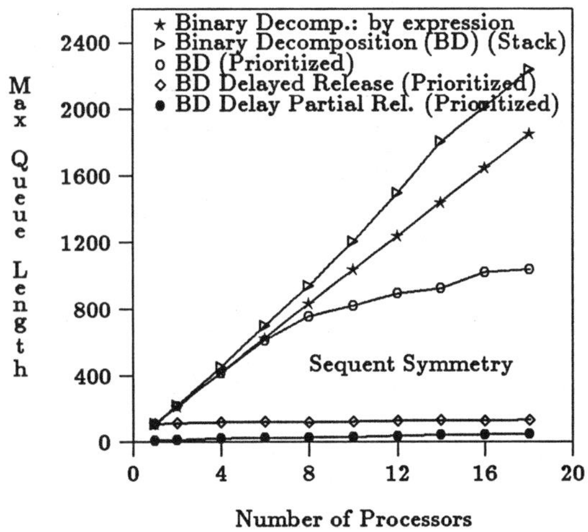

Figure 6: 126-Queens: Maximum Queue Lengths.

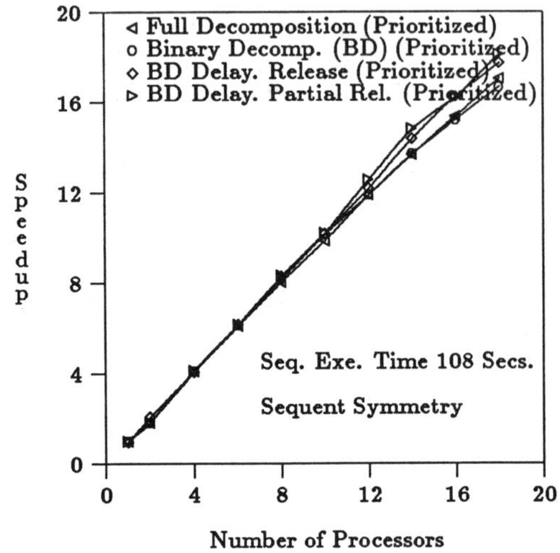

Figure 7: 8X8 Knights-Tour: 1st Solution Speedups

mance data is obtained from a single run of the 126-Queens problem and is highly consistent over different runs. The multiple stack strategy yields speedups that varies from run to run, as documented by Kumar et al. in [Kumar & Rao 1987]. The speedups with the shared stack also varied wildly between highly super-linear (few seconds) to extreme sublinear (aborted after few hours) and so are not reported here. Table I shows the total number of nodes expanded for the three schemes using bit vector priorities. It shows that (a) with priorities, the work with P processors is not significantly more than with 1 processor (e.g. an increase of 3.57% node expansions over sequential search with $P = 18$ using delayed release technique.) and (b) the wasted work is reduced with delayed release techniques. The plots in Figure 6 show that for a *LIFO* stack the maximum queue length (thus, the memory usage) increase proportionately to the number of processors P. This dependence on P is eliminated with the delayed release technique. With delayed partial release technique, the queue length decreases further (the memory usage remains unchanged for reasons explained in Section 3).

In a **Knights-Tour** problem, the knight must visit each position on a NXN chess board *once* and return to its starting position. Many solutions exist for the knights-tour problem. Speedups obtained were highly consistent from run to run, and increase linearly, as shown in Figure 7.

In the **Magic Square** problem the goal is to place integers from *1 to* N^2 on a NXN square board such that the sum of the integers along any row, column or diagonal is identical. Figure 8 gives the speedups to first solution to the problem with $N = 6$. The speedups improve with delayed release strategies. Again, the data reflects performance from a single run and is very consistent over different runs.

5 Discussion

We demonstrated the effectiveness of priority based parallel search techniques to eliminate anomalies and obtain consistent linear speedups to first solution in state-space searches. To the best of our knowledge, no other method proposed to date consistently achieves monotonically increasing speedups for a first solution. Our techniques also reduce the memory usage and it does not increase with the number of processors. It may be argued that this is unimportant as the amount of memory available grows linearly with the number of processors. However, this argument misses the point: on a P processor system our scheme requires a small fraction of the memory required by a stack based scheme. With 18 processors, ***126-Queens*** required 0.4 MBytes of memory compared to 1.8 MBytes with a shared stack. With a large number of processors and large problems, our scheme will be able to solve problems that the stack based scheme cannot solve due to a memory overflow.

An advantage of our scheme is that it adheres to local value-ordering heuristic, which are very important for first solution searches. However, even when good ordering heuristic is not available, our scheme is still valuable, because of its consistent and monotonic speedups.

Recently, Rao and Kumar have derived an interesting result in [Rao & Kumar 1988] concerning the multiple-stack model for parallel search, where the solution density are highly non-uniform across the search space. Although the speedups are anomalous, they show that *on the average* (i.e. averaged over several runs), the speedups tend to be larger than P, compared with the standard backtracking search, where P is the number of processors. In such types of search spaces our result is still valuable for the following rea-

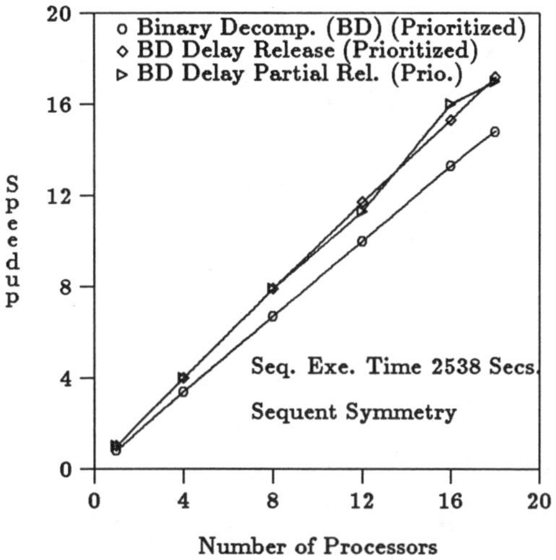

Figure 8: 6X6 Magic Squares: 1st Solution Speedups.

sons. First, the prioritizing scheme we presented *ensures* speedups close to P in all runs, and for varying values of P (assuming, of course, that there is enough work available in the part of the search tree to the left of the solution). Second, their results also show that the 'superlinearity' of speedup is not further enhanced beyond a few processors. Therefore, in a system with many processors we can exploit the non-linear solution densities better by setting the priorities of the top few nodes in the search tree to be null (i.e. empty bit vectors). This retains the advantage of exploring different regions of the search-space, hoping to exploit the non-uniform solution densities (probabilities) while still focusing the processors within these regions for more consistent speedups.

The use of priorities effectively *decouple* the parallel search *algorithm* from the scheduling strategy [Kale & Saletore 1989]. (In contrast, schemes such as [Lusk et al. 1988] for OR-parallel execution of Prolog use an explicit tree representation shared by all processors). This decoupling has several advantages. Scheduling strategies can be chosen independently of the search algorithm itself and synchronisation is much simpler. Most important, the prioritisation strategies can be extended to distributed memory machines such as the Intel iPSC/2 and BBN Butterfly, by providing a priority-balancing strategy in conjunction with the load balancing scheme. We are developing such a strategy.

We have extended these techniques for for Parallel IDA* in [Kale & Saletore 1989]. The extensions were needed because IDA* involves a series of increasing depth-first searches. Problem reduction based problem solving and Logic Programming are related areas in which, frequently, one is looking for one solution while many solutions may exist. However, this is substantially more complex situation than the pure state-space (OR-tree) search, if AND-parallelism is also to be exploited. The techniques developed in this paper can be incorporated beneficially in such schemes with appropriate modifications.

Acknowledgements

We would like to thank anonymous referees for improving the quality of the paper. We also thank Ross Overbeek at Argonne National Lab. for providing access to the Sequent Symmetry multiprocessor.

References

[Halstead 1986] Halstead R. 1986. Parallel Symbolic Computing, *IEEE Computer.*

[Hausman et al. 1987] Hausman B., Ciepielewski A. and Haridi S. 1987. OR-Parallel Prolog Made Efficient on Shared Memory Multiprocessors, *Proceedings of the Symposium on Logic Programming.*

[Kale 1990] Kale L.V. 1990. The Chare-Kernel Parallel Programming Language and System, *Proceedings of the International Conference on Parallel Processing.* Forthcoming.

[Kale & Saletore 1989] Kale L.V. and Saletore V. A. 1989. Parallel State-Space Search for a First Solution with Consistent Linear Speedups, Technical Report UIUCDCS-R-89-1549, Dept. of Comp. Sc., Univ. of Illinois at Urbana-Champaign.

[Korf 1988] Korf R. E. 1988. Optimal Path-Finding Algorithms, *Search in Artificial Intelligence*, 223-276. Kanal L.K., Kumar V. eds.

[Kumar & Rao 1987] Kumar V. and Rao V. N. 1987. Parallel Depth First Search, *International Journal of Parallel Programming.* 479-519.

[Lai & Sahni 1984] Lai T.H. and Sahni S. 1984. Anomalies in Parallel Branch-and-Bound Algorithms, *Communications of the ACM.* 594-602.

[Li & Wah 1986] Li G.J. and Wah B.W. 1986. How Good are Parallel and Ordered Depth-First Searches, *Proceedings of the International Conference on Parallel Processing.*

[Lusk et al. 1988] Lusk E., Warren D.H.D, Haridi S. *et. al* 1988. The Aurora OR-parallel Prolog System, *Fifth Generation Computer Systems.* 819-830.

[Pearl 1985] Pearl J. 1985. Heuristics: Intelligent Search Strategies for Computer Problem Solving, Addison-Wesley, Inc.

[Rao & Kumar 1988] Rao V.N. and Kumar V. 1988. Superlinear Speedup in State-Space Search, *Proceedings of the Foundation of Software Technology and Theoretical Computer Science.*

Inductive Synthesis of Equational Programs

Nachum Dershowitz
Department of Computer Science
University of Illinois
Urbana, IL 61801, U.S.A.
nachum@cs.uiuc.edu

Eli Pinchover
Department of Mathematics
and Computer Science
Bar-Ilan University
Ramat-Gan 52100, Israel

Abstract

An equational approach to the synthesis of functional and logic programs is taken. Typically, a target program contains equations that are only true in the standard model of the given domain rules. To synthesize such programs, induction is necessary. We propose heuristics for generalizing from a sequence of deductive consequences. These are combined with rewrite-based methods of inductive proof to derive provably correct programs.

Introduction

Various approaches to the automated synthesis of computer programs have been taken; see (Barr & Feigenbaum 1981–1982, Chap. X). In particular, deductive methods have been used to derive executable programs from formal specifications; early examples of such an approach include (Burstall & Darlington 1977; Manna & Waldinger 1979). Inductive, example-based methods have also been applied to this task; a survey of this approach is (Smith 1980); more recent work includes (Shapiro 1983). In this paper, we employ both deductive and inductive methods of inferring provably correct programs. This work differs from most others in combining syllogistic and heuristic approaches and in using mathematical induction to formally verify hypotheses drawn by inductive inference. It is similar in spirit to some methods used in automated deduction, notably (Boyer & Moore 1977).

In (Dershowitz 1982; Dershowitz 1985a), it was proposed that equations be used both as specification language and as target programming language within a synthesis system. In the equational paradigm, programs are expressed as sets of directed equations, called *rewrite systems*, and are executed using two mechanisms: *rewriting* (reduction) for the functional aspect and *narrowing* (a restricted form of paramodulation) for the "logic" aspect. As inference engine, these papers suggested using the *completion procedure* (Knuth & Bendix 1970). This completion-based approach to synthesis has since been pursued in (Kodratoff & Picard 1983; Perdix 1986; Reddy 1989) and has been compared to the fold/unfold method of (Burstall & Darlington 1977) in (Fronhöfer & Furbach 1986). For a survey of rewriting, see (Dershowitz & Jouannaud 1990); for completion and its applications, see (Dershowitz 1989).

Consider the following toy system S for addition and doubling (d) of natural numbers in unary notation:

$$\begin{aligned} x+0 &\rightarrow x \\ x+s(y) &\rightarrow s(x+y) \\ d(x) &\rightarrow x+x \end{aligned}$$

Such a pattern-directed program is used to compute by replacing instances of a left-hand side pattern (the x and y are variables) with the corresponding instance of the right-hand side. The term $d(s(0))+s(0)$, representing the expression $2*1+1$, may be rewritten by one application of one rule to $(s(0)+s(0))+s(0)$, since the third rule matches the subterm $d(s(0))$, with $x=s(0)$. It could alternatively be reduced to $s(d(s(0))+0)$, applying the second rule to the whole term, with $x = d(s(0))$ and $y=0$. Continuing in any manner (we treat rewrite systems as nondeterministic programs), eventually results in the irreducible term $s(s(s(0)))$, standing for the numeral 3. We say that $s(s(s(0)))$ is a *normal form* of the input term $d(s(0))+s(0)$.

Consider now the following recursive program R, which does not use addition for doubling:

$$\begin{aligned} x+0 &\rightarrow x \\ x+s(y) &\rightarrow s(x+y) \\ d(0) &\rightarrow 0 \\ d(s(x)) &\rightarrow s(s(d(x))) \end{aligned}$$

System R enjoys four important properties, two intrinsic and two vis-a-vis its specification S: (1) R is *terminating,* i.e. for no input term is an infinite sequence of rewrites possible; (2) R is *ground confluent*, i.e. any variable-free term has at most one normal form; (3) R is *correct* with respect to S, in the sense that terms are only rewritten to terms that are "equal" according to S; (4) R is *complete* with respect to S, in the sense that any two variable-free terms that are equal according to S are also equal according to R. In general, we demand that all synthesized programs meet these requirements.

Section 2 describes the synthesis of deductive consequences of a specification like S. As we will see, deduction alone may produce an infinite program for

S. This leads, in Section 3, to the use of rewriting-based induction techniques to derive the finite program R from a finite subset of the deductive consequences of S. Rewriting-based inductive proofs, called "proofs by consistency" or "inductionless induction", were pioneered by (Musser 1980). It is the use of heuristics for generalizing from a sequence of deductive consequences and then establishing the correctness of the conjectured program by formal inductive techniques that distinguishes this work from previous deductive approaches to program synthesis. A similar approach has independently been taken in (Jantke 1989b).

Deductive Synthesis

The programs we consider in this paper are all in the form of systems of rewrite rules. Rewrite rules are given to the Prolog system as assertions, like `rule(add(X,0),X)` for the rule $x + 0 \rightarrow x$. A simple Prolog interpreter of rewrite programs finds normal forms of input terms. (For things to work right, we take it for granted that "occur-checks" are performed whenever necessary, as can be done in PTTP (Stickel 1986).) With asserted rules corresponding to the program S given earlier, Prolog solves goals like `rewrite(add(d(s(0)),s(0)),Z)`, meaning, "What are the terms `Z` to which the input term `add(d(s(0)),s(0))` rewrites?" The final answer in this case is the normal form `Z = s(s(s(0)))`. Moreover, Prolog can solve goals like `rewrite(add(d(Y),s(0)),s(s(s(0))))`, in which a free ("logic") variable occurs in the term being rewritten, to obtain a solution `s(s(0))` as a value of `Y` that makes `add(d(Y),s(0))` rewrite to `s(s(s(0)))`.

The same program S may be used for subtraction or halving, much like Horn-clause programs may be used to solve for free variables. Instead of using just pattern-matching to locate a potential rewrite, unification is used to make the rewrite possible. To solve the goal equation $d(z) + s(0) = s(s(s(0)))$ for z, one looks for a (nonvariable) subterm of the goal that unifies with a left-hand side of S. (Variables in goals and rules are always treated as disjoint.) After applying the most general unifying substitution to the goal, the enabled step is made. This two-step (unify-rewrite) process is called *narrowing*. The use of narrowing as operational semantics for programming with equations was first suggested in (Dershowitz 1984) and is compared with other approaches in (Reddy 1986).

In our case, the subterm $d(z)$ is an instance of the left-hand side of the third rule, and the goal is rewritten to $(z + z) + s(0)$. (Rewriting is a special case of narrowing in which unification is "one-way" and no substitutions need be made in the goal.) Rewriting twice more, with the second rule followed by the first, gives $s(z + z) = s(s(s(0)))$. Letting $z = 0$ allows the first rule to fire, narrowing the goal to the irreducible, un-narrowable, and unsatisfiable subgoal $s(0) = s(s(s(0)))$. Hence, alternative narrowings must be explored. In this case, we can let $z = s(u)$, instead, yielding the subgoal $s(s(s(u) + u)) = s(s(s(0)))$. Letting $u = 0$, now, gives $s(s(s(0))) = s(s(s(0)))$, the two sides of which are identical. Thus, the solution discovered by narrowing is $z = s(u) = s(0)$.

The basic deductive mechanism we employ in synthesis is *completion* (Knuth & Bendix 1970). *Critical pairs* are equations that are deductive consequences of pairs of rules, formed by unifying one (renamed) left-hand side with a nonvariable subterm of the same or another left-hand-side. The idea in completion is to make new rules out of critical pairs that do not simplify to identity. To generate critical pairs, we use a Prolog predicate `subst(S,L,R,T)` which holds if `T` is the result of applying `rule(L,R)` once at a nonvariable subterm of `S`. The goal solving capabilities of PROLOG allow us to solve for a minimal instance of `S` that makes the rule applicable, yielding—after unification—a critical pair `eq(S,T)`. A terminating system is confluent (a stronger property than ground confluence) if for each critical pair $s = t$, both s and t reduce to the same term v. Some other methods for establishing ground confluence (an undecidable property even of terminating systems) are available; see, for example, (Küchlin 1989).

Completion was programmed as a predicate `kb(Ei,EO)` that applies the basic inference rules described in (Bachmair *et al.* 1986) to `EO` to generate a sequence of sets of equations `EO`, `E1`, etc. One inference rule generates new critical pairs; another reduces them to normal form; a third deletes trivial ones; two inference rules orient critical pairs into uni-directional rewrite rules. Rules are oriented according to a given well-founded ordering on terms, so that applying the rule to any term reduces the term in the ordering, ensuring thereby that the system of generated rules is always terminating (an undecidable property). Completion typically includes additional mechanisms for simplifying rules that have already been generated. (Our implementation does not, and therefore leads to variants of the rules that might be obtained with a full-fledged system like REVE (Lescanne 1983).)

For our purposes, the most useful ordering is the *lexicographic path ordering* (Kamin & Lévy 1980); see (Dershowitz 1987). This ordering $\succ_{lpo}$ is based on a given partial ordering, called a *precedence*, $\succ$ between function symbols. In the induced ordering $\succ_{lpo}$, a term is always greater than each of its subterms, terms with the same leading function symbol are compared lexicographically (from left-to-right, say), and a term with more significant leading symbol needs only be greater than the immediate subterms of a term with less significant leading symbol.

Consider the following specification S:

$$\begin{array}{rcl} x + 0 & \rightarrow & x \\ x + s(y) & \rightarrow & s(x + y) \\ s(x) + y & \rightarrow & s(x + y) \\ x + x & \rightarrow & d(x) \end{array}$$

We choose a precedence that ensures that specification symbols (+) are greater than the synthesized functions (d), which in turn are greater than the primitive operations (s,0). The query `kb([],[])` produces the following equations and rules R:

$$\begin{array}{rcl} d(0) & \to & 0 \\ d(s(x)) & = & s(s(x)+x) \\ d(s(x)) & = & s(s(x+x)) \\ d(s(x)) & \to & s(s(d(x))) \end{array}$$

The first rule, for instance, is the result of orienting the two normal forms of $0+0$ (in the only direction possible). The latter term is obtained by unifying the left-hand sides of the specification and first rule for addition. For more details of completion-based synthesis, see (Dershowitz 1985b).

We need to show that the two generated rules form a correct and complete system for doubling. To define correctness, we need to make precise what was meant earlier by "equal according to S." There are two notions of equality that are relevant: (a) *deductive equality*, meaning provable by substitution of equals for equals; and (b) *inductive equality*, meaning that all variable-free instances of the equation are deductively equal. To symbolize that every equation in R is a deductive equality with respect to S, we write $S \vdash R$; to symbolize that they are inductive equalities, we write $\mathcal{I}nd(S) \models R$. For example, $S \vdash x+y = y+x$ is *not* true, though for every variable-free instance it is; for example, $S \vdash s(s(0)) + s(0) = s(0) + s(s(0))$. The weaker notion, inductive equality, suffices in programming contexts, so we will say that R is correct with respect to specification S if $\mathcal{I}nd(S) \models R$. When completion is used, correctness is guaranteed in the stronger, deductive sense.

Completeness is similar to correctness, but with the roles of R and S reversed. Actually, we split S into $A \cup D$, where A contains domain information and D expresses properties of the defined functions in terms of domain entities. Then, we require only that $\mathcal{I}nd(A \cup R) \models D$. In the doubling example, A would consist of the three rules for addition and D would be the equation $x + x = d(x)$. The two generated rules for d are complete, since both sides of any ground instance of D (happen to) reduce (under $A \cup R$) to domain values constructed from s and 0. Since R is correct (that is, it follows from $A \cup D$), and D is a conservative extension of A (hence does not equate unequal constructor terms), the two reduced sides of D must be equal in A. So, we have $A \cup R \vdash t + t = d(t)$ for all ground terms t. For a discussion of correctness of synthesized rewrite programs, see (Reddy 1989).

In (Reddy 1989) it is pointed out that full completion is unnecessary and a weaker inference engine suffices; in other words, only a subset of the critical pairs need to be generated for synthesis of ground confluent programs. On the other hand, the additional equations generated by full completion occasionally come in handy. Furthermore, we need not be concerned with the potential completion has of generating an infinite number of irrelevant equations, since—for the purposes of synthesis—completion may be arrested as soon as enough rules R have been generated for completeness.

Ordinary completion will fail if it reaches a point where all critical pairs have been generated, and all equations are nontrivial, in normal form, and unorientable. Unfailing extensions of completion have been designed and perform better; see, for example, (Bachmair *et al.* 1989).

Regardless of which version of completion is employed, it may generate an infinite number of *relevant* program rules. What to do in such a case, is the subject of the next section.

Inductive Synthesis

In (Dershowitz 1985b) and (Reddy 1989), it was argued that—with an appropriate ordering—completion will always generate a program from a given specification. The catch is that the "guaranteed" program may be of infinite length. Indeed, running completion *without* the third addition rule, $s(x) + y \to s(x+y)$, instead of the desired program, generates an infinite set of rules:

$$\begin{array}{rcl} d(0) & \to & 0 \\ s(s(x)) + x & \to & d(s(x)) \\ d(s(0)) & \to & s(s(0)) \\ s(s(s(s(x)))) + x & \to & d(s(s(x))) \\ & \vdots & \end{array}$$

There is, of course, little one can do with the resultant *infinite* table lookup: $\{d(s^i(0)) \to s^{2i}(0) \ : \ i \geq 0\}$. What is needed is some way of guessing the more general rule $d(s(x)) \to s(s(d(x)))$.

We use two processes to generate hypotheses. The first involves generating critical pairs between *right-hand* sides of rules; the second is a syntactic form of generalization, à la (Boyer & Moore 1977). The intuition is that once we are dissatisfied with the rules, we look for equations between terms containing the defined function symbol, in the hope of discovering a pattern.

For the first step, we generate critical pairs between inverted rules of the current partial program. That is, we use a precedence $+ \succ s, 0 \succ d$, so that patterns involving d are brought to the fore. Given the above rules for d, we get the following equations

$$\begin{array}{rcl} d(s(0)) & = & s(s(d(0))) \\ d(s(s(0))) & = & s(s(d(s(0)))) \\ & \vdots & \end{array}$$

For the second step, we generate *most specific generalizations* of pairs of equations, by replacing conflicting subterms by a new variable; see (Plotkin 1970). We implemented a predicate `msg(S,T,U,M)` that gives the least general term `U` (i.e. the glb of `S` and `T` in the subsumption lattice) such that `S` and `T` are both instances of U; M is the list of conflicts between S and T used to construct U, which is needed to ensure that the same conflicts result in the same new variable. (This process is called "anti-unification" nowadays.)

From the above two equations, msg generates the hypothesis $d(s(x)) = s(s(d(x)))$. Given a hypothesized rule (such as this equation oriented from left to right), we must apply the inductive proof method to prove that it is consistent with the domain rules and specification. Once proved, it can be used to reduce (away) special cases already generated.

To prove correctness in the inductive sense, we make use of the following fact: $\mathcal{I}nd(S) \models R$ if and only if $\mathcal{I}nd(S) \models dp(R)$, where $dp(R)$ is the set of all equations obtained by using S to narrow the left side of a rule in R. In proving $dp(R)$, the hypothesis R may be taken for granted. This process may be repeated for each of the equations in $dp(R)$ until only deductive consequences of S remain. In a manner similar to generation of critical pairs, we implemented a predicate dp(D,E) that generates equations E obtained by narrowing D. Thus, to prove an equation eq(S,T) we first reduce its two sides to normal form, then consider it proved if it has been shown already, if the two sides are identical, or if it can be oriented into a rule and each equation E such that dp(eq(S,T),E) is itself provable. This is the essence of the improved proof-by-consistency method in (Fribourg 1989). Refinements of this method include (Bachmair 1988) and (Reddy 1990).

Returning to our example, the hypothesis $d(s(x)) \rightarrow s(s(d(x)))$ is narrowed by $d(x) \rightarrow x + x$, giving $s(x) + s(x) = s(s(d(x)))$. Note that the rule for d is used for verification in the opposite direction of its use for synthesis. This is so that the specification itself is (ground) confluent. The above equation simplifies to $s(s(x) + x) = s(s(x + x))$, using the rule $x + s(y) \rightarrow s(x + y)$, but no further (in the absence of $s(x) + y \rightarrow s(x + y)$). Were this equation provable by deductive means, we would be finished; it isn't, so the inductive proof method continues in the same manner, generating an infinite sequence of oriented hypotheses:

$$\begin{array}{rcl} s(s(x) + x) & \rightarrow & s(s(x + x)) \\ s(s(s(y)) + y)) & \rightarrow & s(s(s(y) + y))) \\ & \vdots & \end{array}$$

Clearly, we need to substitute the (missing) lemma $s(x)+y \rightarrow s(x+y)$ for these instances. We employ the same generalization methods as for synthesis (cf. (Jantke 1989a; Lange 1989)). An additional helpful technique is *cancellation*, as used in deduction, for example, by (Stickel 1984). In particular (Huet & Hullot 1982), we can take advantage of "constructors," replacing hypotheses of the from $c(s_1, \ldots, s_n) = c(t_1, \ldots, t_n)$ with n hypotheses $s_i = t_i$, when there are no rules for c in S. In the above case, we are free to strip off matching outer s's from the generated hypotheses:

$$\begin{array}{rcl} s(x) + x & \rightarrow & s(x + x) \\ s(s(y)) + y & \rightarrow & s(s(y) + y) \\ & \vdots & \end{array}$$

Using the same msg procedure as before leads to the more general hypothesis $s(x) + y = s(x + y)$, exactly what we were looking for.

With this added as a rule to S, the recursive program

$$\begin{array}{rcl} d(0) & \rightarrow & 0 \\ d(s(x)) & \rightarrow & s(s(d(x))) \end{array}$$

for d is finally proved correct. The first rule is a deductive consequence of S; the second is an inductive consequence. (Actually, the synthesis procedure would already have suggested the missing equation from the sequence of rules $d(s^i(0)) \rightarrow s^{2i}(0)$, leading to the same result.)

Having succeeded in producing a program for doubling, a recursive program for halving can be generated from the *implicit* definition

$$\begin{array}{rcl} h(d(x)) & \rightarrow & x \\ h(s(d(x))) & \rightarrow & x \end{array}$$

The following sequence of rules is produced:

$$\begin{array}{rcl} h(0) & \rightarrow & 0 \\ h(s(0)) & \rightarrow & 0 \\ h(s(s(0))) & \rightarrow & s(0) \\ h(s(s(s(0)))) & \rightarrow & s(0) \\ h(s(s(s(s(0))))) & \rightarrow & s(s(0)) \\ & \vdots & \end{array}$$

These rules suggest at least two hypotheses, namely:

$$\begin{array}{rcl} h(x) & = & h(s(x)) \\ s(h(x)) & = & h(s(s(x))) \end{array}$$

The former generalizes the equations

$$\begin{array}{rcl} h(0) & = & h(s(0)) \\ h(s(s(0))) & = & h(s(s(s(0)))) \end{array}$$

but is disproved, since (taking $x = s(0)$) it implies that $s(0) = 0$. The second hypothesis is obtained by looking at different pairs of rules (first and third, second and fourth, etc.) and generalizes the equations

$$\begin{array}{rcl} s(h(0)) & = & h(s(s(0))) \\ s(h(s(s(0)))) & = & h(s(s(s(s(0))))) \end{array}$$

It is proved immediately by induction, yielding the correct and complete program

$$\begin{array}{rcl} h(0) & \rightarrow & 0 \\ h(s(0)) & \rightarrow & 0 \\ h(s(s(x))) & \rightarrow & s(h(x)) \end{array}$$

When a program R contains symbols not appearing in its specification S, such as symbols for auxiliary functions, we need to replace inductive truth with the notion of "conservative extension." That is, we require that there exist no terms s and t in the vocabulary of S such that $S \not\vdash s = t$, but $R \cup S \vdash s = t$. One heuristic for introducing auxiliary functions is simply to look for nontrivial subterms that appear (some number of times) in program rules.

For example, suppose we have all three rules for addition, and wish to manufacture a program $q(x)$ for squaring from the following rules for multiplication:

$$\begin{array}{rcl} x * 0 & \rightarrow & 0 \\ x * s(y) & \rightarrow & (x * y) + x \\ s(x) * y & \rightarrow & (x * y) + y \\ x * x & \rightarrow & q(x) \end{array}$$

Suppose, further, that we do not wish to allow addition in the synthesized program, so we order the symbols $* \succ + \succ q \succ s, 0$. Completion will generate the following rules (among others):

$$\begin{array}{rcl} q(0) & \rightarrow & 0 \\ s((q(x) + x) + x) & \rightarrow & q(s(x)) \\ s(s(s((q(s(y)) + y) + y))) & \rightarrow & q(s(s(y))) \end{array}$$

Noting the repeating left-hand side pattern $(y + x) + x$ suggests the introduction of an ancillary function:

$$(x + z) + z \quad \rightarrow \quad p(x, z)$$

Synthesizing p in the same manner as we synthesized d, gives

$$\begin{array}{rcl} p(x, 0) & \rightarrow & x \\ p(x, s(y)) & \rightarrow & s(s(p(x, y))) \end{array}$$

Interpolating p in the precedence after q (since it is alright for q to be defined in terms of p) turns all the above rules for q into just:

$$\begin{array}{rcl} q(0) & \rightarrow & 0 \\ q(s(x)) & \rightarrow & s(p(q(x), x)) \end{array}$$

Together, the rules for p and q constitute the desired program.

Discussion

We have shown how—in the equational framework—both deductive and inductive methods may be applied to the task of program synthesis. We have witnessed the need for heuristics that suggest inductive theorems for incorporation in a developing program, as well as for forming the lemmas needed in the inductive proofs. We have been pleasantly surprised by the success of just these few, simple heuristics.

Not all target programs fall under the purview of the automated techniques we have discussed. For example, suppose the specification is

$$\begin{array}{rcl} k(d(x)) & \rightarrow & f(d(x)) \\ k(s(d(x))) & \rightarrow & g(s(d(x))) \end{array}$$

where f and g are primitive operations, and we are given all the facts we have derived about d and h. This is an indirect program for k, requiring narrowing to first solve the goal $y = d(x)$ (or $y = s(d(x))$) for a given number y *before* rewriting $k(y)$ to $f(y)$ (or $g(y)$). Thus, the first rule applies to even y and the second in the odd case. An alternative program, requiring only rewriting would be

$$\begin{array}{rcl} d(h(y)) = y \mid \ k(y) & \rightarrow & f(y) \\ d(h(s(y))) = y \mid \ k(y) & \rightarrow & g(y) \end{array}$$

where the first part is a conditional "guard," which when satisfied for a particular number y allows $k(y)$ to be rewritten. In general, conditional rewrite systems and conditional narrowing provide a better combination of functional and logic programming; see, for instance, (Dershowitz & Plaisted 1988). Conditional synthesis, however, would necessitate more powerful deductive and inductive methods for handling conditional equations, such as have been investigated in (Ganzinger 1987; Kounalis & Rusinowitch 1990). More elaborate generalization methods would also be required, perhaps along the lines of (Kirchner 1989; Lange 1989). This is an area for further research.

References

Bachmair, L. Proof by consistency in equational theories. In *Proceedings of the Third Symposium on Logic in Computer Science*, pp. 228–233, Edinburgh, Scotland, July 1988.

Bachmair, L., Dershowitz, N., and Hsiang, J. Orderings for equational proofs. In *Proceedings of the Symposium on Logic in Computer Science*, pp. 346–357, Cambridge, MA, June 1986.

Bachmair, L., Dershowitz, N., and Plaisted, D. A. Completion without failure. In Ait-Kaci, H. and Nivat, M., eds., *Resolution of Equations in Algebraic Structures*, vol. 2: Rewriting Techniques, chap. 1, pp. 1–30, Academic Press, New York, 1989.

Barr, A. and Feigenbaum, E. A., eds. *The Handbook of Artificial Intelligence.* William Kaufmann, 1981–1982. Three volumes.

Boyer, R. S. and Moore, J. S. A lemma driven automatic theorem prover for recursive function theory. In *Proceedings of the Fifth International Joint Conference on Artificial Intelligence*, pp. 511–519, Cambridge, MA, 1977.

Burstall, R. M. and Darlington, J. A transformation system for developing recursive programs. *J. of the Association for Computing Machinery*, 24(1):44–67, January 1977.

Dershowitz, N. Applications of the Knuth-Bendix completion procedure. In *Proceedings of the Seminaire d'Informatique Theorique*, pp. 95–111, Paris, France, December 1982.

Dershowitz, N. Equations as programming language. In *Proceedings of the Fourth Jerusalem Conference on Information Technology*, pp. 114–124, IEEE Computer Society, Jerusalem, Israel, May 1984.

Dershowitz, N. Computing with rewrite systems. *Information and Control*, 64(2/3):122–157, May/June 1985.

Dershowitz, N. Synthesis by completion. In *Proceedings of the Ninth International Joint Conference on Artificial Intelligence*, pp. 208–214, Los Angeles, CA, August 1985.

Dershowitz, N. Termination of rewriting. *J. of Symbolic Computation*, 3(1&2):69–115, February/April 1987. Corrigendum: *4*, 3 (December 1987), 409–410.

Dershowitz, N. Completion and its applications. In Ait-Kaci, H. and Nivat, M., eds., *Resolution of Equations in Algebraic Structures*, vol. 2: Rewriting Techniques, chap. 2, pp. 31–86, Academic Press, New York, 1989.

Dershowitz, N. and Jouannaud, J. Rewrite systems. In van Leeuwen, J., ed., *Handbook of Theoretical Computer Science B: Formal Methods and Semantics*, chap. 6, North-Holland, Amsterdam, 1990. In press; available as Rapport 478, LRI, Univ. Paris-Sud, France.

Dershowitz, N. and Plaisted, D. A. Equational programming. In Hayes, J. E., Michie, D., and Richards, J., eds., *Machine Intelligence 11: The logic and acquisition of knowledge*, chap. 2, pp. 21–56, Oxford Press, Oxford, 1988.

Fribourg, L. A strong restriction of the inductive completion procedure. *J. Symbolic Computation*, 8(3):253–276, 1989.

Fronhöfer, B. and Furbach, U. Knuth-Bendix completion versus fold/unfold: A comparative study in program synthesis. In Rollinger, C. and Horn, W., eds., *Proceedings of the Tenth German Workshop on Artificial Intelligence*, pp. 289–300, 1986.

Ganzinger, H. A completion procedure for conditional equations. In Kaplan, S. and Jouannaud, J., eds., *Proceedings of the First International Workshop on Conditional Term Rewriting Systems*, pp. 62–83, Orsay, France, July 1987. Vol. 308 of *Lecture Notes in Computer Science*, Springer, Berlin (1988).

Huet, G. and Hullot, J. Proofs by induction in equational theories with constructors. *J. of Computer and System Sciences*, 25:239–266, 1982.

Jantke, K. P. Algorithmic learning from incomplete information: Principles and problems. In Dassow, J. and Kelemen, J., eds., *Machines, Languages, and Complexity (Selected Contributions of the 5th International Meeting of Young Computer Scientists, Smolenice, Czechoslovakia, November 1988)*, pp. 188–207, 1989. Vol. 381 of *Lecture Notes in Computer Science*, Springer, Berlin.

Jantke, K. P. *Inductive program synthesis by problem proving and term rewriting.* Technical Report, Humbolt Univ. Berlin, Berlin, 1989.

Kamin, S. and Lévy, J. J. *Two generalizations of the recursive path ordering.* Unpublished note, Department of Computer Science, University of Illinois, Urbana, IL, February 1980.

Kirchner, H. Schematization of infinite sets of rewrite rules generated by divergent completion processes. *Theoretical Computer Science*, 67(2,3):303–332, October 1989.

Knuth, D. E. and Bendix, P. B. Simple word problems in universal algebras. In Leech, J., ed., *Computational Problems in Abstract Algebra*, pp. 263–297, Pergamon Press, Oxford, U. K., 1970. Reprinted in *Automation of Reasoning 2*, Springer, Berlin, pp. 342-376 (1983).

Kodratoff, Y. and Picard, M. Complétion de systèmes de réécriture et synthèse de programmes à partir deleurs spécifications. *Bigre*, 35, October 1983.

Kounalis, E. and Rusinowitch, M. Inductive reasoning in conditional theories. In Okada, M., ed., *Proceedings of the Second International Workshop on Conditional and Typed Rewriting Systems*, Montreal, Canada, June 1990. *Lecture Notes in Computer Science*, Springer, Berlin; to appear.

Küchlin, W. Inductive completion by ground proof transformation. In Ait-Kaci, H. and Nivat, M., eds., *Resolution of Equations in Algebraic Structures*, vol. 2: Rewriting Techniques, pp. 211–244, Academic Press, New York, 1989.

Lange, S. Towards a set of inference rules for solving divergence in Knuth-Bendix completion. In Jantke, K. P., ed., *Proceedings of the International Workshop on Analogical and Inductive Inference*, pp. 304–316, October 1989. Vol. 397 of *Lecture Notes in Computer Science*, Springer, Berlin.

Lescanne, P. Computer experiments with the reve term rewriting system generator. In *Proceedings of the Tenth ACM Symposium on Principles of Programming Languages*, pp. 99–108, Austin, TX, January 1983.

Manna, Z. and Waldinger, R. J. Synthesis: Dreams → programs. *IEEE Transactions on Software Engineering*, SE-5(4):294–328, July 1979.

Musser, D. R. On proving inductive properties of abstract data types. In *Proceedings of the Seventh ACM Symposium on Principles of Programming Languages*, pp. 154–162, Las Vegas, NV, 1980.

Perdix, H. Program synthesis from specifications. In Jorrand, P. and Sgurev, V., eds., *AIMSA*, pp. 13–21, North-Holland, 1986.

Plotkin, G. *Lattice theoretic properties of subsumption.* Technical Report MIP-R-77, University of Edinburgh, Edinburgh, Scotland, 1970.

Reddy, U. S. On the relationship between logic and functional languages. In DeGroot, D. and Lindstrom, G., eds., *Logic Programming: Functions, Relations, and Equations*, pp. 3–36, Prentice-Hall, Englewood Cliffs, NJ, 1986.

Reddy, U. S. Rewriting techniques for program synthesis. In Dershowitz, N., ed., *Proceedings of the Third International Conference on Rewriting Techniques and Applications*, pp. 388–403, Chapel Hill, NC, April 1989. Vol. 355 of *Lecture Notes in Computer Science*, Springer, Berlin.

Reddy, U. S. Term rewriting induction. In Stickel, M., ed., *Proceedings of the Ninth International Conference on Automated Deduction*, Kaiserslautern, West Germany, July 1990. *Lecture Notes in Computer Science*, Springer, Berlin; to appear.

Shapiro, E. Y. *Algorithmic Program Debugging.* MIT Press, Cambridge, MA, 1983.

Smith, D. R. A survey of synthesis of Lisp programs from examples. In *International Workshop on Program Construction*, Bonas, France, September 1980.

Stickel, M. E. A case study of theorem proving by the Knuth Bendix method discovering that $x^3 = x$ implies ring commutativity. In Shostak, R. E., ed., *Proceedings of the Seventh International Conference on Automated Deduction*, pp. 248–259, Napa, CA, May 1984. Vol. 170 of *Lecture Notes in Computer Science*, Springer, Berlin.

Stickel, M. E. A Prolog technology theorem prover: Implementation by an extended Prolog compiler. In Siekmann, J. H., ed., *Proceedings of the Eighth International Conference on Automated Deduction*, pp. 573–587, Oxford, England, July 1986. Vol. 230 of *Lecture Notes in Computer Science*, Springer, Berlin.

Mechanizing inductive reasoning

Emmanuel Kounalis and Michaël Rusinowitch
CRIN, 54506 Vandœuvre les Nancy, BP239 (France)
e-mail: {kounalis,rusi}@loria.fr

Abstract

Automating proofs by induction is important in many computer science and artificial intelligence applications, in particular in program verification and specification systems. We present a new method to prove (and disprove) automatically inductive properties. Given a set of axioms, a well-suited induction scheme is constructed automatically. We call such a scheme a test-set. Then, for proving a property, we just instanciate it with terms from the test-set and apply pure algebraic simplification to the result. This method avoids completion and explicit induction. However it retains their positive features, namely the completeness of the former and the robustness of the latter.

1 Introduction

Inductive reasoning consists in performing inferences in domains where there exists a natural well-founded relation on the objects. It is fundamental when proving properties of numbers, data-structures or programs axiomatized by a set of conditional axioms. As opposed to deductive theorems, inductive theorems are usually valid only in some particular models of the axioms, for instance Herbrand models or the initial model, which fits nicely the semantics of data-type specifications, logic and functional programming.

As everybody knows from his experience, it might be difficult, not only to find an appropriate well-founded relation to support inductive inferences, but also to guess suitable induction hypothesis. Two main approaches have been proposed to overcome these difficulties. The first applies explicit induction arguments on the structure of terms [1,3,2,4,14]. The second one involves a proof by consistency: this is the *inductionless induction* method [10,5,6]. However, both methods have many limitations either on the theorems to be proved or on the underlying theory. For instance, explicit induction techniques is unable to provide us automatically with induction schemes, and cannot help to disprove false conjectures. On the other hand, the inductionless induction technique often fails where explicit induction succeeds. Moreover, there does not exist any realistic inductionless induction procedure for conditional theories.

In this paper, we present an alternative proof system for automatizing inductive reasoning in theories defined by conditional axioms. We show how to prove (and disprove) equations and more generally clauses in the initial model and Herbrand models respectively. Our method combines the full power of explicit induction and inductionless induction. It is refutationally complete in the following sense : any positive clause which is not valid in the initial model will be disproved in finite time, provided that no negative literals are introduced by the procedure. This method relies on the notion of *test-set* (which, in essence, is a finite description of the initial model) and applies only pure algebraic simplification. The key-idea of the simplification strategy is to use axioms, previously proved conjectures, and instances of the conjecture itself as soon as they are smaller than the currently examined proposition with respect to a well-founded relation. This last point captures the notion of Induction Hypothesis in the proof by induction paradigm. The refutational aspect of our procedure requires a convergence property of the axiomatization and, also, suitable test-sets. The convergence can be obtained either by a Knuth-Bendix like procedure [9] or semantic techniques specific to hierarchical axiomatizations(see [12] and section 5.2 of this paper). On the other side, building a test-set requires itself some theorem proving. Whereas the computation of test-sets is generally undecidable, in the last section, we propose a method to obtain test-sets in conditional theories over a free set of constructors. Our method can also be viewed as a **real automatization** of explicit induction: indeed the test-set computation yields automatically induction schemes which are well-adapted to the axioms. In addition, we show how the method applies to proofs of properties of some recursive programs and elementary arithmetic.

2 Overview of our approach: an example

Before discussing the technical details of the method we propose for mechanizing proofs of inductive theorems, we first describe our inference system on a simple example, namely positive integers with cut-off and *gcd* functions and the less predicate. The arrow $\rightarrow$ just indicates how to apply a (conditional) equation for simplification:

(1) $x - 0 \rightarrow x$
(2) $0 - x \rightarrow 0$
(3) $s(x) - s(y) \rightarrow x - y$
(4) $(0 < s(x)) \rightarrow tt$
(5) $(x < 0) \rightarrow ff$
(6) $x < y = tt \Rightarrow s(x) < s(y) \rightarrow tt$
(7) $x < y = ff \Rightarrow s(x) < s(y) \rightarrow ff$
(8) $x < y = tt \Rightarrow gcd(x, y) \rightarrow gcd(y - x, y)$
(9) $x < y = ff \Rightarrow gcd(x, y) \rightarrow gcd(x - y, x)$
(10) $gcd(x, 0) \rightarrow x$
(11) $gcd(0, x) \rightarrow x$

Consider the conjectures:

(12) $x - x = 0$
(13) $x < x = ff$
(14) $x < s(x) = tt$
(15) $x < y = tt \vee x < y = ff$
(16) $x < y = ff \vee y < z = ff \vee x < z = tt$
(17) $gcd(x, x) = x$
(18) $gcd(x, y) = gcd(y, x)$
(19) $x < s(x) = ff$
(20) $x < y = ff \vee y < x = tt$

Except the two last ones all these propositions are valid in the standard arithmetic:note that 13,15 and 16 state that $<$ is a total ordering on integers, and 18 is the commutativity of *gcd*. This suggests to prove them by induction. With our method the first step consists in computing a test-set (see def. 4.1). By using techniques of section 6,we get the test-set $\{0, s(x), tt, ff\}$. The next step consists in replacing variables of the conjecture by the elements of the test-set and checking these instances by using pure simplification. *The simplification strategy may use axioms, previously proved conjectures, and instances of the conjecture itself as soon as they are smaller (w.r.t. a noetherian relation which contains the rewriting relation) than the currently examined proposition. This last point captures the notion of Induction Hypothesis in the proof by induction paradigm (see th. 4.1,4.2).* For the equation 12, two instances need to be checked: $0 - 0 = 0$ and $s(x) - s(x) = 0$. The first one reduces immediately to a trivial identity. For the second one consider the reduction (notice the use of 12 as an induction hypothesis): $s(x) - s(x) \rightarrow_3 x - x \rightarrow_{12} 0$ For 13, the only non-trivial instance is $s(x) < s(x) = ff$. However, $s(x) < s(x) \rightarrow_{13,7} ff$. For the last derivation, we have used an induction hypothesis to satisfy the condition of 7 (cf th. 4.1). For 14, the same argument can be employed. For 15, there are four instances by terms from the test-set. The only non-trivial case is $s(x) < s(y) = tt \vee s(x) < s(y) = ff$. By using case rewriting (cf def. 3.3), we can split this formula into the conjunction:

(21) $\neg x < y = tt \vee tt = tt \vee s(x) < s(y) = ff$
(22) $x < y = tt \vee s(x) < s(y) = ff$

Now, 21 is trivial and 22 is split again in:

(23) $x < y = tt \vee \neg x < y = ff \vee ff = ff$
(24) $x < y = tt \vee x < y = ff \vee s(x) < s(y) = ff$

23 is trivial again and 24 is subsumed by the initial conjecture: this is the induction step (cf th. 4.2). The 16,17,18 are proved exactly in the same way. Consider now 19. To disprove it, we are going to use the convergence properties of the initial system. Note that the saturation technique (see section 5) can prove the convergence property for 1-7 and th. 5.1 for the whole axiomatization. The instances to be considered are : $0 < s(0) = ff, s(x) < s(s(x)) = ff$ The first one reduces to $tt = ff$ whose members are irreducible and different. By th. 4.3 the conjecture is false. For 20, consider the following instance $0 < s(x) = ff \vee s(x) < 0 = tt$. It can be reduced to $tt = ff \vee ff = tt$ and therefore 20 is not valid.

3 Preliminaries

3.1 Definitions and notations

Let F be a signature of function symbols, and X a set of variables. We shall denote by $T(F, X)$ the set of terms built from F and X. We write $s[t]_n$ to mean that the term t is a subterm of s at position n. The set of ground terms is denoted by $T(F)$. A conditional equation is an equation or an expression of one of the types: $e_1 \wedge \ldots \wedge e_n \Rightarrow e$ or $e_1 \wedge \ldots \wedge e_n \Rightarrow$ or $\Rightarrow$ where $e, e_1, \ldots e_n$ are equations, $e_1, \ldots e_n$ are *conditions*, a positive literal e in a conditional equation is a *conclusion* and $\Rightarrow$ is the empty clause. In this paper, axiomatizations are built from conditional equations and goals to be proved are clauses (i.e. disjunction of equational literals, since $=$ is the only predicate, here [1]). Given a binary relation $\rightarrow$, $\rightarrow^*$ denotes its reflexive transitive closure. Given two binary relations, R, S, RoS denotes their composition. A relation R is noetherian if there is no infinite sequence $t_1\ R\ t_2\ R\ \ldots$. In the following, we suppose given a *reduction ordering* $\succ$ on the set of terms, that is, a transitive irreflexive relation which is noetherian, monotonic ($s \succ t$ implies $w[s] \succ w[t]$) and stable ($s \succ t$ implies $s\sigma \succ t\sigma$). A reduction ordering can be extended to literals by comparing the multiset of their members with the multiset extension of $\succ$. Formula are compared by using the multiset extension of this last ordering to the multiset of their atomic subformulas. Since there is no ambiguity, all these extensions will also be denoted by $\succ$. An equation $s = t$ will be written $s \rightarrow t$ if for all ground substitution $s\sigma \succ t\sigma$; in that case we say that the equation is *orientable*.

[1] we shall identify a conditional equation and its corresponding representation as a clause

3.2 Inductive theorems

Given a set of conditional equations Ax on the signature F, we recall that a Herbrand model of Ax is a model of Ax whose domain is $T(F)$ (axioms for equality are implicitly assumed to be valid, too). A formula $\mathcal{F}$ is a *deductive theorem of* Ax if it is valid in any model of Ax. This will be denoted by $Ax \models$ F. The notion of inductive theory can be related to several kinds of models: Herbrand models or initial models (i.e least Herbrand models). These relations are discussed in [11]. We have chosen to study the initial and Herbrand model approaches:

Definition 3.1 *Let H be a set of conditional equations on the signature F. A clause e is an* inductive theorem of H *iff for any ground substitution σ, $H \models e\sigma$.*

For clauses, validity in all Herbrand models differs, in general, from validity in the initial model. However these two notions of validity coincide for unconditional equations as it is proved in [11].

3.3 Conditional rewriting

The idea of rewriting is to impose a direction when using equations in proofs. This direction is indicated by an arrow when it is independent from the instanciation: $l \rightarrow r$ means that, we can replace l by r in some context. When an instance of a conditional equation is orientable and has a valid conditional part, it can be applied as a rule. The conditions are checked by a recursive call to the theorem-prover. Termination of such calls is ensured by requiring the conditions to be smaller (w.r.t. the reduction ordering $\succ$) than the conclusion:

Definition 3.2 *Let H be a set of clauses. Let A be a term or a clause, and n an occurrence of A. Then $A[s\sigma]_n \rightarrow_H A[t\sigma]_n$ if σ is a substitution and there is a conditional equation $c \Rightarrow s = t$, in H such that $s\sigma \succ t\sigma$* and $H \models c\sigma$ and $(s = t)\sigma \succ c\sigma$..

A term A is reducible w.r.t. $\rightarrow_H$, if there is a term B such that $A \rightarrow_H B$. Otherwise we say that A is H-irreducible. The system H will be qualified as *convergent* if for all ground terms a,b such that $H \models a = b$ there exists a ground term c such that $a \rightarrow_H {}^* c$ and $b \rightarrow_H {}^* c$. One can easily see that it is also equivalent to the property that every ground term possesses a unique irreducible form. Note that the conditional rewriting relation may be undecidable. The relation $\rightarrow_H$ will be extended to sets of clauses in a natural way: by definition, $S \cup \{c\} \rightarrow_H S \cup \{d\}$ whenever $c \rightarrow_H d$.

3.4 Case rewriting

Case reasoning is a very powerful technique which is the basis of many theorem proving strategies. It is a most important rule in the context of inductive theorem proving where case splitting arises naturally from induction hypothesis. We propose here a notion of case rewriting which is well-suited to inductive reasoning.

Definition 3.3 *Let H be a set of conditional equations and $c \Rightarrow s = t$ a conditional equation in H. Let $A[s\sigma]_n$ be a clause (where σ is a substitution) and let S be a set of clauses. The case rewriting rule can be stated as follows*

$S \cup \{A[s\sigma]_n\} \rightharpoonup_H S \cup \{(c\sigma \vee A[s\sigma]_n), (\neg c\sigma \vee A[t\sigma]_n)\}$

if $c\sigma$ is not a subclause of $A[s\sigma]_n$, n occurs in a maximal literal of A, $s\sigma \succ t\sigma$ and $(s = t)\sigma \succ c\sigma$

Let us denote $\rightharpoonup_H \cup \rightarrow_H$ by $\hookrightarrow_H$. The following propositions is the base for proving (or disproving) clausal theorems.

Proposition 3.1 *The case rewriting rule is sound (the derived set of clauses is logically equivalent to the initial set). The relation $\hookrightarrow_H$ is noetherian.*

4 How to prove and disprove inductive theorems

In this section, we propose general methods to prove (or disprove) automatically that clauses are inductive consequences of theories axiomatized by a set of conditional equations. These techniques allow us to replace inductive reasoning by pure simplification. Such a mechanization of inductive proofs is based on the notion of *test-set*, which, in essence, provides us with a finite description of the initial model.

4.1 Test sets

First, let us define the height of a term as the height of the tree representation of this term. The height of a set of conditional equations will be the maximal height of the terms occurring in this set. The height of an object x will be denoted by $|x|$.

Definition 4.1 *A* **test-set for a set of conditional equations H** *is a finite subset $S(H)$ of $T(F,X)$ such that the following properties hold:*

completeness: *for any H-irreducible ground term s, there exists a term t in $S(H)$ and a substitution σ such that $t\sigma = s$.*

soundness: *for any term t in $S(H)$ there exists an H-irreducible ground term s and a substitution σ such that $t\sigma = s$.*

transnormality: *every non-ground term in $S(H)$ has infinitely many ground instances which are H-irreducible.*

coveredness: *any non-ground term t in $S(H)$, $|t| \geq l$ where $l = |H| - 1$ if every variable in the left-hand side of the positive literals in H occurs once and*

$l = |H|$ if H contains a rule whose left-hand side has multiple occurrences of the same variable.

Definition 4.2 *A* **test-substitution w.r.t. S(H)** *is a substitution which applies every variable to an element of the test-set $S(H)$*

Example 4.1 *Let us come back to the introductory example. Let H be the set of axioms $1, 2, \ldots, 10$. As we pointed out, $S(H) = \{0, s(x), tt, ff\}$ may be considered as a test-set. Note that the four properties of the definition are verified.*

The construction of test-sets for equational theories is decidable and may be performed in relatively efficient way. The algorithm is based on pumping lemmas in tree languages and is detailed in [8]. Such an algorithm does not exist for conditional theories. However, in the last section, we shall give a method to derive test-sets in theories defined over a free set of constructors.

4.2 Inductive proofs by simplification

Our notion of induction refers to a noetherian ordering on ground terms, which contains the conditional rewriting relation. **We can use as an inductive hypothesis any instance of the theorem we want to prove, as soon as this instance is smaller (w.r.t. $\succ$)than the one that is currently considered.** In Theorem 4.1 we propose two rewriting relations which are sound, with regard to the use of induction hypothesis. Both of them allow to utilize the conjecture after a first *normal* simplification step has been applied. However, if the first step is conditional, we can also use the conjecture when attempting to satisfy the conditions of the rule (case a). The following notations will be useful:

Definition 4.3 *Let $u = v$ be an equation, then $\overset{u=v}{\longleftrightarrow}$ denotes the symmetric closure of $\rightarrow_{\{u=v\}}$ and $\rightarrow_{H/u=v}$ denotes the relation $(\overset{u=v}{\longleftrightarrow})^* o(\rightarrow_H) o(\overset{u=v}{\longleftrightarrow})^*$. Let H be a set of conditional equations, let A be a term and n an occurrence of A. Then we write $A[s\sigma]_n \rightarrow_{H[u=v]} A[t\sigma]_n$ if σ is a substitution and there is a conditional equation $a_1 = b_1 \wedge \cdots \wedge a_n = b_n \Rightarrow s = t$ in H, such that:*
1. $s\sigma \succ t\sigma$ and $(s = t)\sigma \succ (a_1 = b_1 \wedge \cdots \wedge a_n = b_n)\sigma$
2. $\forall i, \exists c \;\; a_i\sigma \rightarrow_{H\cup\{u=v\}}{}^* c$ and $b_i\sigma \rightarrow_{H\cup\{u=v\}}{}^* c$

The following theorem shows how to prove equations in the initial model of conditional theories.

Theorem 4.1 (see [9]) *Let H be a set of conditional equations, $S(H)$ a test-set, and $u = v$ an equation. We suppose that one of the following hypothesis is verified:*

a. *$\rightarrow_{H\cup\{u=v\}}$ is noetherian. In this case we define $\rightsquigarrow$ as the reflexive closure of the relation: $(\rightarrow_{H[u=v]}) o (\rightarrow_{H\cup\{u=v\}})^*$*

b. *$\rightarrow_{H/u=v}$ is noetherian. In this case we define $\rightsquigarrow$ as the reflexive closure of the relation: $(\rightarrow_H) o (\rightarrow_{H/u=v})^*$*

If, for all test-substitution ν there is a term α such that $u\nu \rightsquigarrow \alpha$ and $v\nu \rightsquigarrow \alpha$ then $u = v$ is an inductive theorem for H (and therefore is valid in the initial model of H by proposition 3.2).

Example 4.2 *Consider the following conditional axioms for integers with $+$, odd and even.*

(24) $x + 0 \rightarrow x$
(25) $x + s(y) \rightarrow s(x + y)$
(26) $even(0) \rightarrow tt$
(27) $even(s(0)) \rightarrow ff$
(28) $even(s(s(x))) \rightarrow even(x)$
(29) $even(x) = tt \Rightarrow odd(s(x)) \rightarrow tt$
(30) $even(x) = ff \Rightarrow odd(s(x)) \rightarrow ff$

Here the test-set is $\{0, s(0), s(s(z)), tt, ff\}$. Let us prove first the commutativity of $+$. We apply case b. of th. 4.1. We just consider the non-trivial case, which is an instantiation by the last scheme: $s(s(x)) + s(s(y)) = s(s(y)) + s(s(x))$. After simplification, we have to consider the goal: $s(s(s(s(x)) + y)) = s(s(s(s(y)) + x))$. Commutativity can be applied strictly inside *the equation, since it is supposed to be true for smaller instances (induction hypothesis). We get: $s(s(y + s(s(x)))) = s(s(x + s(s(y))))$ and then, simplification finishes the job. By assuming now the commutativity of $+$, we can prove in the same way : $odd(x + s(x)) = tt$. First, $odd(s(s(x)) + s(s(s(x)))) \rightsquigarrow odd(s(s(s(s(s(x + x)))))) \rightsquigarrow tt$. To justify the last rewriting step we need to prove as a lemma $even(s(s(s(s(x + x))))) = tt$ or its simplified form $even(x + x) = tt$. This is achieved by the same technique.*

It is straightforward to generalize the previous method to proving that clauses are inductive theorems. However, in this general situation, case analysis is crucial:

Theorem 4.2 *Let H be a set of conditional equations, $S(H)$ a test-set, and C a clause. If, for all test-substitution ν, $\{C\nu\} \hookrightarrow_H{}^* \{p_1, p_2 \cdots, p_n\}$, and every clause p_j is either a tautology (contains two complementary literals or an instance of $x{=}x$) or is subsumed by an axiom or contains an instance of C which is strictly smaller w.r.t. $\succ$ than $C\nu$, then C is an inductive theorem of H*

Example 4.3 *Let us prove now the transitivity of $<$ (see axioms in the introductory example): $x < y = ff \vee y < z = ff \vee x < z = tt$. The only non-trivial instance by a test-substitution among the eight of them is: $s(x) < s(y) = ff \vee s(y) < s(z) = ff \vee s(x) < s(z) = tt$. After three steps of case-rewriting, we get only one clause which is not a tautology, namely:*

$$x < y = ff \vee y < z = ff \vee x < z = tt \vee s(x) < s(y) = ff \vee s(y) < s(z) = ff \vee s(x) < s(z) = tt$$

This clause contains a subclause which is a strictly smaller instance of the one to be proved. Hence by th. 4.2, the proof is achieved. In the same way we could prove in the example 4.2 that $even(x) = tt \vee odd(x) = tt$.

4.3 Disproving inductive theorems

The notion of test-set is particularly useful for refuting inductive properties. The next definition provides us with criteria to reject such conjectures.

Definition 4.4 *We suppose that we are given a set of conditional equations* H, *and a test-set* $S(H)$. *Let* H' *be the set of positive literals of* H. *Then, a clause* $\neg e_1 \vee \ldots \vee \neg e_m \vee g_1 = d_1 \vee \ldots \vee g_n = d_n$ *is* **quasi-inconsistent** *with respect to* H *if there is a test-substitution* σ *such that, for all* $i \leq m$, $e_i\sigma$ *is an inductive theorem and for all* $j \leq n$ *at least one of the following is verified:*

- $g_j\sigma \not\equiv d_j\sigma$ *and* $g_j\sigma$ *and* $d_j\sigma$ *are irreducible by* H'.
- $g_j\sigma \succ d_j\sigma$ *and* $g_j\sigma$ *is irreducible by* H'.
- $g_j\sigma \prec d_j\sigma$ *and* $d_j\sigma$ *is irreducible by* H'.

The next result shows that, when the set of axioms is convergent, a quasi-inconsistent clause cannot be inductively valid. This is proved by building a well-chosen ground instance of the clause, which is false in some Herbrand model of the axioms. In particular, if the clause is an equation then it is not valid in the initial model.

Theorem 4.3 *Let* H *be a convergent set of conditional equations and* $S(H)$ *a test set for* H. *If* C *is quasi-inconsistent w.r.t.* H *then* C *is not an inductive theorem of* H.

Example 4.4 *The axioms are as in example 4.2. (note that they satisfy the convergence property). Consider the conjecture* $even(x) = tt \vee odd(x) = ff$. *It is quasi-inconsistent as shown by the following instance:*

$$even(s(0)) = tt \vee odd(s(0)) = ff$$

The theorems 4.1,4.2 and 4.3 can be combined into an inductive theorem-proving procedure which is complete for positive clauses, in the sense that it will disprove every positive clause which is not an inductive theorem, provided that no negative literals are introduced by the procedure. However, in the general case, the procedure allows to disprove many false conjectures.

5 How to get convergence

Convergent systems of equations have the property that two terms are equal if and only if they simplify to identical ones. In this section, we recall several methods to obtain the convergence property which is crucial for disproving conjectures.

5.1 The saturation technique

The saturation technique generalizes Knuth and Bendix procedure [7] to conditional theories. It is based on a refutationally complete set of inference rules. These rules have been discussed in [13].

5.2 Hierarchical techniques

Hierarchical axiomatizations are natural tools for building structured specifications. They are obtained by incremental extensions of a base theory with new function definitions. For hierarchical axiomatizations [12] , ground confluence can be obtained by semantic methods. The next theorem underlies Plaisted's work [12]:

Theorem 5.1 *Let* H *be a convergent set of conditional equations on the signature* $F - \{f\}$, *and let* H' *be an extension of* H *with conditional equations where the symbol* f *occurs. Assume that* H' *has the same initial model than* H. *If for every ground term* $f(t_1, \ldots, t_n)$ *there exists* $t' \in T(F - \{f\})$ *such that* $f(t_1, \ldots, t_n) \ (\rightarrow_{H'})^* \ t'$ *then* H' *is convergent.*

Verification of inductive properties often involves the proof of some lemmas. Adding these lemmas to the initial axiomatization does not destroy the convergence property as stated in the following result:

Theorem 5.2 *If* H *is convergent and* C *is a conditional equation which is an inductive theorem of* H. *Then* $\rightarrow_{H \cup \{C\}}$ *is convergent.*

For instance, in the introductory example 1-11 and 12,13,14,17,18 is convergent.

6 How to get test-sets

In this section, we propose a method of constructing test-sets for conditional theories whose signature F can be partitionned into a set C of constructors and a set D of defined functions. Therefore, we assume that every left-hand side of an orientable instance of a conclusion has a symbol from D. This corresponds to the well-known principle of definition of [5]. In order to simplify our presentation we shall suppose that $D = \{f\}$.

Definition 6.1 *Let* CS *be the set* $\{g(x_1, \ldots, x_n); g \in C\}$, *a* **pattern tree** T *of* $f(x_1, \ldots, x_n)$, *where* $f \in D$ *is a tree whose nodes are terms. The root is* $f(x_1, \ldots, x_n)$. *Every successor of a node* s *is obtained by replacing a variable of* s *by an element of* S *whose variables have been renamed.*

Example 6.1 Let CS be $\{0, s(x)\}$. Here is a pattern tree of $x < y$:

$x < y$

$x < 0$ $\quad$ $x < s(y)$

$0 < s(y)$ $\quad$ $s(x) < s(y)$

In the following, we describe a procedure for deriving a pattern-tree such that a test-set can be extracted from its leaves arguments. Hence, we suppose given a set of conditional equations defining a function f. To construct a suitable pattern tree of $f(x_1, \ldots, x_n)$, the next definition tells us how to identify the nodes to be expanded and the variables to be replaced.

Definition 6.2 *A term t is* **extensible at position u** *w.r.t. H if t/u is a variable and there is a rule $c \Rightarrow l \rightarrow r \in H$ such that l/u is a function symbol or a variable occurring more than once in l. A term t is* extensible *w.r.t. H if it is extensible at some position u.*

Definition 6.3 *Given a set H of conditional equations, we say that t is* **pseudo-reducible** *by H if there is a set of rules $\{c_1 \Rightarrow l_1 \rightarrow r_1, \ldots, c_n \Rightarrow l_n \rightarrow r_n\}$ in S such that $t/u_1 = l_1\sigma_1, \ldots, t/u_n = l_n\sigma_n$ and $C_1\sigma_1 \vee \ldots \vee C_n\sigma_n$ is an inductive theorem of H.*

Note immediately that if a term is pseudo-reducible, all its ground instances are reducible. Also, proving that a node is pseudo-reducible amounts to prove some inductive theorems. To avoid any vicious circle, either we can use a different method to prove these particular properties or we can use our method itself with a less refined test-set than the one we are trying to build. Let H be a set of conditional equations and let T be a pattern tree for $f(x_1, \ldots, x_n)$. If each leaf of T is either pseudo-reducible or not-extensible then we say T is complete for H. The tree in example 6.1 is complete for the axioms of the preliminary example. The previous definitions provides us with a procedure to derive complete pattern-trees. Starting from the tree $T = f(x_1, ..., x_n)$, we iterate the following operations:

- Select non-deterministically a leaf t which is extensible at some position u and not pseudo-reducible
- For any c in CS, rename c in c' with new variables and add $t[c']_u$ as a son of t.

When the previous procedure halts with success (as it did on all the examples we have tested), it provides immediately a test-set:

Theorem 6.1 *Given a set of conditional equations H, if there is a finite complete pattern-tree for $f(x_1, \ldots, x_n)$ whose all leaves are pseudo-reducible then a test-set for H can be computed.*

Given a finite complete pattern-tree, let G' be the set of its leaves arguments. We define G to be a subset of G' such that every element of G' has an instance in G and no element of G is an instance of another element of G. In the example 6.1, $G' = \{0, s(x), s(y)\}$ and $G = \{0, s(x)\}$.

7 Conclusion

We have presented new methods for inductive reasoning. These methods try to capture as much as possible the power of simplification. Moreover, when the axioms are convergent, test-sets give an efficient strategy to disprove theorems. We also feel that this method should generalize easily to the case of conditional equations with negative literals in the conditions.

References

[1] R. Aubin. Mechanizing structural induction. In *Theoretical Computer Science 9*, pp. 329–362, 1979.

[2] R.S. Boyer and J.S. Moore. *A Computational Logic.* Academic Press, New York, 1979.

[3] R-M. Burstall. Proving properties of programs by structural induction. In *Computer Journal 12*, pp. 41–48, 1969.

[4] S.J. Garland and J.V. Guttag. An overview of LP, the Larch Prover. In N. Dershowitz, ed., *Proc. of the 3rd RTA Conf., USA*, pp. 137–151, LNCS 355, 1989.

[5] G. Huet and J-M. Hullot. Proofs by induction in equational theories with constructors. *J. of Computer and System Sciences*, 25(2):239–266, 1982.

[6] J.P. Jouannaud and E. Kounalis. Proof by induction in equational theories without constructors. In *Proc. of 1st Symp. on Logic In Computer Science*, pp. 358–366, Boston (USA), 1986.

[7] D.E. Knuth and P.B. Bendix. Simple word problems in universal algebras. In J. Leech, ed., *Computational Problems in Abstract Algebra*, pp. 263–297, Pergamon Press, Oxford, 1970.

[8] E. Kounalis. Pumping lemmas in tree languages. in *Mathematical Foundations of Computer Science*, 1990.

[9] E. Kounalis and M. Rusinowitch. A mechanization of conditional reasoning. In *First International Symp. on Artificial Intelligence and Mathematics*, Fort Lauderdale, Florida, 1990.

[10] D.L. Musser. On proving inductive properties of abstract data types. In *Proc. 7th ACM POPL*, pp. 154–162, 1980.

[11] P. Padawitz. *Computing in Horn Clause Theories.* Springer-Verlag, 1988.

[12] D. Plaisted. Semantic confluence tests and completion methods. In *Journal Information and Control 65*, pp. 182–215, 1985.

[13] M. Rusinowitch. Theorem-proving with resolution and superposition. In *Proc. of the International Conference on Fifth Generation Computer Systems*, 1988.

[14] H. Zhang, D. Kapur, and M.S. Krishnamoorthy. A mechanizable induction principle for equational specifications. In E. Lusk and R. Overbeek, ed., *Proc. 9th CADE*, pp. 162–181, LNCS 310, 1988.

Skolem Functions and Equality in Automated Deduction *

William McCune

Mathematics and Computer Science Division
Argonne National Laboratory
Argonne, Illinois 60439-4801
mccune@mcs.anl.gov

Abstract

We present a strategy for restricting the application of the inference rule paramodulation. The strategy applies to problems in first-order logic with equality and is designed to prevent paramodulation into subterms of Skolem expressions. A weak completeness result is presented (the functional reflexive axioms are assumed). Experimental results on problems in set theory, combinatory logic, Tarski geometry, and algebra show that the strategy can be useful when searching for refutations and when applying Knuth-Bendix completion. The emphasis of the paper is on the effectiveness of the strategy rather than on its completeness.

1 Introduction

Most inference rules and strategies for guiding or restricting searches in automated deduction are syntactic in spirit. Examples are inference rules that generate positive clauses only, unrestricted back-chaining searches, restriction strategies that consider orderings on terms, and guidance strategies that focus on clauses with few symbols. Notable exceptions, which use interpretations or the intended meaning of the symbols, are semantic inference rules, inference rules with built-in knowledge of the intended domain, the set of support strategy for starting the search with specific clauses, and ad hoc weighting methods for controlling searches.

We present a paramodulation strategy which has a semantic motivation in that a distinction is made between Skolem functions and ordinary functions. The strategy is to prevent paramodulation (equality substitution) into proper subterms of Skolem terms. Human reasoners tend to treat the objects corresponding to Skolem terms as atomic, and it appears that programs can benefit by making a related distinction.

One can easily show the completeness of the strategy for otherwise-unrestricted paramodulation in the presence of the functional reflexive axioms. The proof rests on the (not well-known) fact [BKS85, Ben89] that equality axioms are not required for Skolem functions. The focus of this work is to try to determine the practical effectiveness of the strategy.

The restriction strategy was added to the deduction system OTTER [McC90], and experiments were conducted on problems in set theory, combinatory logic, Tarski geometry, and Knuth-Bendix completion. The completeness result does not yet apply to Knuth-Bendix completion problems, but our experiments indicate that the strategy can be valuable for those problems anyway.

Preliminary work on this topic appeared in [McC89].

2 Preliminaries

We assume a resolution/paramodulation refutation system for first-order logic with equality. If the formula representing the problem in question involves existentially quantified variables or is not in conjunctive normal form, it is preprocessed. A standard way to preprocess consists of three steps: conversion to negation normal form, Skolemization, then conversion to conjunctive normal form. The Skolemization procedure is the interesting step. Existentially quantified variables are replaced with new *Skolem functions* and *Skolem constants*. Arguments of the Skolem functions are the universally quantified variables in whose scope the existential quantifier occurs. A term is a *Skolem*

*This work was supported by the Applied Mathematical Sciences subprogram of the Office of Energy Research, U.S. Department of Energy, under Contract W-31-109-Eng-38.

expression if its leading function symbol is a Skolem function symbol, and $Sk(F)$ is any Skolemization of a formula F.

The result of preprocessing is a conjunction of clauses, whose variables are implicitly universally quantified. (Variables in clauses start with 'u'–'z'.) The key property of Skolemization is that unsatisfiability is preserved: $Sk(F)$ unsatisfiable (E-unsatisfiable) if and only if F is unsatisfiable (E-unsatisfiable).

If the problem in question involves equality, one can either apply resolution inference rules with the equality axioms, or apply specialized inference rules that operate on equalities. The *equality axioms* for a set of function and relation symbols are reflexivity, symmetry, transitivity, and a substitution axiom for each argument position of each function symbol and relation symbol.

$$x = x$$
$$x \neq y \lor y = x$$
$$x \neq y \lor y \neq z \lor x = z$$
$$x \neq y \lor f(\ldots, x, \ldots) = f(\ldots, y, \ldots)$$
$$x \neq y \lor \neg P(\ldots, x, \ldots) \lor P(\ldots, y, \ldots)$$

$EqAx(F)$ is the set of equality axioms for the function and relation symbols of a formula F. Although equality substitution axioms for Skolem functions have traditionally been included, it is known [BKS85, Ben89] that they are not necessary.

The most widely used inference rule for equality is *paramodulation* [WOLB84], which generalizes equality substitution to include unification and extra literals in the spirit of resolution. Let N and L be disjunctions of literals, and let M be a literal containing a term t_2. Paramodulation applies *from* clause $t_1 = r \lor L$ *into* clause $M[t_2] \lor N$ if t_1 and t_2 have most a general unifier σ. The paramodulant is $(M[r] \lor N \lor L)\sigma$.

The *functional reflexive axioms* for a set of function symbols consists of an equality $f(x_1, \ldots, x_n) = f(x_1, \ldots, x_n)$ for each n-ary function symbol f.

Let S be a set of clauses involving equality. The following are basic results in logic and automated theorem proving.

- S is E-unsatisfiable if and only if $S \& EqAx(S)$ is unsatisfiable.
- Paramodulation is a complete inference rule for equality. In particular, if S is an E-unsatisfiable set of clauses, there is a paramodulation/resolution/factoring refutation of S & $(x = x)$. (Some useful restrictions of paramodulation, such as the set of support strategy, require the presence of the functional reflexive axioms for completeness. Even when required for completeness, they are rarely used in practice.)

3 The Restriction Strategy

Although the following result is basic in logic, it appears in just one [Lov78] (as far as we can tell) of the standard texts on resolution-based automated theorem proving, and it is not widely used by the automated theorem proving community. A first-order formula F is E-unsatisfiable if and only if $F \& EqAx(F)$ is unsatisfiable. (Note that F is not necessarily Skolemized.)

An immediate consequence of that result is that the equality substitution axioms can be fixed before Skolemization occurs; in particular, equality substitution axioms are not required for the Skolem functions. In fact, the following five statements are equivalent.

(1) F is E-unsatisfiable.

(2) $F \& EqAx(F)$ is unsatisfiable.

(3) $Sk(F)$ is E-unsatisfiable.

(4) $Sk(F \& EqAx(F))$ is unsatisfiable.

(5) $Sk(F) \& EqAx(Sk(F))$ is unsatisfiable.

Research in automated theorem proving with equality has focused on the equivalence (3) iff (5), because clause sets rather than the first-order formulas are usually taken as given. For example, the widely used and cited problem set [MOW76] presents clauses, including equality axioms for Skolem functions.

The fact that equality axioms are not needed for Skolem functions can be turned into a strategy for restricting paramodulation, because paramodulation into a term corresponds to a sequence of resolution steps with equality axioms. For example, let f be a 3-place function symbol, and consider a term $f(t_1, t_2, t_3)$. Paramodulation into t_2 or one of its subterms corresponds to a sequence of resolution steps with equality axioms. One of the equality axioms is $x \neq y \lor f(x_1, x, x_3) = f(x_1, y, x_3)$, because paramodulation is into the second argument of f. If f is a Skolem function, that equality axiom need not be present, indicating that the paramodulation inference need not be made.

The Strategy. *Never paramodulate into a proper subterm of a Skolem expression.*

An Outline of the Completeness Proof. If one assumes unrestricted paramodulation as a starting point, it is not difficult to show the completeness of the restriction. Let S be an E-unsatisfiable set of clauses; let F be the set of function and relation symbols, *excluding Skolem function symbols*, of S; let $EqAx$ be the equality axioms for F; and let FRA be the functional reflexive axioms for F. Let R be a hyperresolution/factoring refutation of $S\&EqAx$. Such a refutation exists because $S\&EqAx$ is unsatisfiable and hyperresolution/factoring is complete. R can be transformed—as in [CL73, pp. 171-172]—into a hyperresolution/factoring/paramodulation refutation of $S\&\ (x = x)\ \&FRA$. Each hyperresolution inference with an equality axiom can be directly transformed into a paramodulation inference that satisfies the restriction.

Motivation. The restriction strategy has intuitive appeal as well. The arguments of Skolem functions should serve as place holders for the objects on which the "existing" object depends—equality substitution should not be applied to them. For an example in set theory, if $A \not\subseteq B$ is assumed, one can conclude that there is an object c in A that is not in B. In clauses, c is a Skolem function applied to A and B. If A and B are complicated expressions, one might wish to reason about them by applying equality substitutions, but not to the occurrences in the Skolem expression representing c—those should be fixed when c is "chosen". If A and B are not ground when c is chosen, further inferences should be free to instantiate the Skolem expression. With this view, the arguments of Skolem functions serve as constraints on unification and constraints on inference.

4 Applications and Experiments

OTTER [McC90] is a resolution/paramodulation theorem prover for first-order logic with equality. The paramodulation restriction strategy was installed in OTTER, and a number of experiments were conducted to try to determine the value of the strategy.

Four application areas were chosen for study: several versions of a problem in set theory, two problems in combinatory logic, a problem in Tarski geometry, and a benchmark algebra problem in complete sets of reductions. The set theory and geometry problems are non-Horn and require a mixture of resolution and paramodulation; in addition, the set theory problems use defined concepts. The combinatory logic and algebra problems require no resolution because they are presented as equality units; the algebra problem requires demodulation (term rewriting) and is not a search for a refutation.

4.1 Set Theory

The problem, to show that the composition of two functions is also a function, is the naive version of one of the lemmas in [BLM+86]. It is an easy problem, but OTTER has difficulty with defined concepts, non-Horn clauses, and mixtures of equality and other relations, all of which occur in this kind of set theory problem.

Definitions of relation, single-valued set, function, and composition.

$$\forall R(relation(R) \leftrightarrow \forall u(u \in R \rightarrow \exists x \exists y(u = \langle x, y\rangle)))$$

$$\forall S\left(singval(S) \leftrightarrow \forall x \forall y \forall z\left(\left[\begin{array}{c}\langle x, y\rangle \in S\& \\ \langle x, z\rangle \in S\end{array}\right] \rightarrow y = z\right)\right)$$

$$\forall F(function(F) \leftrightarrow relation(F)\ \&\ singval(F))$$

$$\forall u \forall F \forall G\left(u \in F \circ G \leftrightarrow \exists x \exists y \exists z\left[\begin{array}{c}u = \langle x, z\rangle\ \& \\ \langle x, y\rangle \in G\ \& \\ \langle y, z\rangle \in F\end{array}\right]\right)$$

Property of ordered pair.

$$\forall x \forall y \forall z \forall w(\langle x, y\rangle = \langle z, w\rangle \rightarrow x = z\ \&\ y = w)$$

Theorem.

$$\forall F \forall G(function(F)\&function(G) \rightarrow function(F \circ G))$$

Four versions of the theorem were considered. Versions ST-1 and ST-2 use the clauses shown below. Version ST-3 does not use the defined relations *relation*, *singval*, or *function* (the theorem is stated in terms of the *composition*, *ordered pair*, and equality). Version ST-4 is entirely in terms of *ordered pair* and equality. Table 1 contains a summary of the results.

Clause form of the denial of the theorem. (Function symbols starting with the letter f are Skolem function symbols.)

1. $x = x$
2. $\neg relation(z) \lor u \notin z \lor u = \langle f7(z,u), f8(z,u)\rangle$
3. $relation(z) \lor f9(z) \in z$
4. $relation(z) \lor f9(z) \neq \langle x, y\rangle$
5. $\neg singval(x) \lor \langle u,v\rangle \notin x \lor \langle u,w\rangle \notin x \lor v = w$
6. $singval(x) \lor \langle f1(x), f2(x)\rangle \in x$
7. $singval(x) \lor \langle f1(x), f3(x)\rangle \in x$
8. $singval(x) \lor f2(x) \neq f3(x)$
9. $\neg function(x) \lor relation(x)$
10. $\neg function(x) \lor singval(x)$
11. $function(x) \lor \neg relation(x) \lor \neg singval(x)$
12. $z \notin y \circ x \lor z = \langle f4(z,x,y), f6(z,x,y)\rangle$
13. $z \notin y \circ x \lor \langle f4(z,x,y), f5(z,x,y)\rangle \in x$
14. $z \notin y \circ x \lor \langle f5(z,x,y), f6(z,x,y)\rangle \in y$
15. $z \in y \circ x \lor z \neq \langle u,w\rangle \lor \langle u,v\rangle \notin x \lor \langle v,w\rangle \notin y$
16. $\langle x,y\rangle \neq \langle u,v\rangle \lor x = u$
17. $\langle x,y\rangle \neq \langle u,v\rangle \lor y = v$
18. $function(F)$
19. $function(G)$
20. $\neg function(F \circ G)$

Table 1: Set Theory

Version	Time	Time with restriction
ST-1	319 seconds	32 seconds
ST-2	93 seconds	45 seconds
ST-3	53 seconds	11 seconds
ST-4	52 seconds	35 seconds

4.2 Combinatory Logic and Fragments

Combinatory Logic (CL) is closely related to the untyped λ-calculus. There are two constants S and K, and one binary operator *apply*. Terms are normally written without the operator, and when parentheses are omitted, association to the left is assumed. For example, the term $apply(apply(a,b), apply(c,d))$ is normally written $ab(cd)$. Many interesting first-order equational theorems in CL can be found in [Smu85].

Problem W, *versions* W-1 *and* W-2. In combinatory logic, find a combinator W with the property $Wxy = xyy$. Version W-1 uses a finely tuned search strategy for problems of this type, and W-2 uses a more naive search strategy.

$\forall x \forall y \forall z (Sxyz = xz(yz))$
$\forall x \forall y (Kxy = x)$

Theorem. $\exists W \forall x \forall y (Wxy = xyy)$

Denial of the theorem in clauses, with explicit function symbol for apply (f and g are Skolem functions, and Ans(z) is an answer literal).

1. $a(a(a(S,x),y),z) = a(a(x,z),a(y,z))$
2. $a(a(K,x),y) = x$
3. $a(a(z,f(z)),g(z)) \neq a(a(f(z),g(z)),g(z)) \lor Ans(z)$

If axioms different from those for S and K are used, the system is in general weaker than CL and is called a fragment of CL.

Problem FP, *versions* FP-1 *and* FP-2. Find a fixed point combinator in the fragment $\{Q, M\}$, with $Qxyz = y(xz)$ and $Mx = xx$. Version FP-1 uses a finely tuned search strategy for problems of this type, and FP-2 uses a more naive search strategy.

$\forall x \forall y \forall z (Qxyz = y(xz))$
$\forall x (Mx = xx)$

Theorem. $\exists \Theta \forall x (\Theta x = x(\Theta x))$

Denial of the theorem in clauses, with explicit function symbol for apply. (f is a Skolem function).

1. $a(a(a(Q,x),y),z) = a(y,a(x,z))$
2. $a(M,x) = a(x,x)$
3. $a(z,f(z)) \neq a(f(z),a(z,f(z))) \lor Ans(z)$

Table 2: Combinatory Logic

Version	Time	Time with restriction
W-1	9 seconds	9 seconds
W-2	(no proof)	12 seconds
FP-1	1 second	1 second
FP-2	50 seconds	3 seconds

4.3 Complete Sets of Reductions

By setting the appropriate options, OTTER can be made to search for a complete set of reductions with the Knuth-Bendix procedure. The completeness argument as presented does not directly apply in this context, because the goal is a canonical term-rewriting system rather than a refutation. However, the restriction strategy can be directly applied, because the computation of critical pairs is itself a restricted form of paramodulaion.

A benchmark completion problem [Chr89]. Given an associative system with 24 left identities and 24 right inverses, find a complete set of reductions. The 24 inverses can be clearly interpreted as Skolem functions. Paramodulation into proper subterms of inverse expressions was prevented, but simplification of those subterms was allowed.

$$f(f(x,y),z) = f(x,f(y,z))$$

$$\begin{array}{ll} f(e_1,x) = x & f(x,g_1(x)) = e_1 \\ f(e_2,x) = x & f(x,g_2(x)) = e_2 \\ \vdots & \vdots \\ f(e_{24},x) = x & f(x,g_{24}(x)) = e_{24} \end{array}$$

The time required to find a complete set of reductions was 474 seconds without the restriction and 56 seconds with it. The same set was found.

4.4 Tarski Geometry

Tarski developed and studied several first-order axiomatizations of elementary geometry—we used the version reproduced in [Wos88]. The domain is points in the plane, and the primitives are a 3-place relation "between" and a 4-place relation "equidistance of 2 pairs of points". We experimented with test problem 10 in [Wos88], the five point theorem. Even though equality relation and several Skolem functions are present, the restriction strategy had little or no effect in any of the comparisons we made. Part of the reason is that there are few occurrences of equality in the axioms and equality plays a small role in the proof of the theorem.

4.5 Summary of Experimental Results

It is difficult to evaluate the effectiveness and generality of new ideas in automated theorem proving. The fact that a new strategy performs well on a particular problem is little indication of its performance on semantically or syntactically similar problems. The Skolem function restriction strategy had a positive effect in three of the four areas that were considered. In *none* of the experiments did the strategy have a negative effect. In particular, we have not found any cases in which the strategy blocks a refutation or interferes in any other way with the search for a refutation (even though the functional reflexive axioms are never included and other restrictions are sometimes applied).

The consequences and completeness of the restriction strategy have not yet been analyzed for Knuth-Bendix completion. However, the algebra completion experiment shows that the restriction can be useful in practice even if it is not complete. When the restricted procedure terminates, we do not in general know whether the resulting set is canonical. However, the unrestricted procedure can then be applied to the resulting set to check whether it is canonical; the cost of such a check is very small.

5 Remarks

Researchers in automated deduction usually start with or are presented with clauses rather than the fully quantified formulas from which they came (for example [MOW76]). In the algebra completion problem, it is clear that the 24 inverses can be interpreted as Skolem functions, but it is not always obvious whether a function symbol is a Skolem function symbol. A partial solution is presented in [McC88], which contains a procedure that attempts to "un-Skolemize" a set of clauses—that is, eliminate function symbols by introducing existentially quantified variables, while maintaining unsatisfiability. Such function symbols can be interpreted as Skolem functions, and the strategy can be applied to them.

We conclude with several points on enhancements and related work.

- We believe that the strategy can be shown to be complete without the presence of the functional reflexive axioms. One attack, suggested by Dan Benanav [Ben90], is to define paramodulation so that all occurrences of the instantiated "into" term are replaced and use a version of the lifting lemma that does not require the functional reflexive axioms.
- A refinement of the strategy was suggested, also by Benanav [Ben90], in which the relevant functions are the ones with just variables as arguments in the input clauses, rather than Skolem functions. This is analogous to the unnecessary equality axioms studied in [Ben89].
- Should demodulation (term rewriting, simplification) be prohibited inside of Skolem expressions when searching for a refutation?
- Is the strategy compatible with the Knuth-Bendix completion procedure? In particular, can critical pair computation and/or simplification be prevented inside of Skolem expression? If not, is there a related restriction that is compatible?
- Can the restriction shed any light on the problem of searching for models/counterexamples of clauses containing Skolem functions?

References

[Ben89] Dan Benanav. *Recognizing Unnecessary Inference.* PhD thesis, Rensselaer Polytechnic Institute, 1989.

[Ben90] Dan Benanav, January 1990. communication.

[BKS85] W. Bledsoe, K. Kunen, and R. Shostak. Completeness results for inequality provers. *Artificial Intelligence*, 27:255–288, 1985.

[BLM+86] Robert Boyer, Ewing Lusk, William McCune, Ross Overbeek, Mark Stickel, and Larry Wos. Set theory in first-order logic: Clauses for Gödel's axioms. *Journal of Automated Reasoning*, 2(3):287–327, 1986.

[Chr89] Jim Christian. Fast Knuth-Bendix completion: A summary. In N. Dershowwitz, editor, *Proceedings of the 3rd International Conference on Rewriting Techniques and Applications, Springer-Verlag Lecture Notes in Computer Science, Vol. 355*, pages 551–555, New York, 1989. Springer-Verlag.

[CL73] C.-L. Chang and R. C.-T. Lee. *Symbolic Logic and Mechanical Theorem Proving.* Academic Press, New York, 1973.

[Lov78] Donald Loveland. *Automated Theorem Proving: A Logical Basis.* North-Holland, Amsterdam, 1978.

[McC88] William McCune. Un-skolemizing clause sets. *Information Processing Letters*, 29:257–263, November 1988. An early version appears as Argonne National Laboratory Tech. Memo ANL/MCS-TM-93, 1987.

[McC89] William McCune. Skolem functions and equality. Association for Automated Reasoning Newsletter no. 12, Argonne National Laboratory, May 1989.

[McC90] William McCune. OTTER 2.0 users guide. Tech. Report ANL-90/9, Argonne National Laboratory, Argonne, Ill., March 1990.

[MOW76] John McCharen, Ross Overbeek, and Larry Wos. Problems and experiments for and with automated theorem-proving programs. *IEEE Transactions on Computers*, C-25(8):773–782, August 1976.

[Smu85] Raymond Smullyan. *To Mock a Mockingbird.* Knopf, New York, 1985.

[WOLB84] Larry Wos, Ross Overbeek, Ewing Lusk, and James Boyle. *Automated Reasoning: Introduction and Applications.* Prentice-Hall, Englewood Cliffs, N.J., 1984.

[Wos88] Larry Wos. *Automated Reasoning: 33 Basic Research Problems.* Prentice-Hall, Englewood Cliffs, N.J., 1988.

Automatically Generating Universal Attachments Through Compilation

Karen L. Myers
Department of Computer Science
Stanford University
Stanford, California 94305
myers@neon.stanford.edu

Abstract

Universal attachment is a general-purpose mechanism for integrating diverse representation structures and their associated inference programs into a framework built on logical representations and theorem proving. The integration is achieved by links, referred to as universal attachments, that connect logical expressions to these structures and programs. In this paper, we describe a compilation-based method for automatically generating new programs and new universal attachments to those programs given a base set of existing programs and universal attachments. The generation method provides the means to obtain large collections of attachments and attached programs without the traditional specification overhead. As well, the method simplifies the task of validating that a collection of attachments is *correct*.

1 Introduction

Universal attachment [Myers, 1990] is a mechanism for integrating diverse representation and reasoning techniques into a framework based on logic and theorem proving. The motivations for using universal attachment are increased inferential efficiency and expanded representational capabilities. Following in the tradition of previous attachment methods [Green, 1969] [Weyhrauch, 1980], universal attachment centers on the notion of 'attaching' procedures and data structures to logical expressions. When expressions having attachments are encountered during theorem proving, the attached procedures are executed on the attached data to directly evaluate the logical expressions rather than relying on further deduction. Universal attachment is a more expressive mechanism for merging procedures and data structures into a theorem prover than previously defined attachment techniques, and as such supports a much broader class of attachments.

This paper describes a method for automatically generating both new programs and new universal attachments to those programs. The general problem of automatically producing attachments and attached programs is extremely difficult. We present a method that relies on the existence of a base set of attachments and attached programs. The method exploits the idea that concepts are often hierarchically defined. In particular, if a given logical expression ϕ is defined in terms of subexpressions $\phi_1, \ldots, \phi_n$ all having attachments, then compilation techniques can be used to generate an attached program for ϕ that calls the attached programs for the ϕ_i's. Attachments to these newly generated programs are obtained by appropriately combining the attachments defined for the ϕ_i's.

An automated generation mechanism is important for several reasons. Such a mechanism can be used to create a large collection of attachments and attached programs, thus providing the computational advantages associated with such a collection but without the specification overhead. Another benefit relates to the *correctness* of attachments, where correctness means that the attached programs and the data upon which the programs operate embody the appropriate semantics for the expressions to which they are attached. Provided that the generation process is sound, the task of validating the correctness of a collection of automatically generated attachments reduces to that of validating the smaller initial set of attachments.

We begin in Section 2 by describing universal attachment. Section 3 outlines the generation process and conditions for its applicability, while Section 4 evaluates the approach taken. The automatic generation method has been implemented as part of a universal attachment system built on top of the KADS theorem prover [Stickel, 1988].

2 Universal Attachment

Before presenting the compilation-based generation method, we first summarize universal attachment and describe the condition of *factorability* required for the method to succeed.

2.1 A Definition of Universal Attachment

Definition 1 (Universal Attachment) *A universal attachment is a five-tuple represented as*

$$\langle \phi[x_1, \ldots, x_n], \mathsf{F} \rangle \rightarrow \langle \mathsf{p}, \mathsf{A}, \mathsf{D} \rangle \qquad (1)$$

where $\phi[x_1,\ldots,x_n]$ *is the attachment pattern,* F *is the filter set,* p *is the attached program,* A *is the attachment map and* D *is the detachment map.*

The *attachment pattern* $\phi[x_1,\ldots,x_n]$ is a logical expression (a relational, functional, quantified or boolean expression in some logical language $\mathcal{L}$) defined over the *distinguished variables* $x_1,\ldots,x_n$. Distinguished variables are schema variables ranging over the terms in the logical language being employed. As a matter of convenience, we will assume that the distinguished variables for an attachment pattern are simply the variables appearing in the pattern (*i.e.* the distinguished variables for the term *plus(x,y)* are x and y).

The *filter set* F is a collection of constraints or *filters* on bindings to the distinguished variables in ϕ, represented as $\mathsf{f}[x_1,\ldots,x_n]$. The language for expressing filters can be defined independently of the universal attachment framework, thus a different filter language can be utilized according to the nature of the applications being considered. We present a sample filter language and its corresponding definition of filter satisfaction later in this section.

The *domain* of the universal attachment, namely the set of logical expressions for which the universal attachment is defined, is determined jointly by the attachment pattern and the filter set. For $\mathsf{F} = \{\mathsf{f}_1[x_1,\ \ldots,\ x_n],\ldots,\mathsf{f}_m[x_1,\ldots,x_n]\}$, the domain of the attachment (1) is the set of logical expressions $\{\phi[t_1,\ldots,t_n]\}$ where $\mathsf{f}_1[t_1,\ldots,t_n],\ldots,\mathsf{f}_m[t_1,\ldots,t_n]$ are satisfied.

The *attached program* p is the name of the program to be used in the attachment process. The *attachment map* A takes the list of bindings to the distinguished variables as input and generates the appropriate set of parameters for p (the *attached data*). The *detachment map* translates the result of evaluating p on the attached data to the appropriate expression in the logical language (the *value* of the universal attachment). The attachment and detachment maps provide a very important service in that they translate between logical terms and structures used to represent those terms outside of the theorem prover. For this reason, we refer to them as the *translation maps.*

The interpretation of the attachment (1) is that a logical expression α in its domain will be *evaluated* by first executing p on the parameters obtained by applying the attachment map to the bindings of the distinguished variables, then translating the result according to the detachment map, and finally substituting that value back in for α.

2.2 The Filter Language $\mathcal{F}_\mathcal{L}$

Before considering an example of universal attachment, we first describe a sample filter language, $\mathcal{F}_\mathcal{L}$, defined for a logical language $\mathcal{L}$. More information on both alternative filter languages and the advantages of using filter languages can be found in [Myers, 1990].

The metalevel filter language $\mathcal{F}_\mathcal{L}$ is built on the assumption that filters can be specified for a distinguished variable independently of all other distinguished variables, *i.e.* filters can be written in the form $\mathsf{f}[x_i]$. The language consists of the predicates atomic(x), sort(x,s), and standard-name(x,s), with their satisfaction defined as follows:[1]

Definition 2 (Filter Satisfaction in $\mathcal{F}_\mathcal{L}$) *A term t satisfies a filter* f *in $\mathcal{F}_\mathcal{L}$ iff:*

1. f *is* atomic(t) *and t is a logical constant symbol in $\mathcal{L}$.*
2. f *is* sort(t,s) *and t has sort* s.
3. f *is* std-name(t,s) *and t is a standard name for sort* s.

The filter atomic requires t to be a constant symbol in $\mathcal{L}$. The filter sort dictates that t be of sort s; the corresponding sort information is included as part of $\mathcal{L}$. Standard name filters are used to make syntactic distinctions within sorts. The user can associate a set of standard names with a sort by making the appropriate specifications in $\mathcal{L}$. For example, we might specify that all numeric representations of integers within our logical language are standard names for the sort int of integers. The filter std-name(t,s) dictates that t must be a member of the set of standard names for sort s. To appreciate the need for standard names filtering, consider the logical constant *the-pope's-favourite-integer.* Although this constant is of sort int, we would not want to attach to expressions in which this constant is bound to a distinguished variable since we don't know the specific number that this constant denotes. We can eliminate such attachments by excluding this constant from the standard names for int.

2.3 A Graph Example

The following example illustrates how universal attachments can be applied.

Example 1 (Path Connectivity)
Consider a directed graph whose edges are described by the axiom

$$edge(a,b) \wedge edge(a,c) \wedge edge(b,c) \wedge edge(c,d) \wedge edge(d,b)$$

Here, the constants a, b, c and d denote particular nodes in the graph.

Now suppose we define a logical relation $path(x,y)$ in terms of the relation *edge* such that *path(x,y)* holds exactly when there is a sequence of edges connecting x to y. To answer queries about paths in the graph we can create a universal attachment. First, we define the LISP structure `gr` to be the following edge-based representation of the graph described by *edge*:

[1] Throughout this document, sans-serif font is used for expressions in $\mathcal{F}_\mathcal{L}$, *italicized* text indicates expressions in the logical language $\mathcal{L}$, and `typewriter-style` font indicates an attached program or data.

```
(defvar gr
  '((a (b c)) (b (c)) (c (d)) (d (b)))) .
```

We also need a LISP function connp that takes two nodes and an edge-based representation of a graph as parameters; the function call (connp n1 n2 g) returns t if n1 and n2 are connected by a path in g, and nil otherwise. Finally, we require a metalevel function h that maps logical representations of nodes onto the LISP representation of those nodes (*i.e.* $\mathsf{h}(a) = \mathtt{a}$, $\mathsf{h}(b) = \mathtt{b}$, *etc*). Using these components, we can create the universal attachment:

$$\langle path(x,y), \mathsf{F}^{path}\rangle \rightarrow \langle \mathtt{connp}, \mathsf{A}^{path}, \mathsf{D}^{tf}\rangle \qquad (2)$$

$$\mathsf{F}^{path} = \{\mathsf{std\text{-}name}(x, \mathsf{node}), \mathsf{std\text{-}name}(y, \mathsf{node})\}$$

$$\mathsf{A}^{path}((x,y)) = (\mathsf{h}(x), \mathsf{h}(y), \mathtt{gr}) \ .$$

The domain of this universal attachment is the set of instances of *path(x,y)* where x and y are bound to standard names of sort node. The attachment map A^{path} maps a pair of logical terms denoting nodes into the triple consisting of the LISP representation of those nodes and the LISP representation of our graph, gr. The detachment map D^{tf} translates the LISP atoms t to the logical truth value *true* and nil to *false*. The attachment (2) states that instances of *path(x,y)* where x and y are bound to standard names for sort node should be evaluated by applying connp to the arguments $\mathsf{h}(x)$, $\mathsf{h}(y)$ and gr.

2.4 Factorable Attachment Maps

The general definition of an attachment map A presented above, whereby A translates the list of bindings to distinguished variables into the list of parameters for the attached program, is very broad. In order to facilitate the automatic generation process, we impose the restriction of *factorability* on attachment maps.

Definition 3 (Factorability) *An attachment map is* factorable *iff it can be represented as a collection of unary and zeroary functions on bindings to distinguished variables.*

The attachment map A^{path} in Example 1 is factorable, being composed of the unary function h applied to bindings to x, h applied to bindings to y, and the constant function gr with value gr. We will refer to the individual unary and zeroary functions as the *component translations* of the attachment map. Factorability guarantees that attachment maps are definable in terms of bindings to individual distinguished variables, independent of all other bindings. As will be seen in Section 2, this independence is important for the compilation process. The factorability requirement is not burdensome; virtually all standard applications of universal attachments use factorable attachment maps.

For this document, we assume a standardized representation of attachment maps. Each map consists of a list of ordered pairs, where the first entry of the pair is a component translation function and the second entry is the distiniguished variable for which the component translation is defined. If the component translation is zeroary, than the second entry is simply $\emptyset$. Using this notation, we would represent the attachment map in Example 1 as $((\mathsf{h}, x)\ (\mathsf{h}, y)\ (\mathsf{gr}, \emptyset))$.

3 The Generation Method

In this section we describe both the *generation method* and the *compilation criteria* that a logical expression must satisfy for the method to apply. For simplicity, we assume that all attached programs are written in LISP.

The generation method derives from the observation that concepts are often hierarchically defined. Given a logical expression ϕ defined in terms of subexpressions having attachments, the method employs compilation techniques to produce an attached program for ϕ that calls the programs attached to ϕ's subexpressions.[2] A universal attachment from ϕ to the generated program is obtained by merging the subexpressions' attachments in a manner that depends on the logical structure of ϕ.

We begin by stating a concise definition of the compilation criteria. This definition will serve as a reference for the remainder of the section. Following the definition, we provide a thorough explanation of its parts (in particular the concepts of *weak satisfaction*, *nesting constraints*, *preserving truth values* and *enumerability* used in the criteria are defined) as well as a full description of the generation process.

Definition 4 (Compilation Criteria) *A logical expression ϕ satisfies the* compilation criteria *iff one of conditions* **C1**, **C2**, *or* **C3** *is met:*

C1 *There is an attachment* $\langle \alpha[x_1, \ldots, x_k], \mathsf{F}^\alpha\rangle \rightarrow \langle \mathsf{p}^\alpha, \mathsf{A}^\alpha, \mathsf{D}^\alpha\rangle$ *such that:*

- **C1.1** $\alpha[x_1, \ldots, x_k]$ *unifies with ϕ, producing bindings* $x_1 : t_1, \ \ldots, \ x_k : t_k$.
- **C1.2** *For each filter* $\mathsf{f}[x_i] \in \mathsf{F}^\alpha$, $\mathsf{f}[t_i]$ *is* weakly satisfied.
- **C1.3** *Each non-atomic t_i satisfies the compilation criteria.*
- **C1.4** *The detachment maps in the attachments defined by* **C1.3** *satisfy the* nesting constraints.

C2 ϕ *is a boolean expression, either* $\neg\beta_i$, $\bigwedge_{i=1}^{n}\beta_i[t_1^i, \ldots, t_{k_i}^i]$, *or* $\bigvee_{i=1}^{n}\alpha_i[t_1^i, \ldots, t_{k_i}^i]$, *where:*

- **C2.1** *Each β_i satisfies the compilation criteria.*

[2] This form of compilation is stronger than that associated with logic programming [Warren, 1977]. First of all, logic programming compilation is limited to Horn clauses. Furthermore, the compilation of a logic program produces an encoding in terms of pre-defined primitives (such as unifications and stack manipulations) of the search process followed by the interpreter, while the compilation we propose builds code from arbitrary attached programs.

C2.2 *The attachments defined by* **C2.1** *for each* β_i *have detachment maps that* preserve truth values.

C3 ϕ *is a quantified expression of the form* $\exists z.\ \alpha$ *or* $\forall z.\ \alpha$ *such that:*

C3.1 α *satisfies the compilation criteria.*

C3.2 z *is bound to a distinguished variable in the attachment pattern of the attachment defined by* **C3.1**.

C3.3 *The terms satisfying the filters specified for* z *in the attachment defined by* **C3.1** *are* enumerable.

C3.4 *The attachment defined by* **C3.1** *has a detachment map that* preserves truth values.

C1: Base Case

C1 constitutes the base case of the definition. For a logical expression ϕ to be compilable in the base case, condition **C1.1** requires the existence of an attachment

$$\langle \alpha[x_1, \ldots, x_k], \mathsf{F}^\alpha \rangle \rightarrow \langle \mathsf{p}^\alpha, \mathsf{A}^\alpha, \mathsf{D}^\alpha \rangle \qquad (3)$$

where ϕ unifies with $\alpha[x_1, \ldots, x_k]$. Condition **C1.2** further requires that if $\mathsf{f}[x_i]$ is in F^α and x_i is bound to t_i in the unification for **C1.1**, then $\mathsf{f}[t_i]$ must be *weakly satisfied.* In contrast to the notion of satisfaction from Definition 2, weak satisfaction only requires that the nonvariable components of a term satisfy a given filter. This relaxation of the satisfaction criteria accounts for variables in the expression being compiled. For the filter language $\mathcal{F}_\mathcal{L}$, a term t weakly satisfies atomic(t) iff t is a variable or logical constant name, and t weakly satisfies std-name(t,s) iff t unifies with a standard name for sort s. Weak satisfaction is identical to standard satisfaction for the filter sort(t,s).

The condition **C1.3** accounts for the binding of distinguished variables to non-atomic functional expressions in ϕ. In general, an expression ϕ that satisfies **C1.1** will have the form

$$\alpha[\beta_1[t_1^1, \ldots, t_{n_1}^1], \ldots \beta_k[t_1^k, \ldots, t_{n_k}^k]] \qquad (4)$$

where each $\beta_i[t_1^i, \ldots, t_{n_i}^i]$ is either a variable, a constant, or a non-atomic functional expression. A program that evaluates ϕ must necessarily include code to evaluate every non-atomic $\beta_k[t_1^k, \ldots, t_{n_k}^k]$. Thus the nesting of functional expressions in ϕ invalidates the compilability of ϕ unless an attached program exists to evaluate these expressions, or an appropriate program can be created through compilation. In either case, the nested expressions must satisfy the compilability criteria, prompting condition **C1.3**.[3]

If we let the set $\mathcal{I}$ index the non-atomic $\beta_i[t_1^i, \ldots, t_{n_i}^i]$, condition **C1.3** guarantees the existence of the attachments:[4]

$$\langle \beta_i[x_1, \ldots, x_{m_i}], \mathsf{F}^{\beta_i} \rangle \rightarrow \langle \mathsf{p}^{\beta_i}, \mathsf{A}^{\beta_i}, \mathsf{D}^{\beta_i} \rangle, \qquad i \in \mathcal{I}. \quad (5)$$

C1.4 requires that these attachments satisfy certain *nesting constraints.* The nesting constraints ensure the soundness of consolidating programs attached to nested functional terms with p^α from (3) into a single attached program for the entire expression ϕ. We can express the nesting constraints as follows:

Definition 5 (Nesting Constraints) *For every* $i \in \mathcal{I}$:

NC1 *The range of* D^{β_i} *must satisfy the filters in* F^α *defined for* x_i.

NC2 *If* $(\mathsf{m}, x_i) \in \mathsf{A}^\alpha$ *and* $i \in \mathcal{I}$, *then* $\mathsf{m}(\mathsf{D}^{\beta_i}(\mathsf{c})) = \mathsf{c}$ *for every* c *in the range of the function* p_{β_i}.

Condition **NC1** states that if $\beta_i[t_1^i, \ldots, t_{n_i}^i]$ is a non-atomic expression bound to the distinguished variable x_i then the range of the detachment map D^{β_i} must satisfy the filters defined for x_i. This constraint ensures that substituting the values produced by the attachments in (5) for the corresponding nested expressions in $\alpha[\beta_1[t_1^1, \ldots, t_{n_1}^1], \ldots \beta_k[t_1^k, \ldots, t_{n_k}^k]]$ yields an expression in the domain of the attachment (3). Condition **NC2** requires that the composition of the component attachment map m defined for a distinguished variable x_i and the detachment map D^{β_i} for the nested expression $\beta_i[t_1^i, \ldots, t_{n_1}^i]$ is the identity map. This constraint ensures that the attachments in (5) and (3) have the same interpretation for attached symbols that they both utilize.

The program generated for ϕ is simply an application of p^α with nested function applications of the p^{β_i} for $i \in \mathcal{I}$ used to evaluate the non-atomic $\beta_i[t_1^i, \ldots, t_{n_i}^i]$. Defining the parameter list for the new program is somewhat complex. In particular, a parameter must be defined for each distinct component translation map applied to a distinguished variable binding. The factorability of the attachment maps makes it possible both to identify these translations and to build the required new attachment map that accounts for all such translations; details are in [Myers, 1990]. The detachment map is simply D^α from (3) while the new filter set is obtained by 'merging' the filter sets for the nested expressions and F^α. The merging process is an enhanced union operation that eliminates filters subsumed by other filters in the union. For example, sort(t,s1) subsumes sort(t,s2) if sort s2 contains sort s1.

Example 2 Let int and rat be functions that map logical representations of integers and rationals onto appropriate LISP representations of those numbers. Using

[3] Note that **C1.3** makes the base case of the definition itself recursive. The well-definedness of the criteria is ensured since the base case recursion parallels the logical structure of ϕ and hence must be finite.

[4] These attachments may be in the set of predefined attachments or may be generated recursively by the compilation process. The guaranteed attachments for subexpressions in the recursive cases **C2** and **C3** also have this characteristic.

int and rat we can specify attachments for the expressions *add(x,y)* and *div(x,y)*, which have the intended interpretations of integer addition and rational division. Let add and div be LISP programs of two inputs that compute integer addition and rational division, and int and rat be the sorts of integer and rational numbers. By defining $\mathsf{A}^{\mathsf{int}} = ((\mathsf{int}, x), (\mathsf{int}, y))$ and $\mathsf{D}^{\mathsf{int}} = \mathsf{int}^{-1}$, along with $\mathsf{A}^{\mathsf{rat}} = ((\mathsf{rat}, x), (\mathsf{rat}, y))$ and $\mathsf{D}^{\mathsf{rat}} = \mathsf{rat}^{-1}$, we can create the attachments:

$$\langle add(x,y), \{\text{std-name}(x,\mathsf{int}), \text{std-name}(y,\mathsf{int})\}\rangle \rightarrow \langle \mathtt{add}, \mathsf{A}^{\mathsf{int}}, \mathsf{D}^{\mathsf{int}}\rangle$$

$$\langle div(x,y), \{\text{std-name}(x,\mathsf{rat}), \text{std-name}(y,\mathsf{rat})\}\rangle \rightarrow \langle \mathtt{div}, \mathsf{A}^{\mathsf{rat}}, \mathsf{D}^{\mathsf{rat}}\rangle \ .$$

Now consider the logical definition

$$\forall xy.\ avg(x,y) = div(add(x,y), 2)\ .$$

The expression *div(add(x,y))* satisfies the base case of the compilation criteria. Using the generation method, we obtain the following program and attachment:

```
(defun avg-lisp (n1 n2)
  (div (add n1 n2) 2)))
```

$$\langle avg(x,y), \{\text{std-name}(x,\mathsf{int}), \text{std-name}(y,\mathsf{int})\}\rangle \rightarrow \langle \mathtt{avg\text{-}lisp}, \mathsf{A}^{\mathsf{int}}, \mathsf{D}^{\mathsf{rat}}\rangle \ .$$

C2: Boolean Expressions

If ϕ is a boolean expression that doesn't satisfy **C1**, ϕ is still compilable provided that condition **C2** is satisfied. All boolean expressions share the same compilation criteria and generation method; here we restrict attention to conjunctive expressions, where ϕ has the form $\wedge_{i=1}^{n} \alpha_i[t_1^i, \ldots, t_{k_i}^i]$.

Compilation condition **C2.1** guarantees the existence of attachments

$$\langle \alpha_i[x_1, \ldots, x_{k_i}], \mathsf{F}^{\alpha_i}\rangle \rightarrow \langle \mathsf{p}^{\alpha_i}, \mathsf{A}^{\alpha_i}, \mathsf{D}^{\alpha_i}\rangle, \quad i = 1, \ldots, n.$$

These attachments provide the programs used to construct the new attached program for ϕ.

To motivate **C2.2**, we consider the nature of the program to be generated for ϕ. The form of this program will mirror the logical structure of ϕ: the program consists of an application of the LISP function and to the results obtained by evaluating the attached programs p^{α_i}. This strategy is sound only if the values produced by the p^{α_i} 'match' the notion of truth values utilized in LISP. In particular, when an attached program p^{α_i} returns `t` (or `nil`), then the truth (or falsity) of the corresponding conjunct should be established. The need for this semantic correspondence motivates the following definition.

Definition 6 (Truth Value Preservation) *A function* g *from a representation language* $\mathcal{L}_1$ *to a representation language* $\mathcal{L}_2$ preserves truth values *iff* g *maps truth and falsity in* $\mathcal{L}_1$ *onto truth and falsity, respectively, in* $\mathcal{L}_2$.

Example 3 The detachment map D^{tf} defined in Example 1 preserves truth values from LISP to our logical language: it maps `t` to *true* and `nil` to *false*.

Although there may be many functions that preserve truth values from one language to another, we will designate D^{tf} as the *canonical* truth preserving function from LISP to our logical language. Verifying that a detachment map D preserves truth values thus reduces to checking that $\mathsf{D} = \mathsf{D}^{tf}$.

As noted above, the new attached program for $\wedge_{i=1}^{n} \alpha_i[t_1^i, \ldots, t_{k_i}^i]$ consists of an application of the LISP function and to the values obtained by evaluating the p^{α_i}. In analogy with programs generated for the base case **C1**, a parameter is required for each unique translation applied to a distinguished variable binding and the new attachment map is the collection of these translations. The new filter set is the union of the filter sets for the individual conjuncts where subsumed filters are once again removed. The detachment map is the canonical truth value preserving function, D^{tf}.

C3: Quantified Expressions

Condition **C3** constitutes the compilation criteria for a quantified expression $\forall z.\ \alpha$ or $\exists z.\ \alpha$ that fails to satisfy **C1**.

C3.1 requires the existence of an attachment

$$\langle \alpha[x_1, \ldots, x_k], \mathsf{F}^{\alpha}\rangle \rightarrow \langle \mathsf{p}^{\alpha}, \mathsf{A}^{\alpha}, \mathsf{D}^{\alpha}\rangle \qquad (6)$$

for the matrix of the quantified expression. The underlying idea for compiling quantified expressions is to apply the program p^{α} from the attachment (6) to the attached LISP representations of all possible bindings to the quantified variable z.

To make this approach feasible, the quantified variable must be bound to a distinguished variable x_i in $\alpha[x_1, \ldots, x_k]$ (**C3.2**), and the set of terms satisfying the filters in F^{α} defined for x_i must be *enumerable* (**C3.3**). With standard names filters, enumerability is obtained by using the list of standard names defined for the sort of the quantified variable. More complex mechanisms for achieving enumerability are described in [Myers, 1990]; these mechanisms use attached structures directly to determine the domain of quantification. For example, with quantified expressions defined relative to a graph, the domain of iteration can be limited to the set of standard names for nodes in that graph rather than the set of standard names for all nodes appearing in any graph.

The new attached program consists of an iteration whose domain is the set of LISP objects obtained by applying the component translation map m defined for x_i (*i.e.* $(\mathsf{m}, x_i) \in \mathsf{A}^{\alpha}$) to the enumeration of terms satisfying the filters for x_i in F^{α}. At each step, p^{α} is called. For existential quantifiers, the program returns `t` only if p^{α} evaluates to `t` for some value in the domain. For universal quantifiers, the program returns `nil` if a value is found for which p^{α} evaluates to `nil` and returns `t` otherwise. As with the compilation of boolean expressions, we require that the detachment map D^{α} preserve truth values (**C3.4**) to ensure that the semantics of the iteration process match the semantics of the logical quantifier.

The parameters for the new program are identical to those of p^{α} except that the parameter corresponding to the variable of quantification is replaced by a parameter representing the domain of the iteration. Correspondingly, the new attachment map is obtained from A^{α} by replacing the pair (m, x_i) by a function that returns the domain of the iteration. The new filter set is obtained from F^{α} by removing filters defined on x_i. The new detachment map is D^{tf}.

Example 4 Consider the logical expression

$$\forall z.\ incycle(z) \equiv \exists y.\ path(z,y) \wedge path(y,z)\ .$$

Given the attachment (2) defined in Example 1, the expression $\exists y.\ path(z,y) \wedge path(y,z)$ satisfies the compilation conditions in **C3**. The compilation process produces the program `incycle-lisp` defined by

```
(defun incycle-lisp (u v domain)
  (some #'(lambda (item)
            (and (connp u item v)
                 (connp item u v)))
        domain)).
```

The formal parameters `u` and `v` to `incycle-lisp` correspond to a node and a graph, respectively. The parameter `domain` is the list of values over which the iteration is defined. During each step of the iteration, the current iterated value `item` is tested to see if the code fragment `(and (connp u item v) (connp item u v)))` evaluates to `t`. This code fragment is produced by recursively compiling the logical expression $path(z,y) \wedge path(y,z)$.

The following attachment for *incycle(z)* is also created, according to the principles described above:

$$\langle incycle(z), \{\mathsf{std\text{-}name}(x, \mathsf{node})\}\rangle \longrightarrow \langle \mathtt{incycle\text{-}lisp}, A^{incycle}, D^{tf}\rangle$$

$$A^{incycle}((z)) = (\mathsf{h}(z), \mathtt{gr}, \mathtt{'(a\ b\ c\ d)})\ .$$

4 Closing Remarks

This paper has presented a compilation-based method for generating new programs and universal attachments to those programs from a base set of existing programs and universal attachments. We have tested an implementation of the method in the domain of graph theory. The class of new attached programs and attachments produced by the implementation method has proven to be quite rich. In addition, the generated attachments appear to provide significant gains in the run-time efficiency of the theorem prover.

For non-quantified expressions, the compilation process consolidates all relevant attachments into a single program. This consolidation eliminates repeated transitions between the theorem prover and the attached computational mechanism, thus reducing the total overhead for translations. The programs constructed for quantified expressions can provide efficiency gains for a different reason: by limiting the domain of iteration for these programs to the relevant terms, the attached programs can be much faster than theorem proving.

The only previous attempt at automating the generation of attachments was Aiello's work on producing new semantic attachments through compilation [Aiello, 1980a] [Aiello, 1980b]. Because universal attachments subsume semantic attachments, Aiello's work is necessarily less ambitious than that reported here. In particular, the compilation of quantified expressions is not addressed. Her work also fails to delimit sufficient restrictions on the class of expressions that are compilable, leading to situations where her method generates programs that are incorrect for the expressions they are designed to evaluate.

Acknowledgements

I would like to thank Jens Christensen, Nils Nilsson, Eunok Paek and Carolyn Talcott for many useful discussions related to this work. The author is supported by an IBM Graduate Fellowship.

References

[Aiello, 1980a] Luigia Aiello. Automatic generation of semantic attachments in FOL. In *Proceedings of the First National Conference on Artificial Intelligence*, 1980.

[Aiello, 1980b] Luigia Aiello. Evaluating functions defined in first order logic. In *Proceedings of the Logic Programming Workshop, Debrecen, Hungary*, 1980.

[Green, 1969] Cordell Green. Application of theorem proving to problem solving. In *Proceedings of the First International Joint Conference on Artificial Intelligence*, pages 219–239, 1969.

[Myers, 1990] Karen L. Myers. Universal attachment. Forthcoming Ph.D. dissertation, Stanford University.

[Stickel, 1988] Mark E. Stickel. The KLAUS automated deduction system. In *Proceedings of the Ninth International Conference on Automated Deduction*, pages 750–751, 1988.

[Warren, 1977] David Warren. Implementing PROLOG — Compiling predicate logic programs. Technical Report 39, University of Edinburgh, 1977.

[Weyhrauch, 1980] Richard W. Weyhrauch. Prolegomena to a theory of mechanized formal reasoning. *Artificial Intelligence*, 13:133–170, 1980.

Solving Term Inequalities

Gerald E Peterson†

225/105/2/206 mailcode 106 5165
McDonnell Douglas Corporation
P. O. Box 516, St. Louis, MO 63166
peterson@mdc.com

Abstract

This work pertains to the Knuth-Bendix (KB) algorithm which tries to find a complete set of reductions from a given set of equations. In the KB algorithm a term ordering is employed and it is required that every equation be orientable in the sense that the left-hand side be greater than the right. The KB algorithm halts if a non-orientable equation is produced. A generalization of the KB algorithm has recently been developed in which every equation is orientable and which halts only when a complete set is generated. In the generalization a constraint is added to each equation. The constraint governs when the equation can be used as a reduction. The constraint is obtained from the equation by "solving" the term inequality *left-hand side* > *right-hand side*. To understand what it means to solve a term inequality, consider the analogy with algebra in which solving term equalities, i.e. *unification*, is analogous to solving algebraic equalities. Then solving term inequalities is analogous to solving algebraic inequalities. Thus, the solution of term inequalities relates to unification as the solution of algebraic inequalities relates to the solution of algebraic equalities. We show how to solve term inequalities when using the lexicographic path ordering.

Introduction

In a landmark paper, Knuth and Bendix (Knuth & Bendix 1970) described a technique for attempting to generate a complete set of reductions from the axioms of an equational theory. If a complete set of reductions could be found, then it embodied a decision procedure for equations provable from the axioms. In particular they generated a complete set of reductions for groups.

In their theory a term ordering was introduced and it was necessary for every equation to be orientable in the sense that one side be larger than the other in the ordering. Equations such as commutativity which could not be oriented would cause the process to fail. Knuth and Bendix were well aware of this limitation of their method. In fact, they proposed using an approach in which a non-orientable equation would be made into two reductions, one which rewrites the left-hand side to the right-hand side and another which rewrites the right-hand side to the left-hand side and in which a method is available to "make sure that no infinite looping occurs when reducing words to a new kind of irreducible form." This proposed approach has been effected (in (Peterson 1990) and forthcoming publications) by adding a *constraint* to each reduction. For example, commutativity is represented as $x \cdot y \rightarrow y \cdot x$ **if** $x > y$.

By using constraints such as these we are able to generalize the entire Knuth-Bendix process. In fact, complete sets of constrained reductions are now known for common equational theories including Abelian groups, rings, and Boolean algebras, and there is an analogue of the Knuth-Bendix procedure which begins with the axioms of an equational theory and attempts to generate a complete set of reductions. This constrained version of the Knuth-Bendix process will never fail because a non-orientable equation shows up—every equation can be oriented. It may, of course, fail because it runs forever trying to find a complete set. The process reduces to that of Knuth and Bendix when presented with equations which are orientable without the use of constraints.

As an example, the following three reductions taken collectively is a complete set equivalent to associativity and commutativity.

1. $(x \cdot y) \cdot z \rightarrow x \cdot (y \cdot z)$
2. $x \cdot y \rightarrow y \cdot x$ **if** $x > y$
3. $x \cdot (y \cdot z) \rightarrow y \cdot (x \cdot z)$ **if** $x > y$.

In reduction 1 there is no constraint. This means that the left-hand side is always greater than the right. In each of the other two reductions there is a constraint which is a necessary and sufficient condition that the left-hand side be greater than the right. In order to find the constraint we must solve the inequality *left-hand side* > *right-hand side*. Looking back at the example, we see

† This work was supported by the McDonnell Douglas Independent Research and Development Program.

that $x > y$ is the solution to $x \cdot y > y \cdot x$ and $x > y$ is also the solution to $x \cdot (y \cdot z) > y \cdot (x \cdot z)$. The manner in which these kinds of solutions are obtained is the subject of the present work.

It will be helpful to consider how the solution of term inequalities relates to unification. In unification, a term equality, such as $(x \cdot y) \cdot (x \cdot a) = (w \cdot z) \cdot y$ is given and it is required to find a most general substitution for the variables which makes the equality true. In this case, the substitution is $\{x \leftarrow w, y \leftarrow w \cdot a, z \leftarrow w \cdot a\}$. This process could be named *solving term equalities* but *unification* has been chosen instead. The problem of solving term inequalities is similar. Given a term inequality, such as $x \cdot (y \cdot z) > z \cdot y$, find the region in term space where the inequality is true. In this case it turns out to be where $x > z$ or $x = z$ or $y > z$ or $y = z$. Consider an analogy to algebra. The solution in real numbers of a polynomial equation is a finite (possibly empty) set analogous to the single most general unifier of a term equation. The solution of a polynomial inequality, however, consists of a region, possibly with several disjoint intervals, such that the inequality is true if and only if the variable is in the region. For example, $x^2 - 5x + 4 > 0$ if and only if $x > 4$ or $x < 1$. Thus we may expect the solution of a term inequality to be a similar type of region in term space.

So far we have been implicitly assuming that an underlying term ordering existed. Throughout this paper we use the *lexicographic path ordering*. Knuth and Bendix used an ordering which has since become known as the *Knuth-Bendix ordering* (Dershowitz 1987). However, it has a more complex definition than the lexicographic path ordering and is, therefore, presumed more difficult to work with. A possible research problem is to figure out how to solve term inequalities when using the Knuth-Bendix ordering.

Related Work

In (Kirchner & Kirchner 1989) a theoretical overview of constrained equational reasoning is presented. They work modulo an equational theory such as associativity and commutativity. However, they assume that constraints are based on term equalities, wheras we assume constraints are based on term inequalities. In (Comon 1990) it is shown than the question of the existence of solutions to term inequalities based on the lexicographic path ordering, such as those herein, is decidable, but NP-hard.

The automatic solution of algebraic inequalities has a similar goal (i.e. the isolation of variables) to that of solving term inequalities, but is accomplished by completely different methods. A good beginning reference to the solution of algebraic inequalities is (Sacks 1987).

An Example

In order to provide further motivation for the introduction of a technique for solving term inequalities, we present an example of the operation of the constrained Knuth-Bendix algorithm. We emphasize those places in which term inequalities are solved. Details of how the constrained Knuth-Bendix algorithm works in general will be described elsewhere. The reader is assumed familiar with the ordinary Knuth-Bendix algorithm throughout this section.

The following problem is from page 91 of (Monthly 1968).

Suppose S is a semigroup in which $x^2 = x^3$ *and* $x^2y = yx^2$ *for all* x, y *in S. Then* $(xy)^2 = x^2y^2$.

We will describe how a solution can be mechanically obtained using the constrained Knuth-Bendix algorithm. We present only the part that directly leads to the desired equation. Other equations will be generated in an actual implementation.

A semigroup has one associative operation. Thus, the first reduction is

1. $(x \cdot y) \cdot z \to x \cdot (y \cdot z)$.

The equation $x^2 = x^3$ is orientable because $x \cdot (x \cdot x) > x \cdot x$ for every x. So the second reduction is

2. $x \cdot (x \cdot x) \to x \cdot x$.

The equation $x^2y = yx^2$, i.e., $x \cdot (x \cdot y) = y \cdot (x \cdot x)$, is not orientable, so the ordinary KB algorithm does not apply to this problem. However, the inequality $x \cdot (x \cdot y) > y \cdot (x \cdot x)$ may be solved and the solution is $x > y$. Thus the equation $x^2y = yx^2$ may be represented as the two reductions

3. $x \cdot (x \cdot y) \to y \cdot (x \cdot x)$ **if** $x > y$,
4. $y \cdot (x \cdot x) \to x \cdot (x \cdot y)$ **if** $y > x$.

If we unify the left-hand side of 2 with the $x \cdot y$ subterm of 1 and proceed as in the ordinary KB process, we obtain the new reduction

5. $x \cdot (x \cdot (x \cdot y)) \to x \cdot (x \cdot y)$.

Unifying the left-hand side of 3 with the subterm $x \cdot (x \cdot y)$ of 5 and applying 3 and 5 once each to the result gives the equality

$$x \cdot (y \cdot (x \cdot x)) = x \cdot (x \cdot y)$$

which is produced only if the constraint of 3, i.e. $x > y$, holds. Now we try to reduce this equality under the assumption $x > y$. Since $x > y$ implies the constraint of reduction 3, the right-hand side can be reduced by 3 giving

$$x \cdot (y \cdot (x \cdot x)) = y \cdot (x \cdot x).$$

No further reductions are possible. At this point, the inequality $x > y$ which came from one of the parents is discarded and the new equality is oriented on its own merits. In this case the equality is orientable and we add

6. $x \cdot (y \cdot (x \cdot x)) \rightarrow y \cdot (x \cdot x)$

as a new reduction.

Similarly, if we unify the left-hand side of 4 with the $x \cdot y$ subterm of 1, we obtain the equation $x \cdot (x \cdot (y \cdot z)) = y \cdot (x \cdot (x \cdot z))$. We now find $x > y$ as the solution of the term inequality $x \cdot (x \cdot (y \cdot z)) > y \cdot (x \cdot (x \cdot z))$ and add the reductions

7. $x \cdot (x \cdot (y \cdot z)) \rightarrow y \cdot (x \cdot (x \cdot z))$ **if** $x > y$,
8. $y \cdot (x \cdot (x \cdot z)) \rightarrow x \cdot (x \cdot (y \cdot z))$ **if** $y > x$.

Finally, unifying the left-hand side of 7 with the left-hand side of 2 and reducing once with 7 and 2, respectively, yields the equation

$$y \cdot ((y \cdot z) \cdot ((y \cdot z) \cdot z)) = (y \cdot z) \cdot (y \cdot z)$$

under the always valid constraint $y \cdot z > y$. We now reduce this equality to normal form using 1, 6 and 5, and obtain

$$y \cdot (y \cdot (z \cdot z)) = y \cdot (z \cdot (y \cdot z))$$

which is the equality we are trying to prove. Note that if this were now added as a reduction, the solution of a term inequality would again be required.

The Lexicographic Path Ordering

Recall that terms are formed from function symbols (including constants) and variables. The definition of the lexicographic path ordering depends on a given linear ordering on the function symbols. Therefore, we assume there are only a finite number of function symbols and they are put into a linear order. This ordering of function symbols and the lexicographic path ordering on terms will both be denoted by $>$ because either it is possible to figure out from the context whether $>$ is the term ordering or the function symbol ordering, or they are both true simultaneously.

Ground terms contain no variables. Two ground terms are equal if and only if they are identical.

The lexicographic path ordering (lpo) is defined only for ground terms. It is defined recursively as follows (Dershowitz 1987):

Definition. *Suppose*

$$s = f(s_1, \cdots, s_m) \text{ and } t = g(t_1, \cdots, t_n)$$

are ground terms. (We may have $m = 0$ and/or $n = 0$ for a constant.) Then $s > t$ if and only if

L1 *$s_i \geq t$ for some i, $1 \leq i \leq m$, or*

L2 *$f > g$ and $s > t_j$ for every j, $1 \leq j \leq n$, or*

L3 *$f = g$ and for some k, $1 \leq k \leq n$, we have $s_i = t_i$ whenever $1 \leq i < k$, $s_k > t_k$, and $s > t_i$ whenever $k < i \leq n$.*

Note that the first inequality in **L2** is from the function symbol ordering, and in the last part of **L3** we do mean $s > t_i$, not $s_i > t_i$. The two examples given next should help clear up any confusion related to this definition. First, however, we note that it is possible to prove (Dershowitz 1987) that the lpo is a well-ordering of the set of ground terms and it satisfies the *subterm property*, i.e., if s is a strict subterm of t, then $t > s$.

For the first example, suppose the function symbol order is $\cdot > a > b$ and it is required to show that $a \cdot b > b \cdot a$. According to **L1** and **L3** of the definition, this will be so if and only if

$$a \geq b \cdot a \text{ or} \quad (1)$$
$$b \geq b \cdot a \text{ or} \quad (2)$$
$$a > b \text{ and } a \cdot b > a \text{ or} \quad (3)$$
$$a = b \text{ and } b > a. \quad (4)$$

In line (3) the first predicate is true by the given function symbol order and the second predicate is true by the subterm property. Thus we have shown what is required. Incidently, lines (1), (2) and (4) are all false.

As the second example let's determine the larger of $a \cdot (b+c)$ and $a + (b \cdot c)$ when the function symbol order is $+ > \cdot > a > b > c$. Since these two terms are not equal, one must be larger than the other. We can use the definition above to test $a \cdot (b + c) > a + (b \cdot c)$. Since $+ > \cdot$, **L2** and **L3** do not apply. By **L1**, we have $a \cdot (b + c) > a + (b \cdot c)$ if and only if

$$a \geq a + (b \cdot c) \text{ or} \quad (5)$$
$$b + c \geq a + (b \cdot c). \quad (6)$$

But (5) is false by the subterm property. By **L1** and **L3**, (6) is true if and only if

$$b \geq a + (b \cdot c) \text{ or}$$
$$c \geq a + (b \cdot c) \text{ or}$$
$$b > a \text{ and } b + c > b \cdot c \text{ or}$$
$$b = a \text{ and } c > b \cdot c.$$

But all of these are clearly false. Thus we do not have $a \cdot (b + c) > a + (b \cdot c)$. So we must have $a + (b \cdot c) > a \cdot (b + c)$.

Solving Term Inequalities

Using the definition of the lexicographic path ordering, we can determine the larger of any two *ground* terms. Suppose, however, that a given inequality contains variables, and the question is to determine where it is satisfied. This can be done by recursively applying the definition of the lpo and gathering all the bottom-level expressions which cannot be simplified. To clarify the meaning of this, let's do a couple of examples.

Example 1. *Solve* $x \cdot y > y \cdot x$. By **L1** and **L3** of the definition, $x \cdot y > y \cdot x$ if and only if

$$x \geq y \cdot x \text{ or} \tag{1}$$
$$y \geq y \cdot x \text{ or} \tag{2}$$
$$x > y \text{ and } x \cdot y > x \text{ or} \tag{3}$$
$$x = y \text{ and } y > x. \tag{4}$$

But (1) and (2) are false by the subterm property and the fact that no term equals a subterm of itself. Also (4) is false since it consists of two incompatible statements. In (3), the second predicate is true by the subterm property. This leaves only the first predicate of (3). Thus the answer is $x > y$.

In order to simplify the presentation we will from now on omit the *or* from the end of each line and we will replace each *and* with a comma.

Example 2. *Solve* $x \cdot y > y \cdot a$ *given that* $a > \cdot$ *in the function symbol ordering*. This example will begin to show the complexity that can arise. By **L1** and **L3**, $x \cdot y > y \cdot a$ if and only if

$$x > y \cdot a \tag{5}$$
$$x = y \cdot a \tag{6}$$
$$y > y \cdot a \tag{7}$$
$$y = y \cdot a \tag{8}$$
$$x > y,\ x \cdot y > a \tag{9}$$
$$x = y,\ y > a. \tag{10}$$

By the subterm property, (7) is false. Since y and $y \cdot a$ are not unifiable, (8) is false. Replacing the equalities by equivalent unifiers and expanding the second predicate in (9) using **L1** gives the following form for the solution

$$x > y \cdot a \tag{11}$$
$$\{x \leftarrow y \cdot a\} \tag{12}$$
$$x > y,\ x > a \tag{13}$$
$$x > y,\ x = a \tag{14}$$
$$x > y,\ y > a \tag{15}$$
$$x > y,\ y = a \tag{16}$$
$$\{x \leftarrow y\},\ y > a. \tag{17}$$

However, note that (11), (12), (15) and (16) each implies (13) by the subterm and transitive properties of $>$. Thus (11), (12), (15) and (16) can be eliminated from the above leaving

$$x > y,\ x > a$$
$$\{x \leftarrow a\},\ a > y$$
$$\{x \leftarrow y\},\ y > a.$$

as the solution.

We now present an algorithm which can be used to solve any given term inequality. It is presented as a person would use it with pencil and paper. From a machine standpoint it is not very efficient as presented. It can be made more efficient at the expense of greater complexity and less understandability. Because of limited space, efficiency considerations will be deferred to a later paper.

Begin with the given inequality on a line by itself. As we proceed, each intermediate stage will consist of a table of one or more lines of the form

$$\theta, e_1, e_2, \cdots, e_n$$

where θ is a substitution (possibly empty) and each element e_i is either an equality or an inequality. An inequality is *fully reduced* if it has one of the forms $v > t$ or $t > v$, where v is a variable and t is a term which does not contain v. A line is a *component* if it consists of a substitution θ followed by 0 or more fully reduced inequalities which do not contain the variables that are replaced in θ.

Algorithm. *Repeat steps 1 to 3 below until each line is a component.*

1. *Move down the table to the first line which is not a component and across this line from left to right to the first element which is not a fully reduced inequality. Call this element e and its line ℓ.*
2. *If e is an equality, unify the two sides. If unification is impossible, delete line ℓ. If the table is now empty,* stop; *the answer is* false. *If unification is possible, let σ be the mgu. Delete e in line ℓ, replace the substitution θ at the beginning of ℓ with θ composed with σ, and apply σ to the rest of ℓ.*
3. *If e is an inequality, then*
   i. *if e has the form $v > t$ where v is a variable which occurs in term t, delete line ℓ; if the table is now empty,* stop; *the answer is* false;
   ii. *if e has the form $t > v$ where v is a variable which occurs in t, delete e from ℓ; if ℓ is now empty,* stop; *the answer is* true;
   iii. *otherwise, the lpo definition will apply to e; delete line ℓ; add to the end of the table several lines corresponding to the results of applying the lpo definition to e; each of these lines will be identical to ℓ except that the position formerly occupied by e will be replaced by one possible way in which e might be true.*

   Now do the following.
4. *Delete each line which is inconsistent.*
5. *For each line ℓ, if ℓ implies another line, delete ℓ.*
6. *Delete the redundant elements in each line. An element e is redundant in ℓ if $\ell - \{e\} \Rightarrow e$.*

Steps 4 to 6 may be interleaved with 1 to 3 in order to keep the table as simple as possible. Steps 4–6 will be automated in the next section.

Example 2 above was performed using essentially these steps. The answers to three other examples are now presented. The reader may go through the above steps to verify these.

Example 3. *Solve $x+(y\cdot z) > x\cdot(y+z)$ given that $+ > \cdot$ in the function symbol ordering.* The solution is

$$x > y$$
$$\{x \leftarrow y\}.$$

Example 4. *Solve $x\cdot(y\cdot z) > y\cdot(z\cdot x)$.* The solution is

$$x > y,\ x > z$$
$$\{x \leftarrow z\},\ z > y$$
$$\{x \leftarrow y\},\ y > z.$$

Example 5. *Solve $(y+z)+(y+w) > x+(z+w)$.* The solution is

$$y + z > x$$
$$\{x \leftarrow y+z\},\ y > z.$$

Reasoning with Components

In the previous section we have seen that every term inequality can be solved and the solution has the form $C_1 \vee C_2 \vee \cdots \vee C_n$ where each C_i is a component. In order to complete the automation of the solution process we need to have algorithms for determining when a component is inconsistent, when one component implies another, and when an element in a component is redundant.

The purpose of this section is to describe these algorithms.

Note first that even without steps 4–6, the algorithm of the previous section would generate a solution of the given inequality. The purpose of steps 4–6 is to render the solution in a simple form. This simplification is a practical necessity because without it solutions to even simple inequalities would be unwieldy. However, validity is not compromised if we do not find every possible way in which steps 4–6 can be performed. Thus, we do not attempt to find *every* possible way in which simplification can be effected by steps 4–6. We will find the common ones, however.

We first show how to decide if a conjunction of fully reduced inequalities implies another fully reduced inequality. Let $e_1, e_2, \cdots, e_n$ and e be fully reduced inequalities. Let $e_i = (\ell_i > r_i)$ for each i and let $e = (\ell > r)$. To decide whether or not

$$e_1, e_2, \cdots, e_n \Rightarrow e$$

we consider all possible inequality sequences of the form

$$\ell \geq \ell_1 > r_1 \geq \ell_2 > r_2 \geq \cdots \geq \ell_k > r_k \geq r \quad (1)$$

where each $\ell_j > r_j$ is one of the e_i. In the above display, each $\geq$ is shown by the subterm property; each $>$ is present in the e_i. If we can find such a sequence, then we have proved e; otherwise we assume a proof is not possible. For example, suppose we wish to show that $\{x > y,\ y > z\} \Rightarrow x > z$. We have

$$x = x > y = y > z = z$$

as an expression of form (1). Thus it is proved.

Now suppose C and D are components and it is required to determine whether $C \Rightarrow D$. Let

$$C = \{\theta, e_1, \cdots, e_n\} \text{ and } D = \{\phi, f_1, \cdots, f_m\}$$

where $\phi = \{v_1 \leftarrow t_1, \cdots, v_n \leftarrow t_n\}$. Then $C \Rightarrow D$ is equivalent to

$$e_1, \cdots, e_n \Rightarrow \phi\theta, f_1\theta, \cdots, f_k\theta \quad (2)$$

where $\phi\theta = \{v_1\theta = t_1\theta, \cdots, v_n\theta = t_n\theta\}$ because substitution of equals for equals is logically valid, and after θ is used in this way it can no longer contribute to the required implication. Normally inequalities cannot prove equalities, so if the implication is to be true, we must have $\phi\theta$ true. That is, we must have $v_1\theta \equiv t_1\theta, \cdots, v_n\theta \equiv t_n\theta$. We are left with the problem of determining the validity of

$$e_1, \cdots, e_n \Rightarrow f_1\theta, \cdots, f_m\theta.$$

To do this, consider the proof of each $f_i\theta$ separately and conjoin the results. Thus, we must be able to solve the problem

$$e_1, \cdots, e_n \Rightarrow f\theta$$

where f is fully reduced. If $f\theta$ is fully reduced, use the procedure of the previous paragraph. Otherwise, solve the inequality $f\theta$ using the procedure of Section 4 and obtain $C_1 \vee \cdots \vee C_k$, where each C_i is a component. We will determine the validity of $e_1, \cdots, e_n \Rightarrow C_i$ separately for each i and disjoin the results. For $e_1, \cdots, e_n$ to imply the component $\{\phi, e'_1, \cdots, e'_p\}$, ϕ must be empty and $e_1, \cdots, e_n$ must imply each e'_i separately as detailed in the previous paragraph.

For example, in Section 4 it was required to show that $\{x > y\cdot a\} \Rightarrow \{x > y,\ x > a\}$. To do this, we show

$x > y \cdot a \Rightarrow x > y$ and $x > y \cdot a \Rightarrow x > a$ separately. The first follows from

$$x = x > y \cdot a > y$$

and the second from

$$x = x > y \cdot a > a,$$

each of which has the form (1).

In order to show that a component $\{\theta, e_1, \cdots, e_n\}$ is inconsistent, we let i run from 1 to n, $e_i = (\ell_i > r_i)$ and test

$$e_1, \cdots, e_{i-1}, e_{i+1}, \cdots, e_n \Rightarrow r_i > \ell_i.$$

If this is so for some i, then the component is inconsistent. Otherwise it is presumed consistent. For example, suppose $\{x > y,\ y > x\}$ is the component. Try $x > y \Rightarrow x > y$. This is easily proved by the above method. Thus this component is inconsistent.

Similarly, in order to test an element e of a component C for redundancy, check $C - \{e\} \Rightarrow e$.

References

Comon, H. 1990. Solving Inequations in Term Algebras. In Proceedings of the Fifth Annual IEEE Symposium on Logic in Computer Science.

Dershowitz, N. 1987. Termination of rewriting. *Journal of Symbolic Computation* 3:69-116.

Kirchner, C., and Kirchner, H. 1989. Constrained Equational Reasoning, Technical Report, CRIN 89-R-220, Centre de Recherche en Informatique de Nancy.

Knuth, D., and Bendix, P. 1970. Simple word problems in universal algebras. *Computational Problems in Abstract Algebras*. J. Leech, ed. Oxford, England: Pergamon Press, 263-297.

Monthly 1968. *The American Mathematical Monthly* 75.

Peterson, G. 1990. Complete Sets of Reductions with Constraints. In Proceedings of the Tenth International Conference on Automated Deduction.

Sacks, E. 1987. Hierarchical Reasoning about Inequalities. In Proceedings of the Sixth National Conference on Artificial Intelligence, 649-654. American Association for Artificial Intelligence.

Exploiting locality in a TMS

Johan de Kleer
Xerox Palo Alto Research Center
3333 Coyote Hill Road, Palo Alto CA 94304 USA
Email: deKleer@xerox.com

Abstract

This paper presents a new approach for exploiting Truth Maintenance Systems(TMSs) which makes them simpler to use without necessarily incurring a substantial performance penalty. The basic intuition behind this approach is to convey the locality of the knowledge representation of the problem solver to the TMS. The TMS then uses this locality information to control and restrict its inferences. The new TMSs accept arbitrary propositional formulae as input and use general Boolean Constraint Propagation(BCP) to answer queries about whether a particular literal follows from the formulae. Our TMS exploits the observation that if the set of propositional formulae are converted to their prime implicates, then BCP is both efficient and logically complete. This observation allows the problem solver to influence the degree of completeness of the TMS by controlling how many implicates are constructed. This control is exerted by using the locality in the original task to guide which combinations of formulae should be reduced to their prime implicates. This approach has been implemented and tested both within Assumption-Based Truth Maintenance Systems and Logic-Based Truth Maintenance Systems.

1 Introduction

This paper presents a new practical approach for exploiting Truth Maintenance Systems which makes them simpler to use without necessarily incurring a substantial performance penalty. The basic intuition behind this new approach is to convey the locality of the knowledge representation of the problem solver to the TMS. Many AI problem solvers, particularly those which reason about the physical world, are inherently local — each constituent of the problem (e.g., a process such as flowing, a component such as a pipe, etc.) has a fixed behavioral model. Much of the reasoning can be viewed as propagation: whenever some new signal is inferred to be present the models of the components on which it impinges are consulted to see whether further inferences are possible from it. Many of these AI problem solvers either exploit TMSs to do much of this propagation, or use TMSs to represent the results of propagations. Although widely used, anyone who has used these strategies can attest that current TMSs manifest some surprising logical incompleteness when used in this way. These blind spots result from the fact that locality present in the original model is often completely lost within the TMS.

The TMS framework we present is fully expressive accepting arbitrary propositional formulae as input. Provided with advice from the overall problem solver it is, if needed, logically complete. Propositional satisfiability is NP-complete, but nevertheless often much of the cost of logical completeness can be avoided by exploiting locality. For example, conjunctions of formulae in the model library can be precompiled into their prime implicates to reduce run-time cost. Also, the TMS uses locality information at run-time to determine which combinations of formulae are worth analyzing.

We have implemented our framework and used it with both Assumption-Based Truth Maintanence Systems (ATMSs) [2; 7] and Logic-Based Truth Maintenance Systems (LTMSs) [2; 19; 20; 21]. We have used it to compile models from constraints, confluences, order-of-magnitude reasoning axioms and processes. A longer paper [10] explores the role of this framework in qualitative physics in more detail.

1.1 Encoding models as formulae

Most problem solvers wish to represent arbitrary propositional formulae many of which derive from local constituents of the problem (e.g., component or process models). However, most TMSs lack the expressive power to represent arbitrary formulae. Therefore, one is typically forced to encode the propositional formulae in terms the TMS accepts. For example, [4] provides a variety of ways of encoding propositional formulae for the Assumption-Based Truth Maintenance Systems (ATMSs). Techniques like these are widely used in QPE [13; 14]. Unfortunately, these encodings tend to be extremely cumbersome. The TMSs which accept arbitrary clauses (such as LTMSs) seem to be more powerful because any propositional formula can easily be converted into an equivalent set of clauses by putting it into conjunctive normal form CNF[1].

Unfortunately, complete LTMSs based on clauses are rarely used because they are too inefficient. Instead, all common LTMS implementations use Boolean Constraint Propagation(BCP)[2; 19; 20; 21] on clauses. BCP is a sound, incomplete, but efficient inference procedure. BCP is inherently local considering only one propositional formula (i.e., boolean constraint) at a time. This locality is the source of both its incompleteness and efficiency. Unfortunately, converting a formula to its CNF clauses loses the locality of the original formula. Consider the formula:

$$(x \Rightarrow (y \vee z)) \wedge (x \vee y \vee z) \tag{1}$$

If y were false, then considering this formula alone, in isolation, we can infer z must be true (this can be seen by the fact that if z were false, the first conjunct $x \Rightarrow (y \vee z)$ requires x to be false, and the second conjunct $(x \vee y \vee z)$ requires x to be true). However, this information is lost in converting the formula to its two CNF clauses:

$$\neg x \vee y \vee z, \quad x \vee y \vee z.$$

Neither of these two clauses can, individually, be used to infer z from $\neg y$. Taken together, of course, they can.

Consider QPE as an example [13; 14]. QPE encodes every qualitative process model as a set of formulae which are eventually encoded as a set of ATMS horn clauses. Within QPE, this set of horn clauses represents a fixed local module, but within the ATMS each clause is treated independently. As some of the formulae cannot be converted to purely horn clauses, the basic ATMS algorithms are incomplete with respect to the original formulae, and the ATMS is therefore incapable of making some simple local inferences which follow from the model alone. QPE deals with this difficulty by adding more clauses (than conversion to CNF would indicate) so that the basic ATMS algorithms can make more inferences than they otherwise would. Part of our proposal is that the set of formulae representing a model be conveyed to the TMS as a single module and the TMS use a complete inference procedure locally on modules. As a result we achieve the kind of functionality that is desired, without incurring substantial performance degradation and without burdening QPE with needless encoding details. This process can be made efficient by recognizing that each model type instantiates the same set of formulae and therefore most of the work can be done at compile time once per model type.

Conceptually, the new TMSs are supplied a set of arbitrary propositional formulae and use general BCP to answer queries whether a particular literal follows from the formulae. BCP is usually applied to clauses but can be applied to arbitrary formulae as well. As input the TMS can accept new propositional formulae to define a module, conjoin two existing modules, or accept a new formula to be conjoined with an existing module. Locally, within each module, the TMS is logically complete. As a consequence, the problem solver can dynamically control the trade-off between efficiency and completeness — if completeness is required, all the modules are conjoined, if efficiency is is required, each formula is treated as an individual module. Later in this paper we present a number of techniques to guide the order in which modules should be conjoined in order to minimize computational cost.

Consider the example of two pipes in series (Fig. 1). Each pipe is modeled by the qualitative equation (or confluence, see [3] for precise definitions) $[dP_l]-[dP_r] = [dQ]$ where P_l is the pressure on the left, P_r is the pressure on the right and Q is the flow from left to right. ($[dx]$ is the qualitative (+, 0, −) value of $\frac{dx}{dt}$). Thus, the attached pipes can be completely modeled by three confluences:

$$[dP_A] - [dP_B] = [dQ_{AB}], \tag{2}$$

$$[dP_B] - [dP_C] = [dQ_{BC}], \tag{3}$$

$$[dQ_{AB}] = [dQ_{BC}]. \tag{4}$$

Suppose we know that the pressure is rising at A (i.e, $[dP_A] = [+]$) and the pressure is fixed at C (i.e., $[dP_C] = [0]$). Considering each component or confluence individually we cannot infer anything about the flows. We only know one of the three variables in confluences (2) and (3), and none of the variables in confluence (4). Therefore, none of the confluences, individually, can be used to infer a new variable value. The only way to determine the behavior is to somehow solve the confluences — but that requires global reasoning over the confluences.

If the individual qualitative equations are converted to their propositional equivalents for a TMS (as many qualitative physics systems do), then $[dP_B]$, $[dQ_{AB}]$ and $[dQ_{BC}]$ remain unknown due to the incompleteness of most TMS's. However, in our TMS if the formulae representing the individual components are merged then $[dQ_{AB}] = [dQ_{BC}] = [+]$ is inferred. As such component combinations reoccur in many systems, this combining can be done once in the model library. To compile this combination, our TMS merges the propositional encoding of the confluences but without the specific inputs ($[dP_A] = [+]$ and $[dP_C] = [0]$). The result is identical to the propositional encoding of the confluence:

$$[dP_A] - [dP_C] = [dQ_{AB}] = [dQ_{BC}].$$

After compiling this combination, and applying the inputs our TMS infers that $[dQ_{AB}] = [dQ_{BC}] = [+]$ far more efficiently than before (i.e., in one step).

A device can always be analyzed by first compiling it without knowledge of any input or outputs. However, compiling a full device model is expensive — it is only useful if we expect to put it in the model library or need to consider many input value combinations. When analyzing a device our TMS does not force the problem-solver to decide whether or not to compile the device beforehand. Our TMS lazily compiles the propositional formulae it is supplied — it only compiles enough to answer queries for the givens it is supplied. When the givens are changed the TMS, if necessary, incrementally compiles more pieces of the device to answer the query. If all possible givens and queries are applied, then the compiled result will be the same as having compiled the full device beforehand.

After developing our approach Section 8 expands on these observations and analyzes its relationship with the qualitative resolution rule [11; 12].

2 BCP on formulae and clauses

As our approach draws on the intuitions underlying BCP, we give a synopsis of it here. (Note that BCP

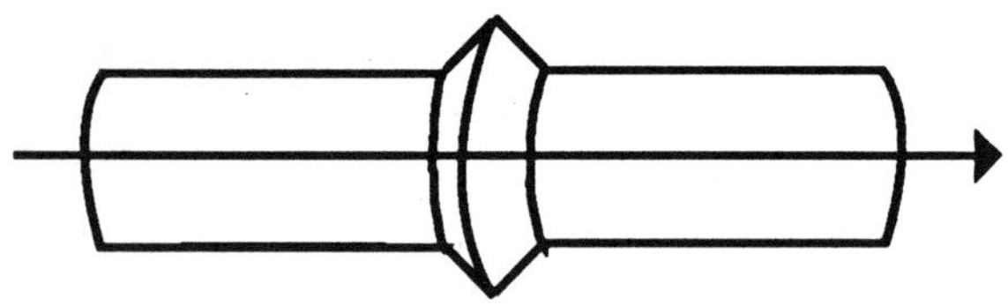

Figure 1: Assembling the qualitative models of the two joined pipes is equivalent to merging the formulae modeling the two pipes.

achieves similar results to unit resolution.) BCP operates on a set of propositional formulae (not just clauses) $\mathcal{F}$ in terms of propositional symbols $\mathcal{S}$. A formula is defined in the usual way with the connectives $\neg, \Rightarrow, \equiv, \vee, \wedge$ and *oneof*. (*oneof* is a useful connective requiring that exactly one of its arguments be true.) For the purposes of this paper a clause is a disjunction of literals with no literal repeated and not containing complementary literals.

BCP labels every symbol **T** (i.e., true), **F** (i.e., false) or **U** (i.e., unknown). BCP is provided an initial set of assumption literals $\mathcal{A}$; if $x \in \mathcal{A}$, then x is labeled **T**, and if $\neg x \in \mathcal{A}$, then x is labeled **F**. $\mathcal{A}$ may not contain complementary literals. All remaining symbols are initially labeled **U**. The reason for distinguishing $\mathcal{A}$ from $\mathcal{F}$ is that $\mathcal{F}$ is guaranteed to grow monotonically while assumptions may be added and removed from $\mathcal{A}$ at any time.

BCP operates by relabeling symbols from **U** to **T** or **F** as it discovers that these symbols logically follow from $\mathcal{F} \cup \mathcal{A}$. A labeling which does not label any symbol **U** is *complete*. Conversely a labeling which labels some symbols **U** is *partial*. A *completion* of a partial labeling is one which relabels all the **U** symbols **T** or **F**. Given any labeling each BCP constraint (in the BCP literature propositional formulae are called constraints) is in one of 4 possible states.

- The labeling *satisfies* the constraint: for every completion of the current labeling the constraint is true. For example, labeling x **T** satisfies the constraint $x \vee y$.
- The labeling *violates* the constraint: there is no completion of the current labeling which satisfies the constraint. Consider two examples: (1) if the constraint is $x \vee y$ and both x and y are labeled **F**, then the constraint is violated, and (2) if the constraint is $(x \vee y) \wedge (x \vee \neg y)$ and x is labeled **F**, then there is no way to satisfy the constraint.
- A constraint *forces* a symbol's label if in every completion of the current labeling which makes the constraint true that symbol is always labeled **T** or always **F**. There may be multiple such symbols. For example, if x is labeled **T**, then the constraint $x \equiv (y \wedge z)$ forces y and z to be labeled **T**. Consider the example from the introduction: $(x \Rightarrow (y \vee z)) \wedge (x \vee y \vee z)$. If y is labeled **F**, then the label of z is forced to be **T**.
- Otherwise a constraint is *open*.

BCP processes the constraints one at a time monotonically expanding the current labeling. The behavior of BCP depends on the condition the constraint is in:

- If the current labeling satisfies the constraint, then the constraint is marked as satisfied and is no longer considered.
- If the current labeling violates the constraint, then a global contradiction is signaled.
- If the current labeling forces the label of some other symbol, then that symbol is labeled and all unsatisfied and unviolated constraints mentioning that symbol are scheduled for reconsideration. If the current constraint is now satisfied it is so marked.
- Otherwise the constraint remains open and BCP reconsiders it when some (other) symbol it references is labeled **T** or **F**.

If this BCP is applied purely to clauses, then the resulting behavior is identical to the clausal BCP dicussed in the LTMS literature.

If the constraints are arbitrary formulae, then determining whether a constraint forces a symbol label is complex to implement and computational expensive execute. However, if the constraints are clauses, then BCP can be implemented simply and efficiently. In particular, we store a count with each clause indicating the number of symbols which are labeled **U** or whose label satisfies the clause. For example, given the clause $x \vee \neg y$ where x is labeled **U** and y is labeled **T**, the count for the clause is 1. Whenever this counter is reduced to 1, then the clause forces the label of a single remaining symbol (i.e., in this case x is forced to **T**). If the count is reduced to 0, then the clause is violated and a contradiction is signaled. As a consequence of this encoding, BCP on clauses can be implemented simply by following pointers and decrementing counters. Conversely, the process of removing an assumption from $\mathcal{A}$ can be efficiently implemented by following pointers and *incrementing* counters. (See [7] for details.) BCP on clauses is equivalent to the circuit value problem and therefore is P-complete (see also [15]). Its worse case complexity is the number of literals in the clauses.

BCP is logically incomplete in that it sometimes fails to label a symbol **T** or **F** when it should. For example, consider the two clauses from the introduction:

$$\neg x \vee y \vee z, \quad x \vee y \vee z.$$

If y is labeled **F**, then BCP on the clauses does not label z **T**. (Note that BCP is also logically incomplete in that it sometimes fails to detect contradictions.)

3 Compiling into prime implicates

The previous example (the encoding of formula (1)) shows that running BCP on the original formulae is usually not the same as running BCP on the clauses produced by converting the formulae to CNF. (BCP on the original formulae is usually much stronger or, at worst, equivalent.) Hence, we cannot directly use the efficient BCP algorithms that have been developed for clauses for arbitrary formulae and no correspondingly efficient BCP algorithm is known. This section shows that if each individual formula is encoded by its prime implicates[16; 17; 22], then BCP on the resulting clauses is equivalent to running BCP on the original formulae.

We use the following definitions. Clause A is subsumed by clause B if all the literals of B appear in A. Therefore if A subsumes B, then B is true wherever A is. An implicate of a set of propositional formulae $\mathcal{F}$ is a clause entailed by $\mathcal{F}$ not containing complementary literals. A prime implicate of a set of formulae $\mathcal{F}$ is an implicate of $\mathcal{F}$ no proper subclause of which is an implicate of $\mathcal{F}$.

Consider the simple example of the introduction. Using the conventional conversion to CNF the formula,

$$(x \Rightarrow (y \vee z)) \wedge (x \vee y \vee z), \qquad (5)$$

is equivalent to the conjunction of the clauses,

$$\neg x \vee y \vee z, \quad x \vee y \vee z.$$

However, there is only one prime implicate,

$$y \vee z.$$

This example illustrates that there may be fewer prime implicates of a formula than the conjuncts in the CNF of a formula. Unfortunately, the reverse is usually the case. Consider the clause set:

$$\neg a \vee b, \quad \neg c \vee d, \quad \neg c \vee e, \quad \neg b \vee \neg d \vee \neg e.$$

In this case, these 4 are all prime implicates, but there are 3 more (for a total of 7):

$$\neg a \vee \neg d \vee \neg e, \quad \neg b \vee \neg c, \quad \neg a \vee \neg c.$$

There are a variety of different algorithms for computing prime implicates (see [6; 7; 9; 16; 22; 23]). Stripped of all the efficiency refinements discussed in the next section, our basic approach is to use a variation of the consensus method to compute prime implicates. First, the formula is converted into CNF to produce an initial set of clauses. Then we repeatedly take two clauses with exactly one pair of complementary literals and construct a resulting clause with both those literals removed. All clauses subsumed by others are removed. This process continues until no new unsubsumed clause is producible.

Using the preceeding definitions, the following theorems are key to an efficient implementation of BCP on constraints:

Theorem 1 *Given a set of clauses $\mathcal{I}$ which are the set of prime implicates of some set of propositional formulae and a set of assumptions $\mathcal{A}$, then if $\mathcal{I} \cup \mathcal{A}$ is inconsistent, then BCP will detect a violation.*

Proof. If $\mathcal{I} \cup \mathcal{A}$ is inconsistent, then there must be a clause,

$$\neg A_1 \vee \cdots \vee \neg A_n,$$

entailed by $\mathcal{I}$ where $A_i \in \mathcal{A}$. This clause is an implicate of $\mathcal{I}$ and thus subsumed by some clause S of $\mathcal{I}$. As all the $\neg A_i$ are labeled **F**, BCP will detect that clause S is violated. □

Theorem 2 *Given a set of clauses $\mathcal{I}$ which are the set of prime implicates of some set of propositional formulae and a set of assumptions $\mathcal{A}$ such that $\mathcal{A} \cup \mathcal{I}$ is consistent, then BCP computes the correct label for every node.*

Proofs for the remaining theorems can be found in [10].

Theorem 3 *Let $\mathcal{A}$ be a set of literals, $\mathcal{F}$ a set of propositional formulae and $\mathcal{I}$ is the union of the prime implicates of each of the formulae of $\mathcal{F}$ individually. If BCP on $\mathcal{A} \cup \mathcal{F}$ does not detect any violations, then BCP on $\mathcal{A} \cup \mathcal{F}$ produces the same symbol labels as BCP on $\mathcal{A} \cup \mathcal{I}$.*

Theorem 4 *Let $\mathcal{A}$ be a set of literals, $\mathcal{F}$ a set of propositional formulae, and $\mathcal{I}$ is the union of the prime implicates of each of the formulae of $\mathcal{F}$ individually. BCP on $\mathcal{A} \cup \mathcal{F}$ detects a violation exactly when BCP on $\mathcal{I} \cup \mathcal{F}$ detects a violation.*

The first two theorems tell us that we can make BCP complete if we need to. The second two theorems tell us that running BCP on the prime implicates of the individual formulae is the same as running BCP on the formulae. Thus, we can exploit the efficient implementations of clausal BCP.

Note that the prime implicates, by themselves, do not solve the task — they represent a family of solutions each characterized by a distinct assumption set $\mathcal{A}$. Computing the prime implicates is analogous to compiling a propositional formula (or set of them) so that it is easy to compute the resulting solution once some input, i.e., $\mathcal{A}$ is provided.

Fig. 2 illustrates some of the options engendered by the theorems. Although replacing the entire set of formulae with their equivalent set of prime implicates allows BCP to be logically complete, the required set of prime implicates can be extremely large. This large set is both difficult to construct and, its very size makes it hard for BCP to work on. Therefore it is usually impractical to exploit this strategy directly.

4 Basic LTMS transactions

Our basic formula LTMS permits the following transactions:

`(add-formula formula)`: This adds an individual formula to the TMS. Section 2 outlines the allowed connectives.

`(add-assumption symbol label)`: This labels the symbol **T** or **F**. This retracts any previous `add-assumption` for this symbol.

`(retract-assumption symbol)`: This removes the initial label for the symbol. Note that the symbol will retain a non-**U** if it follows from $\mathcal{A} \cup \mathcal{F}$.

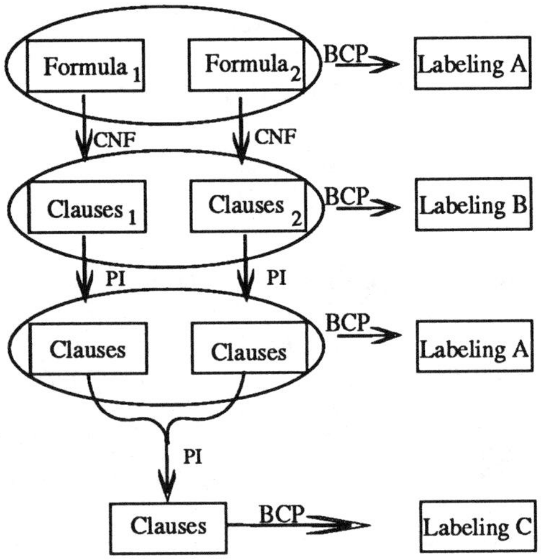

Figure 2: This figure illustrates the different ways BCP can be used. BCP on arbitrary formulae (expensive) produces labeling A. If the formulae encoded as their CNF clauses, then an efficient clausal BCP produces an (unfortunately weaker) labeling B. If formulae are individually converted into their prime implicates, then the efficient clausal BCP finds the same labeling A as the inefficient formula BCP on the original constraints. Finally, if the prime implicates of all the formulae are constructed, then clausal BCP is logically complete.

`(label? symbol)`: This returns the label for the symbol.

`(inconsistent?)`: Tests whether $\mathcal{A} \cup \mathcal{F}$ is inconsistent.

5 Lazy compilation

Using the results of the section 3 a complete formula LTMS algorithm can be implemented as follows. The algorithm always maintains the set of prime implicates $\mathcal{F}'$ of $\mathcal{F}$. Whenever a new formula f is added to $\mathcal{F}$, $\mathcal{F}'$ is updated by computing the prime implicates of the old $\mathcal{F}'$ and the new formula f thus avoiding recomputing the same prime implicates from scratch each time. Whenever $\mathcal{A}$ is changed, we execute the usual clausal BCP algorithm on $\mathcal{F}'$. Therefore, the major cost is paid up front when a formula is added to $\mathcal{F}$ and not when $\mathcal{A}$ is changed.

The algorithm just sketched out is needlessly expensive. In the next few sections we present techniques which substantially improve its performance in most circumstances. The basic intuition behind these techniques to to delay the construction of additional implicates until absolutely necessary because constructing and storing implicates is the most expensive aspect of our framework. In all these techniques $\mathcal{F}'$ is no longer a set of prime implicates of $\mathcal{F}$, but simply a set of implicates of $\mathcal{F}$ none of which is subsumed by another.

Experience has shown that problem solvers often supply a sequence of formulae without making any intervening queries. Thus, calls to `add-formula`, `add-assumption` and `retract-assumption` are not be acted upon until an actual query is made. When the problem solver requests a label of a symbol the following steps are performed:

1. Update $\mathcal{A}$.
2. Perform clausal BCP.
3. If BCP supplies a label for the symbol, we are done.
4. Take the first queued formula f. If there isn't one, then go to step 7.
5. Add each of its prime implicates to the LTMS clause set $\mathcal{F}'$ and mark each such clause as unprocessed.
6. Go to step 2
7. Consider all unprocessed clauses u. Remove all other clauses subsumed by u from $\mathcal{F}'$. Mark u as processed.
8. For two clauses u and v in $\mathcal{F}'$ which contain exactly one complementary pair of literals, which have not been resolved before, compute the consensus of u and v, add it to $\mathcal{F}'$, and remove the clauses it subsumes from $\mathcal{F}'$.
9. If no new clause was added in the previous step and no formulae additions are queued, the the label is **U**.
10. Go to 2.

Although in the naive algorithm which initially computes all prime implicates, retracting an assumption is very simple, in this algorithm retracting an assumption can later provoke further implicate construction because some symbol might lose its **T**/**F** label. Checking for inconsistency is nearly identical. If at any point clausal BCP reports an inconsistency, then no further processing is necessary.

The basic intuition behind this algorithm is to run the efficient clausal BCP before constructing new implicates. This is analogous to the familiar unit-preference strategy except that the initial unit clauses (i.e, $\mathcal{A}$) can be retracted.

The preceeding algorithm still computes far too many implicates than is necessary for a particular $\mathcal{A}$. We can exploit BCP labels to further delay the construction of new implicates. In particular, computing the consensus of two clauses where the complementary literals are labeled **T**/**F** cannot provide new information (for the current $\mathcal{A}$). Therefore, we can add this restriction to the algorithm. This yields substantial performance improvements if not all possible $\mathcal{A}$ are explored.

Many efficiency improvements are possible on this basic scheme. An important one results from distinguishing between the two different reasons a symbol can be labeled **T**/**F**: (1) a symbol can be labeled because it follows via BCP from $\mathcal{F}$ alone (we call this a *fixed* label), or (2) a symbol can be labeled because it follows via BCP from $\mathcal{F} \cup \mathcal{A}$ but not from $\mathcal{F}$ alone (we call this a *variable* label). The important difference is that the fixed labels cannot change as $\mathcal{A}$ changes. If a fixed literal label satisfies a clause, then that clause is removed from $\mathcal{F}'$. If a variable literal label satisfies a clause, then the clause is temporarily set aside. If a fixed literal label violates a clause, then the literal is removed from the clause. These results happen anyway as a consequence of constructing implicates. However, BCP achieves them earlier and more efficiently. Note that as variable labels change, clauses which were previously set aside need to be reanalyzed to compute further implicates.

6 Pre-compiling formulae

Many AI problem solvers operate with a knowledge base or component library. Given a particular task, pieces of this knowledge base are instantiated as needed. For example, in Qualitative Process Theory most processes are instantiated with the same fixed set of formulae (but with different symbols). Hence, the schemas for the prime implicates for each model in the library can be constructed a priori, and many implicate constructions can be thus avoided run time.

A single propositional formula may yield a very large number of prime implicates. If some of the symbols of a formula are internal (i.e., appear only in the formula, are guaranteed never to be referenced by any new input formula and are of no further interest to the problem solver), then all the clauses mentioning that symbol can be discarded without affecting the functionality of the TMS. As a result BCP need not stumble over these needless clauses.

The basic formula LTMS transactions which support this insight are:

`(compile-formula schema internal-symbols)`: Used at *compile* time. This converts the formula schema into a set of prime implicate schemas. This is designed to be used when constructing the knowledge base or the model library. **`internal-symbols`** is a set of internal symbols which are guaranteed not to appear again. Therefore, after computing prime implicates, all clauses mentioning internal symbols are discarded.

`(load-formula schema)`: This takes the prime implicate schemas and communicates them to the TMS.

7 Exercising problem solver control

In many cases, even lazily constructing sufficient implicates of $\mathcal{F}'$ to ensure completeness for the given $\mathcal{A}$ is too costly. In this circumstance the problem solver provides external guidance to control which prime implicates should be constructed and to choose when to give up completeness.

One way to limit the computational cost of the algorithm is instead of running the algorithm on the entire set of formulae, only apply the algorithm to subsets of the formulae. This locality is captured by the notion of *module.* A module is a set of formulae and the LTMS data base consists of a set of modules. The algorithm is restricted to perform subsumption tests and consensus constructions only within modules. But the clausal BCP is run across all clauses of all modules. The problem solver is provided an additional interface to control when to modules are to be merged. This requires the following additional transactions:

`load-formula*` and **`add-formula*`**: These create modules initially containing only their formula argument.

`(merge-modules module1 module2)`: This tells the TMS to conjoin the two modules, by computing the necessary implicates of the combination.

`(internal symbol)`: Used at run time. This informs the TMS that the symbol is internal. If all occurrences of this symbol appear in the same module, than all clauses mentioning this symbol can be discarded. This greatly reduces the number of clauses the TMS needs to consider.

At the one extreme every formula is an individual module and the problem solver never merges modules. In this case the result is equivalent to running BCP on formulae. As all the formulae may be pre-compilable, this may require no implicate construction at run time.

If the problem solver is exercising control to achieve completeness, we must examine more carefully when completeness is achieved for a particular $\mathcal{A}$. Just because some symbol is labeled **U** is no indication of incompleteness — no one guarantees that every literal or its negation should follow from $\mathcal{F} \cup \mathcal{A}$. However, if every clause is individually satisfied, then we know that the clause set is consistent and we can complete the labeling by arbitrarily changing every **U** to **T** or **F**. (Of course, this observation is implicit in the lazy algorithm which stops resolving clauses when they are satisfied.)

This last observation provides two fundamental techniques for coping with incompleteness. First, the problem solver can introduce additional assumptions to attempt to satisfy open constraints, in effect, performing a backtrack search. (This has the disadvantage of extending $\mathcal{A}$ which may not be desired.) Second, the problem solver controls which modules should be merged and in which order. Merging has two important effects: (a) merging can enable the construction of new implicates which yield relabelings, and (b) if each of the modules are either satisfied (we define a module to be satisfied if every one of its clauses is satisfied) or merged into one common unsatisfied module, then we know that BCP is complete. This tradeoff of whether to use backtracking or merging to construct a solution is analogous to the one faced by CSP [8; 18] solvers.

Both approaches to coping with incompleteness can be improved with various tactics. We focus here on tactics to improve the performance of merging. If an internal symbol is labeled **U**, then the modules which mention it are candidates for early merging. Whether or not this relabels the internal symbol, after the merge all clauses mentioning an internal symbol can be discarded. Modules sharing no symbols can be trivially merged as the implicates of the conjunction is the union of the antecedent implicates. If all modules are merged and BCP has not detected a violated clause, then by a slight extension of theorem 1 $\mathcal{F} \cup \mathcal{A}$ is satisfiable. When used in this way our TMS is yet another way to test for propositional satisfiability.

Our implementation also includes an automatic facility which systematically merges those two modules which would produce a module with the fewest number of symbols (determined directly by counting the non-internal symbols). This exploitation of locality often avoids intermediate implicate bloat.

8 Modeling

The user of this style of TMS must make a fundamental tradeoff whether all the formulae should be in one module (and hence be logically complete), or whether the formulae should all be in individual modules (more efficient but incomplete). Suppose all the formulae are in one module. For those symbols which were not provided any initial labels, the same set of implicates will now suffice for any labeling for them. This ideally matches the requirements of problem solving tasks which require the inputs to be changed while the input formulae remain constant. In other words, by computing the implicates we have made it easy to solve exponentially many problems via BCP on these implicates.

One clearcut example of this occurs in qualitative simulation. Typically qualitative analysis uses propagation to determine the qualitative behavior of a system, however, it is well known that simple propagation is incomplete and therefore that additional techniques are needed (feedback heuristics, feedback analysis, etc.) One such technique is the qualitative resolution rule [11] which assembles individual component models into larger assemblages so that (a) the entire device can be repeatedly simulated on different inputs by simple propagation alone and (b) larger devices can be analyzed by building it out of known assemblages.

Our TMS framework achieves the analogous effect. The qualitative resolution rule (sometimes called the qualitative Gauss rule) is implemented using our TMS. [11] presents an example where two pipes (Fig. 1) connected together produce a model for a single pipe. Consider the following instance of the qualitative resolution rule. Let x, y and z be qualitative quantities such that (we drop [...] when unambiguous),

$$x + y = 0, \quad -x + z = 0$$

From these two confluences we can infer the confluence,

$$y + z = 0. \tag{6}$$

(To those unfamiliar with qualitative physics this may not seem that surprising, but it is important to remember that qualitative arithmetic does not obey the usual field axioms and thus the equations cannot be manipulated as in conventional arithmetic.) The qualitative resolution rule is analogous to binary resolution. Two confluences can be usefully combined only if they share at most one symbol in common, otherwise the result is meaningless.

Our TMS achieves the effect of the qualitative resolution rule by conjoining the formulae of the two individual pipes. One way to expand $x + y = 0$ into clauses is to encode all the value combinations disallowed by the confluence:

$$\neg(x{=}+) \vee \neg(y{=}+),$$
$$\neg(x = +) \vee \neg(y = 0),$$
$$\neg(x = 0) \vee \neg(y = +),$$
$$\neg(x = 0) \vee \neg(y = -),$$
$$\neg(x = -) \vee \neg(y = 0),$$
$$\neg(x = -) \vee \neg(y = -).$$

Expanding $-x + z = 0$ into clauses includes:

$$\neg(x = -) \vee \neg(z = +),$$
$$\neg(x = -) \vee \neg(z = 0),$$
$$\neg(x = 0) \vee \neg(z = +),$$
$$\neg(x = 0) \vee \neg(z = -),$$
$$\neg(x = +) \vee \neg(z = 0),$$
$$\neg(x = +) \vee \neg(z = -).$$

If we add the clause,

$$(x = +) \vee (x = 0) \vee (x = -),$$

compute prime implicates and consider $\{x = +, x = 0, x = -\}$ internal symbols, then the result is exactly the prime implicates of the result of the qualitative resolution rule (i.e., of $y + z = 0$). This encoding might appear cumbersome, but the clauses are easily analyzed with BCP. As we have argued earlier, propagation on clauses (i.e., BCP) is efficiently implemented by following pointers and manipulating counters. Thus, by 'Assembling' the device, we obtain a set of prime implicates with which it is easy to determine a system's outputs from its inputs.

Dormoy [12] points out that applying the qualitative resolution rule sometimes produces a combinatorial explosion. This is analogous to the explosion that can occur in expanding a formula to its prime implicates. In his paper Dormoy proposes a joining rule for controlling this explosion. The joining rule applies the qualitative resolution only to components which share an internal variable — it is equivalent to our TMS heuristic of combining modules which share internal symbols.

Consider the two pipe problem of the introduction again. Suppose we know that $[dP_A] = [+]$ and $[dP_B] = [0]$. We have, in effect, two choices how to solve the problem. We could first inform the TMS of these values and then ask it to merge the modules of the two pipes; or we could first merge the two modules and then add these values. Although the answer $[dQ] = [+]$ remains the same, the resulting TMS data base is quite different. If we start with $[dP_A] = [+]$ and $[dP_C] = [0]$, then most of the prime implicate constructions can be avoided because these initial values provide initial BCP labels to 6 symbols (i.e., the symbols representing the possible qualitative values for dP_A and dP_B). On the other hand, if the modules are merged first without initial values, then all prime implicates are constructed, and although only a few of them are necessary to solve for the given inputs it is now much easier to solve problems when the inputs are changed.

Although computing all the prime implicates for a full device may be expensive, it often may be very useful to incur this cost. Once the prime implicates of a device are constructed, the input-output behavior is completely characterized. From the resulting data base of prime implicates one can construct the inputs from the outputs just as easily as outputs from the inputs without constructing any additional prime implicates. So the same data base can be efficiently utilized for a variety of distinct tasks.

9 Conclusion

We have shown a simple example of using our framework for simple qualitative physics analysis tasks. The applicability of these techniques extends to any problem-solving paradigm for which finite propositional encodings exist and there is some notion of locality in the original task which can be conveyed to the TMS. Many tasks for which TMS's are normally used are candidates for this approach. One obvious one which we are currently exploring is model-based diagnosis [5].

10 Acknowledgments

Daniel G. Bobrow, John Lamping, Olivier Raiman and Vijay Saraswat provided extensive insights on early drafts.

References

[1] Chang, C. and Lee R.C., Symbolic Logic and Mechanical Theorem Proving, (Academic Press, New York, 1973).

[2] de Kleer, J., An assumption-based truth maintenance system, *Artificial Intelligence* **28** (1986) 127–162. Also in *Readings in NonMonotonic Reasoning*, edited by Matthew L. Ginsberg, (Morgan Kaufman, 1987), 280–297.

[3] de Kleer, J. and Brown, J.S., A qualitative physics based on confluences, *Artificial Intelligence* **24** (1984) 7–83; also in: D.G. Bobrow (Ed.), *Reasoning About Physical Systems* (MIT Press and North Holland, 1985) 7-83; also in: J.R. Hobbs and R.C. Moore (Eds.), *Formal Models of the Common-Sense World* (Ablex, Norwood, NJ, 1985) 109–183.

[4] de Kleer, J., Extending the ATMS, *Artificial Intelligence* **28** (1986) 163–196.

[5] de Kleer, J. and Williams, B.C., Diagnosing multiple faults, *Artificial Intelligence* **32** (1987) 97-130. Also in *Readings in NonMonotonic Reasoning*, edited by Matthew L. Ginsberg, (Morgan Kaufman, 1987), 372–388.

[6] de Kleer, J., A practical clause management system, SSL Paper P88-00140, Xerox PARC.

[7] de Kleer, J., Forbus, K., and McAllester D., Tutorial notes on truth maintenance systems, IJCAI-89, Detroit, MI, 1989.

[8] de Kleer, J., A comparison of ATMS and CSP techniques, *Proceedings of the Eleventh International Joint Conference on Artificial Intelligence*, Detroit, MI (August 1989).

[9] de Kleer, J., A Clause Management System based on Boolean Constraint Propagation and clause synthesis, 1990.

[10] de Kleer, J., Compiling Devices, submitted for publication, 1990.

[11] Dormoy, J. and Raiman, O., Assembling a device, in: *Proceedings AAAI-88*, Saint Paul, Minn (1988) 330–336.

[12] Dormoy, J-L., Controlling qualitative resolution, in: *Proceedings AAAI-88*, Saint Paul, Minn (1988) 319–323.

[13] Forbus, K.D., Qualitative process theory, *Artificial Intelligence* **24** (1984) 85-168.

[14] Forbus, K.D., The qualitative process engine, University of Illinois Technical Report UIUCDCS-R-86-1288, 1986.

[15] Dowling and Gallier, Linear time algorithms for testing the satisfiability of propositional horn formulae, *Journal of Logic Programming* **3** 267–284 (1984).

[16] Kean, A. and Tsiknis, G., An incremental method for generating prime implicants/implicates, University of British Columbia Technical Report TR-88-16, 1988.

[17] Kohavi, Z., *Switching and Finite Automata Theory* (McGraw-Hill, 1978).

[18] Mackworth, A.K., Constraint satisfaction, *Encyclopedia of Artificial Intelligence*, edited by S.C. Shapiro, (John Wiley and Son, 1987) 205-211.

[19] McAllester, D., A three-valued truth maintenance system, S.B. Thesis, Department of Electrical Engineering, Cambridge: M.I.T., 1978.

[20] McAllester, D., An outlook on truth maintenance, Artificial Intelligence Laboratory, AIM-551, Cambridge: M.I.T., 1980.

[21] McAllester, D., A widely used truth maintenance system, unpublished, 1985.

[22] Reiter, R. and de Kleer, J., Foundations of Assumption-Based Truth Maintenance Systems: Preliminary Report, in: *Proceedings AAAI-87*, Seattle, WA (July, 1987), 183–188.

[23] Tison, P., Generalized consensus theory and application to the minimization of boolean functions, *IEEE transactions on electronic computers* **4** (August 1967) 446-456.

Computing Stable Models By Using the ATMS

Kave Eshghi
Hewlett Packard Laboratories,
Filton Road,
Stoke Gifford,
Bristol BS12 6QZ,
England.
Email:ke@hplb.hpl.hp.com

Abstract

An algorithm is described which computes stable models of propositional logic programs with negation as failure using the Assumption Based Truth Maintenance mechanism. Since stable models of logic programs are closely connected to stable expansions of a class of auto-epistemic theories, this algorithm points to a link between stable expansions of a class of auto-epistemic theories and ATMS structures

Introduction

In this paper an algorithm is described which computes stable models of propositional logic programs with negation as failure [1], using the Assumption Based Truth Maintenance mechanism [2]. Since stable models of logic programs are closely connected to stable expansions of a class of auto-epistemic theories, this algorithm points to a link between stable expansions of a class of auto-epistemic theories and ATMS structures.

Stable Models of Logic Programs

Stable models of logic programs with negation as failure were introduced in [1] as a means of specifying the semantics of logic programs. They are defined as follows:

A logic program is a set of clauses of the type

$$p \leftarrow p_1, p_2, \ldots \sim q_1, \sim q_2 ..$$

where $\sim$ indicates negation as failure. In this paper we only consider propositional logic programs, where $p_1, p_2, ..q_1, q_2..$ are propositions. We do not place any other restriction on the structure of the clasues.

Definition 1 *The answer set of a propositional Horn Clause program is the set of all propositions provable from it. We use* $Answer(\Pi)$ *to denote the answer set of the program* Π

Definition 2 *Let P be a propositional logic program with negation as failure, and I a set of propositions. The negation-free program* P_I *is derived from P by*

- *Deleting all the clauses in P which have a negative conditions such as* $\sim q$ *where* $q \in I$
- *Deleting all the negative conditions in all the remaining clauses of P.*

I is a stable model of P iff $I = Answer(P_I)$

Example: let P be the program

$$a \leftarrow \sim b$$

$$b \leftarrow \sim c$$

Then $P_{\{b\}} = \{b \leftarrow\}$, and therefore $\{b\}$ is a stable model of P.

In general, a logic program may have any number of stable models. The algorithm described here computes all of them.

Stable models of logic programs are closely connected to stable expansions of auto-epistemic theories. In fact, as observed in [1], if we replace every negative condition $\sim p$ in the program P with the condition $\neg B(p)$, where B is the belief operator of auto-epistemic logic, the stable expansion of the resulting auto-epistemic theory is the same as the stable model of P. As such, the algorithm described in this paper can be considered to be a theorem prover for a restricted class of auto-epistemic theories.

The ATMS

We are only concerned with a subset of the capabilities of the ATMS, which we define below.

Let N be a set of propositions, called *nodes*, and S a distinguished subset of N, called *assumptions.* Let J be a set of propositional Horn Clauses, called justifications, in which all propositional symbols are from N. When we transmit S and J to the ATMS, it computes the following structures:

- All the minimal sets of assumptions ϵ such tht $J \cup \epsilon$ is inconsistent. These sets are called nogoods.
- for every node n, all the minimal sets of assumptions e such that $J \cup e \vdash n$. e is called an *environment* of n, and the set of all environments of a node n is called the *label* of n.

For example, let J be

$a \leftarrow b^*$

$\leftarrow b, b^*$

$b \leftarrow c^*$

$\leftarrow c, c^*$

and $S = \{b^*, c^*\}$. Then the ATMS will compute the only nogood to be $\{b^*, c^*\}$, and the following labels for each node:

$a : \{\{b^*\}\}$

$b : \{\{c^*\}\}$

$c : \{\}$

(Note: $\leftarrow c, c^*$ is an alternative syntax for $\neg(c \wedge c^*)$, where $\neg$ signifies classical negation)

Notation: we will use $nogood^{J,S}(\epsilon)$ to indicate that ϵ is a nogood given the justifications J and assumptions S. We will use $env^{J,S}(n, e)$ to indicate that e is an environment of n given justifications J and assumptions S.

The Algorithm

To compute the stable models of a logic program P, we proceed as follows:

1. From the program P derive the set of Horn clauses P^* and the set of assumptions S;
2. Add the elements of S to the ATMS as assumptions, and add the clauses in P^* to the ATMS as justifications;
3. From the data structures computed by the ATMS (environments and nogoods) compute the stable model of P.

Each one of these steps is described below.

Deriving P^* and S

Given a propositional logic program P, P^* and S are derived as follows: for every clause such as

$$p \leftarrow p_1, p_2, .. \sim q_1, \sim q_2 ... \sim q_n$$

in P, add the assumptions $q_1^*, q_2^*, ...q_n^*$ to S, where $q_1^*, q_2^* ... q_n^*$ are propositional symbols not occuring in P, and add the Horn clauses

$p \leftarrow p_2, p_2 .., q_1^*, q_2^* ... q_n^*$

$\leftarrow q_1, q_1^*$

$\leftarrow q_2, q_2^*$

....

$\leftarrow q_n, q_n^*$

to P^*. (We call q and q^* the *complements* of each other. In the rest of this paper, an assumption indicated as q^* will always be the complement of the propositional symbol q).

For example, let P be

$a \leftarrow\sim b$

$b \leftarrow\sim c$

Then P^* is

$a \leftarrow b^*$

$\leftarrow b, b^*$

$b \leftarrow c^*$

$\leftarrow c, c^*$

and $S = \{b^*, c^*\}$.

The relationship between P and P^*

As mentioned before, the stable models of P are related to the environments and nogoods returned by the ATMS when it is presented with the assumptions in S and the justifications in P^*. To explore this relationship, first we define the notion of *stable generator*.

Definition 3 *A set of assumptions σ is a stable generator of P iff*

$P^* \cup \sigma$ *is consistent*

$\forall n^* \in S, (n^* \notin \sigma \rightarrow P^* \cup \sigma \vdash n)$

(Note: n is the complement of n^*)

The following two theorems establish the link between stable generators and stable models:

Theorem 1 *Let σ be a stable generator of P. Then the set*

$$I = Answer(P^* \cup \sigma) \setminus \sigma$$

is a stable model of P.

Theorem 2 *Let I be a stable model of P. Then the set*

$$\sigma = \{q^* : q^* \in S \wedge q \notin I\}$$

is a stable generator of P.

From these theorems it follows that for every stable model of P, there is a unique stable generator. Furthermore, given a stable generator, it is straightforward to compute the corresponding stable model. The algorithm described in this paper computes stable generators of a progam P from the environments and nogoods computed by the ATMS when it is given the assumptions S and justifications P^*. To do this, we need the following lemma.

Lemma 1 *A set of assumptions σ is a stable generator of P iff*

$\forall \epsilon, nogood^{P^*,S}(\epsilon) \rightarrow \epsilon \not\subset \sigma$

$\forall n^* \in S, (n^* \notin \sigma \rightarrow \exists e, (env^{P^*,S}(n, e) \wedge e \subset \sigma))$

(Note: n is the complement of n^*)

This lemma directly follows from the definiton of stable generators and the properties of ATMS nogoods and environments.

Example: When the S and P^* computed in example 1 are transmitted to the ATMS as assumptions and justifications, $\{b^*, c^*\}$ will be the only nogood. The nodes in the ATMS, with their labels, will be:

$$a : \{\{b^*\}\}$$

$$b : \{\{c^*\}\}$$

$$c : \{\}$$

In this situation, $\{c^*\}$ is the only set of assumptions satisfying the definition of a stable generator, i.e. it is the generator of the only stable model of P. $\{b^*\}$ is not a stable generator because it does not safisfy the second requirement of the definition of stable generators, for $c^* \notin \{b^*\}$ but $P^* \cup \{b^*\} \not\vdash c$.

Computing Stable Generators

In this section, an algorithm is described which, given the environments and nogoods returned by the ATMS, computes all stable generators of P. The algorithm computes a stable generator by finding a set of assumptions, τ, such that $S \setminus \tau$ is a stable generator. (We call τ an acceptable culprit set if $S \setminus \tau$ is a stable generator)

The intuition behind the algorithm is as follows: find a set of assumptions τ such that by removing them from S, the remaining set of assumptions σ satisfies the requirements of lemma 1. The first requirement, that no nogood set should be a subset of σ, can be satisfied by choosing one assumption from each nogood and including them in τ. (This is similar to computing diagnoses from a set of conflict sets [9][3]). However, if we remove an assumption q^* from S where q does not have any environment which is a subset of the remaining set of assumptions we violate the second requirement of lemma 1. For example, consider the only nogood set for the example program above, $\{b^*, c^*\}$. If we choose b^* as the culprit, we will satisfy the requirements of lemma 1, because b has an environment, $\{c^*\}$, which is a subset of the remaining set of assumptions, $\{c^*\}$. But if we choose c^* as the culprit, we violate the second requirement of lemma 1, because c does not have any environment which is a subset of the remaining set of assumptions $\{b^*\}$.(In fact, c does not have any environments at all).

We call the environment e a complement environment of the assumption q^* if it is an environment of q. We call the set of all complement environments of q^* the complement label of q^*. In order to make sure that the second requirement of lemma 1 is satified, the algorithm keeps with each chosen culprit q^* the set of all its complement environments which do not include any of the other culprits. We call this set of complement environments the companion of assumption q^*. Every time a new culprit is chosen, the companions of all the other culprits are updated to remove the environments which include the chosen culprit. If we can choose a culprit from each nogood without making the companion of any other culprit empty, this will be an acceptable culprit set, because the remaining set of assumptions will satisfy lemma 1, and will therefore be a stable generator. The details of this process are given below.

Data Structures and Procedures

The data structure used to keep assumptions together with their companions is the augmented assumption. An augmented assumption is a tuple (q^*, E) where q^* is an assumption, and E is a list of complement environments of q^*. We call q^* the main assumption of (q^*, E).

The list of augmented assumptions

$$[(n_1^*, E_1), (n_2^*, E_2)..(n_k^*, E_k)]$$

is an augmented nogood when its main assumption set, i.e. $\{n_1^*, n_2^*....n_k^*\}$, is a nogood (as returned by the ATMS) and for all i, E_i is the complement label of n_i^* (i.e. the list of *all* complement environments of n_i^*). The augmented nogood list relating to example 1 is

$$[(b^*, [[c^*]]), (c^*, [])]$$

At the heart of the algorithm is the procedure stablecomp. If A is the list of all augmented nogoods of P^*, stablecomp(A, Tau) succeeds iff Tau is a set of acceptable culprits (i.e. $S \setminus Tau$ is a stable generator of P).

We have presented the algorithm in Prolog because it is a non-deterministic algorithm. Prolog handles the non-determinism by its built-in backtracking.

Below is the top level definition of stablecomp.

```
stablecomp(A,Tau):-
   stcomp(A,[],Comp),
   main_assumptions(Comp,Tau).
```

stablecomp is defined in terms of stcomp, which recursively chooses one assumption from each nogood as the next culprit, maintaining the list of culprits chosen so far with their companions in the argument Culprits_sofar.

```
stcomp([],X,X).
stcomp([Nogood|Nogoods],Culprits_sofar,Comp):-
   choose(Nogood,(Node*,Label)),
   filter1(Culprits_sofar,Label,Label1),
   filter2(Node*,Culprits_sofar,Culprits1),
   filter3(Node*,Nogoods,Nogoods1),
   stcomp(Nogoods1,[(Node*,Label1|Culprits1],Comp).
```

To explain the behaviour of stcomp, first we describe the data structures in its argument places, then we describe the recursion invariant of the above clauses, and then the constituent predicats choose, filter1,filter2 and filter3.

- The first argument of stcomp is a list of augmented nogoods.
- Its second argument is a list of augmented assumptions $[(a_1^*, E_1), (a_2^*, E_2)...]$, where a_i^* are the chosen assumptions sofar, and E_i are their companions.
- The third argument of stcomp is the variable that is used to return the result of the computation

The following is the recursion invariant for the definition of stcomp. It holds when stcomp is initially called by stablecomp, and whenever it is subsequently called in the recursion.

Invariant 1
Let τ be the main assumptions set $\{a_1^*, a_2^*, ..\}$ of Culprits_sofar. *Then the following will always hold whenever* stcomp(Augmented_nogoods,Culprits_sofar,Comp) *is called.*

1. *For every augmented assumption (n_i^*, E_i) in* Culprits_sofar, *E_i is not empty, and it is the list of all complement environments of n_i^* whose intersection with τ is empty,*
2. Augmented_Nogoods *is a list of all augmented nogoods of P^* the intersection of whose main assumption set with τ is empty.*

These conditions are clearly satisfied when stcomp is initially invoked. Let τ be the set of main assumptions of Culprits_so_far when the base case of recursion is reached. Then it will be the case that

- Every assumption a^* in τ will have at least one complement environment whose intersection with τ is empty,
- Every nogood will have at least one element from *tau*

Thus τ will be an acceptable culprit set, and $S \setminus \tau$ will be a stable generator.

The constituent procedures of stcomp

Below we discuss the function of the choice procedure and the three filter procedures.

choose The call choose(Nogood,(Node*,Label)) non-deterministically chooses an augmented assumption (Node*,Label) from the augmented nogood Nogood.

filter1 Let τ be the main assumption set of Culprits_sofar. The function of the filter1 procedure is to remove from the complement-label of the chosen assumption all the environments which include an assumption which occurs on τ. Thus, if

filter1(Culprits_sofar,Label,Label1)

is successful, Label1 will be the list of all the environments in Label whose intersection with τ is empty. If all the environments in Label include an assumption from τ, then filter1(Culprits_sofar,Label,Label1) fails.

filter2 The function of this procedure is to remove from the companions of all assumptions on Culprits_sofar those environments which include the chosen assumption. Let Culprits_sofar be the list $[(n_1^*, E_1), (n_2^*, E_2)..]$. Then if

filter2(Node*,Culprits_sofar,Culprits1)

is successful, Culprits1 will be the list $[(n_1^*, E_1'), (n_2^*, E_2')...]$ where E_i' is the subset of E_i with all the environments in E_i which include Node* removed. If there is an E_i which would be empty after removing all environments which contain Node*, filter2 fails.

filter3 Let Nogoods be a list of augmented nogoods. Then the procedure call

filter3(Node*,Nogoods,Nogoods1)

removes from Nogoods all the augmented nogoods whose main assumption set includes Node*, returning the result in Nogoods1.

Generating all stable generators

The procedure stablecomp described above returns one acceptable culprit set when invoked, from which the corresponding stable generator can be computed by the set complement operation. To find all stable generators, the Prolog findall procedure can be used to find all the acceptable culprit sets.

Related work

The relationship between truth maintenance and non-monotonic reasoning formalisms is close, and there is an extensive literature on it. Of direct relevance to us is the work reported in [7], where an algorithm (different from the one presented here) is presented for computing stable models of propositional logic programs. The major difference between our work and the one reported in [7] is that they compute stable models directly, and advocate their use as an *alternative* to the ATMS, whereas the work presented here derives the stable models from ATMS structures, and sheds some light on the relationship between stable expansions of auto-epistemic theories and ATMS structures.

In [6] and [8] the semantics of Doyle's TMS [4] are related to auto-epistemic expansions. Their work can be considered complimentary to ours, because they start from a given truth maintenance system (Doyle's TMS) and give its semantics in terms of auto-epistemic expansions, whereas we start from a class of auto-epistemic theories and relate their expansions to ATMS structures.

The two theorems stated above are a special case of a more general theorem proved in [5], in which a link was established between stable models of logic programs and abductive hypotheses generation.

References

[1] Gelfond,M. & Lifschitz,V: "The stable model semantics for logic programming", Proceeding Fifth International Conference on Logic Programming, MIT Press 1988

[2] DeKleer, J: "An assumption based truth maintenance system", Artificial Intelligence Journal 28, 1986

[3] DeKleer, J. & Williams, B.C.: "Diagnosing multiple faults", Artificial Intelligence Journal 32, 1987

[4] Doyle, J: "A truth maintenance system", Artificial Intelligence Journal 12, 1979

[5] Eshghi,K & Kowalski, R.A. "Abduction compared with negation as failure", Proceedings of the Sixth International Conference on Logic Programming, MIT Press 1989

[6] Fujiwara, Y & Honiden, S: "Relating the TMS to auto-epistemic logic", Proceedings IJCAI 89, Morgan Kaufman inc., 1989

[7] Pimental, S.G. & Cuadraro, J.L.: "A truth maintenance system based on stable models", Proceedings of the North American Conference on Logic Programming, MIT Press 1989

[8] Reinfrank,M. et.al.: "On the relation between truth maintenance and auto-epistemic logic", Proceedings IJCAI 89, Morgan Kaufman inc., 1989

[9] Reiter,R: "A theory of diagnosis from first principle", Artificial Intelligence Journal 32, 1987

Appendix

In this appendix the two theorems are proved. First, a few preliminaries.

Definition 4 *Let P be a propositional logic program. Let P^* and S be derived as described in the paper. Let σ be a subset of S. Then P^*_σ is the horn clause program derived from P^* by:*

1. *Removing every clause which has a condition q^* where $q^* \in S \setminus \sigma$*
2. *From the remaining clauses in P^*, removing every condition q^* where $q^* \in \sigma$*

Lemma 2 *For a program P^*_σ defined as above,*

$$Answer(P^*_\sigma) = Answer(P^* \cup \sigma) \setminus \sigma$$

Proof Easily follows from the definition of P^* and P^*_σ

Proof of Theorem 1

From the definiton of I in theorem 1, the definition of P^*_σ and *lemma*2 it follows that

$$I = Answer(P^*_\sigma)$$

Below we prove that $P^*_\sigma = P_I$, thus proving that

$$I = Answer(P_I)$$

which proves that I is a stable model of P.

Proof of $P_I = P^*_\sigma$

1. Let $c = p \leftarrow p_1, p_2, ...$ be a clause in P_I. If c occurs in P, since it does not have any negative conditions it will be in P^*_σ as well.
   Otherwise, there is a clause
   $$p \leftarrow p_1, p_2, ..., \sim q_1, \sim q_2 ...$$
   in P where $q_1, q_2 ... \notin I$.
   Let q_n be any of $q_1, q_2 ....$ Since $\sim q_n$ occurs as a condition of a clause in P, $q^*_n \in S^*$. Since σ is a stable generator of P, $q^*_n \in \sigma \leftarrow P^* \cup \sigma \not\vdash q_n$. But since $q_n \notin I$, by definition of I $P^* \cup \sigma \not\vdash q_n$ which shows that $q^*_n \in \sigma$.
   Now, since $p \leftarrow p_1, p_2, ..., \sim q_1, \sim q_2 ...$ is in P, by definition of P^* there is a clause $p \leftarrow p_1, p_2, ... q^*_1, q^*_2 ..$ in P^*. Since, as proved above, $q^*_1, q^*_2, .. \in \sigma$, from the definition of P^*_σ it follows that $p \leftarrow p_1, p_2 ...$ is in P^*_σ, i.e. c is in P^*_σ
2. Let $c = p \leftarrow p_1, p_2 ..$ be a clause in P^*_σ. If c occurs in P, since it does not have any negative conditions it will be in P_I as well.
   Otherwise, there is a clause $p \leftarrow p_1, p_2, ... q^*_1, q^*_2 ..$ in P^* where $q^*_1, q^*_2 .. \in \sigma$. Now, let q^*_n be any of $q^*_1, q^*_2 ...$ Since σ is a stable generator of P, $P^* \cup \sigma$ is consistent. Furthermore, by definition P^* contains a clause $\leftarrow q_n, q^*_n$. Thus $P^* \cup \sigma \not\vdash q_n$, for otherwise $P^* \cup \sigma$ would be inconsistent. Thus, by definiton of I, $q_n \notin I$.
   Now, since there is a clause $p \leftarrow p_1, p_2, ... q^*_1, q^*_2 ..$ in P^*, there is a clause $p_1, p_2, ... \sim q_1, q_2 ..$ in P, where as shown above, $q_1, q_2, ... \notin I$. Thus $p \leftarrow p_1, p_2, ...$ belongs to P_I, i.e. $c \in P_I$.

Proof of Theorem 2

First, we prove that $P^*_\sigma = P_I$

1. Let $c = p \leftarrow p_1, p_2 ..$ be a clause in P_σ.
   If c occurs in P, since it does not have any negative conditions it will be in P_I as well.
   Otherwise, there is a clause
   $$p \leftarrow p_1, p_2, .. q^*_1, q^*_2 ..$$
   in P^* where $q^*_1, q^*_2, .. \in \sigma$. Let q^*_n be any of $q^*_1, q^*_2 ....$ Since $q^*_n \in \sigma$, by definiton of σ, $q_n \notin I$.
   Since
   $$p \leftarrow p_1, p_2, .. q^*_1, q^*_2 ..$$
   is in P^*, there is a clause
   $$p \leftarrow p_1, p_2, .. \sim q_1, \sim q_2 ..$$
   in P where $q_1, q_2 ... \notin I$. Thus $p \leftarrow p_1, p_2 ..$ is in P_I, i.e. $c \in P_I$.
2. Let $c = p \leftarrow p_1, p_2 ..$ be a clause in P_I. Then there is a clause
   $$p \leftarrow p_1, p_2, .. \sim q_1, \sim q_2 ..$$
   in P, where $q_1, q_2, .. \notin I$. Let q_n be any of $q_1, q_2 ....$ Since $\sim q_n$ occurs as a condition in P, $q^*_n \in S$. Thus, since $q_n \notin I$, by definiton of σ, $q^*_n \in \sigma$.

Since

$$p \leftarrow p_1, p_2, .. \sim q_1, \sim q_2 ..$$

is in P, there is a clause

$$p \leftarrow p_1, p_2, ..q_1^*, q_2^* ..$$

in P^* where $q_1^*, q_2^* ... \in \sigma$. Thus $p \leftarrow p_1, p_2 ..$ is in P_σ, i.e. $c \in P_\sigma$.

Now we show σ is a stable generator by showing that it satisfies the two requirements of stable generators.

1. We prove that $P^* \cup \sigma$ is consistent by contradiction. Suppose $P^* \cup \sigma$ is inconsistent. Then, the proof of inconsistency would involve a denial of the form $\leftarrow p, p^*$, where $P^* \cup \sigma \vdash p$ and $P^* \cup \sigma \vdash p^*$. But since, due to the definiton of P^*, assumptions do not occur at the head of clauses, the only way p^* can be provable from $P^* \cup \sigma$ is for it to be a member of σ. But, due to the definiton of σ, this means that $p \notin I$, which means that $P_I \not\vdash p$, i.e, since $P_I = P_\sigma^*$, $P_\sigma^* \not\vdash p$. Thus, by definiton of P_σ^*, $P^* \cup \sigma \not\vdash p$, leading to a contradiction.

2. To prove that $\forall n^* \in S, (n^* \notin \sigma \rightarrow P^* \cup \sigma \vdash n)$, assume that $n^* \in S$ and $n^* \notin \sigma$. Then by definition of σ, $n \in I$, which, since I is a stable model of P, means that $P_I \vdash n$. Since $P_I = P_\sigma^*$, this means that $P_\sigma^* \vdash n$, i.e. that $P^* \cup \sigma \vdash n$

Computing the Extensions of Autoepistemic and Default Logics with a Truth Maintenance System

Ulrich Junker
GMD, F3-HIS
Postfach 1240
5205 St. Augustin 1, F.R.G.
unido!gmdzi!junker@uunet.uu.net

Kurt Konolige
Artificial Intelligence Center
SRI International
333 Ravenswood Ave.
Menlo Park, California 94025/USA
konolige@ai.sri.com

Abstract

In this paper we develop a proof procedure for autoepistemic (AEL) and default logics (DL), based on translating them into a Truth Maintenance System (TMS). The translation is decidable if the theory consists of a finite number of defaults and premises and classical derivability for the base language is decidable. To determine all extensions of a network, we develop variants of Doyle's labelling algorithms.

Introduction

We seek proof methods for autoepistemic logic (AEL) [11] and default logic (DL) [14]. Most existing techniques are too restrictive in terms of the language allowed. Reiter's original proof procedure is restricted to closed normal defaults [14]. Etherington handles only ordered network theories, a special class of general defaults which are suitable for inheritance [4]. Kautz and Selman are mainly interested in complexity results and restrict their attention to disjunction-free default theories [7]. Brewka's prover handles modal implications having no preconditions of the form Lq [1]. Moore's procedure for AEL is restricted to a propositional language [12], just as Niemelä's work [10]. Closer to our approach is the work of Levesque on quantified AEL [9], which has a proof procedure under the same conditions as ours; however Levesque's proof theory is a Hilbert-style axiomatization, without an efficient implementation.

We want to develop a more general proof procedure for AEL and DL which profits from efficient truth maintenance (TMS) techniques. To this end, we translate an AEL or DL theory into a TMS network, and relate the admissible labeling of the network to extensions of the original theory. It is already known from the work of Reinfrank, Dressler, and Brewka [13] that the TMS can be given a semantics by mapping to a restricted form of AEL or DL; here we give the inverse transformation. Our approach has only two limits: 1) We do not handle infinite sets of defaults and premises. 2) Derivability has to be decidable for the base language. If both requirements are satisfied our procedure is able to determine all extensions and to detect incoherence, i.e., non-existence of an extension. To achieve this goal we tackle three problems:

1. Extensions of autoepistemic and default theories are defined as infinite fixed points of monotonic operators, while the TMS is finite. Are there computable, finite conditions for extensions?

2. Doyle's TMS lacks complete first-order derivability. What first-order derivations must be encoded by justifications to get all needed conclusions?

3. TMS labeling algorithms (cf. [2], [5]) are incomplete because they compute only one extension and can stop without a definite result if there are odd loops. How can we get all extensions?

In outline the strategy of the paper is as follows. We concentrate initially on DL because its fixed-point condition is close to that of the TMS. First we identify all formulas which are relevant for the fixed point conditions, and develop alternative operators whose fixed points consist of relevant formulas. This set of formulas is finite for a finite number of defaults and allows reconstruction of every extension. The appropriate TMS can then be constructed by considering only the relevant formulas as nodes, with justifications coming from the defaults and from appropriate first-order proofs relating the relevant formulas. Admissible labelings of the TMS provably correspond to extensions of the DL theory.

For AEL the story is slightly more complicated. Because of the relation between DL and strongly-grounded extensions of AEL, the above method can be transferred directly. However, in the case of weakly-grounded extensions, the definition of admissible labeling must be changed to allow circular support in the TMS.

Finally, we sketch a complete version of Doyle's labeling algorithm. As in [6], it introduces choice points for loops and performs backtracking if it runs into an odd loop.

Closures of operators

In this paper, we use extensively operators that apply defaults or justifications. Here we give notation and properties for these operators. Let U be a domain and $apply : 2^U \mapsto 2^U$ be a monotonic and compact operator:

$$\begin{array}{ll} \text{if } X \subseteq Y \text{ then } apply(X) \subseteq apply(Y) & \\ \text{if } q \in apply(Y) \text{ then } \exists X \subseteq Y : X \text{ is finite and} & (1) \\ \quad q \in apply(X) & \end{array}$$

Repeated application of *apply* leads to an operator $apply^i$ which is also monotonic and compact. If we apply it to the empty set it satisfies $apply^i(\emptyset) \subseteq apply^{i+k}(\emptyset)$. Now we define the transitive and reflexive closure of *apply*:

Definition 1 *Let apply* $: 2^U \mapsto 2^U$ *be a monotonic and compact operator. The closure* $apply^*(X)$ *is the minimal set that contains* X *and is closed w.r.t. apply, i.e.* $apply(apply^*(X)) \subseteq apply^*(X)$.

We mention some alternative characterizations of $apply^*$ in Lemma 1. Minimality of $apply^*$ can be ensured by iterating *apply* or by finite derivation chains.

Lemma 1 *Let apply* $: 2^U \mapsto 2^U$ *be a monotonic, and compact operator. The following conditions are equivalent:*

1. $T = apply^*(\emptyset)$.
2. $apply(T) = T \subseteq apply^*(\emptyset)$.
3. $T = \bigcup_{i=0}^{\infty} apply^i(\emptyset)$
4. $apply(T) \subseteq T$ *and* $\forall q \in T\ \exists q_1, \ldots, q_k : q = q_k$ *and* $q_i \in apply(\{q_1, \ldots, q_{i-1}\})$ *for* $i = 1, \cdots, k$.

Very often, we consider sets being closed w.r.t. two operators $apply_1$ and $apply_2$. For this purpose, we write $(apply_1 \cup apply_2)(X)$ for $apply_1(X) \cup apply_2(X)$. Consider $(apply_1 \cup apply_2)^*(\emptyset)$. Here, both operators are applied in parallel. Sometimes, a sequential view yields more insights: We first use $apply_2$ and then determine the closure w.r.t. $apply_1$. Thus, we get a concatenated operator $apply_1^* \circ apply_2$.

Lemma 2 *Let* $apply_1, apply_2 : 2^U \mapsto 2^U$ *be two monotonic and compact operators. Then* $(apply_1 \cup apply_2)^*(\emptyset) = (apply_1^* \circ apply_2)^*(\emptyset)$.

A reduced fixed point condition for DL

In this section we reduce the infinite fixed-point extensions of DL to finite ones, which are called the *extension bases*. Let $\mathcal{L}_0$ be a first-order language containing a contradiction formula $\bot$. A default theory Δ is a pair (D, W) consisting of a set D of defaults and a set of first-order premises $W \subseteq \mathcal{L}_0$. Each default has the form $(a : b_1, \cdots, b_k/c)$ where $a, b_1, \cdots, b_k, c$ are ordinary formulas. Informally, we say that the default is *applied* if its prerequisite a is provable and $b_1, \cdots, b_k$ are consistent, i.e. all $\neg b_i$ are not provable. We abbreviate the set of prerequisites, the set of negated consistency assumptions (i.e. exceptions), and the set of conclusions by

$$\begin{array}{lcll} P_D & = & \{a \mid (a : b_1, \cdots, b_k/c) \in D\} & \\ E_D & = & \{\neg b_i \mid (a : b_1, \cdots, b_k/c) \in D, i \in \{1, \ldots, k\}\} & \\ C_D & = & \{c \mid (a : b_1, \cdots, b_k/c) \in D\} & (2) \end{array}$$

Let $Th(X)$ be the set of first-order conclusions of X. We also introduce a special operator that applies defaults. We use different sets X, Y to check both kinds of preconditions. Our operator applies a default $(a : b_1, \cdots, b_k/c)$ if $a \in X$ and $\neg b_i \notin Y$:

$$\begin{array}{l} apply_{D,Y}(X) := \{c \mid (a : b_1, \cdots, b_k/c) \in D, a \in X, \\ \quad \text{and } \neg b_i \notin Y \ \text{ for } i = 1, \cdots, k\} \end{array} \quad (3)$$

To be more precise, we have defined a unary operator for every Y. These operators have nice properties: they are monotonic and compact and we can apply the results of the previous section in reformulating Reiter's operator Γ. $\Gamma(T)$ is the smallest set that contains W and is closed w.r.t. the first-order closure Th and our operator $apply_{D,T}$. Hence, $\Gamma(T) = (Th \cup apply_{D,T})^*(W)$. An extension is defined using Γ:

Definition 2 *(Reiter): Let* $\Delta = (D, W)$ *be a closed default theory. A first-order set* T *is an extension of* Δ *iff* $\Gamma(T) = T$.

We now discuss two problems:

1. What are the relevant formulas to establish the fixed point condition?
2. How can we reduce the argument of Γ to a finite domain?

Every extension is an infinite set and it is difficult to find a set T satisfying the fixed point condition. What part of T is really needed for determining extensions? The operator $apply_{D,T}$ checks $\neg b_i \notin T$ for every default $(a : b_1, \cdots, b_k/c)$ and ignores the rest of T. In addition to these negated consistency assumptions, the prerequisites of defaults are relevant because derived prerequisites are needed to apply further defaults. Thus our test domain is defined by

$$\mathcal{L}_D := P_D \cup E_D.$$

The relevant part of a set T is $B = T \cap \mathcal{L}_D$ and satisfies following properties: $apply_{D,T} = apply_{D,B}$ and $\Gamma(T) = \Gamma(B)$. If T is an extension then $B = T \cap \mathcal{L}_D = \Gamma(T) \cap \mathcal{L}_D = \Gamma(B) \cap L_D$. Thus, we have obtained a fixed point condition for a test domain $\mathcal{L}_D$ which is finite if there are a finite number of defaults. We can now define a reduced extension, called the extension base, as follows.

Definition 3 *Let* $\Delta = (D, W)$ *be a closed default theory.* B *is an extension base of* Δ *iff* $B = \Gamma(B) \cap \mathcal{L}_D$.

Hence, if T is an extension then $T \cap \mathcal{L}_D$ is an extension base. Conversely, if B is an extension base then $\Gamma(B) = \Gamma(\Gamma(B) \cap \mathcal{L}_D) = \Gamma(\Gamma(B))$ and $\Gamma(B)$ is an extension, giving the following theorem.

Theorem 3 *Let $\Delta = (D, W)$ be a closed default theory. There exists a bijective mapping of the set of extensions of Δ to the set of extension bases of Δ.*

There is at most one inconsistent extension of Δ. If B is the extension base of an inconsistent extension then $\bot \in \Gamma(B)$ and $B = \mathcal{L}_D$ since an inconsistency implies every formula. We can check $\bot \in \Gamma(\mathcal{L}_D)$ to detect an inconsistent extension base.

Now, we simplify $\Gamma(B) \cap \mathcal{L}_D$ which is needed in Definition 3. We want to reduce the necessary first-order derivations as much as possible. First, we introduce a new operator that inserts W and then derives first-order consequences. We write it down using a lambda-expression, namely $\lambda(X).Th(X \cup W)$. Then $\Gamma(B)$ is the minimal set that is closed w.r.t. $\lambda(X).Th(X \cup W)$ and $apply_{D,B}$. By Lemma 2, we get:

$$\Gamma(B) = ((\lambda(X).Th(X \cup W)) \circ apply_{D,B})^*(\emptyset) \quad (4)$$

Since $apply_{D,B}$ expects only prerequisites which are in $\mathcal{L}_D$ and $\lambda(X).Th(X \cup W)$ is only supplied with consequents which are in C_D we can show

$$\begin{aligned} &\Gamma(B) \cap \mathcal{L}_D = \\ &\quad ((\lambda(X).(X \cup (Th((X \cap C_D) \cup W) \cap \mathcal{L}_D))) \circ \\ &\quad apply_{D,B})^*(\emptyset) \cap \mathcal{L}_D \end{aligned} \quad (5)$$

consistency assumptions from consequents and premises. Equation 5 allows a simple translation to TMS.

Compact fixed point conditions for the TMS

Doyle's TMS maintains a network $\nu := (N, J)$ consisting of a set N of nodes and a set J of justifications. A justification $\langle in(I), out(O) \to c\rangle$ for a node c consists of a finite in-list $I \subseteq N$, a finite out-list $O \subseteq N$, and a consequent c. A justification is applied if all members of its in-list are believed, but no member of its out-list. As for default logic, we introduce an operator $apply_{J,Y}$ which is monotonic and compact:

$$apply_{J,Y}(X) := \begin{array}{l} \{c \mid \langle in(I), out(O) \to c\rangle \in J, \\ \quad I \subseteq X \text{ and } O \cap Y = \emptyset\} \end{array} \quad (6)$$

Another property of $apply_{J,Y}$ is important for computing extensions, namely:

$$\text{if } X \subseteq Y \text{ then } apply_{J,X}(T) \supseteq apply_{J,Y}(T) \quad (7)$$

T is an extension of a justification network if T is the minimal set closed w.r.t. $apply_{J,T}$:

Definition 4 *Let $\nu = (N, J)$ be a justification network. T is an extension of ν iff $T = apply^*_{J,T}(\emptyset)$.*

Using the results of the section on operators, we find alternatives to definition 4. We split the set J of all justifications into a set M of monotonic justifications and a set NM of non-monotonic justifications. Monotonic justifications have an empty out-list and we write $apply_M(X)$ for $apply_{M,\emptyset}(X)$ which is equal to $apply_{M,T}(X)$ for all T. Then we obtain

$$apply_{J,T}(X) = apply_{NM,T}(X) \cup apply_M(X). \quad (8)$$

Lemma 4 *Let $\nu = (N, J)$ be a justification network, $M \subseteq J$ be a set of monotonic justifications and $NM := J - M$. The following sentences are equivalent:*

1. *T is an extension of ν, i.e. $T = apply^*_{J,T}(\emptyset)$.*
2. *$apply_{J,T}(T) \subseteq T$ and $\forall q \in T\ \exists q_1, \ldots, q_k : q = q_k$, and $q_i \in apply_{J,T}(\{q_1, \ldots, q_{i-1}\})$ for $i = 1, \cdots, k$.*
3. *$T = (apply^*_M \circ apply_{NM,T})^*(\emptyset)$.*

Property (2) agrees with usual definitions of extensions as closed and grounded sets (cf. [3], [13]). The third alternative allows a clear translation of AEL and DL to TMS. We map first-order derivations to monotonic justifications and defaults or modal formulas to non-monotonic justifications.

First-order derivations

We need to derive TMS justifications for the first-order operator $\lambda(X).Th(X \cup W)$. To limit the generated justifications, we use subsets of X which are in a domain U and we are interested in theorems contained in a range R. For default logic, we choose $U := C_D$ and $R := \mathcal{L}_D = P_D \cup E_D$.

To realize $Th((X \cap U) \cup W) \cap R$, we try to find all minimal proofs for elements of the range R. More precisely, we determine all minimal subsets Q of U inferring a $q \in R$ in conjunction with W (i.e. $Q \cup W \models q$ and $Q' \cup W \not\models q$ for every proper subset Q' of Q).[1] For this purpose, we apply a proof method that returns a goal q as well as the premises Q used to prove q; LR-resolution would work here. The proof is translated into a monotonic justification $\langle in(Q) \to q\rangle$. Let $M_W(U, R)$ be the set of all justifications obtained by this method:

$$M_W(U, R) := \begin{array}{l} \{\langle in(Q) \to q\rangle \mid Q \text{ is a minimal subset} \\ \quad \text{of } U \text{ s.t. } Q \cup W \models q \text{ for } q \in R\} \end{array} \quad (9)$$

in question and we get:

$$apply_{M_W(U,R)}(X) = Th((X \cap U) \cup W) \cap R \quad (10)$$

w.r.t. $apply_{M_W(U,R)}$. Hence we obtain the closure of $apply_{M_W(U,R)}$ if we add the input:

$$apply^*_{M_W(U,R)}(X) = X \cup (Th((X \cap U) \cup W) \cap R) \quad (11)$$

Here, we translated complete proofs into justifications. Other encodings of first-order derivations including intermediate steps are conceivable.

Finding all minimal proofs is not computable in general. Therefore, our approach works only when W is a decidable subset of $\mathcal{L}_0$ (e.g., clauses with a finite herbrand universe). However, the source of the non-semi-decidability of DL is the non-decidability of classical logic, not the infinite fixed points.

[1] In fact, it is not necessary to determine minimal subsets: we can use any subset that infers q. But the minimal subsets give the minimal sufficient set of justification rules.

Translating default theories to a TMS

We are now in a position to translate both the defaults and first-order part of a default theory into a TMS network. We translate each default $(a : b_1, \cdots, b_k/c)$ of D into a non-monotonic justification $\langle in(a), out(\neg b_1, \ldots, \neg b_k) \rightarrow c\rangle$. This justification is applied if and only if the default is applied. We put all these justifications into a set NM and get

$$apply_{NM,T}(X) = apply_{D,T}(X) \quad (12)$$

Furthermore, we supply enough monotonic justifications for first-order derivations. As pointed out in the previous section, we take $M := M_W(C_D, \mathcal{L}_D)$.

Definition 5 *Let $\Delta = (D, W)$ be a default theory. Its TMS-translation is $\nu_\Delta := (\mathcal{L}_D \cup C_D, NM \cup M)$ where $M := M_W(C_D, \mathcal{L}_D)$ and $NM := \{\langle in(a), out(\neg b_1, \ldots, \neg b_k) \rightarrow c\rangle \mid (a : b_1, \cdots, b_k/c) \in D\}$.*

Now we concatenate $apply^*_M$ and $apply_{NM,T}$ and relate them to Γ using equation 5:

$$\begin{aligned}&(apply^*_M \circ apply_{NM,T})^*(\emptyset) = \\ &\quad(\lambda(X).(X \cup (Th((X \cap C_D) \cup W) \cap \mathcal{L}_D)))\circ \quad (13)\\ &\quad apply_{D,T})^*(\emptyset)\end{aligned}$$

$$(apply^*_M \circ apply_{NM,T})^*(\emptyset) \cap \mathcal{L}_D = \Gamma(T) \cap \mathcal{L}_D \quad (14)$$

If T is an extension of ν_Δ then $T \cap \mathcal{L}_D = \Gamma(T) \cap \mathcal{L}_D = \Gamma(T \cap \mathcal{L}_D) \cap \mathcal{L}_D$ and $T \cap \mathcal{L}_D$ is an extension base of Δ. Conversely, if B is an extension base of Δ consider $T := (apply^*_M \circ apply_{NM,B})^*(\emptyset)$. Then $T \cap \mathcal{L}_D = \Gamma(B) \cap \mathcal{L}_D = B$ and $apply_{NM,T} = apply_{NM,T\cap\mathcal{L}_D} = apply_{NM,B}$, and T is an extension of Δ.

Theorem 5 *Let $\Delta = (D, W)$ be a default theory and ν_Δ its TMS-translation. There exists a bijective mapping of the set of extension bases of Δ to the set of extensions of ν_Δ.*

This is the main result. We discuss some examples.

1) If $D = \{(a : /a)\}$ and $W = \emptyset$ then the test domain $\mathcal{L}_D = \{a\}$ consists of a single element. There are no interesting first-order derivations, and the network consists simply of a single justification, $\langle in(a) \rightarrow a\rangle$. Its single extension is empty.

2) If $D = \{(: a/b)\}$ and $W = \{b \supset \neg a\}$ then the test domain $\mathcal{L}_D = \{\neg a\}$ again consists of a single element. There is one minimal first-order derivation from the domain $C_D = \{b\}$ to the range $\mathcal{L}_D$, namely $b \cup W \models \neg a$. The network consists of a two justifications ($\langle out(\neg a) \rightarrow b\rangle$ and $\langle in(b) \rightarrow \neg a\rangle$), and has no extensions because of the odd loop.

3) $D = \{(: \neg a/b), (: \neg b/a)\}$, $W = \{a \supset b\}$ is a more complex theory. Here, $\mathcal{L}_D = \{a, b\}$. There is one minimal first-order derivation, $a \cup W \models b$. The resulting justification network ($\langle out(a) \rightarrow b\rangle$, $\langle out(b) \rightarrow a\rangle$, and $\langle in(a) \rightarrow b\rangle$) has a single extension, $\{b\}$.

Thus, we have translated default theories into finite justification networks. Using this translation, we get a proper criterion for incoherence: if a theory has no extension then its TMS-translation contains an odd loop.

Our translation makes no special use of a contradiction node. Therefore, standard labeling routines are also sufficient to determine inconsistent extensions. However, a high price is paid because a lot of justifications are needed for this purpose. If a subset Q of the domain U is inconsistent then $\langle in(Q) \rightarrow q\rangle$ is included for every element q of our range R. If we handle inconsistent extensions separately we can reduce this effort and replace the set $\{\langle in(Q) \rightarrow q\rangle \mid q \in R\}$ by a single justification $\langle in(Q) \rightarrow \bot\rangle$. Consistent extensions of this modified network correspond to consistent extension bases of the theory.

Autoepistemic logic

We now turn to AEL. The results of the previous section carry over to strongly-grounded extensions of AEL theories, by first translating to DL, and then to a TMS. In this section we treat weakly-grounded extensions. The development is similar to that of the previous two sections. The only real difference is in the definition of extension for TMS networks: we must allow circular justifications for some nodes.

We discuss autoepistemic logic using the terminology and concepts in [8]. Hence, we have a first-order language $\mathcal{L}_0$ containing a contradiction formula $\bot$. Extending $\mathcal{L}_0$ by a modal operator L leads to a modal language $\mathcal{L}_{ael}$. If q is a closed formula of $\mathcal{L}_{ael}$ the modal literal Lq is also in $\mathcal{L}_{ael}$. We use some abbreviations from [8]. Two operators apply L and $\neg L$ to each element of a set; T_0 contains the ordinary formulas of T; and $\bar{T}$ is the complement of T:

$$\begin{aligned}LT &= \{Lq \mid q \in T\}\\ \neg LT &= \{\neg Lq \mid q \in T\}\\ T_0 &= T \cap \mathcal{L}_0\\ \bar{T} &= (\mathcal{L}_{ael} - T)\end{aligned}$$

We must be careful in using these terms: $\bar{T}_0$ means $(\mathcal{L}_{ael} - T) \cap \mathcal{L}_0$, but not $\mathcal{L}_{ael} - T_0$. There is a normal form for sentences of $\mathcal{L}_{ael}$, in which there are no nested modal operators. From now on we assume that every sentence is in this form.

From [8], the extensions of a premise set $P \subset \mathcal{L}_{ael}$ are given by:

Theorem 6 *(Konolige): A subset T of $\mathcal{L}_{ael}$ is an extension of P iff $T = \{q \in \mathcal{L}_{ael} \mid P \cup LT_0 \cup \neg L\bar{T}_0 \models_{K45} q\}$.*

$K45$ is the modal logic of weak $S5$. By this theorem, the original fixed point condition is reduced to ordinary sets. From this, we can show that a set $U \subseteq \mathcal{L}_0$ is the kernel of an extension of P if and only if it satisfies $U = \{q \in \mathcal{L}_0 \mid P \cup LU \cup \neg L\bar{U} \models q\}$, so the fixed-point condition is over first-order implication.

We now concentrate on the problem of reducing U in this fixed-point equation to a finite set. Define as a test domain:

$$\mathcal{L}_P := \{q \mid Lq \text{ occurs in a formula of } P\} \quad (15)$$

Since P is in normal form every Lq in P refers only to ordinary formulas q. Hence, $\mathcal{L}_P$ is a subset of $\mathcal{L}_0$. Furthermore, if P is finite $\mathcal{L}_P$ is also finite. We define Γ_P for a set Γ as $\Gamma_P := \Gamma \cap \mathcal{L}_P$. For subsets of the test domain we can derive a reduced fix-point form, the extension base:

Definition 6 *Let P be in normal form. A subset B of $\mathcal{L}_P$ is an extension base of P iff $B = \{q \in \mathcal{L}_P \mid P \cup LB_P \cup \neg L\bar{B}_P \models q\}$*

If T is an extension then T_P is an extension base. We also regain an extension from each extension base B: Consider $U = \{q \in \mathcal{L}_0 \mid P \cup LB_P \cup \neg L\bar{B}_P \models q\}$ which is fo-closed and satisfies $U_P = B_P$. Then $U = \{q \in \mathcal{L}_0 \mid P \cup LU_0 \cup \neg L\bar{U}_0 \models_{K45} q\}$ and U is the kernel of the extension $\{q \in \mathcal{L}_{ael} \mid P \cup LU_0 \cup \neg L\bar{U}_0 \models_{K45} q\}$.

Theorem 7 *Let P be in normal form. Then there is a bijective mapping of the set of extensions of P to the set of extension bases of P.*

As an example, consider $P = \{\neg La \supset b, \neg Lb \supset a\}$. Our test domain $\mathcal{L}_P = \{a, b\}$ has four subsets two of which are extension bases:

if $B = \emptyset$
  then $\{q \in \mathcal{L}_P \mid P \cup \{\neg La, \neg Lb\} \models q\} = \{a, b\} \neq B$
if $B = \{a\}$
  then $\{q \in \mathcal{L}_P \mid P \cup \{La, \neg Lb\} \models q\} = \{a\} = B$
if $B = \{b\}$
  then $\{q \in \mathcal{L}_P \mid P \cup \{\neg La, Lb\} \models q\} = \{b\} = B$
if $B = \{a, b\}$
  then $\{q \in \mathcal{L}_P \mid P \cup \{La, Lb\} \models q\} = \emptyset \neq B$

Finally, we briefly discuss inconsistent extension bases. Suppose a subset B of $\mathcal{L}_P$ satisfies $P \cup LB_P \cup \neg L\bar{B}_P \models \perp$. Since an inconsistency implies all formulas, B is an extension base if and only if $B = \mathcal{L}_P$. Hence, it is easy to find out whether P has an inconsistent extension: just check whether $P \cup L\mathcal{L}_P$ is inconsistent. In the sequel we consider just the consistent extensions of P.

The translation to a TMS is similar to that of DL theories. For every modal sentence $La \wedge \neg Lb_1 \cdots, \neg Lb_n \supset c$ of P, we supply a set of nonmonotonic justifications $\langle in(a), out(b_1, \cdots, b_n) \rightarrow c\rangle$. We also give a set of monotonic justifications over $\mathcal{L}_P$ taking consequents of modal sentences as input.

Definition 7 *Let P be a subset of $\mathcal{L}_{ael}$ in normal form. The TMS-translation of P is $\nu_P = (\mathcal{L}_P \cup C_P, M \cup NM)$ where $M := M_{P \cap \mathcal{L}_0}(C_P, \mathcal{L}_P)$, $NM := \{\langle in(a), out(b_1, \cdots, b_n) \rightarrow c\rangle \mid La \wedge \neg Lb_1 \cdots, \neg Lb_n \supset c \in P - \mathcal{L}_0\}$ and $C_P := \{c \mid La \wedge \neg Lb_1 \cdots \supset c \in P - \mathcal{L}_0\}$.*

Unlike in the strongly-grounded case, the translated TMS network does not behave in the same way as the extensions of P, because P may have expressions like $La \supset a$ that generate circular arguments. However, we must still avoid circular first-order proofs. So we modify the definition of extensions of the TMS. Let $\mathcal{L}_P^+ \subseteq \mathcal{L}_P$ be the set of ordinary sentences $\{a \mid La \wedge \neg Lb_1 \cdots \supset c \in P\}$, i.e., only the arguments of *negative* occurrences of modal atoms. Define a new monotonic, compact operator:

$$apply{+}_{J,Y}(X) := apply_M(X) \cup apply_{NM,Y}(X \cup (Y \cap \mathcal{L}_P^+)) \quad (16)$$

All the results for *apply* hold as well for *apply+*. We call consistent network labelings (those where $\perp$ is not believed) defined by the new operator +-extensions.

Theorem 8 *Let P be a subset of $\mathcal{L}_{ael}$ in normal form and ν_P its TMS-translation. Then there exists a bijective mapping of the set of consistent extension bases of P to the set of +-extensions of ν_P.*

We discuss some examples for autoepistemic logic:

1) If $P = \{La\}$ (that is, $\neg La \supset \perp$ in normal form) our test domain $\mathcal{L}_P = \{a\}$ consists of a single element, and $\mathcal{L}_P^+$ is empty. There are no interesting first-order proofs. The network contains one justification, $\langle out(a) \rightarrow \perp\rangle$, which leads to an inconsistency. It has no +-extension.

2) The premise set $P = \{\neg La\}$ (in normal form, $La \supset \perp$) is similar. However, we get $\mathcal{L}_P^+ = \{a\}$. There is one justification, $\langle in(a) \rightarrow \perp\rangle$, and one +-extension, $\{a\}$.

3) $P = \{\neg La \supset b, \neg Lb \supset a\}$ is a more complex theory. Here, $\mathcal{L}_P = \{a, b\}$, $\mathcal{L}_P^+ = \emptyset$. The resulting justification network ($\langle out(a) \rightarrow b\rangle$ and $\langle out(b) \rightarrow a\rangle$) contains an even loop and has two extensions $\{a\}$, $\{b\}$.

We get the same TMS network for weakly and strongly grounded extensions. The major difference between them is the inclusion of circular justifications in the definition of *apply+*. Moderately-grounded extensions have so far resisted analysis in terms of the *apply* operators, although we are still working on the problem.

Computing TMS-extensions

After translating autoepistemic and default theories into justification networks a single algorithm, with slight variations, is sufficient to compute both extensions and +-extensions. We use a complete variant of Doyle's TMS to compute all extensions of a justification network. It additionally introduces choice points and considers an OUT-label, as well as an IN-label for a node of every loop. This algorithm is also able to detect incoherence, i.e. non-existence of an extension. The algorithm is NP-complete, and we have alternatively been experimenting with stochastic constraint-satisfaction methods to achieve good average time complexity.

We use two disjoint sets, I and O, to denote all nodes that are labeled IN, or OUT, respectively. Above, we mentioned that nodes in a loop may have a chosen label which is unconfirmed and may fail in presence of odd loops. For this purpose, we introduce a third set U containing all unlabeled and unconfirmed nodes. For strongly grounded derivations, we may only use elements of $I - U$.

Similar to TMS, our algorithm uses two rules to determine an IN-label and an OUT-label of a node. The first rule looks for a justification whose in-list members have confirmed IN-labels and whose out-list members are labeled with OUT, i.e. are not contained in any solution. If there is such a justification its consequent gets a confirmed IN-label. The second rule checks whether there is still a justification which may be applied if further unlabeled nodes get an IN-label. If there is none the consequent gets a confirmed OUT-label. If the algorithm cannot proceed with propagation it chooses an arbitrary node contained in a loop and tries an IN-label, as well as an OUT-label. However, these labels may fail and therefore are unconfirmed. A failure occurs if a node is added to I and O. Finally, there is a termination rule. If the algorithm cannot find any justification whose in-list members have a confirmed IN-label then it stops and adds all remaining nodes to O. The precise algorithm is listed below:

Algorithm 1 $Ext_J(I,O,U) \equiv$

1. *if* $I \cap O \neq \emptyset$ *then* $\{\}$ *else*
2. *if* $U = \emptyset$ *then* $\{I\}$
3. *if* $U \neq \emptyset$ *then*
   (a) *if* $U \cap \text{apply}_{J,I}(I - U) = \emptyset$ *then* $Ext_J(I, O \cup U, \emptyset)$
   (b) *if* $\exists q \in U \cap \text{apply}_{J,N-O}(I - U)$ *then* $Ext_J(I \cup \{q\}, O, U - \{q\})$
   (c) *if* $\exists q \in U - \text{apply}_{J,I}(N - O)$ *then* $Ext_J(I, O \cup \{q\}, U - \{q\})$
   (d) *if* $\exists q \in U - (I \cup O)$ *then* $Ext_J(I, O \cup \{q\}, U) \cup Ext_J(I \cup \{q\}, O, U)$

The algorithm terminates if it is supplied with a finite set of nodes. Calling $Ext_J(\emptyset, \emptyset, N)$ results in the set of all extensions of $\nu = (N, J)$. A slight variation of the algorithm is sufficient to get +-extensions, too. Justification in *NM* may be applied to nodes in I even if their label is not confirmed. This change affects lines 3a and 3b.

Conclusion

We have developed a translation of AEL and DL to the finite constraint networks of the TMS. The advantage of doing so is that efficient constraint-satisfaction methods can be exploited in the TMS to produce the extensions of the logics. There are two areas in which we wish to develop further results. The first is in the translation process, which unfortunately is correct only for finite sets of defaults and a decidable base language. The extension to infinite sets of defaults seems attainable, but the base language complexity must remain a problem, because the TMS labelling is always decidable. Rather, we can view the TMS as an *approximation* to the original (undecidable) AEL or DL theory. The question then becomes, under what conditions are we certain to have added enough justifications to the TMS so that its extensions are extensions of the original theory?

The second area is the development of constraint-satisfaction methods for the TMS that allow the efficient computation of whether a node is in all extensions of the network or not. As mentioned above, we are currently interested in stochastic methods, in which the answer is approximate, but improves with time.

Acknowledgements

Ulrich Junker was supported by the West German Ministry for Research and Technology within project TASSO (Grant No. ITW8900A7); Kurt Konolige was supported by the Office of Naval Research Contract No. N00014-89-C-0095.

References

[1] Brewka, G., Nonmonotonic Reasoning: From Theoretical Foundation Towards Efficient Computation. Dissertation, University of Hamburg (1989)

[2] Doyle, J., A Truth Maintenance System. Artificial Intelligence 12 (1979)

[3] Doyle, J., The Ins and Outs of Reason Maintenance. Proc. IJCAI 83

[4] Etherington, D.W., Formalizing Nonmonotonic Reasoning Systems. Artificial Intelligence 31 (1987)

[5] Goodwin, J.W., A Theory and System for Non-Monotonic Reasoning. PhD Dissertation, University of Linköping 1987

[6] Junker, U., A Correct Non-Monotonic ATMS. Proc. IJCAI 89

[7] Kautz, H., Selman, B., Hard Problems for Simple Default Logics. Proc. KR'89

[8] Konolige, K., On the Relation between Default and Autoepistemic Logic. Artificial Intelligence 35 (1988)

[9] Levesque, H. J., All I Know: an Abridged Report. Proc. AAAI87.

[10] Niemelä, I., Decision Procedure for Autoepistemic Logic. Conference on Automated Deduction (1988)

[11] Moore, R.C., Semantical Considerations on Nonmonotonic Logic. Artificial Intelligence 25 (1985)

[12] Moore, R.C., Autoepistemic Logic, in: Smets, P.,Mamdani, E.H., Dubois, D., Prade, H. (eds), Non-Standard Logics for Automated Reasoning, Academic Press (1988)

[13] Reinfrank, M., Dressler, O., Brewka, G., On the Relation between Truth Maintenance and Autoepistemic Logic. Proc. IJCAI 89

[14] Reiter, R., A Logic for Default Reasoning. Artificial Intelligence 13 (1980)

Maintaining Consistency in a Stratified Production System Program

Louiqa Raschid
Department of Information Systems and
Institute for Advanced Computer Studies
University of Maryland
College Park, MD 20742
louiqa@secd.cs.umd.edu

Abstract

We present our research on defining a correct semantics for forward chaining production systems (PS) programs. A correct semantics ensures that the execution of the program will not produce incorrect answers and execution will terminate; it also ensures that the answers are consistent. We define a class of *stratified* PS programs, and propose an operational semantics for these programs. We define an operator T_{PS}, which computes the operational fixpoint for the productions of the stratified PS program; the fixpoint captures the meaning of the PS program. The theory that can be derived from the productions of the PS program may be inconsistent with the constraints that are also derived from the PS program. We can then view the constraints as modifying the theory so that the modified theory $\overline{PS}$ is consistent with the constraints. However, the same answers are obtained in the operational semantics of the stratified PS program or from the modified theory $\overline{PS}$.

1. Introduction

In recent years, much AI research and development has focused on forward chaining rule-based systems which follow the *production sytem* (PS) paradigm (Hayes-Roth 1985). Large production rule-based expert systems have been successfully developed in diverse domains such as engineering design databases, trouble-shooting in telephone networks, and configuring VAX computer systems.

This research was sponsored partially by the National Science Foundation under Grant DMC8814989 and by the University of Maryland Institute for Advanced Computer Studies.

The author would like to thank Timos Sellis, Anne Litcher and Arcot Rajasekar.

In these domains, the expert system programs often have to reason with large quantities of data. As the production rule base and the database grow larger, these programs have to access information stored on disk. Thus, for performance reasons, it is important that PS programs be implemented using database technology. Research in this area is reported in Delcambre and Etheredge 1988, Maindreville and Simon 1988, Raschid, Sellis and Lin 1988, Simon and Mandreville 1988, Sellis, Lin and Raschid 1988 and Widom and Finkelstein 1989.

If large production systems (PS) are to be implemented successfully to interface with large (relational) databases, then it is critical that the semantics of PS be well understood. Unfortunately, most PS have an incomplete operational semantics defined for them. This can result in non-terminating execution of productions and inconsistent answers.

In this paper, we describe our research on defining a *correct* semantics for PS programs. This paper is organized as follows: In section 2, we introduce the operational semantics of OPS5, an example of a PS (Forgy 1981 and Forgy 1982) and motivate this research using some example OPS5 programs. We also define how a logical theory can be derived from the productions of the PS program. In section 3, we define a class of *stratified* PS programs and define an operational semantics for stratified PS programs. A stratified PS program is a stratified program, and comprises an extensional database (EDB) of facts, a stratified intensional database (IDB) of rules, and a stratified set of integrity constraints (IC). Both rules and integrity constraints correspond to productions in the PS program. We show that processing is guaranteed to terminate upon reaching the operational fixpoint of a defined operator T_{PS}. The fixpoint captures the meaning of the PS program and is correct and consistent.

The theory of the PS program, comprising the EDB facts and the IDB rules that are derived from the productions, may be inconsistent with the integrity constraints (IC) that are also derived from the productions. We can view the IC as modifying the theory so that the modified stratified theory $\overline{PS}$ will be consistent with IC. This is described in section 4. We also show the equivalence between the answers obtained in the operational fixpoint and the minimal model for the theory $\overline{PS}$.

2. The OPS5 Production System

In this section we introduce the operational semantics defined for the OPS5 production system language and highlight some of its problems. We chose the OPS5 production system language (Forgy 1981 and Forgy 1982) as an example.

Operational Semantics of OPS5

An OPS5 knowledge base comprises a set of productions and an extensional database (EDB) of ground positive unit clauses which may be stored in relations. There will be one relation corresponding to each predicate.

An OPS5 production consists of (1) the symbol **p**, (2) the **name** of the production, (3) the **antecedent** or the left hand side (LHS), (4) the symbol →, and (5) the **consequent actions** or the right hand side (RHS), enclosed within parentheses.

The **antecedent** is a conjunction of first order positive literals of the form:
$\forall\, x_1, x_2,..\, x_n\ P(a_1, a_2,..a_m, x_1, x_2,..x_n)$
or negative literals of the form:
$\forall\, x_1, x_2,..\, x_n\ \neg Q(a_1, a_2,..a_m, x_1, x_2,..x_n)$. P and Q are (n+m)-ary predicates corresponding to the EDB relations, $a_1, a_2,...a_m$ are constants and $x_1, x_2,..x_n$ are variables. Assume that all variables are *range-restricted*, i.e., any variable that occurs in a literal must appear in a positive literal. The advantages of this restriction have been discussed in Sadri and Kowalski 1988 and correspond to the safety of evaluating queries.

The antecedent of each production is interpreted as a query against the EDB relations. For example, for each of the positive literals, $P(a_1, a_2,..a_m, x_1, x_2,..x_n)$, relation P is queried, and a set of *instantiated* tuples of P satisfying each positive literal in the antecedent is retrieved. For each of the negative literals, Q, the query corresponding to the first order formula, $\neg\, (\, \exists\, x_1, x_2,..x_n\ Q(a_1, a_2,..,a_m, x_1, x_2,..,x_n)\,)$, is verified against the relation Q. Note that since the variables are range-restricted, the queries corresponding to the negative literals can always be verified. The antecedent of a production is *satisfied* if the relations contain instantiated tuples corresponding to each of the positive literals and the relations do not contain tuples corresponding to the negative literals.

The *consequent actions* are of the form: (**make** $R(a_1, a_2,..,a_m,x_1, x_2,..,x_n)$) or (**remove** $P(a_1, a_2,..,a_m,x_1, x_2,..,x_n)$), where P and R are relations. Again, we assume that all variables $x_1, x_2, \ldots, x_n$ are range restricted. The interpretation of the **make** action is to insert the corresponding tuple into the R relation. Similarly, the **remove** action deletes the existing tuple from the P relation. This requires that the expression $P(a_1, a_2,..,a_m,x_1, x_2,..,x_n)$ that is referred to by the **remove** action must occur as a positive literal in the antecedent of that production.

We note that the OPS5 language has many additional features that are not described here; we have not considered the effect of such features in our research.

The operational semantics of an OPS5 program has been defined as follows: The initial state of the PS corresponds to an initial EDB, corresponding to all the tuples of the EDB relations, and a set of productions. Processing in a production system repeatedly cycles through the following sequence:

Match
For each production, the antecedent, interpreted as above, is queried against the tuples of the corresponding relations. Each production whose antecedent is satisfied, together with its *instantiated* tuples is placed in a *conflict set.*

Select
Select one satisfied production from the conflict set. If there is no such production, halt execution.

Act
For this selected production, execute the **make** or **remove** action, interpreted as above. As a result of the **Act** phase, the EDB relations are updated. Consequently, the next **Match** phase may produce a new conflict set.

There is no concept of a query that retrieves information, in a PS program. Processing will continue as long as productions are executed and the EDB relations are updated. Processing terminates when an operational fixpoint is reached, i.e., when there are no longer any productions that can update the EDB relations. This operational fixpoint (or the updated relations) corresponds to the meaning of the PS program.

Shortcomings of the Operational Semantics

The operational semantics for OPS5 are incompletely defined. Consequently, an initial EDB of relations and a set of productions can produce different answers. In some cases, an operational fixpoint is never reached.

Example 1

Consider a PS whose initial EDB has two tuples, {Employee(Mike). GoodWorker(Mike).}, and the following set of productions:

(p p_1 (Employee(X), GoodWorker(X)) → (**make** Manager(X)))
(p p_2 (Manager(X)) → (**make** HasOffice(X)))
(p p_3 (Employee(X), HasOffice(X)) → (**make** PoorWorker(X)))
(p p_4 (Manager(X), PoorWorker(X)) → (**remove** Manager(X)))

Given this initial EDB and corresponding set of productions, p_1, p_2 and p_3 will execute in that sequence and the tuples Manager(Mike), HasOffice(Mike) and PoorWorker(Mike) will be added to the corresponding EDB relations. Next, p_4 executes and the tuple Manager(Mike) will be deleted from the Manager relation. Subsequently, p_1 and p_4 will execute, first inserting the tuple Manager(Mike) and then deleting this tuple from the Manager relation. Processing of p_1 and p_4 will continue but an operational fixpoint is not reached.

Example 2

The initial EDB = {Employee(Mike).} and the productions are as follows:

(p p_1 (Employee(X)) → (**make** GoodWorker(X)))
(p p_2 (Employee(X), GoodWorker(X)) → (**make** Manager(X)))
(p p_3 (Employee(X), ¬ GoodWorker(X)) → (**make** PoorWorker(X)))

If productions execute in the sequence p_1 followed by p_2, then the final EDB will contain the set of tuples {Employee(Mike). GoodWorker(Mike). Manager(Mike).}. If the execution sequence were p_3 followed by p_1 and p_2, then, the final EDB would include the tuples, {Employee(Mike). GoodWorker(Mike). Manager(Mike). PoorWorker(Mike).}. Thus, in this case there are two fixpoints.

A Corresponding Logical Theory

In order to understand the shortcomings of the operational semantics, and to define a *correct semantics*, we define how a logical theory can be obtained from the productions in the PS program.

Definition

Every production that has a **make** action in its **consequent** corresponds to a rule of an intensional database (IDB).

For example, the following production:
(p p_1 (P(x), ¬ Q(x)) → (**make** R(x))) corresponds to the rule
P(x), ¬ Q(x) → R(x).

Every production that has a **remove** action in its consequent corresponds to an integrity constraint (IC). General forms of integrity constraints and their treatment are discussed in Kowalski and Sadri 1989; we delay a detailed discussion of constraints to a later section 4.

Definition

Every production that has **(remove P(x))** in the consequent is a constraint. The literal P(x) is retracted literal to restore consistency.

Thus, the following production:
(p p_2 (P(x), ¬ Q(x)) → (**remove** P(x)))
corresponds to the following IC:
P(x), ¬ Q(x) → .
P(x) is retracted to maintain consistency and the database must not prove
$\forall x\ P(x) \wedge \neg Q(x)$.

The meaning of treating some productions as integrity constraints will be discussed in section 4.

The following logical theory will be obtained, corresponding to the productions of Example 1:

EDB = { Employee(Mike). GoodWorker(Mike). }
IDB = {Employee(X), GoodWorker(X) → Manager(X).
Manager(X) → HasOffice(X) .
Employee(X), HasOffice(X) →PoorWorker(X).}
IC = {Manager(X), PoorWorker(X) → . }

We can see that the logical theory of the PS is inconsistent with the constraints. Thus, there can be no model for the theory which is also a model for the constraints (Lloyd 1987). In the case of Example 2, there is a negative literal in the antecedent of a rule. With Horn theories (including stratified theories), the modus ponens rule of inference is insufficient to prove negative information. To do so one uses the closed world rule of inference or the closed world assumption (CWA). The correct interpretation, based on the CWA, is that a tuple, $<a_1, a_2,... a_n>$ is not true if and only if the IDB ∪ EDB viewed as a logical theory cannot prove $P(a_1, a_2,... a_n)$. In our example, it is clear that the theory can prove GoodWorker(Mike), and ¬ GoodWorker(Mike) cannot be proved. Thus, the interpretation of negative literals in the operational semantics of OPS5 is incorrect.

3. Stratified Production Systems

We identify a class of stratified PS programs, and we define an operational semantics for these programs. Stratification is an extension of Horn programs to more general Horn programs that allow negative literals in the antecedent of a rule; recall that productions in OPS5 have the same feature. Our research draws upon existing research in stratified databases (Apt, Blair and Walker 1988).

The Operational Semantics

A stratified production system program is viewed as a stratified program, and comprises an extensional database (EDB) of facts, a stratified intensional database (IDB) of rules, and a stratified set of integrity constraints (IC). Both rules and integrity constraints correspond to productions in PS.

The initial PS program comprises the following:

(1) an intensional database of rules (IDB), where each rule corresponds to a production that has a **make** action as its consequent,

(2) a set of integrity constraints (IC), where each integrity constraint corresponds to a production that has a **remove** action as its consequent, and

(3) an initial extensional database of facts (EDB_0).

In the operational semantics, there must exist a partition so that PS is a stratified database. Thus,

$$PS = PS_0 \cup PS_2 \ldots \cup PS_n.$$

Each of the partitions PS_i comprises a set of rules IDB_i, and a set of integrity constraints IC_i, each of which may be possibly empty. Partition PS_0 comprises the initial extensional database EDB_0; IDB_0 and IC_0 are null. The following conditions hold for the stratification:

(1) $IDB = IDB_1 \cup \ldots \cup IDB_n$

(2) $IC = IC_1 \cup \ldots \cup IC_n$

(3) For every positive literal in the body of a rule in IDB_i, or in the body of an integrity constraint in IC_i, the definition of that literal must be contained within $\bigcup_{j \leq i} IDB_j$. The definition of a literal is all productions in which the literal occurs in the **make** action.

(4) For every positive literal in the body of a rule in IDB_i, or in the body of an integrity constraint in IC_i, all *other* integrity constraints where the literal occurs in the **remove** action must be contained within $\bigcup_{j < i} IC_j$.

(5) For every negative literal in a rule in IDB_i, or in an integrity constraint in IC_i, the definition of that literal must be contained within $\bigcup_{j < i} IDB_j$.

(6) For every negative literal in a rule in IDB_i, or in an integrity constraint in IC_i, all integrity constraints where the literal occurs in the **remove** action must be contained within $\bigcup_{j \leq i} IC_j$.

The Operator T_{PS}

Once such a partition has been obtained for the stratified PS program, then, for each partition PS_i, we define an operator T_{PS_i} as follows:

Definition

U_{PS} is a Herbrand universe for the stratified PS comprising predicates (**make** P), (**remove** P), where P ranges over all propositional variables in the PS.

If we consider a PS program where the propositional variables are the set {A, B, C}, then U_{PS} is the set of predicates {(**make A**), (**remove A**), (**make B**), (**remove B**),(**make C**), (**remove C**)}.

In the case of predicate variables, we will use relations to represent U_{PS}, two for each predicate symbol. Thus, for predicate P, relation makeP will contain all tuples P(.,.,...) which are added by some action (**make** P(.,.,...)) and relation removeP will contain all tuples P(.,.,...) which are removed by some action (**remove** P(.,.,...)).

Definition

For each proposition P (or ground positive literal P(.,.,...)), in EDB_0, we replace it with (**make** P), (or we add the tuple P(.,.,...) to the relation makeP).

Definition

The interpretation of the predicates of U_{PS} (for the propositional variable P), is defined as follows:

(1) (**make** P) $\wedge \neg$ (**remove** P) $\models$ P

(2) (**make** P) $\wedge$ (**remove** P) $\models \neg$ P

(3) $\neg$ (**make** P) $\wedge \neg$ (**remove** P) $\models \neg$ P

(4) $\neg$ (**make** P) $\wedge$ (**remove** P) is not allowed in the operational semantics and represents an inconsistency.

Definition

T_{PS_i} is a mapping from a subset of U_{PS} to U_{PS}, such that for any rule in IDB_i or any integrity constraint in IC_i, if there exists an interpretation of EDB_{i-1}, as described above, such that the literals in the antecedent of the corresponding production are true, then, the operator adds the **action** in the head of the production to EDB_i.

Each EDBi is computed as follows:

$$EDB_1 = EDB_0 \cup T_{PS_1} \uparrow \omega \ (EDB_0)$$
$$EDB_2 = EDB_1 \cup T_{PS_2} \uparrow \omega \ (EDB_1)$$

$$EDB_n = EDB_{n-1} \cup T_{PS_n} \uparrow \omega \ (EDB_{n-1})$$

Obtaining an Operational Fixpoint for T_{PS_i}

Processing for each partition PS_i should terminate when an operational fixpoint is reached, i.e., when there are no longer any satisfied productions that can update EDB_i. Processing for PS terminates when the operational fixpoint for PS_n is reached and EDB_n is computed.

Theorem

$T_{PS_i} \uparrow \omega \ (EDB_{i-1})$ is a fixpoint for $PS_i = IDB_i \cup IC_i$.

We refer the reader to (Rasc89) for the proof.

Example 3

Consider a PS whose initial EDB has two tuples, {Employee(Mike). GoodWorker(Mike).}, and the following set of productions:

(p p_1 (Employee(X), GoodWorker(X)) →
(**make** Manager(X)))
(p p_2 (Employee(X)) → (**make** HasOffice(X)))
(p p_3 (PoorWorker(X), HasOffice(X)) →
(**remove** HasOffice(X)))
(p p_4 (Employee(X), HasOffice(X)) →
(**make** Manager(X)))

The stratification conditions will place productions p_3 in a higher stratum, say PS_2, while the other three productions are placed in PS_1. The operational fixpoint EDB_1 is as follows: {makeEmployee(Mike). makePoorWorker(Mike). makeHasOffice(Mike). removeHasOffice(Mike).} EDB_1 is interpreted to prove $\neg$ HasOffice(Mike) and Manager(Mike) will not be an answer.

4. Maintaining Consistency with Integrity Constraints

We now try to understand the meaning of maintaining consistency with respect to integrity constraints in a stratified PS program. Informally, a database must satisfy its integrity constraints as it changes over time. Usually, an update to the database (more precisely an update to facts in the EDB) may cause the violation of an integrity constraint; such updates are rejected or modified. Sometimes, the database itself, i.e., the facts and the rules may be inconsistent with the constraints and must be modified, to maintain consistency. In Kowalski and Sadri 1989, such a method is presented for transforming a theory which is inconsistent with respect to a set of integrity constraints into a transformed theory which is consistent with the constraints. The transformation is syntactic. Although the transformation works for more general constraints, we restrict the discussion to *denial* constraints of the form
A(t), Conj→.
where Conj is a conjunction of positive or negative literals (and may be empty). The denial, or the body of the constraint, should not be true in the database. The atom A is the *retractable* atom that restores consistency, if the constraint is violated.

Thus, if we consider the theory {C. C → A} and the constraint A, ¬B →, where the retractable atom is A, then, the theory is inconsistent with the constraint. However, the transformed theory {C. C, B →A} is consistent with the constraint.

If we apply a similar transformation to the theory obtained from the productions of Example 3, we obtain the following consistent theory:
EDB = {Employee(Mike). GoodWorker(Mike). }
IDB={Employee(X), GoodWorker(X)→Manager(X).
Employee(X) ¬PoorWorker(X)→ HasOffice(X).
Employee(X), HasOffice(X) → Manager(X).}

We see that this theory will not prove Manager(Mike), just as in the operational semantics. In general, we can prove that if the PS program is stratifiable as defined, then the following hold: (1) the logical theory derived from the stratified PS program, modified to be consistent with the constraints (also derived from the program), is a stratified theory. (2) the operational fixpoint of the stratified PS program is identical to the model for the modified consistent theory that is derived from the program.

5. Summary

A class of stratified PS programs and an operational semantics for these programs have been defined. The theory derived from the productions is modified so that it forms a consistent theory, $\overline{PS}$, with the integrity constraints that are also derived from the productions. The operational fixpoint of PS is identical to the model for $\overline{PS}$. A formal presentation of this research is in Raschid 1989. Future research includes extending the semantics of PS programs to include PS programs that exhibit non-deterministic behaviour when executing productions.

6. References

Apt, K.R., Blair, H.A. and Walker, A. 1988. Towards a Theory of Declarative Knowledge. In (Minker 1988).

Delcambre, L.M.L. and Etheredge, J.N. 1988. A Self-Controlling Interpreter for the Relational Production Language. In Proceedings of the ACM Sigmod International Conference on the Management of Data.

Forgy, C.L. 1981. OPS5 User's Manual, Technical Report CMU-CS-81-135, Carnegie-Mellon University.

Forgy, C.L. 1982. Rete: A Fast Algorithm for the Many Pattern/Many Object Pattern Match Problem. *Artificial Intelligence* (19).

Hayes-Roth, F. 1985. Rule Based Systems. *Communications of the ACM* (28) 9.

Kowalski, R. and Sadri, F. 1989. Knowledge Representation without Integrity Constraints. Technical Report, Imperial College, London, England.

Lloyd, J.W. 1987. *Foundations of Logic Programming*, Second, Extended Edition. Springer Verlag.

Maindreville, C. de and Simon, E. 1988. A Production Rule Based Approach to Deductive Databases. In Proceedings of the Fourth International Conference on Data Engineering.

Minker. J., ed. 1988. *Foundations of Deductive Databases and Logic Programming.* Morgan Kaufmann Publishers, Inc.

Raschid, L. 1989. Defining a Semantics for Production Systems based on Stratified Databases and Integrity Constraints, Technical Report 89-103, University of Maryland.

Raschid, L., Sellis, T. and Lin, C-C. 1988. Exploiting Concurrency in a DBMS Implementation for Production Systems. In Proceedings of the International Symposium on Databases in Parallel and Distributed Systems.

Sadri, F. and Kowalski, R. 1988. A Theorem-Proving Approach to Database Integrity. In (Minker 1988).

Sellis, T., Lin, C-C. and Raschid, L. 1988. Implementing Large Production Systems in a DBMS Environment: Concepts and Algorithms. In Proceedings of the ACM Sigmod International Conference on the Management of Data.

Simon, E. and Maindreville, C. de, 1988. Deciding Whether a Production Rule is Relational Computable. In IProceedings of the International Conference on Database Theory.

Widom, J. and Finkelstein, S.J. 1989. A Syntax and Semantics for Set-Oriented Production Rules in Relational Database Systems, IBM Research Report, IBM Almaden Research Center.

Cognitive Modeling

Integrating Planning and Acting in a Case-Based Framework.*

Kristian Hammond **Timothy Converse** **Charles Martin**

The University of Chicago
Department of Computer Science
Artificial Intelligence Laboratory
1100 East 58th Street
Chicago, IL 60637
ai@tartarus.uchicago.edu

Abstract

This paper presents an outline of a theory of *agency* that seeks to integrate ongoing understanding, planning and activity into a single model of representation and processing. Our model of *agency* rises out of three basic pieces of work: Schank's structural model of memory organization (Schank, 1982), Hammond's work in case-based planning and dependency directed repair (Hammond, 1989d), and Martin's work in Direct Memory Access Parsing (Martin 1990). We see this paper as a first step in the production of a memory-based theory of *agency*: the active pursuit of goals in the face of a changing environment, that can exist within the computational constraints of a computer model.

Planning as Understanding

Research in planning has recently made a dramatic change in course. Planning researchers have begun to acknowledge that the world is too complex and uncertain to allow a planner to plan exhaustively for a set of goals prior to execution (Chapman, 1985). More and more, the study of planning is being cast as the broader study of planning, action and understanding (Agre and Chapman, 1987, and Alterman, 1986).

The particular cast of this relationship that we have been studying is a view of planning as embedded within an understanding system connected to the environment. The power of this approach lies in the fact that it allows us to view the planner's environment, plan selections, decisions, conflicts and actions through the single eye of situation assessment and response. Because of our further commitment to the use of episodic memory as the vehicle for understanding, it also provides us with a powerful lever on the problem of learning from both planning and execution. In this paper, we draw an outline of *agency*, our model of the relationship between planning and action.

*This work was supported in part by the Defense Advanced Research Projects Agency, monitored by the Air Force Office of Scientific Research under contract F49620-88-C-0058, and the Office of Naval Research under contract N0014-85-K-010.

Memory and Agency

Our model of planning and understanding rises out of three pieces of work: Schank's structural model of memory organization (Schank, 1982), our own work in case-based planning and dependency directed repair (Hammond, 1986), and the work of Martin and Riesbeck in Direct Memory Access Parsing (Martin 1989). Our model has been articulated in two programs, TRUCKER and RUNNER (Hammond, Converse, and Marks, 1988 and Hammond, 1989).

The model was first developed to deal with the problem of recognizing execution-time opportunities in the context of a resource-bound agent that is forced to suspend planning in order to attend to execution (Hammond, 1989). The goal of this model was to capture the ability of an agent to suspend goals, yet still recognize execution-time opportunities to satisfy them.

To accomplish this goal, we use a single set of memory structures both to store suspended goals and to understand the agent's circumstances in the world. In response to a blocked goal, an agent's first step is to do a planning-time analysis of the conditions that would favor the satisfaction of the goal. The agent then *suspends* the goal in memory, indexed by a description of those conditions. For example, a goal to buy eggs that was blocked during planning would be placed in memory associated with the condition of the agent being at a grocery store.

During execution, the agent performs an ongoing "parse" of the world in order to recognize conditions for action execution. Following DMAP (Martin, 1989), this parse takes the form of passing markers through an existing episodic memory. Because suspended goals are indexed in the memory used for understanding the world, the goals are activated when the conditions favoring their execution are recognized. Once active, the goals are then reevaluated in terms of the new conditions. Either they fit into the current flow of execution or they are again suspended.

We called the initial model *opportunistic memory* because the agent's recognition of opportunities depends on the nature of its episodic memory structures. Having turned to the broader issues of integrating planning and action, we now refer to our work as the study of *agency*.

Initial Results

Our initial implementation of opportunistic memory, TRUCKER, exhibited exactly the behavior we wanted. A combined scheduling planner and executive, TRUCKER was able to suspend blocked goals and then recognize later opportunities to satisfy them. It also learned plans for goal combinations that it determined would occur again. The recognition of opportunity and the resulting learning of specific optimizations rose naturally out of the agent's ongoing understanding of its environment.

Our model of planning is case-based. Both of our planners, TRUCKER and RUNNER, plan by recalling existing plans that are indexed by a set of currently active goals. Our initial model of this indexing (Hammond, 1986) was based on the notion that a planner could amortize its planning efforts by caching plans in memory under descriptions of the goals that they satisfied and the problems (in the sense of interactions between steps of a plan) that they avoided. In TRUCKER, we worked on the idea that this method of indexing could itself be cast as a problem of characterizing the situations in the world under which a plan could be run. Retrieval then became a process of recognition, similar to that used in the understanding of the world. The result of this was that plans were cached in the same memory organization used to suspend blocked goals and to understand the changing states of the world.

In TRUCKER, and later in RUNNER, we tried to address the specific problem of recognizing execution-time opportunities. In the process, however, we actually built a general mechanism to control planning and action. That is, to achieve the desired execution-time opportunism, we had to build a general model of planning and action based on embedding the knowledge of plans and goals, as well as the control of action itself, in a memory-based understanding system.

A Model of Agency

We use the term *agency* to comprise the spawning of goals, selection of plans, and execution of actions. Our process model of agency is based on Martin's DMAP understander as well as its antecedent, Schank's *Dynamic Memory*. DMAP uses a memory organization defined by part/whole and abstraction relationships. Activations from environmentally supplied features are passed up through abstraction links and predictions are passed down through the parts of partially active concepts. Subject to some constraints, when a concept has only some of its parts active, it sends predictions down its other parts. When activations meet existing predictions, the node on which they meet becomes active. Finally, when all of the parts of a concept are activated, the concept itself is activated.

Direct Memory Access Processing

The DMAP architecture provides a computational mechanism for specifying and applying domain-dependent information to a general memory search process. Concepts are represented in the abstraction and packaging hierarchies familiar to artificial intelligence researchers. This hierarchy is not only a store of content, but also provides the structure for the indexing and application of process knowledge.

Operational features

In general terms, we can associate *operational* features of the world with the memory structures to which they refer. In language understanding, such features may include words or phrases; for planning, they may comprise detectable states of the world. We call these features *operational* because they can be derived from the input with little reliance on the use of memory. In general, an operational feature cannot be a necessary or sufficient condition for recognizing any particular memory structure.

For example, the RUNNER project (Hammond, 1989) associates "being near the coffee pot" and "the coffee pot is empty" with the FILL-POT action of the MAKE-COFFEE plan. These two conditions are presumed to be easily detectable features of the environment, relying on the planner's location and a capacity for object identification. These features are in no sense equivalent to the FILL-POT action but they are *operational* in that they serve to recognize the applicability of that action to the achievement of the MAKE-COFFEE plan.

Memory search strategies

Operational features are the primitive elements out of which memory search strategies are composed. A search strategy is the specification *relative to a memory structure* of how concepts in memory may become active. In general, a search strategy specifies other memory structures and features along with some ordering information to direct the search. Because memory search involves recognizing a sequence of concepts, we call these search strategies *concept sequences.*

For example, in language analysis, the original domain of the DMAP work, two simple concept sequences associated with the memory structure for the communication event MTRANS are the following.

> { ⟨*actor*⟩ "says" ⟨*info*⟩ }, representing that an MTRANS concept can be recognized as a result of recognizing, in sequence, a concept filling *actor* role of the MTRANS, the lexical item "says" (an operation feature for a language analyzer), and a concept filling the *info* role of the MTRANS.

> { "I" } → ⟨*actor*⟩, representing that the *actor* of an MTRANS concept can be recognized as a result of recognizing the referring lexical item "I".

The organization of memory

Because DMAP associates search strategies with specific concepts in memory, those concepts serve as the points of organization for expectations generated by the system. For example, RUNNER places expectations for the FILL-POT action on the *memory structures* for "being near the coffee pot" and "the coffee pot is empty".

Because these memory structures *already exist* in the system and serve as the organizing point for these expectations, the memory itself provides the medium for disambiguating which expectations are relevant in any situation. Expectations from existing memory structures prime other existing memory structures. Activation of an existing memory structure allows the system to focus on those and only those expectations that primed that particular memory structure.

Accomodating action

To accommodate action, we have added the notion of PERMISSIONS. PERMISSIONS are handed down the parts of plans to their actions. The only actions that can be executed are those that are PERMITTED by the activation of existing plans. Following McDermott (McDermott, 1978), we have also added POLICIES. POLICIES are statements of ongoing goals of the agent. Sometimes these take the form of maintenance goals, such as "Glasses should be in the cupboard." or "Always have money on hand." The only goals that are actively pursued are those generated out of the interaction between POLICIES and environmental features. We would argue that this is, in fact, the only way in which goals can be generated.

Most of the processing takes the form of recognizing circumstances in the external world as well as the policies, goals and plans of the agent. The recognition is then translated into action through the mediation of PERMISSIONS that are passed to physical as well as mental actions.

Goals, plans, and actions interact as follows:

- Features in the environment interact with POLICIES to spawn goals.

  For example, in RUNNER, the specific goal to HAVE COFFEE is generated when the system recognizes that it is morning. The goal itself rises out of the recognition of this state of affairs in combination with the fact that there is a policy in place to have coffee at certain times of the day.

- Goals and environmental features combine to activate plans already in memory.

  Any new MAKE-COFFEE plan is simply the activation of the sequence of actions associated with the existing MAKE-COFFEE plan in memory. It is recalled by RUNNER when the HAVE-COFFEE goal is active and the system recognizes that it is at home.

- Actions are **permitted** by plans and are associated with the descriptions of the world states appropriate to their performance. Once a set of features has an action associated with it, that set of features (in conjunct rather than as individual elements) is now predicted and can be recognized.

  Filling the coffee pot is **permitted** when the MAKE-COFFEE plan is active; it is associated with the features of the pot being in view and empty. This means not only that the features are now predicted but also that their recognition will trigger the action.

- Actions are specialized by features in the environment and by internal states of the system. As with Firby's RAPs (Firby, 1989), particular states of the world determine particular methods for each general action.

  For example, the specifics of a GRASP would be determined by information taken from the world about the size, shape and location of the object being grasped.

- Action level conflicts are recognized and mediated using the same mechanism that recognizes information about the current state of the world.

  For example, when two actions are active (such as filling the pot and filling the filter), a mediation action selects one of them. During the initial phases of learning a plan, this can in turn be translated into a specialized recognition rule which, in the face of a conflict, will always determine the ordering of the specific actions.

- Finally, suspended goals are associated with the descriptions of the states of the world that are amenable to their satisfaction.

  For example, the goal HAVE-ORANGE-JUICE, if blocked, can be placed in memory, associated with the conjunct of features that will allow its satisfaction, such as being at a store, having money and so forth. Once put into memory, this conjunct of features becomes one of the set that can now be recognized by the agent.

The Study of Agency

We do not see this model as a solution to the problems of planning and action. Instead, we see this as a framework in which to discuss exactly what an agent needs to know in a changing world. Advantages of this framework include:

1. A unified representation of goals, plans, actions and conflict resolution strategies.
2. Ability to learn through specialization of general techniques.
3. A fully declarative representation that allows for meta-reasoning about the planner's own knowledge base.
4. A simple marker-passing scheme for recognition that is domain — and task — neutral.

5. Provision for the flexible execution of plans in the face of a changing environment.

The basic metaphors of action as permission and recognition, and planning as the construction of descriptions that an agent must recognize prior to action, these fit our intuitions about agency. Under this metaphor, we can view research into agency as the exploration of the situations in the world that are valuable for an agent to recognize and respond to. In particular, we have examined and continue to explore content theories of:

- The conflicts between actions that rise out of resource and time restrictions as well as direct state conflicts and the strategies for resolving them.
- The types of physical failures that block execution and their repairs.
- The types of knowledge-state problems that block planning and their repairs.
- The circumstances that actually give rise to goals in the presence of existing policies.
- The possible ways in which existing plans can be merged into single sequences and the circumstances under which they can be applied.
- The types of reasoning errors that an agent can make and their repairs.
- The trade-offs that an agent has to make in dealing with its own limits.
- The different ways in which a goal can be blocked and the resulting locations in memory where it should be placed.

Our goal is a content theory of agency. The architecture we suggest is simply the vessel for that content.

RUNNER

Most of our activity in studying this architecture has been within the context of the RUNNER system. The RUNNER project is aimed at modeling the full spectrum of activity associated with an agent—goal generation, plan activation and modification, action execution, and resolution of plan and goal conflict—not just the more traditional aspect of plan generation alone.

RUNNER's world

The agent in RUNNER currently resides in a simulated kitchen, and is concerned with the pursuit of such goals as simulated breakfast and coffee. Such commonplace goals and tasks interest us in part because they are repetitive and have many mutual interactions, both negative and positive. We are interested in how plans for recurring conjuncts of goals may be learned and refined, as part of view of domain expertise as knowledge of highly specific and well-tuned plans for the particular goal conjuncts that tend to co-occur in the domain (Hammond, Converse, and Marks, 1988). We are also interested in the issue of exactly how these plans can be used in the guidance of action.

RUNNER's Representation

The knowledge and memory of the agent is captured in the conjunction of three types of semantic nets, representing knowledge of goals, plans and states. Nodes in these networks are linked by abstraction and packaging links, as in DMAP. In addition, we propose an additional SUSPEND link, which connects suspended goals to state descriptions that may indicate opportunities for their satisfaction. For example, the goal to have eggs would be suspended in association with the description of the agent being at a grocery store. In addition to being passed to abstractions of activated concepts, activation markers are always passed along SUSPEND links.

In general, the only other way in which these nets are interconnected is via *concept sequences.* A node may be activated if all of the nodes in one of its concept sequences is activated – a concept sequence for a given node can contain nodes from any of the parts of memory. The following is a partial taxonomy of the types of concept sequences we currently allow:

- Activation of a goal node can activate a node representing a default plan.
- Activation of a plan node and some set of state nodes can activate a further specialization of the plan.
- Activation of a goal node and some set of state nodes can activate a further specialization of the goal.
- Activation of any state node that has a SUSPEND link will activate the associated goal.

An Example: Making Coffee

The above discussion of representation may make more sense in the context of an example, currently implemented in RUNNER, of how a particular action is suggested due to conjunction of plan activation and environmental input.

One of the objects in RUNNER's simulated kitchen is a coffeemaker, and one of the plans it has available is that of making coffee with this machine. This plan involves a number of subsidiary steps, some of which need not be ordered with respect to each other. Among the steps that are explicitly represented in the plan are: fetching unground beans from the refrigerator, putting the beans in the grinder, grinding the beans, moving a filter from a box of filters to the coffeemaker, filling the coffeemaker with water from the faucet, moving the ground beans from the grinder to the coffeemaker, and turning the coffeemaker on.

The subplans of the coffee plan are associated with that plan via packaging links. In this implemented example, the agent starts out with a node activated which represents knowledge that it is morning. This in turn is sufficient to activate the goal to have coffee (this is as close as the program comes to a theory of addiction). This goal in turn activates a generic plan to have coffee. This turns out to be nothing but an abstraction of several plans to acquire coffee, only one of which is the plan relevant to our kitchen:

```
Sending initial activations to memory
sending activation marker to [morning]
Activating concept: [morning]
concept sequence ([morning])
for node [GOAL: drink-coffee] is completed.
sending activation marker to
   [GOAL: drink-coffee]
Activating concept: [GOAL: drink-coffee]
Asserting new goal: [GOAL: drink-coffee]
sending activation marker to
   [PLAN: coffee-plan]
Node [PLAN: coffee-plan] has both permission
and activation:
   ((MARKER [GOAL: drink-coffee]))
    (TOP-LEVEL-PLAN)
Activating concept: [PLAN: coffee-plan]
Asserting new plan: [PLAN: coffee-plan]
Plan has no steps -- insufficiently specific
```

"Visual" input, in terms of atomic descriptions of recognizable objects and their proximities, is passed to memory. For example, the agent "sees" the following visual types:

`countertop, white wall, box of filters`

Among sets of possible visually recognized objects are concept sequences sufficient for recognition that the agent is in the kitchen. The recognition of the white wall and the countertop completes one of these sequences. The "kitchen" node in turn passes activation markers to its abstractions, activating the node corresponding to the agent being at home:

```
------------------------------------------------
Straight ahead I see:
 a countertop, up close;
 a countertop, fairly close;
 a green square filter-box, up close;
 a countertop, fairly close;
 a countertop, far away;
 a white wall, far away;
 a countertop, fairly close;
 a countertop, far away;
 a white wall, far away
To the left is a countertop, up close
To the right, there's a countertop, up close
Straight ahead, there's a countertop, up close
------------------------------------------------
MEMORY:
Active plans: coffee-plan
sending activation marker to [wall]
Activating concept: [wall]
sending activation marker to [filter-box]
Activating concept: [filter-box]
sending activation marker to [countertop]
Activating concept: [countertop]
concept sequence ([wall] [countertop])
for node [in-kitchen] is completed.
sending activation marker to [in-kitchen]
Activating concept: [in-kitchen]
sending activation marker to [at-home]
Activating concept: [at-home]
```

The activation of this node in conjunction with the activation of the generic coffee goal completes the concept sequence necessary for the goal for making coffee at home, which in turn activates the default plan for that goal. In this way a specialized plan is chosen in response to a conjunction of a recognized state and a more generic goal:

```
MEMORY:
concept sequence
    ([GOAL: drink-coffee] [at-home])
for node
     [GOAL: drink-coffee-at-home] is completed.
sending activation marker to
     [GOAL: drink-coffee-at-home]
Activating concept:
     [GOAL: drink-coffee-at-home]
Asserting new goal:
     [GOAL: drink-coffee-at-home]
sending activation marker to
     [PLAN: make-coffee-at-home]
Node [PLAN: make-coffee-at-home]
has both permission and activation:
     ((MARKER [GOAL: drink-coffee-at-home]))
     (TOP-LEVEL-PLAN)
Activating concept:
     [PLAN: make-coffee-at-home]
```

The activation of the coffee-plan causes permission markers to be sent down packaging links to the nodes representing the parts of the plan. The activation of the other object concepts from the "visual" input in turn have sent activation markers to the actions that contain them in their concept sequences. Among these is the plan step for taking a filter from the box and installing it in the coffeemaker, which is activated by seeing box of filters itself. In this way a sub-plan is suggested by the intersection of permission from its parent plan and cues from the environment that indicate that it is easily satisfiable:

```
Asserting new plan:
     [PLAN: make-coffee-at-home]
Sending permissions to steps of plan
Sending permission markers from
     [PLAN: make-coffee-at-home]
to steps
     FILL-CARAFE
     PUT-BEANS-IN-GRINDER
     MOVE-GROUNDS-TO-COFFEE-MAKER
     TURN-ON-COFFEE-MAKER
     GRIND-BEANS
     PUT-IN-FILTER
     GET-COFFEE-BEANS
concept sequence
     ([filter-box]
      [PLAN: make-coffee-at-home])
for node [PLAN: put-in-filter] is completed.
sending activation marker to
     [PLAN: put-in-filter]
Node [PLAN: put-in-filter]
has both permission and activation:
     ((MARKER ([filter-box]
               [PLAN: make-coffee-at-home])))
```

```
     ((MARKER [PLAN: make-coffee-at-home]))
Activating concept:
     [PLAN: put-in-filter]
Asserting new plan: [PLAN: put-in-filter]
Sending permissions to steps of plan
Sending permission markers from
     [PLAN: put-in-filter]
to steps
     PUT-FILTER-IN-COFFEEMAKER
     GET-FILTER
concept sequence
     ([filter-box]
      [PLAN: put-in-filter])
for node [PLAN: get-filter] is completed.
sending activation marker to
     [PLAN: get-filter]
Node [PLAN: get-filter]
has both permission and activation:
     ((MARKER ([filter-box]
               [PLAN: put-in-filter])))
     ((MARKER [PLAN: put-in-filter]))
Activating concept: [PLAN: get-filter]
```

After another level of passing permission markers to sub-plans, the process "bottoms out" in the suggestion of the primitive action of picking up the box of filters. With no suggestions to the contrary, the action is taken:

```
Asserting new plan:
     [PLAN: get-filter]
Sending permissions to steps of plan
Sending permission markers from
     [PLAN: get-filter]
to steps
      TAKE-OUT-FILTER
      PICK-UP-BOX
      LOOK-FOR-FILTER-BOX
concept sequence
     ([filter-box] [PLAN: get-filter])
for node [PLAN: pick-up-box] is completed.
sending activation marker to
     [PLAN: pick-up-box]
Node [PLAN: pick-up-box]
has both permission and activation:
     ((MARKER ([filter-box] [PLAN: get-filter])))
     ((MARKER [PLAN: get-filter]))
Activating concept: [PLAN: pick-up-box]
Suggesting action: (GRASP 'FILTER-BOX)
----------------------------------------------
ACTION:
Performing action: (GRASP 'FILTER-BOX)
----------------------------------------------
To the left is a countertop, up close
To the right, there's a countertop, up close
Straight ahead, there's a countertop, up close
Result of action: I'm holding on to a filter-box
----------------------------------------------
```

The final action is chosen both on the basis of active plans and goals, and in response to the immediate circumstances in which the agent finds itself. Given a change in either the top-down guidance or the bottom-up recognition, the selection of plan and action will change in response.

Conclusion

We've presented a sketch of an architecture for memory that we believe will be of use in exploring various issues of opportunism and flexible plan use. We do not view the architecture as a solution to the problems of interest, but instead as a framework that may be useful in exploring content theories of plan types, action suggestion and arbitration. As we said before, our goal is a content theory of agency. The architecture we suggest is simply the vessel for that content.

Acknowledgements

This work is the first stage of a collaborative effect at the University of Chicago. As such this paper owes much to Christopher Owens and Phil Agre as well as to Mitchell Marks and the others students at the University of Chicago's Artificial Intelligence Laboratory.

References

Phil Agre and David Chapman. Pengi: An implementation of a theory of activity. In *Proceedings of the Sixth Annual Conference on Artificial Intelligence*, pages 268–72. AAAI, 1987.

L. Birnbaum and G. Collins. Opportunistic planning and freudian slips. In *Proceedings of the Sixth Annual Conference of the Cognitive Science Society*, Boulder, CO, 1984.

David Chapman. Nonlinear planning: A rigorous reconstruction. In *Proceedings of the Ninth International Joint Conference on Artificial Intelligence*, pages 1022–24. IJCAI, 1985.

R. J. Firby. Adaptive execution in complex dynamic worlds. Research Report 672, Yale University Computer Science Department, 1989.

Kristian J. Hammond. *Case-Based Planning: Viewing Planning as a Memory Task*, volume 1 of *Perspectives in Artificial Intelligence.* Academic Press, 1989.

Kristian J. Hammond. Opportunistic memory. In *Proceedings of the Eleventh International Joint Conference on Artificial Intelligence.* IJCAI, 1989.

Kristian J. Hammond. Explaining and repairing plans that fail. *Artifical Intelligence Journal*, In Press.

Kristian J. Hammond, Tim Converse, and Mitchell Marks. Learning from opportunities: Storing and reusing execution-time optimizations. In *AAAI 1988*, pages 536–40. AAAI, 1988.

Charles E. Martin. *Direct Memory Access Parsing.* PhD thesis, Yale University Department of Computer Science, 1989.

D. McDermott. Planning and acting. *Cognitive Science*, 2, 1978.

Roger C. Schank. *Dynamic Memory: A Theory of Reminding and Learning in Computers and People.* Cambridge University Press, 1982.

A Method of Calculating the Measure of Salience in Understanding Metaphors

IWAYAMA Makoto and **TOKUNAGA Takenobu** and **TANAKA Hozumi**
Tokyo Institute of Technology
O-OKAYAMA, 2-12-1
MEGURO-KU, TOKYO, 152, JAPAN
iwa@cs.titech.ac.jp

Abstract

This paper presents a computaional method of calculating the measure of salience in understanding metaphors. We mainly treat metaphors in the form of "A is (like) B," in which "A" is called *target concept*, and "B" is called *source concept*. In understanding a metaphor, some properties of the source concept are transferred to the target concept. In the transfer process, we first have to select the properties of the source concept that can be more preferably transferred to the target concept. The measure of salience represents how typical or prominent the property is and is used to measure the transferability of the property. By introducing the measure of salience, we have to consider only the high salient properties after the selection. The measure of salience was calculated from Smith & Medin's probabilistic concept[12, 13] according to Tversky's two factors[14]. One is intensity which refers to signal-to-noise ratio; this is calculated from the entropy of properties. The other is diagnostic factor which refers to the classificatory significance of properties; this is calculated from the distribution of the property's intensity among similar concepts. Finally we briefly outline the whole process of understanding metaphors using the measure of salience.

Introduction

Natural language is a rich source of metaphors, and metaphors have strong relationship with the conceptual structure that has been acquired through our everyday life[7]. For this reason, we should consider metaphors to develop a better natural language understanding system.

In this paper, we mainly treat metaphors in the form of "A is (like) B," in which "A" is called *target concept*, and "B" is called *source concept*. We consider the understanding metaphor as a transfer process of properties from the source concept to the target concept. For example, in the case of "A man is a wolf," some properties of "wolf" — "being vicious, dangerous, fierce, etc." are transferred to "man." As a consequence of the transfer, "man's" properties "being vicious, dangerous, fierce, etc." are highlighted.

This transfer process consists of the following three steps. First, we have to select properties of the source concept that can be transferred to the target concept. We call this step *selection step*. Secondly, we have to find the properties of the target concepts which correspond to the properties selected in the selection step. We call this step *mapping step*. Finally, we have to highlight or downplay the properties of the target concept according to the corresponding properties of the source concept. We call this step *variance step*. These steps are very similar to that of analogical reasoning[4]. In this paper, we focus on the selection step and show how this step is achieved.

In the selection step, we have to select the properties of the source concept that can be more preferably transferred to the target concept. We introduce *the measure of salience* that measures the transferability of the property. Generally, the measure of salience represents how typical or prominent the property is. By introducing the measure of salience, we have to consider only the high salient properties after the selection step. There are many properties that play little importance during the whole process of understanding metaphors. With respect to the above example, "wolf's" properties "being vicious," "being fierce," "being dangerous" are high salient properties and are more likely to be transferred to "man." On the other hand, "having two eyes," "having four legs," etc. are low salient properties and cut off at the selection step.

Many researchers have used salience in the process of understanding metaphors[10, 9, 15], but they have not described precisely how salience is calculated. It is necessary to show the foundation which salience was based on and the method of calculating salience based on the foundation. In this paper, we propose a method to calculate the measure of salience from Smith & Medin's probabilistic concept[12, 13] which has a grounding in probability theory. According to Tversky[14], we calculate the measure of salience in terms of two factors. One is intensity which refers to the signal-to-noise ratio; this is calculated from the entropy of properties. The other is diagnostic factor which refers to the classificatory significance of properties; this is calculated from the distribution of the property's intensity among similar concepts. Finally we briefly outline the whole process of understanding metaphors using the measure of salience.

Probabilistic concept and the Measure of Salience

In this section, we describe our method of calculating the measure of salience. First, we briefly review *probabilistic concept* that Smith & Medin have proposed[12, 13]. Our measure of salience is calculated based on the probabilistic concept.

Probabilistic Concept

Probabilistic concept is composed of a set of properties, each of which has an attribute with a set of possible values. Probability is attached to each value. We use probabilistic concept as our concept representation form, because:

- Probabilistic concept is not "all or none" concept, and this feature is necessary to calculate the measure of salience as ranging from 0 to 1.
- Once probabilities are attached to attribute's values, they can be treated formally based on probability theory.

We give a definition of concept, which is slight different from Smith & Medin's original definition.

Definition 1 Concept
A *Concept* denoted by *(C) is a set of *properties* S_i.

$$*(C) = \{S_1, S_2, \ldots, S_n\}$$

A property S_i is a pair of an *attribute* a_i and its *possible value set* V_i.

$$S_i = a_i : V_i$$

The possible value set V_i is a set whose element is a pair of a_i's *possible value* $v_{i,j}$ and its *probability* $w_{i,j}$ among the V_i.

$$V_i = \{v_{i,1}\#w_{i,1}, \ldots, v_{i,j}\#w_{i,j}, \ldots, v_{i,m}\#w_{i,m}\}$$

That is,

$$\sum_{j=1}^{m} w_{i,j} = 1$$

Most Likelihood Value(MLV) $v_{i,max}$ is the value with the highest probability among a possible value set V_i, and *Most Likelihood Property(MLP)* $S_{i,max}$ is the pair of attribute a_i and its MLV $v_{i,max}$ and is denoted by $a_i : v_{i,max}$.

Following is an example of *(Apple).

Example 1 Definition of *(Apple)

$$*(\text{Apple}) = \left\{ \begin{array}{ll} color : & \left\{ \begin{array}{l} red\#0.8 \\ green\#0.15 \\ brown\#0.05 \end{array} \right\} \\ shape : & \left\{ \begin{array}{l} round\#0.95 \\ cylindrical\#0.05 \end{array} \right\} \\ texture : & \left\{ \begin{array}{l} smooth\#0.9 \\ rough\#0.1 \end{array} \right\} \\ \vdots & \end{array} \right\}$$

"$color : \{red\#0.8, green\#0.15, brown\#0.05\}$" is a property, and "$\{red\#0.8, green\#0.15, brown\#0.05\}$" is its possible value set, where each real number is the probability of the value. "*red*" is the MLV and "*color* : *red*" is the MLP.

The probability attached to the each value can be understood as the rate of the concept's instances which was observed to have the value. For example, one who has the above representation observed 80% of the "apples" as "red apples."

The Measure of Salience

Each property has a measure of salience which is a real number ranging from 0 to 1. 0 and 1 represents the lowest and the highest salience respectively. The measure of salience represents the typicality of a property and is used in understanding metaphors to decide which properties of a source concept might be more preferably transferred to a target concept. Many researchers have used the measure of salience in the same way as mentioned above[10, 9, 15], but they have not shown the precise method to calculate the measure of salience.

In the field of cognitive psychology, Tversky have pointed out the qualitative nature of salience[14]. Tversky says that salience is determined by two types of factors; intensitive and diagnostic. The former refers to the signal-to-noise ratio and the later refers to the classificatory significance of properties. In the following sections, we show the method of calculating the measure of salience according to Tversky's two factors. Intensitive factor is calculated based on the entropy in information theory, and we call this measure *the Amount of Information of Property(AIP)*. Another diagnostic factor is calculated based on the distribution of a property's AIP among similar concepts, and we call this measure *the Difference of Property(DP)*.

The Amount of Information of Property(AIP)
The first factor in calculating the measure of salience is the amount of information which a property has. This is calculated by the entropy of a possible value set V_i. Because the entropy is a measure of randomness, the lower the entropy is, the less random a possible value set V_i is, that means V_i has more redundant information. Intuitively, more redundant V_i means that its MLV $v_{i,max}$ occurs more frequent comparing with other values of V_i. It follows that the property S_i with more redundant V_i is the more typical and salient property.

For example, compare the following two properties, $S_1 = color : V_1$ and $S_2 = color : V_2$.

V_1={red#0.6,$green$#0.1,$yellow$#0.1,$blue$#0.1,$brown$#0.1}

V_2={red#0.6,$green$#0.4}

In these two possible value sets, probability of each MLV "*red*" are the same 0.6. But if we take account of the distribution of all elements in each possible value set, MLV of V_1 occurs more redundantly than that of V_2 because, the degree of concentration of V_1 is higher than that of V_2. In fact entropy (relative entropy) of V_1 (i.e. 0.7627 according to the definition below) is lower than that of V_2 (i.e. 0.9705), and it shows that V_1 is more redundant and has more information than V_2.

Definition 2 The amount of information of property(AIP)
Given a property $S_i = a_i : V_i$, in which

$$V_i = \{v_{i,1}\#w_{i,1}, v_{i,2}\#w_{i,2}, \dots, v_{i,m}\#w_{i,m}\}$$

the AIP of S_i is denoted by $r(V_i)$ and calculated by the following expression:

$$r(V_i) = 1 - h(V_i)$$

where $h(V_i)$ is

$$h(V_i) = \begin{cases} 0 & \text{if } m = 1 \\ \frac{H(V_i)}{\log_2 m} & \text{otherwise.} \end{cases}$$

$H(V_i)$ is

$$H(V_i) = \sum_{j=1}^{m} w_{i,j} \log_2 \frac{1}{w_{i,j}}$$

$r(V_i)$, $h(V_i)$ and $H(V_i)$ are called "redundancy," "relative entropy," and "entropy" respectively in the information theory[8].

The AIP ranges from 0 to 1 depending on the diversity of a possible value set. If the diversity of a possible value set concentrates on only one value — for example x : $\{a\#1, b\#0, c\#0, d\#0\}$, the property has the highest AIP 1, because all instances has the value a. To the contrary, if the diversity of a possible value set is averaged — for example x : $\{a\#0.25, b\#0.25, c\#0.25, d\#0.25\}$, the property has the lowest AIP 0, because one can not successfully predict which value a instance has.

Example 2 Calculation of AIP
Consider the following three possible value sets which are the value of attribute "*color*" of some fruits.

$V_{Color\_of\_Apple}$={red#0.8,$green$#0.15,$brown$#0.05}

$V_{Color\_of\_Strawberry}$={red#0.9,$purple$#0.1}

$V_{Color\_of\_Grape}$={$violet$#0.7,$green$#0.2,red#0.1}

Each AIP becomes,

$$r(V_{Color\_of\_Apple}) = 1 - \frac{0.8 \times \log_2 \frac{1}{0.8} + 0.15 \times \log_2 \frac{1}{0.15} + 0.05 \times \log_2 \frac{1}{0.05}}{\log_2 3} = 0.4421$$

$$r(V_{Color\_of\_Strawberry}) = 1 - \frac{0.9 \times \log_2 \frac{1}{0.9} + 0.1 \times \log_2 \frac{1}{0.1}}{\log_2 2} = 0.5310$$

$$r(V_{Color\_of\_Grape}) = 1 - \frac{0.7 \times \log_2 \frac{1}{0.7} + 0.2 \times \log_2 \frac{1}{0.2} + 0.1 \times \log_2 \frac{1}{0.1}}{\log_2 3} = 0.2702$$

The Difference of Property(DP) The second factor in calculating the measure of salience is the difference of a property among similar concepts. It is the distribution of a property's AIP among similar concepts. Intuitively, the more distinguished property from other similar concepts has the higher value of DP and this property becomes higher salient.

Definition 3 The Difference of Property(DP)
Given a concept $*(C)$'s property $S_i = a_i : V_i$ and a set of similar concepts $Sim(*(C))$ including $*(C)$, the DP of the S_i is denoted by $d(S_i)$ and calculated by the following expression:

$$d(S_i) = \frac{r(V_i)}{\sum^{*(C_j) \in Sim(*(C))} \sum^{S_k \in *(C_j)} r'(S_k, S_i)}$$

where $r'(S_k, S_i)$ is calculated by the following expression:

$$r'(S_k, S_i) = \begin{cases} r(V_k) & \text{if } S_{k,max} = S_{i,max} \\ 0 & \text{otherwise.} \end{cases}$$

In this paper, we define the similar concepts as the concepts that has the same parent node in the IS-A hierarchy.

For example, the DP of "color of apple" becomes

$$\frac{\text{The AIP of "color of apple"}}{\sum \text{The AIP of "color of fruit" whose MLP is "color:red"}},$$

because similar concepts of "apple" are "fruits," and the MLP of "color of apple" is "color:red,"

Example 3 Calculation of DP
In this example we calculate the DPs of *(Apple)'s properties, $S_{color\_of\_apple}$ and $S_{shape\_of\_apple}$. Both property's MLPs are "*color : red*" and "*shape : round*" respectively. Figure 1 shows the similar concepts of *(Apple) — these are the child concepts of *(Fruit) — and the AIPs of "color of fruit" whose MLP is "color:red" and the AIPs of "shape of fruit" whose MLP is "shape:round." Blank spaces represent that the concepts do not have the property whose MLP is "*color : red*" or "*shape : round.*". For example the MLP of $S_{color\_of\_lemon}$ is "*color : yellow*" and so the place corresponding to this property is blank space. This is because such a property plays no role in calculation of the DP of $S_{color\_of\_apple}$.

The DPs of $S_{color\_of\_apple}$ and $S_{shape\_of\_apple}$ are calculated as follows.

$$d(S_{color\_of\_apple}) = \frac{0.4421}{0.4421 + 0.5310} = 0.4543$$

$$d(S_{shape\_of\_apple}) = \frac{0.7136}{0.7136 + 0.8586 + 1 + 0.7577 + 0.7577 + 0.1181} = 0.1697$$

Note that because there are less "red fruits" than "round fruits," the DP of "color of apple" has higher score than that of "shape of apple."

		shape:round	color:red
*(Fruit)	*(Apple)	0.7136	0.4421
	*(Strawberry)		0.5310
	*(Watermelon)	0.8586	
	*(Lemon)		
	*(Melon)	1	
	*(Orange)	0.7577	
	*(Banana)		
	*(Grape)		
	*(Pear)	0.7577	
	*(Peach)	0.1181	

Figure 1: *(Apple)'s similar concepts

The DP ranges from nearly equal to 0 to 1. If a MLP of a property is the unique MLP among similar concepts, this property is the most distinguished property and the DP of this property becomes 1. For example the MLP of penguin "*can_fly* : *no*" is in this case, because all other birds have the different MLP "*can_fly* : *yes*." To the contrary, if every similar concepts has the same MLP, the DP of the property which has the MLP become nearly equal to 0. For example, because all fruits have the MLP "*have_seed* : *yes*," the DP of this property of apple becomes nearly equal to 0.

The measure of salience of properties The measure of salience of a property is calculated by the following definition.

Definition 4 The measure of salience of a property The measure of salience of a property S_i is calculated by the following expression:

$$salience(S_i) = r(V_i) \times d(S_i)$$

Because $d(S_i)$ is the rate of $r(V_i)$ occupying among similar concepts, $salience(S_i)$ represent the apparent AIP in similar concepts. For example, if $d(S_i)$ is 1, S_i is the most distinguished property and the apparent AIP is the same as the net AIP (i.e. $r(V_i)$) itself. If $d(S_i)$ is much lower, there are many similar concept that have the same MLP of S_i and the apparent AIP becomes lower than the net AIP.

Example 4 Calculation of the measure of salience Using the results obtained by example 2 and 3, we can calculate the measure of salience of properties $S_{color\_of\_apple}$ and $S_{texture\_of\_apple}$.

$$salience(S_{color\_of\_apple}) = 0.4421 \times 0.4543 = 0.2008$$

$$salience(S_{shape\_of\_apple}) = 0.7136 \times 0.1697 = 0.1211$$

While the net AIP of $S_{shape\_of\_apple}$ (i.e. 0.7136) is higher than that of $S_{color\_of\_apple}$ (i.e. 0.4421), the apparent AIP — that is the measure of salience — of $S_{shape\_of\_apple}$ becomes lower. This is because the effect of the lower DP of $S_{shape\_of\_apple}$.

Using the Measure of Salience in Understanding Metaphors

In this section we describe the overview of our metaphor understanding system AMUSE and explain how the measure of salience is used in AMUSE.

The Overview of AMUSE

The process of understanding metaphors is very similar to analogical reasoning[4]. There are four steps in understanding metaphors. In these four steps, the last three steps correspond to the property transfer process.

1) **Extraction step**: Extracts a Source concept and a Target concept from surface sentence.
2) **Selection step**: Selects the properties of the source concept that are transferable to the target concept. (Calculating salience of source concept's properties)
3) **Mapping step**: Finds the properties of the target concept that correspond to the selected properties in the selection step.
4) **Variance step**: Highlight and downplays the properties of the target concept that are found in the mapping step.

As to analogical reasoning, step 1), step 2), step 3) 4) are corresponding to *Retrieval step*, *Elaboration step*, *Mapping and justification step* respectively[5].

We have focused on the step 2) and shown the method of calculating the measure of salience. We think that the higher salient the property is, the more preferably the property can be transferred.

Now, we show the other steps briefly in understanding the following metaphor.

(1) Mary's cheeks are like apples.

Form this sentence, AMUSE first extract a *viewpoint expression*. This process corresponds to step 1). The viewpoint expression is denoted by $*$(Target) \ $*$(Source) and means the *(Target) viewed from *(Source). In this case $*$(Cheek) \ $*$(Apple) is extracted.

In the selection step, AMUSE calculates the measure of salience of the properties of *(Apple). For the limitation of space we consider only the following five properties.

$$salience(S_{color\_of\_apple}) = 0.2008$$

$$salience(S_{shape\_of\_apple}) = 0.1211$$

$$salience(S_{taste\_of\_apple}) = 0.1153$$

$$salience(S_{texture\_of\_apple}) = 0.1062$$

$$salience(S_{has\_seed\_of\_apple}) = 0.06244$$

These five properties are rated according to the measure of salience, and AMUSE send the properties to the mapping step in this order. AMUSE has the parameter of threshold which cut off the lower salient properties. In this example if we set the value of threshold to 0.1, then only the first four properties are sent to the mapping step.

The mapping step finds the property of *(Cheek) which corresponds to the property of *(Apple) selected in the previous step. If both property have the same attribute name and the same value which is equal to the MLV of a property of *(Source), AMUSE finds there is a correspondence between both properties. For example, $S_{color\_of\_apple}$ and $S_{color\_of\_cheek}$ are

$$S_{color\_of\_apple} = \{red\#0.8, green\#0.15, brown\#0.05\}$$

$$S_{color\_of\_cheek} = \{yellow\#0.8, pale\#0.1, red\#0.1\}$$

Since these two possible value sets have the same value "*red*" which is the MLV in $S_{color\_of\_apple}$, there is a correspondence between $S_{color\_of\_cheek}$ and $S_{color\_of\_apple}$. Among selected four properties $S_{color\_of\_apple}$, $S_{shape\_of\_apple}$, $S_{texture\_of\_apple}$ and $S_{taste\_of\_apple}$, the $S_{taste\_of\_apple}$ is dropped at the mapping step because there is no corresponding property in *(Cheek). In this case *(Cheek) does not have the attribute "taste."

In the variance step, AMUSE changes the diversity of the properties of *(Cheek) found in the mapping step. For example, in the most simplest version of AMUSE, $S_{color\_of\_cheek}$ shown above is changed to

$$S_{color\_of\_cheek} = \{yellow\#0, pale\#0, red\#1\}$$

The value of $S_{color\_of\_cheek}$ — "*red*" which corresponding to the MLV of $S_{color\_of\_apple}$ is highlighted and the other values — "*yellow*" and "*pale*" are downplayed.

Finally, we get the following representation of ∗(Cheek) \ ∗(Apple) as the result of understanding the metaphor (1).

$$*(\text{Cheek}) \setminus *(\text{Apple}) = \left\{ \begin{array}{ll} color: & \left\{ \begin{array}{l} yellow\#0 \\ pale\#0 \\ \underline{red}\#1 \end{array} \right\} \\ shape: & \left\{ \begin{array}{l} \underline{round}\#1 \\ plane\#0 \end{array} \right\} \\ texture: & \left\{ \begin{array}{l} \underline{smooth}\#1 \\ rough\#0 \end{array} \right\} \\ \vdots & \end{array} \right\}$$

In the representation, underlined value is highlighted and others are downplayed according to the high salient properties of *(Apple).

The role of salience in understanding metaphors

There are two advantages to use the measure of salience in understanding metaphors. One is as the measure of preference used in the selection step, which has been described in this paper. The other is as the measure to discern three types of sentences — literal sentences, metaphors and anomalies.

AMUSE is a system which can understand not only metaphors but also literal sentences and anomalies based on the same framework. Many systems have a special device for understanding metaphors, and it is necessary to determine whether an input sentence is a metaphor or not before processing[1, 2]. But there does not exist the clear boundary between metaphors and literal sentences, anomalies. AMUSE does not discern the three types of sentences before processing and all of these are processed in terms of the same transfer process. For example in the case of a literal sentence

(2) I saw the girl with a telescope.,

two viewpoint expressions ∗(Telescope) \ ∗(Tool) and ∗(Telescope) \ ∗(Thing) are extracted. In the case of a anomaly

(3) Mary's cheeks are like bananas.,

the viewpoint expression ∗(Cheek) \ ∗(Banana) is extracted. In the case of the metaphor (1), the viewpoint expression ∗(Cheek) \ ∗(Apple) is extracted. In processing these viewpoint expressions, high salient properties of the source concept can be transferred to the target concept as described in the previous section. Considering the percentage of the actually transferred properties among the selected properties in the selection step, almost all properties are transferred in processing ∗(Telescope) \ ∗(Tool) and ∗(Telescope) \ ∗(Thing). To the contrary, almost all properties are not transferred in processing ∗(Cheek) \ ∗(Banana). We define the *Comprehensibility of Viewpoint expression(CV)* as representing this percentage. Following is the definition of the CV.

Definition 5 The Comprehensibility of Viewpoint expression(CV)

The CV of the ∗(A) \ ∗(B) is calculated by the following expression.

$$\frac{\sum \begin{array}{c}\text{The AIP of the property of *(B)} \\ \text{which is actually transferred to *(A)}\end{array}}{\sum \text{The AIP of the selected property of *(B) in the selection step}}$$

The CV is the flowing rate of information of the properties in the transfer process. Some properties selected at the selection step are cut off at the mapping step. In literal sentences, the CV of its viewpoint expression is almost 1. In anomalies, the CV of its viewpoint expression is almost 0, because almost all selected properties in the source concept have not corresponding properties in the target concept. So the higher the value of CV a viewpoint expression has, the more literal the viewpoint expression is.

There needs another measure that distinguish metaphors from other types of sentences. The CV measures only the degree of literal or anomalous of viewpoint expressions. From the Ortony's view[10, 9]: in the case of metaphors, transferred properties are high salient in the source concept and low salient in the target concept. In literal sentences, both are high salient. In anomalies, both are low salient. There is an experimental evidence about the Ortony's view[6]. While the CV only considers the properties in the source concept, Ortony's measure considers the properties in both the source concept and the target concept. To formulate the Ortony's measure in AMUSE, we have to make both the mapping step and the variance step more precise. This is out of the scope of this paper.

Conclusion

In this paper, we have proposed a method of calculating the measure of salience.

The measure of salience represents typicality of a property and can be used in various inferences as a measure of preference. This is an aspect of the utility of salience, and the understanding metaphors is one of them. Our metaphor understanding system AMUSE uses the measure of salience to guide which properties can preferably be transferred from a source concept to a target concept.

It is also significant to show the foundation which salience is based on and the method of calculating salience based on the foundation. This is the aspect of how the salience is calculated. To compare with the aspect of the utility, this aspect has not been so enlighten. But both aspects are necessary to accomplish the theory of salience. The measure of salience proposed in this paper is based on the probability attached to attribute's values, and we have shown the precise method how the measure of salience is calculated from the probability. Our measure of salience is based on the entropy in information theory and more formal than other system's score of salience.

But there remains some questions. We have not shown the effect of the context to the measure of salience. There are two relations between contextual information and two factors of the measure of salience. The first one is the diversity change of a possible value set, which causes the change of the first factor — the amount of information of properties. The second one is the variety of selecting similar concepts, which causes the change of the second factor — the difference of properties. Precise analysis of these relations is left as our future work.

Finally, there is a question how the probabilistic concept is constructed. We think Fisher's incremental concept clustering system COBWEB[3] gives us one answer, because COBWEB also uses probabilistic concept as its representation form and constructs probabilistic concepts and their hierarchy incrementally. Fisher proposed the measure of *Category utility* to control the construction of concept hierarchy. Category utility is the measure calculated by two factors — intra-class similarity and inter-class similarity. Roughly speaking, COBWEB incrementally construct concept hierarchy so as to increase intra-class similarity and decrease inter-class similarity. This strategy reflects *basic-level effect* and *typicality effect*[11] observed in human's categorization. Our measure of salience and Fisher's measure of Category utility are similar, that is intra-class similarity and inter-class dissimilarity corresponding to the amount of information and the difference of properties respectively. Therefore we think COBWEB can be incorporated into our metaphor understanding system AMUSE as constructing probabilistic concepts.

References

[1] J. G. Carbonell. Metaphor: An inescapable phenomenon in natural-language comprehension. In W. G. Lehnert and M. H. Ringle, editors, *Strategies for natural language processing*, pages 415–434. Erlbaum, 1982.

[2] D. Fass. Metonymy and metaphor: What's the difference? In *COLING '88*, pages 177–181, 1988.

[3] D. Fisher. Knowledge acquisition via incremental conceptual clustering. *Machine Learning*, 2:139–172, 1987.

[4] R. P. Hall. Computational approaches to analigical reasoning: A comparative analysis. *Artificial Intelligence*, 39(1):39–120, 1989.

[5] S. T. Kedar-Cabelli. Analogy – from a unified perspective. In D. H. Helman, editor, *Analogical Reasoning*, pages 65–103. Kluwer Academic Publishers, 1988.

[6] T. Kusumi. Effects of categorical dissimilarity and affective similarity between constituent words on metaphor appreciation. *Journal of Psycolinguistic Research*, 16(6):577–595, 1987.

[7] G. Lakoff and M. Johnson. *Metaphors we live by*. Chicago University Press, 1980.

[8] H. Miyagawa. *Information Theory*. CORONA Publishing CO., LTD., Tokyo, Japan, 1979. (in Japanese).

[9] A. Ortony. Beyond literal similarity. *Psychological Review*, 86(3):161–180, 1979.

[10] A. Ortony. The role of similarity in similes and metaphors. In A. Ortony, editor, *Metaphor and Thought*. Cambridge University Press, 1979.

[11] E. Rosch and C. B. Mervis. Family resemblances : Studies in the internal structure of categories. *Cognitive Psychology*, 7:573–605, 1975.

[12] E. E. Smith and D. Medin. *Categories and Concepts*. Harvard University Press, Cambridge, MA, 1981.

[13] E. E. Smith, D. N. Osherson, L. Rips, and M. Keane. Combining prototypes : A selective modification model. *Cognitive Science*, 12(4):485–527, 1988.

[14] A. Tversky. Features of similarity. *Psycological Review*, 84(4):327–352, 1977.

[15] E. J. Weiner. A knowledge representation approach to understanding metaphors. *Computational Linguistics*, 10(1):1–14, 1984.

Distributed Cases for Case-Based Reasoning; Facilitating Use of Multiple Cases

Michael Redmond*
School of Information and Computer Science
Georgia Institute of Technology
Atlanta, Georgia 30332-0280
(404) 853-9382
E-mail: redmond@pravda.gatech.edu

Abstract

A case-based reasoner can frequently benefit from using pieces of multiple previous cases in the course of solving a single problem. In our model, case pieces, called *snippets*, are organized around the pursuit of a goal, and there are links between the pieces that preserve the structure of reasoning. The advantages of our representational approach include: 1) The steps taken in a previous case can be followed as long as they are relevant, since the connections between steps are preserved. 2) There is easy access to all parts of previous cases, so they can be directly accessed when appropriate.

Introduction

Case-based Reasoning (CBR) (Kolodner and Simpson 1984) is a method of using previous episodes to suggest solutions to new problems. CBR allows a reasoner to solve problems efficiently when previous similar experiences are available. Problem solving using case-based reasoning usually involves retrieving relevant previous cases, adapting the solution(s) from the previous case(s), if necessary, to solve the new problem, and storing the current episode as a new case to be used in the future.

A case-based reasoner can frequently benefit from using pieces of multiple previous cases in the course of solving a single problem. For example, in protocols taken by Lancaster (Lancaster and Kolodner 1988), mechanics doing a troubleshooting task used pieces of different cases to suggest different hypotheses to consider and tests to perform.

An annotated example from our program CELIA (Cases and Explanations in Learning; an Integrated Approach) (Redmond 1989b), which solves problems in the domain of automobile troubleshooting, illustrates the successful use of multiple cases. In this example, the car is stalling. In forming an initial hypothesis, the reasoner retrieves part of a previous case with the same symptoms that suggests that the idle speed is low and that the mechanic should test whether the engine stalls when it is cold. After carrying out the test the mechanic finds that the engine stalls when warm. Since the results of this test are different than in the previous case, the rest of that case is not useful for further diagnosis.

```
***** Relevant Case Snippet Retrieved ****
  The HYPOTHESIS that Case 101, Snippet Case-Generate-
Hypothesis-316 suggests is:
        (LOW IDLE-SPEED)
**** Continue with Linked Case Snippet ****
  The TEST that Case 101, Snippet Case-Test-Hypothesis-318
suggests is: (TEMPERATURE ENGINE-SYSTEM
                    (WHEN (STALLS ENGINE-SYSTEM)) COLD)
  The TEST-RESULT predicted is:
        (TEMPERATURE ENGINE-SYSTEM (COLD))
  Result: (TEMPERATURE ENGINE-SYSTEM (WARM))
***** Abandoning Case 101 *****
```

CELIA recognizes that the first case must be abandoned, and retrieves another case to help it interpret the test result. The new case shares hypotheses and test results with the current situation, rather than just symptoms. It suggests that the problem is a low idle mixture.

```
***** Continuing with Case 105, Snippet Case-Interpret-Test-505
  The RULE-IN that Case 105, Snippet Case-Interpret-Test-505
suggests is: (LOW IDLE-MIXTURE)
  The RULE-OUT that Case 105, Snippet Case-Interpret-Test-505
suggests is: (LOW IDLE-SPEED)
...
*** Continuing with Case 102, Snip. Case-Generate-Hypothesis-289
  The hypothesis that Case 102, Snippet Case-Generate-
Hypothesis-289 suggests is:
        (SMALL (DISTANCE THROTTLE-DASHPOT-STEM
                THROTTLE-LEVER))
  The TEST that Case 102, Snippet Case-Test-Hypothesis-287
suggests is: (DISTANCE THROTTLE-DASHPOT-STEM
                THROTTLE-LEVER)
  The TEST-RESULT predicted is:
    (NOT (SMALL (DISTANCE THROTTLE-DASHPOT-STEM
                THROTTLE-LEVER)))
...
```

It further suggests actions to take to fix the problem (not shown), but after carrying out those actions, the car still stalls. This case, too, is abandoned. Another

*This research has been supported by the Army Research Institute for the Behavioral and Social Sciences under Contract No. MDA-903-86-C-173, and by DARPA contract F49620-88-C-0058 monitored by AFOSR. The author wishes to thank Janet Kolodner for her guidance, Ray Bareiss, and Ashwin Ram for helpful discussions, and Tom Hinrichs, Steve Robinson, Louise Penberthy, and Joel Martin for helpful comments on earlier versions of the paper.

case is retrieved that suggests a new hypothesis: the throttle dashpot is out of place. It suggests checking if the distance between the throttle dashpot and the throttle lever is too short. This hypothesis proves to be correct, the fix it suggests is carried out and the problem is fixed.

The process we are describing is one of using pieces of several cases to solve a problem. We have observed this happening in automobile troubleshooting (Lancaster and Kolodner 1988), medical diagnosis, and meal planning (Hinrichs 1988). We suspect that it is common to any problem solving task that is solved by addressing subgoals individually. It is especially evident when planning and execution are interleaved, where the results of execution are not always as predicted. In order for several cases to be used efficiently in combination with each other, several issues must be addressed.

- How to retrieve a case when some part of it could prove useful.
- How to find and isolate the parts of the previous case that will be useful in the current context.
- How to form generalizations to reflect commonalities in parts of the problem solving experiences.

In this paper we discuss a case representation that enables effective combination of multiple cases by making each part of a case directly accessible, while retaining the links between the parts.

Case Representation

When more than one case is used to solve a problem, frequently only parts of each case will be useful in the synthesis. These parts might be buried within an extended sequence of actions serving many goals. For example, when a reasoner is trying to find a test for a particular hypothesis, the relevant test part of a case is all he needs to focus on. The actions taken and the other hypotheses are not important at that time. Cases must therefore be represented such that their parts can be efficiently accessed.

Traditionally, cases used by case-based reasoners have been treated as monolithic entities [1]. That is, an episode is stored as a single instantiation of a single knowledge structure. Aspects of a case are specified as slots in the representation. Although many of these representations have structured representation within slots and reasoning can be applied to parts of a case, indexing, in general, retrieves the case as a whole.

Treating a situation as a monolithic case and embedding everything in it creates problems for using parts of multiple cases to solve one problem:

- Retrieval of the parts of the case that can be helpful in a given situation has to be a two step process. First, the appropriate case must be accessed, then the currently useful parts hidden inside the case must be found. It can take a lot of effort to find them within the case, even given the right indices to the situation. A one step process allowing direct access to the useful parts of cases would be more efficient.
- Monolithic cases contain too much information for a system to be able to do useful generalization. Since cases have many parts, some of which should be generalized with parts of other cases, but others of which are unique, generalization of commonalities may be delayed.

[1] See Related Work section for some exceptions.

In order for the appropriate part of a case to be accessed when it can be useful, in the middle of problem solving, it is advantageous to divide cases into pieces. In our model,

- Cases are stored in pieces, or ***snippets*** (Kolodner 1988). This allows the reasoner to use small fragments of cases in its reasoning rather than having to wade through large monolithic cases.
- Each snippet is organized around one particular goal, and contains information pertaining to the pursuit of that goal.
- Each snippet contains the current problem solving context at the time the goal was initiated, including the initial problem description and results of actions taken so far.
- There are links between the snippets that preserve the structure of the diagnosis. Each snippet is linked to the snippet for the goal that suggested it and to the snippets for the goals it suggests.

Content of Snippets

Each snippet can be thought of as a scene of the larger episode. A snippet has three main types of information. First, is the problem solving context at the time of the snippet's occurrence. Second is information related to the goal that the snippet is centered around. Last is information linking the snippet to other related snippets. Figures 1, 2, and 3 together comprise an example of the internal representation of a snippet representing the goal of testing the hypothesis that the carburetor float bowl had too high a fuel level.

Context. Problem solving context includes actions and results of actions taken earlier in the problem solving, as well as features of the problem. *Global context* is the features given for the overall problem situation, *internal context* is the circumstances, state or knowledge established by the actions already taken as part of the problem solving. In the automobile troubleshooting domain, internal context includes tests that have been done and their results; information or hypotheses that have been ruled out or ruled in during problem solving; fixes that have been made during problem solving; and the current hypothesis. The global context includes the chief complaint; other symptoms; how frequently the symptoms occur; how long the problem has been going on; any particular ambient temperature range when failure occurs; any particular weather conditions when failure occurs; the car model; the customer; the mechanics involved; and where and when the problem solving occurred. Global context remains the same across snippets of a case, but internal context changes.

Figure 1 shows an example of the problem solving context part of a snippet.

```
CASE-TEST-HYPOTHESIS-130

CONTEXT

Internal
  Ruled-In    (Lean (Position (Idle-Mixture-Screw)))
  Ruled-Out   (Low (Position (Idle-Speed-Screw)))
              (Lean (Position (Idle-Mixture-Screw)))
              (Incorrect (Position (Throttle-Dashpot)))
  Tests-Done-N-Results
          (Temperature Engine-System
                   (When (Stalls Engine-System)) Cold)
              (Hot (Temperature Engine-System))
          (Stalls Engine-System)
              (Stalls Engine-System)
          (Small (Distance Throttle-Dashpot-Stem Throttle-Lever))
              (Not (Small
                   (Distance Throttle-Dashpot-Stem Throttle-Lever))
  Fixes-Done    (Increase (Position (Idle-Mixture-Screw)))
  Solution: NIL
  Current-Hypoth   (High (Contains Carburetor-Float-Bowl Fuel))

Global
  Complaint            (Stalls Engine-System)
  Other-Sympt          (Rough (Run Engine-System))
  Frequency            Weekly
  How-Long             2months
  Amb-Temp-@-Fail      Any
  Weath-@-Fail         Rainy
  Car-Type             (1981 Ford Granada)
  Car-Owner            Davis Cable
  Participants         Mark Graves, David Wood
  Location             Mikes-Repair-Shop
  When                 2843569149
```

Figure 1: Example Case Snippet Context.

The problem solving context of a snippet is used for matching during retrieval. As Barletta and Mark (1988) have suggested, both internal and global problem solving context are necessary to maintain coherence and consistency of actions. Since snippets include both internal and global problem solving context, retrieval results in *usefully* similar case pieces.

This form of context creates advantages for combining multiple cases to find a solution. When there is a need to access part of another case, having the internal context available allows matching on results of previous problem solving. Thus a snippet which followed from similar steps and results can be favored. In this way both access issues are addressed: accessing a case that is relevantly similar, and accessing the part of the previous case that will be useful in the current context. An appropriately relevant snippet can be directly accessed. With monolithic cases the internal context at each point in the problem solving would not be available to make accessing parts easy. By saving the context with each piece we are trading space for flexibility. Any method, in order to be as flexible, would have to either represent the internal context at each point, or be able to recompute it at retrieval time, an expensive proposition.

In addition, though not currently implemented, representing the internal context enables analytical reasoning that could determine that the current context is incompatible with something already done prior to the snippet in the previous situation, thus averting failure.

Pursuit of Goal. Each snippet is centered around the pursuit of one goal. It is here that the actions taken in pursuit of a goal and the results of those actions are recorded. When a snippet is retrieved during problem solving, these slots suggest the actions to take and the results to expect if the situation is the same as in the previous case. We have identified 7 types of goals involved in troubleshooting, Table 1 lists those goal types and their associated slots. Figure 2 shows the slots for a test: the test that was done, the method of carrying it out, the tools used, and the result. In general, the goal-related part of a snippet needs to include the actions carried out to achieve the goal and the effects of the actions.

```
CASE-TEST-HYPOTHESIS-130

PURSUIT OF GOAL

Goal      G-TEST-HYPOTHESIS
Test      (High (Contains Carburetor-Float-Bowl Fuel))
Test-Method
          (Turn-Off Engine-System)
          (Remove Carburetor-Air-Horn-Screw)
          (Remove Carburetor-Air-Horn)
          (Ask (Level Fuel Carburetor-Float-Bowl)
                     Scale-On-Carburetor-Float-Bowl)
Test-Tools        Screw-Driver
Test-Result       (High (Level Fuel Carburetor-Float-Bowl))
```

Figure 2: Example Case Snippet Pursuit of Goal.

Goal Type	Slots for Goal Type
Generating a hypothesis	hypothesis generated
Clarifying a complaint	actions taken, information gathered
Verifying a complaint	actions taken
Testing a hypothesis	test that was done, method of carrying it out, tools used, result
Interpreting a test (either of hypotheses or repairs)	hypotheses ruled out, hypotheses suggested or ruled in
Making a fix or replacement	replacement or fix done, method of carrying it out, tools used
Testing a fix or replacement	test that was done, method of carrying it out, tools used, result

Table 1: Goal Types and Their Slots.

Linkage. While it is important to divide cases into snippets so that parts of cases can be easily and directly accessible, it is also important to be able to reconstruct the case. Sometimes a number of steps in the same case can provide useful guidance. A hypothesis suggests a test, the result suggests an interpretation, the interpretation suggests a fix, and the fix is associated with a test of the fix. As long as the expectations from a previous case are upheld in the new situation, the reasoner can benefit by following the sequence of reasoning steps from the recalled case. In order to enable such reconstruction, snippets include links to the snippets for the goals they follow from and the goals that follow from them. Briefly, the idea is, first, retain the links so that in the future use of the snippet, the step that it suggested will be suggested. Second, save the value of the main slot of the preceding snippet to facilitate making generalizations involving the previous step taken. Note that the portion of the snippet shown in Figure 3 has a slot for the previous *hypothesis* because it was preceded by a generate hypothesis snippet, whose main slot was a hypothesis.

CASE-TEST-HYPOTHESIS-130

LINKAGE

Link-Down	CASE-INTERPRET-TEST-140
Link-Up	CASE-GENERATE-HYPOTHESIS-125
Prev-Hypothesis	(High (Contains Carburetor-Float-Bowl Fuel))

Figure 3: Example Case Snippet Linkage.

Links Between Snippets

As mentioned above, snippets are linked together in a manner that preserves the underlying structure of the goals pursued in the case. Figure 4 shows the linkages between snippets for a case of a stalling car. This case illustrates the differences that can occur between temporal order and the underlying structure of which snippets follow from which. Each node represents a case snippet for a particular goal pursued in the case. Each link represents a relationship between goals in the case. Arrows point from a snippet to the snippets that it suggests.

Preserving these intra-case links is important for future use of the case. For example, in diagnosis, the case structure preserves which hypothesis suggested a test, and what test result suggested a hypothesis, even if they were not contiguous in the processing. To demonstrate this, in Figure 4, step 6 follows from step 3, since it is a refinement of the previous hypothesis. Step 7 follows from step 4, since it is a test of the hypothesis. Step 11 does not follow from any of the previous hypotheses or tests, it is the start of a new direction after a dead end was reached. This means that the important structure in a case is not the temporal order of the actions taken. Rather, it is which goals follow from which other goals.

For example, in automobile troubleshooting, a hypothesis that the alternator belt is loose could follow from a hypothesis that the battery is not charging since it is a potential root cause. Or a hypothesis that the radiator hose is leaking could follow from a hypothesis that there is a leak in the cooling system, since it is a narrowing of a hypothesis.

Preserving this linkage enables a case to provide guidance as to what to pursue next as long as the results continue to be the same as in the previous case. In troubleshooting, this allows retrieval of a case fragment with a particular hypothesis to yield a connection to the test to do next. The guidance is not affected by any idiosyncratic temporal ordering that does not reflect the underlying structure of the previous case.

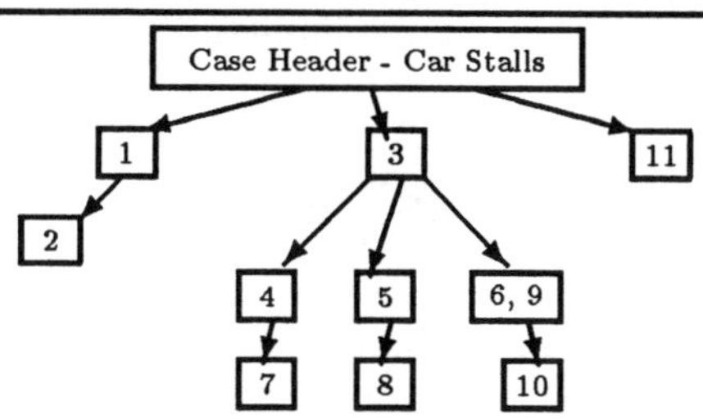

Diagnosis Actions (in order presented)

1. Hyp - Loose Connected Spark Plug
2. Test - Loose Connected Spark Plug (Neg.)
3. Hyp - Malfunction Carburetor
4. Hyp - Lean Idle Mixture
5. Hyp - Low Idle Speed
6. Hyp - High Float Level
7. Test - Lean Idle Mixture (Neg.)
8. Test - Low Idle Speed (Neg.)
9. Hyp - High Float Level (restate)
10. Test - High Float Level (Neg.)
11. Hyp - Malfunction Control System

Figure 4: Case Structure.

Snippet Access

Snippets can be accessed two ways:

- Directly, through retrieval, matching the current situation to the snippet's goal and context.
- Sequentially, by following links between snippets.

In CELIA, retrieval via direct access is first restricted to snippets that are centered around the goal type being considered. Then a weighted similarity metric is used, with matching occurring for all features within both the internal and global context. An empirical adjustment of the weight on a feature's importance is made based on the success or failure of prediction during learning (Redmond 1989b). As would be hoped, the similarity metric quickly comes to favor many of the features in the internal context, and give less importance to features in the global context that seem spurious, such as the car owner, the participants, and the location. These, however, are not eliminated, so they can play a part in some unusual situation in which they are important. Further work will investigate using some form of explanation based indexing (Barletta and Mark 1988) in conjunction with this.

Retrieval by sequential access is easy given our case representation. Snippets have links to other snippets that follow from them. When a snippet has been used to suggest an action, if the result is the same as in the snippet's execution, the reasoner can follow the link to the next goal and its actions. Retrieval by sequential access is favored over direct access when it is appropriate. This retains coherence and avoids unnecessary processing.

Advantages of the Approach

Our system, CELIA, learns from observing an expert's actions (Redmond 1989b, 1989a). It uses parts of multiple cases for two tasks

- To predict and explain the instructor's actions as it is learning. The experience is then saved in the distributed form we have described here. Redmond (1989c) explains how this distributed case representation can be constructed from observing raw input.
- To provide guidance during problem solving.

The distributed case representation has advantages for both processes. Here we discuss the advantages for problem solving.

- There is easy access to all parts of previous cases, so they can be directly accessed when a snippet's goal is to be pursued.
- The structure of the case is retained so it can be reconstructed as a whole or in part when necessary. The actions taken in the previous case can continue to provide guidance as long as the situation remains usefully similar to that of the previous case. Operationally, in the current system this means as long as the same results are obtained in the step as in the corresponding step in the previous case.
- Generalizations of case snippets can be formed for the pursuit of a particular goal, but not hindered by the pursuit of other goals in the cases.

While empirical measures of the learning part of the system have been made, our evaluation of the representational approach is based on the fact that it enables, without much cost, flexible problem solving that would otherwise be difficult. With monolithic cases, not only might the reasoner not have the right indices for the case, finding the right part of a case to use for the current task situation is effortful. Even if the case is indexed so that it will be accessed when any of its parts are relevant (*e.g.* by important features of the internal context at each and every point during the case – the tests done and their results, the fixes done ...), once that case is accessed it is necessary to find the point in the case's problem solving where its context best matches the current context. Making this process as simple as CELIA's process would require including all the same information that CELIA's cases have – the context at each point during the case (for indices), directly associated with the step in the case. This case representation content would not be distinguishable from our theory except that our representation preserves the underlying order of the steps.

The ideas discussed raise some issues. First, as snippets become smaller, the distinction between cases and situation/action rules may seem to blur. If problem solving does not benefit from the overall context provided by a whole case, then the case representation might be equivalent to individual decision rules. A related question one might ask is whether problem solving behavior constructed from relatively local decisions can be globally consistent, or will unforeseen interactions between goals creep in. An advantage of traditional case-based reasoning techniques is that a whole case has a coherency that holds together the problem solving behavior. We do not want to lose coherency when we break cases into pieces. We have discussed a number of important ways in which our snippet representation differs from decision rules. First, the links between actions are retained, so a case can be followed as long as the results of actions are as predicted by the previous case. Sequential access of snippets leads to a goal-directed coherence that is not inherent in a set of individual decision rules. Second, snippets include in their context both the initial problem description and the results of actions taken up to that point. This means that when direct access is used the choice of actions to take is directly influenced by the problem solving that has already occurred. Third, the case snippet can provide useful suggestions even when there is only a partial match to the current situation (*i.e.* when a rule may not apply).

Another issue we must address is what size snippet is most useful for problem solving. There is a trade-off between the efficiency of being able to match and use a single case as the solution to the problem, and the generality of matching to the parts that are applicable in the current situation. We have suggested that the appropriate division is for each snippet to concern a single goal. We should clarify that this means that they are concerned with a *leaf* goal. A high level goal such as *explain anomaly* would be broken down into subgoals using knowledge of goals and subgoals. The lowest level goals are the ones that the reasoner would look for guidance in achieving. It is this level of goals that the case snippets are organized around. Applying this to the advantages suggested above, the approach has these advantages:

- Direct access is to the parts of previous cases involved in the pursuit of the types of goals that the problem solver seeks guidance in achieving.
- When generalization of case snippets is added, it can be done for the pursuit of a particular low-level goal for which the reasoner might later want guidance.

It might be argued that the number of indices necessary increases as the cases are divided into smaller chunks and each chunk requires indices. However, if parts of the larger chunks are to be accessible, then equivalent numbers of indices are necessary in order to be able to get an indication that some part of the larger chunk would be of value in the current circumstances. Thus, snippet size and number of indices are independent of each other.

This division of cases into multiple snippets based on goals pursued is important when multiple cases are used to solve different parts of a problem. When changes lead to the need to access a different case to get help pursuing a goal, the part of the case that should be accessed is available such that it can be found in a timely manner. Such division would not be important in a domains in which cases can *only* be considered as a whole (as in *e.g.* HYPO (Ashley & Rissland 1987)).

Related Work and Conclusions

Most CBR approaches have represented cases as single units and reasoned based on one case. MEDIATOR (Simpson 1985) made use of parts of multiple cases in coming to a solution. However, MEDIATOR had to first choose a case, then access the relevant part. More recently, several CBR approaches have separated cases into pieces.

JULIA's (Kolodner 1989; Hinrichs 1988) case pieces represent scenes that are related partonomically and taxonomically. Its snippets, like CELIA's, facilitate synthesizing parts of multiple cases to form a solution, and effective generalization. JULIA does not need the type of links used in our representation, however, because of the relatively low amount of difference in structure of cases, and a relatively static set of goals across problems, with limited need to pursue them in any particular order.

Derivational Analogy (Carbonell 1986) is somewhat similar to our approach in that it saves the problem trace, including generation of subgoal structures and generation of alternatives. A key difference is that our approach provides both direct and sequential access to parts of the problem solving. Derivational Analogy only accesses a trace at the beginning of a problem. If a case can no longer provide guidance a different case must be accessed from the top and the reasoning followed from there. The start of the problem trace is accessed when it shares a subgoal chain with the current situation. Therefore, derivational analogy cannot retrieve a case or part of a case with a similar current subgoal but a different way of getting to it.

Barletta and Mark (1988) group their cases into pieces such that the actions that are used to recover from each of the hypothesized faults are in the same piece. This serves part of the purpose of dividing the cases into pieces, direct access to relevant actions. It appears to be specific to the particular goal of fixing a known fault, however. It is not as flexible as organization by goals, in that it serves a particular goal type, fixing a problem, but does not allow easy direct access to all the goals pursued in the previous case.

Kopeikina, Bandau, and Lemmon (1988a, 1988b) suggested the need for cases that represent how a situation develops over time. Their approach was to divide a case into problem description; action plan; description of effect of implemented action; description of the 'no need for treatment state'; remove controls; and description of a 'no problem state'. Such a case is always accessed at the beginning, and all of the main actions are within the second piece. If the results are not as expected, another case can be used to recover from that *new* problem, however, it is accessed from the beginning as a whole case. They argue against dividing cases up into unconnected individual cases, but do not consider an approach such as ours. Our use of snippets which retain both the internal context, and the internal structure of the case addresses this need.

The use of parts of multiple cases, and the division of cases into linked, goal-centered fragments provides flexibility to recover from changes or unexpected results, while retaining goal-driven processing. The case representation enables direct access to usefully similar parts of previous cases, while retaining the opportunity to follow significant portions of a previous case. When generating a multi-step solution and the solution can be synthesized from multiple cases, our distributed case representation provides significant flexibility advantages. This is important in numerous domains, including automobile troubleshooting, medical diagnosis, many design problems, and we suspect any problem solving task that is solved by addressing subgoals individually.

References

K. Ashley and E. Rissland 1987. Compare and contrast, a test of expertise. In *Proceedings of the National Conference on Artificial Intelligence (AAAI-87)*, San Mateo, CA. Morgan Kaufmann.

R. Barletta and W. Mark 1988. Breaking cases into pieces. In *Proceedings of Case-Based Reasoning Workshop*, St. Paul, MN.

J. Carbonell 1986. Derivational analogy: A theory of reconstructive problem solving and expertise acquisition. In R. Michalski, J. Carbonell, and T. Mitchell, editors, *Machine Learning: An Artificial Intelligence Approach, Volume II*. Morgan Kaufmann, Los Altos, CA.

T. R. Hinrichs 1988. Towards an architecture for open world problem solving. In *Proceedings of a Workshop on Case-Based Reasoning*, San Mateo, CA. Morgan Kaufmann.

J. Kolodner and R. Simpson Jr. 1984. A case for case-based reasoning. In *Proceedings of the Sixth Annual Conference of the Cognitive Science Society*, Hillsdale, NJ. Lawrence Erlbaum Associates.

J. Kolodner 1988. Retrieving events from a case memory: a parallel implementation. In *Proceedings of a Workshop on Case-Based Reasoning*, San Mateo, CA. Morgan Kaufmann.

J. Kolodner 1989. Judging which is the "best" case for a case-based reasoner. In *Proceedings of the Second Workshop on Case-Based Reasoning*, San Mateo, CA. Morgan Kaufmann.

L. Kopeikina, R. Bandau, and A. Lemmon 1988a. Case-based reasoning for continuous control. In *Proceedings of a Workshop on Case-Based Reasoning*, San Mateo, CA. Morgan Kaufmann.

L. Kopeikina, R. Bandau, and A. Lemmon 1988b. Extending cases through time. In *Proceedings of Case-Based Reasoning Workshop*, St. Paul, MN.

J. Lancaster and J. Kolodner 1988. Varieties of learning from problem solving experience. In *Proceedings of the Tenth Annual Conference of the Cognitive Science Society*, Hillsdale, NJ. Lawrence Erlbaum Associates.

M. Redmond 1989a. Combining case-based reasoning, explanation-based learning and learning from instruction. In *Proceedings of the Sixth Annual International Workshop on Machine Learning*, San Mateo, CA. Morgan Kaufmann.

M. Redmond 1989b. Combining explanation types for learning by understanding instructional examples. In *Proceedings of the Eleventh Annual Conference of the Cognitive Science Society*, Hillsdale, NJ. Lawrence Erlbaum Associates.

M. Redmond 1989c. Learning from others' experience: creating cases from examples. In *Proceedings of the Second Workshop on Case-Based Reasoning*, San Mateo, CA. Morgan Kaufmann.

R. L. Jr. Simpson 1985. *A Computer Model of Case-Based Reasoning in Problem Solving*. PhD thesis, Georgia Institute of Technology, Atlanta, GA.

Validated Retrieval in Case-Based Reasoning

Evangelos Simoudis
Computer Science Department
Brandeis University
Waltham, MA 02254
and
Digital Equipment Corporation

James Miller
Computer Science Department
Brandeis University
Waltham, MA 02254
and
Digital Equipment Corporation

Abstract

We combine simple retrieval with domain-specific validation of retrieved cases to produce a useful practical tool for case-based reasoning. Based on 200 real-world cases, we retrieve between three and six cases over a wide range of new problems. This represents a selectivity ranging from 1.5% to 3%, compared to an average selectivity of only 11% from simple retrieval alone.

Introduction

We have combined simple retrieval (based on the similarity of surface features) with domain-specific validation of retrieved cases to produce a useful practical tool for case-based reasoning. Starting with a case base of 200 real-world cases, we have narrowed our consideration to between three and six cases over a wide range of new problems. This represents a selectivity ranging from 1.5% to 3%, compared to an average selectivity of only 11% from this same case base using retrieval without validation. We are applying the same technology to a larger case base in a different domain, and have deployed a related tool with a much larger case base for actual use in the field.

Our work begins with a real-world problem: a computer manufacturer's diagnosis of system software failures. In this domain, diagnostic knowledge exists in several forms: manuals, courses, production rule systems, and knowledge bases. But the predominant starting point in current use is a set of data bases created by recording successfully diagnosed error conditions. In order to diagnose a new failure, non-expert specialists retrieve from a data base previously solved cases that appear superficially similar to the new problem. They then attempt to verify the similarity by performing tests on the new problem and comparing the results with those of each retrieved case. When they become convinced that a previous case is substantially the same as the new problem, they examine the resolution of the old case and report it (possibly amended or edited to more closely fit the new problem) to the customer. Only in rare cases are experts requested to examine problems — most are resolved from the existing data base — and the solutions are then added to the data base.

This existing human system is a conscious use of case-based reasoning (CBR) techniques; we have improved the system by adding to it an automated tool using results from AI case-based reasoning systems. In order to produce a tool of practical value we were forced to examine more closely the task of retrieval in case-based reasoning. Based on our experience we propose an extension to current systems, validated retrieval, that dramatically reduces the number of cases presented to the reasoning component (human or automated) of a case-based system. Validated retrieval relies on domain-specific knowledge about tests used to compare cases retrieved from the case base with newly presented problem cases. Knowledge about the relationships among the various tests is captured in a validation model which we implement as a semantic network[Quillian, 1968]. In order to build our validation model we are faced with a classic knowledge acquisition task. By perusing existing data bases used by specialists we are able to acquire this knowledge with a reasonable amount of effort — and with only a small investment of specialists' time.

Retrieval in CBR

CBR systems first retrieve a set of cases from a case base and then reason from them to find a solution to a newly posed problem. Existing systems ([Bareiss *et al.*, 1988], [Hammond, 1986], [Kolodner, 1983], [Kolodner *et al.*, 1985], [Rissland and Ashley, 1986] and [Stanfill and Waltz, 1986]) make two assumptions about the initial retrieval of cases from the case base:

1. Very few cases will be retrieved from the case library.
2. The retrieved cases are relevant to the problem being solved.

In many practical applications, retrieval alone is sufficient to solve the difficult part of a task. For example, in our domain of diagnosis of computer software failures, specialists can easily respond to customer problems if they can quickly locate a few similar cases from their collective past experience. For this reason, we have concentrated on the retrieval aspect of case-based reasoning. In MBRTALK[Stanfill and Waltz, 1986], also, the essential task is retrieval; the "reasoning" component consists of merely passing the retrieved information directly to an output unit.

Related Work

Closest to our own work is the work of Koton on CASEY[Koton, 1988], a CBR system which has been applied in the domain of medical diagnosis. CASEY has a justification component whose goal is to determine whether the causal explanation of a retrieved case applies to a new problem. This frequently allows CASEY to avoid invoking its causal model when creating an explanation for a new case. CASEY's justification phase is similar to our validation phase. But there is an important difference between these two systems arising from different assumptions about tests. CASEY relies on precisely two tests (EKG and X-rays), both of which are inexpensive and non-invasive. Both of these tests are performed prior to the retrieval phase and the results are used to provide surface features for the retrieval algorithm. By contrast, there are literally hundreds of tests to be performed in our domains and it is far too expensive to perform all of them in advance of initial case retrieval. As a result, our systems devote attention to minimizing the number of tests that are performed. We not only perform tests incrementally and cache the results, but also employ knowledge about the tests themselves to reduce the number of tests performed.

The CBR system CHEF[Hammond, 1986], whose domain is Chinese cooking, also uses retrieval followed by justification to identify the most appropriate plans (recipes) to solve a new problem. In order to identify a relevant recipe it performs simple tests, similar to our surface feature comparisons, during the retrieval phase. Once retrieved, a recipe may fail to completely satisfy the requirements of the new problem. In this case, CHEF consults a causal model of the domain in order to determine the cause of the mismatch and effect repairs. We have found that we can efficiently achieve our goal (retrieval of relevant cases) without recourse to a causal model by using a validation model that is significantly easier to construct. Our contribution is largely one of *scale*: if CHEF had a larger set of basic recipes from which to choose, our approach would almost certainly improve the performance of CHEF by limiting the number of recipes that must be repaired before a successful solution is found.

The SWALE[Leake, 1988] system concentrates primarily on modifying the explanation (contained in an explanation packet or XP) of a retrieved case to match a new problem. Nonetheless, it has a subcomponent, XP ACCEPTER, that justifies the application of a retrieved XP to a current situation. The ACCEPTER verifies an XP by determining if it can believe the applicability checks that are packaged with each XP. Each such test is similar to the tests associated with our validation model. Because of the small number of cases (eight, by our count) XP ACCEPTER never addressed the issues of scale which are our major concern. Thus, SWALE never developed a justification model to relate the various applicability checks to one another.

Finally, in the more recent case-based reasoning systems PRIAR[Kambhampati, 1989], KRITIK[Goel and Chandrasekaran, 1989], and CYCLOPS[Sycara and Navinchandra, 1989] also use both surface features and deeper knowledge, although in these systems the deeper knowledge is in the form of causal explanations. PRIAR and KRITIK use the causal explanations during case reasoning to adapt existing solutions to fit new problems — an important area, but one that our work does not explore. CYCLOPS concentrates on the reverse of our problem: we are concerned with retrieving too many cases for careful scrutiny, while in CYCLOPS the concern is that no relevant cases may be retrieved. CYCLOPS uses deep knowledge to modify the indices used during the retrieval phase, an approach that meshes nicely with ours to produce an automated method for improving the performance of surface feature retrieval.

Two Phases: Retrieval and Validation

Our goal is to take a sizable pre-existing case base along with a new problem and produce a small number of relevant cases. Like our human specialists, our systems perform diagnosis in two phases:

Retrieval: it poses a query to the case base using a subset of the features that describe the new problem.

Validation: it follows the validation procedure from each retrieved case to determine if it applies to the problem at hand.

The goal of the retrieval phase is to extract from the case base those cases that appear to be relevant to the new case. Since the case base is large, and we have been interested primarily in sequential implementations, it is important that the case base be organized in a way that permits efficient search based on surface similarities. For this reason, we organize the cases into a generalization hierarchy (using UNIMEM[Lebowitz, 1987]). The retrieval phase consists of traversing the generalization hierarchy to find a close match to the new problem. The result of this traversal is either an individual case (a leaf node) or a set of cases (an internal node in the hierarchy, returned as all of the cases indexed under that node). Unlike those systems that rely exclusively on UNIMEM for case retrieval, we don't fine tune UNIMEM to reduce the number of cases retrieved.

The validation phase then considers each of the retrieved cases and attempts to show that the case is relevant to the problem at hand. Associated with each case in the case base is a set of tests and their result values that must be met for the stored case to be valid. We call the set of tests and values a validation procedure, and each element of this set (i.e. a single test/value pair) is called a validation step. The tests are applied to the actual problem and the results are compared with the results in the case. Based on this comparison both the current case and other retrieved cases can be removed from further consideration. Only when all of the tests for a given case are successfully matched against the current problem is the case reported as a candidate for a reasoning component's consideration. (In other domains, it may be possible to assign weights to individual test results and use a threshold or averaging scheme for deciding whether or not to reject the case.)

The Validation Model

The validation phase of our method is straightforward if the individual validation tests are simple and self-contained. Unfortunately, in our domains, and probably in most real-world domains, this is not the case. In each domain we have studied, we have found that the tests are interrelated in a way that is not evident in advance, and we have been forced to face the knowledge acquisition task head-on. In Section we describe a methodology for acquiring this knowledge about tests. We have successfully used this methodology to develop validation models: structures that capture much of an expert's knowledge in a way that makes it easy for the validation phase to process the tests it requires.

What is a validation model?

The test space, which we represent with a validation model, is rich and complex. Not only are there the individual tests themselves, but the tests can often be grouped together to represent methods for testing larger components. Furthermore, performing one test may either require information gathered from earlier tests or generate information that modifies the meaning or need to perform subsequent tests. Thus, there are precedence constraints among the tests, conceptual groupings of tests, and a body of inferential knowledge involving the various tests.

For example, if we want to know why a house is hot (the problem), we may first want to see if the air conditioner is working. But before performing these actions we need to find out if the house *has* an air conditioner. In this example, the desired test (is the air conditioner working?) uses the output of another test (is there an air conditioner?). It is this knowledge, as well as knowledge about the important outcomes and implications of a test, that is captured by the validation model. We have chosen to represent this knowledge in the form of a semantic network whose nodes correspond to sets of tests and whose arcs indicate relationships between these sets.

This richness is reminiscent of causal models and naturally leads us to ask about the relation between causal and validation models. The two forms of models encapsulate different kinds of knowledge, serve to answer different questions, and facilitate different forms of reasoning. Causal models, like declarative programming languages, provide a base for detailed reasoning, theorem proving, and logical deduction — they try to efficiently answer "why?" questions. Validation models, like functional or imperative programming languages, provide control structures and efficient directed search mechanisms — they try to efficiently answer "how to?" questions. [Davis, 1984] argues that causal models can be used to answer the "how to?" questions of diagnosis. We agree, but the argument is similar to an argument from the programming language community: a logic program that clearly declares the meaning of square roots *can* be used to calculate their values, but a functional or imperative program is likely to do so far more efficiently. Similarly, we believe that a validation model is both easier to construct and more efficient to use than a causal model for, at least, diagnostic tasks.

Creating a Validation Model

We build our validation models by first examining *existing* data bases that are used by human specialists. These data bases may be either formalized (as in the case of our WPS-PLUS[1] system) or merely informal notes prepared by the specialists for their own perusal (as in the case of our VAX/VMS system). In our two case-based systems, the existing data contains a textual description of the steps that the specialists used to verify a hypothetical explanation of the problem. In constructing the validation model, it is our goal to capture the interrelationships between the validation tests. As a result, we have built validation models that correspond to a particular case base by:

1. Reading the validation procedures of each case and building a list of all the validation steps used in the entire data base. In the process of reading the data base and preparing this list, the implementor develops a sense of the underlying (but unstated) relationships between tests that are mentioned in the data base.

2. Examining the resulting list, looking for groups of tests that appear to form related sets. Organizing the list provides a basis for discussion with domain experts, who help "debug" the proposed organization.

3. Refining the structure of the list through knowledge acquisition sessions with domain experts. During these sessions, significant ranges of test results are identified, as are inferences from these results that eliminate the need to perform other tests. That is, a dependency graph based on test results is developed.

4. Iterating the above two steps after consulting additional information such as manuals and code documentation. The structure of the domain becomes clearer at each iteration. (We have found that three iterations are sufficient to produce a useful structuring.) The final validation model consists primarily of entries corresponding directly to information that appears in the original data base.

[1] DEC, VAX, VMS and WPS-PLUS are registered trademarks of Digital Equipment Corporation.

5. Integrating the test sets into the structure derived in the previous step. This integration makes explicit the prerequisites of each test, as well as providing alternative ways of obtaining information ordinarily provided by a particular critical test in cases where that test cannot be performed.

An Extended Example

In order to understand the validated retrieval process, consider the following example from the domain of automobile diagnosis and repair We have chosen a simple example from this domain because it allows the reader to understand the details of our approach. An example from either of our practical domains would require the reader to acquire a detailed understanding of a complicated software system. For our example we assume an existing case base with its associated validation model. We are given the following new problem:

NEW CASE			
make:	MAZDA	**model:**	626
engine:	2.0L EFI	**miles:**	50,000
year:	1985		
problem:	engine does not start.		

The retrieval phase uses the make, model, problem, and approximate year of manufacture to search through a case base of previous automobile problems. Based on these surface features, we retrieve three cases to be validated before presentation to a reasoning component:

CASE 1			
make:	MAZDA	**model:**	626
engine:	2.0L EFI	**miles:**	10,000
year:	1988		
problem:	engine does not start.		
validation:	The fuel injector was clogged. Fuel was not delivered to the combustion chamber for the engine to ignite. For this reason the engine could not start.		
solution:	cleaned the fuel injector.		

CASE 2			
make:	MAZDA	**model:**	626
engine:	2.0L	**miles:**	60,000
year:	1984		
problem:	engine does not start.		
validation:	The car had a faulty gas pump. Fuel could not be delivered to the combustion chamber. For this reason the engine could not start.		
solution:	Replaced the gas pump.		

make:	MAZDA	**model:**	626
engine:	1.8L	**miles:**	20,000
year:	1987		
problem:	engine does not start.		
validation:	A leak existed in the gas line. Fuel could not be delivered through the fuel line. For this reason the engine could not start.		
solution:	Fixed the leak.		

The validation model contains (at least) the three tests that are referenced by these cases: "check if a fuel injector is clogged", "check if the gas pump is working", and "check if there is a leak in the fuel line". The first of these is actually composed of two simpler tests: a test for fuel present in the reservoir of the injector and a test for fuel exiting the injector's nozzle. If there is no fuel in the injector then we can deduce that the injector is *not* at fault. Rather, the problem lies earlier in the fuel system — either in the pump or the fuel line.

The system first attempts to validate Case 1 by repeating the validation steps from that case. That is, we wish to test if the fuel injector is clogged. In the process of performing this two-step test we actually acquire knowledge that is relevant to Cases 2 and 3: if the fuel reservoir is not empty we can eliminate both cases; if it *is* empty, we can eliminate Case 1. This relationship is encoded in the semantic network that represents our validation model and is used in the validation phase.

In the best case, this validation model allows us to reduce the work required to validate cases from four tests to two tests and simultaneously reduces the number of cases to be considered by the reasoner from three to one (selectivity of 33.3%). The first test is for an empty fuel reservoir; if the reservoir is full then Cases 2 and 3 are eliminated. We then test the nozzle for fuel exiting. If no fuel leaves the nozzle, then Case 1 is presented to the reasoner; but if fuel *is* leaving the nozzle we, unfortunately, eliminate Case 1 as well and leave the reasoning component to its own resources. The worst case requires all four tests and provides either zero or one case to the reasoner.

Recent Results

An Operating System: VMS

The first system we developed is used for the diagnosis of device driver induced crashes of Digital's VMS operating system. The knowledge about surface features was obtained primarily from DEC internal publications and was complemented by an expert from the VMS support team during three knowledge acquisition sessions. It took a total of 84 hours to acquire the domain specific knowledge about surface features. Based on this information, the domain knowledge used by UNIMEM in order to organize the cases into a generalization hierarchy was implemented in five days.

It took an additional four days of reading validation procedures in the data base to develop a validation model for device drivers. In addition, four more knowledge acquisition sessions, lasting 40 hours, were needed to refine and improve the validation model. Encoding the actual validation model took about 80 additional days. We estimate that it took roughly 20 person-days to acquire the necessary knowledge and about 85 person-days to do the full system development.
Since this was our first attempt to build a case base and validation model, these numbers are much larger than we expect for subsequent systems. Our work to date on the system described in Section appears to confirm this expectation.

The system was evaluated using a case base of 200 cases that were obtained from notes written by specialists. The surface feature retrieval phase of the system was evaluated by presenting each of the 200 cases to the retriever (as new problems) and preparing a histogram of the number of cases retrieved. UNIMEM provides a mechanism, known as retrieval weights, for tuning its retrieval capabilities. After some experimentation, we discovered that the use of larger retrieval weights (i.e. more stringent matching criteria) caused the retriever to miss many relevant cases and, in many occasions, to fail to retrieve any cases at all. With less stringent criteria this problem was rectified. However, many of the retrieved cases were not relevant to the problem. With the optimal weighting, we were able to retrieve on average 22 cases per retrieval (11%). The validation phase, however, was able to reduce this number of cases to an average of 4.5 cases out of 200 (2.25%).

In addition, we presented three new cases to the system. Based on surface features alone, we retrieved 20, 25, and 16 cases (10, 12.5, and 8% selectivity). The validation phase reduced this to 3, 5 and 3 cases, respectively (1.5, 2.5, and 1.5% selectivity). Our experts confirm that these validated cases are the only ones relevant to the problems presented.

A Word Processing System: WPS-PLUS

The second system performs diagnosis of customer problems with the word processing component of an office automation product. During 15 hours of knowledge acquisition sessions, the knowledge about surface features was obtained from a support engineer for the product. It then took an additional five days to encode the domain knowledge for use by UNIMEM.

The validation model was obtained from the validation procedures of the cases in the data base, an internal publication, and 10 hours of knowledge acquisition with the same enginer. While the work is not yet complete (only 50 out of 340 cases have been encoded), it has taken only 10 days to implement the validation model.

This system was evaluated using a case base of 340 cases. Repeating the same experiment performed with the VMS case base led to an average of 26 cases per retrieval, or 7.6% selectivity. The validation phase reduced this to two cases, or 0.58% selectivity. Since the validation model for this case base is not yet fully encoded, we have not presented new problems to the system.

Scope of Work

Our validated retrieval method can be applied in many types of tasks. The basic requirements are: an existing data base of previous practical experience; a set of quick tests that serve to reduce the search space at low cost; a set of more expensive tests that can further reduce the search space; and an understanding of the relationships between the expensive tests.

We have identified four areas of potential interest, but we have limited our implementation work to the first of these:

- **Diagnostic tasks**. As shown in the example, we use the symptoms of a problem as the surface features for the retrieval phase. The validation procedure describes which tests to perform in order to determine if the case is relevant to the new problem.
- **Design tasks**. The surface features are specifications that a design must satisfy. The validation procedure for a stored design describes how to verify that its key parts meet the requirements specification.
- **Sales tasks**. The technique can be used to help identify sales prospects for a new product. The surface features are the characteristics of a customer such as: size of business, type of business, location of business. Each validation procedure describes the customer's requirements that were satisfied in a previous sale. The validation model includes tests that determine whether or not a customer needs a particular type of product.
- **Management tasks**. These tasks include accounting, credit analysis, investment decisions, and insurance underwriting. In each of these areas, specialists can identify easily recognized features in their problem domain (type of company, size, etc.) that allow rapid retrieval of similar situations encountered in the past. They then have more detailed tests that can be applied (debt/equity ratio, payment history, type of client, balance sheets, etc.).

Conclusions

Our work has concentrated exclusively on the issue of case retrieval. A careful study of two applications in which people consciously use case retrieval has shown that retrieval based solely on surface features is not sufficiently discriminating for use with large case bases. It results in large numbers of cases returned to the reasoner, each of which must then be further examined at great expense. Adding a validation phase that uses knowledge of domain-specific tests to prune the retrieved cases dramatically reduces the number of cases that must be examined by the reasoner.

We have found that acquiring knowledge about domain-specific tests is aided by an initial perusal of the existing data base used by specialists. With a reasonable amount of effort, and with only a small investment of specialists' time, this information can be captured in a validation model represented as a semantic network. We have used this methodology to produce two systems. One of these systems has been successful in practice, and the other (incomplete) system is likely to be equally useful.

While the burden of knowledge acquisition in our methodology is small compared with other methods, it is not negligible. Automating this work by combining a natural language system to analyze existing data bases with AI-assisted statistical comparison of surface features provides a fertile area for further investigation. Furthermore, we suspect that a careful study of such a system in practice will reveal validation tests that are sufficiently common that it may be reasonable to promote them to surface features, leading to a system with better retrieval capabilities. This analysis, which must first be performed manually to validate our assumption, is itself an excellent area for the application AI methods. In fact, the work on CYCLOPS appears to be directly applicable to this problem.

Finally, we feel that the kind of knowledge embodied in a validation model has received little serious attention. Yet this is the critical component of many knowledge-based tasks in the real world. The relationship between the "practical how-to" knowledge of our validation models and the more thoroughly explored "conceptually why" knowledge of causal models will bring important insights into the nature of knowledge itself. A reasonable first step in this direction would be to either make this distinction more precise or carefully argue that it is unnecessary.

Acknowledgements

The authors wish to thank David Waltz for his help with this research. In addition, we have received helpful comments from Candy Sidner, Andrew Black, Mark Adler, and Rose Horner.

References

[Bareiss *et al.*, 1988] Ray Bareiss, Karl Branting, and Bruce Porter. The role of explanation in exemplar-based classification and learning. In *Proceedings of Case-Based Reasoning Workshop*, 1988.

[Davis, 1984] Randall Davis. Didagnostic reasoning based on structure and behavior. *Artificial Intelligence*, 24, 1984.

[Goel and Chandrasekaran, 1989] A. Goel and B. Chandrasekaran. Use of device models in adaptation of design cases. In *DARPA Workshop on Case-Based Reasoning*, pages 100–109, 1989.

[Hammond, 1986] Kristian Hammond. *Case-Based Planning: An Integrated Theory of Planning, Learning, and Memory.* PhD thesis, Yale University, 1986.

[Kambhampati, 1989] S. Kambhampati. Representational requirements for plan reuse. In *DARPA Workshop on Case-Based Reasoning*, pages 20–23, 1989.

[Kolodner *et al.*, 1985] Janet L. Kolodner, Jr. Robert L. Simpson, and Katia Sycara-Cyranski. A process model of case-based reasoning in problem solving. In *Proceedings of the International Joint Conference on Artificial Intelligence*, 1985.

[Kolodner, 1983] Janet L. Kolodner. Reconstructive memory: A computer model. *Cognitive Science Journal*, 7:281–328, 1983.

[Koton, 1988] Phyllis Koton. *Using experience in learning and problem solving.* PhD thesis, Massachussetts Institute of Technology, 1988.

[Leake, 1988] David Leake. Evaluating explanations. In *Proceedings of the Seventh National Conference on Artificial Intelligence*, 1988.

[Lebowitz, 1987] Michael Lebowitz. Experiments with incremental concept formation: Unimem. *Machine Learning*, 2:103–138, 1987.

[Quillian, 1968] M.R. Quillian. Semantic memory. In Marvin Minsky, editor, *Semantic Information Processing*, pages 227–270. MIT Press, 1968.

[Rissland and Ashley, 1986] Edwina Rissland and Kenneth Ashley. Hypotheticals as heuristic device. In *Proceedings of the Fifth National Conference on Artificial Intelligence*, 1986.

[Stanfill and Waltz, 1986] Craig Stanfill and David Waltz. Toward memory-based reasoning. *CACM*, 29:1213–1228, 1986.

[Sycara and Navinchandra, 1989] Katia P. Sycara and D. Navinchandra. Index transformation and generation for case retrieval. In *DARPA Workshop on Case-Based Reasoning*, pages 324–328, 1989.

Commonsense Reasoning

MODEL-BASED DIAGNOSIS OF PLANNING FAILURES

Lawrence Birnbaum, Gregg Collins, Michael Freed, and Bruce Krulwich

Northwestern University
The Institute for the Learning Sciences and
Department of Electrical Engineering and Computer Science
Evanston, Illinois

Abstract

We propose that a planner should be provided with an explicit model of its own planning mechanism, and show that linking a planner's expectations about the performance of its plans to such a model, by means of explicit justification structures, enables the planner to determine which aspects of its planning are responsible for observed performance failures. We have implemented the ideas presented in this paper in a computer model. Applied to the game of chess, the model is capable of diagnosing planning failures due to incomplete knowledge of the rules, improper or overly optimistic focus of attention, faulty projection, and insufficient lead time for warning about threats, and is therefore able to learn such concepts as *discovered attack* and the *fork*.

1 Introduction

Learning by debugging, or *failure-driven learning,* has historically been the most prominent approach to learning how to plan in AI (see, e.g., Sussman, 1975; Schank, 1982; Hayes-Roth, 1983; Kolodner, 1987; Chien, 1989; Hammond, 1989). In much of this work, particularly in its early stages, no real distinction was made between the diagnosis methods used to uncover planning errors, and the repair strategies used to correct them. The hope was that relatively superficial descriptions of planning errors could be used to index directly to repair strategies that were likely to be useful in eliminating those errors. More recently, efforts have been made to tease these apart so that relatively general *model-based* methods for diagnosis can be applied to the task of finding bugs in faulty plans (see, e.g., Simmons, 1988). Such methods, derived originally from work in circuit debugging (see, e.g., Stallman and Sussman, 1977; Davis, 1984; DeKleer and Williams, 1987), depend upon having an explicit representation of how a plan is intended to function given certain assumptions. The task of the diagnosis component is then to determine which of these assumptions are faulty when a plan fails to operate as expected. We have been developing such an approach within the context of learning to plan in competitive situations (see, e.g., Birnbaum and Collins, 1988; Collins, Birnbaum, and Krulwich, 1989).

Many assumptions made during planning, obviously, concern the state of the world in which the plan will be executed. In addition, however, plans often depend upon assumptions about the capacities or properties of the agent executing them. Because this agent is often the planner itself, a planner needs some degree of self-knowledge in order to plan correctly. For example, if a robot planner were unaware of its lifting power, it might build plans requiring it to lift objects that were too heavy; if it were unaware of its width, it might build plans requiring it to squeeze through openings that were too narrow; and so on.

Perhaps less obviously, plans do not draw only on the physical capabilities of a planner: They also depend on its *cognitive* capabilities. Thus, a planner will require some knowledge of its mental and perceptual processes in addition to knowledge about its physical properties (Collins and Birnbaum, 1990). For example, chemists often put a stopper in a test tube in which they are boiling something, so that the "Pop!" that occurs when rising pressure forces the stopper out will alert them to the fact that it is time to remove the test tube from the heat.[1] This is a simple instance of a powerful and general strategy often employed by human planners, namely, setting an external alarm to alert the planner when some task needs his attention, thus freeing him to attend to other

[1]Thanks to Ken Forbus for this example.

matters in the interim. The success of such a plan depends upon two things: First, the planner must actually notice the alarm, and second, he must recall the task which is supposed to be resumed when the alarm goes off. In order for a robot planner to successfully apply this strategy, therefore, it will need to know something about the kinds of events that attract its attention—and which can therefore function as an alarm—and something about the reasoning processes that occur when its attention is drawn to such an event. The planner's theory of its cognitive machinery might, for example, specify that flashing lights, loud noises, and quick movements attract its attention; that once its attention is so attracted, the planner will attempt to explain the cause of the event; and that if the cause is due to the planner itself, the planner will recall its purpose in setting up the event. Armed with this theory, the planner can decide whether to attribute to itself the ability to be alerted by a particular type of event, for instance the "Pop!" of a stopper being disgorged from a test tube.

When faulty assumptions in a planner's model of itself cause planning errors, failure-driven learning can be invoked to enable the planner to identify and alter these assumptions, and thus improve its model of itself just as it would its model of anything else. However, in dealing with assumptions about its own capabilities as a planner there is another possibility: For in many cases, these assumptions about the planner are represented in terms of parameters that are *under the planner's own control*. Thus, *rather than changing the model to reflect the way the planner functions, the planner may be able to change the way it functions to conform with the model.*

2 Modelling the planner

Developing a model-directed approach to the diagnosis of planning failures, as discussed above, requires developing explicit models of the planning and plan-execution mechanisms employed, and of how the agent's plans depend upon those mechanisms. In this section, we describe models of two portions of a simple planner, dealing with threat detection and with execution scheduling.

2.1 A model of threat detection

Every planning domain presents a planner with a variety of threats against its goals. In coping with any particular class of threats in some domain, the planner has a choice of either attempting to permanently insulate itself from all instances in that class—i.e., of removing some necessary precondition for all instances of that sort of threat—or of attempting to deal with threats individually as they arise. We refer to these two approaches as the "Great Wall of China" paradigm, and the "Firefighting" paradigm, respectively. It is in the second of these two general strategies that the necessity for threat detection arises.

We model threat detection as a simple rule-based process: For each known type of threat, there is a rule that is able to detect instances of that threat if it is evaluated at some point in time prior to the realization of the threat. The planner must take account of a variety of constraints in formulating and deploying such rules. For example, in order to fulfill the function of threat detection within the Firefighting paradigm, each rule must be capable of detecting its threat in time to permit the planner to carry out an effective counterplan. Moreover, the planner must formulate a control regimen for checking its threat detection rules that ensures that whenever a threat arises, the appropriate threat detection rule will in fact be checked in time. We have previously argued (Collins, Birnbaum and Krulwich, 1989) that, all else being equal, the planner's task is simplified by attempting to detect threats as late as possible. In chess, that point is one move before the threat is carried out. A novice chess planner, then, starts out with a model in which it checks its threat rules at each turn, looking for threats that may be executed on the next turn.

Having decided upon this control regimen, the planner is faced with another choice: It can recompute the set of outstanding threats each time it checks its rules, or it can incrementally compute this set by looking only for changes that have occurred since the previous check. The latter approach is generally more efficient when the number of new threats arising per detection cycle is small compared to the total number of threats outstanding, provided that an effective method for focussing on threats that result from changes can be devised. In turn-taking games such as chess, incremental detection of threats means computing the threats added and removed by each move. Given the rule-based framework for threat-detection described above, focussing on threats resulting from changes can be implemented as a set of restrictions on the domain of application of the threat detection rules. In our model these restrictions are themselves implemented as a set of *focus rules* that specify the domain over which the threat detection rules will be applied. A portion of the model is shown in Figure 1.

$\forall x \exists t \; t \leq ert(x) \,\&\, detect(x, t) \rightarrow added\text{-}to(x, T, t)$

$\forall x, t_1, t_2 \; added\text{-}to(x, T, t_1) \,\&\, t_2 \leq ert(x) \,\&$
$\sim\exists t_r \; (t_1 \leq t_r \leq t_2 \,\&\, removed\text{-}from(x, T, t_r))$
$\rightarrow member\text{-}of(x, T, t_2)$

$\forall x \; \exists r, f, \theta, t \;\; t \leq ert(x) \,\&\, detects(r, x) \,\&\, active(x, t) \,\&$
$(evaluate\text{-}rule(r, \theta, t) \rightarrow detect(x, t)) \,\&$
$\theta \in focus\text{-}results(f, t)$

$\forall r, f, t, \theta \;\; \theta \in focus\text{-}results(f, t) \rightarrow evaluate\text{-}rule(r, \theta, t)$

$\forall x, t \;\; remove\text{-}from(x, T, t) \leftrightarrow member\text{-}of(x, T, t) \,\&$
$\sim active(x, t)$

Figure 1: Partial model of threat-detection[2]

2.2 A model of execution scheduling

Since a planner has limited resources, the formulation of a viable plan in service of an active goal is not, by itself, enough to guarantee that the plan will be carried out. Thus, another important aspect of any planner is a priority-based scheduling mechanism for determining which plans should be executed when. While such a mechanism could, in principle, be arbitrarily complex, we have chosen to model execution scheduling using a simple priority queue, assuming discrete time (which is sufficient for the turn-taking games we are currently investigating). Given such an approach, the basic model of execution scheduling is as follows: Once a goal is formed, a plan is chosen for that goal, assigned a deadline and a priority, and placed on the priority queue. At each time increment, the queue is checked, and the highest priority plan on the queue is chosen for execution. Thus a plan will be successfully executed if and only if there is a time before its deadline when it is the highest priority plan on the queue. A portion of the model appears in Figure 2.

$\forall p, t, g \;\; execute(p, t) \,\&\, t \leq deadline(p) \,\&\, plan\text{-}for(p, g)$
$\rightarrow achieve(g)$

$\forall p, t \;\; execute(p, t) \leftrightarrow member\text{-}of(p, Q, t) \,\&$
$\sim\exists p_a \; (member\text{-}of(p_a, Q, t) \,\&$
$priority(p) < priority(p_a))$

$\forall p, t_s, t_e \;\; added\text{-}to(p, Q, t_s) \,\&\, t_s \leq t_e \,\&$
$\sim\exists t_r \; (t_s \leq t_r \leq t_e \,\&\, removed\text{-}from(p, Q, t_r))$
$\rightarrow member\text{-}of(p, Q, t_e)$

$\forall g, t \;\; goal(g, t) \,\&\, call\text{-}planner(g, t) \,\&\, planner(g, t) = p$
$\rightarrow added\text{-}to(p, Q, t)$

Figure 2: Partial model of execution scheduling

3 Case study: The fork

The models described above were developed as part of an account of learning in competitive situations—in particular, chess. We will now consider their application to the acquisition of a classic chess tactic, the *fork*. In our account, the novice chess player initially notices the fork when it fails to block a threat against one of its pieces. Such a failure leads the planner to search for a fault in the planning and execution mechanisms involved in its ability to block threats—either, that is, in its mechanisms for detecting the threat, for formulating counterplans to the threat, or for executing such counterplans. This search employs the models described in the last section, along with certain other assumptions that specify how the mechanisms they describe are being deployed in order to block threats in chess. For example, one of these assumptions states that for each threat against materiel that is detected, a goal to block that threat will be formulated. In general, these assumptions can be derived by regressing (see, e.g., Manna and Waldinger, 1979) a specification of the desired behavior of the planner through the rules that specify its planning mechanisms.

Consider a situation in which white's rook and knight are under attack from a black pawn. Though it is white's turn to play, there is no move that would protect both pieces. Rooks are more valuable than knights, so white will save the rook, and black will capture the knight. If our planner is

[2]The predicate "ert" stands for earliest realization time, i.e., the earliest time at which the threatened action can be expected to occur.

placed in this situation, the capture of the knight will cause a failure of its expectation that all threats to its pieces will be blocked. We now give an informal account of how fault diagnosis must proceed in this case. (A more detailed description of the process is contained in the next two sections.)

By the first two axioms of execution scheduling (see Figure 2), the planner's ability to block a threat depends upon there being a time such that a counterplan for the threat is on the queue, it is before the deadline, and there is no higher priority plan on the queue. Thus, for blocking to have failed, it must have been the case that there was no such time, i.e., some necessary condition for execution must have been missing at each time when the plan might, in principle, have been executed. Thus we can group all of the times into equivalence classes depending upon which necessary condition failed to hold.

The diagnostic process has now reached a point at which the planner is presented with a choice of ways to fix the problem, since it can choose the time for which it wants to reinstate the missing condition. For example, execution could occur at an earlier time if the planner could find a way to schedule the plan earlier; execution could occur at a later time if the planner could find a way to postpone the carrying out of the threat, say, by putting the opponent in check; and execution could occur at a time in between if the planner could make the plan for saving the knight a higher priority than the plan for saving the rook. In the particular instance that we are considering, the only possible approach is to try to execute the blocking plan earlier. However, by the axioms describing the execution scheduling and threat detection mechanisms, this requires adding the blocking plan to the priority queue earlier, which in turn requires formulating a goal to block the threat earlier, which in turn requires detecting the threat earlier. Our approach, then, makes it possible for a planner to determine for *itself* that the way to cope with forks is to detect them sooner, rather than needing this piece of advice to be built in.

4 Diagnosing faults in plan justification structures

The goal of fault diagnosis is to explain the failure of an expectation as a consequence of the failure of some set of underlying assumptions. In our model the connections between underlying beliefs and consequent expectations are represented in terms of explicit justification structures (see, e.g., DeKleer *et al.*, 1977; Doyle, 1979). These justification structures, as alluded to above, record how the planner's expectations about the performance of its plans are inferred from the policies it has adopted, in conjunction with the axioms that constitute its model of the planning and execution mechanisms it employs. For instance, the justification structure underlying the expectation that the planner will block the threat to its knight in the fork example above is a conjunction of three antecedent expectations: That moving the knight will block the threat, that the move will be executed, and that such execution will take place before the opponent takes the knight. The expectation that the knight move will be executed is in turn justified by the conjunction of two prior expectations that the move appears on the plan queue and that it is the highest priority item on the queue; and so on. Diagnosing the fault thus involves "backing up" through these justification structures, recursively explaining the failure of an expectation as the result of a failure of one or more of its immediately antecedent expectations. This approach is similar to that proposed by Smith, Winston, Mitchell, and Buchanan (1986) and Simmons (1988).

More generally, a justification structure links an expectation with a set of supporting beliefs. The justification may be either *conjunctive*, meaning all the supporters must be true to justify the expectation, or *disjunctive*, meaning at least one of the supporters must be true to justify the expectation. When an expectation fails, the diagnosis algorithm attempts to determine which of its supporters should be faulted. If the support set is conjunctive, then at least one supporter must be faulted. If the support set is disjunctive, then all of the supporters must be faulted. The basic algorithm nondeterministically expands the set of faulted expectations according to these simple rules until a stopping criterion is met. However, when faulting conjunctive supports, the degree of arbitrary choice required can be reduced by checking whether a proposition in the support set was observed to be true during the execution of the plan, and if so removing it from consideration.

Since the goal of the diagnosis process is to provide enough information to allow a repair to be effected, the process should, in principle, continue until a repair is actually generated. Because of this, the diagnostic module in our system calls the repair module at each step, checking to see if the current set of faulted expectations provides enough information for a repair to be generated. This is particularly important for reducing the effort entailed in propagating a fault through a disjunctive justification. Although, in principle, every proposition in such a support set must be faulted when the supported proposition is faulted, it does not necessarily follow that the diagnostic procedure must explain the failure of each disjunct. Since the overarching goal of the process is to *fix* the problem, and since the repair of a single disjunct will suffice to restore the supported expectation, it may be enough to explain the failure of one disjunct. In other words, the attempt to fault a disjunctive justification results in the goal to *unfault* one of the disjuncts.

One additional point deserves special mention. There will be many instances in which the planner expects that the execution of a plan will involve some entity that meets a particular set of constraints, but does not know in advance the exact identity of this entity. This may be true, for example, of objects that will be found in the planning environment, including tools, raw materials, obstacles, and other agents. In our model, it is also true of execution times for plans, since the planner leaves the execution scheduler some latitude in determining when the plan should actually be carried out. The upshot is that some of the assumptions underlying the expectation that a plan will succeed are existentially quantified: They assert that a time, tool, or material meeting certain constraints will actually exist. Faulting such expectations causes special problems, stemming from the fact that the faulting of an existentially quantified proposition implies the faulting of an infinite set of disjuncts, one for each object over which the existential ranges. Of course, even in principle, the diagnostic engine cannot consider why the assertion failed for each instance of the variable. One solution is to partition the set of instances into classes in such a way that the elements of each class have all failed to meet exactly the same constraint or constraints, while meeting all others. This organizes the set of faulted instances in such a way that the unfaulter need only consider one instance of each type of failure, rather than repeatedly trying to unfault instances that have failed for the same reason about which it can do nothing. In the case of the fork, for example, the planner's expectation that there will be a time at which it will be able to carry out the plan to save the knight depends on there being a time before the deadline when the plan is on the schedule queue, and is of higher priority than anything else on the queue. Each of these three constraints defines a class of times, namely, those at which the expectation failed because that particular constraint was not met.[3]

5 Conclusions

We have proposed that a planner should be provided with an explicit model of its own planning mechanism, and have shown that linking a planner's expectations about the performance of its plans to such a model, by means of explicit justification structures, enables the planner to determine which aspects of its planning are responsible for observed performance failures. We have implemented the models of threat detection and execution scheduling described above in our test-bed system for failure-driven learning in planning domains (Collins, Birnbaum, and Krulwich, 1989). Applied to the game of chess, the model is capable of diagnosing planning failures due to incomplete knowledge of the rules, improper or overly optimistic focus of attention, faulty projection, and insufficient lead time for warning about threats, and is therefore able to learn such concepts as *discovered attack* and the *fork*. In other work (see, e.g., Collins, Birnbaum, and Krulwich, 1989), we have addressed the issue of how to use such diagnoses as a basis for repairing the planner's procedures in order to avoid such failures in the future.

We are currently developing explicit models of other aspects of planning, including plan formulation and optimization. In addition, we have identified a number of common sense planning concepts that could be acquired given richer models of threat detection and execution scheduling. For example, one possible reason for a planning system's failure to detect a threat in time might be that it does not evaluate its threat-detection rules often enough. In general, the frequency with which these rules should be evaluated must be a function of the

[3]In fact, there are several other equivalence classes, since multiple constraints may fail for a given time. However, since the goal of fault diagnosis given disjunctive justifications is to find something to *unfault*, we start with those classes corresponding to a single failed constraint on the grounds that these are likely to prove easier to fix.

speed with which threats develop in a particular environment. It is therefore possible that a planner could learn the need to alter this frequency in different domains by applying failure-driven methods. Thus, extending the model of threat detection presented in this paper will allow us to provide a computational account of the acquisition of the common-sense planning heuristic that when things are happening quickly, a planner should pay closer attention.

Acknowledgments: We thank Matt Brand, Kris Hammond, and Dick Osgood for many useful discussions. This work was supported in part by the Office of Naval Research under contract N00014-89-J-3217, and by the Defense Advanced Research Projects Agency, monitored by the Air Force Office of Scientific Research under contract F49620-88-C-0058. The Institute for the Learning Sciences was established in 1989 with the support of Andersen Consulting, part of The Arthur Andersen Worldwide Organization.

References

Birnbaum, L., and Collins, G. 1988. The transfer of experience across planning domains through the acquisition of abstract strategies. *Proceedings of the 1988 Workshop on Case-Based Reasoning,* Clearwater Beach, FL, pp. 61-79.

Birnbaum, L., Collins, G., and Krulwich, B. 1989. Issues in the justification-based diagnosis of planning failures. *Proceedings of the Sixth International Workshop on Machine Learning,* Ithaca, NY, pp. 194-196.

Chien, S. 1989. Using and refining simplifications: Explanation-based learning of plans in intractable domains. *Proceedings of the Eleventh IJCAI,* Detroit, MI, pp. 590-595.

Collins, G., and Birnbaum, L. 1990. Problem-solver state descriptions as abstract indices for case retrieval. *Working Notes of the 1990 AAAI Spring Symposium on Case-Based Reasoning,* Palo Alto, CA, pp. 32-35.

Collins, G., Birnbaum, L., and Krulwich, B. 1989. An adaptive model of decision-making in planning. *Proceedings of the Eleventh IJCAI,* Detroit, MI, pp. 511-516.

Davis, R. 1984. Diagnostic reasoning based on structure and behavior. *Artificial Intelligence,* vol. 24, pp. 347-410.

DeKleer, J., Doyle, J., Steele, G., and Sussman, G. 1977. AMORD: Explicit control of reasoning. *Proceedings of the ACM Symposium on Artificial Intelligence and Programming Languages,* Rochester, NY, pp. 116-125.

DeKleer, J., and Williams, B. 1987. Diagnosing multiple faults. *Artificial Intelligence,* vol. 32, pp. 97-130.

Doyle, J. 1979. A truth maintenance system. *Artificial Intelligence,* vol. 12, pp. 231-272.

Hammond, K. 1989. *Case-Based Planning: Viewing Planning as a Memory Task.* Academic Press, San Diego.

Hayes-Roth, F. 1983. Using proofs and refutations to learn from experience. In R. Michalski, J. Carbonell, and T. Mitchell, eds., *Machine Learning: An Artificial Intelligence Approach, Vol. 1,* Tioga, Palo Alto, CA, pp. 221-240.

Kolodner, J. 1987. Capitalizing on failure through case-based inference. *Proceedings of the Ninth Cognitive Science Conference,* Seattle, WA, pp. 715-726.

Manna, Z., and Waldinger, R. 1979. A deductive approach to program synthesis. *Proceedings of the Sixth IJCAI,* Tokyo, pp. 542-551.

Schank, R. 1982. *Dynamic Memory: A Theory of Reminding and Learning in Computers and People.* Cambridge University Press, Cambridge, England.

Simmons, R. 1988. A theory of debugging plans and interpretations. *Proceedings of the 1988 AAAI Conference,* St. Paul, MN, pp. 94-99.

Smith, R., Winston, H., Mitchell, T., and Buchanan, B. 1985. Representation and use of explicit justifications for knowledge base refinement. *Proceedings of the Ninth IJCAI,* Los Angeles, CA, pp. 673-680.

Stallman, R., and Sussman, G. 1977. Forward reasoning and dependency-directed backtracking in a system for computer-aided circuit analysis. *Artificial Intelligence,* vol. 9, pp. 135-196.

Sussman, G. 1975. *A Computer Model of Skill Acquisition.* American Elsevier, New York.

Characterizing Diagnoses

Johan de Kleer
Xerox Palo Alto Research Center
3333 Coyote Hill Road, Palo Alto CA 94304 USA
Alan K. Mackworth[1]
University of British Columbia
Vancouver, B.C. V6T 1W5, Canada
Raymond Reiter[1]
University of Toronto
Toronto, Ontario M5S 1A4, Canada

Abstract

Most approaches to model-based diagnosis describe a diagnosis for a system as a set of failing components that explains the symptoms. In order to characterize the typically very large number of diagnoses, usually only the minimal such sets of failing components are represented. This method of characterizing all diagnoses is inadequate in general, in part because not every superset of the faulty components of a diagnosis necessarily provides a diagnosis. In this paper we analyze the notion of diagnosis in depth exploiting the notions of implicate/implicant and prime implicate/implicant. We use these notions to propose two alternative approaches for addressing the inadequacy of the concept of minimal diagnosis. First, we propose a new concept, that of kernel diagnosis, which is free of the problems of minimal diagnosis. Second, we propose to restrict the axioms used to describe the system to ensure that the concept of minimal diagnosis is adequate.

1 Introduction

The diagnostic task is to determine why a correctly designed system is not functioning as it was intended — the explanation for the faulty behavior being that the particular system under consideration is at variance in some way with its design. One of the main subtasks of diagnosis is to determine what could be wrong with a system given the observations that have been made.

Most approaches to model-based diagnosis [4] characterize all the diagnoses for a system as the minimal sets of failing components which explain the symptoms. Although this method of characterizing diagnoses is adequate for diagnostic approaches which model only the correct behavior of components, it does not generalize. For example, it does not necessarily extend to approaches which incorporate models of faulty behavior [24] or which incorporate strategies for exonerating components [19]. In particular, not every superset of the faulty components of a diagnosis necessarily provides a diagnosis. In this paper we analyze the notion of diagnosis in depth and propose two approaches for addressing the inadequacy of minimal diagnoses. First, we propose an alternative notion, that of kernel diagnosis, which is free of the problems of minimal diagnosis. Second, we propose to restrict the axioms used to describe the system to ensure that the concept of minimal diagnosis is adequate.

The extended version of this paper [10] expands on the results, includes proofs for all the theorems, develops restrictions on the system description that allow the use of minimal diagnosis, and uses the approach to analyze current model-based diagnostic systems in more detail.

2 Problems with minimal diagnosis

Insofar as possible we follow Reiter's [20] framework.

Definition 1 *A system is a triple (SD,COMPS,OBS) where:*

1. *SD, the system description, is a set of first-order sentences.*
2. *COMPS, the system components, is a finite set of constants.*
3. *OBS, a set of observations, is a set of first-order sentences.*

Most model-based diagnosis papers [7; 8; 13; 19; 20; 24] define a diagnosis to be a set of failing components with all other components presumed to be behaving normally. We represent a diagnosis as a conjunction which explicitly indicates whether each component is normal or abnormal. This representation of diagnosis captures the same intuitions as the previous definitions but generalizes more naturally.

We adopt Reiter's [20] convention that $AB(c)$ is a literal which holds when component $c \in$COMPS is behaving abnormally. (Some of the model-based diagnosis literature uses $\neg OK(c)$ instead of $AB(c)$ but this is just terminology and does not affect the results of this paper.) Depending on the exact definition of fault for the diagnostic task being addressed, abnormality will mean something different. This is reflected in how AB is used in the sentences of SD. For example, in GDE [7], being

[1]Fellow, Canadian Institute for Advanced Research.

abnormal does not restrict the possible behaviors in any way since AB only appears in the form $\neg AB(x) \rightarrow M$ where M is the correct behavior of component x. In [19] being abnormal means that component behavior necessarily deviates from correct behavior since AB only appears in the form $\neg AB(x) \equiv M$.

Definition 2 *Given two sets of components $C1$ and $C2$ define $\mathcal{D}(C1, C2)$ to be the conjunction:*

$$\Big[\bigwedge_{c \in C1} AB(c)\Big] \wedge \Big[\bigwedge_{c \in C2} \neg AB(c)\Big].$$

A diagnosis is a sentence describing one possible state of the system, where this state is an assignment of the status normal or abnormal to each system component.

Definition 3 *Let $\Delta \subseteq COMPS$. A diagnosis for (SD,COMPS,OBS) is $\mathcal{D}(\Delta, COMPS - \Delta)$ such that $SD \cup OBS \cup \{\mathcal{D}(\Delta, COMPS - \Delta)\}$ is satisfiable.*

The following important observation follows directly from the definition (similar to proposition 3.1 of [20]):

Remark 1 *A diagnosis exists for (SD,COMPS,OBS) iff $SD \cup OBS$ is satisfiable.*

Unfortunately, there may be $2^{|COMPS|}$ diagnoses. Therefore we seek a parsimonious characterization of the diagnoses of a system.

Definition 4 *A diagnosis $\mathcal{D}(\Delta, COMPS - \Delta)$ is a minimal diagnosis iff for no proper subset Δ' of Δ is $\mathcal{D}(\Delta', COMPS - \Delta')$ a diagnosis.*

Thus a minimal diagnosis is determined by a minimal set of components which can be assumed to be faulty, while assuming the remaining components are functioning normally.

Note that these definitions subsume Reiter's [20]. Reiter's definition of the concept of diagnosis corresponds to our notion of *minimal* diagnosis. Reiter provides no definition corresponding to our notion of a diagnosis. All the results of [20] therefore apply to our concept of a minimal diagnosis.

The following is an easy consequence of the above definitions:

Remark 2 *If $\mathcal{D}(\Delta, COMPS - \Delta)$ is a diagnosis, then there is a minimal diagnosis $\mathcal{D}(\Delta', COMPS - \Delta')$ such that $\Delta' \subseteq \Delta$.*

Most previous approaches to model-based diagnosis have assumed that the converse holds, i.e., if $\mathcal{D}(\Delta', COMPS - \Delta')$ is a minimal diagnosis and if $\Delta' \subseteq \Delta$, then $\mathcal{D}(\Delta, COMPS - \Delta)$ is a diagnosis. However, as we relax the commonly made assumptions, for example by allowing fault models or exoneration axioms, the converse fails to hold and we must explore alternative means for parsimoniously characterizing all diagnoses.

Remark 3 *If $\mathcal{D}(\Delta', COMPS - \Delta')$ is a minimal diagnosis and $\Delta' \subset \Delta$, then $\mathcal{D}(\Delta, COMPS - \Delta)$ need not be a diagnosis.*

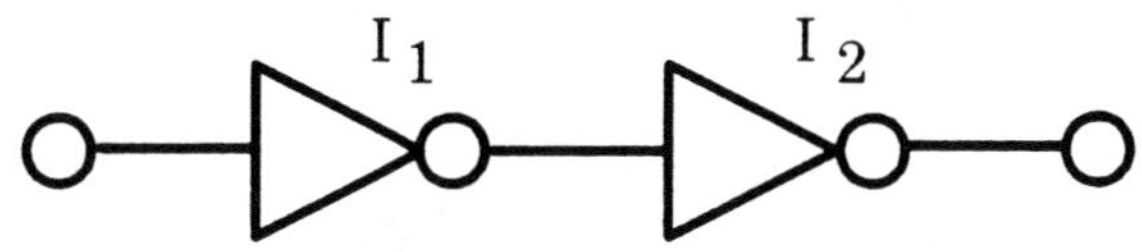

Figure 1: Two inverters

Thus, not every superset of the faulty components of a minimal diagnosis need provide a diagnosis. To see why, consider the following two simple examples. The first example arises if we presume we know all the possible ways a component can fail such as in [24].

Example 1 Consider the simple two inverter circuit of Fig. 1. If we are considering making observations at different times, then we must represent this in SD in some way. One scheme is to introduce observation time t as a parameter. Thus the model for an inverter is:
$INVERTER(x) \rightarrow$
$$\neg AB(x) \rightarrow [in(x,t) = 0 \equiv out(x,t) = 1].$$
We assume that SD is extended with the appropriate axioms for binary arithmetic, etc. Suppose the input is 0 and the output is 1: $in(I_1, T_0) = 0, out(I_2, T_0) = 1$. There are three possible diagnoses: $AB(I_1) \wedge \neg AB(I_2)$, $AB(I_2) \wedge \neg AB(I_1)$ and $AB(I_1) \wedge AB(I_2)$; these are characterized by the first two diagnoses, which are minimal. Suppose we know that the inverters we are using have only two failure modes: they short their output to their inputs or their output becomes stuck at 0. We model this as:

$$INVERTER(x) \wedge AB(x) \rightarrow [SA0(x) \vee SHORT(x)],$$

$$SA0(x) \rightarrow out(x,t) = 0,$$

$$SHORT(x) \rightarrow out(x,t) = in(x,t).$$

From these models we can infer that it is no longer possible that both I_1 and I_2 are faulted. Intuitively, if I_2 is faulted and producing the observed 1, then it cannot be stuck at 0, and must have its input shorted to its output. But then I_1 must be outputting a 1 and there is no faulty behavior of I_1 which produces a 1 for an input of 0. Thus, $AB(I_1) \wedge AB(I_2)$ is no longer a diagnosis, but the minimal diagnoses (remain) unchanged.

The only way to determine which of I_1 or I_2 is actually faulted is to make additional observations. For example, if we observed $out(I_1, T_0)$, we could distinguish whether I_1 or I_2 is faulted. Suppose I_1 is faulted such that $out(I_1, T_0) = 0$. To identify the actual failure mode of I_1 we have to observe $out(I_1, T_1)$ or $out(I_2, T_1)$ given $in(I_1, T_1) = 1$.

This example shows that the use of exhaustive fault models such as in [24] leads to difficulties with the usual definition of diagnosis. One way to avoid this difficulty is not to presume all the faulty behaviors are known as in [8]. However, if we do not know all the faulty behaviors, then nothing useful can ever be inferred from a component being abnormal which defeats the purpose of fault modes in the first place (this is addressed in [8]) by introducing probabilities).

Example 2 The usual definition of diagnosis encounters similar difficulties with the TRIAL framework of [19]. In this framework a component is considered faulty if it is actually manifesting a faulty behavior given the current set of inputs. If we are only concerned with one set of inputs, then every component is modeled as a biconditional. Thus, the inverters of Fig. 1 are instead described by:

$$INVERTER(x) \rightarrow \neg AB(x) \equiv [in(x) = 0 \equiv out(x) = 1].$$

Suppose the input and output are measured to be 0. There are only two diagnoses (the second of which is minimal):

$$AB(I_1) \wedge AB(I_2), \quad \neg AB(I_1) \wedge \neg AB(I_2).$$

It is not possible that one inverter is faulted and the other not. Each inverter exonerates the other. In terms of [19], each inverter is an alibi for the other. Thus, although $\neg AB(I_1) \wedge \neg AB(I_2)$ is a minimal diagnosis, neither $\neg AB(I_1) \wedge AB(I_2)$ nor $AB(I_1) \wedge \neg AB(I_2)$ are diagnoses. Again, we see that by including axioms which restrict faulty behavior in any way, the usual definition of diagnosis is inadequate to characterize all diagnoses.

In the remainder of this paper we explore two approaches to address this problem: (1) find an alternative means to characterize all diagnoses, and (2) restrict the form of $SD \cup OBS$ such that the notion of minimal diagnosis does characterize all diagnoses. We first require some preliminaries.

3 Minimal diagnoses

The minimal diagnoses are conveniently defined in terms of the familiar [17] notions of implicates and implicants (see [16; 21] for similar uses of these notions).

Definition 5 *An AB-literal is $AB(c)$ or $\neg AB(c)$ for some $c \in COMPS$.*

Definition 6 *An AB-clause is a disjunction of AB-literals containing no complementary pair of AB-literals. A positive AB-clause is an AB-clause all of whose literals are positive.*

Note that the empty clause is considered a positive AB-clause.

Definition 7 *A conflict of (SD, COMPS, OBS) is an AB-clause entailed by $SD \cup OBS$. A positive conflict is a conflict all of whose literals are positive.*

If $SD \cup OBS$ is propositional, then a conflict is any AB-clause which is an implicate of $SD \cup OBS$.

The conflicts provide an intermediate step in determining the diagnoses and are central to many diagnostic frameworks. The reason for this can be understood intuitively as follows. The diagnostic task is to determine malfunctions, and therefore the primary source of diagnostic information about a system are the discrepancies between expectations and observations. A conflict represents such a fragment of diagnostic information. For example, the conflict $AB(A) \vee AB(B)$ might result from the discrepancy between observing $x = 1$ while expecting it to be 2, if components A and B were normal. As a consequence, we infer that at least one of A or B is abnormal, i.e., the conflict $AB(A) \vee AB(B)$. Most researchers have focused only on positive conflicts. (As most previous research has focused on the positive conflicts, they usually represented conflicts as sets of abnormal components.) However, as we see in Section 4, the non-positive conflicts are important when modeling faults and doing exoneration.

Remark 4 *A diagnosis exists for (SD, COMPS, OBS) iff the empty clause is not a conflict of (SD, COMPS, OBS).*

Theorem 1 *Suppose (SD, COMPS, OBS) is a system, Π is its set of conflicts, and $\Delta \subseteq COMPS$. Then $\mathcal{D}(\Delta, COMPS - \Delta)$ is a diagnosis iff $\Pi \cup \{\mathcal{D}(\Delta, COMPS - \Delta)\}$ is satisfiable.*

Definition 8 *A minimal conflict of (SD, COMPS, OBS) is a conflict no proper subclause of which is a conflict of (SD, COMPS, OBS).*

Thus, if $SD \cup OBS$ is propositional, then a minimal conflict is any AB-clause which is a prime implicate of $SD \cup OBS$.

Theorem 2 *Suppose (SD, COMPS, OBS) is a system, Π is its set of minimal conflicts, and $\Delta \subseteq COMPS$. Then $\mathcal{D}(\Delta, COMPS - \Delta)$ is a diagnosis iff $\Pi \cup \{\mathcal{D}(\Delta, COMPS - \Delta)\}$ is satisfiable.*

Remark 5 *If all the minimal conflicts of (SD, COMPS, OBS) are non-empty and positive, then $\mathcal{D}(COMPS, \{\})$ is a diagnosis.*

As the minimal conflicts determine the diagnoses, they play a central role in most diagnostic frameworks.

Example 3 Consider the familiar circuit of Fig. 2. Suppose the component models are:

$$ADDER(x) \rightarrow [\neg AB(x) \rightarrow out(x) = in1(x) + in2(x)]$$

$$MULTIPLIER(x) \rightarrow [\neg AB(x) \rightarrow out(x) = in1(x) \times in2(x)].$$

As before we assume that SD is extended with the appropriate axioms for arithmetic, etc. With the given inputs, there are two minimal conflicts:

$$AB(A_1) \vee AB(M_1) \vee AB(M_2),$$

$$AB(A_1) \vee AB(M_1) \vee AB(M_3) \vee AB(A_2),$$

and four familiar minimal diagnoses:

$\mathcal{D}(\{A_1\}, \{A_2, M_1, M_2, M_3\})$:
$AB(A_1) \wedge \neg AB(A_2) \wedge \neg AB(M_1) \wedge \neg AB(M_2) \wedge \neg AB(M_3)$

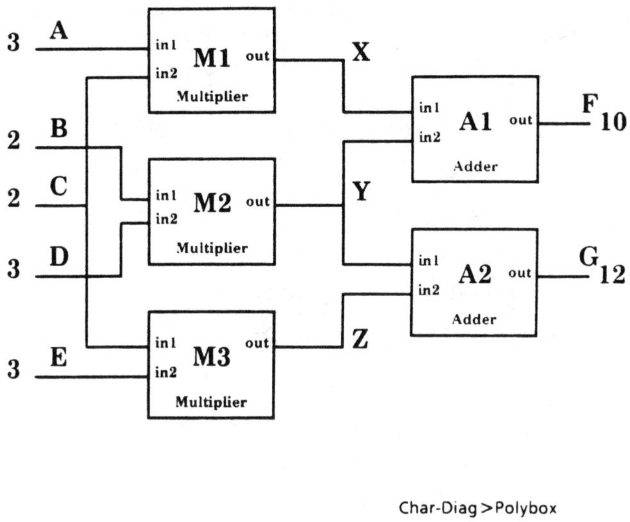

Figure 2: $F = AC + BD, G = CE + BD$

$\mathcal{D}(\{M_1\}, \{A_1, A_2, M_2, M_3\})$:
$AB(M_1) \wedge \neg AB(A_1) \wedge \neg AB(A_2) \wedge \neg AB(M_2) \wedge \neg AB(M_3)$

$\mathcal{D}(\{M_2, M_3\}, \{A_1, A_2, M_1\})$:
$AB(M_2) \wedge AB(M_3) \wedge \neg AB(A_1) \wedge \neg AB(A_2) \wedge \neg AB(M_1)$

$\mathcal{D}(\{A_2, M_2\}, \{A_1, M_1, M_3\})$:
$AB(A_2) \wedge AB(M_2) \wedge \neg AB(A_1) \wedge \neg AB(M_1) \wedge \neg AB(M_3)$.

Definition 9 *A conjunction C of literals covers a conjunction D of literals iff every literal of C occurs in D.*

Definition 10 *Suppose Σ is a set of propositional formulas. A conjunction of literals π containing no pair of complementary literals is an implicant of Σ iff π entails each formula in Σ. π is a prime implicant of Σ iff the only implicant of Σ covering π is π itself.*

Theorem 3 *(Characterization of minimal diagnoses) $\mathcal{D}(\Delta, COMPS - \Delta)$ is a minimal diagnosis of (SD,COMPS,OBS) iff $\bigwedge_{c \in \Delta} AB(c)$ is a prime implicant of the set of positive minimal conflicts of (SD,COMPS,OBS).*

This theorem underlies many model-based diagnostic algorithms. The first step, conflict recognition, finds positive minimal conflicts, and the second step, candidate generation, finds prime implicants. Clearly, if we were only interested in minimal diagnoses, then we would only be interested in identifying the positive minimal conflicts, but, in general, we must consider the non-positive minimal conflicts as well.

We now have the machinery to state precisely when the minimal diagnoses characterize all diagnoses.

Theorem 4 *The following are equivalent:*

1. *If $\mathcal{D}(\Delta', COMPS - \Delta')$ is a minimal diagnosis for (SD,COMPS,OBS), then $\mathcal{D}(\Delta, COMPS - \Delta)$ is a diagnosis for (SD,COMPS,OBS) for every Δ such that $COMPS \supseteq \Delta \supseteq \Delta'$ (i.e., every superset of the faulty components of a minimal diagnosis provides a diagnosis).*
2. *All minimal conflicts of (SD,COMPS,OBS) are positive.*

In Example 1, $AB(I_1) \wedge \neg AB(I_2)$ was a diagnosis, but $AB(I_1) \wedge AB(I_2)$, which has more faulty components, was not. By theorem 4 this must arise because one of the minimal conflicts is not positive. In this example, the negative clause, $\neg AB(I_1) \vee \neg AB(I_2)$, is a minimal conflict, which follows directly from the fault models of I_1 and I_2.

4 Partial diagnoses

Suppose we have the following two diagnoses for a three component system: $AB(c_1) \wedge AB(c_2) \wedge AB(c_3)$ and $AB(c_1) \wedge AB(c_2) \wedge \neg AB(c_3)$. We can interpret this as saying that c_1 and c_2 are faulty, and that c_3 may or may not be faulty. Thus, the two diagnoses may be represented more compactly by $AB(c_1) \wedge AB(c_2)$. In fact, we can view this as a 'partial' diagnosis in which we are uncommitted to the status of c_3; no matter what that status is, it leads to a diagnosis. This is the basis for Poole's observation [18] that a diagnosis need not commit to a status for each component whenever that status is a 'don't care'. Accordingly, we introduce the concept of a partial diagnosis. This concept also has the nice side effect of providing a convenient representation characterizing the set of all diagnoses.

Definition 11 *A partial diagnosis for (SD,COMPS, OBS) is a satisfiable conjunction P of AB-literals such that for every satisfiable conjunction of AB-literals ϕ covered by P, $SD \cup OBS \cup \phi$ is satisfiable.*

The following is an easy consequence of this definition:

Remark 6 *If P is a partial diagnosis of (SD,COMPS, OBS) and C is the set of all components mentioned in P, then $P \wedge \bigwedge_{c \in COMPS - C} A(c)$ is a diagnosis, where each A(c) is AB(c) or $\neg AB(c)$.*

Thus, a partial diagnosis P represents the set of all diagnoses which contain P as a subconjunct. It is natural then to consider the minimal such P's, which we call kernel diagnoses.

Definition 12 *A kernel diagnosis is a partial diagnosis with the property that the only partial diagnosis which covers it is itself.*

The following easy result provides exactly the characterizing property we have been looking for:

Theorem 5 *(Characterization of diagnoses) $\mathcal{D}(\Delta, COMPS - \Delta)$ is a diagnosis iff there is a kernel diagnosis which covers it.*

Consider the example of Fig. 1. Without the introduction of fault models there were three diagnoses: $AB(I_1) \wedge \neg AB(I_2)$, $\neg AB(I_1) \wedge AB(I_2)$, $AB(I_1) \wedge AB(I_2)$ which are characterized by the two kernel diagnoses: $AB(I_1)$ and $AB(I_2)$. With the addition of the fault models, the kernel diagnoses become: $AB(I_1) \wedge \neg AB(I_2)$ and $\neg AB(I_1) \wedge AB(I_2)$.

Partial and kernel diagnoses can be particularly easily characterized in terms of prime implicants and minimal conflicts. Recall that a conjunction of literals π containing no pair of complementary literals is an implicant of Σ iff π entails each formula in Σ.

Theorem 6 *The partial diagnoses of (SD,COMPS, OBS) are the implicants of the minimal conflicts of (SD,COMPS,OBS).*

Corollary 1 *(Characterization of kernel diagnoses) The kernel diagnoses of (SD,COMPS,OBS) are the prime implicants of the minimal conflicts of SD ∪ OBS.*

As a consequence of this corollary and theorem 3, if all minimal conflicts are positive, then there is a simple one-to-one correspondence between minimal diagnoses and kernel diagnoses.

Corollary 1 provides a direct way of computing the kernel diagnoses. One way of doing this is to convert the CNF-form of the minimal conflicts to DNF and simplify as follows (we omit the proof):

1. 'Multiply' the minimal conflicts to give a disjunction of conjunctions.
2. Delete any conjunction containing a complementary pair of literals.
3. Delete any conjunction covered by some other conjunction.
4. The remaining conjunctions are the prime implicants of the original minimal conflicts, and hence the kernel diagnoses.

Example 4a Consider Example 3. There are two minimal conflicts:

$$AB(A_1) \vee AB(M_1) \vee AB(M_2),$$

$$AB(A_1) \vee AB(M_1) \vee AB(M_3) \vee AB(A_2),$$

and four kernel diagnoses:

$$AB(A_1), \quad AB(M_1),$$

$$AB(M_2) \wedge AB(M_3), \quad AB(M_2) \wedge AB(A_2).$$

As all minimal conflicts are positive, these diagnoses correspond one-to-one to the familiar minimal diagnoses.

Example 4b If we considered a component to be faulted only if it manifested a faulty behavior under the current set of inputs (such as in [19]), then we would use slightly different component models:

$$ADDER(x) \rightarrow \left[\neg AB(x) \equiv [out(x) = in1(x) + in2(x)]\right]$$

$$MULTIPLIER(x) \rightarrow \neg AB(x) \equiv [out(x) = in1(x) \times in2(x)].$$

In this case the minimal conflicts become:

$$AB(A_1) \vee AB(M_1) \vee AB(M_2),$$

$$AB(A_1) \vee AB(A_2) \vee AB(M_1) \vee AB(M_3),$$

$$AB(A_2) \vee \neg AB(M_2) \vee AB(M_3),$$

$$AB(A_2) \vee AB(M_2) \vee \neg AB(M_3)$$

$$\neg AB(A_2) \vee AB(M_3) \vee AB(M_2),$$

and the kernel diagnoses become:

$$\neg AB(A_2) \wedge AB(M_1) \wedge \neg AB(M_2) \wedge \neg AB(M_3),$$

$$AB(A_2) \wedge AB(M_1) \wedge AB(M_3),$$

$$AB(A_1) \wedge \neg AB(A_2) \wedge \neg AB(M_2) \wedge \neg AB(M_3),$$

$$AB(A_1) \wedge AB(A_2) \wedge AB(M_3),$$

$$AB(A_2) \wedge AB(M_2), \quad AB(M_2) \wedge AB(M_3).$$

Note that because the positive minimal conflicts are unchanged, the set of minimal diagnoses remains unchanged.

In this example there are only a few more kernel diagnoses than minimal diagnoses (6 vs. 4). However, one possible disadvantage of this approach is that there may be exponentially more kernel diagnoses than diagnoses.

It is interesting to note that the set of minimal conflicts may be redundant. In Example 4b, the first and third minimal conflicts entail the second:

$$\frac{\begin{array}{l} AB(A_1) \vee AB(M_1) \vee AB(M_2) \\ AB(A_2) \vee \neg AB(M_2) \vee AB(M_3) \end{array}}{AB(A_1) \vee AB(A_2) \vee AB(M_1) \vee AB(M_3)}$$

Therefore, the second minimal conflict is redundant. Such redundancy can only occur if there are non-positive minimal conflicts. Unfortunately, these observations do not seem to be of much practical use because there is no easy way to tell whether there are enough minimal conflicts without first finding them all.

Definition 13 *A set of kernel diagnoses is irredundant iff it is a smallest cardinality set with the property that every diagnosis is covered by at least one of its elements.*

Theorem 7 *If all minimal conflicts are positive there is exactly one irredundant set of kernel diagnoses, namely the set of minimal diagnoses.*

Note that a system can have multiple irredundant sets of kernel diagnoses.

Example 5 Consider a circuit having three components A, B, C and the two minimal conflicts:

$$AB(A) \vee AB(B) \vee AB(C), \quad \neg AB(A) \vee \neg AB(B) \vee \neg AB(C)$$

These have six prime implicants (i.e., kernel diagnoses).

$$AB(A) \wedge \neg AB(B), \quad \neg AB(A) \wedge AB(C), \quad AB(B) \wedge \neg AB(C),$$

$$\neg AB(A) \wedge AB(B), \quad AB(A) \wedge \neg AB(C), \quad \neg AB(B) \wedge AB(C).$$

There are two irredundant sets of kernel diagnoses:

$\{AB(A) \wedge \neg AB(B), \neg AB(A) \wedge AB(C), AB(B) \wedge \neg AB(C)\}$

$\{\neg AB(A) \wedge AB(B), AB(A) \wedge \neg AB(C), \neg AB(B) \wedge AB(C)\}$.

Our analysis of kernel diagnoses corresponds exactly to the classical analysis in switching theory of so-called two level minimization of boolean functions (e.g., the Quine-McCluskey algorithm [14; 17]). The problem there is to synthesize a circuit realizing a given function as a disjunction of conjunctions of literals in such a way as to minimize the number of and-, or- and not-gates. Such circuits are characterized by irredundant sets of prime implicants of the given function. In the case of diagnosis, the given boolean function is specified by Π, the set of conflicts of $SD \cup OBS$. The kernel diagnoses are the prime implicants of Π, and the minimal sets of kernel diagnoses sufficient to cover every diagnosis are the irredundant sets of prime implicants of Π. It is well known from switching theory experience that the minimization problem is computationally intractable; there may be too many prime implicants, and even if there aren't, finding an irredundant subset of them is NP-hard. Designers of VLSI circuits have developed various approximation techniques [1]. Because of the exact correspondence with diagnosis, we can expect to profit from these techniques.

5 Prime diagnoses

Raiman [19] proposes a notion of prime diagnosis to characterize diagnoses. In his TRIAL architecture components are individually incriminated and exonerated. Therefore, he characterizes the diagnoses of a system in terms of the diagnoses involving its individual components. The following is a generalization of his definition.

Definition 14 *Given (SD, COMPS, OBS), a prime diagnosis for* $c \in COMPS$ *is a minimal diagnosis for* $(SD, COMPS, OBS \cup \{AB(c)\})$

Prime diagnoses characterize all diagnoses as follows.

Theorem 8 (Raiman) *Suppose* $\mathcal{D}(\Delta, COMPS - \Delta)$ *is a diagnosis. Then for each* $c_i \in \Delta$ *there is a prime diagnosis* $\mathcal{D}(\Delta_i, COMPS - \Delta_i)$ *for* c_i *such that* $\Delta = \bigcup_i \Delta_i$.

Unfortunately, Example 1 shows that not every union leads to a diagnosis. The prime diagnoses are:

$$P(I_1) = \{AB(I_1) \wedge \neg AB(I_2)\},$$

$$P(I_2) = \{AB(I_2) \wedge \neg AB(I_1)\}.$$

However, $AB(I_1) \wedge AB(I_2)$ is not a diagnosis. Thus, prime diagnoses are inadequate to characterize diagnoses.

Raiman [19] implicitly assumes all minimal conflicts contain at most one negative literal. In this case Raiman shows that the converse of Theorem 8 holds which makes prime diagnoses adequate for characterizing diagnoses. This useful property holds if $SD \cup OBS$ is horn, but we do not know of any more general practical condition on $SD \cup OBS$ which ensures it.

6 Restricting the system description

Our overall objective is to find methods of characterizing all diagnoses. We saw that minimal diagnoses were inadequate for this task in general and we examined kernel and prime diagnoses as alternatives. Another approach is to restrict the form of the system such that minimal diagnoses do characterize all diagnoses. We know from Theorem 4 that a necessary and sufficient condition ensuring that every superset of the faulty components of a minimal diagnosis provides a diagnosis is that all minimal conflicts be positive. Unfortunately, we are not aware of any simple necessary and sufficient condition on the syntactic form of a system which ensures that all minimal conflicts are positive. Clearly both OBS and SD need to be restricted because definition 1 allows non-positive AB-clauses to be part of OBS and SD. In the extended paper we explore some commonly used practical restrictions on OBS and SD that suffice to ensure that the minimal diagnoses are adequate to characterize all diagnoses.

7 Summary

The notions of minimal and prime diagnosis are inadequate to characterize diagnoses generally. We argue that the notion of kernel diagnosis which designates some components as normal, others abnormal, and the remainder as being either, is a better way to characterize diagnoses. We avoid significant complexity if kernel diagnoses contain only positive literals (i.e., all minimal conflicts are positive). This can be achieved by limiting the description of the system to ensure this. Most current model-based techniques take this approach[10].

There are usually a large number of minimal conflicts and kernel diagnoses (or minimal diagnoses). Therefore, the brute-force application of the techniques suggested in this paper is not practical. The contribution of this paper is that it provides a clear logical framework for characterizing the space of diagnoses in the general case. It thus provides the specification for an ideal diagnostician. In practice, some focusing strategy must be brought to bear. One approach is to exploit hierarchical information as in [13]. Another approach is to focus the reasoning to identify the most relevant conflicts in order to find the most probable diagnoses [8; 11]. However, both of these approaches require additional information: the structural hierarchy and probabilistic information.

8 Acknowledgments

The contents of this paper benefitted from many discussions with Olivier Raiman. Daniel G. Bobrow, Brian C. Williams, Vijay Saraswat and Jeffrey Siskind provided extensive insights on early drafts.

References

[1] Brayton, R.K., Hachtel, G.D., McMullen, C.T. and Sangiovanni-Vincentelli, A.L., *Logic minimization algorithms for VLSI Synthesis*, (Kluwer, 1984).

[2] Brown, J.S., Burton, R. R. and de Kleer, J., Pedagogical, natural language and knowledge engineering techniques in SOPHIE I, II and III, in: D. Sleeman and J.S. Brown (Eds.), *Intelligent Tutoring Systems*, (Academic Press, New York, 1982) 227–282.

[3] Davis, R., Diagnostic Reasoning based on structure and behavior, *Artificial Intelligence* **24** (1984) 347-410.

[4] Davis, R., and Hamscher, W., Model-based reasoning: Troubleshooting, in *Exploring artificial intelligence*, edited by H.E. Shrobe and the American Association for Artificial Intelligence, (Morgan Kaufmann, 1988), 297–346.

[5] de Kleer, J., An assumption-based truth maintenance system, *Artificial Intelligence* **28** (1986) 127–162. Also in *Readings in NonMonotonic Reasoning*, edited by Matthew L. Ginsberg, (Morgan Kaufmann, 1987), 280–297.

[6] de Kleer, J., Extending the ATMS, *Artificial Intelligence* **28** (1986) 163–196.

[7] de Kleer, J. and Williams, B.C., Diagnosing multiple faults, *Artificial Intelligence* **32** (1987) 97-130. Also in *Readings in NonMonotonic Reasoning*, edited by Matthew L. Ginsberg, (Morgan Kaufmann, 1987), 372–388.

[8] de Kleer, J. and Williams, B.C, Diagnosis with behavioral modes, in: *Proceedings IJCAI-89*, Detroit, MI (1989) 1324–1330.

[9] de Kleer, J., A comparison of ATMS and CSP techniques, *Proceedings of the Eleventh International Joint Conference on Artificial Intelligence*, Detroit, MI (August 1989) 290–296.

[10] de Kleer, J., Mackworth, A.K. and Reiter, R., Characterizing Diagnoses and Systems, SSL Paper P89-00193, Xerox PARC, 1990. Also available as University of British Columbia Department of Computer Science TR90-8.

[11] Dressler, O., and Farquhar, A., Focusing ATMS-based problem solvers, Siemens Report INF-2-ARM 13, 1989.

[12] Genesereth, M.R., The use of design descriptions in automated diagnosis, *Artificial Intelligence* **24** (1984) 411–436.

[13] Hamscher, W.C., Model-based troubleshooting of digital systems, Artificial Intelligence Laboratory, TR-1074, Cambridge: M.I.T., 1988.

[14] Hill, F.J. and Peterson, G.R., *Introduction to Switching Theory and Logical Design* (John Wiley and Sons, New York, 1974).

[15] Kohavi, Z., *Switching and Finite Automata Theory* (McGraw-Hill, 1978).

[16] Kean, A. and Tsiknis, G., An incremental method for generating prime implicants/implicates, University of British Columbia Technical Report TR88-16, 1988.

[17] Kohavi, Z., *Switching and Finite Automata Theory* (McGraw-Hill, 1978).

[18] Poole, D., Representing knowledge for logic-based diagnosis, *Proc. Int. Conf. on Fifth Generation Computer Systems* (1988) 1282–1290.

[19] Raiman, O., Diagnosis as a trial: The alibi principle, IBM Scientific Center, 1989.

[20] Reiter, R., A theory of diagnosis from first principles, *Artificial Intelligence* **32** (1987) 57–95. Also in *Readings in Non-Monotonic Reasoning*, edited by Matthew L. Ginsberg, (Morgan Kaufmann, 1987), 352–371.

[21] Reiter, R. and J. de Kleer, Foundations of Assumption-Based Truth Maintenance Systems: Preliminary Report, *Proceedings of the National Conference on Artificial Intelligence*, Seattle, WA (July, 1987), 183–188.

[22] Slagle, J.R., C.L. Chang, and R.C.T. Lee, A new algorithm for generating prime implicants, *IEEE Transactions on Computers* **C-19**(4) (April 1970) 304–310.

[23] Struss, P., Extensions to ATMS-based Diagnosis, in: J.S. Gero (ed.), *Artificial Intelligence in Engineering: Diagnosis and Learning* (Elsevier, Amsterdam, 1988) 3–28.

[24] Struss, P., and Dressler, O., "Physical negation" — Integrating fault models into the general diagnostic engine, in: *Proceedings IJCAI-89* Detroit, MI (1989) 1318-1323.

Physical Impossibility Instead of Fault Models

Gerhard Friedrich, Georg Gottlob, Wolfgang Nejdl
Christian Doppler Laboratory for Expert Systems
Technical University of Vienna, Paniglgasse 16,
A-1040 Vienna, Austria — friedrich@vexpert.at

Abstract

In this paper we describe the concept of *physical impossibility* as an alternative to the specification of fault models. These axioms can be used to exclude impossible diagnoses similar to fault models. We show for Horn clause theories while the complexity of finding a first diagnosis is worst-case exponential for fault models, it is polynomial for physical impossibility axioms. Even for the case of finding all diagnoses using physical impossibility axioms instead of fault models is more efficient, although both are exponential in the worst case. These results are used for a polynomial diagnosis and measurement strategy which finds a final sufficient diagnosis.

1 Introduction

Model-based diagnosis has traditionally been based on the use of a correct behavior model. Faulty components were assumed to show arbitrary behavior modeled by an *unknown fault* mode.

An interesting extension to this approach is the inclusion of specific fault models, which have been introduced in [3] and [6]. [3] retains an *unknown fault* mode and uses fault models to assign different probabilities to different behavior modes. [6] shows how to exclude impossible diagnoses ("the light of a bulb is on although no voltage is present") by deleting the *unknown fault* mode. However, in this case the fault models have to be complete to find the correct diagnoses. While the correct model behavior can often be expressed as a Horn clause theory (with polynomial consistency checking[1]) the introduction of fault models leads to a non Horn clause theory in any case and thus to a computationally more complex algorithm for finding diagnoses.

[1] In this paper we assume a system model guaranteeing a restricted term depth of all arguments and a restricted number of argument positions. Otherwise the problem would of course be undecidable or exponential.

In this paper we investigate a third approach, which excludes impossible diagnoses by specifying physical impossibility axioms in the form of negative clauses. This approach does not enlarge the diagnosis complexity compared to a correct behavior based system, but usually excludes the same diagnoses as fault models. Starting from a Horn clause description of the correct behavior, the introduction of physical impossibility axioms retains the Horn property. On the other hand the introduction of fault models leads to a non Horn theory resulting in an exponential algorithm for finding even a first diagnosis. Our approach is therefore advantageous in cases where the additional information which can be expressed by specific fault models (like probabilities of different behavior modes) is not needed or not available.

In Section 2 we describe the concept of physical impossibility and discuss the relationship between physical impossibility and fault models. Section 3 shows the computational advantages of our approach and discusses the worst-case complexity of finding diagnoses. A polynomial algorithm for finding a final sufficient diagnosis is given which is not possible if we use fault models.

Because of the space limitations formal definitions and complete proofs are given in a longer version of this paper.

2 Physical Impossibility

To describe the notion of physical impossibility, let us first analyze the possible behavior of the components of a device. This behavior can be represented by specifying constraints between the state variables describing the component. We assume a finite domain for these variables. Each state variable can have only one value.

The domain of a component can be specified by a finite set of value tuples denoting all possible value combinations which can be assigned to the state variables of the component. The arity of a tuple is equal to the number of variables describing a component.

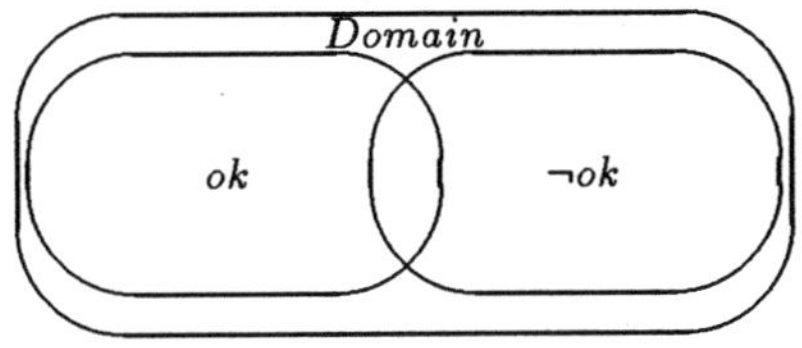

Figure 1: Tuple domain of a component including correct behavior and fault model tuples.

To diagnose a system various subsets of this domain may be specified. The relations of these sets are depicted in Figure 1. We will discuss the following sets (using $S_1 \setminus S_2$ to denote S_1 minus S_2):

- correct behavior set denoted by *ok*
- fault model set $\neg ok$
- physical impossibility set $(Domain \setminus (\neg ok \cup ok))$

In the following paragraphs we will describe how to represent correct, faulty, and impossible behavior. For each definition we show the appropriate rules used for the bulb example which has been introduced in [6]. Note, that the specific formalism used for describing a system model depends on the inference mechanism used. The general concepts defined here do not depend on it.

In Figure 2 a simple circuit is shown, consisting of a power supply and three bulbs. Wires connect these components in parallel. The domain theory specifies the correct behavior of the circuit as usual, as described below. The literal $ok(X)$ denotes that the component X works correctly.

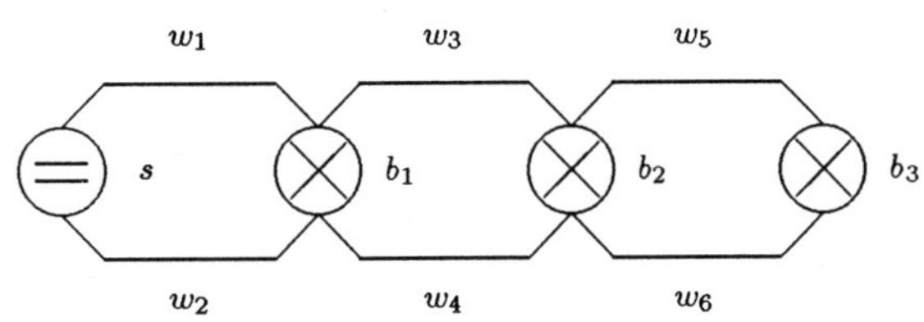

Figure 2: Three bulbs and one voltage supply in parallel

The following axioms describe the *correct behavior* of our components. Variables are stated by capital letters and are universally quantified. In order to achieve a clear and simple presentation, we assume without losing generality that wires always behave correctly.

(1) bulb(X) ∧ ok(X) ∧ val(port(X),+)
→ val(light(X),on).
(2) bulb(X) ∧ ok(X) ∧ val(port(X),0)
→ val(light(X),off).
(3) bulb(X) ∧ ok(X) ∧ val(light(X),off)
→ val(port(X),0).
(4) bulb(X) ∧ ok(X) ∧ val(light(X),on)
→ val(port(X),+).
(5) supply(X) ∧ ok(X)
→ val(port(X),+).

Values are propagated along connections, each state variable can have only one value.

val(Port1, Val) ∧ conn(Port1,Port2)
→ val(Port2, Val).
val(Port1, Val) ∧ conn(Port2,Port1)
→ val(Port2, Val).
val(Port, Val1) ∧ val(Port, Val2)
→ Val1 = Val2.

$supply(s)$.	$conn(port(s),port(b_1))$.
$bulb(b_1)$.	$conn(port(s),port(b_2))$.
$bulb(b_2)$.	$conn(port(s),port(b_3))$.
$bulb(b_3)$.	

Additionally the following observations are made:

$val(light(b_1),off)$. $val(light(b_3),on)$.
$val(light(b_2),off)$.

The construction of conflict sets leads to four minimal conflict sets $\langle s,b_1\rangle$, $\langle s,b_2\rangle$, $\langle b_1,b_3\rangle$ and $\langle b_2,b_3\rangle$ which determine two diagnoses $[s,b_3]$ and $[b_1,b_2]$.

Now usually one would not consider b_1 and b_2 to be correct while b_3 and s are faulty producing light when there is no power supply. The additional information a diagnosis expert uses in this case is the knowledge about what is physically possible. If this knowledge is omitted (because only the correct behavior is modeled), "miracles" are possible.

Using the principle of *physical impossibility*, we simply exclude all tuples which are impossible. This can always be done by completely negative clauses and thus without adding a non Horn clause to the description of the correct behavior. In our case:

¬ (bulb(X) ∧ val(light(X),on) ∧ val(port(X),0)).

Using domain closure axioms stating that a light can be *on* or *off* and that the voltage can be 0 or +, we get the following rules, which subsume rule 2 and 4 of our correct behavior rules. They can be used instead of the physical impossibility axiom.

bulb(X) ∧ val(light(X),on)	→	*val(port(X),+).*
bulb(X) ∧ val(port(X),0)	→	*val(light(X),off).*

On the other hand, a *fault model* consists of the following axiom to eliminate the undesirable diagnosis $[s, b_3]$:

$$bulb(X) \wedge \neg\ ok(X)$$
$$\rightarrow\ (val(port(X),0) \wedge val(light(X),off)) \vee$$
$$(val(port(X),+) \wedge val(light(X),off)).$$

This axiom can be simplified to

$$bulb(X) \wedge \neg\ ok(X) \quad \rightarrow \quad val(light(X),off).$$

The introduction of fault models into a Horn theory describing the correct behavior always leads to a non Horn theory. (If we use the literal $ab(X)$ denoting abnormal behavior, we have to include the additional axiom $ab(X) \leftrightarrow \neg ok(X)$).

Both approaches reduce the conflict sets $\langle s, b_1\rangle$, $\langle s, b_2\rangle$ to $\langle b_1\rangle$ and $\langle b_2\rangle$. This results in the elimination of diagnosis $[s, b_3]$. The reason for the conflict set reduction using the fault model approach is that $ok(b_3)$ can be deduced without assuming it, since the light is *on*. Therefore each single assumption $ok(b_1)$ and $ok(b_2)$ is inconsistent with the system description and the observations. By using physical impossibility, we simply exclude the possibility, that a light is *on* with no voltage present. Transforming the physical impossibility axiom using the domain axioms even lets us directly deduce the presence of voltage. (Note, that we use the domain axioms only during transformation, not for the final generation of the model.)

This example suggests an equivalence between fault models and physical impossibility axioms. This equivalence can be formally described by the following theorem:

Theorem 1 If the domain and the model of correct behavior is represented and $\neg ok(X)$ only appears in the clauses representing the correct behavior (e.g., $ok(c_i) \rightarrow \ldots$) then the additional specification of a fault model is equivalent to the additional specification of the physical impossibility axioms for the task of diagnosis.

We use the usual component oriented description and the assumption that faults are independent from each other. Rules like $\neg ok(c_i) \rightarrow \neg ok(c_j)$ are excluded.

Proof (informal): Using domain axioms and the axioms describing correct and faulty behavior we can deduce the physical impossibility axioms. No additional conflict will result if we add the physical impossibility axioms to the system model.

On the other hand using domain axioms, correct behavior and physical impossibility axioms (which are specified by negative clauses), we can deduce the possible behavior. Additionally for each component c_i in a diagnosis we can deduce $\neg ok(c_i)$ otherwise the diagnosis would not be minimal. This can be deduced only by using the correct behavior clauses, as $\neg ok(c_i)$ does not appear in any other clauses. Therefore every correct behavior tuple leads to a contradiction. Using the possible behavior, we can now derive at least a subset of the faulty behavior subsuming the fault model.

Let us denote the correct behavior axioms as $\mathcal{B}_C$, the faulty behavior axioms as $\mathcal{B}_F$, the physical impossibility axioms as $\mathcal{B}_I$ and the domain axioms as $\mathcal{D}$.

Then we can write the equivalence of fault models and physical impossibility axioms for the purpose of finding all diagnoses somewhat informally as

$$\mathcal{B}_C \cup \mathcal{D} \cup \mathcal{B}_I \cong \mathcal{B}_C \cup \mathcal{D} \cup \mathcal{B}_F$$

In most systems (especially those based on value propagation) only Horn clauses are used for describing correct and faulty behavior modes. Explicit domain axioms are not included in the system model. Notwithstanding the potential incompleteness caused by this omission, we usually use such a simplified theory to avoid combinatorial explosion. Its incompleteness with respect to diagnosis decreases with an increasing set of measurements.

What we would therefore like to prove is the following equivalence of physical impossibility and fault models (without domain axioms):

$$\mathcal{B}_C \cup \mathcal{B}_I \cong \mathcal{B}_C \cup \mathcal{B}_F$$

Although this is indeed valid in many cases it is possible to construct situations where the addition of Horn clause fault models yields a more complete theory than the addition of physical impossibility. If domain axioms are omitted physical impossibility axioms can therefore only be a reasonable approximation. However, although Horn clause fault models yield better results in some cases, they are themselves an approximation (except if completely unrestricted clauses are used).

In Section 3 we will show that physical impossibility axioms do not degrade the efficiency of the diagnosis algorithm. We can still construct a polynomial algorithm finding a final sufficient diagnosis for such a theory. On the other hand we show that fault models are intractable, something we wanted to avoid when we excluded the domain axioms initially. So we are faced once again with the well-known completeness/efficiency tradeoff often encountered in AI.

3 Efficiency and Complexity

3.1 Efficiency Considerations

To allow efficient consistency checking and diagnosis generation, we use Horn clauses for our system model as much as possible. This corresponds to the use of value propagation as inference engine. Usually only the subset of the correct behavior which can be expressed by functional dependencies is used in the system model.

It is clear that by extending such a Horn clause theory by physical impossibility axioms (which are negative or definite clauses) we do not increase the complexity of the diagnosis process, while even the inclusion of Horn clause fault models automatically makes the theory non Horn, leading to the well-known combinatorial explosion.

Example 1 We use the standard d74 circuit depicted in Figure 3.1 with six different behavior modes (as used in [4], see Figure 3.1).

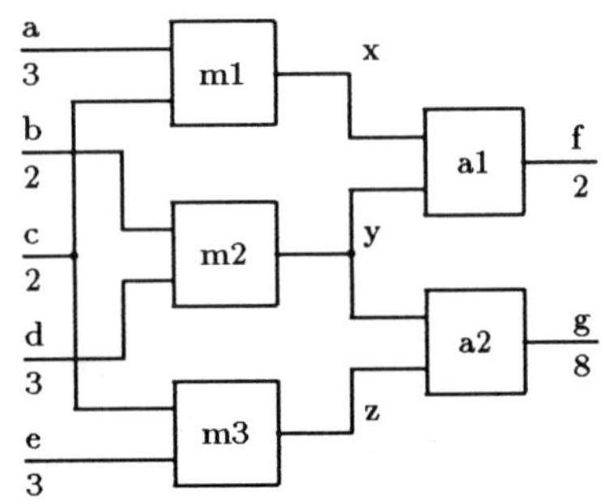

1. output is correct
2. output is zero
3. output is left input
4. output is right input
5. output is one
6. output is shifted left one bit

Figure 3: D74-circuit

We do not use an *unknown fault* mode, as such a mode would allow any possible behavior. Such a fault mode is therefore only interesting if we rely on probability ranking.

Initial measurements are $a = d = e = 3$, $b = c = 2$, $f = 2$ and $g = 8$. The two double fault diagnoses for these measurements are $[(a1, right), (m2, left)]$ and $[(m1, zero), (m2, left)]$. Using physical impossibility we get the same diagnoses as using fault models, without the additional fault mode information. However, if we just want to change the faulty components, the exact fault mode is irrelevant. (In this example, the physical impossibility axioms define that any behavior not covered by the behavior modes is inconsistent.)

Using the MOMO system described in [5] we got the following normalized model generation times (for finding all diagnoses):

- physical impossibility (4 or 6 modes): 1
- fault models (first 4 modes): 7.6
- fault models (all 6 modes): 22.9

In this example we achieved a runtime improvement factor of 22.9 by using physical impossibility axioms instead of fault models. Note, that this does not depend on our algorithm, but simply mirrors the combinatorial explosion caused by the non Horn theory (see also [4]). Each fault model introduces alternative rules used for value propagation and we have exponentially many combinations of fault models.

On the other hand physical impossibility is barely affected by the introduction of additional fault models, as only the checks to exclude impossible diagnoses get slightly more complicated. No new values are deduced because of the physical impossibility axioms. Consistency has to be checked only for a Horn clause theory.

3.2 Complexity

In the following we will concentrate on Horn clause theories for the correct and faulty behavior and the physical impossibility axioms. This is sufficient for most cases and usually used by value propagation systems. It also allows us to capture all functional dependencies.

For consistency based model-based diagnosis we can state the following complexity theorems. They are independent of the inference strategy used.

Theorem 2 Assume a description of the correct behavior by a (propositional) Horn clause theory, a set of observations and a set of (already found) diagnoses $\mathcal{D}$. The complexity of deciding whether ***a next diagnosis*** exists which is not in $\mathcal{D}$ is $\mathcal{NP}$-complete.

Proof (informal): The problem is obviously in $\mathcal{NP}$. By reduction to SAT we can show that it is also $\mathcal{NP}$-complete.

Let C be a set of propositional clauses in SAT form. Let U be the set of variables used in C. Assume further for each x $(\neg x)$ that there exists at least one clause $c \in C$ such that x $(\neg x)$ does not occur in c. We use the following instance of the next diagnosis problem $ND = \langle COMP, SD, OBS, D\rangle$ consisting of a set of components, a system description, a set of observations and of diagnoses.

$$\begin{aligned}
COMP &= \{x, \bar{x} \mid x \in U\} \\
SD &= G_1 \cup G_2 \cup G_3 \cup G_4 \\
OBS &= \{\neg z\} \\
D &= \{\{x, \bar{x}\} \mid x \in U\} \\
G_1 &= \{[\textstyle\bigwedge_{x \in c} ok_x \wedge \bigwedge_{\neg x \in c} ok_{\bar{x}}] \rightarrow f \mid c \in C\} \\
G_2 &= \{ok_x \rightarrow \hat{x}, ok_{\bar{x}} \rightarrow \hat{x} \mid x \in U\} \\
G_3 &= \{\textstyle\bigwedge_{x \in U} \hat{x} \rightarrow a\} \\
G_4 &= \{a \wedge f \rightarrow z\}
\end{aligned}$$

For a diagnosis $\Delta \notin D$ the following truth value assignment satisfies C:

$$\forall u \in U : \varphi(u) = \begin{cases} true & if\ u \in \Delta \\ false & otherwise \end{cases}$$

Using this assignment we can show

$$C\ satisfiable \iff \exists \Delta \notin D\ for\ ND$$

This complexity theorem is valid if the system description includes just a model of correct behavior consisting of propositional Horn clauses. Extending the model by fault models or physical impossibility axioms can not decrease the complexity.

Sometimes it is sufficient to find just one initial diagnosis, especially if we take various repair or measurement strategies into account. Let us therefore compare the complexity of this problem for physical impossibility and fault models.

While both physical impossibility and fault models exclude impossible diagnoses, the difference between them is, that the use of a fault model also influences the candidate space and the use of physical impossibility does not. This is expressed by the following theorem:

Theorem 3 If we add physical impossibility axioms to the correct behavior model, each superset of a diagnosis is consistent.

Proof (informal): No clause from the description of the correct behavior and the physical impossibility axioms contains the positive literal $ok(c)$. Only negative literals $\neg ok(c)$ appear in the clauses describing the correct behavior. Therefore adding $\neg ok(c)$ for some component c to a diagnosis can not lead to a contradiction as we cannot derive $ok(c)$ from the given theory.

We can define a polynomial algorithm for a system description consisting of correct behavior and physical impossibility axioms to find a diagnosis:

Algorithm 1 (Finding the First Diagnosis)

1. Take the candidate which assumes all components to be faulty. This candidate has to be correct otherwise the system description itself is inconsistent.
2. Now remove an arbitrary component from the candidate, i.e. assume the component to be correct. The component has to be chosen in such a way that the remaining candidate is consistent. Components need only be checked once. In a value propagation system new values may be deduced for each component which is assumed to be correct. If the theory proves to be inconsistent, these values have to be retracted.
3. Do this until no more components can be removed from the candidate (i.e. all components have been tried). The (minimal) candidate found can be output as first diagnosis.

Proof (informal): As the candidate space is contiguous, algorithm 1 always finds a minimal candidate. The inclusion of $ok(C)$ is monotonous so the algorithm performs exactly n consistency checks.

Note, that checking consistency of all single faults by a simple algorithm exhibits also a worst-case complexity of n and a average case complexity of $n/2$, if we set the cost for a consistency check to 1. If we use conflict sets to compute the single faults the complexity is exponential in the worst case. (Consider the case, where we have exponential many conflict sets.)

Finding the first diagnosis using a system description with several incompatible behavior modes is exponential in general. For fault models which do not exclude any diagnosis compared to the correct behavior model alone (e.g. if the *unknown fault* mode is included), we can find the first diagnosis in polynomial time simply by deleting all fault model axioms.

Theorem 4 Let us assume, that we extend the description of the correct behavior by clauses describing the faulty behavior and that these clauses include the positive literal $ok(c_i)$ for the described components c_i, which appears in negative form in the correct behavior clauses. Then deciding whether a first diagnosis exists is $\mathcal{NP}$-complete.

Proof (informal): The proof is very similar to the *next diagnosis problem*. We transform sets of assumptions which are inconsistent (like $\{ok(c_i), \neg ok(c_i)\}$) into already found diagnoses. (By the way, even deciding whether there exists an arbitrary consistent candidate is $\mathcal{NP}$-complete.)

Similar results to theorem 2 and 4 have been shown in an interesting paper of Bylander et al ([1]) in the context of abductive reasoning. However, the transformation from a consistency-based diagnosis problem into an abductive one sketched in their paper using conflict sets is not preferable, as the number of conflict sets can grow exponentially resulting in an exponential algorithm for the transformed problem.

3.3 Polynomial Diagnosis Strategies

The results described in the previous section indicate the complexity of the consistency based diagnosis problem. However, it is still possible to define a polynomial diagnosis algorithm for finding a sufficient[2] diagnosis

[2]By *sufficient* we mean a correct diagnosis we want to accept as the final one depending on some termination criterion.

by using our first diagnosis algorithm for correct behavior and physical impossibility axioms.

Unfortunately, a measurement selection function derived from entropy (e.g. [2], [3]) tries only to minimize the number of measurements (and therefore measurement costs). What is not included in the minimization process are the inference costs which, however, can get exponential. We have to use measurement selection heuristics, which need to compute only one diagnosis.

Algorithm 2 Polynomial algorithm for finding a sufficient diagnosis (if correct behavior and physical impossibility rules are given):

1. Find the first diagnosis using all available observations (algorithm 1).
2. If the diagnosis found fulfills the termination criterion, then exit. This could be the case if we can prove the components included in the diagnosis to be faulty without assuming the correctness of other components. In other cases, an immediate repair may be more cost efficient than further testing.
3. Take additional actions to get new information such as
   - Take one or more additional measurements.
   - Try to prove a component to be correct or faulty.
   - Replace a component by a good one, etc.

   Which strategy we take and which measurements we choose may depend on the conflicts found so far, the failure probability of the components, cost of testing etc. Trying to prove or disprove the current diagnosis is also a good heuristic. If we can prove a component c_i to be correct for the given exogenous variables (i.e. by measuring its direct inputs and outputs), it can be excluded from a diagnosis. We can assume $ok(c_i)$ for such a component. This might also be done by using an internal test. Replacing a component by a good one has usually the same effect.
4. goto 1

The difference to the algorithm used in [2] and similar algorithms is that only one diagnosis is computed at each iteration. As only polynomially many measurement points exist and the number of consistency checks is polynomial, the algorithm halts in polynomial time.

4 Conclusion

We have described the concept of physical impossibility as an alternative to fault models. Compared to fault models physical impossibility axioms result in a more efficient computation of diagnoses. We also described a polynomial algorithm for finding the first diagnosis using physical impossibility axioms. The inclusion of fault models even into a Horn clause system model was shown to lead to a $\mathcal{NP}$-complete decision procedure to check for a first diagnosis. For both finding the next diagnosis is exponential in general. By relaxing the optimality criterion for measurement selection as defined in [2] we are able to define a simple algorithm for finding a final sufficient diagnosis in polynomial time using correct behavior and physical impossibility axioms.

Acknowledgements

We thank Peter Struss, Oskar Dressler, Hartmut Freitag, Olivier Raiman, and Johan de Kleer for their comments to a previous version of this paper.

References

[1] Tom Bylander, Dean Allemang, Michael C. Tanner, and John R. Josephson. Some results concerning the computational complexity of abduction. In *Proceedings of the International Conference on Principles of Knowledge Representation and Reasoning*, pages 44–54, Toronto, May 1989. Morgan Kaufmann Publishers, Inc.

[2] Johan de Kleer and Brian C. Williams. Diagnosing multiple faults. *Artificial Intelligence*, 32:97–130, 1987.

[3] Johan de Kleer and Brian C. Williams. Diagnosis with behavioral modes. In *Proceedings of the International Joint Conference on Artificial Intelligence*, pages 1324–1330, Detroit, August 1989. Morgan Kaufmann Publishers, Inc.

[4] Oskar Dressler and Adam Farquhar. Problem solver control over the ATMS. In *Proceedings of the German Workshop on Artificial Intelligence*, pages 17–26, Eringerfeld, September 1989. Springer-Verlag.

[5] Gerhard Friedrich and Wolfgang Nejdl. MOMO — Model-based diagnosis for everybody. In *Proceedings of the IEEE Conference on Artificial Intelligence Applications*, Santa Barbara, March 1990.

[6] Peter Struss and Oskar Dressler. Physical negation — Integrating fault models into the general diagnostic engine. In *Proceedings of the International Joint Conference on Artificial Intelligence*, pages 1318–1323, Detroit, August 1989. Morgan Kaufmann Publishers, Inc.

On the Role of Coherence in Abductive Explanation*

Hwee Tou Ng
Raymond J. Mooney
Department of Computer Sciences
University of Texas at Austin
Austin, Texas 78712
htng@cs.utexas.edu, mooney@cs.utexas.edu

Abstract

Abduction is an important inference process underlying much of human intelligent activities, including text understanding, plan recognition, disease diagnosis, and physical device diagnosis. In this paper, we describe some problems encountered using abduction to understand text, and present some solutions to overcome these problems. The solutions we propose center around the use of a different criterion, called *explanatory coherence*, as the primary measure to evaluate the quality of an explanation. In addition, explanatory coherence plays an important role in the construction of explanations, both in determining the appropriate level of specificity of a preferred explanation, and in guiding the heuristic search to efficiently compute explanations of sufficiently high quality.

1 Introduction

Finding explanations for properties and events is an important aspect of text understanding and of intelligent behavior in general. The philosopher C.S. Peirce defined abduction as the process of finding the best explanation for a set of observations; i.e. inferring cause from effect. The standard formalization of abductive reasoning in artificial intelligence defines an explanation as a set of assumptions which, together with background knowledge, logically entails a set of observations [Charniak and McDermott, 1985].

Natural language understanding has recently been studied in terms of abduction [Charniak, 1986, Hobbs *et al.*, 1988]. Specifically, abduction has been used to solve problems ranging from resolving anaphoric references and syntactic ambiguity [Hobbs *et al.*, 1988] to recognizing characters' plans in a narrative [Charniak, 1986].

*This research is supported by the NASA Ames Research Center under grant NCC-2-429. The first author was also partially supported by a University of Texas MCD fellowship.

We have built an understanding system called ACCEL (Abductive Construction of Causal Explanations for Language) that is capable of constructing deep, causal explanations for natural language text (both narrative and expository text) through the use of abduction. In this paper, we focus on several problems that arise when applying abduction to text understanding. These problems include: (1) the inadequacy of the frequently used simplicity criterion, i.e. "Occam's Razor", in selecting the preferred abductive explanation; (2) the determination of an abductive proof of the appropriate level of specificity; and (3) the computational intractability of abduction. The solutions we propose to these problems center around the use of a different criterion, called *explanatory coherence*, to construct and evaluate abductive explanations.

2 The Basic Abductive Mechanism

A generic abductive inference procedure operates as follows. The background knowledge is encoded in Horn clause axioms. Given a conjunction of positive literals which encodes the input sentences, the abductive inference procedure computes all possible abductive proofs by backward-chaining on the input literals using the Horn clause axioms in the knowledge base, much like Prolog. However, when there is no fact or consequent of a rule in the knowledge base that unifies with a subgoal in the current partial proof, instead of the proof failing, the abductive procedure has the choice of making that subgoal an assumption, if it is consistent to do so. Inconsistency is detected by calling a theorem prover to try to deduce a contradiction. Since consistency checking is undecidable in general, we impose a depth bound in the theorem prover such that it only tries to search for a proof of inconsistency within the depth bound.

Hence, an abductive proof is a proof of the conjunction of the input literals using Horn clause rules and facts in the knowledge base, together with a set of assumptions. An abductive proof is considered an explanation, or an interpretation of the input sentences.

3 Problems and Solutions

The basic abductive mechanism has several problems. These problems and their solutions are described below.

3.1 Occam's Razor Isn't Sharp Enough

Most previous research on abduction, whether applied to plan recognition, language understanding, disease diagnosis, or physical device diagnosis, only uses "Occam's Razor", i.e. the simplicity criterion, as the basis for selecting the best explanation. For instance, in [Charniak, 1986], the best interpretation is one that maximizes $E - A$, where $E =$ the number of explained observations, and $A =$ the number of assumptions made. The work of [Hobbs *et al.*, 1988] also adopts a similar simplicity criterion. In [Reiter, 1987], he proposed a simplicity criterion based on subset-containment minimality. Other related work, though not explicitly utilizing abduction, also relies on some kind of simplicity criterion to select the best explanation. For example, [Kautz and Allen, 1986] explicitly incorporates the assumption of minimizing the number of top level events in deducing the plan that an agent is pursuing.

Though an important factor, the simplicity criterion is not sufficient by itself to select the best explanation. We believe that some notion of explanatory coherence is more important in deciding which explanation is the best. This is especially true in the area of language understanding and plan recognition. Consider the sentences: "John was happy. The exam was easy." The sentences translate into the conjunction of the following literals:[1] `(name j john)`, `(happy j)`, `(exam e)`, `(easy e)`. A knowledge base of axioms relevant to these input literals are:

```
(happy ?x) <- (optimist ?x)
(happy ?x) <- (succeed ?x ?y)
(succeed ?x ?y) <- (exam ?y) (easy ?y)
                   (study ?x ?y) (take ?x ?y)
```

Based on these axioms, there are two possible interpretations of these sentences, as shown in Figure 1a and 1b. Relying on the simplicity metric results in selecting the interpretation that John was happy because he is an optimist, someone who always feels good about life in general (Figure 1b). This is in contrast with our preferred interpretation of the sentence — John was happy because he did well on the easy exam (Figure 1a).[2]

Intuitively, it seems that the first interpretation (Figure 1a) is better because the input observations are connected more "coherently" than in the second interpretation (Figure 1b). We manage to connect "John was happy" with the "easy exam" in the first interpretation, whereas in the second interpretation, they are totally unrelated. This is the intuitive notion of what we mean by *explanatory coherence*. It is clear that "Occam's Razor", i.e. making the minimum number of assumptions, is not the dominant deciding factor here at all. Rather, we select an explanation based on its coherence, i.e. how well the various observations are "tied together" in the explanation.[3]

That sentences in a natural language text are connected in a coherent way is reflected in the well known "Grice's conversational maxims" [Grice, 1975], which are principles governing the production of natural language utterances, such as "be relevant", "be informative", etc. Although the notion that natural language text is coherently structured has long been recognized by researchers in natural language processing (see for example [Allen, 1987]), previous work on abduction applying to the tasks of text understanding and plan recognition has not included this criterion in its evaluation of explanations. The use of explanatory coherence here attempts to remedy this problem.

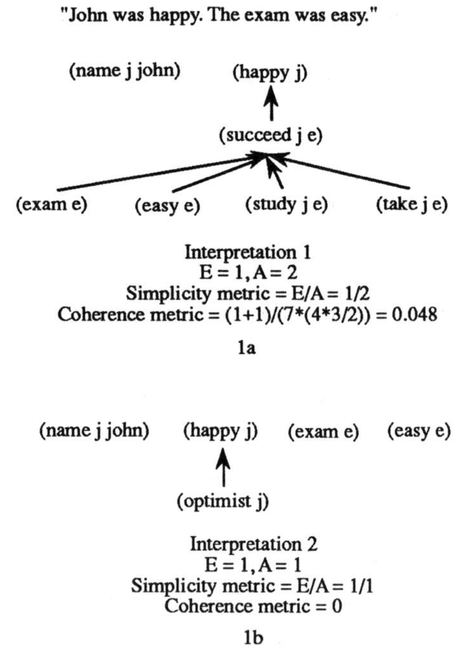

Figure 1: The importance of explanatory coherence

[1] Since we do not focus on the parsing aspect of language understanding, we assume the existence of some appropriate parser that translates the given set of input sentences into a logical representation consisting of a set of literals.

[2] Note that the simplicity criterion of [Reiter, 1987] based on subset minimality also does not work well for this example — it is indifferent towards both interpretations, instead of choosing the preferred one.

[3] [Thagard, 1989] has independently proposed a computational theory of explanatory coherence that applies to the evaluation of scientific theories. However, his theory of explanatory coherence consists of seven principles — symmetry, explanation, analogy, data priority, contradiction, acceptability, and system coherence. Independent criteria like simplicity and connectedness have been collapsed into one measure which he termed "explanatory coherence".

We would like to formulate our coherence metric so as to possess several desirable properties. In particular, explanations with more connections between any pair of observations, as well as those with fewer disjoint partitions are more coherent. Also, a coherence metric with values lying in a unit range 0–1 will facilitate the comparison of explanations.

We have developed a formal characterization of what we mean by explanatory coherence in the form of a coherence metric that satisfies the above mentioned properties. The metric is defined as follows :

$$\mathcal{C} = \frac{\sum_{1 \leq i < j \leq l} N_{i,j}}{N \binom{l}{2}}$$

where
l = the total number of observations;
N = the total number of nodes in the proof graph;
$\binom{l}{2} = l(l-1)/2$;
$N_{i,j}$ = the number of distinct nodes n_k in the proof graph such that there is a (possibly empty) sequence of directed edges from n_k to n_i and a (possibly empty) sequence of directed edges from n_k to n_j, where n_i and n_j are observations.

The numerator of this metric is a measure of the total number of nodes in the explanation connecting pairs of observations. This measure is constructed so that it increases with the number of nodes in the explanation which simultaneously lend support to a given connection. The denominator of the metric simply scales the result according to the size of the explanation so that the final value falls between 0 and 1.

To illustrate the computation of the coherence metric, consider the explanation in Figure 1a. Let n_1 = (name j john), n_2 = (happy j), n_3 = (exam e), n_4 = (easy e), n_5 = (succeed j e), n_6 = (study j e), and n_7 = (take j e). In this explanation, the total number of nodes $N = 7$, and the total number of observations $l = 4$. $N_{2,3} = 1$, since there is exactly one node (namely n_3) such that there is a directed path from n_3 to n_2 and also a directed path from n_3 to n_3 (the trivial empty path). Similarly, $N_{2,4} = 1$. All other $N_{i,j} = 0$. This results in the coherence metric $\mathcal{C} = 0.048$, as shown in Figure 1a.

The coherence metric as defined above can be efficiently computed. Using a standard depth-first search graph algorithm[4], it can be readily shown that $\mathcal{C}$ can be computed in time $O(l \cdot N + e)$, where l = the total number of observations, N = the total number of nodes in the proof graph, and e = the total number of directed edges in the proof graph [Ng and Mooney, 1989]. Based on the coherence metric, ACCEL has successfully selected the best interpretation for a half dozen examples of expository and narrative text that we have tested. (See [Ng and Mooney, 1989] for the list of examples successfully processed by ACCEL.)

We note here some additional advantages of our coherence metric. One observation is that coherent explanations also tend to be simple explanations. This is because in a coherent explanation, propositions tend to be more tightly connected. This increases the likelihood of assumptions being unified, and leads to a reduction in the number of assumptions made and thus a simpler explanation.

In addition, compared to the simplicity metric, the coherence metric is less vulnerable to changes in the underlying representation of the knowledge base. It is relatively easy to encode the axioms in a knowledge base in a slightly different way so as to change the number of assumptions made in an explanation. However, connections between propositions are less dependent (relatively speaking) on such changes. For example, suppose we change the axioms in the given example slightly so that as long as one takes an easy exam, one will succeed in the exam without having to study for it. Also, suppose one has to be wealthy as well as an optimist to be happy. Given this modified set of axioms, the first interpretation now only requires one assumption, while the second interpretation requires two. So all of a sudden, the first interpretation becomes the simpler explanation of the two. However, the coherence metric of the first interpretation (= (1+1)/(6*(4*3/2)) = 0.056) is still higher than that of the second (which remains at zero).

3.2 Deciding on the Appropriate Level of Specificity of Explanations

Another problem in constructing a good explanation is determining the appropriate level of specificity of an abductive proof. Previous approaches fall into one of three categories : most specific abduction, least specific abduction, and weighted abduction.[5]

In most specific abduction, the assumptions made must be *basic*, i.e. they cannot be "intermediate" assumptions that are themselves provable by assuming some other (more basic) assumptions. This is the approach used in the diagnosis work of [Cox and Pietrzykowski, 1987]. In least specific abduction, the only allowable assumptions are literals in the input observations. [Stickel, 1988] claims that least specific abduction is best suited for natural language interpretation. He argues that what one learns from reading a piece of text is often close to its surface form, and that assuming deeper causes is unwarranted. In weighted abduction [Hobbs *et al.*, 1988], weights (or costs) are assigned to the antecedents of

[4] We assume here that the proof graph contains no cycles, since circular justification is not considered a good trait of an explanation.

[5] [Stickel, 1988] describes yet another form of abduction known as predicate specific abduction, which has been used primarily in planning and design-synthesis tasks. In predicate specific abduction, the predicate of any assumption made must be one of a pre-specified set of predicates.

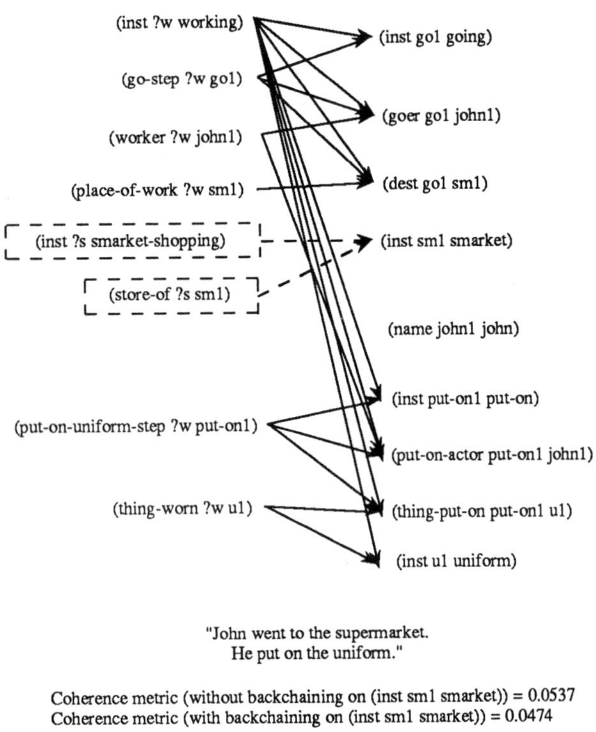

Figure 2: The level of specificity of explanation

backward-chaining rules in order to influence the decision on whether to backchain on a rule. In this case, the best interpretation is the one with assumptions that have the lowest combined total cost.

However, none of these approaches is completely satisfactory. Consider the sentences "John went to the supermarket. He put on the uniform." Both least specific and most specific abduction fail to generate the preferred interpretation in this case, which is that John is working at the supermarket. Figure 2 shows the proof graph of the preferred interpretation of this example (excluding the dashed lines and boxes). (See [Ng and Mooney, 1989] for the details of the relevant axiomatization.)

Note that nowhere in the input sentences is the concept of "working" mentioned at all. It has to be *inferred* by the reader. Since this preferred interpretation includes making the assumptions that there is a working event, that John is the worker of this working event, etc, it is evident that least specific abduction, in which the only allowable assumptions are input literals, is incapable of arriving at this explanation.

On the other hand, most specific abduction will not do the job either. Recall that most specific abduction always prefers backchaining on rules to prove a subgoal if possible rather than making that subgoal an assumption. Thus, applying most specific abduction to this example results in backchaining on the input literal (inst sm1 smarket) to the assumptions (inst ?s smarket-shopping) and (store-of ?s sm1), since in the present knowledge base, this is the *only* backchaining rule with a consequent that unifies with (inst sm1 smarket).[6] That is, we explain the going action, its agent and its destination by assuming that John is working there, and we are also forced to assume, by the requirement of most specific abduction, that there is some supermarket shopping event to explain the supermarket instance! This is because most specific abduction requires that we have an explanation for why John went to the supermarket as opposed to some other workplace. This is clearly undesirable.

However, determining the level of specificity of an explanation based on coherence produces the desired interpretation. That is, we backchain on rules to prove the subgoals in an explanation only if doing so increases its overall coherence, and thus we make assumptions just specific enough to connect the observations. In the current example, backchaining on (inst sm1 smarket) results in a decrease in the coherence metric value, since the total number of nodes in the proof graph increases by two but there is no increase in the number of connections among the input observations. Intuitively, explaining the supermarket instance by assuming a supermarket shopping event is completely unrelated to the rest of the explanation that John is working there. The coherence metric has been successfully used in ACCEL to determine the appropriate level of specificity of explanations, where the desired specificity is one which maximizes coherence.

The weighted abduction of [Hobbs *et al.*, 1988] would presumably arrive at the correct interpretation given the "appropriate" set of weights. However, it is unclear how to characterize the "semantic contribution" of each antecedent in a rule in order to assign the appropriate weights. In contrast, our method does not rely on tweaking such weights, and it produces the preferred interpretation with the desired level of specificity in all of our examples. We believe that allowing arbitrary weights on rules is too much of a burden on the knowledge engineer. It also provides too many degrees of freedom, which can lead to the knowledge engineer "hacking up" arbitrary weights in order to get the system to produce the desired explanation.

3.3 Taming the Intractability Problem

Finding a simplest abductive explanation has been shown to be NP-hard [Reggia *et al.*, 1985, Bylander *et al.*, 1989]. However, an optimal explanation in our system is one with the highest coherence, as opposed to the simplest explanation, and so none of the proofs in the above research applies directly. Nonetheless, we have a proof that finding a maximally coherent explanation that satisfies simple contradiction restrictions in a two-level, propositional abduc-

[6] (inst sm1 smarket) denotes "sm1 is an instance of a supermarket"; (inst ?s smarket-shopping) denotes "?s is an instance of a supermarket shopping event; and (store-of ?s sm1) denotes "the store of the shopping event ?s is sm1".

tion model is NP-hard. As such, the use of heuristic search to explore the vast space of possible solutions seems to be a good strategy to adopt. In fact, we have implemented a form of beam search that has successfully computed the preferred interpretation of all of our examples very efficiently.

We use a beam search algorithm with two beam widths, called *inter-observation beam width* (β_{inter}) and *intra-observation beam width* (β_{intra}), in order to reduce the explored search space. A queue of best explanations is kept by the beam search procedure, forming the "beam" of the beam search. At all times, explanations in the queue are sorted by coherence, where the best explanation is the one with the highest coherence.[7] Only at most β_{inter} number of the best explanations are kept in the queue after completing the processing of each input observation. Within the processing of an input observation, at most β_{intra} number of best explanations are kept in the queue. We have adopted two beam widths instead of one as in a typical beam search algorithm since we have found out empirically that optimal solutions can be computed most efficiently using two beam widths of different sizes.

Figure 3 shows how the quality of the best explanation varies with run time for the supermarket working example with different values of β_{inter} and β_{intra}. We use the ratio of the coherence metric value of an explanation over that of the optimal explanation to represent the quality of an explanation. All the run times reported in this paper are the actual execution times on a Texas Instruments Explorer II Lisp machine.

Each data point in the Figure represents a quality-time pair obtained by using some specific values of β_{inter} and β_{intra}. Each curve connects all the data points with the same β_{inter} but different β_{intra}. Without using any heuristic search (i.e., if a complete search is made), it takes more than 3 hours to compute the optimal solution, while setting $\beta_{inter} = 3$ and $\beta_{intra} = 8$ yields the optimal solution in 0.89 min, which represents a speed up of over 200 times! Also, fixing $\beta_{inter} = 4$ and $\beta_{intra} = 13$, the optimal explanations are computed in about one minute on average for the half dozen examples of expository and narrative text that we have tested.

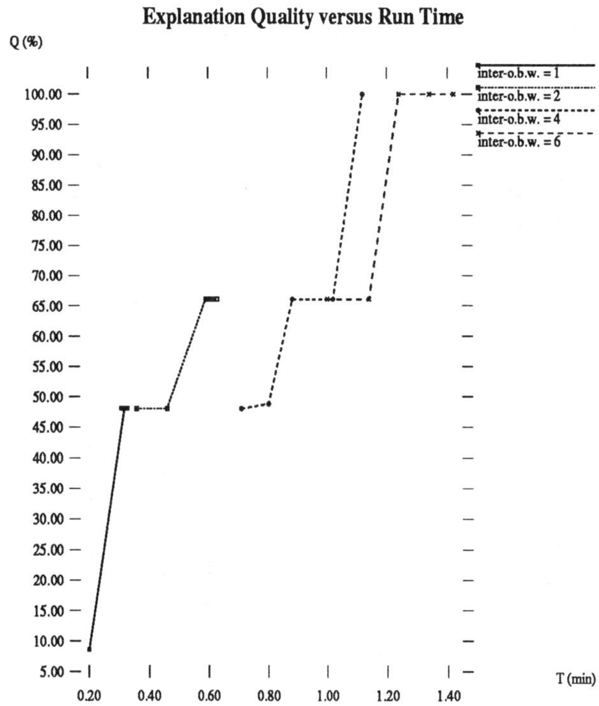

Figure 3: Explanation Quality versus Run Time

4 Related Work

Several research efforts have focused on abduction as an important inference process in plan recognition [Charniak, 1986], natural language understanding [Hobbs *et al.*, 1988], disease diagnosis [Pople, 1973], and physical device diagnosis [Cox and Pietrzykowski, 1987]. In the area of natural language understanding, [Hobbs *et al.*, 1988] describes the use of abduction in solving the four local pragmatics problems of text understanding. This work differs from ours in that unlike their emphasis on mostly linguistics issues like reference resolution and syntactic ambiguity resolution, ACCEL is concerned with constructing deep, causal explanations of the input text. The work of [Charniak, 1986] and [Charniak and Goldman, 1989] are most similar to ours. However, they are primarily concerned with recognizing characters' plans and goals in narrative stories, whereas ACCEL is also capable of constructing causal explanations for expository text. For example, a complete understanding of an encyclopedia text describing animals requires understanding the purpose or reason for the various features of the animals. (See [Ng and Mooney, 1989] for a list of expository text sentences that can be processed by ACCEL.) Also, explanations are evaluated based on their explanatory coherence in our work, as opposed to the simplicity criterion of [Charniak, 1986] and the probability criterion of [Charniak and Goldman, 1989]. Furthermore, the work of [Charniak, 1986] used marker passing to restrict the search for explanations, whereas we used a form of beam search for the efficient construction of explanations.

The Bayesian probabilistic approach to plan recognition and text understanding has been proposed by [Charniak and Goldman, 1989]. Besides the problem of engineering the numerous prior and posterior probabilities of the nodes in a Bayesian network, this approach does not take into account the importance of text coherence. For instance, in the sentences "John got a gun. He entered the grocery store.", one can set

[7] Ties are broken based on the simplicity metric of E/A, where E is the number of observations explained and A is the number of assumptions made.

up reasonable probability estimates such that the conditional probability that John was both hunting and shopping is higher than that of John robbing the store (given the propositions stated in the text). However, selecting an interpretation based solely on the probability of propositions about the situation being described is ignoring the fact that these propositions are adjacent sentences in a natural language text, not just random facts observed in the world. As illustrated by this example, text coherence dominates and results in the reader selecting the more coherent interpretation that John was robbing the store.

5 Future Research

We plan to investigate the efficiency gain which may be brought about by incorporating an ATMS (Assumption-based Truth Maintenance System) into the abductive inference procedure, so as to efficiently keep track of the dependency among the assumptions and propositions of various competing explanations.

Since uncertainty and likelihood information is needed in order to achieve a complete understanding of natural language text, and because a straightforward application of Bayesian probability theory does not give a completely satisfactory solution (as we have illustrated here), an approach that will integrate both the importance of text coherence and likelihood information is an important issue in future research.

6 Conclusion

In summary, we have described some problems encountered using abduction to understand text, and have presented some solutions to overcome these problems. The solutions we propose center around the use of explanatory coherence to evaluate the quality of explanations, to determine the appropriate level of specificity of explanations, and to guide the heuristic search to efficiently compute explanations of sufficiently high quality. These solutions have proven to be very effective on a range of examples in text understanding.

References

[Allen, 1987] James F. Allen. *Natural Language Understanding.* Benjamin/Cummings, Menlo Park, CA, 1987.

[Bylander *et al.*, 1989] Tom Bylander, Dean Allemang, Michael C. Tanner, and John R. Josephson. Some results concerning the computational complexity of abduction. In *Proceedings of the First International Conference on Principles of Knowledge Representation and Reasoning*, pages 44–54, Toronto, Ontario, Canada, 1989.

[Charniak and Goldman, 1989] Eugene Charniak and Robert P. Goldman. A semantics for probabilistic quantifier-free first-order languages, with particular application to story understanding. In *Proceedings of the Eleventh International Joint Conference on Artificial Intelligence*, 1989.

[Charniak and McDermott, 1985] Eugene Charniak and Drew McDermott. *Introduction to Artificial Intelligence.* Addison Wesley, Reading, MA, 1985.

[Charniak, 1986] Eugene Charniak. A neat theory of marker passing. In *Proceedings of the National Conference on Artificial Intelligence*, pages 584–588, Philadelphia, PA, 1986.

[Cox and Pietrzykowski, 1987] P. T. Cox and T. Pietrzykowski. General diagnosis by abductive inference. In *Proceedings of the 1987 Symposium on Logic Programming*, pages 183–189, 1987.

[Grice, 1975] H. P. Grice. Logic and conversation. In P. Cole and J. Morgan, editors, *Syntax and Semantics 3 : Speech Acts*, pages 41–58. Academic Press, New York, 1975.

[Hobbs *et al.*, 1988] Jerry R. Hobbs, Mark E. Stickel, Paul Martin, and Douglas Edwards. Interpretation as abduction. In *Proceedings of the 26th Annual Meeting of the Association for Computational Linguistics*, pages 95–103, Buffalo, New York, 1988.

[Kautz and Allen, 1986] Henry A. Kautz and James F. Allen. Generalized plan recognition. In *Proceedings of the National Conference on Artificial Intelligence*, pages 32–37, Philadelphia, PA, 1986.

[Ng and Mooney, 1989] Hwee Tou Ng and Raymond J. Mooney. Abductive explanation in text understanding : Some problems and solutions. Technical Report AI89-116, Artificial Intelligence Laboratory, Department of Computer Sciences, The University of Texas at Austin, October 1989.

[Pople, 1973] Harry E. Pople, Jr. On the mechanization of abductive logic. In *Proceedings of the Third International Joint Conference on Artificial Intelligence*, pages 147–152, 1973.

[Reggia *et al.*, 1985] James A. Reggia, Dana S. Nau, and Pearl Y. Wang. A formal model of diagnostic inference. I. problem formulation and decomposition. *Information Sciences*, 37:227–256, 1985.

[Reiter, 1987] Raymond Reiter. A theory of diagnosis from first principles. *Artificial Intelligence*, 32:57–95, 1987.

[Stickel, 1988] Mark E. Stickel. A prolog-like inference system for computing minimum-cost abductive explanations in natural-language interpretation. Technical Note 451, SRI International, September 1988.

[Thagard, 1989] Paul Thagard. Explanatory coherence. *Behavioral and Brain Sciences*, 12(3):435–467, September 1989.

Abductive and Default Reasoning: A Computational Core

Bart Selman and Hector J. Levesque*
Dept. of Computer Science
University of Toronto
Toronto, Canada M5S 1A4

Abstract

Of all the possible ways of computing abductive explanations, the ATMS procedure is one of the most popular. While this procedure is known to run in exponential time in the worst case, the proof actually depends on the existence of queries with an exponential number of answers. But how much of the difficulty stems from having to return these large sets of explanations? Here we explore abduction tasks similar to that of the ATMS, but which return relatively small answers. The main result is that although it is possible to generate some non-trivial explanations quickly, deciding if there is an explanation containing a given hypothesis is NP-hard, as is the task of generating even one explanation expressed in terms of a given set of assumption letters. Thus, the method of simply listing all explanations, as employed by the ATMS, probably cannot be improved upon. An interesting result of our analysis is the discovery of a subtask that is at the core of generating explanations, and is also at the core of generating extensions in Reiter's default logic. Moreover, it is this subtask that accounts for the computational difficulty of both forms of reasoning. This establishes for the first time a strong connection between computing abductive explanations and computing extensions in default logic.

Introduction

Of all the possible ways of computing abductive explanations, the procedure employed by an assumption-based truth-maintenance system (ATMS) is one of the most popular (de Kleer 1986a; Reiter and de Kleer 1987). It is therefore somewhat surprising that so little effort has gone into understanding in precise terms the nature of the computational task performed by an ATMS, that is, the *what* for which an ATMS is a *how*.

What do we know in general about this task? It has been known since at least 1985 that in the worst case, any procedure that computes what the ATMS computes will need time that is exponential in the length of its input (McAllester 1985). This is because there are problems for which the desired set of answers (where intuitively, each answer is a set of assumptions that would *explain* a given condition) is exponentially large. Perhaps this simple fact has discouraged further theoretical analysis into the worst-case difficulty of computing explanations.

But it doesn't tell the whole story. Is the fact that an ATMS can take exponential time *only* due to cases where an exponential number of answers need to be returned? What if instead of generating all the answers, we only required a procedure to reply to simple yes/no questions about them, such as whether or not there is an explanation containing a given assumption? Furthermore, in many (if not most) applications, we expect to be dealing with a very small number of explanations. For example, in circuit diagnosis, explanations involve sets of possibly faulty components (Reiter 1987; Poole 1988), and one would not expect k components to break down independently, for large k. Is it still the case that generating a small number of explanations is hard? In other words, if an ATMS still runs in exponential time for problems like this (as it apparently does (Provan 1987)), should we be looking for a different procedure, or is this the best that can be expected?

In this paper, we attempt to answer these questions. In particular, we show that certain natural variations of the ATMS task that do not require listing all the answers are nonetheless NP-hard. In our view, this provides concrete evidence that the ATMS is doing as well as can be expected.

But something more fundamental came out of the analysis. We were surprised to discover a strong connection between computing explanations on the one hand, and computing extensions in Reiter's default logic (Reiter 1980), on the other. It turns out that both tasks share a common computational core. Moreover, it is this common subtask that leads to the computational difficulty of both abductive and default reasoning. Apart from the fact that both forms of reasoning use the word "assumption," this is the first result that we know of to show a clear relationship between the

*Fellow of the Canadian Institute for Advanced Research.

computational properties of these two apparently very different forms of reasoning.

The rest of the paper is organized as follows. In the next section, we review Reiter and de Kleer's analysis of the ATMS. Next, we show that while it is always easy to find at least one non-trivial explanation, determining if there is one containing a given assumption, or finding one that is expressed only in terms of a given assumption set is NP-hard. In section 4, we consider a weaker version of the ATMS task (which we call the Support Selection Task), where explanations are not required to be minimal, and show that it too is NP-hard. In section 5, we briefly review the definitions from Reiter's default logic, and show that the problem of computing an extension is a variant of the Support Selection Task where we care about maximality instead of minimality. It turns out that making a support set minimal or maximal is easy; it's finding one in the first place that is hard. Finally, some conclusions are drawn.

Abduction

In this section, we formally define what constitutes an explanation as computed by the ATMS (Reiter and de Kleer 1987). We will assume a standard propositional language $\mathcal{L}$ with propositional letters from the set P. We will use p, q, r, s, and t (possibly with subscripts) to denote propositional letters. A *clause* is a disjunction of literals (a *literal* is either a propositional letter, called a positive literal, or its negation, called a negative literal). We will represent a clause by the set of literals contained in the clause. A clause is called a *unit* clause if it only contains a single literal. A clause is *Horn* if and only if it contains at most one positive literal. A set of Horn clauses will be called a *Horn theory*.

Definition 1 [Explanation] *Given a set of clauses Σ, called the background theory, and a letter q, an explanation for q is a minimal set of unit clauses α such that*

1. $\Sigma \cup \alpha \models q$, and

2. $\Sigma \cup \alpha$ is consistent.

For a discussion on the desirability of the above properties, see Levesque (1989).[2] Instead of expressing explanations as sets of unit clauses, we will often give the logical equivalent form consisting of the conjunction of the literals occurring in the clauses, *e.g.*, we write $p \wedge q \wedge r$ instead of $\{\{p\}, \{q\}, \{r\}\}$.

Example: Let Σ be the set $\{\{p\}, \{q\}, \{\overline{p}, \overline{r}, \overline{s}, t\}\}$. The conjunctions $r \wedge s$ and t are explanations for t. We call t the trivial explanation for t; our interest lies of course in the other, non-trivial explanations.

The notion of explanation defined above, is somewhat more general than the one employed in the ATMS. The ATMS only computes a certain subset of these explanations, namely those drawn from a distinguished subset of the propositional letters, called *assumptions*. Assumptions stand for the hypotheses that we are willing to consider in the explanations, such as the possible failure of a component in circuit diagnosis.

Definition 2 [Formal Specification of the ATMS] *Given a set of Horn clauses Σ, a set of assumptions $A \subseteq P$, and a letter q, called the query, the ATMS procedure computes the following set:*

$$\mathcal{A}[\Sigma, A, q] = \{\alpha \mid \alpha \text{ is an explanation for } q \text{ containing only letters from } A\}.$$

The explanations in $\mathcal{A}[\Sigma, A, q]$ will be called *assumption-based* explanations. Note that when the assumption set includes all symbols in the language, every explanation is also an assumption-based one.

Computing explanations

We will now consider the computational cost of generating explanations. As is well-known, there may be exponentially many explanations for a given letter (McAllester 1985; de Kleer 1986b); and therefore, listing all of them may require exponential time.[3] However, this leaves open the question of what the complexity of finding some explanation is. In particular, what is the complexity of finding a non-trivial one?

In case Σ contains arbitrary clauses, finding any explanation is easily shown to be NP-hard.[4] However, the following theorem shows that when Σ is a Horn theory, a non-trivial explanation (if one exists) can be computed efficiently.

Theorem 1 *Given a set of Horn clauses Σ and a letter q, a non-trivial explanation for q can be computed in time $O(kn)$, where k is the number of propositional letters and n is the number of occurrences of literals in Σ.*

Here we only give an outline of the algorithm. Consider a clause in Σ of the following form: $\{\overline{q}_1, \ldots, \overline{q}_k, q\}$ with $k \geq 0$ (if no such clause exists, return "no non-trivial explanation"). Now, clearly $q_1 \wedge \ldots \wedge q_k$ with Σ implies q. Subsequently, try removing a letter from this conjunction while ensuring that the remaining conjunction together with Σ still implies q (testing can be done in linear time, using the Dowling and Gallier (1984) procedure). Repeat this process until no more letters can be removed. If the remaining conjunction is non-empty and combined with Σ is consistent, return that one; otherwise consider another clause containing q and repeat the above procedure. When all clauses

[2] For a quite different definition of explanation, see Reggia (1983) and Allemang et al. (1987).

[3] In fact, there may be exponentially many assumption-based explanations, and therefore the worst case complexity of the ATMS, which lists all of them, is clearly exponential.

[4] Since explanations only exist when Σ is consistent, an explanation procedure can be used to test the satisfiability of a set of clauses.

containing q have been explored and no explanation is found, return "no non-trivial explanation."

It is clear that the above algorithm only generates certain, very particular explanations — which ones depend on the way the background knowledge Σ is expressed. But if there are *some* non-trivial explanations that are easy to find, could it be that in some sense they are *all* easy to find, even if there are too many to list? One way to look at this question is to consider a procedure that generates only a single explanation, but must return different ones for different arguments. For example, if we can ask for an explanation containing the letters in S_1 but not containing those in S_2, clearly we can generate arbitrary explanations.[5] Unfortunately, the following theorem show that there can be no efficient procedure for this form of "goal-directed" abduction, even if the set S_1 contains only a single literal, and S_2 is empty.[6]

Theorem 2 *Given a set of Horn clauses Σ and letters p and q, the problem of generating an explanation for q that contains p is NP-hard.*

The proof of this theorem is based on a reduction from the NP-complete decision problem "path with forbidden pairs" (or PWFP) defined by Gabow, Maheshwari, and Osterweil (1976). An instance of PWFP consists of a directed graph $G = (V, E)$, specified vertices $s, t \in V$, and a collection $C = \{(a_1, b_1), ..., (a_n, b_n)\}$ of pairs of vertices from V. The question is: does there exist a path from s to t in G that contains at most one vertex from each pair in C? This problem remains NP-complete even if we only consider acyclic graphs.

Given an instance of this restricted version of PWFP, we now construct a background theory Σ. Identifying the vertices of the graph with propositional letters, Σ contains the following clauses: (1) for each directed edge (x, y), the clause $\{\overline{x_y}, \overline{x}, y\}$ where x_y is a new propositional letter, and (2) for each forbidden pair (a_i, b_i), the clause $\{\overline{a}_i, \overline{b}_i\}$. Now, consider an explanation for t that contain s. It can be shown that if such an explanation exists, it will consist of a set of propositional letters of the form x_y that uniquely identify a path from s to t in the original graph (Selman 1990). Moreover, because of the clauses in group (2), such a path goes through at most one vertex of each forbidden pair. Thus, we can reduce the PWFP problem to goal-directed abduction.

Intuitively speaking, theorem 2 shows that certain explanations will be hard to find, even if our background theory Σ is Horn. And, as can be seen from the reduction, this result also holds when Σ consists of an acyclic Horn theory.[7]

Finally, we consider the influence of an assumption set as used in the ATMS. Recall that the assumption set A is a distinguished subset of the propositional letters and that given a query q, the ATMS will generate only explanations that contain letters from among those in A. Note that the assumption set again allows one to select a certain subset of all possible explanations. This way of of selecting certain explanations is related, but *not* identical, to the notion of goal-directed abduction. The following theorem shows that the use of such an assumption set dramatically increases the complexity of finding a non-trivial explanation (compare with theorem 1):

Theorem 3 *Given a set of Horn clauses Σ, a set of assumptions A, and a query letter q, finding an assumption-based explanation for q is NP-hard.*

The proof of this theorem is based on a modification of the reduction used in the proof of theorem 2: add the clause $\{s\}$ to the background theory, and let the assumption-set contain all letters of the form x_y. Now, an assumption-based explanation will consist of a subset of the letters in the assumption set, and as above, this set will uniquely identify a path from s to t not containing any forbidden pair. Again, the problem remains NP-hard even for acyclic theories.

This theorem shows that apart from the fact that the ATMS may have to list an exponential number of explanations, merely finding one of them may require exponential time.

Finally, we consider the experimental observation, reported by Provan (1987), that the ATMS can exhibit exponential behaviour even if the background theory is such that there are only a few assumption-based explanations for the query letter. Provan argues that such restricted theories have practical significance, for example, in scene interpretation. We can now show that in fact the intractability is *inherent* in the task, and not simply caused by the particular procedure employed in the ATMS:

Theorem 4 *Given a set of assumptions A, a query q, and a set of Horn clauses Σ such that q has at most one assumption-based explanation, finding this explanation is NP-hard under randomized reductions.*

To prove this theorem we use a result by Vazirani and Valiant (1988), who show that determining propositional satisfiability remains hard (unless NP = RP, considered to be very unlikely) even if one guarantees that the given instances of SAT has at most one satisfying truth assignment. Since the reduction from SAT to

[5]The set S_1 could be used, for example, to identify components that have a high failure rate when doing circuit diagnosis. For a related approach, see de Kleer and Williams (1989).

[6]For the purpose of this paper, and to keep the provisos to a minimum, we assume that P≠NP. An excellent introduction to the basic concepts of computational complexity theory can be found in Garey and Johnson (1979).

[7]Given a Horn theory Σ, let G be a directed graph containing a vertex for each literal in Σ and an edge from any vertex corresponding to a letter on the left-hand side of a Horn rule to the vertex corresponding to the letter on the right hand-side of that rule. A Horn theory is *acyclic* if and only if the associated graph G is acyclic.

PWFP and the reduction from PWFP to assumption-based explanations are parsimonious (*i.e.*, the number of solutions is preserved), it follows that even if we guarantee that there is at most one assumption-based explanation for the query letter, finding it still remains hard. So, the problem of generating assumption-based explanations even for such special restricted background theories remains intractable, and therefore the ATMS procedure is doing as well as can be expected.

One remaining question is whether the problem is still hard if we are guaranteed that there are only a few explanations overall (including the non-assumption-based ones) for the query. Note that we can always generate at least one non-trivial explanation (see theorem 1); we conjecture however that generating $O(n)$ of them is again NP-hard (possibly under randomized reductions), where n is the number of propositional letters in the language.

The Computational Core

We have shown that finding an assumption-based explanation is intractable, even when the background theory Σ is an acyclic set of Horn clauses. In this section, we will isolate a subtask, called the Support Selection Task, which lies at the core of the computational difficulties.

Definition 3 [Support Selection Task] *Given a set of Horn clauses Σ, a set of letters $A \subseteq P$, and a letter q, find a set of unit clauses α, called a support set, such that the following conditions hold:*

1. $\Sigma \cup \alpha \models q$,
2. $\Sigma \cup \alpha$ *is consistent, and*
3. α *contains only letters form A.*

Note that an assumption-based explanation is simply a *minimal* support set. We first consider the complexity of the Support Selection Task:

Theorem 5 *Given a Horn theory Σ, a set $A \subseteq P$, and a letter q, finding a support set for q is NP-hard.*

This result follows directly from a generalization of the reduction used in the proof of theorem 3. Since the reduction does not rely on finding a minimal set of assumptions to support the query, any support set for the query will identify a path that goes from s to t containing at most one vertex from each forbidden pair.

Because an assumption-based explanation is a minimal support set, finding such an explanation is at least as hard as finding support sets. Hence, the intractability of finding an assumption-based explanation is in fact a direct consequence of theorem 5. Stated differently, in order to establish the intractability of finding an assumption-based explanation, one need not use the fact that explanations are minimal.

Furthermore, the minimality requirement does not further increase the computational difficulty of the task, as can be seen from the following argument. Consider a support set α for q. We can minimize this set by removing clauses from it while each time verifying that the reduced set combined with Σ still implies q. Since Σ is a Horn theory this can be done in polynomial time. Finally, note that the Support Selection Task can be shown to be no harder than any problem in NP, and thus neither is generating an assumption-based explanation.

To summarize, the Support Selection Task is at the core of the ATMS-style abduction task. In the next section, we will see how this task also is at the core of goal-directed default reasoning, thereby establishing a computational connection between abductive and default reasoning.

Default Reasoning

Default Logic, introduced by Reiter (1980), is one of the more prominent formal proposals for representing and reasoning with default information. We will first briefly define Default Logic (see Reiter (1980) and Etherington (1986) for further details), and subsequently consider the complexity of default logic theories.

Reiter formalized default reasoning by extending first-order logic with default rules. A ***default theory*** is a pair (D, W) where D is a set of default rules and W a set of ordinary first-order formulas. A rule is of the form:

$$\frac{\alpha : \beta}{\gamma}$$

where α is the ***prerequisite***, γ the ***conclusion***, and β the ***justification*** of the rule, each of them formulas. A rule is intuitively understood as meaning that if α is known, and β is consistent with what is known, then γ may be inferred.

An *extension* is a *maximal* set of conclusions that can be drawn from a theory. But care must be taken that none of the justifications of the rules used in the construction of an extension conflict with its final contents, and that every formula in the extension can in fact be derived from W and the rules. The formal definition of an extension (from Reiter (1980), Theorem 2.1) is therefore rather complex:

Definition 4 [Extension] *A set of formulas E is an extension for the theory (D, W) if and only if it satisfies the following equations:*[8]

$$\begin{aligned} E_0 &= W, \text{ and for } i \geq 0 \\ E_{i+1} &= Th(E_i) \cup \\ &\quad \left\{ \gamma \,\middle|\, \frac{\alpha : \beta}{\gamma} \in D, \ \ \alpha \in E_i, \ \ \text{and } \neg\beta \notin E \right\} \\ E &= \bigcup_{i=0}^{\infty} E_i \end{aligned}$$

Note the explicit reference to E in the definition of E_{i+1}. Th denotes logical closure.

[8] We assume that all formulas are closed, *i.e.*, they do not contain free variables.

Computing Extensions

Kautz and Selman (1989) give a detailed analysis of the computational complexity of default reasoning based on Reiter's proposal. They consider a partially ordered space of more and less general propositional default logic theories. For each theory the complexity is determined of the following tasks: finding an extension (*credulous* reasoning), generating an extension that contains a given set of propositions (*goal-directed* reasoning), and the problem of determining what holds in all extensions of a default logic theory (*skeptical* reasoning). To avoid the difficulty of the consistency check needed to determine whether a rule can be applied, Kautz and Selman restrict the default theories to ones in which the set of facts W, the prerequisites, the justifications, and the consequences each consist of a set of literals. Here we will consider a relaxation of these restrictions. In particular, we will allow W to contain Horn clauses.

We will show that even for extremely simple default rules and a Horn theory W goal-directed default reasoning is intractable, and that the computational difficulty is again appropriately characterized by the Support Selection Task.[9] To facilitate our discussion, a rule of the form $:p/p$ will be called an *elementary* default — these rules are the simplest possible defaults.[10]

We have the following result concerning goal-directed default reasoning:

Theorem 6 *Given an acyclic Horn theory W, a set of elementary defaults D, and a letter q, finding an extension of (D,W) that contains q is NP-hard.*[11]

This result strengthens a recent result by Stillman (1989), who showed the task is NP-hard for arbitrary Horn theories with general normal unary defaults. But aside from strengthening Stillman's result, our interest in this result arises from the fact that the Support Selection Task lies again at the root of the computational difficulty of the problem, as we will see below.

To prove theorem 6, we first consider the relation between goal-directed default reasoning and the Support Selection Task. Note that if Σ is a Horn theory and D a set of elementary defaults involving letters from a set A, then each extension of (D, Σ) is of the form $Th(\Sigma \cup \alpha)$, where α is a set of unit clauses drawn from A. Intuitively, α is the set of letters that are added to Σ via the rules in D. We have the following theorem:

Theorem 7 *Let Σ be a Horn theory, q be a letter, $A \subseteq P$ be a set of letters, and let $D = \{:p/p \mid p \in A\}$. Then, $Th(\Sigma \cup \alpha)$ is an extension of (D, Σ) that contains q if and only if α is a* maximal *support set of q.*

This theorem follows from a more general result by Reiter (1987). It follows that finding extensions of the default logic theory that contains a given letter q, is at least as hard as finding a support set for q. Thus, theorem 6 follows directly from the fact that the Support Selection Task is NP-hard (theorem 5).

Furthermore, the fact that extensions correspond to *maximal* support sets does not further add to the difficulty of computing extensions: given a support set, one can simply try adding additional letters from the assumption set while maintaining consistency, until a maximal set is obtained. Thus, as for assumption-based explanations, the Support Selection Task is the difficult part of goal-directed default reasoning.

It is suggested in Kautz and Selman (1989) that goal-directed reasoning could be of use in resolution theorem provers that incorporate default information. Our results here suggest that such an integration will most likely run into computational difficulties. Much more promising, are credulous reasoners that search for an arbitrary extension. This task remains tractable for relatively expressive default rules combined with Horn theories (Selman 1990). By contrast, skeptical default reasoning, *i.e.*, determining what holds in all extensions of a theory, can be shown to be strictly harder than goal-directed reasoning, and thus our intractability result carries over to skeptical reasoning.

Conclusions

In this paper, we have examined the problem of computing abductive explanations. We have shown that given a Horn theory and a letter q, some non-trivial explanation for q can be calculated in polynomial time. However, goal-directed abduction or the use of an assumption set renders the problem intractable, even for acyclic Horn theories. Thus, the exponential worst-case complexity of the ATMS is not just a consequence of having to return an exponential number of answers; generating even one explanation containing letters from the assumption set is inherently difficult. It appears unlikely, therefore, that the efficiency of the ATMS algorithm can be significantly improved.

This work also shows that there is a strong connection between computing explanations and computing extensions in default logic. Our Support Selection Task is at the core of both assumption-based abductive reasoning and goal-directed default reasoning. We need to minimize support sets for the former, and maximize them for the latter, but neither is hard for Horn theories. In both cases, the difficult task is deciding on an appropriate set of assumptions to make.

Finally, given the difficulty of dealing with acyclic Horn theories, this work suggests that we may not be

[9] Determining the complexity of goal-directed reasoning for such theories was given as one of the central open problems in Kautz and Selman (1989).

[10] Using the terminology of Kautz and Selman (1989), they are normal unary defaults with empty prerequisites and positive consequences.

[11] Since an extension consists of an infinite set of formulas because of the logical closure, we are only looking for a set of unit clauses that represents an extension, as described below.

able to trade expressiveness for tractability in abductive reasoning. It may turn out that there are *no* interesting restrictions on the background theory that could guarantee efficient abduction (for some class of queries). This is quite unlike the situation with deductive reasoning, where there is a linear time algorithm for propositional Horn theories (Dowling and Gallier 1984), and with default reasoning, where there are polynomial algorithms for certain acyclic default theories (Selman and Kautz 1988; Kautz and Selman 1989). If we want to produce explanations automatically, in a timely fashion, and over a wide class of inputs, there may be no alternative to some notion of "approximate" explanation, or perhaps some principled form of unsound or incomplete abduction (a proposal for which is suggested in Levesque (1989)).[12]

Acknowledgments

This research was supported in part by a grant from the Natural Sciences and Engineering Research Council of Canada. We thank Ray Reiter for bringing to our attention the close relation between default reasoning and the ATMS, and for useful suggestions and discussions.

References

Allemang, D., Tanner, M.C., Bylander T., and Josephson, J.R. (1987) On the computational complexity of hypothesis assembly. *Proceedings IJCAI-87*, Milan, Italy, 1987, 1112-1117.

de Kleer, J. (1986a) An assumption-based TMS, *Artificial Intelligence*, Vol. 28, #2, 1986, 127–162.

de Kleer, J. (1986b) Problem solving with the ATMS, *Artificial Intelligence*, Vol. 28, #2, 1986, 197–224.

de Kleer, J. and Williams, B.C. (1989) Diagnosis with behavioral modes. *Proceedings IJCAI-89*, Detroit, MI, 1989, 1325-1330.

Dowling, W.F. and Gallier, J.H. (1984). Linear-time algorithms for testing the satisfiability of propositional Horn formulae. *Journal of Logic Programming*, **3**, 1984, 267–284.

Gabow, H.N., Maheshwari S.N, and Osterweil L. (1976). On two problems in the generation of program test paths. *IEEE Trans. Software Engineering,* 1976, 227–231.

Garey, M.R. and Johnson, D.S. (1979). *Computers and Intractability, A Guide to the Theory of NP-Completeness.* New York: W.H. Freeman, 1979.

Kautz, H.A. and Selman, B. (1989) Hard problems for simple default logics. *Proceedings of the First International Conference on Knowledge Representation and Reasoning (KR-89)*, Toronto, Ont., 1989, 189–197.

Levesque, H.J. (1989). A knowledge-level account of abduction. *Proceedings IJCAI-89*, Detroit, MI, 1989, 1061–1067.

McAllester, D. (1985). A widely used used truth-maintenance system. MIT, AI-lab memo, 1985.

Poole, D. (1988). A methodology for using a default and abductive reasoning system. Technical report, Dept. of Computer Science, University of Waterloo, Waterloo, Ont., 1988.

Provan, G.M. (1987). Efficiency analysis of multiple-context TMSs in scene representation. *Proceedings AAAI-87*, Seattle, WA, 1987, 173–178.

Provan, G.M. (1988). The Computational Complexity of Truth Maintenance System. Technical Report 88-11, University of British Columbia, Department of Computer Science, 1988.

Reggia, J. (1983) Diagnostic expert systems based on a set-covering model. *International Journal of Man Machine Studies*, 19(5), 1983, 437–460.

Reiter, R. and de Kleer, J. (1980). Foundations of assumption-based truth maintenance systems. *Proceedings AAAI-87*, Seattle, WA, 1987, 183–188.

Reiter, R. (1987). A theory of diagnosis from first principles. *Artificial Intelligence*, 32(1), 1987, 57–96.

Selman, B. and Kautz, H.A. (1988) The Complexity of Model-Preference Default Theories. *Proceedings of the Seventh Biennial Conference of the Canadian Society for Computational Studies of Intelligence (CSCSI-88)*, Edmonton, Alberta, 1988, 102–109. Extended version to appear in *Artificial Intelligence.*

Selman, B. (1990) Tractable default reasoning. Ph.D. Thesis, Dept. of Computer Science, University of Toronto, Toronto, Ont. (forthcoming.)

Stillman (1989) The complexity of Horn theories with normal unary defaults. Technical report, General Electric Research and Development Center, Schenectady, N.Y., 1989.

Valiant, R.G. and Vazirani V.V. (1986) NP is as easy as detecting unique solutions. *Theoretical Computer Science*, #47, 1986, 85–93.

[12]Recently, it has been brought to our attention that Provan (1988) has independently obtained complexity results for the ATMS which are similar to our results, but somewhat weaker.

Interaction-based Invention: Designing Novel Devices from First Principles

Brian C. Williams*
System Sciences Laboratory
Xerox Palo Alto Research Center
3333 Coyote Hill Road, Palo Alto CA 94304
bwilliams@xerox.com

Abstract

An inventor who is skilled at constructing innovative designs is distinguished, not just by the first principles he knows, but by the way he uses these principles and how he focusses the search for novel devices among an overwhelming space of possibilities. We propose that an appropriate focus for design is the network of qualitative interactions between quantities, (called an *interaction topology*), used by a device to achieve its desired behavior. We present an approach, called *interaction-based invention*, which views design as a process of building interaction topologies — in this paper directly from first principles. The program *Ibis*, which embodies this approach, designs simple hydro-mechanical regulators, analogous to devices that were fundamental to the development of feedback control theory.

1 Introduction

In highly competitive markets with rapid technology shifts a designer must continually exploit new technologies and existing technologies in nonobvious ways. Current AI design research focuses on heirarchical refinement using libraries of design fragments [McDermott 1977; Roylance 1980; Mitchell *et al.* 1983; Ressler 1984; Mitchell *et al.* 1985; Mittal *et al.* 1986). While library-based techniques like configuration [McDermott 1982] have been highly successful for some "routine tasks," they ignore these innovative aspects of the design process.

To achieve the generality necessary to maintain a competitive edge, the designer might have to consider, not just what is in the routine library, but any possible device structure. Evaluating the behavior of any structure requires reasoning from first principles. The generality afforded by these principles presents the designer with an overwhelming space of possibilities. To avoid being lost the inventor must use every means at his disposal to focus the search. This is the ability to innovate. Thus a robust theory must capture, not only techniques for routine design, but the process of innovation from first principles. We refer to this as invention.

Innovation is a multi-faceted process that researchers are only beginning to explore [Murthy & Addanki 1987; Ulrich 1988; Joskowicz & Addanki 1989]. This paper explores one such facet — the process of innovation when reasoning from first principles alone. Specifically we present a theory that captures key aspects of a process that can be used to construct novel devices like the one shown to the left in figure 1 (from Mayr [1970]). This device (developed by Heron of Alexandria in the first century AD) automatically fills a cup k with fluid from a vase v, and maintains the fluid at a specified level:

> If the fluid level in the cup is too low, then the volume of fluid is too small, the cup will be too light, and the weight at the end of the balance will move downward. Through a set of linkages the disk lifts off of the end of the pipe. When the gap appears, fluid flows out of the vase, through the pipe, and into the cup. As a result the cup's fluid height and weight increases. Eventually the fluid reaches the desired height, at which time the balance tips, closing the gap.

This device was innovative in its time for the use of a balance to sense fluid height via weight and for its explicit use of feedback control.

More generally, we explore the design of lumped-parameter devices (i.e., networks of components and connections) whose desired behavior is described by transitions in a qualitative state diagram, and whose behavior is governed by the laws of physical system dynamics [Shearer *et al.* 1971] or circuit theory [Bose 1965].

Our work begins with the intuition that this and similar devices can be constructed *by focussing on qualitative differences between how alternative devices work.* The first part of this paper teases apart this intuition through a series of questions. This results in three concepts that we believe are central to focussing the design process: the interaction topology, interaction-based invention, and the topology of potential interactions. We then use a simple fluid regulation example to demonstrate how these concepts are embodied in a program called *Ibis*.

2 Design as Focussing on Interactions

How do devices work?

Our research takes the perspective that a device "works" by establishing a network of interactions between quantities and orchestrating these interactions over time. We call this network an *interaction topology.* A simplified

*Discussions with my advisor Randy Davis and committee Patrick Winston and Tomas Lozano-Perez had a tremendous impact on this research. Johan de Kleer, Brian Falkenhainer, Leo Joskowicz and Mark Shirley provided valuable comments on earlier drafts. This research was performed both at the MIT AI Lab and Xerox PARC. MIT support was provided by an Analog Devices Fellowship, DEC, Wang, and DARPA under Office of Naval Research contract N00014-85-K-0124.

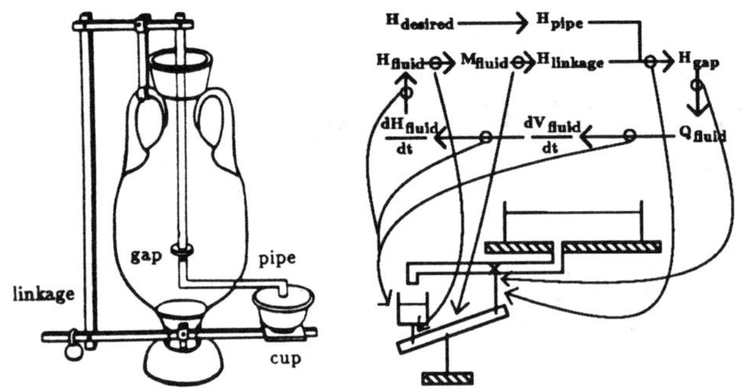

Figure 1: Heron's weight regulator from [Mayr 1970] (left) and interaction-based invention (right). The graph at the upper right is an interaction topology, constructed to relate dH_{fluid}/dt to H_{fluid} and $H_{desired}$. The topology is built from interactions, each producible by a single component or connection (downward arrows).

example for Heron's regulator[1] is depicted by the graph in figure 1 (top right), where H, M, Q and V denote fluid height, mass, flow and volume. The explanation in the introduction traced a path through this topology. In addition to connectivity, the topology must capture exactly those features of interactions that directly contribute to how a device achieves its behavioral specification. Initially a designer ignores many details of the specification like delay and power dissipation, instead focussing on the basic shape of a device's behavior. In our case this is the rise and fall of fluid levels or, more generally, state transitions in a qualitative state diagram [Bobrow (ed.) 1984]. The salient features of interactions are exactly those necessary to achieve each transition. In [Williams 1988, 1989] we argue that this is captured by a combination of qualitative and quantitative features, expressible by equations in Q1 — a hybrid algebra on signs and reals.[2]

How do these observations impact invention? We claim that, because the interaction topology captures qualitative features of how devices work, it is an appropriate central focus of invention. Specifically:

> Invention involves constructing a topology of interactions that both produces the desired behavior and makes evident a topology of physical devices that implements those interactions (figure 1, right).

This approach, called *Interaction-based Invention*, has three major components: building the interaction topology, building the corresponding physical structure, and verifying that the interactions produce the desired behavior. To ensure that the topology "makes evident" the physical structure, the topology is built from interactions that are producible by a single component or physical connection. The producible interactions are identified using the first principles of the current domain and technology, and interactions are interconnected through shared variables. The topology is verified by algebraically "composing" interactions and comparing the result with the desired interaction.

A strategy for proposing the interconnection of interactions is faced with an enormous space of possibilities. To cope, Ibis generates candidate solutions by focussing first on the most constraining features of interactions ...

What qualitative features are most important? Rarely do primitives directly relate the types of variables were interested in. For example, the purpose of Heron's regulator is to relate height change to height difference, but there is no way to achieve this directly. Instead the device uses a lengthy chain of interactions that successively transform a signal from one variable type to another. This difficulty is highlighted by the *connectivity of interactions*, conveyed in the graph of figure 1 (top right), independent of the behavior each interaction produces. The importance of connectivity is further supported by a detailed historical analysis [Mayr 1970] which uses similar diagrams to highlight the innovative aspects of feedback control devices developed over a period of 1800 years. For example, Heron's innovation is a path of interactions that uses force to sense height. The end of this paper shows several other innovations that exploit alternative paths. To summarize, qualitative features that are particularly important are the connectivity of interactions and the types of variables involved.

How are devices composed from first principles? We conjecture that, for simple devices, new innovations are constructed in a manner similar to how existing inventions are understood. To understand how a device works, we first imagine all the interactions produced by every component and every connection in the device, and then trace out a path that identifies interactions contributing to the behavior of interest. Analogously, to invent a device, we use our first principles to imagine *all* possible interactions producible by every type of component and every type of connection available in the current technology, and *all ways* that these interactions can be connected. The resulting structure we call a *topology of potential interactions.* A device is proposed by tracing a path through the potential interaction topology that connects variables in the desired interaction. The device's interaction topology are those variables and interactions that lie along the path. We call this process *imagining potential interactions.* Interesting alternatives correspond to distinct paths through this topology. Of course it would be unreasonable to explicitly represent all producible interactions and interconnections, since the space would be infinite. Compactness is achieved by representing *types* rather than instances. The topology of potential interactions is built from the types of interactions producible, connected wherever it is consistent for them to share a variable. These interaction types are those produced by each type of component and physical connection.

1 A more representative example of an interaction topology is shown in figure 5.

2 For more complex topologies, in [Williams 1989] we argue for the importance of capturing an interaction's causal and temporal features at a level of abstraction expressible in the representations of [Williams 1984, 1986].

To maximize function sharing — the use of a single component for several functions — it is important wherever possible to exploit interactions produced by existing structure (structure already introduced in the design). This helps to reduce design costs and parasitic effects. In some cases variables in a desired interaction are only accessible through existing interactions — function sharing is then an absolute necessity. To this end we augment our space with a ***topology of existing interactions***, representing the interactions of a partially constructed design, that are produced by structure already introduced. This is interconnected with the topology of potential interactions wherever it is consistent to share variables. A candidate solution is proposed by tracing a path through the combined topology, for example, minimizing the number of potential interactions traversed (figure 2, top of upper half).

This combined topology is the key to our approach. It is an interaction topology and thus focuses the search within the realm of how devices work. It makes physical structure evident — each interaction is produced by a type of component or connection. It can be searched quickly — path tracing in a small graph is fast. It captures the first principles — that's what the topology is built from. And it highlights connectivity between variable types — one of the most constraining, and potentially innovative aspects of alternative solutions. Together these features allow us to make good on the claim that we are able to construct innovative devices from first principles.

3 Ibis: Interaction-based Invention System

For simplicity of presentation we demonstrate our approach using the punch bowl example of [Williams 1988] (e.g., as opposed to heron's regulator):

> Suppose you are throwing a large party that includes beverages. Having waiters manually refill the punch bowl from a large vat would intrude on the ambiance of the event; thus, you decide to use Ibis to construct a device that restores the punch bowl automatically. At Ibis' disposal is an array of pipes, containers and lids. The vat, v, and bowl, b, are sitting on a table, both open to the air. For aesthetics the vat is hidden, and connections are only allowed to the bottom of the vat and bowl. For simplicity you decide the level of punch in the bowl should be the same as that in the vat.

The desired behavior is specified by a qualitative state diagram. Using a process roughly analogous to finite state machine design [Hill & Peterson 1974], Ibis maps the diagram into interactions. As discussed in [Williams 1989], in our example Ibis infers that the desired interaction is to change the bowl's fluid height in the direction of the vat/bowl height difference ($[\,]$ denotes an expression's sign $\{+,0,-\}$):

$$[H(v) - H(b)] = [dH(b)/dt]$$

Our focus here is on how Ibis maps a single desired interaction into an interaction topology. Ibis' basic steps are numbered on the top half of figure 2. First, Ibis

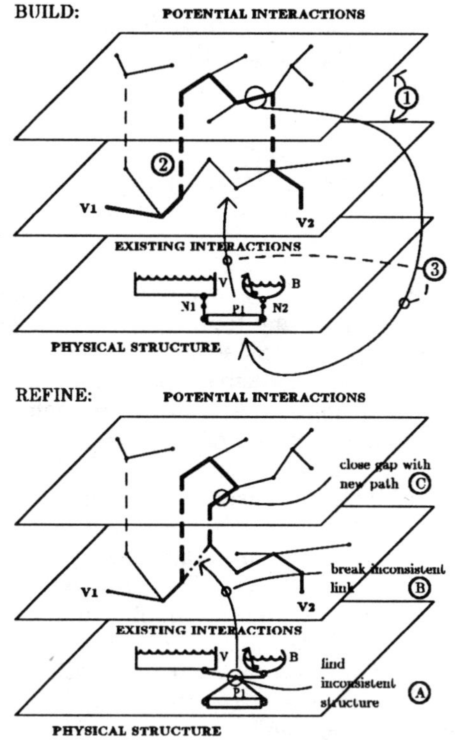

Figure 2: Major steps Ibis performs to build (upper) and refine (lower) an interaction topology.

builds the space of all interactions: the topology of potential interactions for the domain and technology, and the topology of existing interactions for the initial structure and interactions. Second, Ibis proposes a candidate by identifying a path through the two topologies, connecting the variables in the desired interaction. Third, Ibis augments the device structure in order to instantiate the potential interactions along the path (and links connecting these interactions). Finally, Ibis verifies that the path produces the behavior of the desired interaction.

Ibis may fail on two accounts: either because the structure introduced in the third step is inconsistent, or because the behavior verified in the fourth step is incorrect. In either case Ibis has the choice of exploring a topology corresponding to an alternative path, or refining the current candidate (bottom half, figure 2). In the latter case Ibis A) identifies one or more links causing inconsistencies, B) breaks these links to remove all inconsistencies, (preserving the consistent links and interactions), and C) tries to close the gaps where these links have been broken, by tracing additional paths through the topology of potential interactions. Finally, Ibis repeats the process of introducing structure and verifying behavior (steps 3 and 4).

To support this process, Ibis exploits two reasoning components described elsewhere: the symbolic algebra system, called *Minima*, for the hybrid qualitative quantitative algebra Q1 [Williams 1988], and the hybrid terminological reasoning and congruence closure system called

Iota [Williams 1989]. The remaining sections describe Ibis' inputs and demonstrate the first four steps of the building process on our example. Refinement is demonstrated in [Williams 1989].

4 Ibis' Inputs and Outputs

Ibis takes as input the desired interaction, initial constraints on the physical structure and interactions, and terminological definitions and physical principles characterizing the domain and technology. It produces from these a consistent physical structure whose interaction topology produces the desired interaction. First consider inputs involving structure. The terminological definitions describe the classes of valid physical structures (e.g., pipes, containers), quantities (e.g., H, P) and their interrelationships for a given domain and technology. The initial and final structures describe particular instances of these classes (called individuals) and their interrelationship. Each is described in a terminological language, called Iota, roughly similar in style to languages like Klone [Brachman & Schmolze 1985]. Iota's syntax and semantics is presented in [Williams 1989]. Our example uses a device-centered model. That is, each component communicates externally through a set of *terminals*, and a physical structure is a network of components whose terminals are connected to common points called *nodes*. Two example definitions are shown below, the left is for nodes and the right is for pipes:

```
node are_unique constituent;
t1_of(node) are terminal;
t2_of(node) are terminal;
P(node) are pressure;
1-1_function(t1_of);
1-1_function(t2_of);
1-1_function(P);
t1_of(node) disjoint t2_of(node);
forall (n) node(n) implies nt1_of(n) ≡ n;
forall (n) node(n) implies nt2_of(n) ≡ n;
```

```
pipe are_unique device;
t1(pipe) are_unique terminal;
t2(pipe) are_unique terminal;
R(pipe) are fluid_resistance;
1-1_function(t1);
1-1_function(t2);
1-1_function(R);
```

The left says roughly that a node is a unique type of physical constituent, and each node has a unique P, t1_of and t2_of, where P is a pressure, and t1_of and t2_of are distinct terminals. Also, a terminal which is the t1_of or t2_of some node has that node associated with it.[3] The right definition says roughly that a pipe is a unique type of device, and has a unique R, t1 and t2, where R is a fluid resistance, and t1, t2 are distinct terminals. See [Williams 1989] for the complete set of definitions and their semantics.

A structural description specifies the individuals that a device is composed of, their types, and their interrelationship through equivalences (≡) and inequivalences (≢). For example, the following describes a solution to the punch bowl problem that connects a pipe between the vat and bowl. The corresponding schematic uses open circles to denote terminals, and closed circles to denote nodes:

[3] nT is an abbreviation for node_of(T), where T is a terminal. We also abbreviate bottom with b and top with t.

```
vat(v);              b(v) ≡ t1_of(N1);
bowl(b);             t2_of(N1) ≡ t1(P1);
pipe(P1);            t2(P1) ≡ t2_of(N2);
node(N1);            t1_of(N2) ≡ b(b);
node(N2);
```

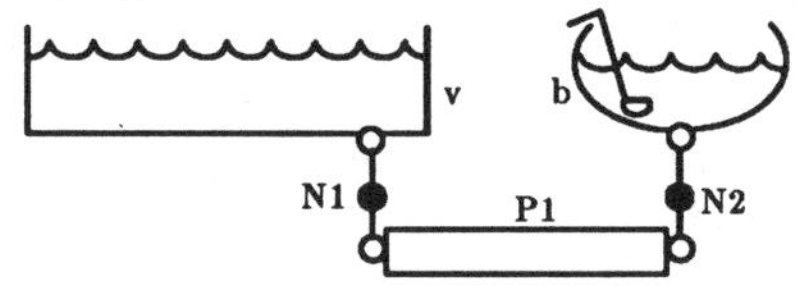

The description introduces a distinct vat v, bowl b, pipe P1, and two nodes N1 and N2. A component is connected to a node by sharing a terminal. For example, "b(v) ≡ t1_of(N1)" says that the terminal at the bottom of v is one of $N1$'s terminals. The above description says that the bottom of v is connected to the $t1$ end of $P1$ through node $N1$, and the $t2$ end of $P1$ is connected to the bottom of b through node $N2$. The declarations "vat(v)" and "bowl(b)" specify the initial structure for our example.

Next consider the inputs that are specified as interactions: the initial and desired interactions, and physical principles. An interaction is a qualitative (or quantitative) relationship between variables. In this paper it is an equation in the Q1 algebra [Williams 1988]. Initial interactions specify interactions enforced by the problem statement. In our example, no fluid can flow into the top of the bowl; that is, $Q(t(b)) = 0$. Desired interactions are interactions that the design must satisfy — in our example $[H(v) - H(b)] = [dH(b)/dt]$. The physical principles describe the types of interactions (called *potential interactions*) producible by classes of physical constituents. In a device-centered approach these are interactions produced by classes of components (the device models) and connections (the connection laws). A potential interaction is an interaction over classes of variables (called *variable types*). It is expressed as a universally quantified horn clause. The antecedents restrict each quantifier to range over defined classes. The consequent is an interaction (here a Q1 equation) on variables and variable types (terms containing quantifiers). For example, the pipe model consists of three potential interactions:

```
forall (pi) pipe(pi) implies Q(t1(pi)) + Q(t2(pi)) = 0;
forall (pi) pipe(pi) implies Pd(nt1(pi),nt2(pi)) = R(pi) × Q(t1(pi));
forall (pi) pipe(pi) implies R(pi) = [+]
```

The first says that what flows into one end of the pipe flows out the other end. The second relates a pipe's pressure difference (Pd) to its fluid resistance (R) and flow (Q). The third says that R is always positive.

5 Building the Space of Interactions

Recall that the topology of potential interactions represents all producible interactions and all ways they interconnect. The topology of existing interactions represents interactions produced by the current structure and is updated as the structure is modified. To build the first topology, Ibis creates an undirected hyper-edge for each potential interaction that connects the interaction's variables. For example, consider two interactions

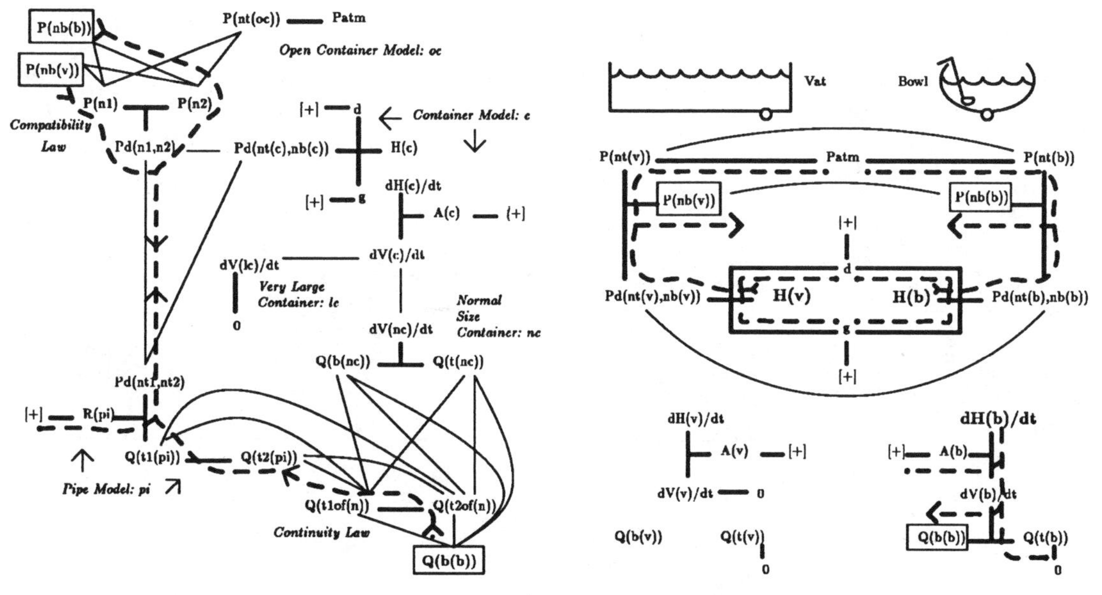

Figure 3: The topology of potential (left) and existing (right) interactions for the punch bowl problem. Thick lines denote interactions and thin lines denote links. Dashed lines show a path through the two topologies between desired variables: H(v), H(b) and dH(b)/dt. Boxed variables indicate where branches of the path jump between topologies.

— the first is from the pipe model and the second is the continuity law for nodes (Pd is pressure difference, Q flow and R resistance):

forall (pi) pipe(pi) implies Pd(nt1(pi),nt2(pi)) = Q(t1(pi)) × R(pi);
forall (n) node(n) implies Q(t1_of(n)) = – Q(t2_of(n))

Hyper-edges representing these two interactions are shown below by thick lines to the far left and right:

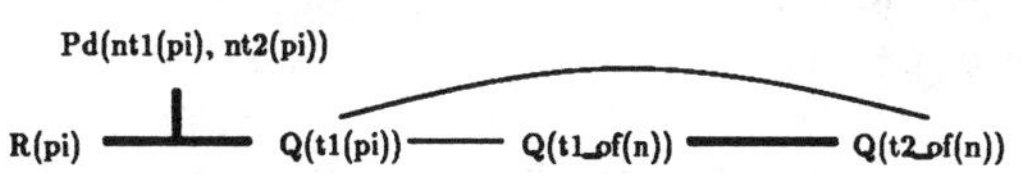

Each edge tells us which quantities interact directly, while suppressing the algebraic properties of the interaction. The complete set of hyper-edges for the example are shown as thick lines in figure 3, left half.

Next the hyper-edges are combined into a graph. Interactions communicate through shared variables. Possible sharings are represented by thin lines, called *links*, between pairs of unifiable variables (i.e., variable types that aren't necessarily disjoint and thus can share an individual). Unification is semantic rather than syntactic, and is determined by Iota from the terminological definitions. The pipe and continuity interactions shown earlier are connected by two links. For example, variable types Q(t1(pi)) and Q(t1_of(n)) are linked — by definition Q is a 1-1 function; thus, for an individual Q(i) to be an instance of both variable types, i must be an instance of both t1(pi) and t1_of(n). This is consistent with the definitions for pipe and node given earlier. In contrast Q(t1_of(n)) and Q(t2_of(n)) are not linked, since from the definition of node t1_of(n) and t2_of(n) are disjoint. The complete set of links are shown in figure 3, left half.[4]

Next the topology of existing interactions is constructed, corresponding to the initial structure. This involves instantiating the applicable potential interactions and combining them with the initial interactions. Common vertices denote shared variables, where sharing is determined by Iota through congruence closure. Links are added to this topology between variables that are unifiable (and not already equivalent). The complete topology of existing interactions for the punch bowl problem is shown on the right side of figure 3. The vat's interactions are to the left and the bowl's are to the right.

Once the topology of potential and existing interactions are created, they are interconnected by linking each variable and variable type that are unifiable. Variables of interest that link the two topologies are highlighted in figure 3 by boxes.

6 Proposing a Candidate Topology

Next, Ibis uses these topologies to identify a candidate solution — an interaction topology that has a simple mapping to physical structure and which may combine to produce a desired interaction (step two of figure 2). A candidate solution is a minimal set of interactions and links that *relates those and only those variables in the desired interaction* (called *desired variables*). In our example these variables are H(v), H(b) and dH(b)/dt. A candidate C is identified by tracing a (multi) path between the desired variable through both interaction topologies. C consists of every interaction and link touched by the

[4]This topology is overly simple for presentation purposes. A more representative topology, for example, combining hydraulic and mechanical properties might contain several types of connections and a few dozen device types.

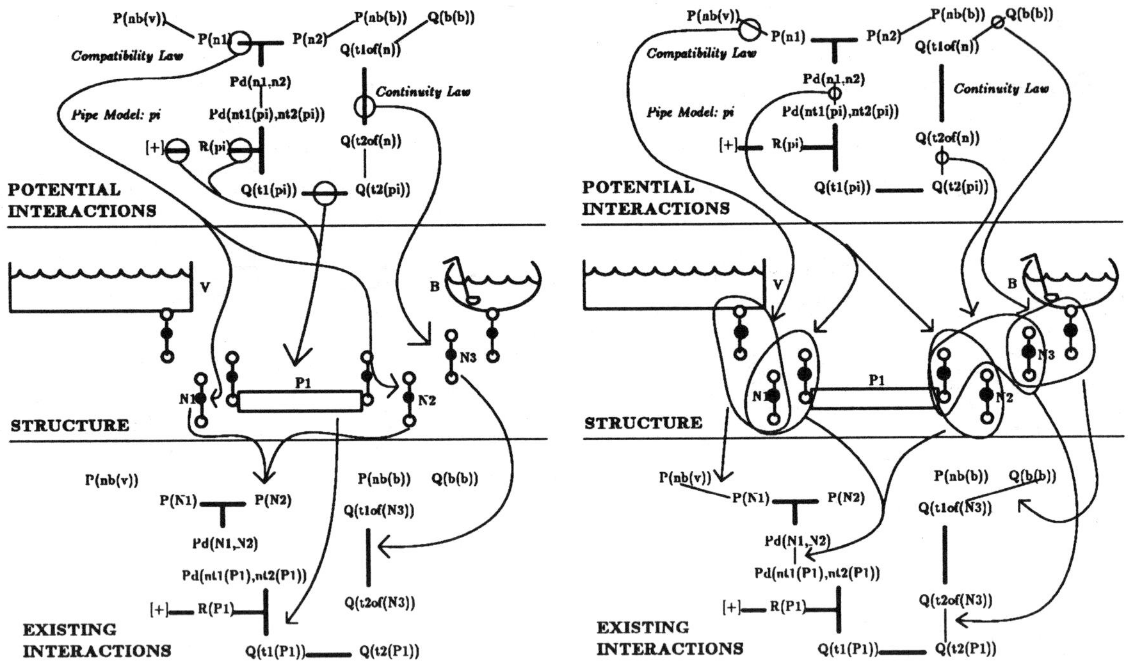

Figure 4: Instantiating the candidate potential interactions (left) and links (right). On the left, a downward arrow points to the structure and existing interaction that result from instantiating a potential interaction. On the right each points to the unifications of structure and variables resulting from instantiating a link.

multi path. To *relate the desired variables,* C should contain a path P going between the variables that has no intervening constants. To *relate only the desired variables*, every branch off of P should terminate on a constant, unless it leads to a desired variable. Intuitively, a branch terminating on another variable represents an undesired influence (see [Williams 1989] for details).

A path corresponding to a candidate for the punch bowl problem are shown as dashed lines in figure 3. It begins as three separate paths starting at the desired variables, H(v), H(b) and dH(b)/dt, and tracing out through the topology of existing interactions (right half, figure 3). One branch of each path reaches P(nb(v)), P(nb(b)) and Q(b(b)), respectively, which are linked to the potential interaction topology. The other branches terminate on constants (denoted by paths ending with black dots). After crossing links at P(nb(v)), P(nb(b)) and Q(b(b)), the paths trace through the potential interaction topology, where they come together as a single path (left half, figure 3). In so doing the path traverses five links and five potential interactions: the three interactions of the pipe model, and one each for the continuity and compatibility laws (governing the behavior of connections at nodes).[5]

[5]Note that a single path introduces a component of each type at most once. Several instances of the same type are introduced either during the refinement process (figure 2, bottom), or when multiple desired interactions are specified.

7 Adding Interactions and Structure

Next Ibis augments the topology of existing interactions with the potential interactions and links in the candidate (step three of figure 2). Potential interactions and links are introduced through analogous operations on physical structure. Interactions are instantiated by introducing physical parts (e.g., pipes, nodes, terminals) — the parts specified in the first principles corresponding to each potential interaction. Links are instantiated by unifying physical parts. This in turn unifies existing variables, thereby connecting the interactions together.

The top left of figure 4 shows the candidate potential interactions and links for our example. Next to each interaction is the name of the corresponding model or law. The vat v and bowl b in the middle left of the figure are part of the initial structure. P(nb(v)), P(nb(b)) and Q(b(b)) at the bottom left are variables of the existing interactions that the augmentations connect to.

Ibis instantiates five potential interactions: the interaction from the compatibility law, three interactions from the pipe model, and the interaction from the continuity law. First, the compatibility law:

```
forall (n1,n2) node(n1) and node(n2) implies
        Pd(n1,n2) = P(n1) - P(n2)
```

applies to any pair of nodes; thus, Ibis instantiates the law by introducing two nodes with unique names – call them $N1$ and $N2$. Similarly, introducing $N1$ and $N2$ results in a single interaction being added to the topology of existing interactions, as is shown by the downward arrow at the far left of figure 4. The remaining four interactions are introduced in a similar manner, as depicted in the figure: a pipe $P1$ for the three interactions of the pipe model, and a node $N3$ for the continuity law.

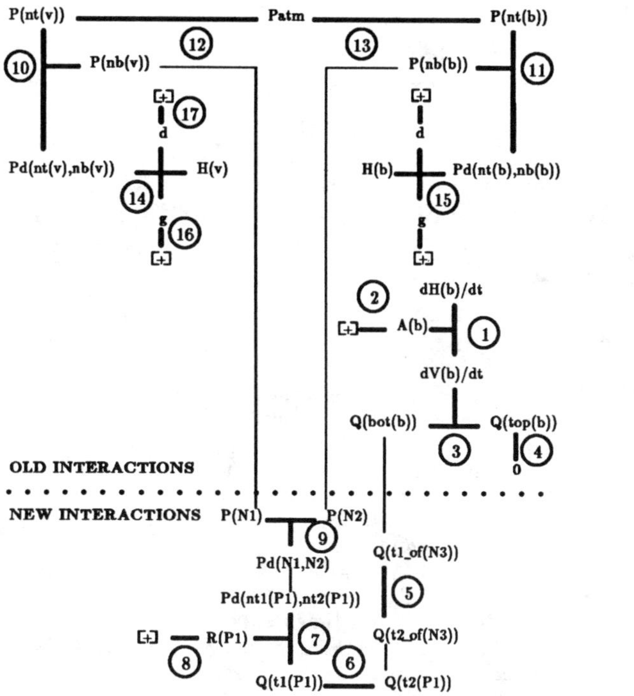

Figure 5: The augmented topology of interactions. Numbers indicate the sequence in which interactions are combined during verification.

Next, to complete the interaction topology Ibis "glues" the interactions together by instantiating the candidate links. This involves unifying the variables of interactions and is accomplished by unifying pieces of device structure. For example, consider the link between Q(t1_of(n)) and Q(b(b)), shown in the upper right corner of figure 4. To instantiate this link we want to equate Q(t1_of(N3)) and Q(b(b)). To enforce this equivalence the bottom of bowl b must be connected to N3. That is, t1_of(N3) and b(b) must refer to the same terminal, and N3 and nb(b) must refer to the same node. This is inferred by Iota through congruence closure from the definitions and structural description. The remaining four links are instantiated in a similar manner. The resulting unifications of structure and variables are depicted by downward arrows in the right half of figure 4. The net effect of the instantiations is to connect the pipe between the vat and bowl. The augmented interaction topology is shown in figure 5.

Although the above structure is consistent with the definitions, this is not always the case. The reason is that the topology of potential interactions ensures only that the links are pairwise consistent — the instances of several links may be globally inconsistent. When this happens the inconsistent links are broken, and the solution is refined as sketched earlier ([Williams 1989] provides detailed examples). Several refinements are normally required for complex structures, like Heron's regulator and the fluid regulators at the end of this paper.

8 Verifying the Desired Interaction

The remaining step is to determine whether or not the combined behaviors of the interactions in the candidate produce the desired interaction $[H(v) - H(b)] = [dH(b)/dt]$. The composition process involves qualitative symbolic algebra on Q1 equations, and is performed by Minima [Williams 1988]. To compose interactions, Ibis starts with the expression involving the variable being controlled, in our example $[dH(b)/dt]$. It walks back along the path traced when constructing a candidate, accumulating a symbolic expression. Ibis then tests whether the accumulated expression matches the other expression in the desired behavior, $[H(v) - H(b)]$. The sequence of interactions walked through during the accumulation are numbered in figure 5, with the corresponding expressions at each step shown below. The initial and final expressions (lines 0, 17) match the desired interaction; thus, connecting the pipe solves the punch bowl problem.

0) $[dH(b)/dt]$
1) $[dV(b)/dt] \otimes [A(b)]$
2) $[dV(b)/dt]$
3) $[Q(b(b)) + Q(top(b))]$
4) $[Q(b(b))]$
5) $\ominus[Q(t2\_of(N3))]$
6) $[Q(t1(P1))]$
7) $[Pd(nt1(P1), nt2(P1))] \otimes [R(P1)]$
8) $[Pd(nt1(P1), nt2(P1))]$
9) $[P(N1) - P(N2)]$
10) $[(Pd(nt(v), nb(v)) - P(nt(v))) - P(N2)]$
11) $[Pd(nt(v), nb(v)) + P(nt(b)) - P(nt(v)) - Pd(nt(b), nb(b))]$
12) $[Pd(nt(v), nb(v)) + P(nt(b)) - P_{atm} - Pd(nt(b), nb(b))]$
13) $[Pd(nt(v), nb(v)) - Pd(nt(b), nb(b))]$
14) $[H(v)/(d \times g) - Pd(nt(b), nb(b))]$
15) $[H(v) - H(b)] \otimes [d] \otimes [g]$
16) $[H(v) - H(b)] \otimes [d]$
17) $[H(v) - H(b)]$

Note that the resulting design is quite compact in part because the device exploits a substantial set of interactions produced by the initial structure. The complete set of interactions directly contributing to the desired behavior is extensive — all those shown in figure 5. Ibis' use of the topology of existing interactions when proposing candidates is central to how it achieves this type of function sharing. [6]

9 Discussion

Consider briefly the complexity and completeness of our approach. A simple mapping exists between propositional formulas and Q1 equations; thus, verifying an interaction topology is at least as difficult as 3-Sat, and is in fact NP-hard. Design introduces bounded quantification into the equations (the potential interactions), raising the problem to first order satisfiability. It is at

[6] In [Ulrich 1988] a device is initially designed without function sharing, and then functions are later collapsed. In contrast, for problems like our example, some function sharing must be considered immediately, since a solution can only control the desired variables through existing interactions (e.g., H through P).

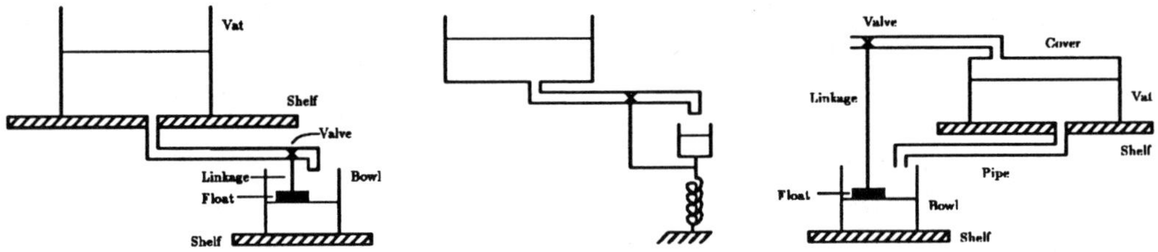

Figure 6: Analogues to early feedback devices, constructed by Ibis.

best semi-decidable. Our aspiration then has been to make the individual steps of interaction-based invention efficient and to develop a more sophisticated coordination of these steps through future research. Building the space of interactions, identifying a candidate path, elaborating structure, and testing consistency are at worst quadratic in the number of individuals and classes introduced. We are working on proving whether Ibis generates all candidates; the other steps are complete. As discussed above, the verification step is NP-hard. The set of compositions is linear in the number of interactions, but the cost is in canonicalization and factoring. As argued in [Williams 1988] Q1 has a number of unique properties that tend to make these operations efficient in practice. Verification is sound but incomplete. Ibis has been demonstrated on several simple devices. Also, it has been walked through the design and verification of the devices in figure 6, which are analogous to regulators that were fundamental to the development of feedback control theory [Mayr 1970]. Although we haven't experimented with this, Ibis should also work with analog designs, since quantitative equations are a subset of Q1.

Ibis' initial focus on the connectivity of interactions bares a loose similarity to Ulrich's [1988] use of bond graphs (i.e., graphic depictions of n ports). However Ulrich's approach is very different. Bond graphs are initially proposed by arbitrarily composing bonds, device behavior, excepting connectivity, is never considered, and there are no analogues to Ibis' topologies of existing and potential interactions, Q1, Iota or Minima.

The approach of imagining potential interactions is one piece of a larger project on interaction-based design (see [Williams 1990]). We are currently exploring a more robust causal-temporal representation of interactions and are embedding our approach within evolutionary and library-based design. In addition [Joskowicz & Addanki 1989] is suggestive of a promising avenue for combining interaction-based and geometric design.

This work is best summarized by the initial intuition and series of questions raised in the introduction — *innovative devices can be constructed by focussing on qualitative differences between how alternative devices work:*

How do devices work? By constructing an interaction topology and orchestrating it over time.

How does this impact invention? Invention involves constructing a topology of interactions that both produces the desired behavior and makes evident a physical structure that implements those interactions.

What qualitative features are most important? The connectivity of interactions and their variable types.

How are simple devices composed out of first principles? By tracing paths through a topology of potential interactions.

10 References

Bobrow, D. G. (Ed.) [1984], "Special Issue on Qualitative Reasoning," *Artificial Intelligence*, **24**.

Bose, A. G., and K. N. Stevens [1965], *Introductory Network Theory*, Harper and Row, New York.

Brachman, R. J., and J. G. Schmolze [1985], "An Overview of the KL-ONE Knowledge Representation System," *Cognitive Science*, volume 9, pages 171-216.

Hill, F. J., and G. R. Peterson [1974], *Introduction to Switching Theory and Logical Design*, Wiley, New York.

Joskowicz, L., and S. Addanki [1989], "Innovative Design of Kinematic Pairs," Report RC14507, IBM T.J.Watson Research Center, Yorktown Heights, N.Y.

Mayr, O. [1970], *The Origins of Feedback Control*, MIT Press, Cambridge, MA.

McDermott, D. [1977], "Flexibility and Efficiency in a Computer Program for Designing Circuits," MIT AITR-402.

McDermott, J. [1982], "R1: A Rule-based Configurer of Computer Systems," *Artificial Intelligence*, volume 19, number 1, pages 39-88.

Mitchell, T. M., *et al.* [1983], "An Intelligent Aid for Circuit Redesign," AAAI.

Mitchell, T. M., S. Mahadevan, and L. I. Steinberg [1985], "LEAP: A Learning Apprentice for VLSI Design," IJCAI, pages 573-80.

Mittal, S., C. M. Dym, and M. Morjaria [1986], "PRIDE: An Expert System for the Design of Paper Handling Systems," *Computer*.

Murthy, S. S., and S. Addanki [1987], "PROMPT: An Innovative Design Tool," AAAI, pages 637-42.

Ressler, A. [1984], "A Circuit Grammar for Operational Amplifier Design," MIT AI Lab TR-807.

Roylance, G. [1980], "A Simple Model of Circuit Design," MIT AI Lab TR-703.

Shearer *et al.* [1971], *Introduction to System Dynamics*, Addison-Wesley, Reading, Mass.

Ulrich, K. [1988], "Computation and Pre-Parametric Design," MIT AI Lab TR-1043.

Williams, B. C. [1984], "Qualitative Analysis of MOS Circuits," *Artificial Intelligence*, **24**, pages 281-346.

Williams, B. C. [1986], "Doing Time: Putting Qualitative Reasoning on Firmer Ground," AAAI, pages 105-112.

Williams, B. C. [1988], "MINIMA: A Symbolic Approach to Qualitative Reasoning," AAAI, pages264-269.

Williams, B. C. [1989], "Invention from First Principles via Topologies of Interaction," PhD Thesis, MIT.

Williams, B. C. [1990], "Invention from First Principles: An Overview," P. Winston and S. Shellard (Eds.), *Artificial Intelligence at MIT: Expanding Frontiers*, MIT Press.

Efficient Diagnosis of Multiple Disorders Based on a Symptom Clustering Approach

Thomas D. Wu
MIT Laboratory for Computer Science
545 Technology Square, Cambridge, Massachusetts 02139
tdwu@lcs.mit.edu

Abstract

Diagnosis of multiple disorders can be made efficient using a new representation and algorithm based on symptom clustering. The symptom clustering approach partitions symptoms into causal groups, in contrast to the existing candidate generation approach, which assembles disorders, or candidates. Symptom clustering achieves efficiency by generating aggregates of candidates rather than individual candidates and by representing them implicitly in a cartesian product form. Search criteria of parsimony, subsumption, and spanning narrow the symptom clustering search space, and a problem-reduction search algorithm explores this space efficiently. Experimental results on a large knowledge base indicate that symptom clustering yields a near-exponential increase in performance compared to candidate generation.

Introduction

Many challenges in artificial intelligence derive from the intractability of reasoning. One ubiquitous but computationally hard reasoning task is diagnosis, especially when it involves multiple disorders. The success of multidisorder diagnosis depends heavily on the efficiency of the algorithm employed. This paper augments the capabilities of diagnostic reasoning by developing an efficient representation and algorithm based on a symptom clustering approach.

The current approach to multidisorder diagnosis is based on candidate generation. A candidate is a set of disorders that explains a given set of symptoms. Set-covering approaches to diagnosis [5] explore a "candidate space" [1], also called a "hypothesis graph" [4] or "hitting set tree" [6]. In contrast, the approach introduced in this paper is based on symptom clustering. Whereas a candidate assembles disorders, a symptom clustering partitions symptoms into clusters. It structures symptoms into causal groups, with symptoms in the same cluster hypothetically caused by the same disorder. Experience with our implemented system SYNOPSIS indicates that the symptom clustering approach offers increased efficiency for multidisorder diagnosis.

In the rest of the paper, we develop the symptom clustering representation and show how it is related to candidate generation. We introduce search criteria to help narrow the symptom clustering search space and then devise a problem-reduction search algorithm that explores this space efficiently. Finally, we verify the performance gains of the symptom clustering approach empirically on a large, real-world knowledge base.

The Candidate Generation Approach

In set-covering approaches to diagnosis, the task is to find minimal candidates that explain a case, where a case is a set of symptoms to be explained. Each symptom has a set of possible causes, which is called a conflict set. In this paper, we will usually refer to this conflict set as the *causes relation*, represented as Causes(s) for symptom s. A candidate explains a symptom if it contains a disorder in Causes(s). A candidate is *valid* for a case if it explains every symptom in the case. A candidate is *minimal* for a case if it is valid and none of its subsets is also valid for that case.

Minimal candidates can be generated recursively. Suppose we already have a minimal candidate for some symptoms S and consider a new symptom s. If the candidate explains s, no change is necessary since the candidate is already minimal for $(S \cup \{s\})$. Otherwise expand the candidate by creating, for each element of Causes(s), a new candidate that includes that element. Finally, prune any candidates that are nonminimal.

An example of the candidate generation algorithm, taken from [1], is shown in Figure 1. There are two features of the candidate generation process worth noting. First, candidates are generated individually, so that each node in the search tree has only one candidate. Second, candidates often share elements; for example, the candidates $[A_2M_2]$ and $[M_3M_2]$ share M_2. These two features are notable in contrast to the symptom clustering approach. In symptom clustering, candidates are generated aggregately rather than individually, and these aggregates are represented implicitly rather than explicitly. By *implicit representation*,

This research was supported in part by National Institutes of Health grant R01 LM04493 from the National Library of Medicine and by National Research Service Award T32 GM07753. I am grateful to Ramesh Patil, Peter Szolovits, and Randy Davis for their helpful discussions and to Randolph Miller for generously allowing use of the INTERNIST/QMR knowledge base for testing purposes.

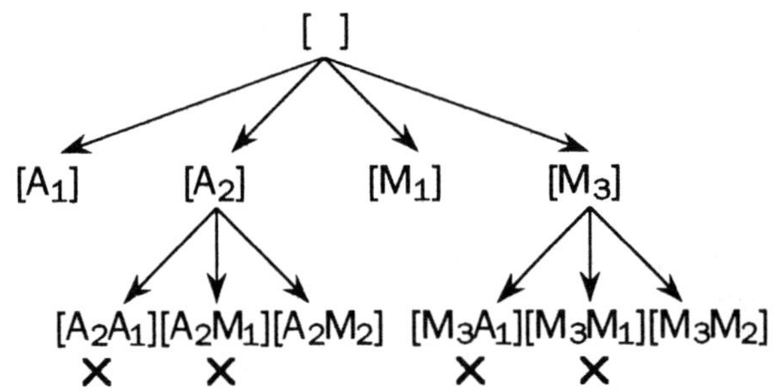

Figure 1: Candidate generation algorithm for a faulty circuit with two symptoms. One symptom can be explained by adders A_1 or A_2 or multipliers M_1 or M_3. The other symptom can be explained by A_1, M_1, or M_2. Pruned candidates, shown with ×'s, are nonminimal.

we mean that shared elements are factored completely into a cartesian product form. For instance, the explicit representation, $[A_2M_2]$ and $[M_3M_2]$, can be represented implicitly as a cartesian product: $\{A_2M_3\} \times \{M_2\}$. For this small example, the difference may seem minor, but it can become critical for large knowledge bases. The implicit representation is much more compact than the explicit representation and helps reduce one source of combinatorial explosion.

The Symptom Clustering Approach

The symptom clustering approach [8] changes the search space from subsets of disorders to clusterings of symptoms. A symptom clustering is a partition of symptoms into clusters. It denotes a possible interpretation of a case, hypothesizing which symptoms are caused by a common disorder and which by separate disorders. A disorder explains a cluster if it can cause every symptom in that cluster. For example, the symptom clustering (ABD)(C) indicates that two disorders are present: one that explains A, B, and D, and one that explains C.

The sets of disorders that meet this interpretation are called *differential diagnoses*, or simply differentials. Each differential contains disorders that can explain one cluster. Differential diagnoses are usually subject to parsimony criteria, which means that they may be shaped by the symptoms in other clusters as well as their own clusters. The cartesian product of the differential diagnoses implicitly represents an aggregate of candidates. A more precise definition of differentials will be presented later in this paper.

The symptom clustering approach offers a novel view of diagnosis. Whereas candidate generation views diagnosis as the *assignment of cause*, symptom clustering views it as the *assignment of structure*. It tries to determine the best way to decompose a problem, since a symptom clustering essentially represents a problem reduction. Its clusters represent the subproblems and its differentials contain solutions to each subproblem. Specifically, a symptom clustering may be expressed as a two-level AND/OR graph, since it contains a conjunction of clusters, and the differential associated with each cluster contains a disjunction of disorders.

Thus, diagnosis becomes primarily a matter of finding the correct structure for a problem and secondarily a matter of finding the correct causes. Focusing on structure in diagnosis opens a rich source of heuristics which might be called *structural heuristics*; these seem to be used commonly in everyday reasoning. Detectives often begin by piecing together evidence rather than trying to identify a culprit for each piece of evidence. In medical diagnosis, problem solving is facilitated by compiled knowledge about clusters of commonly co-occurring symptoms called *syndromes*. Another structural heuristic that ties symptoms together is temporal co-occurrence: symptoms that occur simultaneously are usually related. Structural heuristics such as these appear to be powerful and widely available. However, exploiting them requires viewing problem solving as the search for structure, a view that is inherent to the symptom clustering approach.

Relations between Representations

In a sense, candidates and symptom clusterings are duals, since candidates group disorders, while clusterings group symptoms. This duality can be expressed formally as a satisfaction relation from candidates to symptom clusterings. Formally, we say that candidate D *satisfies* clustering C if there exists a complete matching between clusters in C and disorders in D that can explain them.

For example, let us postulate a knowledge base containing four symptoms (A, B, C, and D) and seven disorders (d_1, d_2, ..., d_7). The causes for each symptom are given below:

Symptom	Causes
A	$\langle d_1d_2d_3d_4\rangle$
B	$\langle d_1d_3d_5d_7\rangle$
C	$\langle d_1d_2d_5\rangle$
D	$\langle d_1d_3d_4d_6\rangle$

Then the candidate $[d_3d_5]$ satisfies the clustering (ABD)(C) because d_3 can explain A, B, and D, while d_5 can explain C.

The inverse of the satisfaction relation is the entailment relation: C *entails* D if and only if D satisfies C. We are interested in knowing the set of clusterings that a given candidate satisfies and the set of candidates that a given clustering entails. In the next two subsections, we see how to compute these sets.

Computing the Satisfaction Relation

The satisfaction relation for a given candidate and case can be computed as follows. List the possible effects for each disorder in the candidate. Then select each symptom in the case once, making sure to select at least one effect in each list. The selected symptoms from each list form a cluster in the clustering. For example, consider the candidate $[d_3d_5d_6]$:

$$\begin{array}{llcccc} d_3 & \rightarrow & \mathbf{A} & \mathbf{B} & & \mathrm{D} \\ d_5 & \rightarrow & & \mathrm{B} & \mathbf{C} & \\ d_6 & \rightarrow & & & & \mathbf{D} \end{array} \left(\text{or} \quad \begin{array}{cccc} \mathbf{A} & \mathrm{B} & & \mathrm{D} \\ & \mathbf{B} & \mathbf{C} & \\ & & & \mathbf{D} \end{array} \right)$$

There are two ways to select the symptoms A, B, C, and D, as shown in boldface in each of the above matrices. These selections correspond to the two clusterings satisfied by $[d_3d_5d_6]$, namely, (AB)(C)(D) and (A)(BC)(D).

In addition to the satisfaction relation, the validity or minimality of a particular case can be determined. Validity testing is simple: Each symptom in the case must appear in the effects matrix; otherwise, some symptom cannot be explained. Minimality testing is a bit trickier. Each disorder must have a *justification*, a symptom in the case that appears in exactly one effects list. When each disorder has a justification, the candidate is minimal. For instance, the candidate $[d_3d_5d_6]$ shown above is not minimal, because d_6 lacks a justification. (Its only effect, D, appears also as a possible effect of d_3.) However, removing d_6 yields a minimal candidate:

$$\begin{array}{llcccc} d_3 & \rightarrow & \mathrm{A}^* & \mathrm{B} & & \mathrm{D}^* \\ d_5 & \rightarrow & & \mathrm{B} & \mathrm{C}^* & \end{array}$$

Each disorder has a justification (shown as starred), so $[d_3d_5]$ is minimal.

Computing the Entailment Relation

The inverse of satisfaction is entailment: Given a symptom clustering, what are all candidates that satisfy it? Actually, we may be interested in finding either valid candidates or minimal candidates that satisfy the clustering. Thus, we need two entailment relations: V-entailment to obtain valid candidates and M-entailment to obtain minimal candidates.

The V-entailment relation can be computed as follows. Given a clustering, find the *causal intersection* for each cluster c, by intersecting the possible causes for each symptom s in that cluster:

$$\mathrm{Int}(c) = \bigcap_{s \in c} \mathrm{Causes}(s)$$

The valid candidates are then the cartesian product of the causal intersections, excluding sets with duplicate elements. This exclusion ensures that the number of disorders (cardinality) in the candidate equals the number of clusters (dimension) in the clustering. For example, consider the clustering (AC)(B)(D). The causal intersections of the three clusters are $\{d_1d_2\}$, $\{d_1d_3d_5d_7\}$, and $\{d_1d_3d_4d_6\}$, respectively, yielding 22 valid candidates:

V-entails((AC)(B)(D)) =
$[d_1d_3d_4], [d_1d_3d_6], [d_1d_5d_3], [d_1d_5d_4], [d_1d_5d_6], [d_1d_7d_3], [d_1d_7d_4], [d_1d_7d_6], [d_2d_1d_3], [d_2d_1d_4], [d_2d_1d_6], [d_2d_3d_1], [d_2d_3d_4], [d_2d_3d_6], [d_2d_5d_1], [d_2d_5d_3], [d_2d_5d_4], [d_2d_5d_6], [d_2d_7d_1], [d_2d_7d_3], [d_2d_7d_4], [d_2d_7d_6]$

To compute M-entailment, we use *exception filtering*. This process removes *exceptions* from causal intersections to yield differential diagnoses. An exception is a disorder that does not appear in any of the minimal candidates entailed. To find and remove exceptions from causal intersections, we use *filters*. A filter is essentially a cross-cluster constraint: A filter for each cluster identifies exceptions in other clusters. A filter is composed of subfilters, each subfilter deriving from a symptom in the associated cluster. The subfilter represents a situation where its corresponding symptom is a justification; it contains disorders inconsistent with this assumption. However, we may discover that some symptoms cannot be justifications; they impose such strong constraints that they would eliminate all disorders in some other cluster. The subfilters for these symptoms are called *infeasible*. Hence, an exception is a disorder appearing in every feasible subfilter of some filter. The algorithm for exception filtering follows:

1. Initialize: For each cluster c, initialize its differential to be its causal intersection. For each symptom s in c, initialize its subfilter to be the intersection of s with all disorders in other differentials:

$$\begin{aligned} \mathrm{Diff}(c) &\leftarrow \mathrm{Int}(c) \\ \mathrm{Subfilter}(s) &\leftarrow \mathrm{Causes}(s) \cap \bigcup_{c' \neq c} \mathrm{Diff}(c') \\ \mathrm{Filter}(c) &\leftarrow \{\mathrm{Subfilter}(s) \mid s \in c\} \end{aligned}$$

2. Remove infeasible subfilters: A subfilter f for a cluster c is infeasible if it subsumes another differential. Remove infeasible subfilters from each filter:

$$\begin{aligned} \mathrm{Infeasible}(f) &\iff \exists c' \neq c.\ f \supseteq \mathrm{Diff}(c') \\ \mathrm{Filter}(c) &\leftarrow \mathrm{Filter}(c) - \{f \mid \mathrm{Infeasible}(f)\} \end{aligned}$$

   At this point, every filter must have at least one feasible subfilter. If not, then the clustering entails no minimal candidates.

3. Remove exceptions: Find exceptions for each filter by taking the intersection of its subfilters. Remove these exceptions from all differentials and subfilters:

$$\begin{aligned} \mathrm{Exc}(c) &\leftarrow \bigcap_{f \in \mathrm{Filter}(c)} f \\ \mathrm{Diff}(c) &\leftarrow \mathrm{Diff}(c) - \bigcup_{c} \mathrm{Exc}(c) \\ \mathrm{Subfilter}(s) &\leftarrow \mathrm{Subfilter}(s) - \bigcup_{c} \mathrm{Exc}(c) \\ \mathrm{Filter}(c) &\leftarrow \{\mathrm{Subfilter}(s) \mid s \in c\} \end{aligned}$$

4. Terminate: If no exceptions were found in the last step, halt. Else repeat step 2, since the smaller differentials may have made more subfilters infeasible.

   An example of this process for the cluster

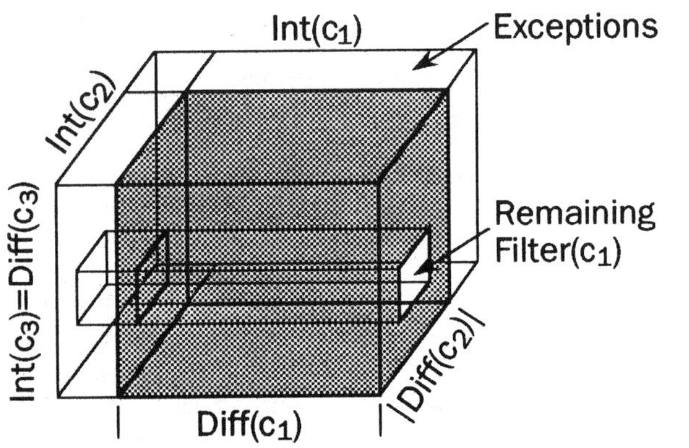

Figure 2: Geometric interpretation of symptom clusterings. A symptom clustering with n clusters bounds a region in n-dimensional candidate space. Minimal candidates entailed by a clustering are points within the shaded region. Causal intersections define the outer boundary; differentials define the inner boundary. Exception filtering removes exterior regions of nonminimality and represents interior regions implicitly.

(AC)(B)(D) is shown below:

	Clusters		
	(AC)	(B)	(D)
Diff:	$\{d_1 d_2\}$	$\{d_1 d_3 d_5 d_7\}$	$\{d_1 d_3 d_4 d_6\}$
Filter:	$((\{d_1 d_3 d_4\}\{d_1 d_5\}))$	$((\{d_1 d_3\}))$	$((\{d_1 d_3\}))$
Exc:	$\{d_1\}$	$\{d_1 d_3\}$	$\{d_1 d_3\}$
Diff:	$\{d_2\}$	$\{d_5 d_7\}$	$\{d_4 d_6\}$
Filter:	$((\{d_4 d_5\}))$	$((\{\}))$	$((\{\}))$
Exc:	$\{\}$	$\{\}$	$\{\}$

The minimal candidates are contained within the cartesian product of these differentials. Here, the differentials are $\{d_2\}$, $\{d_5 d_7\}$, and $\{d_4 d_6\}$, with a cartesian product of $[d_2 d_5 d_4]$, $[d_2 d_5 d_6]$, $[d_2 d_7 d_4]$, $[d_2 d_7 d_6]$. But the remaining exception filter $((\{d_4\}\{d_5\}))$ specifies that candidate $[d_2 d_5 d_4]$ is nonminimal because it contains an element from each subfilter. The minimal candidates are therefore

$$\text{M-entails}((\text{AC})(\text{B})(\text{D})) = [d_2 d_5 d_6], [d_2 d_7 d_4], [d_2 d_7 d_6]$$

Note that these three candidates cannot be factored into a single implicit representation. Exception filtering handles this by representing minimal candidates in two implicit parts: differentials and filters. Although differentials may contain some nonminimal candidates in their cartesian product, this enables them to represent the minimal candidates more economically. Thus, exception filtering achieves efficient representation by ignoring details about minimality that would fragment aggregates of candidates.

Geometric Interpretation

The relationship between symptom clusterings and candidates is shown geometrically in Figure 2. As illustrated, the efficiency of symptom clustering results from three sources. First, candidates are generated *aggregately* instead of individually. This allows entire sets of candidates to be pruned simultaneously. Second, these aggregates are represented *implicitly*. Analogously, we compute the *boundaries* of a candidate region, rather than every point in the volume. Finally, minimal candidates are computed *convexly*. This allows internal regions of nonminimality to remain in the differentials, thereby maintaining the n-dimensional cubic shape of the aggregates.

To a first approximation, we expect symptom clustering to achieve exponential time and space savings over candidate generation. If each symptom clustering has n clusters and each differential has a geometric mean of $\mathcal{D}$ disorders, each clustering entails approximately $\mathcal{D}^n$ candidates. However, the exact savings are difficult to determine, because some of the candidates are not minimal and because a candidate may satisfy more than one symptom clustering. Nevertheless, experimental results presented later lend support to a near-exponential increase in performance.

Search Criteria

Even with an more efficient representation, the symptom clustering search space can still grow rapidly. Thus, we impose additional criteria to help prune the search space, namely, parsimony, subsumption, and spanning. Parsimony is a preference for simplicity, subsumption minimizes unwarranted constraints, and spanning avoids redundant solutions.

Parsimony

Parsimony is a preference for simplicity in explanations. In candidate generation, the criterion of parsimony typically used is minimality. Likewise, the symptom clustering approach can adopt parsimony criteria, such as validity and minimality, to help reduce search. We define a symptom clustering to be valid (likewise minimal) if it V-entails (M-entails) at least one candidate:

$$\begin{aligned} \text{Valid}(C) &\iff \text{V-entails}(C) \neq \emptyset \\ \text{Minimal}(C) &\iff \text{M-entails}(C) \neq \emptyset \end{aligned}$$

Determining whether a clustering is valid or minimal can be accomplished by the entailment procedures given previously.

Subsumption

In addition to parsimony, symptom clustering can reduce search by exploiting subsumption. Subsumption occurs when a more general model or concept contains a more specific one. Subsumption applies in symptom clustering because the candidates entailed by one clustering may be a subset of those entailed by another clustering. Since both clusterings represent valid interpretations of the data, the more specific clustering is constrained unnecessarily by having its symptoms allocated to the "wrong" clusters. In the absence of any other information, we should therefore prefer the more general clustering, because it represents only constraints that are minimally necessary.

We say that clustering C_1 ***subsumes*** C_2 if there exists a complete matching between their causal intersections under the superset relation, that is, if each causal intersection in C_1 is a superset of some corresponding causal intersection in C_2. Clusterings C_1 and C_2 are *equigeneral* if there exists a complete matching under set equality. Finally, C_1 ***properly subsumes*** C_2 if C_1 subsumes C_2 but they are not equigeneral. These definitions lead to the subsumption criterion of generality: A clustering is *general* for a given case if no other valid clustering properly subsumes it. In the geometric interpretation given above, a clustering is general if its outer boundary is not enclosed by any other clustering.

This definition of generality can be computed readily using a process of *symptom rearrangement.* In symptom rearrangement, if a clustering is not already general, symptoms are moved between clusters until it is general. The conditions for moving a symptom between clusters can be expressed in terms of the following concepts. We say that a symptom s *constrains* a cluster c if it directly reduces its causal intersection, that is, if the possible causes for s do not subsume the causal intersection of $(c - \{s\})$:

$$\text{Constrains}(s, c) \iff \text{Causes}(s) \not\supseteq \text{Int}(c - \{s\})$$

A contrary notion is covering. We say that a symptom s *covers* a cluster c if its possible causes subsume the causal intersection of that cluster:

$$\text{Covers}(s, c) \iff \text{Causes}(s) \supseteq \text{Int}(c)$$

Finally, a symptom s in cluster c_1 is *movable* to another cluster c_2 if it constrains c_1 and covers c_2. (For definitional purposes, a symptom cannot move out of a singleton cluster.)

The key to symptom rearrangement is this theorem: A cluster is general if and only if all of its symptoms are not movable. This theorem yields a procedure to turn nongeneral clusterings into general ones: Simply move all movable symptoms until generality is obtained. This process must terminate because each movement of s from c_1 to c_2 has no effect on the causal intersection of c_2 but enlarges the causal intersection of c_1. At some point, the growth of causal intersections must halt.

For example, consider the clustering (AB)(CD) which has causal intersections $\{d_1\}$ and $\{d_1 d_3\}$. This is not general because A is movable from c_1 to c_2 and D is movable from c_2 to c_1. If we move A forward, we get (B)(ACD), which is general (but not minimal). If we move D backward, we get (ABD)(C), which is also general (and minimal). This example reveals that the rearrangement procedure is nondeterministic, a fact we will account for when we devise an algorithm to explore the search space.

Spanning

Spanning attempts to find a representative group of solutions by eliminating those that are redundant. Redundancy occurs in symptom clustering because some symptoms may be placed in several clusters without affecting the set of candidates entailed. Whenever the causes for a symptom are broad enough to covers more than one cluster, that symptom can be placed arbitrarily; each placement results in an equigeneral clustering. This redundancy is especially undesirable because broad symptoms have little discriminatory power. We seek to avoid this redundancy by generating only one clustering from each class of equigeneral clusterings. This yields a ***spanning set*** of general clusterings.

For example, suppose symptom E has possible causes $\langle d_1 d_3 d_4 d_5 \rangle$. Consider clustering (AD)(BC), which has causal intersections of $\{d_1 d_3 d_4\}$ and $\{d_1 d_5\}$. Symptom E covers either cluster, so that (ADE)(BC) and (AD)(BCE) are equigeneral. A spanning set would include either (ADE)(BC) or (AD)(BCE) but not both.

Problem-Reduction Search

The criteria given above define a set of clusterings that we would like to generate, namely a spanning set of general, minimal clusterings for a given case. We now present an algorithm that generates these clusterings. This algorithm is called problem-reduction search because it is a state-space search with each node of the search tree being one possible symptom clustering. As we mentioned before, a symptom clustering represents a problem-reduction, so this algorithm combines the features of both the problem-reduction and the state-space representations.

The algorithm processes one symptom in the case at a time. The first symptom can be clustered in only one way, a single cluster, yielding a frontier with a single clustering. The clusterings in each frontier are then expanded by another symptom from the case until all symptoms have been processed. Expansion consists of three steps: allocating a symptom to a cluster, rearranging the symptoms to achieve generality, and pruning nonminimal and equigeneral clusterings.

Allocating Symptoms

Symptom s may be allocated to a cluster in four ways:

Covering: Put s into a cluster c that it covers. Precondition: Covers(s, c).

Restricting: Put s into a cluster c that it would constrain. Precondition: Constrains(s, c).

Adding: Add a cluster consisting only of s. Precondition: $\text{Causes}(s) - \bigcup_c \text{Int}(c) \neq \emptyset$.

Extracting: Add a cluster consisting of s and a symptom s' already in some cluster c' that would constrain it. Precondition: $\text{Constrains}(s', c') \wedge \text{Constrains}(s', \{s\})$.

Only some of these allocations need be performed for a given symptom and clustering. If some covering allocation is possible, the allocation process is finished. Else, all restrictions, additions, and extractions meeting the preconditions are invoked.

For example, Figure 3 shows problem-reduction search for symptoms A, B, C, and D in our running example. All four types of allocation, shown on each arc, are illustrated for symptom D. Node (ABCD) comes from covering (ABC); (AD)(BC) from restricting (A)(BC); (A)(BC)(D) from adding to (A)(BC); and (C)(B)(AD) from extracting A from (AC)(B).

Rearranging Symptoms

After allocating symptoms, they may need to be rearranged. However, as we mentioned previously, rearrangement can be nondeterministic. This presents problems in creating a spanning set of clusterings. Two sibling clusterings in the same frontier could rearrange to form the same clustering, thereby duplicating one clustering while failing to generate another one. We can eliminate this nondeterminism and create a spanning set by specifying exactly how symptoms should be rearranged. These techniques are called incremental and coordinated rearrangement.

Incremental rearrangement assumes that a clustering is general before allocating a new symptom and that nongenerality may be introduced during allocation. The specific source of nongenerality can then be repaired. Nongenerality can be introduced in three ways: (1) Reducing a causal intersection for cluster c enables symptoms in other clusters to move into c. (2) Adding a cluster c enables symptoms in other clusters to move into it. (3) Enlarging a causal intersection for c enables to symptoms in c to move to other clusters.

Thus, allocating a symptom can introduce nongenerality as follows: Covering has no effect; restricting or adding a cluster enables that cluster to import symptoms from other clusters; and extracting a symptom from cluster c' to create cluster c enables c' to export symptoms and c to import symptoms. We must also consider the secondary effects of moving symptoms. Moving a symptom from c_1 to c_2 enlarges the causal intersection of c_1, enabling c_1 to export symptoms, but has no effect on c_2.

Incremental rearrangement is performed in two stages: an importing stage and exporting stage. Suppose that cluster c has been restricted, added, or newly created by extraction. In the importing stage, c imports all symptoms that are eligible to move to it. Then in the exporting stage, any cluster that has exported a symptom exports any other symptom that can now move out. For extraction, the cluster with the extracted symptom originally also counts as an exporting cluster.

Figure 3 illustrates an example of rearrangement, indicated by the starred arc. Symptom D initially restricts clustering (AC)(B) to give (AC)(BD). Incremental rearrangement imports symptom A to the restricted cluster, giving (C)(ABD). In the exporting stage, cluster (C) has no symptoms to export, so rearrangement is complete.

Incremental rearrangement handles most cases of nondeterminism. Nevertheless, the exporting stage may still be nondeterministic, because exporting from c_1 to c_2 may preclude an export from c_3 to c_1. We say that these two movements *conflict*. Movement conflicts can be resolved by a coordinated rearrangement strategy. Coordinated rearrangement assumes that clusters are maintained in order of their creation. When two movements conflict, we favor a forward movements (from earlier clusters to later ones) over backward ones. Thus, in our example, if c_1 is before c_3, then movement $c_3 \rightarrow c_1$ is backward, and $c_1 \rightarrow c_2$ takes precedence. If c_3 is before c_1, then conflict can be avoided by performing $c_3 \rightarrow c_1$ before $c_1 \rightarrow c_2$.

This bias for forward movements depends on other parts of the search tree to explore missed opportunities that would have been generated by backward movements. To avoid foreclosing these opportunities prematurely, we also need a least-commitment strategy, whereby symptoms are moved to the earliest cluster possible, if there is more than one. Covering allocations must also adhere to the least-commitment strategy, so a symptom is allocated to the first cluster it covers, if any.

Coordinated rearrangement can be implemented easily. In the exporting stage, export from clusters in forward chronological order. For each constraining symptom in an exporting cluster, move it to the first cluster that it covers, if any. This may mean that a symptom moves backward, but this backward movement will not conflict with any forward movements, since earlier clusters will have already exported.

Pruning

After a clustering has been expanded and rearranged if necessary, its differentials are computed using the exception filter procedure discussed previously. If any filter lacks a feasible subfilter or any differential becomes null, that clustering is pruned.

In addition to nonminimal clusterings, redundant equigeneral clusterings must also be pruned. This can be done by comparing clusterings pairwise to check for equigeneral clusterings. This comparison will also uncover any duplicate clusterings that can arise. For example, in Figure 3, the clustering (ABD)(C) is generated twice, so one duplicate can be removed.

Experimental Results

Candidate generation and symptom clustering algorithms were implemented in Common Lisp on a Symbolics Lisp Machine and applied to the INTERNIST/QMR knowledge base [3]. This knowledge base contains 600 diseases and 4300 symptoms, covering 70% of the knowledge in internal medicine. To

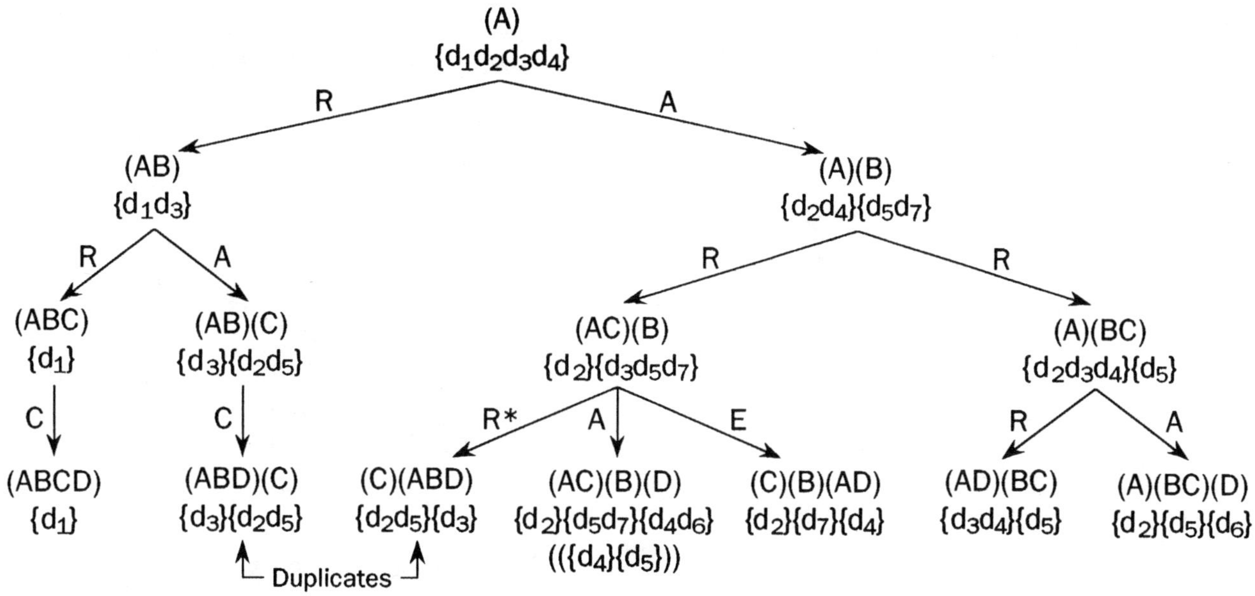

Figure 3: Problem-reduction search algorithm. The four symptoms, A, B, C, and D, correspond to the example given in the text. Each node shows a clustering and its differentials, along with any remaining exception filter. Arcs are labeled with the type of allocation: Covering, Restricting, Adding, or Extracting. A star indicates that rearrangement was performed.

control for effects of case variation and symptom ordering, we decided to analyze a single disease profile in depth. Prerenal azotemia was chosen because it generated relatively few symptoms (14, excluding age and sex), and these triggered various numbers of possible causes. The sets of possible causes ranged in size from 2 to 76, with a median of 29. The union of possible causes contained 147 diseases, meaning that a subgraph of 147 diseases and 14 symptoms was selected for this experiment.

Ten test cases were generated stochastically, by randomly selecting from the 14 symptoms for prerenal azotemia. These test cases contained 7–12 symptoms each. The probability of selecting a symptom depended on its frequency value: a frequency value of 1 resulted in a 3% chance of selection; 2, 20%; 3, 50%; 4, 80%; and 5, 98%. Contextual symptoms of age and sex were excluded, since the knowledge base lists all 600 disease as possible "causes", which would have severely penalized the candidate generation algorithm. However, we made no other checks for medical accuracy. In particular, some test cases contained two values for the same test, such as a blood urea nitrogen level of both 30–59 and 60–100 mg/dl, or a creatinine level of both 1.5–2.9 and 3–10 mg/dl. A reasonable interpretation of these readings is the common situation of testing a patient multiple times.

Solving each of the ten test cases for minimal candidates, we obtain six categories of solutions, ranging from 27 to 39101 minimal candidates. Although cases were generated from a single disease, minimal candidate solutions contained 1 to 5 disorders, with the following distributions:

	Candidates by Cardinality					
Category	1	2	3	4	5	Total
A	1	1	25			27
B	1	0	39	33		73
C	1	0	11	100		112
D	1	0	6	165	165	337
E	1	11	85	435	15	547
F	1	21	769	8985	29325	39101

The number of minimal clustering solutions ranged from 3 to 10, with the following size distributions:

	Clusterings by Dimensions					
Category	1	2	3	4	5	Total
A	1	1	1			3
B	1	0	3	1		5
C	1	0	2	1		4
D	1	0	1	3	1	6
E	1	2	2	1	1	7
F	1	1	3	4	1	10

We generated ten runs for each case by randomly permuting the order of the symptoms, and running times and search tree sizes were measured for each run. Any candidate generation run requiring more than 10^5 seconds (27.8 hours) was terminated. This eliminated 3 of the 40 runs in category A, 6 of the 20 runs in D, and all 10 runs in F. These cases are not shown on our graphs, but were solved by the symptom clustering algorithm in an average of 161 seconds. Figure 4 compares run times and search tree sizes.

We see that symptom clustering is substantially faster and more space-efficient than candidate generation. The roughly linear relationship on a log-linear scale indicates a near-exponential increase in performance, agreeing with the theoretically predicted re-

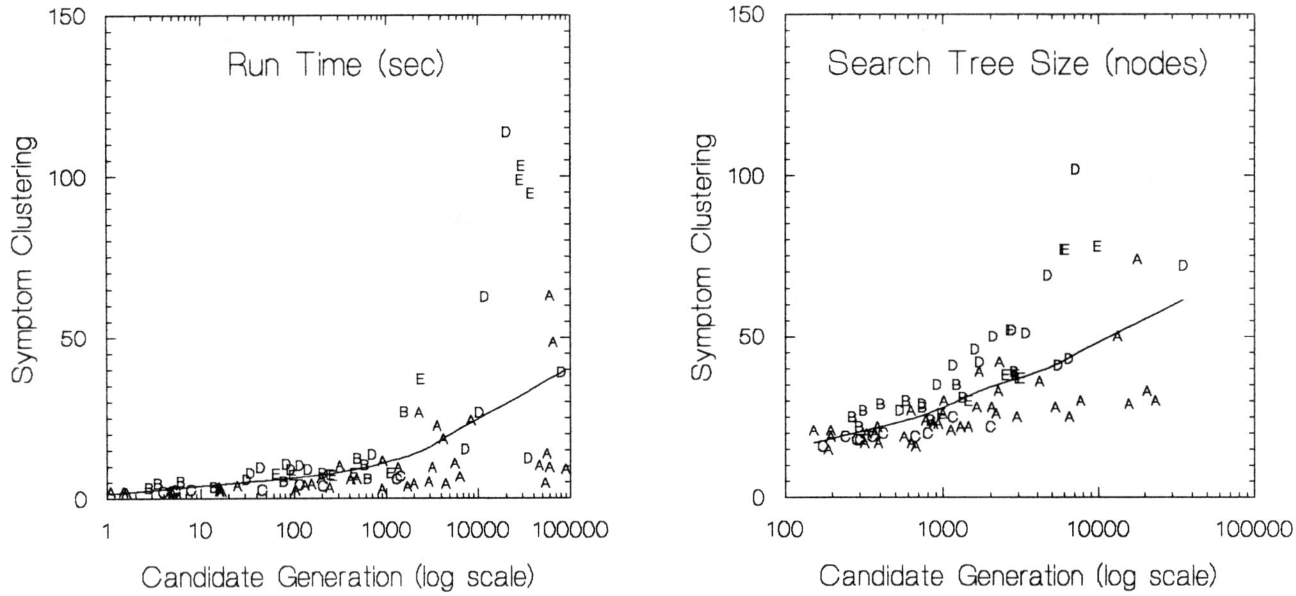

Figure 4: Comparison of candidate generation and symptom clustering for run times and search tree size. Search tree size is the total nodes over all frontiers after pruning. Letters correspond to the case category. Lines represent locally weighted scatterplot smoothing.

sults. As the problems become more difficult, however, these savings diminish somewhat, perhaps indicating the overhead of symptom clustering or other sources of computational complexity.

Conclusions and Further Research

This paper shifts the problem representation for multidisorder diagnosis from candidates to symptom clusterings. It establishes satisfaction and entailment relations between candidates and symptom clusterings, and defines criteria of minimality, generality, and spanning. The paper then devises an efficient algorithm to compute all symptom clusterings satisfying these criteria. Finally, the theoretical work is supplemented with empirical results that suggest a near-exponential increase in performance for symptom clustering.

This work presents several opportunities for further research. It offers a new representation for exploring novel types of search strategies, probabilistic theories, and heuristic sources. In particular, symptom clustering could potentially exploit "structural heuristics"—information about plausible groupings of evidence—which constitute a promising source of domain-specific knowledge.

Other fields of artificial intelligence besides diagnosis might benefit from the concepts here. For instance, previous research on learning and discovery systems [2] has also investigated clustering representations. Multidisorder diagnosis is closely related to the problems of multiple constraint satisfaction, conjunctive-goal planning and truth maintenance. Thus, some analogous notion of "constraint clustering" or "goal clustering" might be used effectively for these problems. Artificial intelligence deals primarily with problems that are ill-structured [7]. This paper suggests, at least for the domain of diagnostic problem solving, how the explicit assignment of structure might facilitate the solution of ill-structured problems.

References

[1] J. de Kleer and B. C. Williams. Diagnosing multiple faults. *Artificial Intelligence*, 32:97–130, 1987.

[2] D. Fisher and P. Langley. Approaches to conceptual clustering. In *Proceedings, Ninth International Joint Conference on Artificial Intelligence*, pages 691–697, 1985.

[3] R. A. Miller, M. A. McNeil, et al. The Internist-1/Quick Medical Reference project—status report. *Western Journal of Medicine*, 145:816–822, 1986.

[4] Y. Peng and J. A. Reggia. A probabilistic causal model for diagnostic problem solving. *IEEE Transactions on Systems, Man, and Cybernetics*, 17:146–162 and 395–406, 1987.

[5] J. A. Reggia, D. S. Nau, and P. Y. Wang. Diagnostic expert systems based on a set covering model. *Intl. Journal of Man-Machine Studies*, 19:437–460, 1983.

[6] R. Reiter. A theory of diagnosis from first principles. *Artificial Intelligence*, 32:57–96, 1987.

[7] H. A. Simon. The structure of ill-structured problems. *Artificial Intelligence*, 4:181–201, 1973.

[8] T. D. Wu. Symptom clustering and syndromic knowledge in diagnostic problem solving. In *Proceedings, Thirteenth Symposium on Computer Applications in Medical Care*, pages 45–49, 1989.

QPC: A Compiler from Physical Models into Qualitative Differential Equations*

James Crawford, Adam Farquhar, and **Benjamin Kuipers**
Department of Computer Sciences
University of Texas at Austin
Austin, Texas 78712
jc@cs.utexas.edu, farquhar@cs.utexas.edu, and kuipers@cs.utexas.edu

Abstract

Qualitative reasoning can, and should, be decomposed into a *model-building* task, which creates a qualitative differential equation (QDE) as a model of a physical situation, and a *qualitative simulation* task, which starts with a QDE, and predicts the possible behaviors following from the model.

In support of this claim, we present QPC, a model builder that takes the general approach of Qualitative Process Theory [Forbus, 1984], describing a scenario in terms of views, processes, and influences. However, QPC builds QDEs for simulation by QSIM, which gives it access to a variety of mathematical advances in qualitative simulation incorporated in QSIM.

We present QPC and its approach to Qualitative Process Theory, provide an example of building and simulating a model of a non-trivial mechanism, and compare the representation and implementation decisions underlying QPC with those of QPE [Falkenhainer and Forbus, 1988; Forbus, 1990].

Introduction

There have been a variety of productive approaches to qualitative reasoning about physical systems [Bobrow, 1985; Weld and de Kleer, 1990]. Alternate approaches (e.g. [de Kleer and Brown, 1984; Forbus, 1984; Kuipers, 1984; Kuipers, 1986; Williams, 1989; Williams, 1988]) frequently differ in emphasis and content, and can seem incompatible. However, we believe that the common themes underlying these different approaches can be clarified by decomposing qualitative reasoning into two tasks:

	Model Building		Qualitative Simulation	
Physical Situation	→	QDE	→	Behaviors

- *Model-building* creates a qualitative differential equation (QDE) as a model of a physical situation.
- *Qualitative simulation* starts with a QDE, and predicts the possible behaviors following from the model.

The QSIM research effort (surveyed in [Kuipers, 1989]) has focussed primarily on the qualitative simulation task: predicting the possible qualitative behaviors consistent with a given QDE and initial state:

$$\text{QSIM} \vdash (\text{QDE} \ \& \ \text{State}(t_0) \rightarrow \text{or}(\text{Beh}_1, \ldots \text{Beh}_n))$$

Research into the mathematics underlying the simulation of qualitative differential equations has been very fruitful, yielding higher-order derivative constraints, phase space representations, integral representations, energy constraints, algebraic and quantitative reasoning methods, and more [Weld and de Kleer, 1990].

Qualitative reasoning methods based on component-connection descriptions [de Kleer and Brown, 1984] or view-process descriptions [Forbus, 1984] also lead to behavioral predictions, but in ways that mix elements of the model-building and model-simulation tasks, obscuring their relationship.

This paper describes QPC, which assembles a QDE model of a physical situation by drawing on a library of model-fragments (e.g. views and processes); QSIM is then used to predict the behaviors consistent with the model.[1] QPC is based on the model-building aspects of Qualitative Process Theory [Forbus, 1984; Forbus, 1990; Falkenhainer and Forbus, 1988], a major approach to the creation and simulation of qualitative models. (Franke and Dvorak have previously reported on *CC*, a compiler from component-connection models into QSIM QDEs [Franke and Dvorak, 1989].)

Algernon, our implementation of Access-Limited Logic [Crawford and Kuipers, 1989], serves as the knowledge representation language for implementing QPC. It combines the clarity, rigor, and expressive

*This work has taken place in the Qualitative Reasoning Group at the Artificial Intelligence Laboratory, The University of Texas at Austin. Research of the Qualitative Reasoning Group is supported in part by NSF grants IRI-8602665, IRI-8905494, and IRI-8904454, by NASA grants NAG 2-507 and NAG 9-200, and by the Texas Advanced Research Program under grant no. 003658–175.

[1]This approach was originally proposed by Kuipers in his 1986 AAAI Tutorial on Qualitative Reasoning, and was explored in [Vincent, 1988].

power of predicate logic with the efficiency and intuitive appeal of a frame-based semantic network. Such a foundation will be necessary for the application of qualitative reasoning to non-trivial scenarios and large knowledge bases with a realistic library of views and processes.

There are several benefits which we hope QPC will provide. First, comparison and contrast between QPC and QPE will shed additional light on the model-building ideas in Qualitative Process Theory. Second, a clear decomposition at the QDE representation allows qualitative reasoning generally to benefit from independent advances in model-building and qualitative simulation. Third, the incremental model-building capability provided by QPC avoids the use of total envisionments, which can be intractable in some cases. This is especially important in tasks such as monitoring and control where many "possible" situations need never be examined because knowledge about the state of the system is available [Dvorak and Kuipers, 1989].

After describing the model-building methods in QPC, its relationship with QSIM, and presenting a detailed example, we discuss the differences in philosophy and implementation between QPC and QPE, Forbus' [1989] implementation of Qualitative Process Theory.

Overview of QPC

The basic QPC algorithm consists of four steps:

1. Assemble a view-process structure from a description of the scenario.
2. Apply the closed world assumption and build the QDE.
3. Form an initial state.
4. Simulate using QSIM.

Two kinds of complexity add iterative paths to this simple sequence (figure 1). First, when the initial state is formed, additional variable values are learned which may activate additional views and processes. This may necessitate re-building the QDE. Second, when simulation reaches a boundary of the QDE being simulated, control is returned to QPC so that a new model can be created.

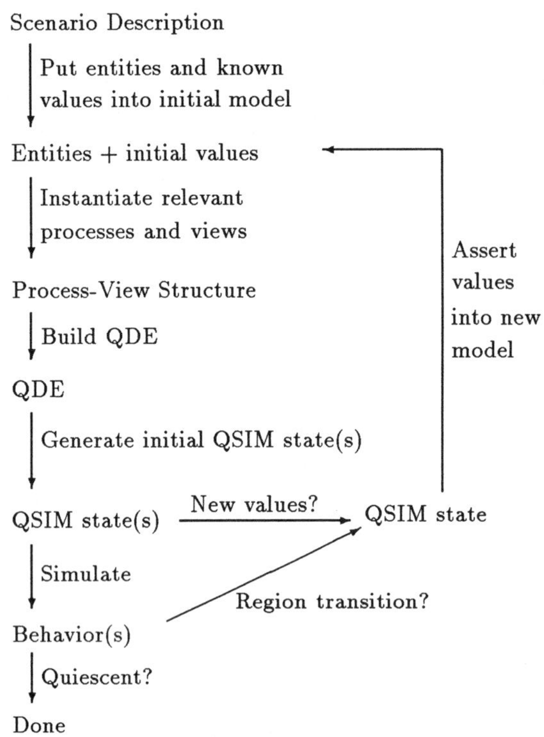

Figure 1: Flow of control in QPC

Representing Views and Processes

The QPC knowledge-base has three components. The first consists of background knowledge about scenarios, models, views, and processes, as well as basic information about the physical world (e.g. that materials can be in three possible states: solid, gas, or liquid). The second component is a domain library of processes and views. The third contains instantiated processes and views for specific entities in the world.

In QPC, both processes and views are represented by rules which create their instances. A user syntax like that of QPE could easily be provided, but in this paper we focus on the underlying representation used by QPC. We refer to both views and processes by the general term *model fragment*. A model fragment is created only once, and can then be included in a variety of models. Figures 2 and 3 shows rules representing the physical view of a physical object and the fluid-flow process, respectively.

Building the View-Process Structure

Model-building starts with a *scenario* which identifies the entities in the world one is interesting in modeling, and specifies their initial conditions. The entities in the scenario become part of the initial model of the scenario (but may or may not be part of subsequent models of the scenario, as entities can be created or destroyed by region transitions). QPC builds the view-process structure for the initial model by first adding, to the initial model, any entities needed to complete it, and then determining which instances of views and processes are relevant [Forbus, 1990; Falkenhainer and Forbus, 1988].

We illustrate QPC with the scenario depicted in figure 4. It consists of two containers, `A` and `B`, connected by a fluid path. `B` has a *portal* located part way up one side. Initially there is fluid in container `A`.

```
((physical-view ?x ?view)
 (mass ?x ?mx) (volume ?x ?vx) (pressure ?x ?px)
 ->
   ;; link a view to its variables
   (variable ?view ?mx) (variable ?view ?vx)
   (variable ?view ?px)
   ;; cd-ineqs are inequalities indexed by view
   ;; Mass not less zero
   (not (cd-ineq ?view less ?mx zero))
   ;; Volume not less zero
   (not (cd-ineq ?view less ?vx zero))
   ;; Mass=0 <-> Volume=0
   (correspondence ?view ?mx zero ?vx zero))
```

Figure 2: A rule to fill in the physical view of a physical object.

The scenario is set up in QPC by creating (in the Algernon KB) frames for the containers A and B, the open fluid path connecting them, and then asserting that there is fluid in A and a portal in B. We also assert that A is an *entity* in the initial model of the scenario, but do not explicitly link B into the scenario (as QPC will do so automatically). The Algernon assertions to establish the scenario are shown in figure 4.

QPC then applies rules to complete the set of entities in the initial model. For example, if a container is part of a model and it is connected, via an open connection, to another container, then the second container should be considered part of the model. Instantiated for fluid-connections this rule reads:

```
((fluid-connection ?obj1 ?path1 ?obj2)
 (open ?path1 true)
 (part-of ?obj1 ?model1)
  ->
  (entity ?model1 ?obj2))
```

where the relation `entity` links a model to its objects.

QPC deduces that B, the portal in B, and the contents of A must be included in the initial model. Instantiation of a fluid flow from A to B implies the need for a frame for the contents of B, which is created and added to the model (along with a frame for its physical view). The initial model thus consists of the physical views of A, B, the portal, the contents of A and B, and the fluid flow process. The influences, relations, correspondences and inequalities of these views and processes are shown in figure 5. Notice that, as yet, no process or region transition for portal flow has been added. Neither the process nor the region transitions are set up until the relationship between the fluid level of B and the portal height is learned.

```
((fluid-connection ?can1 ?path ?can2)
 (part-of ?can1 ?model) (isa ?model models)
 (flow-rate ?path ?flow-rate)
 (pressure-difference ?path ?pressure-diff)
 (contents ?can1 ?liquid1)
 (isa ?liquid1 contained-liquids)
 (mass ?liquid1 ?mass1)
 (open ?path true)
 (pressure ?can1 ?pressure-can1)
 (pressure ?can2 ?pressure-can2)
 ->
 ; Find the process OR Create a new one.
 (:forc ?process
      (cd ?model ?process)
      (isa ?process fluid-flow-processes)
      (path ?process ?path))
 (variable ?process ?flow-rate)
 (variable ?process ?pressure-diff)
 (correspondence ?process ?flow-rate zero
                          ?pressure-diff zero)
 ;; pressure-diff = c1.pressure - c2.pressure
 (ADD ?process ?pressure-can2 ?pressure-diff ?pressure-can1)
 (influence ?process Q+ ?pressure-diff ?flow-rate)
 (influence ?process I- ?flow-rate ?mass1)
 (:forc ?liquid2
       (contents ?can2 ?liquid2)
       (same-material ?liquid1 ?liquid2)
       (same-state ?liquid1 ?liquid2))
 (influence ?process I+ ?flow-rate (mass ?liquid2)))
```

Figure 3: The rule to instantiate the fluid-flow process. The relation `fluid-connection` links a container, a path, and another container. The relation `cd` links a model to a view or process.

Applying the Closed-World Assumption and Building the QDE

At this point, QPC has created a view-process structure comprising a collection of influences, relations, inequalities, and correspondences. The next step is to convert to a QDE which consists of constraints, quantity spaces, landmarks, and corresponding values.

The key step is to transform a collection of influences into constraints. If X *influences* Y then Y will change as a result of a change in X, *all else being equal.* A *constraint* between X and Y is a universal law, limiting the possible joint behaviors of X and Y, *independent of context.* Thus, in order to transform influences into constraints, we require a Closed World Assumption, asserting that we know *all* the relevant influences.

Intuitively, the indirect influence or "qualitative proportionality" $Q^+(X_1, Y)$, means that an increase in X_1 will tend to increase Y. More formally:

$$Q^+(X_1, Y) \equiv Y = f(X_1, X_2, \ldots X_n) \text{ and } \frac{\partial f}{\partial X_1} > 0,$$

```
;; The U-Tube Scenario
(:create ?utube) (current-scenario global-context ?utube)
;; Create A, B, and the pipe between them.
(:create ?A) (isa ?A containers) (entity ?utube ?A)
(:create ?B) (isa ?B containers)
(:create ?pipe) (open ?pipe true)
(fluid-connection ?A ?pipe ?B)
;; The contents of A has mass greater than zero.
(:create ?A-contents) (contents ?A ?A-contents)
(state ?A-contents liquid-state)
(:create ?A*) (greater ?A* zero)
;; (tmag var model time mag) → var = mag at time in model.
(tmag (level ?A-contents) ?utube (initial-time ?utube) ?A*)
;; B has a portal.
(:create ?port) (isa ?port portals) (portal b ?port) (open ?port true)
;; ...and forms to assert that the bottoms of A and B
;; are at zero, and the top heights are positive.
```

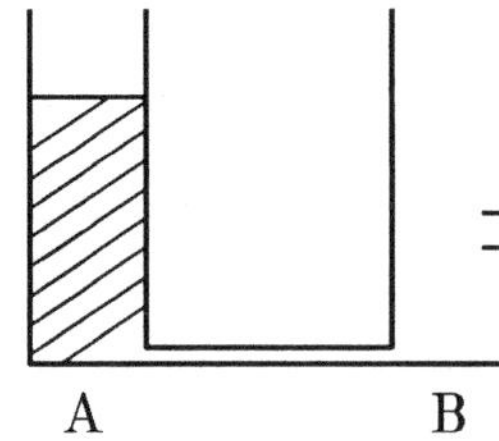

Figure 4: Scenario description for the u-tube with portal. `(:create ?x)` creates a new frame and binds `?x` to it.

A Physical View:
top-height $\geq$ fluid-level $\geq$ bottom-height

A-Contents Physical View:
mass $\geq$ zero; volume $\geq$ zero
volume $\leq$ (volume A)
mass Q^+ volume Q^+ level Q^+ pressure

mass = zero $\leftrightarrow$ volume = zero $\leftrightarrow$
level = zero $\leftrightarrow$ pressure = zero

level = (bottom-height A) $\leftrightarrow$ volume = zero
level = (top-height A) $\leftrightarrow$ volume = (volume A)

Fluid Flow Process:
pressure-diff = (pressure A) - (pressure B)
pressure-diff Q^+ flow-rate
flow-rate I^- (mass (contents A))
flow-rate I^+ (mass (contents B))
flow-rate = zero $\leftrightarrow$ pressure-diff = zero

B-Portal Physical View:
(bottom-height B) < height < (top-height B)
height $\geq$ zero

Figure 5: Highlights of the initial views and processes for the u-tube with portal. The physical views of `B` and `B-Contents` are similar to those of `A`.

for some functional relationship f (with an indefinite number of arguments). The direct influence is similar:

$$I^+(X_1, Y) \equiv \frac{dY}{dt} = f(X_1, X_2, \ldots X_n) \text{ and } \frac{\partial f}{\partial X_1} > 0.$$

Influence resolution on a variable Y identifies the sets P and N of variables that positively and negatively influence Y. Based on the CWA, this determines the number of arguments to the function f. Qualitative Process Theory makes the additional assumption that f can be approximated by a linear combination of single-variable functional relationships. This allows us to assert QSIM *constraints* to capture the set of indirect influences on Y:

$$Y = \sum_{X_i \in P} M^+(X_i) - \sum_{X_j \in N} M^+(X_j).$$

Resolution of direct influences is similar.

QPC helps clarify the role of the linear decomposition assumption in model-building. This assumption does not cause problems durring purely qualitative simulation, but as we attempt to incorporate quantitative information into the model [Kuipers and Berleant, 1988], cases where it is invalid will raise difficulties. Such cases will require a qualitative theory of multivariate functional relations.

Inequality information in the view-process structure is represented in several ways in the QDE. Inequality relations between magnitudes are used to order the quantity spaces. Inequalities between variables and variables, or variables and magnitudes, are represented in the QDE as boundary conditions triggering operating region transitions. For example, if the fluid-level reaches the level of the portal and is increasing, then the portal-flow process must be made active (adding additional influences and relations to the model).

Highlights of the initial QDE for the u-tube example are shown in figure 6.

Building the Initial State

At this point, we have created a QDE which reflects the current view-process structure, but we do not have initial values for all the variables in the model. We calculate initial values in three steps:

```
(define-qde utube-initial-model
  (quantity-spaces
   (a-contents-level (minf 0 a* a-top inf))
   (b-contents-level (minf 0 b-top inf))
   ...)
  (constraints
   ((m+ a-contents-mass a-contents-volume) (0 0))
   ((m+ a-contents-volume a-contents-level)
        (frame23 a-top) (0 0))
   ((m+ a-contents-level a-contents-pressure)
        (0 0))
   ((= a-contents-level a-fluid-level))
   ((= a-contents-pressure a-pressure))
   ((add b-pressure pipe-ab-pressure-diff a-pressure))
   ((m+ pipe-ab-pressure-diff pipe-ab-flow-rate)
    (0 0))
   ((minus var-1 pipe-ab-flow-rate))
   ((d/dt a-contents-mass var-1))
   ((d/dt b-contents-mass pipe-ab-flow-rate))
   ((constant b-portal-height)) ...)
  ...)
```

Figure 6: Highlights from the initial QDE for the example. Constraints on B are similar to those on A.

1. Propagate known values through the QDE.
2. Apply default assumptions.
3. Generate possible completions.

Propagation Frequently, initial values are given for only some of the variables, but other values follow easily from the constraints and relations in the QDE. It would be possible to build rules into the knowledge-base to calculate such values, but this would unnecessarily duplicate the knowledge already in QSIM. Instead, we use QSIM itself as an efficient special purpose reasoning tool to propagate the known values through the QDE. In the u-tube example, propagation concludes, among other values, that the mass of the contents of A is greater than zero (but concludes nothing about the mass of the contents of B).

Default Assumptions During automatic model building, it may be impossible to establish values for enough variables to uniquely determine an initial state. Our solution to this problem is to make default assumptions which are appropriate for the model. E.g, in the u-tube no initial value is known for the mass of the contents of B, and it is not possible to determine a value through propagation. However, QPC assumes that the mass of any newly created liquid is zero. Such values are explicitly tagged as assumptions in the knowledge-base so that they can be withdrawn if they lead to a contradiction. In the examples we have looked at, propagating known values before making default assumptions has been sufficient to avoid such contradictions.

Finding All Completions Even after propagation and the default assumptions, there may be variables which do not have known values. At this point we again use QSIM as a special purpose reasoner to construct *all* possible completions of the current state. In simple cases, such as the u-tube, there is only one possible completion. If there are multiple completions, a separate model must be created for each of them.[2]

In either case it is possible for the new values (from propagation, default assumptions or state completion) to require additional region transitions, new views, or new processes. To handle this problem, the resulting completed state information is asserted back to the knowledge-base, causing the appropriate rules to fire. In the u-tube example, the default assumptions lead QPC to assume that the fluid level in B is zero. This sets up a region transition that will instantiate the portal flow process if the fluid level ever reaches the portal height and is increasing.[3]

Simulation and Region Transitions

Once a complete initial state has been created, QSIM is used to simulate the possible behaviors. In the u-tube example, QSIM predicts three behaviors: one in which equilibrium is reached below the portal-height, one in which equilibrium is reached exactly at the portal height, and a third in which the fluid level in tank B reaches the portal and continues to increase. The first two behaviors can be simulated using only the initial model. The third behavior, however, triggers a region transition and the building of a new model.

When a behavior ends in a region transition, QPC attempts to construct a new set of models. This is done by creating an empty model and asserting the quantity spaces and variable values of the final state of the behavior into it. The new model is then linked to its predecessor. QPC checks the previously active process and view instances to determine which remain active in the new model. QPC then determines whether new entities need to be included, and whether new views or processes need to be activated. Finally, the QDE and initial state(s) are built as before.

In the u-tube example, after the region transition, QPC is able to retain pointers to the old model fragments for A, B, **B-portal**, and **Fluid-flow-AB**. A new

[2]This is the first "choice point" in QPC (the second being the case in which a simulation produces several behaviors ending in region transitions). In such cases the possibilities are queued, and we use a simple search strategy to select the one to follow next.

[3]In complex models, the additional views and processes activated at this point may invalidate the closed world assumption; new views and processes may add influences on some variable v previously assumed to be constant. In such cases, we must return to the original view-process structure and assert the new influence on v, rebuild the QDE, and recalculate the initial values.

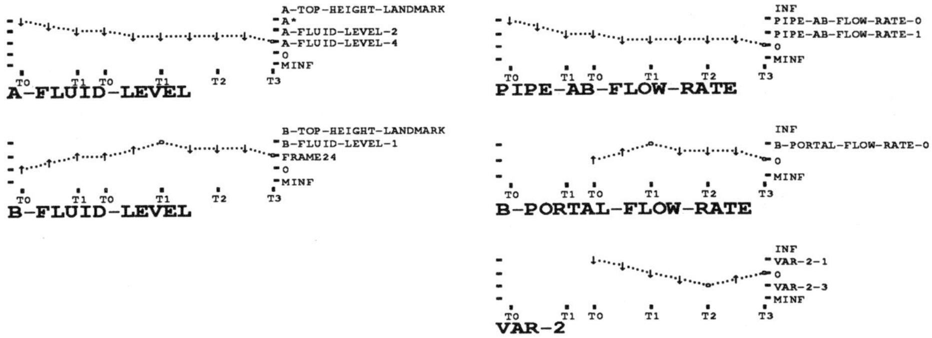

Figure 7: A QSIM behavior for the u-tube example which spans two models. The time step begins again at zero for the second model. `B-portal-flow-rate` and `var-2` are not present in the initial model, but are defined by the portal-flow process. `Var-2` is the netflow into `B`, i.e. `pipe-ab-flow-rate - B-portal-flow-rate`.

portal flow process is created, since its precondition, that the fluid level in `B` is greater than or equal to the portal height, is now satisfied. This results in an additional influence on `B-contents-mass`.

The expected behavior is, of course, that the level of liquid in `B` will increase until the flow in from `A` and the flow out of the portal equalize, and then the liquid will drain out of the portal until a final equilibrium is reached, with the level of `B` even with the portal. This type of behavior is difficult for qualitative simulators to reason about because `B-net-flow` is the difference between two positive and decreasing values. Simple qualitative subtraction is ambiguous, and the result can become negative, zero, or positive any number of times. This behavior is known as *chatter*, and results in an infinite number of qualitatively distinct behaviors.

Fortunately, there is a solution. QSIM automatically derives constraints based on the second derivatives of the variables [Kuipers and Chiu, 1987]. It is this sort of advance in qualitative mathematics which we were hoping to take advantage of! Instead of producing an infinite tree of behaviors, QSIM produces a small number: `B-contents-level` reaches a maximum somewhere above the portal, or it reaches a maximum at the top-height, or B overflows, triggering a region transition. The first two behaviors drop down to our expected equilibrium state; the third causes a new model to be constructed. Figure 7 shows a QSIM plot for a behavior spanning two models and ending in the final equilibrium state in which the level in `B` is at the height of the portal.

Comparison with QPE

While we are following the Qualitative Process Theory approach to model-building, QPC differs in numerous ways from QPE [Forbus, 1990] and its predecessor, GIZMO [Forbus, 1984]. For simplicity, we will use the term QPE for both versions.

Influences and Constraints

Simulation requires a CWA to assert that all influences on all variables are known. Automatic model-building, on the other hand, requires an open-world assumption, so that models can be build by composing model fragments which are stated independently of context.

In QPE, the meanings of Q^+ and I^+ are context dependent, with an open world assumption holding in the view-process library, and a closed-world assumption holding after influence resolution. We believe that this use of the same symbols for semantically distinct concepts has been a source of confusion in the literature.

In QPC, influences belong only to the model-building phase, while a QDE consists only of constraints. Since influences and constraints are semantically distinct, we make them syntactically distinct as well, using Q^+ and I^+ for influences, and M^+ and d/dt for constraints.

Total Envisionment versus Incremental Model-Building

QPE simulates the possible behaviors of a mechanism by producing a *total envisionment*: a graph of all possible states, linked by the transitions between them. The total envisionment representation has several advantages, including a finite representation for infinite behaviors, and support for certain global operations such as cycle detection and state aggregation.

On the other hand, it also raises significant problems of both semantics and efficiency. Semantically, the total envisionment representation depends on the fact that all qualitatively important landmark values are known statically when simulation begins. Dynamically created landmarks are critical to making many important distinctions among behaviors, such as the distinction between increasing and decreasing oscillations [Kuipers, 1985; Kuipers, 1986].

Efficiency can also be a problem. Creation of all possible states of the mechanism is an up-front cost of the total envisionment, required before the transition graph can be constructed. For a very complex model, or worse an "unboundedly creative" one [Forbus, 1989], creation of the set of states is intractable. We minimize this problem in QPC by building models and creating states incrementally, as needed by the simulation. This makes a critical difference when external constraints, such as observations, can focus the simulator's attention to a tractable "beam search" within a potentially infinite behavior tree. In particular, in applications such as monitoring and control, many "possible" states of the system need never be considered and only limited look-ahead is needed [Dvorak and Kuipers, 1989].

The QPE implementation is based on an ATMS [de Kleer, 1986], whereas QPC is built in Algernon, a frame-based knowledge representation language based on Access-Limited Logic [Crawford and Kuipers, 1989]. The ATMS is used in QPE as an efficient tool for implementing several exhaustive search or generation tasks, such as creation of all possible states for the total envisionment, or search for a combination of `consider` statements capable of answering a given question. However, as discussed above, we believe that the total envisionment is often more difficult to compute, and less useful, than the set of possible behaviors. We also believe that the inference involved in model-building will require the service of a full knowledge representation language.

A Layered Representation for Model Revision

Since QPC builds models incrementally, we must deal with a version of the frame problem: what must change and what remains the same after a region transition? Rather than build the new model from scratch, we have structured the representation so that chunks of the old model may be incorporated in the new model. The representation is structured in layers, as shown below, so that each layer changes more slowly than the one below it.

Individuals and their Relationships
Views and Processes
Models (QDEs)
Variable Values

- At the lowest level are the values of variables in the model. These values generally change at every step of the simulation.
- One step up are the models (QDEs) built by QPC. Models are likely to remain valid for several simulation steps, but still change whenever a region transition occurs.
- Changing more slowly, are the views and processes. When region transitions occur, they generally cause one or more view or process instances to become invalid and one or more new ones to be activated. In general, however, most of the views and processes from the previous model are still valid. For example, in the u-tube example, when the portal flow begins, a new "portal flow" process is created, but the views of the containers, and the old fluid flow process, are unchanged.
- Finally, the set of individuals and their relationships change the most slowly. For example, initiation of a boiling process would create a new individual to represent the steam produced. Our framework handles the creation or deletion of individuals naturally.

Conclusion

We have demonstrated QPC as a model-building tool that takes the Qualitative Process Theory view of the modeling task, and compiles models into QDEs for simulation by QSIM.

This approach clarifies several aspects of the structure of qualitative reasoning. First, the tasks of model-building and qualitative simulation can be treated as essentially independent, communicating in the language of qualitative differential equations. Second, the comparison between QPC and QPE helps us distinguish between the fundamental ideas in Qualitative Process Theory and the design decisions of QPE.

In addition to theoretical clarity, QPC provides us with several more tangible benefits. First, we believe that a history-based approach to model-building as well as simulation will be essential for qualitative reasoning about complex mechanisms that would overwhelm a total-envisionment-based approach. Second, we believe that the mathematical methods developed for use with the QSIM representation are essential to reasoning qualitatively about models of complex systems. Finally, QPC provides a bridge between Algernon, a general-purpose knowledge representation language designed for large-scale knowledge bases, and QSIM, an efficient special purpose reasoning system in the domain of qualitative simulation. We expect to exploit this combination to work in the following areas:

- Answering questions and explaining the predicted behaviors. We expect QPC to support explanations which draw on descriptions of the system at multiple levels of detail: the scenario description, the view-process structure, the QDE, and the predicted behaviors of the system.
- Resolving discrepancies between prediction and observation by considering alternative views of the objects in the model. For example, the nail does not fall (as predicted by the physical view) because it is attracted by the magnet.
- Using QPC (and thus QSIM and model-based reasoning) as a component of very large knowledge-bases [Porter *et al.*, 1988; Lenat and Guha, 1990].

References

[Bobrow, 1985] D. G. Bobrow, editor. *Qualitative Reasoning about Physical Systems.* Bradford Books/MIT Press, Cambridge, MA, 1985.

[Crawford and Kuipers, 1989] J. M. Crawford and B. J. Kuipers. Toward a theory of access-limited logic for knowledge representation. In *Proceedings of the First International Conference on Principles of Knowledge Representation and Reasoning (KR'89)*, Los Altos, CA, 1989. Morgan Kaufman.

[de Kleer and Brown, 1984] J. de Kleer and J. S. Brown. A qualitative physics based on confluences. *Artificial Intelligence*, 24:7–83, 1984.

[de Kleer, 1986] J. de Kleer. An assumption-based truth maintenance system, Extending the ATMS, Problem solving with the ATMS. *Artificial Intelligence*, 28(2):127–224, 1986.

[Dvorak and Kuipers, 1989] D. Dvorak and B. J. Kuipers. Model-based monitoring of dynamic systems. In *Proceedings of the Eleventh International Joint Conference on Artificial Intelligence (IJCAI–89)*, pages 1238–1243, Los Altos, CA, 1989. Morgan Kaufman.

[Falkenhainer and Forbus, 1988] B. Falkenhainer and K. D. Forbus. Setting up large-scale qualitative models. In *Proceedings of the National Conference on Artificial Intelligence (AAAI-88)*, Los Altos, CA, 1988. Morgan Kaufman.

[Forbus, 1984] K. D. Forbus. Qualitative process theory. *Artificial Intelligence*, 24:85–168, 1984.

[Forbus, 1989] K. D. Forbus. Pushing the edge of the (QP) envelope. 3rd Qualitative Physics Workshop, Stanford, CA, 1989.

[Forbus, 1990] K. D. Forbus. The qualitative process engine. In *Readings in Qualitative Reasoning about Physical Systems*, pages 220–235. Morgan Kaufman, 1990.

[Franke and Dvorak, 1989] D. Franke and D. Dvorak. Component connection models. Model-Based Reasoning Workshop, Eleventh International Joint Conference on Artificial Intelligence (IJCAI–89), Detroit, Michigan, 1989.

[Kuipers and Berleant, 1988] B. J. Kuipers and D. Berleant. Using incomplete quantitative knowledge in qualitative reasoning. In *Proceedings of the Seventh National Conference on Artificial Intelligence (AAAI-88)*, pages 324–329, Los Altos, CA, 1988. Morgan Kaufman.

[Kuipers and Chiu, 1987] B. J. Kuipers and C. Chiu. Taming intractable branching in qualitative simulation. In *Proceedings of the Tenth International Joint Conference on Artificial Intelligence (IJCAI-87)*, 1987.

[Kuipers, 1984] B. J. Kuipers. Commonsense reasoning about causality: deriving behavior from structure. *Artificial Intelligence*, 24:169–204, 1984.

[Kuipers, 1985] B. J. Kuipers. The limits of qualitative simulation. In *Proceedings of the Ninth International Joint Conference on Artificial Intelligence (IJCAI-85)*, Los Altos, CA, 1985. William Kaufman.

[Kuipers, 1986] B. J. Kuipers. Qualitative simulation. *Artificial Intelligence*, 29:289–338, 1986.

[Kuipers, 1989] B. J. Kuipers. Qualitative reasoning: modeling and simulation with incomplete knowledge. *Automatica*, 25:571–585, 1989.

[Lenat and Guha, 1990] D. B. Lenat and R. V. Guha. *Building Large Knowledge-Based Systems.* Addison-Wesley, Reading, MA, 1990.

[Porter *et al.*, 1988] B. W. Porter, J. Lester, K. Murray, K. Pittman, A. Souther, L. Acker, and T. Jones. AI research in the context of a multifunctional knowledge base: the botany knowledge base project. Technical Report AI TR-88-88, University of Texas at Austin, 1988.

[Vincent, 1988] T. C. Vincent. Model building using qualitative process theory. Master's thesis, UT Austin, May 1988.

[Weld and de Kleer, 1990] D. S. Weld and J. de Kleer. *Readings in Qualitative Reasoning About Physical Systems.* Morgan Kaufman, Los Altos, CA, 1990.

[Williams, 1988] B. Williams. Minima: A symbolic approach to qualitative algebraic reasoning. In *Proceedings of the Seventh National Conference on Artificial Intelligence (AAAI-88)*, pages 264–269, Los Altos, CA, 1988. Morgan Kaufman.

[Williams, 1989] B. Williams. Qualitative analysis of MOS circuits. *Artificial Intelligence*, 24:281–346, 1989.

Availability of Code

The code for QSIM may be obtained for research purposes from Benjamin Kuipers. We plan to have distributable versions of Algernon and QPC available shortly after AAAI-90.

Dynamic Across-Time Measurement Interpretation

Dennis DeCoste *
Qualitative Reasoning Group
Beckman Institute, University of Illinois
405 North Mathews Avenue, Urbana, Illinois 61801
email: decoste@cs.uiuc.edu

Abstract

Incrementally maintaining a qualitative understanding of physical system behavior based on observations is crucial to real-time process monitoring, diagnosis, and control. This paper describes the DATMI theory for dynamically maintaining a *pinterp-space*, a concise representation of the local and global interpretations consistent with observations over time. Each interpretation signifies an alternative path of states in a qualitative envisionment. DATMI can use domain-specific knowledge about state and transition probabilities to maintain the best working interpretation. By maintaining the space of alternative interpretations as well, DATMI avoids the need for extensive backtracking to handle incomplete or faulty data.

1 Introduction

Efficient incremental interpretation of observations is essential for real-time process monitoring, diagnosis, and control. A consistent interpretation of what is happening, along with alternatives, should continually be available. Since data can be incomplete and faulty, interpretations must be efficiently revised as new data arrives or inconsistencies are discovered. For example, the original hypothesis during the Three Mile Island incident was that the reactor core had too much water. The correct failure hypothesis was triggered once it was noticed that the symptoms remained even after a lot of water was removed. Capturing this kind of reasoning is clearly important for engineering-oriented applications of qualitative physics.

This paper describes the DATMI theory and algorithm for efficient dynamic across-time measurement interpretation. DATMI is an extension of the ATMI theory of measurement interpretation [7]. Like ATMI, we assume the input includes a *total envisionment* representing the qualitative states and transitions which characterize all the possible behaviors of the system being observed. This envisionment serves as a finite-state transition graph for "parsing" the observations. Each interpretation identifies the behavior as a path through the envisionment. However, ATMI did not allow incremental updating of its interpretation and made no provision for handling faulty data. DATMI overcomes these limitations by using a concise representation of the space of possible interpretations, called the *pinterp-space*. A vocabulary of dependency relations allows DATMI to dynamically adjust to changing data and to provide efficient hypothesis revision. Furthermore, DATMI can exploit two kinds of domain-specific information, when available: probabilities specified for states and transitions and duration bounds specified for states and paths. DATMI has been fully implemented and successfully tested on a variety of envisionments and data sets.

Section 2 describes DATMI's theoretical foundation and Section 3 explains its basic algorithm. Section 4 presents an example of DATMI handling faulty data. Section 5 summarizes how additional domain-specific knowledge is used. Finally, Section 6 notes some limitations and discusses related and future work.

2 DATMI Theory

As in ATMI, we assume that data consists of *measurements* of numeric variables (such as temperature) and *observations* of symbolic properties (such as whether a switch is ON or OFF and whether the temperature of one object is greater than, less than, or equal to that of another). We also assume that the measurements have been smoothed to reflect their qualitative trends. Discarding data at the fringes of each qualitative change, to account for the temporal imprecision of smoothings, is allowed since DATMI handles incomplete data.

DATMI conservatively converts measurements at time points into observations over time intervals, using probabilities and disjunctive values to express uncertainty in the sensor readings. This requires: (1) converting numerical values into qualitative ones by comparing them with limit points and (2) aggregating measurements with identical qualitative values into observations. Each property which signifies the ordering between a variable and a limit point has an associated *conversion table*. Each table maps ranges of distance from the limit

*This research was supported by the Office of Naval Research under Contract No. N00014-85-K-0225.

point into qualitative values having discrete probability assignments. Figure 1 gives an example. DATMI provides no means for determining these tables; it assumes that domain-specific information provides them, perhaps based on *a priori* sensor precisions and reliabilities. In lieu of probabilistic assignments, DATMI assumes each disjunctive value is equally probable; Section 5.1 explains how these discrete probabilities are used.

For comparison between variable A and limit point B:

$(A-B)/|B| \in [-\infty, -0.2)$ ⇒ $(A < B$, with probability p=1.0)
$(A-B)/|B| \in [-0.2, -0.01)$ ⇒ $(A < B$, p=0.6) ∧ $(A = B$, p=0.4)
$(A-B)/|B| \in [-0.01, 0.01]$ ⇒ $(A = B$, p=1.0)
$(A-B)/|B| \in (0.01, 0.2]$ ⇒ $(A > B$, p=0.6) ∧ $(A = B$, p=0.4)
$(A-B)/|B| \in (0.2, \infty]$ ⇒ $(A > B$, p=1.0)

(If $B = 0$ then $(A-B)/|B|$ is replaced by $(A-B)$)

Figure 1: A simple example conversion table

As the overview in Figure 2 shows, the observations are concisely represented as properties of *global segments*. As in ATMI, each segment represents the interval of maximal temporal extent over which all of its properties are identical. The interval of each segment *meets* [1] the interval of each of its two neighboring segments. Thus, the history of segments is temporally totally-ordered. *Gap-fill* segments represent intervals over which no observations are available. Since DATMI maintains the segments as observations are gathered, it splits and merges segments appropriately.

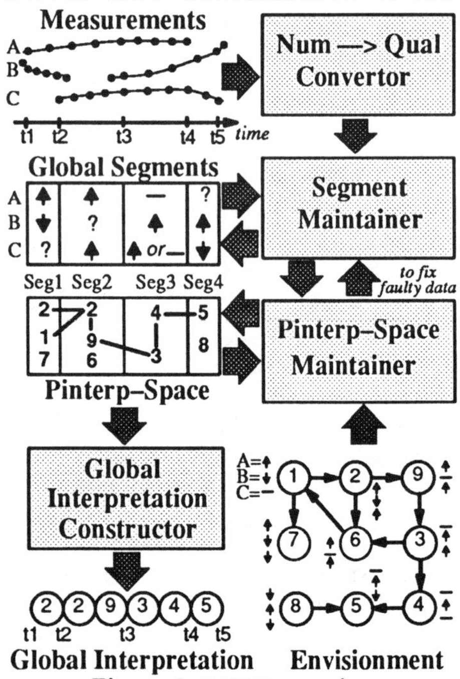

Figure 2: DATMI overview

ATMI introduced the notion of a *pinterp*: an envisionment state which can possibly occur during a particular segment. Let $P(G,S)$ be the pinterp which indicates whether state S can occur during global segment G. $P(G,S)$ is considered COMPATIBLE exactly when all the properties describing S are compatible with all the properties of G. $P(G,S)$ is also considered ACTIVE exactly when all constraints allow S to occur during G.

Clearly, an ACTIVE pinterp must be COMPATIBLE, to satisfy the constraints of its own segment. An ACTIVE pinterp must also satisfy the constraints of the other segments and the envisionment transitions. In particular, a pinterp is ACTIVE exactly when it is COMPATIBLE and there is a *transition consistency relation* between it and each neighboring segment. Alternatively, a pinterp is INACTIVE exactly when it is COMPATIBLE but not ACTIVE. Thus, each pinterp is either INCOMPATIBLE, INACTIVE, or ACTIVE. Figure 3 illustrates DATMI's five types of transition consistency relations. A relation between a pinterp $P(G,S)$ and a neighboring segment N indicates a path of ACTIVE pinterps which starts at $P(G,S)$ and reachs an ACTIVE pinterp of N. Each relation signifies a consistent way to be in S during G and also be in a state during N.

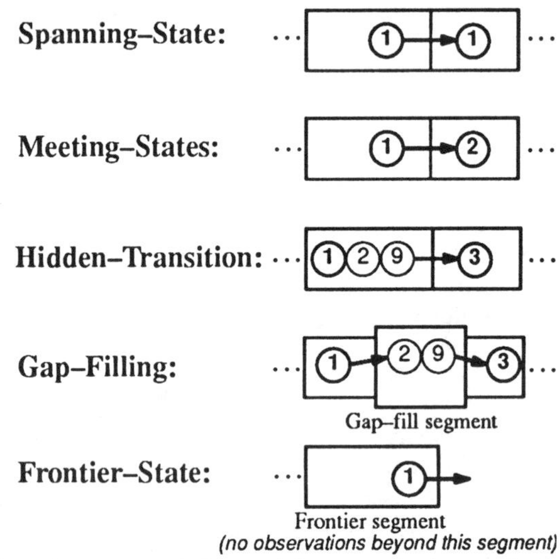

Figure 3: Types of transition consistency relations
These paths through the envisionment of Figure 2 illustrate the five types of ways a pinterp can lead to a pinterp of the next observed segment.

Identifying hidden-transition and gap-filling paths allows DATMI to interpret even very incomplete data. For simplicity, DATMI considers only acyclic paths of pinterps for these two relations. Thus, it will misinterpret behaviors where the system returns to the same state during a single segment. However, unless duration constraints invalidate all acyclic relation paths, this simplification will not prevent DATMI from finding some interpretation which is at least simple, if not best.

Each global interpretation is a chain of relation paths across all segments. For example, the global interpretation given in Figure 2 is a global chain of some of the relation paths indicated in its pinterp-space. We do not show the INCOMPATIBLE pinterps of the pinterp-space; so, the INACTIVE ones are exactly those for which no relation paths are shown.

3 The DATMI algorithm

DATMI dynamically maintains the pinterp-space by keeping track of the status of each pinterp (INCOMPATIBLE, INACTIVE, or ACTIVE) as segment properties are asserted and retracted. It determines which pinterps are COMPATIBLE the same way as ATMI did; it uses a lookup-table precomputed from the envisionment that indicates every state compatible with a given property. It determines whether a COMPATIBLE pinterp is ACTIVE by using graph search through the envisionment to find the *best* relation path between the pinterp and each neighboring segment. As shown in this section, breadth-first graph search suffices to find the *simplest* paths. Section 5.1 explains how least-cost graph search finds the *most-probable* paths. In both cases, the best global paths are built from the best local (relation) paths.

After determining a relation path between a pinterp and a neighboring segment, DATMI caches that path as a *dependency path* for that pinterp. Each ACTIVE pinterp is assigned exactly two dependency paths: a *b-dependency path* reaching a pinterp of the backward neighboring segment and a *f-dependency path* reaching a pinterp of the forward neighboring segment. Since global chains of relation paths indicate global interpretations, so do global chains of b-dependency paths or f-dependency paths.

By finding dependency paths using breadth-first graph search which expands each state at most once, the interpretation indicated by a chain of b-dependency paths is the simplest (i.e. shortest) one. This search through the envisionment starts at the pinterp $P(G,S)$ whose dependency path is sought and finds the simplest path (if any) to each ACTIVE pinterp of the neighboring segment by expanding only from $P(G,S)$ and ACTIVE pinterps of G. To ensure finding the simplest b-dependency chains, DATMI records the cost (i.e. number of transitions) of the chain of b-dependency paths leading up to each pinterp $P(G,S)$ when its b-dependency path is found. This allows b-dependency path search for each pinterp $P(F,f)$ of the forward neighboring segment F to sum $P(G,S)$'s recorded cost with the cost of the relation path found from $P(F,f)$ to $P(G,S)$. DATMI compares that sum against the sums for the simplest paths found to other ACTIVE pinterps of G, to decide which one offers the simplest chain of b-dependency paths to $P(F,f)$.

The above discussion assumes that each gap-fill segment is treated as an ordinary segment whose pinterps all happen to be COMPATIBLE. For efficiency, however, DATMI does not actually maintain pinterps for gap-fill segments. It uses a lookup-table precomputed from the envisionment that indicates the best path through the envisionment between any two particular states. This table, along with the recorded b-dependency chain costs, suggests the best b-dependency path across the gap-fill segment which connects a particular pinterp of the forward neighboring segment with an ACTIVE pinterp of the backward neighboring segment. (This is why the gap-fill path in Figure 3 involves three segments.) If desired, one can determine if a particular pinterp of a gap-fill segment is ACTIVE – by checking this table to see if paths exist from it to ACTIVE pinterps of the neighboring segments.

As explained below, dependency paths play one other key role: they indicate which pinterps must find new relation paths when a pinterp of a neighboring segment ceases to be ACTIVE. In that sense, they are analogous to TMS justifications [5]. However, for our task, caching alternative dependency paths would not lead to the efficiencies that one might expect. As explained in [4], if the alternative path is short, it is more efficient to find it as needed; if it is long, it is not likely to be best or even consistent (i.e. contain only ACTIVE pinterps) when the current best path becomes inconsistent.

Asserting properties for a segment can make some pinterps of that segment cease to be ACTIVE because they are no longer COMPATIBLE. These changes can cause other pinterps to become INACTIVE if they depend on those newly INCOMPATIBLE pinterps. So, a replacement dependency path must be sought for each pinterp which has a newly INCOMPATIBLE pinterp in its dependency path. A pinterp which fails to find replacements becomes INACTIVE, which then affects the pinterps depending on it. Loss of activation is thus globally propagated in two segment-wise sweeps out from the segment with new properties. To ensure that the recorded cost of b-dependency chains (as mentioned above) is propagated correctly, the backward sweep is performed before the forward one.

When asserting the initial properties for a new frontier segment or what was a gap-fill segment, initial relation paths from the COMPATIBLE pinterps of that segment to the neighboring segments must be sought. All of these COMPATIBLE pinterps are first assumed to be ACTIVE, to allow them to be expanded during breadth-first searches to find these initial dependency paths. Each one is considered INACTIVE only if dependency paths cannot be found for it. All ACTIVE pinterps of both neighboring segments then seek (initial) dependency paths to that segment, propagating loss of activation as before.

As explained in the next section, pinterps can also become ACTIVE when dubious properties are retracted from a segment. For this to happen, some pinterps of that segment must first become newly COMPATIBLE with the reduced set of properties. The newly COMPATIBLE pinterps which find dependency paths (i.e. become ACTIVE) can allow other (INACTIVE) pinterps to become ACTIVE as well. Furthermore, newly ACTIVE pinterps can allow some ACTIVE pinterps to obtain better b-dependency paths. An inefficient technique would be to start from the first segment and re-compute dependency paths from scratch. However, by allowing intermediate steps to temporarily create dependency paths involving INACTIVE pinterps, efficient incremental propagation of activation is achieved (see [4]).

3.1 Handling Faulty Data

DATMI's conservative conversion from measurements to disjunctive qualitative values cannot always avoid the effects of faulty data. Inconsistencies due to faulty data can only be prevented if the conversion tables never assert any qualitative value to have zero probability. However, in that case, each path through the envisionment would be a consistent global interpretation. So, DATMI provides a means for modifying segment properties to recover from faulty data which do sneak past the conservative conversions.

DATMI detects inconsistencies between the envisionment and the observations as soon as all of some segment's pinterps cease to be ACTIVE. That segment is called an *inconsistent segment.* Since DATMI assumes that the envisionment itself is sound and complete, it attempts to recover from inconsistency by generating and testing sets of property changes to remove hypothesized faulty data. Associated with each hypothesis are: 1) a set of property changes, 2) its plausibility, and 3) the conditions under which it remains valid.

Because the faulty data might not be in an inconsistent segment's own properties, all segment properties are suspect. To avoid considering the power set of possible property changes, DATMI currently limits itself to an especially common subset of these. In particular, it considers forgetting properties that could arise from non-intermittent *sensor failures.* An example of such a failure is when a flow-rate seems constant because its sensor has gotten stuck.

Each DATMI sensor failure hypothesis suggests forgetting (i.e. retracting) all recent segment properties having the most-recent value for one type of property. This assumes that each sensor only contributes to one type of property. So, in the above example, it would forget all the recent observations of that flow-rate being constant, back until it was last observed to be changing. For simplicity, DATMI considers the plausibility of a sensor failure hypothesis to be the *a priori* probability that the particular most-recent value is due to that sensor failure. Determining these probabilities is outside of our theory; we currently use arbitrary values reflecting commonsense intuitions. Finally, the hypothesis holds as long as that type of property is not observed to have a different value at later times, since the hypothesized failure is non-intermittent.

DATMI generates these hypotheses in order of plausibility and then tests each by propagating any pinterp activations due to the reduced number of segment properties, as explained earlier. A useful aspect of forgetting properties, without asserting any replacements, is that no new inconsistencies can be introduced during this test. If all segments are not consistent after propagating activation, the forgotten properties are reasserted. By resorting to such reassertions, to avoid excessive removal of constraints on the interpretation space, DATMI cannot recover from an inconsistency caused by multiple sensor failures.

The generate-and-test process continues until there are no inconsistent segments or each hypothesis has been tried. If an inconsistent segment still remains, the pinterp-space is partitioned by that segment and each part is interpreted separately. In any case, if the conditions of a successful hypothesis are later violated, it must be retracted by reasserting the forgotten properties. Inconsistencies will then be redetected and rehandled unless some later successful hypothesis (that fixed some later arising inconsistencies) happened to fortuitously fix those inconsistencies as well. In the case of our sensor failure hypotheses, such fortuitous fixes can occur if the earlier hypothesis recovered solely from the early inconsistencies arising from a sensor failure.

4 Example

We now highlight an implemented example of DATMI handling incomplete and faulty data. This example uses a pump-cycle system of two containers of water connected by a valved path and a pump, as illustrated in Figure 4. The QPE [8] envisionment (not shown here due to space limitations) consists of 42 states and 61 transitions. This envisionment differentiates states by ten types of properties, of which the following five are observed: P3 (the comparison between L1 and L2) P4 (the ON/OFF status of PUMP), P7 (the direction of change in L1), P8 (the direction of change in L2), and P10 (the direction of change in FR). Partial, perturbed results of a numeric simulation provided the incomplete, faulty measurements for determining those five types of properties.

As Figure 4 shows, DATMI interprets the measurements for the first 15.0 seconds with no problem. Note that properties are not asserted for every segment, as indicated by the "?" values. This is because the conservative conversions did not specify exact times for changes between qualitative values, since they are indeterminate from the sampled data. The arrows in the pinterp-space show the backward and forward dependency paths. The best working global interpretation for the first 15.0 seconds is found by following the chain of b-dependency paths starting at state 40 in Seg30 and ending at state 39 in Seg1.

However, no COMPATIBLE pinterps exist for the properties observed for Seg32. Thus, when those properties are asserted, Seg32 becomes inconsistent because it has no ACTIVE pinterps. To fix this inconsistency, DATMI considers five sensor failure hypotheses, one for each of the five types of observed properties.

DATMI first tries forgetting properties for P10; for this example, each hypothesis is considered equally plausible. Since P10's most-recent observed value is INCREASE in Seg24 and its last different value is STEADY in Seg11, the sensor failure hypothesis is to forget all properties for P10 after Seg11. DATMI quickly finds that forgetting P10 from Seg18, Seg22, and Seg24 fails to fix the pinterp-space. Indeed, in this case forgetting P10 could not possibly help since the pinterps of Seg32 are

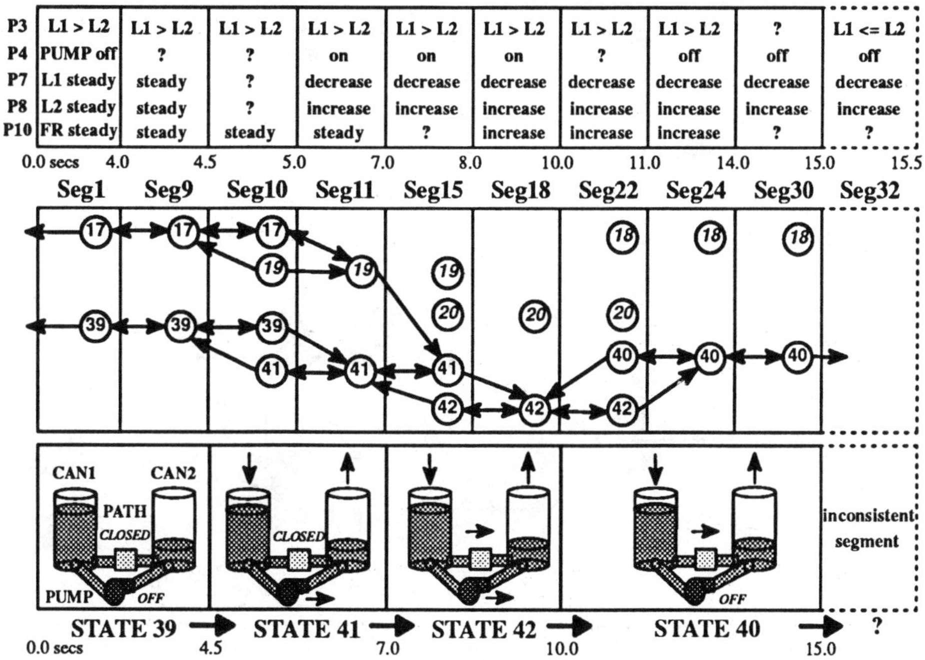

Figure 4: The pinterp-space when inconsistency first detected
L1=(FLUID-LEVEL CAN1), L2=(FLUID-LEVEL CAN2), and FR=(FLOW-RATE PATH).

all INCOMPATIBLE, which requires changing the properties of Seg32 itself. However, to illustrate the general case, we do not treat this case specially for this example. Even hypotheses which modify only properties of consistent segments are generally useful since they may allow INACTIVE pinterps of an inconsistent segment to become ACTIVE. In any case, DATMI then tests hypotheses to forget P8 (after Seg9) and forget P7 (after Seg9), also with no success.

DATMI succeeds by forgetting P4 after Seg18, as shown in Figure 5. This reflects the hypothesis that the pump indicator failed sometime after Seg18 and continues to indicate that the pump is OFF, perhaps because the indicator light burnt out. The OFF values for P4 are shown in parenthesis since they are now forgotten and do not constrain the pinterps. While propagating activation due to these forgotten properties, the dependency paths are updated appropriately, yielding a new simplest global interpretation where the pump is never OFF after Seg9. Of course, the pinterp-space also allows interpretations where the pump is OFF after Seg18. However, the pump must become ON again in Seg32 because its pinterps are INCOMPATIBLE otherwise. So, those alternative interpretations involve more state changes than DATMI's (simplest) working interpretation does.

5 Using Additional Knowledge

5.1 Probabilities

DATMI can use numeric probabilities associated with the envisionment states and transitions to maintain the most-probable working global interpretation, instead of the simplest one. This requires that those probabilities have been estimated by some external means, such as the stochastic analysis technique of [6]. DATMI composes these probabilities using Bayes' chain rule by assuming independent events [12]. Thus, the *a priori* probability of a chain of b-dependency paths is considered the product of the *a priori* probability of the earliest state and the conditional probabilities of all the transitions in that chain.

This composition is valid assuming that each transition is truly independent of which states occurred earlier in the chain, which is typically the case for paths through sufficiently detailed envisionments. It overestimates the probability of spanning-state dependency paths relative to other types, since other types involve more transitions during the same period of time. Since spanning-state paths provide simpler interpretations, this is usually acceptable.

To reflect uncertainty in the measurements, the segment property probabilities from the conversion tables (e.g. Figure 1) can also be included in this composition. DATMI assumes that a segment's properties are independent, which is most reasonable when the observations are never redundant. The total property probability for a particular pinterp is then the product of the probabilities of the segment property values with which its state is compatible. Thus, DATMI multiplies the *a priori* probability of a chain of b-dependency paths by the product of the property probabilities for each pinterp in that chain to get a more accurate probability for that chain. Furthermore, to accurately reflect the probability of a b-dependency chain that is conditional on

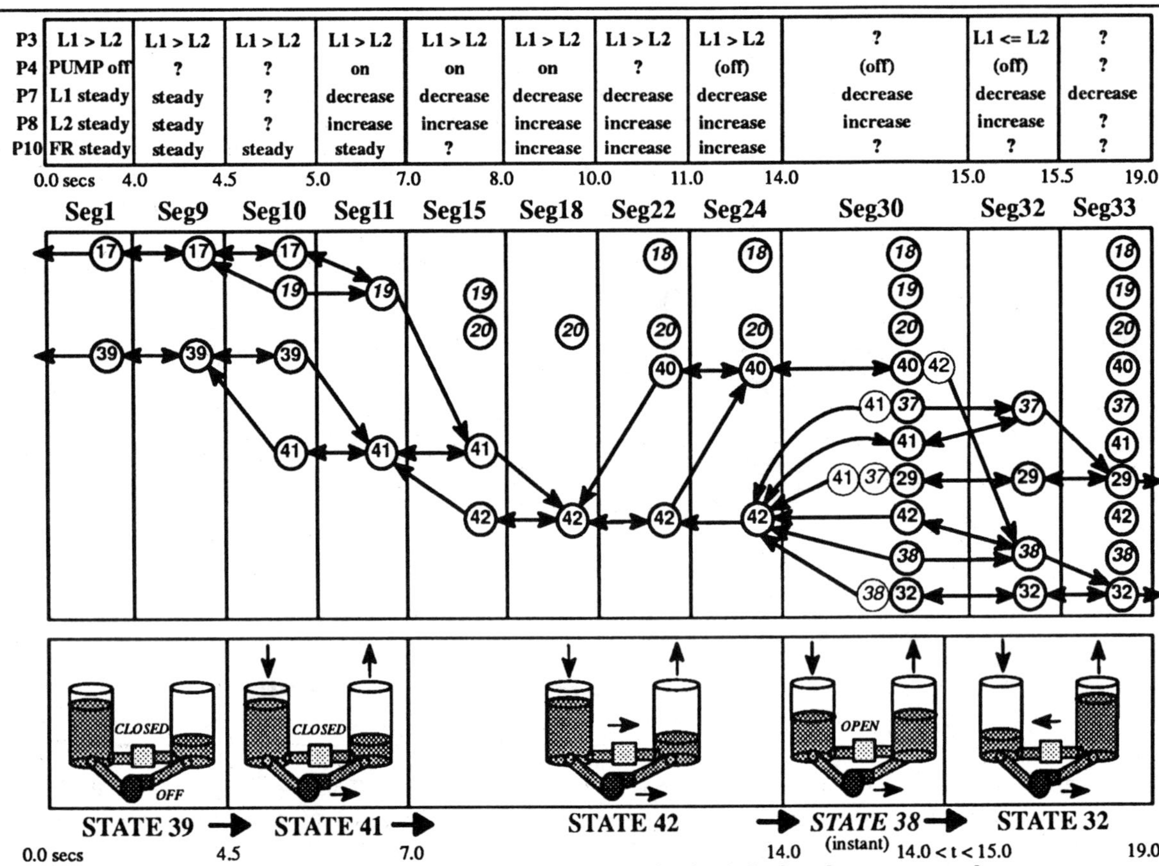

Figure 5: The pinterp-space when hypothesized faulty data retracted

the set of observations, one must redistribute the *a priori* probability associated with pinterps which are not ACTIVE to the ACTIVE ones, as described in [4].

Standard exhaustive graph search for least-cost paths between all pairs of nodes [11] suffices for finding the most-probable b-dependency paths. DATMI records the composed probability of the chain of b-dependency paths leading up to each pinterp when its b-dependency path is found. It finds the most-probable paths from each COMPATIBLE pinterp of a segment G to each ACTIVE pinterp of the backward neighboring segment B using least-cost path search over all those pinterps, with the following cost assignments. The cost of each pinterp of B is the inverse of its (recorded) composed probability. The cost of each pinterp of G is the inverse of its property probability. The cost of each transition is the inverse of its conditional probability. The total cost of a path is thus the product of the costs it entails.

Actually, DATMI avoids the cubic time cost of exhaustive least-cost path search by performing efficient best-first search for each pinterp, resorting to least-cost search only when some cubic function of states have been examined without success, as detailed in [4].

5.2 Durations

Space limitations do not permit an explanation of how DATMI uses duration bounds to prune candidate b-dependency paths during best-first search. However, it is important to realize that such bounds can be incorporated into the DATMI framework to avoid interpretations which are inconsistent with those constraints. One simple example is indicated by the b-dependency paths in Figure 5. The b-dependency path for state 19 in segment Seg11 includes state 17 in segment Seg10 instead of state 19 in Seg10. State 19 cannot span from Seg10 to Seg11 because it is an instantaneous state.

6 Discussion

DATMI incrementally maintains a concise interpretation space, which allows it to quickly detect faulty data and then efficiently recover by doubting observations. It provides a framework for integrating domain-specific knowledge, such as probability and duration estimates, with the causal constraints given by qualitative simulation. Its use of dependency paths makes maintenance efficient and provides the best working global interpretation at all times. Furthermore, it indicates which states can consistently occur during each segment, making it suitable for monitoring tasks and providing strong focus for finding alternative global interpretations. DATMI has been fully implemented and tested on several examples from both QPE and FROB [9] domains, suggesting that it is applicable to any system of qualitative physics.

To avoid intractable temporal reasoning during interpretation, DATMI accepts two key limitations. First, global interpretations are not always most appropriately represented by DATMI's linear sequences of states. For example, partial orderings provide more general explanations, but DATMI's use of global segmentation and local dependency paths precludes them. Second, DATMI requires an appropriate envisionment as input. By referring to an available envisionment, DATMI's pinterp-space maintenance requires time at most cubic in the number of envisionment states. This bound is based on the cubic worst-case time cost for finding the most-probable b-dependency paths; DATMI's overall cubic worst-case complexity is analyzed in [4].

Although envisioning itself can be exponential in the number of system variables, we suspect that it is more efficient to cleanly separate envisioning from interpreting for tasks where a large fraction of the envisionment states are likely to occur or where observations are very sparse. This intuition is based on the efficient techniques developed for total envisioning, such as those described in [8]. To handle the other cases, we are currently developing incremental envisioning techniques which could provide DATMI with previously unavailable states and transitions when suitable interpretations cannot be found using a working partial envisionment.

By not accepting DATMI's two key limitations, related approachs allow other gains while sacrificing the ability to interpret incomplete, faulty data as efficiently and robustly as DATMI. For example, Q2 [10] can exploit more of the quantitative information in the measurements as it generates consistent histories. However, to ensure that it can always offer some interpretation, Q2 must be able to follow every branch during history generation, which can be exponential in the number of states. Although the number of paths through an envisionment is also exponential in the number of states, DATMI never needs to consider more than a cubic number of them (during dependency path search) because of the factorization of the problem provided by global segmentation.

GDE [3] provides an alternative means for handling inconsistencies between the measurements and the model. It is not directly suited for our problem because its focus is on determining faults in the system itself, not the observations. Although it acknowledges sensor failure rates, it does not attempt to reason about the nature of such failures, as DATMI does with sensor failure hypotheses. Also, GDE does not reason over time. The consequences of using TCP [13] with GDE to allow across-time reasoning, which deKleer and Williams suggest as future work, are not clear. Although TCP's *concise histories* could represent partially-ordered interpretations, that approach would suffer from overhead that DATMI's globally-segmented pinterp-space avoids.

The DATMI framework suggests future research in several directions. Continued progress in qualitative modelling, along with incremental envisioning, is needed. Multiple faults might be handled by not always retracting a hypothesis when it fails to recover from all the inconsistencies by itself. Also, more formal, general techniques for generating fault-recovery hypotheses are needed, perhaps based on *knowledge groups* as in [2]. Finally, the data selection problem (i.e. using the most informative data first) might be addressed by preferring observations at times nearest the segments having the most ACTIVE pinterps.

Acknowledgements

Thanks to Ken Forbus, John Collins, Brian Falkenhainer, and Janice Skorstad for useful comments.

References

[1] James F. Allen. Maintaining knowledge about temporal intervals. *Communications of ACM*, 26(11):832–843, November 1983.

[2] B. Chandrasekaran and W. F. Punch III. Data validation during diagnosis, a step beyond traditional sensor validation. In *Proceedings of AAAI-87*, pages 778–782, July 1987.

[3] Johan de Kleer and Brian Williams. Reasoning about multiple faults. In *Proceedings of AAAI-86*, pages 132–139, August 1986.

[4] Dennis DeCoste. *Dynamic Across-Time Measurement Interpretation: Maintaining Qualitative Understandings of Physical System Behavior.* Master's thesis, University of Illinois at Urbana-Champaign, Urbana, Illinois, October 1989. (Technical Report UIUCDCS-R-90-1572, February 1990).

[5] Jon Doyle. A truth maintenance system. *Artificial Intelligence*, 12:231–272, 1979.

[6] Jon Doyle and Elisha P. Sacks. Stochastic analysis of qualitative dynamics. In *Proceedings of IJCAI-89*, pages 1187–1192, August 1989.

[7] Kenneth D. Forbus. Interpreting measurements of physical systems. In *Proceedings of AAAI-86*, pages 113–117, August 1986.

[8] Kenneth D. Forbus. The qualitative process engine. In Daniel S. Weld and Johan de Kleer, editors, *Readings in Qualitative Reasoning about Physical Systems*, pages 220–235, Morgan Kaufmann, 1990.

[9] Kenneth D. Forbus. *A Study of Qualitative and Geometric Knowledge in Reasoning about Motion.* Technical Report TR-615, AI Lab, MIT, 1981.

[10] Benjamin Kuipers and Daniel Berleant. Using incomplete quantitative knowledge in qualitative reasoning. In *Proceedings of AAAI-88*, pages 324–329, August 1988.

[11] Kurt Mehlhorn. *Graph Algorithms and NP-Completeness.* Volume 2 of *Data Structures and Algorithms*, Springer-Verlag, 1984.

[12] Judea Pearl. *Probabilistic Reasoning In Intelligent Systems: Networks of Plausible Inference.* Morgan Kaufmann, 1988.

[13] Brian C. Williams. Doing time: putting qualitative reasoning on firmer ground. In *Proceedings of AAAI-86*, pages 105–112, August 1986.

Self-Explanatory Simulations: An integration of qualitative and quantitative knowledge

Kenneth D. Forbus
Qualitative Reasoning Group
Beckman Institute, University of Illinois
405 N. Mathews Street, Urbana IL 61801

Brian Falkenhainer
System Sciences Laboratory
Xerox Palo Alto Research Center
3333 Coyote Hill Road, Palo Alto CA 94304

Abstract

A central goal of qualitative physics is to provide a framework for organizing and using quantitative knowledge. One important use of quantitative knowledge is numerical simulation. While current numerical simulators are powerful, they are often hard to construct, do not reveal the assumptions underlying their construction, and do not produce explanations of the behaviors they predict. This paper shows how to combine qualitative and quantitative models to produce a new class of *self-explanatory simulations* which combine the advantages of both kinds of reasoning. Self-explanatory simulations provide the accuracy of numerical models and the interpretive power of qualitative reasoning. We define what self-explanatory simulations are and show how to construct them automatically. We illustrate their power with some examples generated with an implemented system, SIMGEN. We analyze the limitations of our techniques, and discuss plans for future work.

1 Introduction

A central goal of qualitative physics is to provide a framework for organizing and using quantitative knowledge. One important use of quantitative knowledge is numerical simulation. With recent advances in computational power, numerical simulations are playing an ever increasing role in science and engineering. Yet they have important limitations. Most of today's simulations are built by hand, with the long development time and travails associated with custom software. The physical assumptions underlying the simulation are at best only made explicit in technical reports or documentation, and cannot be accessed by the simulation engine or other reasoning systems using its results. And while numerical simulations are superb at producing sets of numbers representing predictions of system behavior over time, they do not incorporate any mechanism for interpreting their results (save graphics). This paper introduces a new class of *self-explanatory simulations* which integrates methods from qualitative physics to directly address these limitations.

By tightly integrating qualitative knowledge with numerical simulations, we hope to achieve three advantages: *increased automation*, *improved self-monitoring*, and *better explanations*. We describe each in turn.

Increased automation: In most engineering domains numerical simulations are still built by hand. With some exceptions (e.g. SPICE and similar systems for electronic circuits), most simulation tools leave the formulation of physical models to the user. For example, PC-DYSIM [5] supports modeling of dynamic systems [24] by providing a generic simulation engine and standardized graphics routines but lacks a well-tested, standard parts library for building system models. In fact, we have been unable to find any such library describing fluid and thermal systems for engineering thermodynamics. Engineers we talk to agree that such a library would be useful, but they lack ways to organize it. Qualitative physics provides such formalisms for organizing knowledge, so that general model libraries can be built and used by simulation compilers to take on more of the modeling burden.

Improved self-monitoring: One unfortunate consequence of the predominance of hand-crafted simulations is sporadic detection of errors and inconsistencies. Many numerical simulations are designed for a narrow range of behaviors, but often such limitations are only recorded in the mind of the programmer. This can lead to erroneous results for unsuspecting users, such as negative water levels in tanks. By making modeling assumptions explicit, the simulator itself should be able to ensure that its numerical predictions are consistent with the qualitative intuitions.

Better explanations: Computer-based tutors like STEAMER [17; 28] and RBT [31] use a combination of numerical simulators to provide students with a "feel" for a system's dynamics and hand-crafted explanation facilities to tie observed behaviors to principles [16; 11; 31]. We hope to help automate the production of such tutors. Other engineering tasks could benefit from self-explanatory simulations. A designer, for instance, could find what range of parameters leads to the desired set of behaviors, and ascertain what needs to be changed if the desired behaviors are unachievable.

Section 2 describes the structure of self-explanatory simulators and outlines how they can be automatically constructed. Section 3 illustrates these ideas with examples from some simulators generated by SIMGEN, our implemented simulator compiler. Section 4 analyzes our compilation technique. We close with related research and our plans for future work.

2 Self-explanatory Simulations

A self-explanatory simulation integrates qualitative and numerical models to produce accurate predictions and causal explanations of the behavior of continuous physical systems. Self-explanatory simulators produce numerical simulations of behavior, just as traditional systems do. However, they also can describe what is happening in qualitative terms, and provide a causal explanation of the parameters' behavior at any time during the simulation. In addition, all the modeling assumptions involved in creating the qualitative and numeric models are completely explicit, and hence subject to inspection, review, and revision.

Writing self-explanatory simulators requires knowing a system's qualitatively distinct regions of behavior and the ability to construct mathematical models for each region. These models must then be embedded in a control structure which switches between them as appropriate, and keeps the qualitative and quantitative accounts of behavior in sync to generate useful explanations and detect clashes. We have developed a program which compiles such simulators automatically, to relieve the modeler from this complex chore. Our program, called `SIMGEN`, takes as inputs (1) a qualitative domain model, (2) a corresponding math-model library, and (3) a specific physical system to model.

Roughly, `SIMGEN` works like this. The qualitative domain model is used to produce a total envisionment for the physical system. Next the math-model library is used to construct a set of ordinary differential equations for each qualitatively distinct region of behavior identified in the envisionment. A simulation program is written for each set of equations, using the causal account from the qualitative model. The state transitions in the envisionment are used to construct procedures which detect when the set of relevant equations changes. Collectively, these procedures constitute a simulator capable of producing predictions and explanations starting from any valid initial condition of the physical system.

This section describes self-explanatory simulations and how they are built. We begin by examining the domain knowledge required, define an appropriate, integrated notion of state, and describe both their architecture and how they are compiled.

2.1 Integrating qualitative and numerical domain knowledge

For a given physical system and task, a relevant qualitative model can be automatically built from the constructs of a general QP (qualitative process) domain model (c.f. [12; 9; 10]). An envisionment using this model determines the space of possible behaviors to consider. Suppose we design a corresponding quantitative domain model that satisfies the following constraints: (1) All parameters that can change during a behavior must be mentioned in the QP model; (2) all behaviors generated by the numerical model must be predicted and thus explained by the qualitative model (requiring the converse is difficult [22]); and (3) every state-space boundary where the set of governing equations changes is marked by a transition in the qualitative model.[1] In this case the envisionment identifies the set of potentially relevant numerical models, with each qualitative state being governed by a single set of equations. We define a *math model library* to be an association of numerical models to (combinations of) the qualitative proportionalities in a QP domain model. For example, a contained liquid description typically includes the relationship [2]

`Level(?cl)` $\propto_{Q+}$ `Amount-of(?cl)`

The corresponding numeric entry for cylindrical containers might be (assuming `?cl = (c-s ?sub liquid ?can)`)

```
(= (A (level (c-s ?sub liquid ?can)))
   (/ (A (amount-of (c-s ?sub liquid ?can)))
      (* PI (A (density ?sub))
         (expt (A (radius ?can)) 2))))
```

where `density` and `radius` are numerical constants not appearing in the QP model. Models like these are composed to produce simulation code, as described below.

2.2 State in self-explanatory simulations

Integrating qualitative and quantitative state is a key idea of self-explanatory simulations. For concreteness, consider an envisionment produced by `QPE`, an envisioner for QP theory [14]. Each qualitative state is defined by a set of assumptions (e.g., an ATMS *environment*), whose consequences are what is true in that state. These assumptions are drawn from classes of statements gleaned from an automatic analysis of the scenario model. For example, if the model for a scenario includes a container `can`, then the possibility of liquid or gas being in `can` is important, and hence one of the possible relationships between `Amount-of-in(water,gas,can)` and `ZERO` must be included in each qualitative state. Similarly, if a pair of containers is connected by a fluid path, then the possible relationships between their pressures becomes one of the constituents of state, since this information is needed (along with other facts) to ascertain whether or not a liquid flow is occurring between them. In addition to inequalities, other classes of assumptions needed to establish state properties are identified and included as well. For example, an assumption about whether or not the fluid path is blocked is essential to knowing if flow can occur, and hence must be included in a state.

The constituents of a qualitative state are thus a set of propositions, drawn from a set of choices that can be considered the *basis set* for qualitative states. Many (indeed, most) of these propositions are ordinal relationships between continuous parameters. A traditional numerical state, on the other hand, consists of a

[1] Enforcing the converse, that every qualitative transition corresponds to a change in equations, would be useful for minimizing complexity but cannot always be done. Modeling an indicator turning on at 10% below a critical value, for instance, requires a transition without any change of equations.

[2] In QP theory [12], $a \propto_{Q+} b$ is an *indirect influence* and reads "a is qualitatively proportional to b". It indicates a positive monotonic relationship between a and b. $I+(a, b_i)$ is a *direct influence* and indicates that the derivative of a is equal to the sum of all b_i's actively influencing it.

vector of numerical values for the continuous parameters. Call this vector $\mathcal{N}_f$. We define a new notion of state by linking these two notions. First, for each non-ordering proposition class in the basis set, we add to $\mathcal{N}_f$ a boolean variable whose value is *true* or *false* according to whether the corresponding statement is true or false in a given state. For example, `Blocked(Pipe1)` becomes an explicit parameter in $\mathcal{N}_f$. (This extension is common, at least in training simulators.) Second, we define state as a pair $< \mathcal{N}_f, \mathcal{Q}_f >$, where $\mathcal{Q}_f$ ranges over the set of states in the envisionment. A state is *consistent* if and only if the values of $\mathcal{N}_f$ satisfy the propositions of the qualitative state corresponding to the value of $\mathcal{Q}_f$. Otherwise, it is *inconsistent*. Checking the consistency of a state is straightforward. For each non-ordinal proposition in $\mathcal{Q}_f$, check that its corresponding boolean parameter has the appropriate value. For each ordinal relationship in $\mathcal{Q}_f$, check if the same relationship holds between the corresponding numerical parameters.[3]

Determining the components of $\mathcal{N}_f$ for a system requires analyzing the envisionment in concert with the math-model library. A boolean parameter must be included for each class of non-ordering propositions in the basis set. A numeric parameter must be included for each continuous property in the QP model, as well as for each constant introduced by the corresponding numerical models (such as `Density` and `Radius` in the entry for `Level` above).

2.3 The architecture of self-explanatory simulators

A self-explanatory simulation consists of a tightly integrated set of qualitative and numerical representations. Such simulations are generated by self-explanatory simulators, which in turn are constructed by a *simulator compiler*. The compiler takes as input an envisionment of a specific system and a math model library, and produces a simulator, consisting of a set of procedures and datastructures which support prediction and explanation concerning the classes of behaviors described by the envisionment.

There are three crucial components in a self-explanatory simulator: (1) a set of *evolvers*, procedures which specify for each qualitative state how to update its numerical parameters over time; (2) a set of *state transition procedures* (STP's) which detect qualitative changes in state, and (3) an *explanation facility* which uses information from the envisionment to provide causal accounts and characterize possible behaviors. These components interact during simulation as follows. The value of $\mathcal{Q}_f$ is used to fetch the corresponding evolver. The evolver is executed to update $\mathcal{N}_f$. The STP corresponding to $\mathcal{Q}_f$ is fetched and executed to see if a transition has occurred. If it has, then $\mathcal{Q}_f$ is updated to this new state. The cycle repeats until no more simulation is required. The explanation facility can be used during or after simulation to better understand the results.

SIMGEN works by first computing the constituents of $\mathcal{N}_f$ and $\mathcal{Q}_f$. Next it writes the evolvers and state transition procedures. Finally, it caches information from the envisionment to support explanation. The rest of this section describes these components in more detail, and how **SIMGEN** builds them.

2.3.1 Evolvers

An evolver is a procedure which, given a state vector and Δt, produces a new state vector representing the evolution of the modeled system over Δt. Roughly, traditional simulations operate by identifying a small set of state variables, estimating derivatives for them, computing their new values, and then calculating new values for any relevant dependent variables. This organization can be easily translated into QP terms. In a QP model, the directly influenced parameters correspond to state variables, since direct influences comprise an integral connection [12]. The indirectly influenced parameters, that is, those linked by some chain of qualitative proportionalities to the directly influenced parameters, form the dependent variables. Any parameters not mentioned in the QP model are constants, and hence cannot change.

A key problem in writing simulation programs is establishing an order of computation for a given set of equations. In QP theory, a qualitative proportionality represents both a functional and a causal relationship. Since entries in the math-model library correspond to combinations of qualitative proportionalities, we can use the *causal ordering* [18] induced by the influences in the qualitative model to construct an order of computation for any consistent set of numeric equations. In particular, (1) estimate the derivatives of directly influenced parameters (e.g., the state variables), (2) update the amounts (`A`) of directly influenced parameters, (3) recompute amounts of indirectly influenced parameters, and (4) estimate derivatives of indirectly influenced parameters by subtracting old values from new.

The individual updates within steps 1, 2, and 4 can be performed in any order (our current system uses Euler integration for simplicity). The order of computation in step 3 can be determined by a simple search of the influence graph. Notice that QP theory requires the subgraph of qualitative proportionalities to be loop-free in any legal state; feedback is represented by explicit integral connections (e.g., direct influences) only. This has the effect of demanding that any loop contain at least one state variable, a common constraint in numeric simulators. For example, Figure 1 illustrates the graph of influences for a simple two-container liquid flow. Given the current values for the `Amount-Ofs` and `Heats`, the `Levels` are computed next, followed by the `Pressures` and then `Flow-Rate`, while the `Temperatures` can be computed in any order (in this situation). The math-model library must contain at least one model for each consistent combination of qualitative proportionalities.[4]

[3] The finite precision of floating point requires using a "fuzz" parameter to detect equality.

[4] If there is more than one model, currently one is selected

Figure 1: The influence graph for a two-container flow problem. The graph of influences that holds at any moment in a QP description indicates a causal ordering between the parameters it describes. The state variables are given by the direct influences.

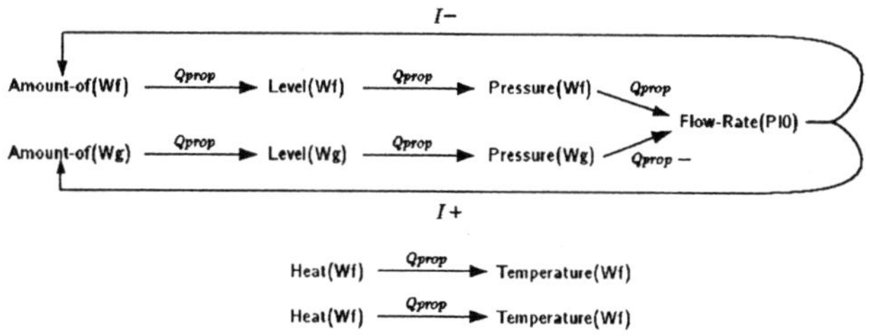

The model is tested to ensure that all parameters it mentions have already been computed in the current situation, using the order constraints of the influence graph.

Conceptually, an evolver could be supplied for each qualitative state. However, it is more practical to divide states into equivalence classes, grouping together those governed by a common set of equations and writing only a single evolver for each group. In QP models two states can share an evolver when they have the same set of active processes and views, since the set of qualitative proportionalities for each state is identical, and hence the corresponding equations will be the same.

An important opportunity for self-monitoring occurs when setting up states. The strategy used for writing evolvers is also used to write *initialization routines*, which obtain values for independent variables from the user, calculate dependent parameters and estimate derivatives, and check the resulting state's consistency.

2.3.2 State Transition Procedures

Traditional mathematical formalisms do not provide a comprehensive, formal language for describing when an equation holds. By using QP theory as the basis for a modeling language, such conditions can be stated formally and used in reasoning. Given a particular qualitative state, we can ascertain what conditions must be monitored to detect when a transition occurs, and write STP's that sense such transitions and determine the new qualitative state.

The parameters that must be monitored for each state are determined by analyzing the envisionment's transitions. Recall that *limit hypotheses* indicate possible changes in ordinal relationships [12]. All of the changes possible in the current situation must be monitored. Usually the result of a limit hypothesis is unique, but not always – underconstrained properties of objects coming into existence or actions which cause discontinuous changes [15] can result in multiple next states. In such cases the STP must also perform enough extra tests to discriminate between the possibilities. Importantly, these tests are all inexpensive numerical inequality tests, and typically only a handful are needed for each state, so the overhead of transition finding is quite small.

Handling transitions where a numerical relationship changes to equality requires special care, since the equality may only hold for an instant and hence could be missed. We call this the *numerical transition skip* (NTS) problem. We detect when NTS has occurred by noting when one of the monitored relationships undergoes a discontinuous change (e.g., when $N_1 < N_2$ holds at one tick but $N_1 > N_2$ holds at the next). This causes the run-time system to "roll back" the simulation, performing binary search to find a value for Δt that hits the transition. Once the numerical values at the transition are computed, the simulation proceeds with the original Δt.

STP's also share the burden of self-monitoring. Assuming that the initial state vector is consistent, inconsistencies can only arise when the evolution $\mathcal{N}_f$ "drifts away" from the subspace consistent with $\mathcal{Q}_f$. The procedure outlined above already catches cases where the result of a transition is not a state the envisionment predicted. However, inconsistencies involving unmonitored relationships are not detected by default. What level of error checking is reasonable depends on circumstances. For example, if the domain models are well-tested, only the minimal testing described so far may be needed. When more stringent self-monitoring is required, such as developing a new domain model, the numerical component of state can be re-classified as often as desired. Reclassifying at every clock tick, for instance, ensures that any misalignments between qualitative and quantitative models is caught as early as possible. (Such tests can be made reasonably efficient by using a discrimination tree to peform the classification, but since the overhead is still substantially higher, these extra tests are not performed by default in our implementation.)

2.3.3 Supporting Explanation Generation

Using qualitative models to ground and generate simulation procedures supports a variety of explanation generation tasks. The qualitative model provides a causal account for all changes in every state. The inclusion of $\mathcal{Q}_f$ in the state vector provides access to the appropriate account for any (simulated) time. Furthermore, this causal explanation is not simply a post-hoc reconstruction – given the organization of evolvers above, it is literally the way the simulation of the system is evolved! Similarly, information about classes of possible futures is available through the transitions of the envisionment. At any simulated time, one can find out what events might happen, or could have happened instead with other choices for $\mathcal{N}_f$.

We make two stipulations concerning the run-time system. First, we require that it includes access to information from the envisionment. How much information is needed and how it is accessed varies according to task requirements. If the run-time system cannot be

at random. Clearly, this is an opportunity for a reasoned choice, based on criteria such as desired accuracy and performance requirements.

compute-intensive, the simulation compiler might identify in advance what information is needed about each envisionment state and create a database to serve as a cache for the run-time system. Alternately, relevant portions of an envisionment or history could be generated incrementally, on demand. (Currently we simply include pointers to the envisionment in the simulator itself.)

The second stipulation is that the run-time system must maintain a *registration* [13], which describes the history of the system in terms of occurrences of states of the envisionment. Each episode in this history includes the corresponding state of the envisionment, a numerical value for its temporal beginning, and if it ends, a numerical value for its end along with the limit hypothesis which occurred. (It is straightforward to compute STP's that provide this information.) This history provides the temporal framework required to relate simulated time to a path of qualitative states, and hence provide access to the appropriate qualitative knowledge.

3 Examples

Here we show some interactions with simulators produced by `SIMGEN`, our compiler of self-explanatory simulations. The QP domain models used are similar to those in [12], but are slightly enhanced to better model the interaction of heat and mass flows [6]. The questions were posed using a formal query language, and the English output was generated automatically by the default explanation facility.

Simple Liquid Flow: The two-container example in Figure 2 shows that the simulation can provide a variety of information about parameters and possible behaviors.

Boiling: In Figure 3, the simulator detects that boiling has begun, and changes evolvers appropriately. Furthermore, it enforces the semantics of existence, by refusing to provide information about properties of objects at times when they don't exist.

Spring/Block Oscillator: As Figure 4 illustrates, `SIMGEN` is not limited to thermodynamic systems. Here a naive user attempts to provide a negative spring constant (a "perturbing force", rather than a restoring force). This is inconsistent with the user's presumed starting state, and after examining the equations and the assumptions, the user makes a more reasonable choice.

4 Analysis

What are the limits of `SIMGEN`? Given a QP domain model, a math model library that provides appropriate expressions for each instance of indirectly influenced quantities (e.g., one that follows the causal ordering represented by the graph of influences), `SIMGEN` can compile a self-explanatory simulator for any system that can be successfully envisioned with that domain model. Issues of scale and numerical stability are important, of course, as noted below. But more fundamentally, when can we have the appropriate domain models?

Figure 2: A simple example of liquid flow. Questions about specific points in time establish the temporal context for subsequent questions.

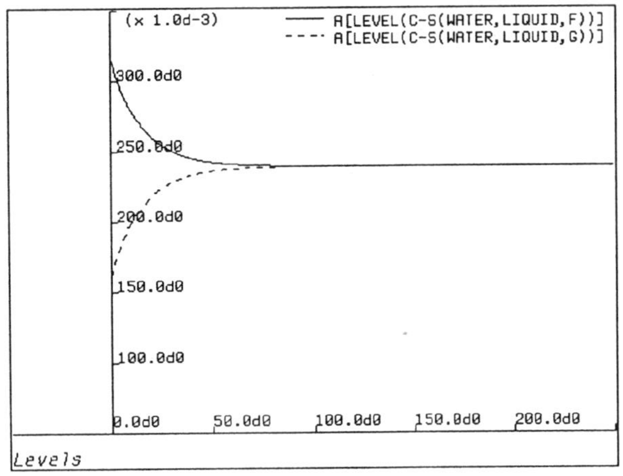


```
Q: What is happening at t = 50.0 seconds?
A: A flow of water from F to G.

Q: What is A[LEVEL(C-S(WATER,LIQUID,F))]?
A:The level of the water in F is 0.24224941.

Q: How is LEVEL(C-S(WATER,LIQUID,F)) changing?
A: The level of the water in F is decreasing.

Q: What affects LEVEL(C-S(WATER,LIQUID,F))?
A:The level of the water in F is changing as a
  function of the amount of the water in F.

Q: What happens next?
A: At 130.5 seconds the pressure of the water
   in F and the pressure of the water in G
   become equal.  Then, nothing is happening.

Q: What else might have happened?
A: The transition at 130.5 seconds was inevitable.

Q: What is happening at t = 200.0 seconds?
A: Nothing is happening.

Q: What happens next?
A: This behavior continues forever.
```

Just as no single traditional engineering technique for organizing knowledge has proven adequate for all domains, we should not expect any single ontology to suffice for qualitative physics. [5] The process-centered view works best for domains like thermodynamics [27] and chemistry, where explicit reasoning about processes is crucial. The device-centered view [7; 29] works best when the idealizations of network theory hold. For example, analyzing a voltage divider can give rise to simultaneous equations, which cannot be solved via propagation alone. `SIMGEN` could not handle this system. It

[5] [8] makes a similar point comparing engineering to economics.

Figure 3: Changes in regime and existence are automatically detected.

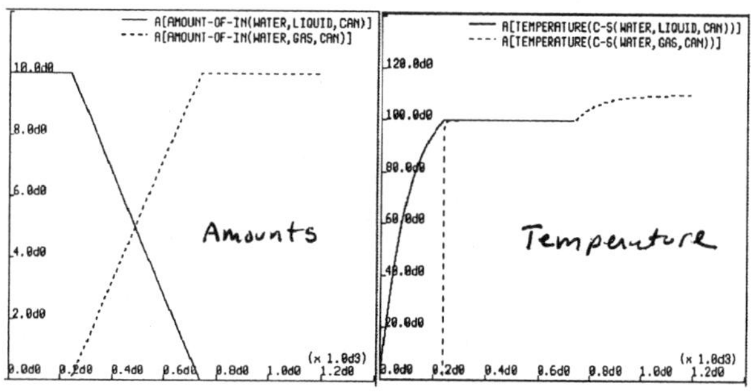


```
Q: Summarize the behavior
A: The initial state is S3. In S3 there is heat is
   flowing from STOVE to the water in CAN.

   The boiling temperature of WATER and the
   temperature of the water in CAN become equal,
   which leads to S1.  In S1, heat is flowing from
   STOVE to the water in CAN and the water in CAN
   is boiling.

   The amount of steam in CAN becomes positive,
   which leads to S16.   In S16, heat is flowing
   from STOVE to the water in CAN, heat is flowing
   from STOVE to the steam in CAN, and the water
   in CAN is boiling.

   The amount of water in CAN becomes zero,
   which leads to S4. In S4, heat is flowing
   from STOVE to the steam in CAN.

   The temperature of the steam in CAN and the
   temperature of STOVE become equal, which leads
   to S5.   In S5, nothing is happening.

Q: What is happening at t = 100.0 seconds?

A: Heat is flowing from STOVE to the water in CAN.

Q: What is the temperature of the steam?

A: Sorry, the temperature of the steam in CAN
   does not exist at 100.0 seconds.

Q: What happens next?

A: At 238.6 seconds the boiling temperature of WATER
   and the temperature of the water in CAN become
   equal.   Then, heat is flowing from STOVE to the
   water in CAN and the water in CAN is boiling.

Q: What else might have happened?

A: The only other possibility was: The temperature
   of the water in CAN and the temperature of STOVE
   become equal, which leads to S2.   In S2, nothing
   is happening.
```

Figure 4: Clashes between qualitative and quantitative models are detected.

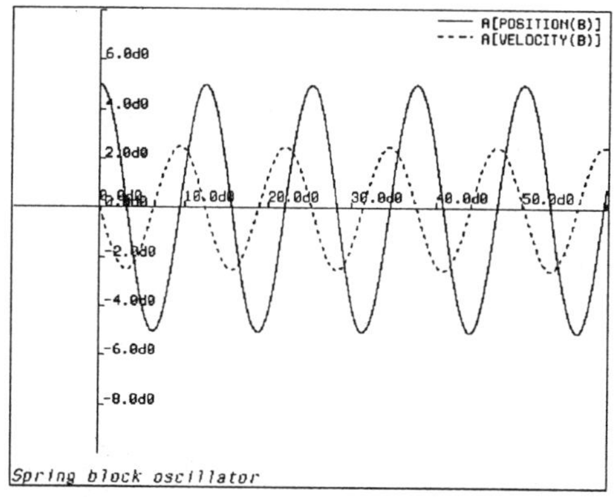


```
Q: Set up a run starting from S5 for 120.0 seconds,
   with dt = 0.001, using these parameters:
      VELOCITY(B) = 0.0
      REST-LENGTH(SPR) = 5.0
      POSITION(B) = 5.0
      MASS(B) = 1.0
      K(SPR) = -0.1
A: The values provided do not match S5.
   The differences are:
   (A (FORCE B)) is greater than zero,
   should be less than. No legal state.

Q: Show the equations for S5.
A: (= (ACC PIO) (/ (FORCE B) (MASS B)))
   (= (FORCE B) (FORCE SPR))
   (= (LENGTH SPR) (+ (POSITION B)
                      (REST-LENGTH SPR)))
   (= (FORCE SPR) (* (- (K SPR))
                     (- (LENGTH SPR)
                        (REST-LENGTH SPR))))
   (= (D (VELOCITY B)) (ACC PIO))

Q: Change K to be 0.1 and simulate.
A: Okay.
```

could handle the analogous fluid system, however. Modeling the nodes of a system as containers, and charge as something that flows between them, provides the basis for a QP-style causal account. Conversely, when the "stuff" flowing in a system has behaviors that cannot be captured in System Dynamics (such as phase changes and chemical properties), the device ontology is unsuitable. SIMGEN provides the most leverage where QP theory works best. For domains where time-varying differential equations are only part of the relevant mathematics, such as aerodynamic analyses, stability of structures, and other heavily geometric analyses, SIMGEN obviously provides little leverage.

So far we have discovered two kinds of difficulties in building math model libraries. First, we found ourselves using ever more sophisticated qualitative models in order to provide enough functional dependencies to yield reasonable numerical models. Second, many engineering formulations have evolved under the constraint of simplifying algebraic analyses, rather than supporting causal reasoning. For instance, heat is often not used as an explicit variable in today's formal thermodynamic analyses (those which refer directly to temperature), although textbooks often revert to employing heat in its commonsense usage when discussing difficult points. In any case, we believe the discipline imposed by supporting self-explanatory simulations should be viewed as an invigorating challenge, which will ensure that one's domain models will be both powerful and accurate.

Importantly, while an envisionment is needed to generate self-explanatory simulators, no new qualitative reasoning needs to occur during simulation. The qualitative knowledge is compiled into a set of procedures expressing its implications for the particular system. Given good optimization techniques, it seems self-explanatory simulators could become asymptotically close in speed to the best hand-written numerical simulators, despite their increased transparency and robustness.

5 Related Work

Several recent projects have focused on the relationship between qualitative and quantitative knowledge [23; 30; 27; 32]. None of these efforts focus on automatically constructing numerical simulators or explanation generation. The closest in spirit is [3], which also argues for a unification of qualitative and numerical simulation. We differ in most specifics, however: Berleant augments a `QSIM` representation with interval values for parameters to restrict behavior generation, while we co-evolve qualitative and numerical states. We generate simulations automatically, whereas `QSIM` models are hand-crafted, and we also focus on generating causal explanations, while Berleant focuses on constraining a-causal predictions.

Sussman's *Dynamicist's Workbench* project, which uses AI techniques to develop efficient numerical simulations from equational models, shares several of our concerns, including generating efficient code and producing understandable results. Their work complements ours in several ways. They have focused on sophisticated reasoning about numerical techniques [1] maximizing efficient computation [4], including compiling to special-purpose hardware [2]. But while the behaviors of the systems they are analyzing are subtle, they start with a single set of equations which governs the system for all time. By contrast, we have downplayed reasoning about numerical methods in favor of understanding how to automatically generate a system's equations from a physical model, including situations where the relevant set of equations changes over time, and on producing understandable explanations. We believe our work will benefit from their advances in numerical reasoning, while theirs will benefit from our use of qualitative reasoning to guide simulation construction and improved techniques for detecting clashes between qualitative and quantitative models.

Our compilation of qualitative knowledge into simulation procedures finds echos in [21], which describes the compilation of diagnosis and redesign rules from a general-purpose knowledge base of device models. In fact, the KSL group has proposed a *simulation foundry* which could create simulations from a knowledge base of physical models and structural equations [19]. `SIMGEN` can be viewed in part as an instantiation of this idea, although they did not anticipate our notion of self-explanatory simulations.

6 Discussion

We introduced a new kind of simulation, self-explanatory simulations, which blend qualitative and quantitative knowledge to provide several of the advantages of each. By using qualitative analysis to represent when different sets of equations are appropriate, we gain increased automation. By incorporating knowledge of what behaviors are reasonable into simulation code and co-evolving numerical and qualitative states we achieve improved self-monitoring. And by incorporating "compiled" knowledge from an envisionment, we are able to produce understandable explanations. Importantly, complex, first-principles reasoning can occur off-line – self-explanatory simulations can run at speeds which asymptotically approach standard numerical simulations.

While this method of integrating qualitative and quantitative knowledge is by no means the only one, we believe it is particularly important. For design, it is important to ensure that reasonable parameter values can result in the desired behaviors. For training, the value of numerical simulators is already well-established, but the incorporation of inexpensive explanation facilities can make them even more valuable. In developing models, either qualitative or numerical, of a new phenomena, checking the match between the model and your intuitions is an important task. By formulating intuitions explicitly in the form of qualitative models, self-explanatory simulations can help detect whether or not the behaviors predicted by a numerical model make sense.

6.1 Future Work

This research suggests several new possibilities:

Scaling up: Envisioning is not the only qualitative simulation technique which could support self-explanatory simulations. For example, given an incremental envisioner and simulation compiler, states and simulation procedures could be generated on the fly, just one step ahead of the current qualitative state. Or, if the structure of the system is extremely large and the run-time system must be kept simple, the simulator could be decomposed into subsystems. Q_f would be a vector of Q_f's for the subsystems, and the evolvers for the subsystems would be executed in concert to provide the effect of an evolver for the whole system. These and other alternatives need exploration.

Self-explanatory simulations for other kinds of qualitative physics: SIMGEN might be adapted to the device ontology. SIMGEN relies critically on two features of QP theory: the causal account provides the order of computation for parameters, and the use of quantified descriptions allows explicit modeling assumptions. The causal account in device ontologies is based on an identified input perturbation or signal, which is consistent with the use of specified inputs to drive numerical device-centered simulators such as SPICE [20]. It also seems possible to adapt many of the representational techniques of QP theory to give device-centered models the same ability to explicitly encode modeling assumptions. However, we leave such extensions for advocates of this ontology.

Tutor Compilers: Self-explanatory simulators could become a core component in a variety of computer-based tutors. By using SIMGEN with action-augmented envisionments [15], it may be possible to automatically construct a class of training simulators (such as STEAMER) automatically. By caching envisionment information and "cross-compiling", self-explanatory simulators could be built for delivery on inexpensive target hardware. Actually building a tutor compiler will require a great deal of work, including developing powerful domain models, developing better explanation generation systems, and support software such as graphical systems. However, we are very excited by the possibility of semi-automating the production of computer-based tutors.

7 Acknowledgements

This work was supported by the National Aeronautics and Space Administration Contract No. NAG 9408, and an equipment grant from IBM. We thank Gerald Sussman and Brian Williams for useful comments on this work and its presentation.

References

[1] Abelson, H. and Sussman, G. J. The Dynamicist's Workbench: I Automatic preparation of numerical experiments MIT AI Lab Memo No. 955, May, 1987.

[2] Abelson, H. et. al. Intelligence in Scientific Computing *Communications of the ACM* 32:546-562, 1989.

[3] Berleant, D. A unification of numerical and qualitative model simulation. *Proceedings of the 1989 Workshop on Model-Based Reasoning at IJCAI-89.*

[4] Berlin, A. A Compilation strategy for numerical programs based on partial evaluation MIT AI Lab Technical Report No. 1144, July, 1989.

[5] Christensen, P, Kofoed, J. and Larsen, N. PC-DYSIM - A program package for simulation of continuous dynamic processes: User's manual Technical Report Riso-I-342, Riso National Laboratory, DK-4000 Roskilde, Denmark, February, 1988

[6] Collins, J and Forbus, K. Building qualitative models of thermodynamic processes. Technical report in progress.

[7] deKleer, J. and Brown, J. S. A qualitative physics based on confluences. *Artificial Intelligence*, 24:7–83, 1984.

[8] deKleer, J. and Brown, J. S. Theories of causal ordering *Artificial Intelligence*, 29:33-62 1986.

[9] Falkenhainer, B and Forbus, K. D. Setting up large-scale qualitative models. In *Proceedings of AAAI-88.*

[10] Falkenhainer, B. and Forbus, K. D. Compositional Modeling: Finding the right model for the job *Submitted for publication*, February, 1990.

[11] Forbus, K. An interactive laboratory for teaching control system concepts BBN Tech Report No. 5511, 1984.

[12] Forbus, K. D. Qualitative process theory. *Artificial Intelligence*, 24, 1984.

[13] Forbus, K. The logic of occurrence. *Proceedings of IJCAI-87.*

[14] Forbus, K. D. The qualitative process engine in *Readings in Qualitative Reasoning about Physical Systems*, Weld, D. and de Kleer, J. (Eds.), 1989.

[15] Forbus, K. D. Introducing actions into qualitative simulation. *Proceedings of IJCAI-89.*

[16] Forbus, K. and Stevens, A. Using qualitative simulation to generate explanations. *Proceedings of the Third Annual Conference of the Cognitive Science Society*, 1981.

[17] Hollan, J, Hutchins, E, and Weitzman, L. STEAMER: An interactive inspectable simulation-based training system. *AI Magazine*, Summer 1984.

[18] Iwasaki, I. and Simon, H. "Causality in device behavior", *Artificial Intelligence*, **29**, 1986.

[19] Iwasaki, Y., Doshi, K.,Gruber, T.,Keller, R., and Low, C. M. Equation model generation: Where do equations come from? *Proceedings of the 1989 Workshop on Model-Based Reasoning at IJCAI-89.*

[20] Katzenelson, J. AEDNET: A simulator for nonlinear networks *Proceedings of the IEEE*, Vol 54, No. 11, November, 1966.

[21] Keller, R., Baudin, C.,Iwasaki, Y., Nayak, P. and Tanaka, K. Compiling special-purpose rules for general-purpose device models Stanford Knowledge Systems Laboratory Report No. KSL 89-50, June, 1989.

[22] Kuipers, B. Qualitative simulation. *Artificial Intelligence*, 29:289–338, 1986.

[23] Kuipers, B. and Berleant, D. Using incomplete quantitative knowledge in qualitative reasoning Proceedings of AAAI-88, St. Paul, Minnesota, 1988.

[24] Larsen, N. Simulation model of a PWR power plant Technical Report Riso-M-2640, Riso National Laboratory, DK-4000 Roskilde, Denmark, March, 1987

[25] Roberts, B. and Forbus, K. The STEAMER mathematical simulation. BBN Tech Report No. 4625, 1981.

[26] Shearer, J., Murphy, A. and Richardson, H. *Introduction to System Dynamics*, Addison-Wesley, 1971.

[27] Skorstad, G. G and Forbus, K. D. Qualitative and quantitative reasoning about thermodynamics. In *Proceedings of the Eleventh Annual Conference of the Cognitive Science Society*, Ann Arbor, MI, August 1989.

[28] Stevens, A., Roberts, B., Stead, L. Forbus, K., Steinberg, C., Smith, B. "STEAMER: Advanced computer-aided instruction in propulsion engineering", BBN Technical report, July, 1981

[29] Williams, B. Qualitative analysis of MOS circuits. *Artificial Intelligence*, 24:281–346, 1984.

[30] Williams, B. MINIMA. A symbolic approach to qualitative algebraic reasoning. *Proceedings of AAAI-88.*

[31] Woolf, B., Blegen, D., Jansen, J., and Verloop, A. Teaching a complex industrial process *AAAI-86.*

[32] Yip, K. Generating global behaviors using deep knowledge of local dynamics *Proceedings of AAAI-88.*

Obtaining Quantitative Predictions From Monotone Relationships

Joseph Hellerstein

IBM T. J. Watson Research Center
P.O. Box 704
Yorktown Heights, New York 10598
jlh@ibm.com

Abstract

Quantitative predictions are typically obtained by characterizing a system in terms of algebraic relationships and then using these relationships to compute quantitative predictions from numerical data. For real-life systems, such as mainframe operating systems, an algebraic characterization is often difficult, if not intractable. This paper proposes a statistical approach to obtaining quantitative predictions from monotone relationships -- non-parametric interpolative-prediction for monotone functions (NIMF). NIMF uses monotone relationships to search historical data for bounds that provide a desired level of statistical confidence. We evaluate NIMF by comparing its predictions to those of linear least-squares regression (a widely-used statistical technique that requires specifying algebraic relationships) for memory contention in an IBM computer system. Our results suggest that using an accurate monotone relationship can produce better quantitative predictions than using an approximate algebraic relationship.

1. Introduction

Numerical or quantitative predictions of system behavior are frequently required in tasks such as forecasting, diagnosis, and planning. Typically, quantitative predictions are obtained by characterizing a system in terms of algebraic relationships and then using these relationships to compute quantitative predictions from numerical data. Unfortunately, for real-life systems an algebraic characterization is often difficult, if not intractable. This paper describes an approach to obtaining quantitative predictions from monotone relationships, and applies this approach to predicting memory contention in an IBM computer system.

Why is it often so difficult to obtain accurate algebraic characterizations of real-life systems? Our experience with analyzing measurements of computer systems, in particular the IBM operating system Virtual Machine/System Product (VM/SP), suggests that the major impediment to an algebraic characterization is the absence of sufficiently detailed information about the system's operation. For example, the performance of VM/SP systems is often constrained by contention for the first sixteen megabytes of main memory (referred to as **low memory**), even though there may be sixty-four megabytes or more of main memory. Low-memory contention is a consequence of the operating system using twenty-four bit addressing and requiring that many system services use memory that is directly addressable by the operating system. A key indicator of low-memory contention is the rate at which pages below sixteen megabytes are taken from users in the multi-programming set. Constructing an algebraic relationship between this measure and parameters such as the virtual machine input/output rate and the number of logged-on users requires using these parameters to quantify the frequency and execution times of operating-system service-requests (e.g., spool operations, messages exchanged through the inter-user communication vehicle, and file opens) as well as the low-memory demands of each service requested (e.g., bytes required, page and/or cache alignments, and algorithm used when fixed-sized pools are empty). Unfortunately, such detailed information is rarely available.

When we are unable to construct algebraic relationships, we often have qualitative knowledge in the form of monotone relationships. For example, in VM/SP intuition and experience strongly suggest that low-memory contention increases with the virtual machine input/output rate and the number of logged-on users. Another example in CPU-bound VM/SP systems is the relationship between response time and a workload characterized by CPU utilization and the rate of small transactions. Again, an algebraic characterization appears to be intractable; however, we expect response time to decrease with the rate of small transactions (since more small transactions means fewer large ones, in a resource-constrained system) and to increase with CPU utilization. Still other examples where monotone relationships apply but algebraic relationships are difficult to construct include the following: relating lock contention to user activity, relating disk operations to the virtual machine input/output rate, and relating working set size to the virtual machine input/output rate and CPU demands.

If an accurate algebraic characterization of the system is unavailable, how can we obtain quantitative predictions? One approach is to approximate the unknown algebraic relationship by a simple function, such as a polynomial. Herein, we present an alternative approach in which quantitative predictions are computed directly from monotone relationships. Our experience with this approach, as shown in section 3, suggests that using an accurate monotone relationship frequently results in better predictions than using an approximate algebraic relationship.

Our approach to prediction is statistical. Referred to as *non-parametric interpolative-prediction for monotone functions (NIMF)*, our approach assumes the existence of historical data, which is appropriate for domains such as computer performance, financial analysis, and demographic studies. Often, the historical data is highly variable; indeed, providing a point estimate (e.g., an expected value) may be meaningless. For this reason, NIMF produces *prediction intervals* at a user-specified *confidence level* (e.g., 75%). A prediction interval consists of a lower bound (y_L) and an upper bound (y_H), with the following interpretation: The probability that the predicted value lies between y_L and y_H is at least as large as the confidence level. NIMF uses monotone relationships to search the historical data for y_L and y_H.

Monotone relationships have been used in many contexts, such as predicting changes in qualitative state (e.g., (Forbus, 1984), (Kuipers, 1986), and (DeKleer84)), monitoring dynamic systems (Dvorak and Kuipers, 1989), and explaining quantitative predictions produced by algebraic relationships (e.g., (Apte and Hong, 1986)). More recently, there has been interest in the probabilistic semantics of qualitative influences (Wellman, 1987) and probabilistic considerations in qualitative simulation ((Dvorak and Sacks, 1989)). Our work further extends the application of monotone relationships by demonstrating their use in quantitative, statistical prediction for situations in which numerical data are available but an algebraic characterization is intractable.

The remainder of this paper is organized as follows. Section 2 describes the NIMF technique. Section 3 evaluates NIMF by comparing its predictions to those of least-squares regression, a widely-used statistical technique that requires specifying algebraic relationships. Our conclusions are contained in section 4.

2. Approach

Our approach to obtaining quantitative predictions from monotone relationships was motivated by observations of performance analyst who tune VM/SP computer systems. One aspect of tuning is workload assignment, in which users of computing services are assigned to one of several computer systems in a manner so that computing resources (e.g., CPU, input/output bandwidth, and memory) are utilized within prescribed guidelines. Clearly, this task requires an ability to predict the resource utilizations of an assignment. The most common approach to predicting the performance of computer systems is based on queueing theory (Kleinrock, 1975). Queueing theory characterizes computer systems in terms of stochastic processes, which permits deriving algebraic relationships between measurement variables. While queueing theory has proven effective for modeling "active" resources (e.g., CPU, input/output operations), it has not been particularly effective for modeling "passive" resources, such as memory. In large VM/SP computer systems, contention for low memory is often the primary performance bottleneck.

How then do performance analysts predict low-memory contention? Lacking a formal approach to the problem, analysts often use an informal approach. We illustrate this by predicting **LOSTEALRAT** (the rate at which pages in low memory are taken from users in the multi-programming set) from **LOGGED** (the number of logged-on users) and **VIO** (virtual machine input/output rate). (All three variables can be obtained from the Virtual Machine Monitor Analysis Program (VMMAP) (IBM, 1985).) Suppose that a workload assignment would result in a computer system having an average of 500 logged-on users with an average aggregate VIO rate of 500. Although we know of no algebraic equation that relates LOSTEALRAT to LOGGED and VIO, we do have an excellent understanding in terms monotone relationships. Specifically, for each logged-on user, data structures are allocated in low memory to describe the virtual address space; so we expect LOSTEALRAT to increase with LOGGED. Further, each VIO re-

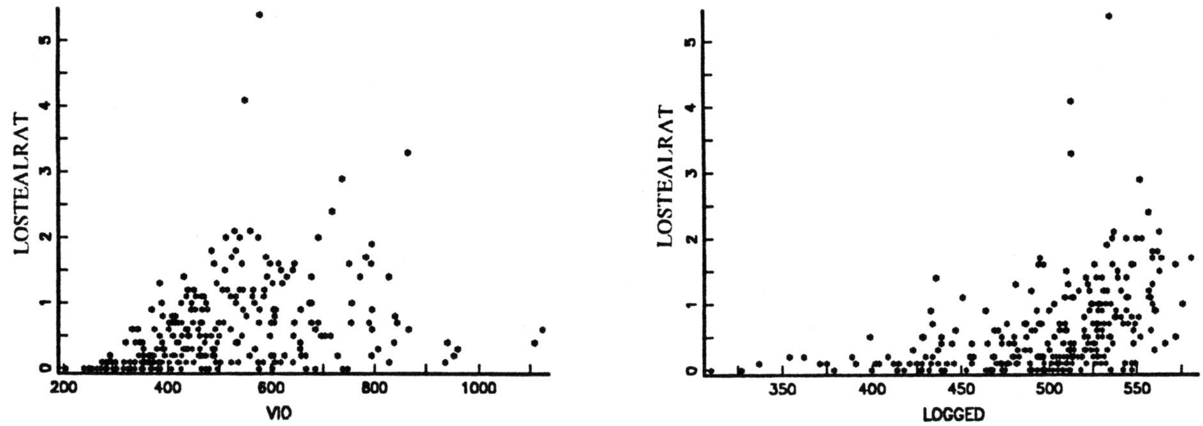

Figure 1. Scatter plots

quires that transient data structures be allocated in low memory, and so LOSTEALRAT should increase with VIO as well. That is,

MR_1: `LOSTEALRAT increases with VIO and LOGGED.`

MR_1 provides analysts with an approach to searching historical data for potential bounds. For example, to find a lower bound for the point VIO = 500 and LOGGED = 500, the analyst considers data for which VIO $\leq$ 500 and LOGGED $\leq$ 500. Similarly, finding an upper bound involves examining data for which VIO $\geq$ 500 and LOGGED $\geq$ 500.

Once the sets of potential bounds are identified, analysts often resort to heuristics, such as setting y_L to the largest element in the set of potential lower bounds and y_H to the smallest element in the set of potential upper bounds. Unfortunately, such heuristics do not indicate the confidence level of the resulting prediction interval, and they certainly do not permit choosing bounds so that a particular confidence level is achieved.

Translating the above approach into a formal statistical technique requires that we address randomness in the measurement data. For example, Figure 1 displays scatter plots of LOSTEALRAT vs. LOGGED and LOSTEALRAT vs. VIO for measurements taken from a VM/SP computer system; these plots suggest a high degree of randomness. We say that a monotone relationship exists between the **response variable** y (e.g., LOSTEALRAT) and the **explanatory variables** $x_1, \ldots, x_J$ (e.g., x_1 = VIO and x_2 = LOGGED) if, and only if, there is a monotone function g such that

$$y_i = g(\mathbf{x}_i) + \varepsilon_i, \tag{1}$$

where y_i is the i-th measurement of the response variable, $\mathbf{x}_i = (x_{i,1}, \ldots, x_{i,J})$ is the i-th measurement of the explanatory variables, and ε_i is the i-th error term. Randomness is handled by the ε_i, which are assumed to be realizations of continuous, independent, and identically distributed random variables. We make no assumption about g's functional form. However, we do assume that g's **directional effects** are known; that is, for the j-th explanatory variable (x_j), we know if g is non-increasing or non-decreasing. (If g is differentiable, this is equivalent to knowing the sign of g's first derivatives.) Since we do not assume that error terms are drawn from a specific distribution and we make no assumption about g's functional form, our approach is *non-parametric*. Further, the approach that we will describe is appropriate only if there are existing measurements within the region in which a prediction is desired; that is, our approach provides interpolation, not extrapolation. These characteristics of our approach as well as its being applicable only to monotone functions motivate the name *non-parametric interpolative-prediction for monotone functions (NIMF)*.

The NIMF procedure takes as input

- $\mathbf{x}^*$ - values of explanatory variables at which a prediction is desired
- a description of g in terms of its directional effects
- $(\mathbf{x}_1, y_1), \ldots, (\mathbf{x}_I, y_I)$ - historical data containing values of explanatory variables paired with the corresponding value of the response variable

NIMF computes prediction intervals by finding a lower bound (y_L) and an upper bound (y_H) for the unknown response (Y^*) such that

$$P(y_L \leq Y^* \leq y_H) \geq 1 - \alpha, \tag{2}$$

where $1 - \alpha$ is the desired confidence level. Typical values for $1 - \alpha$ are 75%, 90%, or 95%.

NIMF consists of three steps. The first step selects sets of potential bounds by using the monotone relationship that describes g. This is accomplished by observing that a monotone relationship imposes a partial order on values of explanatory variables. Specifically, given $\mathbf{x}_1$ and $\mathbf{x}_2$, the partial order $\mathbf{x}_1 \prec \mathbf{x}_2$ holds if, and only if, the following relationship is present for all explanatory variables (x_j):

- $x_{1j} \leq x_{2j}$, if g is non-decreasing in x_j
- $x_{1j} \geq x_{2j}$, if g is non-increasing in x_j

The **set of potential lower bounds**, S_L, is the subset of $\{y_i \mid \mathbf{x}_i \prec \mathbf{x}^*\}$ that consists of the M y_i whose $\mathbf{x}_i$ are closest to $\mathbf{x}^*$. ("Closest to" is defined as the Euclidean distance measure normalized by standard deviation.) By picking $\mathbf{x}_i$ close to $\mathbf{x}^*$, we hope to reduce $|g(\mathbf{x}_i) - g(\mathbf{x}^*)|$ and hence reduce the width of prediction intervals. The **set of potential upper bounds**, S_H, is a subset of $\{y_i \mid \mathbf{x}^* \prec \mathbf{x}_i\}$, and is chosen in the same manner as S_L.

NIMF's second and third steps select y_L from S_L and y_H from S_H in a manner so that at least a $1 - \alpha$ confidence level is obtained. Our approach is similar to that taken by Bradley (1968) to obtain confidence intervals for distribution percentiles. Assuming that $y_L \leq y_H$, it suffices to pick y_L and y_H such that

$$P(y_L \leq Y^*) \geq 1 - \frac{\alpha}{2}$$
$$P(y_H \geq Y^*) \geq 1 - \frac{\alpha}{2}$$

To find y_L, we proceed by considering its components. Let $y_i \in S_L$, with $y_i = g(\mathbf{x}_i) + \varepsilon_i$. If g is monotone and we know the directional effect of each x_j, then $g(\mathbf{x}_i) \leq g(\mathbf{x}^*)$ (by construction). So

$$\begin{aligned} P(y_i \leq Y^*) &= P(g(\mathbf{x}_i) + \varepsilon_i \leq g(\mathbf{x}^*) + \varepsilon^*) \\ &\geq P(\varepsilon_i \leq \varepsilon^*) \\ &= .5. \end{aligned}$$

(The last step is a result of the error terms being continuous, independent, and identically distributed.) Let $N_L = size(S_L)$, and let $E_{L,k}$ be the event that at least k elements in S_L are smaller than Y^*. Since the ε_i are realizations of independent and identically distributed random variables, the binomial distribution applies:

$$P(E_{L,k}) \geq \sum_{k=n}^{N_L} \binom{N_L}{n} .5^{N_L}$$

Let $y_{L,k}$ be the k-th smallest element in S_L. A key observation is that the event $E_{L,k}$ is equivalent to the event that $y_{L,k} \leq Y^*$(Waite, 1987) . Hence,

$$P(y_{L,k} \leq Y^*) \geq \sum_{k=n}^{N_L} \binom{N_L}{n} .5^{N_L}.$$

NIMF's second step finds k_L such that

$$P(y_{L,k_L} \leq Y^*) \geq 1 - \frac{\alpha}{2},$$

and k_H such that

$$P(y_{H,k_H} \geq Y^*) \geq 1 - \frac{\alpha}{2}.$$

To minimize the width of prediction intervals, NIMF finds the largest k_L and the smallest k_H that satisfy the above inequalities. In its third step, NIMF selects the prediction interval bounds; $y_L = y_{L,k_L}$ and $y_H = y_{H,k_H}$.

We illustrate the second and third steps of the NIMF procedure by computing a prediction interval for LOSTEALRAT when VIO = 500 and LOGGED = 500. Let $1 - \alpha = 75\%$, and assume that the following potential-bounds sets have been constructed:

$$\begin{aligned} S_L &= \{0, .1, .2, .3, .6, 1.2\} \\ S_H &= \{.5, .7, 1.1., 1.4, 1.5, 1.6\} \end{aligned} \tag{3}$$

From Eq. (3), we see that both sets have six elements, so $N_L = N_H = 6$. Let $\phi(N, \alpha)$ be defined as follows

$$\phi(N, \alpha) = \max \{k \mid \sum_{n=k}^{N} \binom{N}{n} .5^N \geq 1 - \frac{\alpha}{2}\}. \tag{4}$$

Then,

$$\begin{aligned} k_L &= \phi(N_L, \alpha) \\ &= \phi(6, .25), \end{aligned}$$

Or,

$$\phi(6, .25) = \max \{k \mid \sum_{n=k}^{6} \binom{6}{n} .5^6 \geq .875\}.$$

Performing the necessary computations, we determine that $k_L = 2$. For k_H, we have

$$\begin{aligned} k_H &= N_H - \phi(N_H, \alpha) + 1 \\ &= 6 - 2 + 1 \\ &= 5. \end{aligned}$$

We use these indexes to find the prediction interval bounds; y_L is the second smallest element in S_L, and

y_H is the fifth smallest element in S_H. That is, $y_L = .1$, and $y_H = 1.5$.

NIMF's ability to produce prediction intervals depends on the historical data provided and the monotone relationships used. When NIMF cannot compute a lower bound, $y_L = -\infty$; when an upper bound cannot be computed, $y_H = \infty$. One situation in which NIMF cannot produce a bound is when there is insufficient historical data; that is, N_L (N_H) is so small that $k_L = 0$ ($k_H = N_H + 1$) at the $1 - \alpha$ confidence level. In most computer installations, data are cheap to collect and plentiful; so a missing bound can often be obtained by simply including more data. Alternatively, the analyst can reduce the confidence level.

There is a second situation in which NIMF can produce prediction intervals, but the results are inconsistent with the monotone relationship. This situation occurs when $y_L > y_H$. A statistically valid prediction interval can be produced by taking y_L to be the smaller bound and y_H to be the larger bound. However, our feeling is that this situation suggests an error in the underlying model, which should be surfaced to the user.

3. Case Study

This section presents a case study in which NIMF's predictions are compared to those of linear least-squares regression (hereafter, just *regression*), a widely-used statistical technique that requires an algebraic specification of variable relationships (Draper and Smith, 1968). We compare NIMF and regression by using the data in Figure 1 as the historical data from which NIMF potential-bounds sets are obtained and regression constants are estimated. Prediction intervals are then constructed at values of VIO and LOGGED (the $\mathbf{x}^*$ variables) contained in separately acquired test data; the test data also include measurements of LOSTEALRAT at each $\mathbf{x}^*$, which we use to evaluate the prediction intervals.

Prediction intervals are typically evaluated based on two criteria:

- coverage (percent of LOSTEALRAT values in the test data that lie in their prediction interval)
- prediction interval width

Since confidence level is a user-specified parameter, coverage is viewed as a constraint rather than an optimization criteria. So, the preferred technique is the one that minimizes prediction interval width subject to the constraint that coverage is at least as large as the specified confidence level.

First, we briefly describe the regression procedure. A regression model takes the same form as Eq. (1), but stronger assumptions are made: g's functional form must be known, and (to obtain prediction intervals) ε_i must be normally distributed. A functional form is an algebraic relationship with unknown constants. For example,

$$\hat{y}_i = b_0 + b_1 L_i + b_2 V_i \tag{5}$$

Where:

$\hat{y}_i$ = i-th estimated LOSTEALRAT
L_i = i-th measured LOGGED
V_i = i-th measured VIO

Here, the unknown constants are the b_j. In essence, regression is a curve-fitting technique: Unknown constants are estimated by using the historical data to find values that minimize the total squared error, where $\varepsilon_i = y_i - \hat{y}_i$. The quality of a regression model can be evaluated by R^2, which is the fraction of the response variability that is accounted for by the regression model.

To compare NIMF and regression, we need to construct models using both approaches. A NIMF model is a monotone relationship; we use MR_1. For regression, the choice of model is more difficult since we must specify an algebraic relationship for an unknown g. Our approach is to approximate g by an n-degree polynomial. We choose n by considering polynomials of increasing degree until there is no improvement in R^2. Equation 5 is a first degree polynomial. Below are second and third degree polynomials.

$$\hat{y}_i = b_0' + b_1' L_i + b_2' V_i + b_3' L_i^2 + b_4' L_i V_i + b_5' V_i^2 \tag{6}$$

$$\hat{y}_i = b_0'' + b_1'' L_i + b_2'' V_i + b_3'' L_i^2 + b_4'' L_i V_i + b_5'' V_i^2 + b_6'' L_i^3 + b_7'' L_i^2 V_i + b_8'' L_i V_i^2 + b_9'' V_i^3 \tag{7}$$

For the data in Figure 1, the R^2 for Eq. (5) is .26; for Eq. (6), .34; and for Eq. (7), .37. A fourth degree polynomial showed no increase in R^2; so we use Eq. (7).

Figure 2 plots 75% prediction intervals for the test data, both for regression and for NIMF[1]. The plots show the measured value of LOSTEALRAT for each

1 We use $M = 20$.

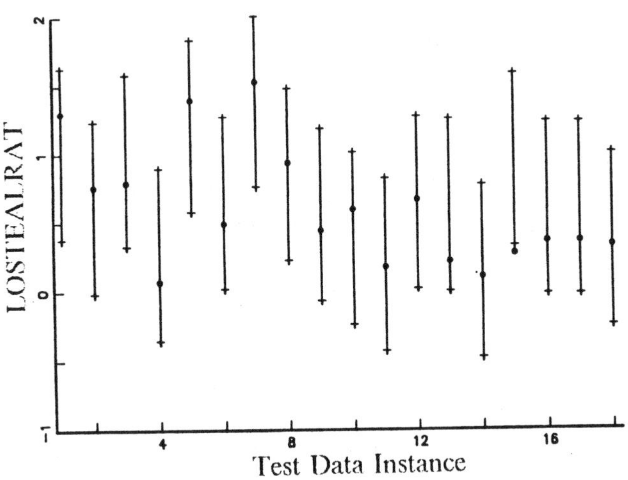

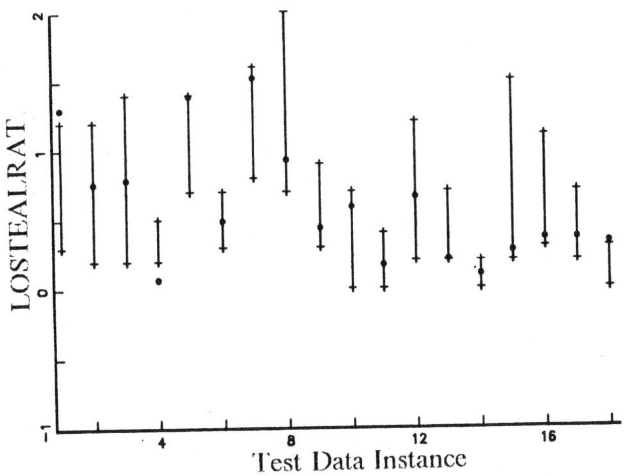

Figure 2. Prediction Intervals

test-data instance (depicted by a dot) and the associated prediction interval (indicated by a vertical line with a horizontal bar at each end). Both techniques achieve adequate coverage: 94% for regression and 83% for NIMF. However, the average width of NIMF prediction intervals (.58) is less than half that of the regression prediction intervals (1.25). Also, in several instances the regression prediction interval includes negative values, which is impossible for LOSTEALRAT (a rate). In contrast, NIMF prediction intervals are constrained to lie within the measured data; so NIMF predicts only non-negative values for LOSTEALRAT.

The foregoing is one of eighteen case studies in which we compared NIMF to regression using measurements of VM/SP computer systems (Hellerstein, 1987). The results of the other studies parallel those contained in Figure 2: In all cases adequate coverage is provided by both techniques, but NIMF consistently (17 out of 18 case studies) produces smaller prediction intervals.

Why does NIMF produce smaller prediction intervals? One reason is that regression assumes a specific algebraic relationship between the response and explanatory variables. If the wrong equation is chosen, then the fit is poor and prediction intervals are large. This shortcoming can, in part, be avoided by using other curve fitting techniques (e.g., cubic splines), which consider families of curves. However, these techniques still implicitly assume algebraic relationships, and are complex to apply to multivariate data. *NIMF avoids these problems by not making any assumption about the form of the unknown monotone function.* Instead, NIMF uses the function's monotonicity to construct sets of potential bounds from which prediction-interval end-points are selected.

4. Conclusions

Frequently, we require quantitative predictions for systems in which numerical data are available but the following situation exists:

- There is no known algebraic characterization for the system.
- The system can be characterized easily in terms of monotone relationships.

One could obtain quantitative predictions by approximating the unknown algebraic relationship by a simple function, such as a polynomial. This paper presents an alternative approach: generating quantitative predictions directly from monotone relationships.

Our approach, non-parametric interpolative-prediction for monotone functions (NIMF), is statistical, and hence assumes the presence of historical data (which is reasonable for domains such as computer performance, financial analysis, and demographic studies). NIMF uses the partial order imposed by a monotone relationship to construct sets of potential bounds; S_L is the set of potential lower bounds, and S_H is the set of potential upper bounds. A simple technique based on non-parametric statistics is then employed to select the lower bound of the prediction interval (y_L) from S_L, and the upper bound (y_H) from S_H.

Do we obtain better predictions by using an accurate monotone relationship instead of an approximate algebraic relationship? Although the answer depends on many factors (e.g., the system being studied and the approximation used), our experience with predicting low-memory contention in VM/SP suggests that using an accurate monotone relationship with the NIMF procedure can produce significantly better predictions than using a polynomial approximation of the unknown algebraic relationship and employing least-squares regression. Admittedly, NIMF's superior results are not solely a consequence of using monotone relationships instead of algebraic relationships, since NIMF also makes weaker assumptions about the distribution of error terms. However, avoiding unnecessary assumptions about algebraic relationships is clearly an advantage in terms of predictive accuracy. Also, using monotone relationships simplifies model building and greatly facilitates explaining predictions.

NIMF has been implemented in APL and Prolog; the results presented here are from the Prolog implementation. Prolog is a particularly good implementation language for NIMF since monotone relationships are easily expressed as facts, and simple predicates can be used to find the sets of potential bounds.

Acknowledgements

We wish to thank Robert Berry and William W. White for their helpful comments.

References

Chidanand Apte & Se June Hong. (1986) Using Qualitative Reasoning to Understand Financial Arithmetic. *Proceedings of the Fifth National Conference on Artificial Intelligence*, pages 942-948.

James Bradley. (1968) *Distribution-Free Statistical Tests*. Prentice-Hall.

Johan De Kleer and John Seely Brown. (1984) A Qualitative Physics Based on Confluences. *Artificial Intelligence*, **24**, 7-83.

N. R. Draper & H. Smith. (1968) *Applied Regression Analysis*. John Wiley & Sons.

Daniel Dvorak & Benjamin Kuipers. (1989) Model-Based Monitoring of Dynamic Systems. *Proceedings of the Eleventh International Joint Conference on Artificial Intelligence*, pages 1238-1243.

Daniel Dvorak & Elisha P. Sacks. (1989) Stochastic Analysis of Qualitative Dynamics. *Proceedings of the Eleventh International Joint Conference on Artificial Intelligence*, pages 1187-1192.

Kenneth D. Forbus. (1984) Qualitative Process Theory. *Artificial Intelligence*, **24**, 85-168.

Joseph Hellerstein. (1987) An Intuitive Approach to Performance Prediction with Application to Workload Management in VS SP/HPO. *Proceedings of the Computer Measurement Group*, **December**, 53-63.

IBM. (1985) *Virtual Machine Monitor Analysis Program: User's Guide and Reference*. IBM Corporation, (SC34-2166).

Leonard Kleinrock. (1975) *Queueing Systems, Volume 1*. John Wiley.

Benjamin Kuipers. (1986) Qualitative Simulation. *Artificial Intelligence*, **29**, 289-338.

Norman Waite. (1987) Two Non-Parametric Confidence Intervals. Yorktown Heights, New York: IBM Corp. RC 13268.

Michael P. Wellman. (1987) Probabilistic Semantics for Qualitative Influences. *Proceedings of the Sixth National Conference on Artificial Intelligence*, pages 660-664.

Shifting Ontological Perspectives in Reasoning about Physical Systems

Zheng-Yang Liu & Arthur M. Farley
Department of Computer and Information Science
University of Oregon, Eugene, OR 97403
liu@cs.uoregon.edu art@cs.uoregon.edu

Abstract

Commitment to an ontological perspective is a primary aspect of reasoning about the physical world. For complex analytic tasks, the ability to switch between different ontologies to represent the same target system can be critical. Supplementing the standard device ontology for electronic circuits, we outline elements of a charge-carrier (CC) ontology for reasoning about electronics. Having two ontologies extends our range of reasoning, but raises the issue of how to control their application. We propose a set of ontological-choice rules to govern the process of ontological shift and demonstrate its effectiveness with examples involving the two ontologies in reasoning about electronic circuits.

Introduction

In order to reason about a physical system, we must be able to describe the structure and behavior of the system within some representational language. Such a description is generally called a model of the system (de Kleer & Brown 1984, Davis & Hamscher 1988). Whatever representational language we use, a model embodies separate entities which we use to designate the "things" in the world, the conceptions which we have about them, and the interrelationships that exist among them. We refer to the individual entities - terms, predicates, and axioms - as organized in the representational language as an ontology. An ontology determines "what there is" in the world (Munitz 1974). The world is initially unlabeled. Division into conceptual entities is made by us with respect to specific ontological choices.

It follows that a physical system can be described from several, distinct ontological perspectives. For example, Hayes (1985) identifies two distinct ontologies for reasoning about liquids. He notices that sometimes an engineer thinks of "the liquid in the container" as an object (the contained-stuff ontology) while at other times thinking about a hypothetical collection of molecules traveling together through the system as an object (the piece-of-stuff ontology). Consequently, the two ontologies involve different language forms as terms, predicates, and axioms. When one uses the contained-stuff ontology for liquids, the terms available include "volume", "pressure" and so on. These terms are not applicable to the piece-of-stuff ontology for liquids, which refers to "fixed mass", "spatiotemporal position", "velocity", etc.

Employing a particular language form to describe a physical object is equivalent to committing to a particular ontological choice (Munitz 1974, Hayes 1985). If we require a term as an important means for reasoning, then whatever type of universe is needed to define this term is the universe to which we are committed. For example, as soon as we use the term "pressure" to describe a liquid, we have committed to the contained-stuff ontology for liquids with "pressure" defined by the set of predicates and axioms therein. Such an ontological commitment leads to a particular perspective for modeling and subsequent analysis of the real world systems. We just cannot analyze a physical system in the world without committing ourselves to an ontological choice. This is an inherent fact of reasoning: true for us and true for artificial systems.

The purpose of this paper is to present an outline of a theory for ontological shift in reasoning about the physical world. While the theory we develop is domain-independent, the discussion here focuses on reasoning about electronic circuits. Below, we first introduce a charge-carrier (CC) ontology that supplements the standard device ontology for modeling and reasoning about electronic circuits. We then discuss how ontological shift is made possible through bridging relations. Finally, we present ontological-choice rules that guide the selection of proper ontological perspectives when generating qualitative causal explanations of circuit behavior in an automated qualitative simulation environment.

Two Ontological Choices for Circuits

Drawing on the rich literature from qualitative physics of electronic circuits, we find that most work has focused on the device ontology (de Kleer & Brown 1984). This is largely due to the need to describe each individual device and its connections with other devices in the circuit. Mirroring the engineering paradigm of system dynamics (Shearer, et al. 1971), the approach is to model a system in terms of its component devices and their interconnections with qualitative differential equations (confluences) involving macroscopic concepts such as "voltage", "current", and "resistance". The axioms at this level essentially represent aspects of Ohm's Law and Kirchoff's Laws.

The device ontology of electronic circuits can generate a wide range of causal explanations. We do not cover details of this ontology here. They are well discussed in (de Kleer & Brown 1984, de Kleer 1984, Williams 1984, White & Frederiksen 1986, Douglas & Liu 1989).

Unfortunately, device-ontology models of electronic circuits cannot answer some basic questions that relate structures to behaviors, such as "Why does the current through a resistor increase when the voltage across it increases?" or "Why changing the length or cross-sectional area of a resistor affect the current through it, even if the voltage across it remain constant?" Although a device-ontology model correctly describes what the device's behavior is, it typically cannot explain why it behaves the way it does. In short, it represents "compiled knowledge" about the circuit components' behaviors.

To explain why an electronic device behaves in a certain way requires an appreciation of the forces that act upon charge carriers inside the device and the effects on charge-carrier movements from externally applied bias voltages. The explanation process of a qualitative and causal analysis program should have the alternative of shifting to this form of reasoning. Below, we introduce a charge-carrier ontology to reason about electronics to address these issues.

In the charge-carrier (CC) ontology, the basic function of an electronic device is viewed as that of controlling the movement of electric charge carriers, such as electrons (or holes). The primitives for the CC ontology include concepts such as "field", "force", "velocity", "charge-flow", etc. The central notion in the CC ontology is the charge-carrier collection. Considering individual charge carriers would be prohibitive and unnecessary since all positive or negative charge carriers act alike. Considering an anonymous collection of charge carriers as one individual greatly reduces the complexity of modeling their behavior. Thus, a CC collection is similar in spirit to Collins and Forbus's (1987) molecular collection (MC).

We introduce the notion of *region* as a common level of structural description for both the device ontology and the CC ontology. Being a conceptual structural unit, a region is denoted as $\mathbb{R}(p,n)$, where p and n stand for the positive and negative poles of the region, respectively. Structural aggregation can be performed over regions as needed. Specifically, two regions are in series when they share a common pole, one using it as its positive pole and the other as its negative pole. Two regions are in parallel if they share the same two poles. Thus, a region may consist of any number of sub-regions, connected either in series, or parallel, or in mixed ways. By definition, the behavior of a region is a composition of the behaviors of its sub-regions.

When considered as occupying a cylindrical piece of space, a region $\mathbb{R}(p,n)$ has two features that capture its physical shape: length, $L(p,n)$, and cross-sectional area, $A(p,n)$. Likewise, a pole, p, when considered as a two-dimensional surface, has two features: surface area, Sp, and unit charge, Qp. Figure 1 shows a region's field description. A subset of the axioms of the CC ontology is presented as follows (a more detailed description of the CC ontology is available in (Liu 1989)):

CC-Axiom 1: (Field, Charge, and Region's length)
$$\partial E(p,n) = \partial Qp - \partial L(p,n).$$
CC-Axiom 2: (Electric force and Field)
$$\partial F(p,n) = \partial E(p,n).$$
CC-Axiom 3: (CC motion velocity and Electric force)
$$\partial v(p,n) = \partial F(p,n).$$
CC-Axiom 4: (Charge flow, Region's cross-section, and CC Velocity)
$$\partial C(p,n) = \partial A(p,n) + \partial v(p,n).$$

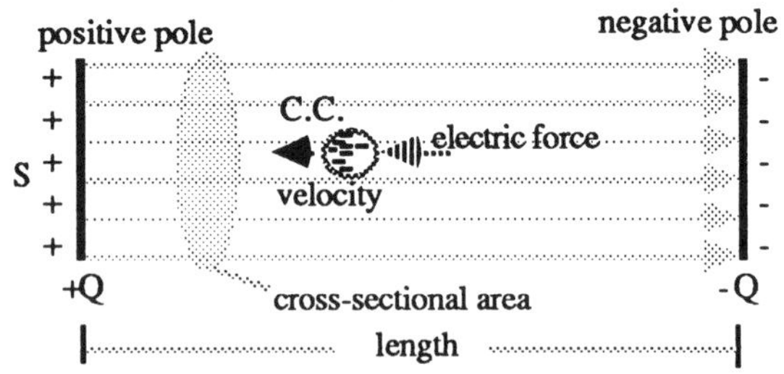

Figure 1: A Region's Electric Field.

Qualitative and causal reasoning about circuits can be carried out in the CC ontology. As a simple example, the following derivation explains why increasing the length of a resistor causes the charge-flow through it to decrease (Figure 2):

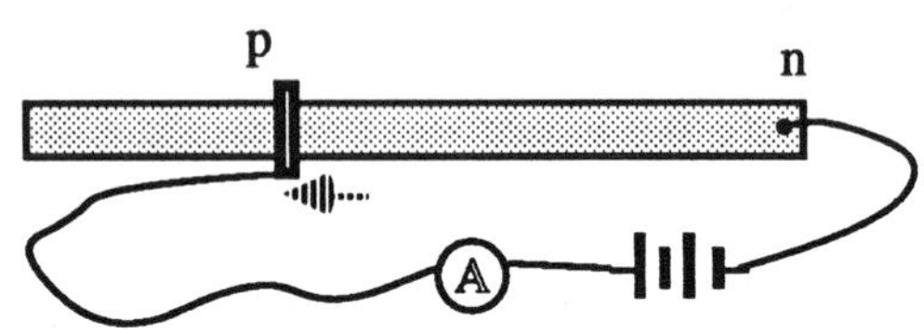

Figure 2: Changing the length of a resistor.

Precondition:	Derivation:	Justification:
	$\partial L(p,n) = +$	Given.
$\partial Qp=0,$	$\Rightarrow \partial E(p,n) = -$	CC-Axiom 1.
	$\Rightarrow \partial F(p,n) = -$	CC-Axiom 2.
	$\Rightarrow \partial v(p,n) = -$	CC-Axiom 3.
$\partial A(p,n)=0,$	$\Rightarrow \partial C(p,n) = -$	CC-Axiom 4.

"When the length of the resistor increases, the electric field of its region decreases, causing the electric force on the charge carriers inside the region to decrease. The decrease of the force causes the velocity of the charge carriers to decrease. As a result, the charge flow through the resistor decreases."

One may suggest that the CC-ontology axioms could be simply lumped into the device-ontology models for modeling and reasoning. However, there is ample evidence that models embodying a jumble of interrelated ontologies produce more harm than good (Winograd & Flores 1987). An ontologically consistent model of a physical system is the basis for the kind of simplicity and understandability that makes our analytic program robust and usable.

Bridging Relations

The CC ontology is at a microscopic level when compared to the device ontology. For circuit analysis, the CC ontology supplements the device ontology, but is not "parasitic" to it, as the above example has shown. Causal reasoning can be carried out independently in either ontology. To enable ontological shift between the two, we introduce the notion of bridging relations that link elements from the two ontologies.

Notice that the basic structural elements in the device ontology are the component devices and their interconnections in the system topology of a circuit. In contrast, the basic structural elements in the CC ontology are electric fields. For coherence of causal explanation, we argue that ontological shift must preserve the spatiotemporal continuity of causal propagation. This requires that both the device ontology and the CC ontology have compatible structural views of electronic circuits. The notion of ***region*** provides this common view. This observation is expressed in the following principle:

> **Structural Compatibility Principle:** In order to preserve spatiotemporal continuity during ontological shift, multi-ontological perspectives of a target physical system must be compatible to a common structural view of the system.

The importance of this principle is two folds. First, bridging relations between distinct ontologies can be formulated with respect to the common structural view. Second, spatiotemporal continuity of causal propagation is maintained when different aggregated constructs are involved in causal reasoning. As the compatible structural view between the device ontology and the CC ontology, a region refers to a structural entity between two chosen poles through which the current or the movement of electric charge is of interest.

Macroscopic concepts and microscopic concepts can relate to each other through regions via bridging relations. Three sample bridging relations are shown as follows:

DC-Bridge 1: (Voltage, Field, and Length)

$$\partial V_{p,n} = \partial E(p,n) + \partial L(p,n).$$

DC-Bridge 2: (Resistance and Field's physical features)

$$\partial R_{p,n} = \partial L(p,n) - \partial A(p,n).$$

DC-Bridge 3: (Current and Charge flow)

$$\partial I_{p,n} = \partial C(p,n).$$

Bridging two different ontologies, these relations provide a simple means for shifting ontological perspective during causal reasoning about the physical world while maintaining the spatiotemporal continuity of causal propagation from one ontological perspective to another.

Now, since an analytic task can often be carried out in or require more than one ontological perspective, how do we control their applications? In the next section, we show that selection of ontological choices is task-dependent, i.e., the decision as to which ontology to use and when to shift perspective depends on the specific analytic task at hand.

Shifting Ontological Perspective

Our interest in qualitative analysis of a physical system is to be able to generate causal explanations for behavior resulting from input perturbations to the system. This reasoning process follows a specific analytic task defined by specifying the input and desired output of the task with respect to a specific target system under analysis.

We have designed a task definition language (TDL). Three parts comprises a task definition: the target system topology, the specification of input perturbation, and the specification of output desired. Using TDL, one can manipulate the circuit at some equilibrium state through either *parameter perturbation* or *structural perturbation.* The former means changing the value of a system parameter to cause change. The latter means adding a new device either in series or parallel with an existing construct in the system topology to cause change. In either case, we ask for causal explanations of related system variables' behavior as a result. A complete discussion of TDL is beyond the scope of this paper. Instead, we will present task definitions in English. Based on a given specific task, proper ontological perspectives are selected using the ontological-choice rules.

Ontological choice rule 1: If the input is a parameter perturbation, then if the output variable is of the same ontology and the analysis requires justification for one of the axioms of the ontology, then shift to a related ontology for explanation.

Consider the analytic task: "Why does the current through a resistor increase when the voltage across it increases?" This task directly questions the component model of the resistor in the device ontology. Since a component model contains primitive axioms of the ontology, which cannot be derived in the same ontology, we shift between the device ontology and the CC ontology, generating the following explanation of why "$\partial V_{p,n} \Rightarrow \partial I_{p,n}$".

Precondition:	Derivation:	Justification:
	$\partial V_{p,n} = +$	Given.
$\partial L(p,n)=0,$	$\Rightarrow \partial E(p,n) = +$	*DC-Bridge 1.*
	$\Rightarrow \partial F(p,n) = +$	CC-Axiom 2.
	$\Rightarrow \partial v(p,n) = +$	CC-Axiom 3.
$\partial A(p,n)=0,$	$\Rightarrow \partial C(p,n) = +$	CC-Axiom 4.
	$\Rightarrow \partial I_{p,n} = +$	*DC-Bridge 3.*

"When the voltage across the resistor increases, (shifting to the CC ontology) the resistor's region, with its length and cross-sectional area unchanged, experiences a stronger electric field than before. This increases the electric force on the charge carriers in the field and speeds up their movement. As a result, more charge carriers move through the field in unit time. The increased charge-carrier movement in the region (shifting back to the device ontology) reflects the current increase through the resistor." Figure 3 illustrates the ontological shifts involved.

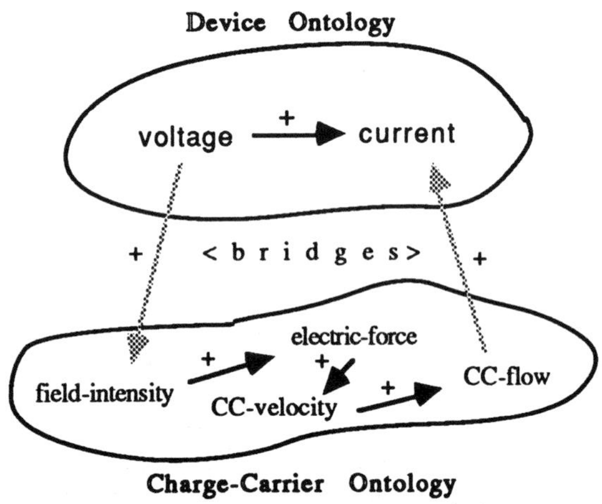

Figure 3: Ontological Shift.

Ontological Choice Rule 2: If the input is a parameter perturbation, then if the output variable is of the same ontology and the analysis does not require justification of any of the axioms in the ontology, then select that ontology.

For example, "Given the circuit in Figure 4, when the voltage between *a* and *d* decreases, what happens to the voltage between *b* and *c*?"

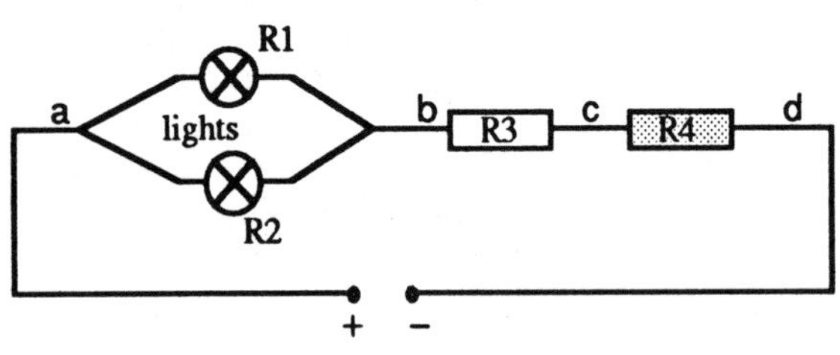

Figure 4: Light-bulb Circuit.

In this task, both the input and output variables are in the device ontology and the question does not directly concern a specific axiom in the ontology. The explanation thus stays in the device ontology.

Precondition:	Derivation:	Justification:
	$\partial Va,d = -$	Given.
$\partial Ra,d = 0,$	$\Rightarrow \partial Ia,d = -$	Ohm's Law.
$Ia,d = Ib,c,$	$\Rightarrow \partial Ib,c = -$	(KCL).
$\partial Rb,c = 0,$	$\Rightarrow \partial Vb,c = -$	Ohm's Law.

"When the voltage between *a* and *d* decreases, the current between *a* and *d* decreases. As a result the current through *b* and *c* (R3) decreases. This causes the voltage across *b* and *c* to decrease."

Ontological Choice Rule 3: If the input is a parameter perturbation, then if the output variable is from a different ontology, proceed with the input ontology until causal propagation comes to the region of the output variable and then shift to the output ontology to complete the reasoning.

For example, "Given the light-bulb circuit in Figure 4, when the voltage between nodes *a* and *d* increases, what happens to the charge flow between nodes *b* and *d*?" For this task, the following explanation is generated:

Precondition:	Derivation:	Justification:
	$\partial Va,d = +$	Given.
$\partial Ra,d = 0,$	$\Rightarrow \partial Ia,d = +$	Ohm's Law.
$Ia,d = Ib,d,$	$\Rightarrow \partial Ib,d = +$	(KCL).
$\partial Rb,d = 0,$	$\Rightarrow \partial Vb,d = +$	Ohm's Law.
$\partial L(b,d) = 0,$	$\Rightarrow \partial E(b,d) = +$	*DC-Bridge 1.*
	$\Rightarrow \partial F(b,d) = +$	CC-Axiom 2.
	$\Rightarrow \partial v(b,d) = +$	CC-Axiom 3.
$\partial A(b,d) = 0,$	$\Rightarrow \partial C(b,d) = +$	CC-Axiom 4.

"When the voltage Va,d increases, the current Ia,d increases, which causes current Ib,d to increase. This causes the voltage across *b* and *d* to increase. (shifting to the CC ontology) This voltage increase causes the field between *b* and *d* to increase, resulting in more force pushing the charge carriers in the region to move. Therefore, the charge carriers' velocity increases, causing the charge-flow between nodes *b* and *d* to increase."

Ontological Choice Rule 4: If the input is a structural perturbation, then select the ontology of the output variable specification.

When a resistor is added to an existing construct in the target system, either in series or parallel, a new region is created. The following two heuristics are used to account for the underlying structural perturbation to the system:

P-Heuristic (parallel-heuristic):
For all R and R', R(x, y), R'(x', y'), **to-parallel!**(R, R')
=> there exists $\mathbb{R}$(p, p'), p=x=x', p'=y=y',
$\partial L(p,p') \leq 0, \partial A(p,p') = +.$
S-heuristic (series-heuristic):
For all R and R', R(x, y), R'(x', y'), **to-serialize!**(R, R')
=> there exists $\mathbb{R}$(p, p'), p=x, p'=y',
$\partial L(p,p') = +, \partial A(p,p') \leq 0.$

When a structural perturbation is made to the target circuit in the simulation, the change can be viewed in either the device ontology or the CC ontology, as illustrated in Figure 5. The selection of an ontology depends on the specification of the output desired.

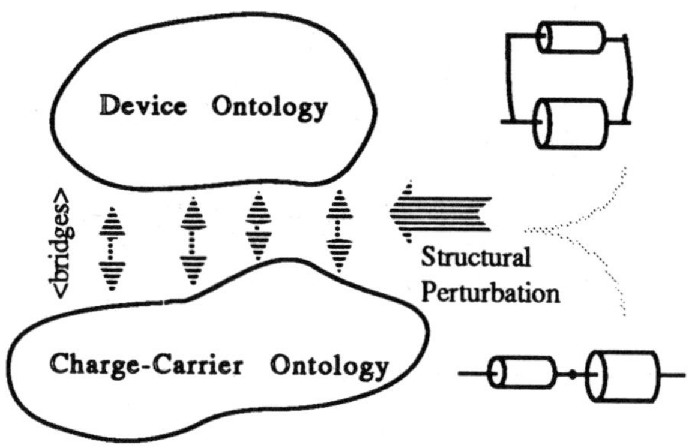

Figure 5: Structural Perturbations.

For example, "Given the light-bulb circuit in Figure 4, will the current through the two lights (R1, R2) increase or decrease when one adds a new resistor R5 to the circuit as shown in Figure 6?"

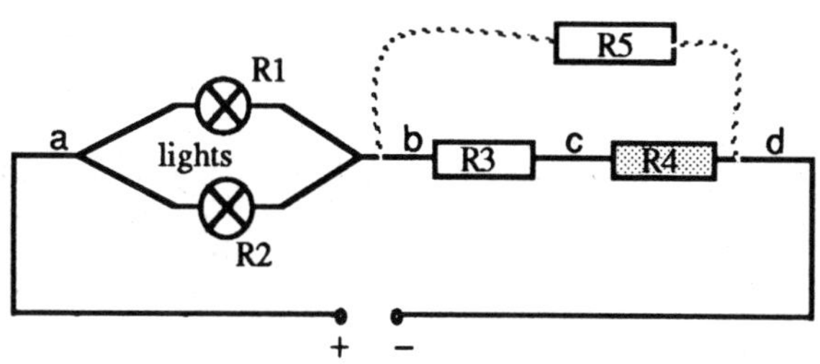

Figure 6: Structural Perturbation by Adding a Device.

In this example, since the output specification is of the device ontology, the following explanation is generated:

Precondition:	Derivation:	Justification:
	to-parallel!$(R5, R(b,d))$	Given.
	$\Rightarrow \partial L(b,d) \leq 0, \partial A(b,d)=+$	P-Heuristic.
	$\Rightarrow \partial Rb,d = -$	*DC-Bridge 2.*
$\partial Ra,b = 0,$	$\Rightarrow \partial Ra,d = -$	Compatibility.
$\partial Va,d = 0,$	$\Rightarrow \partial Ia,d = +$	Ohm's Law.
$Ia,d = Ia,b,$	$\Rightarrow \partial Ia,b = +$	(KCL).
$\partial Ra,b = 0,$	$\Rightarrow \partial Va,b = +$	Ohm's Law.
$\partial R1 = 0,$	$\Rightarrow \partial I(R1) = +$	Model of R1.
$\partial R2 = 0,$	$\Rightarrow \partial I(R2) = +$	Model of R2.

"As a result of the parallel construction, the parallel-heuristic indicates that the cross-sectional area of the region $R(b,d)$ increases, causing the resistance of the region to decrease. As a result, the total resistance of the circuit decreases, causing the current through the whole circuit as well as the region $R(a,b)$ to increase. This current increase causes the voltage through the region $R(a,b)$ to increase, which in term causes the current flow through both the light-bulbs (R1, R2) to increase." Therefore, the two lights in the circuit become brighter.

If, instead, the output specification of this task asks about what happens to the "charge flow" from *a* and *b* as a result of the structural change, then the explanation will be generated in the CC ontology because "charge flow" is a concept in the CC ontology. We omit this derivation here.

Discussion

The approach presented here is based on two insights regarding modeling in general and work in qualitative physics in particular. First, all model-based reasoning is only as good as the model and no single model can be adequate for a wide range of tasks (Davis & Hamscher 1988). Second, model generation and selection is an integral part of a human engineer's reasoning process about complex physical systems. The work described here is part of our on-going effort to automate qualitative and causal analysis of physical systems from multiple perspectives, including structural aggregation, dynamic configuration, as well as ontological shift (Farley and Liu 1990). We recognize that ontological perspective is of a more fundamental nature than the other two because it provides the underlying organizing structure of the problem world.

Related work includes Collins and Forbus's (1987) system that reasons about liquids from both a contained-stuff ontology and a molecular-collection (MC) ontology. They state that the MC ontology is parasitic to the contained-stuff ontology. Specifically, the predicates and axioms of the MC ontology itself are not represented. Their bridging relations consist of rules for one-way conversion of process descriptions into MC descriptions. As a result, the overall reasoning is done only in the contained-stuff ontology. The system "peeps" into the MC ontology from active processes through the bridging rules and draws conclusions about the corresponding molecular-collection behaviors.

In contrast, the CC ontology is not parasitic on the device ontology. Instead of one-way conversion, the framework presented in this paper allows two-way conversions during causal analysis. Reasoning can potentially proceed in either ontology. The decision as to which ontology to use and when to shift perspectives is based on the specific analytic task at hand. When a shift is necessary from one ontology to another, reasoning follows one of the bridging relations, formulated according to a common structural view of the world.

The representation of charge carriers as pieces of stuff is rather limited in our system. Complex analytic tasks may require additional spatial and temporal reasoning about the behavior of charge carriers as pieces of stuff. The parallel and series heuristics only cover resistors for structural perturbations. When one adds other types of devices such as a capacitor or a battery as a structural perturbation, the underlying configuration of the circuit may change as a result, triggering generation of a new model of the circuit for analysis.

The ontological choice rules presented in this paper are novel. Exploratory in nature, they provide a way to control ontological choices to carry out an analytic task and generate causal explanations. We assume that a task can be either formulated by the user or generated by another program, such as the tutoring module in an intelligent tutoring system. Based on task specifications in TDL, these rules are straightforward to automate. We are aware that for complex tasks in design, diagnosis, and tutoring, more knowledge will be incorporated into deciding which ontological choice to take.

Other related work on reasoning from multiple perspectives include the paradigm of graph of models (Weld 1989, Addanki, et al. 1989) and query-guided local model generation (Falkenhainer & Forbus 1988). The former use a lattice of predefined models. Each edge connecting two models is labeled with a set of simplifying assumptions for model selection. The latter is to generate models according to the tasks or queries by activating (or deactivating) pertinent pieces of a large-scale model of a complex physical system. Recent progress has been made. However, the bulk of the work in these approaches involves only a single ontology.

Conclusion

We have presented a framework for shifting ontological perspectives in qualitative and causal reasoning about physical systems. We illustrate how reasoning with multi-ontological perspectives provides significant advantages over using a single ontology. The examples presented are implemented, based upon our previous system that generates causal explanations in a constructive simulation environment (Douglas & Liu 1989). Work is in progress to create a framework that generates and selects qualitative models to reason about electronic circuits. Capabilities for ontological shift are combined with means for identifying dynamic configurations to handle nonlinear devices and aggregating structural components for structural abstraction. Although our discussion has focused on electronic circuits, our approach to how and when to shift ontological perspectives is domain-independent. Such a framework that is capable of reasoning from multiple perspectives is essential to many types of application programs that require qualitative analysis, from automated design and diagnosis to intelligent tutoring systems.

References

Addanki, S., Cremonini, R., and Penberthy, J. S. 1989, "Reasoning about assumptions in graphs of models". In *Proceedings IJCAI-89*, pp. 1432-1438, Detroit, MI.

Collins, J. W. and Forbus, K. D. 1987, "Reasoning about fluids via molecular collections". In *Proceedings AAAI-87*, pp. 590-594, Seattle, WA.

Davis, R. and Hamscher, W. 1988, "Model-based reasoning: Troubleshooting". In H. E. Shrobe, editor, *Exploring Artificial Intelligence*, chapter 8, pp. 297-346, Morgan Kaufmann, San Mateo, CA.

de Kleer, J. and Brown, J. S. 1984, "A qualitative physics based on confluences". *Artificial Intelligence*, 24:7-83.

de Kleer, J. 1984, "How circuits work". *Artificial Intelligence*, 24:205-280.

Douglas, S. and Liu, Z. Y. 1989, "Generating causal explanation from a cardio-vascular simulation". In *Proceedings IJCAI-89*, Detroit, MI.

Falkenhainer, B. and Forbus, K. D. 1988, "Setting Up Large Scale Qualitative Models". In *Proceedings AAAI-88*, pp. 301-306, Saint Paul, Minn.

Farley, A. M. 1988, "Cluster-based representation of hydraulic systems". In *Proceedings of the 4th Conference on Artificial Intelligence Applications*, pp. 358-364, San Diego, CA.

Farley, A. M. and Liu, Z. Y. 1990, "Automated analysis of physical systems from multiple perspectives". Forthcoming.

Hayes, P. 1985. "Naive physics I: Ontology for Liquids". In J. R. Hobbs and R. C. Moore, editors, *Formal Theories of the Commonsense world*, chapter 3, pp. 71-107, Ablex, Norwood, NJ.

Liu, Z. Y. 1989, "A charge-carrier ontology for reasoning about electronics" In *Proceedings of the 3rd Int. Qualitative Physics Workshop*, Palo Alto, CA.

Munitz, M. K. 1974, *Existence and Logic*. New York University Press, NY.

Shearer, J., Murphy, A., and Richardson, H. 1971, *Introduction to System Dynamics*. Addision-Wesley.

Smith, B. and Davis, R. 1989, "Expert systems: How far can they go?" *AI Magazine*, 10(2):65-77, Summer. (A panel session at IJCAI-85 in Los Angeles.)

Weld, D. S. 1989, "Automated model switching". In *Proceedings of the 3rd Int. Qualitative Physics Workshop*, Palo Alto, CA.

White, B. Y. and Frederiksen, J. R. 1986, "Intelligent tutoring systems based upon qualitative model evolutions". In *Proceedings IJCAI-86*, pp. 313-319.

Williams, B. C. 1984, "Qualitative analysis of MOS circuits". *Artificial Intelligence*, 24:281-346.

Winograd, T. and Flores, F. 1987, *Understanding Computers and Cognition - A New Foundation for Design*. Addison-Wesley, reading, MA.

Qualitative Reasoning with Microscopic Theories

Shankar A. Rajamoney and **Sang Hoe Koo**
Computer Science Department
University of Southern California
Los Angeles, CA 90089

Abstract

A model of the elementary particles of a domain and their rudimentary interactions is essential for sophisticated reasoning about the macroscopic behavior of physical system. A microscopic theory can make explicit the deeper mechanisms underlying causal models, collapse a great variety of macroscopic phenomena into a few rudimentary interactions, elaborate upon or validate macroscopic explanations, and so forth. This paper describes a qualitative representation for microscopic theories and, a method for reasoning with microscopic particles to obtain the macroscopic behavior. The representation and reasoning are illustrated using implemented examples from the fluids domain.

Introduction

A central goal of Artificial Intelligence (AI) is to build systems that are capable of expert performance. Early expert systems were based on domain models that encoded empirically observed associations as rules (for example, MYCIN [Shortliffe 76]). However, these shallow models failed to capture the causal relations underlying the rules; consequently, they were severely limited in their explanatory capabilities. Later AI methods, model-based reasoning [Davis 88] and, more specifically, qualitative reasoning [Forbus 84, de Kleer & Brown 84, Kuipers 86], use a deeper model of the domain that captures many of the underlying causal relations in the form of incompletely specified constraints. While qualitative reasoning systems demonstrate improved performance, the explanations they provide are often inadequate since they lack a deeper theory underlying their causal models.

A profound understanding of the domain in terms of a theory of the elementary particles comprising the domain and their interactions is a prerequisite to superior explanatory performance since these rudimentary interactions define the observed macroscopic behavior. A theory of elementary particles can make explicit the deeper mechanisms underlying the causal relations; collapse a great variety of macroscopic phenomena into a few rudimentary interactions; determine the effect of perturbations on factors affecting the causal relations; elaborate upon or validate macroscopic explanations; explain phenomena such as Brownian motion that are direct manifestations of the microscopic world; and so forth.

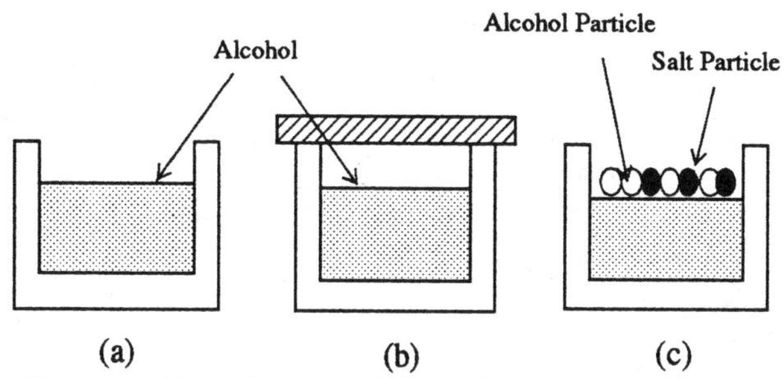

Figure 1: Situations involving microscopic reasoning.

This paper describes a qualitative representation for microscopic theories and a method for reasoning with them. The representation carves the macroscopic world into a small number of hypothetical particles representative of collections of actual particles. Reasoning considers the effect of rudimentary interactions on these hypothetical particles, and extends the results to the collections associated with them in accordance with the laws pertaining to the distribution of the particles. Finally, the computed microscopic behavior is mapped back to the macroscopic world to provide explanations for the observed macroscopic behavior. Implemented examples from the fluids domain are used to illustrate the representation of, and the reasoning with, microscopic theories.

Motivating Examples

This section describes several situations that require reasoning with microscopic theories. These examples illustrate the importance and the utility of microscopic theories.

Profound Explanations. Consider the simple situation shown in Figure 1a in which some alcohol is placed in an open container. Why does the temperature of the alcohol drop? A simple explanation is:

> The contained alcohol is exposed to the external atmosphere; consequently, it evaporates. Evaporation leads

to the drop in the temperature of the alcohol.

A more profound explanation is:

The kinetic theory of fluids [Lee 70] postulates that the molecules of the alcohol contained in the open bowl are continually in random motion, and are held together by intermolecular forces of attraction. According to the random distribution of energies, some of the molecules may have high kinetic energy. Some of these molecules may possess sufficient energy to conquer the forces of attraction. If some of them are on the surface and have outward velocity, they escape from the liquid and are lost to the external atmosphere. The constant loss of such high energy molecules leads to a drop in the average kinetic energy of the molecules. Since the macroscopic property, temperature, is directly proportional to the average kinetic energy of liquid particles, the temperature of the alcohol will drop.

The first explanation is based on empirically observed relations such as "evaporation occurs when a liquid is exposed to the external atmosphere, and it results in a drop in the temperature of the evaporating liquid." The second explanation is a deeper explanation that involves more fundamental concepts, and displays a profound understanding of the nature of matter, its constituents, and the interactions among them.

Dynamic Equilibria. Consider what happens when the bowl of alcohol is closed completely (Figure 1b). Eventually, the level and the temperature of the enclosed alcohol become constant; outwardly, it appears as though all activity has ceased. However, the picture at the microscopic level is one of continuous raging activity; but, in this case, the escape of high-energy molecules is matched by the capture of molecules from the atmosphere. The understanding of such dynamic equilibria at the microscopic level is instrumental in explaining many otherwise mysterious phenomena like diffusion and osmosis.

Mechanisms of Processes. What is the effect of dissolving a salt in the alcohol (Figure 1c)? How does the rate of evaporation vary with the concentration of the solution? A microscopic theory makes explicit the mechanism underlying evaporation. A microscopic model for evaporation will describe it as the escape of liquid molecules from the surface, and will predict a drop in the rate of evaporation with dissolving since the solute[1] particles deprive the solvent particles of many escape sites by occupying a portion of the alcohol's surface. Therefore, as the concentration of the solution increases the rate of evaporation will drop.

The Architecture of MRE

Figure 2 shows the architecture of the implemented microscopic reasoning system, MRE[2]. The inputs to the system are the macroscopic description of a situation of interest from the domain (whose behavior is to be determined) and, macroscopic and microscopic theories of the domain that describe the objects in the domain, their interactions, and the relationship between the two theories. The outputs of the system are the macroscopic and microscopic behavior of the situation,[3] and explanations for the behavior. The system converts the macroscopic scenario into a microscopic representation involving representative particles, reasons about the interactions among these particles, extends the results to the collections of particles associated with them and, finally, computes the macroscopic changes due to these microscopic changes.

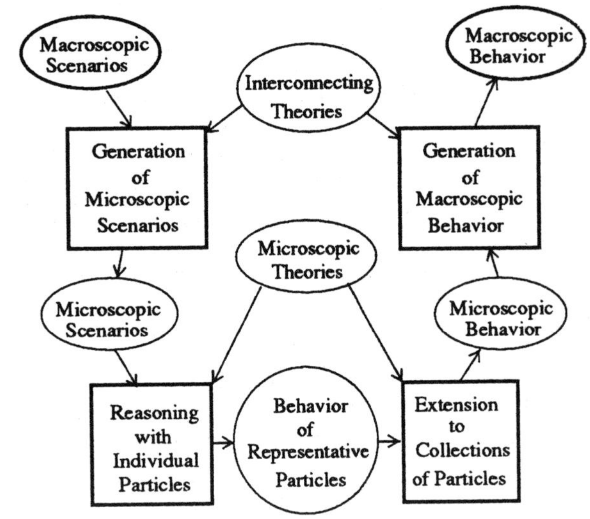

Figure 2: Architecture of the MRE system

Representation of Microscopic Theories

The representation of microscopic theories includes the representation of the microscopic particles, their interactions, and the relationship between the macroscopic and microscopic theories. Despite the seemingly unnerving complexity of the billions and billions of particles at the microscopic level, reasoning at this level is not impossible because there are only a few qualitatively different interactions, and each interaction involves a few particles belonging to qualitatively distinct groups. Therefore, an important function of a representation of microscopic theories is to identify and distinguish between these particles.

Microscopic Particles. We define three types of hypothetical particles that serve as representatives for groups of microscopic particles: (a) *Average Particle.* An average particle represents the entire collection of

[1] A solution consists of two components: a liquid *solvent* and a solid *solute*.

[2] The MRE system is a rule-based qualitative simulator with an underlying ATMS [de Kleer 86].

[3] The current implementation of the system obtains only the behavior for the initial state. It does not compute the *envisionment* [de Kleer & Brown 84, Forbus 84] or how the behavior evolves over time. We are in the process of extending the implementation to obtain the envisionment too.

particles that make up a macroscopic object. Often, this hypothetical particle suffices for many situations, for instance, a flow of a liquid through a pipe under external pressure. (b) *Qualified Particle.* An average particle is further qualified to take into account its type. A macroscopic object may be composed of various kinds of particles. For example, a solution consists of solute particles and solvent particles. Qualified particles are necessary to reason about phenomena such as osmosis that preferentially involve one type of particle. (c) *Quantified Particle.* An average particle of a particular type need not describe a group of uniform particles. The particles within each group may have widely differing values for properties such as kinetic energy, velocity, and momentum. Quantified particles capture the qualitative differences in the values of these properties. The particles are divided along the dimensions of the quantity spaces [Forbus 84] for each continuous quantity and the property spaces for other properties (such as *outward-velocity* and *on-surface*) and a quantified particle is associated with each division. Quantified particles are useful in reasoning about phenomena such as evaporation that involve particles with kinetic energy greater than the forces of intermolecular attraction (barrier energy).

Consider the situation shown in Figure 1c. The macroscopic object, the contained solution consisting of some salt dissolved in the alcohol, will have one representative, hypothetical particle—*contained-solution-average-particle.* This average particle is divided into two kinds of qualified particles, solvent and solute particles. The solvent particle is further divided into several kinds of quantified particles: for example, a *high-kinetic-energy-particle* (with kinetic energy greater than the barrier energy) and a *low-kinetic-energy-particle* (with kinetic energy less than the barrier energy).

Rudimentary Interactions. The representation of rudimentary interactions includes a description of the particles that may participate, the conditions that the particles must satisfy, and the effects of the interaction. Our representation is similar to the *process* representation in QP theory; however, in our case, the effects may include discrete changes, such as a phase transition from a liquid particle to a gas particle with escape, in addition to continuous changes like a decrease in kinetic energy of a particle. Table 1 shows the representation for the rudimentary interaction **escape** of a liquid particle.

We define two additional quantities for reasoning about many instances of the same interaction on different particles drawn from the groups associated with the representative particles: (1) *Population.* The population of a particle (average, quantified, or qualified) represents the population of the group of particles associated with the representative particle. The population of the average particle of a macroscopic object represents the entire collection of particles that constitute the object. (2) *Frequency.* Frequency corresponds to

```
Rudimentary Interaction: Escape (?liq-particle)
Individuals :
    ?liq-particle   ; a representative particle of the contained-liquid
QuantityConditions :
    kinetic-energy(?liq-particle) > barrier-energy(?liq-particle)
Preconditions :
    outward-velocity(?liq-particle)
    on-surface(?liq-particle)
Results :
    phase-transition      (?liq-particle, liquid, gas)
    location-transition   (?liq-particle, on-surface, in-gas)
```

Table 1: Rudimentary interaction **Escape**.

the number of instances of an interaction that are active. It is analogous to the macroscopic quantity, the *rate* of a process, in Forbus' QP theory. As is normally the case in qualitative reasoning, we are not concerned with the numerical values of these quantities, but only with their relative magnitudes.

The frequency of an interaction and the population of the pools from which the participating particles are drawn are related. Consider the **escape** interaction previously described. The frequency of **escape** is qualitatively proportional to three quantities: the population of the high-kinetic-energy liquid particles, the population of the liquid particles on the surface, and the population of the liquid particles with outward velocity. Dissolving a substance in the liquid will decrease the population of the liquid particles on the surface leading to a decrease in the frequency of **escape** (manifested as a decrease in the rate of evaporation in the macroscopic world). **Escape** results in a decrease in the population of the high-kinetic-energy particles, and this too will lead to a decrease in the frequency of **escape**.

The Interconnecting Theory. The interconnecting theory describes the relationship between the macroscopic and microscopic worlds, and is needed to obtain the microscopic description of the scenario from the given macroscopic description, and to obtain the macroscopic behavior from the computed microscopic behavior. For the former task, the interconnecting theory must specify the composition of the macroscopic objects in terms of microscopic particles, and the quantity relations among the populations of the different types of particles constituting the object. For the latter task, the interconnecting theory must specify the relationship between the macroscopic and the microscopic quantities.

Table 2 shows the parts of the interconnecting theory required to generate the microscopic descriptions for the contained alcohol in the situation shown in Figure 1a. The theory specifies that a liquid consists of liquid particles, some of which are on the surface and some of which are in the interior. At any time, the number of

```
Macroscopic-Object: Contained-Liquid(?contained-alcohol)
Average-Particle :average-particle
Quantified-Particles :
  outward-particle              ; a particle with outward velocity
  inward-particle               ; a particle with inward velocity
  on-surface-particle           ; a particle located on surface
  interior-particle             ; a particle located inside the liquid
  high-kinetic-energy-particle  ; a high kinetic energy particle
  low-kinetic-energy-particle   ; a low kinetic energy particle
  ....
Relations :
  population(on-surface-particle) = constant
  population(average-particle) Q= population(outward-particle)
                           + population(inward-particle)
  population(average-particle) Q= population(on-surface-particle)
                           + population(interior-particle)
  kinetic-energy(average-particle) Q+
                           population(high-kinetic-energy-particle)
  kinetic-energy(average-particle) Q-
                           population(low-kinetic-energy-particle)
  temperature(?contained-alcohol) Q+ kinetic-energy(average-particle)
  amount(?contained-alcohol) Q+ population(average-particle)
  ....
```

Table 2: The interconnecting theory corresponding to the macroscopic entity *contained-alcohol.*

particles on the surface is constant[4]—so if a particle escapes, a particle from the interior must occupy its space. In addition, it specifies that at a given time, half the particles will have outward velocity and the remaining half will have inward velocity. The description also specifies the relationships between the amount of the contained liquid and the population of the average particle, and between the temperature of the contained liquid and the kinetic energy of the average particle.

Microscopic Reasoning

The qualitative simulation of a given macroscopic scenario proceeds in four steps:

1. *Moving down to microscopic world.* The given macroscopic scenario is first converted into a microscopic representation. For each macroscopic object, the corresponding hypothetical particles: average, qualified, and quantified are created, and the relations due to these particles are asserted. Also, in this step, the quantity relations among the populations of the different types of particles are also asserted.
2. *Reasoning with the representative particles.* The representative particles are examined to check if a group of representative particles satisfies the requirements of any of the rudimentary interactions. If a given group does satisfy the requirements, the rudimentary interaction is asserted to be active, and all the effects of the interaction are asserted.
3. *Extending the reasoning to collections of particles.* Using the notions of population and frequency, the results of the previous stage are extended to the collections of particles associated with each of the representative particles. The frequency of each of the active rudimentary interactions is determined based on the populations that affect it, and the changes to the frequency are determined by computing the changes to the populations due to the interactions. At the end of this step, the microscopic behavior of the scenario is fully determined.
4. *Moving back to macroscopic world.* Finally, the microscopic behavior is converted into observable macroscopic behavior using the relations postulated by the interconnecting theory. At the end of this step, the macroscopic behavior of the given scenario is determined, and profound, microscopic-level explanations are available for each of the predicted changes.

Consider the situation shown in Figure 1a involving the evaporation of the contained alcohol. The MRE system is given a macroscopic description of the situation: in this case, there are two macroscopic entities—the contained alcohol and the contained vapor.[5] The first step generates the representative particles corresponding to each of the macroscopic entities. The second step examines collections of particles to check if they can participate in a rudimentary interaction. In this case, an alcohol particle that is on the surface, has outward velocity, and possesses kinetic energy greater than the barrier energy participates in the **escape** interaction. The interaction results in a phase transition of the particle from the liquid to the gaseous state. The third step computes the effects of many such interactions. The frequency of **escape** depends on the populations of three types of particles: the alcohol particles on the surface, the alcohol particles with outward velocity, and the alcohol particles with kinetic energy greater than the barrier energy. Since **escape** results in a decrease in the population of the last group, the frequency of **escape** gradually drops. The last step maps the changes at the microscopic level onto macroscopic quantities. A decrease in the population of the average particle for alcohol corresponds to a decrease in the amount of the alcohol. Likewise, a decrease in the kinetic energy of the average particle results in a drop in the alcohol temperature. Table 3 shows the (truncated) explanation for the decrease in the temperature of the alcohol.

Additional Examples

In this section, we briefly describe two additional implemented examples involving the situations shown in Figures 1b and 1c that were described in Section 2.

[4]This model assumes that the amount of liquid is at all times sufficient to form a complete surface spanning the width of the container. A small drop of liquid in the container will not be consistent with this model as its surface will change with evaporation.

[5]As in [Hayes 85, Forbus 84], we use the Contained-Liquid ontology to specify macroscopic objects.

```
(⇓ (temperature alcohol))
    (Q+ (temperature alcohol) (KE aver-alcohol-p))
        (Active contained-alcohol)
    (⇓ (KE aver-alcohol-p)))
        (Q+ (KE aver-alcohol-p) (pop high-KE-alcohol-p))
            (Active aver-alcohol-p)
        (⇓ (pop high-KE-alcohol-p))
            (Q+ (pop high-KE-alcohol-p) (pop escape-p))
                (Active high-KE-alcohol-p)
            (⇓ (pop escape-p))
                (> (A (freq (escape escape-p))) 0)
                    (phase-transition escape-p liquid gas)
                        (Active (escape escape-p))
                (I- (pop escape-p) (A (freq (escape escape-p))))
                    (Active (escape escape-p))

Description of particles involved in explanation.
aver-alcohol-p = (aver-p (CL alcohol))
high-KE-alcohol-p = (quantified-p (aver-p (CL alcohol))
                    (> (A (KE (aver-p (CL alcohol))))
                       (A (BE (aver-p (CL alcohol))))))
escape-p = (quantified-p (aver-p (CL alcohol))
                    (on-surface (aver-p (CL alcohol)))
                    (outward-velocity (aver-p (CL alcohol)))
                    (> (A (KE (aver-p (CL alcohol))))
                       (A (BE (aver-p (CL alcohol))))))

*note :  ⇓ (decreasing)
         ⇑ (increasing)
         p (particle)
         KE (kinetic-energy)
         BE (barrier-energy)
         CL (contained-liquid)
         pop (population)
         freq (frequency)
```

Table 3: The explanations for a drop in the alcohol temperature. The explanations for why the particles are active is not shown.

```
(⇑(freq (capture capture-p)))
    (Q+ (freq (capture capture-p)) (pop aver-gas-p))
        (active (capture capture-p))
    (⇑(pop aver-gas-p))
        (Q+ (pop aver-gas-p) (pop capture-p))
            (active aver-gas-p)
        (⇓ (pop capture-p))
            (> (A (freq (capture capture-p))) 0)
                (phase-transition capture-p gas liquid)
                    (active (capture capture-p))
            (I- (pop capture-p) (A (freq (capture capture-p))))
                (active (capture capture-p))
        (Q- (pop aver-gas-p) (pop escape-p))
            (active aver-gas-p)
        (⇓ (pop escape-p))
            (> (A (freq (escape escape-p))) 0)
                (phase-transition escape-p liquid gas)
                    (active (escape escape-p))
            (I+ (pop aver-gas-p) (A (freq (escape escape-p))))
                (active (escape escape-p))
        (>  (pop escape-p) (pop capture-p))

(⇓ (freq (escape escape-p)))
    (Q+ (freq (escape escape-p)) (pop on-surface-alcohol-p)))
        (active (escape escape-p))
    (⇓ (pop on-surface-alcohol-p))
        (Q+ (pop on-surface-alcohol-p) (pop escape-p))
            (active on-surface-alcohol-p)
        (⇓ (pop escape-p))
            (> (A (freq (escape escape-p))) 0)
                (phase-transition escape-p liquid gas)
                    (active (escape escape-p))
            (I- (pop escape-p) (A (freq (escape escape-p))))
                (active (escape escape-p))
```

Table 4: Explanations for some of the changes in the situations shown in Figures 1b and 1c.

The first explanation in Table 4 describes the tendency of the rates of evaporation and condensation to attain equilibrium in a closed container (please refer to the situation shown in Figure 1b). It is initially assumed that the rate of evaporation is greater than that of condensation. The explanation describes why the frequency of the **capture** of the gas particles gradually increases due to an increase in the population of gas particles (which in turn is due to evaporation dominating condensation). A similar explanation for why the frequency of the **escape** of the alcohol particles gradually drops is constructed by the system. As yet, the current implementation of MRE does not perform *limit analysis* [Forbus 84], therefore, it cannot describe the attainment of the dynamic equilibrium.

The second explanation in Table 4 describes why the rate of evaporation gradually drops in the situation of Figure 1c. In this case, alcohol particles satisfying the requirements of the **escape** interaction: namely, they must be on the surface, have outward velocity, and possess sufficient kinetic energy to overcome the barrier, are constantly lost. The frequency of **escape** depends on the populations of the collections of particles satisfying these requirements. The explanation shown in the table describes why the frequency of **escape** drops because the population of the alcohol particles on the surface drops (the additional explanation for the drop in frequency due to the depletion of high-kinetic-energy alcohol particles is not shown). Note that the population of the particles on the surface is maintained constant by a corresponding increase in the population of the salt particles on the surface.

Related Research

Research on qualitative reasoning has traditionally focused on reasoning with macroscopic theories [Forbus 84, de Kleer & Brown 84, Kuipers 86]. Hayes [Hayes 85] has developed two types of ontologies to describe the behavior of liquids: the *contained-liquid* ontology and the *piece-of-stuff* ontology. Collins and Forbus [Collins & Forbus 87] have further expanded the piece-of-stuff ontology to their *molecular collection* ontology. The contained-stuff and the piece-of-stuff ontologies reason with complementary perspectives of a phenomenon at the macroscopic level: the former reasons about the changes to a liquid defined by its containment in a vessel, and the latter reasons about changes to a liquid during its movement through a system. The MRE system, on the other hand, reasons about a physical phenomenon with two theories at different levels of abstraction—the macroscopic and the microscopic levels. Unlike our quantified-particles representation, the piece-of-stuff and molecular collection ontologies assume a distribution of uniform pieces and, consequently, cannot explain phenomena like evaporation that involve reasoning about the differences in the pieces. Collins and Forbus compute the behavioral description of their molecular collections from the macroscopic behavior and from annotations to macroscopic processes, whereas the MRE system uses separate representations for the microscopic theories and macroscopic theories, and links the two theories using an interconnecting theory.

A number of researchers have used multiple theories or levels of abstraction in reasoning and learning. For example, Doyle [Doyle 86] describes a learning system that uses multiple theories at different levels of generality. Weld [Weld 86] describes a system that forms abstractions via aggregation. However, these researchers have not dealt with microscopic theories which have unique problems due to the large number of particles and the transitory nature of their individual behavior.

Discussion

Microscopic theories are of considerable importance in the understanding and explication of many physical phenomena. This paper has described an initial step towards the qualitative representation of, and the reasoning with, microscopic theories. The representation defines a small number of hypothetical representative particles for a macroscopic object. Reasoning commences by converting the given macroscopic representation into a microscopic one by identifying the representative particles for each macroscopic object, and by asserting the relationships among the particles that hold in the given situation. Next, the rudimentary interactions that are active are determined and their results are asserted. Reasoning then extends these results for the collections of particles associated with each of the representative particles to obtain the microscopic behavior. The final step involves converting the microscopic behavior into the macroscopic behavior using the interconnecting theory. The implemented system, MRE, was demonstrated on several examples from the fluids domain.

The present framework suffers from many limitations that restrict the types of microscopic theories that can be represented and reasoned with: for example, it lacks a sophisticated geometric reasoner, a good representation for motion (including random motion, vibration, etc.), and a good representation for forces (including intermolecular forces of attraction in liquids). Apart from addressing these limitations, we envisage several important directions for future research: (1) Envisionment: We are currently extending the current implementation to construct an envisionment at the microscopic level. This will enable us to reason about phenomena involving dynamic equilibria such as the one described in Section 2. (2) Integrated reasoning: We plan to draw on the strengths of macroscopic and microscopic reasoning to overcome their respective limitations. (3) Learning: We plan to extend our earlier research on learning macroscopic theories of physical phenomena [Rajamoney 90] by incorporating microscopic theories to validate and extend the learned macroscopic theories.

References

[Collins & Forbus 87] John Collins and Ken Forbus. Reasoning About Fluids Via Molecular Collections. In *Proceedings of AAAI-87*, 1987.

[Davis 88] R. Davis. Model-Based Reasoning: Troubleshooting. *Exploring Artificial Intelligence.* Morgan Kaufmann Publishers, 1988.

[de Kleer & Brown 84] J. de Kleer and J. S. Brown. A Qualitative Physics Based on Confluences. *Artificial Intelligence,* 1984.

[de Kleer 86] John de Kleer. An Assumption-Based Truth Maintenance System. *Artificial Intelligence,* 1986.

[Doyle 86] Richard Doyle. Constructing and Refining Causal Explanations from an Inconsistent Domain Theory. *Proceedings of AAAI-86,* 1986.

[Forbus 84] Ken Forbus. Qualitative Process Theory. *Artificial Intelligence,* 1984.

[Hayes 85] Patrick Hayes. Naive Physics 1: Ontology for Liquids. In *Formal Theories of the Commonsense World.* Ablex Publishing, 1985.

[Kuipers 86] Benjamin Kuipers. Qualitative Simulation. *Artificial Intelligence,* 1986.

[Lee 70] Garth L. Lee. *Principles of Chemistry: A Structural Approach.* International Textbook Company, 1970.

[Rajamoney 90] Shankar A. Rajamoney. Towards a Computational Model of Theory Revision. In *Computational Models of Discovery and Theory Formation.* Lawrence Erlbaum Associates, 1990 (in press).

[Shortliffe 76] E. Shortliffe. *MYCIN: Computer-Based Medical Consultation.* American Elsevier, New York, 1976.

[Weld 86] Daniel Weld. The Use of Aggregation in Qualitative Simulation. *Artificial Intelligence,* 1986.

Approximation Reformulations

Daniel S. Weld*
Department of Computer Science and Engineering, FR-35
University of Washington
Seattle, WA 98195
weld@cs.washinton.edu

Abstract

Although computers are widely used to simulate complex physical systems, crafting the underlying models that enable computer analysis remains difficult. When a model is created for one task, it is often impossible to reuse the model for another purpose because each task requires a different set of simplifying assumptions. By representing modeling assumptions explicitly as approximation reformulations, we have developed qualitative techniques for switching between models. We assume that automated reasoning proceeds in three phases: 1) model selection, 2) quantitative analysis using the model, and 3) validation that the assumptions underlying the model were appropriate for the task at hand. If validation discovers a serious discrepancy between predicted and observed behavior, a new model must be chosen. We present a domain independent method for performing this model shift when the models are related by an approximation reformulation and describe a Common Lisp implementation of the theory.

Introduction

Although the bulk of work in model-based reasoning has focussed on problems of analysis in the framework of a single model, we believe that no single model can be adequate for a wide range of tasks. Imagine trying to diagnose a misbehaving auto with a flat molecular-level description of the whole system. Quantum mechanics may be the right level to reason about bond angle in impure hydrocarbon fuels, but it does not provide a useful model of the spark plugs or transmission.

To achieve robust performance when reasoning about complex systems, analytic programs must do what human experts do: switch between models, dynamically choosing perspectives and simplifying assumptions that are appropriate to the task at hand. Since different assumptions are warranted depending on the analytic question being answered, a program that uses multiple models should validate its choice in the context of the problem at hand. Thus the critical step is enabling the program to reason explicitly about modeling assumptions.

In this paper we address the problem of INTER-MODEL COMPARATIVE ANALYSIS: qualitatively computing the differences in the behaviors predicted by two different models. As input, inter-model comparative analysis takes two models and a mapping (called a reformulation) that links vocabulary terms in the two models. As output, inter-model comparative analysis predicts the how the time-varying behavior predicted by one model differs qualitatively from that predicted by the other. The next section explains how inter-model comparative analysis enables model-switching in tasks such as theory formation and innovative design.

Although inter-model comparative analysis is very difficult in general, we show that it can be efficiently solved when the mapping between models is of a restricted type (called an APPROXIMATION REFORMULATION). Intuitively, a simple model approximates a more complex model when the complex model has an exogenous parameter (called a FITTING PARAMETER) such that the quantitative behaviors predicted by the two models get arbitrarily close as the fitting parameter tends towards a limit. If models are related by approximation reformulations then the inter-model comparative analysis problem reduces to an *intra*-model comparative analysis problem and can be efficiently solved by the existing techniques of DQ analysis [Forbus, 1984, Weld, 1988a, Chiu and Kuipers, 1989] and exaggeration [Weld, 1990]. For example, consider the simple system of figure 1.

One can imagine many models of this system, each incorporating different simplifying assumptions, but for now consider two models that differ only in their treatment of the rope. Suppose model $\mathcal{A}$ considers the rope to be inelastic, while $\mathcal{B}$ models the stretching rope as a stiff spring (via Hooke's law $f = -kx$). One can show that $\mathcal{A}$ approximates $\mathcal{B}$, because $\mathcal{B}$'s parameter k is a fitting parameter. As the spring constant k tends towards infinity, the rope approaches the stretchless

*This research was funded in part by National Science Foundation Grants IRI-8902010 and IRI-8957302, and a cash donation from the Xerox corporation.

into a corresponding state in the ontology of the system system: $\Psi(\vec{q})$. The π_i projection functions extract the i-th parameter value from the two states and the difference is called the PDIFF.

Definition 5 *Let $\mathcal{A}$ and $\mathcal{B}$ be models with* PARAM$(\mathcal{A})$ $= (P_1, \ldots, P_n)$. *Let Ψ be a reformulation such that $\mathcal{A} \preceq_\Psi \mathcal{B}$. Let $\vec{q}$ be an internal state of $\mathcal{B}$ representing a set of initial conditions. Let $\vec{p}$ be the internal state of $\mathcal{A}$ corresponding to the state $\Psi(\mathcal{B}_{\vec{q}}(0))$. Define the* BEHAVIOR DIFFERENCE BETWEEN $\mathcal{A}$ *and* $\mathcal{B}$ USING Ψ OVER THE TIME INTERVAL $[t_s, t_f]$ GIVEN $\vec{q}$ *as* BDIFF$(\mathcal{A} \preceq_\Psi \mathcal{B}, \vec{q}, t_s, t_f) =$

$$\max_{1 \leq i \leq n} \left(\sup_{t \in [t_s, t_f]} |\text{PDIFF}(P_i, \Psi, \mathcal{A}_{\vec{p}}(t), \mathcal{B}_{\vec{q}}(t))| \right)$$

In other words, for each parameter in the simple model, we compare corresponding values in the complex model for all times and take the least upper bound of the absolute differences. The behavior difference is the maximum value of the suprema. It is important to recognize that while the PDIFF must be measured in the simpler model, the initial conditions must be specified in the more complex model to ensure that both models can be simulated.

Approximation Reformulations

Intuitively, one model approximates another when the behavior difference between them can be brought arbitrarily close to zero.

Definition 6 *Let $\mathcal{A}$ and $\mathcal{B}$ be models, and suppose there exists a reformulation Ψ such that $\mathcal{A} \preceq_\Psi \mathcal{B}$. Say that $\mathcal{A}$* APPROXIMATES $\mathcal{B}$ UNDER Ψ *if there exists a parameter $Q_f \in$* INDEP$(\mathcal{B})$ *and an endpoint l of the closure of* RANGE(Q_f) *such that for all internal states $\vec{q}$ of $\mathcal{B}$, and forall times t,*

$$\lim_{\pi_f(\vec{q}) \to l} \text{BDIFF}(\mathcal{A} \preceq_\Psi \mathcal{B}, \vec{q}, 0, t) = 0$$

In this case, the parameter Q_f is called the FITTING PARAMETER *of Ψ and l is called its* APPROXIMATION LIMIT.

Since a fitting parameter is independent by definition, it is constant over time; this is why the definition refers to only its initial value $\pi_f(\vec{q})$. The idea behind the definition is that $\mathcal{A}$ approximates $\mathcal{B}$ if sending $\mathcal{B}$'s fitting parameter to a limit squeezes the behavior difference to zero. As a simple example, see figure 2.

At time zero the block is released at the top of the θ-degree inclined plane; under the force of gravity, it moves downward (and to the left, but both models ignore the horizontal component of movement). Let $\mathcal{A}$ be a model of this system with parameters θ, G, Y, V, A denoting angle, gravity, height, and the vertical components of velocity and acceleration respectively. Let $\mathcal{B}$ be a model with all these parameters plus an additional parameter, μ, denoting the coefficient of friction. Let Ψ be the projection function:

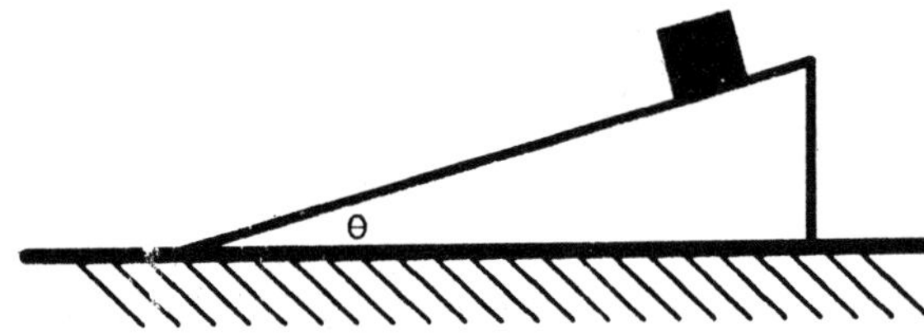

Figure 2: Block slides down an inclined plane.

$\Psi(\theta, g, y, v, a, \mu) = (\theta, g, y, v, a)$. Since Ψ is a reformulation, $\mathcal{A} \preceq_\Psi \mathcal{B}$.

Suppose INDEP$(\mathcal{A})$=$\{G, \theta\}$ and BOUND$(\mathcal{A}) = \{G, \theta, Y, V\}$; $\mathcal{A}$'s ODE's are: $(V = \frac{d}{dt}Y) \wedge (A = G\cos(\theta) = \frac{d}{dt}V)$ while $\mathcal{B}$ has an extra independent parameter μ and ODEs: $(V = \frac{d}{dt}Y) \wedge (A = G\cos(\theta) - \mu G\sin(\theta) = \frac{d}{dt}V)$. As the coefficient of friction μ tends to zero, the frictional force diminishes and the first equation of $\mathcal{B}$ gets arbitrarily close to the first equation of $\mathcal{A}$. When there is no friction then the equations are identical so it is clear that the behavior difference is zero. Thus, we can say that $\mathcal{A}$ approximates $\mathcal{B}$ with fitting parameter μ and approximation limit 0. But while this system provides a clear example of an approximation, it is a bit misleading. The case where the fitting parameter can actually take on the limiting value (i.e., where it is legal for $\mathcal{B}$ to have zero friction) is really a degenerate case of the approximation definition. In general, this is not the case, which is why the definition allows l to be in the closure of the parameter's range; this was illustrated with the elastic string example of figure 1.

Exploiting Approximations

We seek a qualitative characterization of the difference in behavior that two models predict. By assuming one model as 'current' and considering a shift in models, we can phrase this question as comparative analysis: "What is the effect on predicted behavior of shifting from the current model to a different one?" Since this comparison is based on a switch in models, rather than a perturbation to the boundary parameters of a single model, we call it *inter*-model comparative analysis, rather than the *intra*-model case that has been studied in the past [Weld, 1988a]. Space considerations preclude precise definitions of the following terms; see [Weld, 1989]:

- A behavior TRANSITIONS whenever a parameter moves to or from a LANDMARK VALUE. A model's TIME-FUNCTION, $\mathcal{T}$, maps from transitions (the i-th being written γ_i) to the time when they occur.
- An input to intra-model comparative analysis is a perturbation δ to the initial values of boundary parameters. Since δ can be thought of as a vector of qualitative values, $\pi_f(\delta) = [+]$ means that the perturbation specifies an increase in the fitting parameter.

$1 \leq i \leq k$. *A* STATE *of $\mathcal{A}$ is an n-tuple such that the values $p_1, \ldots, p_k$ are an internal state, $p_{k+1}, \ldots, p_n$ are in their ranges, and $p_1, \ldots, p_n$ satisfy the model's quantitative constraints. A set of* INITIAL CONDITIONS *for $\mathcal{A}$ is an internal state of $\mathcal{A}$. The* BEHAVIOR *of $\mathcal{A}$ given initial conditions $\vec{p}_0$ is the unique function*

$$\mathcal{A}_{\vec{p}_0} : \Re \rightarrow \text{RANGE}(P_1) \times \ldots \times \text{RANGE}(P_n)$$

defined by $\mathcal{A}_{\vec{p}_0}(t) = (P_1(t), \ldots, P_n(t))$ where the P_i are closed-form solutions to the model's ordinary differential equations given the boundary values $\vec{p}_0$.

Thus a model $\mathcal{A}$ is an abstract description of a system, a state is a snapshot of the values of all the model's parameters at a given time, and an internal state is a compact representation of a state. Combining a model $\mathcal{A}$ and a set of initial conditions $\vec{p}$ specifies a behavior $\mathcal{A}_{\vec{p}}$ that maps from times to states. Given a behavior or a state, one can use a projection function to isolate the parameter or parameter value of interest. For example, to extract the closed-form solution i-th parameter from the $\mathcal{A}_{\vec{p}}$ behavior, one would write $\pi_i(\mathcal{A}_{\vec{p}})$. If mnemonic names are used then the parameter name may be substituted in place of the index. For example, to determine the velocity (parameter V) specified by a state $\vec{p}_i$, one would write $\pi_V(\vec{p}_i)$.

The definition above describes the relationship between a model, initial conditions and the resulting behavior but it deliberately does not say anything about how to compute the behavior; our objective is a general theory of model shifting that is independent of particular simulation, symbolic solution, or numeric approximation methods.

Reformulations

Since two models may describe a physical system using different parameters, some work is necessary to enable behavioral comparison. In this section, we introduce REFORMULATION FUNCTIONS to define a correspondence between the ontologies of different models. Next we discuss how to measure the difference in the predicted behavior of two models that are connected by a reformulation. Finally, we consider a restricted class of reformulations, called APPROXIMATIONS, that have useful properties regarding this behavior difference. In the next section we show that inter-model comparative analysis can be efficiently solved if one of the models approximates the other.

The basic idea behind reformulations is that a complex model $\mathcal{B}$ can be compared to a simpler one $\mathcal{A}$ if an internal state of $\mathcal{B}$ allows us to construct a complete description of an internal state of $\mathcal{A}$. Although this notion is very general (almost any continuous function, meaningful or not, is a reformulation), it provides a useful foundation. Later, we refine the idea to a useful class of reformulations called approximations.

Definition 3 *Let $\mathcal{A}$ and $\mathcal{B}$ be models with n and m parameters such that* BOUND$(\mathcal{A}) = \{P_1 \ldots P_k\}$ *and* BOUND$(\mathcal{B}) = \{Q_1 \ldots Q_l\}$. *If there exists a continuous function Ψ' from* RANGE$(Q_1) \times \ldots \times$ RANGE(Q_l) *onto* RANGE$(P_1) \times \ldots \times$ RANGE(P_k) *then say that Ψ* COMPARES *$\mathcal{B}$ to $\mathcal{A}$ (written $\mathcal{A} \preceq_\Psi \mathcal{B}$) where Ψ is an extension of Ψ' that maps from states (rather than internal states) of $\mathcal{B}$ to states of $\mathcal{A}$ in the obvious way. Ψ is called a* REFORMULATION FUNCTION *from $\mathcal{B}$ to $\mathcal{A}$. For any state $\vec{q}$ of $\mathcal{B}$, if $\vec{p} = \Psi(\vec{q})$ then $\vec{p}$ is said to be the* CORRESPONDING STATE *of $\vec{q}$.*

For example, let $\mathcal{B}$ be a model of the two dimensional motion of a billiard ball using polar coordinates and let $\mathcal{A}$ be a model of the same system using rectangular coordinates. In this case $\mathcal{A} \preceq_\Psi \mathcal{B}$ because a reformulation function exists. Let Ψ be defined from $\{\theta\} \times \{R\}$ to $\{X\} \times \{Y\}$ with $\Psi(\theta, R) = (R \cos\theta,\ R \sin\theta)$

For the rest of this paper, however, we assume that all reformulation functions are defined in terms of simple arithmetic operations (addition, subtraction, multiplication, and division). In fact, for many examples it suffices to specify trivial reformulations that equate parameters pairwise in the two models.

Proposition 1 *Let $\mathcal{A}$ and $\mathcal{B}$ be models with k and l boundary parameters respectively. $\mathcal{A} \preceq_\Psi \mathcal{B}$ iff $k \leq l$.*

Proof: This is an easy corollary of the Borsuk-Ulam theorem [Massey, 1967, p170]. □

Proposition 2 *The compared-to relation $\preceq_\Psi$ is reflexive and transitive but not symmetric.*

Proof: See [Weld, 1989]. □

Intuitively this means that one can compare a "large" model to a "smaller" one but not vice versa. The lack of symmetry results from a reformulation function being onto, but not necessarily invertible. Note that our definition allows many possible reformulations between two nonempty models, most of which are uninteresting or irrelevant. Meaningful comparison between two models requires a good choice of Ψ, hence much of this paper is concerned with characterizing useful classes of reformulations.

Behavior Difference

To perform model switching we are interested in a qualitative measure of behavior difference. However, a quantitative measure also proves useful. In both cases we define difference in terms of the parameters of the simpler of the two models (i.e., in terms of $\mathcal{A}$ if $\mathcal{A} \preceq_\Psi \mathcal{B}$) because of the inherent asymmetry of reformulations.

Definition 4 *Let $\mathcal{A}$ and $\mathcal{B}$ be models with* PARAM$(\mathcal{A})$ $= (P_1, \ldots, P_n)$. *Let $\vec{p}$ be a state of $\mathcal{A}$ and $\vec{q}$ be a state of $\mathcal{B}$. Suppose that Ψ is a reformulation such that $\mathcal{A} \preceq_\Psi \mathcal{B}$. Define the* DIFFERENCE IN P_i BETWEEN $\vec{p}$ AND $\vec{q}$ USING Ψ *as*

$$\text{PDIFF}(P_i, \Psi, \vec{p}, \vec{q}) = \pi_i(\Psi(\vec{q})) - \pi_i(\vec{p})$$

In other words the difference in the value of a parameter in the two states is calculated by using the reformulation Ψ to convert the complex-system state $\vec{q}$

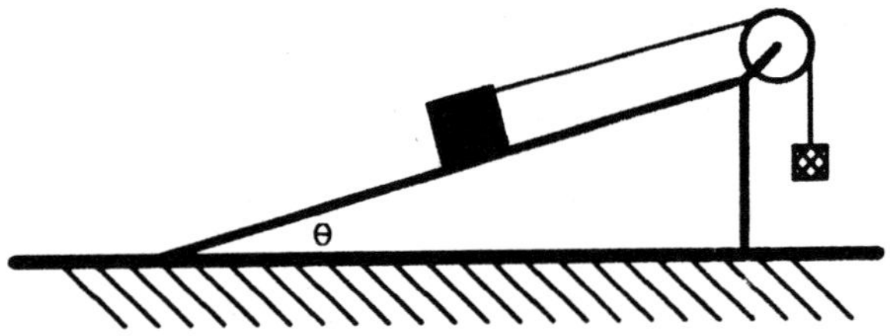

Figure 1: A pulley, two weights and an inclined plane.

ideal and the difference in the time-varying behavior predicted by the two models vanishes.

Since $\mathcal{A}$ approximates $\mathcal{B}$, one can solve an inter-model comparative analysis problem such as "Will model $\mathcal{B}$ predict a higher terminal velocity than $\mathcal{A}$?" by solving an intra-model comparative analysis problem about the fitting parameter in model $\mathcal{B}$, i.e. "Will terminal velocity increase if k decreases?" This reduction from an inter-model to an intra-model comparative analysis problem means that the well-studied techniques of DQ analysis and exaggeration may be used to solve model switching problems.

Motivation

Inter-model comparative analysis allows one to use behavioral discrepancies to guide shifts in modeling detail. We expect this to have application to the problems of (among others) theory formation and the evaluation of design modifications — each of these problems can be thought of as improving a given model or determining that no better model exists.

- The goal of theory revison is to improve a theory that fails to account for all observations. This fits into our paradigm by considering a theory of the world as a model and the failure as a discrepancy between observed and predicted values. Inter-model comparative analysis allows the learner to compare alternate theories to see if they account for the discrepancy.
- If a proposed design fails to meet a behavioral specification (e.g. the power consumption is too great), then a new design must be found that alleviates the discrepancy. If one considers the two designs as models, then inter-model comparative analysis evaluates the effect of the proposed change.

The rest of the paper is couched within the objectives of the first application. Given a set of discrepancies between the predictions of a model and observations of the actual system, determine if a model exists that will predict a behavior which is in closer agreement to the observations. We assume reasoning proceeds in three phases: choice of a model, analysis of the model, and validation that the model is appropriate. If validation instead shows that the model was an inappropriate choice then a new model must be selected. We assume that the analysis performed on each model is quantitative, behavioral prediction (i.e., numerical simulation), but our model-switching technique is qualitative; it works for approximation reformulations.

Models and Behaviors

We consider a model to be a description of a physical system in terms of one or more PARAMETERS, continuous, continuously-differentiable functions from an interval of $\Re$ into an interval of $\Re$ that have only a finite number of points where the derivative crosses zero in any bounded interval [Kuipers, 1986]. To specify the interdependence between parameters in a physical system, models contain qualitative and quantitative constraints. By quantitative constraints we mean simply a system of ordinary differential equations (ODEs). A model's qualitative constraints are a finite set of instantiations of the six constraints used by QSIM — ADD, MINUS, MULT, M^+, M^-, and $\frac{d}{dt}$ — see [Kuipers, 1986] for the details. Naturally, it is important that the quantitative and qualitative descriptions are consistent. We say that A set of qualitative constraints AGREES with a set of ordinary differential equations (ODEs) iff every solution to the ODEs satisfies the constraints.

Definition 1 *Let $(P_1, \ldots, P_n)$ be an ordered list of parameters. Let* C *be a set of qualitative constraints defined over $\{P_i\}$. Let* D *be a set of ordinary differential equations over $\{P_i\}$. Say that $\mathcal{A} = ((P_1, \ldots, P_n), \mathrm{C}, \mathrm{D})$ is a* MODEL *if* C *agrees with* D *and* D *specifies a unique (closed form) solution. Let* PARAM *be a function taking a model to the list of parameters for the model. Let* BOUND *be a function taking a model to the sublist $(P_1, \ldots, P_l)$ of boundary parameters. Let* INDEP *be a function taking a model to the sublist $(P_1, \ldots, P_k)$ of independent parameters, where $1 \leq k \leq l \leq n$.*

Parameters whose values must be known for all time to determine the model's behavior are called independent; we assume that they are constant. In addition to these independent parameters, many models have dependent parameters whose value must be known at at least one time point to specify a unique behavior; the union of these and the independents are called boundary parameters by analogy to the boundary conditions of an ODE. We use calligraphic letters to denote models, lower case letters to denote real numbers, and capitals to denote parameters. All parameters are numbered so we will frequently talk about the i-th parameter of a model as P_i, but when discussing a particular model we may use mnemonic names like V for velocity.

A behavior describes a model's changing state over time. Both qualitative and quantitative descriptions are necessary. We use the QSIM representation [Kuipers, 1986] as a qualitative description; the quantitative behavioral representation is defined below.

Definition 2 *Let $\mathcal{A}$ be a model with parameters $P_1, \ldots, P_n$ of which the first k are boundary parameters. An* INTERNAL STATE *of $\mathcal{A}$ is a k-tuple $\vec{p} = (p_1, \ldots, p_k)$ such that $p_i \in$ RANGE(P_i) forall i such that*

- The output of intra-model comparative analysis is an array of relative change values for all parameters for all transitions. $\text{RCS}(\mathcal{B}_{\vec{q}}, \delta, \gamma_i)$ denotes a vector of relative change values for all parameters in model $\mathcal{B}$, given initial condition $\vec{q}$ and perturbation δ, formed by slicing through this array at transition γ_i.
- A reformulation Ψ, can be trivially extended to map qualitative values as well as real numbers. Thus if $\mathcal{A} \preceq_\Psi \mathcal{B}$, then $\pi_j(\Psi(\text{RCS}(\mathcal{B}_{\vec{q}}, \delta, \gamma_i)))$ denotes the relative change value of the j-th paramter of $\mathcal{A}$, which corresponds to the predicted change of $\mathcal{B}$ at γ_i given perturbation δ.
- The *inter*-model statement $\text{RC}(P, \mathcal{A} \preceq_\Psi \mathcal{B}, \vec{q}, \gamma_i) = [+]$ means that a model switch along the reformulation Ψ (i.e. from model $\mathcal{A}$ to $\mathcal{B}$) given initial conditions $\Psi(\vec{q})$ and $\vec{q}$ respectively, will cause P to have a higher predicted value at transition γ_i. This can be abbreviated ${}^{\vec{q}}_{\Psi}P{\Uparrow}_i$.

Proposition 3 *(CA Reduction Theorem). Let $\mathcal{A}$ and $\mathcal{B}$ be models such that* $\text{PARAM}(\mathcal{A}) = (P_1, \ldots, P_n)$, $\text{PARAM}(\mathcal{B}) = (Q_1, \ldots, Q_m)$, *and $\mathcal{B}$ has k boundary parameters. Let Ψ be a reformulation such that $\mathcal{A} \preceq_\Psi \mathcal{B}$. Suppose that $\mathcal{A}$ approximates $\mathcal{B}$ under Ψ with fitting parameter Q_f and approximation limit l where l is the greatest lower bound of* $\text{RANGE}(Q_f)$. *Suppose the two time functions are equal: ${}_{\mathcal{A}}T = {}_{\mathcal{B}}T$. Let δ denote a perturbation that increases the fitting parameter, $\pi_f(\delta) = [+]$, and holds all other boundary parameters constant, $\forall i, 1 \leq i \leq k \wedge i \neq f \rightarrow \pi_i(\delta) = [0]$. Let $\vec{q}$ denote an internal state of $\mathcal{B}$ such that $\pi_f(\vec{q}) = l$, and let $\vec{p}$ be the internal state of $\mathcal{A}$ corresponding to $\vec{q}$. For any parameter $P_j \in$* $\text{PARAM}(\mathcal{A})$ *and for any transition γ_i,*

$$\pi_j(\Psi(\text{RCS}(\mathcal{B}_{\vec{q}}, \delta, \gamma_i))) = \text{RC}(P_j, \mathcal{A} \preceq_\Psi \mathcal{B}, \vec{q}, \gamma_i)$$

For example, if $\pi_j(\Psi(\text{RCS}(\mathcal{B}_{\vec{q}}, \delta, \gamma_i))) = [+]$ then switching from $\mathcal{A}$ to $\mathcal{B}$ will increase the predicted value of P_j at γ_i: ${}^{\vec{p}}_{\Psi}P_j{\Uparrow}_i$. Thus while inter-model comparative analysis appears quite difficult in general, the previous theorem shows that it can be performed easily in certain cases. If the reformulation linking the two models is an approximation, then inter-model comparative analysis reduces to an intra-model comparative analysis problem in the more complex model, with an initial RC of the fitting parameter away from the approximation limit.

Implementation

To test the ideas of model shifting with approximation reformulations, we have implemented a Common Lisp program, SAM, that embodies our theory of inter-model comparative analysis. As input SAM is given a GRAPH OF MODELS (GoM) [Penberthy, 1987, Addanki *et al.*, 1989]. Each edge in the GoM is an approximation reformulation labeled with the fitting parameter and approximation limit. For simplicity, SAM's GoM representation only allows reformulations that can be expressed as projection functions.

SAM solves an analysis task by reasoning in three phases. First a model is chosen; by default, the simplest model is used. The user enters data values for some number of parameters at an observed event. Next, the model's quantitative ODE description is integrated using a fourth-order Runge-Kutta algorithm with adaptive stepsize control [Press *et al.*, 1986]. Once quantitative simulation is complete, SAM compares the predictions with observations and computes discrepancies. If any discrepancies exceed the user-specified threshold, SAM seeks to switch models. It does this by generating a list of GoM models that differ from the current model by the elimination of one assumption. For each candidate model, SAM performs inter-model comparative analysis as follows.

1. The candidate model is simulated using the QSIM qualitative simulator [Kuipers, 1986]. If more than one qualitative behavior results, the user is consulted to disambiguate.
2. An initial perturbation, δ, is created by choosing a change for the fitting parameter that is in the direction away from the approximation limit, and constraining all other boundary parameters not to change.
3. DQ analysis is applied to determine the relative changes resulting from the perturbation.
4. The GoM's reformulation function converts the intra-model RC values to inter-model RC values.

If the RC values predicted by inter-model comparative analysis match the observed discrepancy, the candidate model is accepted and the Runge-Kutta integrator is called on this model. Otherwise, the next candidate is considered. Since DQ analysis is incomplete [Weld, 1988a], it is not guaranteed to deduce all RC values for every parameter. As a result, it is critical that SAM's matcher considers both agreement (RC predicted matches discrepancy) and agnosticism (no RC predicted) as an acceptable match. The current implementation warns when a switch is taken as a result of DQ agnosticism; an alternative approach for future investigation would be to select the candidate model with the best match (least agnosticism) rather than the first acceptable match.

If none of the candidate models matches the discrepancy, SAM complains that the observations were noisy. This is the likely cause, but other problems are also possible; for example, the GoM could be incomplete. Since DQ analysis is sound [Weld, 1988a] and since the matcher accepts agnosticism, the intra-model comparative analysis routine will never miss a valid model switch. However, SAM uses a generalization of proposition 3 that weakens the constraints on fitting parameter value and time function equality. Since this generalization has not been proven sound, the problem could be that intra-model comparative analysis was performed too far from the approximation limit resulting in an incorrect value for the inter-model RC value [Weld, 1989]. Although theoretically possible, we have been unable to construct an example which would cause this error. Thus we feel that the conclusion of noisy data is a reasonable one.

Since this control algorithm causes each model switch to move upwards in the $\preceq_\Psi$ lattice, SAM's analysis is guaranteed to terminate either by producing an acceptable prediction or by failing at the most complex model. This does not mean, however, that the optimal model (in the sense of an accuracy vs computational cost tradeoff) will be found.

SAM has been tested on about five problems, all using a simple (2 model) GoM corresponding to the example in figure 2.

Conclusion

We view the theory presented in this paper as a promising first step towards automating the types of model switching that occur during problem solving. Since our technique only works when models are related by an approximation reformulation, an important question is whether these relations are common. While we have no general answer to this question, we did enumerate as many assumptions for the simple mechanics domain as we could (17). Of these seventeen, all but the assumption of unbreakable rope could be expressed as approximation reformulations. This suggests the generality of our approach. However, we have yet to demonstrate that our theory can be extended to handle systems with multiple operating regions.

We also hope to increase the speed of model switching. The approach we are taking is to combine our ideas with Falkenhainer and Forbus's scheme for compositional modeling [Falkenhainer and Forbus, 1988]. The goal here is to switch models based on intra-model comparative analysis as performed in the complex model of a single component rather than of the system as a whole. In a sense, this means switching the modeling focus to enable a change of modeling detail.

Another idea is to perform explanation-based generalization on the results of inter-model comparative analysis to build up a library of parameter-change rules (as used by PROMPT [Addanki *et al.*, 1989]).

Our general agenda is to develop a comprehensive approach to automated model management that facilitates integrated reasoning with models of differing focus [Falkenhainer and Forbus, 1988], ontology [Collins and Forbus, 1987, Amador and Weld, 1990], and temporal granularity [Kuipers, 1987, Weld, 1986] — as well as varying accuracy. This paper supplies the mathematical foundation for part of this theory.

Acknowledgements

This work benefited from conversations with Olivier Raiman, J. Scott Penberthy, Dorothy Neville, Ben Kuipers, Rich Keller, Leo Joskowicz, Walter Hamscher, Steve Hanks, Paul Beame, Tony Barrett and Franz Amador. Elisha Sacks kindly provided the Common Lisp code for the Runge-Kutta algorithm, and Ben Kuipers supplied QSIM; both of these are used in SAM.

References

[Addanki *et al.*, 1989] S. Addanki, R. Cremonini, and J. S. Penberthy. Reasoning about Assumptions in Graphs of Models. In *Proceedings of IJCAI-89*, August 1989.

[Amador and Weld, 1990] F. Amador and D. Weld. Multi-Level Reasoning about Populations. In *Proceedings of the 4th Qualitative Physics Workshop*, July 1990.

[Chiu and Kuipers, 1989] C. Chiu and B. Kuipers. Comparative Analysis and Qualitative Integral Representations. In *Proceedings of the 3rd Qualitative Physics Workshop*, August 1989.

[Collins and Forbus, 1987] J. Collins and K. Forbus. Reasoning About Fluids Via Molecular Collections. In *Proceedings of AAAI-87*, July 1987.

[Falkenhainer and Forbus, 1988] B. Falkenhainer and K. Forbus. Setting up Large Scale Qualitative Models. In *Proceedings of AAAI-88*, August 1988.

[Forbus, 1984] K. Forbus. Qualitative Process Theory. *Artificial Intelligence*, 24, December 1984.

[Kuipers, 1986] B. Kuipers. Qualitative Simulation. *Artificial Intelligence*, 29, September 1986.

[Kuipers, 1987] B. Kuipers. Abstraction by Time-Scale in Qualitative Simulation. In *Proceedings of AAAI-87*, July 1987.

[Massey, 1967] W. Massey. *Algebraic Topology: An Introduction*. Springer-Verlag, 1967.

[Penberthy, 1987] J.S. Penberthy. Incremental Analysis and the Graph of Models: A First Step towards Analysis in the Plumber's World. MS Thesis, MIT Laboratory for Computer Science, January 1987.

[Press *et al.*, 1986] W. Press, B. Flannery, S. Teukolsky, and W. Vetterling, editors. *Numerical Recipes*. Cambridge University Press, Cambridge, England, 1986.

[Weld, 1986] D. Weld. The Use of Aggregation in Causal Simulation. *Artificial Intelligence*, 30(1), October 1986.

[Weld, 1988] D. Weld. Comparative Analysis. *Artificial Intelligence*, 36(3), October 1988.

[Weld, 1989] D. Weld. Automated Model Switching: Discrepancy Driven Selection of Approximation Reformulations. Technical Report 89-08-01, University of Washington, Department of Computer Science and Engineering, October 1989.

[Weld, 1990] D. Weld. Exaggeration. *Artificial Intelligence*, 43(2), 1990.

Finding the average rates of change in repetitive behavior

Alexander Yeh*
MIT Laboratory for Computer Science
545 Technology Sq., NE43-413
Cambridge, MA 02139 USA
ay@zermatt.lcs.mit.edu

ABSTRACT

The repetitive behavior of a device or system can be described in two ways: a detailed description of one iteration of the behavior, or a summary description of the behavior over many repetitions. This paper describes an implemented program called AIS that transforms the first type of description into the second type. AIS deals only with behavior where each repetition changes parameters by the same amounts. At present, the summary consists of the symbolic average rates of change in parameter values and information on how those rates would be different if various constants and functions had been different. Unlike some other approaches, AIS does not require that a repeating behavior be described in terms of a set of differential equations. Two examples of running AIS are given: one concerns the human heart, the other a steam engine.

INTRODUCTION: I have implemented a program called AIS (short for Analyzer of Iterated Sequences) that when given a continuous state-description of a system and a sequence of actions or transformations on that state, symbolically finds some of the time-averaged effects of continually iterating that sequence. The specific effects found at present include 1) the symbolic average rate of change in parameters that have a net increase or decrease in value with each iteration, and 2) how those rates of change would be different with different values of various constants and functions (sensitivity analysis). The sequences handled by AIS are ones which have the following "constancy": the sequence always has the same actions in the same order and each occurrence of a particular action changes the parameters by the same amounts. An example of such an iterated action sequence is the one taken by a heart in going through a beat cycle at steady-state. Effects to be found include the average rate at which blood enters the heart and how increasing the pressure of that entering blood affects that rate.

A motivation for finding such effects is that while modeling some system, there may be some sub-system β which iterates a sequence of actions at such a fast rate that the rest of the system only responds to β's behavior averaged over many iterations. Then a steady-state model for the entire system would only need a description of β's averaged behavior; β can be modeled as constantly iterating the same sequence of parameter value changes. Examples of such sub-system and system combinations include 1) the heart and the human circulatory system, and 2) an engine and a car.

Some other approaches of finding the behaviors of a continually iterating sequence have combined qualitative simulation with cycle detection [1]. For complicated systems (such as the heart), these simulations predict many possible sequences of actions besides the actual sequence. If the actual sequence can be isolated, one can use *aggregation* [10] to find which parameters change as the sequence repeats and use *comparative analysis* [11] to find the effects of perturbing model constants.

Another approach [6] uses piecewise-linear approximations of differential equations. This approach requires that one describe a system with a single set of always applicable differential equations. Creating such a description may often be hard, such as when describing a human heart or a steam engine. In contrast, the input for both the qualitative simulation approaches and AIS can have many sets of simple equations along with the conditions to determine when a particular set is applicable.

The next section describes the form of input for AIS. Following this are sections on how AIS processes that input and on what AIS can output. Afterwards are sections that give examples of AIS running on a description of a heart and a steam engine, respectively. The paper ends with a summary.

*Supported by the National Institute of Health through grant R01-LM04493 from the National Library of Medicine and grant R01-HL33041 from the National Heart, Lung, and Blood Institute.

AIS INPUT: An input description consists of three parts: the parameters which describe the system state, static conditions on those parameters, and the sequence of actions (transformations) that gets iterated. The description only has to try to describe what happens in a sequence of actions, not necessarily how or why that sequence occurs or repeats.

Parameters are divided by the model-builder into four types. The first three types are classified by how a parameter behaves as the action sequence is iterated:

1. *Constant parameters* do not change in value at all during the iterations.

2. *Periodic parameters* change in value, but the sequence of values repeats exactly with each new action sequence iteration.

3. *Accumulating parameters* monotonically increase or decrease in value with each sequence iteration.

In general, parameters are represented by symbols. The constant parameter type also includes numbers and arbitrary functions of expressions of constant parameters such as $f[x+3, g[5]]$, where x is a constant. The fourth type of parameter is the rate at which the action sequence iterates. At present, the rate must be expressed as a constant parameter that is a symbol or number.

The second part of the input are static conditions between constant parameters. These conditions are inequalities between numbers and expressions made up of constant parameters. The expressions can have algebraic and the more common transcendental functions. Also permissible are (partial) derivatives of constant parameters which are arbitrary functions.[1] The inequalities can be either definitions that are always true or conditions that are required for the given action sequence to iterate. An example of a definition is to say that some volume is ≥ 0. An example of a necessary condition is to say that for a normal sequence of actions in the heart, (input pressure) < (output pressure).[2]

The last part of the input gives the sequence of actions (transformations) that is iterated. The sequence is partitioned into *phases* so that each part of a sequence is put into exactly one phase and each part where different actions are occurring is put in a separate phase. What is desired is that all the important and possibly extreme parameter values appear at the end of some phase. The specific requirements are that the phases must be chosen so that 1) every part of a sequence (including all the parts with parameter value changes) is put in exactly one phase, and 2) during each phase, every parameter's value is either monotonically non-decreasing or non-increasing.

Beyond these two requirements, a model-builder is free to divide a sequence into as few or many phases as desired. Also, a model-builder might violate the above requirements if the violation's consequences are judged to be negligible.

For each phase, the input description needs to supply an expression for every parameter that changes in value during that phase. For a periodic parameter π, the corresponding expression gives π's value at the end of the phase.[3] For an accumulating parameter α, the expression gives the change in α's value each time that phase occurs. An expression may have algebraic and the more common transcendental functions. The expression's arguments can consist of constant parameters, periodic parameters' values at the beginning or end of that phase, and/or accumulating parameters' change in values[4] each time that phase occurs.

The limitations on describing parameter changes are to assure that each occurrence of a phase alters the parameters by the same constant amount. Without some restrictions on how phases alter parameters, it will be hard to impossible for AIS to determine the effects of steadily iterating the sequence of actions. There are at least two interesting alternatives to having constant alterations. The first is a generalization of constant alterations and has as what stays constant be the *change* in the amount changed (or an even higher order of change). The second is having the alterations form a converging series [9, Ch. 18]. Neither of these alternatives has been needed so far to model a "steadily running" device.

It is sometimes difficult to provide expressions for the periodic parameter values at the end of a phase. For example, one might not be able to explicitly give the pressure at any point in a water pipe circuit. Unfortunately, if one provides only changes to the periodic parameter values, finding their actual values during the sequence would be impossible or hard, involving symbolically solving simultaneous (nonlinear) equations. With only changes in their value solved for, periodic parameters would be just like accumulating parameters that have a zero net change on each sequence iteration.

[1] Such a condition only makes a statement of the derivative with respect to the symbol mentioned. For example, mentioning that $0 < d^2f(x)/dx^2$ says nothing about $d^2f(y)/dy^2$. The derivative of a constant parameter here makes sense and may need to be described because: 1) the function itself is not constant, only the arguments are; and 2) one may need to describe how an argument's value being different would affect the function's "output".

[2] Otherwise, all the heart valves will open, letting blood flow freely through the heart.

[3] Due to the requirements on choosing phases, a periodic parameter's value at a phase's beginning and the preceding phase's end is the same. And because the sequence iterates, the last phase in the sequence is also considered to "precede" the first phase.

[4] Only the change in value can be referred to because it stays the same from one iteration of the sequence to the next. The actual value changes with each iteration of the sequence.

Each phase also has a list of the conditions that either are true by definition or need to be true for the phase to occur as stated. The conditions are inequalities between expressions and numbers. Note that the definitions of phase expressions and conditions are slightly different from the definitions given earlier for static conditions between constant parameters.

AIS makes the "closed world" assumption that all changes are mentioned. So if some phase's description does not mention a new value for a parameter α, α is assumed not to change in value during that phase.

Here is an example of an input description for a phase. Let X_B stand for parameter X's value at the beginning of a phase, X_E for the value at the end, and X_C for X's change in value when the phase occurs. Furthermore, let a be an accumulating parameter, q and r be periodic parameters, and c be a constant parameter. The sample phase description is:

$$(5 \leq q_E), \quad q_E = (c + a_C), \quad a_C = (q_B \cdot r)$$

Whenever this phase occurs: r's value is constant, q is ≥ 5 at the phase's end, a changes by the product of q's value at the phase's beginning and r's value during the phase, and q ends with c's value plus a's change in value.

AIS PRELIMINARY PROCESSING: Before producing output, AIS needs to solve the equations given in the phase description and to check for obvious inconsistencies between the equations and given conditions.

To solve the equations, AIS computes for each phase: the change in value for each accumulating parameter, and the beginning and end values for each periodic parameter. These values and changes are expressed in terms of constant parameters. The beginning value of each periodic parameter is taken from that parameter's value at the end of the previous phase.[5] The solver currently handles only simple substitutions of the solved for the unsolved. Complicated equations like quadratics are left unsolved.

As an example of equation solving, suppose the equations

$$V_E = Y, \quad A_C = (V_E - V_B), \quad W_C = (P \cdot A_C)$$

are given, where Y is a constant and P is a periodic parameter that does not change during the phase. Let AIS find $V_B = Z$ and $P = Pi$ by looking at the values of V_E and P_E in the previous phase (Z and Pi are constants). Then AIS derives $V_E = Y$, $P = Pi$, $A_C = Y - Z$, $W_C = Pi \cdot (Y - Z)$.

To check for obvious inconsistencies, AIS enters the solved equations, the assumption that the rate of sequence repetition is positive, and the conditions given in the input (with periodic and accumulation parameter values substituted by the appropriate expression of constants) into the Bounder system [6]. This system checks for consistency by deriving an upper and lower numeric bound for every constant parameter. An inconsistency is declared if some parameter's lower bound is greater than its upper bound. Bounder derives the bounds with the *bounds propagation* and *substitution* methods. The former method reasons over numeric bounds. The latter method will also perform substitutions of symbolic expressions for symbols. For example, if $c > d + 5$, then the latter can find a lower bound on $(c - d)$ of $c - (c - 5) = 5$. In addition to these methods, the Bounder system uses an algebraic simplifier. These methods are also used to perform the bounding and inequality testing needed in the steps described below to produce the output.

AIS OUTPUT: After performing the above equation solving and inconsistency checking, AIS can infer the following about continually repeating the input sequence: 1) the average rate of change in an accumulating parameter including numeric bounds on that rate and the relative contribution of each phase to that rate, and 2) how that rate would differ if a constant symbol or function had a different value (sensitivity analysis).

To derive the average rate of change in an accumulating parameter a, AIS locates the change in that parameter's value (a_C) during each phase of a sequence, adds all those changes together, and then multiplies the sum by the rate of cycle repetition. Next AIS finds numeric bounds on this rate. Then AIS tries to determine which phases helped to increase or decrease this rate by observing which phases have a_C values that are bounded above and/or below by zero. As an example of deriving a rate of change, let A be an accumulating parameter and R be the rate of sequence repetition. Furthermore, let two phases in this sequence alter A's value. One phase has $A_C = C$ and the other has $A_C = K$, where C and K are constant parameters. Then the average rate of change in A is $dA/dt = R \cdot (C + K)$.

After deriving an average rate for a, AIS can observe how that rate would be different if any one constant symbol or function were different. For each symbol, AIS takes the first two (symbolic) derivatives of the rate with respect to that symbol, obtains numeric bounds on those derivatives, and tries to determine which phases helped to increase or decrease each derivative. Each constant symbol is considered to be independent of all

[5] The reason is given in a previous footnote. Also mentioned there is the consideration of the last phase in the sequence as "preceding" the first.

other symbols. AIS performs the phase determination task by looking at the derivatives (with respect to the symbol) of each phase's contribution to the rate (the phase's a_C value multiplied by the sequence repetition rate) and observing which are bounded above and/or below by zero. Those phases with a derivative of a_C that is > 0 made a positive contribution to the derivative, etc.

At present, AIS also tries to plot a "qualitative" graph of the rate versus each constant symbol. The first derivative described above provides slope information and the second provides convexity information. AIS makes the assumption that the rate versus constant function is smooth (differentiable). If the second derivative can be both more or less than zero, AIS gives up. Otherwise, depending on how the second derivative is bounded by zero and on how the first derivative's bounds relate to zero, AIS determines which of the following shapes the curve may possibly have:

╲, —, ╱, ╰─, ╰╯, ─╯, ╭─, ╭╮ and/or ─╮.

For example, if the 1st derivative is < 0 and the 2nd is $= 0$ (such as when the rate is $-3x$ and the symbol is x), then the curve shape is ╲. However, if the 2nd is instead > 0 (such as when the rate is $\exp[-x]$) then the shape is ╰─. If the 1st derivative has no bounds, but the 2nd is < 0, then the possible shapes are ╭─, ╭╮ or ─╮.

In the future, the QS system [6] will probably be used to perform the plotting. The advantage of QS is that it can detect complications like discontinuities and sketch curves with such complications. However, before QS can be used, it needs to be extended to handle functions for which derivative and smoothness information exists, but where the exact analytic form is unknown. Such functions are often used in system descriptions.

Besides deriving the effects of symbols having different values on a rate, AIS also derives the effects of functions having different values. One cannot take a derivative with respect to a function. But if one wants to observe how rates would be different if function f were larger in value, one can substitute $f(x) + e(x)$ for every occurrence of $f(x)$ in the rate (making the side assumption that $\forall x : [e(x) > 0]$), symbolically subtract the original rate from this altered rate, and bound the difference. If the difference is > 0, then if f were larger, the rate would be also, and so on.

HEART EXAMPLE: This section describes the current version of AIS running on a model of the beating of the part the human heart called the left ventricle.[6]

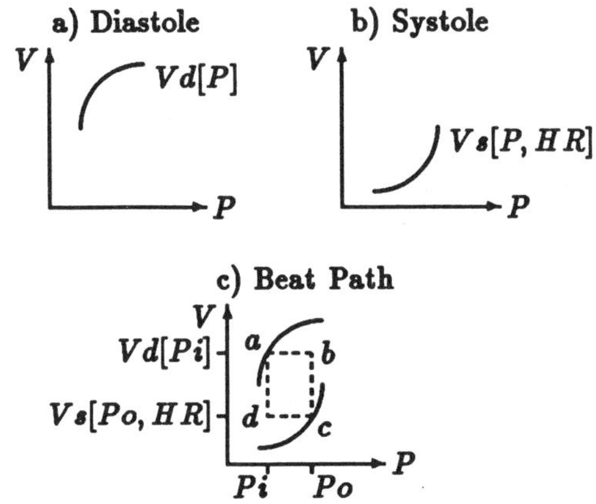

Figure 1: Curves for a Left Ventricle

The ventricle is a chamber with two one-way valves: one valve lets in blood from the lungs at a pressure of Pi, and the other valve lets out blood going to the rest of the body at a pressure of Po. The chamber consists of muscle which can either relax or contract. When relaxed (*diastole*), the ventricle volume (V) versus pressure (P) curve ($Vd[P]$) is roughly as shown in Figure 1a. When contracted (*systole*), the V versus P curve ($Vs[P, HR]$) is roughly as shown in Figure 1b. The symbol HR appears because with Vs, V decreases as the rate at which the ventricle contracts and relaxes increases. This rate is known as the heart rate (HR). Figure 1c shows with a dashed line the V versus P path that ventricle takes as it contracts and relaxes once (a beat sequence): 1) The ventricle contracts, but no blood moves. So, V stays the same while P increases to Po. Move from a to b in the diagram. 2) The ventricle continues contracting, but now, blood is ejected out the output valve. P stays the same while V decreases to $Vs[Po, HR]$. Move from b to c. 3) The ventricle now starts to relax and the blood movement stops. V becomes constant as P decreases to Pi. Go from c to d. 4) The ventricle continues relaxation, but now blood enters from the input valve. P stays the same while V increases to $Vd[Pi]$. Go from d back to a.

The input to AIS has the following: The symbol HR gives the rate at which the ventricle beat sequence repeats. The constants are Pi, Po, $Vd[Pi]$ and $Vs[Po, HR]$.[7] The periodic parameters are P and V. The accumulating parameters are the amount of work done by the blood in moving through the ventricle (W), and the amount of blood that has entered the ventricle (Bi) and left the ventricle (Bo). The static conditions on the constants are:

[6] The description is based on various texts and articles [5, 8] and makes many assumptions. One assumption is that blood is an incompressible fluid without inertia.

[7] Pi and Po are assumed to be constant during the ventricle beats. These assumptions then force $Vd[Pi]$ and $Vs[Po, HR]$ to be also constant during the beats.

$$Pi < Po, \quad Vd[Pi] > Vs[Po, HR], \quad 0 \leq Vd[Pi],$$
$$0 \leq Vs[Po, HR], \quad 0 < d(Vd[Pi])/d(Pi),$$
$$0 > d^2(Vd[Pi])/d(Pi)^2, \; 0 > \partial(Vs[Po, HR])/\partial(HR),$$
$$0 < \partial(Vs[Po, HR])/\partial(Po),$$
$$0 < \partial^2(Vs[Po, HR])/\partial(Po)^2.$$

Most of the conditions help describe the shape of $Vd[Pi]$ and $Vs[Po, HR]$. There are four phases in the sequence. Each phase has a name, condition(s), and equation(s) for value changes. In order, the phases are:

1. Isovolumetric Contraction: $0 \leq V$, $P_E = Po$.
2. Ejection: $0 \leq V_B$, $0 \leq V_E$, $V_E = Vs[Po, HR]$, $W_C = -P \cdot Bo_C$, $Bo_C = V_B - V_E$.
3. Isovolumetric Relaxation: $0 \leq V$, $P_E = Pi$.
4. Filling: $0 \leq V_B$, $0 \leq V_E$, $V_E = Vd[Pi]$, $W_C = P \cdot Bi_C$, $Bi_C = V_E - V_B$.

After solving these phases' equations, AIS discovers the following average rates of change for the accumulating parameters and bounds on those rates:

$$\begin{aligned} d(W)/dt &= ((Pi \cdot (Vd[Pi] - Vs[Po, HR])) \\ &\quad + (-Po \cdot (Vd[Pi] - Vs[Po, HR]))) \cdot HR \\ d(Bi)/dt &= HR \cdot (Vd[Pi] - Vs[Po, HR]) > 0 \qquad (1) \end{aligned}$$

Also, $d(Bo)/dt = d(Bi)/dt$. One can show that $dW/dt < 0$, but the bounding mechanism cannot pick this up. In looking at the contributions of the phases to these rates, AIS discovers that the *ejection* phase is the only phase to affect $d(Bo)/dt$, making it as positive as it is. Similarly, the *filling* phase is the only phase to affect $d(Bi)/dt$. AIS can deduce that the *ejection* and *filling* phases are the ones that affect $d(W)/dt$, but cannot deduce how they affect $d(W)/dt$.

After finding the rates, AIS derives and bounds the first two derivatives of those rates with respect to each constant symbol, and tries to give the shape of the curve of each rate versus each constant. For $d(Bi)/dt$, its 1st derivative with respect to HR is > 0, but no bounds are found for the 2nd derivative. No curve shape is deduced. With respect to the constant Pi, the 1st derivative is > 0 but the 2nd is < 0. Assuming smoothness, AIS deduces a 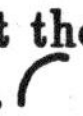 shape for $d(Bi)/dt$ versus Pi. With respect to Po, both derivatives are < 0, so the curve has a  shape. These results also apply to $d(Bo)/dt$. As a check on the ventricle model, these rate shape results are compared to experimental results. The results for Pi and Po agree [7]. For HR, the AIS and experimental results are incomparable because the latter came from intact systems where changing HR can change Pi and Po.

For the rate dW/dt, the only bound AIS can derive is that this rate's second derivative with respect to either Pi or Po is > 0. So for dW/dt versus either Pi and Po, the possible curve shapes are ,  or .

For the Vd and Vs functions, AIS deduces that if Vd were larger, both the $d(Bi)/dt$ and $d(Bo)/dt$ rates would be also. But if Vs were larger, these rates would be smaller. These results agree with the description in [8].

When modeling a circulatory system that has been averaged over many heart beats and is in a steady-state, such as done in [3, 8], most of the system's mechanics can be modeled by using direct current electrical circuit analogies (such as [pressure drop] = [resistance]·[flow]). Too complicated to be modeled this way is the part of the mechanics that relates the Pi, Po, HR, Vs, and Vd for each ventricle to the rate at which blood flows through that ventricle ($d(Bi)/dt = d(Bo)/dt$). Current modeling efforts either directly use empirically derived relationships (like [7]) or derive the needed equations by hand from an AIS-input-like description (done in [8]). AIS can perform the latter derivations automatically: equation (1) found by AIS for $d(Bi)/dt$ provides the desired relationship for the left ventricle. The right ventricle is similar. Actually, to use this relationship numerically, one must be more specific about the Vs and Vd curves, such as specifying that $Vd[x] = \log x$.

Other than needing more specific curve shapes, the AIS $d(Bi)/dt$ equation is similar to the equations derived by others. The differences are caused by modeling with slightly different sets of assumptions and beliefs on what relationships exist and are important.

STEAM ENGINE EXAMPLE: This next example of running AIS concerns a simple steam engine (simplified version of the ones in [2]). This engine has one cylinder and a piston that slides back and forth along the inside of that cylinder. The piston also covers the main opening in the cylinder. The sequence of actions is that the piston slides further out in the cylinder and then back in. As piston slides out, the volume contained by the cylinder and piston combination (V) increases, moving from a low value of Vl to a high of Vh. Steam (at a pressure of Pi and a temperature of Ti) is let into the cylinder from $V = Vl$ to $V = Vex$. From $V = Vex$ to $V = Vh$, no steam is let in or out (steam in the cylinder expands adiabatically [4]). At $V = Vh$, a flywheel (connected to the piston via a crankshaft) pushes the piston back into the cylinder. As the piston slides back in, V decreases from a value of Vh back to Vl. From $V = Vh$ to $V = Vcp$, steam is let out of the cylinder via an exhaust port (at a pressure of Po). From $V = Vcp$ to $V = Vl$, no steam is let in or out (steam in the cylinder is compressed adiabatically). At $V = Vl$, the sequence repeats. The model makes many assumptions, including one that steam behaves almost like an ideal gas.

The parameters are: The symbol RPM (for revolutions per minute) gives the rate of sequence repetition. The constants are Pi, Ti, Po, Vl, Vex, Vcp, Vh, R and k. R is the constant in the ideal gas law $PV = nRT$, and kR is the molar specific heat of steam at constant volume [4]. The periodic parameters are V and the pressure inside the cylinder (P). The accumulating parameters are the amount of work done in driving the piston (W), the energy of all the steam entering the cylinder (Ei) and leaving the cylinder (Eo), and the amount of steam that has entered the cylinder (Ai).

Static conditions on the constants are:

$$0 < Po < Pi,\ 0 < Vl < Vex < Vh,\ Vl < Vcp < Vh,$$
$$0 < Ti,\ 0 < R,\ 3/2 \leq k$$

The sequence has six phases, each with a set of phase equations. After AIS solves these phase equations, it deduces the average rates of change for the accumulating parameters. For example,

$$\begin{aligned} d(Ei)/dt &= (k \cdot Vl \cdot (Pi - Po \cdot (Vcp/Vl)^{(1+1/k)}) \\ &\quad + Pi \cdot (Vex - Vl) \cdot (1 + k)) \cdot RPM \end{aligned}$$

AIS can determine which phases affect these rates, but cannot always determine how these phases affect the rates. A reason for this is that the bounding algorithms do not always find the tightest bounds on a given expression. This reason also causes AIS' inability to put numeric bounds on any of the rates.

In addition, this general shortcoming affects AIS' ability to bound the derivatives of the rates with respect to various constants. AIS cannot bound the 1st derivatives of any rate with respect to RPM, nor bound any of the 1st derivatives of the W rate. For the Ai, Ei and Eo rates, AIS can do better. For example, the 1st derivative of $d(Ei)/dt$ with respect to Pi is > 0 and the 2nd is $= 0$, so the $d(Ei)/dt$ versus Pi curve has a / shape.

SUMMARY: A program called AIS has been implemented and tested. It takes in a description of a sequence of actions and tries to find information associated with the symbolic average rate of change in various parameters.

Compared to some other work on automatically analyzing dynamic systems, AIS is limited in that it only analyzes systems which steadily repeat a fixed sequence of parameter value changes. In exchange for this limitation, AIS does not get lost trying to find the iterated sequence, nor is AIS limited to descriptions in the form of a single set of differential equations. So work on AIS helps further the ability to automatically analyze dynamic systems, a goal of much work in artificial intelligence.

ACKNOWLEDGMENTS: Peter Szolovits and Jon Doyle helped in formally describing AIS' abilities. Elisha Sacks programmed and maintained the Bounder system. Members of the lab's CDMG group helped with modeling the heart and proof reading.

References

[1] D. G. Bobrow, ed.. *Qualitative Reasoning about Physical Systems.* MIT Press, 1985. Reprinted from *Artificial Intelligence*, vol. 24, 1984.

[2] Terrell Croft, editor. *Steam-Engine Principles and Practice.* McGraw-Hill Book Co., Inc., New York, 2nd edition, 1939. Revised by E. J. Tangerman.

[3] C. V. Greenway. Mechanisms and quantitative assessment of drug effects on cardiac output with a new model of the circulation. *Pharmacological Reviews*, 33(4), 1982.

[4] David Halliday and Robert Resnick. *Physics.* John Wiley and Sons, Inc., New York, 1960.

[5] J. Ross. Cardiovascular system. In *Best and Taylor's Physiological Basis of Medical Practice.* Williams & Wilkins, Baltimore, 11th ed., 1985.

[6] E. Sacks. Automatic qualitative analysis of ordinary differential equations using piecewise linear approximations. TR 416, MIT, Lab. for CS, 545 Tech. Sq., Cambridge, MA, 02139, 1988. Most of the material appears in *Artificial Intelligence*, 41(3), Jan. 1990.

[7] K. Sagawa. Analysis of the ventricular pumping capacity as a function of input and output pressure loads. In E. Reeve & A. Guyton, ed., *Physical Bases of Circulatory Transport: Regulation and Exchange.* W. B. Sanders Co., Philadephia, 1967.

[8] T. Sato, *et. al.* Computer assisted instruction for therapy of heart failure based on simulation of cardiovascular system. In *MEDINFO 86: Proceedings of the Fifth Conference on Medical Informatics*, p. 761–765, Washington, Oct. 1986. North-Holland.

[9] G. Thomas, Jr. *Calculus and Analytic Geometry, 4th edition.* Addison-Wesley Publishing Co., 1968.

[10] D. S. Weld. The use of aggregation in causal simulation. *Artificial Intelligence*, 30(1):1–34, 1986.

[11] Daniel S. Weld. Theories of comparative analysis. AI-TR 1035, MIT, AI Lab., 545 Tech. Sq., Cambridge, MA, 02139, May 1988.

Education & Artificial Intelligence

Towards a System Architecture Supporting Contextualized Learning

Gerhard Fischer,[1] Andreas C. Lemke,[1] and Raymond McCall[2]

Dept. of Computer Science,[1] College of Environmental Design,[2] and Inst. of Cognitive Science[1,2]
Engineering Center ECOT 7-7, University of Colorado, Boulder, CO 80309-0430
{gerhard, andreas}@boulder.colorado.edu, mccall_r@cubldr.colorado.edu

Abstract

We have developed a conceptual framework and a demonstration system that contextualize (or situate) learning in the context of real-world work situations. The conceptual framework is based on the following requirements: the choice of tasks and goals must be under the control of the user, not the system. The environment must be able to situate learning, allow situations to "talk back," support reflection-in-action, identify the instructional information relevant for tasks at hand, and turn breakdowns from disasters into opportunities for learning. Learning must not disrupt or interfere with solving a problem, and new information to be learned must help to accomplish the task at hand.

Our demonstration system JANUS (developed for the domain of architectural design) is built on an *integrated architecture*: a knowledge-based construction component, a hypermedia-based argumentation component, a set of critics, and a catalog of precedent solutions. Contextualized learning is supported by the critics that link construction and argumentation, and precedent solutions from the catalog that situate argumentation. Evaluation of JANUS and the underlying conceptual framework have shown that this approach combines some of the best features of open-ended learning environments and tutoring systems.[1]

Introduction

We have developed a prototype and an architecture for knowledge-based design environments that contextualize learning. Our system uses knowledge-based construction kits and hypermedia to contextualize learning, i.e., to enable users *to learn within the context of their work on real-world problems*. With such systems, learning does not take place in a separate phase and in a separate place but is integrated into the work process. The system lets users construct solutions to their own problems, advises them when they are getting into trouble, and provides directly relevant information. By letting users see for themselves the usefulness of new knowledge for actual problem situations, the system improves the motivation to learn.

In this paper, we discuss the necessity and rationale to support contextualized learning, develop a conceptual framework for the problem and describe JANUS as a demonstration system illustrating the approach. From the specific system we derive a generalized architecture for such systems. Our evaluations of our effort identified the limitations of our current work and suggested a number of extensions for future research.

The Need to Contextualize Learning

Doing problem solving and design well has always been difficult, but the explosive growth of technology is greatly magnifying this difficulty. In technologically oriented design fields, the knowledge base needed for design is growing and changing at an alarming rate (Draper, 1984; Fischer, 1988). Learning everything in advance is impossible because there are too many things to learn. Humans cannot keep up with developments in their own fields, much less in other fields of potential relevance. The large and growing discrepancy between the amount of potentially relevant knowledge and the amount an individual can know and remember puts a limit on progress in design. Overcoming this limit is a central challenge for developers of support systems.

Designers can no longer depend on learning everything they need to know before they enter the world of work. They must be able to learn on demand and learning must be contextualized. At least two things are required of a system that allows learning to take place within the context real problem-solving situations. First of all, instruction must relate to and serve the actual task situation at hand where the choice of tasks is primarily under the control of the problem solver, not the system. Secondly, learning must not disrupt or otherwise interfere with solving the problem. The system must avoid the "production paradox," (Carroll, Rosson, 1987) where learning is inhibited by lack of time and working is inhibited by lack of knowledge. The designer must regard the time and effort invested in learning to be immediately worthwhile for the task at hand — not merely for some putative long-term gain.

Contextualizing learning shares goals with the concept of "cognitive apprenticeship" of (Collins, Brown, Newman, 1989). They characterize their approach as follows:

> Perhaps as a byproduct of the relegation of learning to schools, skills and knowledge have become abstracted from their uses in the world. In apprenticeship learning, on the other hand, target skills are not only continually in use by skilled practitioners, but are instrumental to the accomplishment of meaningful tasks.

Contextualizing learning requires more support than *tutoring systems* or *open learning environments* can provide. The strength of tutoring systems (Anderson, Reiser, 1985; Psotka, Massey, Mutter, 1988; Polson, Richardson, 1988; Wenger, 1987) lies in their ability to teach basic concepts and skills of a problem domain. However, they cannot be designed to closely match the concrete problem solving situations of users. Problems

[1]This research was partially supported by grants No. DCR-8420944 and No. IRI-8722792 from the National Science Foundation, grant No. MDA903-86-C0143 from the Army Research Institute, and grants from the Intelligent Interfaces Group at NYNEX and from Software Research Associates (SRA), Tokyo.

presented by tutoring systems are often well-defined and prespecified by the system rather than ill-structured and arising out of real-world contingencies. With tutoring systems, learners are left to acquire task application knowledge on the job, after the completion of formal training. It is left to the learner to relate such training to real-world problem situations.

Open learning environments (e.g., LOGO (Papert, 1980)) do not suffer from the problem that presentation of instructional material is system-controlled without regard to the learner's situation, but these systems provide limited support in helping learners detect mistakes or overcome breakdowns. Misconceptions may accumulate into chains in which each later misconception is based on a previous one. Learners get trapped on suboptimal plateaus because they fail to discover the knowledge needed for better design.

Contextualized learning has the potential to overcome these shortcomings. Since the learning context is triggered by the actual working context, applicability of the knowledge is clear. Elaboration of new knowledge and inferential recall is facilitated by the familiarity of the working situation. Learning in work situations fosters efficient impasse-driven learning (VanLehn, 1988). Computer-based contextualized learning environments could tailor instruction to the special learning needs of different users and could monitor users' success in applying knowledge.

A Conceptual Framework for Contextualized Learning

Our understanding of contextualized learning is based on an analysis of learning as situated and of seeing reflection-in-action as a crucial process in design.

Situated Learning. Situating learning requires integrating learning into situations for which that learning is useful. Instructional information needs to be related to the specific tasks which it serves and doing so while those tasks are being undertaken. General concepts and principles have to be mapped onto specific instances.

A growing number of researchers (Lave, 1988; Schoen, 1983; Schoen, 1987; Suchman, 1987; Winograd, Flores, 1986) argue that no amount of knowledge of principles suffices to account for successful action in real-world problem situations. An additional skill is needed: *contextual elaboration*, i.e., the ability to go beyond general procedural prescriptions to devise specific courses of action and to make intelligent exceptions to principles. Learning is not truly situated unless the learner can perform such contextual elaboration.

Reflection-in-Action. Underlying the *reflection-in-action* approach (Schoen, 1983) is an "action-breakdown-repair model" of the relationship between action and rational thought. Design is seen as repeated alternation between situated action and reflection. The former is governed by a non-reflective thought process and proceeds until it breaks down. A breakdown occurs when the designer realizes that non-reflective action has resulted in unanticipated consequences — either good or bad. Schoen describes this feedback as "the situation talking back." Reflection is used to repair the breakdown, and then (non-reflective) situated action continues. Reflection-in-action is different from pre-planning and post-mortem analysis because it takes place within the *action present*, i.e., the time period during which the decision to act has been made but the final decision about how to act has not. This is the period during which reflection can still make a difference to what action is taken. Schoen gives extensive arguments and examples that it is during reflection-in-action that instructional information can best be presented.

Integrating Construction and Argumentation. The concepts of situated learning and reflection-in-action need to be further operationalized and augmented if they are to provide a basis for a system architecture. We have done this conceptual elaboration in conjunction with the building and testing of a prototype which provided an "object-to-think-with." These efforts led us to interpret action as construction and reflection as argumentation. Construction is the process of shaping the solution — e.g., manipulating the form of a building. Argumentation is the reasoning about the problem and its solution.

The problem of contextualizing design learning thus becomes one of integrating construction and argumentation. In particular, the system must help designers to do the following:

- to see where their construction knowledge is inadequate (to perceive breakdowns, to "let the situation talk back");
- to find the argumentative knowledge they need for such situations (ideally, all the knowledge and only the knowledge needed for the tasks at hand);
- to understand how generalized principles of design relate to their particular construction situations;
- to understand how to perform the contextual elaboration needed to go beyond principles — i.e., to make intelligent exceptions and perform detailed situated construction.

A Demonstration System: JANUS

JANUS (Fischer, McCall, Morch, 1989) is a integrated design environment comprising two subsystems: JANUS-CRACK (see Figure 1), a knowledge-based construction component and JANUS-VIEWPOINTS (see Figure 2), a hypermedia argumentation component. The former consists of a domain-oriented construction kit, a set of rule-based critics that "judge" the object under construction, and a catalog of completed designs. The domain of JANUS is architectural design, specifically kitchen design. The critics (Fischer et al., 1990) in JANUS-CRACK evaluate design decisions and provide feedback when design principles are violated.

JANUS supports the construction of an artifact either "from scratch" by combining the primitives from the palette or by modifying an already constructed artifact from its catalog of previously designed kitchens. The designer can browse through this catalog until an interesting design is found. This can then be brought into the

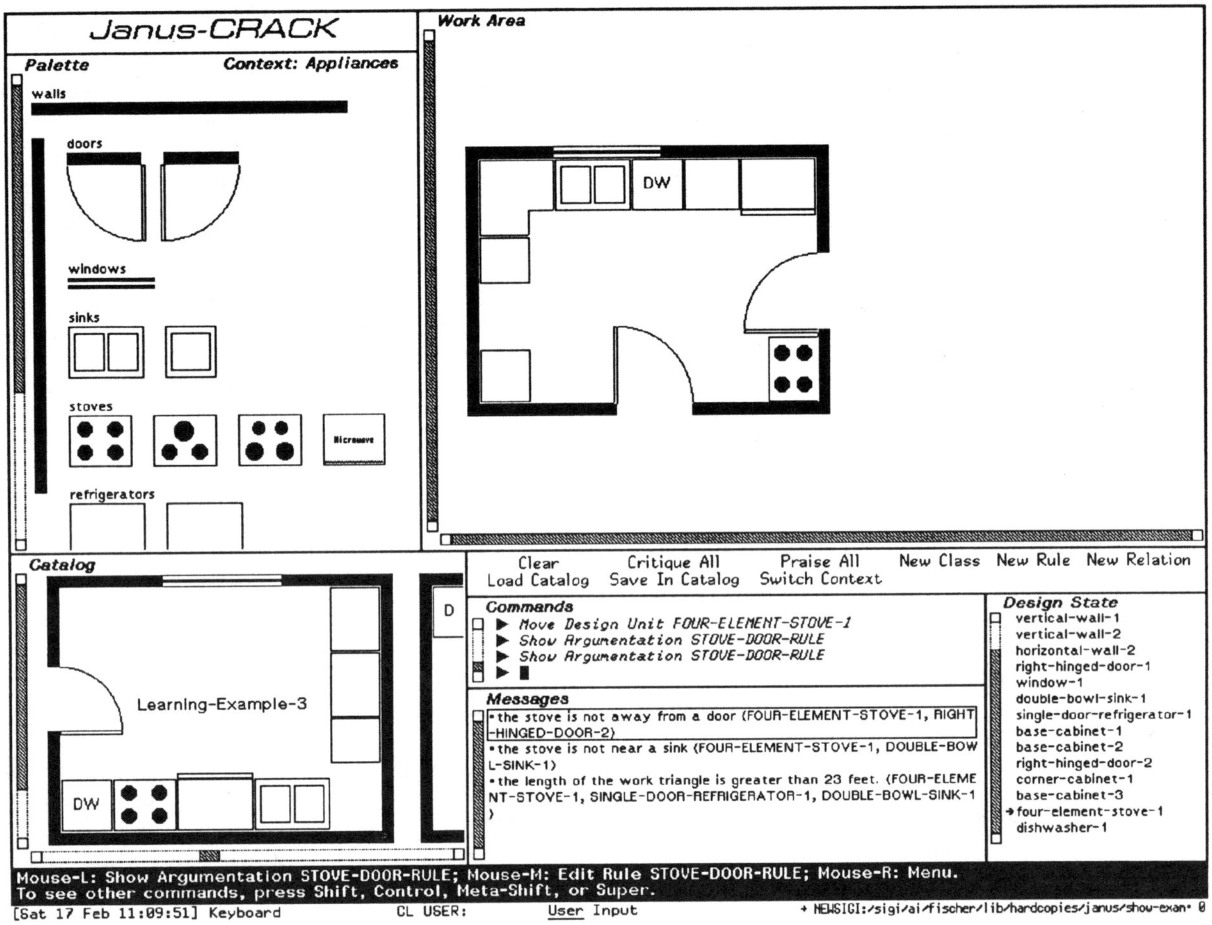

Figure 1: JANUS-CRACK

This screen image shows JANUS-CRACK, the construction component of JANUS. Building blocks (design units) are selected from the *Palette* and moved to desired locations inside the *Work Area*. Designers can reuse and redesign complete floor plans from the *Catalog*. The *Messages* pane displays critic messages automatically after each design change that triggers a critic. Clicking with the mouse on a message activates JANUS-VIEWPOINTS and displays the argumentation related to that message.

work area and modified to the designer's liking.

JANUS-VIEWPOINTS (see Figure 2) is an issue-based hypermedia system (McCall, 1987) containing answers, arguments and subissues. Its arguments use design knowledge ranging from building codes describing safety rules to work flow rules such as the work triangle rule. The system allows designers to learn about what issues have to be resolved, about possible answers to these issues, and why and when these answers are appropriate.

The knowledge-based critiquing mechanism is the main means for bridging the gap between construction and argumentation. This means that JANUS-CRACK and JANUS-VIEWPOINTS are coupled by using JANUS's critics to provide the designer with immediate entry into the exact place in the hypermedia network where the argumentation relevant to the current construction task lies. This solves two problems: It greatly enriches the argumentative information for construction, it allows hypermedia-based argumentation to be used during construction and it contextualizes learning by exposing designers to directly relevant knowledge.

The catalog contains both positive and negative "learning examples" (see Figure 1). The positive examples in the catalog can be used to learn design principles and explore their argumentative background by bringing them into the work area and applying the *Praise All* command to them. This results in the critics pointing out design principles that are *not* violated. The negative examples violate design principles embedded in JANUS. After such an example is brought into the work area, critics will fire providing the learner a list of the violated design principles. Both praise and criticism provide the users with entry points into the hypermedia system, where the argumentative background of the principles can be explored by navigation.

The integrated system supports contextualized learning by providing argumentative information for construction effectively, efficiently and without designers' having to (1) realize they need information, (2) suspect that needed in-

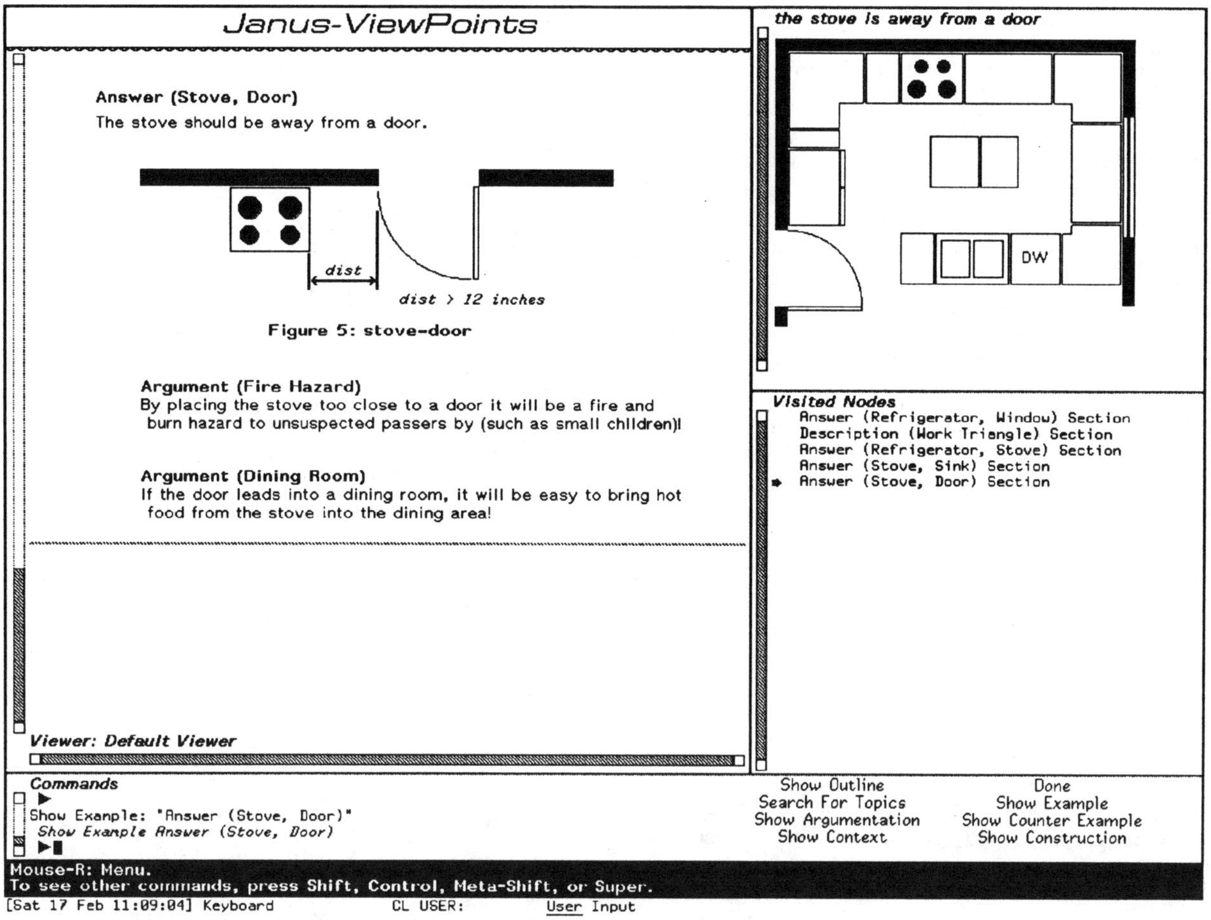

Figure 2: JANUS-VIEWPOINTS

This screen image of JANUS-VIEWPOINTS shows an answer to the issue of where to locate the kitchen stove with respect to doors and graphically indicates the desirable relative positions of the two design units. Below this is a list of arguments for and against the answer. The example in the upper right corner (activated by the "Show Example" command in the "Commands" pane) contextualizes an argumentative principle in the context of a specific design (retrieved by the system from the catalog).

formation is in the system or (3) know how to retrieve it. The system also contextualizes the general principles contained in the hypermedia system by dynamically showing examples illustrating these principles in the context of specific designs.

A System Architecture to Contextualize Learning

The system building effort around JANUS served as a starting point for a generalized architecture for design environments in support of contextualized learning. The major components of such an architecture are (see Figure 3): a construction kit, argumentative hypermedia, critics, and a catalog.

Construction Kit. The construction kit provides a palette of domain abstractions for construction of artifacts. The domain abstractions preserve the situatedness of work in the problem domain. Designers can think about problem situations without the distraction of having to think about communicating with the computer.

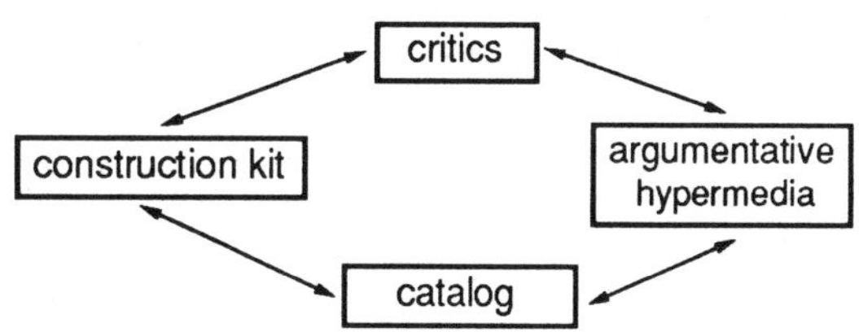

Figure 3: A System Architecture Supporting Contextualized Learning

Critics. Successful design requires that the *situation talks back* (Schoen, 1983). However, for designers who do not have extensive experience in the domain, the situation is often mute unless the learning environment has a component that speaks up and points out issues that the designer may otherwise not consider. Critics can fulfill this role. Critics point out suboptimal aspects of the artifact and retrieve relevant issues in the issue base. Critics thus contextualize learning in two ways: by identifying learning needs through real-time analysis of actual construction situations and by presenting just the argumentative information useful for those needs.

Argumentative Hypermedia. Contextualized learning can only be effective if the flow of work is not disrupted. This requires rapid and timely access to relevant information in the issue base, a collection of argumentation on recurring issues in the problem domain. Issue-based hypermedia (McCall, 1987) make designers aware of issues, possible answers, and argumentation, and allows them to incrementally specify personal design constraints at various levels.

The PHI (Procedural Hierarchy of Issues) approach to issue-based hypermedia structures information according to its relevance to design tasks (issues). It contains principles of design together with the argumentative background necessary for contextual elaboration. The rich connectivity of hypermedia allows immediate access to explanatory, elaborative and other types of information. Hypermedia also accommodates individual differences in prior knowledge and learning styles — crucial contextual factors. Users with little knowledge can explore the hypermedia network in depth, while knowledgeable users can ignore links to known information.

Catalog. The catalog is an evolving collection of artifacts accumulated by the actual use of the system. It illustrates the space of possible designs in the domain. For instructional purposes, the catalog can be enriched with positive and negative learning examples (see Figure 1). The catalog examples are contextualized that the system dynamically selects and presents those examples that not only illustrate the concept but most closely correspond to the construction situation at hand (see Figure 2). Catalog examples provide a link back from argumentation to construction by making abstract principles concrete and ready to be integrated into the artifact under construction. Catalog examples support *case-based reasoning* (Riesbeck, Schank, 1989; Rissland, Skalak, 1989) to complement the generalized argumentative reasoning in the issue base. To this end, catalog examples are annotated with design rationale that allows designers to assess the relevance of the example to the situation at hand. This allows them to provide examples for how to make intelligent exceptions to design principles and to do other types of contextual elaboration — which by definition go beyond what can be stated in principles. The user can independently analyze catalog examples with the critics to discover design principles in the context of specific construction situations.

Evaluation, Limitations, and Future Work

Evaluation. Our evaluation using professional and amateur designers showed that contextualized learning can be supported by JANUS. Users extend their knowledge in a demand-driven way and breakdowns in the systems were perceived as learning opportunities. Users were able to understand the purposes and uses of the new knowledge encountered. The different components of the architecture enabled users to learn new knowledge in multiple contexts: tied to the contexts of its uses and independent of any particular context.

Limitations. Our evaluation also showed several shortcomings of the current system. One is that JANUS allows views of the artifact only at the individual room level and not at a higher or lower level of aggregation. A second is that it does not support functional simulation. This is a technique frequently used by designers to understand the consequences of design decisions — increasing the possibilities of *letting the situation talk back* — by simulating use of the design. A third is that JANUS does not allow designers to volunteer their goals, preferences, and specifications (Fischer, Stevens, 1987) and therefore fails to realize the full potential of critics and the argumentation component to give advice tailored to the actual problem situation.

Extended Architecture. In order to overcome these limitations we are in the process of developing an extended architecture containing the following components:

- *Specification component.* Design is a process of trading off competing goals such as minimizing cost or maximizing reliability or extensibility, and the final artifact depends on which tradeoffs are acceptable. Without knowing and adapting to such characteristics of the specific problem situation, the system's appearance will remain abstract. A specification component would allow the designer to input these characteristics, and the system can use them to better situate its information structures by filtering out argumentation, critics, and catalog examples that are not relevant to the specified problem situation.
- *Simulation component.* Evaluations of the JANUS system by expert designers have demonstrated a need for simulating usage scenarios with the artifact being designed. Such functional simulations can take the form of deterministic mathematical models as well as informal what-if games. Functional simulation enhances further the capability of the construction situation to talk back to the designer.
- *Dynamic Recomputation of Hypermedia Networks.* To situate the issue and argumentation structure, the issue base must be *active*, that is, it must filter out information that is irrelevant to the current construction situation, even if that information is relevant for other hypothetical situations. The situated information structure then is much more manageable. Concretely, an issue base can be better situated by suppressing issues that are made irrelevant by answers to other issues, and, secondly, by inferring answers from information the designer has previously specified and from design decisions that have already been made.

New Application Domains. In order to test the generality of our architecture, we will test this approach with other application domains. Our previous work has concentrated on the domain of kitchen design. A first test of the generality was conducted by designing and implementing with the same basic architecture a system for user interface design (Lemke, 1989). We are currently in the planning stage to apply the approach to more general architectural design issues (e.g., design of buildings) *in combination* with a technical domain (e.g., the design of high-speed digital communication networks within these buildings).

Future Issues for Investigation. With these new features added to our design environments, we will be able to investigate issues such as the following: (1) Will there be substantial differences in performance if the system is used with and without critics, catalog, and simulation component? (2) What are the most important components in our architecture that enable situated learning? How should these components be structured? (3) What intervention strategies should the system use for displaying enough information at the right time without disrupting the work process? (4) When are designers willing to suspend the construction process to access relevant information? (5) When will designers challenge or extend the knowledge represented in the system? and (6) When are subjects willing to enhance the knowledge structures (Fischer, Girgensohn, 1990)?

Conclusions

In order for designers to cope with the deluge of knowledge for design they must integrate learning into their everyday work. With the described research, we have created an initial conceptual framework for such contextualized learning. This framework was illustrated with a prototype system utilizing argumentative hypermedia and knowledge-based critics. From this a preliminary architecture for integrated knowledge-based design environments was developed. Evaluation has shown the benefits and limitations of this approach and, in particular, showed that additional components are needed to contextualize learning more fully. In our future research we will develop and test these new components. Our goal is to develop systems which become means for lifelong learning. Ultimately, such environments for contextualized learning might allow learning to become a more personal, less alienating process not separate from the rest of our life.

Acknowledgements. The authors would like to thank Andreas Girgensohn, Anders Morch, Kumiyo Nakakoji, and Jonathan Ostwald who have made major contributions to the JANUS system.

References

J.R. Anderson, B.J. Reiser (1985). The LISP Tutor. *BYTE, 10*(4), 159-175.

J.M. Carroll, M.B. Rosson (1987). Paradox of the Active User: In J.M. Carroll (Ed.), *Interfacing Thought: Cognitive Aspects of Human-Computer Interaction* (pp. 80-111). Cambridge, MA: The MIT Press.

A.M. Collins, J.S. Brown, S.E. Newman (1989). Cognitive Apprenticeship: Teaching the Crafts of Reading, Writing, and Mathematics: In L.B. Resnick (Ed.), *Knowing, Learning, and Instruction* (pp. 453-494). Hillsdale, NJ: Lawrence Erlbaum Associates.

S.W. Draper (1984). The Nature of Expertise in UNIX. *Proceedings of INTERACT'84, IFIP Conference on Human-Computer Interaction*, 182-186. Amsterdam: Elsevier Science Publishers.

G. Fischer (1988). Enhancing Incremental Learning Processes with Knowledge-Based Systems: In H. Mandl, A. Lesgold (Eds.), *Learning Issues for Intelligent Tutoring Systems* (pp. 138-163). New York: Springer-Verlag.

G. Fischer, A.C. Lemke, T. Mastaglio, A. Morch (1990). Using Critics to Empower Users. *Human Factors in Computing Systems, CHI'90 Conference Proceedings (Seattle, WA)*, 337-347. New York: ACM.

G. Fischer, A. Girgensohn (1990). End-User Modifiability in Design Environments. *Human Factors in Computing Systems, CHI'90 Conference Proceedings (Seattle, WA)*, 183-191. New York: ACM.

G. Fischer, R. McCall, A. Morch (1989). JANUS: Integrating Hypertext with a Knowledge-Based Design Environment. *Proceedings of Hypertext'89*, 105-117. New York: ACM.

G. Fischer, C. Stevens (1987). Volunteering Information -- Enhancing the Communication Capabilities of Knowledge-Based Systems. *Proceedings of INTERACT'87, 2nd IFIP Conference on Human-Computer Interaction (Stuttgart, FRG)*, 965-971. Amsterdam: North-Holland.

J. Lave (1988). *Cognition in Practice*. Cambridge, MA: Cambridge University Press.

A.C. Lemke (1989). *Design Environments for High-Functionality Computer Systems*. Unpublished doctoral dissertation, Boulder, CO: Department of Computer Science, University of Colorado.

R. McCall (1987). PHIBIS: Procedurally Hierarchical Issue-Based Information Systems. *Proceedings of the Conference on Architecture at the International Congress on Planning and Design Theory*. New York: American Society of Mechanical Engineers.

S. Papert (1980). *Mindstorms: Children, Computers and Powerful Ideas*. New York: Basic Books.

M.C. Polson, J.J. Richardson (Eds.). (1988). *Foundations of Intelligent Tutoring Systems*. Hillsdale, NJ: Lawrence Erlbaum Associates.

J. Psotka, L.D. Massey, S.A. Mutter (Eds.). (1988). *Intelligent Tutoring Systems: Lessons Learned*. Hillsdale, NJ: Lawrence Erlbaum Associates.

C. Riesbeck, R.C. Schank (1989). *Inside Case-Based Reasoning*. Hillsdale, NJ: Lawrence Erlbaum Associates.

E.L. Rissland, D.B. Skalak (1989). Combining Case-Based and Rule-Based Reasoning: A Heuristic Approach. *Proceedings of the Eleventh International Joint Conference on Artificial Intelligence*, 524-530.

D.A. Schoen (1983). *The Reflective Practitioner: How Professionals Think in Action*. New York: Basic Books.

D.A. Schoen (1987). *Educating the Reflective Practitioner*. San Francisco, CA: Jossey-Bass Publishers.

L.A. Suchman (1987). *Plans and Situated Actions*. New York: Cambridge University Press.

K. VanLehn (1988). Toward a Theory of Impasse-Driven Learning: In H. Mandl, A. Lesgold (Eds.), *Learning Issues for Intelligent Tutoring Systems* (pp. 19-41). New York: Springer-Verlag.

E. Wenger (1987). *Artificial Intelligence and Tutoring Systems*. Los Altos, CA: Morgan Kaufmann Publishers.

T. Winograd, F. Flores (1986). *Understanding Computers and Cognition: A New Foundation for Design*. Norwood, NJ: Ablex Publishing Corporation.

Backward Model Tracing: An Explanation-Based Approach for Reconstructing Student Reasoning

Danilo Fum (*), Paolo Giangrandi(°), Carlo Tasso (°)

(*) Dipartimento di Psicologia, Università di Trieste
Via dell'Università 7, I-34123 Trieste, Italy - fum@uts882.units.infn.it.bitnet
(°) Laboratorio di Intelligenza Artificiale, Università di Udine
Via Zanon 6, I-33100 Udine, Italy - tasso@uduniv.infn.it.bitnet

Abstract

An original methodology, called *backward model tracing* to model student performance which features a profitable integration of the bug collection and bug construction techniques is presented. This methodology has been used for building the modelling module of a new version of ET (English Tutor), an ITS aimed at supporting the learning of the English verb system. Backward model tracing is based on the idea of analyzing the reasoning process of the student by reconstructing, step by step and in reverse order, the chain of reasoning (s)he has followed in giving his/her answer. In order to do this, both correct domain specific knowledge and a catalogue of stereotyped errors (malrules) are utilized. When the system is unable to explain the student behavior by exploiting its previous knowledge, new malrules are generated dynamically, by utilizing explanation-based learning techniques. The overall process is based on a deep modelling of the student problem solving and the discrimination among possible explicative hypotheses about the reasons underlying the student behavior is carried on non-monotonically through a truth maintenance system. The proposed approach has been fully implemented in a student modelling module developed in PROLOG.

1. Introduction

One of the most important features an intelligent tutoring system (ITS for short) should provide, is the capability to adapt its behavior to the specific traits of the student. To this purpose, a fundamental contribution is given by the component aimed at building and maintaining the student model. The student model describes the knowledge and beliefs of the student in the specific subject domain and is used for designing and taking appropriate tutorial and remedial actions, tailored to the peculiarities of the student.

Building an ITS with a student modelling component is hindered by several problems concerning both theoretical and practical issues. There is a sufficiently general agreement on the fact that the modelling activity cannot be based only on the knowledge provided by an expert in the domain but it is better performed by relying on an explicit description of possible student (mis)behaviors.

Unfortunately, no agreed-upon solution exists on this topic and the three main approaches adopted for building student modelers (i.e., overlay, bug collection and bug construction: Wenger 1987) directly reflect this situation. In fact, each technique has been generally used alone and no clear ways have been proposed to combine these techniques in order to exploit their respective advantages. Considered by itself, each technique has known drawbacks and falls short of constituting an ideal tool for building cognitively adequate and computationally sufficient student models: overlay is generally considered as not sufficiently powerful to perform sophisticated modelling, collecting catalogues of bugs is notoriously a dull and labor-intensive endeavor, while bug construction has not yet proved to be a reliable and sufficiently comprehensive approach.

In this paper we present an original methodology, called *backward model tracing* to model student performance which features a profitable integration of the bug collection and bug construction techniques. This methodology has been used for building the modelling module of a new version of ET (English Tutor), an ITS aimed at supporting the learning of the English verb system. Backward model tracing is based on the idea of analyzing the reasoning process of the student by reconstructing, step by step and in reverse order, the chain of reasoning (s)he has followed in giving his/her answer. In order to do this, both correct domain specific knowledge and a catalogue of stereotyped errors (malrules) is utilized. When the system is unable to explain the student behavior by exploiting its previous knowledge, new malrules are generated dynamically, by utilizing explanation-based learning techniques.

The overall process is based on a deep modelling of the student problem solving and the discrimination among possible explicative hypotheses about the reasons underlying the student behavior is carried on non-monotonically through a truth maintenance system.

Backward model tracing seems a promising approach to tackle the hard problem of student modelling (Self 1988) for the following reasons:

- it shares the benefits of the model tracing methodology (Anderson 1987);
- it exploits the respective advantages of bug collection and bug construction without the limitation of the exclusive usage of a single technique;

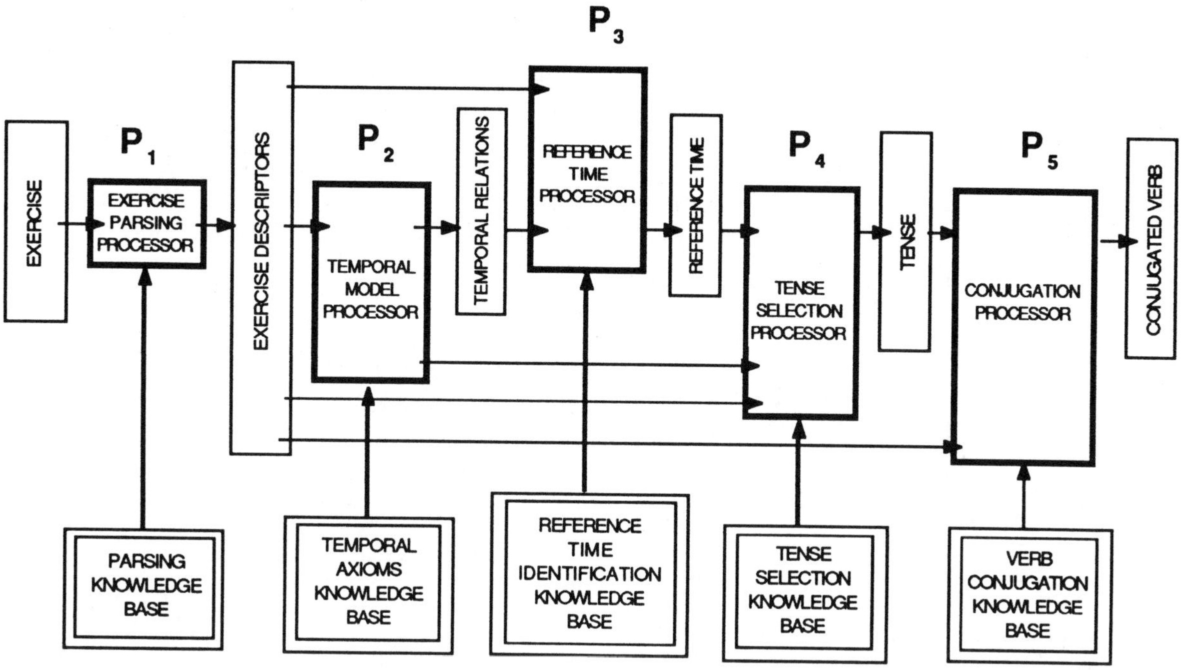

Figure 1. The tense generation process.

- it exploits a sophisticated technique such explanation-based learning to push the limits of the bug construction methodology.

The paper is organized as follows: The following section briefly presents the ET system where backward model tracing has been applied. Section 3 illustrates the general criteria upon which the methodology is grounded. Section 4 and 5 describe the technical details of the modelling process focusing on the generation of explanatory hypotheses about the causes of the student erroneous behavior and on the discrimination among the formed hypotheses, respectively. Section 6 presents the conclusions of the work.

2. Second Language Tutoring in ET

The backward model tracing methodology has been utilized in the new version of the ET system (Fum, Giangrandi, & Tasso 1988), an ITS aimed at supporting Italian students in the learning of the English verb system. ET comprises an articulated knowledge-based domain expert (Fum, Giangrandi, & Tasso 1989), devoted to tense generation, capable to solve fill-in exercises constituted by one or more sentences in which some verbs have to be conjugated into the appropriate tenses. The operation of the domain expert is organized around a sequence of five phases (illustrated in figure 1), each devoted to a specific (sub)process, namely:

- parsing the exercise sentence(s);
- recognizing the temporal relations among the events described in the sentence(s);
- identifying the reference time for every clause in the sentence(s);
- selecting the correct tense to be used for each verb;
- conjugating the verb(s) into the appropriate tense.

Each process is carried out by a dedicated processor, which is supported by a knowledge base encoding the knowledge usually exploited by humans for that subtask. The main representation paradigm utilized in the knowledge bases is constituted by production rules. The generation expert produces also a precise track of the reasoning performed and of the knowledge utilized for solving the exercises.

The second fundamental module of ET is the tutor which is devoted to define the modalities of the teaching activity. More particularly, the tutor assigns the exercises according to a given syllabus, cooperates with the modeler in order to discriminate among alternative hypotheses about the student erroneous behavior, and manages the dialogue with the student.

The student modeler is the module which implements the backward model tracing methodology. The general goal of this module is to discover the domain specific knowledge the student has utilized in order to derive her/his answer(s). The modelling process aims at constructing a model of the students beliefs in which both correct knowledge and misconceptions are explicitly represented. The student model, which is partitioned into different parts, one for each computational phase, contains therefore a collection of facts and rules that have been utilized in order to interpret the student behavior and that are supposed to mirror what the student knows/beliefs about the subject domain. The student model supplies the basis for remedial activity which is aimed at correcting the student misconceptions. The structure and the functioning of this module constitutes the subject of this paper.

3. Modelling Student Performance

Backward model tracing relies on two basic assumptions:

(i) in achieving the solution, the student follows a process akin to that used by the expert module i.e., it goes through the same phases and performs essentially the same kind of computations, and

(ii) the student mistakes can be modelled by appropriately perturbing the knowledge utilized by the expert module.

Some words are needed in order to justify these assumptions. It could be claimed that assumption (i) is unrealistic: in fact it is easy to find evidence that novices solve problems by using strategies that are different from those utilized by experts (e.g., diSessa 1982; Reif 1987). While this cannot be denied, it is also true that, in order to be able to model possible student misbehaviors, a model of the correct performance is required. The student behavior needs thus to be compared with that of an 'expert', being this a real domain expert, a teacher or an 'ideal student' (Anderson 1987). The general philosophy followed in ITS development is to locate the domain specific knowledge in the expert module which plays therefore a twofold role: it acts as the *source* for the knowledge to be presented and, at the same time, it serves as the *standard* for evaluating the student's performance" (Wenger 1987). In our context we assume that a student, trying to figure out the correct answer for an exercise, follows the same reasoning steps of the expert module, i.e. after interpreting the meaning of the exercise sentences (s)he computes the temporal relations between the states/events described in the sentence, calculates the reference times for every clause of the sentence, chooses the tense for the verb and, finally, conjugates the verb in that tense. Assumption (i) implies that the errors the student makes could derive only from the fact that some of the rules (s)he applies are 'bugged', not from the fact that (s)he can follow computational paths different from those of the expert. Assumption (ii), (shared by other authors: Brown & Burton 1980; Sleeman 1983; Bonar & Soloway 1985) states that it is possible to model these bugs by assuming more or less severe deviations from the knowledge base actually utilized by the expert module.

Backward model tracing is grounded on the idea of trying to reconstruct, step by step and in reverse order, the chain of reasoning the student has followed in building the answer. Backward model tracing is triggered by the discovery of a mismatch between the answer given by the student and that provided by the expert module. The goal of the modelling process is to identify the phase(s) where the reasoning process of the student and of the expert differ, and the specific erroneous rules *(malrules)* applied by the student. Backward model tracing analyzes the reasoning process performed by the student starting from the last phase and going back toward the first ones. For each phase, the modeler tries to determine the input to the phase and the knowledge the student has utilized in order to produce the corresponding output. If a mismatch between the student and the expert output is discovered, it could mean that: (a) some of the rules contained in the knowledge base utilized by the student in that phase, or (b) some of the data utilized as input for that phase or, (c) both some of the rules and the data differ from those utilized by the expert.

The goal of the diagnostic process performed by the modeler is to realize which of the above alternatives holds. Case (a) is true when both the expert and the student work with the same input data but their output is different because some of the rules contained in the student knowledge base are actually bugged. In this case a remedial activity could be planned in order to clarify the student misconceptions. As an example of case (a) let us consider the case when both the student and the expert have to form the present perfect of 'to study' and the student produces as an answer 'has studyied'. If (b) is true, then at least one of the previous phases should be blamed for producing the erroneous data and the diagnostic process is repeated focusing on the phase immediately preceding the current one. As an example of (b) let consider the case of the student answering 'has studied' when in fact the correct verb tense is the past perfect. If (c) is true, then both the above mentioned activities occur, i.e., the malrules responsible for the mistake made in that phase are identified and the diagnostic process continues with the preceding phases. An example of case (c) is the answer 'has studyed' given when the past perfect is required.

Backward model tracing shares all the features of the model tracing methodology (Anderson 1987), i.e. it tries to simulate dynamically a student's problem solving and uses that simulation to interpret the student behavior. Differently from Anderson's approach:

- it does not rely only on a-priori established catalogue of correct and incorrect productions but it is able to dynamically generate the malrules necessary to explain the student performance;
- the tracing occurs *after* the student has produced his/her performance and it is not used to monitor the student during the solution process just to assure that the correct path will be followed.

As a result, backward model tracing possibly represents a less intrusive modelling methodology and a more general diagnostic procedure.

Having established the general features of our approach to student modelling, we concentrate now on the technical details of the diagnostic process as it is performed within a single phase.

4. Explaining the Student Answer

The diagnostic process aimed at reconstructing the student reasoning for each single phase can be divided in two activities: the first is aimed at generating all the possible lines of reasoning which constitute putative explanations of how the student determined his solution in that phase; the second is aimed at discriminating among the different candidate explanations trying to discover the one(s) that best account(s) for the actual student reasoning. The present section explains how the first activity is performed; section 5 deals with the hypotheses discrimination activity.

In order to formulate possible explanations for the student behavior, the modeler operates in backward chaining and generates a derivation tree containing the rules and facts used to produce the output of the phase. More precisely, the output is considered as explained if it is possible to prove it by exploiting the production rules contained in the knowledge base the student utilizes for that phase. As a result of the diagnostic process, the modeler will be able to identify the input data for that phase and the possible malrules utilized by the student.

In order to give a more comcrete idea of the diagnostic process, let us follow the system operation through a worked out example, restricted for simplicity only to the last verb conjugation phase. The student, requested to conjugate into the appropriate tense the verb 'to study', gives as an answer 'is studyed' while the output given by the expert module is 'has studied'. As a first step, the modeler transforms the student answer into the following clause

verb(Verb, Tense, Person, Number, [is, studyed]/[])

which represents the goal to be proven and whose first four arguments will be instantiated at the end of the diagnostic process with the input data for the phase. The modeler then tries to construct one or more derivation trees for that goal. To this purpose, the system tries to find, among the rules contained in the student knowledge base, that whose right hand side matches the current goal (if several rules match the goal, the modeler constructs several derivation trees in parallel) and it tries to prove each antecedent clause in the left hand side of the rule. If a clause constitutes a primitive goal (for example a fact contained in the dictionary) it is considered as proven and the modeler goes on to analyze a new clause, otherwise the modeler proceeds recursively by trying to build a derivation (sub)tree for that clause.

The main improvement of our algorithm in comparison with similar approaches (e.g. classic backward chaining, the resolution plus oracle method reported in (Costa, Duchenoy, & Kodratoff 1988), and the technique utilized in (Sleeman 1983)), concerns the treatment of the failing situations. In fact, when the modeler finds a subgoal which is unprovable (i.e. which is neither a primitive goal nor can be demonstrated by applying the rules contained in the student knowledge base) it tries to recover from this situation by exploiting two different modelling strategies. First, it can resort to the bug collection technique by selecting in a catalogue of malrules, representing instances of stereotyped errors students generally make, an appropriate malrule which could be used to prove the current goal. This malrule is then imported as a hypothetical misconception into a/the derivation tree for the student answer. Second, if none of the available malrules is suitable to prove the current goal, the modeler tries to generate a new malrule by perturbing an expert rule; in other words a rule representing certain domain knowledge is purposely modified and made incorrect in order to use it to prove the original goal. This malrule is also imported into the derivation tree.

While the first strategy simply utilizes the classic bug collection approach, the second strategy (bug construction) exploits machine learning techniques in order to generate new malrules. Among the possible machine learning techniques usable for generating new malrules, we have adopted an explanation-based approach (Mitchell, Keller, & Kedar-Kabelli 1986; DeJong & Mooney 1986). This approach, which has been already exploited in the field of ITS (Bar-On & Or-Bach 1988), seems particularly promising to be utilized for student modelling for the following reasons:

- differently from other machine learning techniques, it requires only a few training instances (possibly only one) to be applied and it seems therefore particularly suitable for modelling when only a few student answers are available;
- it is an intensive knowledge-based technique and it seems therefore suitable in a field where a lot of domain-dependent knowledge is available in terms of both the expert knowledge base and of diagnostic knowledge (i.e. knowledge about possible student errors).

Bug construction thus constitutes the major tool when no a-priori information about a specific student (mis)behavior is available, i.e. when a student makes an error not contained in the bug library. The generative capability of the bug construction methodology, however, can be improved by taking into account other useful kinds of diagnostic knowledge. For this reason, we have generalized the bug catalogue approach in order to be able to represent any kind of misconception a student could possibly have about expert knowledge. The solution adopted is to allow the bug library to specify not only the malrules but also to describe possible perturbations of them (Hirsh 1985). To perturb a rule, the modeler uses the knowledge contained in the so-called *meta-bug library* of rules which specifies the kinds of perturbations that could be applied to a rule. This knowledge, which forms a theory of the possible errors students can make, is represented with general diagnostic rules whose condition part specifies a failing situation (a general pattern for a goal that cannot be proved) and whose conclusion part specifies a clause that could be used to replace the failing condition.

Coming back to our example, the spelling error contained in the student answer can be explained by the following stereotyped malrule (MR1):

IF add_string(V,ed,V_ed)
THEN form_ed(V,[V_ed |X]/X).

which says that to form the ed-form of a verb it is sufficient to add the suffix 'ed' to the root form of the verb.

Two rules of the meta-bug library (MB1 and MB2) utilized by the system are the following:

IF verb(have,T,P,N,V1/V2) *% Failure*
THEN verb(be,T,P,N,V1/V2). *% Repair*

IF regular(Verb, Tense) *% Failure*
THEN true. *% Repair*

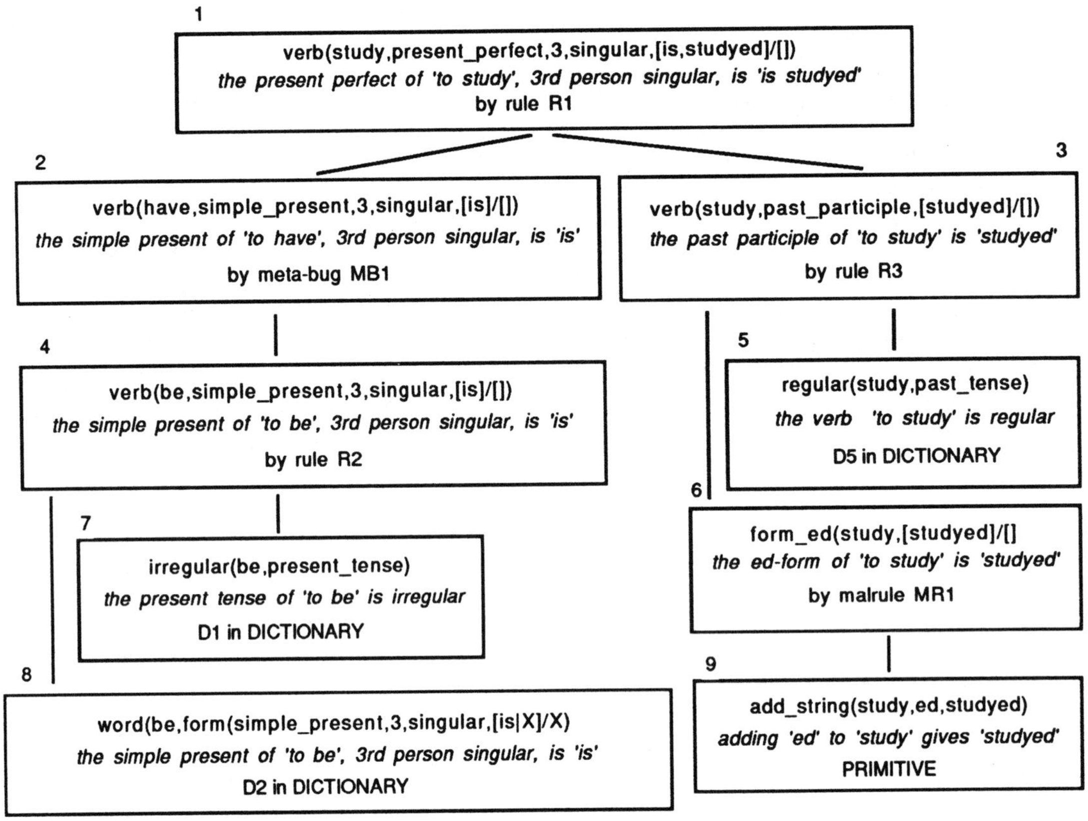

Figure 2. A derivation tree.

The first rule takes care of the case in which a student could use the auxiliary 'to be' instead of 'to have' (auxiliary inversion represents a typical error made by Italian students) by saying that, in order to prove a failing clause containing the verb 'to have', it is possible to replace it with a clause containing 'to be'. The second rule takes care of the case in which the student may forget the constraint that, in order to use a given conjugation rule, a regular verb is required, by relaxing that constraint and considering the clause to be proven as true.

In our example, the first meta-rule allows to explain the incorrect use of the auxiliary. In fact, when the modeler tries to prove the original goal

verb(Verb, Tense, Person, Number, [is, studyed]/[])

it finds a match with the consequent of the following conjugation rule (R1):

IF verb(have,simple_present,Person,Number,V1/V2),
verb(V,past_participle,V2/V3)
THEN verb(V, present_perfect,Person,Number, V1/V3).

(the present perfect of a verb is formed by joining the simple present of 'have' and the past participle of the verb). To prove this goal it tries to prove the two antecedent clauses. It fails with the first one since nowhere it can find a rule that enables it to deduce that

verb(have, simple_present, Person, Number, [is]/[])

(i.e. that the simple present of have is 'is'). But now the meta-bug MB1 can be applied to this clause thus obtaining

verb(be,simple_present,Person, Number, [is]/[])

which can be proven by looking at another rule (R2). By introducing this new clause it is possible to positively conclude the building of the derivation tree. Figure 2 illustrates a complete example of a derivation tree for the above discussed goal while figure 3 shows both a PROLOG and a natural language version of the knowledge utilized. Each node of the derivation tree (with the exception of the root) specifies a (partial) conclusion produced during the hypothesized reasoning process of the student, while the root represents the final output. In the specific case, the student built incorrectly the present perfect as a combination of the simple present of the verb 'to be' (rule R1) and the ed-form of the verb 'to study'. His wrong answer has been caused by the mistakes made in producing the present perfect and the ed-form of 'to study' (this mistake is represented in the bug catalogue by the malrule MR1).

Since each derivation tree describes the reasoning of the student applied to a very specific situation, in order to be able to extract more general malrules it is necessary to generalize the derivation tree containing the mistake.

```
CONJUGATION RULES
%% R1: The present perfect is formed with the simple present of the verb
%% 'to have' and the past participle of the verb.
  IF verb(have,simple_present,Person,Number,V1/V2),
     verb(Vb,past_participle,V2/V3),
  THEN verb(Vb,present_perfect,Person,Number,V1/V3).
%% R2: The simple present of an irregular verb is contained in the dictionary.
  IF irregular(Vb,present_tense),
     word(Vb,form(simple_present,Person,Number,V1/V2)),
  THEN verb(Vb,simple_present,Person,Number,V1/V2).
%% R3: The past participle of a regular verb is formed with the ed-form
%% of the verb.
  IF regular(Vb,past_participle),
     form_ed(Vb,V1/V2),
  THEN verb(Vb,past_participle,V1/V2).

VERB DICTIONARY
%% D1: The simple present of the verb 'to be' is irregular.
  irregular(be,present_tense).
%% D2: The simple present of the verb 'to be', 3rd singular, is 'is'.
  word(be,form(simple_present,3,singular,[is|X]/X)).
%% D3: The simple present of the verb 'to have' is irregular.
  irregular(have,present_tense).
%% D4: The simple present of the verb 'to have', 3rd singular, is 'has'.
  word(have,form(simple_present,3,singular,[has|X]/X)).
%% D5: The verb 'to study' is regular.
  regular(study,past_tense).

BUG LIBRARY
%% MR1
  IF add_string(V,ed,V_ed)
  THEN form_ed(V,[V_ed|X]/X).

META BUG LIBRARY
%% MB1
  IF verb(have,T,P,N,V1/V2)
  THEN verb(be,T,P,N,V1/V2).
%% MB2
  IF regular(Verb,Tense)
  THEN true.
```

Figure 3. Domain and diagnostic knowledge.

For this purpose, the modeler considers a more general structure, called *explanation structure*, which highlights the various rules (domain rules and possible diagnostic rules) applied during the construction of the derivation tree. Figure 4 illustrates the explanation structure originating from the derivation tree of figure 2. Each box contains the pair of rule clauses unified during the construction of the derivation tree.

At this point, while the standard explanation-based learning technique works on the whole structure in order to extract a single general concept, our algorithm proceeds instead focussing on the subtrees containing some meta-bugs; more precisely, it considers those rules who have clauses linked to the meta-bugs. From a single derivation tree it is thus possible to infer more than one malrule. In our example, illustrated in figure 4, the modeler concentrates upon the subtree constituted by rule R1 and the meta-bug MB1. For each subtree, the modeler unifies the rule clauses to which a meta-bug has been applied with the left hand side of the meta-bug and then it applies the substitution to the right hand side of the meta-bug. In our example, the antecedent clause of R1

verb(have, simple_present,P1,N1,V1/V2)

is unified with the left hand side of meta-bug MB1

verb(have, T2, P2, N2, V4/V5)

and the substitution {T2 ⇔ simple_present, P2 ⇔ P1, N2 ⇔ N1, V4 ⇔ V1, V5 ⇔ V2} is then applied to the right hand side of the meta-bug. The resulting right hand side of meta-bug MB1 is thus:

verb(be,simple_present,P1,N1,V1/V2)

Now, the final step consists in substituting this clause to the antecedent of rule R1. The final resulting malrule is therefore:

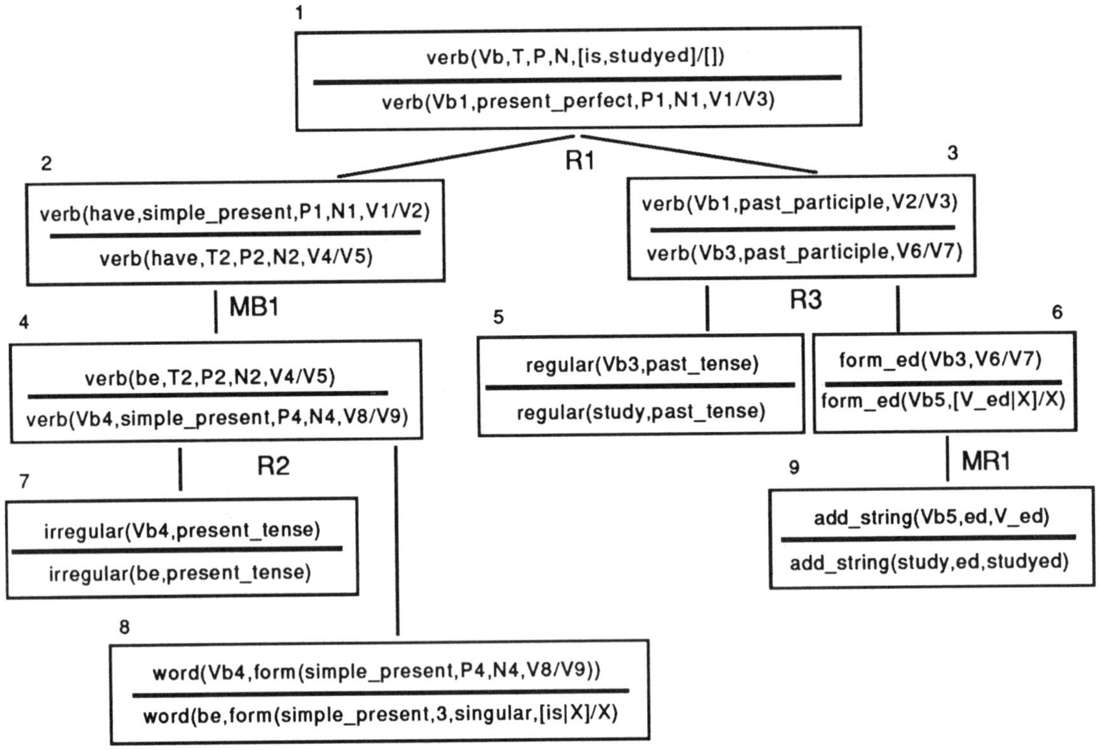

Figure 4. An explanation structure.

IF verb(be,simple_present,P1,N1,V1/V2),
verb(Vb1,past_participle,V2/V3)
THEN verb(Vb1,present_perfect,P1,N1, V1/V3),

meaning that the present perfect could be erroneously formed with the simple present of the verb 'to be' and the past participle of the verb.

5. Discriminating among Explanations

In general, the result of the first modelling activity is a collection of derivation trees which represent different possible reasoning processes followed by the student. The second basic activity of the modelling process has the goal to test all the generated hypotheses in order to select the best one(s) which account(s) for the student performance. During this operation the modeler behaves non monotonically discarding contradictory or very unlikely hypotheses, retracting the disconfirmed assumptions and transforming hypotheses into certified facts.

More particularly, in order to discriminate among the different candidate explanations the modeler has built, two strategies are followed. On one hand, some heuristic criteria are utilized to eliminate unplausible hypotheses or to derive new assertions about the student. On the other hand, the hypotheses about the reasons of the student behavior are maintained by utilizing a justification-based truth maintenance system (Doyle 1979; McAllester 1982).

Some of the heuristic criteria utilized to discriminate among the different hypotheses are the following:

- *If the student answer is explained by a single derivation tree, the rules and the facts contained in the tree are inserted into the student model.*
- *If a hypothesized malrule appears in all the alternative derivation trees, it can be taken for sure and inserted into the student model.*
- *If a derivation tree contains a number of perturbations which is greater than an established threshold, the derivation tree and its hypothesized malrules are discharged.*
- *If a hypothesized malrule, applied to simulate the student behavior in an exercise different from that by which it was originally derived, produces an answer different from that given by the student, then it is considered as unplausible and discharged.*

The hypotheses the modeler makes about the student are managed through a justification-based truth maintenance system. In particular, the hypotheses are organized into a network (called *dependency network*) which describes the dependency relations among different hypotheses. For example, the rules and the dictionary facts R1, R2, R3, D1, D2, and D5 support the derivation tree of figure 2 and this derivation tree supports both the stereotyped malrule MR1 and the newly constructed one. If some node of the network is deleted during the modelling process, then all the nodes that are dependent on it are also cancelled. This operation is achieved by following the edges of the dependency network. On the other hand, when a previously constructed hypothesis is confirmed, it is introduced into the student model and, furthermore, the consequences of this change are propagated through the dependency network thus influencing the truth of the other hypotheses supported by it.

The diagnostic process requires generally also the cooperation of the tutoring module. When the information the system has about the student is insufficient to discriminate among the different alternative hypotheses generated by the modeler, the tutor can (i) assign new exercises in order to gather data to confirm or disconfirm them or (ii) can start an interactive (menu-driven) dialogue with the student. More precisely, the tutor selects from the exercise database the exercises related to the hypothesized misconceptions and, for each of them, the system determines the answers corresponding to these misconceptions. An exercise is considered as discriminating if it gives different answers for every different hypothesized misconception. The tutor then can select the most discriminating exercise. If no discriminating exercises are available, it is necessary to use the dialogue in order to establish which misconception reflects the student knowledge. It must be pointed out that the tutor considers not only the derivation tree(s) related to the last exercise but it also analyzes the derivation trees of the previous exercises in order to examine the remaining hypotheses. The analysis of a student misconception cannot therefore generally be completed in a single exercise but it requires a sequence of exercises.

6. Conclusions

A new methodology for modelling student performance has been presented which could be used for making diagnosis in those systems that, like ET are based on processes decomposable into a finite number of subtasks related to each other through producer-consumer dependencies. It is claimed, in other words, that the deep modelling process illustrated in the paper has general significance beyond the domain of second language teaching and can constitute an attempt to deal with the problem of finding the reasons of and giving a satisfactory explanation to the student performance. Some features of the proposed approach that we find particularly original are: (i) the integration of the bug collection and bug construction techniques, (ii) the use of diagnostic knowledge contained in the meta-bug library in order to help the process of bug construction, and (iii) the use of explanation based learning techniques in the domain of modelling students' misconceptions. The proposed approach has been fully implemented in a student modelling module written in QUINTUS PROLOG and running on a SUN 3 workstation.

References

Anderson, J. 1987. Production Systems, Learning, and Tutoring. In D. Klahr, P. Langley, and R. Neches eds. *Production System Models of Learning and Development.* Cambridge, MA: The MIT Press.

Bar-On, E.; and Or-Bach, R. 1988. Explanation-Based Learning in Intelligent Tutoring Systems. In P. Ercoli, and R. Lewis eds. *Artificial Intelligence Tools in Education.* Amsterdam, NL: Elsevier Science Publ.

Bonar, J.G.; and Soloway, E.M. 1985. Pre-Programming Knowledge: A Major Source of Misconceptions in Novice Programmers. *Human-Computer Interaction* 1(2): 133-161.

Brown, J.; and Burton, R. 1980. Diagnostic Models for Procedural Bugs in Mathematical Skills. *Cognitive Science* 4: 379-426.

Costa, E.; Duchenoy, S.; and Kodratoff, Y. 1988. A Resolution Based Method for Discovering Students' Misconceptions. In J.A. Self ed. *Artificial Intelligence and Human Learning.* London, UK: Chapman and Hall.

DeJong, G.F.; and Mooney, R.J. 1986. Explanation-Based Learning: An Alternative View. *Machine Learning* 1: 145-176.

diSessa, A.A. 1982. Unlearning Aristotelian Physics: A Study of Knowledge-Based Learning. *Cognitive Science* 6: 37-75.

Doyle, J. 1979. A Truth Maintenance System. *Artificial Intelligence* 12: 231-272.

Fum, D.; Giangrandi, P.; and Tasso, C. 1988. ET: An Intelligent Tutor for Foreign Language Teaching. In Proceedings of ITS-88, 462-468. Montreal, Canada.

Fum, D.; Giangrandi, P.; and Tasso, C. 1989. Tense Generation in an Intelligent Tutor for Foreign Language Teaching: Some Issues in the Design of the Verb Expert. In Proceedings of the 4th Conference of the European Chapter of the Association for Computational Linguistics, 124-129. Manchester, UK: Association for Computational Linguistics.

Hirsh, H. 1985. Modeling Problem Solving Performance. Master's thesis, Stanford Univ.

McAllester, D.A. 1982. Reasoning utility package user's manual. Technical Report, AIM-667, Artificial Intelligence Laboratory, M.I.T.

Mitchell, T.M.; Keller, R.; and Kedar-Kabelli, S. 1986. Explanation-Based Generalization: A Unifying View. *Machine Learning* 1: 47-80.

Reif, F. 1987. Interpretation of Scientific or Mathematical Concepts: Cognitive Issues and Instructional Implications. *Cognitive Science* 11: 395-416.

Self, J.A. 1988. Bypassing the Intractable Problem of Student Modelling. In Proceedings of ITS-88, 18-24. Montreal, Canada.

Sleeman, D. 1983. Inferring (Mal) Rules from Pupils' Protocols. In Proceedings of the Second International Machine Learning Workshop, 221-227. Chicago, IL.

Wenger, E. 1987. *Artificial Intelligence and Tutoring Systems.* Los Altos, CA: Morgan Kaufman.

A Blackboard-based Dynamic Instructional Planner

William R. Murray

Artificial Intelligence Department
FMC Corporate Technology Center
1205 Coleman Avenue, Box 580
Santa Clara, California 95052
murray@ctc.fmc.com

Abstract[1]

The Blackboard Instructional Planner is a blackboard-based dynamic planner for intelligent tutoring systems. It generates a sequence of lesson plans customized to a student's background, and adaptively replans to handle student requests and unexpected changes to the student model or time remaining. The planner is designed to be generic to tutors that teach troubleshooting for complex physical devices. It controls the Lower Hoist Tutor, a prototype tutor for the Mark-45 naval gun mount. This tutor teaches troubleshooting of the lower hoist, a complex hydraulic-electronic-mechanical assembly of the Mark-45. The tutor implementation demonstrates the planner's operation and means of integration.

This research contributes to an understanding of dynamic instructional planners, planner-controlled tutors, and ITS control architectures. The planner implementation shows precisely how a blackboard architecture can be used to realize a dynamic instructional planner. Although experimental, the tutor implementation demonstrates how such a planner can be embedded in an intelligent tutoring system and what the respective roles of the different components of a planner-controlled tutor are. Finally, the analysis of the planner's use of the blackboard architecture clarifies requirements for control architectures in intelligent tutoring systems and trade-offs made in choosing alternatives.

Introduction

The Blackboard Instructional Planner (BB-IP) is a blackboard-based dynamic planner for intelligent tutoring systems. Although experimental, the planner demonstrates key plan generation and replanning capabilities required to handle common tutorial situations. It generates a sequence of lesson plans customized to a student model inferred from a pre-instruction questionnaire. The content, sequencing, and length of lessons are determined by the inferred student model, by the time allotted for lessons, by the target skill to be taught, and by the subject domain. These lesson plans are revised during instruction in response to student questions and requests, changes in time remaining for lessons, and modifications to the student model.

The goal of this research is to increase the flexibility and effectiveness of computer-based tutoring systems by applying dynamic planning techniques to control the tutor's actions. Traditional CAI systems do not plan at all although they can deliver very well-crafted lesson plans. Typically, however, they have no domain expertise, customize only via branching or problem selection, and cannot use opportunistic teaching methods. They must limit student questions and requests since they cannot reason about the domain or the student's lesson plan during instruction. On the other hand, most intelligent tutoring systems incorporate domain expertise and student modeling so that they can apply opportunistic teaching approaches in the course of student problem-solving or a dialog about the subject matter. These tutors tend to be used as adjuncts to classroom instruction since they assume primary instruction is delivered elsewhere. Generally, lesson planning is not done although recent systems have focused on sophisticated local discourse planning. The purpose of the Blackboard Instructional Planner is to integrate these two complementary means of instruction - plan-based and opportunistic - for tutors and domains where this is most appropriate.

Our approach to this control problem is called *dynamic instructional planning*. In this approach, an initial instructional plan is generated by the planner. This plan is customized to an inferred student model. It takes into account the resources available to the tutor (e.g., time). The tutor interprets this plan to control its delivery of instruction. The planner is dynamic since it can later revise this plan during instruction as the tutorial situation changes. The tutorial situation changes as the student model changes, the amount of time available changes, and as student-initiated interactions interrupt the tutor's plan.

The planner operates as the control element of an intelligent tutoring system, as shown in Figure 1 (arrows indicate data flow). The planner generates an initial instructional plan customized to the inferred student model. The actions in the instructional plan are procedures that control the text, highlighting, and animation displayed on the student interface. The interface also accepts student input, including student-initiated questions and requests that can interrupt these instructional procedures. The library of possible instructional procedures the planner can draw upon is part of the courseware. The courseware includes curriculum

[1]This project was sponsored jointly by the Manpower, Personnel and Training R&D Committee of the Office of the Chief of Naval Research (under contract N00014-86-C-0487); the Air Force Human Resources Laboratory; the Naval Training Systems Center; and the Naval Personnel Research and Development Center.

materials such as test questions and troubleshooting cases. The domain expert evaluates student performance on these cases, demonstrates correct troubleshooting, and provides answers to student questions about the domain. These evaluations update the student model. Changes to the student model cause replanning if student progress is much better or worse than expected.

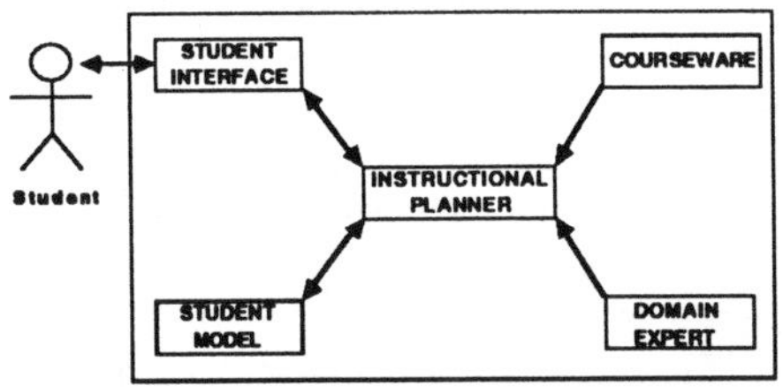

Figure 1: The planner and other ITS components

The planner is designed to be generic to tutors that teach troubleshooting for complex physical devices. It has been implemented as the controller for the Lower Hoist Tutor, a prototype tutor for the Mark-45 naval gun mount, to demonstrate the planner's operation and means of integration. The tutor teaches troubleshooting of the lower hoist assembly, a complex hydraulic-electronic-mechanical assembly of the Mark-45, by first imparting a mental model of the device and its operation. A STEAMER-based (Hollan, Hutchins, & Weitzman 1984) display of the lower hoist schematic has been adapted for use in exposition, assessment, and troubleshooting practice.

Overview of Operation

Figure 2 provides an overview of the operation of the Blackboard Instructional Planner. The *generic skills knowledge base* is a graph with nodes representing device-independent troubleshooting skills for complex hydraulic-electronic-mechanical devices. Arcs represent prerequisite relationships among these skills. The planner interprets this graph as a very high level strategy for teaching troubleshooting.[1] Structure and operation of the device must be taught along with possible faults and a troubleshooting strategy. The *domain knowledge base* is a semantic network that provides the particulars of the structure and operation of the lower hoist assembly of the Mark-45. It includes a parts breakdown and the sequence of events (part state changes) that occur in normal operation. The circled X in Figure 2 means that a cartesian product of the two knowledge bases is formed to produce the graph of *domain-specific skills*. For example, one skill in the generic skills knowledge base specifies that the student should understand the role of each part in the device. So for the lower hoist's 42 parts, 42 domain-specific skills result. Each corresponds to understanding the role of one particular part.

[1]This strategy is not based on any cognitive theory, rather it was inferred from the subject matter expert's approach to classroom instruction.

The graph of domain-specific skills acts as a machine-generated curriculum graph for the skill of troubleshooting the particular device. A three-level instructional plan is produced by selecting out skills from this graph to teach the student, selecting abstract methods to teach the skills, and then selecting specific LISP routines consistent with these methods. The plan generation process also involves sequencing the lessons and lesson plan steps, selecting appropriate parameters for the instructional procedures, critiquing the plan as it is developed, and revising it to improve discourse flow. The result is an *instructional plan*, which is further broken down into a sequence of *lesson plans*, corresponding to individual tutorial sessions.

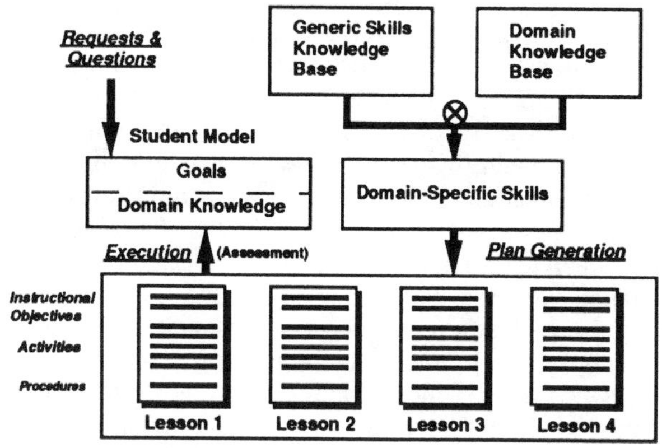

Figure 2: Overview of BB-IP Planning

The plan is executed by interpreting the instructional procedures. Some of the procedures assess student ability through tests or by monitoring task performance. This assessment updates the student model, which can in turn cause replanning to occur. Replanning occurs when student performance is unexpectedly good or bad. It can also be initiated when much less time or more time is available than expected, or when student questions or requests interrupt the tutor's plan. During replanning the plan is edited to add plan steps, remove them, or to alter the procedure parameters. Then execution resumes.

Examples of Plan Customization

Consider two different student backgrounds and the different plans that are generated. Suppose the first student is deficient in the background area of electronics and learns more slowly than the average student. The second student has the expected knowledge of hydraulics, electronics, and mechanics and learns rapidly. The tutor labels the first as *Electronics-Deficient, Low-Aptitude* and the second as *Has-Prerequisites, High-Aptitude* based on the results of a short pre-instruction questionnaire covering prerequisite material and general student background. The inferred cognitive stereotypes (Rich 1979) are used to initialize an overlay student model (Carr & Goldstein 1977) that is an overlay of the domain-specific skills.

The tutor generates quite different plans for these two students although the high-level teaching strategy, derived from the common generic skills knowledge base, is the same. Both plans cover structure and operation of the lower hoist and discuss a general troubleshooting strategy. Then correct troubleshooting is demonstrated and student performance monitored in troubleshooting cases selected by the tutor. But the first plan is much longer than the second since it provides more layered instruction on lower hoist structure and operation, more discussion of how to troubleshoot, and specific remedial instruction covering the operation of electrically-controlled parts.

The instructional plan for the *Electronics-Deficient, Low-Aptitude* student consists of five lessons and 51 steps (instructional procedures). In the first lesson an introduction to lower hoist structure and operation is given, followed by a detailed description of the lower hoist parts, their location, and their role in lower hoist operation. The second lesson explains how solenoids operate and then provides a detailed explanation of all the part state changes that occur in a normal cycle of operation of the lower hoist. This detailed explanation interleaves text explaining part state changes with animation showing the changes discussed. In the third lesson the student must demonstrate his understanding of normal operation by successively pointing to the next part that should change state and indicating what the new state should be. Essentially, the student leads the simulation. In the fourth lesson, the tutor discusses the possible faults that can occur in the lower hoist. It also discusses how to reason from symptoms to possible faults. Then it presents a troubleshooting strategy that takes into account part change cost, malfunction probability, and split-half testing. Finally, troubleshooting is demonstrated for a particular case. The last lesson is devoted to letting the student practice troubleshooting for various cases with the tutor's assistance.

The instructional plan for the *Has-Prerequisites, High-Aptitude* student is quite different. Instead of five lessons and 51 steps there are only three lessons and 26 steps. This plan omits much of the layered instruction given to the first student. For example, the procedures that introduce the structure and operation of the lower hoist in a layered fashion are omitted. Similarly, procedures that introduce troubleshooting in a layered fashion are omitted along with topics that the tutor judges to be of lower priority, such as part locations and descriptions. Procedure parameters also differ for the procedure that monitors student troubleshooting. In the second instructional plan the parameters are set to provide hints later, tolerate more incorrect actions, and provide less assistance with selecting test codes than in the first instructional plan.

Examples of Dynamic Replanning

Consider an example where a question is asked that interrupts the tutor's presentation. Assume the tutor is executing an instructional procedure called *Explain-Subcycles* that explains the detailed sequence of changes that occur during the operation of lower hoist. Midway through the procedure, when a change happens to the UVK4 piston, the student interrupts and asks what the role of that particular part is. The interruption and specification of the question is handled by a menu interface. Question templates are used to restrict questions to those that can be answered by executing one of the tutor's instructional procedures.

The tutor can either defer or directly answer the question. In this case the tutor chooses to answer the question now since the material being asked about will not be covered later. To answer the question the current procedure is suspended and a step to answer the question is inserted. The step *Explain-Subcycles* is suspended and two steps are spliced in after it:

Explain-Subcycles **[subcycles hoist]**
Patch-1:Part-Roles(to-ans-Ques#1) **[UVK4]**
Patch-1:Explain-Subcycles(cont) **[subcycles hoist** ***cont*****]**

The parameters of each procedure are indicated in boldface after the procedure name. They are shown here in a more readable format than the internal representation. The first step after the interrupted *Explain-Subcycles* procedure answers the question. The second continues *Explain-Subcycles* where it was interrupted. But this is not all that happens since the student model is affected simply by the student asking the question.

When the student asks a question about material that was covered earlier, the tutor's belief that the student knows that material is diminished. In this case the tutor covered the roles of the lower hoist parts earlier. The tutor detects that its prior goal, that the student knows the roles of these parts, is no longer satisfied and still should be. To reachieve this goal it splices in a review of the roles of the lower hoist parts before resuming *Explain-Subcycles*. Now the affected portion of the plan, after both plan patches have been added, appears as:

Explain-Subcycles **[subcycles hoist]**
Patch-1:Part-Roles(to-ans-Ques#1) **[UVK4]**
Patch-2:Part-Roles(to-review) **[all hoist parts]**
Patch-2:Multiple-Choice-Quiz **[role each hoist part]**
Patch-1:Explain-Subcycles(cont) **[subcycles hoist** ***cont*****]**

The multiple choice quiz has been added to check that the tutor's review is successful.

Now plan critics are applied to improve the tutorial discourse. There is an abrupt context shift from the review of the roles of the lower hoist parts back to the detailed discussion of the lower hoist cycle. This shift in discourse is smoothed out by adding a step: *Patch-2:Transition* **[part roles, subcycles hoist]**. Another plan critic attempts to remove redundant discussions. It ensures that only the first *Part-Roles* procedure discusses UVK4 by removing UVK4 from the list of parts discussed by the second *Part-Roles* procedure. After all the edits, the affected portion of the lesson plan appears as shown below:

Explain-Subcycles **[subcycles hoist]**
Patch-1:Part-Roles(to-ans-Ques#1) **[UVK4]**

Patch-2:Part-Roles(to-review) **[all parts except UVK4]**
Patch-2:Multiple-Choice-Quiz **[role each hoist part]**
Patch-2:Transition **[part roles, subcycles hoist]**
Patch-1:Explain-Subcycles (cont) **[subcycles hoist** ***cont*****]**

Requests are handled similarly. New steps are inserted to handle requests. Furthermore, future lesson plan steps may be *omitted.* For example, suppose the tutor grants a student request to use the device simulation. The tutor monitors the student's actions. If it believes the student has learned material it plans to cover then it will omit pending procedures to cover this material.

Dynamic replanning can also be initiated by unexpected changes to the student model. For example, as the tutor monitors student troubleshooting performance it updates the student model. Each troubleshooting action the student selects is compared to an expert's to compute its utility. Repeated inappropriate actions and hint requests cause the tutor to revise its belief that the student can troubleshoot the device downwards. When the belief value falls below a certain threshold, the procedure for monitoring student troubleshooting is suspended and replanning begins.

A diagnosis phase is entered where the tutor decides why its instruction has been ineffective. It could be that it assumed too much of the student, or that an earlier method of instruction was inappropriate. Once it has decided the cause of the problem it edits the instructional plan to address the problem and continues. Only a few diagnosis methods have been implemented. One is to collect the prerequisites for the skill not learnt and then to assess the student's knowledge of the prerequisites, one by one, until a prerequisite is found that the student does not understand. Then a review for that prerequisite is spliced into the plan prior to the suspended procedure for monitoring student troubleshooting. Execution resumes with the review before troubleshooting practice continues.

Other kinds of planning functionality have also been implemented, as discussed in detail in (Murray 1990b). If there is insufficient time to finish all the activities of a lesson then some activities may be deferred until the next lesson. All the remaining lesson boundaries may also be affected. If there is extra time a useful activity is added to take advantage of the time remaining. Incremental planning has also been demonstrated. Only abstract activities are specified for lesson plan steps with the choice of procedure deferred until the step is reached.

In the implementation of the examples above specific decisions had to be made about how to customize plans, how to handle student questions, and how to diagnose and correct ineffective plans. The claims made in this paper are not about these specific decisions, since at present there is little guidance from the educational psychology literature specific enough to be applied in these situations. Other approaches can be implemented that would customize plans differently and make different decisions about when and exactly how to replan. The claim made is that the planner framework - the plan representation, the use of blackboard architecture, and the kinds of plan editing that can be performed - would support these alternative pedagogical approaches as well.

Plan Representation

This section presents the hierarchical instructional plan representation. There are three levels:

1. *Instructional objectives* - goals of the tutor. These are domain specific skills which the tutor intends for the student to acquire (e.g., **can-predict-normal-behavior-hoist**).
2. *Activities* - abstract methods for achieving these goals. The most common activities are to cover a topic (e.g., **cover-topic-part-role-uvk4**) or to perform assessment for a skill (e.g., **assess-understands-structure-hoist**).
3. *Procedures* - instructional routines that implement specific activities.

Multiple procedures are available for the same activity. For example, different kinds of tests can be used for student assessment.

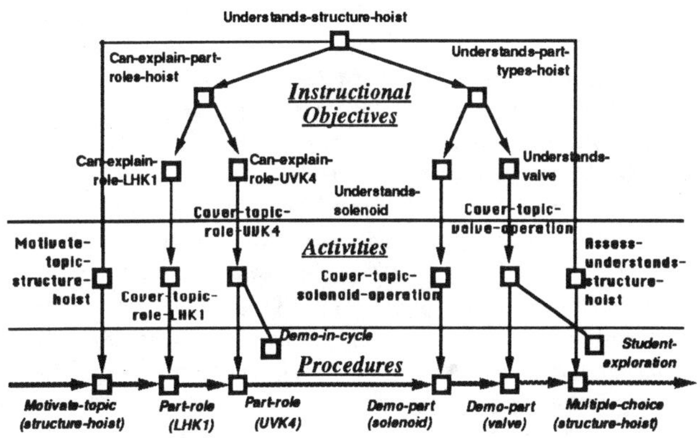

Figure 3: A simple instructional plan

Figure 3 shows a small instructional plan for teaching the structure of the lower hoist, assuming that it only had two parts. The top level is the *instructional objectives level.* On it, the top-level instructional objective has been broken down into two subordinate (i.e., prerequisite) objectives. First, that the student can explain the roles of the parts of the lower hoist. Second, that the student understands how the different part types operate. These objectives are broken down still further. First, the student must understand the role of each of the two parts. Then since LHK1 is a solenoid assembly the student needs to understand how solenoids operate. Similarly, since UVK4 is a hydraulic valve the student needs to understand how hydraulic valves operate.

The reason that the instructional objectives level is important is that it supports replanning. BB-IP needs to know why it was doing a procedure to determine what to do if that procedure fails. This representation of plan rationale supports replanning when previously satisfied instructional objectives are no longer maintained, or when pending instructional objectives are discovered to be already satisfied.

The next level, the *activities level*, supports incremental planning by allowing methods for carrying out the objectives to be represented, without committing to specific actions to carry out these methods. There is one activity for each terminal skill node plus additional activities to improve discourse flow and monitor plan progress. The activities **cover-topic-role-lhk1** and **cover-topic-role-uvk4** simply present text describing the role of the two lower hoist parts. The activity **motivate-topic-structure-hoist** has been added to improve discourse flow. It explains to the student that it is important to understand lower hoist structure in order to perform effective troubleshooting. The activities **cover-topic-solenoid-operation** and **cover-topic-valve-operation** present material explaining the operation of solenoids and valves. The final activity **assess-understands-structure-hoist** tests the student to determine if the plan has had its intended effect.

The final level, representing a sequence of directly executable plan actions, is the *procedures level*. For each activity a single procedure has been chosen to carry it out. For example, to cover UVK4's role the tutor can use either *Part-Role* or *Demo-in-Cycle*. *Part-Role* presents a textual description of UVK4's role. It also highlights and labels it in the device simulation. *Demo-in-Cycle* demonstrates the part's operation in the lower hoist cycle by animating the STEAMER device simulation. Similarly, the topic of hydraulic valve operation can be taught either by *Student-Exploration* or by *Demo-Part*. The first procedure asks the student to use the device simulation to explore the operation of a particular valve. The second demonstrates different valve states and how they affect connecting parts.

Each procedure is broken down into steps called *procedure steps*. A procedure can be interrupted between procedure steps and then resumed later. Typically, a procedure step displays another paragraph of text, or makes an incremental change to the device simulation shown on the student interface. For assessment procedures, each procedure step asks a question. Procedures are written this way so the student can ask questions or make requests between procedure steps. Another reason is to monitor procedure execution and student progress since the tutor can assess progress or lack of progress between procedure steps. If progress is insufficient then the tutor can interrupt the procedure to adjust its parameters or abandon it altogether.

Plan Generation, Execution, and Repair

Figure 4 shows the resources used in plan generation. The *activities library* is a set of generic activities (e.g., **cover-topic**, **assess-topic**, **demo-skill**) that can be used to achieve objectives. The *procedures library* is a set of instructional routines that can be used to achieve activities (e.g., *Explain-Subcycles*). These libraries are part of the courseware for the domain, although most of the activities and procedures can apply to other similar domains. The student model is a resource since it is used to filter out those objectives, activities, and procedures that are inappropriate for the student. Another resource is the library of *discourse critics* that are used to critique and revise the plan during plan generation, and immediately after plan editing. Once the plan has been generated, time estimates and a simple hill-climbing procedure are used to place lesson partitions (see (Murray 1990b) for details).

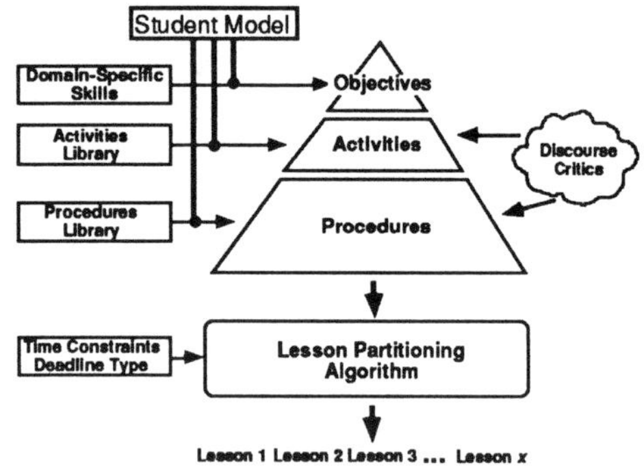

Figure 4: Plan generation

Plan generation and execution occur in phases called *control phases*. These are states where only certain kinds of planning actions are performed. BB-IP's control phases are shown in Figure 5. Phases on horizontal lines are next to the planning level they affect. Planning actions that occur in these phases either add to or modify a partially refined instructional plan. The special *Meta-Level* phase decides what plan phase to jump to next.

Consider plan generation first, assuming complete top-down plan elaboration. The basic sequence of phases is:

1. *Refine Objectives*- The top-level instructional objective is refined by copying prerequisite objectives from the domain specific skills.
2. *Assess Objectives* - The student is given a pre-instruction questionnaire to initialize the student model.
3. *Propose Activities* - Activities to achieve the objectives are proposed.
4. *Prioritize Activities* - Numerical priorities are assigned to each activity to indicate its importance.
5. *Filter Activities* - Only those activities above a threshold are retained.
6. *Sequence Activities* - These activities are now sequenced.
7. *Critique Activities* - Improvements in the discourse flow are made.
8. *Propose Actions* - Candidate procedures for each activity are proposed.
9. *Select Actions* - Heuristics are used to select the best procedure for each activity. Parameters are set for the procedures.
10. *Sequence Actions* - Procedures are

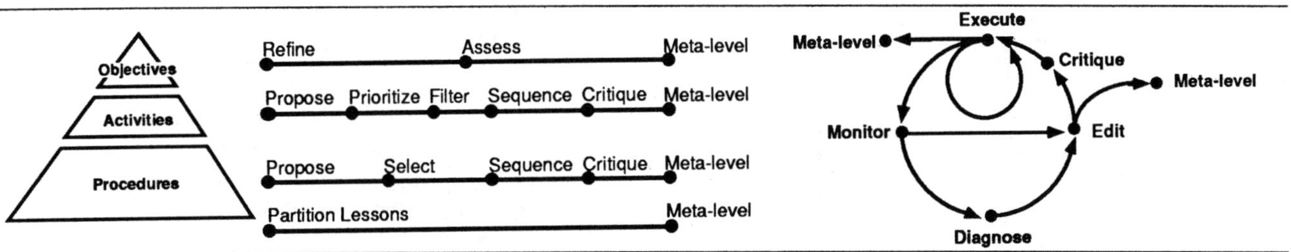

Figure 5: Control phases in plan generation and execution

sequenced in the same order as their parent activities.

11. *Critique Actions* - The plan is again critiqued and improved.
12. *Partition Lessons* - Partitions are laid down, breaking the instructional plan up into lesson plans.

The *Meta-Level* phases at the end of each horizontal line in Figure 5 were not mentioned since they just produce the sequencing above. However, when incremental planning occurs phases 8, 9, 10, and 11 are skipped.

After the *Partition Lessons* phase execution begins. The *Meta-Level* phase moves the planner into the execution loop shown at the right of Figure 5, starting with the *Execute* phase. The planner stays in the *Execute* phase as long as the instructional plan is executing smoothly. Interruptions occur when the student model or time do not change as expected or if there are student-initiated questions or requests. The planner enters the *Monitor* phase and the reason for the plan's interruption is recorded.

A question or a request is deferred if it will be handled later in the instructional plan anyway. Otherwise it is granted immediately. In the former case the tutor explains why the request is being deferred and continues with the *Execute* phase. In the latter case a step performing the procedure that answers the question or grants the request is spliced into the lesson plan in the *Edit* phase. The *Critique* phase adds a transition step then execution resumes. The next step to be executed is the step satisfying the student's request.

An unexpected change to time remaining or the student model means that the plan has some flaw. The *Diagnose* phase attempts to infer what is wrong. This phase ends when a decision has been made about what the problem is. Then the *Edit* phase either adds or deletes lesson plan steps, or alters procedure parameters, according to the kind of problem diagnosed. The steps added may only be at the activity level, requiring a digression back to the plan generation process to select procedures. Then this new plan patch is critiqued and execution resumes.

Planning and execution are interleaved through the use of control phases and in particular the *Meta-level* control phase. The *Meta-level* phase allows suspending the execution cycle to return to any point in the plan generation process. It also determines when execution should resume. This kind of interleaving of control phases occurs in incremental planning, in diagnosing plan execution problems, in generating initial assessment plans, and in elaborating, splicing in, and then executing plan repair patches.

The Blackboard Architecture and its Role

BB-IP is built on the BB1 Blackboard Architecture (Hayes-Roth 1984), which allows multiple blackboards, rather than just one. These are the main blackboards used by BB-IP:

- *Instructional Plan* - represents the three-level instructional plan.
- *Student Model* - represents the student model.
- *Device* - represents the structure and operation of the device.
- *Planner Control* - represents meta-level decisions such as whether to continue planning or start execution. Problems noted in the plan's execution and decisions about their cause are also recorded.

The *Device* blackboard is not updated during execution; the others are.

The knowledge sources of BB-IP are planning actions. They primarily modify the *Instructional Plan* blackboard. The kinds of actions performed are:

- *Plan generation* - new objects are added to the instructional plan and linked to the objects they refine. These objects represent objectives, activities, or procedures.
- *Plan execution* - a step in a procedure is executed.
- *Plan monitoring* - some problem in plan execution is noted. For example, the time available or student model is not as it should be.
- *Plan diagnosis* - a decision is made regarding a plan failure.
- *Plan revision* - part of the plan is modified. New activities or procedures may be added or others deleted.

The execution cycle of BB-IP is shown in Figure 6. Changes to the blackboards are caused either by the execution of planning actions, or by student interaction. These changes are called *events*. They trigger *knowledge sources* creating activation records which are placed on the agenda. These *knowledge source activation records* or *KSARs* record the knowledge sources and their variable bindings when triggered. The *scheduler* selects the next KSAR to run. Then the next KSAR is interpreted. Its execution may cause changes to the student interface, the instructional plan, or both. This cycle continues until the instructional plan has been completed.

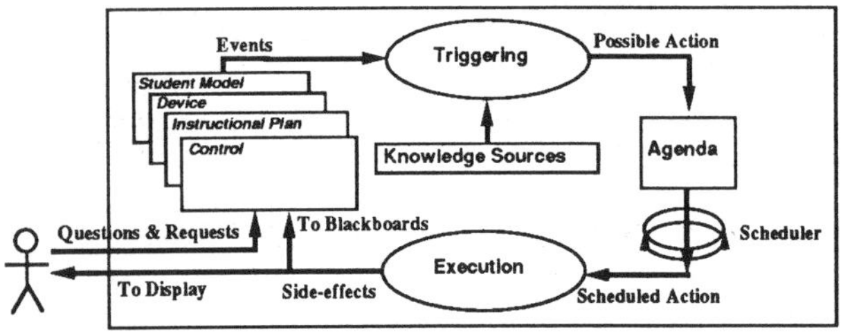

Figure 6: BB-IP Execution Cycle

The blackboard architecture facilitates the implementation of dynamic instructional planners by supporting an explicit plan representation, meta-level reasoning, interruptibility, and rapid prototyping. The explicit instructional plan representation supports dynamic planning by representing plan rationale, future unexecuted actions, global resource allocation, and constraints on partially refined plans. The use of plan critics is also supported. These issues are explained in more detail in (Murray 1990b). Other reasons cited (Hayes-Roth 1987a) for using blackboard architectures such as integrating uncertain data, island driving, and providing opportunistic control appear more relevant to interpretation applications (e.g., HEARSAY-II (Erman et al. 1980)) than this planning application.

Related Work

This section considers related work in control for intelligent tutoring systems. We consider:

1. *Reactive systems having no plans at all.*
2. *Tutors that follow a single fixed plan.*
3. *Tutors that can only select dynamically from stored plans.*
4. *Tutors that generate and interpret an explicit instructional plan.*

Reactive systems recognize and act upon opportunities to provide instruction but do not plan any sequence of actions. WEST (Burton & Brown 1979) and SOPHIE-I (Brown, Burton, & Bell 1975) are examples. Reactive systems such as these are limited to coaching or opportunistic tutoring strategies. The student's actions determine the course of the instructional session, not a stored or generated plan. Simulated microworlds that only allow discovery learning can also be considered reactive systems, but it is arguable whether such systems are intelligent tutoring systems, although they do apply artificial intelligence techniques to education.

Traditional CAI tutors rely on a single fixed plan. The instruction produced may be very good but these systems cannot be readily extended to new domains or instructional strategies since they procedurally encode domain knowledge and teaching methods. To make program development practical (i.e., less time consuming), their flexibility is quite limited. The tutor controls the instructional session, rather than the student. Student questions and requests are restricted or disallowed. For example, the student typically cannot pose a problem for the tutor to solve.

A considerable increase in flexibility results when tutors can dynamically select discourse plans from a plan library. MENO-TUTOR (Woolf & McDonald 1984) provides these capabilities with pre-stored skeletal plans, encoded as default state transitions in an ATN-like discourse management network. The network is augmented with meta-rules that allow transitions from the execution of one skeletal plan to the execution of another. Another tutor, WHY (Stevens & Collins 1977), also provides Socratic question and answer dialogs, but it uses rules to generate its dialogs. GUIDON (Clancey 1987) provides more sophisticated capabilities than either WHY or MENO-TUTOR. Its t-rules (tutorial rules) are used both as pre-stored discourse plans and as meta-rules to control the selection and operation of other t-rules. GUIDON's capabilities are still limited by the lack of an explicit instructional plan even though it provides very sophisticated dialog management. GUIDON's dialog can be verbose since it does not plan its dialog to determine which topics should be stressed and which should be deemphasized. Although the user can interrupt GUIDON at any time some requests may be disallowed since they would invalidate assumptions underlying the t-rule currently executing. These and other limitations are discussed in more detail in (Murray 1990a).

Tutors that generate and revise explicit instructional plans during instruction are intended to overcome these limitations, and support both lesson and discourse planning. This paper has described one approach; others are described briefly below. A planner-based approach to instruction based on applying classical (i.e., STRIPS-based (Fikes & Nilsson 1971)) planning techniques is presented in (Peachey & McCalla 1986). The focus is on planning lesson content. Unlike the Blackboard Instructional Planner, this planner does not address issues in resource management, incremental planning, handling mixed-initiative instruction, and integrating lesson planning and discourse management. Another tutor, IDE-Interpreter (Russell 1988), also adopts a planner-based approach to instruction to interpret an instructional design developed in IDE (Russell, Moran, & Jordan 1988), the Instructional Design Environment. It does not rely on classical planning techniques but uses a top-down plan elaboration approach similar to that presented here. However, it does not address issues in procedure interruption and the diagnosis of failed plans. The handling of mixed initiative instruction is also more limited. Finally, the work presented here builds on research by MacMillan and Sleeman (MacMillan & Sleeman 1987). Their work focused on implementing general planner and ITS architectures. The subsequent work by the author has focused on the implementation of a dynamic instructional planner for a realistic application, rather than developing generic ITS architectures.

The planner presented here is actually the second version of the Blackboard Instructional Planner. The first version was much simpler and focused more on discourse management and less on lesson planning. Instructional actions were simulated and resource management not addressed. It was implemented using a high-level language describing instructional actions. The implementation was modeled after the PROTEAN (Hayes-Roth et al. 1987b) blackboard application and its ACCORD (Hayes-Roth et al. 1987c) language framework using Hayes-Roth's BB* environment as described in (Murray 1989a).

Research Contributions

The first major contribution of this research is its analysis of architectural and planning issues in ITS. (Murray 1990b) presents a more detailed analysis of the role of the blackboard architecture than can be provided here. Alternative approaches to planning for ITS, and trade-offs made between them, are considered in (Murray 1989b). Two particular architectures for intelligent tutoring systems, discourse management networks and blackboard architectures, are analyzed in (Murray 1990a). That paper concludes that blackboard architectures provide greater support for the implementation of dynamic instructional planners, although discourse management networks are sufficient for sophisticated dialog management where only local planning is required.

A second research contribution is the implementation of the Lower Hoist Tutor. This prototype tutor shows how a dynamic instructional planner such as BB-IP can be integrated with other ITS components to form a complete system. A realistic naval training application, teaching troubleshooting of the lower hoist assembly of the Mark-45 naval gun mount, has been selected to test the planner. Although not yet appropriate for classroom use, all instructional actions have been implemented and the tutor can deliver about two hours worth of instruction on the lower hoist.

The major research contribution of this work is the implementation of the Blackboard Instructional Planner. This planner shows precisely how a dynamic instructional planner can be implemented in the blackboard architecture. The Blackboard Instructional Planner generates an instructional plan customized to student background and time constraints, then adaptively replans to support mixed-initiative instruction, and to handle changes to the student model and time remaining.

Acknowledgements. I would like to thank Kurt Steuck (AFHRL) and Susan Chipman (ONR) for their technical advice and guidance. I am also grateful to Perry Thorndyke, Barbara Hayes-Roth, N. S. Sridharan, Stuart MacMillan, and Lee Brownston for their help on this project.

References

Brown, J. S.; Burton, R. R.; and Bell, A. G. 1975. SOPHIE: a Step towards a Reactive Learning Environment. *IJMMS* 7:675 - 696.

Burton, R. R.; and Brown, J. S. 1979. An Investigation of Computer Coaching for Informal Learning Activities. *IJMMS* 11:5 - 24.

Carr, B; and Goldstein, I. P. 1977. Overlays: a Theory of Modeling for Computer-aided Instruction, Technical Report, AI Lab Memo 406, MIT.

Clancey, W. 1987. *Knowledge-based Tutoring: The GUIDON Program*. The MIT Press.

Erman, L. D.; Hayes-Roth, F.; Lesser, V. R.; and Reddy, D. R. 1980. The Hearsay-II Speech-understanding System: Integrating Knowledge to Resolve Uncertainty. *Computing Surveys* 12:213 - 253.

Fikes, R. E.; and Nilsson, N. J. 1971. STRIPS: a New Approach to the Application of Theorem Proving to Problem Solving. *Artificial Intelligence* 2:189-208.

Hayes-Roth, B. 1984. BB1: An Architecture for Blackboard Systems that Control, Explain, and Learn about their own Behavior, Tech Report HPP 84-16, KSL, Stanford.

Hayes-Roth, B. 1987a. Blackboard Systems. In *Encyclopedia of Artificial Intelligence*, 73 - 80. Wiley-Interscience Publication.

Hayes-Roth, B.; Buchanan, B.; Lichtarge, O.; Hewett, M.; Altman, R.; Brinkley, J.; Cornelius, C.; Duncan, B.; and Jardetzky, O. 1987b. PROTEAN: Deriving Protein Structure from Constraints. In *Blackboard Systems*, 417 - 431. Addison-Wesley.

Hayes-Roth, B.; Garvey, A.; Johnson, M. V.; and Hewett, M. 1987c. A Modular and Layered Environment for Reasoning about Action, Technical Report KSL 86-38, KSL, Stanford.

Hollan, J. D.; Hutchins, E. L.; and Weitzman, L. 1984. STEAMER: an interactive inspectable simulation-based training system. *AI Magazine* 5(2):15 - 27.

MacMillan, S. A.; and Sleeman, D. H. 1987. An Architecture for a Self-improving Instructional Planner for Intelligent Tutoring Systems. *Computational Intelligence* 3(1):17 - 27.

Murray, W. R. 1989a. Dynamic Instructional Planning in the BB1 Blackboard Architecture. In *Blackboard Architectures and Applications*, 455 - 480. Academic Press, Inc.

Murray, W. R. 1989b. Control for Intelligent Tutoring Systems: a Blackboard-based Dynamic Instructional Planner. Proceedings 4th International Conference on AI and Education, 150 - 168. IOS.

Murray, W. R. 1990a. Control for Intelligent Tutoring Systems: A Comparison of Blackboard Architectures and Discourse Management Networks. *Machine-Mediated Learning* 3(1), 1990.

Murray, W. R. 1990b. A Blackboard-based Dynamic Instructional Planner. Tech Report R-6376, FMC Corporation. ONR final report.

Peachey, D. R.; and McCalla, G. I. 1986. Using Planning Techniques in Intelligent Tutoring Systems. *IJMMS* 24:77 - 98.

Rich, E. 1979. User Modeling via Stereotypes. *Cog. Sci.* 3:355 - 366.

Russell, D. M. 1988. IDE: The Interpreter. In *Intelligent Tutoring Systems: Lessons Learned*, 323 - 349. Lawrence Erlbaum Associates.

Russell, D. M.; Moran, T. P.; and Jordan, D. S. 1988. The Instructional-Design Environment. In *Intelligent Tutoring Systems: Lessons Learned*, 203 - 228. Lawrence Erlbaum Associates.

Stevens, A. L.; and Collins, A. 1977. The Goal Structure of a Socratic Tutor. Proceedings National ACM Conference, 256 - 263. ACM.

Woolf, B. P.; and McDonald, D. D. 1984. Building a Computer Tutor: Design Issues. *IEEE Computer* 17(9):61 - 73.

Intelligent Interfaces

Coordinating Text and Graphics in Explanation Generation*

Steven K. Feiner
Kathleen R. McKeown

Department of Computer Science
Columbia University
New York, New York 10027
Feiner@cs.columbia.edu
Mckeown@cs.columbia.edu

Abstract

To generate multimedia explanations, a system must be able to coordinate the use of different media in a single explanation. In this paper, we present the architecture that we have developed for COMET (*COordinated Multimedia Explanation Testbed*), a system that generates directions for equipment maintenance and repair, and we show how it addresses the coordination problem. COMET includes a single content planner that produces a common content description used by multiple media-specific generators, and a media coordinator that performs a fine-grained division of information among media. Bidirectional interaction between media-specific generators allows influence across media. We describe COMET's current capabilities and provide an overview of our plans for extending the system.

Introduction

A number of researchers have begun to explore the automated generation of multimedia explanations [Arens, Miller, and Sondheimer 88, Feiner 88, Neal and Shapiro 88, Roth, Mattis, and Mesnard 88, Wahlster et al. 89]. One common concern is how to coordinate the use of different media in a single explanation. How are the communicative goals that the explanation is to satisfy and the information needed to achieve those goals to be determined? How is explanation content to be divided among different media, such as pictures and text? Once divided, how can material in each medium be generated to complement that of the other media? In this paper, we describe an architecture for generating multimedia explanations that we have developed for COMET (*COordinated Multimedia Explanation Testbed*), a system that generates directions for equipment maintenance and repair. We use sample explanations produced by COMET to illustrate how its architecture provides some answers to these questions.

*This work is supported in part by the Defense Advanced Research Projects Agency under Contract N00039-84-C-0165, the Hewlett-Packard Company under its AI University Grants Program, the Office of Naval Research under Contract N00014-82-K-0256, the National Science Foundation under Grant IRT-84-51438, and the New York State Center for Advanced Technology under Contract NYSSTF-CAT(88)-5.

COMET's architecture includes a single content planner, a media coordinator, bidirectional links between the text and graphics generators, and a media layout component. The content planner determines communicative goals and information for an explanation in a media-independent fashion, producing explanation content in a common description language used by each media-specific generator [Elhadad et al. 89]. Using the same description language allows for more flexible interaction among media, making it possible for each generator to query and reference other generators. The media coordinator annotates the content description, noting which pieces should be conveyed through which media. Our coordinator is unique in its ability to make a fine-grained division between media. For example, COMET may generate a sentence accompanied by a picture that portrays just the modifiers of one of the sentence's referents, such as its location. The annotated content description will allow our media layout component to lay out text and pictures appropriately.

Bidirectional interaction between the media-specific generators makes it possible to address issues in how media can influence each other. For example, informal experiments that we performed when designing our current media coordinator showed that people strongly prefer sentence breaks that are correlated with picture breaks. This influence requires bidirectional interaction, since graphical constraints on picture size may sometimes force delimitation of sentences, while grammatical constraints on sentence construction may sometimes control picture size. Other influences that we are currently investigating include reference to pictures based on characteristics determined dynamically by the graphics generator (e.g., ''the highlighted dial'' vs. ''the red dial'') and coordination of style (e.g., whether the graphics generator designs a composite picture or sequence of pictures to represent a process can influence whether the text generator uses past or progressive tense).

In the following sections, we provide a system overview of COMET, discuss the production of explanation content in the common description language, describe our media coordinator, and preview our ongoing work on allowing the media to influence each other.

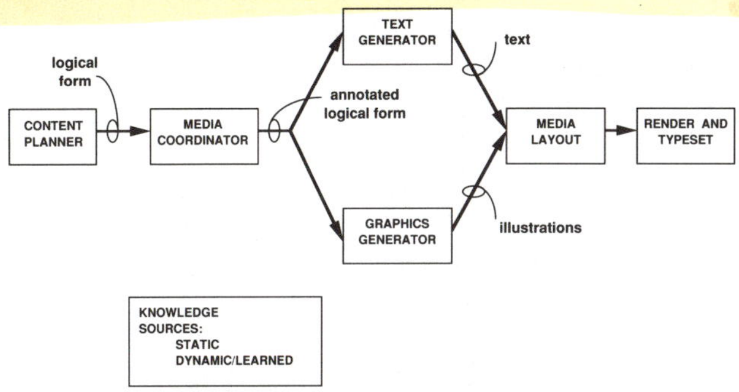

Figure 1: COMET system architecture.

System Organization and Domain

COMET, shown below in Fig. 1, features a single *content planner* which uses text plans, or *schemas*, to determine which information from the underlying *static knowledge sources*, encoded in LOOM [MacGregor & Brill 89], should be included in the explanation. The content planner produces the full content for the explanation, represented as a hierarchy of logical forms (LFs) [Allen 87], which are passed to the *media coordinator*. The media coordinator annotates the LFs to indicate which portions are to be produced in each medium.

COMET currently includes text and graphics generators. The *text generator* and *graphics generator* each process the same LFs, producing fragments of text and graphics that are keyed to the LFs they instantiate. Text and graphics fragments are passed to the *media layout* component, which lays them out on the screen.

Much of our work on COMET has been done in a maintenance and repair domain for the US Army AN/PRC-119 portable radio receiver-transmitter [DOA 86]. An underlying expert system determines which problems the radio is experiencing, which components are suspect, and which tests would be most useful in identifying the causes. The generation facilities create multimedia explanations of how to test and fix the radio. A user interacts with COMET using a menu interface through which the expert system can be invoked and requests for explanations made.

Figure 2, which we will refer to later, shows a simple example of the text and 3D graphics that COMET generates to describe how to clear the radio's display.

A Common Content Description for Multiple Media Generators

In COMET, explanation content is produced by a single content planner that does not take into account which media will be used for presentation. The content planner outputs a hierarchy of LFs that represent the content for the entire explanation. Content is later divided among the media by annotating the LFs. As a result, the system maintains a single description of the content to be generated, which is annotated and accepted as input by both the text generator (FUF [Elhadad 88]) and the graphics generator (IBIS [Seligmann and Feiner 89]). Thus, both FUF and IBIS share a common description of what is to be communicated. Just as both generators accept input in the same formalism, they may both annotate the description as they carry out its directives. This design

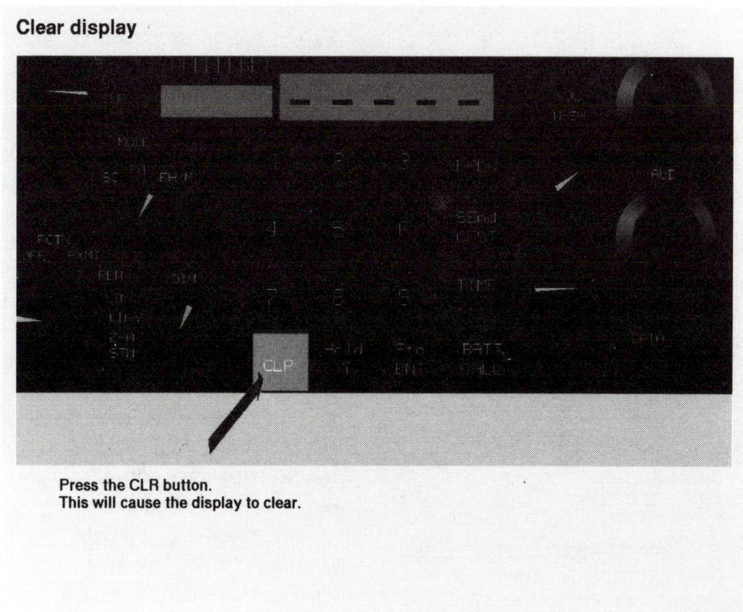

Figure 2: Text and graphics produced by COMET to explain how to clear the AN/PRC-119 display.

has several ramifications for the system:

Single content planner

COMET contains only one component dedicated to determining the communicative goals and subgoals needed to produce an explanation. COMET's content planner uses a schema-based approach that was originally used for text generation [McKeown 85, Paris 87], and which has proved successful for multimedia explanations as well. Keeping the content planner media-independent means that it only has to determine what information must be communicated to the user, without worrying about how. If it did select information with a specific medium in mind, it would have to carry out the media coordinator's task simultaneously.

Separation of goals from resources

The specification of content must be made at a high enough level that it is appropriate as input for all generators. We have found that by expressing content as communicative goals and information needed to achieve those goals, each generator can select the resources it has at hand for achieving the goals. In text, this means the selection of specific syntactic or lexical resources (e.g., passive voice to indicate focus), whereas in graphics, it means the selection of a conjunction of visual resources (e.g., to highlight an object, IBIS may change its color, outline it, and center it).

Text and graphics can influence each other

Since both FUF and IBIS receive the same annotated content description as input, they know which goals are to be expressed in text, which in graphics, and which in both. Even when a media-specific generator does not realize a piece of information, it knows that information is to be conveyed to the user and thus, it can use this information to influence its presentation.

Text and graphics generators can communicate with each other

Since both generators understand the same formalism, they can decide to provide more information to each other about the resources they have selected to achieve a goal, simply by annotating the content description. For example, if IBIS has decided to highlight a knob by changing its color to red, it might note that decision in the description, and FUF could ultimately generate the reference "the red knob", instead of "the highlighted knob". Communication requires bidirectional interaction and is discussed further below.

Single mechanism for adding annotations

Since different system tasks (e.g., dividing information between text and graphics, and communication between text and graphics generators) are achieved by adding annotations, the same mechanism can be used to make the annotations throughout the system. COMET uses FUF for this task. This simplifies the system and provides more possibilities for bidirectional interactions between components, as discussed below.

```
((cat lf)
 (directive-act substeps)
 (substeps
  [((process-type action)
    (process-concept c-push)
    (mood non-finite)
    (speech-act directive)
    (roles
     ((medium
       ((object-concept c-button-clr)
        (roles
         ((location ((object-concept c-location)))
          (size     ((object-concept c-size)))))
        (quantification ((definite yes)
                         (countable yes)
                         (ref-obj singular)
                         (ref-set singular)))
        (ref-mode description))))))])
 (effects
  [((process-type action)
    (process-concept c-clear)
    (mood non-finite)
    (speech-act assertive)
    (roles
     ((agent
       ((object-concept c-display)
        (roles
         ((location ((object-concept c-location)))
          (size     ((object-concept c-size)))))
        (quantification ((definite yes)
                         (countable yes)
                         (ref-obj singular)
                         (ref-set singular)))
        (ref-mode description))))))]))
```

Figure 3: Content planner output (LF 1): Press the CLR button. This will cause the display to clear.

Examples

Clearing the display

To see how these points relate to COMET, consider how it generates the response shown in Fig. 2. The content planner selects one of its schemas, the *process schema* [Paris 87], and produces content by traversing the schema, which is represented as a graph, producing an LF (or piece of an LF) for each arc it takes. For this simple example, it produces one simple LF.

Figure 3 shows the LF produced by the content planner for this example. It contains several communicative goals. The main goal is to describe an action (`c-push`) and its role (`medium`). Subgoals include referencing an object (e.g., `c-button-clr`, the clear button) and conveying its `location`, `size`, and `quantification`. IBIS and FUF use different resources to achieve these goals. For example, FUF selects a lexical item, the verb "press", to describe the action. "Press" can be used instead of other verbs, because of the characteristics of the medium, `c-button-clr`. If the medium were a slider, a verb such as "push" or "move" would be required. In contrast, IBIS uses a meta-object, an arrow, to depict the action of pushing. To refer to the clear button, FUF uses a

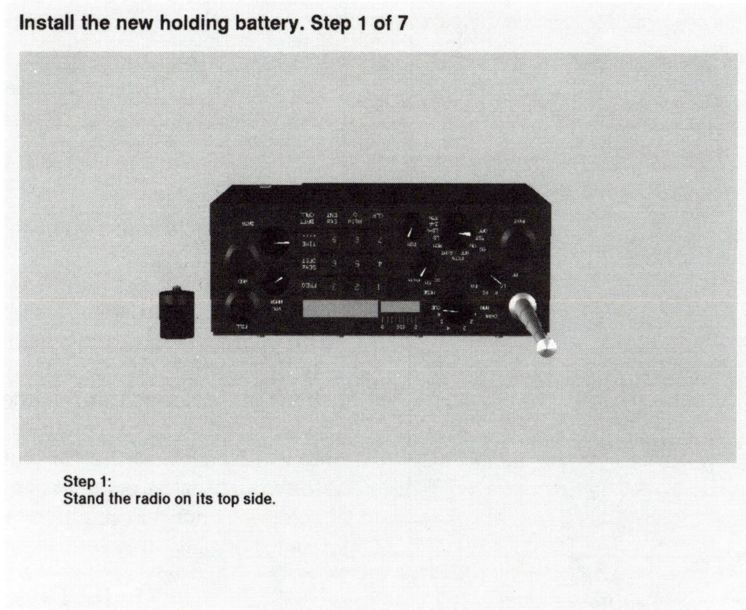

(a)

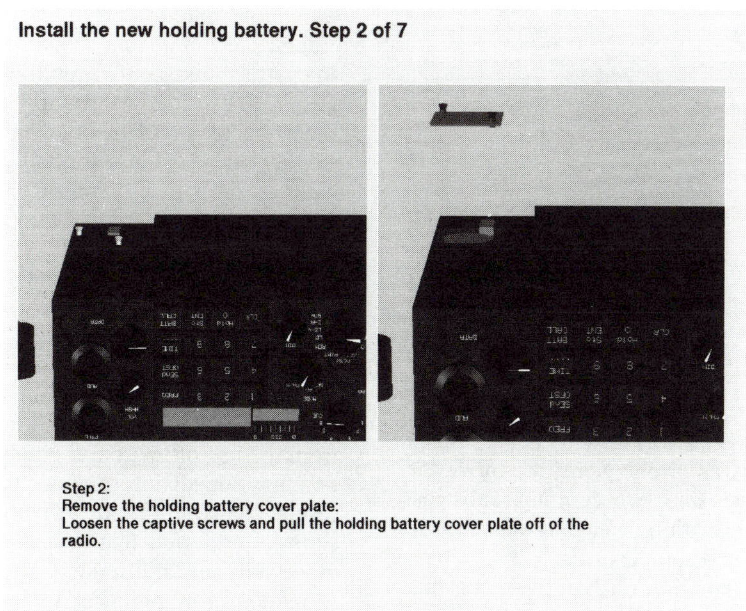

(b)

Figure 4: Part of an explanation produced by COMET for installing the holding battery.

definite noun phrase, whereas IBIS highlights the object in the picture.

To portray its location, IBIS uses a combination of techniques: it selects a camera position that locates the button panel (of which the button is part) centrally in the picture; it crops the picture so that additional, surrounding context is included; it highlights the button; and it subdues the surrounding objects, since it determines that the text on the button cannot be made any brighter than the surrounding text. If FUF were to convey location, it would use a prepositional phrase. Here, COMET's media coordinator has determined that location information appears in graphics only, while the causal relation between the action and the display clearing is realized only in text. In general, COMET performs a mapping from communicative goals to text and graphics resources, using media-specific knowledge about the resources available to achieve the goals. A discussion of communicative goals and the associated media-specific resources that can achieve them can be found in [Elhadad et al. 89].

```
((cat lf)
  (directive-act goal)
  (goal
   ((distinct
     ((car
       ((process-type action)
        (process-concept c-remove)
        ...
        (roles
         ((medium
           ((object-concept c-hb-cover-plate)
            ....))))))))))
  (substeps
   ((distinct
     ((car
       ((process-type action)
        (process-concept c-loosen)
        ...
        (roles
         ((medium
           ((object-concept c-captive-screw)
            ...))))))
      (cdr
       ((car
         ((process-type action)
          (process-concept c-pull)
          ...
          (roles
           ((medium
             ((object-concept c-hb-cover-plate)
              ...))
            (from-loc
             ((object-concept c-rt)
              ....))))))))
  ...)))))
```

Figure 5: Content planner output (LF 2): Step 2: Remove the holding battery cover plate: Loosen. . . .

Installing the holding battery

COMET produces seven LFs as part of an explanation of how to install the "holding battery" (which provides power for the memory when the main battery has been removed). The first LF, which corresponds to the generated explanation shown in Fig. 4(a) is a simple LF. The second, which corresponds to Fig. 4(b) is a complex LF. The complex LF consists of one goal (to remove the holding battery cover plate) and two complex substeps. The remainder of the explanation, which is not shown, contains additional simple and complex LFs.

This example illustrates how information in the LF that is *not* realized by a medium can influence that medium's generator. The second LF of this explanation, shown in outline form in Fig. 5, contains one goal and two substeps that carry out that goal. As can be seen in Fig. 4, the media coordinator determines that the goal is to be generated in text ("Remove the holding battery cover plate:") and that the substeps are to be shown in both media. Although IBIS is to depict just the substeps of the LF, it receives the entire annotated LF as input. Since it receives the full LF, and not just the pieces earmarked for graphics, IBIS knows that the actions to be depicted are steps that achieve a higher-level goal. Although the higher-level goal is not actually realized in graphics, IBIS uses this information to create a composite picture. If IBIS were to receive only the substeps, it would have no way of knowing that in the explanation as a whole these actions are described in relation to the goal, and it would produce two separate pictures, just as it does for each simple LF, such as that in part (a) of the figure. Thus, information that is being conveyed in the explanation as a whole, but not in graphics, is used to influence how graphics depicts other information.

location information	graphics only
physical attributes	graphics only
simple actions	text and graphics
compound actions	text and graphics
conditionals	text for connectives, text and graphics for actions
abstract actions	text only

Figure 6: Division of information.

Media Coordinator

The media coordinator receives as input the hierarchy of LFs produced by the content planner and determines which information should be realized in text and which in graphics. Our media coordinator does a fine-grained analysis, unlike other multiple media generators (e.g., [Roth, Mattis, and Mesnard 88]), and can decide whether a portion of an LF should be realized in either or both media. Based on informal experiments and on work reported on in the literature, we distinguish between six different types of information that can appear in an LF, and have categorized each type as to whether it is more appropriately presented in text or graphics, as shown in Fig. 6 [Lombardi 89].

Our experiments involved hand-coding displays of text/graphics explanations for situations taken from the radio repair domain. We used a number of methods for mapping media to different kinds of information, ranging from the use of text only, graphics only, and both text and graphics for all information, to several variations on the results shown in Fig. 6. Among the results, we found that subjects preferred that certain information appear in one mode only and not redundantly in both (e.g., location information in graphics, and conditionals in text). Furthermore, we found that there was a strong preference for tight coordination between text and graphics. For example, readers much preferred sentence breaks that coincided with picture breaks.

The media coordinator is implemented using our functional unification formalism (see the following section), and has a grammar that maps information types to media. This grammar is unified with the input LFs and results in portions of the LF being tagged with the attribute value pairs `(media-text yes)` and `(media-graphics yes)`, with a value of `no` used when the information is not to be presented in a given medium. The media coordinator also annotates the LFs with indications of the type

```
((cat lf)
 (directive-act substeps)
 (substeps
  [((process-type action)
    (process-concept c-push)
    (mood non-finite)
    (speech-act directive)
    (function ((type substeps)
               (media-text yes)
               (media-graphics no)))
    (roles
     ((medium
       ((object-concept c-button-clr)
        (roles
         ((location ((object-concept c-location)
                     (media-graphics yes)
                     (media-text no)))
          (size     ((object-concept c-size)
                     (media-graphics yes)
                     (media-text no))))))
        (quantification ((definite yes)
                         (countable yes)
                         (ref-obj singular)
                         (ref-set singular)))
        (ref-mode description)
        (cat role)))))
    (cat lf)
    (media-graphics yes)
    (media-text yes))
 (effects
  [((process-type action)
    (process-concept c-clear)
    (mood non-finite)
    (function ((type effects)
               (media-text yes)
               (media-graphics no)))
    (speech-act assertive)
    (roles
     ((agent
       ((object-concept c-display)
        (roles
         ((location ((object-concept c-location)
                     (media-graphics yes)
                     (media-text no)))
          (size     ((object-concept c-size)
                     (media-graphics yes)
                     (media-text no)))))
        (quantification ((definite yes)
                         (countable yes)
                         (ref-obj singular)
                         (ref-set singular)))
        (ref-mode description)
        (cat role)))))
    (cat lf)
    (media-text yes)
    (media-graphics yes))]))
```

Figure 7: Media coordinator output (LF 1 with annotations).

of information (e.g., simple action vs. compound action), as this information is useful to the graphics generator in determining the style of the generated pictures. Portions of the resulting annotated output for the first LF are shown below in Fig. 7, with the annotations that have been added for the media generators in boldface.

The explanation shown in Fig. 4 illustrates how COMET can produce a fine-grained division of information between text and graphics. In both of the segments (a) and (b), location information is portrayed in the picture only (as dictated by annotations such as those shown in Fig. 7), while the entire action is realized in both text and graphics. In contrast, the overview in part (b) is realized in text only.

Bidirectional Interaction between Components

We have been able to achieve a good level of coordination between text and graphics through a common content description and the media coordinator. The use of a common description language allows each media generator to be aware of the goals and information the other is realizing and to let this knowledge influence its own realization of goals. The media coordinator performs a fine-grained division of information between media, allowing for a tightly integrated explanation. There are certain types of coordination between media, however, that can only be provided by incorporating interacting constraints between text and graphics. Coordination of sentence breaks with picture breaks, references to accompanying pictures (e.g., "the knob in the lower left hand corner of the picture"), and coordination of pictorial and textual style are all examples that require bidirectional interaction between text and graphics components.

Coordinating sentence breaks with picture breaks

Consider the task of coordinating sentence breaks with picture breaks. IBIS uses a variety of constraints to determine picture size and composition, including how much information can easily fit into a single picture, the size of the objects being represented, and the position of the objects and their relationship to each other. Some of these constraints cannot be overridden. For example, if too many objects are depicted in a single picture, individual objects may be rendered too small to be clearly visible.

This situation suggests that constraints from graphics should be used to determine sentence size and thereby achieve coordination between picture and sentence breaks. However, there are also grammatical constraints on sentence size that cannot be overridden without creating ungrammatical, or at the least, very awkward text. Verbs each take a required set of inherent roles. For example, "put" takes a medium and to-location. Thus, "John put." and "John put the book." are both ungrammatical. Once a verb is selected for a sentence, this can in turn constrain minimal picture size; the LF portion containing information for all required verb roles should not be split across two pictures. Therefore, we need two-way interaction between text and graphics.

Our proposed solution is to treat the interaction as two separate tasks, each of which will run independently and annotate its own copy of the LF when a decision is made. The text generator will produce text as usual, but once a verb is selected for a sentence, the text generator will annotate its copy of the LF by noting the roles that must be included to make a complete sentence. At the same time, the graphics generator will produce pictures as usual, creating a hierarchical picture representation incorporating pieces of the LF. This representation indicates where picture breaks are planned. The graphics generator will annotate its LF with pointers into the picture hierarchy, indicating these tentative picture breaks.

When there is a choice among different possible sentence structures, the text generator will use the graphics generator's annotations to make a choice. The text generator can read the graphics generator's annotations by using unification to merge the graphics generator's annotated LF with its own, or can examine the relevant portions of the LF. Similarly, *when there is a choice* among different possible picture breaks, the graphics generator can use the text generator's annotations on minimal sentence size when making the decision. When there are real conflicts between the two components, either one component will generate less than satisfactory output or coordination of sentence breaks with picture breaks must be sacrificed.

Coordination through unification

While there are clearly many difficult problems in coordinating the two tasks, our use of FUF for annotating the LF allows for some level of bidirectional interaction quite naturally through unification. We use FUF in our system for the media coordination task, for the selection of words, for the generation of syntactic structure (and linearization to a string of words), and for the mapping from communicative goals to graphics resources. Each of these components has its own ''grammar'' that is unified with the LF to enrich it with the information it needs. For example, the lexical chooser's ''grammar'' is a Functional Unification Lexicon, which contains domain concepts as keys and associated attribute-value pairs that enrich the input LF with selected words, their syntactic category, and any syntactic features of the selected words. The result is a cascaded series of FUF ''grammars,'' each handling a separate task.

Currently, the unifier is called separately for each grammar, as we are still developing the system. We plan to change this, eventually calling the unifier once for the combined series of grammars, thus allowing complete interaction through unification among the different types of constraints. In this scenario, a decision made at a later stage in processing can propagate back to undo an earlier decision. For example, selection of syntactic form can propagate back to the lexical chooser to influence verb choice. Similarly, selection of a verb can propagate back to the grammar that maps from goals to graphics resources, to influence the resource selected.

There are many problems that must be addressed for this approach to work. We are currently considering whether and how to control the timing of decision making. Note that a decision about where to make a picture break, for example, should only affect sentence size when there are no reasonable alternatives for picture division. Unresolved issues include at what point decisions can be retracted, when a generator's decisions should influence other generators, and what role the media coordinator should play in mediating between the generators.

Conclusions and Future Work

We have focused on three features of COMET's architecture that allow the dynamic generation of integrated multimedia explanations: a common content description, the fine-grained assignment of information to media, and bidirectional interaction among components. The use of an annotated common content description allows each media-specific generator to be aware of all information to be communicated in the explanation, and to use that information to influence the realization of segments for which it is responsible. Our media coordinator allows for small portions of the same LF to be realized in different media. For example, location modifiers of an object may be expressed in graphics only, while the remainder of the LF is expressed in both text and graphics. Similarly, conditionals may be expressed in text only, while the conjoined actions may be expressed in both text and graphics. Finally, our proposed approach for accomplishing bidirectional interaction between components will make it possible for the text and graphics generators to communicate with each other. This will allow decisions made by each generator to influence the other.

We are pursuing a number of different research directions, in addition to our work on bidirectional interaction. Our media coordinator is currently more of a dictator than a coordinator. We are interested in developing strategies for those situations in which the media generators determine that the assignments made by the media coordinator are unsatisfactory. In these cases, the generators could provide feedback to the coordinator, which could in turn modify its plan. We are also interested in situations where context influences the selection of media. Finally, although a single media-independent content planner has definite advantages, there are situations in which it, too, should accept feedback from the generators and modify the content specification.

Acknowledgements

The development of COMET is an ongoing group effort and has benefited from the contributions of Michelle Baker (plan execution component), Cliff Beshers (menu interface), Andrea Danyluk (learned rule base), Michael Elhadad (FUF), Laura Gabbe (static knowledge base and content planner), David Fox (text formatting component for media layout), Jong Lim (static knowledge base and content planner), Jacques Robin (lexical chooser), Doree Seligmann (IBIS), Tony Weida (static knowledge base), Matt Kamerman (user model), and Christine Lombardi and Yumiko Fukumoto (media coordinator).

References

[Allen 87] Allen, J. *Natural Language Understanding.* Benjamin Cummings Publishing Company, Inc., Menlo Park, CA, 1987.

[Arens, Miller, and Sondheimer 88] Arens, Y., Miller, L., and Sondheimer, N. Presentation Planning Using an Integrated Knowledge Base. In *Proc. ACM SIGCHI Workshop on Architectures for Intelligent Interfaces*, pages 93-107. Monterey, March 29-April 1, 1988.

[DOA 86] Department of the Army. *TM 11-5820-890-20-1 Technical Manual: Unit Maintenance for Radio Sets AN/PRC-119, . . .* Headquarters, Department of the Army, June, 1986.

[Elhadad 88] Elhadad, M. *The FUF Functional Unifier: User's Manual.* Technical Report, Columbia University, June, 1988.

[Elhadad et al. 89] Elhadad, M., Seligmann, D., Feiner, S., and McKeown, K. A Common Intention Description Language for Interactive Multi-media Systems. In *A New Generation of Intelligent Interfaces: Proceedings of IJCAI89 Workshop on Intelligent Interfaces*, pages 46-52. Detroit, MI, August 22, 1989.

[Feiner 88] Feiner, S. An Architecture for Knowledge-Based Graphical Interfaces. In *Proc. ACM SIGCHI Workshop on Architectures for Intelligent Interfaces*, pages 129-140. Monterey, April, 1988.

[Lombardi 89] Lombardi, C. Experiments for determining the assignment of information to media in COMET. 1989. Columbia University, New York, NY.

[MacGregor & Brill 89] MacGregor, Robert and David Brill. *LOOM Reference Manual.* Technical Report, USC-ISI, Marina del Rey, CA, 1989.

[McKeown 85] McKeown, K.R. *Text Generation: Using Discourse Strategies and Focus Constraints to Generate Natural Language Text.* Cambridge University Press, Cambridge, England, 1985.

[Neal and Shapiro 88] Neal, J. and Shapiro, S. Intelligent Multi-Media Interface Technology. In *Proc. ACM SIGCHI Workshop on Architectures for Intelligent Interfaces*, pages 69-91. Monterey, March 29-April 1, 1988.

[Paris 87] Paris, C.L. *The Use of Explicit User models in Text Generation: Tailoring to a User's Level of Expertise.* PhD thesis, Columbia University, 1987.

[Roth, Mattis, and Mesnard 88] Roth, S., Mattis, J., and Mesnard, X. Graphics and Natural Language as Components of Automatic Explanation. In *Proc. ACM SIGCHI Workshop on Architectures for Intelligent Interfaces*, pages 109-128. Monterey, March 29-April 1, 1988.

[Seligmann and Feiner 89] Seligmann, D.D., and Feiner, S. Specifying Composite Illustrations with Communicative Goals. In *Proc. UIST89 (ACM SIGGRAPH Symposium on User Interface Software and Technology)*, pages 1-9. Williamsburg, VA, November 13-15, 1989.

[Wahlster et al. 89] Wahlster, W., Andre, E., Hecking, M., and T. Rist. *WIP: Knowledge-based Presentation of Information.* Technical Report WIP-1, German Research Center for Artificial Intelligence, Saarbruecken, FRG, May, 1989.

Avoiding Unwanted Conversational Implicatures in Text and Graphics

Joseph Marks and Ehud Reiter†

Aiken Computation Laboratory
Harvard University
Cambridge, Mass 02138
marks@harvard.harvard.edu
reiter@aipna.edinburgh.ac.uk

Abstract

We have developed two systems, FN and ANDD, that use natural language and graphical displays, respectively, to communicate information about objects to human users. Both systems must deal with the fundamental problem of ensuring that their output does not carry unwanted and inappropriate conversational implicatures. We describe the types of conversational implicatures that FN and ANDD can avoid, and the computational strategies the two systems use to generate output that is free of unwanted implicatures.

Introduction

We have developed a natural-language generation system (FN) and an automatic graphic-design system (ANDD) that use their respective media to communicate facts about objects to users. Both systems address the *surface content-determination* problem: given as input a set of predicates about objects in the discourse domain that need to be communicated to the user, FN and ANDD are expected to produce output that either directly informs, or allows the user to infer, that the predicates in the input set are true. One of the most important conceptual and computational problems that both systems face is generating output that is free of unwanted *conversational implicatures* (Grice 1975). Generating syntactically and semantically correct communications (utterances and diagrams) that convey the target predicates is relatively straightforward for both FN and ANDD; what is difficult is the pragmatic problem of ensuring that the utterances and diagrams do not mislead the user into making incorrect conversational implicatures (Hirschberg 1984).

More precisely, FN and ANDD produce (respectively) *attributive descriptions of individuals* and *network diagrams*. Attributive descriptions of individuals are natural-language object descriptions that are intended to inform a hearer that a particular object has certain properties: they differ from *referring expressions*, which are object descriptions that are intended to identify particular objects in the current discourse context (Donnellan 1966). *Network diagrams* (Bertin 1983) are graphical displays that are used to depict *network models*. A network model is an attributed graph, i.e., a graph in which the vertices and edges have nominal and quantitative attribute values associated with them. Network models are useful abstractions for many complex systems, including computer, communication, and command-and-control systems.

The FN system determines the words that will best communicate to the user that the object in question has the relevant properties; however, it does not decide which properties are important in the current discourse context and need to be communicated to the user. The ANDD system designs a network diagram that depicts a given network model: it does not decide what information the network model should contain, or how a real-world system is modeled as a network model. Both systems are intended to be used as components of a larger collaborative system, in which a discourse analysis subsystem that is based on the SharedPlan framework (Grosz & Sidner 1990; Lochbaum, Grosz, & Sidner 1990) will be used to solve the *information content-determination* problem, i.e., the problem of deciding what information is important in the current discourse context and needs to be communicated to the user. The full system may also use *media coordination* (Feiner & McKeown 1990) to tie FN and ANDD together, but such coordination has not been investigated to date.

Conversational Implicatures

Implicatures in Text

Suppose a speaker is given the communicative goal of informing a human hearer that a particular object is a *computer network* with the attributes {*data-rate:10Mbit/sec, circuit-type:packet-switched*}. Consider two possible descriptions that might be used to convey this information:

1a)"*10Mbit/sec packet-switched computer network*"

1b)"*Ethernet*"

One might think that (1a) and (1b) convey the same information, provided that the hearer knows that *Ethernets* are *computer networks* that have the attributes {*data-rate:10Mbit/sec, circuit-type:packet-switched*}. However, if the hearer does in fact have this domain knowledge, the use of utterance (1a) might lead her to draw the conversational implicature (i.e., to interpret the utterance as implicating) that the object being described is *not* an Ethernet — because if it were, the hearer would reason, then the speaker would have uttered (1b).

† Ehud Reiter is currently at the Department of Artificial Intelligence, University of Edinburgh, 80 South Bridge, Edinburgh EH1 1HN, Scotland.

A similar phenomenon occurs in referring expressions: consider, for example, the difference between

2a) "Sit by *the table*"

2b) "Sit by *the brown wooden table*"

If there was only one visible table (which was brown and made of wood), then utterances (2a) and (2b) would both fulfill the referring goal, because a hearer who heard them would have no trouble picking out the object being referred to. However, a hearer who heard utterance (2b) would probably draw the additional conversational implicature that it was somehow important that the table was brown and made of wood, i.e., that the speaker was trying to do more than just identify the table. If the speaker did not have this intention, and only wanted to tell the hearer where to sit, then the hearer would have drawn an incorrect conversational implicature.

Implicatures in Graphics

Figure 1 shows a typical network diagram that depicts a network-model abstraction of a computer-disk system. The topology of the network model is communicated directly by the connectivity of the network diagram, and the nominal and quantitative attributes of the model are communicated directly by the graphical properties (e.g., shape, pen width) of symbols, by text labels, and by diacritical symbols (e.g., enclosures), as indicated in the diagram legend.

Given that Figure 1 conveys precisely the desired information, Figures 2 and 3 are variants of Figure 1 that might be said to carry unwanted conversational implicatures. For example, in Figure 2 the pen-width used in drawing the channel-facility queue symbol differs from the pen-width used for all other queue (and server) symbols in the diagram. A viewer of this diagram might conclude that the channel-facility queue is somehow different from the other queues (and the servers), because otherwise the diagram designer could simply have used the same pen width to draw the symbol. Other unwanted conversational implicatures in Figure 2 result from perceptual grouping. For example, the way the disk symbols are perceptually grouped by proximity to form two 'gestalts' might lead the viewer to conclude that there is some semantic basis to the perceived grouping, because otherwise the designer would not have positioned the disk symbols in this way. In addition, the layout of the device-queue symbols violates the Gestalt Principle of Good Continuation (Kaufman 1974), resulting in the implicature that one of the device queues is uniquely different, because otherwise the designer could have positioned the symbols as in Figure 1, for example.[1] Finally, in Figure 3 there is an ordering (by size) of the node symbols: this ordering implicates that there must be a similar ordering relation among the vertices in the network model, which is not true (given Figure 1).

A thorough analysis that relates these graphical phenomena to known linguistic phenomena is a topic for future research. For now, we note that in each instance described above information is conveyed that differs from what is communicated directly by the symbols in the diagram. Furthermore, the ultimate source of implicature is the assumption that the designer and viewer are following Grice's Cooperative Principle (Grice 1975) in their discourse, i.e., that the designer is not trying to mislead the viewer, and that his design decisions can therefore be considered as appropriate contributions to the discourse.

Analysis and Discussion

Grice (1975) proposed a number of maxims of conversation that cooperative communicating agents usually obey (cooperative agents might disobey the maxims to achieve a particular communicative goal). These maxims fall into four categories: *Quality, Quantity, Relation*, and *Manner*. We consider how these maxims can be applied to avoid unwanted conversational implicatures in text and graphics. Although Grice's maxims apply to both information-content determination and surface-content determination, we will consider here only their application to the surface-content-determination tasks performed by the FN and ANDD systems.

Quality: Grice's maxims of Quality require utterances to be truthful. For our purposes, these maxims translate into a constraint that everything that is explicitly communicated to the user must be true.

Quantity: The maxims of Quantity require utterances to be neither more or less informative than is necessary for the purpose of the exchange. For natural language, these maxims forbid utterances from containing elements that are irrelevant, can be inferred from other parts of the utterance, or are otherwise redundant. For instance, in the referring expression example of Section 2.1, the adjectives "brown" and "wooden" are unnecessary for fulfilling the referring goal, and hence their inclusion in utterance (2b) leads to false implicatures.

The application of Grice's Quantity maxims to surface-content determination in graphics is less clear. In some cases extra information in graphical diagrams leads to false implicatures: for example, communicating the same network-model attribute via two distinct graphical properties (e.g., using both symbol color and shape to communicate the same information) could lead to unwanted implicatures, because the viewer might conclude that there must have been some reason the designer used two graphical properties instead of one. In other cases, however, extra information is acceptable and even desirable: for example, if the communicative goal is to identify the overloaded servers in the disk subsystem, the network diagram in Figure 1 (which depicts not only the overloaded servers, but also servers that are not overloaded, various other objects and how they interconnect,

[1] Implicatures that result from perceptual-grouping phenomena do not occur in chart graphics and maps, because symbol location in these kinds of graphical display is completely determined by the display semantics.

and subsystem affiliation) is preferable to a diagram that depicts only the two overloaded servers and nothing else. In yet other cases, the inclusion of 'redundant' information may actually be necessary to avoid leading the user to make unwanted implicatures: for example, the use of perceptual grouping to reinforce information communicated in other ways is sometimes essential (in Figure 1 the perceptual groupings of the node symbols reinforce the subsystem-affiliation information, whereas in Figure 2 they do not), even though the perceptual grouping is in some sense redundant.

Relation: The maxim of Relation requires utterances to be relevant to the discourse. This maxim primarily affects the information-content determination task, but it also has some impact on surface-content determination. For example, natural-language utterances should not contain irrelevant elements, and graphical displays should avoid the use of spurious graphical-property values (the use of a distinct pen-type for the channel-facility queue symbol in Figure 2 is an example of a spurious or irrelevant graphical-property value that can lead to an unwanted conversational implicature.)[2]

Manner: Grice's maxims of Manner concern obscurity, ambiguity, brevity, and orderliness. The concept that probably has the most impact on natural-language generation is brevity: shorter descriptions are preferred over longer ones, because the use of an unnecessarily long utterance may implicate that a shorter utterance could not be used (e.g., the use of utterance (1b) implicates that utterance (1a) could not have been used). The category of Manner is also important for graphics, but some additional concepts are needed to cover issues that are unique to graphic design. Two important concepts are *appropriate perceptual organization* and *perceptual limits*. To achieve appropriate perceptual organization spurious perceptual organizations that are orthogonal to the information being conveyed in a diagram should be avoided. This is necessary to avoid the kinds of unwanted implicatures caused by perceptual grouping and ordering that are illustrated in Figures 2 and 3. The concept of perceptual limits also concerns human visual perception: a designer should limit the number of graphical-property values used in a diagram so that the values may be easily distinguished, and to ensure that the values are perceptually dissimilar (well-known design heuristics that concern perceptual limits can be found in (Bertin 1983)).

Basic Level: An additional source of conversational implicature, which was proposed by Cruse (1977) and Hirschberg (1985), is the failure to use *basic-level* classes (Rosch 1978) in an utterance. For example, consider the utterances

3a)"I have *a red shirt*"

3b)"I have *a red T-shirt*"

3c)"I have *a red piece of clothing*"

3d)"I have *a carmine shirt*"

Red and *shirt* are probably basic-level for most urban Americans. Accordingly, utterance (3b) carries the conversational implicature that it is important that the object is a *T-shirt* and not some other kind of *shirt*; utterance (3c) carries the conversational implicature that the speaker was not able to categorize the object as a *shirt* or any other type of commonly used clothing; and utterance (3d) carries the conversational implicature that it is relevant that the object is *carmine* and not some other shade of *red*. If none of these implicatures are desired, then utterance (3a) should be generated.

A similar phenomenon can occur in the design of graphical displays. For example, a network diagram in which all the symbols are blinking will likely cause the viewer to conclude that there is some reason why the diagram could not be drawn with non-blinking symbols. Similarly, a network diagram in which all the node symbols are tiny (or huge) will lead to the conclusion that symbols of 'normal' size could not be used. In other words, some graphical-property values seem to be preferred, and the use of a non-preferred value in a graphical display may implicate that the preferred value could not have been used.

The FN System

The FN system (Reiter 1990a) generates natural-language descriptions that are attributive descriptions of individuals, i.e., that communicate to the hearer that a particular object has certain attributes. Utterances (1a) and (1b) are examples of such descriptions. [Note that FN does not generate referring expressions such as (2a) or (2b).] FN assumes that the user has some domain knowledge, and takes advantage of this domain knowledge to form better descriptions. For instance [cf. utterances (1a) and (1b)], if FN wished to inform a user that a certain object is a *computer network* that had the attributes {*data-rate:10Mbit/sec, circuit-type:packet-switched*}, and the object being described is in fact an *Ethernet*, then FN would generate (1b) if it believed that the user knew that Ethernets were networks that had these attributes, and (1a) otherwise.

FN formalizes the problem of avoiding unwanted conversational implicatures by requiring generated utterances to be *maximal elements* under a *preference function*. More precisely, let $\gg$ be a preference function that prefers utterances that do not contain unnecessary elements, that use basic-level classes, and so forth. Let D be the set of utterances that are truthful and that successfully fulfill the system's communicative goal (e.g., inform the hearer that the object is a *computer network* with the attributes {*data-rate:10Mbit/sec, circuit-type:packet-switched*}). Then, an utterance in D is said to be *free of false implicatures* if it is a maximal element of D with respect to $\gg$. Hence, an utterance B in D is free of false

[2] The use of spurious graphical-property values might alternatively be considered a violation of one of the maxims of Manner.

this approach assumes info. about user beliefs

implicatures if there is no utterance A in D, such that A ≫ B. The preference-function formalization of conversational implicature is similar to the *partially-ordered sets* that Hirschberg (1984, 1985) used to formalize scalar implicatures (Gazdar 1979).

FN's overall preference function consists of three separate preference rules: *No Unnecessary Components*, *Lexical Preference*, and *Local Brevity*. We make the assumption that there are no conflicts between these preference rules, i.e., that it is never the case that utterance A is preferred over utterance B by one preference rule, but B is preferred over A by another preference rule.

No Unnecessary Components: The No Unnecessary Components rule is motivated by Grice's Quantity maxim. Formally, it states that A ≫ B if A uses a subset of the modifiers (e.g., adjectives, prepositional phrases, relative clauses) that B uses. Hence, a 'free-of-false-implicatures' description cannot contain any unnecessary modifiers.

Utterance (2b) is an example of a referring expression that contains unnecessary components (the adjectives "brown" and "wooden") and hence carries false implicatures. An example of an attributive description that contains an unnecessary component is the following:

1c)"*packet-switched Ethernet*"

If the user knows that *Ethernets* have the attribute *circuit-type:packet-switched*, the modifier "*packet-switched*" is redundant, and hence utterance (1b) is preferred over utterance (1c) by the No Unnecessary Components preference rule. Therefore, FN will not generate utterance (1c) for such a knowledgeable user, since it might lead her to draw incorrect conversational implicatures (e.g., that there were some Ethernets that did not have the attribute *circuit-type:packet-switched*).

Lexical Preference: The Lexical Preference rule is an extension of the basic-level implicature principle. This rule assumes there is a *lexical preference hierarchy* among the different lexical units that can be used in an utterance; the lexical-preference hierarchy always marks basic-level classes as preferred over other lexical units, and it may include other preference relations as well. The Lexical Preference rule then states that A ≫ B if A and B have the same syntactic and semantic structure, and every lexical unit used in A is equal to or lexically preferred over the corresponding lexical unit in B. Thus, free-of-false-implicatures descriptions need to use preferred lexical units whenever possible. An example of Lexical Preference is that utterance (3a) is preferred over utterances (3b), (3c), and (3d), because (3a) uses basic-level classes.

Local Brevity: This rule states that it should not be possible to generate a shorter description by introducing a single new classification or modifier and then eliminating old modifiers that are no longer necessary. Formally, say A ⋙ B if length(A) < length(B), and size(components(A)-components(B)) = 1 (i.e. A has exactly one component not present in B; B can have an arbitrary number of components not present in A). Then, ≫ is defined as the transitive closure of ⋙. FN uses the number of open-class words as its measure of description length.

This rule is an approximation to the more powerful rule of requiring descriptions to be as short as possible. The latter rule is rejected for complexity-theoretic reasons: it is impossible to find the shortest description with a polynomial-time algorithm (Reiter 1990b). An example of Local Brevity is that utterance (1b) is preferred over utterance (1a), if the user has appropriate domain knowledge, because the single class *Ethernet* in utterance (1b) replaces both the class *computer network*, and the attributes {*data-rate:10Mbit/sec*, *circuit-type:packet-switched*}, in utterance (1a).

The generation algorithm used by FN is described in Reiter (1990a). The algorithm works by incremental improvement: it starts with an initial description, and then repeatedly replaces the current description by a preferred description, as long as such a description can be found. The algorithm terminates when it reaches a point where there are no descriptions that are preferred over the current one: this means the current description must be maximal and hence free of false implicatures.

The ANDD System

The ANDD (Automated Network-Diagram Designer) system automatically designs network diagrams.[3] Its input is a network model and a list of relations that describe the information to be communicated to the user. These relations indicate which attribute values need to be communicated, whether the actual values of the quantitative attributes or just their relative ordering are important, and which aspects of the network interconnection should be emphasized (e.g., source-sink paths, feedback loops, hub structures).

The ANDD system uses an original formulation of syntax and semantics for network diagrams (Marks 1990) to relate graphical-display symbols to elements and attributes of the network model. This formulation is crucial to ANDD's ability to automatically design network diagrams that are free of unwanted conversational implicatures. It also leads to a natural breakdown of the overall design problem into distinct *design tasks*. We first provide an overview of syntax and semantics, and then describe the various design tasks, how they are automated, and the ways in which they try to eliminate unwanted conversational implicatures.

The Syntax of Network Diagrams: The syntax of network diagrams used by ANDD describes the symbols, graphical properties, and perceptual-organization phenomena that a designer can use to communicate infor-

[3] Previous research on automating the generation of graphical displays of data can be found in (Friedell, Barnett, & Kramlich 1982), (Friedell 1984), (Feiner 1985), and (Mackinlay 1986).

mation. The morphological elements of network diagrams aré node symbols, link symbols, text labels, and diacritical symbols. Symbols from each class have their own set of graphical properties (e.g., node symbols have the graphical properties of shape, size, pen color, and fill color). The most novel aspect of the syntax used by ANDD is the inclusion of relations that describe the perceptual organization of symbols, such as sequential layout (top-to-bottom or left-to-right), proximity grouping, alignment, symmetry, similarity, and ordering.

The reason for including perceptual grouping and ordering relations in the syntax is that perceptual organization is a property of the human visual system that we cannot disable: it is virtually impossible to design meaningful network diagrams for which no perceptual organization will occur. Instead, the ANDD system tries to actively exploit this property of the visual system (and thereby satisfy the maxim of Manner) by designing diagrams that contain appropriate perceptual groupings and orderings that communicate or emphasize certain information. The two vertical, evenly spaced node alignments in Figure 4 (designed by ANDD) are an example of this technique: the node interconnections are clear from the links in the diagram, but two special paths in the network are visually emphasized by the active use of perceptual grouping.

The Semantics of Network Diagrams: A major difference between language and graphics is that language has a fixed vocabulary (the English lexicon), while graphics, in general, does not. The meaning of a graphical property such as shape or color usually changes from one graphical display to the next; a graphic designer decides what information is to be communicated by each graphical property, and uses the diagram legend to inform the viewer of his design decisions.

In the ANDD system, the semantics of a network diagram is described in terms of an *expressive mapping*, which relates the network-model information to be communicated to a syntactic description of the network diagram. An expressive mapping includes the obvious direct mapping from vertices and edges in a network model to node and link symbols in a network diagram. In addition, it maps network-model attributes and relations onto network-diagram graphical properties and perceptual-organization relations.

The expressive mapping for the network diagram in Figure 4 maps vertex names onto text labels, vertex types onto node-symbol shapes, and edge types onto link pen types. In addition, node fill intensity is used to visually emphasize some nodes relative to others (emphasis is one of the vertex quantitative attributes in the network model). Finally, relations of sequential layout and alignment are used to help distinguish the two significant source-to-sink paths in the network model.

Automating the Design Tasks: ANDD's syntactic and semantic formulation leads naturally to two central design tasks: (i) creating an expressive mapping, and (ii) instantiating a diagram that conforms to the expressive mapping.

ANDD uses a rule-based system to construct expressive mappings: the rules encode the conditions under which the various network-model attributes and relations should be mapped onto certain graphical properties and syntactic relations. The rules incorporate a limited amount of graphic-design expertise to enable the system to avoid the kind of unwanted conversational implicature shown in Figure 3: for example, no rule maps a non-quantitative attribute onto a graphical property that will be perceived as ordered. In addition, the rules avoid violations of the maxims of Quantity (e.g., the use of multiple graphical properties to communicate a single network-model attribute), and other well-known design flaws that qualify as violations of the maxims of Manner (e.g., the use of too many colors, intensities, or shapes).

Once an expressive mapping is created, ANDD extracts the set of syntactic relations that must appear in the network diagram to communicate the desired information. It then attempts to instantiate a network diagram in which exactly these required syntactic relations appear. The diagram-instantiation task can be thought of as a constraint-satisfaction problem, in which the constraints are the required syntactic relations.

The diagram-instantiation task has two subtasks: picking locations for the symbols, and choosing suitable values for the other graphical properties. The latter task is performed first, by another rule-based system, which chooses graphical-property values to satisfy syntactic relations governing the perceptual-organization phenomena of similarity and ordering. The various symbol shapes, node fill intensities, and link pen types shown in Figure 4 were chosen from a palette of graphical-property values by these rules. Again, the rules must encode a certain degree of graphic-design expertise to avoid unwanted conversational implicatures due to violations of various maxims of Lexical Preference and Manner, e.g., the inappropriate use of preferred graphical-property values, or graphical-property values that are hard to distinguish visually.

Computing diagram layout is computationally much more difficult. The ideal algorithm for this task would compute a diagram layout with exactly the required syntactic relations governing such things as proximity grouping, alignment, and symmetry. However,, such an algorithm appears to be computationally prohibitive. As a reasonable tradeoff between speed and performance (the eventual context is that of an interactive system), the current ANDD system uses a third rule-based system that heuristically picks locations for symbols based on the desired syntactic constraints and the existing layout of local regions of the nascent diagram. In principle, this heuristic approach will not always produce a network diagram with exactly the desired syntactic characteristics (and consequent absence of unwanted conversational implicatures); in practice, the system has worked well in many cases. We continue to refine our current approach to the layout task, and to investigate possible alternative approaches, including the use of mathematical-programming and simulated-annealing techniques.

It is interesting to note that FN and ANDD seem to face similar computational-tractability problems. For both systems, some of the most obvious formalizations of the unwanted-conversational-implicature problem (requiring NL descriptions to be as short as possible; requiring network diagrams to contain certain perceptual organizations) result in computationally intractable solutions. This has been formally proven for FN (Reiter 1990b); a formal complexity-theoretic analysis has not yet been carried out for ANDD, but it seems likely that such an analysis would show that the idealized version of the diagram-instantiation task is NP-Hard.

Conclusion

Grice observed that conversational implicatures are not just a linguistic phenomenon, but that they can occur in all modes of human communication. People expect communications that are directed towards them to follow certain stylistic/pragmatic rules (e.g., NL descriptions should not contain irrelevant components; network diagrams should not contain spurious perceptual groupings), and a computer system that violates these rules may lead its users, in an attempt to explain the violations, to draw unwanted and incorrect implicatures. The task of avoiding unwanted implicatures is central for both the FN natural-language generation and the ANDD automated graphic-design systems, and it seems likely that it will be a fundamental problem for any system that engages in complex computer-human communication, regardless of the communication medium.

Acknowledgments

Many thanks to Cecile Balkanski, Mark Friedell, Barbara Grosz, Julia Hirschberg, Sandeep Kochhar, Candy Sidner, and Bill Woods for their help. The first author was partially supported by a contract from U S West Advanced Technologies; the second author was partially supported by a National Science Foundation Graduate Fellowship, an IBM Graduate Fellowship, and a contract from U S West Advanced Technologies. Any opinions, findings, conclusions, or recommendations are those of the authors and do not necessarily reflect the views of the National Science Foundation, IBM, or U S West Advanced Technologies.

References

Bertin, J. 1983. *Semiology of Graphics: Diagrams, Networks, Maps.* Univ. of Wisconsin Press.

Cruse, D. 1977. The pragmatics of lexical specificity. *Journal of Linguistics* **13**:153-164.

Donnellan, K. 1966. "Reference and Definite Description." *Philosophical Review* **75**:281-304.

Feiner, S. 1985. APEX: An Experiment in the Automated Creation of Pictorial Explanations. *IEEE Computer Graphics and Applications*, Nov. 1985, pp. 29-37.

Feiner, S., and McKeown, K. 1990. Generating Coordinated Multimedia Explanations. In Proc. of the Sixth IEEE Conf. on Artificial Intelligence Applications. Santa Barbara, CA.

Friedell, M., Barnett, J., and Kramlich, D. 1982. Context-sensitive, Graphic Presentation of Information. *Computer Graphics* **16, 3**:181-188.

Friedell, M. 1984. Automatic Synthesis of Graphical Object Descriptions. *Computer Graphics* **18, 3**:53-62.

Gazdar, G. 1979. *Pragmatics: Implicature, Presupposition, and Logical Form*, New York: Academic Press.

Grice, H. 1975. Logic and conversation. In Cole, P., and Morgan, J. eds. *Syntax and Semantics: Vol 3, Speech Acts*, pp. 43-58. New York: Academic Press.

Grosz, B., and Sidner, C. 1990. Plans for Discourse. In Cohen, P., Morgan, J., and Pollack, M. eds. *Intentions in Communication*, Cambridge, Mass.: MIT Press. Forthcoming.

Herring, B., and Prather, W. 1986. A simulation model for analyzing service times in a rotational position sensing disk system. *Simulation* **46**:185-191.

Hirschberg, J. 1984. Anticipating False Implicatures: Cooperative Responses in Question-Answer Systems. In Proc. of the First International Workshop on Expert Database Systems, (2):456-466.

Hirschberg, J. 1985. A Theory of Scalar Implicature. Ph.D. diss., Report MS-CIS-85-56, LINC LAB 21, Dept. of Computer and Information Science, Univ. of Pennsylvania.

Kaufman, L. 1974. *Sight and Mind: An Introduction to Visual Perception*, New York: Oxford University Press.

Lochbaum, K., Grosz, B., and Sidner, C., Models of Plans to Support Communication: an Initial Report. In Proc. of AAAI-1990, Boston, MA.

Mackinlay, J. 1986. Automating the Design of Graphical Presentations of Relational Information. *ACM Transactions on Graphics* **5**:110-141.

Marks, J. 1990. Automating the Design of Network Diagrams, Technical Report, TR 02-90, Center for Research in Computing Technology, Harvard Univ.

Reiter, E. 1990a. Generating Descriptions that Exploit a User's Domain Knowledge. In Dale, R., Mellish, C., and Zock, M. eds. *Current Research in Natural Language Generation*. London: Academic Press. Forthcoming.

Reiter, E. 1990b. The Computational Complexity of Conversational Implicature. In Proc. of the 28th Annual Meeting of the Association for Computational Linguistics. Forthcoming.

Rosch, E. 1978. Principles of Categorization. In Rosch, E., and Lloyd, B. eds. *Cognition and Categorization*, pp. 27-48. Hillsdale, NJ: Lawrence Erlbaum.

Sanden, B. 1989. An Entity-Life Modeling Approach to the Design of Concurrent Software. *CACM* **32**:330-343.

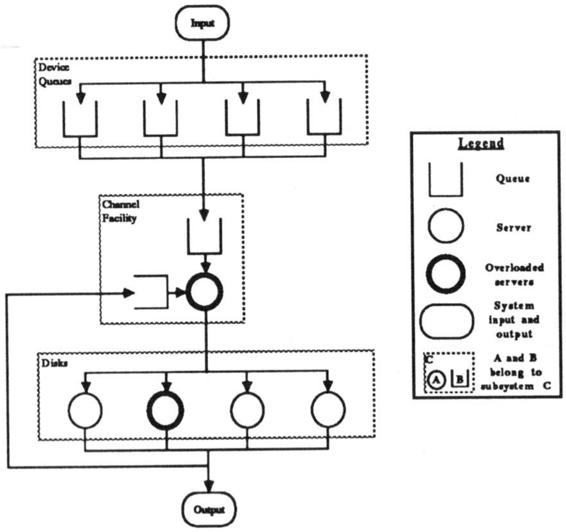

Figure 1 The disk subsystem of a computer [after Herring & Prather (1986)].

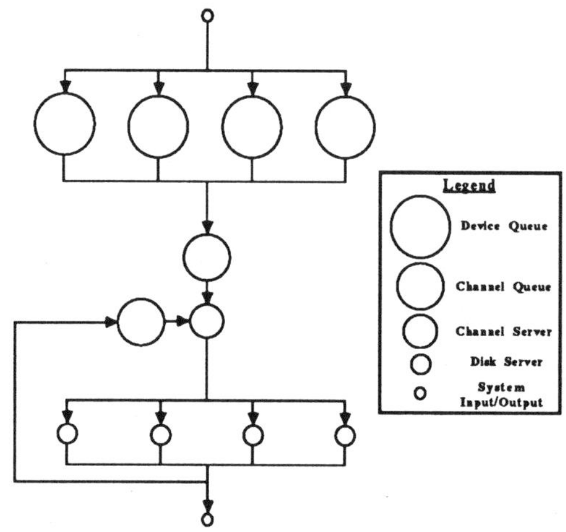

Figure 3 Another variation of Figure 1.

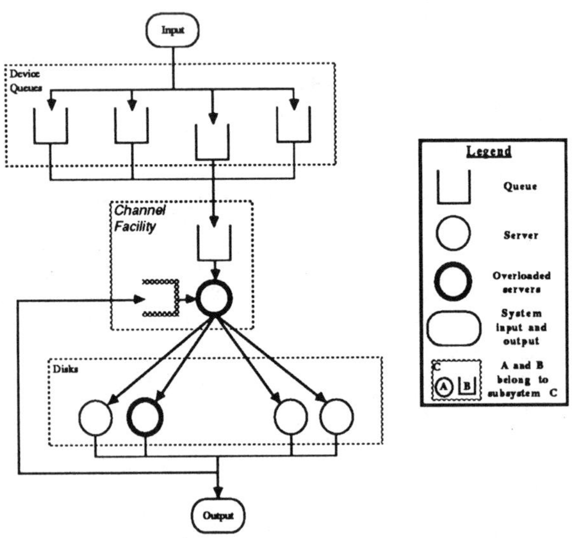

Figure 2 A variation of Figure 1.

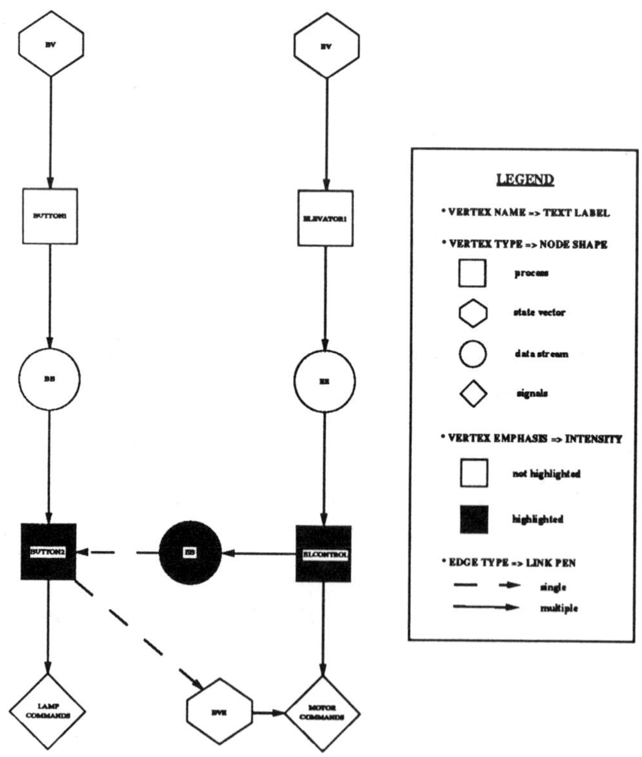

Figure 4 A network diagram designed by ANDD [after Sanden (1989), p.337].

Pointing: A Way Toward Explanation Dialogue*

Johanna D. Moore
Department of Computer Science
and
Learning Research and Development Center
University of Pittsburgh
Pittsburgh, PA 15260

William R. Swartout
USC/Information Sciences Institute
4676 Admiralty Way
Marina del Rey, CA 90292-6695

Abstract

Explanation requires a dialogue. Users must be allowed to ask questions about previously given explanations. However, building an interface that allows users to ask follow-up questions poses a difficult challenge for natural language understanding because such questions often intermix meta-level references to the discourse with object-level references to the domain. We propose a hypertext-like interface that allows users to point to the portion of the system's explanation they would like clarified. By allowing users to point, many of the difficult referential problems in natural language analysis can be avoided. However, the feasibility of such an interface rests on the system's ability to understand what the user is pointing at; i.e., *the system must understand its own explanations.* To solve this problem, we employ a planning approach to explanation generation which records the design process that produced an explanation so that it can be used in later reasoning. In this paper, we show how synergy arises from combining a "pointing-style" interface with a text planning generation system, making explanation dialogues more feasible.

Introduction

It has been argued extensively that natural language interaction is critical to the effective use of expert and advisory systems (for example, see [Finin *et al.*, 1986]). Further, we have argued that explanation requires a dialogue [Moore and Swartout, 1989]. In particular, systems must be able to clarify misunderstood explanations, elaborate on previous explanations, and respond to follow-up questions in the context of the on-going dialogue. Moreover, systems must be able to provide further explanations even when the user cannot ask a well-formulated follow-up question.

In [Moore and Swartout, 1989] we described a system that implements a reactive approach to explanation – one that can participate in an on-going dialogue and employs feedback from the user to guide subsequent explanations. Our system explicitly plans the explanations it produces using a set of explanation strategies. The planning process is recorded to capture the "design" of the explanation. This design record tells the system what it was trying to explain, how it explained it, and what alternative ways could have been used to explain the same thing. When a user indicates that he doesn't understand an explanation, the design record is used to provide the conversational context needed in planning a clarifying response. This system demonstrates that dialogue can be supported effectively by explicitly representing and reasoning about the "design" of the system's explanations.

However, building an interface that allows users flexibility in asking follow-up questions poses a difficult challenge. If the system allows users to pose their questions in natural language, it must be able to handle questions or statements that refer to previously given explanations, e.g.:

> *"Could you please elaborate on the part about applying transformations that enhance maintainability?"*
>
> *"Could you please explain that last part again?"*

This type of question poses a serious problem for a natural language understander. The difficulty arises because such questions make reference to items in the domain of discourse as well as to the discourse itself, so that the natural language analysis system must be capable of understanding both comments made at the object level (about the domain) and comments made at the meta-level (about the discourse). Further, as the first sentence shows, the two levels may be intermixed in a single question. To our knowledge, these referential problems are beyond the capabilities of current natural language understanding systems. Such difficulties mean that it will be hard to achieve dialogue-based explanation capabilities if we rely solely on natural language understanding techniques for accepting feedback from the user.

Fortunately, there is another approach, which we describe in this paper. The idea is to provide the user

*The research described in this paper was supported by the Defense Advanced Research Projects Agency (DARPA) under a NASA Ames cooperative agreement number NCC 2-520.

with a hypertext-style interface, i.e., an interface that allows the user to point to the portion of the system's explanation that he doesn't understand or wants further clarified and then provides a menu of questions that may be asked about the highlighted text. By allowing the user to point to the text he doesn't understand, many of the difficult referential problems in understanding natural language can be avoided. However, for such an interface to be feasible, the system must be able to understand what the user is pointing at; i.e., *the system must understand its own explanations.* Because our system explicitly plans its explanations and records the planning process, it retains the intent behind the explanation, and thus can understand what the user is pointing at.

It is important to note that while we are drawing on a hypertext-like *interface*, the system is not a hypertext system in the traditional sense; i.e., it is not organized as a collection of canned pieces of text interconnected by typed links. Our system differs from a hypertext system in several important ways. First, our system creates text dynamically in response to the user's need for explanations. This text can therefore be tailored to a particular user and situation. A hypertext system would have all the text pre-canned and the user would have to browse through it to find the information he requires. The text cannot be tailored to a particular context.

In a hypertext system, all the things that can be pointed at have to be worked out in advance. It is easy to imagine that users may have questions about items in the texts that were not envisioned, and hence not provided for, by the hypertext designers. In our system, what can be pointed at is determined dynamically, and the links are not worked out in advance. (Indeed, since the texts are not written in advance, it would be difficult to create the links in advance.)

Moreover, as we will see in a later example, what follow-up questions are meaningful is also highly context-dependent. Therefore, the precoded and fixed interconnections employed in a traditional hypertext system would offer the user many possible "links" (corresponding to follow-up questions) that the user might find superfluous. Since one of the main problems with hypertext systems is that users get lost in the network and may even forget what it was they were originally seeking [Carando, 1989, Halasz, 1988], it seems especially important to present a confused user with a small set of pertinent follow-up questions as opposed to a very large set of questions, many of which are irrelevant or even ridiculous. Presenting a user with a follow-up question that the user thinks has just been answered may cause the user to think that he's even more confused than he actually is. In our system, dialogue context (provided by the text plan record) and a user model are used to prune the list of possible questions down to those that appear most relevant.

In this paper, we describe the "pointing" interface we have implemented and combined with our text planning generation system. This combination acts in synergy to support explanation dialogues. The pointing interface allows us to avoid some difficult problems in natural language understanding, while the text planning approach to generation allows us to achieve greater flexibility and sensitivity to context than can be provided with the pre-canned links and text strings of traditional hypertext systems.

Overview of the Reactive Approach

Our explanation facility is part of the Explainable Expert Systems (EES) framework, an architecture for building expert systems that facilitates both explanation capabilities and system maintenance [Neches *et al.*, 1985]. Using EES, we constructed the Program Enhancement Advisor (PEA), an advice-giving system intended to aid users in improving their Common Lisp programs by recommending transformations that enhance the user's code.[1] The user supplies PEA with the program to be enhanced. PEA begins the dialogue with the user by asking what characteristics of the program he would like to improve. The user may choose to enhance any combination of readability, maintainability, and efficiency. PEA then recommends transformations that would enhance the program along the chosen dimensions. After each recommendation is made, the user may accept, reject, or ask questions about the recommendation.

An overview of the explanation generator and its relationship to other components in the system is shown in Figure 1. When the user provides input to the system, the *query analyzer* formulates a discourse goal (e.g., make the hearer know a certain concept, persuade the hearer to perform an action) representing an abstract specification of the response to be produced and posts this goal to the *text planner*. The planner then searches its library of explanation strategies looking for candidates that could achieve the current goal. In general, there may be many strategies capable of achieving a given goal and the planner employs a set of *selection heuristics* to determine which of the candidate strategies is most appropriate in the current situation. These selection heuristics take into account information about the hearer's knowledge state (as recorded in the *user model*), the conversation that has occurred so far (as recorded in the *dialogue history*), and information about whether or not a strategy requires assumptions to be made. Once a strategy is selected, it may in turn post subgoals for the planner to refine. Planning continues in a top-down fashion until the entire plan is refined into primitive operators, which in our system are speech acts ([Searle, 1979]) such as `INFORM` and `RECOMMEND`.

[1] PEA recommends transformations that improve the "style" of the user's code. It does not attempt to understand the content of the user's program.

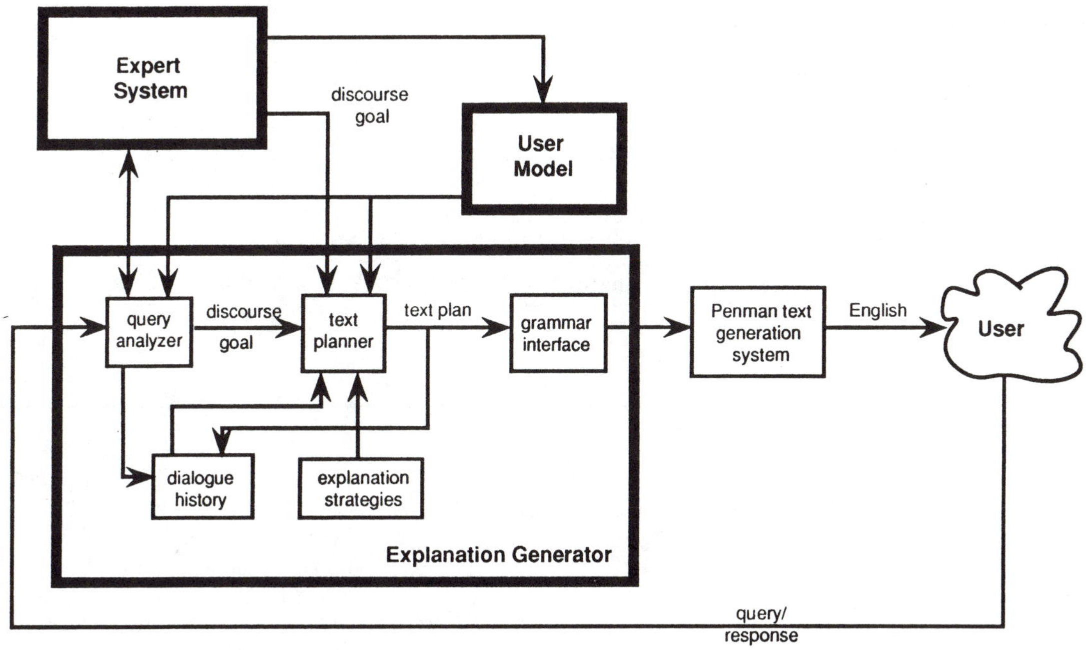

Figure 1: Architecture of Explanation System

As the system plans explanations to achieve its discourse goals, it records the goal/subgoal structure of the response being produced. In addition, it keeps track of any assumptions it makes about what the user knows, as well as alternative strategies that could have been chosen at any point in the planning process. Once a text plan is completed, it is recorded in the dialogue history and passed to the *grammar interface* to be transformed into a form suitable to be passed, a sentence at a time, to the Penman text generation system [Mann and Matthiessen, 1983] for translation into English. After producing an utterance, the system awaits the user's feedback. The user may provide feedback in several ways. He may indicate that the explanation was understood and therefore that the system can move to a new topic. He may ask one of a prescribed set of follow-up questions. In addition, in cases where the user cannot formulate a question, he can type "Huh?" and the system will provide an elaborating or clarifying response. Alternatively, he can use the "pointing" interface which is the topic of this paper, and point to the portion (noun phrase, clause, or sentence) of the explanation that he finds problematic, and a menu of follow-up questions the system can answer about that portion of text will appear.

The completed text plans stored in the dialogue history provide the dialogue context the system needs to respond appropriately to the user's feedback. A completed text plan is an explicit representation of the planning or "design" process that produces an explanation. As described in [Moore and Paris, 1989], a completed text plan represents the roles individual clauses in the resulting text play in achieving discourse goals, as well as how the clauses relate to one another rhetorically. In addition, information about what entities are salient at each point in the explanation (attentional information) can be derived from a text plan. In previous work, we have demonstrated that this context can be used to disambiguate follow-up why-questions [Moore and Swartout, 1989], to select perspective when describing or comparing objects [Moore, 1989a], to avoid repeating information that has already been communicated [Moore and Paris, 1989], and to allow the system to recover from failures when feedback from the user indicates that he hasn't understood the system's utterance [Moore, 1989b]. In this paper we show how a completed text plan allows the system to provide an intelligent hypertext-style interface, one that provides a context-sensitive menu reflecting the ongoing dialogue.

An Example Dialogue

We have found that having the text plans of the system's responses recorded in the dialogue history makes it possible to automatically generate a menu of possible follow-up questions the user may wish to ask about an utterance. Because the text plans provide information about the context in which the highlighted text appears, questions that would appear redundant to the

SYSTEM	What characteristics of the program would you like to enhance?	[1]
USER	Readability and maintainability.	[2]
	⋮	
SYSTEM	You should replace (SETQ X 1) with (SETF X 1).	[3]
USER	Why?	[4]
SYSTEM	I'm trying to enhance the maintainability of the program by applying transformations that enhance maintainability. SETQ-TO-SETF is a transformation that enhances maintainability.	[5]

Figure 2: Sample Dialogue

user can be ruled out.

For example, consider the sample dialogue with our system shown in Figure 2. In this dialogue, the system recommends that the user perform an act, namely replace (SETQ x 1) with (SETF x 1) (line [3]). The user, not immediately convinced that this replacement should be made, responds by asking "Why?" (line [4]). Because the user's why-question follows a recommendation, the query analyzer interprets it as a request by the user to be persuaded to do the recommended act. In our text planning formalism, discourse goals are represented in terms of the effects that the speaker (the PEA-system) wishes to have on the hearer (the user). In this case, the discourse goal posted to the text planner is: (PERSUADED USER (GOAL USER (DO USER REPLACE-1))) where REPLACE-1 is the act of replacing (SETQ x 1) with (SETF x 1). This goal expression can be paraphrased by saying that the system now has the goal to achieve the state where the hearer is persuaded to adopt the goal of performing the replacement.

Figure 3 shows the final result of the planning process, i.e., the completed text plan for achieving the goal (PERSUADED USER (GOAL USER (DO USER REPLACE-1))).[2] Basically this text plan does the following. To persuade the user to do an act, the system motivates that act in terms of a mutual domain goal that the act is a step towards achieving. In this case, the system persuades the user to replace SETQ with SETF (REPLACE-1) by motivating this act in terms of the shared domain goal to enhance the maintainability of the program. Thus, the discourse subgoal (MOTIVATION REPLACE-1 ENHANCE-MAINTAINABILITY) is posted.

One strategy for achieving this discourse subgoal is to inform the user of the domain goal that the system is trying to achieve and then to establish that the act in question is part of the method for achieving that domain goal. Applying this strategy to achieve the discourse goal (MOTIVATION REPLACE-1 ENHANCE-MAINTAINABILITY) in turn gives rise to two discourse subgoals, one for informing the user of the domain goal the system is trying to achieve ((INFORM SYSTEM USER (GOAL SYSTEM ENHANCE-MAINTAINABILITY))), and one to establish that the act being persuaded is indeed part of the method for achieving this goal ((MEANS REPLACE-1 ENHANCE-MAINTAINABILITY)). Speech acts, such as INFORM, are achieved by operators that construct an input specification for the sentence generator. From the text planner's perspective they are considered primitive.

However, the discourse subgoal (MEANS REPLACE-1 ENHANCE-MAINTAINABILITY) requires further refinement. To establish a MEANS relation between the goal just mentioned and the recommended act, the planner has chosen a strategy that informs the user of the method used for achieving the goal (here APPLY-TRANSFORMATIONS-THAT-ENHANCE-MAINTAINABILITY) and then posts a discourse subgoal of making the hearer believe that the recommended act is a step in this method, i.e., (BEL USER (STEP REPLACE-1 APPLY-TRANSFORMATIONS-THAT-ENHANCE-MAINTAINABILITY)).

PEA's domain knowledge contains the information that the domain goal APPLY-TRANSFORMATIONS-THAT-ENHANCE-MAINTAINABILITY is achieved by applying each of the individual maintainability-enhancing transformations known to the system in turn. The appropriate rhetorical strategy for expressing this domain reasoning is ELABORATION-GENERAL-SPECIFIC, in which a general concept is elaborated by citing a specific instance of it. Making the hearer believe that REPLACE-1 is a step in achieving the goal APPLY-TRANSFORMATIONS-THAT-ENHANCE-MAINTAINABILITY thus boils down to informing him that SETQ-TO-SETF is one of the maintainability-enhancing transformations.

The text plan shown in Figure 3 produces the system's response appearing on line [5] in the sample dialogue of Figure 2. After this utterance is produced, the user wishes to ask a follow-up question about an

[2] A complete discussion of the plan language and planning mechanism is beyond the scope of this paper and has been reported elsewhere; see [?].

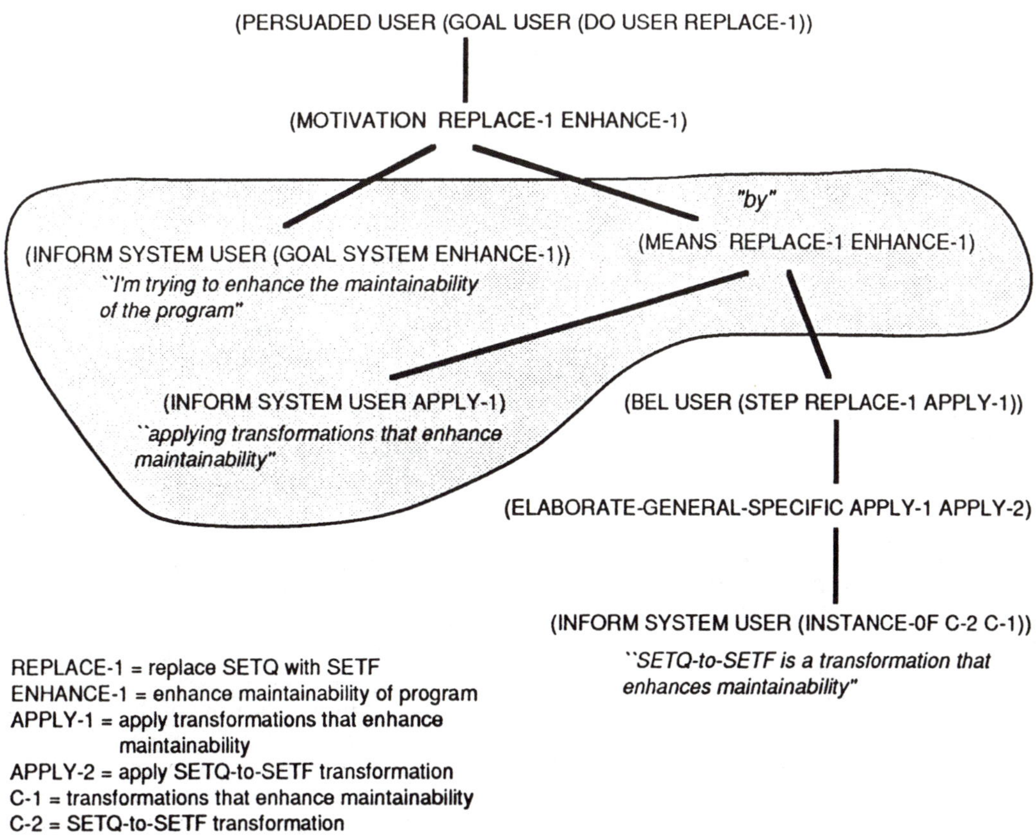

Figure 3: Completed Text Plan for Persuading User to Replace SETQ with SETF

aspect of the system's response and has positioned the mouse so that the sentence

> I'm trying to enhance the maintainability of the program by applying transformations that enhance maintainability.

is highlighted. To ask a follow-up question about this text, the user clicks the mouse and a menu of possible follow-up questions appears. In this context, the follow-up questions that will be contained in the menu are shown in Figure 4. Note that there are many questions that could be asked about this text that are not included in this menu. For example,

Q1: Why are you trying to enhance the maintainability of the program?

Q2: How do you enhance the maintainability of the program?

Q3: Why are you applying transformations that enhance maintainability?

However, given the dialogue that has already taken place, it is very likely that the user already knows the answers to these questions, and therefore they should not be included in the menu. In the next section we show how our system generates candidate menu items and eliminates those such as Q1–Q3 which are almost certainly inappropriate in this context and therefore only clutter the menu and may confuse the user.

Generating Follow-up Questions for Menu

In the example under consideration, the user has highlighted a complex clause corresponding to the shaded region of the text plan shown in Figure 3. When the user selects a complex clause, there are three sources of follow-up questions: the two simple clauses that make up the complex, and the relation between the two simple clauses. For example, in this case where the user selected the text

> (1) I'm trying to enhance the maintainability of the program **by** (2) applying transformations that enhance maintainability.

the system generates follow-up questions from each of the simple clauses (1) and (2), but must also consider follow-up questions that arise because of the MEANS relation that exists between (1) and (2), here explicitly

Q4: How do you apply transformations that enhance maintainability?

Q5: Why are you trying to enhance the maintainability of the program by applying transformations that enhance maintainability?

Q6: What are transformations that enhance maintainability?

Figure 4: Follow-up Question Menu After Eliminating Superfluous Questions

expressed by the term "by".

Generating Menu Entries for Simple Clauses. In our system, simple clauses arise from the leaf nodes of a completed text plan tree, i.e., speech act nodes. For each simple clause, the system generates two types of follow-up questions: questions about the entire clause, and questions about the objects that are participants in the clause. The system currently considers two types of questions that can be asked about speech acts: why-questions and how-questions. We have found that the interpretation of why and how-questions asked about a speech act is dependent on the type of speech act and that in some cases it is not possible to form both a why and how-question from a given speech act.[3]

In the current example, clause (1) informs the user of a goal the system is trying to achieve. From this type of `INFORM` speech act, the system can form both a how and a why-question, namely

Q1: Why are you trying to enhance the maintainability of the program?

Q2: How do you enhance the maintainability of the program?

Clause (2) informs the user of the method the system is currently applying. Again, both a how and a why-question can be formed, namely

Q3: Why are you applying transformations that enhance maintainability?

Q4: How do you apply transformations that enhance maintainability?

Each simple clause in the text produced by the system is made up of a process (e.g., a relation or an action), and the participants and circumstances associated with that process. So, for example, the simple clause "I (the system) apply transformations that enhance the maintainability of the program" consists of a process, `APPLY`, whose actor is the concept `PEA-SYSTEM` and whose object is a complex concept that is expressed as "transformations that enhance the maintainability of the program". This expression includes mention of another process `ENHANCE` and the concepts `TRANSFORMATIONS`, `MAINTAINABILITY` and `PROGRAM`. Since each of these concepts is expressed in the final text, the user may have questions about any of them. To generate candidate follow-up questions for the concepts mentioned in a single speech act, the system examines the complete specification of the sentence passed to the text generator by the grammar interface. This specification contains an entry for each of the concepts that will be uttered in the final text. Each concept appearing in that specification becomes a potential questioned item and the system considers generating a question of the form "What is a ...?" for each.

Generating Menu Entries for Complex Clauses. Because the user has highlighted a complex clause, the system must also consider follow-up questions that arise because of the relation that exists between the two simple clauses, in this case `MEANS`. Currently the system attempts to formulate only why-questions from complex clauses. In the current example, the system formulates the question:

Q5: Why are you trying to enhance the maintainability of the program by applying transformations that enhance maintainability?

In other words, why is the system using this particular method (applying transformations that enhance maintainability) to achieve the goal in question (enhancing the maintainability of the program) as opposed to trying some other strategy?

Although not illustrated in this example, there is one additional source of questions to be included in the follow-up menu. As we stated earlier, the planner records any assumptions it makes about the user's knowledge during the planning process. In addition to the questions that come from the highlighted text itself, the system also generates questions if any assumptions were made in planning the text. If there are any assumptions recorded at the plan nodes that

[3] For example, the `ASK` speech act causes a question to be posed to the user. If the user points at text that was generated as the result of an `ASK` speech act, a sensible why-question can be formed. The user may wish to understand why the system needs to know the answer to its question in order to perform its task; i.e., he would like to ask "Why are you asking me this question?". However, it is not possible to form a meaningful how-question for text produced by an `ASK` speech act. It does not make sense for the user to ask "How are you asking me this question?" For a more thorough discussion of the types of speech acts used in our system and what questions can be formed, see [Moore, 1989a].

created the highlighted text or at any of their ancestor nodes higher up in the text plan tree, the system will generate questions for the follow-up menu that serve to check these assumptions. Note that an assumption could have led to the user's need to ask a follow-up question at this point.

Eliminating Candidate Menu Entries. If we simply used the rules described above for generating menu entries when the user selected a piece of text, the menu for our current example would include all of the questions shown in Figure 5. However, many of these questions are questions that the user would probably not wish to ask. As we have argued above, presenting the user with a menu uncluttered by superfluous entries is desirable.

Note that in the context of the current dialogue, the user is almost certainly not asking any of the questions Q1 – Q3, or Q8 – Q10. The user would not ask Q1 because earlier in the sample dialogue, the system asked what characteristics of the program should be enhanced and the user responded that he would like the system to enhance readability and maintainability. Therefore, the user would not ask why the system is achieving the goal of enhancing maintainability. Q8 – Q10 are questions about basic concepts that almost any user of the system would be familiar with. The reason the user is not likely to ask Q2 or Q3 is because both of these questions were answered when the system said

> I'm trying to enhance the maintainability of the program by applying transformations that enhance maintainability.

Our system can detect these various conditions and omit these superfluous options from the menu using the context provided by the text plans recorded in its dialogue history and the knowledge it has about the current user stored in its user model. The system eliminates candidate menu entries using three heuristics:

1. Don't pose questions that have recently been answered.
2. Don't pose questions to justify shared goals.
3. Don't pose questions to which the user knows the answers.

Let us see how these three heuristics are applied in this example. When the user highlights the text shown in Figure 2, mouse-handling code returns a pointer to the portion of the text plan for the previous response that caused this piece of text to be generated. This corresponds to the shaded area in Figure 3.

The system eliminates Q2 and Q3 using the first heuristic. The semantics of the rhetorical relation MEANS[4] are that the MEANS relation associates the statement of a goal with a statement of the method used to achieve that goal. Thus, since the act APPLY-TRANSFORMATIONS-THAT-ENHANCE-MAINTAINABILITY appears in the second position of a MEANS relation, the system determines that it has just told the user why it is using this method, namely to achieve the goal ENHANCE-MAINTAINABILITY. Therefore, the system determines that the user is almost certainly not asking Q3 and hence it can be omitted from the menu. Similarly, the system can determine that it has just answered the how-question of Q2. Again, from the MEANS relation, the system determines that it has just told the user how it is achieving the goal ENHANCE-MAINTAINABILITY, namely by employing the method APPLY-TRANSFORMATIONS-THAT-ENHANCE-MAINTAINABILITY. Therefore, Q2 is not added to the menu.

Q1 is eliminated using the second heuristic. When the system asks the user what characteristics are to be enhanced, the user's responses are recorded in the user model (see lines [1] and [2] of Figure 2). Thus, when the system considers forming a question asking why it is achieving a goal, it first checks to see if that goal is a mutual goal of both the user and the system. If so, the candidate question is eliminated.

Finally, the system can eliminate many of the "What is a ...?" questions using the third heuristic and the information contained in the user model. Recall that all of the concepts that will be mentioned in an utterance become potential questioned items. When selecting questions for inclusion in the menu, the system compares the list of potential items against the user model and eliminates all of those concepts that the user model indicates the user already knows. In this way, the follow-up question menu will not be cluttered with questions about concepts the user already knows.

In the current example, suppose that the only concept not indicated to be known to the user is the complex concept MAINTAINABILITY-TRANSFORMATIONS. Thus only the question

Q6: What are transformations that enhance maintainability?

will be included in the menu.

After pruning out the follow-up questions that can be ruled out by the dialogue context and the user model, the menu of follow-up questions would include only the three questions shown earlier in Figure 4. This menu is uncluttered by questions the user is almost certainly not asking and therefore presents the user with a concise set of the most meaningful follow-up questions that the system can handle in this context. A user who is confused to begin with will be greatly facilitated by being presented with a small set of the most relevant questions.

[4] MEANS is one of 25 rhetorical relations whose semantics are defined in Rhetorical Structure Theory (RST) [Mann and Thompson, 1987], a descriptive theory of the organization of English text that has identified the relations that normally occur between portions of coherent text.

Q1: Why are you trying to enhance the maintainability of the program?
Q2: How do you enhance the maintainability of the program?
Q3: Why are you applying transformations that enhance maintainability?
Q4: How do you apply transformations that enhance maintainability?
Q5: Why are you trying to enhance the maintainability of the program by applying transformations that enhance maintainability?
Q6: What are transformations that enhance maintainability?
Q7: What are transformations?
Q8: What is maintainability?
Q9: What is a PEA-system?
Q10: What is a program?

Figure 5: Follow-up Question Menu without Eliminating Superfluous Questions

Conclusions

Explanation requires a dialogue, where the user can formulate questions about previously given explanations. However, the follow-up questions a user is likely to ask are difficult for natural language understanding systems to process because they mix meta-level references to the discourse with object-level references to the domain. In this paper, we have argued that some of the difficult natural language understanding issues can be avoided through the use of a hypertext-like "pointing" interface that lets a user indicate what parts of the system's explanations should be elaborated by pointing at them with a mouse. To respond appropriately to the user's pointing, the system needs to know what it was trying to say in the text the user highlighted. Our approach to explanation generation uses a text planner that captures the intent behind an explanation so that the system can reason with it. Because the text in our system is dynamically generated, it is much more flexible than the pre-canned texts of traditional hypertext systems. Further, by recording the text planning process, important aspects of the dialogue context are captured. This dialogue context can be used to prune irrelevant or unnecessary options out of the pop-up menu of follow-up questions. Our system demonstrates the synergistic support for dialogue that can be achieved by combining a "pointing" interface with a text planning generation system.

References

Patricia Carando. Shadow: Fusing hypertext with AI. *IEEE Expert*, 4(4):65–78, 1989.

Timothy W. Finin, Aravind K. Joshi, and Bonnie Lynn Webber. Natural language interactions with artificial experts. *Proceedings of the IEEE*, 74(7), July 1986.

Frank G. Halasz. Reflections on NoteCards: Seven issues for the next generation of hypermedia systems. *Communications of the Association for Computing Machinery*, 31(7):836–870, 1988.

William C. Mann and Christian Matthiessen. Nigel: A systemic grammar for text generation. Technical Report RR-83-105, USC/Information Sciences Institute, February 1983.

William C. Mann and Sandra A. Thompson. Rhetorical Structure Theory: A theory of text organization. In Livia Polanyi, editor, *The Structure of Discourse.* Ablex Publishing Corporation, Norwood, N.J., 1987.

Johanna D. Moore and Cécile L. Paris. Planning text for advisory dialogues. In *Proceedings of the Twenty-Seventh Annual Meeting of the Association for Computational Linguistics*, Vancouver, B.C., Canada, June 26-29 1989.

Johanna D. Moore and William R. Swartout. A reactive approach to explanation. In *Proceedings of the Eleventh International Joint Conference on Artificial Intelligence*, Detroit, MI, August 20-25 1989.

Johanna D. Moore. *A Reactive Approach to Explanation in Expert and Advice-Giving Systems.* PhD thesis, University of California, Los Angeles, 1989.

Johanna D. Moore. Responding to "huh?": Answering vaguely articulated follow-up questions. In *Proceedings of the Conference on Human Factors in Computing Systems*, Austin, Texas, April 30 - May 4 1989.

Robert Neches, William R. Swartout, and Johanna D. Moore. Enhanced maintenance and explanation of expert systems through explicit models of their development. *IEEE Transactions on Software Engineering*, SE-11(11), November 1985.

John R. Searle. *Expression and Meaning: Studies in the Theory of Speech Acts.* Cambridge University Press, Cambridge, England, 1979.

Understanding Natural Language with Diagrams

Gordon S. Novak Jr.
Department of Computer Sciences
University of Texas at Austin
Austin, Texas 78712
novak@cs.utexas.edu

William C. Bulko
IBM Corporation
11400 Burnett Road
Austin, Texas 78758
bulko@cs.utexas.edu

Abstract

We describe a program, BEATRIX, that can understand textbook physics problems specified by a combination of English text and a diagram. The result of the understanding process is a unified internal model that represents the problem, including information derived from both the English text and the diagram. The system is implemented as two opportunistic co-parsers, one for English and one for diagrams, within a blackboard architecture. A central problem is establishing *coreference*, that is, determining when parts of the text and diagram refer to the same object. Constraints supplied by the text and diagram mutually reduce ambiguity in interpretation of the other modality.

Introduction

Natural language is a versatile means of communication, but it is difficult to describe complex spatial relationships using natural language. Diagrams are frequently used to supplement natural language when spatial relationships need to be described. One of us has previously written a program that could understand textbook physics problems stated in English [14, 15]; however, most textbook physics problems are specified by a combination of English text and a diagram, neither of which is a complete description by itself. In understanding such a problem, the human reader must produce a single, unified model of the problem that incorporates information from both input modalities; to do so, it is essential to establish *coreference*, that is, to determine when different forms of description refer to the same object in the situation that is being described and, therefore, in the model of the situation that is being constructed by the reader.

Both natural language and diagrams can be highly ambiguous. A line in a diagram might represent an edge of a large object (such as the surface of the earth), part of a single object, a shared boundary between two objects, or an object in itself (such as a cable). Ambiguity can be reduced by knowing what things are expected to be in the diagram from reading the English text. As some objects are identified, the set of possible identifications of the remaining objects is reduced. Inferences based on common-sense physical principles can further reduce ambiguity; for example, an object is expected to be supported by something, and a rope is expected to be attached to something. Understanding the diagram can likewise reduce ambiguity in interpretation of the English description.

The process of understanding text and diagram together must be opportunistic: it is important to use all the clues that are available, but it is not possible to predict which clues will be present for a particular problem or what order of interpretation will cause all the pieces to fall into place. For this reason, the BEATRIX system [2, 3] has been implemented within a blackboard architecture, using the BB1 blackboard system [5] and GLISP [13].

Examples of the kinds of problems understood by BEATRIX are shown in Figures 1 and 2. The result of the understanding process is a representation of the problem suitable for input to a physics problem solver such as that of Kook [9, 10].

Diagram Input

Diagrams are entered by means of a user interface that allows drawings to be constructed easily by selecting drawing components and moving, scaling, and rotating them as desired. The interface also allows entry of bits of text within the diagram, as well as entry and editing of the English problem statement. The drawing is displayed in a window as it is constructed. As a side effect, a symbolic description of the items in the diagram is constructed; it is this description that serves as input to the understanding program.

If the input to the diagram understander were in terms of components such as blocks, ropes, and pulleys, understanding it would be trivial. Instead, we have taken care to make the input consist of "neutral"

*This research was supported by the U.S. Army Research Office under contract DAAG29-84-K-0060. Computer equipment used in this research was donated by Xerox Corporation and Hewlett Packard.

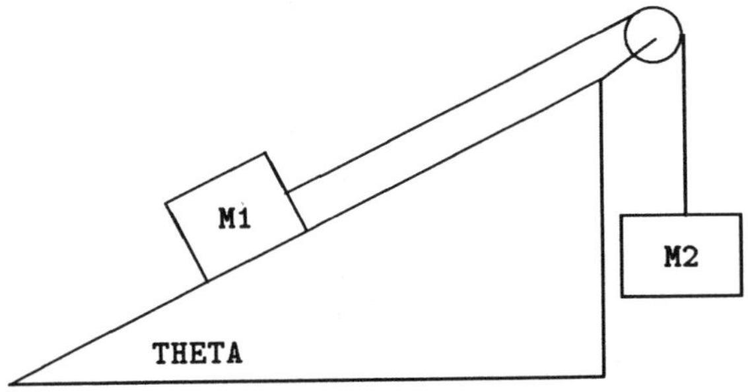


```
((TWO MASSES ARE CONNECTED BY A LIGHT STRING
  AS SHOWN IN THE FIGURE)
 (THE INCLINE AND PEG ARE SMOOTH)
 (FIND THE ACCELERATION OF THE MASSES AND
  THE TENSION IN THE STRING FOR
  THETA = 30 DEGREES AND M1 = M2 = 5 KG))
```

Figure 1: Test Problem P3 (Tipler 11)

components such as lines, circles, and rectangles – a form of input that could reasonably be produced automatically from a printed diagram by a vision preprocessor [1]. Diagram items are represented by property-value pairs; for example,

```
(class LINE endpt1 (129 . 142)
            endpt2 (354 . 173)
            dashed T   ah1 T   ah2 NIL)
```

represents a dashed line with an arrowhead at its first endpoint (**ah1**).

Co-parsing English and Diagram

A human who is solving a physics problem will not read all of the text, and only then look at the diagram, or *vice versa*; instead, the human will typically look briefly at the picture, read some text, look back at the picture, and so forth until the problem has been understood. It is unlikely that any fixed order of processing would suffice for a broad selection of problems, especially since a given problem could be specified entirely by text, entirely by a diagram, or by a combination of the two. For this reason, BEATRIX is organized using *co-parsing* of the two input modalities. Parsing of the English text and parsing of the diagram proceed in parallel; the final interpretation of objects takes into account information from both parsed text and parsed diagram. This kind of control strategy allows understanding to be opportunistic, taking advantage of clues to understanding that arise from diverse knowledge sources; such a control strategy has been found to be advantageous in other perceptual domains such as speech understanding [8] and sonar signal interpretation [12].

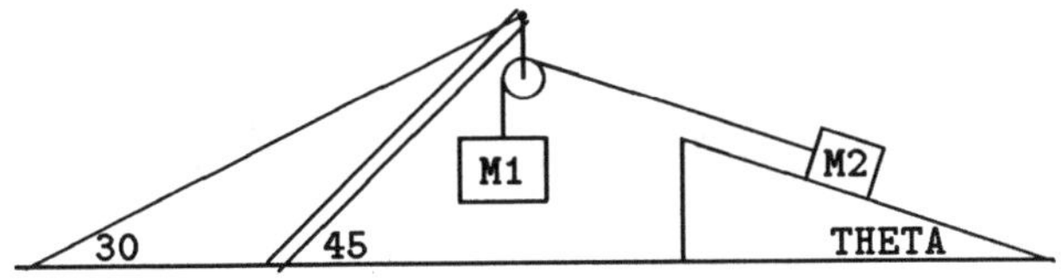


```
((TWO MASSES ARE CONNECTED BY A CABLE AS
  SHOWN IN THE FIGURE)
 (THE STRUT IS HELD IN POSITION BY A CABLE)
 (THE INCLINE IS SMOOTH , AND THE CABLE
  PASSES OVER A SMOOTH PEG)
 (FIND THE TENSION IN THE CABLE FOR
  THETA = 30 DEGREES AND M1 = M2 = 20 KG)
 (NEGLECT THE WEIGHT OF THE STRUT))
```

Figure 2: Test Problem A2

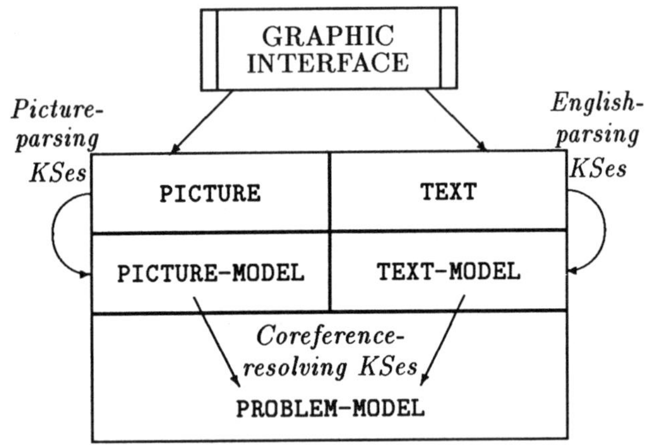

Figure 3: Domain Blackboard Organization

Blackboard Organization

The domain blackboard of the system is organized into five levels, as shown in Figure 3.

The lowest levels of the blackboard are called **TEXT** and **PICTURE**. **TEXT** contains the English sentences of the problem statement; each sentence has a sequence number indicating its order of occurrence. **PICTURE** contains symbolic descriptions of the diagram elements, such as **BOX**, **LINE**, or **CIRCLE**. In addition, the **PICTURE** level contains a set of objects created by a preprocessor that represent contact points between diagram elements.

The intermediate blackboard levels, **TEXT-MODEL** and **PICTURE-MODEL**, represent hypotheses created by the parsing of the text and diagram. Objects on the **PICTURE-MODEL** level represent elementary physical objects, such as **MASS** or **PULLEY**, that are possibly contained in the diagram; these are recognized independently from the text, before coreference resolution takes place. **TEXT-MODEL** objects represent physical objects and relations tentatively identified from the TEXT by the English parser.

The most abstract level of the blackboard is the PROBLEM-MODEL level. Objects at this level represent physical objects in the final interpretation of the problem; these objects have links connecting them to their corresponding objects on the TEXT-MODEL and PICTURE-MODEL levels.

Knowledge Sources

BEATRIX contains 53 knowledge sources (*KS's*); each is a specialist in understanding a particular part of a problem description. Table 1 shows the knowledge sources used and classifies them into groups. The Control KS, *Define-Reliability,* is used to set up code for calculating execution priorities of the other KS's. The Identify KS's operate between the PICTURE and PICTURE-MODEL levels; they perform syntactic recognition of related groups of diagram elements. The single Parse KS calls an ATN parser written in Lisp to parse the sentences of the English text. Match KS's perform coreference matching, finding objects on the PICTURE-MODEL and TEXT-MODEL that correspond and making objects on the PROBLEM-MODEL level that encompass them. KS's whose names begin with *Retrieve-* serve to move information to higher levels of the blackboard when other KS's fail to do so, such as when an object appears in the diagram but is not mentioned in the text. Semantic KS's modify existing objects and make inferences; for example, if the angle between a horizontal surface and another surface is known, *Propagate-Angle-ROTN* will cause the rotation of the other surface to correspond to that angle. Of the Special KS's, *Post-the-Problem* initiates blackboard action by placing the text and diagram on their respective blackboard levels; the remaining KS's perform default reasoning for those cases where no more specific KS was able to act.

English Parsing

English sentences are parsed using an augmented transition network grammar [17] written in a meta-language similar to that described by Charniak and McDermott [4]. Figure 4 shows the grammar function for a noun phrase; the grammar is simple and defers most semantic processing to the understanding module that considers text and diagram together. The ATN parser is invoked by a single knowledge source, *Parse-the-Sentences.* A sentence is syntactically parsed top-down, resulting in a parse tree and a list of tokens of the objects mentioned in the sentence on the TEXT-MODEL blackboard level. This forms the natural language input to the understanding module, which performs semantic processing of the natural language input and diagram together.

Control:	**Match:**
Define-Reliability	*Match-Incline*
	Match-Mass-to-Mass
Identify:	*Match-Mass-to-Object*
Identify-Angles	*Match-Normal-Arrow*
Identify-Arrows	*Match-Normal-Force*
Identify-Line	*Match-Pivot*
Identify-Mass-Labels	*Match-Pulley*
Identify-Masses	*Match-Rope*
Identify-Pulley	*Match-Struts*
Identify-Pulley-System	*Match-Surface*
Identify-Struts	*Match-Tension*
Identify-Surfaces	*Match-Tension-Arrow*
Propagate-Touches	*Match-Variable*
	Propagate-PM-Contact
Parse:	*Propagate-PSt-Contact*
Parse-the-Sentences	*Propagate-RM-Contact*
	Propagate-RP-Contact
Semantic:	*Propagate-RS-Contact*
Add-Contact-Locs	*Propagate-RSt-Contact*
Add-Contact-Objects	*Propagate-SM-Contact*
Assign-Value-to-Variable	*Propagate-SP-Contact*
Correct-Floor-to-Table	*Propagate-SS-Contact*
Find-COEF	*Propagate-SSt-Contact*
Get-Mass-Value	
Neglect-TM-Weight	**Special:**
Propagate-Angle-ROTN	*Default-Mass-ROTNs*
Propagate-Rope-ROTN	*Default-Rope-ROTNs*
Propagate-Touch-ROTN	*Post-the-Problem*
Translate-BE-ADJ	*Retrieve-Mass*
Translate-LET-BE	*Retrieve-Pulley*
	Retrieve-Rope

Table 1: Classes of BEATRIX Knowledge Sources

```
(DEFINEQ (NP (LAMBDA ()
  (CHAIN NP
    (EITHER
      (CAT QWORD)
      (SEQ (OPTIONAL (CAT DET))
           (OPTIONAL (CAT NUMBER))
           (OPTIONAL* (CAT ADJ))
           (OPTIONAL (MEAS))
           (CAT NOUN)
           (SETQ NN1 (THAT NOUN))
           (OPTIONAL (AND (SETQ LABEL-ARC
                                (CAT NOUN))
                          (EQ (GETPROP
                                (THAT NOUN)
                                'TYPE))
                              'VARIABLE)
                          LABEL-ARC))
           (OPTIONAL (VCLAUSE))
           (OPTIONAL (PREPP NN1))))))
```

Figure 4: Noun Phrase ATN Grammar Function

Diagram Parsing

The diagram is parsed by a set of knowledge sources that recognize combinations of picture elements that have special meaning. In effect, these KS's act as grammar productions of a picture grammar [7]; [6] describes the use of a blackboard system for scene interpretation that uses a grammar-like representation of components of a scene.

Local analysis of combinations of diagram elements often allows a combination to be interpreted as a larger and meaningful grouping. For example, if two lines touch at an acute angle and contain text between the lines and close to the vertex, and the text is a number or is a variable name that is typically used to denote an angle (such as **THETA**), then the two lines will be collected on the **PICTURE-MODEL** level as an **ANGLE**, and the number or variable will be associated with the **ANGLE** as its magnitude. An arc connecting the two lines is associated with the **ANGLE** if present, but is not required. The following examples show two angles, one containing text that is not part of the angle.

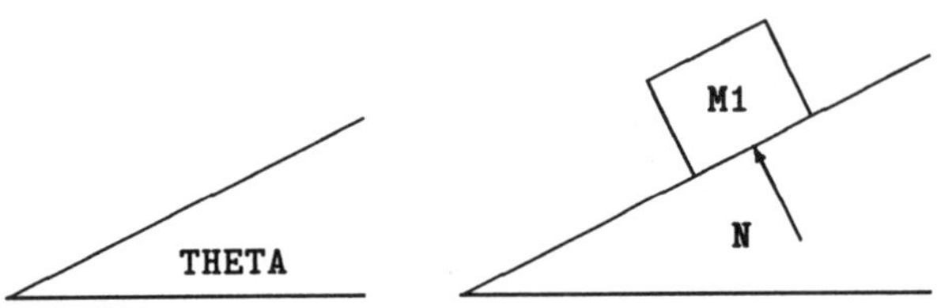

As parts of the diagram are interpreted, they trigger additional KS's that are associated with the interpretations. For example, after a small circle with a line to its center is interpreted as a **PULLEY**, the KS *Identify-Pulley-System* is triggered to look for the lines tangent to the pulley that represent the rope passing around the pulley. This results in the two lines that represent the rope being collected as a single **ROPE** object, with their endpoints away from the pulley being identified as the ends of the rope. This, in turn, triggers additional inferences, since the ends of a rope are expected to be attached to objects or surfaces. When a KS can make a clear interpretation of a part of the diagram, it ***obviates*** other KS's involving alternative interpretations of the object that might have been triggered.

In addition to triggering interpretations of other parts of the diagram, the diagram parsing KS's trigger expectations for later stages of processing. For example, identification of a **CONTACT** between a mass and a surface sets up an expectation that a normal force and coefficient of friction for the **CONTACT** may be specified by the English text.

The process of diagram "parsing" continues until no further interpretations can be made at that level; this results in a substantial degree of interpretation of the diagram. Figure 5 schematically illustrates the interpretation of an example after diagram parsing; most of the **TOUCH** relations and some **CONTACT** relations are omitted for readability.

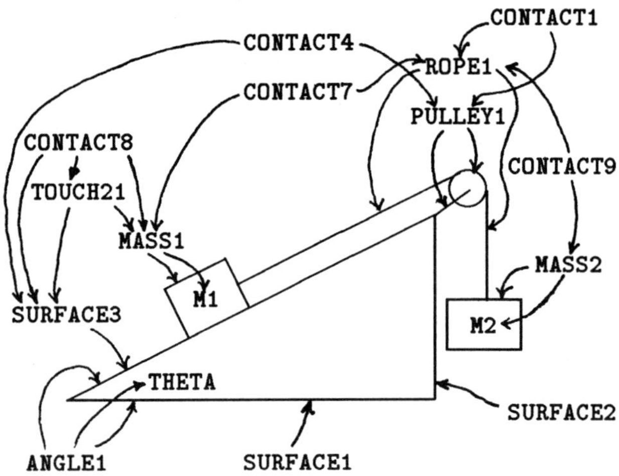

Figure 5: Interpretation after Diagram Parsing

The Understanding Module

The understanding module controls the parsing of the text and diagram and performs the majority of the semantic processing. Its inputs are the "parsed" diagram on the **PICTURE-MODEL** level of the blackboard and the parsed sentences, represented as semantic networks or case frames, on the **TEXT-MODEL** level. It produces as output a unified model of the problem, incorporating information from both modalities.

Establishing Coreference

In order to produce a unified model, a major task is to establish coreference between the two input modalities. Each object that appears in either text or diagram must be present on the **PROBLEM-MODEL** blackboard level; if features of an object appear in both text and diagram, the features must be collected on the *same* object in the model, to which the text and diagram *corefer*. For example, the text could say "the coefficient of friction is 0.25", referring to a contact between a block and an inclined plane that is shown in the diagram but not mentioned in the text. In order to correctly understand the problem, the friction value from the text must be associated in the problem model with the contact relation between block and plane that was derived from the diagram.

The knowledge sources (*KS's*) that perform coreference resolution are triggered when their corresponding types of objects are posted on the **PICTURE-MODEL** or **TEXT-MODEL** blackboard levels. For example, in the problem shown in Figure 1, parsing the phrase "the string" will cause an object representing the string to be added to the **TEXT-MODEL** level, and this will trigger the *Match-Rope* KS to attempt to find a corresponding object in the **PICTURE-MODEL**. In some cases, establishing coreference is fairly trivial, such as resolving a reference to "the mass" when only one item that could be a mass is present in the diagram. In other cases, however, the presence of parsed diagram elements on PICTURE-MODEL is necessary to resolve the referent of a phrase that would otherwise be incoherent. The text may contain a definite reference to an object ("the incline") or to a feature of a relationship ("the coefficient of friction") that is not otherwise mentioned in the text and could not be understood properly without the presence of the corresponding elements from the diagram. In effect, forward inferences are made to attempt to match things that might occur in the other modality; for example, in Figure 1 the contact between the mass and the inclined plane in the diagram causes the KS's *Match-Normal-Force* and *Find-COEF* to be triggered to look for corresponding references that might appear in the text.

Inference of Properties

The KS's of the understanding module also perform inferences that flesh out the representation of the problem; in some cases these can be considered to be based on common-sense physics. For example, BEATRIX will infer that the rotation of an object is the same as the rotation of the object on which it rests and that an object that is hanging from a rope hangs directly below it. Contact between an object and a surface is assumed to be a frictional touch contact, while contact between a rope and an object it supports is assumed to be an attachment. Such inferences are important for understanding, since natural language text often omits things that an intelligent reader is assumed to be able to infer.

Control of Processing

Control of processing in understanding text and diagrams must be flexible, since no fixed order of processing is likely to succeed for a wide variety of problems. Some problems contain all of the necessary information in the text; for example, ISAAC [14] handled problems that had diagrams in the textbooks from which they were taken, but had English descriptions sufficiently complete that diagram understanding was not necessary. Other problems rely heavily on the diagram; for example, in one example handled by BEATRIX the entire text is: ((WHAT IS THE TENSION IN THE CORD IN THE FIGURE)).

Control needs to be opportunistic, so that clear identifications can be made first; as some identifications are made, others that had been ambiguous often can be resolved uniquely. Expectations must be posted so that they can be matched with corresponding references that will appear later. Defaults need to be performed when no other knowledge source can operate.

A blackboard architecture provides a scheduling mechanism that allows many knowledge sources to be *triggered*, or scheduled for execution; the same KS can be triggered multiple times on different data. In the BB1 blackboard system [5], a dynamically calculated priority is associated with each triggered KS; the KS with the highest priority is executed first. If a KS makes a clear identification, it can *obviate* (remove from the schedule) any remaining KS's for the same task. These methods are used to achieve opportunistic control. Bulko [2] describes the processing of an example problem in step-by-step detail; the following summarize the control strategies used:

1. Knowledge sources are triggered, based on the possibility of a match, when objects are placed on the blackboard. For example, a CIRCLE element placed on the PICTURE level will trigger a KS to determine whether it represents a pulley. The initial objects are placed on the blackboard by the special KS's *Post-the-Problem* and *Parse-the-Sentences*. Other KS's implement expectations, as when identification of contact between an object and a surface in the diagram triggers KS's to look for a coefficient of friction and a normal force in the text.
2. Priority ratings are used to cause KS's with the best input data to execute first. For example, *Identify-Masses* gives itself a high rating if there is only one mass against which to match. The priority rating is done dynamically, so that the priority of a KS is raised as its prospects improve; thus, *Identify-Masses* can receive a better rating when one of the masses it might have matched becomes matched with a different object.
3. Default KS's are triggered automatically, but at a very low priority level, to provide default values for unmentioned features or to move objects mentioned in only one input modality to the PROBLEM-MODEL level. If another KS makes an identification for which a default KS exists, the default KS is obviated.
4. Flow of control from low-level KS's to higher-level ones occurs naturally because the low-level KS's are triggered by the problem statement and diagram, while the high-level KS's are triggered by the output of the low-level KS's.

Conclusions and Future Work

Understanding information from different perceptual modalities about a single situation is an important area of A.I. research. The task of understanding English text and diagrams together is nontrivial but simple enough for useful progress to be made. In addition, a clear test of the validity of the results is available, since the output must be sufficient to allow solving of the physics problem; the output of BEATRIX has been used as input to the physics problem solver of Kook [9].

Potential Applications

Humans find graphical interfaces convenient. Most present graphical interfaces are special-purpose: the graphical primitives that are used, and the ways in which they can be connected and combined, are specialized to the application. The ability to understand diagrams input by the user as free-form drawings would allow the same interface to be used for multiple applications; special-purpose knowledge sources would be needed for particular application areas. With input of line drawings using an optical scanner and computer vision pre-processing, existing drawings (such as blueprints) could be understood without having to be entered by hand.

Drawings alone are not sufficient for complete specification; in many cases, blueprints contain blocks of text as well as drawings. The ability to understand text and drawings together would be needed for successful applications.

Future Work

It is possible to imagine cases in which the diagram would allow resolution of ambiguity in parsing the English sentences and in which the semantics of the English itself would be insufficient. In the well-known example sentence, "I saw the man on the hill with the telescope," several different parses are possible and correspond to different meanings; a diagram could indicate which meaning was correct. Likewise, the English text might allow resolution of an ambiguity in "parsing" the diagram. No cases of either type were found in the examples used in testing BEATRIX. There were many potential ambiguities in matching objects in the diagram and text, but none that would have changed the "phrase structure" of either. Nevertheless, this is a possibility, so we identify it as an area for further work. Implementation of the natural language parser within the blackboard framework would make it possible for natural language and diagram parsing to proceed in parallel at the lowest level and to influence each other.

The present system builds only a single interpretation of a problem. A more advanced system should allow representation of alternative interpretations, perhaps like that of [16] with certainty factors to indicate the goodness of an interpretation.

Understanding of larger diagrams, such as mechanical drawings or circuit diagrams, is an interesting area for additional research.

References

[1] Ballard, D. H. and Brown, C. M., *Computer Vision*, Prentice-Hall, 1982.

[2] Bulko, W., *Understanding Coreference in a System for Solving Physics Word Problems*, Ph.D. dissertation, Tech. Report AI-89-102, A.I. Lab, CS Dept., Univ. of Texas at Austin, 1989.

[3] Bulko, W., "Understanding Text With an Accompanying Diagram", *Proc. First International Conference on Industrial and Engineering Applications of AI and Expert Systems*, Tullahoma, TN, 1988, pp. 894-898.

[4] Charniak, E. and McDermott, D. V., *Introduction to Artificial Intelligence*, Addison-Wesley, 1985.

[5] Garvey, A., Hewett, M., Schulman, R., and Hayes-Roth, Barbara, "BB1 User Manual – Interlisp Verison", working paper KSL 86-60, Knowledge Systems Lab, Stanford Univ., 1986.

[6] Hanson, A. R. and Riseman, E. M., "Visions: A Computer System for Interpreting Scenes", in Hanson and Riseman (eds.), *Computer Vision Systems*, Academic Press, 1978.

[7] Fu, K. S., *Syntactic Methods in Pattern Recognition*, Academic Press, 1974.

[8] Erman, L. D., *et al.*, "The Hearsay-II Speech-Understanding System: Integrating Knowledge to Resolve Uncertainty", *ACM Computing Surveys*, vol 12, no. 2 (June 1980), pp. 213-253.

[9] Kook, Hyung Joon, *A Model-Based Representational Framework for Expert Physics Problem Solving*, Ph.D. dissertation, Tech. Report AI-89-103, A.I. Lab, C.S. Dept., Univ. of Texas at Austin, 1989.

[10] Kook, Hyung Joon and Novak, G., "Representation of Models for Solving Real-World Physics Problems", *Proc. IEEE Conf. on Applications of A.I.*, Santa Barbara, CA, March 1990.

[11] Larkin, J., J. McDermott, D. Simon and H. A. Simon. "Expert and Novice Performance in Solving Physics Problems", *Science*, 208 (20 June 1980), pp. 1335-1342.

[12] Nii, H. P. *et al.*, "Signal-to-symbol Transformation: HASP/SIAP Case Study", *A.I. Magazine*, vol. 3, no. 2 (Spring 1982), pp. 23-35.

[13] Novak, G., "GLISP: A LISP-Based Programming System With Data Abstraction", *A.I. Magazine*, vol. 4, no. 3 (Fall 1983), pp. 37-47.

[14] Novak, G., "Computer Understanding of Physics Problems Stated in Natural Language", *Am. J. Computational Linguistics*, Microfiche 53, 1976.

[15] Novak, G., "Representations of Knowledge in a Program for Solving Physics Problems", *IJCAI*, 1977, pp. 286-291.

[16] Seo, J. and Simmons, R. F., "Syntactic Graphs: A Representation for the Union of All Ambiguous Parse Trees", Tech. Report AI-87-64, A.I. Lab, C.S. Dept., Univ. of Texas at Austin, 1987.

[17] Woods, W. A., "Transition Network Grammars for Natural Language Analysis", *Comm. ACM*, vol. 13, no. 10 (Oct. 1970), pp. 591-606.

Incorporating Default Inferences into Plan Recognition

Sandra Carberry
Department of Computer and Information Sciences
University of Delaware
Newark, Delaware 19716
carberry@dewey.udel.edu

Abstract[1]

This paper presents a process model of plan inference for use in natural language consultation systems. It includes a strategy that can both defer unwarranted decisions about the relationship of a new action to the user's overall plan and sanction rational default inferences. The paper describes an implementation of this strategy using the Dempster-Shafer theory of evidential reasoning. Our process model overcomes a limitation of previous plan recognition systems and produces a richer model of the user's plans and goals, yet one that can be explained and justified to the user when discrepancies arise between it and what the user is actually trying to accomplish.

Introduction

During task-oriented interactions with an expert consultation system, a user is engaged in seeking information in order to construct a plan for accomplishing a task. A number of researchers have demonstrated the importance of inferring the user's partially constructed domain plan and tracking his focus of attention in the plan structure[1, 9, 12, 13, 14, 17, 21], and models of plan inference have been used to address problems in language understanding and response generation. Unfortunately, current models of plan inference encounter difficulty when there are several possible explanations for an agent's action. They cannot use a priori knowledge about the domain to make default choices among plans that might be inferred from an observed action, nor can they revise incorrect beliefs about an agent's plan. For example, suppose an agent asks how late the Super-Saver Supermarket is open. Current systems are unable to make the default inference that the agent intends to purchase groceries since there are other high-level actions, such as cashing a check, that might motivate his query.

Analysis of naturally occurring dialogue suggests that human information-providers often make default inferences about the plans and goals of the information-seeker, use the resulting beliefs to generate helpful responses, and can explain, rationally justify, and revise their beliefs when they are in error. If natural language consultation systems act in the same manner, their responses will appear intelligent and natural to their human users. If they fail to make these inferences, they will often be forced to engage in lengthy clarification dialogues in order to ascertain with certainty what the user is trying to do, and will therefore appear unintelligent, obtuse, and uncooperative.

We have been investigating how the behavior exhibited by human information-providers can be captured in an intelligent natural language system. This paper presents a process model of plan recognition that is motivated by an analysis of naturally occurring dialogues and by psychological studies of human inference. It includes a strategy for incrementally updating the system's model of the user's plan that can both defer unwarranted decisions about the relationship of a new action to the user's overall plan and sanction rational default inferences. The paper describes an implementation of this strategy using the Dempster-Shafer theory of evidential reasoning. Our process model overcomes a limitation of previous models of plan recognition and produces a richer model of the user's plans and goals, yet one that can be explained and justified to the user when discrepancies arise between it and what the user is actually trying to accomplish.

Intended versus Keyhole Recognition

Default inferencing plays a role in both intended and keyhole plan recognition. Intended recognition is the recognition of those goals and plans that an agent intends to convey and is essential in identifying the intended meaning of a speaker's utterance[3]. Allen[13] was the first to model intended recognition. When n mutually exclusive higher-level goals could be inferred from a given subgoal, he used a branching heuristic that reduced the ratings of the alternative inferred partial plans to *1/n* of the rating of the partial plan from which they were inferred; he justified this heuristic by arguing that the speaker would have realized that the hearer would have difficulty identifying which

[1] This material is based upon work supported by the National Science Foundation under Grant No. IRI-8909332. The Government has certain rights in this material.

inference he was intended to choose. In [1] and [20], upward inference of higher-level goals was terminated once a choice among several possible but mutually exclusive plans had to be made. We contend that if the speaker believes that the mutual domain knowledge suggests that one goal is substantially more likely than the other possible alternatives to be the motivation for his actions, he may *intend* the listener to recognize it by virtue of default inferencing.

Keyhole recognition is the inference of an agent's goals and plans by unobtrusively observing the agent, as if through a keyhole, and is useful in generating cooperative, helpful responses[3]. A natural language consultation system's ability to provide useful advice will be directly related to how well it is able to recognize what the user is trying to do. Since an action can generally play a role in many different plans, some of them a priori far more likely than others to be the motivation for the action, the system must be able to make appropriate default inferences if it is to develop a rich and tractable model of the user's plans and goals. Thus default inferencing is important in both intended and keyhole plan recognition. Although a number of researchers have studied default reasoning and developed formal models of default inference[4, 15, 16], little attention has been given to incorporating default inferencing into incremental plan recognition in natural language advisement systems.

Motivation for Our Process Model

Our objective is a plan inference framework that will produce a rich model of the user's underlying task-related plan. What requirements should be placed on this model? We contend that rather than be the *best* model in the sense of being the model with the greatest mathematical probability of representing the user's intended plan, the model should represent intelligent, rational decisions about the user's intentions — decisions that can be explained and justified to the user when questions about them arise. Although various strategies could be devised for constructing a model with the highest probability of occurrence[2, 7, 8], these schemes require that the system perform a great deal of time-consuming and complicated computation. In addition, even if the system's model of the user's plan is the one *most likely* to be correct, it *can* still be wrong. Analysis of naturally occurring dialogue indicates that although human information-providers occasionally make incorrect inferences during a dialogue, they can rationally justify them to the information-seeker when errors arise. Unfortunately, complex probability computations are extremely difficult to explain and justify to a lay person. Yet if an information system is to be viewed by users as intelligent and cooperative, it must appear rational and must be able to explain its reasoning; otherwise its users will not have confidence in the system's ability to intelligently assimilate a dialogue and provide helpful advice.

We contend that an advisement system should model the user's plans and goals by following strategies that not only produce a rich set of beliefs about what the user is trying to do but also capture the kind of behavior exhibited by intelligent human information-providers. If the system does this, then when it finds that its model of the user's plan is in error, it can explain its reasoning to the user and the user is likely to accept as reasonable the system's decisions and bases for making them. The user will come to expect the system to make the kinds of inferences human information-providers generally make and a naturally appearing dialogue can ensue. Note that our intent is not to simulate a particular individual or group of individuals, but rather to produce behavior that can be justified to a human observer and which the observer would regard as intelligent, rational, and natural.

Research by psychologists has provided insight on prediction and inference by humans. In [18], it was found that humans tend to develop a hypothesis explaining a planning agent's actions, expand their beliefs about the agent's plan as much as possible without making unwarranted assumptions about subactions and parameter bindings, and then revise this hypothesis as necessary to accommodate new actions. In [6], it is argued that humans do not reason with large numbers of alternative scenarios and make inferences from these possibilities by complex combinations of uncertain information. Instead, the *As-if* model[6], proposed to explain human behavior in multi-stage inferencing, hypothesizes that humans gather additional information until their confidence in an intermediate conclusion exceeds a threshold, then adopt this conclusion as certain evidence in the next stage of inferencing.

Our model of plan inference incorporates these aspects of human inferencing. It develops a rational hypothesis about an agent's plan by both sanctioning appropriate default inferences and deferring unwarranted decisions until further evidence is available. It reasons about the support that evidence about the user's intended actions gives to alternative conclusions about his goals, has a confidence threshold at which a conclusion is accepted and added to the system's beliefs about the user's plan, views actions that are representative parts of performing a higher-level action as confirming the latter's presence in the system's beliefs about the user's plan, and revises the model when contradictions are detected.

The Process Model

System Overview

Dynamic plan recognition requires that the user's plan be built incrementally as the dialogue progresses. We use a tree structure called a context model[1] to represent the system's beliefs about the user's plan as inferred from the preceding dialogue. Each node in the tree represents an action that the system believes

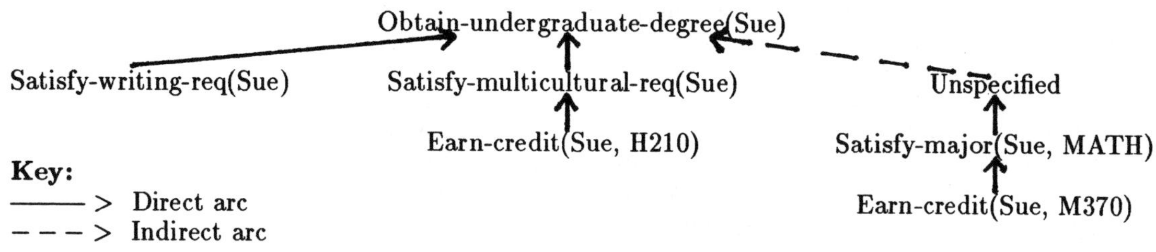

Figure 1: A sample context model

the user wants to perform, along with a set of beliefs that have been ascribed to the user in inferring the action[14]. The arcs connecting nodes are of two types: 1) a direct arc from action A_i to A_j indicates that A_i plays a direct role in performing A_j — ie., A_i is part of an operator description for A_j in the system's plan library, and 2) an indirect arc from A_i to A_j indicates that A_i is part of an expanded plan for A_j, but exactly what role it plays in that plan is as yet ambiguous — ie., there is more than one plausible way to expand the operator for A_j so that it includes A_i and a decision about which expansion represents the user's intentions is unwarranted at the current time. In addition, direct arcs are divided into three classes, representing a generation[14], enablement, or subaction relationship between the actions they connect. Figure 1 illustrates a sample context model containing both direct and indirect arcs. It indicates that earning credit in H210 (an Asian history course) is a subaction in Sue's plan for satisfying the multicultural requirement for getting an undergraduate degree. In addition, it indicates that the system believes that Sue wants to take M370 as part of fulfilling a math major, but that there is insufficient evidence for deciding exactly how satisfying the requirements for a math major fits into her overall plan (ie., whether it is part of obtaining a BA, BS, or Liberal Studies degree).

As each new utterance occurs, the context model must be adjusted and expanded to reflect an updated hypothesis about the information-seeker's plans and goals. We use plan identification heuristics to hypothesize domain actions that might motivate the user's new utterance and focusing heuristics to identify the most coherent relationship between a hypothesized action and the user's current focus of attention in the context model. These are described in [1] and will not be repeated here. If there is only one expansion of the context model that captures the relationship identified by the focusing heuristics, that expansion becomes the updated context model. However, there may be more than one way to expand the context model to include the new action in the specified way. Dynamically computed preference rules are used to represent alternative inferences that might be made from given evidence and order them according to plausibility. The decision to sanction a default inference is based on the conclusion's plausibility with respect to the plausibility of alternative competing conclusions, as estimated by their respective plausibility factors.

Preference Rules

Although our model of plan recognition does not rely on any particular representation scheme, we do need a means for representing how individual pieces of evidence lend support to alternative hypotheses about the user's plans and goals and for reasoning about the combined support offered by several items of evidence. We are using the Dempster-Shafer theory[10, 19] for this purpose. One advantage of the Dempster-Shafer theory over other approaches to evidential reasoning is that belief is distributed over subsets of the possible hypotheses, thereby allowing belief to be attributed to a hypothesis H without all remaining belief being attributed to $\neg H$. In addition, the result of combining evidence in the Dempster-Shafer theory models how the set of plausible hypotheses shrinks as additional evidence is evaluated and taken into consideration[10]. These features are useful for incorporating default inferencing into incremental plan recognition. They will allow us to view several competing conclusions as totally plausible without completely ruling out other conclusions and enable us to model how several pieces of information incrementally gleaned from an ongoing dialogue tend to single out one conclusion as far more plausible than the other possibilities.

In the Dempster-Shafer theory, the set of mutually exclusive alternative possible conclusions is called the *frame of discernment* Θ. A basic probability assignment m represents the impact of given evidence on belief in the alternative conclusions by distributing probability mass among the subsets of Θ. Dempster's rule of combination provides a method for combining evidence by computing a new basic probability assignment from the basic probability assignments associated with individual pieces of evidence.

We are using Dempster-Shafer basic probability assignments to represent the support that evidence about the user's actions gives to alternative conclusions about his goals. The frame of discernment Θ is the set of mutually exclusive higher-level goal actions that might be inferred as the reason that a user wants to perform the actions comprising the evidence E. We are assuming that an agent has only one immediate primary goal as his reason for wanting to perform the actions in E; thus the elements of Θ are mutually exclusive as motivation for the actions in E. *Others* is included as a subset of Θ in order to make it exhaustive and to account for user misconceptions and novel plans. The semantics of an entry $m(X) = k$ in a basic probability assignment is that evidence E commits a portion k of belief to the hypothesis that the user wants to perform some higher-level action in the set X; however, other entries may distribute extra portions of belief to subsets of X.

We contend that default recognition of user goals should be based on a goal's plausibility with respect to other competing goals. In order to do this, we need the notion of a default inference rule in which alternative possible conclusions are ordered by levels of plausibility. We capture this in *preference rules*[2] which have the form **IF** $< E >$ **P-THEN** $<$ *p-list* $>$ where

$< E >$	::=	actions comprising the evidence
$<$ *p-list* $>$	::=	$<$ *p-pair* $>$|$<$ *p-pair* $><$ *p-list* $>$
$<$ *p-pair* $>$	::=	$< A_g >< PF_p(A_g) >$
$< A_g >$	::=	an element of Θ
$< PF_p(A_g) >$	::=	plausibility factor for $< A_g >$

The preference rule P associated with evidence $< E >$ is constructed from the basic probability assignment m associated with $< E >$ by using its frame of discernment Θ and computing plausibility factors $PF_p(A_g)$ as $Plausible_m(\{A_g\}) = 1 - \sum_{(Y \subseteq \Theta) \wedge (Y \cap \{A_g\} = \emptyset)} m(Y)$. This last formula measures the extent to which the inconclusive evidence accumulated thus far makes A_g plausible by failing to refute it[19]. Thus the *plausibility factor* for a goal action A_g captures what Reiter[16] calls the intuitive plausibility of a default. Figure 2 illustrates several basic probability assignments (bpa's) and the preference rules compiled from them.

Sanctioning Default Inferences

If the system believes that the user wants to perform a set of actions E and that there is more than one action A_g whose performance would include all the actions in E, then the system must be able to decide whether one of these actions should be identified as the user's goal. We contend that this decision should be based on the plausibility of a goal action with respect to the alternative possible goal actions — namely, if one action is extremely plausible as the user's goal and far more plausible than the other possibilities, then it should be recognized as part of the user's plan. We are modeling this decision-making by maintaining a *threshold plausibility level* ϵ_{pl} and a *threshold difference level* ϵ_d, and sanctioning inference of a goal action A_g by default from the actions comprising the evidence E if A_g is the most plausible goal that might motivate the actions in E, A_g's plausibility factor exceeds the threshold plausibility level ϵ_{pl}, and no other action suggested by the evidence E has a plausibility factor within the threshold difference level ϵ_d of A_g. If A_g can be inferred from E, either with certainty or by default, then we say that $Infer(E) = A_g$. More formally, if P is the preference rule associated with evidence E, then

$Infer(E) =$

A_g if A_g is the only action whose associated operator contains the actions in E

A_g if $(A_g \in \Theta_p) \wedge (PF_p(A_g) > \epsilon_{pl})$
$\wedge[\neg\exists A_k \text{ s.t. } (PF_p(A_k) > PF_p(A_g)$
$\vee PF_p(A_g) - PF_p(A_k) < \epsilon_d)]$

$\emptyset$ otherwise

The threshold settings are determined by the criticality of the interaction (medical versus travel domain).

Building the Context Model

Although our processing strategy and heuristics are domain-independent, the system must be provided with domain knowledge representative of that required by a capable human information-provider. This knowledge consists of the set of actions that a user might pursue in the domain, operators that describe how to perform these actions, and basic probability assignments representing how individual actions lend support to alternative conclusions about the user's goals. Preference rules are computed dynamically from combinations of one or more basic probability assignments. Since operator descriptions contain subactions which also have associated operators, a plan for an action can be expanded to any desired degree of detail by starting with the operator for the action and repeatedly replacing subactions with their own operator descriptions.

Each new utterance must be assimilated into the context model to produce an updated hypothesis about the user's plans and goals. As described earlier, plan identification heuristics are used to hypothesize domain actions that might motivate a user utterance and focusing heuristics are used to identify the most coherent relationship between a hypothesized action and the user's current focus of attention in the context model. The preceding sections showed how preference rules rank alternative conclusions by plausibility and can be used to sanction default inferences. This section presents some of our rules for incorporating default inferences into a model of plan recognition, along with examples illustrating the rules. The examples are taken from a student advisement domain; the relevant basic probability assignments are shown in Figure 2. We will assume a threshold plausibility level of $\epsilon_{pl} = .9$ and a threshold difference level of $\epsilon_d = .7$.

If there is only one expansion of the context model that captures the relationship identified by the focusing heuristics, the context model should be updated to include it. When more than one expansion satisfies the constraints of the focusing heuristics, Rule-D1 captures the notion of making default inferences that

[2] The initial work on preference rules was done with Kathy Cebulka.

Basic Probability Assignments

1) Evidence: {Earn-credit(_user, M370)}
$m_1(\{A_3\}) = .85$
$m_1(\{A_2, A_3\}) = .12$
$m_1(\Theta_1) = .03$

2) Evidence: {Earn-credit(_user, EE202)}
$m_2(\{A_1\}) = .15$
$m_2(\{A_1, A_2\}) = .80$
$m_2(\{A_1, A_2, A_3\}) = .04$
$m_2(\Theta_1) = .01$

3) Evidence: {Earn-credit(_user, CS321)}
$m_3(\{A_2, A_3\}) = .95$
$m_3(\{A_1, A_2, A_3\}) = .02$
$m_3(\Theta_1) = .03$

4) Evidence: {Satisfy-major(_user, CS)}
$m_4(\{A_4\}) = .74$
$m_4(\{A_4, A_5\}) = .25$
$m_4(\Theta_2) = .01$

5) Evidence: {Satisfy-major(_user, MATH)}
$m_5(\{A_5\}) = .15$
$m_5(\{A_4, A_5\}) = .84$
$m_5(\Theta_2) = .01$

Preference Rules

IF {Earn-credit(_user, M370)}
P-THEN A_3 1.000
A_2 .150
Other .030

IF {Earn-credit(_user, EE202)}
P-THEN A_1 1.000
A_2 .850
A_3 .050
Other .010

IF {Earn-credit(_user, CS321)}
P-THEN A_2 1.000
A_3 1.000
A_1 .050
Other .030

IF {Satisfy-major(_user, CS)}
P-THEN A_4 1.000
A_5 .260
Other .010

IF {Satisfy-major(_user, MATH)}
P-THEN A_5 1.000
A_4 .850
Other .010

A_1 = Satisfy-major(_user, EE)
A_2 = Satisfy-major(_user, CS)
A_3 = Satisfy-major(_user, MATH)
A_4 = Earn-degree(_user, BS)
A_5 = Earn-degree(_user, BA)

Figure 2: Sample bpa's and Preference Rules for a University Advisement Domain

coherently mesh with the user's current focus of attention in his plan, while deferring unwarranted decisions until further evidence is accumulated. Note that the context model can now contain indirect arcs, indicating an incompletely specified relationship between actions.

Rule-D1: Suppose that the focusing heuristics have determined that the new action A_{new} associated with the user's utterance is part of a plan for performing an action A_c in the context model, but that there is more than one way of constructing a plan for A_c that includes A_{new}. If $Infer(\{A_{new}\}) = A_j$ and A_j can play a role in a plan for A_c, then add A_j to the context model, with a direct arc from A_{new} to A_j, and repeat Rule-D1 with A_j in place of A_{new}; otherwise add an uninstantiated node with a direct arc from A_{new} to this new node and an indirect arc from the new node to A_c.

Example-1:
Suppose that Sue has asked about satisfying such university requirements as a writing project and a multicultural course, leading the system to believe that she wants to get an undergraduate degree, and that Sue then asks about taking M370 (probability theory). The plan identification heuristics identify α = Earn-credit(Sue, M370) as the domain action motivating Sue's query. Since the system's domain knowledge includes an operator for earning an undergraduate degree and that operator can be expanded to produce a plan that includes taking M370, the focusing heuristics determine that Sue wants to take M370 as part of earning an undergraduate degree. However, there are several ways that taking M370 fits into such a plan, including satisfying the requirements for a math or a CS major, or merely filling a free elective. Since the first preference rule in Figure 2 produces Infer($\{\alpha\}$) = Satisfy-major(Sue, MATH) and fulfilling a math major can be part of a plan for getting an undergraduate degree, Rule-D1 results in the default inference that Sue wants to satisfy the requirements for a

math major. Since the fifth preference rule in Figure 2 produces Infer({Satisfy-major(Sue, MATH)})=$\emptyset$, a decision about precisely how satisfying a math major fits into her plan — ie., about whether she intends to fulfill a math major as part of a BA or a BS degree — is deferred until further evidence is accumulated. The resulting context model was shown in Figure 1.

Since a single piece of evidence may be insufficient to warrant a default inference, a plan recognition system must have the ability to combine individual pieces of evidence. The next rule addresses the problem of recognizing actions from an accumulation of evidence.

Rule-D2: Suppose that the context model indicates that one or more actions $A_1, \ldots, A_k$ are part of some as yet unspecified higher-level action and suppose that the focusing heuristics determine that A_{new} is also part of this action. Add A_{new} and a direct arc from A_{new} to this as yet unspecified action, construct a preference rule for $\{A_1, \ldots, A_k, A_{new}\}$ from the bpa produced by combining the bpa's associated with the individual actions $A_1, \ldots, A_k, A_{new}$ (using Dempster's rule of combination), and if $Infer(\{A_1, \ldots, A_k, A_{new}\}) \neq \emptyset$, then instantiate the previously unspecified parent action with $Infer(\{A_1, \ldots, A_k, A_{new}\})$.

Example-2:
Suppose that the system believes that Al wants to take EE202 as part of a plan to perform some as yet unspecified higher-level action A_u. (Note that the second preference rule in Figure 2 produces Infer({Earn-Credit(Al, EE202)}) = $\emptyset$.) Now suppose that Al asks about the preconditions for taking CS321 and that Earn-credit(Al,CS321) is identified as the action motivating his new utterance. The focusing heuristics must now determine the most coherent relationship between this new action and the existing context model. Since taking CS321 and taking EE202 are both possible actions for earning majors in math, computer science, and electrical engineering, the focusing heuristics suggest that taking CS321 and taking EE202 are both actions that will be executed as part of a plan to perform the unspecified higher-level action A_u. Rule-D2 applies. Using Dempster's rule of combination[19], the bpa associated with taking EE202 is combined with the bpa associated with taking CS321 (Figure 2) to produce

Combined basic probability assignment

$m(\{A_1\})$	$= .0088$	$m(\{A_2, A_3\})$	$= .0554$
$m(\{A_2\})$	$= .8862$	$m(\{A_1, A_2, A_3\})$	$= .0026$
$m(\{A_1, A_2\})$	$= .0467$	$m(\Theta_1)$	$= .0003$

Preference Rule

IF {Earn-credit(Al,EE202), Earn-credit(Al,CS321)}

P-THEN	A_2	.9912
	A_1	.0584
	A_3	.0583
	Other	.0003

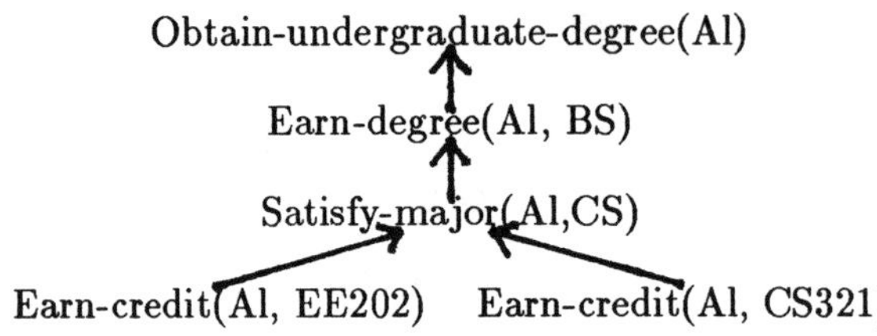

Figure 3: Extended Context Model

In this case, Infer({Earn-credit(Al,EE202),Earn-credit(Al,CS321)}) = Satisfy-major(Al, CS), resulting in the default inference that Al is trying to satisfy the requirements for a CS major. This produces the lower half of the context model in Figure 3.

The next rule addresses the problem of default recognition of higher-level actions motivating the actions that are currently part of the system's beliefs about the user's plan.

Rule-D3: If A_r is the action at the root of the context model and $Infer(\{A_r\}) \neq \emptyset$, then add $Infer(\{A_r\})$ to the context model along with a direct arc from A_r to $Infer(\{A_r\})$; otherwise, add an uninstantiated node with a direct arc from A_r to this new node, indicating that the user may be intending to execute A_r in order to perform some other action whose identify is as yet unknown.

Example-3:
Consider the situation at the end of Example-2, in which the top-level action that has been inferred as part of Al's plan is Satisfy-major(Al, CS). Rule-D3, with this conclusion as evidence, leads to the default inference that he is pursuing a Bachelor of Science degree. Since pursuing a Bachelor of Science degree only plays a role in obtaining an undergraduate degree, this higher-level action is added to the system's beliefs about his overall plan, producing the context model shown in Figure 3.

With the inclusion of default inferences into the context model, new utterances not only can cause the context model to be expanded, but may also confirm, contradict, or call into question components of the model previously added by default. The next two rules accumulate evidence confirming an action added by default to the user's plan; this evidence is being used in our current research to hypothesize the source of disparity when errors in the context model are suspected.

Rule-D4: Suppose that A_d is an action added by default to the context model and that the new utterance either explicitly confirms A_d or is equated with an action that can only be part of a plan for accomplishing A_d — ie., there are no other high-level actions that can account for the domain action motivating the user's utterance. Then mark A_d's status as confirmed and note the type of confirmation.

Rule-D5: Suppose that 1) the focusing heuristics determine that the most coherent relationship between the existing context model and the action A_{new} associated with the current utterance is that A_{new} will be executed as part of a plan to perform an action A_d added by default to the context model, and 2) A_{new} is a plausible action in a plan for A_d (ie., it is representative of what one might expect an agent to do to perform A_d). Then record the occurrence of A_{new} as confirming the presence of A_d in the user's plan.

We contend that representativeness should be used in plan recognition to confirm existing beliefs about what the user wants to do, but that it should not be used as the basis for default inferences. Rule-D5 allows the action of *going to the post office* to confirm a previous default inference that the user wants to *register for the Selective Service*, since going to the post office is representative of (ie., a typical part of a plan for) registering for the Selective Service. However, it avoids the error of using representativeness to make default inferences[11] — ie., when an agent is observed going to the post office, representativeness should not be used to sanction the default inference that he must be registering for the Selective Service.

The user's utterance can also contradict an action A_{d_3} added by default to the context model. Not only must A_{d_3}, along with all higher-level actions inferred from it, be removed, but also a decision must be made about whether to retain the components of the context model that led to inference of A_{d_3}. If A_{d_3} was inferred by default from another action A_{d_2} also inferred by default from an action A_1 and current world knowledge contradicts all plausible conclusions that might result from adopting A_{d_2}, then confidence that A_{d_2} is really part of the user's plan diminishes and it should be removed from the context model. On the other hand, if A_{d_2} is retained in the context model, then A_{d_3} may be replaced with a new action inferred by default once A_{d_3} is removed from consideration. Our method in the case where A_{d_2} has not been confirmed by other evidence is the following:

Rule-D6: Suppose that A_{d_3} was inferred by default from another default action A_{d_2}, A_{d_2} has not been confirmed by other evidence, and A_{d_3} is contradicted and must be removed from the context model.

1. If one of the alternatives to A_{d_3} has at least some minimal plausibility in the preference rule associated with A_{d_2}, then revise this preference rule by recomputing its plausibility factors from the bpa produced by combining $m(\Theta - \{A_{d_3}\}) = 1.0$ with the bpa from which the preference rule was formed. If $Infer(\{A_{d_2}\}) \neq \emptyset$ using this revised preference rule, then add $Infer(\{A_{d_2}\})$ as the new parent of A_{d_2} in the context model.
2. If none of the alternatives to A_{d_3} has at least some minimal plausibility in the preference rule associated with A_{d_2}, then retract A_{d_2} from the context model.

Example-4:

Suppose that the system believes that Al's plan contains the actions shown in Figure 3 and that the system then finds that Al is not pursuing a BS degree.[3] Rule-D6 applies. The default inference that Al is pursuing a BS degree, and therefore an undergraduate degree, is withdrawn. This default inference resulted from the fourth preference rule in Figure 2, using as evidence the belief that Al wanted to major in computer science. Since the alternative conclusion that he is pursuing a BA degree is not implausible, the belief that he wants to major in computer science is retained in the context model and the bpa from the fourth preference rule in Figure 2 is combined with $m(\Theta_2 - \{A_4\}) = 1.0$, producing a revised bpa in which $m(\{A_5\}) = .96$, $m(\{A_4\}) = 0$, and $m(\Theta_2 - \{A_4\}) = .04$. This leads to the revised preference rule

IF {Satisfy-major(USER, CS)}
P-THEN A_5 1.00
Other .04

and Infer({Satisfy-major(Al,CS)})=A_5, thus producing the default inference that Al is pursuing a BA degree instead of a BS degree. From this the system again infers that he wants to get an undergraduate degree.

Future Research

This paper has described a process model for incorporating default inferences into plan recognition and has presented rules for inferring higher-level actions that are the motivation for observed actions. We are also formulating rules that apply when the user is already believed to be pursuing a particular higher-level action. These rules take into account the relative plausibility of alternative possible subactions in the plan for that action and even default inferences about these. In addition, we are working on extending our process model to make generalized inferences[12] about higher-level goal actions that are not the immediate parent of an existing action in the context model.

We are also developing an overall strategy for revising the system's context model when the user's utterances suggest possible disparity between it and what the user is actually trying to accomplish. This strategy will use the system's relative confidence in components of the context model, along with meta-knowledge about how utterances were related to one another using focusing heuristics and how default goals were inferred, to justify and explain the system's beliefs to the user, formulate an intelligent hypothesis about the source of

[3]This might happen in several ways. The simplest case would be a direct statement to this effect by Al. A more realistic scenario would be a query from Al about satisfying a foreign language requirement, where it is mutually believed that BS degrees do not have such a requirement.

error, and guide a negotiation dialogue to remedy the error[5].

Conclusions

This paper has presented a process model of plan inference that is motivated by an analysis of naturally occurring dialogues and by psychological studies of human inference and plan recognition. It includes a strategy for incrementally updating the system's model of the user's plan that can both sanction appropriate default inferences and defer unwarranted decisions until further evidence is available. In this strategy, dynamically computed preference rules are used to rank alternative conclusions according to plausibility, and the decision to sanction a default inference is based on the conclusion's plausibility with respect to the plausibility of alternative competing conclusions. We have presented a set of rules that incorporate appropriate default inferences into the system's model of the user's plan and update and revise the model as the dialogue progresses. Our process model overcomes a limitation of previous plan recognition systems and will produce a rich model of the user's plans and goals that is rational and can be explained and justified to the user when questions about it arise.

References

[1] Sandra Carberry. Modeling the user's plans and goals. *Computational Linguistics*, 14(3):23–37, 1988.

[2] Peter Cheeseman. A method of computing generalized bayseian probability values for expert systems. *Proceedings of the Eighth International Joint Conference on Artificial Intelligence*, 1983.

[3] Philip R. Cohen, C. Raymond Perrault, and James F. Allen. Beyond question answering. In W. Lehnert and M. Ringle, editors, *Strategies for Natural Language Processing*, pages 245–274, Lawrence Erlbaum Associates, 1981.

[4] James P. Delgrande. An approach to default reasoning based on a first-order conditional logic. In *Proceedings of the Sixth National Conference on Artificial Intelligence*, pages 340–345, Seattle, Washington, 1987.

[5] Rhonda Eller and Sandra Carberry. A meta-rule approach to dynamic plan recognition. In *Proceedings of the Second International Workshop on User Modeling*, Honolulu, Hawaii, 1990.

[6] Charles F. Gettys, Clinton Kelly III, and Cameron R Peterson. The best-guess hypothesis in multistage inference. In Daniel Kahneman, Paul Slovic, and Amos Tversky, editors, *Judgment Under Undertainty: Heuristics and Biases*, pages 370–377, Cambridge University Press, 1982.

[7] Robert Goldman and Charniak. A probabilistic approach to plan recognition and text understanding. In *Proceedings of the 1989 Workshop on Plan Recognition*, Detroit, Michigan, 1989.

[8] Robert Goldman and Eugene Charniak. A probabilistic atms for plan recognition. In *Proceedings of the AAAI Workshop on Plan Recognition*, Saint Paul, Minnesota, 1988.

[9] Bradley Goodman and Diane Litman. Plan recognition for intelligent interfaces. In *Proceedings of the Sixth Conference on Artificial Intelligence Applications*, 1990.

[10] Jean Gordon and Edward H. Shortliffe. A method for managing evidential reasoning in a hierarchical hypothesis space. *Artificial Intelligence*, 26:323–357, 1985.

[11] Daniel Kahneman and Amos Tversky. On the psychology of prediction. In Daniel Kahneman, Paul Slovic, and Amos Tversky, editors, *Judgment under Uncertainty: Heuristics and Biases*, pages 48–68, Cambridge University Press, 1982.

[12] Henry Kautz and James Allen. Generalized plan recognition. In *Proceedings of the Fifth National Conference on Artificial Intelligence*, pages 32–37, Philadelphia, Pennsylvania, 1986.

[13] R. Perrault and J. Allen. A plan-based analysis of indirect speech acts. *American Journal of Computational Linguistics*, 6(3-4):167–182, 1980.

[14] Martha Pollack. A model of plan inference that distinguishes between the beliefs of actors and observers. In *Proceedings of the 24th Annual Meeting of the Association for Computational Linguistics*, pages 207–214, New York, New York, 1986.

[15] D. L. Poole. A logical framework for default reasoning. *Artificial Intelligence*, 36(1):27–47, 1988.

[16] Raymond Reiter. A logic for default reasoning. *Artificial Intelligence*, 13:81–132, 1980.

[17] Roger C. Schank and Robert P. Abelson. *Scripts, Plans, Goals and Understanding.* Lawrence Erlbaum Associates, Hinsdale, New Jersey, 1977.

[18] C. F. Schmidt, N. S. Sridharan, and J. L. Goodson. The plan recognition problem: an intersection of psychology and artificial intelligence. *Artificial Intelligence*, 11:45–82, 1978.

[19] G. Shafer. *A Mathematical Theory of Evidence.* Princeton University Press, Princeton, New Jersey, 1976.

[20] Candace L. Sidner. Plan parsing for intended response recognition in discourse. *Computational Intelligence*, 1:1–10, 1985.

[21] Robert Wilensky. *Planning and Understanding.* Addison-Wesley, 1983.

A Cooperative Problem Solving System for User Interface Design

Andreas C. Lemke and Gerhard Fischer

Department of Computer Science and Institute of Cognitive Science
Engineering Center ECOT 7-7, University of Colorado, Boulder, CO 80309-0430
{andreas, gerhard}@boulder.colorado.edu

Abstract

Designing a user interface is an ill-defined problem making cooperative problem solving systems a promising approach to support user interface designers. Cooperative problem solving systems are modular systems that support the human designer with multiple, independent system components. We present a system architecture and an implemented system, FRAMER, that demonstrate the cooperative problem solving approach. FRAMER represents design knowledge in formal, machine-interpretable knowledge sources such as critics and dynamic specification sheets, and in semi-formal knowledge sources such as a palette of user interface building blocks and a checklist. Each of these components contributes significantly to the overall usefulness of the system while requiring only limited resources to be designed and implemented.[1]

Cooperative Problem Solving

Artificial intelligence research has traditionally focused on building systems that autonomously solve complex problems (e.g., R1/XCON (McDermott, 1982) and MYCIN (Buchanan, Shortliffe, 1984)). This approach is however not easily applicable in ill-defined problem domains, such as user interface design. Consistency (Grudin, 1989), learnability, and many other concepts of user interface design cannot be adequately formalized in a precise way.

Alternatively, one can design cooperative problem solving systems (Fischer, 1988) that work in conjunction with human problem solvers rather than replacing them. Cooperative problem solving systems are located between systems that design with human guidance (e.g., UofA*, (Singh, Green, 1989)) and passive CAD tools (e.g., MENULAY, (Buxton et al., 1983)).

A desirable characteristic of practical cooperative problem solving systems is a modular, incremental architecture with simple but extensible components. In contrast, many intelligent support systems that have been proposed carry a heavy weight of complex system components. For example, a natural language based help system requires a natural language understanding component, a problem solver, and a natural language generator. Each of these components is large and complex, and all three components have to exist for the whole system to function properly. A system with an incremental architecture, however, can be gradually improved by extending its components and by adding new components. There is a low threshold for creating a low-end system and quickly introducing it into practical use.

To build effective cooperative problem solving systems, the limitations of both autonomous expert systems and human problem solvers must be understood. This knowledge will enable us to complement intelligent machines where they are limited, and to augment the human intellect where it needs support. Contributions from the machine must enable the human to proceed in ways that were not possible without them and vice versa.

Among the limitations of autonomous intelligent machines are the difficulty of capturing a sufficiently complete store of domain knowledge, the opaqueness of expert decision making process, the specification problem, and issues of conflicting and subjective practice. Of these, the specification problem is one of the hardest to overcome. It refers to the fact that, for ill-defined problems (Eastman, 1969; Simon, 1973), specification and solution are developed hand in hand and not in sequence (Rittel, 1972; Swartout, Balzer, 1982). At the start of a design process, a specification may be lacking in at least two ways. First, the specification may be incomplete, i.e., certain characteristics of the artifact have been left unspecified although they are important. For example, the behavior of computer systems in exceptional situations is often left unspecified. Second, for some characteristics, the desired values may yet be unknown, for example, because their consequences have not been evaluated. For these problems, an interactive approach is necessary because the human is unable to specify all the relevant information and preferences in advance and because specifying the problem is itself a problem solving process.

Human problem solving is limited by fundamental cognitive limitations such as short term memory capacity, forgetting, and slow long term memory access. At a higher level, it has been found that inexperienced problem solvers

[1]This research was partially supported by grants No. DCR-8420944 and No. IRI-8722792 from the National Science Foundation, grant No. MDA903-86-C0143 from the Army Research Institute, and grants from the Intelligent Interfaces Group at NYNEX and from Software Research Associates (SRA), Tokyo.

do not consider and deliberate enough alternatives but rather use the first one they find (Jeffries et al., 1981). Humans do not search for information of whose existence they are unaware (Fischer, 1989), and they are unable to keep all relevant factors in mind when making decisions.

The purpose of our systems is to reduce the knowledge needed to design and to help less experienced designers achieve better results by providing external knowledge sources. Cooperative problem solving systems must be able to communicate design knowledge to the user. Typical AI knowledge representation formalisms, such as rules or frames, are designed to be efficiently executable by inference engines but are not necessarily applicable in cooperative problem solving systems where the knowledge must be interpreted by humans as well. Our approach is based on a combination of formal, machine-interpretable and semi-formal knowledge sources that can only partially used by the system to control its actions. The kinds of semi-formal knowledge structures we are employing are easier to acquire and modify than formal knowledge structures (Peper, MacIntyre, Keenan, 1989). Semi-formal knowledge structures are also useful in ill-defined problem domains where concepts and relationships cannot always be captured in a complete, executable way. Semi-formal knowledge structures alone, however, can not give users sufficient support—they have to do "all the work." Thus, we complement them with formal knowledge structures that allow the system to solve well-defined subproblems for the user.

In the following section, we describe a system architecture for cooperative problem solving systems that addresses these questions. The architecture employs system components that serve as formal and semi-formal knowledge sources.

Framer: A Cooperative User Interface Design Environment

Our research has focussed on devising methods and tools to support the above-mentioned design activities. We describe our results using the example of the FRAMER design environment. FRAMER (Figure 1) is a knowledge-based design environment for program frameworks, which are high-level building blocks for window-based user interfaces. Program frameworks consist of a window frame of nonoverlapping panes and an event loop for processing mouse clicks, keyboard input, and other input events. Program frameworks also manage the update of information displayed on the screen. The current Framer system and its architecture is the result of an iterative development process that has gone through three major stages: tool kits, construction kits, and knowledge-based design environments. In this sequence, each later stage is an extension of its predecessor. We describe version 2 of the FRAMER system, which is based on experience with FRAMER1.

Tool Kits

The first stage, tool kits, aims at providing domain-oriented building blocks, such as windows and menus. Examples of tool kits are Xlib, NextStep, and the Macintosh toolbox. Tool kits enable designers to work in terms of concepts of their domain of expertise rather than at the level of a general-purpose programming language. FRAMER uses the Symbolics user interface toolkit, specifically program frameworks and different kinds of windows and menus. Tool kits represent a limited amount of design knowledge that was used in the design of the building blocks.

Construction Kits

Toolkits provide domain-oriented building blocks, but they do not support the processes of finding and combining the blocks—designers have to know what blocks exist and how they are used. Construction kits address this problem by providing a *palette* and a *work area* (see Figure 1). The palette displays representations of the building blocks and thus shows what they are and makes them easily accessible. The palette provides an answer to the question what the possible components of the design are. The work area is the principal medium for design and construction in the FRAMER design environment. This is where the designer builds a window layout by assembling building blocks taken from the palette. Examples of user interface construction kits are the Symbolics FrameUp system, MENULAY (Buxton et al., 1983), the NeXt user interface builder, and WIDES and TRIKIT (Fischer, Lemke, 1988).

Design Environments

Knowledge-based design environments address shortcomings that we have found in construction kits. Construction kits support design of interfaces at a syntactic level only, and our experience with this class of systems has shown that it is easy to create a functioning interface, but creating a *good* interface requires a great deal of additional knowledge that is not provided by construction kits. Design environments provide additional design knowledge through critics, checklists, and other means described below.

Critics. Critics are a formal knowledge source in FRAMER. Critics (Fischer et al., 1990) are demons that evaluate the evolving artifact. When the system detects a suboptimal aspect of the artifact, it displays a message describing the shortcoming in the critic window entitled "Things to take care of" (Figure 1) The critics trigger as soon as the designer makes an inferior design decision and they update the critic window continuously.

FRAMER2 distinguishes between *mandatory* and *optional* suggestions. Mandatory suggestions must be carried out by the designer. They represent system requirements for the construction of a functioning program framework. For example, a frame must be completely covered with panes if correct LISP code is to be generated,

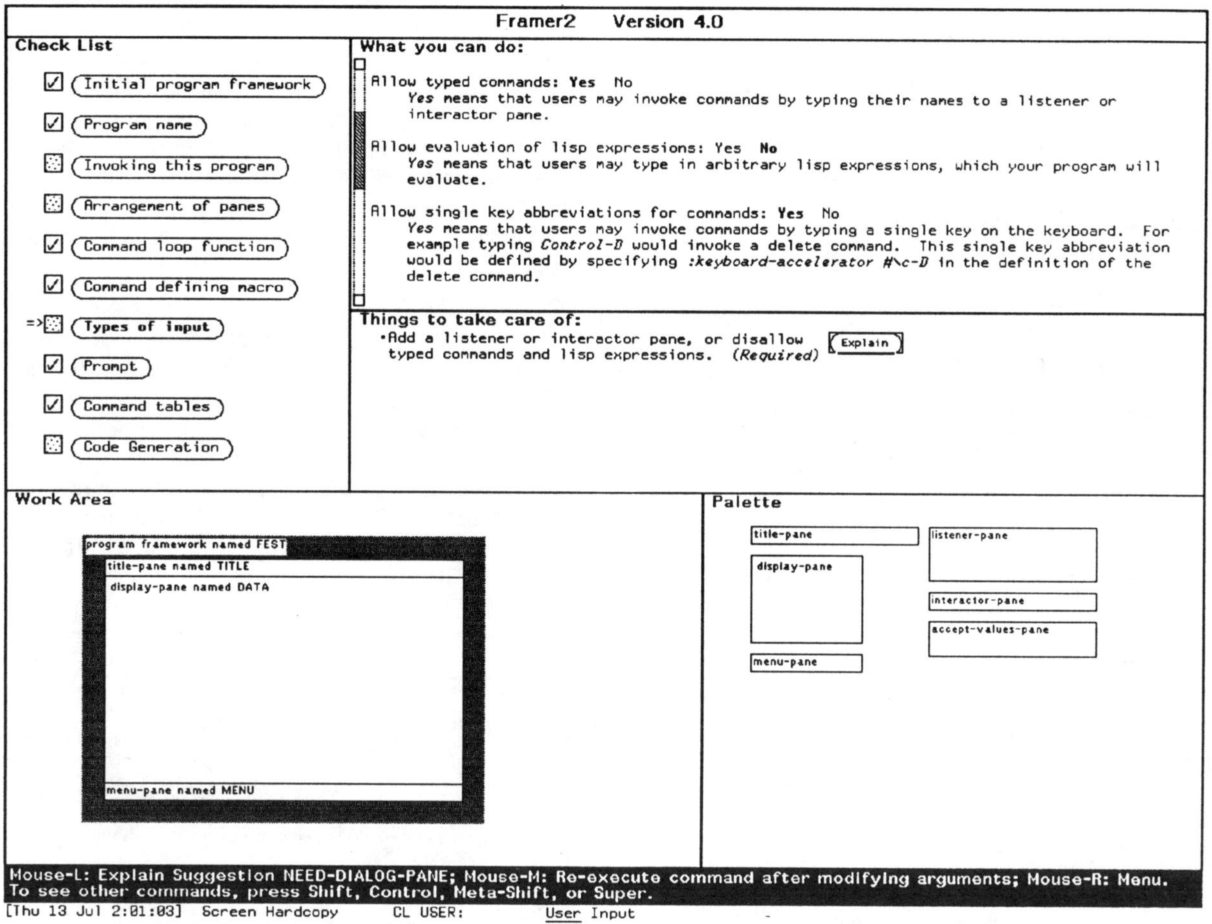

Figure 1: FRAMER

In the situation shown in the figure, the designer makes a decision about what types of user input should be supported in the interface. The system responds to this decision by displaying a critic message in the critic window entitled "Things to take care of." The critic message identifies a discrepancy between the specification sheet (entitled "What you can do") and the work area. The designer can either modify the window layout in the work area or change the specification sheet.

and the suggestion to take care of this is mandatory. Optional suggestions recommend typical design choices, but they can be ignored by the designer if desired. The *Explain* button accesses prestored explanations of why the system critiques and what the designer can do about it. Designers can indicate their intent to disregard the suggestion through the *Reject* operation. For some critic messages, a *Remedy* operation is available; that is, FRAMER can provide a default solution for a problem it has detected.

Critics provide heuristics to decide design questions and point out interactions between different subproblems. The critic knowledge base contains rules about naming the program, arranging window panes, specific knowledge about title panes, dialog panes, and menu panes, and knowledge about invoking a program and selecting interaction modes. These rules are based on a study of existing systems in our computing environment. We interviewed the system designers and elicited the rules they were using. Some of the rules represent system constraints, for example, that a window frame must be completely divided up into panes. Other rules concern the consistency among different applications and functional grouping.

Figure 2 shows a typical critic rule. This rule contains knowledge about the relationship of interaction mode and configuration of window panes in the interface. If the *mouse-and-keyboard* interaction mode is selected, then the rule suggests adding a dialog pane. A *Remedy* action is also defined. Invoking the *Remedy* operation associated with this rule causes the system to add a listener pane at the bottom of the window frame.

The critics in FRAMER1 were passive, i.e., had to be explicitly invoked by the designer. FRAMER1 was tested in a video-taped thinking-aloud study, which showed that the critics substantially improved the performance of user interface designers when compared to a construction kit. But the passive critics failed to be effective in some cases. Subjects invoked the critics only after they thought they

```
;; A critic rule named need-dialog-pane.
(define-critic-rule need-dialog-pane
  ;; Applicability condition. This rule is applicable if the
  ;; interaction mode is mouse-and-keyboard.
  :applicability (equal $interaction-mode
                        mouse-and-keyboard)

  ;; The rule is violated if there is no pane of type dialog-pane
  ;; in the set on inferiors of a program framework.
  :condition
     (not (exists x (type x dialog-pane)))

  ;; The Remedy operation adds a listener-pane.
  :remedy
   (let ((pane(make-instance 'listener-pane
               :x (+ x 20) :y (+ y 184)
               :superior self)))
          (add-inferior self pane)
          (display-icon pane))

  ;; Text of the suggestion made to the user if critic is
  ;; applicable.
  :suggestion
  "Add a listener or interactor pane, or
   set the interaction mode to mouse-only."

  ;; Text for Praise command.
  :praise
  "There is a listener or interactor pane."

  ;; Text for Explain command.
  :explanation "Since the interaction mode
   is mouse-and-keyboard, a dialog pane is
   required for typing in commands.")
```

Figure 2: An Example of a Critic Rule

This is a slightly paraphrased FRAMER critic rule that applies to program frameworks. The rule suggests adding a listener or interactor pane if the interaction mode *mouse-and-keyboard* was specified.

had completed the design. Thus, the critics were not activated early enough to prevent designers from going down garden paths. In FRAMER2, the system described here, an active critiquing strategy has been chosen and has proved to be much more effective.

Specification Sheets. The window layout of an interface has a natural graphical representation as shown in the work area. This is, however, not true of all characteristics of an interface. Behavioral characteristics, for instance, must be described in a different way. In the FRAMER system, these other characteristics are described in a symbolic way as fillers in the fields of a specification sheet (see the "What you can do" window in Figure 1). Through the sheet, the system brings design issues and their possible answers to the user's attention. Associated texts explain the significance and consequences of the different design choices.

In the example of Figure 1, the designer makes a decision about what types of user input should be supported in the interface. The system responds to this decision by displaying a critic message in the critic window entitled "Things to take care of." The system can also respond by modifying the construction situation in the work area. This is accomplished through procedural demons attached to the fields of the specification sheet. The specification sheet is dynamic in that the set of fields in the sheet is dynamically determined based on information that the designer has previously specified.

Catalog. The catalog is a collection of predesigned artifacts illustrating the space of possible designs in the domain. Rather than starting from scratch, the designer starts the design process by invoking the catalog (Figure 3) and selecting a suitable program framework in the catalog. The selected framework is inserted into the work area, and the designer modifies and adapts it to fit the requirements of the problem. Our experiments have shown that use of the catalog can substantially reduce the difficulties in using the design environment. The catalog provides design knowledge in the form of concrete examples that allow reuse and case-based design.

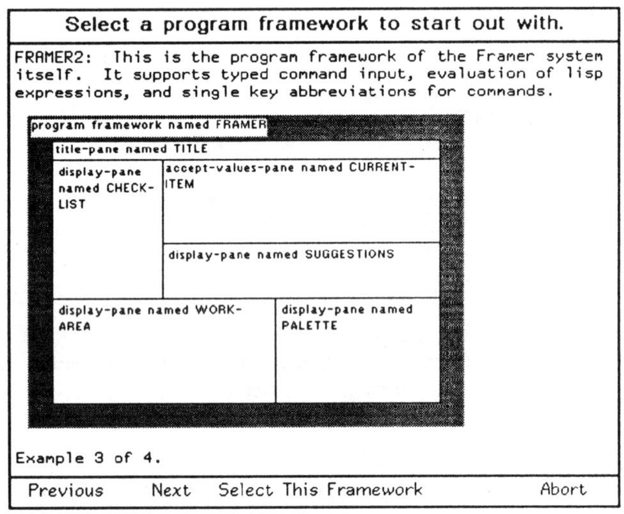

Figure 3: The FRAMER2 Catalog

Users of FRAMER1 tended to design frameworks from scratch without using the catalog. In FRAMER2, the use of the catalog has been made mandatory, which eliminated many low-level tasks. Making the use of the catalog mandatory is not really a restriction because designers can choose very generic frameworks that are almost equivalent to starting from scratch. However, subjects did use more complex examples from the catalog.

Checklist. Another problem in FRAMER1 was that designers who were not familiar with the program framework abstraction were unable to decide what steps had to be done to create a complete functional program framework. The checklist in FRAMER2 addresses this problem by providing the designers with an explicit problem decomposition that is appropriate for the design of program

System Component	User communicates to system	System communicates to user (uninterpreted knowledge)	System communicates to user (interpreted knowledge)
checklist	current focus of attention	how to decompose design problem	raise subproblems depending on information from designer
palette	What primitive components are used in the artifact?	What are the primitive components?	-
specification sheets	User symbolically specifies answers to design issues.	System brings design issues to the designer's attention. System presents potential answers. System explains significance and consequences of different design choices.	System raises design issues depending on information from the designer. System updates artifact according to specified information.
critics	User may reject the system's critique.	-	System points out suboptimal design decisions. System explains why it objects. Critics provide heuristics for making decisions.
catalog	User selects an artifact to reuse and modify.	System provides design knowledge in the form of examples, allows "case-based" design.	-
code generator	-	-	System generates an executable representation of the designated artifact.

Table 1: Components of Cooperative Problem Solving Systems

frameworks.

The checklist serves as the main organizing tool for the interaction with FRAMER. With the checklist, the system indicates to the user how to decompose the problem of designing a program framework, and it helps to ensure that designers attend to all necessary issues, even if they do not know about them in advance. Each item in the checklist is one subproblem of the total design process. By selecting a checklist item, designers tell the system their current focus of attention in the design process.

When the designer selects an subproblem in the checklist, the system responds by displaying the corresponding options in the specification sheet shown in the neighboring "What you can do" window and, thus, provides further detail about the subproblem. The critics are grouped according to the checklist items. The critic pane always displays exactly those critic messages that are related to the currently selected checklist item.

When designers believe that the topic of one checklist item has been completed, they indicate this fact to the system by checking off the associated check box. This causes the system to verify whether all constraints represented in the active critics are satisfied. Only then does the system insert a check mark into the check box. By showing check marks for completed subproblems, the checklist is also a tool for the designer to keep track of which issues have or have not been resolved.

The exact set of checklist items displayed depends on the designer's previous design decisions. The system displays only those items that are currently relevant (i.e., it is context-sensitive); for example, the prompt item is only displayed if command-based interaction is specified.

Code Generator. The ultimate goal of user interface design is the generation of an executable program code, and the design activity supported by FRAMER can be viewed as creating a specification for the code. The code generator component of FRAMER is an formal knowledge source that takes care of creating syntactically correct, executable code.

An Architecture for Cooperative Problem Solving Systems

FRAMER cooperates with the user in a structured dialog mediated through the following system components: checklist, palette, specification sheets, critics, catalog, and code generator. Table 1 shows how these different components contribute to the cooperative problem solving process.

The cooperative system architecture of FRAMER was designed to cope with the ill-structured nature of the user interface domain. Most cooperative design support systems operate in well-defined domains. For example, PRIDE (Mittal, Araya, 1986) operates in the well-defined domain of paper path design for copiers. In this domain, the design problem can be completely specified and decomposed in advance, and for each design question there is a well-known set of possible answers. These premises are not true for the user interface domain. The challenge for the FRAMER system was to define an architecture that can support designers effectively even if the system's knowledge is incomplete.

Conclusions and Ongoing Research

The goal of this work is to build a cooperative support system for user interface design. For cooperative systems, not only internal representation and reasoning mechanisms but, in particular, the external presentation and communication of that knowledge to the user is of crucial importance. The proposed architecture provides a migration path from simple tool kits to sophisticated design environments. By incrementally adding relatively simple components such as critics and checklists, the utility of a support system can be significantly improved.

Our approach was driven by the needs of designers, i.e., their needs for support in decomposing the problem, finding applicable building blocks, and understanding the effects of design decisions. Knowledge-based design environments are unique in addressing these needs with a rich set of semi-formal and formal knowledge sources.

The FRAMER system is an object of ongoing research in several directions. The existence of the knowledge sources in FRAMER does not guarantee that users find and take advantage of them, and the control of the user's attention to the great variety of available information becomes a problem. We are investigating ways to control attention using a cognitive modeling approach using the construction integration model of cognition (Kintsch, 1989).

Another active research area is the design of generalizations of the checklist and the specification sheets. These two components taken together represent a two level hierarchy of design issues. We are extending this to an unlimited number of levels by using the concept of issue-based information systems (IBIS) in the form of (McCall, 1987). Issue-based information systems represent argumentative design knowledge as hierarchies of issues, answers, and arguments for or against choosing those answers. To make an IBIS component more responsive, we are adding active mechanisms similar to the ones found in the checklist and the specification sheets.

References

B.G. Buchanan, E.H. Shortliffe (1984). *Rule-Based Expert Systems: The MYCIN Experiments of the Stanford Heuristic Programming Project.* Reading, MA: Addison-Wesley Publishing Company.

W.A.S. Buxton, M.R. Lamb, D. Sherman, K.C. Smith (1983). Towards a comprehensive user interface management system. *Computer Graphics, 17*(3), 35-42.

C.M. Eastman (1969). Cognitive Processes and Ill-Defined Problems: A Case Study from Design. *Proceedings of the International Joint Conference on Artificial Intelligence,* 669-675. Los Altos, CA: Morgan Kaufmann Publishers.

G. Fischer (1988). Cooperative Problem Solving Systems. *Proceedings of the 1st Simposium Internacional de Inteligencia Artificial (Monterrey, Mexico),* 127-132.

G. Fischer (1989). Human-Computer Interaction Software: Lessons Learned, Challenges Ahead. *IEEE Software, 6*(1), 44-52.

G. Fischer, A.C. Lemke, T. Mastaglio, A. Morch (1990). Using Critics to Empower Users. *Human Factors in Computing Systems, CHI'90 Conference Proceedings (Seattle, WA),* 337-347. New York: ACM.

G. Fischer, A.C. Lemke (1988). Construction Kits and Design Environments: Steps Toward Human Problem-Domain Communication. *Human-Computer Interaction, 3*(3), 179-222.

J. Grudin (1989). The Case Against User Interface Consistency. *Communications of the ACM, 32*(10), 1164-1173.

R. Jeffries, A.A. Turner, P.G. Polson, M. Atwood (1981). The Processes Involved in Designing Software: In J.R. Anderson (Ed.), *Cognitive Skills and their Acquisition* (pp. 255-283). Hillsdale, NJ: Lawrence Erlbaum Associates.

W. Kintsch (1989). The Representation of Knowledge and the Use of Knowledge in Discourse Comprehension: In R. Dietrich, C.F. Graumann (Eds.), *Language Processing in Social Context* (pp. 185-209). Amsterdam: North Holland.also published as Technical Report No. 152, Institute of Cognitive Science, University of Colorado, Boulder, CO.

R. McCall (1987). PHIBIS: Procedurally Hierarchical Issue-Based Information Systems. *Proceedings of the Conference on Architecture at the International Congress on Planning and Design Theory.* New York: American Society of Mechanical Engineers.

J. McDermott (1982). R1: A Rule-Based Configurer of Computer Systems. *Artificial Intelligence.*

S. Mittal, A. Araya (1986). A knowledge-based framework for design. *Proceedings of AAAI-86,* 856-865. Los Altos, CA: Morgan Kaufmann.

G. Peper, C. MacIntyre, J. Keenan (1989). Hypertext: A New Approach for Implementing an Expert System. *Proceedings of Expert Systems ITL Conference.*

H.W.J. Rittel (1972). On the Planning Crisis: Systems Analysis of the First and Second Generations. *Bedriftsokonomen*(8), 390-396.

H.A. Simon (1973). The Structure of Ill-Structured Problems. *Artificial Intelligence*(4).

G. Singh, M. Green (1989). A high-level user interface management system. *Human Factors in Computing Systems, CHI'89 Conference Proceedings (Austin, TX),* 133-138. New York: ACM.

W.R. Swartout, R. Balzer (1982). On the Inevitable Intertwining of Specification and Implementation. *Communications of the ACM, 25*(7), 438-439.

Models of Plans to Support Communication: An Initial Report*

Karen E. Lochbaum
Barbara J. Grosz
Harvard University
Cambridge, MA 02138
kel@pandora.harvard.edu

Candace L. Sidner
DEC Cambridge Research Lab
Cambridge, MA 02139
sidner@crl.dec.com

Abstract

Agents collaborating to achieve a goal bring to their joint activity different beliefs about ways in which to achieve the goal and the actions necessary for doing so. Thus, a model of collaboration must provide a way of representing and distinguishing among agents' beliefs and of stating the ways in which the intentions of different agents contribute to achieving their goal. Furthermore, in collaborative activity, collaboration occurs in the planning process itself. Thus, rather than modelling plan recognition, per se, what must be modelled is the *augmentation* of beliefs about the actions of multiple agents and their intentions. In this paper, we modify and expand the SharedPlan model of collaborative behavior (Grosz & Sidner 1990). We present an algorithm for updating an agent's beliefs about a partial SharedPlan and describe an initial implementation of this algorithm in the domain of network management.

Introduction

Agents collaborating to achieve a goal bring to their joint activity different beliefs about ways in which to achieve the goal and the actions necessary for doing so. Each agent may have incomplete or incorrect beliefs. In addition, their beliefs about each other's beliefs and capabilities to act may be incorrect. As a result, collaborative activity cannot be modelled by simply combining the "plans"[1] of individual agents. Even when the agents' beliefs are the same, a simple combination is not possible (Grosz & Sidner 1990). An adequate model of collaboration must provide a way of representing and distinguishing among agents' beliefs and of stating the ways in which the intentions of different agents contribute to achieving their goal.

In this paper, we modify and expand the SharedPlan model of collaborative behavior originally proposed by two of the authors (Grosz & Sidner 1990), present an algorithm for updating an agent's beliefs about a partial SharedPlan, and describe an initial implementation of this algorithm in the domain of network management. This work is being done in the context of a project to investigate the development of systems that support coordination of graphical and linguistic means of communication between agents involved in collaborative activities [see also (Reiter 1990; Marks 1990; Marks & Reiter 1990; Balkanski *et al.* 1990)]. This paper sets forth an initial framework for modelling particular aspects of collaborative activity and identifies several key problems.

The sample dialogue in Figure 1 illustrates collaboration in the network management domain. In this discourse, the network manager (NM) and the network presenter (NP) are working together to determine what type of maintenance to perform on a particular switching node that can no longer handle the amount of traffic flowing through it. NM begins by stating the problem and then proceeds to ask for information that would be useful in solving it. NP supplies that information, both verbally and graphically, while also making further suggestions. A goal of our work is to provide the basis for a computer system to assume the role of NP.

(1) NM: It looks like we need to do some maintenance on node39.
(2) What kind of switch is it?
(3) NP: It's an XYZ, but it's at full capacity.
(4) NM: OK, then let's replace it with an XYZ+.
(5) First, we'll have to divert the traffic to another node.
(6) Which nodes could be used?
(7) NP: *[puts up diagram]*
(8) Node41 looks like it could temporarily handle the extra load.
(9) NM: I agree.
(10) Let's go ahead and divert the traffic to node41 and do the replacement.

Figure 1: Sample discourse

Most previous models of plan recognition (Allen & Perrault 1980; Kautz 1990; Sidner 1985) are inadequate for modelling collaboration because they make assumptions appropriate for single agent plans, or the

*This research has been supported by a contract from U S WEST Advanced Technologies and by a Bellcore Graduate Fellowship for Karen Lochbaum.

[1] We have scare quotes around "plan" because it has been given a variety of meanings in the AI literature.

plans of multiple independent agents, but not for the plans of collaborating agents. These assumptions include a data-structure model of plans as well as a master/slave relationship between all-knowing agents. In particular, these models treat plans as sequences of steps to be performed; as each step occurs, it is filled into a particular plan schema. These models also assume that one agent, the speaker, is a controlling agent, while the other agent, the hearer, is simply a reactive agent, inferring and cooperating with the plan of the speaker. Because the hearer and speaker are assumed to have the same complete and correct knowledge of the domain, the systems do not distinguish between the speaker's and hearer's beliefs about actions.

Pollack, in modelling how an inferring agent reasons about another agent's invalid plans, differentiates each agent's individual beliefs and intentions regarding actions and the relations among them from other agents' (Pollack 1986; Pollack 1990). Her model thus provides a useful base on which to define a model of collaborative activity. However, she also makes the assumptions that the inferring agent has complete and accurate knowledge of domain actions and that that agent is recognizing the plans of another. In collaborative activity, collaboration occurs in the planning process itself. Thus, rather than modelling plan recognition, per se, what must be modelled is the *augmentation* of beliefs about the actions of multiple agents and their intentions.

In the next section, we present the modified definition of SharedPlan and describe two new constructs: recipes and the Contributes relation. We then present an augmentation algorithm and give examples of its use. Finally, we describe future directions of this work.

Definition of SharedPlan

The definition of SharedPlan follows Pollack's work on single agent plans (Pollack 1986; Pollack 1990) in taking the notion of "having a plan" to be central and to consist of being in a certain mental state, namely, holding certain beliefs and intentions regarding acts and their executability. This stance differs from other work in planning which takes a plan to be a data structure encoding a sequence of actions. The mental state view is crucial to the ability to model plans constructed and carried out collaboratively.

SharedPlans are defined in terms of *act-types* and relations among them. We distinguish types of actions, act-types (or *acts*), from individual tokens of the type (for which we will use the term *action*). An act-type is a triple, $\langle\gamma(P_1 \ldots P_n),G,T\rangle$, where the P_i are parameters of the activity $\gamma(P_1 \ldots P_n)$[2], G is the agent who performs the activity, and T the time interval over which the activity occurs (Balkanski *et al.* 1990)[3]. Act-type relations include generation [CGEN (Pollack 1986; Pollack 1990)] and enablement. In addition, complex act-types, for example, ones involving sequences of acts or simultaneous acts, may be built from simpler ones using act-type constructor functions (Balkanski *et al.* 1990).

Two agents, G_1 and G_2, are said to have a SharedPlan during time T1 to accomplish an action of type **A** during time T2 if and only if they hold the beliefs and intentions listed below:

SharedPlan(G_1,G_2,A,T1,T2) $\Longleftrightarrow$

1. $MB(G_1,G_2,EXEC(\langle\alpha_j,G_{\alpha_j},T_{\alpha_j}\rangle),T1)$
2. $MB(G_1,G_2,$R:recipe-for-**A**$,T1)$
3. $MB(G_1,G_2,INT(G_{\alpha_j},\langle\alpha_j,G_{\alpha_j},T_{\alpha_j}\rangle,T1),T1)$
4. $MB(G_1,G_2,INT(G_{\alpha_j},\langle\alpha_j,G_{\alpha_j},T_{\alpha_j}\rangle \wedge$ $\text{Contributes}(\langle\alpha_j, G_{\alpha_j}, T_{\alpha_j}\rangle, \mathbf{A}), T1), T1)$
5. $INT(G_{\alpha_j},\langle\alpha_j,G_{\alpha_j},T_{\alpha_j}\rangle,T1)$
6. $INT(G_{\alpha_j}, \langle\alpha_j,G_{\alpha_j},T_{\alpha_j}\rangle \wedge$ $\text{Contributes}(\langle\alpha_j, G_{\alpha_j}, T_{\alpha_j}\rangle, \mathbf{A}), T1)$

In this definition, the index j ranges over the act-types in the recipe R for doing **A**. For each α_j, G_{α_j} denotes the agent who performs the activity, and T_{α_j} denotes the time interval over which the activity is performed. Each T_{α_j} is a subinterval of T2 which is the interval over which **A** is performed. The predicate MB holds of two agents, a proposition, and a time just in case the two agents mutually believe the proposition over the time interval. The predicate INT holds of an agent, an act-type, and a time if the agent intends to perform an action of that type during the time interval. EXEC holds if the agent is able to perform an action of the appropriate type (Pollack 1990).

This definition provides a framework in which to further evaluate and explore the roles that particular beliefs and intentions play in collaborative activity. Currently, the definition only provides for recipes in which each constituent act is performed by one of two agents. However, we are currently investigating act-types performed by multiple agents (i.e. G_{α_j} is a set of agents) and extensions of the definitions of INT and EXEC to multiple agents.

The two most complex portions of the definition of SharedPlans are the recipe-for-**A** in Clause (2) and the Contributes relation in Clauses (4) and (6). Recipes were not part of the original SharedPlan definition (Grosz & Sidner 1990) and Contributes was only informally defined; both of these are discussed in more detail below.

SharedPlans are constructed incrementally. When agents G_1 and G_2 have some partial set of beliefs and intentions from the SharedPlan definition (or even simply have a mutual desire to achieve a SharedPlan), but have not yet completed the building of such a

[2]When the parameters of an activity are not at issue, we will simply use the activity name, γ, as an abbreviation for $\gamma(P_1 \ldots P_n)$.

[3]We follow the Prolog convention of specifying variables using initial uppercase letters and constants using initial lowercase letters.

plan, they are considered to have a partial SharedPlan, which we will denote by *SharedPlan**. Each utterance of a discourse contributes some information about beliefs and intentions to this evolving jointly-held plan. As opposed to a SharedPlan*, a SharedPlan for a particular **A** specifies all of the beliefs and intentions necessary for performing **A**. It is not necessary, however, for the SharedPlan to be fully specified before any actions may take place. On the contrary, performance of actions may be interleaved with discussion of those and other actions.

Recipes

Following Pollack (Pollack 1990), we use the term *recipe* to refer to what agents know when they know a way of doing something. Clause (2) of the SharedPlan definition thus states that when agents have a SharedPlan for doing some act, they must hold mutual beliefs about the way in which to perform that act. Recipes are specified at a particular level of detail. Hence, Clause (2) only requires the agents to have mutual beliefs about acts specified at the particular level of detail of the recipe and does not require them to have mutual beliefs about all levels of acts that each agent will perform. In our earlier work (Grosz & Sidner 1990), we considered only simple recipes; each recipe consisted of only a single act-type relation. However, for any interesting activity, recipes include many different types of relations.

Recipes, more formally stated, are aggregations of act-types and relations among them. Act-types, rather than actions, are the main elements in recipes because the regularities about which agents can have beliefs must necessarily be stated in terms of types and not tokens. A recipe for performing a particular act, Γ[4], encodes constraints on constituent acts and their interrelationships. Performing all of the constituent acts in the recipe, following any ordering stipulated by the act-type relations, will result in the performance of Γ.

Figure 2 contains two sample recipes from the network management domain. Recipe1 indicates that one way to upgrade a particular switching node, subject to conditions, C_{rs}, is to replace the node by a new node of a different type; i.e. *CGEN(⟨replace_switch(N:node, S:switch_type), G1, T1⟩, ⟨upgrade(N:node), G1, T1⟩, C_{rs})*[5]. However, before that can be done, the switch traffic must be diverted to another node. According to Recipe2, a node may be upgraded by adding more capacity to it; however, there is a generation-enabling condition on this relation which requires that the node still have room for more capacity.

[4] When the specific components of an act-type are not at issue, we will abbreviate the triple by using capital Greek letters.

[5] We assume a typed logic in which *X:type* is used to indicate the *type* of object that may replace the variable *X*. For presentation purposes, the types have been omitted from Figure 2.

Recipe1	*Recipe2*
⟨upgrade(N),G1,T1⟩	⟨upgrade(N),G,T⟩
$\uparrow C_{rs}$	$\uparrow \neg(full(N))$
⟨replace_switch(N,S),G1,T1⟩	⟨add_capacity(N),G,T⟩
$\Uparrow$	
⟨move_traffic(N,D),G2,T2⟩	

$\uparrow c$ indicates generation subject to the condition c
$\Uparrow$ indicates enablement

Figure 2: Two network management recipes

Note that the act-types in these recipes are specified at a fairly high level of detail. For example, although the activity *move_traffic* is further decomposable into activities involving flipping specific switches, such low-level details are not part of this recipe. They may, of course, be part of a recipe for *move_traffic* itself. For example, this more detailed level is necessary for a situation in which a new operator is being taught exactly how to move traffic around a network.

Recipe1 may be used to upgrade any node, but Recipe2 may only be used for types of switches that allow some additional capacity to be added. This condition on applicability of recipes may be modelled by associating recipes with elements of an act-type lattice (Balkanski *et al.* 1990). In such a lattice, act-types are partially ordered according to specialization — more specialized act-types lie below their abstractions. For example, such a lattice might contain the act-types *⟨upgrade(N:node), G, T⟩*, *⟨upgrade(N:node_type1), G, T⟩*, and *⟨upgrade(N:node_type2), G, T⟩*, where the second and third act-types are specializations of the first. The parameter type specialization of *node* to *node_type1* or *node_type2* corresponds to the distinction made by the recipes in Figure 2; switches of *node_type2* allow the addition of extra capacity while switches of *node_type1* do not. Thus, Recipe1 is associated with the lattice element *⟨upgrade(N:node_type1), G, T⟩*, while both Recipe1 and Recipe2 are associated with *⟨upgrade(N:node_type2), G, T⟩*. The distinction made in the use of these two recipes is not modeled in the recipes themselves, but is a consequence of the association of recipes with lattice elements.

Upon completion of a SharedPlan, the recipe-for-**A** in Clause (2) of the definition will be of the same form as the recipes in Figure 2. During the construction of a SharedPlan, however, the agents are establishing mutual beliefs about act-types relevant to performing **A**. Thus, at any time during this construction, the recipe-for-**A** of Clause (2) is only partially specified.

Contributes

Agents' beliefs about recipes may be partial in a number of different ways. Not only might an agent not know all of the act-types involved in performing **A**, but he might not know the exact relations that hold between the act-types. For example, Jack may believe that to replace his oil filter, he has to find the drain plug on his oil pan (perhaps because his friend Carol, who believes that it's good practice to always change your oil and filter together, told him so), but he may not know the specific act-type relations that hold between finding the plug and replacing the filter (e.g. *enable(⟨find(P:drain_plug), G, T1⟩, ⟨remove(P:drain_plug), G, T2⟩),...)*. The Contributes relation used in Clauses (4) and (6) of the SharedPlan definition is a general act-type relation intended to capture this level of knowledge. Thus, Jack's beliefs about replacing his filter, would include an act-type relation of the form, *Contributes(⟨find(P:drain_plug), G, T1⟩, ⟨replace(F:oil_filter), G, T3⟩)*.

Contributes is defined as the transitive closure of the D-Contributes relation where D-Contributes depends upon the act-type relations and constructors defined in (Balkanski *et al.* 1990) and is defined as follows:[6]

D-Contributes (Γ, Δ) $\equiv$

1. $\rho(\Gamma, \Delta)$
   where ρ is one of the primitive act-type relations: generate,enable, facilitate, ...

OR

2. $\Delta = \kappa(\Gamma_1, \Gamma_2, \ldots, \Gamma_n)$, such that $\Gamma = \Gamma_j$ for some j, $1 \leq j \leq n$, and
   κ is one of the act-type constructor functions: sequence, simult, conjoined, or iteration.

That is, D-Contributes holds between act-types Γ and Δ, when Γ stands directly in an act-type relation ρ to Δ or when Γ is a direct component of Δ.

The Contributes relation is used in Clauses (4) and (6) of the SharedPlan definition as a modifier indicating the way in which an act-type is performed. That is, $INT(G_{\alpha_j}, \langle \alpha_j, G_{\alpha_j}, T_{\alpha_j} \rangle \wedge Contributes(\langle \alpha_j, G_{\alpha_j}, T_{\alpha_j} \rangle, \mathbf{A}), T1)$ means that G_{α_j} intends to do the activity α_j *as a way of* contributing to **A** (cf. Pollack's act-type constructor *by* (Pollack 1986; Pollack 1990)). Such a construction is meant to capture the notion that α_j is only being done as a way to achieve A, and hence failures related to it constrain replanning (Bratman 1990).

SharedPlan Augmentation

The process of augmenting a SharedPlan* comprises the adoption of mutual beliefs and intentions related to the clauses of the SharedPlan definition. Such beliefs include those about acts in the recipe of the plan, properties of those acts, and intentions to perform them. A SharedPlan* may thus be affected by utterances containing a variety of information. An individual utterance, however, can only convey information about the beliefs or intentions of the speaker of that utterance. Thus, the algorithm for updating a SharedPlan* includes mechanisms for attributing individual beliefs and intentions and subsequently establishing mutual beliefs based on those individual attitudes and on the discourse and SharedPlan contexts in which the utterance occurs.

The basic algorithm for updating a partial SharedPlan on the basis of information contained in an utterance of a dialogue carried out in support of collaborative activity is given below. G_i and G_j denote the two agents, G_1 and G_2. G_i denotes the speaker of the utterance and G_j the other participant. The algorithm given is for G_j; G_i's differs in some details, e.g. G_i already knows his beliefs about recipes whereas G_j must infer new ones to attribute to G_i. λ*ActProp* is used to denote the proposition (*Prop*) expressed in the current utterance, where *Act* indicates the particular act to which it refers. To simplify the discussion, we will ignore the details of the information about *Act* that *Prop* represents. Utterances (4) through (6) of the dialogue in Figure 1 illustrate the variety of such propositions that utterances may contain.

SharedPlan Augmentation Algorithm:

Assume:
Act is an action of type Γ,
G_i designates the agent who communicates λ*ActProp*,
G_j designates the other agent,
SharedPlan*(G_1, G_2, **A**, T1, T2).

1. As a result of the communication, assert MB(G_1,G_2,BEL(G_i,λ*ActProp*)).
2. Search own beliefs for BEL(G_j,λ*ActProp*).
3. Ascribe BEL(G_i,Contributes(Γ,**A**)).
4. Search own beliefs for Contributes(Γ,**A**) and where possible, more specific information as to how Γ contributes to **A**.
5. If Steps (2) and (4) are successful, signal assent and MB(G_1,G_2,Contributes(Γ,**A**))[7].
6. If Step(2) or Step (4) is unsuccessful then query G_i or communicate dissent.

Each agent brings to the joint activity private beliefs and intentions. As these private attitudes are communicated, they participate in the agents' having a SharedPlan. Steps (3) and (4) reflect this behavior. Namely, G_j, based upon G_i's utterance, *ascribes* beliefs to G_i and then searches his own beliefs with respect to G_i's. Taking "having a plan" to mean having a set of beliefs and intentions about an act is crucial to these steps. The interleaving of the ascription of private plans and of SharedPlans would be much more difficult if plans were taken to be data structures.

The Contributes relation also plays an important role in the ascription process in that it supports partiality during the construction of plans. Without this general relation, plan ascription would have to assert that some much stronger relationship held, one which would not necessarily be supportable (e.g. if information relevant to establishing it were unavailable). Furthermore, when two agents have different recipes for

[6] We assume a theory of mutual belief that allows for belief of a Contributes relationship without necessitating explicit beliefs about all of the supporting D-Contributes relationships.

[7] G_j may, of course, suggest alternatives.

achieving a goal, and are not initially aware of these differences, use of the Contributes relation is critical (see the second example below). If the inferring agent has no beliefs about how an act-type contributes to the goal, he can choose to accept the belief of a Contributes relation on good faith or after checking with the other agent. In the case that the inferring agent has beliefs that suggest that there is no relation between the act-type and the goal, he can dissent to the other agent's beliefs about that act-type.

Typically, only partial information is available to G_j when he is reasoning about G_i's utterances. Thus, an agent can only tentatively ascribe beliefs to other agents and not logically deduce their being held. Upon subsequent information, the agent must be able to retract his beliefs. We are currently investigating the use of defeasible reasoning and direct argumentation for the ascription of belief (Konolige 1988; Konolige & Pollack 1989).

An Example

To illustrate the algorithm, consider its use with respect to the dialogue of Figure 1 with NP as the reasoner in the augmentation algorithm. Using conversational default rules (Grosz & Sidner 1990), from utterance (1) and NP's lack of dissent, the agents may infer *SharedPlan*(nm,np,upgrade(node39))*[8].

Given the context of the SharedPlan, NP must decide how utterance (2), which he could interpret as *Desire(nm,find_out(switch_type(node39)))*, relates to the goal of the SharedPlan, performing the act *upgrade(node39)*. Based on NP's knowledge of act-type specializations, particularly those described above (his utterances indicate that he does indeed have such knowledge), NP recognizes that NM may be asking this question to ascertain which recipes for upgrading a node are applicable. Thus, in his response in utterance (3), NP reports the type of the node. In addition, however, because he believes that NM will recognize that nodes of that type do allow the addition of extra capacity, he adds the caveat that the node is already at full capacity (Reiter 1990). That is, although this type of node usually allows the addition of capacity, the condition that there be available capacity left cannot be met.

Assuming that NM also has similar knowledge about act-type specializations and recipes, one could interpret her "OK" as indicating recognition of the caveat and hence that Recipe2 is not applicable. Because the act-type, $\langle$*upgrade(N:node_type2), G, T*$\rangle$ in the lattice has both Recipe1 and Recipe2 associated with it, however, NM may now proceed using her beliefs about the act-types and their interrelations given in Recipe1[9].

NP could interpret the remainder of utterance (4) as *Desire(nm,replace_switch(node39,xyz+))*. According to the SharedPlan augmentation algorithm, as a result of this communication, NP ascribes *BEL(nm,Contributes(replace_switch(node39, xyz+),upgrade(node39)))*. At this point, NP must search his own beliefs to determine if he also believes such a contributing relation. That is, NP considers the recipes he knows for *upgrade(node39)* (given the previous discourse, only Recipe1 is relevant at this point) and finds specifically that indeed he believes *CGEN(replace_switch(node39,xyz+), upgrade(node39),* C_{rs}*)*. NP can then indicate his belief of this contributing relation by either signaling assent or simply not signaling dissent. Given his lack of dissent, NM can assume that NP believes the action to contribute to the upgrade and thus *MB(nm,np,Contributes(replace_switch(node39, xyz+), upgrade(node39)))* is established.

From NM's next utterance, (5), NP could infer *Desire(nm,move_traffic(node39,D:node))*. To summarize the algorithm's performance, NP will search his own beliefs (i.e. Recipe1) and find that he believes *Contributes(move_traffic(node39, D:node), upgrade(node39))*. This Contributes relation is based upon the enabling relation between *move_traffic(node39,D:node)* and *replace_switch(node39,xyz+)*, which, in turn, was previously found to contribute to *upgrade(node39)*.

Utterances (6) through (9) comprise a sub-dialogue to find an appropriate node to which the traffic may be diverted (Litman & Allen 1990; Sidner 1985; Grosz & Sidner 1986). Finally, with utterance (10) the complete recipe-for-**A** is spelled out.

A More Complicated Example

Unlike the previous example, we now assume that the two agents have different know-how. NM knows Recipe1, but NP knows only Recipe3, which is similar to Recipe1, but does not contain an act for replacing the switch. That is, according to Recipe3, a node may be upgraded by simply moving traffic off of it. We will use the modified dialogue in Figure 3 to illustrate the algorithm's performance in such cases.

From utterance (2), NP infers *Desire(nm,move_traffic(node39,D:node))*. Upon searching Recipe3, NP finds that he believes *CGEN(move_traffic(node39, D:node), upgrade(node39),* C_{mt}*)* and hence *Contributes(move_traffic(node39, D:node), upgrade(node39))*. The specific relationship he believes to hold between these two acts is different from what NM believes; however, this difference has not yet surfaced. After identifying node41 as a possible *D*, NM continues, in utterance (6), with her recipe and indicates a desire to

[8]Throughout this discussion, we will use an abbreviated notation in which only the activity of the act-type is specified; i.e., *SharedPlan*(nm,np,upgrade(node39))* is a shorthand for *SharedPlan*(nm,np,*$\langle$*upgrade(node39),*$\{$*nm,np*$\}$*, T2*$\rangle$*,T1,T2)*.

[9]The current augmentation algorithm only models that portion of the example which follows this point; however, we are investigating extensions which will model the preceding discussion as well.

replace node39. Upon searching his beliefs, NP cannot determine how *replace_switch(node39,xyz+)* contributes to *upgrade(node39)*. He signals his confusion and asks NM to clarify why such an action is necessary.

(1) NM: It looks like we need to do some maintenance on node39.
(2) What node could we divert its traffic to?
(3) NP: *[puts up diagram]*
(4) Node41 looks like it could temporarily handle the extra load.
(5) NM: I agree.
(6) Let's divert the traffic to node41 and replace node39 with an XYZ+ switch.
(7) NP: Huh? Why do you want to replace node39?

Figure 3: Sample discourse

Implementation

An initial version of the augmentation algorithm has been implemented in Prolog in which the system is one of the agents working on a SharedPlan. In the context of a SharedPlan for some act **A**, when presented with a specification of the other agent's (i.e. the user's) desire of some act, Γ, the system searches its recipes for **A** to determine if a Contributes relationship holds between Γ and **A**. In this initial implementation, we have concentrated on the process of searching through recipes to determine whether or not an act-type is a constituent part of a recipe. Unlike previous work (Kautz 1990; Pollack 1990), however, the recipes through which the system searches involve more complex relations than simple step decomposition or generation. In addition, because the system may have multiple recipes for **A**, if no contributing relation can be found between Γ and **A** in a particular recipe, then that recipe is removed from consideration. If the user's recipes differ from the system's, then Γ may not be a constituent part of any of the system's recipes, in which case, the system will respond with "Huh?". The current system is able to model those portions of the above network management examples in which NP ascribes beliefs (both individual and mutual) based on NM's desire for a particular act-type.

Conclusion and Future Directions

In this paper, we have presented a model of collaboration and discussed an algorithm for augmenting an evolving jointly-held plan. We are currently investigating the following extensions: (1) The use of defeasible reasoning and direct argumentation for the ascription of belief (Konolige 1988; Konolige & Pollack 1989); (2) Modelling the agents' abilities to negotiate to an agreed upon act rather than simply assenting or dissenting to each other's suggestions; (3) Extending the formalism to include acts performed by more than one agent.

Acknowledgments

We would like to thank Cecile Balkanski, Joyce Friedman, Martha Pollack, and Stuart Shieber for many helpful discussions and comments on this paper.

References

Allen, J. and Perrault, C. 1980. Analyzing intention in utterances. *Artificial Intelligence*, 15(3):143–178.

Balkanski, C. T., Grosz, B., and Sidner, C. L. February 1990. Act-type relations in collaborative activity. Technical report, Harvard University.

Bratman, M. E. 1990. What is intention. In P. Cohen, J. Morgan, and M. Pollack, eds., *Intentions in Communication*. MIT Press. Forthcoming.

Grosz, B. and Sidner, C. 1986. Attention, intentions, and the structure of discourse. *Computational Linguistics*, 12(3).

Grosz, B. and Sidner, C. 1990. Plans for discourse. In P. Cohen *et al.*, eds., *Intentions in Communication*. MIT Press. Forthcoming.

Kautz, H. 1990. A circumscriptive theory of plan recognition. In P. Cohen *et al.*, eds., *Intentions in Communication*. MIT Press. Forthcoming.

Konolige, K. and Pollack, M. 1989. Ascribing plans to agents: Preliminary report. In *Proceedings of IJCAI-11*, Detroit, Michigan.

Konolige, K. 1988. A direct argumentation system. In *Proceedings of the International Symposium on Machine Intelligence and Systems*, Torino, Italy.

Litman, D. and Allen, J. 1990. Discourse processing and commonsense plans. In P. Cohen *et al.*, eds., *Intentions in Communication*. MIT Press. Forthcoming.

Marks, J. and Reiter, E. 1990. Avoiding unwanted conversational implicatures in text and graphics. In *Proceedings of AAAI-90*, Boston, MA.

Marks, J. January 1990. Automating the design of network diagrams. Technical report, Harvard University.

Pollack, M. E. June 1986. A model of plan inference that distinguishes between the beliefs of actors and observers. In *Proceedings of the 24th Annual Meeting of the ACL*.

Pollack, M. E. 1990. Plans as complex mental attitudes. In P. Cohen *et al.*, eds., *Intentions in Communication*. MIT Press. Forthcoming.

Reiter, E. 1990. Generating action descriptions that exploit a user's domain knowledge. In Dale, R., Mellish, C., and Zock, M., editors, *Natural-language Generation (working title)*. Forthcoming.

Sidner, C. February 1985. Plan parsing for intended response recognition in discourse. *Computational Intelligence*, 1(1):1–10.

A Collaborative Interface for Editing Large Knowledge Bases

Loren G. Terveen and David A. Wroblewski

MCC Human Interface Laboratory
3500 West Balcones Center Drive
Austin, TX 78759
terveen@mcc.com and wroblewski@mcc.com

Abstract

A new generation of knowledge/databases is emerging. These systems contain thousands of objects, densely interconnected and heterogeneously organized, entered from many sources, both human and automated. Such systems present tremendous challenges to their users, who must locate relevant information quickly and add new information effectively. Our research aims to understand and support the knowledge editing task. The HITS Knowledge Editor (HKE) is an interface that supports browsing and modifying the CYC knowledge base (Guha & Lenat 1990). HKE has been designed to be a *collaborative* interface, following a set of principles for sharing tasks between system and user. We describe these principles and illustrate how HKE provides resources built according to those principles that collaborate with its users on a variety of knowledge editing tasks.

Introduction: problems with large knowledge bases

A new generation of knowledge/databases is emerging. These systems contain thousands or tens of thousands of classes and instances, densely interconnected and heterogeneously organized, entered from many sources, both human and automated. Such systems present tremendous challenges to their users, who must locate relevant information quickly and add new information effectively. Left to one's own resources, it is easy to get lost in data space (Carroll et al. 1990 and O'Shea et al. 1986) or make inappropriate or ineffective changes.

CYC (Guha & Lenat 1990) is an example of such systems. CYC consists of a representation language (CYCL) and a knowledge base expressed in that language. The knowledge base currently consists of approximately 35000 units (known in other systems as "frames" "schemata", etc.). Each unit consists of a set of slots containing a set of values. CYC units average 13 slots filled with 2 or 3 values, meaning that each unit bundles around 35 assertions.

Our research aims to understand and support the knowledge editing task. We consider knowledge editing to be a family of related tasks, rather than a single homogeneous task. Knowledge editing is different from ordinary data entry because the user must understand the structure and content of the knowledge base well enough to be able to locate information in a timely manner and add or modify information in harmony with the existing representation conventions; in this way it is much like programming. In this paper we consider two knowledge editing tasks, *browsing* and *entry*. Browsing, at its simplest, consists of determining the truth status of some assertion P; in reality, it involves acquiring a model of the relational structure of the knowledge base and landmarks from which important data elements can be found quickly. Entry, at its simplest, consists of setting the truth status of some assertion P; in reality, it consists of managing a coordinated series of changes to the knowledge base or the creation of a cluster of interrelated units each consisting of many slots and values. Browsing and entry are interleaved throughout a typical knowledge editing session.

Principles of collaboration

The HITS Knowledge Editor (HKE) is an interface that supports browsing and modifying the CYC knowledge base. This paper focuses on several of HKE's capabilities that illustrate our attempts to make it a *collaborative* system. This section defines collaborative systems and puts forth several design principles to which HKE conforms.

In collaborative systems tasks must be shared between systems and users based on their respective capabilities. In some sense, all interfaces at least attempt to be collaborative. What is needed is a set of principles that guide us in deciding *how* to divide tasks between system and user. These principles should emerge from general principles of communication and must acknowledge the highly asymmetrical abilities of people and computers. For this paper, the key principles are:

- do not force users to make decisions in a rigid order,
- provide resources that help users in making decisions,
- let users build their solutions to problems as modifications of prior solutions to similar problems,
- make *relevant* action possibilities apparent when the set of *possible* actions becomes large.

Collaboration on browsing tasks

Users can be overwhelmed with information when browsing complex data spaces. One of the motivating assumptions of our work has been that in such complex data spaces there is no one right way to view all the data, nor even a fixed set of ways. The best browsing display is highly dependent on the topic of the information being displayed, the task being performed with the data, and the experience of the user. We support this approach in HKE by allowing users to create, reuse, and share methods of viewing data.

There are several mechanisms that allow this in HKE; this paper discusses only one – *perspectives* on units. Perspectives are objects that dictate several parameters of tabular slot/value displays, such as attributes to display or suppress and the order in which to display them. Perspectives are constructed collaboratively by the system and the user.

Motivation for customizable perspectives

Several features of large-scale object systems affect browsing. First, each object may have many attributes. In CYC there are over 4000 defined slots, and, on average, 295 of them are relevant to a given unit. This means that users must manage a very large vocabulary for object features. Second, the vocabulary is complicated by the fact that slots often do not represent a simple set of unrelated attributes. Instead, relationships between the slots significantly constrain their semantics. For instance, the slot `parts` is known to be a generalization of the slot `subOrganizations`: any value filling `subOrganizations` automatically fills `parts`. Third, effective browsing hinges on seeing the appropriate subset of slots for the task at hand. Fortunately, entire groups of slots are devoted to specialized tasks such as consistency checking or bookkeeping; thus one may roughly partition the total set of applicable slots for a given unit into more manageable subsets for specialized tasks. This is what perspectives do.

This is clearly non-trivial work. A collaborative system can help by suggesting a reasonable initial perspective and allowing the user to improve it. The initial perspective might be generated from a variety of sources, such as a standard template, the user's past perspective on the same data, another user's perspective, or a model of the task the user is performing. This approach segments the work of browsing into three parts: specifying the format of the initial display, modifying the format of an existing display, and retrieving the format of past displays of the same object. HKE takes on the tasks of generating an initial display, storing modified displays, and retrieving those displays for reuse, while the user modifies the suggested perspective when it is ineffective.

Perspectives follow the principles of collaborative systems. First, HKE doesn't force the specification of perspectives before the act of browsing itself, but rather provides tools to evolve the perspective as the browsing proceeds. Second, HKE lets users build new solutions from previously generated solutions by always putting the user in the position of repairing rather than synthesizing perspectives.

Example: perspectives on Organizations

One section of the CYC knowledge base is devoted to representing organizations. The relevant class hierarchy is displayed in Figure 1.

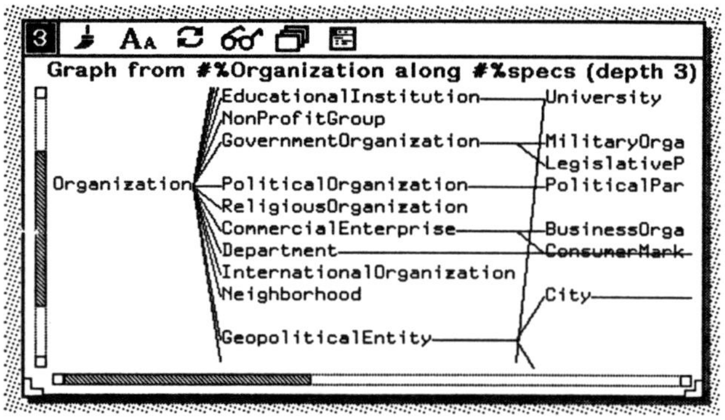

Figure 1: The `Organization` Class Hierarchy

The default perspective of any unit is created by composing the individual perspectives of all the classes of which the object is a member, in order of increasing generality. Thus, the default display of an instance of `CityOfAustinTX` would display the attributes given it because it was an instance of `City`, then those from `GeoPoliticalEntity`, then from `Organization`, and so on. To save space, empty slots are not displayed.

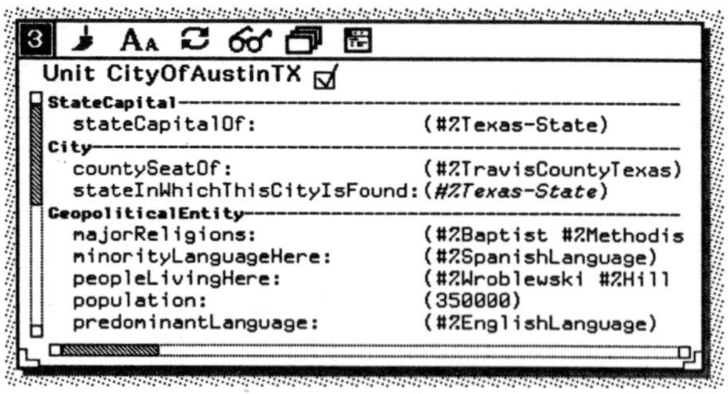

Figure 2: The unit `CityOfAustinTX`

This display may be unsatisfactory either because it is still too complex, eliminates important attributes that don't happen to be filled in the unit, or includes the right attributes in an unintuitive order. Each component of the composite perspective can be edited to change these features of the display.

Suppose after looking at `CityOfAustinTX`, the user decides that a number of slots always should be displayed, including `predominantLanguage`, `majorReligions` and `population`. This is accomplished by clicking on the perspective labelled "GeoPoliticalEntity". Since the user has no custom perspective for GeoPoliticalEntity yet, one is created and initialized with the slots shown in the current display. A special perspective editor pops up to rearrange the new perspective. When the user is done, the new perspective is indexed against the user and the class GeoPoliticalEntity and then the unit CityOfAustinTX is redisplayed. Figure 3 shows the perspective editor and the resulting display of the CityOfAustinTX. All subsequent displays of instances of GeoPoliticalEntity will use this custom perspective.

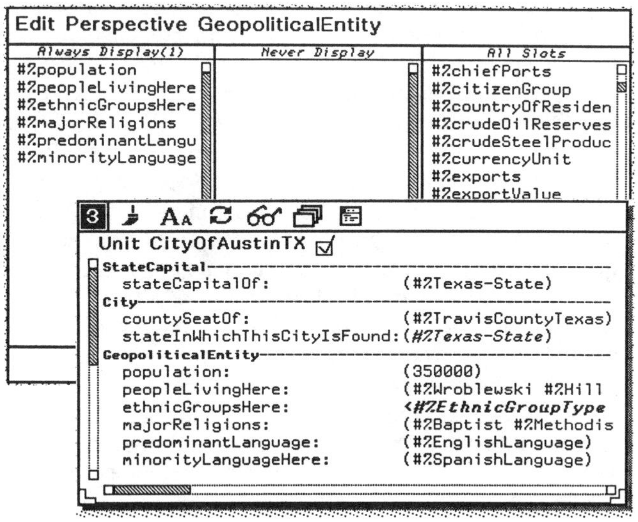

Figure 3: The perspective editor

Collaboration on entry tasks

Motivation

Basic knowledge entry tasks include (1) choosing which slots should appear on a unit, (2) specifying fillers for these slots, and (3) managing the creation of groups of interrelated units. Tasks (1) and (2) are made especially difficult by the sheer size of CYC: it is a formidable task to select 10 or 15 out of the nearly 300 slots that could appear on a unit, then choose several fillers from the hundreds or even thousands of legal values. Task (3) arises from the recursive nature of knowledge entry: when representing the organization MCC, for example, one may well want to create units that represent people employed there, their areas of expertise, etc. Keeping track of related representational tasks is a significant part of the overall entry task. The resources that HKE provides to collaborate on these tasks were designed in accordance with our principles of collaboration:

- *flexible decision making* – checklists package decisions that are relevant when creating a particular type of unit, agendas allow users to do unit creation tasks in whatever order they wish, and several repair facilities bring out information relevant to making a decision,
- *relevant action advertisement* – a display of the slots that a unit could have supports the user in choosing slots that should appear, and
- *build on previous solutions* – a unit is created by copying and editing an existing unit, and other similar units are presented as models from which the user can extract pieces to add to the new unit.

Example

We suppose that the user's task is to represent knowledge about the organization MCC. He has browsed through the section of the knowledge base representing organizations, identified ResearchOrganization as the right class for MCC, and has decided to copy-and-edit the unit UniversityOfTexasAtAustin to create MCC. Editing is initiated by clicking on the check mark displayed in the label line of the unit display (see figure 2). This causes HKE to construct and display a checklist for editing the unit.

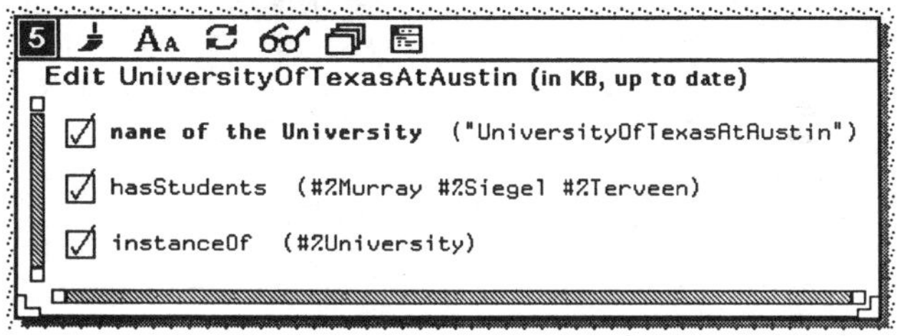

Figure 4: The task of editing UniversityOfTexasAtAustin

The initial resource

A checklist is a computerized version of the everyday to-do list. A checklist helps to organize an activity by reminding one what needs to be done and helping keep track of what already has been done. The checklist for editing a unit contains an *issue* (item) for each slot to appear on the unit. The initial set of issues is derived from the slots of the copied unit, here UniversityOfTexasAtAustin, using perspectives to filter and order the slots.

Checklists support flexible decision-making: the issues can be done in any order and can be revisited and modified any number of times.

Customizing the resource

The system-constructed checklist is a reasonable resource for editing a unit. It contains issues for specifying the value of a fairly small number of slots, filtered and ordered by the perspectives that apply to the unit. The user can access a menu that provides resources for customizing the checklist. These include: (1) **additional slots** – a display of slots the unit could have (in order from most to least specific and with uninteresting slots filtered out). The user can add an issue to the checklist for specifying the value of any of these slots by mousing it. (2) **model units** – a display of units that share characteristics of the unit being edited. The user can browse these units for slots and fillers that should appear on the unit being edited and can add a slot-value pair to the checklist with a mouse gesture, thus customizing the checklist and answering the newly added issue at once.

In our example, the user will want to customize the checklist in several ways.

- Change the type of unit being created from University to ResearchOrganization. He does so by editing the answer to the "instanceOf" issue, replacing University by ResearchOrganization. This causes the "hasStudents" issue to be removed from the checklist, since a ResearchOrganization may not have the slot hasStudents. It also causes the set of **additional slots** to be recomputed.
- Add issues for specifying the subOrganizations and organizationHasActivities slots to the checklist. This has two effects. First, it signals that the user wants to take care of these two items as part of the task of representing MCC. Second, the user can state that he wants these changes to be recorded on the perspective used to construct the checklist, i.e., to add these slots to the Organization perspective. In this way, changes to a particular task resource will affect future browsing and entry of any instance of Organization.
- Customize the issues of the checklist. The text of the question may be changed, whether the issue is necessary or optional in completing the task can be indicated, and a textual explanation of the question can be entered.

After making these changes, the checklist looks like:

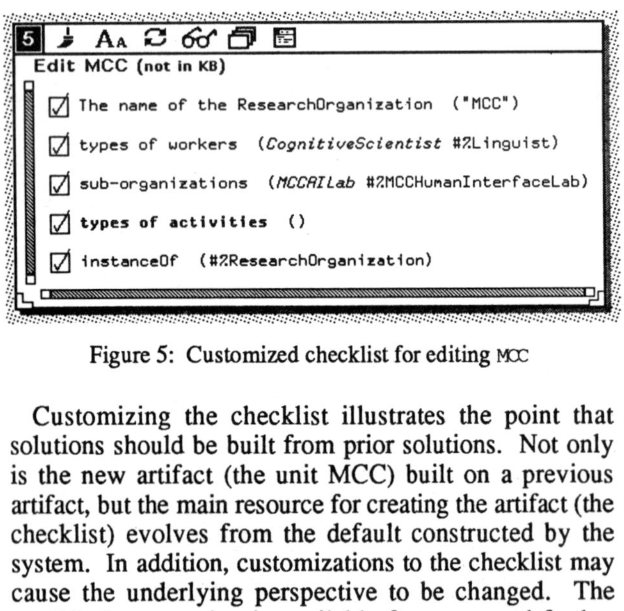

Figure 5: Customized checklist for editing MCC

Customizing the checklist illustrates the point that solutions should be built from prior solutions. Not only is the new artifact (the unit MCC) built on a previous artifact, but the main resource for creating the artifact (the checklist) evolves from the default constructed by the system. In addition, customizations to the checklist may cause the underlying perspective to be changed. The modified perspective is available for reuse and further evolution. This evolution results in knowledge entry resources that are abstractions of the pure example-based method. For example, if the perspective for Organization contains an issue for setting the value of the subOrganizations slot, then, even if the user selects an instance of Organization to copy-and-edit that does not specify a value for this slot, the checklist will contain an issue for it.

Managing the task context

As the user continues to enter knowledge about MCC, he will need to create additional units. For example, none of the sub-organizations of MCC or people who work at MCC are represented yet. When answering an issue, the user can press the HELP key to get a menu of all the units that could answer the issue. If the object the user is seeking does not yet exist, he simply can type in a new name for the unit he wants to create. This causes the system to (1) construct a checklist for creating an instance of the appropriate class, and (2) record this checklist on the task agenda.

The visible representation of a checklist serves as an **implicit agenda** of tasks associated with a checklist. For example, the "types of workers" issue of the "Edit MCC" task might refer to a unit that does not exist yet, CognitiveScientist. Such unmade units are displayed in *italics*, letting the user "read off" related tasks with a glance. These tasks can be worked on in any order and can be interleaved, illustrating the principle of allowing users to make decisions in whatever order they wish. The system manages certain types of dependencies between tasks. If the user performs the "Update" action on the "Edit MCC" task, the unit MCC is created, but the user is notified that since CognitiveScientist does not exist yet, the fact that it is one of the worker types of MCC cannot be asserted. When CognitiveScientist has been created, the system makes this assertion, and notifies the user that it has done so.

Repair

When a person cannot understand a communicative act well enough to respond as expected, he must engage in repair. For example, a user of HKE can have a problem in responding to an issue of a checklist when he does not know what object to supply. A menu of repairs is available for each issue. The repairs index the user into relevant sections of the knowledge base, direct the user to related tasks, or provide remedies for problems the system has detected with the user's answer. For example, if the user begins to represent the people who work at MCC (recorded on the hasWorkers slot), one repair would be to display the class Person, since fillers of hasWorkers must be instances of Person.

If the user chooses to display the collection Person, he can explore related knowledge using all the normal browsing facilities of HKE. One useful action is to find out the specializations of the concept Person using the Inspect Lattice command. This will trace out any relationship from a specified unit to a specified depth. In this case, the user wants to see the lattice constructed by traversing the specs relationship from Person.

However, when a user issues this or any other command, more goes on than meets the eye. First, command interpretation is done using a blackboard architecture (Cohen, McCandless & Rich, 1989). Second, after the command has been fully interpreted but before the application program gets to execute the command, *angels* get a chance to inspect and possibly modify the command. An angel's knowledge consists of *anomalies*, problems that can occur in doing a particular task, and *strategies*, methods for repairing these problems. Thus, the system can repair the user's command specifications.

The angel competent about knowledge editing is named Hank. One of Hank's anomalies is HighBranchingFactor, which detects the condition that some units appearing in a lattice display have too many children. This is problematic because displaying a lattice with many highly branching nodes (1) can take a long time, and (2) can overwhelm the user with too much information. The anomaly is detected by doing a partial traversal of the lattice, locating all the units whose children exceeded the maximum branching factor. (The traversal can be done quite cheaply, so detecting the anomaly does not cause significant overhead.)

Thus, when the user issues the command to inspect the specializations of Person, Hank detects the HighBranchingFactor anomaly before the command is executed, modifies it to mark certain units not-to-be-expanded, and notifies the user what has been done.

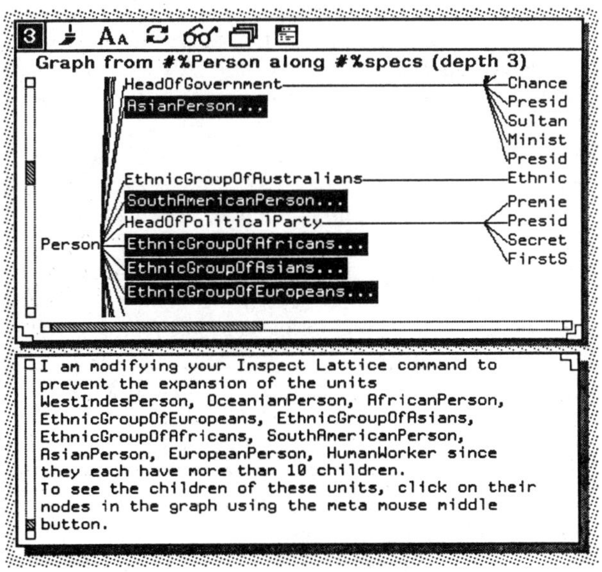

Figure 6: Angel intervening to modify a problematic action

Several comments are in order. First, the resulting lattice took seconds instead of minutes to produce and displays a manageable amount of information. Second, no options are taken away from the user. He still can expand any of the unexpanded units, but now will be aware of the cost of doing so. Third, we once again advertise potential actions, using reverse video to indicate units the user might wish to expand. Finally, we should emphasize that this anomaly could not be avoided by modifying the Inspect Lattice command to take an additional argument specifying units not to expand. Knowing which units not to expand requires knowing the structure of a particular section of the knowledge base, and since the user issued the command to find out about that structure, we cannot expect him to know it already.

Strengths and weaknesses

HKE's strengths are the set of collaborative resources it offers. Perspectives afford selective, task-sensitive, customizable views on complex objects. Checklists provide a flexible knowledge entry scheme and constitute implicit agendas of relevant tasks. Repair facilities help users overcome problems arising in their tasks.

A number of limitations of HKE's current collaborative facilities are not in-principle shortcomings: we "just haven't done them yet." However, there are several in-principle limitations as well.

Perspectives almost always are used to reduce the total information displayed. One possible disadvantage is that this could hide essential but infrequently used slots. In addition, we do not yet have any good schemes for managing large sets of perspectives. Extended use of HKE means generating many perspectives and evolving old perspectives in response to changing task demands.

Checklists are less useful in informal activities. The system can provide assistance in responding to individual issues of the checklist – as HKE does by indexing the user into relevant sections of the knowledge base – only if the issues themselves are relatively formal. Even in less formal activities, however, checklists perform valuable organizational and reminding functions.

Checklists are textual resources; however, many knowledge editing tasks are best expressed in a non-textual fashion. For example, laying out the ontology of a new domain usually consists of graphing out collections, relationships between the collections, and attributes they can have.

Finally, one might consider our reliance on users to customize resources a limitation – aren't we just adding to their burden? We advance four reasons why we expect users to do the customization we have described here.

First and most important, the work is done jointly with the system, in service of and in the context of the user's tasks. Changing the display of an object or adding a new issue to a checklist is done to help the user achieve his comprehension or editing goals and builds from a set of resources supplied by the system. Second, since a user may view or edit particular types of knowledge at infrequent intervals, the work invested in creating customized perspectives is paid off when he once again returns to a section of the knowledge base. Third, since perspectives are distributed along the generalization hierarchy, customizations made for one unit apply to whole classes of related units. Finally, since perspectives are stored in a shared knowledge base, views built up by one user are available to other users, too.

Related work

HKE is not a knowledge acquisition tool. Such systems address issues like techniques for eliciting knowledge from an expert and acquisition of domain or problem-solving method specific knowledge. For example, Protos (Bareiss, Porter, & Murray 1989) acquires knowledge used to do heuristic classification, TDE (Kahn et al. 1987) acquires troubleshooting hierarchies, and Luke (Wroblewski & Rich 1988) acquires linguistic knowledge. HKE provides functionality for browsing, entry, and task management that could be utilized by any of these tools.

RABBIT (Tou et al. 1982) introduced the use of perspectives for browsing; however, our implementation affords more extensive control of the display of information (but makes perspective management a task for the user) and applies perspectives to entry tasks, too. Object Lens (Lai, Malone, & Yu 1988) used checklist-like objects ("templates") for data entry; however, we use perspectives to filter the slots that appear in a checklist and provide repair facilities to help users fill out checklists. KREME (Abrett & Burstein 1987) provides browsing and entry facilities similar to HKE. It uses agenda-like structures to keep track of editing tasks. BACKBORD (Yen, Neches, & DeBellis 1988) focuses on retrieval of objects from knowledge bases and browsing of class hierarchies. It uses checklists to support several simple browsing and entry tasks. The distinguishing mark of our work is to make the system a more active collaborative partner.

Finally, the Framer system (Lemke 1989) is a good example of a collaborative interface. Our implementation of checklists is an adaptation of his.

Future work

Further development will come along three fronts. First, existing resources will be extended and several new types will be added. For example, we will use checklists to support several types of tasks more complicated than editing a single unit. Second, we will refine the principles of collaboration offered here. Finally, we will do empirical studies of users editing knowledge in HKE in order to test these principles. We already have anecdotal evidence that HKE succeeds in its aims, through our own use and through its use by a small community of users within MCC and its shareholder companies. Our work to date has given us a qualitative understanding of the nature of knowledge editing. We now are in a position to carry out empirical studies to test our hypotheses about collaboration for the knowledge editing task.

Acknowledgements

We thank Will Hill, Tim McCandless, Elaine Rich, and Steven Tighe of MCC and Robert Simmons and Bruce Porter of UT-Austin for their thoughtful review and discussion of this paper and the ideas presented in it.

References

Abrett, G., & Burstein, M.H. 1987. The KREME Knowledge Editing Environment. *International Journal of Man-Machine Studies* 27:103-126.

Bareiss, R., Porter, B.W., & Murray, K.S. 1989. Supporting Start-to-Finish Development of Knowledge Bases. *Machine Learning* 4:pp. 259-283.

Carroll, J.M., Singer, J.A., Bellamy, R.K.E., & Alpert, S.R. 1990. A View Matcher for Learning Smalltalk. In Proceedings of the 1990 ACM Conference on Human Factors in Computing Systems, 431-437. Seattle, WA: ACM Press.

Cohen, R.M., McCandless, T.P., and Rich, E.A. 1989. A Problem Solving Approach to Human-Computer Interface Management, MCC Technical Report Number ACT-HI-306-89, Microelectronics and Computer Technology Corporation. Austin, TX.

Guha, R.V. & Lenat, D.B. 1990. *Building Large Knowledge Based Systems.* Reading, MA: Addison-Wesley.

Kahn, G.S., Breaux, E.H., DeKlerk, P., & Joseph, R.L. 1987. A Mixed-Initiative Workbench for Knowledge Acquisition. *International Journal of Man-Machine Studies* 27:167-179.

Lai K.Y., Malone, T.W., & Yu, K.C. 1988. Object Lens: A "Spreadsheet" for Cooperative Work. *ACM Transactions on Office Information Systems.* 6:332-353.

Lemke, A. 1989. Design Environments for High-Functionality Computer Systems. Ph.D. diss., Department of Computer Science, The University of Colorado at Boulder.

O'Shea, T., Beck, K. Halbert, D., & Schmucker, K. 1986. Panel: The Learnability of Object-Oriented Programming Systems. Object-Oriented Programming Systems, Languages, and Applications: OOPSLA 86 Conference Proceedings, 502-503. New York, NY: ACM Press.

Tou, F.N., Williams, M.D., Fikes, R.E., Henderson, D.A., & Malone, T.W. 1982. RABBIT: An Intelligent Database Assistant. In Proceedings of the National Conference of the American Association for Artificial Intelligence, 314-318. Philadelphia, PA: American Association for Artificial Intelligence.

Wroblewski, D.A., & Rich, E.A. 1988. Luke: An Experiment in the Early Integration of Natural Language Processing. In Proceedings of the Second Conference on Applied Natural Language Processing, 186-194. Austin, TX: ACL Press.

Yen, J., Neches, R., & DeBellis, M. 1988. BACKBORD: Beyond Retrieval by Reformulation. In Architectures for Intelligent Interfaces: Elements and Prototypes, 219-235. Monterey, CA.

Knowledge Acquisition

An Experiment in Direct Knowledge Acquisition

Peter W. Mullarkey
Schlumberger Laboratory for Computer Science
P.O. Box 200015, Austin, TX 78720-0015, U.S.A.
mullarkey@slcs.slb.com

Abstract

LQMS is a knowledge-based system that identifies and explains anomalies in data acquired from multiple sensors. The knowledge base was built by a sequence of domain experts. Its prototype performed with a high level of accuracy and that performance has been incrementally and significantly improved during development and field testing. Several points are developed in this paper. (1) The combination of an intuitive model (sufficient for the task) and powerful, graphical development tools allowed the domain experts to build a large, high performance system. (2) The Observation-Situation-Relation representation illustrates an intermediate point on the simplicity-expressiveness spectrum, which is understandable to the domain experts, while being expressive enough for the diagnostic task. (3) The system was designed as a workbench for the domain experts. This enticed them to become more directly involved, and, resulted in a better system. (4) The use of an integrated knowledge base edit-tracking system was important to the project in several ways: it reassured computer-naive experts that they could not damage the overall system, which increased their productivity; and, it also allowed experts located in various places around the world to compare, contrast, and integrate changes in a structured way.

Introduction

LQMS is a knowledge-based system that identifies and explains anomalies in data acquired from multiple sensors [O'Neill and Mullarkey, 1989]. This paper describes its knowledge representation and graphical development tools, which allowed direct involvement of several domain experts in the construction of its knowledge base.

Task Description

The task is to enhance the performance of well-trained field engineers in a demanding environment (oil field exploration). Oil-well logs are made by lowering tools into the borehole and recording measurements made by sensors in the tools as they are raised to the surface. The resulting logs are sequences of values indexed by depth. Logging tools measure a variety of petrophysical properties. The field engineer's task involves data acquisition and interpretation, and is characterized by high data rates, with noisy and uncertain data. Earlier work on some aspects of the interpretation problem is discussed in [Smith, 1984]. In this paper, we concentrate on data acquisition. The quality of the data may be affected by many sources: problems with the tools, problems with the downhole environment (*e.g.*, unusual borehole geometry and fluids, extreme formation conditions), and untoward interactions between the tools and the downhole environment. In normal circumstances, it takes three to five years for a field engineer (with an engineering degree) to become truly competent in this task.

The goal of LQMS is to assure that the field engineers leave the field location with full knowledge of the quality of the data collected. Given the task complexity and the level of training required, it was clear from the outset that the knowledge-based system would need to encompass a large amount of knowledge in order to achieve high performance. This makes the acquisition of domain knowledge critical.

Overview of LQMS

LQMS has two main components: a signal-to-symbol module that identifies anomalous behavior in the signal data and an analysis module that applies explicit domain models to arrive at causal explanations for the anomalies. These two modules are implemented in an object-oriented paradigm, and communicate via asynchronous message-passing. The system was implemented in the HyperClass environment [Smith *et al.*, 1987, Schoen *et al.*, 1988] and Common Lisp and runs on both Sun and VAX workstations.

The overall process can be envisioned as a progression of transformations from the raw data, through a signal-to-symbol module, to the analysis module (which can direct the signal-to-symbol module to search for further evidence about features of interest). Our basic design philosophy is to have small, efficient computational agents (the signal-to-symbol module) whose responsibility is only to find anomalous segments of data, and then use more extensive domain knowledge in the analysis module to discern which anomalies are problems requiring action, and which are explainable in other ways. This decomposition allows the signal-to-symbol module to run real-time, while the analysis module works in background.

A research prototype was deployed over a two-year field test program in several locations (Houston, TX; New Orleans, LA; Cairo, Egypt; Midland, TX; and, Paris, France). It has done an effective job of dealing with the task and providing a model that the users feel is intuitive.

Knowledge Representation Model

The analysis module consists of an inference engine that operates on domain knowledge represented as networks. These networks are composed of Situations that can be used to explain groups of Observations connected by Relations; they are referred to as OSR networks. We will explain via the example shown in Figure 1.

In the example network, Situations are boxed nodes (*e.g.,* LDT-PROBLEM), Observations are unboxed leaf nodes (*e.g.,* RHOB-UNUSUALLY-LOW). Relations are unboxed interior nodes, drawn from the set AND, OR, COMB (a weighted average), NOT, and ANY (essentially an OR that uses breadth-first search).

The example network can be understood (and constructed) from either of two viewpoints.

1. From a symptomatic view, the network has possible explanations for the anomaly RHOB-UNUSUALLY-LOW (highlighted in the middle right section of the network). This observation means that the sensor is measuring a bulk density of the surrounding material that is lower than normally expected, but not so low as to be out of the physical measurement range of the sensor. This anomaly can be explained by a misapplication of the sensor pad to the surrounding rock (LDT-PAD-STANDOFF), allowing lower-density material (*e.g.,* drilling fluid) to exist between the sensor and the material of interest, and/or a problem with the tool that houses the sensor (LDT-PROBLEM).
2. From a "failure model" point of view, there are two subnetworks shown in Figure 1. One describes the observations that would be associated with an LDT sensor pad being out of contact with the borehole wall. The other describes the observations that would be associated with an LDT tool problem.

The various domain experts have found that a choice of different ways of visualizing (and building) the networks allows them to think about their knowledge in the way that is most natural for them. One domain expert prefers the symptomatic perspective, while another prefers the failure model view, and a third seems to be comfortable switching between these views.

The basic components of the knowledge representation scheme were derived by direct observation of the domain experts at work. This recognition that the behavior of the experts is a real expression of the knowledge is discussed in [Musen, 1989] in regard to separating the *knowledge level* from the *symbol level.* The domain experts visually recognize an anomalous data pattern, and attempt to construct a set of conditions that could explain that anomaly. Their "heuristic associations" between anomalies and multiple possible explanations are not through explicit relations, but such relations are implicit in the context. For example, to support an LDT-PAD-STANDOFF there needs to be evidence of both borehole wall roughness (described by the upper subnetwork to the right of the AND in Figure 1) AND an indication of abnormal density borehole fluid (described by the lower subnetwork to the right of the AND in Figure 1). In describing this situation, the AND relation would be obvious to a domain expert from the context. The OSR environment encourages the domain expert to make these implicit relations explicit, both for obvious computability and to make the networks less ambiguous for the next domain expert.

The OSR framework was developed to organize and unify the various concepts that seemed intuitive to the domain experts. These experts clearly had more than a jumble of loosely-connected heuristics, but did not use a complete structural and behavioral model. Our early experience with a rule-based prototype demonstrated that the domain experts had difficulty encoding their knowledge as rules. Furthermore, the prototype did not clearly support the domain experts' model. This was also noted in [Davis and Hamscher, 1988].

We were also led to believe that a "deep model" approach was also not appropriate because:

- No complete model exists for the domain. The lack of a strong domain model is a good reason for using a different approach [Hamscher, 1988, page 19].
- The problem solving must be done in a real-time environment and "deep models" are typically computationally intensive.
- The users do not reason with a deep model; hence, a system using such a model would be less understandable to them.

The inherent simplicity of the OSR framework is a strong asset, since (after three years of successful use) it appears to be expressive enough to cover the domain of interest, while being intuitively comfortable to a set of five geographically distributed domain experts with different backgrounds. Thus, it illustrates an intermediate point on the simplicity-expressiveness spectrum.

Inference

LQMS uses its knowledge base of OSR networks in a way similar to the "cover and differentiate" problem-solving method used in MOLE [Eshelman, 1988]. The signal-to-symbol module notices an anomaly. The

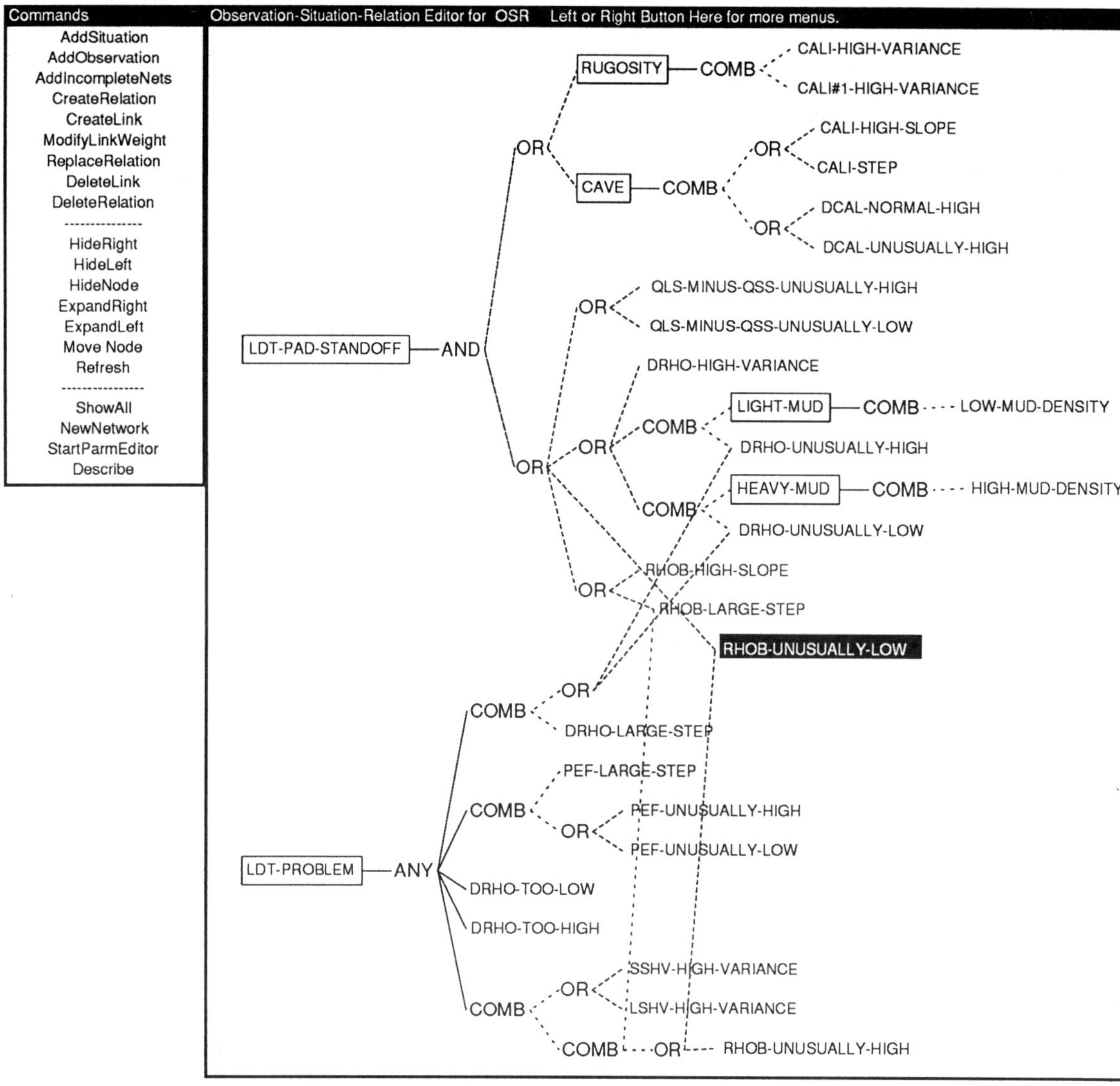

Figure 1: The OSR Network Editor (see text for legend)

analysis module retrieves all situations that can explain the anomaly. It gathers appropriate evidence for discrimination between the possible explanations by traversing the networks. It develops the best explanation(s) for the anomaly from the situations that have the highest belief, based on available evidence. LQMS combines evidence in the OSR networks using an algebra that combines beliefs for the relation types in a conventional manner [Reboh, 1981, Buchanan and Shortliffe, 1984]. Beliefs are represented as a five-valued range with an explicit representation for unknown values. The particular combination rule used is determined by the Relation type. A small set of relations has been found to work well in the LQMS domain.

LQMS can show its reasoning with an animated display of the OSR networks it is processing (highlighting nodes currently being processed, and changing fonts to indicate current belief). The user can also direct the system to explain its conclusions after a session using a mouse-sensitive debriefing report to access the appropriate OSR networks and signal-to-symbol agents. The system's explanation of its results is clear and meaningful to our domain experts. Over the three years of construction, refinement and use, the main debugging tool used has been animated OSR networks.

In addition to the basic framework, the OSR environment offers the domain expert several ways of augmenting the networks with further experiential knowledge.

- `search first` — The domain expert can specify a partial order of situations that are most likely to explain a particular anomaly.

- `relative link weights` — The links between a relation and its operands can be assigned different weights, thus their evidence will be combined based on the specified relative importance.
- `tie breaking` — The domain expert can designate that some situations be preferred. Then if a "preferred" situation is among the equally believed explanations for an anomaly, it is selected as the best explanation.

Knowledge-Acquisition Tools

LQMS has a rich knowledge engineering environment (based on the HyperClass system). These tools have made it possible for domain experts to enter, test, and refine the OSR network knowledge base (which contains 1880 classes) with minimal assistance from the system developers. Like the knowledge editors in ROGET [Bennett, 1985] and MOLE [Eshelman, 1988], the OSR Network Editor takes advantage of knowledge of the problem-solving method used in LQMS to assist the user in entering knowledge. This approach has been referred to as using a *method-oriented conceptual model* to support knowledge acquisition [Musen, 1989].

The "boxes and links" OSR Network Editor (Figure 1) is the main tool for constructing, maintaining, and refining OSR networks. It has an integrated, object-oriented, edit-tracking system to notice, save (and restore) incremental changes to the knowledge base. This allows multiple domain experts to work independently on the knowledge base, making incremental changes. It supports review, comparison, and conflict detection of various changes proposed for the core knowledge base. Aside from indicating when they start and end editing sessions, the domain experts do not notice the presence of edit-tracking in their normal style of development. The edit-tracking capabilities enhanced both speed and consistency of development and inter-developer communication (discussed in the subsequent section, Support for Distributed Development).

Experiences

This section describes some of our experiences during the construction of LQMS. We begin with a timeline that summarizes the main knowledge-acquisition phase of its development. We then describe two episodes from late in the project that illustrate the ease with our domain experts could understand and modify the knowledge base.

Development

The initial domain expert (who will be referred to as DE_1), had an engineering degree, over 15 years of varied field experience, and much exposure to programming. He worked on the project part-time, helped with the analysis of the domain, and prompted the development of the OSR idea. He was followed, with overlap, by a second domain expert (DE_2), working full-time on the project. DE_2 had an engineering degree, over ten years of varied field experience, and much exposure to programming. DE_2, using the early knowledge-acquisition tools, built the first 80 networks, which represented behavior models for four basic tool types. The knowledge base by then included about 800 total classes. DE_2 transferred back to the field after over a year on the project, and there was a 4 month gap before a third domain expert (DE_3) was transferred in from the field to work on the project. During this time, we developed the OSR Network editor, based on observing DE_2 and seeing that while he was able to construct the networks using the object/slot/value linkage editors, he always kept a current graphic display that would show him the developing structure. The new OSR Network editor allowed these activities to be unified, thus increasing the productivity of future network development. This process of knowledge-acquisition tools being developed contemporaneously with the system is discussed in [Smith, 1984]. DE_3 had an engineering degree, over five years of field experience, and very little exposure to programming or workstations. DE_3 reviewed the state of the system, revised fewer than 10% of the networks, and began adding models of three additional tools. These new tools were quite complex, and involved the addition of 200 networks (and tie-ins to many of the existing networks), over one and a half years. The system used during the final field tests and transferred from research to engineering had models of nine tools, with over 280 networks, including 480 Observations, 280 Situations, and 680 Relations.

Refinement

During the later development phase of the prototype, the system was field tested in five locations worldwide. Each of these field tests involved installing the system in an office environment where engineers would use it to replay previously run commercial data acquisition jobs and provide feedback on the utility, ease of use, and performance of the system. The office environment was selected since the commercial logging acquisition trucks work in a very high-cost, time-critical environment while the drilling rig is configured to allow logging; while in the office, the systems and data are still available after normal work hours. Some of the field test sites provided excellent feedback on how naive users might benefit from the system's analyses, while others provided feedback on how a complex, knowledge-based system would react to local modifications. One of these latter (more technically demanding) locations was Cairo, Egypt, where by that time DE_2 was working. During the field test, in addition to the normal use and testing of the system, DE_2 recognized a weakness in the system's coverage, understood the part of the knowledge base that required refinement, made several changes, and tested and validated his new (better) results. All this activity transpired without the support of the developers.

Support for Distributed Development

The next episode illustrates how the edit-tracking system acted as a communication vehicle. When LQMS was transferred to engineering, two more domain experts (DE_4 and later DE_5) became part of the team. After a period of electronic communication, DE_3 met with DE_4. They worked on understanding the current state of the system, and discussed refinements that might be made. After DE_3 returned to his home location, he made several hundred changes (of various sizes) since he was still the principal domain expert. DE_4 then asked if he could find out what had been changed. Since all the changes DE_3 had made were recorded by the edit-tracking system, it was straightforward to generate a transcript of those changes. A single change summary is shown that captures adding a link from a situation (`MULTIPLEXER#1-FAILURE`) to an AND relation (`AND-99`). Although the transcript is very low level, DE_4 found it quite helpful.

```
Updating Object MULTIPLEXER#1-FAILURE
Slot ACCOMPANIEDBY to ADD AND-99
```

These transcripts were also used as a chronicle of knowledge base development. This automatic construction of a record of the construction and refinement of the knowledge base deals with one of the inherent problems in knowledge engineering: "interviewing without a record"[Forsythe and Buchanan, 1989].

Performance

The size of a knowledge base and ease of its construction are interesting only when the system performs well. In this section, we summarize several studies of LQMS's performance.

DE_4 performed a set of case studies on the system. The first set was done in 1988 before he had any knowledge of the internals of the system, while the second set was done in 1989 after DE_4 had become familiar with the system. He was not responsible for the knowledge base development until after these studies were completed. In the earlier studies he found that correct diagnoses of causes of anomalies had been far from perfect (60% correct) but with the testing and refinement activities (done by DE_3 primarily), accuracy steadily improved.

In June, 1989, DE_4 ran eight jobs and compiled the following estimated results. He judged approximately 85% of the explanations to be reasonable. In fact, the system found and explained some problems likely to be missed by a normal field engineer. He believed 15% were wrong, since the given explanation could easily be shown to be inappropriate by anyone with a reasonable level of experience in log interpretation.

All of the grading was done on the basis of information that an engineer would normally have available post-hoc, in the office environment. This level of information is not always available to the field engineer, on location, so these results are very encouraging. Explanations classified as wrong were typically those that reasonably fit with a subset of the observations, but conflicted with other available information. This additional information was missed for any of several reasons. It may have been omitted (or improperly included) in the OSR network. It was sometimes inaccessible because no Observers had been designed to monitor that particular data. We believe that most of these wrong explanations can be corrected through further completion of the knowledge base.

LQMS was estimated by DE_4 to be performing at 85% of the level of an experienced field engineer, and had shown that its performance can be improved incrementally and substantially.

Current Status

The prototype LQMS was transferred to engineering in 1989 after three years of development and field testing. The system is being ported into the commercial environment of the data acquisition system.

Related Work

The idea of using networks to structure the association of observations and situations has some of its roots in Hendrix's partitioned semantic networks [Hendrix, 1979].

The basic architectural approach of abstraction of data by low-level modules with higher-level processing (sometimes directing the low-level modules) is very much like Hearsay-II [Erman *et al.*, 1980]. The MOLE [Eshelman, 1988] system has many similarities to the OSR framework used in LQMS. MOLE has more powerful support for refinement of the knowledge base, although the OSR Network Editor has the capability to discover and display (partial) networks it considers incomplete (Figure 1—*AddIncompleteNets* command). The domain expert has played a more active role in refining the knowledge base in LQMS (with good results). Based on the examples shown in [Eshelman, 1988], MOLE has a less expressive knowledge representation, in that there is only one "relation" called "*covering (explanatory)*", which is visually encoded as a link. Additionally, there is a presumption that *initial symptoms* are different in a significant way from *other symptoms* and that only initial symptoms can be used to prompt a diagnosis. In contrast, OSR has the concept of a *trigger observation*, but this is just an additional characteristic that any observation can have, although intuitively, some observations (*e.g.*, value-out-of-range) are much more likely to be interesting triggers in a diagnosis task. We designed this uniformity into the observations since we believe that if a knowledge base describes a domain, there may be several uses for that knowledge (*e.g.*, data quality diagnosis, pre-interpretation data analysis, training), and the trigger observations for the different uses may not be the same.

There is a problem inherent with the development of ambitious systems: keeping the pace of development fast enough to maintain the domain experts' interest and contribution [Buchanan *et al.*, 1983]. One approach is to use a team of developers, suggested by Reboh [Reboh, 1981, p. 94], one to interview the domain expert and another to implement the knowledge in a prototype. The approach used in LQMS brings the domain expert directly to the center of the action and responsibility. This approach has the additional feature of making the domain expert a real part-owner of the system, with all the positive aspects that "ownership" brings.

Conclusions

LQMS is a system based primarily on knowledge encoded directly by domain experts. Its prototype performed with a high level of accuracy and that performance has been incrementally and significantly improved during development and field testing. Several points have been developed in this paper.

- The combination of an intuitive model (sufficient for the task) and powerful, graphical development tools allowed the domain experts to build a large, high performance system. There was a significant transition from the prototype system based on rules (no direct interaction between domain expert and knowledge base) to the system based on OSR networks built with direct "boxes and links" editing (very productive interaction).
- The OSR representation illustrates an intermediate point on the simplicity-expressiveness spectrum, which is understandable to non-developers, while being expressive enough for the domain.
- The system was a natural workbench for the domain experts, which enticed them to become more directly involved, resulting in a better system.
- The edit-tracking system served many useful purposes. It reassured computer-naive experts that they could not damage the overall system, which increased their productivity. It also allowed experts located in various places around the world to compare, contrast, and integrate changes in a structured way.

Acknowledgments

There have been many people associated with the successful history of the LQMS project without whom these lessons would not have been possible. With respect to the knowledge-acquisition aspects, I would like to acknowledge the efforts of our excellent domain experts: Alistair Cox, Ace Dumestre, Laurent Moinard, and Alan Sibbit. The core development team included Dennis O'Neill, Paul Gingrich, and the user interface work of Ruven Brooks. Although this paper primarily describes work on the research prototype, the engineering team at Schlumberger Austin Systems Center, involved in the technology transfer, provided valuable interactions. Bob Young was a critical resource during the original development of the OSR ideas, provided the spark of motivation to produce this paper, and excellent feedback to make it right. Eric Schoen and Reid Smith supplied insightful comments and helpful pointers. Stan Vestal and SLCS allowed this retrospective activity to occur.

References

[Bennett, 1985] James S. Bennett. ROGET: A knowledge-based consultant for acquiring the conceptual structure of a diagnostic expert system. *Journal of Automated Reasoning*, 1:49–74, 1985.

[Buchanan and Shortliffe, 1984] B. G. Buchanan and E.H. Shortliffe. *Rule-Based Expert Systems: The MYCIN Experiments of the Stanford Heuristic Programming Project*. Addison-Wesley, Reading, Mass., 1984.

[Buchanan *et al.*, 1983] Bruce G. Buchanan, David Barstow, Robert Bechtal, James Bennett, William Clancey, Casimir Kulikowski, Tom Mitchell, and Donald A. Waterman. Constructing an expert system. In Frederick Hayes-Roth, Donald A. Waterman, and Douglas B. Lenat, editors, *Building Expert Systems*, chapter 5, pages 127–168. Addison-Wesley, Reading, Mass., 1983.

[Davis and Hamscher, 1988] Randall Davis and Walter Hamscher. Model-based reasoning: Troubleshooting. In H.E. Shrobe and AAAI, editors, *Exploring Artificial Intelligence*, pages 347–410. Morgan Kaufmann, 1988.

[Erman *et al.*, 1980] L. D. Erman, F. Hayes-Roth, V. R. Lesser, and D. R. Reddy. The Hearsay-II speech-understanding system: Integrating knowledge to resolve uncertainty. *Computing Surveys*, 12(2):213–253, June 1980.

[Eshelman, 1988]
Larry Eshelman. MOLE: A knowledge-acquisition tool for cover-and-differentiate systems. In Sandra Marcus, editor, *Automating Knowledge Acquisition for Expert Systems*, chapter 3, pages 37–80. Kluwer Academic Publishers, Boston, Mass., 1988.

[Forsythe and Buchanan, 1989] Diana E. Forsythe and Bruce G. Buchanan. Knowledge acquisition for expert systems: Some pitfalls and problems. *IEEE Transactions on Systems, Man and Cybernetics*, 19(3):435–442, May/June 1989. Special issue on perspectives in knowledge engineering.

[Hamscher, 1988] Walter C. Hamscher. *Model-based Troubleshooting of Digital Systems*. PhD thesis, MIT AI Lab, 1988.

[Hendrix, 1979] G. G. Hendrix. Encoding knowledge in partitioned networks. In *Associative Networks—The Representation and Use of Knowledge in Computers*, pages 51–92. Academic Press, New York, NY, 1979.

[Musen, 1989] Mark A. Musen. *Automated Generation of Model-Based Knowledge-Acquisition Tools*. Research Notes in Artificial Intelligence. Pitman Publishing, London, 1989. Revision of Stanford University PhD dissertation (STAN-CS-88-1194).

[O'Neill and Mullarkey, 1989] D. M. O'Neill and P. W. Mullarkey. A knowledge-based approach to real time signal monitoring. In *Proceedings of the Fifth Conference on Artificial Intelligence Applications*, pages 133–140, March 1989.

[Reboh, 1981] R. Reboh. Knowledge engineering techniques and tools in the Prospector environment. Technical Report 243, SRI International, Menlo Park, Calif., June 1981.

[Schoen *et al.*, 1988] Eric Schoen, Reid G. Smith, and Bruce G. Buchanan. Design of Knowledge-Based Systems with a Knowledge-Based Assistant. *IEEE Transactions on Software Engineering*, 14(12):1771–1791, December 1988.

[Smith *et al.*, 1987] R. G. Smith, P. S. Barth, and R. L. Young. A substrate for object-oriented interface design. In *Research Directions in Object-Oriented Programming*. MIT Press, Cambridge, MA., 1987.

[Smith, 1984] R. G. Smith. On the Development of Commercial Expert Systems. *AI Magazine*, 5(3):61–73, Fall 1984.

Parametric Engineering Design Using Constraint-Based Reasoning

Niall Murtagh and **Masamichi Shimura**
Department of Computer Science, Tokyo Institute of Technology
2-12-1 O-okayama, Meguro-ku, Tokyo 152, JAPAN
email: niall@cs.titech.ac.jp

Abstract

Conventional methods for the parametric design of engineering structures rely on the iterative re-use of analysis programs in order to converge on a satisfactory solution. Since finite element and other analysis programs require considerable computer resources, this research proposes a general method to minimize their use, by utilizing constraint-based reasoning to carry out redesign. A problem-solver, consisting of constraint networks which express basic relationships between individual design parameters and variables, is attached to the analysis programs. Once an initial design description has been set out using the conventional analysis programs, the networks can then reason about required adjustments in order to find a consistent set of parameter values. We describe how global constraints representing standard design behavioral equations are decomposed to form binary constraint networks. The networks use approximate reasoning to determine dependencies between key parameters, and after an adjustment has been made, use exact relationship information to update only those parts of the design description that are affected by the adjustment. We illustrate the ideas by taking as an example the design of a continuous prestressed concrete beam.

1 Introduction

Parametric design refers to the design of engineering objects, in which the parameters and variables describing the object are known, and the problem is one of finding a consistent set of parameter values which conform to specified requirements. Conventional parametric design algorithms for civil and mechanical engineering structures use finite element and other structural analysis programs to propose an initial solution. If the solution is infeasible, redesign is carried out in iterative fashion in order to converge on a feasible solution. The analysis programs have to be treated as black-boxes with fixed input and output, and hence each redesign iteration requires a complete re-processing, irrespective of how small the change made to the previous design description. Furthermore, these analysis programs are often large and require considerable computer resources [Murthy and Addanki, 1987]. Therefore, any reduction in their usage through the application of intelligent redesign methods is advantageous for design efficiency.

Previous research into structural engineering design has dealt with meta-level control [Orelup et al, 1988], domain independence [Dixon et al, 1987], and innovative design [Murthy and Addanki, 1987], but has not applied intelligent technology to the fundamental analysis part of parametric design. In this research, we replace the analysis programs in redesign with a knowledge-based constraint reasoning process. This provides the double advantage of minimizing the use of expensive analysis programs, and of being able to update only those parameters or variables in the design description which require updating.

Constraint-based techniques have been shown to improve the problem-solving capabilities for applications such as combinatorial problems and vision [Montanari, 1974], [Mackworth, 1977], electrical circuit analysis [Sussman and Steele, 1980], and preliminary structural design [Sriram and Maher, 1986]. A constraint-based approach reflects the view that design is essentially a process of integrating constraints from a variety of sources [Mostow, 1985]. In the present system, however, the constraints considered are restricted to those that can be conveniently handled, i.e., numeric constraints on design parameter values. We explain how constraint networks are formed for the type of application considered here, and we propose an architecture to accommodate a constraint-based problem solver together with structural analysis programs. The actual design process is then detailed, showing how backward reasoning enables dependencies between key parameters to be determined, and how forward propagation through the constraint network obviates the need to re-access analysis modules. We illustrate our techniques by referring to the design of a statically indeterminate prestressed concrete beam.

2 Design Process Model

A conventional parametric design problem is described by parameters and variables, which can be classified according to the following three groups:

Initial Parameters These include the user specification together with certain other unknown parameters whose values must be estimated before processing can be carried out to determine performance parameter values.

Intermediate Variables These are determined as part of the processing of the initial parameters.

Design Performance Parameters These are provided either by the user or by engineering codes, and they determine whether the solution proposed by the initial parameter values is adequate or not.

Since it is not possible to directly determine the unknown parameters from the specification and required performance, conventional design is carried out in an iterative generate-and-test manner, using analysis programs to generate a complete description, before testing the performance parameters. The analysis programs, cannot be fully replaced by more flexible reasoning systems, such as constraint-based problem solvers, because the analysis programs have certain capabilities–for example, the handling of various data types–which constraint-based reasoning systems do not possess, e.g., analysis programs process both single and multi-valued parameters, such as arrays of loads on a multi-span beam, while constraint-based systems can only reason about single valued parameters. Therefore, we use both conventional and constraint-based processing of parameters. Our system initially follows the conventional algorithm using analysis programs to generate an initial complete design description. However, in subsequent redesign, only extreme values need be considered for each parameter, so that constraint-based reasoning alone can complete the design problem.

3 Constraint Network Model

A standard constraint-satisfaction problem is characterized by a set of variables or parameters, each of which has a domain, finite or infinite, of possible values. To this is added a set of domain constraints and a set of inter-parameter constraints.

Domain Constraints are unary constraints, $c(p)$, where c is a function mapping a parameter, p, onto a particular domain of allowable values. In our model, these constraints act on the initial and performance parameters. Intermediate variables do not have unary constraints and will accept any value propagated to them. Two levels of unary constraint exist:

- Unary *limit*-constraints restrict the parameter to a multi-value domain within fixed limits, which cannot be adjusted during design. They may be obtained from a domain expert or textbook, or may be specified by the user.
- Unary *value*-constraints assign a single numerical value to each initial parameter, i.e., they further tighten the limit-constraints so that a single value is associated with the parameter prior to propagation. These value-constraints may be supplied either by the user as part of the design specification, in which case the limit-constraints ensure that the value is in the allowable domain, or they may be supplied by the system, through default or other methods. System-supplied unary value-constraints may be automatically adjusted during redesign, whereas user-supplied constraints are considered as part of the specification and may not be altered.

Inter-Parameter Constraints are "n-ary" constraints, $c(p_1, p_2 ...... p_n)$, where c is a function relating parameters $p_1, p_2 ...... p_n$, $n \geq 2$. These constraints, representing the laws of statics, geometry, mathematics, etc., link all the parameters/variables in the design description. They are used to propagate the value-constraints on the initial parameters, i.e., they force an "n-ary" constraint between the initial and performance parameters. If the constraints cannot be satisfied, adjustments have to be made. This is where the manner of representation of the inter-parameter constraints can have a big influence on the efficiency of the design. We now describe the treatment of these constraints.

3.1 Constraint Decomposition

In conventional engineering design methods, global inter-parameter constraints are represented by behavioral equations contained in the analysis programs which process the input description and check the result against performance requirements. This can be regarded as applying an "n-ary" constraint to the initial and performance parameters, where n is the number of parameters involved.

We convert these "n-ary" constraints into binary constraint networks for the following reasons:

- In conventional methods which use "n-ary" constraints as in Figure 1(a), specific or generalized dependency relations between initial and performance parameters must be explicitly stated, e.g., factor × imposed loading = tensile stress. By linking all parameters together in a binary network, part of which is shown in Figure 1(c), approximate dependency relations can be worked out by the system.
- With a few "n-ary" constraints linking many parameters, as in Figure 1(a), if one parameter is adjusted then a complete re-computation involving all n parameters, is generally required to determine the adjustment necessary for the other parameters. The "n-ary" constraint gives no information regarding

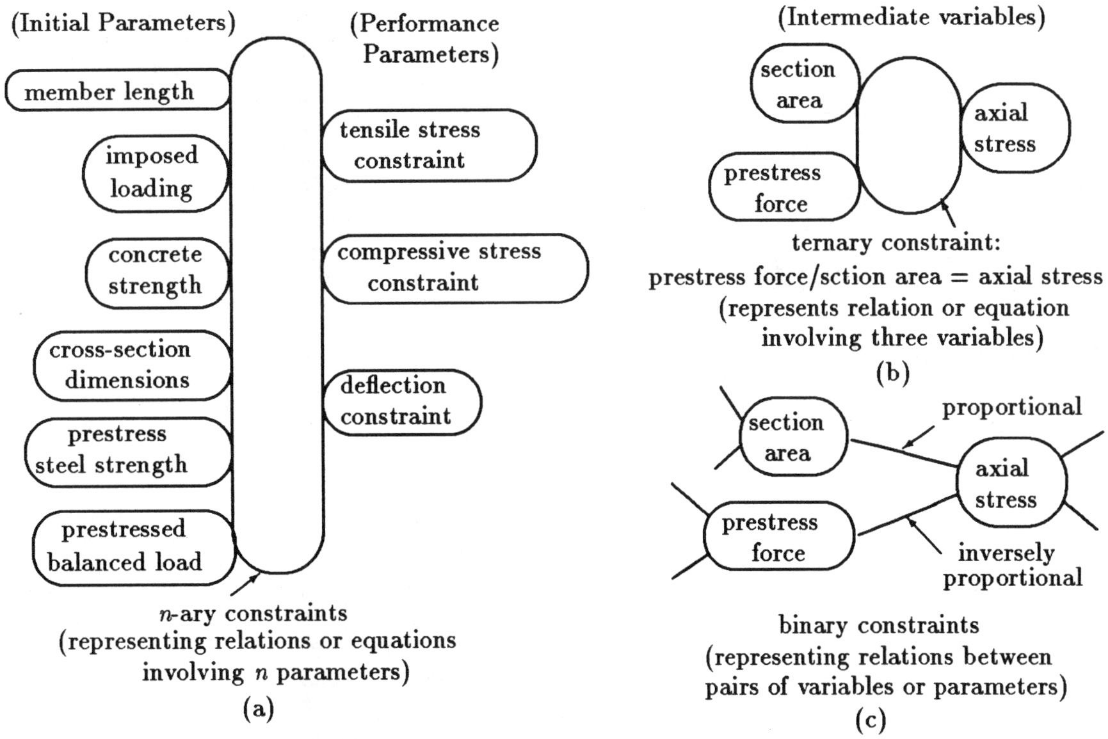

Figure 1: Constraint Decomposition

individual parameter-to-parameter relations, so that partial re-adjustment of the design description is not possible. However, a binary constraint network directly relates individual parameters, enabling local adjustments to be carried out and propagated only to those parameters affected by a change.

The "n-ary" constraints as in Figure 1(a), are decomposed by firstly introducing intermediate variables as "stepping-stones" in the propagation process, i.e., we explicitly represent all steps in the evaluation of the behavioral equations as nodes in the constraint network. This reduces the "n-ary" constraint to simpler forms, e.g., the ternary constraint shown in Figure 1(b), which processes two variable-values to produce one new variable-value. Secondly, these simpler constraints are then further decomposed into binary constraints, or relations between pairs of nodes. After the first step the constraints still represent equations, as in Figure 1(b), but after the second, we only have one-to-one relations between nodes as in Figure 1(c), and we can directly transfer an adjustment from one node to another, without having to consider any more than two nodes at a time. In our system binary relations similar to those shown in Figure 1(c), cater for addition, multiplication, etc., and power operators, as well as the reverse operators. Certain complications that occur in the adjustment transfer process are dealt with in section 4.1.

3.2 System Architecture

An expert system such as the one proposed here will generally be built on top of existing procedural programs, not the other way around. Therefore, it is necessary to adapt constraint-based ideas to suit the demands of conventional programs. As shown in Figure 2, the architecture consists of a 2-level structure, with the constraint network set out in the upper, shallow-knowledge level, and conventional analysis modules located in the lower, procedural knowledge level. The links between nodes in the upper level consist of simplified direct dependency relations, as explained in the previous section, while those which pass through the lower level utilize traditional software tools, such as finite element programs, etc. Unary constraints are shown acting vertically down on the upper level. This separation between top and bottom levels reflects the distinction in conventional engineering terminology between "design" and "analysis". Design concerns initial decisions, outline data, etc., and uses heuristics or shallow knowledge, while analysis concerns precise numerical values and uses procedural knowledge embedded in algorithmic programs. User communication and system output take place through the upper design level, which is also used in redesign to carry out propagation in forward and backward directions. The lower level analysis modules are used in setting out a full initial description, and typically link several nodes together,

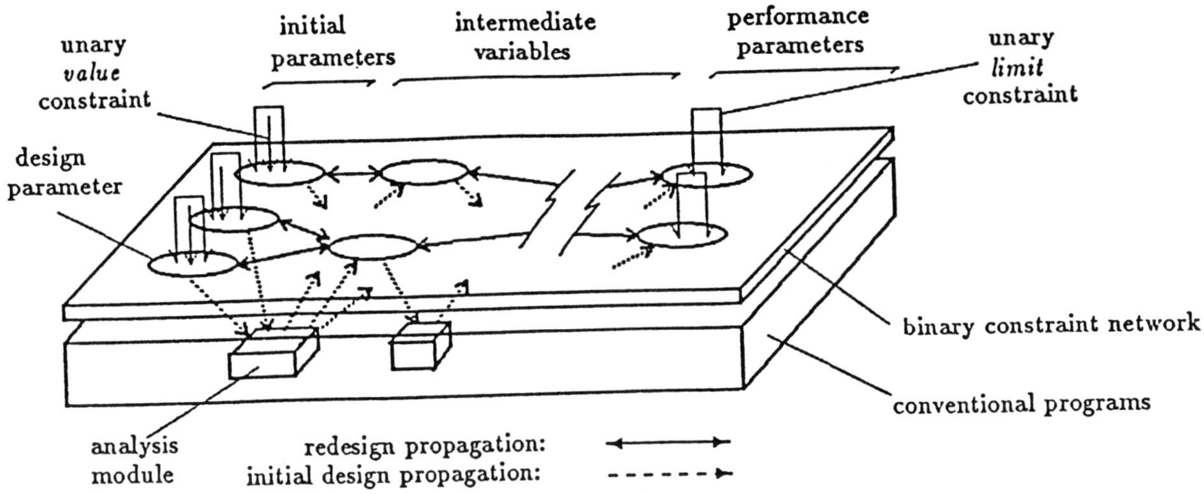

Figure 2: System Architecture

i.e., they form "n-ary" constraints, which, for clarity, we illustrate by dotted-line arrows.

4 Problem-solving Process

4.1 Application of Constraints

A design problem is commenced by the application of unary constraints. Allowable domains and specific values are assigned to the initial parameters, and allowable domains are assigned to the performance parameters. The user specification provides some of these unary constraints and the remainder are supplied by the system. This is done either through system-dependent default values, or through constraint derivation, which generalizes standard textbook heuristics linking certain parameters, e.g., span/depth ratios. (For details of the constraint derivation algorithm, see [Murtagh and Shimura, 1989]).

The values assigned to the initial parameters are then propagated using the "n-ary" constraints. This resembles standard propagation except that in the initial propagation the lower level algorithmic modules are used and multiple parameter values are simultaneously operated on. A complete description is thus obtained, and its validity is tested by the performance parameters. Generally this first complete description will be invalid due to conflict between the propagated constraint values and the allowable domains of the performance parameters, and a redesign phase is automatically commenced.

In the redesign phase, the system first determines the dependency information necessary for redesign, i.e., it back-propagates from the critical performance parameter to determine how much the initial parameters should be adjusted in order to achieve the required alteration in the critical performance parameter. Thus, it obviates the need to set out parameter-to-parameter dependency information, although parameter ordering [Dixon et al, 1987], specifying which parameter to adjust first, is still required.

After the adjustments required in the initial parameters have been established, one initial parameter is selected for adjustment in accordance with the current redesign strategy. The adjustment is carried out, and forward propagation through the network updates the nodes related to the adjusted initial parameter.

While the initial forward propagation can be regarded as a global propagation, the redesign phase is based on local propagation. Local propagation has the advantage that it is fast because it uses only simple relationships and deals only with single-valued nodes. However, it relies on approximate reasoning in back-propagation, due to the presence of loops or cycles in the network. Referring to Figure 3(a), in back-propagation where more than one link lead out of the node *N4*, the required adjustment in *N4* is propagated to both *N2* and *N3*, an adjustment in either one being sufficient to produce the required adjustment in *N4*. Where the two paths subsequently lead into a single node *N1*, a cycle or loop occurs. In general, the two adjustments back-propagated to *N1* along the two paths, will not be the same. In order to combine the values, we propose an empirically derived approximate equivalence equation, supplemented with a self-updating heuristic correction factor, F.

proposed adjustments		executed adjustment
$x,\ y$	$\Longrightarrow$	$F \times [x \times y/(x+y)]$

The heuristic factor, initially set to 1, and updated after adjustment, is used to speed up the adjustment process, i.e., it attempts to move immediately to the top of the current hill. This factor is problem-specific

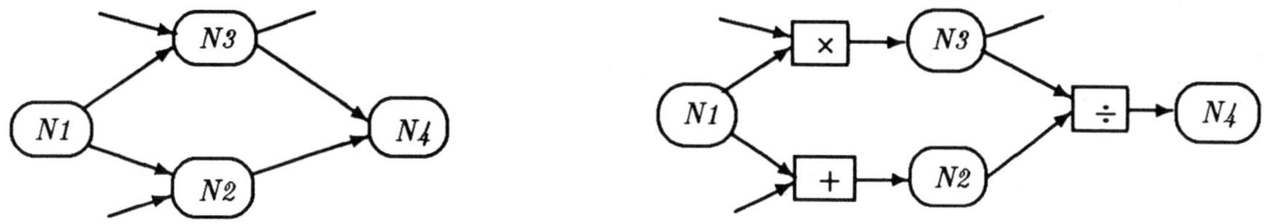

(a) Node relations represented by binary links

(b) Node relations represented by operators

(Arrows show direction of forward propagation)

Figure 3: Loop in Binary Constraint Network

Design Parameter Values		
parameter name	*user specification*	
no of spans	3	
span lengths	10 m, 18 m, 10 m	
end fixities	cantilever, pinned	
dead load	5 kN/m	
live load	6 kN/m	
	computed parameters	
	initial value	*final value*
concrete strength	35 N/mm^2	40 N/mm^2
section width	300 mm	450 mm
section depth	650 mm	800 mm
prestress steel strength	1950 N/mm^2	1950 N/mm^2
cover to steel †	30 mm	103 mm
balanced load factor ‡	0.4	0.486

†Steel cover determines max prestress tendon sag.
‡Proportion of load balanced by prestress.

Table 1: Design Description for Prestressed Beam

and path-specific. Hence, although it has no usefulness in the first adjustment, since its value is 1, it performs better than over-generalized statistical factors and will enable convergence to be quickly obtained in a subsequent adjustment of the same parameter.

In forward propagation, where multiple adjustments are passed to a single node, they are super-imposed to give the exact required adjustment. The difference between forward and backward propagation, while not obvious from Figure 3(a), can be seen more clearly in Figure 3(b), which shows the links passing through operators, which act like ternary constraints.

5 Implementation and Results

The system at present comprises four partially overlapping constraint networks, each network joining the initial parameters with one particular performance parameter. These networks are written in Prolog, while the structural analysis modules are in C. The analysis modules in the current system carry out bending moment and shear computations, prestress system computations, and ultimate strength verification. Table 1 shows the numeric data for the design of a 3-span prestressed concrete beam. The design was carried out using the constraint network for redesign and also using conventional techniques, i.e., using the analysis programs only. The same results were obtained for each case, since the constraint networks exactly reflect the processing of the analysis programs. However, the conventional design method necessitated accessing each of the analysis programs a total of 18 times, while the constraint-based method only required the use of the analysis programs once, in the initial design.

6 Comparison with Related Research

Relaxation [Leler, 1988] involves making an initial guess at the value of an object, estimating the resultant error, and making new guesses in order to converge on a rational value. We have adapted this technique to the demands of engineering design, focusing on how to represent relations between the objects, and how to improve the convergence methods.

In [Chan and Paulson, 1987], constraints are used for determining design descriptions as well as checking proposed descriptions for a structural engineering application. However, procedures are required for each intended use of the constraint. We also use constraints in different ways, but instead of setting out numerous procedures, we avail of simplified relationships represented by constraint networks. One of the ways in which we utilize the constraints, in addition to checking, is in establishing parameter-to-parameter dependency information, using local constraint relationships together with problem-specific heuristic factors. Thus we do not need to set out explicit dependency relationships as in more conventional systems [Dixon et al, 1987].

In [Mackworth, 1977] consistency algorithms are proposed for attaching feasible values to variables, and for filtering infeasible values in constraint networks.

Only unary and binary constraints are treated, and the inter-variable constraints are assumed to be inexpensive, unlike those represented by analysis programs in engineering design. Hence, our research focuses on the nature of the inter-variable constraints.

In [Dechter and Pearl, 1987], the variable-domains consist of a finite number of discrete values, enabling candidate-ordering and/or elimination to be used. These techniques cannot be used in engineering design where the parameters normally have continuous and therefore infinite domains. However, the continuous nature of the domain values permits movement from one candidate value to another, using only information concerning the extent to which the previous value was unsatisfactory, thus avoiding expensive re-computation procedures.

7 Conclusion

This system has shown how a constraint-based problem solver can improve the efficiency of parametric engineering design, by minimizing the use of large analysis programs and updating only the minimum number of parameters and variables in redesign. The fundamental difference between previous work and the present system is the following: in conventional systems the redesign process releases all intermediate variables from their currently assigned values, and after some alteration to the initial parameter(s), re-assigns these variables using the same methods as before. In our system, redesign does not release variables from their current values, but instead automatically adjusts the values of those variables related to the most critical performance parameter, by propagation through the constraint network. Forward propagation is exact, depending only on the binary constraints between the parameters and variables. Back propagation is generally approximate, due to loops or cycles in the constraint networks, and relies on *ad hoc* procedures. At best this will give exact accuracy (for single path, or no-loop dependencies) and good approximations for other multi-path dependencies. At worst, it will rely on the heuristic correction factor to steer the adjustment in the right course. The system at present uses a general hill-climbing strategy. A parametric design system should ideally have a variety of strategies, as shown in [Orelup et al, 1988]. However, this is a separate issue to the one considered in the present research.

The strategy used in this work is applicable to parametric design problems in which basic relationships between parameters and variables can be obtained from the behavioral equations, and in which multi-valued parameters can be rationalized into controlling single values for reasoning purposes. Although the system has been tested in only one domain, parametric design does not differ radically from domain to domain, so that our strategy has the potential to be applied generally.

References

[Brown and Breau, 1986] Brown, D.C., Breau, R., Types of Constraints in Routine Design Problem-Solving, in *Applications of Artificial Intelligence in Engineering Problems, Proceedings of the 1st International Conference*, Southampton U.K., 1986, Springer-Verlag.

[Chan and Paulson, 1987] Chan, W.T., Paulson, B.C. Jr, Exploratory Design using Constraints, in *Artificial Intelligence in Engineering Design, Analysis and Manufacturing* 1, 1987, pp. 59-71.

[Dechter and Pearl, 1987] Dechter, R., Pearl, J., Network Based Heuristics for Constraint-Satisfaction Problems, in *Artificial Intelligence* 34, 1987, pp.1-38.

[Dixon et al, 1987] Dixon, J.R., Howe, A., Cohen, P.R., Simmons, M.K., Dominic I: Progress Toward Domain Independence in Design by Iterative Redesign, in *Engineering with Computers* 2, 1987, pp. 137-145.

[Leler, 1988] Leler, Wm., *Constraint Programming Languages, their Specification and Generation*, 1988, Addison-Wesley Publishing Company.

[Mackworth, 1977] Mackworth, A., Consistency in Networks of Relations, in *Artificial Intelligence* 8, 1977, pp. 99-118.

[Montanari, 1974] Montanari, U., Networks of Constraints: Fundamental Properties and Applications to Picture Processing, in *Information Sciences* 7, 1974, pp. 95-132.

[Mostow, 1985] Mostow, J., Toward Better Models of the Design Process, in *AI Magazine* 6, 1985, Spring.

[Murtagh and Shimura, 1989] Murtagh, N., Shimura, M., A Constraint-Based Hybrid Engineering Design System, in *Proceedings of The Third IFIP WG 5.2 Workshop on Intelligent CAD*, 1989, Osaka, Japan, (to be published by North-Holland).

[Murthy and Addanki, 1987] Murthy, S., Addanki, S., PROMPT: An Innovative Design Tool, in *Proceedings of AAAI*, 1987, pp. 637-642.

[Orelup et al, 1988] Orelup, M.F., Dixon, J.R., Cohen, P.R., Simmons, M.K., Dominic II: Meta-Level Control in Iterative Redesign, in *Proceedings of AAAI*, 1988, pp. 25-29.

[Sriram and Maher, 1986] Sriram, D., Maher, M.L., The Representation and Use of Constraints in Structural Design, in *Applications of Artificial Intelligence in Engineering Problems, Proceedings of the 1st International Conference*, Southampton U.K., 1986, Springer-Verlag.

[Sussman and Steele, 1980] Sussman, G.J., Steele, G.L. Jr, Constraints –a Language for Expressing Almost Hierarchical Descriptions, in *Artificial Intelligence*, 14, 1980 pp. 1-39.

Establishing the Coherence of an Explanation to Improve Refinement of an Incomplete Knowledge Base

Young-Tack Park and **David C. Wilkins**
Computer Science Department
405 North Mathews Ave.
University of Illinois
Urbana, Illinois 61801

Abstract

The power of knowledge acquisition systems that employ failure-driven learning derives from two main sources: an effective global credit assignment process that determines when to acquire new knowledge by watching an expert's behavior, and an efficient local credit assignment process that determines what new knowledge will be created for completing a failed explanation of an expert's action. Because an input (e.g., observed action) to a failure-driven learning system can generate multiple explanations, a learning opportunity to extend the incomplete domain theory can go unobserved. This paper describes a failure-driven learning with a context analysis mechanism as a method to constrain explanations and thereby increase the number of learning opportunities. Experimentation using a synthetic expert system as the observed expert shows that the use of context analysis increases the number of learning opportunities by about 47%, and increases the overall amount of improvement to the expert system by around 10%.

Introduction

Knowledge acquisition is the major bottleneck in the development of expert systems. One promising method to overcome this difficulty is exemplified by the Learning Apprentice System [Mitchell *et al.*, 1985] and other apprenticeship learning programs, which assimilate new problem solving knowledge by observing and analyzing a human expert's actions [Kodratoff and Tecuci, 1987] [Wilkins, 1988a].

Apprenticeship learning involves first recognizing a failure to interpret an expert's actions and then acquiring new knowledge to recover from the failure. The detection of a failure can be done either by outside human experts or by the apprenticeship learning system itself. When outside human experts are used, the humans point out the the expert system's failure and provide the apprenticeship learning system with a learning opportunity [Mitchell *et al.*, 1985] [Kodratoff and Tecuci, 1987]. Hence, in such systems, the global credit assignment as defined in [Dietterich and Buchanan, 1981] is done by a human and is not addressed in the learning process.

In contrast, when an apprenticeship learning system recognizes a failure by watching a human expert's problem solving steps, it must employ a global credit assignment process to determine when to learn. For example, the ODYSSEUS apprenticeship learning program [Wilkins, 1988a] for the HERACLES classification shell [Clancey, 1987] watches an expert and tries to explain the expert's observed actions. An explanation in ODYSSEUS is created by backward chaining the meta-level strategy rules. When ODYSSEUS fails to explain an action, it assumes that relevant facts are missing from its knowledge base.

Apprenticeship learning systems use diverse means to acquire new knowledge from failures [Mitchell *et al.*, 1985; Kodratoff and Tecuci, 1987; Wilkins, 1988a]. The most common approach is to construct an explanation of the failure. ODYSSEUS suggests new knowledge that can complete a failed meta-rule chain when this knowledge is added to the knowledge base.

Therefore, the power of knowledge acquisition systems that employ an apprenticeship learning method derives from two main sources: an effective global credit assignment process that determines when to acquire new knowledge by watching an expert's behavior, and an efficient local credit assignment process that determines what new knowledge will be created for completing a failed explanation of an expert's action.

Because a human's observed action can be explained in many different ways, a learning opportunity can go unnoticed. If the learning system does not filter out implausible explanations, its performance may be seriously hampered. In order to profit fully from watching an expert, the learning system must be able to reason about explanations as well as generate them.

In this paper we present an effective mechanism to avoid masking of learning opportunities by multiple explanations in apprenticeship learning system. The method reasons about the generated explanations and has been demonstrated to improve the performance of the learning system. We also offer an efficient method to suggest missing knowledge to recover from failures through a repair module that employs top-down and bottom-up approaches to infer new knowledge. The repair program reasons about failures, suggests new knowledge based on induction over solved cases, and verifies the suggested knowledge based on the context.

Explanation Generation

When a human expert takes an incomprehensible action and fails to do what a learning system expects him or her to do, failure driven learning attempts to understand the action by generating plausible explanations of the expert's behavior. Understanding is a process that explains the incomprehensible action in a context-sensitive way. Hence, it is important to represent explanations and contexts declaratively.

Experts usually employ problem solving strategy knowledge that is obtained through experience. Therefore, strategy knowledge is an important part of explaining an observed action. We implemented the MINERVA expert system shell [Park *et al.*, 1989] that uses explicit and flexible strategy knowledge. MINERVA is a rule-based expert system shell that is a Prolog reimplementation and enhancement of HERACLES expert system shell [Clancey, 1987]. The enhancement was guided by experience gained from the ODYSSEUS [Wilkins, 1988b] apprenticeship learning program for HERACLES. In MINERVA, the representation of the meta-level strategy knowledge is more explicit, declarative, and modular. This strategy knowledge is a Horn clause. The following is an example:

```
goal(clarify_finding(Finding1)) :-
        new_datum(Finding1),
        not value(Finding1, no),
        clarified_by(Finding1, Finding2),
        not concluded(Finding2),
        goal(findout(Finding2)).
```

The head of this clause consists of name and argument of this strategy knowledge source. The body consists of a sequence of premises followed by a subgoal. A strategy knowledge source is activated only by a new change of problem state and invokes a subgoal that changes problem states. When the premises of an activated knowledge source are satisfied, the subgoal is inserted into the agenda. MINERVA employs explicit schedule knowledge to determine which subgoal to perform next. Subgoals are of two types: actions and tasks. An action refers to a subgoal that tries to find out a symptom. A task refers to a subgoal that invokes another task. For example, a subgoal *apply_rule(Rule)* represents a task that fires a domain rule. It triggers a sequence of tasks that find the values of antecedents of the domain rule, checks if the values satisfy conditions, and evaluates the domain rule. The modular representation and the opportunistic control of strategy knowledge source is suitable both for flexible problem solving and efficient knowledge acquisition.

We view an expert's action as a coproduction of strategy knowledge, domain knowledge, and problem solving state. Finding relevant explanations of an expert's action hinges on the notion of differential modelling, whereby the expert's behavior is compared to the expert system's choices for the same circumstances.

The modular knowledge sources predict all reasonable actions that an expert might take based on the new problem solving states. The problem solving states can be acquired from the expert or by inferring from the expert's problem solving steps. Predicted actions and tasks are justified by the explanations that describe why those are expected by the expert system. And, we will say that apprentice understands an observed action if it can construct an explanation of the same expected action or the relevant task.

Failure Detection

If an apprenticeship learning system fails to generate an explanation of an expert's action, this suggests that the knowledge base is missing a piece of information that the expert knows. This kind of explanation failure is categorized as the *expectation failure* type.

While the detection of the expectation failure is important, it is also important to be able to recognize and learn from situations where explanations are not coherent with a problem solving context. When failure driven learning encounters a situation where all the generated explanations fail to be consistent with the problem solving context, it discards them and tries to understand the action by finding a new explanation that is coherent with the context. This kind of explanation failure is categorized as the *context failure* type.

For example, suppose a human physician asks a question on *headache_duration*. Perhaps she wants to clarify a finding *headache*, because *headache_duration* is a more specific fact. Or, she might intend to differentiate two diseases; the symptom of one disease hypothesis is long *headache_duration* and the other has short duration. Hence, a learning system cannot identify which explanation is a plausible intention of the question without using a bias. However, if the physician asked many questions on the detailed facts of *headache* just before, her intention is more likely to be clarification of *headache*. In contrast, if she asked questions on both diseases, she is probably trying to differentiate between the hypotheses. We need meta level reasoning about generated explanations to judge the quality of these multiple explanations.

Our model of knowledge acquisition includes the detection of both types of failures and the generation of explanations for the failures (see Figure 1). The global and local credit assignment processes are guided by reasoning about strategy knowledge and context analysis.

The scope of this work is limited by the assumption that the strategy knowledge of the expert system is complete, consistent, and correct. Thus, when a discrepancy arises between what the learning system expects and what the human expert apparently does, the learning system is justified in assuming that strategy knowledge is right and domain knowledge is wrong.

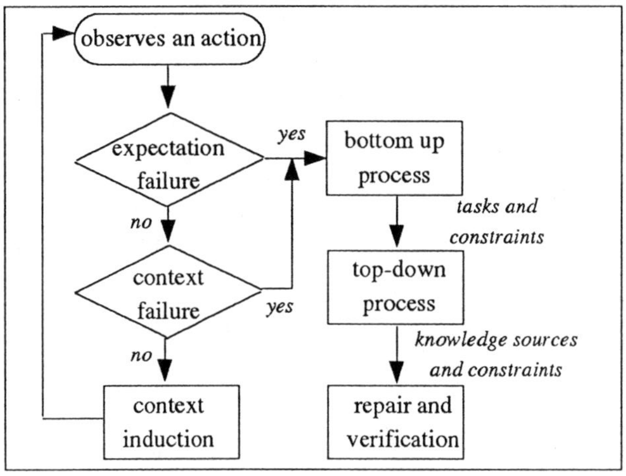

Figure 1: A knowledge acquisition cycle

Using expectations to generate explanations

We use an expect-explain method to understand observed actions (see Figure 1). As the learning program watches the human expert's actions, it builds a problem solving model which contains all the given facts, derived facts, and hypotheses. Whenever the learning program observes an action, it updates the problem solving model and predicts the next possible actions based on the problem solving model and its strategic knowledge (see section).

Expectation failure detection

In order for the learning system to explain an expert's action, it tries to connect the action to one of its expected actions. If the observed action is one of those predicted, then the learning system understands the action. The justification of the expected action is a candidate explanation for the expert's action.

An observed action may be related to an expected task. Suppose the system expects a task that executes a domain rule. If an observed action is one of the antecedents of the domain rule, the explainer assumes the task's explanation as a candidate explanation of the observed action. In order to find the path between the observed action and the task, the learning program runs meta rules backward. A declarative and explicit representation of meta rules makes it easy for the learning program to run the system backward.

When the learning system fails to find a candidate explanation for the observed action, this suggests that the knowledge base is missing the piece of information that prompted the expert to take the observed action. This *expectation failure* triggers the repair module to refine the incomplete knowledge base by finding missing knowledge that will allow a coherent explanation of the expert's actions.

Context analysis

An explanation is relevant to an observed action if it coheres with the problem solving context as well as addresses the action. To understand an action by finding an explanation, it is important to recognize whether an explanation is relevant to the context as well as the observed action. Even if a single goal may prompt the human expert to ask a question, when we try to find reverse mappings from the question to possible explanations, there will be many possible answers. To single out the correct explanation among them requires reasoning about the context where the action is taken.

In general, experts tend to take an action which is coherent with their problem solving context. For example, physicians usually ask follow-up questions on current hypotheses or symptoms. When human apprentices encounter difficulties to understand an expert's actions, they have an urge to find an explanation based on the human expert's problem solving context.

Constrain context failure

The learning program observes a human expert's action one at a time and generates a set of explanations of the action. An explanation consists of a strategy knowledge source name, such as *clarify_finding*, and a focus of attention such as *headache* (see a knowledge source example in section).

The context analysis program maps an observed action on the explanation plane (see Figure 2). The explanation plane has two axes. The strategy axis represents all the predefined strategy knowledge sources. The focus axis represents human expert's actions, derived facts, and hypotheses. An explanation on this plane has a pointer to a set of actions that are explained by the explanation. The context analysis program also keeps track of observed actions until a context failure occurs.

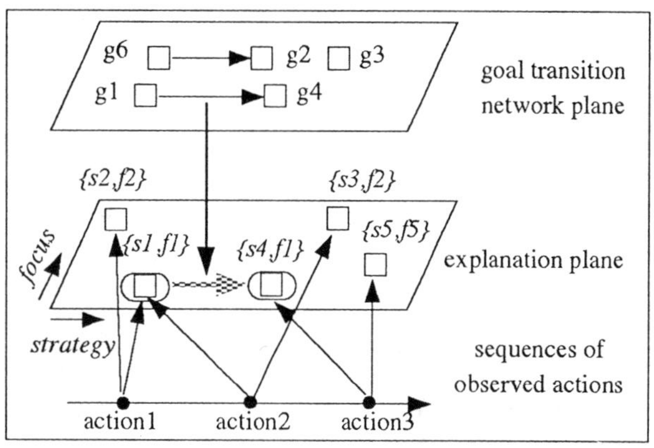

Figure 2: A context transition guided by a goal transition network

Since an action can have multiple explanations, the mapping may be one-to-one or one-to-many. An explanation on the explanation plane becomes a sub-context that explains a subset of observed actions. When the context analysis program inputs the set of explanations of the first action, it creates as many sub-contexts as explanations in the set. As the context analysis program inputs a succession of explanation sets, it creates many sub-contexts that explain a subset of observed actions. Since the context analysis program keeps track of observed actions, it can find a sub-context that explains all the actions. Such a sub-context is considered as the context of the observed actions.

However, this simple method to build a context may produce many redundant context failures even if the human expert changes his or her goal slightly. It is necessary for the context analysis program to understand such change and not to consider it as a context failure. We use a goal transition network to identify a natural goal transition from a context failure (see Figure 2).

There are at least three factors which can be justified as rational bases for people to make causal descriptions: contiguity, similarity, and statistical [Anderson, 1987]. Our context analysis program currently considers contiguity and similarity factors to constrain redundant context failures. By the similarity factor we mean similar contexts. Contexts are similar if their strategy axes are the same and their focus axes can be grouped by a known relation. For example, suppose `context-1` and `context-2` consist of (*clarify_finding, surgery*) and (*clarify_finding, neurosurgery*), respectively. Since *surgery* and *neurosurgery* is defined by a relation *more_specific*, a transition from `context-1` to `context-2` is considered as a natural one. This transition describes a human expert's natural stream of diagnosis that attempts to find out more detailed facts progressively.

By the contiguity factor we mean contiguous transition. A transition from `context-1` to `context-2` is contiguous if their focus axes are the same and the transition between strategy is declared to be plausible. For example, (*clarify_finding, X*) and (*process_finding, X*) [1] are different contexts. When a human expert starts to ask a question that is explained by (*process_finding, X*), after he or she asked questions related to (*clarify_finding, X*), the observed action can not be explained by the current context (*clarify_finding, X*). Hence, the simple context analysis program considers the explanation (*process_finding, X*) as a context failure and tries to repair the failure. However, the transition from (*clarify_finding, X*) to (*process_finding, X*) is a stream of the diagnostic reasoning sequence. This transition describes a human expert's reasoning approach that predicts hypotheses related to a symptom after he or she find out more detailed facts of the symptom.

A transition on the goal transition network plane represents such allowable transitions to guide context transitions. In the current system, the goal transition network is explicitly hand-coded.

[1] The first seeks more specific information and the second applies domain rules related to X.

In Figure 2, `action1` and `action2` are described by a context {*s1,f1*}. Because no transitions are known from {*s2,f2*} to {*s3,f2*} and {*s1, f1*} to {*s3,f2*} in the goal transition network, only {*s1,f1*} becomes the context when `action2` is observed. Then, the context analysis program projects explanations of `action3` for context {*s1,f1*}. If the context {*s1,f1*} were unable to cover any explanation of `action3`, the transition model would guide the induction program in considering the transition from {*s1,f1*} to {*s4,f1*} as a natural one.

Suppose projected explanations of an `action-n` are too far from the current context on the explanation plane and no paths in the goal transition model can explain them. Then the context analysis program considers two possible cases: the expert may have changed his or her goal or the system may be missing a piece of information. When the context analysis program encounters such a situation where no explanation coheres with the context, it saves the current context, restarts the context analysis by posting sub-contexts of `action-n`, and waits to see the next actions. If some of the sub-contexts explain subsequent actions, the context analysis program assumes the expert changed his or her goal. However, if the subsequent actions are explained by the saved context instead of the sub-contexts of `action-n`, the explanations of `action-n` are not coherent with the expert's problem solving behavior. The context analysis program recognizes the explanations of the `action-n` as a context failure. If a failure driven learning system does not employ this context analysis, multiple explanations may mask a learning opportunity in this situation.

Failure Recovery and Constraints

When the global credit assignment program encounters an explanation failure, it triggers a repair module. The repair module employs top-down and bottom-up approaches to infer new knowledge. While the top-down interpretation fires a set of knowledge sources to predict actions and tasks, the bottom-up interpretation accepts observed actions and finds tasks related to the actions by running the meta rules backward.

We employ a combined method (see Figure 1) that first runs meta rules backwards [Wilkins, 1988b] and then runs strategy knowledge sources forward. Both searches will suggest plausible paths which connect the observed action and the strategy knowledge sources, and also post constraints to predicates in the paths. These constraints and the use of the meta-level strategy knowledge enable the repair module to reduce search space.

Construction of explanation and constraints

When the learning system detects expectation failures and context failures, it invokes a bottom-up repair module that drives meta rules backward from an observed action to tasks (see Figure 1). Since in medical di-

Disease	Learning opportunities	Method-1		Method-2		
		expectation failure	multiple masking	expectation failure	context failure	multiple masking
Bacterial Meningitis	40	11	29	11	8	21
Brain Abscess	3	0	3	0	1	2
Cluster Headache	16	16	0	16	0	0
Fungal Meningitis	0	0	0	0	0	0
Migraine	5	0	5	0	2	3
Myco-TB Meningitis	6	6	0	6	0	0
Primary Brain Tumor	1	0	1	0	1	0
Subarach Hemorrhage	34	18	16	18	13	3
Tension Headache	3	0	3	0	3	0
Viral Meningitis	26	15	11	15	3	8
Totals	134	66	68	66	31	37

Table 1: Comparison of failure detection with and without context analysis. *Method-2* and *Method-1* represent the failure detection method with and without context analysis, respectively.

agnosis, the backward search may suffer from combinatorial explosion, the bottom-up repair module runs the meta rules backward from an observed action to tasks that are used as subgoals of strategy knowledge sources. Hence the backward search is not deep and the number of paths from the action to tasks is small. The bottom-up repair module generates constraints of the tasks as well as finds tasks that are related to the observed action. For example, suppose the human expert asks about *seizures* and the learning system fails to find explanations of the action. The bottom-up module runs meta-rules backward from the observed action to a task such as *apply_rule(domain_rule1)* and the constraint that *domain_rule1* must have *seizures* in the antecedent. The tasks and constraints of the argument generated by the bottom-up module are used to determine the subgoals of strategy knowledge sources.

The top-down repair module is run after the bottom-up module and determines the heads of strategy knowledge sources based on the context and sub-contexts. This assumes the human expert diagnoses a case in a context sensitive way. The top-down module instantiates a set of strategy knowledge sources using subgoals, constraints, and instantiated heads generated both repair modules. A strategy knowledge source in MINERVA is designed to be instantiated by the bindings of head and subgoal. Suppose the current context is (*explore_hypothesis*, *primary_brain_tumor*), then the top-down repair module instantiates *explore_hypothesis* strategy knowledge source and adds a constraint that *domain_rule1* must conclude *primary_brain_tumor*. In this example, *domain_rule1* has one antecedent *seizures* and must conclude *primary_brain_tumor*.

The constraints are used to remove an instantiated knowledge source from the candidate explanations of the unexplained action. The top-down repair module first removes an instantiate knowledge source whose constraints of a premise are contradictory.[2] Suppose an instantiated knowledge source has a constraint that *domain_rule1* must have an antecedent *value(headache,yes)*. However, if the patient is known *not* to have a *headache*, the knowledge source contains a contradictory condition and is removed from the candidate set.

If a premise of an instantiated knowledge source is not contradictory and fails to be satisfied, it may be the missing knowledge that is responsible for the failed explanation. Suppose there is no rule that has the desired symptom in the antecedent and the desired disease in the consequent; this means the knowledge base is missing the domain rule. The repair module identifies that a domain rule is missing and induces the domain rule which has the desired disease in the consequent and has the symptom in the antecedent, using the case library. Moreover, the repair module produces new domain rules which have more specific antecedents and also conclude the disease. If this domain rule generates a coherent explanation and its belief value calculated by Pearl's method [Pearl, 1986] over a library of 112 solved cases exceeds the threshold, it will be added to the knowledge base.

Experimental Results

We have completed two experiments using the knowledge refinement method described in this paper. The first experiment tests the performance of the failure detection program. The second experiment tests the repair module which generates new domain knowledge based on the failure, and also tests the diagnostic accuracy of the MINERVA expert system shell [Park *et al.*, 1989] after learning has taken place. We used a collection of 112 solved medical cases that were obtained from records at Stanford Medical Hospital.

The synthetic agent method [Wilkins, 1988a] was used in experiments: MINERVA with complete domain knowledge is used as a synthetic agent. We created ten incomplete knowledge bases. An incomplete knowledge base is missing all the domain rules which conclude a

[2] MINERVA uses a maintenance system to maintain the dependency structure of facts and hypotheses.

Disease	Incomplete KB Perf.1	Refined KB Perf.2	Refined KB Perf.3
Bacterial Meningitis	50	59	61
Brain Abscess	54	54	57
Cluster Headache	55	58	58
Fungal Meningitis	53	53	53
Migraine	57	57	58
Myco-TB Meningitis	57	61	61
Primary Brain Tumor	60	60	77
Subarach Hemorrhage	53	59	60
Tension Headache	53	53	60
Viral Meningitis	60	62	67
All diseases		64	75

Table 2: The performance of MINERVA after failure driven learning and context analysis. Each experiment is done over a library of 112 solved medical cases.

specific disease (see Table 1). In Table 1, *learning opportunity* means that a missing rule is a part of the synthetic agent's explanation. *Multiple masking* represents a case where multiple explanations mask an explanation failure. When the failure detection method without context analysis is applied, it can detect 66 out of 134 missing domain rule applications (49.2% accuracy). When the failure detection method with context analysis is used, it can detect 97 out of 134 missing domain rule applications (72.4%accuracy). Hence, the proposed method increased the number of learning opportunities by 47%.

In Table 2, under performance 1 column, the performance of MINERVA with missing knowledge is reported. Each experiment is done over a library of 112 solved cases with an incomplete knowledge base that is missing all the rules that conclude one designated disease. Under performance 2 column, the improved performance after failure driven learning without context analysis is presented. Each incomplete knowledge base is refined by the failure driven learning method. And each improved knowledge base is used to diagnose the 112 case library. Under performance 3 column, further improved performance after failure driven learning and context analysis is reported. After the system learns new knowledge for each disease, it adds all the knowledge to the existing knowledge base. The results of experiments with these new knowledge bases are shown in the last rows of performance 2 and performance 3 columns.

Conclusion

We have presented an effective and efficient knowledge acquisition method that employs failure driven learning. The failure detection process has been demonstrated to pinpoint the context failure as well as the expectation failure. It enables the learning program to avoid masking of learning opportunities due to the existence of multiple explanations, thereby improving the performance of the knowledge acquisition process. Our failure repair approach generates explanations and constraints using a bottom-up search followed by a top-down instantiation. A subject for future work is to develop a method which can reduce the number of redundant context changes by building a more robust goal transition model.

Acknowledgments

We would especially like to thank Marianne Winslett for providing invaluable comments on this paper. Chip Mayse also provided helpful comments.

We would like to express our deep gratitude to Ziad Najem, Lawrence Chachere, Kok-Wah Tan for their major role in the design and implementation of the MINERVA shell. This research was supported by ONR grant N00014-88K0124.

References

[Anderson, 1987] J.R. Anderson. Causal analysis and inductive learning. In *Proceedings of the Fourth International Workshop on Machine Learning*, Urvine,CA, 1987.

[Clancey, 1987] W.J. Clancey. Acquiring, representing, and evaluating a competence model of diagnostic strategy. In *Contributions to the Nature of Expertise*. Lawerce Erlbaum Press, 1987.

[Dietterich and Buchanan, 1981] T.G. Dietterich and B.G. Buchanan. The role of the critic in learning systems. Technical Report STAN-CS-81-891, Stanford University,CA., 1981.

[Kodratoff and Tecuci, 1987] Y. Kodratoff and T. Tecuci. What is an explanation in disciple? In *Proceedings of the Fourth International Machine Learning Workshop*, pages 160–166, Irvine,CA, 1987.

[Mitchell *et al.*, 1985] T.M. Mitchell, S. Mahadevan, and L.I. Steinberg. Leap: a learning apprentice for vlsi design. In *Proceedings of the National Conference on AI*, pages 573–580, Los Angeles,CA, August 1985.

[Park *et al.*, 1989] Y.T. Park, K.W. Tan, and David Wilkins. *MINERVA: A Knowledge Based System with Declarative Representation and Flexible Control.* Working Paper UIUC-KBS-89-01, Dept. of Computer Science, University of Illinois, Urbana, IL, 1989.

[Pearl, 1986] J. Pearl. On evidential reasoning in a hierarchy of hypotheses. *Artificial Intelligence*, 28:9–15, 1986.

[Wilkins, 1988a] D.C. Wilkins. Apprenticeship learning techniques for knowledge based systems. Technical Report STAN-CS-88-1242, Stanford University,CA., 1988.

[Wilkins, 1988b] D.C. Wilkins. Knowledge base refinement using apprenticeship learning techniques. In *Proceedings of the National Conference on AI*, pages 646–651, St. Paul, MN, August 1988.

A Design Based Approach to Constructing Computational Solutions to Diagnostic Problems

D. Volovik & I. A. Zualkernan
Department of Computer Science
University of Minnesota, Minneapolis, Minnesota USA

P. E. Johnson
Department of Information & Decision Sciences
University of Minnesota, Minneapolis, Minnesota USA

C. E. Matthews
IBM Application Business Systems, Rochester, Minnesota USA

Abstract

Troubleshooting problems in real manufacturing environments impose constraints on admissible solutions that make the computational solutions offered by "troubleshooting from first principles" and the conventional experience based expert systems approaches infeasible. In this paper we present a computational theory for a solution to these problems that is based on the Principle of Locality and exploits the domain specific weak methods of troubleshooters and debugging knowledge of the designers. The computational theory is evaluated by generating focus of attention heuristics for a moderately complex digital device.

1. Computational Problem

We are interested in finding computational solutions to diagnostic problems as they occur in real manufacturing environments [Johnson 89]. This class of problems introduces two constraints on any computational solution: 1) the devices are large and complex, which precludes any solution that relies on a complete simulation or on enumeration of the various fault propagation paths through one or more abstractions of the device (e.g., [Genesereth 84],[de Kleer 87], [Reiter 87]) and 2) the life-cycle of these devices is short, which makes any solution (e.g., [Freiling 85]) that relies on trouble-shooting knowledge specific to a particular device unfeasible.

The first constraint suggests that any computational solution to this class of problems should have a uniform mechanism for handling the order of complexity of these devices. The second constraint precludes the use of any troubleshooting knowledge that is compiled for a specific device as an adaptation to the task of troubleshooting that device.

2. Computational Theory

The task of troubleshooting complex large-scale devices can be viewed as a two step process: 1) Determine an appropriate search space in which the fault is "local" [Davis 84] and 2) Apply weak-troubleshooting methods on this space to locate the fault. A search space is defined by a specification of appropriate 'pathways of interactions" that are exploited by a weak troubleshooting method.

Although the definition of our computational problem precludes the use of device-specific troubleshooting knowledge, device-independent but *domain-specific* troubleshooting methods [Reed 88] developed by troubleshooters can be a valid component of a computational solution. However, a solution that relies solely on these methods, given the constraints of the computational problem is not adequate. There are two difficulties with such a solution:

1) Domain specific weak methods are used by troubleshooters only when the device specific heuristics fail; this means that the best performance one can expect from a solution that relies solely on these methods would be that of a troubleshooter's performance on a new device.

2) The locus of search spaces that can be used by troubleshooters is restricted by device representations available in their task environment. The representations of a device available to troubleshooters in real manufacturing environments, however, often consist of just the physical device itself (which leads to the used of a search space based on physical pathways of interaction) and at most one other level of abstraction (such as schematic for digital designs). This means that any solution that relies solely on weak-methods of troubleshooting will have the restriction that it can only work for faults that are 'local' in search spaces that can be derived from these representations. A large class of interesting faults are not 'local' in a search space derived from the physical representation of a device [Davis 84].

Another source of knowledge that is admitted by the definition of the computational problem is that of designers conducting the task of debugging, which though different from troubleshooting, has components that are similar to the troubleshooting task. Designer's task environment has a rich variety of representations of the device. In any design process, these consist of various by-products of the design. For example, in the case of digital hardware design, the designers may use requirements, functional specifications and block level descriptions in addition to the schematics and the physical representation of a device.

Our solution to the computational problem described above is to exploit the knowledge of how designers debug designs in addition to the device-independent methods and search spaces of the troubleshooters. This solution has the advantage that it can detect faults that are not only 'local' in the search spaces of troubleshooters, but ones that are 'local' in the various spaces that result from the combination of the search spaces used by designers for debugging a class of devices.

This solution is based on a computational theory that can be stated as follows:

1) The task of troubleshooting is to determine the appropriate search space in which a fault is local and then apply *domain dependent* weak troubleshooting method to the search space until the fault is found.

2) The source for domain dependent weak troubleshooting methods is the task of troubleshooting in the domain.

3) The source for appropriate search spaces is task of debugging by designers in the domain during the design phase.

The construction of a computational solution based on the computational theory consist of the following steps:

1) Determine weak trouble-shooting methods used by troubleshooters in a domain.

2) Determine search spaces used by designers in debugging designs in the domain

3) Use the "principle of locality" as an organizational principle to construct a solution that applies weak troubleshooting methods of troubleshooters to search space used by the designers.

3. Experimental Validation of the Computational Theory

To asses the validity of the computational theory described above, we chose the domain of small card digital design. This is an appropriate domain under the definition of the computational problem as the small card designs are fairly complex devices (~ 10^2 - 10^3 components at the schematic level) and the life-cycles of these cards are short; typical life is ~ 2 years.

3.1 Constructing a Computational Solution for Digital Devices

Previous work done in the domain of troubleshooting digital devices indicates that troubleshooters use a variety of domain specific weak troubleshooting methods [Reed 89]. As a first test of the computational theory, we concentrate on a method called *initial focus of attention* method. This is a method that troubleshooters use to initially focus on a sub-set of the device, given certain symptoms. The symptoms in the case of digital design typically consist of test failures on a specific device.

As a first step in the validation process, a designer (with 10 years of experience with constructing small card digital designs) was asked to construct a design for an *Interrupt Control Coprocessor* with the following features:

- One level prioritized Interrupts
- Subroutine handling capabilities
- LIFO stack for return address storage
- Interrupt masking by software and hardware
- Stack full flag

The resulting device consisted of 254 components (LSI's and gates) with approximately 10^4 signals. In addition to the designing the device, the designer was also asked to write tests (see endnote #1) for the device (a normal part of the design process). The designer was asked to think aloud as he conducted the design and these comments (verbal protocols) were tape-recorded along with the various by-products generated by the designer as he constructed the design.

An analysis of the verbal protocols during the process of debugging design indicated that the designer used the search space schema for initial focus of attention shown in Figure 1.

This space is based on pathways of interaction that go across the various representations of design available to the designers (e.g., functional specifications, workbook level design and tests).

Given the nature of the search space used by the designers and the domain specific weak troubleshooting methods of troubleshooters, the principle of locality was used to construct a computational model that used "path following" weak method on the search space.

To apply the principle of locality we identify the types of faults that are local in component spaces of the search space. For example, in the space defined by test specifications, immediately obvious faults are patterns of test failures. These failures are detected in the space through observations of test outcomes generated by the testing equipment. Interactions of tests and specifications establish pathways of interaction between these two spaces. If pathways of interaction map local faults in one space (e.g. specification faults) into local faults in another space (e.g. test failures), propagating the faults from one space into another along the pathway is desirable. This allows detection of specification failures in a specification space by observing test failures in the test space.

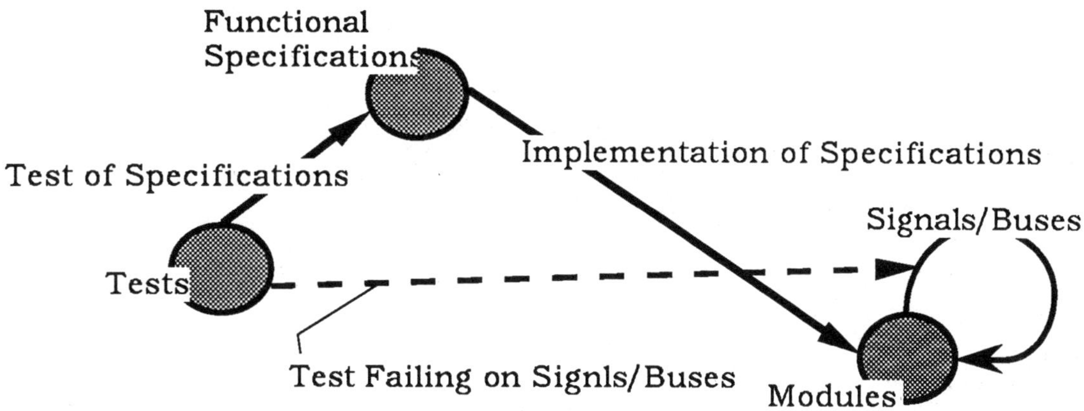

Figure 1. Search Space Schema for Focus of Attention

Similarly, failures of modules in workbook-level specification space are detectable through pathways of interaction between functional specifications and workbook-level modules. Single-stepping from failing tests to failing specifications to failing modules is an example of a weak search method for traversing along the pathways of interaction.

When local faults in one space cannot be mapped along pathways of interaction into local faults in another space, different pathways of interaction are required for successful diagnosis. *The suitable pathway should preserve the locality of faults.*

An instance of search space schema for focus of attention method for the interrupt controller (see Figure 2) demonstrates how the principle of locality is used to identify appropriate pathways of interaction. For example, test T3 verifies specifications C and E and test T8 verifies specifications A and C. Specification C is implemented by module *c*, specification E by modules *d* and *e*, and specification A by module *a*. If tests T3 and T8 both fail at the same time, specifications C and/or E are failing at the same time as specifications A and/or C are failing. Assuming singular faults and disjoint modules, one of modules *c* or *d* or *e* is failing at the same time as one of the modules *a* or *c* is failing. Thus, module *c* is failing and specification C is failing.

On the other hand, test T7 verifies specification B which is implemented by module *b*. If both T7 and T3 fail, *b* is failing at the same time as *c* or *d* or *e* is failing, which is not possible under the assumptions (singular faults and disjoint modules). Fault locality is not preserved along the pathways.

Different pathways of interaction that map test spaces into workbook-level spaces can be constructed by identifying signals (on which tests fail) with modules that generate these signals. In workbook-level spaces, for example, failure of tests T7 or T3 can be due to any of the signals *I, rd, halt, stf, mask, SEQ, pend0* or *SAV* failing. In test spaces, T7 failure is detected on *rd* and T3 on *halt.* In workbook-level spaces *rd* is generated by *d* or *e* and *halt* is generated by *d* or e, thus either *d* or *e*, for example, is faulty.

An application of the path following method to the above search space results in a computational solution that is based on the following heuristics:

(i) Start with a set of failing tests.

(ii) Use interactions of tests and functional specifications to propose a set of failing high level functional specifications, given a set of failing tests.

(iii) Use interactions of specifications via aggregation and decomposition to propose a set of failing low-level functional specifications.

(iv) Use an interaction across representations of low-level functional specifications and high-level workbook modules to propose a set of failing high-level workbook modules.

and

(i) Start with a set of failing tests.

(ii) Use the mapping between interactions of tests and functional specifications they check, and among modules via signals/busses to propose a set of failing high-level workbook modules, given a set of failing tests.

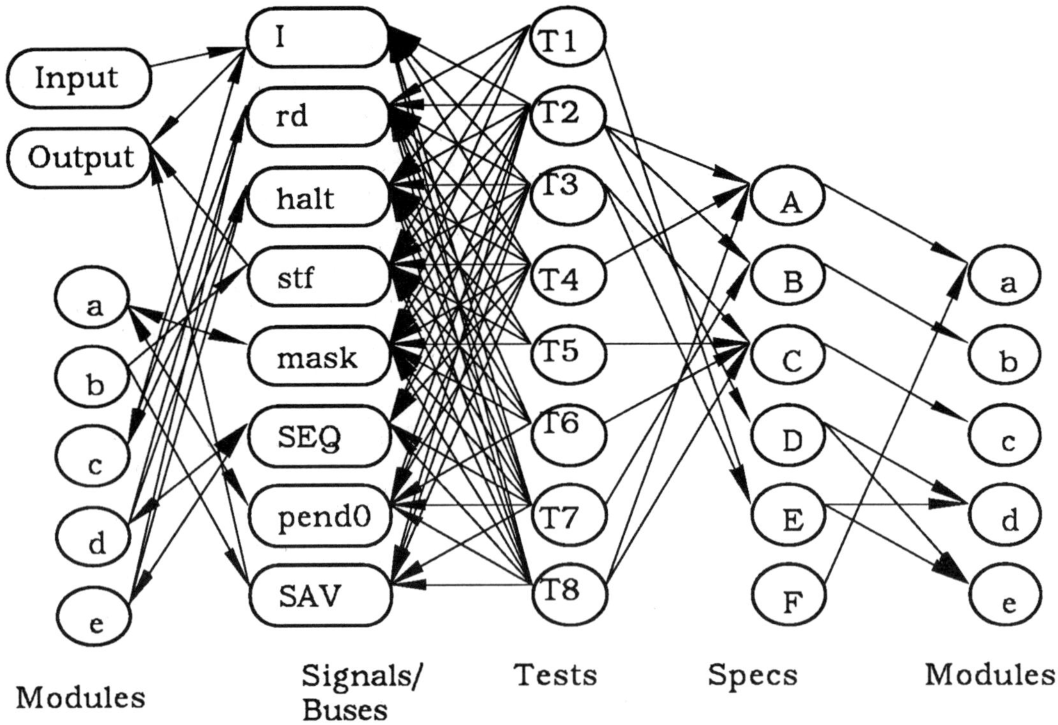

Figure 2: Instance of Search Space Schema for Focus of Attention

The above heuristics can be implemented by the following two rules:

IF
a substantial number of tests fail and a substantial number of test failures are caused by a variety of different test signals
THEN
among all the test that fail and that point to a possible failure of a set of functional units (areas) on the board, chose an area or areas that the majority of tests point to
ACTION
the areas most tests point to are likely to contain a fault.

IF
a substantial number of tests fail and a substantial number of test failures are caused by a small number of different test signals
THEN
among all the functional units or areas on the board that generate this small set of failing signals, chose the area that generates the most such failing signals
ACTION
the areas that generate the most failing signals are likely to contain the fault and the signals are good starting test points

Although in this paper we discuss only the *initial focus of attention* method, the corresponding search spaces for other domain dependent weak troubleshooting methods is given in Appendix A.

3.2 Evaluation of the Computational Solution

The validation of the computational solution was carried out as summarized in Figure 3.

A simulation model of the board as designed by the designers was constructed using a commercially available simulation environment running on IBM-PS/2 Model 70. A variety of faults such as bridge-faults, stuck-at faults and general component failure were introduced in the simulation. Bridge faults arise from shorts (see [Davis 84] for a description). The stuck-at faults consist of input or output of a component held to a constant value. Component failures were simulated by either eliminating the component or substituting one component for another. For example, a failed NOT gate behaves like a wire.

For each fault introduced, tests created by the designer were run on the simulation to produce test results for that fault. Test results for each fault were used as the input to the computational solution that generated the predictions about the area on the board where the fault exists (focus of attention).

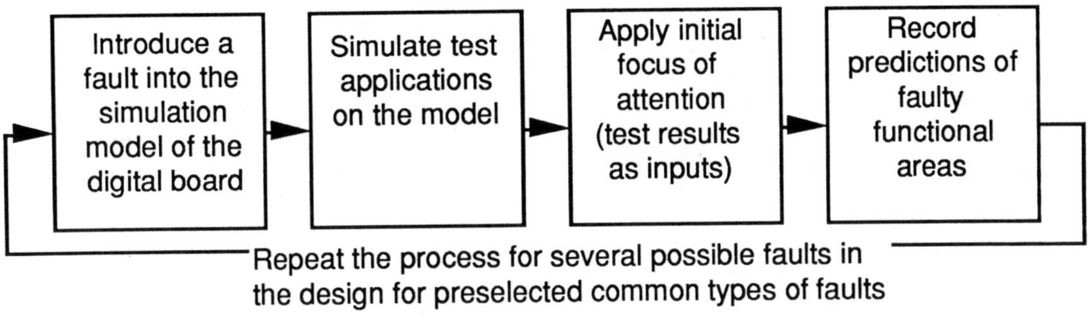

Figure 3. Process used to Evaluate the Computational Solution

3.3 Results

The results from testing the computational solution were evaluated by using the following two criteria:

$$\textit{Effectiveness} = \frac{\textit{Number of Correctly Predicted Faults}}{\textit{Total Number of Faults introduced}}$$

$$\textit{Power} = \frac{\textit{Number of Components in the Predicted Sub-set}}{\textit{Total Number of Components}}$$

Table 1. gives the distribution of the various types of faults introduced on the board.

Of the 27 faults introduced, the overall effectiveness was 77.8 %. The effectiveness measure of computational solution demonstrates that generated troubleshooting heuristics correctly predict a functional area on the board where the fault is located for 77.8% of all faults that were introduced.

The power of the focus of attention method is given in Table 2.

The reduction in search space measure from Table 2. demonstrates that the focus of attention method (on average) reduces the search area on the board where the fault is located to 27.9% of all the components (area) of the board. Comparing the best, worst and average cases in Table 2 demonstrates that computational solution might be imprecise, reducing the search by only to 70.5%, or very accurate, reducing the search to 8.8% of all components.

4. Conclusions

We are attempting to construct solutions to an interesting class of computational problems that impose unique constraints on an admissible solution. In this paper we have proposed a computational theory that exploits designer's knowledge obtained from the process of designing a device, and combines it with domain specific weak-troubleshooting methods by using the principle of locality as the organizational principle. We have also presented results on the feasibility of the computational theory by applying it to the process of designing digital devices to generate focus of attentions heuristics. The initial results, although limited, seem promising. We are in the process of extending the approach to incorporate additional weak methods.

Fault Type	Number of Faults Introduced	Number of Faults Caught
Stuck-at	10	7
Gate Failure	10	8
Bridge Faults	7	6

Table 1. Distribution of Faults Introduced to the Simulation Model

Power	Reduction in Search Space
Worst	70.5%
Best	8.8%
Average	27.9%

Table 2. Power of Focus of Attention Method

Bibliography

[Davis 84] R. Davis, "Diagnostic Reasoning Based on Structure and Behavior," Artificial Intelligence, No. 24, Volumes 1-3, 1984, pp. 347-410.

[Freiling 85] M. Freiling, J. Alexander, S. Messick, S. Rehfuss, and S. Shulman, "Starting a Knowledge Engineering Project: A Step-by-step Approach," The AI Magazine, No. 6, Vol. 3, 1985, pp. 150-164.

[Genesereth 84] M. R. Genesereth, "The Use of Design Descriptions in Automated Diagnosis," Artificial Intelligence, No. 24, 1984, pp. 411-436.

[Johnson 89] P. E. Johnson, D. Volovik, I. A. Zualkernan and C. E. Matthews, "Design Knowledge for Discovering Troubleshooting Heuristics," in Proceedings of IASTED Symposium on Expert Systems Theory and Applications, June 26-28, 1989, Zurich, pp. 17-21.

[de Kleer 87] J. de Kleer and B. C. Williams, "Diagnosing Multiple Faults," Artificial Intelligence, No. 32, 1987, pp. 97-130.

[Reed 88] N. E. Reed, E. R. Stuck, and J. B. Moen, "Specialized Strategies: An Alternative to First Principles in Diagnostic Problem Solving," Proceedings of the Seventh National Conference on Artificial Intelligence, Vol. 1, August 1988, pp. 364-368.

[Reiter 87] R. Reiter, "A Theory of Diagnosis from First Principles," Artificial Intelligence, No. 32, 1987, pp. 57-95.

Endnote #1.

The typical tests written by designers are used by designers for validation and hence are not sufficient for troubleshooting as they only check top level functional specifications.

Appendix A

Domain Dependent Weak methods	Pathways of interactions that define the relevant Search Space	Source of interaction knowledge (from designers doing a debugging task)
Path-following by Easter-egging	(i) Correct interaction of a part with its surrounding at the observation time	(i) Schematic diagrams (e.g. including ground, 'high' and clock signals)
Path-following by single-stepping	(i) Correct interaction of a part with its surrounding at the observation time (ii) Violated high-level interaction to track forward or backward	(i) Block-diagrams showing adjacent block interactions (ii) Block interfaces on the schematic diagrams
Path-following by subdivision	(i) Correct interaction of a part with its surrounding at the observation time (ii) Violated high-level interaction pathway to subdivide (iii) Correct interaction at a remote point along the interaction pathway	(i) Block-diagram showing block interactions and interaction pathways (ii) Block interfaces and interaction pathways on the schematics (iii) Test definitions (sources of stimuli for the initial correct and incorrect interactions along interaction pathways)
Compare-and-conquer	(i) Strong similarity of interactions of two or more parts (e.g. two signals are always 'high' at the same time)	(i) System and sub-system functional level specifications
Stateless analysis	(i) Stable states where the failure occurs (ii) Correct interaction of a part with its surrounding at the time of the failure	(i) System and sub-system functional level specifications (ii) Finite state diagrams (ii) State-control signals on the schematic diagram
Floating	(i) Pathway of interactions forming a feedback loop (ii) Appropriate signal value to force onto the floated part interface	(ii) Finite state diagrams (ii) State-control signal loops on the schematic diagram
Focus-of-attention	(i) Test-to-specification map (ii) Specification-to-subsystem map	(i) Test definitions (ii) System and sub-system functional level specifications (iii) Block-diagrams

Knowledge Representation

Causal Theories for Nonmonotonic Reasoning

Hector Geffner
hector@ibm.com
T. J. Watson Research Center
P. O. Box 704, Room H1-K10
Yorktown Heights, N.Y. 10598

Abstract

Causal theories are default theories which explicitly accommodate a distinction between 'explained' and 'unexplained' propositions. This is accomplished by means of an operator 'C' in the language for which propositions α are assumed explained when literals of the form $C\alpha$ hold. The behavior of causal theories is determined by a preference relation on models based on the minimization of unexplained abnormality. We show that causal networks, general logic programs and theories for reasoning about change can be all naturally expressed as causal theories. We also develop a proof-theory for causal theories and discuss how they relate to autoepistemic theories, prioritized circumscription, and Pearl's C-E calculus.

Introduction

Preferential entailment has emerged as a powerful means for specifying non-monotonic behavior. An order on interpretations determines the preferred models of a given theory, and those models determine in turn the propositions that the theory non-monotonically entails. Shoham [1988], who most clearly articulated the framework, used a preference order on interpretations to specify the behavior of temporal theories dealing with change. Similar proposals have been advanced for logic programs with negation [Przymusinski, 1987] and defeasible inheritance hierarchies [Krishnaprasad *et al.*, 1989] among others.

In all these proposals, the preference order adopted is tailored to the particular task or domain addressed. Still, the appeal of preferential entailment as a unifying framework for non-monotonic inference could be enhanced if a general domain-independent criterion for inferring preferences from theories could be developed. A general proof-theory, for instance, if available, could then be imported by any individual domain as well. Similarly, the resulting framework would subsume the expressive power of individual domains, enabling a user to express, say, theories which combine patterns of inference characteristic of theories for reasoning about change with those of general logic programs.

An attempt in this direction was recently reported in [Geffner, 1989b], where it was shown that non-monotonic inference in several domains of interest in AI could be understood in terms of a model preference criterion based on the minimization of *unexplained* abnormality. 'Explanations' were defined as logical derivations constrained by the *form* of the formulas in the knowledge base. A formula $\neg p \Rightarrow q$, for example, was assumed to permit an explanation of q in terms of an assumption $\neg p$, but to exclude an explanation of p in terms of an assumption $\neg q$. Thus, the different semantics associated with two logically equivalent logic programs $q \leftarrow \neg p$ and $p \leftarrow \neg q$, for instance, could be accounted for.

In this paper we pursue the same goal and intuition as in [Geffner, 1989b] but proceed with a different formalization. Rather than appealing to the syntactic form of the rules in the knowledge base to distinguish between logically equivalent theories, we appeal to a richer language. Such a language includes a new operator 'C' for which propositions α are assumed explained when literals of the form $C\alpha$ hold. Default theories over the new language are called *causal theories*. As we will show, not only causal theories do abide by the principle that equal models imply equal behavior, but they also provide a significant additional expressive power. Causal networks, general logic programs and theories about change can be all naturally expressed as causal theories. Moreover causal theories lend themselves to a simple sound and complete proof-theory.

Causal Theories

A causal theory is a default theory augmented with a 'causal' operator 'C.' Default theories are essentially what McCarthy's [1986] refers to as "abnormality" theories: classical first order theories in which certain literals, abnormalities (resp. assumptions), are expected to be false (resp. true).[1] The language of causal theories is closed under all standard connectives, while ex-

[1]Note that unlike McCarthy, we will be concerned with abnormality *literals* as opposed to abnormal *individuals*. The trade-offs involved in that choice are discussed in [Geffner, 1989a, section 4.3].

cluding expressions with embedded causal operators. We usually denote abnormalities by atoms of the form $\mathbf{ab_i}(a)$, and use the symbol α possibly indexed as a variable ranging over abnormalities. Additionally, we often partition the formulas in a causal theory T into two sets: a background context K containing the formulas which express generic knowledge (e.g. "penguins are birds"), and an evidence set E containing the formulas which express knowledge specific to the situation at hand (e.g. "Tweety is a bird"; see [Geffner and Pearl, 1987]).

The operator C is most commonly used to encode causal or explanatory rules of the form "if a then b" as sentences of the form $a \Rightarrow Cb$ (see [Pearl, 1988a]). A rule such as "rain causes the grass to be wet" may thus be expressed as a sentence **rain** $\Rightarrow$ C**grass_wet**, which can then be read as saying that if **rain** is true, **grass_wet** is explained. We assume that the operator C obeys certain minimal constraints which correspond to the postulates of system T in modal logic [Hughes and Cresswell, 1968]:

[C1] $C\alpha \Rightarrow \alpha$
[C2] $C(\alpha \Rightarrow \beta) \Rightarrow (C\alpha \Rightarrow C\beta)$
[C3] If $\vdash_K \alpha$ then $C\alpha$

[C1] forces every explained proposition to be true, while [C2] and [C3] guarantee the set of explained proposition to be closed under deduction. The expression '$\vdash_K \alpha$' in [C3] is an abbreviation of $K \vdash \alpha$, which says that in any causal theory every proposition that logically follows from its background context is explained.

An interpretation M that satisfies a causal theory T and the constraints [C1]–[C3] will be said to be a model of T. Moreover, we will refer to the set of abnormalities rendered true by an interpretation M as the *gap* of the interpretation and denote it as $A[M]$. Since the preference relation on models will be an exclusive function of the model gaps we will find useful to group models into classes of models. Formally, the *class* $\mathcal{C}$ of T *with a gap* $A[\mathcal{C}]$ will represent the non-empty collection of models M of T with a gap $A[M] \subseteq A[\mathcal{C}]$. Intuitively, since the negation of abnormalities are *assumptions* expected to hold, a class $\mathcal{C}$ with a gap $A[\mathcal{C}]$ represents the collection of models which validate all assumptions logically compatible with $A[\mathcal{C}]$. Models and classes of T with *minimal gaps* will be said to be *minimal*. Moreover, we will say that a proposition p *holds* in a class $\mathcal{C}$ of T, when p holds in every model in $\mathcal{C}$. Proof-theoretically this is equivalent to require that p be derivable from T and a set of assumptions compatible with $A[\mathcal{C}]$.[2]

The operator C is used as a device to order the *classes* of models of the theories T of interest. As in [Geffner, 1989b], such a preference order is defined as a function of the abnormalities and the *explained* abnormalities in the different classes. An abnormality α is *explained* in a class $\mathcal{C}$ when the literal $C\alpha$ holds in $\mathcal{C}$. If we denote the set of explained abnormalities in a class $\mathcal{C}$ by $A^e[\mathcal{C}]$, then the preference relation on classes of a theory T can be described as follows:

Definition 1 *A class* $\mathcal{C}$ *is* as preferred *as a class* $\mathcal{C}'$ *iff* $A[\mathcal{C}] - A^e[\mathcal{C}] \subseteq A[\mathcal{C}']$. $\mathcal{C}$ *is* preferred to $\mathcal{C}'$ *iff* $\mathcal{C}$ *is as preferred as* $\mathcal{C}'$ *but* $\mathcal{C}'$ *is* not *as preferred as* $\mathcal{C}$.

In words, a class $\mathcal{C}$ is preferred to a class $\mathcal{C}'$ when every abnormality in $\mathcal{C}$ but not in $\mathcal{C}'$ has an explanation, but not vice versa. Notice that this preference relation on classes is not necessarily transitive, and thus, certain care is required for defining the propositions which a given theory *causally entails.*

Let us say that a collection $\mathcal{B}$ of classes constitute a *basis* for a theory T if for every class $\mathcal{C}$ of T not in $\mathcal{B}$, there is a class $\mathcal{C}'$ in $\mathcal{B}$ such that $\mathcal{C}'$ is preferred to $\mathcal{C}$. Moreover let us say that a basis $\mathcal{B}$ *supports* a proposition p if p holds in every class in $\mathcal{B}$. Then, we will say that a proposition p is *causally entailed* by a causal theory T when there is a basis for T which supports p.

Most theories T of interest will be well-founded in the sense that for any *non-minimal* model M of T there will be a *minimal* model M' of T such that $A[M'] \subset A[M]$.[3] In such cases, causal entailment can be computed by considering the minimal classes of T only. Indeed, $\mathcal{B}$ will be a basis for a well-founded theory T iff for every *minimal* class $\mathcal{C}$ of T *not* in $\mathcal{B}$, $\mathcal{B}$ includes a *minimal* class $\mathcal{C}'$ preferred to $\mathcal{C}$.

Moreover, T will often possess a single *minimal* basis $\mathcal{B}$. In such cases, we will refer to the classes in $\mathcal{B}$ as the *preferred classes* of T. For such theories causal entailment can be cast in the more familiar form in which a proposition is causally entailed when it holds in all the preferred classes.

Example 1 Let us consider first a simple causal theory T given by the single sentence $\neg\mathbf{ab_1} \Rightarrow C\mathbf{ab_2}$, where $\mathbf{ab_1}$ and $\mathbf{ab_2}$ are two different abnormalities. Such a theory admits two minimal classes: a class $\mathcal{C}_1$, comprised by the models of T which only sanction the abnormality $\mathbf{ab_1}$, and a class $\mathcal{C}_2$, comprised of the models which only sanction the abnormality $\mathbf{ab_2}$. Thus $\mathcal{C}_1$ has an associated gap $A[\mathcal{C}_1] = \{\mathbf{ab_1}\}$, while $\mathcal{C}_2$ has an associated gap $A[\mathcal{C}_2] = \{\mathbf{ab_2}\}$. Both classes represent the minimal classes of T, as there is no model of T that satisfies both $\neg\mathbf{ab_1}$ and $\neg\mathbf{ab_2}$, together with the restriction $C\alpha \Rightarrow \alpha$. The abnormalities α explained in each class $\mathcal{C}$ can be determined by testing which literals $C\alpha$ hold in $\mathcal{C}$. As we said, this amounts checking whether there is a set of assumptions legitimized by $\mathcal{C}$ which together with T implies $C\alpha$. Thus, in the class $\mathcal{C}_2$, the abnormality $\mathbf{ab_2}$ is

[2] The notions of derivability and consistency are to be understood relative to the postulates [C1]–[C3].

[3] A sufficient condition for T to be well-founded is that T gives rise to a finite number of bound assumptions, where an assumption is bound when it is in conflict with other assumptions (see [Geffner, 1989a]).

explained as the literal Cab_2 logically follows from T and the assumption $\neg\mathbf{ab_1}$. On the other hand, the abnormality $\mathbf{ab_1}$ is *not* explained in $\mathcal{C}_1$, as there is no set of assumptions validated by $\mathcal{C}_1$ which supports the literal Cab_1. It follows then, that the class $\mathcal{C}_2$ is preferred to $\mathcal{C}_1$, as $A[\mathcal{C}_2] - A^c[\mathcal{C}_2] = \emptyset \subseteq A[\mathcal{C}_1]$, but $A[\mathcal{C}_1] - A^c[\mathcal{C}_1] = \{\mathbf{ab_1}\} \not\subseteq A[\mathcal{C}_2] = \{\mathbf{ab_2}\}$. Furthermore, since the theory T is well-founded, and $\mathcal{C}_1$ and $\mathcal{C}_2$ are the only minimal classes of T, it follows then that $\mathcal{B} = \{\mathcal{C}_2\}$ is the single minimal basis of T, and thus, that $\mathcal{C}_2$ is the single preferred class of T. As a result, the propositions $\neg\mathbf{ab_1}$ and $\mathbf{ab_2}$ which hold in $\mathcal{C}_2$ are (causally) entailed by T.

Applications

In this section we consider the use of causal theories for reasoning about change and for specifying and extending the semantics of general logic programs. For the use of causal theories for inheritance and abductive reasoning see [Geffner, 1989a].

Reasoning about Change

Theories for reasoning about change need to represent the effects of actions, the conditions which can prevent actions from achieving their normal effects, and the tendency of certain aspects of the world (fluents) to remain stable (see [McDermott, 1982]). Here we will refer to the first type of rules as *change* rules, to the second type as *cancellation* rules, and to the third type as *persistence* rules.

Change, cancellation and persistence rules can interact in various ways. The Yale shooting scenario [Hanks and McDermott, 1987] illustrates a problem that results from spurious interactions between change and persistence rules. We now present general guidelines to locally map general theories for reasoning about change into causal theories which avoid those problems. The guidelines are uncommitted about the particular temporal notation used. For simplicity, we use a simple reified temporal language sufficient to illustrate the relevant issues. Other notations could be used as well. The notation $p(x)_t$ below, where p is a predicate and t is a time point, is used as an abbreviation of the sentence $\text{Holds}(p(x), t)$, to read "fluent $p(x)$ holds at time t." We also assume for simplicity a discrete time where t precedes $t+1$.

First we specify the encoding of rules about change. A rule describing the effect $\mathtt{e}(x)$ of an action $\mathtt{a}(x)$ with precondition $\mathtt{p}(x)$ is encoded as a causal rule of the form:

$$\mathtt{p}(x)_t \wedge \mathtt{a}(x)_t \Rightarrow \text{C}\mathtt{e}(x)_{t+1}$$

where x is a tuple of variables and both x and t are universally quantified. Such a rule can be read as stating that given the precondition $\mathtt{p}(x)$, $\mathtt{a}(x)$ causes or explains $\mathtt{e}(x)$.

Often, however, rules about change are defeasible. Defeasible rules about change are encoded by means of a unique abnormality predicate $\mathbf{ab_i}$ and a *pair* of causal rules:

$$\mathtt{p}(x)_t \wedge \mathtt{a}(x)_t \wedge \neg\mathbf{ab_i}(x)_t \Rightarrow \text{C}\mathtt{e}(x)_{t+1}$$

$$\mathtt{p}(x)_t \wedge \mathtt{a}(x)_t \wedge \text{C}\neg\mathtt{e}(x)_{t+1} \Rightarrow \text{C}\mathbf{ab_i}(x)_t$$

where the second rule simply asserts that the violation of an expected change is explained when there is an explanation for the negation of the expected effect (a similar rule is needed for modeling inheritance hierarchies [Geffner, 1989a]).

The persistence of a fluent f (e.g. $\mathtt{on(a,b)}$), on the other hand, is encoded by the expressions:

$$f_t \wedge \neg\mathbf{ab_i}(f)_t \Rightarrow f_{t+1}$$

$$\text{C}\neg f_{t+1} \Rightarrow \text{C}\mathbf{ab_i}(f)_t$$

where $\mathbf{ab_i}(f)_t$ is an abbreviation of the atom $\mathbf{ab_i}(f, t)$, read "the persistence of f holds at time t." Thus, while the first rule expresses the tendency of fluents to remain stable, the second rule expresses that changes are explained when the negation of the projected fluent is explained.

For the causal encoding of a version of the Yale Shooting problem, see [Geffner, 1989a]. Here we will consider a slightly richer example due to Ginsberg and Smith [1988].

Example 2 Let us assume that there is a room with some ducts that maintain the room ventilated. Moreover, an object sitting on a duct, blocks the duct, and if all ducts get blocked, the room becomes stuffy. This information is encoded in a causal theory with background:

$$\mathtt{duct}(x) \wedge \exists y.\,\mathtt{on}(y,x)_t \Rightarrow \text{C}\mathtt{blocked}(x)_t$$

$$[\forall x.\mathtt{duct}(x) \Rightarrow \mathtt{blocked}(x)_t] \Rightarrow \text{C}\mathtt{stuffy}_{t+1}$$

$$\mathtt{move\_to}(x,y)_t \wedge \neg\mathbf{ab_1}(x,y)_t \Rightarrow \text{C}\mathtt{on}(x,y)_{t+1}$$

$$\mathtt{move\_to}(x,y)_t \wedge \text{C}\neg\mathtt{on}(x,y)_{t+1} \Rightarrow \text{C}\mathbf{ab_1}(x,y)_t$$

The persistence of the fluents $\mathtt{on}(x,y)$, $\mathtt{stuffy}$, and $\mathtt{blocked}(x,y)$, and their negations, is expressed as stipulated above. To keep in mind that all these fluents are really *terms*,[4] we use the notation $\overline{f}$ to denote the fluent which is the complement of f. Thus, for instance, $\overline{\mathtt{on(a,b)}}$ stands for the 'negation' of $\mathtt{on(a,b)}$. Namely, if $\mathtt{on(a,b)}$ holds at time t, $\overline{\mathtt{on(a,b)}}$ will not, and vice versa. This is expressed by a constraint

$$f_t \Rightarrow \neg\overline{f}_t$$

which renders f and $\overline{f}$ incompatible, provided that the complement of $\overline{f}$ is f itself.

Finally, we need to express that an object cannot be on two different places at the same time:

$$\mathtt{on}(x,y)_t \wedge \mathtt{on}(x,z)_t \Rightarrow y = z$$

Given this background K, we consider a theory $T = \langle K, E\rangle$ describing a room with two ducts $\mathtt{d_1}$ and $\mathtt{d_2}$. Furthermore, at time $\mathtt{t} = \mathtt{0}$ it is known that the room

[4] Recall that $\mathtt{blocked}(x,y)_t$ is an abbreviation of the *atom* $\text{Holds}(\mathtt{blocked}(x,y), t)$.

is not stuffy, that a block **a** is sitting on top of duct $\mathtt{d_1}$, and that a block **b** is sitting on a place different than $\mathtt{d_2}$. Namely, $E = \{\mathtt{duct}(x) \Rightarrow x = \mathtt{d_1} \vee x = \mathtt{d_2}, \overline{\mathtt{stuffy_0}}, \mathtt{on(a,d_1)_0}, \overline{\mathtt{on(b,d_2)_0}}\}$.

In the context T, the fluents $\overline{\mathtt{stuffy_0}}$, $\mathtt{on(a,d_1)_0}$, and $\overline{\mathtt{on(b,d_2)_0}}$ project both forward and backward in time. If block **b** is moved to duct $\mathtt{d_2}$ at time $\mathtt{t} = 0$, however, conflicts among these projections arise, resulting in three classes of minimal models: the intended class $\mathcal{C}$ where the action is successful and, as a result, the two ducts get blocked and the room becomes stuffy; the class $\mathcal{C}'$, where the action is successful but somehow the block **a** has been removed from duct $\mathtt{d_1}$; and the class, $\mathcal{C}''$, where the action is unsuccessful and the block **b** remains in a place different than $\mathtt{d_2}$. Nonetheless, the interpretation of causal theories singles out the intended class $\mathcal{C}$ as the only preferred class, capturing the intuition that block **a** stays on $\mathtt{d_1}$ and that the room becomes stuffy. Note that such a behavior arises without the presence of explicit cancellation axioms.

Logic Programming

While the adequacy of the framework presented for reasoning about change rests mainly on empirical grounds —how natural it is to express knowledge about these domains and how closely the resulting behavior resembles the behavior intended by the user— a growing body of work on the semantics of general logic programs will permit us to assess the expressivity and semantics of causal theories on more formal grounds.

As it is standard, we consider only the Herbrand models of programs. Moreover, since for answering existential queries, a program involving variables can be shown to be equivalent to a program without variables, we will be dealing mainly with variable-free logic programs. More precisely, we will analyze the semantics of general logic programs in terms of two mappings $C_i[\cdot]$, $i = 1, 2$, each converting a program P into a causal theory $C_i[P]$. Each mapping associates a different "meaning" with P. For the purposes of logic programming, $C_1[P]$ is the most relevant. The mapping $C_2[\cdot]$ will be used mainly to illustrate the relation between the interpretation of general logic programs and the semantics of causal theories. We assume every atom in a logic program to be an "abnormality" and write $\mathcal{C}_A$ to represent the class of Herbrand models M whose "abnormalities" are among those of A. Namely, if $\mathcal{L}$ denotes the formulas not involving the causal operator, $\mathcal{C}_A$ will stand for the collection of models M such that $M \cap \mathcal{L} \subseteq A$.

We consider first the mapping $C_1[\cdot]$ which converts each rule

$$\gamma \leftarrow \alpha_1, \ldots, \alpha_n, \neg\beta_1, \ldots, \neg\beta_m$$

in P, where $n \geq 0$ and $m \geq 0$, and α's, β's and γ are atoms, into a *causal* rule of the form

$$C\alpha_1 \wedge \ldots \wedge C\alpha_n \wedge \neg\beta_1 \wedge \ldots \wedge \neg\beta_m \Rightarrow C\gamma \ .$$

Example 3 Consider a program P given by the following rules:

$$\mathtt{c} \leftarrow \mathtt{a}, \neg\mathtt{b}$$
$$\mathtt{d} \leftarrow \neg\mathtt{c}$$
$$\mathtt{a} \leftarrow$$

P gives rise to two minimal models: $M_1 = \{\mathtt{a}, \mathtt{c}\}$ and $M_2 = \{\mathtt{a}, \mathtt{b}, \mathtt{d}\}$, the former of which is the single *canonical* or *perfect* model of P [Apt *et al.*, 1987; Przymusinski, 1987].

The mapping $C_1[\cdot]$ maps P into the causal theory $C_1[P]$:

$$\mathrm{Ca} \wedge \neg\mathtt{b} \Rightarrow \mathrm{Cc}$$
$$\neg\mathtt{c} \Rightarrow \mathrm{Cd}$$
$$\mathbf{true} \Rightarrow \mathrm{Ca}$$

$C_1[P]$ gives rise to two minimal classes $\mathcal{C}_{M_1}$ and $\mathcal{C}_{M_2}$, with gaps M_1 and M_2 as above. Furthermore, in the former class, the atoms **a** and **c** are both explained, as $C_1[P], \neg\mathtt{b} \vdash \mathrm{Ca} \wedge \mathrm{Cc}$ holds, and $\neg\mathtt{b}$ is a legitimate assumption in $\mathcal{C}_{M_1}$. On the other hand, only the atom **a** is explained in $\mathcal{C}_{M_2}$. Thus, the class $\mathcal{C}_{M_1}$ is the single preferred class of $C_1[P]$. As a result, the canonical model M_1 of P and the preferred class $\mathcal{C}_{M_1}$ of $C_1[P]$ sanction the same non-causal (free from 'C') literals.

As the example suggests, for *stratified* programs the following correspondence between the canonical model of P and the single preferred class of the theory $C_1[P]$ can be established:[5]

Theorem 1 *M is the canonical model of a stratified program P if and only if $\mathcal{C}_M$ is the single preferred class of $C_1[P]$.*

Moreover, if we say that a class of models is *perfectly coherent* when it explains *every* abnormality that it sanctions, we obtain a correspondence between the *stable* models of a program P [Gelfond and Lifschitz, 1988; Fine, 1989] and the perfectly coherent classes of the causal theory $C_1[P]$, even when P is *not* stratified.

Theorem 2 *M is a stable model of an arbitrary program P if and only if $\mathcal{C}_M$ is a perfectly coherent class of the causal theory $C_1[P]$.*

In spite of this correspondence, however, the semantics of causal theories $C_1[P]$ and the stable semantics of logic programs P diverge outside the family of stratified programs. On the one hand, programs may lack stable models (e.g. $\{\mathtt{p} \leftarrow \neg\mathtt{p}\}$); on the other, causal theories $C_1[P]$ may give rise to multiple preferred classes even when P accepts a single stable model (e.g. $P = \{\mathtt{a} \leftarrow \neg\mathtt{b}, \mathtt{b} \leftarrow \neg\mathtt{a}, \mathtt{p} \leftarrow \neg\mathtt{b}, \mathtt{p} \leftarrow \neg\mathtt{p}\}$).

Logic Programs and Causal Networks We now investigate the semantics associated with a second mapping $C_2[\cdot]$ of logic programs into causal theories.

[5] Proofs can be found in [Geffner, 1989a].

For a logic program P, $C_2[P]$ represents the collection of rules which result from mapping each rule

$$\gamma \leftarrow \alpha_1, \ldots, \alpha_n, \neg\beta_1, \ldots, \neg\beta_m$$

in P, into a causal rule of the form:

$$\alpha_1 \wedge \ldots \wedge \alpha_n \wedge \neg\beta_1 \wedge \ldots \wedge \neg\beta_m \Rightarrow C\gamma$$

The difference with the previous translation is that the positive antecedents of the resulting causal rules do not need to be "causally" established. This renders the models of the causal theory $C_2[P]$ as models of $C_1[P]$, though not the other way around. As a result, the semantics of causal theories of the form $C_2[P]$ differs from that of $C_1[P]$ even within the family of stratified programs.

For instance, the stratified program $P = \{\mathbf{q} \leftarrow \neg\mathbf{p}, \mathbf{p} \leftarrow \mathbf{r}, \mathbf{r} \leftarrow \mathbf{p}\}$, possesses a single canonical model $M = \{\mathbf{q}\}$, and thus C_M is the single causally preferred class of $C_1[P]$. On the other hand, the mapping $C_2[\cdot]$ renders the causal theory $C_2[P] = \{\neg\mathbf{p} \Rightarrow C\mathbf{q}, \mathbf{r} \Rightarrow C\mathbf{p}, \mathbf{p} \Rightarrow C\mathbf{r}\}$ which accepts *two* preferred classes C_M and $C_{M'}$, with $M = \{\mathbf{q}\}$ and $M' = \{\mathbf{p}, \mathbf{r}\}$.

In this example, the 'anomalous' behavior of the theory $C_2[P]$ is a consequence of the circularity relating the atoms $\mathbf{p}$ and $\mathbf{r}$. 'Circular' explanations are precluded in $C_1[P]$ but not in $C_2[P]$. What is interesting, however, is that once these circularities are removed, the 'anomalous' behavior is guaranteed to disappear.

Let us say that a program P is *acyclic* when its dependency graph does not contain cycles. Acyclic programs are thus stratified. Moreover, acyclic programs, not only preclude 'recursion trough negation,' but *every* type of recursion. For acyclic programs, the following result applies.

Theorem 3 *Let P be an acyclic program. Then the class C_M, where M is the canonical model of P, is the unique preferred class of the theories $C_1[P]$ and $C_2[P]$.*

In other words, once recursion is removed the two mappings examined result into an identical behavior, in correspondence with the received semantics of logic programs. While the requirement of acyclicity is unacceptably strong in the domain of programming, it is common among network representational languages, such as inheritance hierarchies [Touretzky, 1986] and Bayesian networks [Pearl, 1988b]. Indeed, causal theories of the form $C_2[P]$ for acyclic programs P, possibly augmented by integrity constraints, provide a sufficiently expressive language for reasoning in *causal networks*. [Geffner, 1989a] discusses the use of such representations for abductive reasoning as well as some of their advantages over the representations resulting from the mapping $C_1[\cdot]$.

Proof-Theory

The proof-theory of causal theories is structured in the form of an argument-based system (e.g. [Loui, 1987]). We assume the theories of interest are well-founded in the sense defined above. The notions of consistency and derivations are to be understood relative to postulates [C1]-[C3].

We start with some terminology. Assumptions are the complements of abnormalities. We denote the complement of a proposition p as $\bar{p}$, thus, if p is an abnormality $\bar{p}$ is an assumption, and vice versa. Furthermore, in a context T, a set Δ of assumptions constitutes an ***argument*** if the set Δ is consistent with T. Moreover, Δ is an argument *for* q, if q is derivable from the causal theory $T + \Delta$, and an argument *against* q, if $\neg q$ is derivable from $T + \Delta$. When the context T is understood, we also say that Δ *supports* q and $\neg q$ respectively. Now, if Δ is not an argument in T, then Δ is said to be a ***conflict set***. Two arguments are ***in conflict*** when their union is a conflict set. In such a case we also say that one argument *refutes* the other.

For instance, in a theory T consisting of the expressions $\neg\mathbf{ab_1} \Rightarrow C\mathbf{ab_2}$ and $\neg\mathbf{ab_3} \Rightarrow C\mathbf{q}$, the arguments $\Delta_1 = \{\neg\mathbf{ab_1}\}$ and $\Delta_2 = \{\neg\mathbf{ab_2}\}$ are in conflict. On the other hand, no argument is in conflict with $\Delta_3 = \{\neg\mathbf{ab_3}\}$.

By the minimality of preferred classes, it easily follows that propositions supported by unrefuted arguments are entailed. Thus, for example, we can safely conclude that propositions $C\mathbf{q}$ and $\mathbf{q}$ above are entailed, as they are supported by the unrefuted argument Δ_3.

Often, however, refuted arguments may also provide legitimate support. Once such example is the proposition $\mathbf{ab_2}$ which is entailed by T in spite of having a single minimal supporting argument Δ_1 which is refuted by Δ_2. Intuitively, what is going on is that Δ_1 not only refutes Δ_2, but also explains its negation. We will say in that case that Δ_1 is *protected* from Δ_2. As we will see, propositions supported by protected arguments may also be entailed.

Formally, let us say that an argument Δ explains a proposition p when Δ is an argument for Cp. Then the notion of ***protection*** can be defined as follows:

Definition 2 *An argument Δ is* protected *from a conflicting argument Δ' iff there is a set $\Delta'' \subseteq \Delta' - \Delta$ such that $\Delta + \Delta' - \Delta''$ is not a conflict set, and every abnormality α, $\bar{\alpha} \in \Delta''$, is explained by $\Delta + \Delta' - \Delta''$.*

Similarly we will say that an argument Δ is ***stronger*** than a conflicting argument Δ' when Δ is protected from Δ' but Δ' is not protected from Δ. In the example above, for instance, Δ_1 is ***stronger*** than the conflicting argument Δ_2. If we say that an argument is ***stable*** when it is stronger than any conflicting argument, we obtain the following sufficient conditions for a proposition to be causally entailed:

Theorem 4 *If a proposition p is supported by an* stable *argument, then p is causally entailed.*

Yet, theorem 4 does not provide *necessary* conditions. For instance, the proposition $\mathbf{ab_3}$ is causally entailed by the theory comprised of the formulas $\neg\mathbf{ab_1} \vee$

$\neg$**ab**$_2$ $\Rightarrow$ **Cab**$_3$ and **ab**$_1$ $\vee$ **ab**$_2$, and yet, **ab**$_3$ is not supported by any stable argument.

A simple extension of the definitions above takes care of such cases. Let us refer to a collection of arguments as a *cover*, and let us say that a cover *supports* a proposition p if every argument in the cover supports p. Furthermore, let us say that an argument is in *conflict* with a cover when the argument is in conflict with every argument in the cover, and that a cover is *stronger* than a conflicting argument Δ when it contains an argument stronger than Δ. Moreover, let us also say that a cover is *stable* when it is stronger than every conflicting argument. Then, the following sound and complete characterization of causal theories results:

Theorem 5 (Main) *A proposition p is causally entailed if and only if it is supported by a stable* cover.

For the theory comprised of the sentences $\neg$**ab**$_1$ $\vee$ $\neg$**ab**$_2$ $\Rightarrow$ **Cab**$_3$ and **ab**$_1$ $\vee$ **ab**$_2$, it is easy to show that the pair of arguments $\Delta_1 = \{\neg \mathbf{ab}_1\}$ and $\Delta_2 = \{\neg \mathbf{ab}_2\}$ constitute a stable cover. Since such a cover supports the proposition of **ab**$_3$, it follows then that **ab**$_3$ is entailed by the theory.

Related Work

Causal theories are an elaboration of ideas in [Geffner, 1989b], where the notions of *explanations*, *classes*, and *coherence* were originally presented. The adoption here of a *causal operator* as part of the object-level language, however, has simplified matters considerably, providing additional expressive power and permitting the construction of a proof-theory. Part of the motivation for the move came from a proposal due to Pearl to explicitly incorporate a causal language into default theories. Pearl's proposal [Pearl, 1988a] draws on work in causal probabilistic networks to suggest a distinction between defaults which *encode* explanations (e.g. `fire` $\rightarrow$ `smoke`) from defaults which *trigger* explanations (e.g. `smoke` $\rightarrow$ `fire`). He calls the former defaults *causal* and the latter *evidential*. He argues that the language of default theories should accommodate such a distinction, and in particular, that explanation 'giving' defaults should be prevented from triggering explanation 'seeking' defaults. Pearl's proposal to preclude such chains consists of three parts. First, he labels every default as either *causal*, e.g. `rain` $\rightarrow_{\mathrm{C}}$ `grass_wet`, or *evidential*, e.g. `grass_wet` $\rightarrow_{\mathrm{E}}$ `sprinkler_on`; second, he distinguishes the status of propositions p established on *causal* grounds, Cp, from those established on *evidential* grounds, Ep; and third, he introduces a calculus for reasoning with causal and evidential rules which purposely precludes deriving q from Cp and an evidential rule $p \rightarrow_E q$.

Though differing in detail and goals, the reading of the operator 'C' in causal theories follows Pearl's intuitions. Pearl, however, focuses on evidential reasoning, while we focus on default reasoning. A proposal for performing evidential reasoning in causal theories is discussed in [Geffner, 1989a].

Causal theories are also related to Moore's [1985] autoepistemic theories. The autoepistemic encoding $L[P]$ of a stratified logic program P [Gelfond, 1987], for instance, turns out to be the "dual" of the causal encoding $C_1[P]$ (i.e. in $L[P]$ every *negated* atom is preceded with the *autoepistemic* operator 'L', while in $C_1[P]$ every *non-negated* atom is preceded with the *causal* operator 'C') and they both legitimize the same behavior. Indeed, it is possible to understand the autoepistemic operator L as an *evidential* operator, with Lα meaning "there is evidence for α." Namely, instead of using the *causal* operator C under the conventions that

$\neg\alpha$ is an assumption
C$\alpha \Rightarrow \alpha$ must hold for every (plain) sentence α, and
α is *explained* in a class when Cα holds,

we could have used an *evidential* operator E under the conventions that

$\neg$Eα is an assumption
$\alpha \Rightarrow$ Eα must hold for every (plain) sentence α, and
Eα is *explained* in a class when α holds.

Under such an approach the *evidential* encoding of a logic program would be identical to the *autoepistemic* encoding, except for the presence of E's instead of L's. Moreover, both encodings would sanction an equivalent semantics for stratified programs. For non-stratified programs, however, as for most default theories, the duality between causal and autoepistemic disappears. First, default theories may lack stable models; second, the prefix $\neg$L, as no causal prefix, "generates" the assumptions needed.

The fact that the operator 'C' establishes a preference for the abnormality **q** over the abnormality **p** in a theory like $\neg$**p** $\Rightarrow$ C**q**, raises the question of whether the semantics of causal theories can be understood in terms of prioritized circumscription [McCarthy, 1986]. The answer is a qualified no: there are causal theories for which no priority order on the abnormalities will render an equivalent behavior. The causal theory $\{\neg\mathbf{a} \wedge \neg\mathbf{b} \Rightarrow \mathrm{C}\mathbf{c} \wedge \mathrm{C}\mathbf{d}, \neg\mathbf{c} \wedge \neg\mathbf{d} \Rightarrow \mathrm{C}\mathbf{a} \wedge \mathrm{C}\mathbf{b}\}$ for abnormalities **a**, **b**, **c**, and **d**, is one such example. Still, the semantics of such theories could in principle be captured by defining priorities for *non-atomic* formulas.

Finally, another family of theories related to those treated in this paper is Shoham's [1988] causal theories. Shoham's causal theories are epistemic theories designed for efficient reasoning about change. They are interpreted by a preference criterion which rewards models in which "as little is known for as long as possible." While there is no direct correspondence between our causal theories and Shoham's, it seems possible to understand the intuition behind Shoham's chronological minimization in terms of the ideas of explanation and coherence. If we recall that we regard an abnormality α as explained in a class C when C validates a set of assumption Δ which supports the truth of $C\alpha$, chronological minimization assumes α explained by Δ instead, when Δ supports the truth of α, without involving assumptions about times past α.

Acknowledgements. For the topic of this paper I have benefited from conversations with many people. I'd like to thank here K. Fine, M. Gelfond, M. Ginsberg, B. Grosof, K. Konolige, J. Pearl and H. Przymusinska.

References

[Apt *et al.*, 1987] K. Apt, H. Blair, and A. Walker. Towards a theory of declarative knowledge. In J. Minker, editor, *Foundations of Deductive Databases and Logic Programming*, pages 89–148. Morgan Kaufmann, Los Altos, CA, 1987.

[Fine, 1989] K. Fine. The justification of negation as failure. *Proceedings of 8th International Congress of Logic Methodology and Philosophy of Science*. North Holland, 1989.

[Geffner and Pearl, 1987] H. Geffner and J. Pearl. A framework for reaasoning with defaults. Technical Report TR-94, Cognitive Systems Laboratory, UCLA, Los Angeles, CA., August 1987. To appear in *Knowledge Representation and Defeasible Inference*, H. Kyburg, R. Loui and G. Carlson (Eds), Kluwer, 1989.

[Geffner, 1989a] H. Geffner. *Default Reasoning: Causal and Conditional Theories.* PhD thesis, UCLA, Los Angeles, CA, November 1989.

[Geffner, 1989b] H. Geffner. Default reasoning, minimality and coherence. *Proceedings of the First International Conference on Principle of Knowledge Representation and Reasoning*, pages 137–148, Toronto, Ontario, 1989.

[Gelfond and Lifschitz, 1988] M. Gelfond and V. Lifschitz. The stable model semantics for logic programming. *Proceedings 1988 Symposium on Logic Programming*, pages 1070–1080, Cambridge, Mass., 1988. MIT Press.

[Gelfond, 1987] M. Gelfond. On stratified autoepistemic theories. *Proceedings AAAI-87*, pages 207–211, Seattle, Washington, 1987.

[Ginsberg and Smith, 1988] M. Ginsberg and Smith. Reasoning about action I: A possible worlds approach. *Artificial Intelligence*, 35:165–195, 1988.

[Hanks and McDermott, 1987] S. Hanks and D. McDermott. Non-monotonic logics and temporal projection. *Artificial Intelligence*, 33:379–412, 1987.

[Hughes and Cresswell, 1968] G. Hughes and Cresswell. *An Introduction to Modal Logic.* Methuen and Co. LTD, London, Great Britain, 1968.

[Krishnaprasad *et al.*, 1989] T. Krishnaprasad, Kiefer, and D. Warren. On the circumscriptive semantics of inheritance networks. In Z. Ras and L. Saitta, editors, *Methodologies for Intelligent Systems 4*. North Holland, New York, N.Y., 1989.

[Loui, 1987] R. Loui. Defeat among arguments: A system of defeasible inference. *Computational Intelligence*, 1987.

[McCarthy, 1986] J. McCarthy. Applications of circumscription to formalizing commonsense knowledge. *Artificial Intelligence*, 28:89–116, 1986.

[McDermott, 1982] D. McDermott. A temporal logic for reasoning about processes and plans. *Cognitive Science*, 6:101–155, 1982.

[Moore, 1985] R. Moore. Semantical considerations on non-monotonic logics. *Artificial Intelligence*, 25:75–94, 1985.

[Pearl, 1988a] J. Pearl. Embracing causality in default reasoning. *Artificial Intelligence*, 35:259–271, 1988.

[Pearl, 1988b] J. Pearl. *Probabilistic Reasoning in Intelligent Systems.* Morgan Kaufmann, Los Altos, CA., 1988.

[Przymusinski, 1987] T. Przymusinski. On the declarative semantics of stratified deductive databases and logic programs. In J. Minker, editor, *Foundations of Deductive Databases and Logic Programming*, pages 193–216. Morgan Kaufmann, Los Altos, CA, 1987.

[Shoham, 1988] Y. Shoham. *Reasoning about Change: Time and Causation from the Standpoint of Artificial Intelligence.* MIT Press, Cambridge, Mass., 1988.

[Touretzky, 1986] D. Touretzky. *The Mathematics of Inheritance Systems.* Pitman, London, 1986.

Decidable Reasoning in First-Order Knowledge Bases with Perfect Introspection

Gerhard Lakemeyer
Department of Computer Science
University of Toronto
Toronto, Ontario, Canada, M5S 1A4
e-mail: gerhard@ai.toronto.edu

Abstract

Since knowledge bases (KBs) are usually incomplete, they should be able to provide information regarding their own incompleteness, which requires them to introspect on what they know and do not know. An important area of research is to devise models of introspective reasoning that take into account resource limitations. Under the view that a KB is completely characterized by the set of beliefs it represents (its *epistemic state*), it seems natural to model KBs in terms of *belief*. Reasoning can then be understood as the problem of computing membership in the epistemic state of a KB. The best understood models of belief are based on possible-world semantics. However, their computational properties are unacceptable. In particular, they render reasoning in first-order KBs undecidable. In this paper, we propose a novel model of belief, which preserves many of the advantages of possible-world semantics yet, at the same time, guarantees reasoning to be decidable, where a KB may contain sentences in full first-order logic. Moreover, such KBs have perfect knowledge about their own beliefs even though their beliefs about the world are limited.

Introduction

Since the information contained in a knowledge base (KB) is usually incomplete, a KB should not only be able to answer queries about the domain in question but also about its own state of incompleteness. In other words, a KB should possess self-knowledge, which it gains by introspection. For the purposes of this paper, we assume that a KB is capable of *perfect* introspection, that is, it knows exactly what it knows[1] and does not know. Perfect introspection is not uncontroversial. For example, one may want to restrict knowledge of what is not known to concepts that one is at least aware of (see [14] for a formalization of this idea). However, we have adopted perfect introspection here simply because it comes at no additional computational cost.

An important area of research is to devise models of introspective reasoning that take into account resource limitations [9]. Under the view that a KB is completely characterized by the set of beliefs it represents (its *epistemic state*), it seems natural to model KBs in terms of *belief*. Reasoning can then be understood as the problem of computing membership in the epistemic state of a KB.

The best understood models of belief are based on possible-world semantics [10, 8]. Most autoepistemic logics, a favorite framework to study introspection (e.g. [20, 17, 18]), specify epistemic states that have possible-world models, as shown in [21, 5, 17]. A big advantage of possible world models is their simplicity. Unfortunately, they also make the assumption that a KB's (or agent's) beliefs are closed under logical consequence, a property often referred to as *logical omniscience*, which renders reasoning undecidable in first-order KBs. An important problem then is to find models of belief with better computational properties.

While there has been some progress in finding computationally attractive models of belief in the propositional case [14], adding quantifiers to the framework in the obvious way leads to undecidability. In this paper, we remedy this situation and propose a new model of belief that preserves much of the simplicity of possible-world semantics yet, at the same time, guarantees that reasoning in first-order KBs is computable.[2]

As in [14, 17], we use an approach that allows us to model the beliefs of a KB directly within the logic. Intuitively, a KB's epistemic state can be characterized as the set of all sentences that are believed given that the sentences in the KB are *all* that is believed or, as we will say for short, *only-believed*. This idea is formalized in a modal logic with two modal operators **B** and **O** for belief and only-believing, respectively. The epistemic state of a KB is characterized by the set of sentences α for which $\mathbf{O}\mathrm{KB} \supset \mathbf{B}\alpha$ is valid.[3] The

[1] Although this paper is concerned with belief rather than knowledge, we nevertheless use both terms interchangeably.

[2] In section "A Decidable KR Service," we also discuss restrictions under which reasoning is in fact tractable.

[3] Whenever KB occurs within a logical sentence, we

complexity of reasoning then reduces to the complexity of determining whether $\mathbf{B}\alpha$ follows logically from $\mathbf{O}$KB for a given KB and α.

The main contribution of this paper lies in the novel model-theoretic account of belief and only-believing. In particular, KBs under this model of belief may contain arbitrary first-order sentences and they have perfect knowledge about what they do and do not believe even though their beliefs about the world are limited. Most importantly, the beliefs of such KBs are computable.

In related work, Konolige [9] also addresses the issue of modeling introspection under resource limitations. However rather than proposing an actual instance of a computationally attractive reasoner, he presents a general framework in which one can be formalized. Work regarding decidable forms of first-order entailment (without introspection) is also relevant [7, 2, 22, 4], since it is a useful starting point when considering limited forms of belief. In particular, Patel-Schneider's [22] and Frisch's [4] notions of entailment, which have a model-theoretic semantics, are good candidates as a basis for belief. Indeed the logic developed in this paper[4] is shown to subsume Patel-Schneider's t-entailment (Theorem 1). By using a more expressive modal language, this paper goes beyond t-entailment by formalizing first-order beliefs *about* beliefs and agents introspecting on their own beliefs. At the same time, we are able to preserve the computational benefits of t-entailment. Finally, belief is formalized in fairly intuitive model-theoretic terms.

The rest of the paper is organized as follows. We begin by defining the syntax and semantics of *OBL*, the logic of belief and only-believing. This is followed by a brief discussion of the properties of belief. The next section formally establishes the decidability result regarding which beliefs follow logically from only-believing a KB. After that, we apply these ideas to the specification of KR service routines **ASK** and **TELL** in the sense of [15]. Finally, we summarize the results and outline extensions of the current framework and future directions.

The Logic *OBL*

The key aspects of this logic are the semantics and properties of belief and only-believing, which ultimately gives us the specification of decidable, introspective reasoning in first-order KBs. Before turning to the technical definitions, we first introduce the two notions of belief informally. (The other logical connectives and quantifiers have the usual meaning.)

Belief Belief is defined in a possible-world fashion. Roughly, an agent is assumed to imagine a set of states of affairs or *situations* M. The agent is then said to believe a sentence α just in case α (or, as we will see below, a slightly modified α) holds in all situations in M. Except for the definition of situations, which are described in more detail below, this framework is very similar to one that defines the logic *weak S5* [6]. In fact, as in *weak S5*, our approach results in agents capable of perfect introspection with respect to what they know and don't know.

In order to avoid the logical omniscience problem, we limit an agent's ability to reason by cases in the following two ways, which follow from the way situations are defined and used. For one, we allow beliefs not to be closed under *modus ponens*. For example, if p, q, and r are atomic facts, we allow an agent to believe $(p \vee q) \wedge (\neg q \vee r)$, yet fail to believe $(p \vee r)$. Another way reasoning by cases is limited is by weakening the link between disjunction and existential quantification in the sense that an agent may believe $\mathtt{P}(a) \vee \mathtt{P}(b)$ for a predicate $\mathtt{P}$ and distinct terms a and b, yet fail to believe $\exists x \mathtt{P}(x)$.

In *OBL*, closure under modus ponens is avoided by decoupling the notions of truth and falsity within situations. Instead of assigning either true or false to atomic facts (predicates applied to individuals), situations are allowed to assign independent *true-support* and *false-support* to atoms. This corresponds to using four truth values $\{\}$, $\{\mathtt{true}\}$, $\{\mathtt{false}\}$, and $\{\mathtt{true}, \mathtt{false}\}$, an idea originally proposed to provide a semantics for a fragment of relevance logic called *tautological entailment* [1, 3].[5] Note that the classical worlds of possible-world semantics are a special kind of situations, namely those where each atomic fact has either true- or false-support but not both. In *OBL*, classical worlds are used to provide the standard notions of *truth* and *validity*. Non-classical situations are only allowed to be part of what agents imagine (defining their beliefs). The fact that an agent's imagination can be incomplete and inconsistent provides some intuition for situations that assign neither true- nor false-support to an atom or both true- and false-support.

In order to weaken the link between disjunction and existential quantification, *OBL* restricts the interpretation of existential quantifiers within belief. Roughly, we require that an agent who believes the existence of an individual with a certain property must be able to name or give a description of that individual, although we do not require the agent to know who the individual is. More concretely, for $\exists x \mathtt{P}(x)$ to be believed there must be a closed term t (e.g. $father(john)$) such that $\mathtt{P}(t)$ is true in all accessible situations. In general, if the existential appears in the scope of universal quantifiers, the corresponding universals may (but need not)

mean the conjunction of all the sentences in the KB.

[4]A preliminary model which addressed neither self-knowledge nor only-believing appeared in [11]. However, ultimately it proved to be too complex and was abandoned in favor of the current, much simpler model.

[5]Levesque [16] was the first to introduce the notion of four-valued situations to model a limited form of belief in a propositional framework.

occur in the description chosen for the existential.

Only-Believing An agent who only-believes a sentence α believes α and, intuitively, believes as little else as possible. In other words, the agent is maximally ignorant while still believing α.

As demonstrated in [14, 17], if belief is modeled by a set of situations, independent of whether they are four-valued or two-valued as in classical possible-world semantics, only-believing has a particularly simple characterization: an agent only-believes a sentence α if he or she believes α and the set of situations M the agent imagines is as large as possible, i.e., if we were to add any other world to M, the agent would no longer believe α.[6]

With the special treatment of existential quantification as outlined above, there is, however, one complication that needs to addressed. Consider the sentence $\alpha = \exists x \mathtt{P}(x)$. What should it mean for an agent, whose beliefs are modeled by a set of situations M, to only-believe α? Since a necessary requirement is that the agent believes α, there must be some closed term a such that $\mathtt{P}(a)$ is believed. It may be tempting to let M be the set of *all* situations where $\mathtt{P}(a)$ holds for some fixed closed term a. But that seems too strong. For example, to say that all the detective believes is that someone is the murderer conveys a lot less information than all the detective believes is that the driver of the red car is the murderer.

One way around this problem is to require the terms that are used when only-believing an existentially quantified sentence to convey no information about the world. In other words, the terms should behave like skolem functions or internal identifiers. For that reason, we introduce a special set of function symbols which must be used when substituting existentials in the context of only-believing. Making sure that these function symbols carry no information about the world is treated as a pragmatic issue when applying the logic to knowledge bases. As we will see in section "A Decidable KR Service," a simple way of dealing with the issue is to enforce that a user interacting with a KB is prevented from asking queries or telling the system sentences containing these special function symbols.

The Language $\mathcal{L}$

The language is a modal first-order dialect with function symbols, which are partitioned into two countably infinite sets $\mathcal{F}_{\text{REG}}$ and $\mathcal{F}_{\text{SK}}$ of every arity. The latter contains the function symbols that will be used to interpret existential quantifiers in the context of only-believing. The members of $\mathcal{F}_{\text{SK}}$ are also referred to as **sk-functions**. The language also contains a countably infinite set N of standard names, which are syntactically treated like constants. Their meaning is explained below.

[6] M need not be unique for the same reasons as there are multiple extensions in autoepistemic logic (see [14, 17]).

Given the usual definitions of **terms** and **atomic formulas**, a **primitive term (formula)** is a term (atomic formula) with only standard names as arguments. We also distinguish a special primitive formula **true** (with the obvious intended meaning).

The **formulas** of $\mathcal{L}$ are constructed in the usual way from the atomic formulas, the connectives $\neg$ and $\vee$, the quantifier $\exists$,[7] and the modal operators **B** and **O** with the restriction that formulas of the form $\mathbf{B}\alpha$ or $\mathbf{O}\alpha$ may not contain free variables. In other words, we ignore the issue of quantifying into belief (*quantifying-in*) as in $\exists x \mathtt{P}(x) \wedge \neg \mathbf{B}\mathtt{P}(x)$. This restriction will be lifted in a forthcoming paper [13]. To simplify the technical presentation below, we also require that no variable is bound more than once in a formula. Formulas without any occurrences of **B** or **O** are called **objective**, formulas without occurrences of **O** are called **basic**, and formulas whose predicate symbols all occur within the scope of a modal operator are called **subjective**. **Sentences** are, as usual, formulas without free variables.

Notation: Sequences of terms or variables are sometimes written in vector notation. E.g., a sequence of variables $\langle x_1, \ldots, x_k \rangle$ is abbreviated as $\vec{x}$. Also, $\exists \vec{x}$ stands for $\exists x_1 \ldots \exists x_k$. If a formula α contains the free variables $x_1, \ldots, x_k$, $\alpha[x_1/t_1, \ldots, x_k/t_k]$ (sometimes abbreviated as $\alpha[\vec{x}/\vec{t}]$) denotes α with every occurrence of x_i replaced by t_i. In the case of one variable, we sometimes write α^x_t instead of $\alpha[x/t]$.

Definition 1 *A quantifier within a formula α occurs at the* **objective level** *of α if it does not occur within the scope of a modal operator.*

Definition 2 *A formula α is* **existential-free** *iff α contains no existential quantifiers at the objective level within the scope of an even number of $\neg$-operators.*

A Formal Semantics

The semantics of *OBL* relies on the notion of situations, which are essentially four-valued extensions of classical (two-valued) Kripke worlds [10]. All situations are defined over a fixed universe of discourse, which we take to be the standard names of the language. None of the results in this paper depends on this choice,[8] but it greatly simplifies the technical presentation. For example, the true- and false-support of predicates can be described by the true- and false-support of primitive formulas. Also, at each situation, the closed terms of the language are interpreted by mapping them into the standard names.

Definition 3 *Denotation Functions*
A **denotation function** *d is a mapping from closed*

[7] Other logical connectives like $\wedge$, $\supset$, and $\equiv$ and the quantifier $\forall$ are used freely and are defined in the usual way in terms of $\neg$, $\vee$, and $\exists$.

[8] The use of standard names as the universe of discourse becomes much more significant in the context of quantifying-in [15, 13].

terms into the standard names such that $d(n) = n$ for all $n \in N$ and $d(f(t_1, \ldots, t_k)) = d(f(d(t_1), \ldots, d(t_k)))$. ($f$ may be 0-ary.)
d is canonically extended to apply to sequences as well, i.e., $d(\langle t_1, \ldots, t_k\rangle) = \langle d(t_1), \ldots d(t_k)\rangle$.

It is easy to see that denotation functions are uniquely determined by the values they assign to primitive terms.

Definition 4 *Situations*
A situation s is a triple $s = \langle T, F, d\rangle$, where T and F are subsets of the set of primitive sentences such that $\mathtt{true} \in T$ *and* $\mathtt{true} \notin F$. *d is a denotation function.*

Definition 5 *Worlds*
A situation $\langle T, F, d\rangle$ is called a **world**, *iff*

$\mathtt{P}(\vec{n}) \in T \Longleftrightarrow \mathtt{P}(\vec{n}) \notin F$ *for all primitive formulas* $\mathtt{P}(\vec{n})$

The following definitions are needed for the semantics of **B** and **O**. In particular, they describe how to substitute terms for existentially quantified variables when interpreting belief (definition 9) and what kinds of terms are eligible in the context of **B** (definition 7) and **O** (definition 8).

Definition 6 *Existentially Quantified Variables*
Let α be a formula in $\mathcal{L}$. A variable x is said to be **existentially (universally) quantified** *in α iff x is bound in the scope of an* **even (odd)** *number of $\neg$-operators.*

Definition 7 *Admissible Terms*
Let α be objective and x existentially quantified in α. A term t is said to be an **admissible** *substitution for x with respect to α iff every variable y in t is universally quantified in α and x is bound within the scope of y.*

If the context is clear, we often say t is admissible *for x or t* is admissible.

Definition 8 *Sk-terms*
Let α be a sentence and x an existentially quantified variable bound at the objective level of α. Let $U(x)$ be a sequence of the universally quantified variables in whose scope x is bound. Let $f \in \mathcal{F}_{\mathrm{SK}}$ be a function symbol of arity $|U(x)|$ occurring nowhere else in α. Then $f(U(x))$ is called an **sk-term** *(for x).*

Note that sk-terms are also admissible.

Definition 9 *Let α be a sentence and let $\vec{x} = \langle x_1, \ldots, x_k\rangle$ be a sequence of the existentially quantified variables bound at the objective level of α. Let $\vec{t} = \langle t_1, \ldots, t_k\rangle$ be a sequence of terms s.t. t_i is admissible for x_i for all i. $\alpha^{\sharp}[\vec{x}/\vec{t}]$ denotes α with all $\exists x_i$ removed and with all occurrences of x_i replaced by t_i.*

To illustrate the previous definition, let $\alpha = \exists x(\neg\exists y(\mathtt{P}(x, y) \vee \neg\exists z\mathtt{Q}(z)))$, $t_1 = a$, and $t_2 = f(y)$. Then both t_1 and t_2 are admissible and $\alpha^{\sharp}[x/t_1, z/t_2] = (\neg\exists y(\mathtt{P}(a, y) \vee \neg\mathtt{Q}(f(y))))$.

We are now in a position to define the semantic rules for the sentences of $\mathcal{L}$. The rules except for **B** and **O** are no different from those in classical logic except that they are somewhat more longwinded because the true- and false-support of sentences have to be considered separately.

Let s be a situation and M a set of situations. The true- ($\models_{\mathrm{T}}$) and false-support ($\models_{\mathrm{F}}$) relations for sentences in $\mathcal{L}$ are defined as: (Let $\mathtt{P}(\vec{t})$ be an atomic sentence. α and β are sentences except in rule 4., where α may contain the free variable x.)

1. $M, s \models_{\mathrm{T}} \mathtt{P}(\vec{t}) \iff \mathtt{P}(d(\vec{t})) \in T$, where $s = \langle T, F, d\rangle$
   $M, s \models_{\mathrm{F}} \mathtt{P}(\vec{t}) \iff \mathtt{P}(d(\vec{t})) \in F$
2. $M, s \models_{\mathrm{T}} \neg\alpha \iff M, s \models_{\mathrm{F}} \alpha$
   $M, s \models_{\mathrm{F}} \neg\alpha \iff M, s \models_{\mathrm{T}} \alpha$
3. $M, s \models_{\mathrm{T}} \alpha \vee \beta \iff M, s \models_{\mathrm{T}} \alpha$ or $M, s \models_{\mathrm{T}} \beta$
   $M, s \models_{\mathrm{F}} \alpha \vee \beta \iff M, s \models_{\mathrm{F}} \alpha$ and $M, s \models_{\mathrm{F}} \beta$
4. $M, s \models_{\mathrm{T}} \exists x\alpha \iff$ for some $n \in N$ $M, s \models_{\mathrm{T}} \alpha^x_n$
   $M, s \models_{\mathrm{F}} \exists x\alpha \iff$ for all $n \in N$ $M, s \models_{\mathrm{F}} \alpha^x_n$

   For the following rules, let $\vec{x} = \langle x_1, \ldots, x_k\rangle$ be a sequence of the existentially quantified variables bound at the objective level of α.
5. $M, s \models_{\mathrm{T}} \mathbf{B}\alpha \iff$
   for all s', if $s' \in M$ then $M, s' \models_{\mathrm{T}} \alpha^{\sharp}[\vec{x}/\vec{t}]$,
   where $\vec{t}$ is a sequence of admissible terms.
   $M, s \models_{\mathrm{F}} \mathbf{B}\alpha \iff M, s \not\models_{\mathrm{T}} \mathbf{B}\alpha$
6. $M, s \models_{\mathrm{T}} \mathbf{O}\alpha \iff$
   for all s', $s' \in M$ iff $M, s' \models_{\mathrm{T}} \alpha^{\sharp}[\vec{x}/\vec{t}_{\mathrm{SK}}]$,
   where $\vec{t}_{\mathrm{SK}}$ is a sequence of distinct sk-terms.
   $M, s \models_{\mathrm{F}} \mathbf{O}\alpha \iff M, s \not\models_{\mathrm{T}} \mathbf{O}\alpha$

Note that, in the definition of **B** and **O**, the same $\vec{t}$ or $\vec{t}_{\mathrm{SK}}$ must be chosen for all $s' \in M$. Also note how the definition of only-believing differs only in two places from that of belief. For one, the terms that can be substituted for existentials are restricted to mention exactly one sk-function (the "internal identifiers"). The only other change involves replacing the "if" in the definition of belief by an "iff". This ensures that the set of situations M is as large as possible.

The notions of truth, logical consequence, validity, and satisfiability are defined with respect to worlds and non-empty sets of situations.

A formula α is *true* at a non-empty set of situations M and a world w if $M, w \models_{\mathrm{T}} \alpha$. α is *false* if $M, w \not\models_{\mathrm{T}} \alpha$. A formula α is *valid* ($\models\alpha$) iff α is true at every world w and every non-empty set of situations M. α is *satisfiable* iff $\neg\alpha$ is not valid.[9]

[9] In [17, 14] it is shown that using arbitrary sets of situations has the unintuitive effect that what is only-believed at an epistemic state (represented by a set of situations) is not completely determined by the basic beliefs at that state. This flaw can be overcome by using so-called *maximal* sets of situations [17, 14]. Since this issue is independent from

Finally, if α is objective, we often write $s \models_T \alpha$ instead of $M, s \models_T \alpha$, since nothing in the interpretation of α depends on M (similar for $s \models_F \alpha$).

Properties of Belief

Apart from belief and only-believing, the logic behaves much like a classical first-order logic. For example, all the substitution instances of sentences that are valid in classical FOL are also valid in *OBL*. In the rest of this section, we present important properties of belief.

The following four examples of *invalid* sentences illustrate in what ways belief is not closed under classical logical implication. Let $\mathtt{P}(a)$ and $\mathtt{Q}(b)$ be distinct atomic formulas.

$\not\models \mathbf{B}(\mathtt{P}(a) \vee \neg\mathtt{P}(a))$ Valid sentences need not be believed

$\not\models \mathbf{B}\mathtt{P}(a) \wedge \mathbf{B}(\mathtt{P}(a) \supset \mathtt{Q}(b)) \supset \mathbf{B}\mathtt{Q}(b)$ No Modus Ponens

$\not\models \mathbf{B}\mathtt{P}(a) \wedge \mathbf{B}\neg\mathtt{P}(a) \supset \mathbf{B}\mathtt{Q}(b)$ Inconsistent beliefs do not imply believing everything

$\not\models \mathbf{B}(\mathtt{P}(a) \vee \mathtt{P}(b)) \supset \mathbf{B}\exists x\mathtt{P}(x)$ No existential generalization from disjunctions

While the first three examples are a direct consequence of the four-valued situations, the fourth is a result of the special treatment of existential quantifiers within belief.

Next we list some of the *valid* sentences concerning belief, which give an indication of what can be concluded from a given belief. Let α and β be arbitrary sentences.

$\models \mathbf{B}\mathtt{true} \wedge \neg\mathbf{B}\neg\mathtt{true}$

$\models \mathbf{B}(\alpha \wedge \beta) \equiv \mathbf{B}\alpha \wedge \mathbf{B}\beta.$

$\models \mathbf{B}\alpha \supset \mathbf{B}(\alpha \vee \beta) \wedge \mathbf{B}(\beta \vee \alpha)$

$\models \mathbf{B}\forall x\alpha \supset \mathbf{B}\alpha^x_t$ for any closed term t.

$\models \mathbf{B}\alpha^x_t \supset \mathbf{B}\exists x\alpha$, where x is free in α and t is any closed term.

$\models \mathbf{O}\alpha \supset \mathbf{B}\alpha$

Believing objective sentences is strongly related to Patel-Schneider's t-entailment:

Theorem 1 *OBL subsumes t-entailment*
Let α and β be objective sentences containing neither standard names nor occurrences of $\mathtt{true}$.[10] *Then*

$$\models \mathbf{B}\alpha \supset \mathbf{B}\beta \quad \text{iff} \quad \alpha \longrightarrow_t \beta.$$

This result is significant in itself, since it can be viewed as providing a new semantics for t-entailment. The original semantics of t-entailment has the peculiar property of interpreting disjunction in a non-standard way. In *OBL*, all the classical connectives including disjunction are interpreted in the usual way and all the non-standard aspects are pushed into the semantics of **B** and **O**.

We conclude this section with a list of properties concerning self-knowledge. Let α and β be arbitrary sentences and let ρ and σ be subjective sentences.

Perfect Introspection:
$\models \mathbf{B}\alpha \supset \mathbf{B}\mathbf{B}\alpha$ and $\models \neg\mathbf{B}\alpha \supset \mathbf{B}\neg\mathbf{B}\alpha$

Self-Knowledge is Accurate: $\models \mathbf{B}\sigma \supset \sigma$

Self-Knowledge is Complete: $\models \sigma \supset \mathbf{B}\sigma$

Self-Knowledge is consistent: $\models \mathbf{B}\sigma \supset \neg\mathbf{B}\neg\sigma$

Self-Knowledge is Closed Under MP:
$\models \mathbf{B}(\rho \wedge (\neg\rho \vee \sigma)) \supset \mathbf{B}\sigma$

The above results show that an agent with this model of belief has *perfect* knowledge about her own beliefs even if her beliefs about the world are limited.

Computing What an Objective KB Knows

The intuition behind only-believing the sentences in a knowledge base has been to capture what a KB knows or what epistemic state the KB represents. Ideally, one would like **O**KB to pick out a unique epistemic state from the range of states defined by the logic (in the form of sets of situations). Unfortunately, this is not the case for arbitrary KBs. For one, if the KB is not objective, **O**KB may be satisfied in multiple epistemic states for the same reason as there are *multiple extensions* in other autoepistemic logics such as [20]. Unlike other autoepistemic logics, **O**KB does not represent a unique epistemic state even if KB is objective. For example, $\mathbf{O}\exists x\mathtt{P}(x)$ is satisfied by $\{s \mid s \models_T \mathtt{P}(a)\}$ for any constant $a \in \mathcal{F}_{SK}$. On the other hand, all those states are isomorphic up to renaming of sk-functions. Moreover, they agree on all beliefs not mentioning sk-functions. In general, we obtain

Theorem 2 *Let* KB *be an objective sentence. Then for any sentence α not containing function symbols from $\mathcal{F}_{SK}$, exactly one of* $\models \mathbf{O}\text{KB} \supset \mathbf{B}\alpha$ *or* $\models \mathbf{O}\text{KB} \supset \neg\mathbf{B}\alpha$ *holds.*

From a KB user's point of view, this result can be explained as follows: the user is not sure which internal identifiers (sk-terms) the KB has chosen for its existentially quantified variables, thus allowing for multiple possible epistemic states. However, the beliefs of the KB that matter to a user are those that are free of sk-terms, and those, according to the theorem, are uniquely determined by the KB. In the next section, this view will be made explicit by defining routines that allow a user to interact with a KB.

In the rest of this section, we prove that it is in fact decidable whether a belief without sk-functions follows from only-believing a KB. Although the decidability result holds for beliefs containing **O**s, we restrict our

the main concern of this paper, we have chosen to ignore it here.

[10] These restrictions are necessary in order to match the language of t-entailment.

attention to *basic* beliefs in order to simplify the presentation.

The idea behind the procedure for deciding whether a KB believes α, i.e., whether $\mathbf{O}$KB $\supset \mathbf{B}\alpha$ is valid, is as follows. First we replace all occurrences of subsentences of the form $\mathbf{B}\gamma$ in α by `true` or $\neg$`true` depending on whether γ is believed or not. This evaluation proceeds from the innermost occurrence of $\mathbf{B}$ to the outermost so that at each step we are asking whether an *objective* sentence is believed, which can be computed using Patel-Schneider's decidable t-entailment [22].

To perform the reduction, we need the following definitions.

Definition 10 *Let* KB *and* α *be objective,* α *without sk-function.*

$$\texttt{RES}[\![\mathrm{KB}, \alpha]\!] = \begin{cases} \texttt{true} & \text{if } \models \mathbf{O}\mathrm{KB} \supset \mathbf{B}\alpha \\ \neg\texttt{true} & \text{if } \models \mathbf{O}\mathrm{KB} \supset \neg\mathbf{B}\alpha \end{cases}$$

Definition 11 *Let* KB *be objective and* α *basic.*

$$\begin{aligned} ||\alpha||_{\mathrm{KB}} &= \alpha, \quad \text{for objective } \alpha \\ ||\neg\alpha||_{\mathrm{KB}} &= \neg\, ||\alpha||_{\mathrm{KB}} \\ ||\alpha \vee \beta||_{\mathrm{KB}} &= ||\alpha||_{\mathrm{KB}} \vee ||\beta||_{\mathrm{KB}} \\ ||\exists x\alpha||_{\mathrm{KB}} &= \exists x\, ||\alpha||_{\mathrm{KB}} \\ ||\mathbf{B}\alpha||_{\mathrm{KB}} &= \texttt{RES}[\![\mathrm{KB}, ||\alpha||_{\mathrm{KB}}]\!] \end{aligned}$$

The following three results are key to establishing decidability.

Lemma 1 *If* KB *is objective and* α *basic without sk-functions, then* $\models \mathbf{O}\mathrm{KB} \supset \mathbf{B}\alpha$ *iff* $\models \mathbf{O}\mathrm{KB} \supset \mathbf{B}\, ||\alpha||_{\mathrm{KB}}$.

Lemma 2 *If* KB *and* α *are objective, then* $\models \mathbf{O}\mathrm{KB} \supset \mathbf{B}\alpha$ *iff* $\models \mathbf{B}\mathrm{KB} \supset \mathbf{B}\alpha$.

Theorem 3 *(Patel-Schneider) t-entailment is decidable.*

With these intermediate results, the main theorem can be proven.

Theorem 4 *The validity problem for sentences of the form* $\mathbf{O}$KB $\supset \mathbf{B}\alpha$ *is decidable, assuming that* KB *is an objective sentence and* α *is a basic sentence not containing sk-functions.*

Proof: Lemma 1 implies that deciding whether a KB believes an arbitrary basic sentence reduces to deciding whether it believes an *objective* sentence. Thus let us assume that both KB and α are objective. Next, without loss of generality, we replace every standard name in KB and α by a new constant occurring nowhere else. In addition, we simplify both sentences in case they contain occurrences of `true` (e.g. $\gamma \vee \neg$`true` reduces to γ). Then $\models \mathbf{O}\mathrm{KB} \supset \mathbf{B}\alpha$ iff $\models \mathbf{B}\mathrm{KB} \supset \mathbf{B}\alpha$ (by lemma 2) iff (a) KB = `false` or (b) α = `true` or (c) KB $\longrightarrow_t \alpha$ (by theorem 1), which is decidable (theorem 3). ■

A Decidable KR Service

In this section, we apply the results of this paper to the specification of a KR service in the sense of [15]. The idea is that a KB can be defined in purely functional terms by two operations **ASK** and **TELL** that allow a user to ask the KB queries and to add new information to it. All a user has to know about is an *interaction language* in which to phrase queries and updates. By defining the interaction language to consist of the basic sentences of $\mathcal{L}$ that do not contain sk-functions, the results of the previous section can be readily applied to define **ASK** and **TELL**. Note that, from a user's point of view, the absence of sk-functions is of no concern since there are an infinite supply of other function symbols ($\mathcal{F}_{\mathrm{REG}}$) at hand.

Definition 12 **ASK** *and* **TELL**
Let KB *be an objective sentence and* α *a basic sentence without sk-functions.*

$$\texttt{ASK}[\![\mathrm{KB}, \alpha]\!] = \begin{cases} \text{YES} & \text{if } \models \mathbf{O}\mathrm{KB} \supset \mathbf{B}\alpha \wedge \neg\mathbf{B}\neg\alpha \\ \text{NO} & \text{if } \models \mathbf{O}\mathrm{KB} \supset \mathbf{B}\neg\alpha \wedge \neg\mathbf{B}\alpha \\ \text{UNK} & \text{if } \models \mathbf{O}\mathrm{KB} \supset \neg\mathbf{B}\alpha \wedge \neg\mathbf{B}\neg\alpha \\ \text{INC} & \text{if } \models \mathbf{O}\mathrm{KB} \supset \mathbf{B}\alpha \wedge \mathbf{B}\neg\alpha \end{cases}$$

$$\texttt{TELL}[\![\mathrm{KB}, \alpha]\!] = \mathrm{KB} \wedge\, ||\alpha||_{\mathrm{KB}}\ .$$

Note that the way **TELL**ing a sentence α to a KB is handled. Any occurrence of a $\mathbf{B}\gamma$ within α is first evaluated with respect to the *old* KB with the effect that an objective KB is always transformed into another objective KB. **ASK** and **TELL** are also implementable, which follows easily from the last section.

Corollary 1 **ASK** *and* **TELL** *are decidable.*

Apart from being decidable, are these routines also *efficient*? To answer this question, note that the complexity for both operations is dominated by the complexity of t-entailment, which follows easily from the way queries are evaluated using definition 10 and 11. Patel-Schneider [22] shows that, while t-entailment is intractable in general, it is indeed tractable under the following assumptions: the KB is in conjunctive normal form (CNF); queries, when converted into CNF, are of size at most $log(|\mathrm{KB}|)$; individual clauses are of constant size; and finally, only $log(|\mathrm{KB}|)$ clauses in the KB subsume a given clause in the query. From a KR point of view, these assumptions seem quite reasonable. The last condition, for example, can be satisfied if the KB uses many different predicates.

Conclusions

In this paper, we have developed a new model of belief and only-believing with perfect introspection for a full first-order language with function symbols. Most importantly, the model of belief has attractive computational properties in that it specifies first-order knowledge bases whose epistemic states are computable and, under certain assumptions, efficiently computable.

There are several ways this framework can be extended. In a forthcoming paper [13], we show how an equality predicate and quantifying-in can be incorporated, which allows us to make important distinctions between "knowing that" and "knowing what."

The deductive component of the current framework is rather weak. One way of increasing its power is by using a sorted logic approach as in [4]. Also, the work by McAllester et. al. [19] seems applicable in this context.

Finally, the logic developed here captures aspects of nonmonotonic reasoning similar to other autoepistemic logics. For example, the default assumption that Tweety flies unless known otherwise is captured by the valid[11] sentence

$$\mathbf{O}[\neg\mathbf{B}\neg\mathtt{Fly}(tweety) \supset \mathtt{Fly}(tweety)] \supset \mathbf{B}\mathtt{Fly}(tweety).$$

In the first-order case, it has so far been very difficult to investigate how default reasoning affects the overall complexity of reasoning because the underlying deductive component is already undecidable. Our framework allows, for the first time, to investigate this issue with a decidable deductive component in hand.

Acknowledgements

I would like to thank Hector Levesque for many stimulating discussions on the subject of modeling belief. His comments on the paper and those of the anonymous referees are greatly appreciated.

References

[1] Belnap, N. D., A Useful Four-Valued Logic, in G. Epstein and J. M. Dunn (eds.), *Modern Uses of Multiple-Valued Logic*, Reidel, 1977.

[2] Davis, M., Obvious Logical Inferences, in *Proceedings of the Seventh International Joint Conference on Artificial Intelligence*, Vancouver, B.C., 1981, pp. 530–531.

[3] Dunn, J. M., Intuitive Semantics for First-Degree Entailments and Coupled Trees, *Philosophical Studies* **29**, 1976, pp. 149–168.

[4] Frisch, A. M., *Knowledge Retrieval as Specialized Inference*, Ph.D. Thesis, University of Rochester, Department of Computer Science, 1986.

[5] Halpern, J. Y. and Moses, Y. O., Towards a Theory of Knowledge and Ignorance: Preliminary Report, in Proceedings of The Non-Monotonic Workshop, New Paltz, NY, 1984, pp.125–143.

[6] Halpern, J. Y. and Moses, Y. O., A Guide to the Modal Logics of Knowledge and Belief, in *Proc. of the Ninth International Joint Conference on Artificial Intelligence*, Los Angeles, CA, 1985, pp. 480–490.

[7] Ketonen, J. and Weyhrauch, R., A Decidable Fragment of Predicate Calculus, *Theoretical Computer Science* **32**, 1984, pp. 297–307.

[8] Hintikka, J., *Knowledge and Belief: An Introduction to the Logic of the Two Notions*, Cornell University Press, 1962.

[9] Konolige, K., A Computational Theory of Belief Introspection. In *Proceedings of the Ninth International Conference on Artificial Intelligence*, Los Angeles, 1985, pp. 502–508.

[10] Kripke, S. A., Semantical Considerations on Modal Logic, *Acta Philosophica Fennica* **16**, 1963, pp. 83–94.

[11] Lakemeyer, G., Steps Towards a First-Order Logic of Explicit and Implicit Belief, in *Proc. of the Conference on Theoretical Aspects of Reasoning about Knowledge*, Asilomar, California, 1986, pp. 325–340.

[12] Lakemeyer, G., Decidable Reasoning in First-Order Knowledge Bases with Perfect Introspection, Technical Report, Department of Computer Science, University of Toronto, in preparation.

[13] Lakemeyer, G., A Model of Decidable, Introspective Reasoning with Quantifying-In, in preparation.

[14] Lakemeyer, G. and Levesque, H. J., A Tractable Knowledge Representation Service with Full Introspection, in *Proc. of the Second Conference on Theoretical Aspects of Reasoning about Knowledge*, Asilomar, California, 1988, pp. 145–159.

[15] Levesque, H. J., Foundations of a Functional Approach to Knowledge Representation, *Artificial Intelligence*, **23**, 1984, pp. 155-212.

[16] Levesque, H. J., A Logic of Implicit and Explicit Belief, Tech. Rep. No. 32, Fairchild Lab. for AI Research, Palo Alto, 1984.

[17] Levesque, H. J., All I Know: A Study in Autoepistemic Logic, *Artificial Intelligence*, North Holland, **42**, 1990, pp. 263–309.

[18] Marek, W. and Truszczyński, M., Relating Autoepistemic and Default Logics. in *Proc. of the First International Conference on Principles of Knowledge Representation and Reasoning*, Morgan Kaufmann, San Mateo, CA, 1989, pp. 276–288.

[19] McAllester, D., Givan, B., and Fatima, T., Taxonomic Syntax for First Order Inference, in *Proc. of the First Int. Conf. on Principles of Knowledge Representation and Reasoning*, Morgan Kaufmann, San Mateo, 1989, pp. 289–300.

[20] Moore, R. C., Semantical Considerations on Nonmonotonic Logic, in *Proc. of the Eighth International Joint Conference on Artificial Intelligence*, Karlsruhe, FRG, 1983, pp. 272–279.

[21] Moore, R. C., Possible World Semantics for Autoepistemic Logic, in *The Non-Monotonic Reasoning Workshop*, New Paltz, NY, 1984, pp. 344–354.

[22] Patel-Schneider, P. F., *Decidable, Logic-Based Knowledge Representation*, Ph.D thesis, University of Toronto, 1987.

[11] Note that, even though *OBL* itself is monotonic, the epistemic states of KBs, which are specified in terms of only-believing, are nonmonotonic.

A Formal Theory of Multiple Agent Nonmonotonic Reasoning

Leora Morgenstern
leora@ibm.com
IBM T.J. Watson Research
P.O. Box 704, Mail Stop H1N08
Yorktown Heights, N.Y. 10598
(914)784-7151

Abstract

This paper presents a formal theory of multiple agent non-monotonic reasoning. We introduce the subject of multiple agent non-monotonic reasoning for inquiry and motivate the field in terms of its applications for commonsense reasoning. We extend Moore's [1985] Autoepistemic Logic to the multiple agent case, and show that the resulting logic is too weak for most applications of commonsense reasoning. We then suggest some possible sets of principles for a logic of multiple-agent non-monotonic reasoning, based on the concept of an agent's *arrogance* towards his knowledge of another agent's ignorance. While the principles of arrogance are in general too strong, we demonstrate that restricted versions of these principles can work quite well for commonsense reasoning. In particular, we show that a restricted form of the principle of arrogance yields results that are equivalent to EMAT [Morgenstern, 1989], a non-monotonic logic which was designed to reason about temporal projection in epistemic contexts.

1. Introduction and Motivation

Past research in non-monotonic reasoning (cf. [Ginsberg, 1987]) has concentrated almost exclusively on the single-agent case. [1] The focus has been either on how a single agent uses default rules of reasoning ([Reiter, 1980], [McDermott and Doyle, 1980]), or how an agent reasons about his own beliefs [Moore, 1985]. In fact, much practical non-monotonic reasoning involves reasoning about multiple agents. An agent who wishes to predict what another agent believes must reason about how the second agent's reasoning is non-monotonic. If I tell Susan that I have just bought a bird, I should be able to predict that Susan will believe that the bird flies. In order to do that, I will have to understand how Susan reasons with default rules and to know the default rules that Susan uses.

The ability to reason about how other agents reason non-monotonically is particularly crucial for multi-agent planning domains. An agent in a multi-agent domain who constructs any complex plan will have to reason about the ways in which other agents' actions interact with his plan. That is, he must be able to predict how other agents will act. This, in turn, entails having some set of beliefs about other agents' beliefs and goals.

For example, suppose that I plan to meet Carol at a restaurant five blocks from my home at 8 P.M. Carol lives 20 miles away, and I know that she assumes that it typically takes 40 minutes to travel that particular stretch of road. I can thus reason that Carol leaves her home at approximately 7:20 P.M. If at 7:40, I turn on the radio and discover that there is a major traffic jam on the route that Carol takes, I can conclude that Carol will be quite late. Most likely, I will not go down to the restaurant at 8, but will postpone going down until sometime later. In order to engage in this sort of reasoning, it is necessary for me to reason about Carol's default beliefs regarding the time it takes her to travel.

Other more complex examples involve the frame problem and temporal projection. Agents who plan must reason about what stays the same when actions are performed. Typically, agents perform temporal projection by doing some sort of non-monotonic reasoning. If I count on someone else to perform an action in my plan, I must be able to reason about how he performs temporal projection. Thus, I must be able to reason about how he reasons non-monotonically. A specific example of this sort of reasoning is given in Section 3.

Another rich source of examples comes from speech acts theory. Gricean theory [Grice, 1957] is best modelled in terms of mutual default assumptions about the other agents' beliefs regarding the conventions that they both hold. Russell [1987] has argued that communication is enabled by a *mutual absence of doubt* on the part of the agents that they have different conven-

[1] A notable exception is the work of [Perrault, 1987] and [Appelt and Konolige, 1988] on speech acts. The emphasis there, however, is on the default assumptions that the speaker [resp. hearer] of a speech act must make about the hearer's [resp. speaker's] beliefs. There is no discussion of the ways in which agents reason about other agent's abilities to reason non-monotonically, the focus of this paper.

tions. This mutual absence of doubt is likewise best modelled by multi-agent non-monotonic reasoning.

2. Extending AEL to MANML

We begin our formalization of a Multiple-Agent Non-Monotonic Logic (which we will call MANML) by extending a standard theory of plausible reasoning to the multi-agent case. There are several candidates for such a theory: Circumscription [McCarthy, 1980], Default Logic [Reiter, 1980], Non-monotonic Logic [McDermott and Doyle, 1980], and Autoepistemic Logic (AEL) [Moore, 1985]. We choose to extend Moore's AEL to the multiple-agent case. [2] This is primarily because the semantics underlying AEL is that of belief, and when we talk about agents engaging in multiple-agent non-monotonic reasoning, we most often talk in terms of knowledge and belief. I believe that Carol believes that it takes 40 minutes to get from her home to my neighborhood; Susan believes that my bird can fly. It is therefore reasonable to formulate such a system of reasoning within a logic that makes explicit reference to an agent's beliefs.

AEL was designed to formalize how an agent reasons about his own beliefs. Sentences of AEL are defined by the following rules:
(1) if ϕ is a formula of the predicate calculus, $\phi \in$ AEL;
(2) if $\phi \in$ AEL, $L\phi \in$ AEL, where L is the standard belief operator;
(3) if ϕ and ψ are sentences of AEL, so are $\phi \wedge \psi$ and $\neg\phi$.

We say a theory T of AEL is a stable set if it obeys the following three rules:
[1] T is closed under logical consequence
[2] if $P \in T$, then $LP \in T$
[3] if $P \notin T$, then $\neg LP \in T$.

That is, AEL models a perfect reasoner who has perfect positive and negative introspection.

Since Moore only considered single agents there was no need to index the belief operator L. Since we are modelling a multiple agent world, we do. We thus state the formation rules of MANML as follows:
(1) if ϕ is a sentence of the predicate calculus, ϕ is a sentence of MANML.
(2) if ϕ is a sentence of MANML, $L_a\phi$ is a sentence of MANML, where a is a constant of the language that represents an agent
(3) if ϕ and ψ are sentences of MANML, so are $\phi \wedge \psi$ and $\neg\phi$

Once we introduce multiple agents into the theory, the stable set formation rules of AEL should no longer hold. If P is in T, we do not necessarily want to say that L_aP is in T, for any a. Just because a formula is true in a theory, we would not want to say that any agent believes that formula.

Nevertheless, we wish to get the effect of these stable set formation rules, so that agents can reason autoepistemically, and so that agents can reason about other agents reasoning autoepistemically. The simplest way to do this is to alter the stable set formation rules by adding an explicit level of indexing in the obvious way. This yields the following set of rules:

0. if $P_1, ..., P_n \in T, P_1...P_n \vdash Q$, then $Q \in T$.
1. if $L_aP_1, ..., L_aP_n \in T, P_1...P_n \vdash Q$, then $L_aQ \in T$
2. if $L_aP \in T$, then $L_aL_aP \in T$
3. if $L_aP \notin T$, then $L_a\neg L_aP \in T$

Note that rule 3. is close, but not identical, to the principle of negative introspection in theories of belief: $\neg L_aP \Rightarrow L_a\neg L_aP$.

If we also assume that agents never believe contradictions, we get the following consequences:

4. if $L_aL_aP \in T$, then $L_aP \in T$
5. if $L_a\neg L_aP \in T$, then $L_aP \notin T$

Default rules must also be indexed appropriately. Bill's belief that he would know if he had an older brother is represented as $L_{Bill}(P \Rightarrow L_{Bill}P)$, where P stands for the sentence: Bill has an older brother. Suppose $L_{Bill}P \notin T$. By 1., $L_{Bill}(\neg L_{Bill}P \Rightarrow \neg P)$. But, since $L_{Bill}P \notin T$, by 3., $L_{Bill}\neg L_{Bill}P \in T$. Thus, by 1., $L_{Bill}\neg P$. Thus, we can see that the MANML stable set formation rules allow an agent to reason from his lack of belief in a particular proposition to the fact that he does not believe a proposition.

The MANML stable set formation rules 1. - 3. were chosen so that agents in MANML could perform autoepistemic reasoning. To show that that this is the case, we must prove a formal connection between AEL's and MANML's stable set formation rules. We begin with some definitions:

Let T be a set of sentences of MANML. T is *single-indexed* if all occurrences of L are indexed by the same constant. T is *epistemically closed* if all sentences in T are of the form $L_\alpha P$ for some α and P. For example, the theory $\{L_B(P \Rightarrow L_BP)\}$ is single-indexed and epistemically closed; the theory $\{P \wedge Q \Rightarrow L_aP)\}$ is single-indexed but not epistemically closed, and the theory $\{L_ap, L_bq\}$ is not single-indexed, but is epistemically closed.

We define the following function on single-indexed theories:

Strip(T) replaces every instance of L_α in T by L.

We then have the following theorem:

[2] Moore's Autoepistemic Logic has in some sense been superseded by Konolige's extensions to it [Konolige, 1987]. We use here Konolige's first extension: his move from propositional to predicate logic. In subsequent extensions, Konolige also gave a stronger notion of groundedness that eliminates circular reasoning. We choose the first extension as a starting point because of its simplicity.

Theorem1: Let T be a single-indexed and epistemically closed collection of sentences of MANML. Let $T_\alpha = \{\phi | L_\alpha \phi \in T\}$. Then, $L_\alpha P$ is a MANML stable-set consequence of T iff P is an AE stable-set consequence of $Strip(T_\alpha)$.

The theorem follows directly from the definitions.

Note that, in restricted cases, MANML seems to permit *other* agents to reason about an individual agent's autoepistemic reasoning. Assume that the principle of negative introspection: $\neg L_a P \Rightarrow L_a \neg L_a P$ holds in T. Let Q stand for the sentence: Alex has an older brother. Now suppose that T contains the following axioms: $L_{Bill} L_{Alex}(Q \Rightarrow L_{Alex} Q))$ (Bill believes that Alex believes that if Alex had an older brother, Alex would know about it) and $L_{Bill}(\neg L_{Alex} Q)$ By negative introspection and rule 1. of MANML, $L_{Bill} L_{Alex} \neg L_{Alex} Q$, and thus, by rule 1. we get $L_{Bill} L_{Alex} \neg Q$.

It should be noticed that in the foregoing example, Bill did not really reason about Alex's autoepistemic reasoning abilities at all. He started with two beliefs about Alex: Alex's default belief that if he had an older brother, he would know about it, and that Alex didn't believe he had an older brother. Given Bill's explicit belief that Alex did not have a belief about having an older brother, he was able to conclude that Alex believed that he did not have an older brother using only the principles of negative introspection and consequential closure. But this goes against the spirit of autoepistemic reasoning. The point is to start out from the positive beliefs in one's data base, use the stable set principles to conclude that there are beliefs that one doesn't have, and to go from there to negative beliefs. One should not have to explicitly ***assume*** the lack of positive beliefs in order to conclude that one has negative beliefs.

Similarly, suppose Susan believes that birds typically fly. Following Konolige's [1987] suggestion for representing default rules in autoepistemic logic, adding the appropriate indexing, and doing universal instantiation, we get:

$L_{Susan}(L_{Susan} Bird(X) \wedge \neg L_{Susan} \neg Fly(X) \Rightarrow Fly(X)),$

where X stands for Tweety. Suppose also that Susan knows that Tweety is a bird:

$L_{Susan} Bird(X)$

and that James knows that Susan has these beliefs:

$L_{James} L_{Susan}(L_{Susan} Bird(X) \wedge \neg L_{Susan} \neg Fly(X) \Rightarrow Fly(X))$

$L_{James} L_{Susan} Bird(X)$

In order for James to conclude that Susan believes that Tweety flies, James must also believe that Susan does ***not*** believe that Tweety cannot fly. That is, there must exist in T the belief:

$L_{James} \neg L_{Susan} \neg Fly(X)).$

Then the desired conclusion:

$L_{James} L_{Susan} Fly(X)$

follows by negative introspection and consequential closure. Again, these constraints go directly against the spirit of non-monotonic reasoning. The whole point is that agents need not have explicit knowledge of the conditions that are assumed to be true by default.

The question, then, at the heart of a system of multiple-agent non-monotonic reasoning is this: How is one agent to reason about a second agent's non-monotonic reasoning abilities? What can any agent coherently conclude about the beliefs that another agent does ***not*** have?

It is crucial to note that the multi-agent case is not at all symmetric with the single-agent case. In the single-agent case the given theory was a complete description of the mind of some agent. In the multi-agent case, agents have at best a partial description of other agents' beliefs.

The core of our approach to modelling multi-agent non-monotonic reasoning is this: Agents reason about how other agents reason non-monotonically by making default assumptions about what these agents ***do not*** believe. We make two important observations: Firstly, one agent may incorrectly assume that a second agent does not believes some statement P. Thus, the first agent's default assumptions are defeasible. In this sense, MANML is very different from AEL, which as Moore pointed out, is not defeasible at all. Secondly, this strategy embodies a certain amount of arrogance. An agent who reasons about a second agent's non-monotonic reasoning process must be arrogant with respect to his beliefs about the ***limitations*** of the second agent's beliefs. That is, he must in some sense believe that he knows all that is important to know about the second agent's beliefs.

Even if necessary, arrogance is not an attractive quality, and in too large doses, will certainly lead to wrong conclusions. Our aim, therefore, is to limit this arrogance as much as possible. For any default rule of the form $L_a \alpha \wedge \neg L_a \beta \Rightarrow \gamma$ let us call $\neg L_a \beta$ the ***negative*** part of the rule, since it deals with an agent's negative beliefs. To enable multi-agent non-monotonic reasoning, we need only assume that agents are arrogant with respect to the negative parts of the default rules.

A first step towards a principle of inference for MANML might therefore be:

If an agent X believes that a second agent Y believes some default rule $L_Y \alpha \wedge \neg L_Y \beta \Rightarrow \gamma$, and X believes that Y believes α and has no reason to believe that Y believes β, X can conclude that Y believes γ.

Formally, suppose

$L_X L_Y(L_Y \alpha \wedge \neg L_Y \beta \Rightarrow \gamma) \in T,$

$L_X L_Y \alpha \in T,$

$L_X L_Y \beta \notin T.$

Then,

$L_X L_Y \gamma \in T.$

Note that the $L_Y\alpha$ part of the rule may be empty; the rule thus covers autoepistemic rules of the form: $P \Rightarrow L_X P$.

We will call the above principle the Principle of Moderate Arrogance (PMA). If Q can be inferred from a theory T using the MANML stable set principles and PMA, we say Q is a PMA-stable-set consequence of T.

It can easily be seen that the Principle of Moderate Arrogance allows us to model in a rational manner how Bill comes to conclude that Alex believes that he has no older brother. In particular, it is an instance of the following theorem:

Theorem 2: Let $T = \{L_X L_Y(P \Rightarrow L_a P)\}$ be a theory of MANML + PMA. Then $L_X L_Y \neg P$ is a PMA-stable-set consequence of T.

Often, even an arrogant agent finds it worthwhile to be more circumspect about ascribing the absence of beliefs to other agents. This is particularly the case when the arrogant agent *does* believe the negative part of some default rule. It is very often difficult to believe that someone knows less than you do - so if you have stumbled across some unexpected circumstance, you would not want to assume that other agents are ignorant of it. This is especially true if the first agent has any reason to mistrust, or fear the actions of, the second agent (e.g., in cases where agents have conflicting goals, such as enemy agents in wartime).

We call this rule of inference the Principle of Cautious Arrogance (PCA). It is formalized as follows:

Suppose
$L_X L_Y(L_Y\alpha \wedge \neg L_Y\beta \Rightarrow \gamma) \in T$,
$L_X L_Y\alpha \in T$,
$L_X L_Y\beta \notin T$, and
$L_X\beta \notin T$.
Then
$L_X L_Y\gamma \in T$.

The PCA may be too cautious at times. There are certainly cases in which one agent knows that another agent is more ignorant than he - as in the restaurant example in section 1 - and in these cases one would rather adopt PMA than PCA. In general, however, both principles are much too permissive. For example, it is reasonable to assume that virtually all agents believe that if they had an older brother, they would know about it. Nevertheless, I would not want to conclude of every new person that I meet that they do not have an older brother, simply because I do not know that they believe that they have an older brother! Yet these conclusions would be sanctioned by both the PMA and PCA.

Clearly, we need restricted versions of the PMA and PCA for different situations. There are two ways to go about formalizing these restrictions: (1) posit that arrogance is a binary relation between agents. Bill may be arrogant about Alex's knowledge but not about Susan's, if he knows Alex very well and Susan only slightly. (2) restrict the types of defaults about which agents are arrogant. In particular, it may be the case that agents do some sort of default reasoning more readily the others. The restrictions should capture these tendencies.

Much research needs to be done on both these fronts in order to develop a realistic system of multiple-agent non-monotonic reasoning. In particular, we believe that it will be instructive to look at specific domains of multiple-agent non-monotonic reasoning in which restricted versions of PMA or PCA do seem reasonable. These exercises should give us insight into the reasons the arrogant rules of inference yield intuitive results in many cases, and ought to point us toward modifying these principles into truly reasonable rules of inference.

3. Epistemic Motivated Action Theory in MANML

A promising domain for the formalization of a restricted version of PMA is that of temporal reasoning, and specifically, of temporal projection. Agents who operate in multi-agent domains must reason about other agents' abilities to predict which facts about the world stay the same, and which change. We examine below a difficult problem in temporal projection, discuss its solution in a model-preference based theory known as EMAT [Morgenstern, 1989], and show that the principle embodied in EMAT can be recast as a restricted form of PMA.

Consider, then, the following problem, which we will call the Chain Request Frame Problem: [3] Suppose Alice wants to open a safe. She knows that the combination of the safe is a sequence of three two-digit numbers, but she does not know which. That is, she knows a finite disjunction of the form: *Comb = N1 or Comb = N2 or .....* The combination of the safe is a fluent; various authorized individuals may change the combination of the safe. However, typically, the combination does not change; this is a fluent with a long persistence. Given the large number of possible combinations, it would not be wise to attempt all of them. Alice knows that Jim knows the combination of the safe, but she is not on good enough terms with him to ask him. However, she knows Susan quite well, and Susan is on good terms with Jim. Alice therefore constructs the following 4-step, multi-agent plan:

1. Alice asks Susan to ask Jim for the combination
2. Susan asks Jim for the combination

[3] The Chain Request Frame Problem is a synthesis and simplification of two variant frame problems, the Third Agent Frame Problem, and the Vicarious Planning Frame Problem, which are discussed in [Morgenstern, 1989]. These frame problems and their solutions in EMAT, were developed in a rich logical language that allowed quantification into epistemic contexts. AEL (even Konolige's extended version) and therefore MANML do not allow quantification into epistemic contexts.

3. Jim tells Susan the combination
4. Susan tells Alice the combination

Unfortunately, Alice cannot prove that this plan will work. The reason is that although Jim knows the combination at the time when Alice begins her plan, Alice does not know that he will still know the combination by the time Susan asks him for it. Frame axioms will not work: since Jim is not involved in the initial stage of the plan, he may not know what happens, and therefore will not be able to apply the frame axioms. For the same reason, neither do standard non-monotonic temporal logics ([Lifschitz, 1987], [Haugh, 1987], and [Baker and Ginsberg, 1988]). Very briefly, the reason these logics will not work is that they are based on the situation calculus, and are therefore *dense* and/or *complete* in the following sense: A theory is *dense* if there are no gaps; for any interval in the past, one always knows of some action or subaction that has occurred during that subinterval. A theory is *complete* if all actions that have occurred are known to have occurred. In cases where a particular chronicle is not dense and/or not complete for a particular agent - as in the case of Jim, above - such logics cannot be used.

Nevertheless, a system capable of commonsense reasoning should be able to conclude that Alice's plan will probably work. Most likely, the combination of the safe will not change. Jim knows this. Therefore, as long as Jim does not know of anything that would indicate that the combination has changed, he will assume that it has not changed; i.e., he will still know the combination. This is true regardless of whether Jim knows what has happened in the initial stage of Alice's plan. Alice does not know of anything that Jim knows that would indicate a change; therefore she reasons that he will know the combination when Susan asks him, and will be able to tell her.

The basic principle underlying the foregoing reasoning is that actions happen only if they have to happen, or are *motivated*. This principle has been formalized in a non-monotonic logic called Motivated Action Theory (MAT) [Morgenstern and Stein, 1988] and is given in terms of a preference criterion over models. We assume a theory of causal and persistence rules TH, and a collection of statements giving a partial description of a chronicle, called a chronicle description CD. $CD \cup TH = TI$, a particular theory instantiation. All rules are monotonic; non-monotonicity is achieved through the preference criterion. A statement is said to be *motivated* if it has to be in all models of TI (is a theorem of TI); a statement is said to be motivated with respect to a particular model if it has to be true, given rules and boundary conditions, within that particular model. More specifically, if TH contains a rule of the form

$$\alpha \wedge \beta \Rightarrow \gamma$$

where α is a conjunction of sentences of the form $True(t, Occurs(act))$, i.e., the *triggering events* of the causal rule, β contains the conditions which must be true for the triggering events to have an effect, and γ is the result of the triggering events, and it is the case that α is motivated, and β is true with respect to some particular model, then γ is *motivated* with respect to that model. We prefer models which minimize statements of the form $True(t, Occurs(act))$; i.e., in which as few unmotivated actions as possible occur. Note that this is not the same as minimizing occurrences; in particular, the two concepts are different for causal chains of events in which the triggering event is motivated.

We have demonstrated that MAT models both forward and backward temporal reasoning, and in particular have shown that it gives intuitive results for the Yale Shooting Problem and a host of related problems. [4]

EMAT extends MAT by parameterizing theory instantiations with respect to agents and times. For example, $TI(a, t1)$ describes a's beliefs at $t1$ with regard to the causal theory and the description of the chronicle that he is in; $TI(a, t1, b, t2) = TI(a, t1)(b, t2)$ describes what a at $t1$ believes b at $t2$ believes. Motivation within a parameterized theory instantiation is analogous to motivation within a standard theory instantiation; similarly, the preference criterion over models of a parameterized theory instantiation is analogous to the preference criterion over models of a standard theory instantiation. The net result is that agents always assume that other agents reason using MAT on the theory instantiations which they ascribe to them.

In the above example, EMAT allows Alice to prove that her 4-step plan will work. The theory instantiation TI(Alice,1,Jim,3) contains the statement that the combination at time 3 is identical to the combination at time 1; thus, Jim knows the combination.

EMAT provides a simple, intuitive solution to the problem of temporal projection in epistemic contexts. It is interesting to note, however, that a very basic assumption of arrogance lies at the foundation of EMAT. By using the inference rules of MAT within a parameterized theory instantiation, agents in EMAT implicitly assume that the partial characterization that they have of the other agents' theory instantiations is sufficient for their purposes. It is implicitly assumed that if $TI(b, t2)$ contained some unexpected action, then $TI(a, t1, b, t2)$ would contain this action as well. That is, agents are arrogant with respect to what they know regarding other agents' beliefs about the course of events.

In fact, it is straightforward to model the basic principle of EMAT as a restricted form of PMA. To see

[4] Specifically, MAT yields the desired results for the Bloodless Yale Shooting Problem [Morgenstern and Stein, 1988], the Stanford Murder Mystery [Baker and Ginsberg, 1988], the Waiting Can Kill You [unnamed problem in [Baker and Ginsberg, 1988], p. 5], and the Message Passing Problem [Morgenstern and Stein, 1988]

this, note that the intuition underlying MAT - actions happen only if they have to happen - can be captured by the following axiom schema of MANML:

$L_a(\neg L_a Occurs(act) \Rightarrow \neg Occurs(act))$

Equivalently,

$L_a(Occurs(act) \Rightarrow L_a Occurs(act))$

That is, a believes that if it is consistent for him to believe that an action has not occurred, then the action has not occurred. In other words, it is assumed by default that unmotivated actions do not occur.

This assumption can be made explicit in the following restricted form of the PMA, which is limited to default rules of causal reasoning. This restricted form of the PMA, (EMAT-PMA) can be stated as follows: [5]

Suppose

$L_X L_Y(L_Y \alpha \wedge \neg L_Y True(t, Occurs(act)) \Rightarrow \gamma) \in T$

$L_X L_Y \alpha \in T$

$L_X L_Y True(t, Occurs, act)) \notin T$

Then

$L_X L_Y \gamma \in T$

This gives us a powerful, but not overly permissive, inference rule for non-monotonic temporal reasoning.

Thus far, we have shown that MANML + EMAT-PMA gives identical results to EMAT for the Chaining Request Frame Problem, and the class of Yale Shooting Problems. We are currently working on a proof of the claim that MANML + EMAT-PMA is equivalent to EMAT, modulo quantification into epistemic contexts.

Naturally, EMAT-PMA models only some of the reasoning power that a genuine theory of commonsense reasoning must have. Nevertheless, the reasonableness of this inference rule suggest the possibility that a group of rules of this sort, each expressing a restriction of PMA for some sort of reasoning, is a good first step toward building a general purpose theory of multi-agent non-monotonic reasoning.

4. Conclusions and Future Work

We have argued that a theory of multiple-agent non-monotonic reasoning is crucial for a realistic theory of commonsense reasoning. We have presented MANML, a logic which is capable of expressing such reasoning, and have suggested two inference rules to allow this type of non-monotonic reasoning, based on the concept of an agent's arrogance towards his knowledge of another agent's ignorance. While they are good first approximations, these rules were shown to be overly permissive. It was suggested that domain-specific restrictions of the principles of arrogance would give a more realistic theory. Finally, we demonstrated that an existing theory of temporal reasoning, which allowed for limited multiple-agent non-monotonic reasoning, could be duplicated by a restricted form of one of the principles of arrogance.

Future work includes investigating further restrictions of the PMA or PCA for specific domains of commonsense reasoning. One promising domain seems to be that of speech acts theory. Gricean theory [Grice, 1957] has argued that a mutual knowledge of convention is a prerequisite for successful communication; Russell [1987] has argued that a more realistic theory would be based on the concept of a mutual absence of doubt on the part of the speakers that they have different conventions. That is, it should be reasonable to assume that the agent with whom you are communicating shares your conventions unless you can prove otherwise. This assumption is predicated on some amount of arrogance towards the other agent; you believe that if he had different conventions (i.e., did *not* believe the accepted conventions), you would know about it. Let us introduce the operator LCL, which we define equivalent to [Cohen and Levesque, 1987] BMB (believe that it is mutually believed) operator. Then, a first pass at modelling this sort of inference rule might be:

Suppose $L_X(\neg LCL_Y(X, Y, Convention_i)) \notin T$. Then $L_X LCL_Y(X, Y, Convention_i) \in T$.

This is clearly a restricted form of PMA. The accuracy and usefulness of this inference rule for formalizing speech acts theory is a topic for further investigation.

Finally, we plan to integrate MANML with various existing theories of multiple-agent commonsense reasoning, starting with a robust theory of planning and action. We can then test the utility of MANML on AI commonsense reasoning problems that thus far have been solvable only within a monotonic logic.

Acknowledgements

This work has benefited from the criticisms, suggestions and comments of Francisco Corrella, Ernie Davis, Hector Geffner, Benjamin Grosof, Daniel Lehmann, Lynn Stein, and Wlodek Zadrozny.

References

[Appelt and Konolige, 1988] Appelt, Douglas and Kurt Konolige: "A Practical Non-monotonic Theory for Reasoning About Speech Acts, " *Proceedings of the 26th Conference of the ACL*, 1988

[Baker, 1989] Baker, Andrew: "A Simple Solution to the Yale Shooting Problem," *Proceedings, First Conference on Principles of Knowledge Representation and Reasoning*, 1988

[Baker and Ginsberg, 1988] Baker, Andrew and Matthew Ginsberg: "Some Problems in Temporal Reasoning," manuscript, 1988

[5] To ensure that theorems of MAT are also theorems of MANML + EMAT-PMA, we must also add the axiom of privileged access [Davis, 1990]: $L_X L_X P \Rightarrow L_X P$. This is of course a consequence of the stable set principles of MANML if we assume that agents do not believe contradictions.

[Cohen and Levesque, 1987] Cohen, Philip and Hector Levesque: "Rational Interaction as the Basis for Communication," *Proceedings, Symposium on Plans and Intentions in Communication and Discourse*, Monterey, 1987

[Davis, 1990] Davis, Ernest: *Representations of Commonsense Knowledge*, Morgan Kaufman, 1990

[Ginsberg, 1987] Ginsberg, Matthew, ed: *Readings in Nonmonotonic Reasoning*, Morgan Kaufman, Los Altos, 1987

[Grice, 1957] Grice, H.P.: "Meaning," *Philosophical Review*, 1957

[Haugh, 1987] Haugh, Brian: "Simple Causal Minimizations for Temporal Persistence and Projection," *Proceedings, AAAI 1987*

[Konolige, 1987] Konolige, Kurt: "On the Relation Between Default Theories and Autoepistemic Logic," *Proceedings, IJCAI 1987*

[Lifschitz, 1987] Lifschitz, Vladimir: "Formal Theories of Action," *Proceedings, IJCAI 1987*

[McCarthy, 1980] McCarthy, John: "Circumscription," *Artificial Intelligence*, Vol. 13, 1980

[McDermott and Doyle, 1980] McDermott, Drew and Jon Doyle: "Non-monotonic Logic I," *Artificial Intelligence*, Vol. 13, 1980

[Moore, 1985] Moore, Robert: "Semantical Considerations on Nonmonotonic Logic," *Artificial Intelligence*, Vol.25, 1985

[Morgenstern, 1989] Morgenstern, Leora: "Knowledge and the Frame Problem," Workshop on the Frame Problem, Pensacola, 1989. To appear in: Kenneth Ford and Patrick Hayes, eds: *Advances in Human and Machine Cognition*, Vol. I: The Frame Problem in Artificial Intelligence, JAI Press, Greenwich, 1990

[Morgenstern and Stein, 1988] Morgenstern, Leora and Lynn Andrea Stein: "Why Things go Wrong: A Formal Theory of Causal Reasoning," *Proceedings, AAAI 1988*

[Perrault, 1987] Perrault, Ray: "An Application of Default Logic to Speech Act Theory," *Proceedings, Symposium on Intentions and Plans in Communication and Discourse,* Monterey, 1987

[Reiter, 1980] Reiter, Ray: "A Logic for Default Reasoning," *Artificial Intelligence*, Vol. 13, 1980

[Russell, 1987] Russell, Stuart: "Rationality as an Explanation of Language?," *Behavioral and Brain Sciences*, Vol. 10, 1987

A Circumscriptive Theory for Causal and Evidential Support

Eunok Paek
Department of Computer Science
Stanford University
Stanford, California 94305
paek@cs.stanford.edu

Abstract

Reasoning about causality is an interesting application area of formal nonmonotonic theories. Here we focus our attention on a certain aspect of causal reasoning, namely *causal asymmetry*. In order to provide a qualitative account of causal asymmetry, we present a justification-based approach that uses circumscription to obtain the minimality of causes. We define the notion of causal and evidential support in terms of a justification change with respect to a circumscriptive theory and show how the definition provides desirable interactions between causal and evidential support.

1 Introduction

Commonsense reasoning has provided a rich application area for nonmonotonic logic. As some researchers have noted, however, certain aspects of causal reasoning which are prevalent in ordinary discourse have not received due treatment by nonmonotonic logic[Pearl, 1988a].

In this paper, we will focus on the phenomenon of *causal asymmetry* which results because two causes of an observation interact differently than two consequences of a common cause. In [Pearl, 1988a], Pearl presents a causal reasoning system as an attempt to provide a qualitative account of such causal directionality shown in his Bayesian analysis[Pearl, 1988b]. His system, however, generates certain counterintuitive conclusions, as Section 3 will illustrate.

Here we introduce a better qualitative account of causal directionality that overcomes the difficulty mentioned in Section 3. Our approach is not as detailed as the probabilistic account of causal directionality, but a qualitative approach has its advantages: it is simpler and more intuitive than the probabilistic approach.

In Section 2, we will briefly describe Pearl's causal reasoning system and clarify a few implicit assumptions made by the system. In the following section, we will look into some difficulty with his framework. In Section 4, we present a simple circumscriptive theory[McCarthy, 1986] that allows us to draw explanatory conclusions. Finally we will give a justification-based account of causal directionality using this circumscriptive theory and also discuss how our approach improves on Pearl's.

2 Pearl's Causal Reasoning System

In [Pearl, 1988a], Pearl states that it is necessary to know whether a given proposition was established by causal or evidential considerations, and that there is a causal asymmetry stemming from the fact that two causes of an observation interact differently than two consequences of a common cause; in the absence of a direct relation between the two, the former *compete* with each other, while the latter *support* each other. For example, when we observe a rash we are more likely to observe fever as well because measles always involves both fever and rash. In contrast, when we know that the cause of a rash is measles, it is less likely that the patient is also suffering from an allergy. In order to produce such an asymmetry, Pearl proposes a reasoning system in which every proposition is labeled as either *causally* or *evidentially established*, every rule is labeled as either *causal* or *evidential*, and inference rules are defined according to these labels. That is, each rule in the system is labeled as C (connoting "causal") or E (connoting "evidential"), and $P \rightarrow_C Q$ means "P causes Q" and $Q \rightarrow_E P$ means "Q is evidence for P". Similarly each proposition is labeled either as E or C where $E(P)$ means that P is believed for evidential reasons and $C(Q)$ means that Q is believed for causal reasons. The semantics of the $C - E$ distinction are defined by the following three inference rules

$$\frac{P \rightarrow_C Q \quad C(P)}{C(Q)} \qquad \frac{P \rightarrow_C Q \quad E(P)}{C(Q)} \qquad \frac{P \rightarrow_E Q \quad E(P)}{E(Q)}$$

while purposely precluding the inference rule

$$\frac{P \rightarrow_E Q \quad C(P)}{Q}$$

Before we explain how these inference rules deal with causal asymmetry, we want to clarify a few assumptions made by Pearl's reasoning system. First, in his reasoning system it is not specified how we initially obtain propositional labels. When we have some labels for certain propositions initially, we can deduce other labeled propositions by using the initially labeled propositions and rules according to the inference rules sanctioned by the system. Without any initial labeling, however, we cannot use the inference rules at all. But from the fact that we can use a causal rule $P \rightarrow_C Q$ together with a proposition P regardless of its label, we can obtain labels for certain propositions without any initial labeling for P. From now on, whenever we have a rule $P \rightarrow_C Q$ and a proposition P without any label, we will assume that $C(Q)$ follows. Secondly, there is an implicit correspondence between causal and evidential rules. That is, the database must have $Q \rightarrow_E P$ whenever it has $P \rightarrow_C Q$. If we can represent evidential rules without assuming the existence of their causal counterparts, some inference rules can be counterintuitive. If there is a strong correlation between two events without any causal connection, sometimes we should allow the inference prohibited by Pearl's reasoning system. For example, suppose that the database has the sentence $\forall x.Take\_cs221(x) \rightarrow_E Brown\_Hair(x)$ together with $C(Take\_cs221(John))$; we can easily imagine a situation in which John is taking cs221 to fulfill his course requirements, hence $Take\_cs221(John)$ is "causally established." It is apparent that we should conclude $Brown\_Hair(John)$. We can justify the reasoning system presented above only when we assume the coexistence of both causal and evidential rules.

With these assumptions in mind, let us look at the following example, which is slightly modified from [Pearl, 1988a].

Example 1
Suppose we have the knowledge about causation that rain causes grass to be wet, that a sprinkler also causes wet grass and that rain causes slippery roads. Its translation into Pearl's representation will be as follows:

$Rain \rightarrow_C WetGrass$;
$Sprinkler \rightarrow_C WetGrass$;
$Rain \rightarrow_C SlipperyRoad$;
$WetGrass \rightarrow_E Rain$;
$WetGrass \rightarrow_E Sprinkler$;
$SlipperyRoad \rightarrow_E Rain$.

If we came to know *WetGrass* because of *Rain*, *WetGrass* would be labeled C according to the assumption mentioned above. When *WetGrass* is labeled C, it cannot be used to infer *Sprinkler* together with the evidential rule $WetGrass \rightarrow_E Sprinkler$, because it is not sanctioned by the system. This shows how two causes of a single effect work *against* each other. On the other hand, if *SlipperyRoad* were labeled E, we would deduce $E(Rain)$ using the evidential rule $SlipperyRoad \rightarrow_E Rain$, and $C(WetGrass)$ would follow from $E(Rain)$ and $Rain \rightarrow_C WetGrass$. In this case, two consequences of a single cause work *for* each other.

3 Difficulty with Pearl's System

With the assumptions mentioned in the previous section in mind, we will now see what can go wrong with Pearl's reasoning system. For instance, when *WetGrass* is established evidentially, it can be used to infer both *Rain* and *Sprinkler*, which is rather counterintuitive. Instead, what we would like to conclude from *WetGrass* is *Rain or Sprinkler*.

One way to overcome this counterintuitive result is to weaken the meaning of the labels (C and E) from that of *acceptance* to that of *support*. That is, we reinterpret the meaning of $E(Sprinkler)$ as *there is evidential support for Sprinkler,* not as *Sprinkler holds for an evidential reason.* Once we reinterpret the E label as support, concluding $E(Rain)$ and $E(Sprinkler)$ from *WetGrass* is no longer counterintuitive. We have reason to believe that it might have rained, and also that the sprinkler might have been on.

Once we weaken the meaning of the E label from acceptance to support, we must also weaken the meaning of the C label. Since one of the three inference rules allows us to infer $C(Q)$ from $E(P)$ and $P \rightarrow_C Q$ and $E(P)$ means only that P is evidentially supported, we are no longer justified in saying that Q holds for a causal reason. Instead, we can say that Q is *causally supported.*

Having a notion of support and making a distinction between causal and evidential support may be useful. However, we still need a mechanism to draw conclusions. If we know it rains, it is clear that we should conclude that the grass is wet, in addition to concluding that there is causal support for the wet grass. In the following sections, we will show how a simple circumscriptive theory can be used to draw conclusions and then see how we can use this circumscriptive theory to define the notion of support.

4 Circumscription for Minimization of Causes

In this section, we propose a simple circumscriptive theory which allows us to draw explanatory conclusions by minimizing causes.

In order to minimize causes, we will reify causal information by using the predicate $causes(P, Q)$. The intended meaning of $causes(P, Q)$ is that P causes Q to hold. We will also use the predicates $holds(P)$ and $holds\_acausally(Q)$, meaning that P is true and that Q is true without any cause being known, respectively. Let the causal theory be divided into two parts, $\mathcal{T} = < R, F >$. R consists of instances of the *causes* predicate together with the following axiom:

$\forall x.holds(x) \equiv$
$[\exists y.causes(y,x) \wedge holds(y)] \vee holds\_acausally(x)$ (1)

F consists of instances of the *holds* predicate[1].

Given a two-part background theory $< R, F >$, we will circumscribe it by minimizing *causes* and *holds_acausally* with *causes* given higher priority. *causes* is given higher priority because we would like to say that something holds acausally only when we cannot find a cause for it from all we know. That is, we are justified in saying that an event holds acausally only when we do not have any information about its cause.

Example 2
Let our background theory be as follows:

R : $\{causes(Rain, WetGrass),$
$causes(Rain, SlipperyRoad),$
$causes(Sprinkler, WetGrass)\}$ with Axiom (1)
F : $\{holds(WetGrass)\}$

If we circumscribe the background theory in this example, we can conclude $holds(Rain) \vee holds(Sprinkler)$. Consider all the minimal models that satisfy the result of circumscription. In all minimal models, nothing holds acausally. By the axiom (1), we know that $holds(WetGrass)$ is true if and only if any of its causes holds. In this example, the only causes for *WetGrass* are *Rain* and *Sprinkler*. Hence $holds(Rain) \vee holds(Sprinkler)$ is true in all minimal models. However, we will not have $holds(Rain) \wedge holds(Sprinkler)$.

Using the circumscribed background theory, we will define the notion of support in the following section.

5 Supports

As we saw in the previous section, circumscription allows us to draw explanatory conclusions without any unintuitive behavior, and that without the burden of specifying propositional labels initially. However, the notion of causal/evidential support may be useful for certain problems. For instance, we may want to know how one event causally/evidentially affects another even if this event does not logically follow from the other.

As a logical abstraction of probabilistic analysis, we will use a *justification-based* notion of support. First, we will define what a justification is. Then we will define causal and evidential support in terms of justification change and compare our notion of support with the propositional labels in Pearl's $C - E$ system.

5.1 Justification

Informally, a justification for a certain proposition is a *reason to believe* that proposition. Let $\mathcal{T}$ be our background theory. We will define $J_\mathcal{T}$ to be a mapping from a well-formed formula to a well-formed formula. If $J_\mathcal{T}(\alpha) = \beta$, then α will be true whenever β (a justification for α) is true in the models of the theory $\mathcal{T}$. That is, $\mathcal{T} \cup \{\beta\} \models \alpha$. A formal definition for a justification follows.

Definition 5.1.1 (Justification):
Given a set of first-order sentences $\mathcal{T}$ and a well-formed formula α, $J_\mathcal{T}(\alpha) = \beta$ if and only if

$$\beta = \bigvee_i \beta_i$$

for each β_j such that
(1) $\mathcal{T} \cup \{\beta_j\}$ is satisfiable;
(2) $\mathcal{T} \cup \{\beta_j\} \models \alpha$; and
(3) β_j is a conjunction of literals.

Our definition of justification is closely connected with the definition of *minimal support* in the Clause Maintenance System (CMS) by Reiter and deKleer [Reiter and de Kleer, 1987]. They define support as a set of literals which satisfies the conditions (1) and (2) in Definition 5.1.1, and minimal support as a minimal such set. Here we obtain minimality of justification by taking a disjunction of all β_i's rather than requiring each β_i to be minimal. That is, we would like to think of justification as a well-formed formula in disjunctive normal form. Viewing justification as a formula allows us to handle disjunctive explanation easily, thus giving us much more flexibility in defining support.

The third condition deserves some attention. Let us see what happens if we don't have this condition. Given an empty background theory, the justification for P will be P itself. That is, it can only be self-justified because we do not know anything about P. Once we add Q, which may have nothing to do with P, justification for P will change to $\neg Q \vee P$. This is equivalent to $Q \supset P$. This is undesirable because Q can be a random proposition which may have no relevance to P. If we don't have the condition (3), $\tau \supset \alpha$ will be a valid β_i for justification of α for any τ in $\mathcal{T}$.

The addition of condition (3) creates another interesting effect. Suppose our initial background theory was $R \equiv (\neg Q \vee P)$, i.e., we explicitly name $Q \supset P$ as R. Now $J_\mathcal{T}(P) = R \wedge Q$. Simply giving a name for $Q \supset P$ causes it to become a part of justification for P. At first glance, it looks rather strange, but in a sense we gave a possibility of using certain literals, in this example R and Q, to express justifications by mentioning them in the background theory. Once we note

[1] How to axiomatize causality is an important problem in and of itself, but it is not what we are interested in. We are interested in how to obtain the proper interaction between causal and evidential support. We believe that the results in the following sections apply independently of the axiomatization used for a causal theory.

this feature, we can use it as a guide for characterizing the terms in which we should express justifications.

Now we will define a partial order on justifications in terms of entailment.

Definition 5.1.2 (Ordering on Justifications): Given two well-formed formulas β_1 and β_2,

(1) $\beta_1 \leq \beta_2$ if and only if $\beta_1 \models \beta_2$, and
(2) $\beta_1 < \beta_2$ if and only if $\beta_1 \leq \beta_2$ and $\beta_2 \not\leq \beta_1$.

Given two different justifications for α, β_1 and β_2, we will say that β_2 is *better* than β_1 if $\beta_1 < \beta_2$, that is, we will say that a semantically weaker justification is better. Essentially a justification for α is a formula we have to add to the background theory so that we can deduce α. If one justification is semantically weaker than others, it means that what we must have in addition to the background theory is weaker. That's why we like a semantically weaker justification better.

We will say that a proposition α is supported when its justification gets better due to the addition of some other proposition β [2]. In the next section, we will define support in terms of an increase in justification, and see how our notion of support is different from Pearl's propositional labels.

5.2 Causal and Evidential Supports

Now we will define causal and evidential supports. In the following, circumscription minimizes *causes* and *holds_acausally* with *causes* given higher priority.

Definition 5.2.1 (Evidential Support): A proposition α is *evidentially* supported with respect to a background theory $\mathcal{T} =< R, F >$ if and only if there is a formula β such that

(1) $\mathcal{T} \models \beta$;
(2) $J_R(\alpha) \not< J_{R\cup\{\beta\}}(\alpha)$;
(3) $J_{CIRC(R\cup F-\{\beta\})}(\alpha) < J_{CIRC(R\cup F)}(\alpha)$.

Definition 5.2.1 says that β evidentially supports α when there is no causal relation between β and α (the second clause), but rather there is evidential relation between them so that the justification for α increases due to circumscription, but not due to the initial background theory.

Definition 5.2.2 (Causal Support): A proposition α is *causally* supported with respect to a background theory $\mathcal{T} =< R, F >$ if and only if there is a formula β such that

(1) β is supported (either evidentially or causally) or $F \models \beta$;
(2) $J_R(\alpha) < J_{R\cup\{\beta\}}(\alpha)$;
(3) $\beta \not\models \alpha$.

β causally supports α when β itself is supported and there is a causal relation between β and α. The third clause is to prevent a circular definition of support. Without it, α may be causally supported if it is either evidentially or causally supported.

Let us work through some examples. Let our background theory have the same R as in Example 2. When F is $\{holds(SlipperyRoad)\}$, $holds(Rain)$ is evidentially supported. In order to see this, we have to compare the justifications for $holds(Rain)$ with and without $holds(SlipperyRoad)$, given a circumscribed background theory. The following relation holds between two different justifications:

$$J_{CIRC(R\cup F-\{holds(SlipperyRoad)\})}(holds(Rain)) < J_{CIRC(R\cup F)}(holds(Rain))$$

Without $holds(SlipperyRoad)$ in the background theory, the justification for $holds(Rain)$ with respect to the circumscribed theory is *unknown* [3]. With $holds(SlipperyRoad)$ in the background theory, the result of circumscription makes the justification for $holds(Rain)$ $True$. Hence we can say that $holds(SlipperyRoad)$ makes the justification for $holds(Rain)$ increase. Also with this background theory, $holds(WetGrass)$ is causally supported because $holds(Rain)$ is evidentially supported and $causes(Rain, WetGrass)$. Here two consequences of a common cause $holds(Rain)$ support each other.

When F is $\{holds(Rain)\}$, $holds(Sprinkler)$ is not evidentially supported because its justification does not increase but rather decreases. Justifications for $holds(Sprinkler)$ with respect to the circumscribed background theory with and without $holds(Rain)$ are as follows:

$$J_{CIRC(R\cup F-\{holds(Rain)\})}(holds(Sprinkler)) = holds(WetGrass) \wedge \neg holds(Rain)$$
$$J_{CIRC(R\cup F)}(holds(Sprinkler)) = unknown$$

This situation arises because if we apply circumscription to the background theory without $holds(Rain)$, we can infer $holds(WetGrass) \supset holds(Rain) \vee holds(Sprinkler)$. With $holds(Rain)$ in the background theory, however, the justification for $holds(Sprinkler)$ becomes *unknown*. Hence, the justification for $holds(Sprinkler)$ decreases due to the addition of $holds(Rain)$ to the background theory. In this case, two causes of an observation do not support

[2] We were inspired by Gardenfors' work on explanation [Gardenfors, 1988] in that we require an increase in justification, hence a decrease in *surprise*, for a proposition to be supported.

[3] When a proposition can only be self-justified, we will refer to its justification as *unknown*.

each other but rather compete with each other.

Our definition of support is different from Pearl's propositional labels in two ways. The first difference is in its partiality. That is, when a conjunction of multiple events E_1, E_2, and E_3 causes another event E_4, any combination of E_1, E_2, E_3 will causally support E_4; this differs from Pearl's system, in which all three events must happen in order to causally support E_4. As for evidential support, Pearl's system is already partial but there still is a subtle difference. To illustrate this, let R be as in Example 2 and F be $\{holds(WetGrass), holds(SlipperyRoad)\}$. According to definition 5.2.1, $holds(Rain)$ is evidentially supported, but $holds(Sprinkler)$ is not. In Pearl's system $E(Sprinkler)$ will follow if $WetGrass$ and $SlipperyRoad$ are evidentially supported. We believe that this is another aspect of causal reasoning that a logical framework should capture (i.e., when a certain cause must hold in order to explain multiple evidence, it *explains away* others). There is one more difference in the way we define support for events in F. For instance, when our background theory has $R : \{causes(P, Q)\}, F : \{holds(Q)\}$, $holds(P)$ is evidentially supported and $holds(Q)$ is causally supported. However, in Pearl's system, neither $E(P)$ nor $C(Q)$ follows from the theory, $\{P \rightarrow_C Q, Q\}$. This again shows the advantage of our approach.

6 Conclusion

We have presented a very simple circumscriptive theory to draw explanatory conclusions from a causal background theory. We have also showed that we can define the notion of causal/evidential support using circumscription and changes in justification. Not only does our approach avoid certain counterintuitive results, but it also serves as a better logical abstraction of the probabilistic account of causality in the sense that various desirable interactions between causal and evidential supports fall out naturally from their semantic definitions. Our approach provides a notion of both acceptance and support of a proposition. It also allows us to define support without any initial labeling of propositions in the background theory. Finally, it handles the phenomenon of causal asymmetry in a more sophisticated way in that one cause explains away others not only when it is directly known, but also when it can be inferred indirectly from some other propositions. Our approach is not as detailed as a probabilistic analysis, but it is an improvement over Pearl's system.

Acknowledgement

The author would like to thank Matt Ginsberg for his interest, criticism and technical help. Thanks also to Kurt Konolige, Karen Myers, Nils Nilsson, and Martha Pollack for valuable discussions. This work has been supported by NSF under grant IRI-89-12188, by NASA under the research contract NCC2-494, and by General Dynamics.

References

[Gardenfors, 1988] Peter Gardenfors. *Knowledge in Flux: Modeling the Dynamics of Epistemic States.* MIT Press, Cambridge, Massachusetts, 1988.

[McCarthy, 1986] John McCarthy. Applications of circumscription to formalizing common sense knowledge. *Artificial Intelligence*, 28:89–116, 1986.

[Pearl, 1988a] Judea Pearl. Embracing causality in default reasoning. *Artificial Intelligence*, 35:259–271, 1988.

[Pearl, 1988b] Judea Pearl. *Probabilistic Reasoning in Intelligent Systems: Networks of Plausible Inference.* Morgan Kaufmann, San Mateo, California, 1988.

[Reiter and de Kleer, 1987] Raymond Reiter and Johan de Kleer. Foundations of assumption-based truth maintenance systems: Preliminary report. In *Proceedings of the Sixth National Conference on Artificial Intelligence*, pages 183–188, 1987.

The Complexity of Closed World Reasoning and Circumscription

Marco Cadoli, Maurizio Lenzerini
Dipartimento di Informatica e Sistemistica
Università di Roma "La Sapienza"
via Buonarroti 12, 00185 Roma, Italia

Abstract

Closed world reasoning is a common nonmonotonic technique that allows for dealing with negative information in knowledge and data bases. We present a detailed analysis of the computational complexity of the different forms of closed world reasoning for various fragments of propositional logic. The analysis allows us to draw a complete picture of the tractability/intractability frontier for such a form of nonmonotonic reasoning. We also discuss how to use our results in order to characterize the computational complexity of other problems related to nonmonotonic inheritance, diagnosis, and default reasoning.

1 Introduction

Closed World Reasoning (CWR) is a common nonmonotonic technique that allows for dealing with negative information in knowledge and data bases.

The simplest form of closed world reasoning is the *(simple) closed world assumption* (CWA), introduced by Reiter [13], which states that a negative ground fact of the form $\neg p$ is inferred from a knowledge base T just in case the corresponding positive fact p cannot be deduced from T. This represents the idea that every positive fact that is not known to be true, should be considered false. A semantic characterization of the CWA can be given in terms of minimal Herbrand models: reasoning with the CWA is equivalent to assuming that every ground fact which is not included in the intersection of all the Herbrand models of T is false.

Starting from the consideration that the simple CWA may lead to inconsistency when the knowledge base contains disjunctive positive assertions, such as $(a \vee b)$, Minker [10] proposed a new form of closed world reasoning, called *generalized closed world assumption* (GCWA), which states that the negative facts to be inferred from a knowledge base T, should be those which do not appear in *any* of the minimal models of T. This principle takes into account that a (non-Horn) theory may have, in general, more than one minimal model, and every such model should be considered in closed world inference.

Gelfond and Przymusinska [4] extend the work of Minker, by allowing the generalized closed world assumption to be applied to a specified set P of (not necessarily all) predicates of the knowledge base. The resulting form of closed world reasoning, called *careful closed world assumption* (CCWA), is shown to be more expressive than the original generalized closed world assumption. In particular, it allows the derivation of new positive facts, which is impossible in both the CWA and the GCWA.

Gelfond, Przymusinska, and Przymusinski [5] deal with an extension of the CCWA, proposing the so-called *extended closed world assumption* (ECWA), which is shown to be the most powerful formalization of closed world reasoning. In particular, they prove the equivalence (at least for propositional theories) between ECWA and circumscription [9].

Although the importance of the above forms of CWR has often been stressed both from a theoretical and a practical point of view, a complete analysis of the computational complexity of CWR is missing. Notice that, on the contrary, such an analysis has been provided for other forms of nonmonotonic reasoning, such as default reasoning [6], abduction [2], and path-based inheritance [17].

The aim of this paper is to present a detailed analysis of the computational complexity of closed world reasoning. In particular, we are interested in exploring the tradeoff between the tractability of the inference problem and the expressive power of the representation language. To this purpose, we concentrate our attention on propositional logic (although our results can be generalized in several ways, as mentioned in Section 4). which provides a representation language which is decidable, and, at least in some case, tractable, and we consider different subclasses of propositional formulae, each one characterized by some syntactic restriction.

In the analysis, we shall refer to the results concerning the computational complexity of CWR which have appeared in the literature since now, namely [1,7,8,16].

The paper is organized as follows. In Section 2 we provide some definitions and results which will be used in the subsequent sections. In Section 3 we present the complexity analysis: the analysis is performed along two directions, one concerning the expressive power of the language, and one concerning the form of CWR. Finally, in Section 4 we discuss possible applications of our results to other reasoning problems.

2 Preliminaries

We always refer to propositional formulae in conjunctive normal form, called CNF formulae or simply formulae. The set of propositional letters appearing in a formula is called its alphabet. A CNF formula is a conjunction of clauses, where a clause is a disjunction of literals, and a literal is either a propositional letter or its negation.

A *closed world reasoning rule* (CWR-rule) is a rule specifying a set of clauses to be conjoined to a formula T in order to obtain the *closure* of T according to some closed world resoning criterion. Some CWR-rule requires the alphabet of the formula to be partitioned into three sets, denoted P, Q, Z respectively. P contains the letters to be minimized, Z contains the letters whose truth value can vary when minimizing the letters in P, and Q contains all the remaining letters. Given a set of letters R, we denote by R^+ (resp. R^-) the set of all positive (resp. negative) literals from R.

All the forms of CWR we consider in this paper can be abstractly characterized as follows.

Definition 1 *Let T be a propositional formula, and $\langle P; Q; Z\rangle$ be a partition of the letters of its alphabet. We define the closure of T with respect to the CWR-rule α as follows:*

$$\alpha(T; P; Q; Z) = T \cup \{\neg K \mid K \text{ is free for negation in } T \text{ with respect to } \alpha\}$$

where K is a formula whose form depends on α.

As a notational convenience, we say that the formula K is α-ffn to mean that it is free for negation with respect to the CWR-rule α in $\langle T; P; Q; Z\rangle$. In order to precisely characterize the different forms of CWR, we now consider every CWR-rule α, specifying what it means for a formula to be α-ffn.

- The CWA-rule corresponds to the (simple) closed world assumption [13]. K is CWA-ffn if K is a positive literal and $T \not\models K$.
- The GCWA-rule corresponds to the generalized closed world assumption [10]. K is GCWA-ffn if K is a positive literal and, for each positive clause B such that $T \not\models B$, it holds that $T \not\models B \vee K$.
- The EGCWA-rule corresponds to the extended generalized closed world assumption [18]. K is EGCWA-ffn if K is a conjunction of positive literals and, for each positive clause B such that $T \not\models B$, it holds that $T \not\models B \vee K$.
- The CCWA-rule corresponds to the careful closed world assumption [4]. The letters of T are partitioned into $\langle P; Q; Z\rangle$. K is CCWA-ffn if K is a positive literal from P and, for each positive clause B whose literals belong to $P^+ \cup Q^+ \cup Q^-$ such that $T \not\models B$, it holds that $T \not\models B \vee K$.
- The ECWA-rule corresponds to the extended closed world assumption [5]. The letters of T are partitioned into $\langle P; Q; Z\rangle$. K is ECWA-ffn if K is an arbitrary formula not involving literals from Z and, for each positive clause B whose literals belong to $P^+ \cup Q^+ \cup Q^-$ such that $T \not\models B$, it holds that $T \not\models B \vee K$.

Notice that in the CWA, GCWA, EGCWA rules, there is no need to partition the letters into P, Q, Z, and therefore, we can simplify the notation and write $CWA(T)$ $GCWA(T)$, and $EGCWA(T)$.

The CWR-rules can also be given a semantical characterization, which is based on the notion of *minimal* model. A model of a formula T is a truth assignment that satisfies T. For any two models M, N of T, we write $M \leq N$ if the set of letters of T which are assigned true by M is a subset of the analogous set for N. Moreover, if $\langle P; Q; Z\rangle$ is a partition of the letters of T, we write $M \leq_{(P;Z)} N$ if M and N assign the same truth value to the letters in Q, and the set of letters of P which are assigned true by M is a subset of the analogous set for N. We say that a model M is minimal for T if there exists no model N of T such that $N \leq M$ and $M \not\leq N$. Analogously, we say that a model M is $(P; Z)$-minimal for T if there exists no model N of T such that $N \leq_{(P;Z)} M$ and $M \not\leq_{(P;Z)} N$. Notice that $(P; Z)$-minimality reduces to minimality when $Q = Z = \emptyset$.

The semantical characterization of freeness for negation is now given by the following properties.

- K is CWA-ffn in T iff there exists a model M of T such that $M \not\models K$.
- K is GCWA-ffn in T iff for each minimal model M of T it holds that $M \not\models K$.
- K is EGCWA-ffn in T iff for each minimal model M of T it holds that $M \not\models K$.
- K is CCWA-ffn in $\langle T; P; Q; Z\rangle$ iff for each $(P; Z)$-minimal model M of T it holds that $M \not\models K$.
- K is ECWA-ffn in $\langle T; P; Q; Z\rangle$ iff for each $(P; Z)$-minimal model M of T it holds that $M \not\models K$.

From the above properties, one can easily show that for any formula F, $EGCWA(T) \models F$ iff for each minimal model M of T it holds that $M \models F$, and $ECWA(T; P; Q; Z) \models F$ iff for each $(P; Z)$-minimal model M of T it holds that $M \models F$. Moreover, it is shown in [5] that for any formula F,

$ECWA(T;P;Q;Z) \models F$ iff $CIRC(T;P;Q;Z) \models F$, where $CIRC(T;P;Q;Z)$ denotes the *circumscription* of P in T with variables Z. In other words, the ECWA is equivalent to circumscription, at least for propositional formulae.

The different forms of CWR are not independent from each other. In the rest of this paper we shall make use of the following facts relating the various CWR-rules.

Fact 1: for each formula F, if T is Horn, i.e. is constituted by clauses with at most one positive literal, then $CWA(T) \models F$ iff $GCWA(T) \models F$ iff $EGCWA(T) \models F$ iff $ECWA(T;P;\emptyset;\emptyset) \models F$ iff $CCWA(T;P;\emptyset;\emptyset) \models F$.

Fact 2: for each formula F, $EGCWA(T) \models F$ iff $ECWA(T;P;\emptyset;\emptyset) \models F$.

Fact 3: for each formula F, $GCWA(T) \models F$ iff $CCWA(T;P;\emptyset;\emptyset) \models F$.

Fact 4: for each literal L belonging to $P^+ \cup P^-$, $CCWA(T;P;Q;Z) \models L$ iff $ECWA(T;P;Q;Z) \models F$.

As we said in the introduction, in this paper we are concerned with CWR in the context of propositional logic (although our results can be generalized in several ways, see Section 4). Since we are interested in the tractability frontier for CWR, we focus our attention on those classes of formulae for which monotonic inference is a polynomial task. The results reported in [15] show that this holds for three classes of formulae, namely, Horn, dual-Horn, and Krom.

In the rest of the paper, we shall refer to various subsets of such classes. A complete classification of all the classes of propositional formulae that we consider is as follows:

- Horn: at most one positive literal per clause
- dual-Horn: at most one negative literal per clause
- Krom: at most two literals per clause – either positive or negative
- Definite: exactly one positive literal per clause
- HornKrom: Horn and Krom
- dual-HornKrom: dual-Horn and Krom
- HornKrom$^-$: HornKrom with no negative clauses having 2 literals
- 2-positive-Krom: exactly two positive literals, and no negative literal, per clause.

The complexity analysis presented in the next section, will be performed along two directions, concerning the expressiveness of the language, and the form of CWR, respectively. For those CWR-rules requiring the letters of a formula T to be partitioned into the three sets P, Q, Z (e.g. CCWA and ECWA), we will consider two special cases, namely $Q = \emptyset$ or $Z = \emptyset$.

3 Complexity Analysis

In this section we consider the different forms of closed world reasoning, and, for each form, we analyze the various classes of formulae, providing lower complexity bounds for the deduction problem (for the sake of brevity, most of the proofs are omitted).

With regard to the upper complexity bounds, we notice that, from the analysis of Schlipf [16] it follows that performing deduction under the CCWA in propositional logic is both an NP-hard and a coNP-hard problem. Hence it is unlikely that the problem is either in NP or in coNP. Obviously, by Fact 4, this applies to the ECWA as well. In fact, we can go one step further, and prove that the deduction problem under the ECWA is in PSPACE, and in particular in the class Π_2^P of the polynomial hierarchy, although we do not know whether the problem is complete for such a class. A simple intuition supporting this fact is that, determining if $ECWA(T;P;Q;Z) \models \gamma$ can be done by checking if γ is satisfied in *all* the truth assignments of T which are $(P;Z)$-minimal models of T, and the problem of checking if a truth assignment M of T is a $(P;Z)$-minimal model is in the class of coNP (it suffices to compare M with *all* the other truth assignments of T). A more detailed analysis of the upper complexity bounds for several classes of propositional formulae is described in [3].

3.1 CWA

The results reported in [13] show that the application of the CWA to Krom and dual-Horn formulae may lead to inconsistency. Moreover, Minker [10] shows that, when the CWA is consistent, it is equivalent to GCWA (see Subsection 3.2).

In [1], it is shown that the deduction problem under CWA for Definite formulae is solvable in polynomial time. Since negative clauses do not contribute to the deduction (see [13]), this property extends to Horn formulae. By Fact 1, one can conclude that, for Horn formulae, the deduction problem under both the GCWA and the EGCWA is polynomial too.

3.2 GCWA

In [7], it is shown that the problem of determining whether $GCWA(T) \models L$, where T is a dual-Horn formula and L is a literal, is coNP-hard. By Facts 1,2, and 3, this holds also for EGCWA, CCWA and ECWA.

The deduction problem under the GCWA for Krom formulae is polynomial; this derives from Fact 3 and from a stronger result which will be presented in Subsection 3.4.

Recently, Rajasekar, Lobo and Minker [12] have proposed a weak form of GCWA, called Weak GCWA (WGCWA), which applies to disjunctive logic programs (i.e. logic programs whose rules have any number of positive literals in the head) and is defined in such a way that every deduction under such a form reduces polinomially to deduction under the CWA on definite logic programs. It is easy to see that the WGCWA yields polynomial time deduction algorithms in the propositional case.

3.3 EGCWA

We already mentioned that the deduction problem under the EGCWA is polynomial for Horn formulae. The following theorem shows that this is the only tractable case.

Theorem 1 *Let T be a 2-positive-Krom formula, and γ any clause. Then determining if $EGCWA(T) \models \gamma$ is a coNP-hard problem.*

PROOF (sketch): We reduce the unsatisfiability problem to our problem by exhibiting a mapping from any CNF formula π to a 2-positive-Krom formula π'' and a clause C such that π is unsatisfiable iff $EGCWA(\pi'') \models C$.

Let π be a CNF formula on the alphabet L. Let L' be the alphabet $L \cup \{\overline{a} \mid a \in L\}$. We define π' on L' as follows: 1. for each letter a of L, there is a clause $\neg a \vee \neg\overline{a}$ in π'; 2. for each clause $\neg w_1 \vee \cdots \vee \neg w_n \vee w_{n+1} \vee \cdots \vee w_{n+m}$ in π, there is a clause $\overline{w_1} \vee \cdots \vee \overline{w_n} \vee w_{n+1} \vee \cdots \vee w_{n+m}$ in π'. Obviously, π' is satisfiable iff π is satisfiable. Let L'' be the alphabet obtained from L' by adding a new letter g_i for each clause γ_i in π. We define π'' on L'' as follows: 1. for each letter a of L, there is a clause $a \vee \overline{a}$ in π''; 2. for each clause $\gamma_i = \neg w_1 \vee \cdots \vee \neg w_n \vee w_{n+1} \vee \cdots \vee w_{n+m}$ in π, there are $n+m$ clauses $g_i \vee \overline{w_1}, \ldots, g_i \vee \overline{w_n}, g_i \vee w_{n+1}, \ldots, g_i \vee w_{n+m}$ in π''. Notice that the above mapping from π to π'' is clearly polynomial, and π'' is a 2-positive-Krom formula. Moreover, given a model M of π', we can build a disjunction B such that $\pi'' \models B \vee K$ and $\pi'' \not\models B$, and, conversely, given a disjunction B such that $\pi'' \models B \vee K$ and $\pi'' \not\models B$, we can build a model M of π'. Therefore, the conjunction $K = g_1 \wedge \cdots \wedge g_h$, where $g_1, \ldots, g_h$ are all the letters of L'' corresponding to the clauses in π, is not EGCWA-ffn in π'' iff π' is satifiable. Taking into account that $\neg K$ is a disjunction, and $EGCWA(\pi'') \models \neg K$ iff K is EGCWA-ffn in π'', it follows that $EGCWA(\pi'') \models \neg K$ iff π is unsatisfiable. □

Taking into account Fact 2, we can conclude that the above result applies to the ECWA too.

3.4 CCWA

In [8] a detailed analysis of CCWA is presented. In particular it is shown that determining if $CCWA(T; P; Q; \emptyset) \models L$, where L is a literal, is coNP-hard for Horn formulae. Moreover, two different problems are shown to be polynomial: $CCWA(T; P; Q; Z) \models \gamma$, where γ is an arbitrary clause and T is HornKrom, and $CCWA(T; P; \emptyset; Z) \models \gamma$, where γ is an arbitrary clause and T is Krom. We complete the analysis of [8] by providing the following result:

Theorem 2 *Let T be a Krom formula, and γ be a clause. Then the problem of determining if $CCWA(T; P; Q; Z) \models \gamma$ is polynomial (see [3] for an $O(|T|^2)$ algorithm).*

Notice that, by Fact 3, the above result on Krom formulae can be extended to the GCWA.

3.5 ECWA

We first present two intractability results concerning HornKrom and Definite formulae, respectively.

Theorem 3 *Let T be a HornKrom formula, γ be a clause and L be a literal. Then both determining if $ECWA(T; P; Q; \emptyset) \models \gamma$ and if $ECWA(T; P; Q; Z) \models L$ are coNP-hard problems.*

Theorem 4 *Let T be a Definite formula, and γ be a clause. Then the problem of determining if $ECWA(T; P; Q; \emptyset) \models \gamma$ is coNP-hard.*

The above theorems can be proven similarly to theorem 1. Moreover, we can strengthen the result of theorem 1, by showing that, as far as 2-positive-Krom formulae are concerned, the problem of deducing literals under the ECWA is a coNP-hard problem, even if $Q = \emptyset$.

Theorem 5 *Let T be a 2-positive-Krom formula, and L be a literal. Then the problem of determining if $ECWA(T; P; \emptyset; Z) \models L$ is coNP-hard.*

The above theorem, together with theorem 2 and Fact 4, allows us to conclude that determining whether a given literal L logically follows from $ECWA(T; P; \emptyset; Z)$ can be characterized as follows: the problem is polynomial for $L \in P^+ \cup P^-$, whereas is coNP-hard for $L \in Z^+ \cup Z^-$. Notice that the same holds for the case when $Q \neq \emptyset$ (see [3]).

In the rest of this subsection, we discuss two tractable cases, concerning Horn and HornKrom$^-$, respectively.

Theorem 6 *Let T be a Horn formula, and γ be a clause. Then $ECWA(T; P; \emptyset; Z) \models \gamma$ iff $CCWA(T; P; \emptyset; Z) \models \gamma$. Hence determining if $ECWA(T; P; \emptyset; Z) \models \gamma$ is a polynomial problem (see [8] for a polynomial algorithm).*

Theorem 7 *Let T be a HornKrom$^-$ formula, and γ be a clause. Then the problem of determining if $ECWA(T; P; Q; Z) \models \gamma$ is polynomial.*

In [3], we present an algorithm that, given a HornKrom$^-$ formula T, and a clause γ, determines if $ECWA(T; P; Q; Z) \models \gamma$. The algorithm uses a graph representation for T, and runs in $O(T^2)$ time.

The above theorem is probably the first tractability result concerning parallel circumscription. For example, it

literal	Horn	Krom	Definite	HornKrom	HornKrom$^-$	2posKrom	dual-Horn	dual-HornKrom
pos	≤1		1	≤1	≤1	2		
neg					≤1	0	≤1	≤1
tot		≤2		≤2	≤2	2		≤2
CWA	P [1]	–	P [1]	P [1]	P [1]	–	–	–
GCWA	P [1]	P	P [1]	P [1]	P [1]	P	coNP [7]	P
WGCWA	–	–	P [12]	–	–	P [12]	P [12]	P [12]
EGCWA	P [1]	coNP	P [1]	P [1]	P [1]	coNP	coNP [7]	coNP
CCWA $Q = \emptyset$	P [8]	P	P [8]	P [8]	P [8]	P	coNP [7]	P
CCWA $Z = \emptyset$	coNP [8]	P	P [8]	P [8]	P [8]	P	coNP [7]	P
CCWA	coNP [8]	P	P [8]	P [8]	P [8]	P	coNP [7]	P
ECWA $Q = \emptyset$	P	coNP	P	P	P	coNP	coNP [7]	coNP
ECWA $Z = \emptyset$	coNP	coNP	coNP	coNP	P	coNP	coNP [7]	coNP
ECWA	coNP	coNP	coNP	coNP	P	coNP	coNP [7]	coNP

Table 1: Summary of the complexity analysis

can be easily shown that the algorithm in [11] for computing circumscription is exponential even for HornKrom$^-$ formulae. This fact shows that in order to develop efficient methods for computing circumscription, it is necessary to look for structural properties of the ECWA-ffn formulae which are relevant to the deduction.

All the complexity results about closed world reasoning for the different classes of propositional formulae are summarized in Table 1, where P means "polynomial time", coNP means coNP-hardness, and symbol "-" means non-applicable. Each entry referring to a result previously known, is marked with the appropriate reference. Entries without references refer to results presented in this paper.

4 Applications

In this section we briefly discuss some possible applications of the complexity analysis developed in Section 3. In general, our results can be used to characterize the complexity of any reasoning problem which can be formalized in terms of CWR on propositional formulae. We concentrate our attention to three of such problems, namely nonmonotonic inheritance, default reasoning, and diagnosis.

As a first observation, notice that we can directly apply all the above results to the problem of performing CWR on a particular class of first order monadic theories, called Inheritance Networks [8]. Moreover, it can be seen that the problem of reasoning under circumscription on an Inheritance Network N can be reduced to the one of performing deduction under the ECWA on a suitable propositional formula obtained from N by means of a polynomial transformation. By virtue of this fact, some of the results presented in Section 3 can be used to give lower bounds to the complexity of performing deduction on circumscriptive Inheritance Networks, i.e. Inheritance Networks with defeasible rules, where the meaning of defeasible rules is formalized in terms of minimization of abnormalities.

With regard to diagnosis, in [14] a general methodology for solving the problem of diagnosing a malfunctioning system is given. The system is described by means of a logical formula SD in which the distinguished unary predicate symbol $ABNORMAL$ is used to model the malfunctioning of a component. Observations about the system behaviour are represented by a further formula OBS. A *diagnosis* is then defined as a minimal set $\Delta \subseteq COMPONENTS$ such that $SD \cup OBS \cup \{\neg ABNORMAL(c) \mid c \in COMPONENTS \setminus \Delta\}$ is consistent, where $COMPONENTS$ is the set of constant symbols of SD representing the system components.

Reiter shows that there is a natural correspondence between the diagnoses of $SD \cup OBS$ and the extensions of the default theory whose first-order part is $SD \cup OBS$, and whose default rules are $\{: \neg ABNORMAL(c)/\neg ABNORMAL(c) \mid c \in COMPONENTS\}$. It is easy to prove that, when $SD \cup OBS$ can be expressed as a propositional formula, for example when the system is a digital circuit, the diagnosis problem can also be formulated as a deduction problem under ECWA. This allows us to apply some of our results to the diagnosis problem. For example, consider a very simple digital circuit made up by only two kinds of components: the wire and the inverter. A way to model (unidirectionally) the behaviour of these components is by means of the clauses $oninput(wire_i) \wedge \neg ab(wire_i) \supset onoutput(wire_i)$ and $oninput(inverter_i) \wedge \neg ab(inverter_i) \supset \neg onoutput(inverter_i)$. Now, based on the result stated in theorem 1, it can be shown that determining whether a given fact is true in all the diagnoses of a system of the above form is coNP-hard.

Finally, we observe that our analysis can be used to obtain complexity results in the context of default logic. The basic observation is that *skeptical reasoning* in default theories (i.e. validity in all the extensions of a default theory–see [6]) can be reduced to ECWA, at least for some propositional default theories where defaults are of the form $: \neg a/\neg a$. In [6] it is shown that for a superclass of this class (namely Normal Unary default theories) skeptical reasoning is polynomial if the first-order part of the theory is a conjunction of literals. By exploiting the results of this paper, it is possible to prove that the problem is coNP-hard for a slight enhancement of the expressive power of the language, namely if the first-order part of the theory is a 2-positive-Krom propositional formula.

References

[1] Apt K.R., "Introduction to Logic Programming", Technical Report TR-87-35, University of Texas, Department of Computer Science, 1987.

[2] Bylander T., Allemang D., Tanner M.C., and Josephson J.R., "Some Results Concerning the Computational Complexity of Abduction", *Proceedings of the 1st KR Conference*, 1989.

[3] Cadoli M., and Lenzerini M., "The Complexity of Closed World Reasoning", Technical Report, Università di Roma "La Sapienza", Dipartimento di Informatica e Sistemistica, 1990.

[4] Gelfond M., and Przymusinska H., "Negation as Failure: Careful Closure Procedure", *Artificial Intelligence*, Vol. 30, 1986.

[5] Gelfond M., Przymusinska H., and Przymusinsky T., "On the Relationship between Circumscription and Negation as Failure", *Artificial Intelligence*, Vol. 38, 1989.

[6] Kautz H.A., and Selman B., "Hard Problems for Simple Default Logics", *Proceedings of the 1st KR Conference*, 1989.

[7] Lenzerini M., "Covering and Disjointness Relationships in Hierarchy Networks", Technical Report RAP.17.88, Università di Roma "La Sapienza", Dipartimento di Informatica e Sistemistica, 1988.

[8] Lenzerini M., "Reasoning about Inheritance Networks", Technical Report RAP.22.88, Università di Roma "La Sapienza", Dipartimento di Informatica e Sistemistica, 1988.

[9] McCarthy J., "Circumscription - A form of Non-Monotonic Reasoning", *Artificial Intelligence*, Vol. 13, 1980.

[10] Minker J., "On Indefinite Databases and the Closed World Assumption", *Proceedings of the 6th CADE Conference*, 1982.

[11] Przymusinsky T., "An Algorithm to Compute Circumscription", *Artificial Intelligence*, Vol. 38, 1989.

[12] Rajasekar A., Lobo J., and Minker J., "Weak Generalized Closed World Assumption", *Journal of Automated Reasoning*, Vol. 5, 1989.

[13] Reiter R., "On Closed World Data Bases", in Gallaire H., and Minker J. (eds), *Logic and Data Bases*, Plenum, New York, 1978.

[14] Reiter R., "A Theory of Diagnosis from First Principles", *Artificial Intelligence*, Vol. 32, 1987.

[15] Schaefer T.J., "The Complexity of Satisfiability Problems", *Proceedings of the 10th ACM STOC*, 1978.

[16] Schlipf J.S., "When is Closed World Reasoning Tractable?", *Proceedings of the 3rd ISMIS*, 1988.

[17] Selman B., and Levesque H.J., "The Tractability of Path-Based Inheritance", *Proceedings of the 11th IJCAI*, 1989.

[18] Yahya A., and Henschen L.J., "Deduction in Non-Horn Databases", *Journal of Automated Reasoning*, Vol. 1, 1985.

ON THE EXPRESSIVENESS OF NETWORKS WITH HIDDEN VARIABLES

Rina Dechter [1]

Computer Science Department
Technion -- Israel Institute of Technology
Haifa, Israel, 32000
e-mail: dechter@techsel.bitnet

Abstract

This paper investigates design issues associated with representing relations in binary networks augmented with hidden variables. The trade-off between the number of variables required and the size of their domains is discussed. We show that if the number of values available to each variable is just two, then hidden variables cannot improve the expressional power of the network, regardless of their number. However, for $k \geq 3$, we can always find a layered network using k-valued hidden variables that represent an arbitrary relation. We then provide a scheme for decomposing an arbitrary relation, ρ, using $\frac{|\rho|-2}{k-2}$ hidden variables, each having k values ($k>2$).

1. Introduction

Hidden units play a central role in connectionist model, without which the model would not represent many useful functions and relations. In the early days of the Perceptrons [Minsky 1969] it was noted that even simple functions like the *XOR* were not expressible in a single layer perceptron; a realization that slowed research in the area until the notion of hidden units had emerged [Rumelhart 1988a, Hinton 1988]. Nevertheless, a formal treatment of the expressiveness gained by hidden units, and systematic schemes for designing systems with hidden units within the neural network paradigm are still not available.

Our intention is to investigate formally the role of hidden units and devise systematic schemes for designing systems incorporating hidden units. Specifically, we address the following task: given a relation on n variables, called visible, we wish to design a network having $n+h$ units whose stable patterns, (relative to the visible units) coincide with the original relation. This task is central to most applications of connectionist networks, in particular to its role as associative memory. The task will be investigated for a connectionist architecture which is different from classic connectionist networks in that it is based on **constraint networks**. The sequential constraint network model is defined next.

A **Network of binary constraints** involves a set of n variables $X_1,...,X_n$, each represented by its domain values, $D_1, . . . ,D_n$, and a set of constraints. A **binary constraint** R_{ij} between two variables X_i and X_j is a subset of the cartesian product $D_i \times D_j$ that specifies which values of the variables are compatible with each other. A solution is an assignment of values to all the variables which satisfy all the constraints, and the **constraint satisfaction problems (CSP)** associated with these networks is to find one or all solutions. A binary CSP can be associated with a **constraint-graph** in which nodes represent variables and arcs connect pairs of variables which are constrained explicitly. Figure 1a presents a constraint network where each node represents a variable having values $\{a, b, c\}$ and each link is associated with a strict lexicographic order (where $X_i < X_j$ iff $i < j$). (The domains and the constraints explicitly indicated on some of the links.)

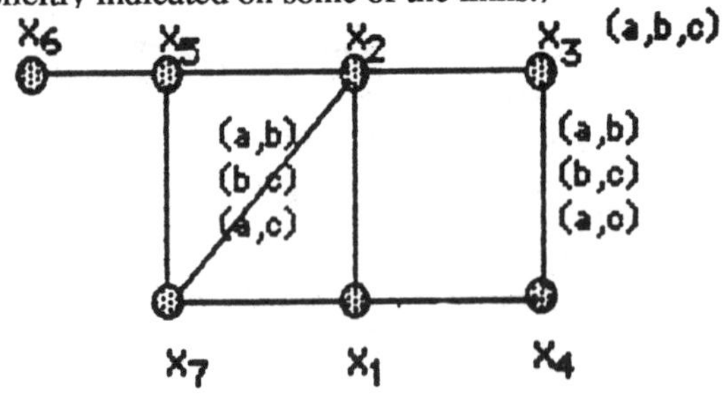

Figure 1: An example of a binary CN

Our constraint-based connectionist architecture assumes that each unit plays the role of a variable having k states, and that the links, representing the constraints, are quantified by compatibility relations between states of adjacent units. Each unit asynchronously updates its state

(1) This research was supported in part by NSF grant #IRI-8821444 and by an Air Force grant #AFOSR 88 0177 while the author was visiting the cognitive systems lab at UCLA.

(i.e., assigns itself one of its values) using a decision function based only on the states of its neighboring units and its compatibility relations with them. In a companion paper we provide a communication protocol for this model which is guaranteed to converge to a global consistent assignment of values [Collin 1990]. Although this constraint-based architecture differs from classical connectionist architectures the resemblance is strong enough to shed interesting light on the latter architectures as well.

The paper is organized as follows. Section 2 continues with definitions and preliminaries. In section 3 we show that bi-valued hidden variables add no expressional power, while, in section 4 we show that if the hidden variables have 3 values or more they can decompose any relation. Bounds on the trade-off between the number of hidden variables and the cardinality of their values are given as well. Section 5 extends the decomposition scheme to those having some initial inner decomposition, section 6 presents examples and section 7 provides concluding remarks. Due to space limitation most results are presented with sketchy or no proofs. For formal proofs see [Dechter 1990].

2. Definitions and preliminaries

Since communication links are pairwise our constraint-based architecture is restricted to expressing **binary** constraint networks only. A general relation on n variables is not necessarily expressible as a binary network of constraints on the same set of variables. The question we pose, therefore, is how to express any relation in a binary constraint network, with the aid of new **hidden** variables.

Let $rel(R)$ denotes the relation associated with network R. (i.e., $rel(R)$ is the set of all solutions to R). Let ρ be an n-ary relation over variables $X = \{X_1, \ldots, X_n\}$, each having k values. We now define the notion of decomposability with hidden variables.

Definition: Relation ρ is ***h*-network-decomposable** if there exist h additional variables, $Y = \{Y_1, \ldots, Y_h\}$, having k values or less, for which there is a binary network $R = R(X,Y)$, on $X \cup Y$, such that

$$\rho = \Pi_X rel(R(X,Y)). \quad (1)$$

$\Pi_U(\rho)$ denotes the projection of relation ρ on subsets of variables U. The projection of variables $X_{i_1}, \ldots, X_{i_l}$ on relation ρ is given by: $\Pi_{X_{i_1},\ldots,X_{i_l}}(\rho) = \{(x_{i_1}, \ldots, x_{i_l}) \mid \exists\, \bar{x} \in \rho \ s.t.\ \forall\, i_j\ \bar{x}_{i_j} = x_{i_j}\}$ When no hidden variables are required for network decomposability we say that the relation is **network decomposable.** Any relation, ρ, can be associated with a unique binary network that is generated by projecting the relation on each pair of its variables. This network is called **the minimal network** [Montanari 1974] and it is known to provide the best approximation to ρ. Namely, $\rho \subseteq rel(M)$ and if R is any other binary network on the original set of variables s.t. $\rho \subseteq rel(R)$ then $\rho \subseteq rel(M) \subseteq rel(R)$. It follows that the minimal network can determine whether a relation is network decomposable or not.

Theorem 1: A relation is network decomposable if and only if its minimal network represents it precisely. Namely, if $\rho = rel(M)$. □

Every non-decomposable relation has a trivial **star-decomposition** using one hidden variable and an **unrestricted** number of values. In this decomposition the hidden variable, Y, needs t values, when t is the cardinality of the relation. Each value of Y is needed to "index" each tuple in the relation. This is achieved by constraining the hidden variable with each original variable as follows. The constraint between the hidden variable, Y, and an original variable X_j makes the ith value of Y compatible with one and only one value of X_j, the value that appears in the ith tuple of the relation. That way each value of Y is made consistent with exactly one tuple (Fig. 2). The resulting constraint network, which has a star shape (hence its name), clearly represents the target relation (i.e. projecting it on all original variables yields the original relation).

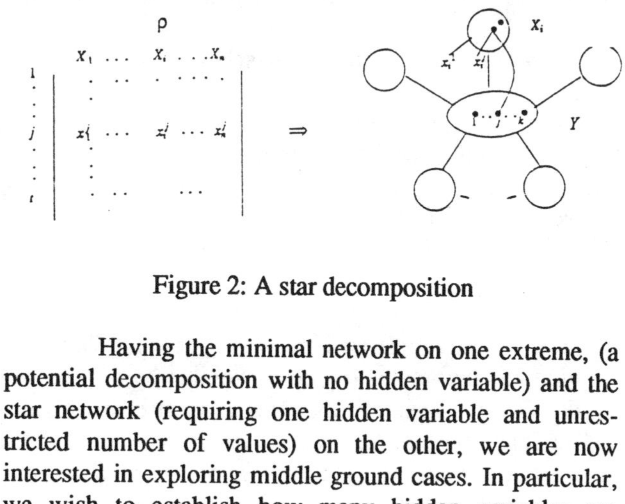

Figure 2: A star decomposition

Having the minimal network on one extreme, (a potential decomposition with no hidden variable) and the star network (requiring one hidden variable and unrestricted number of values) on the other, we are now interested in exploring middle ground cases. In particular, we wish to establish how many hidden variables are required, were we to restrict the size of their domains.

3. Using bi-valued hidden variables

When the hidden variables have only two values we get a surprising negative result:

Theorem 2: Relations which are not network decomposable cannot be decomposed by adding any number of 2-valued hidden variables.

Sketch of proof: Lets ρ be a relation that is not network decomposable and let M be its minimal network. The minimal network, since not representing ρ, allows a tuple $\bar{x}=\bar{x}_1,\ldots,\bar{x}_n$ which is not part of ρ. The task of any hidden variable is to disallow such tuple while at the same time allow all tuples in ρ. Assume Y is such bi-valued hidden variable that when added to the network M it is inconsistent with $\bar{x}$ while consistent with any tuple in ρ. Y has to be consistent with each value of $\bar{x}$ (since $\bar{x}$'s values are generated from the minimal network). Namely, each value of $\bar{x}$ is consistent either with Y's "0" or with Y's "1". We claim, further, that **all** $\bar{x}$'s values are either consistent with the "0" or with the "1". Since if not there is a value, $\bar{x}_i$, not consistent with Y=0 and a value, $\bar{x}_j$, not consistent with Y=1 and the pair $(\bar{x}_i,\bar{x}_j)$ is not consistent with any value of Y. However, since this pair is allowed by the minimal network, excluding it must eliminate a legal tuple of ρ which yields a contradiction. The argument can be extended by induction to any number of hidden variables [Dechter 1990]. □

4. Multi-valued hidden variables

4.1 A conditional decomposition scheme

This section investigates decomposition schemes utilizing multi-valued (i.e., more then 2 values) hidden variables. In particular we wish to explore the trade-off between r, the number of hidden variables, and k, their domain sizes, required for decomposing an arbitrary relation.

We first restrict ourselves to $r = 1$. Clearly, a relation having t tuples is 1-decomposable by the star network. One may expect that when using also the minimal constraints between the original variables as part of the network decomposition the number of values needed by the centered hidden variable can be reduced. It can be shown, however, that for some relations, t, is also the smallest number of values required for decomposition (when using one hidden variable).

Let us define the **unit relation**, U_n, to be the "0-1" relation on n variables whose i^{th} tuple consists of a value "1" for variable X_i and a value "0" for all other variables (Fig. 3a).

$$U_5 = \left\{ \begin{matrix} X_1 & X_2 & X_3 & X_4 & X_5 \\ 1 & 0 & 0 & 0 & 0 \\ 0 & 1 & 0 & 0 & 0 \\ 0 & 0 & 1 & 0 & 0 \\ 0 & 0 & 0 & 1 & 0 \\ 0 & 0 & 0 & 0 & 1 \end{matrix} \right\} \qquad U_{10,3} = \left\{ \begin{matrix} 1 & 0 & 0 & 0 & 0 \\ 2 & 0 & 0 & 0 & 0 \\ 0 & 1 & 0 & 0 & 0 \\ 0 & 2 & 0 & 0 & 0 \\ 0 & 0 & 1 & 0 & 0 \\ 0 & 0 & 2 & 0 & 0 \\ 0 & 0 & 0 & 1 & 0 \\ 0 & 0 & 0 & 2 & 0 \\ 0 & 0 & 0 & 0 & 1 \\ 0 & 0 & 0 & 0 & 2 \end{matrix} \right\}$$

(a) (b)

Figure 3: (a) the unit relation U_5, (b) relation $U_{10,3}$

It can be shown that relation U_n cannot exploit the minimal constraints in order to reduce the value cardinality of the hidden variable:

Theorem 3: The smallest value, k, for which the unit relation U_n is 1-decomposable is k=n.

Sketch of proof: The minimal network of U_n allows the extra all "0" tuple. To exclude it any value of the hidden variable must be inconsistent with at least one $X_i = 0$ and therefore consistent with $X_i = 1$. As such it can "extend" only the ith tuple of U_n hence we need n values. □

Let us define $H_\rho(h)$ to be the the minimum number of values (per variable) required for an h-decomposition of relation ρ. We can conclude:

Corollary 1: For every ρ, $H_\rho(1) \le |\rho|$ and for some ρ's, $H_\rho(1) = |\rho|$. □

A straightforward extension of the star decomposition to two hidden variables presents itself by expressing the $|\rho|$ values of one hidden variable by $|\rho|$ different pairs of values on the pair of hidden variables as follows. All pairs of values are of the form $(i, 0)$ or $(0,i)$, where $\frac{|\rho|}{2} \ge i > 0$, and the value $(i, 0)$ is associated with the ith tuple while the pair $(0,i)$ is associated with the $\frac{|\rho|}{2}+i$ tuple. (For notational convenience we assume that all fractional expressions represent the ceiling integer of that fraction.) Since $|\rho|$ different pairs can be expressed in this way by two $(\frac{|\rho|}{2})$-valued hidden variables, we can infer that $H_\rho(2) \le \frac{|\rho|}{2}$. It can be shown, however [Dechter 1990] that this bound is tight, namely:

Corollary 2: For every ρ, $H_\rho(2) \le \frac{|\rho|}{2}$ and for some ρ'

(e.g., U_n) $H_\rho(2) = \frac{|\rho|}{2}$. □

The above property is extensible to any number of hidden variables and we can show that the unit relation U_n needs at least r, $(\frac{n}{r})$-valued hidden variables in order to be decomposed. We conclude that:

Corollary 3: For some ρ's $H_\rho(r) \geq \frac{|\rho|}{r}$. □

Our approach for systematically decomposing a relation is to start from a star decomposition using a $|\rho|$-valued hidden variable, and then, if only k-valued variables are available, to simulate the star hidden variable by a relation that obeys the value restriction and that can be network decomposed. If the latter relation is not network decomposable we will apply the same principle to it and so on. This approach is detailed in the following paragraphs.

Let us extend the notion of unit relation into a k-valued relation as follows: the k-valued unit relation, $U_{n,k}$ has n tuples and $r = \frac{n}{k-1}$ variables such that the $(i(k-1)+j)^{th}$ tuple, $i \leq r$, $j \leq k-1$, has zero everywhere accept for the ith variable whose value is j (Fig. 3b).

We focus, first, on the decomposition of U_n. The unit relation U_n can be **conditionally star-decomposed** via $\frac{n}{k-1}$ k-valued hidden variables. We first generate the concatenated relation $U_n U_{n,k}$, and then decompose it via a two layered network. The first layer consists of the original variables $X_1, \ldots, X_n$ and the second layer has the hidden variables $Y_1, \ldots, Y_{\frac{n}{k-1}}$. The only constraints in the decomposing network are those relating each hidden variable with an original variable (Fig. 4a). The constraints themselves are generated by projecting the concatenated relation $U_n U_{n,k}$ on the corresponding pairs of variables (Fig. 4b). We say that $U_{n,k}$ "conditionally" decomposes U_n in the following sense: for any instantiation of the hidden variables to a legal tuple in $U_{n,k}$ the network allows only legal tuples among the original variables, namely, those participating in U_n. However, the new appended relation $U_{n,k}$, by itself, is not network decomposable. Namely, even if we add all the minimal constraints between the hidden variables it will not exclude the "0" tuple on the hidden variables which in turn will allow any combination of values on the original variables. As its name indicates it is just a conditional decomposition, i.e. conditioned on our ability to further decompose $U_{n,k}$.

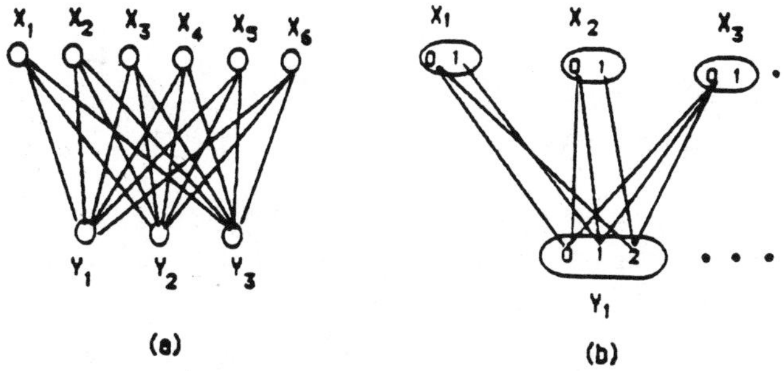

Figure 4: Decomposing U_6 by $U_{6,3}$

Let ρ_1 and ρ_2 be two relations, having the same number of tuples on disjoint sets of variables. Let us denote by $R(\rho_1, \rho_2)$ the two layered network in which the top layer contains ρ_1's variables, the bottom layer contains ρ_2's variables and there are constraints between any variable in ρ_1 and any variable in ρ_2. The constraints themselves are the projection of the concatenated relation $\rho_1\rho_2$ on the corresponding pairs of variables. Using this notation we can say that $R(U_n, U_{n,k})$ is a conditional decomposition of U_n.

4.2. A general decomposition scheme

It seems as though we didn't solve anything! just transferred the decomposability problem from one unit relation (U_n) to another ($U_{n,k}$). Nevertheless, since the number of variables in $U_{n,k}$ is $\frac{n}{k-1} < n$, (for $k > 2$) we can now decompose it with a new k-valued unit "relation", denoted $U^1{}_{n,k}$ having even a smaller number of variables. The unit relation $U^1{}_{n,k}$ is a pseudo-relation since it is a set of tuples which are not necessarily different. $U^1{}_{n,k}$ has $\frac{n}{(k-1)^2}$ variables and it is generated by taking the unit relation, $U_{\frac{n}{2},k}$, and duplicating each tuple in it (Fig. 5). The intention being that each tuple in $U^1{}_{n,k}$ will not distinguish between tuples in $U_{n,k}$ having non-zero values for the same variable. $U^1{}_{n,k}$ can conditionally decompose $U_{n,k}$ in the same manner that $U_{n,k}$ conditionally decomposes U_n using the layered network $R(U_{n,k}, U^1{}_{n,k})$.

This results in having a sequence of "pseudo" unit relations, each with a smaller number of variables and each disallowing a smaller tuple of "0"'s in the preceding relation. The resulting relation is a concatenation of "inflated" unit relations each having a $(k-1)$ fraction of the variables of the preceding relation. Let us denote the resulting relation by $U^*{}_n$ (Fig. 5). Clearly $U_n = \Pi_X U^*{}_n$.

X_1	X_2	X_3	X_4	X_5	X_6	X_7	X_8	X_9	X_{10}	X_{11}	X_{12}	Y_1	Y_2	Y_3	Y_4	Y_5	Y_6	Z_1	Z_2	Z_3	T_1
1	0	0	0	0	0	0	0	0	0	0	0	1	0	0	0	0	0	1	0	0	1
0	1	0	0	0	0	0	0	0	0	0	0	2	0	0	0	0	0	1	0	0	1
0	0	1	0	0	0	0	0	0	0	0	0	0	1	0	0	0	0	2	0	0	1
0	0	0	1	0	0	0	0	0	0	0	0	0	2	0	0	0	0	2	0	0	1
0	0	0	0	1	0	0	0	0	0	0	0	0	0	1	0	0	0	0	1	0	2
0	0	0	0	0	1	0	0	0	0	0	0	0	0	2	0	0	0	0	1	0	2
0	0	0	0	0	0	1	0	0	0	0	0	0	0	0	1	0	0	0	2	0	2
0	0	0	0	0	0	0	1	0	0	0	0	0	0	0	2	0	0	0	2	0	2
0	0	0	0	0	0	0	0	1	0	0	0	0	0	0	0	1	0	0	0	1	0
0	0	0	0	0	0	0	0	0	1	0	0	0	0	0	0	2	0	0	0	1	0
0	0	0	0	0	0	0	0	0	0	1	0	0	0	0	0	0	1	0	0	2	0
0	0	0	0	0	0	0	0	0	0	0	1	0	0	0	0	0	2	0	0	2	0

U_{12} $\qquad$ $U_{12,3}$ $\qquad$ $U^1{}_{12,3}$ $\qquad$ $U^2{}_{12,3}$

Figure 5: $U^*{}_{12}$; the relation generated from decomposing U_{12}

The network that decomposes $U^*{}_n$ is a layered network where each set of new hidden variables are connected to all variables in the preceding layer and the constraints are the projection of $U^*{}_n$ on the corresponding pairs of variables. The bottom layer consists of one or two variables whose allowed tuples can be controlled by a direct constraint. A schematic description of the network decomposition for U_{12} is given in Fig. 6.

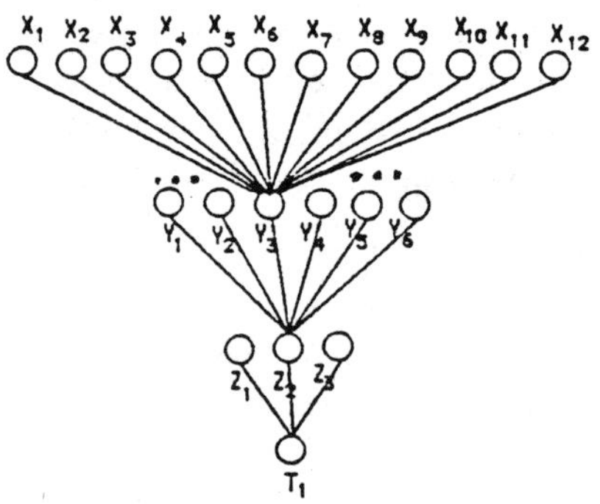

Figure 6: A layered decomposition of $U^*{}_{12}$

To summarize, U_n can be decomposed by intersecting sequences of two layered networks. The resulting network, $R^*{}_n$, is defined by: ("$\cdot$" denotes the intersection operation)

$$R^*{}_n = R(U_n, U_{n,k}) \cdot R(U_{n,k}, U^1{}_{n,k}) \cdot \tag{4}$$

$$R(U^1{}_{n,k}, U^2{}_{n,k}), \cdot \ldots, \cdot R(U^i{}_{n,k}, U^{i+1}{}_{n,k})$$

$$\cdot, \ldots, \cdot R(U^{\log_k n-1}{}_{n,k}, U^{\log_k n}{}_{n,k}).$$

We can now apply the same idea to an arbitrary relation. Namely, in order to decompose a given relation ρ using k-valued hidden variables we will generate the network

$$R^*(\rho) = R(\rho, U_{|\rho|,k}) \cdot R(U_{|\rho|,k}, U^1{}_{|\rho|,k}) \cdot, \ldots, \cdot \tag{5}$$

$$R(U^{\log_k |\rho|-1}{}_{|\rho|,k}, U^{\log_k |\rho|}{}_{|\rho|,k}).$$

Let $H^{-1}{}_\rho(k)$ denotes the minimum number of k-valued hidden variables needed for decomposing ρ. We get the following theorem:

Theorem 4: Any relation is decomposable by $\frac{|\rho|-2}{k-2}$ k-valued hidden variables, when $k > 2$. □

From corollary 3 and from Theorem 4 it follows that the unit relation's decomposition cannot be substantially improved. Namely,

$$\frac{n}{k} \le H^{-1}{}_{U_n}(k) \le \frac{n-2}{k-2}. \tag{6}$$

Therefore, the decomposition scheme presented by (5) is optimal in the sense that for some relations (the U_n's) a better decomposition does not exist. Nevertheless, we still wish to find the minimum number of values needed for the star-decomposition, since it will provide a better bound for any general decomposition, namely:

$$H^{-1}{}_\rho(k) \le \frac{H_\rho(1)-2}{k-2}. \tag{7}$$

5. Decompositions of partially decomposable relations

One way of improving our scheme can be hinted by investigating the level of *inner* decomposition of the relation using only its original variables. We assumed that the relation is not binary network decomposable, however it may be losslessly decomposed to relations having arity greater then 2 yet smaller then n. Let a relation scheme $R = R_1, \ldots, R_l$ be a set of subsets of attributes of the original relation. We say that the scheme R is a **lossless decomposition** of ρ if:

$$\rho = \rho_1 \bowtie \rho_2 \bowtie, \ldots, \bowtie \rho_l. \tag{8}$$

When $\bowtie$ is the relational database *join* operator. We claim that if a lossless decomposition of the relation is available and if we use hidden variables to decompose each component separately without introducing any conflicts between the components, the combined network is a decomposition of the target relation. The general scheme is as follows: given a lossless decomposition $R = R_1, R_2, \ldots, R_l$ of ρ which is defined over variables $X = X_1, \ldots, X_n$, and given a binary network decomposition, R'_i, for each subrelation ρ_i, utilizing a set of hidden variables Y_i, (i.e., $\rho_i = \Pi_X rel(R'_i)$), and denoting by $\rho' = rel(R'_1) \bowtie, \ldots, \bowtie rel(R'_l)$, it is always true that

$$\Pi_X \rho' \subseteq (\Pi_X rel(R'_1)) \bowtie, \ldots, \tag{9}$$

$$\bowtie (\Pi_X rel(R'_l)) = \rho$$

If we take special care to ensure that the hidden variables used in different components will not interfere with each other (by utilizing disjoint subsets, for instance) and will not eliminate a legal tuple of ρ we will have an equality in the left hand side of (9). In that case the combined network $\bigcap_i R'_i$, is a network decomposition of ρ utilizing a set of hidden variables $\bigcup_i Y_i$.

We can associate a star decomposition with each component separately. Namely, if l hidden variables are available, each devoted to a star decomposition of one subrelation, then the hidden variable Y_i of subrelation ρ_i will need $|\rho_i|$ values. We will get therefore that

$$H^{-1}{}_{\rho}(\max_i |\rho_i|) \leq l \tag{10}$$

If only k-valued hidden variables are available we can decompose each component subrelation using disjoint subsets of k-valued hidden variables. This way the non-interfering property is maintained. When applying the bound of Theorem 4 to each component separately and summing over all components we get:

$$H^{-1}{}_{\rho}(k) \leq \sum_{i=1}^{l} \frac{|\rho_i| - 2}{k-2} = \frac{\sum_{i=1}^{l} |\rho_i| - 2l}{k-2} \tag{11}$$

We see, therefore, that the "level" of inner decomposition can affect ρ's decomposability. We further conjecture that if ρ cannot be losslessly decomposed at all then $H_{\rho}(1) = |\rho|$. Examples conforming with this conjecture is the unit relation and the parity relation [Dechter 1990].

6. Examples

The following two examples, taken from chapter 8 of [Rumelhart 1988b], demonstrate the use of inner decompositions once they are available.

Example 1: addition

Consider the problem of adding two-digit numbers, where the digits are 0 or 1. Denote the first number by $X_1 Y_1$, the second number by $X_2 Y_2$, let T stand for the carry and let $Z_1 Z_2 Z_3$ stand for the resulting sum. The *add* relation is given in figure 7a.

add =

X_1	Y_1	X_2	Y_2	T	Z_1	Z_2	Z_3
0	0	0	0	0	0	0	0
0	0	0	1	0	0	0	1
0	0	1	0	0	0	1	0
0	0	1	1	0	0	1	1
0	1	0	0	0	0	0	1
0	1	0	1	1	0	0	0
0	1	1	0	0	0	1	1
0	1	1	1	1	1	0	0
1	0	0	0	0	0	1	0
1	0	0	1	0	0	1	1
1	0	1	0	0	1	0	0
1	0	1	1	0	1	0	1
1	1	0	0	0	0	1	1
1	1	0	1	1	1	0	0
1	1	1	0	0	1	0	1
1	1	1	1	1	1	1	0

(a)

R_2 =

T	X_1	X_2	Z_1	Z_2
0	0	0	0	0
0	0	1	0	1
0	1	0	0	1
0	1	1	1	0
1	0	0	0	1
1	0	1	1	0
1	1	0	1	0
1	1	1	1	1

R_1 =

T	Y_1	Y_2	Z_3
0	0	0	0
0	0	1	1
0	1	0	1
1	1	1	0

(b)

Figure 7: (a) The *add* relation,
(b) A lossless decomposition of *add*

A star decomposition of *add* with one hidden variable requires 16 values, namely $H_{add}(1) \leq 16$. Using 3-valued variables our scheme requires 14 variables (EQ. (7)). Consider now the lossless decomposition of the *add* relation given by $R = R_1, R_2$ where $R_1 = T, Y_1, Y_2, Z_3$ and $R_2 = T, X_1, X_2, Z_1, Z_2$ (see figure 7b.) By decomposing each component separately we get that one 8-valued variable is needed for $rel(R_2)$ and a 4-valued variable is needed for $rel(R_1)$, each of the two can star-decompose its corresponding subrelation. In that case nothing is gained by the inner decomposition since a decomposition of the relation with 8-valued variables can be directly applied to the overall relation using just two variables. However, if only 3-valued variables are permitted, $rel(R_1)$ would require two such hidden variables while $rel(R_2)$ will require 6 variables, resulting in a total of 8, 3-valued variables as in Fig. 8.

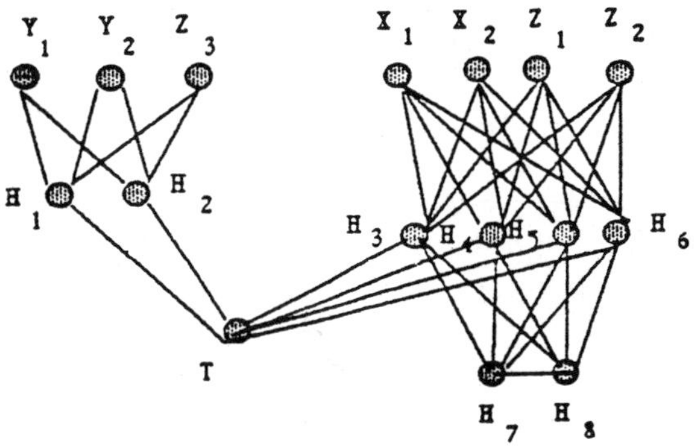

Figure 8: A 3-valued decomposition of *add*.

Example 2: the negation problem:

Consider a situation where the input to a system consists of a pattern of $n+1$ bits and n output bits. One of the input bit is called "the negation bit". When it is "0" the rest of the n input bits should be mapped directly to the output patterns. If it is "1" then each bit should be mapped to its negation. Fig. 9a describes the relation defined over the negation variable N, the input variables X_1, X_2, X_3 and the output variables Y_1, Y_2, Y_3.

neg_3

N	X_1	X_2	X_3	Y_1	Y_2	Y_3
0	0	0	0	0	0	0
0	0	0	1	0	0	1
0	0	1	0	0	1	0
0	0	1	1	0	1	1
0	1	0	0	1	0	0
0	1	0	1	1	0	1
0	1	1	0	1	1	0
0	1	1	1	1	1	1
1	0	0	0	1	1	1
1	0	0	1	1	1	0
1	0	1	0	1	0	1
1	0	1	1	1	0	1
1	1	0	0	0	1	1
1	1	0	1	0	1	0
1	1	1	0	0	0	1
1	1	1	1	0	0	0

(a)

$R_1 =$

N	X_1	Y_1
0	0	0
0	1	1
1	0	1
1	1	0

(b)

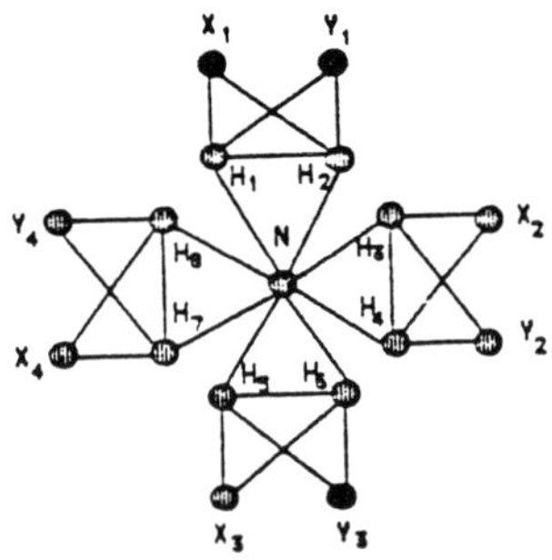

(c)

Figure 9: (a) The neg_3 relation,
(b) Subrealtion R_i, (c) A network decomposition

A direct decomposition of this relation requires 2^n values for a star decomposition and when 3-valued variables are available $2^n - 2$ hidden variables are required. Consider now the following lossless decomposition

$$neg_n = rel(R_1), \bowtie, \ldots, \bowtie rel(R_n) \tag{12}$$

where $rel(R_i)$ is given in figure 9b. Two 3-valued hidden variables can be used for each $rel(R_i)$, resulting in a total of $2n$ 3-valued hidden variables. The constraint graph of this decomposition is given in Fig. 9c.

7. Conclusions

We have shown that any relation can be expressed as a network of binary relations if augmented by hidden variables having three values, while no expressional power is gained by hidden variables having only two values. Specifically, a constructive scheme is presented that decomposes any relation, ρ, into a layered network using $\frac{|\rho|-2}{k-2}$ k-valued hidden variables when $k>2$. We also showed that the scheme is worse-case optimal, meaning that some relations require that many hidden variables. We extended the scheme to exploit an initial lossless decomposition of the relation, if one is available.

Comparing our decomposition scheme with current techniques used in the neural networks community we should consider two systems; those based on the Hebbian rule and those using feedforward networks. The former are restricted to orthogonal vectors, and thus our scheme is more general. The latter have no established theoretical guarantees and often require a long time to converge. In contrast our scheme is complete and it works in time linear in the size of the initial relation. Its drawback, however, is that it requires an a-priori knowledge of the entire relation. Nonetheless, understanding the basic theoretical limitations of architectures using hidden variables should facilitate the development of effective generalizing scheme based on partial relations.

References

[Collin 1990] Collin, Z. and R. Dechter, "A distributed solution to the network consistency problem," Technion., Tech. Rep. Haifa, Israel, 1990.

[Dechter 1990] Dechter, R., "Design of networks with hidden variables.," Technion., Tech. Rep. Haifa, Israel, 1990.

[Hinton 1988] Hinton, G.E. and T.J. Sejnowski, *Learning and relearningin Boltzman machines*, Cambridge, Massachusetts: Parallel Distributed Processing, Vol 1. Ch. 7., 1988.

[Minsky 1969] Minsky, M. and S. Papert, *Perceptrons*, Cambridge, MA: MIT Press, 1969.

[Montanari 1974] Montanari, U., "Networks of Constraints: Fundamental Properties and Applications to Picture Processing," *Information Science*, Vol. 7, 1974, pp. 95-132.

[Rumelhart 1988a] Rumelhart, D.E., G.E. Hinton, and R.J. Williams, *Learning Internal representation by error propagation*, Cambridge, Massachusetts: Parallel Distributed Processing, Vol 1. Ch. 8., 1988.

[Rumelhart 1988b] Rumelhart, D.E. and J.L. McClelland, *Parallel Distributed Processing*, Cambridge Massachusetts, London England: The MIT Press, 1988.

An Optimally Efficient Limited Inference System*

Lokendra Shastri and Venkat Ajjanagadde

Department of Computer & Information Science
University of Pennsylvania
Philadelphia, PA 19104, USA
shastri@cis.upenn.edu

Abstract

This paper describes a knowledge representation and reasoning system that performs a limited but interesting class of inferences over a restricted class of first-order sentences with optimal efficiency. The proposed system can answer *yes-no* as well as *wh*-queries in time that is only *proportional* to the *length* of the shortest derivation of the query and is *independent* of the *size* of the knowledge base. This work suggests that the expressiveness and the inferential ability of a representation and reasoning systems may be limited in unusual ways to arrive at extremely efficient yet fairly powerful knowledge based systems.

Introduction

Research in artificial intelligence has made it abundantly clear that tremendous computational activity underlies even the most commonplace intelligent behavior. For example, language understanding, a task that we usually perform so effortlessly and effectively, depends upon the agent's ability to disambiguate word senses, recover the phrase structure of input sentences, resolve anaphoric references, impose selectional restrictions, recognize speaker's plans, perform numerous predictions, and generate explanations.

Within the knowledge representation and reasoning paradigm, most of the above computations are viewed as *inferences*. Such a view, however, leads to the following paradox: A generalized notion of inference is intractable, yet the human ability to perform cognitive tasks such as language understanding in real-time suggests that we are capable of performing a wide range of inferences with extreme efficiency.

The success of AI critically depends on resolving the above paradox. Fortunately, one is only faced with an *apparent* paradox because humans are not general purpose reasoners — we can only perform a limited (but perhaps a fairly rich) class of inferences with extreme efficiency. This suggests two alternate research strategies for addressing the paradox: One may attempt to characterize the class of inference that people perform with great efficiency and try and discover appropriate representations, algorithms, and computational architectures to perform these inferences with requisite efficiency. Unfortunately, a precise characterization of what humans can infer with ease does not appear to be in sight. An alternate strategy would be to develop a complexity theory of reasoning by identifying what classes of inference can be performed with what degree of efficiency. The work reported in this paper conforms to this latter strategy. Such a strategy has been pursued by several researchers (for example, [6, 10, 13, 9, 14, 7]), and their work has covered a wide band of the complexity spectrum: Thus we have decidability results (e.g., [13]) as well as characterizations of simple knowledge representation systems that merely perform database retrieval [10].

Most of the above results have been surprisingly negative and have shown that even fairly restricted kinds of reasoning turns out to be intractable (for example, refer to [4, 7]). Yet the human ability to understand language in real-time clearly suggests that *there does exist a fairly rich class of reasoning that humans can perform effortlessly and within seconds.* To appreciate the richness of such reasoning, consider the following sentence: "John seems to have suicidal tendencies, he has joined the Columbian drug enforcement agency". Even though the reader would have understood the above sentence spontaneously, and perhaps within a few seconds, a careful analysis would reveal that doing so requires performing a number of fairly elaborate inferences. For convenience let us agree to refer to such spontaneous and fast reasoning as *reflexive* reasoning.[1]

*This work was supported by NSF grants IRI 88-05465, MCS-8219196-CER, MCS-83-05211, DARPA grants N00014-85-K-0018 and N00014-85-K-0807, and ARO grant ARO-DAA29-84-9-0027.

[1] It is as if such reasoning is a *reflex* response of our cognitive apparatus. Clearly, all human reasoning is not reflexive.

Reflexive Reasoning

In evaluating the complexity of reflexive reasoning it must be recognized that such reasoning is performed with reference to an extremely large body of knowledge. We believe that a conservative estimate of the number of 'rules' and 'facts' required to encode all relevant aspects of the domain of common sense will easily run into several million (perhaps, even more).[2] In view of the above it appears that the time complexity of an inference algorithm for reflexive reasoning should *at worst* be *sublinear* in $|KB|$ – where $|KB|$ is the size of the knowledge base – and perhaps even be *independent* of $|KB|$.

Reflexive reasoning introduces a very strong notion of effectiveness, one that seems formidable in view of the negative results cited above. In this paper we report an encouraging result. We identify a class of inference that is computable in time that is not only sublinear in $|KB|$ but is also, in a sense, *optimal*. We describe a knowledge representation and reasoning system that can encode a restricted class of first-order sentences and answer a class of queries in time that is only *proportional* to the *length* of the shortest derivation of the query and is *independent* of $|KB|$. This work suggests that there exist interesting points in the tradeoff-continuum between computational effectiveness and inferential/expressive power. It also demonstrates that it is possible to arrive at extremely efficient yet fairly powerful knowledge representation systems by explicitly recognizing the symbiotic relationship that exists between expressiveness, effectiveness of inference, the choice of representation (data-structures), and the underlying model of computational.

Functional Specification

The knowledge representation system encodes *rules* and *facts* of the following form:

$$\forall x_1, ..., x_m \; [P_1(...) \wedge P_2(...) ... \wedge P_n(...) \Rightarrow \exists z_1, ... z_l \; Q(...)]$$

The arguments of P_i's are elements of $\{x_1, x_2, ... x_m\}$. An argument of Q is either an element of $\{x_1, x_2, ... x_m\}$, or an element of $\{z_1, z_2, ... z_l\}$, or a constant. It is required that any variable occurring in multiple argument positions in the antecedent of a rule must also appear in its consequent.

Facts are assumed to be partial or complete instantiations of predicates. Thus facts are atomic formulae of the form $P(t_1, t_2 ... t_k)$ where t_i's are either constants or distinct existentially quantified variables.

A query has the same form as a fact. A query all of whose arguments are bound to constants, corresponds to a *yes-no* question. On the other hand, a query with existentially quantified variables corresponds to a *wh*-query and answering such a query involves findings variable binding(s) for which the query follows from the rules and facts encoded in the system.

It can be shown that the knowledge representation system responds soundly provided a query satisfies the following conditions:[3]

1. The number of distinct constants specified in the query does not exceed Ω, where Ω is an implementation parameter (see Section 3).
2. Any rule that participates in the derivation of the query must obey the following constraint: Any variable occurring in *multiple* argument positions in the *antecedent* of such a rule must get bound during the reasoning process (this, via backward chaining).
3. During the processing of the query, each predicate may only be instantiated with one set of argument bindings. This restriction, however, only applies to run-time or 'dynamic' instantiations of predicates and not to 'long-term' facts stored in the system. Recently, we have extended the system to allow it to represent up to k – where k is a system parameter – dynamic instantiations of *each* predicate during the processing of a query [11]. (This extension is not discussed in this paper.)

If the above conditions are met, the system answers *yes* to all *yes-no* queries that follow from the encoded rules and facts in time proportional to the *length* of the *shortest* derivation of the query. The system obeys the closed world assumption and produces a *no* answer in time proportional to d, where d equals the diameter of the inferential dependency graph associated with the rule-base (see Section 3). *wh*-queries are also answered in time proportional to d. Finally, the *space* complexity of the system is just *linear* in $|KB|$.

Cognitive Significance

Reflexive reasoning takes place with reference to a large body of knowledge and even though each reasoning episode may involve a large number of rules and facts, there is considerable psychological evidence to suggest that most cognitive tasks performed efficiently without props involve only a *small number of distinct entities*. A reasonable estimate of the maximum number of distinct entities we can deal with at a time is around seven [12]. It must be emphasized that the limit is on the number of distinct entities and not on the number of variable (i.e.,

[2]Thorpe and Imbert [16] argue that even the number of visually identifiable entities is around a hundred thousand!

[3]The system is incomplete and the above conditions characterize its incompleteness.

role) bindings that these entities participate in during an episode of reasoning. We believe that the first condition listed in the previous section is consistent with this aspect of human reasoning and a psychologically plausible value of Ω may be around seven.

We also conjecture that any given episode of reflexive reasoning does not require the same predicate to be dynamically instantiated more than k times, where a psychologically plausible value of k may be as low as three to five (observe that k greater than 1 allows for bounded recursion). Thus the third limitation of the reasoning system is also well motivated.

In our view, the KB underlying reflexive reasoning primarily encodes an agent's *long-term* and *stable* knowledge about the world. Although new rules do get added to an agent's KB, the assimilation of a new rule *in a form that allows its participation in reflexive reasoning* takes time – not seconds, but perhaps minutes, days or even months. It is in this context that one must evaluate the realization of the reasoning system described below.

Finally, the realization of the reasoning system is also biologically plausible in that it strictly adheres to the core features of the connectionist model. At the same time, there exists neurophysiological evidence to suggest that the basic mechanisms used below, namely, the propagation of rhythmic patterns of activity, play a role in the representation and processing of information in the animal brain. For a detailed discussion, refer to [15].

Realization of the Reasoning System

The representation and reasoning system is realized as a massively parallel network of simple processing elements (nodes). A major technical problem that must be solved in realizing such a 'connectionist' reasoning system is the run-time (dynamic) creation and propagation of variable bindings. The proposed system solves this problem while still using extremely simple oscillatory nodes (see next section).

Ballard [2] was the first to propose a massively parallel inference system. He however, required that *all possible variable bindings be explicitly pre-wired* into a network. This requirement is too severe and unrealistic and greatly limits the generality of his system. Touretzky and Hinton's DCPS does represent dynamic bindings [17] but its ability to do so is very limited. First, DCPS can only deal with *single variable* rules. Second, even though DCPS is a parallel system, it allows only *one* rule to fire at a time, and hence, does not satisfy the efficiency requirements of reflexive reasoning. A detailed comparison of our system with other massively parallel reasoning systems (for example, ROBIN, CONPOSIT, and NETL [8, 3, 5]) may be found in [15].

Conceptually, the proposed encoding of the knowledge base amounts to creating a directed *inferential dependency* graph: Each predicate argument is represented by a node in this graph and each rule is represented by links from nodes denoting the arguments of the consequent predicate to nodes denoting the arguments of the corresponding antecedent predicate. Facts are small networks attached to their respective predicates nodes. We describe the encoding with the help of an example. For simplicity we only describe the realization of single antecedent rules without constants and existentially quantified variables in the consequent.

Fig. 1 illustrates the encoding of the following *facts* and *rules*.

1. $\forall x, y, z\ [give(x, y, z) \Rightarrow own(y, z)]$
2. $\forall x, y\ [buy(x, y) \Rightarrow own(x, y)]$
3. $\forall x, y\ [own(x, y) \Rightarrow can\text{-}sell(x, y)]$
4. $give(John, Mary, Book1)$
5. $buy(John, x)$
6. $own(Mary, Ball1)$

The encoding makes use of two types of nodes. These are ρ-btu nodes (depicted as circles) and τ-and nodes (depicted as pentagons). The computational behavior of these nodes is as follows:

A ρ-btu is a phase-sensitive binary threshold unit. When such a node becomes active, it produces an oscillatory output in the form of a pulse train that has a period π and pulse width ω. The timing (or the *phase*) of the pulse train produced by a ρ-btu node is precisely governed by the phase of the input to the node. A τ-and node acts like a *temporal and* node. Such a node also oscillates with the same frequency as a ρ-btu node except that it becomes active only if it receives *uninterrupted* activation over a whole period of oscillation. Furthermore, the width of the pulses produced by a τ-and node equals π. The implementation parameter Ω that governs the maximum number of distinct entities that may participate in the derivation of a *yes-no* query equals ω/π (assume integer divide).

The output pulse of a node propagates along every link emanating from the node. The encoding also makes use of *inhibitory modifiers*. An inhibitory modifier is a link that impinges upon and inhibits another link. Thus a pulse propagating along an inhibitory modifier will block the propagation of a pulse propagating along the link it impinges upon. In Fig. 1, inhibitory modifiers are shown as links ending in dark blobs.

Each constant in the domain is encoded by a ρ-node. An n-ary predicate is encoded by a pair of τ-and nodes and n ρ-btu nodes, one for each of the n arguments. One of the τ-and nodes is referred to as the *enabler* and the other as the *collector*. As a matter of convention, an *enabler* always points upwards and is named *e:[predicate-name]*. A *collector* always points downwards and is named *c:[predicate-name]*.

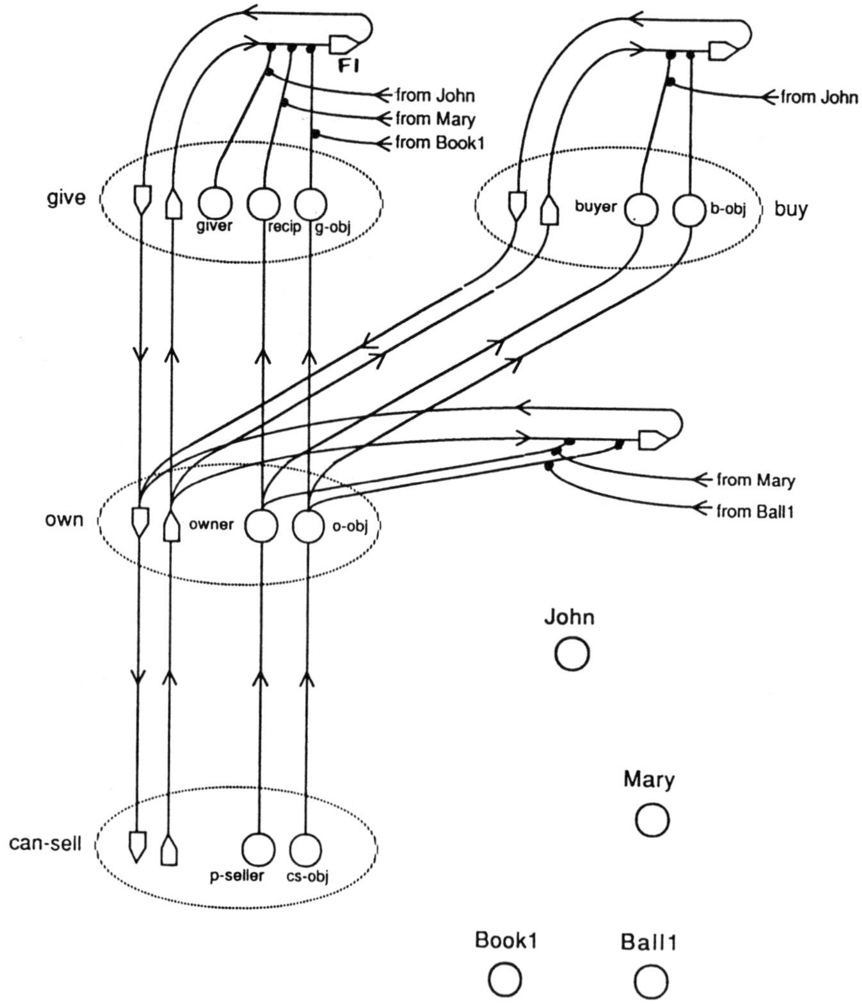

Figure 1: An example encoding of rules and facts

A rule is encoded by connecting the *collector* of the antecedent predicate to the *collector* of the consequent predicate, the *enabler* of the consequent predicate to the *enabler* of the antecedent predicate, and by connecting the argument nodes of the consequent predicate to the argument nodes of the antecedent predicate in accordance with the correspondence between these arguments specified in the rule (refer to Fig. 1.)

A fact is encoded using a τ-and node that receives an input from the enabler of the associated predicate. This input is modified by inhibitory modifiers from the argument nodes of the associated predicate. If an argument is bound to a constant in the fact then the modifier from such an argument node is in turn modified by an inhibitory modifier from the appropriate constant node. The output of the τ-and node is connected to the *collector* of the associated predicate (refer to the encoding of the fact $give(John, Mary, Book1)$ and $buy(John, x)$ in Fig. 1.)

The number of nodes required to encode a knowledge base, (i.e., the space complexity) is only *linear* in $|KB|$. Specifically, the number of nodes required are $O(r+f+a+c)$, where r is the number of rules, f is the number of facts, a is the total number of predicate arguments and c is the number of constants in the domain. The number of links required is also only linear in $|KB|$. Specifically, the number of links required is $O(r1+f1)$, where $r1$ is the number of rules weighted by the number of predicate arguments occurring in each rule, and $f1$ is the number of facts weighted by the number of arguments in the predicate associated with each fact.

Inference Process

Reasoning in the proposed system is the transient but systematic flow of *rhythmic* patterns of activation, where

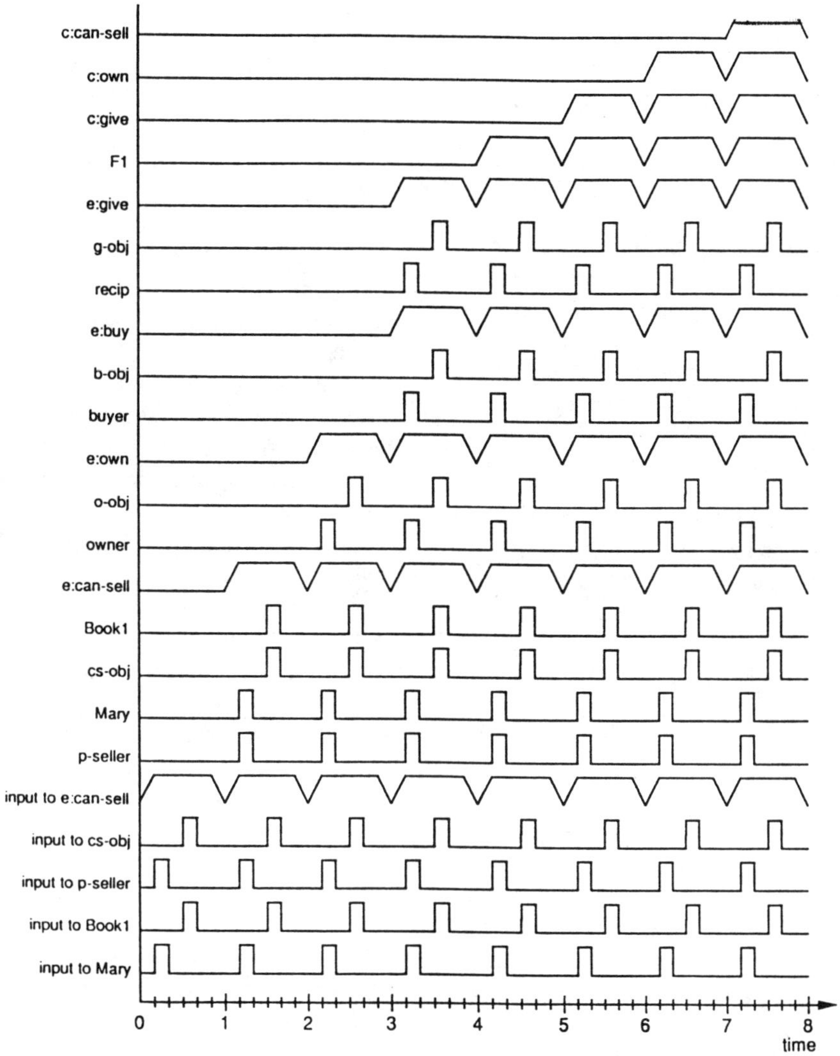

Figure 2: Activation trace for the query *can-sell(Mary, Book1)*?

each *phase* (or time-slice) in the rhythmic pattern corresponds to a distinct *constant* involved in the reasoning process and where variable bindings are represented as the *in-phase* (i.e., synchronous) firing of appropriate argument and constant nodes. A fact behaves as a temporal pattern matcher that becomes 'active' when it detects that the bindings corresponding to it are present in system's pattern of activity. Finally, rules are interconnection patterns that propagate and transform rhythmic patterns of activity. Below we describe the reasoning process in greater detail, complete details may be found in [15].

We first consider *yes-no* queries. The inference process may be thought of as consisting of two overlapping but conceptually distinct stages. The first stage corresponds to a parallel breadth-first exploration of the potentially huge inferential dependency graph. During this stage, all the facts that are relevant to the proof of the query become active. In the second stage the actual proof is constructed: activation from the relevant facts flows downwards along *collector* nodes to produce an answer to the query. A *yes* answer corresponds to the activation of the *collector* node of the query predicate.

Posing a Query: Specifying Variable Bindings

Posing a query to the system involves specifying the query predicate and the argument bindings specified in the query. In the proposed system this is done by simply activating the relevant nodes in the manner described below. In particular, *posing a query to the system does not involve any hidden time or space costs* such as rewiring of the network, or addition of new nodes and links.

Let us choose an arbitrary point in time – say, t_0 – as our point of reference for initiating the query. We assume that the system is in a quiescent state just prior to t_0. The query predicate is specified by activating the *enabler* of the query predicate, with a pulse train of width and periodicity ω starting at time t_0.

The argument bindings specified in the query are communicated to the network as follows:

- Let the argument bindings in the query involve k distinct constants: $c_1, ..., c_k$. With each of these k constants, associate a delay δ_i such that no two delays are within ω of one another and the longest delay is less than $\pi - \omega$. Each of these delays may be viewed as a distinct *phase* within the period t_0 and $t_0 + \pi$.
- The argument bindings of a constant c_i are indicated to the system by providing an oscillatory pulse train of pulse width ω and periodicity π starting at $t_0 + \delta_i$, to c_i and all arguments to which c_i is bound. This is done for each constant c_i $(1 \leq i \leq k)$ and amounts to representing argument bindings by the *in-phase or synchronous activation of the appropriate constant and argument nodes.*

An Example

Once the query is posed, a parallel search for facts that are relevant to the proof of the query ensues. We illustrate this process with the help of an example (refer to Fig. 1.) Consider the query *can-sell(Mary,Book1)*. This query is posed by providing inputs to the constants *Mary* and *Book1*, the arguments *p-seller*, *cs-obj* and the *enabler e:can-sell* as shown in Fig. 2. (In the illustration, Ω has been assumed to be 6.) *Mary* and *p-seller* receive in-phase activation and so do *Book1* and *cs-obj*. Let us refer to the phase of activation of *Mary* and *Book1* as phase-1 and phase-2 respectively. As a result of these inputs, *Mary* and *p-seller* will fire synchronously in phase-1 of every period of oscillation, while *Book1* and *cs-obj* will fire synchronously in phase-2 of every period of oscillation. The node *e:can-sell* will also oscillate and generate a pulse train of periodicity and pulse width π.

The activations from the arguments *p-seller* and *cs-obj* reach the arguments *owner* and *o-obj* of the predicate *own*, and consequently, starting with the second period of oscillation, *owner* and *o-obj* become active in phase-1 and phase-2, respectively. At the same time, the activation from *e:can-sell* activates *e:own* (Refer to Fig. 2). The system has essentially, created dynamic bindings for the arguments of predicate *own*. *Mary* has been bound to the argument *owner*, and *Book1* has been bound to the argument *own-object*. These newly created bindings in conjunction with the activation of *e:own* can be thought of as encoding the query *own(Mary,Book1)* (i.e., 'Does Mary own Book1?')!

Theτ-and node associated with the fact *own(Mary, Ball1)* does not match the query and remains inactive. Observe that during phase-2, the activation from *e:own* going into the τ-and node is blocked by the inhibitory activation from the argument *owner*.

The activations from *owner* and *o-obj* reach the arguments *recip* and *g-obj* of *give*, and *buyer* and *b-obj* of *buy* respectively. Thus beginning with the third period of oscillation, arguments *recip* and *buyer* become active in phase-1, while arguments *g-obj* and *b-obj* become active in phase-2. In essence, the system has created new bindings for the predicates *can-sell* and *buy* that can be thought of as encoding two new queries: *give(x,Mary,Book1)* (i.e., 'Did someone give Mary Book1?'), and *buy(Mary,Book1)* (i.e., 'Did Mary buy Book1?').

The τ-and node associated with the fact *buy(John, x)* does not become active because the activation from *e:buy* is blocked by the inhibitory activations from the arguments *buyer* and *b-obj*. The τ-and node associated with the fact *give(John,Mary,Book1)* (this is the τ-and node labeled F1 in Fig. 1), however, does become active as a result of the uninterrupted activation from *e:give*. The inhibitory inputs from *recip* and *g-obj* are blocked by the in-phase inputs from *Mary* and *Book1*, respectively. The activation from this τ-and node causes *c:give*, the *collector* of *give*, to become active and the output from *c:give* in turn causes *c:own* to become active and transmit an output to *c:can-sell*. Consequently, *c:can-sell*, the *collector* of the query predicate *can-sell*, becomes active resulting in an affirmative answer to the query *can-sell(Mary,Book1)*. (refer to Fig. 2).

Encoding Complex Rules

A rule with conjunctive predicates in the antecedent, i.e., a rule of the form $P_1(...) \wedge P_2(...) \wedge ... P_m(...) \Rightarrow Q(...)$, is encoded using an additional τ-and node that has a threshold of m. The outputs of the *collector* nodes of $P_1, ..., P_m$ are connected to this node which in turn is connected to the *collector* of Q. This additional node becomes active if and only if it receives inputs from the *collector* nodes of all the m antecedent predicates. The interconnections between the argument nodes of the antecedent and consequent predicates remain unchanged.

The encoding of rules and facts described in the previous section assumes that constants or existentially quantified variables do not appear in the consequent of a rule. It also assumes that the same variable does not occur in multiple argument positions in the consequent of a rule. The encoding of such rules can be carried out by very simple mechanisms that involve detecting whether appropriate nodes are firing in synchrony or not. A complete description may be found in [15].

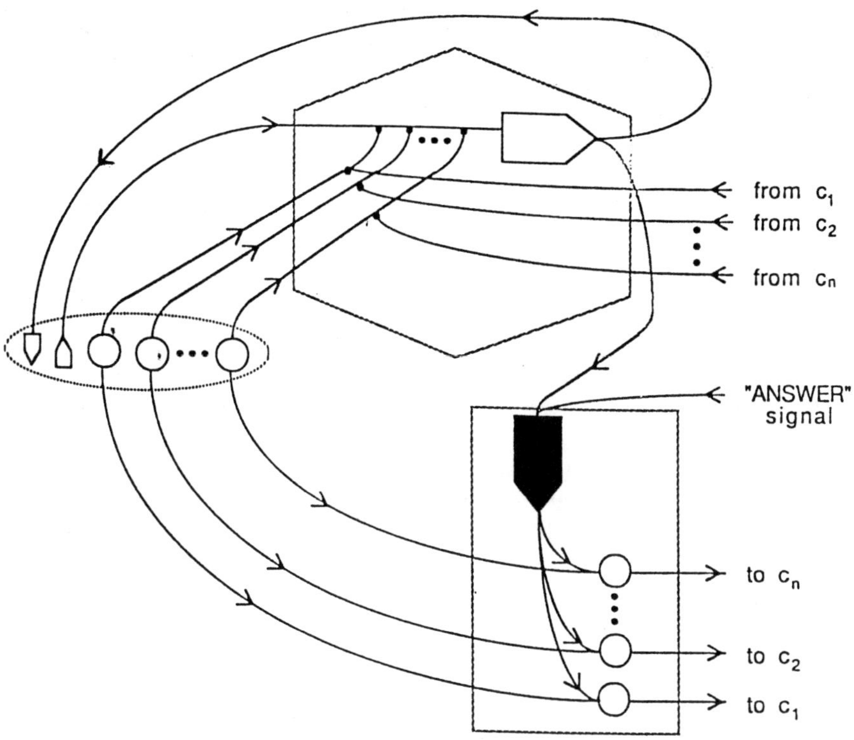

Figure 3: Augmented encoding of a fact in order to support answer extraction

Answering "wh-"queries

In this section, we will discuss a way of extending the system to answer *wh*-queries. Consider the proof of the query *can-sell*$(Mary, x)$ with respect to the network shown in Fig. 1. In the process of proving this query the two relevant facts $own(Mary, Ball1)$ and $give(John, Mary, Book1)$ will become active. The answer to the *wh*-query 'What can Mary sell?', can be obtained by simply identifying the constants that are bound to the arguments *g-obj* and *b-obj*, respectively, of the two active facts. This is not a coincidence — notice that the arguments *g-obj* and *b-obj* are precisely the arguments that map to the unbound argument *cs-obj* of *can-sell* via the rules encoded in the system. The system can easily extract this information by making use of the same binding propagation mechanism it uses to map arguments bound in the query. A straightforward way of doing so is to posit a separate *answer extraction* stage that is carried out after the *yes-no* query associated with the *wh*-query has produced a *yes* answer. For example, given the query 'What can Mary sell?' the system first computes the answer to the *yes-no* query 'Can Mary sell something?' and identifies the facts $own(Mary, Ball1)$ and $give(John, Mary, Book1)$ that lead to a *yes* answer. The answer extraction stage follows and picks out the constants $Ball1$ and $Book1$ as the answers.

The representation of a fact is augmented as shown in Fig. 3. in order to support answer extraction. The representation of a fact involving an n-ary predicate is modified to include $n+1$ additional nodes: for each of the n arguments of the associated predicate there exists a ρ-btu node with a threshold of two. For convenience we will refer to such a node as a *binder* node. The other node (shown as a filled-in pentagon) is like a binder node, except that once active, it remains so — even after the inputs are withdrawn. This node, which we will refer to as a *latch* node, receives an *Answer* input in addition to an input from the τ-and node of the associated fact.

At the end of the first stage, the outputs of the τ-and nodes of all the relevant facts would be active. The output of these τ-and nodes in conjunction with the *Answer* signal will turn on the associated *latch* nodes and provide one of the two inputs to the *binder* nodes. If the associated *yes-no* query results in a *yes* answer, the answer extraction stage is initiated. Inputs relating to the first stage are withdrawn and the relevant *unbound* argument of the query predicate a_i is activated in a distinct phase. In addition a network wide *Answer* signal is also propagated. The activation of unbound query arguments results in a phase-sensitive propagation of activation and eventually leads to the activation of arguments associated with facts relevant to the query. This provides an input to the appropriate *binder* nodes of these facts. As the *binder* nodes were already receiving an input from a *latch* node, they become active and produce a phase-sensitive output that in turn activates the associated constants in-phase with a_i. The answer to the *wh*-query will be precisely those constants that are active in-phase with a_i. The time taken by the answer extraction step is bounded by the depth of the inferential dependency graph.

Extensions

The reasoning and expressive power of the system described in this paper can be enhanced by interfacing it with specialized reasoning modules such as a semantic network or a *IS-A* hierarchy. Such an interface allows *terms* in the rules and facts to be any concept (type/instance) in the *IS-A* hierarchy. Another important extension extends the expressiveness and reasoning power of the system by allowing a limited use of function terms in rules[1].

Conclusion

The paper describes a knowledge representation and reasoning system that performs a limited but interesting class of inferences over a restricted class of first-order sentences with optimal efficiency. This work suggests that extremely efficient yet fairly powerful knowledge representation systems can be obtained by limiting the expressiveness and the inferential ability of a representation and reasoning systems in unusual ways.

References

[1] V. Ajjanagadde. Reasoning with function symbols in a connectionist network. In *Proceedings of the Cognitive Science Conference*, 1990. Submitted for publication.

[2] D.H. Ballard. Parallel logic inference and energy minimization. In *Proceedings of AAAI 86*, Philadelphia, PA, July 1986.

[3] J. Barnden. Neural-net implementation of complex symbol processing in a mental model approach to syllogistic reasoning. In *Proceedings of IJCAI 89*, Detroit, MI, August 1989.

[4] R. Brachman and H. Levesque. The tractability of subsumption in frame-based description languages. In *Proceedings of the 1984 Meeting of AAAI*, pages 34–37, Austin, TX, 1984.

[5] S. Fahlman. *NETL: A System for Representing Real-World Knowledge.* MIT Press, Cambridge, MA, 1979.

[6] A.M. Frisch and J.F. Allen. Knowledge retrieval as limited inference. In D.W. Loveland, editor, *Lecture Notes in Computer Science: Sixth Conference on Automated Deduction*, Springer-Verlag, New York, 1982.

[7] H.A. Kautz and B. Selman. Hard problems for simple default logics. *Artificial Intelligence*, 1989. Submitted.

[8] T.E. Lange and M.G. Dyer. High-level inferencing in a connectionist network. *Connection Science*, 1(2):181 – 217, 1989.

[9] H.J. Levesque. Logic and the complexity of reasoning. *Journal of Philosophical Logic*, 17, 1988.

[10] H.J. Levesque. Making believers out of computers. *Artificial Intelligence*, 30(1), 1986.

[11] D.R. Mani and L. Shastri. *Representing Multiple Dynamic Instantiations of a Predicate in a Connectionist System.* Technical Report, University of Pennsylvania, Dept. of Computer and Information Science, Philadelphia, PA, 1990. To appear.

[12] G.A. Miller. The magical number seven, plus or minus two: some limits on our capacity for processing information. *The Psychological Review*, 63(2):81–97, March 1956.

[13] P. Patel-Schneider. A decidable first-order logic for knowledge representation. In *Proceedings of IJCAI-85*, pages 455–458, Los Angeles, CA, 1985.

[14] L. Shastri. *Semantic Networks: An Evidential Formulation and its Connectionist Realization.* Pitman/Morgan Kaufman, London/Los Altos, 1988.

[15] L. Shastri and V. Ajjanagadde. *From simple associations to systematic reasoning: A connectionist representation of rules, variables and dynamic bindings.* Technical Report MS-CIS-90-05, Dept. of Computer and Information Science, University of Pennsylvania, Philadelphia, PA, January 1990.

[16] S.J. Thorpe and M. Imbert. Biological constraints on connectionist modeling. In R. Pfeiffer, editor, *Connectionism in Perspective*, Springer, 1988.

[17] D. Touretzky and G.E. Hinton. A distributed connectionist production system. *Cognitive Science*, 12(3):423 – 466, 1988.